PAGE 50

ON THE ROAD

YOUR COMPLETE DESTINATION GUIDE
In-depth reviews, detailed listings and insider tips

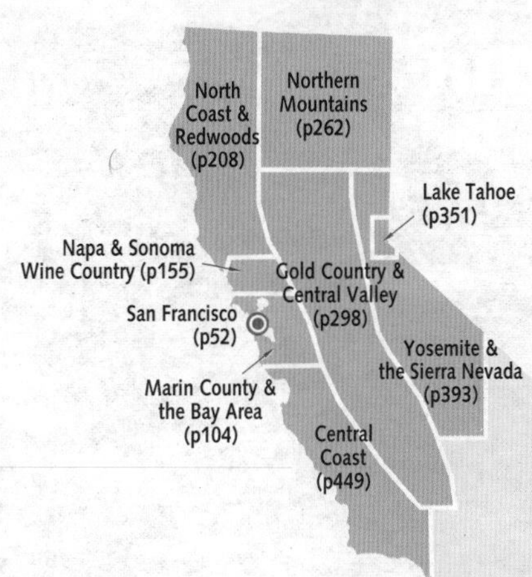

PAGE 553

SURVIVAL GUIDE

VITAL PRACTICAL INFORMATION TO HELP YOU HAVE A SMOOTH TRIP

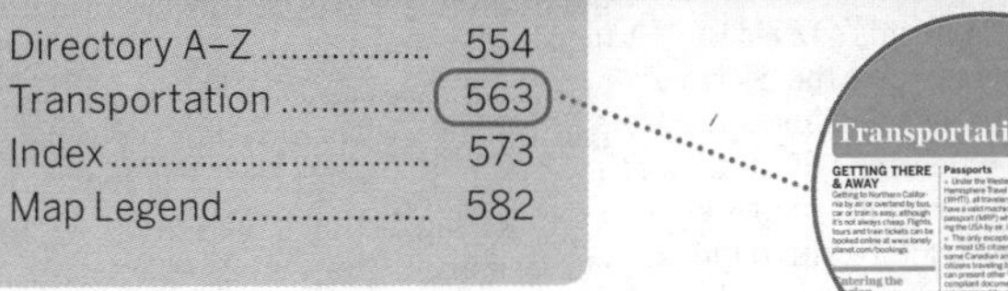

THIS EDITION WRITTEN AND RESEARCHED BY

Nate Cavalieri,

Sara Benson, Alison Bing, Beth Kohn, John A Vlahides

Natural Splendor

Drama is in Northern California's DNA: the edge of the continent between the Sierra Nevada and the sparkling Pacific holds the west's most accessible wilderness. Even the region's major city, San Francisco, shrinks when compared to the scale of surrounding nature, as the towers of the Golden Gate Bridge get enveloped in ethereal fog and a crashing coastline encroaches from north and south along Hwy 1. The region's diversity is evident in its three national parks: steep granite canyons and rushing waterfalls in Yosemite; mist-shrouded prehistoric ferns, spectacular seaside and immense forests in Redwood; and pitch-black lava caves and thermal geysers in Lassen. Add white water rivers that rush out of the mountains, trails that bypass innumerable peaks and the sparkling blue waters of Lake Tahoe, and Northern California's natural beauty leaves visitors gobsmacked. The region's great conservationist John Muir claimed that 'thousands of tired, nerve-shaken, over-civilized people are beginning to find out...that wilderness is a necessity.' A trip here is more necessary than ever.

Food & Drink

How cruel that most people only have an appetite for three meals a day. Bordering America's most agriculturally rich valley and blessed by long growing seasons, the

JOHN ELK III/LONELY PLANET IMAGES ©

Winding paths traverse mist-covered redwood groves, granite canyons and sun-washed vineyards, and lead into the inimitable City by the Bay's wild heart. Nature, culture and adventure exist in abundance.

(left) Coastal cliffs, Marin County
(below) Pots of ceviche, Santa Barbara

BRENT WINEBRENNER/LONELY PLANET IMAGES ©

region offers amazing food. A dinner reservation might be reason enough to book the plane ticket. Even putting aside the fancy digs – revolutionary fine-dining restaurants and famed wine regions – there's *still* a burden of riches. Locals wax poetic about burritos in San Francisco's Mission District, make weekend trips up the north coast for fresh crab and have the pick of hoppy microbrews. It's all part of a food scene that's dedicated to high quality and constant reinvention (have we mentioned the fine-dining food truck trend?) where even baguettes – chewy, perfectly crusty sourdough – are sterling. Have pity on the traveling foodie, this little piece of culinary heaven might be a bit overwhelming. Deep breaths. Deep breaths.

Weekend Escapes

The wonder about hitting the byways of Northern California is that things get better with every winding mile – trees get bigger, picturesque towns get cuter, roadside swimming holes get more inviting. An idyllic escape is constantly within reach. There's the cliffside route on Hwy 1 between Big Sur and Oregon, or a winding jaunt traversing wineries and Gold Country along Hwy 49. There are looping back roads between vineyards and the B&Bs of Napa Valley, organic farm tours in Sonoma and Marin Counties and a weekend drive to the slopes around Lake Tahoe. A lifetime of weekends won't cover it, so consider calling in sick and extending the trip.

Northern California

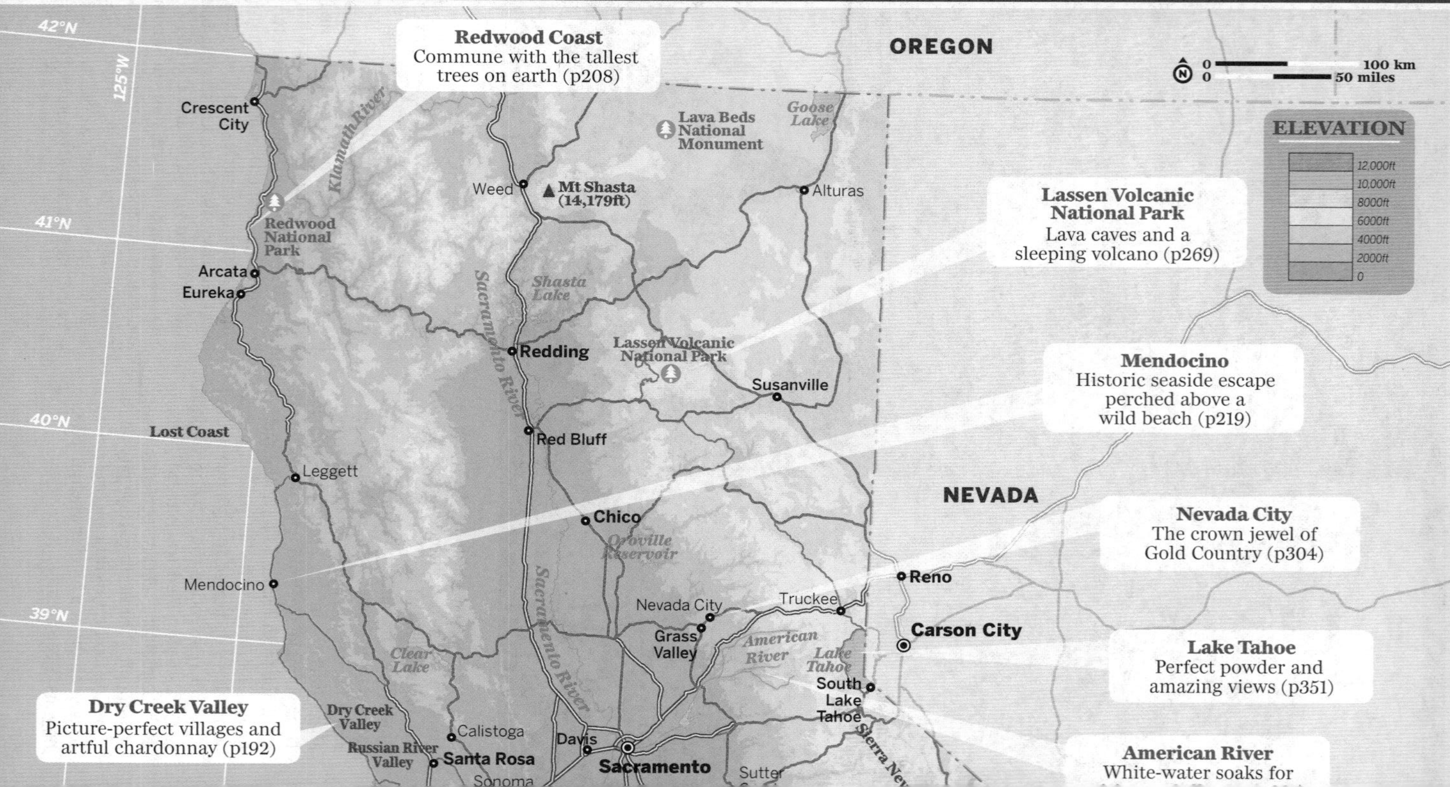

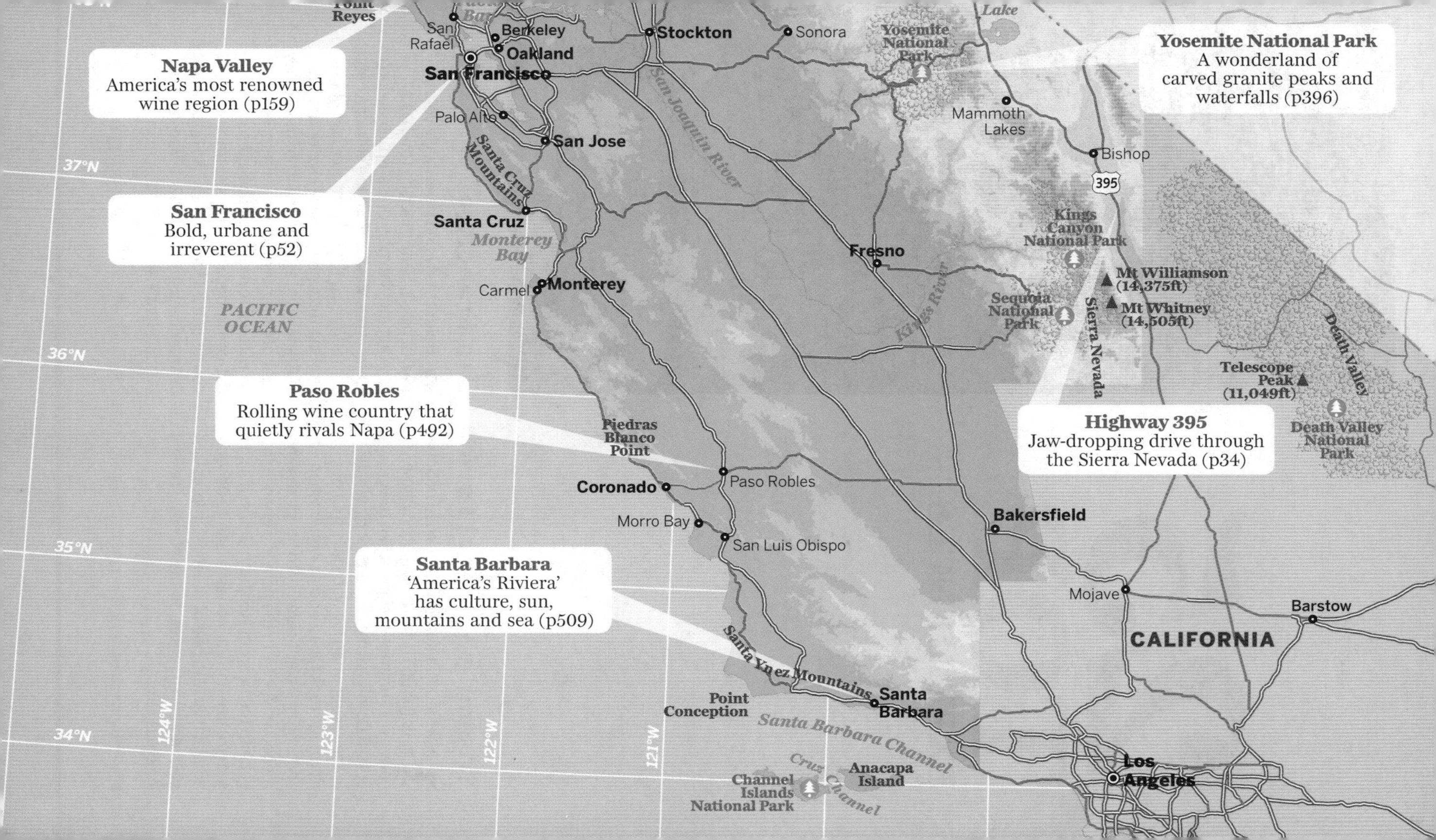

Napa Valley
America's most renowned wine region (p159)
San Francisco
Bold, urbane and irreverent (p52)
Paso Robles
Rolling wine country that quietly rivals Napa (p492)
Santa Barbara
'America's Riviera' has culture, sun, mountains and sea (p509)
Yosemite National Park
A wonderland of carved granite peaks and waterfalls (p396)
Highway 395
Jaw-dropping drive through the Sierra Nevada (p34)
Reyes
San Rafael
Berkeley
Oakland
San Francisco
Stockton
Sonora
Yosemite National Park
Lake
Mammoth Lakes
Bishop
395
Palo Alto
San Jose
Santa Cruz Mountains
San Joaquin River
Santa Cruz
Monterey Bay
Fresno
Kings Canyon National Park
Mt Williamson (14,375ft)
Mt Whitney (14,505ft)
Sequoia National Park
Sierra Nevada
Kings River
Death Valley
Telescope Peak (11,049ft)
Death Valley National Park
Carmel
Monterey
PACIFIC OCEAN
37°N
36°N
35°N
34°N
124°W
123°W
122°W
121°W
Piedras Blanco Point
Paso Robles
Coronado
Morro Bay
San Luis Obispo
Bakersfield
Mojave
Barstow
CALIFORNIA
Santa Ynez Mountains
Santa Barbara
Point Conception
Santa Barbara Channel
Anacapa Island
Cruz Channel
Channel Islands National Park
Los Angeles

25 TOP EXPERIENCES

Yosemite National Park

1 Northern California's cherished national park (p396) is rewarding at any time – early on a summer evening when the granite of Half Dome warms with a pink glow, late in the spring when icy waterfalls thunder down the rock faces, and all winter when snow brings silent serenity to the peaks and meadows. A visit to the park is a chance to get into the heart of Northern California's remarkable natural wonders, and to become acquainted with one of the most impressive mountain ranges on the planet. Above: Yosemite Falls

San Francisco

2 Bold, brassy and perennially young at heart, San Francisco (p52) is a city that loves to play dress-up. It can look iconic while viewed from the side of a cable car rattling up the hills, mysterious while strolling through its fog bridge or the alleys of Chinatown, and urbane from the window seat of its renowned restaurants. The home of '60s holdovers, dreadlocked squatters, dot-com moguls and people from every corner of the globe, it feels like no other city in America. Right: View of the Transamerica Building (architect William L Pereira; p57) and downtown San Francisco

1

EMILY RIDDELL/LONELY PLANET IMAGES ©

2

EMILY RIDDELL/LONELY PLANET IMAGES ©

Lassen Volcanic National Park

3 The rugged peak of Mt Lassen glowers on the horizon as visitors plunge into the inky depths of lava caves, wander to the edge of bubbling thermal fields and ponder geological oddities that seem poised on the brink of a meltdown. Even at the peak of summer, this remote national park (p269) is an uncrowded natural playground. And just when the place starts to resemble the sinister setting of a *Lord of the Rings* battle, a flock of migrating birds adds an elegant flourish to the skies above. Below: Mt Lassen and Manzanita Lake

Mono Lake

4 The haunting gem of the Eastern Sierra, the spectacular, alien, inimitable terrain of Mono Lake (p430) is hard to believe. With millions of migrating birds, an abundance of thermal hot springs and tufa (terrifically bizarre rock formations), this ancient salty lake seems like it was sketched from the pages of a sci-fi novel. It's a visually stunning place, offering solitude, unreal photo opportunities and dramatic sunsets. Plus, the snowy peaks of Yosemite's eastern edge are a constant reminder of the region's limitless possibility for outdoor adventure.

LEE FOSTER/LONELY PLANET IMAGES ©

JERRY ALEXANDER/LONELY PLANET IMAGES ©

JOHN ELK III/LONELY PLANET IMAGES ©

Skiing Tahoe

5 Epic powder, long seasons, fantastic panoramic views and an amazing variety of runs make Lake Tahoe's ski areas (p353) some of the most exciting in the nation. You can go glam and hit upscale slopes at Squaw Valley or Heavenly, or find a down-home local run in the backcountry. It's worth visiting for the view alone: a bird's-eye vista of the lake's shimmering blue water. By the time you snuggle in the glow of a fire back at the lodge, you'll know you've arrived at California's winter wonderland.

Napa & Sonoma Valleys

6 The sun-washed valleys of Napa (p159) and Sonoma (p180) are equally well suited for producing the country's best wine and exploring California's renowned wine region. A weekend in Wine Country lives up to the lore: visitors cruise the quaint back roads on bicycles in search of that perfect bottle, soak in the region's luxuriant spas and order dinner off visionary menus of celebrity chefs. Among the endless fields of grapes and rolling, oak-dotted hills, this is a beautiful place to get pampered. Top right: Napa Valley

Mendocino

7 Perched on a windswept headland and blessed with Northern California's triumvirate charms of wine, wilderness and a thriving local arts and crafts scene, Mendocino (p219) is *the* romantic weekend getaway for folks from the Bay Area. The town's historic shopping district and lacy B&Bs offer all the upscale creature comforts, while the raging waters of the Pacific, whale-watching trips and evergreen trails invite outdoor adventures. When it's time for dinner, count your blessings: Mendocino's fine-dining scene is all about organics, sustainability and elegant culinary experimentation.

IAN DAGNALL/ALAMY ©

Santa Barbara

8 There's good reason that tourist boards like to refer to the breezy Mediterranea-like shores of Santa Barbara (p509) as the 'American Riviera.' Travelers laze on dreamy stretches of sand, chase a twinkling nightlife and roll along with California's yachting set. Sure, it's fancy, but the stately Spanish mission, steaming plates of seafood and rugged spine of the nearby Santa Ynez Mountains add tactile, historic and culinary depth. A quick escape from the grinding gridlock of neighboring cities, Santa Barbara is SoCal's northern playground.

Rafting the American River

9 It's a bit unfair that the American trumps so many other white-water options in California – it's really three rivers in one. Between the North Fork, Middle Fork and South Fork, the American River (p301) has the potential to wow beginners and surly river rats alike. A great weekend for families, expeditions can be short and simple or full-blown, adrenaline-soaked overnighters. And – bonus! – there are plenty of historic towns on the way home where you can pull off for an ice cream.

Dry Creek Valley & Russian River Area

10 Sonoma County offers idyllic wine-tasting weekends. Many of the winemakers here have espoused sustainable practices that are every bit as visionary as the blends. You'll sample some of the state's best pinot noir and chardonnay in the Russian River Area (p190) and a helluva sauvignon blanc in the Dry Creek Valley (p192). Come during the crushing season in autumn, when the leaves explode with color and the smell of fermenting fruit lingers on the breeze.

Opposite top: Alexander Valley (p193)

10

JERRY ALEXANDER/LONELY PLANET IMAGES ©

Big Sur

11 Cruising at the jagged edge of the continent along the cliffs of Hwy 1 to Big Sur (p473) makes for an unforgettable road trip, and an easy, refreshing breather from the bustle of San Francisco. Between the endless expanse of the Pacific and the rolling hills of the coastal mountains, this is a drive that proves that sometimes the journey is more exciting than the destination. When you tire of the breathtaking views (as if!) you can hike inland trails, wander along the moody shore or soak in the area's hot springs. McWay Falls (p477), Julia Pfeiffer Burns State Park

11

DOUGLAS STEAKLEY/LONELY PLANET IMAGES ©

Highway 395

12 In a state filled with great road trips, Hwy 395 (p34), otherwise known as the Eastern Sierra Scenic Byway, might be the ultimate: a north–south route that runs along the east side of the Sierra Nevada and passes offshoots along the way to both the highest and lowest points in the continental US. You'll cross five jaw-dropping mountain passes and a clutch of must-sees: famous destinations like Mono Lake and Mt Whitney and out-of-the-way delights like the ghost town of Bodie and the rugged Alabama Hills. Below: View of Mt Whitney through an arch in the Alabama Hills

Monterey

13 Home to the best aquarium on the west coast (p460), Monterey has transformed from a fishing and canning hub (Steinbeck's *Cannery Row* was set here) to the Central Coast's most family-friendly destination. Apart from the jellyfish, otters and splash pools of the aquarium's 'indoor ocean,' the agenda for a visit includes a saltwater taffy along the touristy Fisherman's Wharf, a boat trip to see some whales, an amazing kids' park, and forts, missions and other historic buildings from California's Mexican and Spanish periods. Bottom: Monterey Bay Aquarium

12

13

PAUL MOUNCE/CORBIS ©

CHRISTIAN BEIER/CBPICTURES / ALAMY ©

ZACH HOLMES/ALAMY ©/LONELY PLANET IMAGES ©

San Luis Obispo & Paso Robles

14 Although new wine regions seem to pop up every harvest, the rolling hills around San Luis Obispo (p494) and Paso Robles (p492) have maintained their low-key insider feel for the past two decades, even while the region's intense, elegant reds have won the highest international acclaim and the viticulture covers three times the ground of Napa Valley. The network of scenic, sunny drives connects one perfect picnic spot after the next and you'll never be far from a vibrant little college town or the Pacific shore. Top left: Paso Robles

Swimming Holes

15 You're traveling California's back roads on a blazing July day when, in the middle of nowhere, you pass a cluster of cars parked at the side of the road. Don't ask questions – just park, strip and plunge. California's byways are dotted with icy swimming holes that offer welcome reprieve from the summer heat, and those who travel without a swimsuit in the trunk will be sorry. Look for a concentration of swimming spots along Hwy 49 in northern Gold Country, or just ask the locals; floating along on cool currents makes a blissful break from the road. Top right: Merced River (p402), Yosemite National Park

Klamath Basin National Wildlife Refuges

16 Not to take all the thrill of pursuit out of it, but bird-watchers who visit this area (p290) are guaranteed a spectacle – this pit stop on the 'avian superhighway' guarantees migrating traffic at all times of the year. If spotting a semi-palmated sandpiper doesn't quicken your pulse, birds are only a fraction of the fauna in this far-northern region. Near the edges of Lava Beds National Monument (p289) is an overwhelming display of wildlife – vesper bats and mule deer, flying squirrels and marmot. Bottom right: Dawn, Klamath Basin National Wildlife Refuge

Sequoia & Kings Canyon National Parks

17 This is a place of superlatives: with a cleft that's deeper than the Grand Canyon, trees whose mass qualify them as the largest living things on the planet, and pristine backcountry that inspires the rapture of hikers and campers. Caving, climbing and walking through granite-carved landscapes draw visitors to these conjoined national parks (p414), which are over 80% wild. No visit is complete without saying howdy to General Sherman, the granddaddy of all the sequoias and the earth's largest tree by volume. Below left: General Grant Tree (p415), Kings Canyon National Park

Lost Coast

18 Those that thrive on getting to the map's blank spaces have their work cut out for them along the Lost Coast (p241), the longest stretch of undeveloped coastline in the state. This ghostly, abandoned territory is where the Kings Range drops so abruptly into the Pacific Ocean that building a road wasn't feasible. Thank goodness; hiking along foggy shores to observe roaming herds of Roosevelt elk, rusting shipwrecks and limitless horizons makes for a brilliant escape from reality.

17

JOHN ELK III/LONELY PLANET IMAGES ©

18

NICHOLAS PAYLOFF/LONELY PLANET IMAGES ©

JOHN ELK III/LONELY PLANET IMAGES ©

Mt Shasta

19 There's no other pile of rock in California that stirs the imagination quite like Mt Shasta (p278), as it suddenly rises from the Central Valley flatlands. Native tribes believed that a god left heaven to live on its summit, John Muir said it made his 'blood turn to wine,' and an early-20th-century explorer reported a city of mummies 11 miles below its surface. So whether it's the 'energy vortex' felt by today's New Age pilgrims or the spine-tingling chills of hikers summiting its wind-blown peak, this mountain is magical.

Nevada City & Gold Country

20 Judging by a trip through Gold Country (p298), you might think that the '49ers stormed California in search of antiques, lacy B&Bs and ice-cream parlors. These are the contemporary complements to a cruise along Hwy 49 through the picturesque Sierra Nevada foothills. An emerging wine and upscale-dining scene completes the journey, which is easily tailored for honeymooners, history buffs and schoolkids. The northern terminus of the trip is the sparkling and well-preserved Nevada City (p304). Bottom: Broad Street, Nevada City

The Redwood Coast

21 Just spend a few minutes staring agape at the world's tallest tree – the magnificent, ancient coast redwood – from the sun-dappled forest floor of prehistoric ferns, and the trifles of the modern world suddenly gain perspective. The Redwood Coast (p208) may be a long drive from Northern California's conveniences, but this land of giant trees and punishing coastline delivers a wallop. When you come in from the forest, the area's idiosyncratic communities offer drive-thru trees, real-life lumberjacks and a culture that thrives off the grid. Above: Redwood National Park (p256)

Point Reyes National Seashore

22 Only an hour away from the 'burbs of San Francisco, Point Reyes National Seashore (p123) has the North Coast's calling cards on full display: roaring ocean breakers and jagged headlands, grasslands that explode with colorful wildflowers, wide beaches and tide pools seething with life. But in terms of animals, the birds, sea lions and deer are merely the supporting cast. If you take the long staircase down to the Point Reyes lighthouse, it offers your best chance to spy a migrating whale.

Santa Cruz & Capitola

23 There's a lot of spunk in the stretch of coast between Santa Cruz and Capitola, home to surfers, college kids and *nuevo* hippies, a clutch of amazing beaches and a fantastic boardwalk. No trip to this area is complete without at least one bone-rattling ride on the Giant Dipper (p451), a National Historic Landmark that's among the oldest such thrill rides in the nation. The wooden seaside monster makes riders gasp with its expansive bird's-eye view of the Pacific...just before it makes them squeal with delight. Bottom right: Santa Cruz Beach Boardwalk (p451)

Muir Woods

24 The pictures don't do justice to a place like Muir Woods (p119), a national monument where the enormous redwoods grow amongst whispers of coastal fog. Rightly named after California's fiercest conversationalist, it can be visited on a half-day trip from San Francisco. Once you get away from the hordes of Bay Area escapees and get lost on the network of trails, you discover a place that seems timeless. If you want something well timed, find an excuse to end the hike at the German Tourist Club (p118).

Wilderness Camping

25 There's no other place in the US where you can sleep in such a variety of elements: from the high mountain forests of the Trinity Alps (p292), to the lake-dotted landscape of Yosemite National Park and Kings Canyon and the lonely shores of the Lost Coast. All are within a day's drive of one another. Add to the mix California's amazing long-distance hiking trails, like the epic Pacific Crest Trail and John Muir Trail – and dedicated backcountry campers will find paradise.
Bottom: Mt Whitney Trail (p444), Sierra Nevada mountains

THOMAS WINZ/LONELY PLANET IMAGES ©

BRENT WINEBRENNER/LONELY PLANET IMAGES ©

need to know

Currency

» US dollars ($)

Language

» English

When to Go?

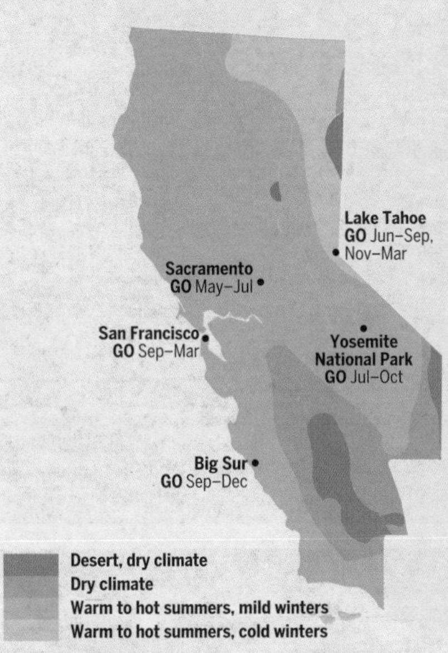

High Season
(Jun–Aug)

» Increased domestic visitors during summer mean accommodations are at their most expensive.

» During holiday weekends prices and competition for accommodations spike.

Shoulder
(Sep–Oct, Mar–May)

» In the fall and spring, prices drop.

» Best time to visit the national parks as they are uncrowded and generally accessible.

Low Season
(Nov–Feb)

» Crowds trickle out in winter as many towns, particularly at higher elevations, are covered with snow.

» Prices spike during winter holidays.

» Lake Tahoe has a high season in mid-November and at end of April.

Your Daily Budget

Budget Less Than

$100

» Fresh, affordable food at farm stands and taco trucks

» Campsites: $20-40; hostels: $25-40

» Look for 'free admission' days at museums

» Use public transportation

Midrange

$100-200

» Two-star motel room: $75-150

» Car rental from $30 per day, plus insurance and gas

Top End More Than

$200

» Single-day rafting trip: $135 per person

» Meal in top restaurant: $60-75 plus wine

» Three-star lodging: from $150

Money

» ATMs and banks widely available. Credit cards required for car and hotel reservations. Checks rarely accepted. Tipping is customary, not optional.

Visas

» Not required for citizens of Visa Waiver Program (VWP) countries with ESTA approval; apply online. Other travelers need a valid US visa.

Cell Phones

» Foreign GSM multiband phones will work in the USA. Prepaid cell phones widely available. Coverage can be spotty in remote areas.

Driving/ Transportation

» Drive on the right; steering wheel is on the left side of the vehicle.

Websites

» **California Travel and Tourism Commission** (www.visitcalifornia.com) Multilingual trip-planning guides.

» **SF Gate Travel** (www.sfgate.com/travel) Travel features and Bay Area getaways.

» **Redwood Hikes** (www.redwoodhikes.com) A guide to walking under old-growth redwood.

» **Lonely Planet** (www.lonelyplanet.com/california) Destination info, travelers' forums and more.

» **California State Parks** (www.parks.ca.gov) Outdoor activities and free e-guides.

Exchange Rates

Australia	A$1	$0.98
Canada	C$1	$0.96
Europe	€1	$1.34
Japan	¥100	$1.29
Mexico	MXN10	$0.71
UK	£1	$1.56

For current exchange rates see www.xe.com.

Important Numbers

Country code	☎1
International access code	☎011
Operator	☎0
Emergency (ambulance, fire & police)	☎911
Directory assistance (local)	☎411

Arriving

» **San Francisco International Airport** (SFO; p102)
BART to downtown ($8.10, 30 minutes)
Door-to-door shuttles ($15 to $20, 24 hours)
Taxis to downtown ($35 to $50, 30 to 50 minutes)

» **Oakland International Airport** (OAK; p132)
AirBART system connects to trains that service the Bay Area
Taxis to downtown SF (about $65)

» **Sacramento International Airport** (SMF; p330)
Good for Yosemite and Gold Country
Capital Corridor trains connect to the Bay Area

The Cloudy Future of California Parks

The future of 70 of California's 278 state parks is in jeopardy due to California's budget crisis. Parks on the list for closure by July 2012 include historic parks such as Jack London State Historic Park and Governor's Mansion State Park, as well as pristine natural parks such a Del Norte Coast Redwoods State Park and Castle Craggs State Park. In September 2011, the State Legislature passed a bill that allows nonprofit organizations to govern the effected parks, allowing public access and providing basic maintenance and infrastructure. Still, barring a miracle, many of the parks on the list will close and travelers should inquire before visiting. See California State Parks website (www.parks.ca.gov) for more information.

if you like...

Majestic Scenery

Thanks to wildly diverse geology and a long history of plucky conservationism, Northern California has a stunning collection of federally protected natural land. From granite spires to geothermic springs, the national parks are among the grandest in the West – and much closer to hand.

Yosemite National Park High meadows and granite domes, this was conservationist John Muir's wonderland (p396)

Lassen Volcanic National Park Find alien lava fields and noxious sulfuric mud pots under the bold, snow-capped Lassen Peak (p269)

Redwood National & State Parks Marvel at trees from prehistory in this patchwork of protected redwoods (p256)

Sequoia & Kings Canyon National Parks Stand agape under canopies of proud, stout sequoia and hike into California's wildest canyon wilderness (p414)

Marin Headlands Within a stones' throw of San Francisco – Northern California's most vibrant city – these dramatic cliffs and foggy shores offer respite from the urban bustle (p105)

History

Northern California's history is fueled by a lust for gold and checkered with dramatic tales of banditry, bravado and utter catastrophe. And who are the storytellers? Heroes, villains and vagabonds from history and literature like Capone, Kerouac, Donner and Twain.

Mission Santa Barbara The 'Queen of the Missions' includes a cemetery with 4000 Chumash graves (p509)

Sutter's Fort State Historic Park Smack dab in the center of the state capital, this historic fort is a glimpse of California's first military settlements (p324)

Alcatraz 'The Rock' – America's first military prison – awaits within tempting distance of the San Francisco skyline (p75)

Angel Island An immigration station, WWII Japanese internment camp and Nike missile site, this windswept island in the Bay is a history buff's treasure trove (p115)

Manzanar National Historic Site Commemorates the Japanese Americans who were interned here during WWII (p442)

Small Towns

Big cities in Northern California may have cultural bustle, but the little one-stop light towns offer deliriously charming main streets, captivating history and enough ice-cream parlors for several lifetimes.

Ferndale Scramble to the top of the historic hilltop cemetery overlooking this charming North Coast dairy capital, home to picturesque Victorian-era 'butterfat mansions' (p245)

Angels Camp Mark Twain's big break came writing about a contest of jumping frogs here, and the town still buzzes with rowdy Gold Rush history (p316)

Weaverville In the shadow of the majestic Trinity Alps, this tiny berg has an ancient Chinese temple, access to rugged outdoors and stunning nature in every direction. Don't expect traffic – there isn't a stop light in the entire county (p292)

Boonville Exquisite food, stylish historic lodging and thriving wineries make a brilliant escape from the Bay Area. Did we mention the killer brewery? Or that the locals invented their own language? (p232)

SABRINA DALBESIO/LONELY PLANET IMAGES ©

» Rainforests of the World dome at the California Academy of Sciences

Lakes

Sure, the moody waters of the Pacific draw throngs of travelers to the NorCal coast, but the region's inland lakes are deep blue treasures which offer a little rare solitude (and sometimes even an icy swim).

Lake Tahoe From the edge of the lapping waves in the summer to the top of a powdery ski run in the winter, Tahoe's unbelievably blue waters make visitors gasp (p351)

Shasta Lake Here you can party with 10 of your best friends on a house boat or find tranquility while hiking along endless miles of shore (p267)

Eagle Lake Want some space to be truly alone? Venture where few others tread, navigating gorgeous two-lane roads to the pristine area surrounding the state's second-largest natural lake (p275)

Mono Lake The alien rock formations of this seething volcanic landscape are dramatic and surreal – forget swimming, there are hot springs! (p430)

Tenaya Lake This sparkling oasis welcomes you to the granite-carved high country of Yosemite National Park, a place some call heaven (p398)

Museums

If the drippy weather drives you inside, the consolation is some exceptional (and exceptionally weird) museums. Northern California's museums house everything from priceless art and Gold Rush folklore to displays on Bigfoot.

MH de Young Memorial Museum Copper-skinned temple to art from around the globe in San Francisco's Golden Gate Park (p70)

California Academy of Sciences San Francisco's natural-history museum and aquarium breathes 'green' in its eco-certified design, with a four-storey rainforest and living roof (p70)

San Francisco Museum of Modern Art (SFMOMA) Cutting-edge photography, including many of the great photographers of the 20th century, and new media works in SoMa (p64)

Laws Railroad Museum Railroad and Old West aficionados love the original 1883 train depot (p438)

Live Music

The summer of love may be long gone, but the sound of Northern California's music makers is still loud and proud. San Francisco enjoys the lion's share of the action, but a lively festival circuit reverberates in every corner of the region.

The Fillmore This is the house that Bill Graham built in the '60s, and one look at the posters of past bills – from The Dead and The Doors to Radiohead and Adele – will blow a music fan's mind (p96)

Yoshi's Locations on both sides of the Bay have doubled the capacity of the best jazz venue on the West Coast (p96)

Cafe du Nord All red velvet and heady drinks, this subterranean club is the classiest place in Northern California to catch acts on the rise (p97)

Buck Owens' Crystal Palace Shine up your boots and don your pressed jeans at this, the premier country venue in the Central Valley. It's a monument to the legendary king of the Bakersfield Sound. (p348)

High Sierra Music Festival Thank goodness this top-notch folk and jam band festival is in the middle of nowhere – if it were any easier to get here it'd be mobbed by fans (p276)

» Gay and lesbian parade in San Francisco during Pride Month

Skinny Dippin'

Don't be shy. There's no place for modesty when it comes to taking a dip in Northern California's amazing collection of au naturel hot springs and swimming spots.

Orr Hot Springs A great place to camp, connect with your inner hippie and soak in thermal waters, this is within a quick drive of the Bay Area (p236)

Esalen Institute Big Sur's blissful retreat is spendy, but the memory of soaking in a bath on a ledge over the crashing Pacific will last a lifetime (p477)

Finnish Country Sauna & Tubs Private open-air redwood tubs and a classy European vibe make this an idyllic North Coast soak (p251)

Baker Beach Global warming be damned; there are goose bumps galore at San Francisco's clothing-optional dip in the Pacific (p64)

Bidwell Park The swimming holes nearby offer a secluded plunge (p335)

Mind-Bending Festivals

Northern Californians love a big party, and the area is host to some of the most wild, wacky and wonderful festivals in the nation. Not for the xenophobic, these festivals are as diverse as the crowds who gather.

Hardly Strictly Bluegrass San Francisco's best free music festival hosts three days of A-list folk, rock, bluegrass and country artists. (p76)

Reggae On the River In the heart of Humboldt County, this music event is all dreadlocks and Jamaican-influenced jams. No, that's not a skunk you smell (p240)

Burning Man The furthest-out of all far-out festivals, this trippy art party in the desert is a dusty, anything-goes affair (p445)

San Francisco Pride Month A delightfully gay affair – in every sense of the word – San Francisco celebrates a month of pride (p75)

Beautiful Coastline

Northern California's coast is a temperamental beauty – astonishingly picturesque, wildly rugged and prone to dramatic mood swings. A visit to the coast offers huge rewards.

Julia Pfeiffer Burns State Park It's tough to pick a favorite among Big Sur's coast sights, but this remote crescent-shaped beach gem is a stunner (p477)

Point Reyes National Seashore Migrating whales and squawking sea birds, excellent hikes and pristine coastline (p123)

Redwood Coast Mysterious and majestic, this wild coast of big trees and brooding surf feels like it is lost in time (p238)

Sonoma State Beaches A road trip up Hwy 1 past these hidden coves could keep a beachcomber busy for years (p213)

Santa Barbara Warm sand beaches with potential for celeb-spotting (p509)

month by month

Top Events

1 **California State Fair**, July

2 **North Lake Tahoe SnowFest**, March

3 **Pride Month**, June

4 **Mendocino Coast Whale Festivals**, March

5 **Burning Man Festival**, August

January

Typically the wettest month, January is a slow time for coastal travel. Mountain ski resorts are busy and skies over the Bay Area are gray.

Chinese New Year

San Francisco's Chinatown sounds like a warzone, as firecrackers announce the lunar new year (p75). Usually in late January or early February, there are parades, lion dances and street vendors.

March

Less rain brings travelers back to the coast searching for whales. Ski season begins to wind down.

North Lake Tahoe SnowFest

Held at the peak of the Tahoe winter season, this wild affair couples excellent powder conditions with costume parties, ski competitions, a parade and an '80s Hot Dog Retro Party.

Mendocino Coast Whale Festivals

As the north-bound winter migration of gray whales peaks, Mendocino (p221), Fort Bragg and the surrounding area fill up three weekends in March with food and wine tasting, art shows, marine-mammal educational exhibits and naturalist-guided walks and talks.

April

Shoulder season in the mountains and along the coast means lower hotel prices, but not during spring break, which is usually around Easter.

Stockton Asparagus Festival

A noteworthy celebration (p341) of stinky little green stalks. Where else on earth are you going to find asparagus ice cream?

San Francisco International Film Festival

The Americas' longest-running film festival (p75) has been lighting up San Francisco since 1957, with over 150 independent-minded films, including provocative premieres from around the globe in late April and early May.

May

Weather heats up statewide, although some coastal areas remain blanketed by fog. The Memorial Day weekend is the official start of summer, and among the year's busiest travel times.

Bay to Breakers

Jog in costume during San Francisco's annual pilgrimage (p75) from the Embarcadero to Ocean Beach on the third Sunday in May. Watch out for participants dressed as salmon, who run 'upstream' from the finish line!

Kinetic Grand Championship

Over Memorial Day weekend, this 'triathlon of the art world' (p251) merits a three-day, 38-mile race from Arcata to Ferndale. Competitors outdo each other in inventing human-powered, self-propelled contraptions to make the journey.

June

With school out for the summer, families travel and everywhere in Northern California gets busy. Some coastal fog lingers, pulled in by the Central Valley's heat.

Pride Month

Out and proud since 1970, San Francisco's big, bawdy celebrations (p75) take place throughout June, with costumed parades, coming-out parties, live music, DJs and more. It's one of the city's most joyful events.

July

In the peak of summer, the trails of Yosemite get crowded and the valley gets scorching hot. July 4th is the summer's peak weekend, and many of the towns in the region have street fairs and fireworks.

California State Fair

A million people come to pet pigs and cheer horse races, browse the blue-ribbons, and taste California wines and microbrews. The special events – like concerts and bull riding – draw huge crowds to Sacramento's State Fair grounds for two weeks at the end of July (p329).

Reggae on the River

Come party with the 'Humboldt Nation' of hippies, Rastafarians, tree huggers and other beloved NorCal eccentrics for two days of live reggae bands, arts and crafts, barbecue, juggling, unicycling, camping and swimming in mid-July (p240).

August

Warm weather keeps beaches busy, even though school summer vacations wind down

Strawberry Festival at Monterey Bay

The messy marquee event (p465) at this Watsonville festival is the pie-eating contest, but live music and tons of fruit entertain families. The food comes fresh from the region which produces almost 90% of the strawberries in the US.

Humboldt County Fair

This is a classic county fair (p245) with a traditionalist flourish. Hosted in the picturesque Victorian village of Ferndale, it's been running annually since 1869.

Burning Man

Although the festival (p445) takes place in the high desert of Nevada, it draws throngs of Northern Californians with a taste for tripping out in an arty, utopian free-for-all. Make arrangements well in advance and be prepared for a mind-bending experience.

September

Summer's last hurrah is the Labor Day holiday weekend; travel peaks. After kids go back to school, cities start seeing fewer visitors.

Monterey Jazz Festival

A roster of iconic artists and young jazz visionaries arrive to play one of the world's longest-running jazz festivals (p465), featuring outdoor concerts and more intimate indoor shows over a long weekend in mid-September.

October

Even with balmy weather, things quieten down. Travel deals abound along the coast and in cities; mountains begin to cool.

Vineyard Festivals

California's wine counties celebrate bringing in the harvest from the vineyards with star chef food-and-wine shindigs, grape-stomping 'crush' parties and barrel tastings, with some events starting earlier in September.

Litquake

San Francisco's edgy literary festival (p76) features readings, storytelling hours, workshops, author appearances, guided walking tours and a 'LitCrawl' in the Mission district.

November

Temperatures drop everywhere, and scattered snowstorms begin. Coastal areas and cities are less busy, except around the Thanksgiving holiday. Ski season starts.

Día de los Muertos

Mexican communities honor ancestors on November 2 with costumed parades, sugar skulls, graveyard picnics and candlelight processions. Join the colorful festivities (p76) in San Francisco's Mission District.

Whether you've got six days or 60, these itineraries provide a starting point for the trip of a lifetime. Want more inspiration? Head online to lonelyplanet.com/thorntree to connect with other travelers.

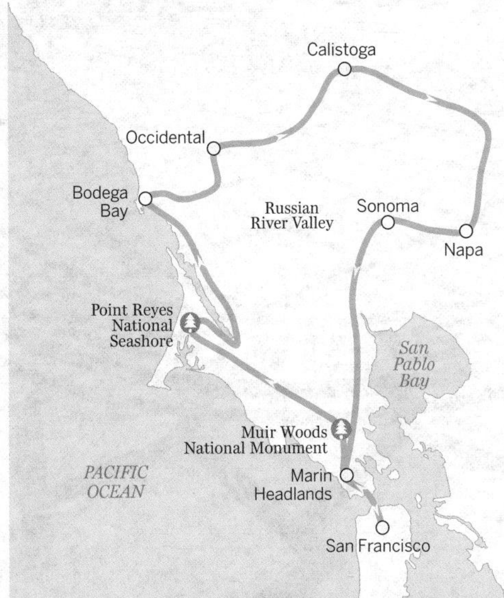

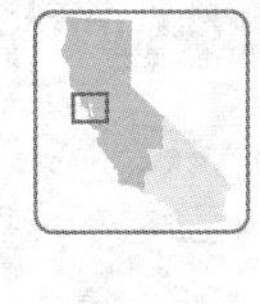

Five Days to One Week

San Francisco, Marin County & Wine Country

With its hills and streetcars, ocean views and vibrant counterculture, **San Francisco** is an instant charmer. Wander though the alleyways of Chinatown and past Beat-poet hangouts in North Beach. Take in boldly colored murals and amazing cheap eats in the Mission District, or Golden Gate Park, where manicured gardens and museums now decorate the trippy epicenter of 1967's Summer of Love.

Cross the iconic **Golden Gate Bridge** to the **Marin Headlands**, where you can hike cliffs above the Pacific and catch the ferry back to the city. Or keep going north, where the region's natural beauty delivers a one-two punch with towering redwoods in **Muir Woods National Monument** and the wildly beautiful **Point Reyes National Seashore**.

Beyond **Bodega Bay** country roads wind through **Occidental** and **Russian River Valley** vineyards. Truck east across Hwy 101 to soak in the thermal waters of **Calistoga**, then head south to meander around the nation's most renowned Wine Country, pausing for a meal in chic **Napa** or its darling country cousin **Sonoma** before looping back to San Francisco.

CAROL POLICH/LONELY PLANET IMAGES ©

» (above) Neptune Pool, Hearst Ca (p481)
» (left) Enjoying the view at Yosemi National Park (p396)

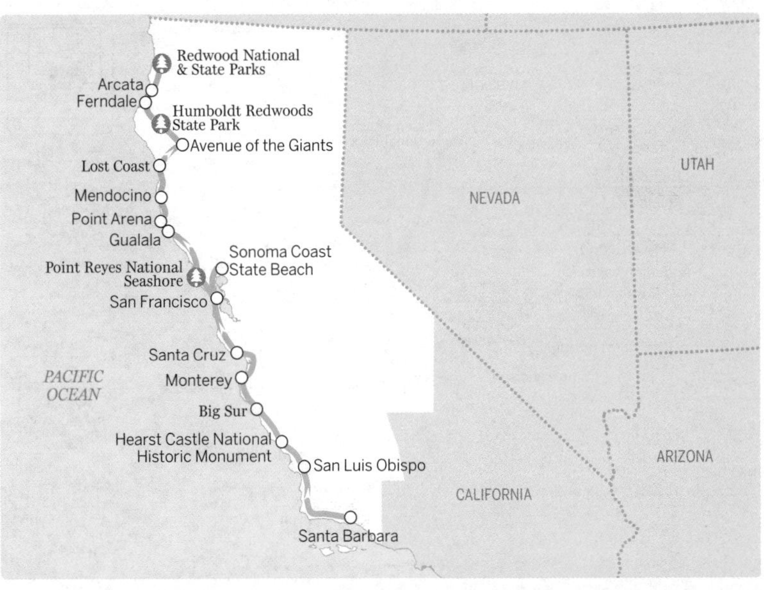

One Week

Up the Coast

The serpentine two-lane stretch of Hwy 1 between Santa Barbara and the Oregon border is among Northern California's most epic escapes, offering cute two-stoplight towns, dramatic cliffs, migrating whales and majestic redwood groves.

Begin tracing the edge of the continent in **Santa Barbara**, pause for a laid-back lunch in the college town of **San Luis Obispo** before touring the stately **Hearst Castle National Historic Monument**. North of the castle is one of America's most famous drives, along the **Big Sur** coast. There's lots of photo ops, so take things slow, being sure to mug for a picture at the **Bixby Bridge**. Now, choose your adventure: either the best aquarium in the west at **Monterey** or a classic, bone-rattling roller coaster on the boardwalk at **Santa Cruz**. Perhaps both.

You've finally reached **San Francisco**, the thrilling urban centerpiece of the trip. When you're ready to get out of town, continue north to **Point Reyes National Seashore** or the **Sonoma Coast State Beach** for a day picnicking by the tide pools and scanning the waters for migrating whales. This is where the coast gets truly wild, with wind-swept bluffs and white-knuckle driving. When you break from the road, you can rough it under redwoods at a campground in **Gualala** or choose the plush option, beside a crackling fire at bed and breakfasts near **Point Arena**.

Over the next few days, make your way north slowly, stopping for at least a day enjoying the boutiques and organic fine dining at the stunning seaside village of **Mendocino**. Those with more time to kill can hike a bit on the **Lost Coast** before heading inland for the region's best short drive, the **Avenue of the Giants**.

From there, travelers are treated to one amazing grove of monstrous trees after another, beginning with **Humboldt Redwoods State Park**, which has the greatest concentration of old-growth trees in the world. Pass through the adorable towns of the far north, like the Victorian village of **Ferndale** and the wild-at-heart, weed-growing hub of **Arcata**, before returning to the patchwork groves of **Redwood National and State Parks**.

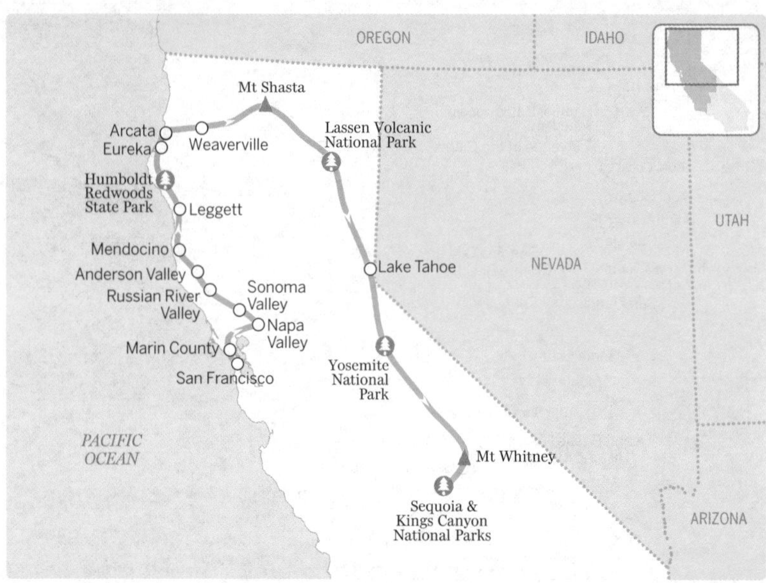

Two to Three Weeks

Northern California Classics

Kick off with a dose of big-city culture in **San Francisco**, sitting proudly on its often foggy bay. Bite into inspiring California cooking at the Ferry Building market, then hop a boat over to infamous Alcatraz prison, aka 'The Rock.' For panoramic bay views, it's all aboard a cable car before getting lost in verdant Golden Gate Park.

Head north over the arched Golden Gate Bridge into outdoorsy **Marin County**. California's most famous grapes grow nearby in the rustic **Russian River Valley**, burgeoning **Sonoma Valley** and chichi **Napa Valley**. Detour west through the boondocks of the hidden **Anderson Valley**, jumping on Hwy 1 north to **Mendocino**, a postcard-perfect Victorian oceanfront town.

Work your way north to rejoin Hwy 101 at **Leggett**, where your magical mystery tour of the Redwood Coast really begins. In **Humboldt Redwoods State Park** encounter some of the tallest trees on earth along the Avenue of the Giants. Relax in harborfront **Eureka**, with its candy-colored Victorian architecture, or its far more funky, radical northern neighbor, **Arcata**.

Turn east on Hwy 299 for a long, supremely scenic trip through Gold Rush–era **Weaverville**, skirting around the lake-studded Trinity Alps. Head north on I-5 to **Mt Shasta**. Pay your respects to this majestic mountain, then cut southeast on Hwy 89 to unearthly **Lassen Volcanic National Park**, a hellishly beautiful world in the volcanic Cascade Range.

Keep trucking southeast on Hwy 89 to **Lake Tahoe**, a four-seasons outdoor playground and mountain resort. Roll down the Eastern Sierra's Hwy 395, taking the back-door route via high-country Tioga Rd (closed in winter and spring) into **Yosemite National Park**. Gape at waterfalls tumbling over soaring granite cliffs.

This whirlwind tour of Northern California ends in befittingly oversized style. Take the scenic drive down Hwy 395, with short detours to the highest and lowest places in the contiguous US: **Mt Whitney** and Death Valley, respectively. Finally, end at **Sequoia & Kings Canyon National Parks**, where visitors wander among groves of giant sequoias, the world's biggest trees.

Road Trips & Scenic Drives

Driving Times & Distances from San Francisco

The following time estimations don't account for traffic or sightseeing detours.

Napa Valley 47 miles, 1¼ hours

Yosemite National Park 165 miles, 3½ hours

Redwood National Park 330 miles, six hours

Sequoia and Kings Canyon National Parks 265 miles, five hours

Point Reyes Lighthouse 55 miles, 2½ hours

South Lake Tahoe 186 miles, 3½ hours

Hearst Castle via Big Sur 213 miles, 4¾ hours

Sacramento 87 miles, 1½ hours

Nevada City via Hwy 49 220 miles, 4½ hours

Bakersfield via Hwy 99 300 miles, 5½ hours

Avenue of the Giants 235 miles, 4½ hours

Oregon border via Hwy 1 426 miles, 10 hours

Northern California is irresistible for road trippers – and this selection below outlines the very best. Gas up and get ready for your jaw to drop, from the coastal drives along Hwy 1 and the sun-washed vineyards of the region's wine countries, to the towering redwoods of the North Coast and the granite monoliths of the Sierra Nevada. Thankfully, that rental car has unlimited miles.

For more drives in a particular region, check the destination chapters.

Big Sur

You know the image from car commercials and daydreams in the cubicle: the winding two-lane strip of pavement that drops into the Pacific and traces the edge of the continent. Ancient forests, rocky cliffs and dizzying views make the drive between San Luis Obispo and Monterey an unforgettable experience.

Why Go

Lean into the endless curves of Hwy 1, scan limitless ocean views and pull over to soak in the sights; if it's your first trip here or your 50th, a trip along the Big Sur coast will blow your mind. Sunny or shrouded in fog, the views are spectacular – the iconic Bixby Creek Bridge, the Point Sur Lighthouse, and endless bluffs, tide pools and rocky islands. Don't dare rush; enjoy each pull-off to let the salty Pacific air rejuvenate your soul.

This is a part of Northern California that is as much a state of mind as it is a geographic location – since the late '40s it's been an irresistible home to artists, writers and alternative lifestylers of every stripe. The prices are not friendly to the starving artist these days, but vigilant protection has allowed Big Sur to keep the stunning nature at center stage: no high-rise hotels, no big cities or subdivisions. Cell-phone service? Forget it. You'll be grateful to coax a couple of $20s from a dial-up ATM.

But who needs cash when the best stuff is free? Visitors scramble along the road's edge to spy lazing sea lions, hike inland hills through old-growth forests and come away rejuvenated.

When to Go

Late September to late November is when the skies are clearest. The summers are dense with fog.

The Route

Although it's only about 135 miles between San Luis Obispo and Monterey, this serpentine drive takes at least three hours. Those who pull over to check out the sights should plan on a full day. North of Monterey, Hwy 1

Road Trips & Scenic Drives

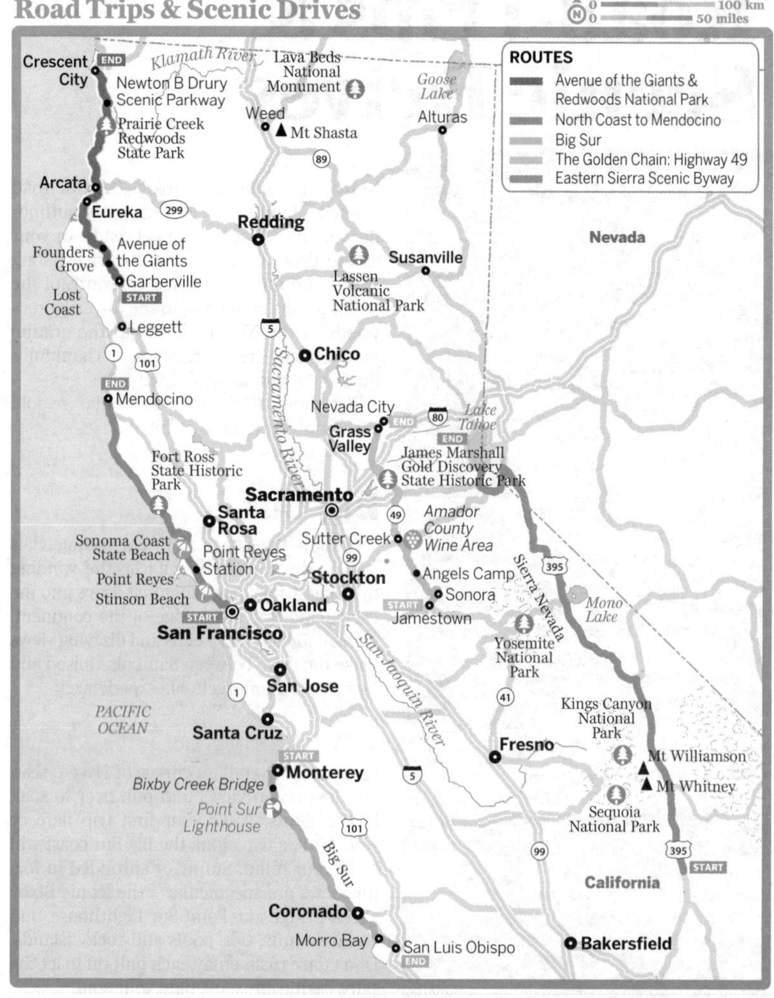

connects to Hwy 101, which cuts inland and connects to San Francisco.

Worthy Detour

Stop in Santa Cruz and take a wild ride on the Giant Dipper, a historic wooden rollercoaster that overlooks the glittering boardwalk and a sea of sunbathers.

Time & Mileage

Distance: 135 miles
Time: At least three hours

North Coast to Mendocino

Sure, everyone wants to take a trip along the Big Sur coast, but the trip north is equally scenic, far less populated and studded with cute little seaside villages. The terrain here is stunning, with fields dotted with dairy cows and dazzling flowers rambling to the edge of cliffs overlooking the ocean. Come at the right time of year and you may also see a whale.

Why Go

The North Coast offers a cultured counterpoint to the coastal drama of a trip along Big Sur, and allows a much more intimate experience. Visitors spend days beachcombing in hidden coves, eat sustainably farmed fine dining and retire at night to fire-warmed cottages with bottles of exceptional local wine.

Just over the Golden Gate Bridge, the wonders of the North Coast begin to show up in spades. There's the rhythmic tide of the Pacific that invites a stroll (or, if the weather is right, some sunbathing) on Stinson Beach. Then there are the boutiques and gourmet eateries of picture-perfect Point Reyes Station and the dense green trails and wildlife of the Point Reyes National Seashore. The view from the Point Reyes lighthouse is a stunner, and it's the best place on the North Coast to spot whales.

Continue north for an endless string of adorable fishing towns and unique hideaways. The Sonoma Coast State Beach has scores of wind-sheltered coves, and other curious detours include Fort Ross State Historic Park, once the southernmost outpost of imperial Russia. End in Mendocino, a historic town that's perched on a stunning bluff over the ocean and packed with plush bed and breakfasts.

When to Go

Weather along the North Coast is fairly consistent, with the clearest skies between late June and early September.

The Route

Take Hwy 101 north across the Golden Gate Bridge and go north on Hwy 1 to Mendocino. For a quicker return to San Francisco, cut inland on Hwy 128 and connect with Hwy 101.

Worthy Detour

Fort Bragg, the somewhat utilitarian sister city to Mendocino, hosts the Mendocino Coast Botanical Garden, where there are beautiful, informative and downright surreal displays on California flora.

Time & Mileage

Distance: 170 miles
Time: One to three days

The Golden Chain: Highway 49

That highway number is no coincidence: it commemorates the '49ers who came to get rich in California's Gold Rush. These days the road connects the historic towns and rolling hills of Gold Country with opportunities to rush Class III white water and sip full-bodied zinfandel.

Why Go

You'll combine a trip to the heart of California's wild youth with some of the state's contemporary treasures: wine, white water and wilderness. An adventure along Hwy 49 traces the turf of gold-rushing '49ers, and when the heat of the blistering sun is too much, you can duck into the region's fascinating (often taxidermy-stuffed) history museums.

Tour the rusting beasts on display at Jamestown's Railtown 1897 State Historic Park, or Angels Camp, where feisty Mark Twain impersonators wander the streets. Amador and El Dorado Counties have California's boldest young wineries: hand over the keys and uncork one of the zinfandels, which thrive in the dry foothills. Spend a few hours in the park where James Marshall discovered gold before taking an afternoon white-water expedition of the American River.

End the trip in Nevada City – the gem of Gold Country is a heady blend of Old West and new-age kitsch. Gas lamps line its narrow streets as a romantic nod to the gilded riches of yesteryear, while a thriving contemporary arts scene reminds visitors of Northern California's enduring riches.

When to Go

Late May to mid-June and September to November. The summer is busy and *very* hot, but it's a perfect opportunity to enjoy the region's icy swimming holes.

The Route

Start in Jamestown and follow Hwy 49 all the way north to Nevada City, or do this trip in reverse. Both ends of the trip have major highways connecting Hwy 49 to the Bay Area and points east.

Time & Mileage

Distance: 127 miles
Time: Half a day to two days

Avenue of the Giants & Redwood National Park

Sure, it's short – only 32 miles – but venturing under the canopy of the tallest trees on earth is anything but underwhelming. This scenic trip parallels Hwy 101 through Humboldt Redwoods State Park and will inspire wonder in even the most road-weary traveler.

Why Go

There are few road trips that confront the traveler with such visceral reminders of nature's splendor. The giant redwoods of Northern California are the largest trees in the world and under their majestic, unfathomable size, it's impossible not to be gobsmacked.

Begin the trip in Garberville, where you can get stick-to-your-ribs fare and chat up the mix of loggers, weed farmers and back-to-the-landers who somehow manage to coexist in this rustic little community. Just north, exit at the Avenue of the Giants, to commune with trees that were seedlings during the Byzantine Empire (the oldest are up to 2000 years old, the young 'uns are merely 500). The half-mile stroll through the Founder's Grove is a great way to cool the engine before connecting to the Newton B Drury Scenic Parkway, which passes under the groves of the Prairie Creek Redwoods State Park, part of the Redwood National & State Parks system. Although ample possibilities for detours exist all the way north to the Oregon border, the trip ends in Crescent City, a perfectly serviceable (if somewhat uninspired) hub for exploring even more old-growth redwood.

When to Go

Year-round, but count yourself lucky if you drive it on a sunny morning, when sunlight glints off dew-laden ferns.

The Route

Take Hwy 101 to the Avenue of the Giants/State Rte 254 exit. Rejoin Hwy 101 just south of Rio Dell. Take Hwy 101 through Eureka and Arcata before taking exit 753 for the

ODDITIES OF THE NORTHERN COAST

Giant Paul Bunyan A gargantuan lumberjack robotically waves hello at Trees of Mystery. On weekends Paul even cracks wise (via a loudspeaker) at visitors ambling in from the parking lot. (p258).

Drive-Thru Trees Conflicted conservationists can still navigate their Chevy through the belly of a redwood. There are – count 'em – *three* opportunities to do so along the North Coast. (p243).

California's Smallest Licensed Bar Order a martini on the open water aboard the *Madaket*, America's oldest continuously operating passenger vessel (p247).

Confusion Hill Bring the camera for this classic stop, a clapper-trap complex of slanting floors, skewed perspectives and corny delights (p238).

20 GREAT TRIPS FROM THE BAY AREA

DESTINATION	APPROXIMATE DISTANCE/TIME FROM SAN FRANCISCO	GOOD FOR	BEST TIME TO GO	PAGE
Arcata	280mi/5hr	Political radicals, redwoods, wild college vibe	Year-round	p250
Bear Valley	160mi/3hr	Skiing, sledding, snowshoeing	Dec-Apr	p413
Big Sur	150mi/3hr	Picturesque coastline, amazing drive	Sep-Nov	p473
Blossom Trail	200mi/3.5hr	Fruit trees in bloom, roadside stands, small farm towns	late Feb–mid-Mar	p346
Gualala	155mi/3hr	B&Bs, beachcombing, whale-watching	Apr-Nov	p216
Lake Tahoe	190mi/3½-5hr to Truckee	Swimming, boating, camping, hiking, gambling	Jun-Sep	p351
Lost Coast	230mi/4.5hr	Hiking, deserted beaches, sea lions	Jun-Oct	p245
Mendocino	155mi/3¼hr	Art, B&Bs, Skunk Train, wine tasting	Jun-Oct	p223
Monterey	115mi/2hr	Aquarium, boutiques & rugged coastline	Year-round	p460
Mt Shasta	276mi/5hr	Climbing, camping, mystical retreats, swimming	Jul-Sep	p278
Murphys	142mi/2¾hr	Old West sites, wine tasting, caverns, near snow in winter	Year-round	p317
Nevada City	148mi/2½hr	Gold Rush sites, wine tasting, swimming holes	May-Sep	p304
Russian River Area	65mi/1.5hr	Wine tasting, cycling, winding road to the Pacific	Year-round	p189
San Luis Obispo & Paso Robles	233mi/4hr	College nightlife, rolling hills, art, Hearst Castle, wine tasting	Sep-Nov	p494
Santa Cruz	75mi/1.5-2hr	Beaches, kids' stuff, wine tasting, roller-coasters	Jun-Oct	p451
Sonoma Coast	45mi/1hr	Hidden coves, surfing, B&Bs	Year-round	p217
Sonoma Valley	45mi/1.5hr	Small wineries, hiking, excellent food	Mar-Nov	p178
South Lake Tahoe ski resorts	186mi/3½hr	Skiing, snowboarding, sledding, snowshoeing	Dec-Apr	p354
Trinity River Scenic Byway	217mi/4hr	Hiking, camping, mountain towns	Jun-Oct	p291
Yosemite Valley	190mi/3½-4hr	Hiking, camping, snowshoe-ing, wildlife-watching	Year-round	p397

Newton B Drury Scenic Parkway. Follow it north, reconnecting with Hwy 101 to Crescent City.

Worthy Detour

The Victorian village of Ferndale is a pastoral beauty with 'butterfat mansions,' cute shops and an amazing annual fair. The village is just a short jog off the Avenue of the Giants.

Time & Mileage

Distance: 155 miles
Time: Two days

Eastern Sierra Scenic Byway

From Lake Tahoe, the mountainous US Hwy 395 traces the rough and rugged back side of the Sierra Nevada, passing the otherworldly tufa columns of Mono Lake, dense pine forests, crystalline alpine lakes and hot springs galore.

Why Go

Forget the heavily traveled routes up and down California's length; the mountains and deserts, boulder-strewn fields and unending pines of this drive are a whole lot prettier than cruising north staring at the back of an 18-wheeler on I-5. You'll skirt the highest and lowest points in the lower 48 states (Mt Whitney and Death Valley, respectively – connected by CA 190) and three national parks.

Along the way is also the heartbreaking Manzanar National Historic Site, which was where 10,000 people of Japanese ancestry were interned during WWII.

The rest of the route is riddled with other stop-offs, from the Ancient Bristlecone Pine Forest, which has some of the oldest living trees on the planet (one named Methuselah has been around over 4750 years) to the bizarre volcanic formations at Mono Lake and Devils Postpile. To unwind from all the action, spend an afternoon soaking in one of the area's hot springs, before climbing up over the glorious ridges of Yosemite's backcountry and back to civilization.

When to Go

To avoid snow and road closures on the high passes, go between July and October.

The Route

Connect with Hwy 395 east of Bakersfield and travel north to reach CA 120, which goes west through Yosemite National Park.

Worthy Detour

Keep going north to end the trip at the brilliantly blue Lake Tahoe.

Time & Mileage

Distance: 250 miles
Time: Three days

Northern California Camping & Outdoors

Best Times to Go

Camping May to September
Cycling and mountain-biking June to October
Hiking April to October
Kayaking, snorkeling and diving June to October
Rock climbing April to October
Surfing September to November
Swimming July to August
Whale-watching January to March
White-water rafting April to October

Northern California's Ultimate Outdoor Experiences

Cycling the Pacific Coast Hwy
Backpacking the John Muir Trail and summiting Mt Whitney
White-water rafting American River, and Cherry Creek on the Upper Tuolumne River
Mountain-biking around Downieville and Marin County
Rock climbing in Yosemite Valley
Whale-watching in Bodega Bay
Surfing Mavericks, Bolinas or Santa Cruz

Mountains, rivers and vast wilderness set the stage for Northern California's all-seasons outdoor adventures. Visitors hike among high alpine meadows in early summer, mountain-bike through fiery fall foliage and schuss down deep powder in the winter. Although the water is too chilly for carefree swimming, hearty souls also take to the North Coast's waters (usually in a wetsuit) to surf, kayak and scout for whales.

Camping

Northern California's camping opportunities are among the best in the country, spoiling campers with an array of riches. Those who get into the backcountry have the biggest rewards – pitching their tents beside alpine lakes and streams with solitary views of snaggle-toothed Sierra Nevada peaks, or taking shelter underneath redwoods, the tallest trees on earth, from Big Sur north to the Oregon border. Those who are car camping or seeing the state by RV (recreational vehicle) have a slightly less private stay in store – California's state-park system is heavily used. Still, there are amazing choices among the region's state, county and nationally managed campgrounds, particularly if you're willing to drive a few extra miles. Even RVs are sometimes accommodated at some of the superbasic (but often free!) national-forest campgrounds. If you didn't bring a tent, you can rent or buy camping gear in most cities – the best deals are at **REI** (www.rei.com) in San Francisco and Sacramento.

Campground Types & Amenities

Primitive campsites The cheapest; many are seldom full. Usually have fire pits, picnic tables and access to drinking water and vault toilets. Most common in USFS-managed national forests and on Bureau of Land Management (BLM) land.

Developed campgrounds Typically found in state and national parks, with more amenities, including flush toilets, barbecue grills and occasionally hot showers and coin-op laundry. May need reservations.

RV hookups and dump stations Available at many privately owned campgrounds, but only a few public-lands campgrounds.

Private campgrounds Cater mainly to RVers. Offer hot showers, swimming pools, wi-fi and family camping cabins; tent sites may be few, exposed and uninviting. Typically more expensive than developed public campgrounds and usually not as nice.

Walk-in (environmental) sites More peace and privacy; a few public-lands campgrounds reserve these for long-distance hikers and cyclists.

Hiker/biker sites Along the coast the 'hiker/biker' sites are the best value for those traveling the slow way along Hwy 1. While occasionally crowded, they reward two-wheel travelers and hikers with excellent sites.

Seasons, Rates & Reservations

Many campgrounds, especially in the mountains and at high elevation, are closed from late fall through early spring. Actual opening and closing dates vary each year, depending on weather. Private campgrounds are often open year-round, especially those closest to cities, beaches and major highways. Unfortunately, these also have the least natural charm.

Many public and private campgrounds accept reservations for all or some of their sites, while a few are strictly first-come, first-served. Overnight rates range from free for the most primitive campsites to $45 or more for pull-through RV sites with full hookups. The best deals are always with USFS campgrounds and in the national forests of the Northern Mountains. Check with a ranger station before plopping down the tent, but an astonishing amount of land in the Plumas, Lassen, Mendocino, Modoc, Trinity and Shasta National Forests allows camping for no fee whatsoever. If you decide to go this route, always have a good supply of water on hand.

These agencies let you search for campground locations and amenities, check availability and reserve campsites online:

Recreation.gov (☎518-885-3639, 877-444-6777; www.recreation.gov) Camping and cabin reservations for national parks, national forests, BLM land etc.

ReserveAmerica (☎916-638-5883, 800-444-7275; www.reserveamerica.com) Reservations for California state parks, East Bay regional parks and some private campgrounds.

Kampgrounds of America (KOA; http://koa.com) National chain private campgrounds offering full facilities (usually a swimming pool) and services for RVs.

ADVANCE RESERVATIONS THAT ARE WORTH IT

» Wrights Beach State Park – Easy car camping, right on a sandy stretch of the North Coast

» Angel Island State Park – Select few enjoy a stunning view of the San Francisco skyline from an island in the bay

» Yosemite backcountry – Trailhead permits for popular backcountry camps fill months in advance

» Limekiln State Park – One of the best camping options on Big Sur, with only 24 sites

Cycling & Mountain-Biking

Strap on that helmet! Northern California is outstanding cycling territory, no matter whether you're off for a leisurely spin along the beach, an adrenaline-fueled mountain ride or a multiday bike-touring coastal adventure. The cycling season runs year-round in most coastal areas, but in the winter the mountains will be snow-covered and bikers have to deal with coastal rain.

Road Rules

» In national and state parks bicycles are usually limited to paved and dirt roads and are not allowed on trails or in designated wilderness areas.

» Most national forests and BLM lands are open to mountain-bikers. Stay on established tracks and always yield to hikers and horseback riders.

» For road-cycling rules, rental rates, purchase tips, emergency roadside assistance and transporting your bike, see p565.

Best Places to Cycle

» In the summer, Hwy 1 is a heavily traveled route for cycle tourism on the **North Coast**, especially the dizzying stretch through **Big Sur**.

» In Northern California's bike-friendly **San Francisco**, you can cruise through Golden Gate Park and over the Golden Gate Bridge, then hop the ferry back across the bay from Sausalito.

» South along the Central Coast, the waterfront **Monterey Peninsula Recreational Trail** and the famously scenic **17-Mile Drive** entice cyclists of all skill levels.

» NorCal's **Wine Country** offers some beautiful bike tours and wine tasting – just don't get too wobbly.

» Up north at Humboldt Redwoods State Park, ride among the world's tallest trees on the winding **Avenue of the Giants**.

» In the Sierra Nevada, **Yosemite National Park** has mostly level, paved recreational paths through a glacier-carved valley overhung by waterfalls.

Best Mountain-Biking Areas

» Serious mountain-bikers should prioritize a stop in **Downieville**, a little Gold Rush town which offers an enormous downhill sweep.

» Just north of San Francisco, the **Marin Headlands** offers a bonanza of trails for fat-tire fans, while **Mt Tamalpais** lays claim to being the sport's birthplace.

» Top-rated single-track rides near **Lake Tahoe** include Mr Toad's Wild Ride and the Flume Trail.

» Speed freaks also sing the praises of the Eastern Sierra's **Mammoth Mountain**, whose summer-only bike park beckons with 70 miles of dirt singletrack.

» More ski areas that open trails and chairlifts to mountain-bikers can be found at some resorts at **Lake Tahoe**.

» State parks especially popular with mountain-bikers include NorCal's **Prairie Creek Redwoods**, the Gold Country's **Calaveras Big Trees**, **Wilder Ranch** outside Santa Cruz, **Andrew Molera** in Big Sur or San Luis Obispo's **Montaña de Oro**.

Maps & Online Resources

Local bike shops can supply you with more cycling-route ideas, maps and advice.

» **California Association of Bicycling Organizations** (www.cabobike.org) offers free bicycle touring and freeway-access information.

» **California Bicycle Coalition** (www.calbike.org) links to free online cycling maps, bike-sharing programs and community bike shops.

» **Adventure Cycling Association** (www.adventurecycling.org) sells long-distance cycling route guides and touring maps, including the Pacific Coast Hwy (PCH).

» Find bicycle specialty shops, local cycling clubs, group rides and other special events with the **League of American Bicyclists** (www.bikeleague.org).

» For online forums and reviews of mountain-biking trails in California, search **DirtWorld.com** (http://dirtworld.com) and **MTBR.com** (www.mtbr.com).

NO RESERVATIONS?

If you can't get a reservation, plan to show up at the campground between 10am and noon, when other campers are leaving. Don't be too choosy, or you may end up with no site at all, especially during summer holidays. Park rangers, visitors centers and campground hosts can often tell you where spaces may still be available, if there are any; otherwise, ask about overflow camping and dispersed camping areas nearby. Note that in popular areas, like the stretch of Big Sur coast on Hwy 1, it's almost impossible to score quality last-minute campsites.

Hiking

Got wanderlust? With epic scenery, California is perfect for exploring on foot. That's true whether you've got your heart set on peak-bagging in the Sierra Nevada, rambling among the world's tallest trees, or simply walking on the beach by booming surf. During spring and early summer, a painter's palette of wildflowers bloom on coastal hillsides, in mountain meadows, on damp forest floors and across endless desert sands.

Northern California Camping & Outdoors

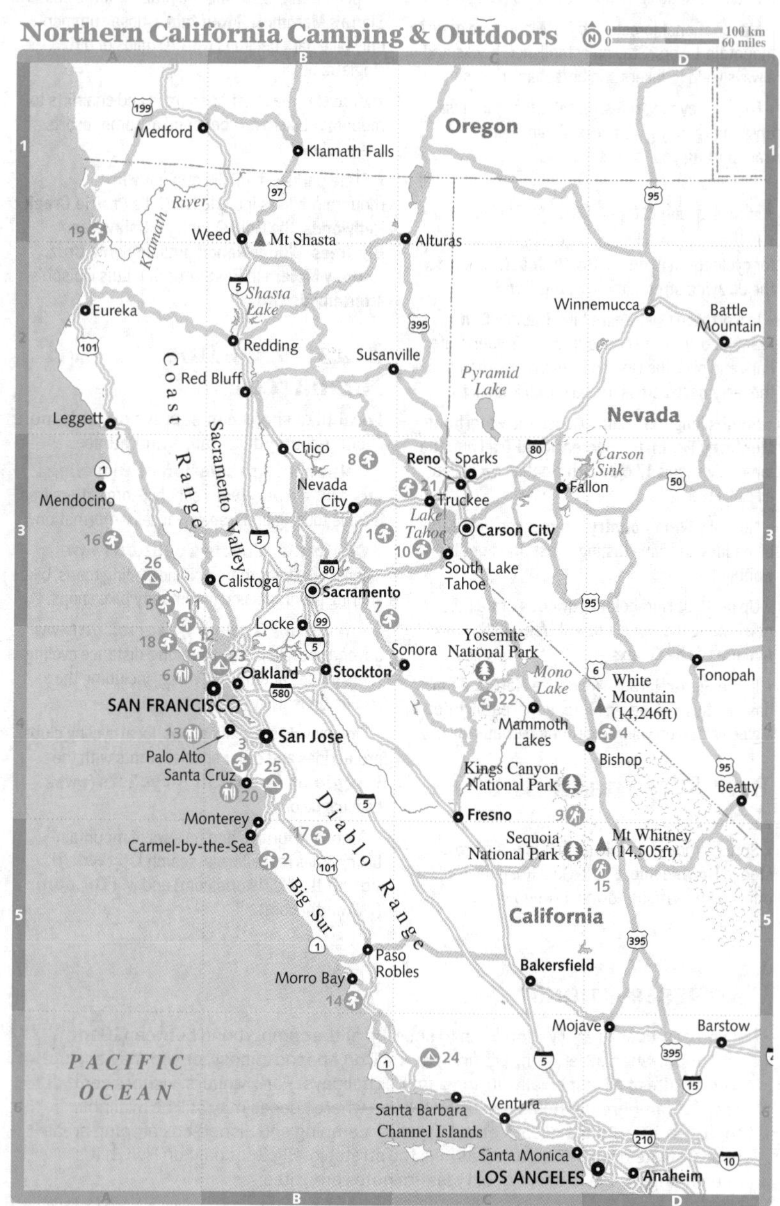

Best Places to Hike

No matter where you find yourself in California, you're never far from a trail, even in busy metropolitan areas. For jaw-dropping scenery, head to national and state parks to choose from a staggering variety of trails, from easy nature walks negotiable by wheelchairs and strollers to multiday backpacking routes through rugged wilderness.

» **Sierra Nevada** In Yosemite, Sequoia and Kings Canyon National Parks, clamber toward waterfalls, wildflower meadows and alpine lakes, tackle mighty granite domes and peaks, or wander among the world's biggest trees – giant sequoias.

» **North Coast** Redwood National & State Parks offer misty walks through groves of old-growth redwoods, or tackle the truly wild beaches of the challenging Lost Coast Trail.

» **San Francisco Bay Area** The Marin Headlands, Muir Woods, Mt Tamalpais, Point Reyes National Seashore and Big Basin Redwoods State Park, all within a 90-minute drive of San Francisco, are crisscrossed by dozens of superb trails.

» **Northern Mountains** Summiting Mt Shasta is a spiritually uplifting experience, while Lassen Volcanic National Park is a bizarre world of smoking fumaroles, cinder cones and craters.

Fees & Wilderness Permits

» Most California state parks charge a daily parking fee of $5 to $15; there's often no charge if you walk or bike into these parks.

» National-park entry averages $10 to $20 per vehicle for seven consecutive days; some national parks are free.

» For unlimited admission to national parks, national forests and other federal recreation lands, buy an 'America the Beautiful' annual pass (see p556).

» Often required for overnight backpackers and extended day hikes, wilderness permits are issued at ranger stations and park visitors centers. Daily quotas may be in effect during peak periods, usually late spring through early fall.

» Some wilderness permits may be reserved ahead of time, and very popular trails (like the ascent to the top of Half Dome) may sell out several months in advance.

» Buy passes from USFS ranger stations and select local vendors such as sporting-goods stores.

Maps & Online Resources

» There are bulletin boards showing basic trail maps and other information at most major trailheads in national, state and regional parks.

» For short, well-established hikes, the free trail maps handed out at visitors centers and ranger stations are usually sufficient.

» A more detailed topographical map may be necessary for longer backcountry hikes. Topo maps are sold at park bookstores, visitors centers, ranger stations and outdoor-gear shops including **REI** (www.rei.com).

Northern California Camping & Outdoors

Activities, Courses & Tours

1	American River	B3
2	Andrew Molera State Park	B5
3	Big Basin Redwoods State Park	B4
4	Bishop	D4
5	Bodega Bay	A3
6	Bolinas	A4
7	Chery Creek	B3
8	Downieville	B3
9	John Muir Trail	C4
10	Lake Tahoe	C3
	Limekiln State Park	(see 2)
11	Marin County	A3
12	Marin Headlands	A4
13	Mavericks	A4
14	Montaña de Oro State Park	B5
15	Mt Whitney	D5
16	Pacific Coast Hwy	A3
17	Pinnacles National Monument	B5
18	Point Reyes National Seashore	A4
19	Prairie Creek Redwoods State Park	A1
20	Santa Cruz	B4
21	Truckee	C3
22	Yosemite Valley	C4

Sleeping

23	Angel Island State Park	B4
24	Los Padres National Forest	C6
25	New Brighton State Beach	B4
26	Wrights Beach State Park	A3

TAKE A (REALLY LONG) HIKE

Famous long-distance trails that wind through California include the 2650-mile **Pacific Crest National Scenic Trail** (PCT; www.pcta.org) that takes hikers from Mexico to Canada. Running mostly along the PCT, the 211-mile **John Muir Trail** links Yosemite Valley and Mt Whitney via the Sierra Nevada high country. Or enjoy inspirational views of Lake Tahoe while tracing the footsteps of early pioneers and Native Americans along the 165-mile **Tahoe Rim Trail** (www.tahoerimtrail.org).

» **US Geological Survey** (USGS; www.store.usgs.gov) offers its topographic maps as free downloadable PDFs, or you can order print copies online.

» **Trails.com** (www.trails.com) lets you search for hundreds of multisport trails throughout California (trail overviews are free).

» **Coastwalk** (www.coastwalk.org) advocates for a long-distance trail along California's 12,100-plus miles of shoreline. Join a group hike, or volunteer to do beach cleanup or trail maintenance.

» Learn how to minimize your impact on the environment while traipsing through the wilderness by visiting the **Leave No Trace Center** (www.lnt.org).

Rock Climbing

Climbers can test their mettle on the big walls, granite domes and boulders of **Yosemite National Park**, where the climbing season runs from April to October. Outfitters offer guided climbs and instruction.

Other prime spots for bouldering and rock climbing include **Sequoia and Kings Canyon National Parks**, south of Yosemite; around **Bishop** in the Eastern Sierra; outside **Truckee**, near Lake Tahoe; and at **Pinnacles National Monument** in central California.

SuperTopo (www.supertopo.com) is a one-stop shop for rock-climbing guidebooks, online forums, free topo maps and route descriptions across the state.

Beaches & Swimming

If you've come to Northern California expecting the idyllic scenes from a Beach Boys song, forget it. The beaches in Northern California are better for strolling than for swimming, as the water can be very cold – bring or rent a wetsuit – and the tides very strong. The water starts getting warmer around Santa Barbara.

The mind-bogglingly detailed *California Coastal Access Guide* (University of California Press, 2003) has comprehensive beach driving directions and maps.

Water quality varies from beach to beach, and day to day. Stay out of the ocean for at least three days after a major rainstorm due to toxic pollutants being flushed out to sea through storm drains. For current water-safety conditions statewide, check the **Beach Report Card** (http://brc.healthebay.org).

For safety tips about riptides, see p560.

Scuba Diving & Snorkeling

All along the coast, rock reefs, shipwrecks and kelp beds teem with sea creatures ready for their close-up.

If you've already got your PADI certification, you can rent one-tank dive outfits for $65 to $100, while two-tank boat dives cost over $100; reserve either at least a day in advance. Snorkel kits can be rented from most dive shops for around $15 to $40 per day. If you're going to be taking the plunge more than once or twice, it's probably worth buying your own mask and fins. Remember not to touch anything while you're out snorkeling, don't snorkel alone and always, always wear sunblock!

Best Scuba-Diving & Snorkeling Spots

» With its national marine sanctuary, **Monterey Bay** offers world-renowned diving and snorkeling, although you'll need to don a wetsuit.

» Further south, **Point Lobos State Natural Reserve** is another gem for scuba divers (snorkeling prohibited); permit reservations required.

» North of San Francisco, dive boats depart from **Bodega Bay**.

Sea Kayaking

Few water sports are as accessible and fun for the whole gang as kayaking. Most outfitters offer a choice between sit-upon (open) kayaks and sit-in (closed-hull) ones, the latter usually requiring some training before you head out. Kayak rentals average $40 to $70 per day, and you'll usually have a choice between single and tandem. A reputable outfitter will make sure you're aware of the tide schedule and wind conditions of your proposed route. Many also give lessons and lead guided paddles (from $50), including full-moon, sunset and sunrise trips. Try to make reservations at least a day ahead. There are dozens of places to launch along the coast.

Surfing

Surf's up! The most powerful swells arrive along the coast during late fall and winter. May and June are generally the flattest months, although they do bring warmer water. Speaking of temperature, don't believe all those images of hot blonds surfing in skimpy bikinis; without a wetsuit, you'll likely freeze your butt off except at the height of summer.

Crowds can be a problem at many surf spots, as can overly territorial surfers. Befriend a local surfer for an introduction before hitting the most famous waves. Sharks do inhabit California waters, but attacks are rare. Most take place in the 'Red Triangle' between Monterey on the Central Coast, Tomales Bay north of San Francisco and the offshore Farallon Islands.

Generally speaking, the north is a bit better for beginners than it is for hardcore pros, who would find more challenge in the breaks of the south. There are a couple notable exceptions: Santa Cruz's **Steamers Lane**, with glassy point breaks and rocky reef breaks, and Half Moon Bay's **Mavericks** (www.maverickssurf.com), which is world-famous for big-wave surfing. Mavericks tops 50ft when the most powerful winter swells arrive.

Best Breaks for Beginners

The best spots to learn to surf are at the beach breaks of long, shallow bays where waves are small and rolling, including:

» **Central Coast** Santa Cruz, Santa Barbara, Cayucos

» **San Francisco Area** Ocean Beach

» **North Coast** Bolinas, Stinson Beach

Rentals & Lessons

You'll find board rentals on just about every patch of sand where surfing is possible. Expect to pay about $20 per half-day for a board, with wetsuit rental another $10.

Two-hour group lessons for beginners start at around $75 per person, while private, two-hour instruction costs over $100. If you're ready to jump in the deep end, many surf schools offer pricier weekend surf clinics and week-long 'surfari' camps.

Stand-up paddle surfing (SUP) is easier to learn, and it's skyrocketing in popularity. You'll find similarly priced board-and-paddle rentals and lessons all along the coast.

Books, Maps & Online Resources

» Plan a coastal surfing adventure using **SurfMaps** (www.surfmaps.net), which even detail seasonal weather and water temperatures.

» Enlightened surfers can join up with **Surfrider** (www.surfrider.org), a nonprofit organization that aims to protect the coastal environment.

White-Water Rafting

California has dozens of kick-ass rivers. Paddling giant white-water rapids swelled by the snowmelt that rips through sheer canyons, your thoughts are reduced to just two simple words: 'survive' and 'damn!' Too much for you? Myriad opportunities are suited to the abilities of any wannabe river rat, even beginner paddlers.

California Whitewater Rafting (www.c-w-r.com) covers all of California's prime river-running spots, with links to outfitters and river-conservation groups. Most of the premier river runs are in the Sierra Nevada and the Gold Country, but the Northern Mountains also offer some rollicking rides, including on the Klamath, Trinity, Sacramento, Smith and California Salmon Rivers.

White-water trips are not without danger, and it's not unusual for participants to fall out of the raft in rough conditions. Serious

CALIFORNIA'S BEST WHITE-WATER RAFTING

NAME	CLASS	SEASON	DESCRIPTION
American River	Class II-IV	Apr-Oct	The South Fork is ideal for families and rafting virgins looking to get their feet wet, while the more challenging Middle and North Forks carve through deep gorges in the Gold Country.
Kern River	Class II-V	Apr-Sep	Staged near Bakersfield, the Upper and Lower Forks offer some of the southern Sierra's best white water.
Kaweah River	Class IV+	Apr-Jul	After steeply dropping through Sequoia National Park, this fast, furious ride is for experienced paddlers craving hair-raising white water.
Kings River	Class III-IV	Apr-Jul	One of California's most powerful rivers cuts a groove deeper than the Grand Canyon; trips begin outside Kings Canyon National Park.
Merced River	Class III-IV	Apr-Jul	Starting outside Yosemite National Park, this canyon run is the Sierra's best one-day intermediate trip.
Stanislaus River	Class II-IV	Apr-Oct	In the Gold Country, the North Fork provides rafting trips for novices and the more adventure-minded.
Truckee River	Class II-IV	Apr-Aug	Near Lake Tahoe, this is a great beginners' run, with a white-water park for kayakers on the river in downtown Reno.
Tuolumne River	Class IV-V	Apr-Sep	Experienced paddlers may prefer a ferocious run on 'the T'; in summer, experts-only Cherry Creek is a legendary Sierra Nevada run.

injuries are rare, however, and most trips are without incident. No prior experience is needed for guided river trips up to Class III, but for Class IV you want to be healthy, active, in good shape and an excellent swimmer, plus have some paddling experience under your life-jacket belt.

Seasons, Rates & Reservations

Commercial outfitters run a variety of trips, from short, inexpensive morning or afternoon floats to overnight outings and multiday expeditions. Expect to pay from $100 for a guided all-day trip. Reservations are recommended, especially for overnight trips.

The main river-running season is from April to October, although the exact months depend on which river you're rafting and the spring snowmelt runoff from the mountains. You'll be hurtling along either in large rafts for a dozen or more people, or smaller ones seating half a dozen; the latter tend to be more exhilarating because they can tackle rougher rapids and everyone paddles.

Whale-Watching

During their annual migration, gray whales can be spotted off the California coast from December to April, while blue, humpback and sperm whales pass by in summer and fall (see also p543). You can try your luck whale-watching (eg from lighthouses) while staying shore-bound – it's free, but you're less likely to see whales and you'll be removed from all the action.

» Just about every port town worth its sea salt offers whale-watching boat excursions, especially during winter. Bring binoculars!

» Half-day boat trips cost from $30 to $45, while all-day trips average $65 to $100; make reservations at least a day ahead.

» Better tour boats limit the number of people and have a trained naturalist or marine biologist on board.

» Some tour companies will let you go again for free if you don't spot any whales on your first trip.

» Choppy seas can be nauseating. To avoid seasickness, sit outside on the boat's second level – but not too close to the diesel fumes in back.

Snow Sports

High-speed modern ski lifts, mountains of fresh powder, a cornucopia of trails ranging from easy-peasy 'Sesame St' to black-diamond 'Death Wish,' skyscraping pristine alpine scenery, luxury mountain cabins – they're all hallmarks of a California vacation in the snow. The Sierra Nevada offers the best slopes and trails for skiers and snowboarders, not to mention the most reliable conditions.

Season, Rates & Lessons

Ski season runs from late November or early December until late March or early April, although this of course depends on specific elevations and weather conditions. All resorts have ski schools and equipment-rental facilities and offer a wide variety of lift tickets, including half-day, all-day and multiday versions. Prices vary tremendously, from $25 to $95 per day for adults. Discounts for children, teens, students and seniors are typically available.

EVEN MORE IN THE OUTDOORS!

ACTIVITY	LOCATION	REGION	PAGE
Bird-watching	Klamath Basin National Wildlife Refuges	Northern Mountains	p290
	Mono Lake	Yosemite & the Sierra Nevada	p430
	Marin Headlands	Marin County & the Bay Area	p105
Caving	Lava Beds National Monument	Northern Mountains	p289
	Crystal Cave	Yosemite & the Sierra Nevada	p421
	Pinnacles National Monument	Central Coast	p491
Fishing*	Shasta Lake	Northern Mountains	p267
	Bodega Bay	North Coast & Redwoods	p211
	Klamath River	North Coast & Redwoods	p257
Horseback riding	Yosemite National Park	Yosemite & the Sierra Nevada	p403
	Wild Horse Sanctuary	Northern Mountains	p272
	Point Reyes National Seashore	Marin County & the Bay Area	p123
Kiteboarding & Windsurfing	San Francisco Bay	San Francisco	p73
	Bodega Bay	North Coast & Redwoods	p211
	Lake Tahoe	Lake Tahoe	p378

*For fishing licenses, regulations and location information, consult the **California Department of Fish & Game** (www.dfg.ca.gov).

'Ski and stay' lodging packages may offer the best value.

Best Places for Snow Sports

For sheer variety, the over a dozen downhill skiing and snowboarding resorts ringing **Lake Tahoe** are unbeatable. Alongside such world-famous places as Squaw Valley USA, host of the 1960 Winter Olympic Games, and Heavenly, you'll find scores of smaller operations, many of them with lower ticket prices, smaller crowds and great runs for beginners and families. Royal Gorge, near Truckee west of Lake Tahoe, is North America's largest cross-country ski resort. For family-friendly **sno-parks** that offer sledding and snow play, visit http://ohv.parks.ca.gov/?page_id=1233.

In the glacier-carved winter wonderland of Yosemite National Park, in the western Sierra Nevada, **Badger Pass** is ideal for beginners and families. One of California's oldest ski resorts, it's also a launching pad for cross-country skiing and snowshoe walks into the wilderness, and kids love the snowtubing hill. In the southern Sierra at **Sequoia and Kings Canyon National Parks**, you can tramp or cross-country ski among giant sequoia trees.

In Northern California, **Mt Shasta Board & Ski Park** is the most popular, with a cool night-skiing operation.

Travel with Children

San Francisco Bay Area

Explore hands-on, whimsical and 'wow!' science museums, hear the barking sea lions at Pier 39, then traipse through Golden Gate Park and along that famous bridge.

Sierra Nevada

Kids will gawk at Yosemite's waterfalls and granite domes and can hike through ancient groves of giant sequoias, the world's biggest trees. Mammoth Lakes is a four-seasons family adventure base camp.

Gold Country

Young imaginations run wild in Gold Country, ignited by tall tales of rough-n-tumble '49ers, ruthless bandits and treasure hunters. Connect with the Wild West in historic towns such as Columbia State Historic Park and Nevada City.

Young travelers love Northern California and it's an excellent, adventurous and safe destination for traveling with kids.

The weather is great for outdoor adventures. Even when the waters are cold, kids don't seem to mind, and there are plenty of decent beaches for a dip. Back on land, you can spend your days bicycling, hiking or horseback riding. In winter when it's cold and rainy or snowing outside, or when fog hugs the coast, you'll find museums and indoor-entertainment galore.

Most of the time, no organized activity is necessary. We've seen young kids thrill at their first glimpse of a palm tree, and teens bliss out over their first taste of heirloom tomatoes at a farmers market or shrimp dumplings at a dim-sum joint.

Northern California for Kids

Children's discounts are available for everything from museum admission to bus fare. The definition of a 'child' varies – in some places anyone under 18 is eligible, while at others the cut-off is age six.

Kids are welcomed at casual restaurants, which often have high chairs, children's menus, and paper placemats and crayons for drawing. On the road, local supermarkets such as Trader Joe's have wholesome, ready-to-eat take-out dishes.

HOW OLD IS OLD ENOUGH?

Naturally some outdoor activities will be easier to master than others. Those as young as five can take part in paddling and skiing. Horseback riding is a good choice for kids aged seven and up, and there are plenty of pleasant hikes easy enough for little legs. Teens will love the challenge of rock climbing, white-water rafting and surfing.

Most women are discreet about breastfeeding in public. Many public toilets have a change table, while places such as airports and museums may have gender-neutral, private 'family' bathrooms.

Children's Highlights

Northern California has ample services and attractions geared towards kids. Throughout this book, look for activities marked with the family-friendly icon (👪). National and state parks often have ranger-led activities and self-guided 'Junior Ranger' programs, in which kids earn a badge. To explore Northern California's urban jungle, see the special 'San Francisco for Children' section in the San Francisco chapter.

Aquariums & Museums

» **San Francisco** The Bay Area is a mind-bending classroom for kids, especially the hands-on Exploratorium, the multimedia Children's Creativity Museum and the eco-friendly California Academy of Sciences.

» **Monterey Bay Aquarium** Get acquainted with the denizens of the deep next door to the Central Coast's biggest marine sanctuary.

» **Seymour Marine Discovery Center** Santa Cruz's university-run aquarium makes interactive science fun, with nearby tide pools for exploring at the beach.

» **Turtle Bay Exploration Park** In Redding, this indoor/outdoor attraction combines an eco-museum with arboretum, botanical and butterfly gardens.

Beaches

» **Central Coast** Laze on Santa Barbara's unmatched beaches, then roll all the way north to Santa Cruz's famous boardwalk and pier.

» **Lake Tahoe** In summer, it's California's favorite high-altitude beach escape: a sparkling diamond tucked in the craggy Sierra Nevada mountains.

» **North Coast** No swimming – the water is too rough – but plenty of chances for beach combing, collecting shells and building sandcastles on uncrowded beaches.

Parks

» **Yosemite National Park** Get a juicy slice of Sierra Nevada scenery, with gushing waterfalls, alpine lakes, glacier-carved valleys and peaks.

» **Golden Gate Park** This gem in the heart of San Francisco has lots of grassy areas for lounging, strolling ice-cream vendors and plenty of space to fly a kite.

» **Redwood National & State Parks** On the misty North Coast, a string of nature preserves protects magnificent wildlife, beaches and the planet's tallest trees.

» **Lassen Volcanic National Park** An off-the-beaten-path destination in the Northern Mountains, with otherworldly volcanic scenery and lakeside camping and cabins.

Planning

When to Go

For tips on the best (and worst) times to visit Northern California and on setting your family's budget, see p18. For Northern California's don't-miss festivals and events, see p23.

A word of advice: don't pack your schedule too tightly. Navigating metro areas such as San Francisco, and the winding back roads to Northern California's natural areas always takes longer than expected.

Accommodations

Motels and hotels often have rooms with two beds or an extra sofa bed, ideal for families. Many also have roll-away beds or cots, typically for a surcharge. Some offer 'kids stay free' promotions, although this may apply only if no extra bedding is required. Some B&Bs don't allow children; ask when booking.

Resorts may have drop-off day camps for kids or on-call babysitting services. At other hotels, the front-desk staff or concierge might be able to help you make babysitting arrangements.

Transportation

Airlines usually allow infants (up to age two) to fly for free, while older children requiring a seat of their own qualify for reduced fares. Children receive substantial discounts on Amtrak and Greyhound. In cars, any child under age six or weighing less than 60lb must be buckled up in the back seat in a child or infant safety seat. Most car-rental agencies rent these for about $10 per day or $50 per trip, but you must book them in advance. Take note: rest stops on freeways are few and far between, and gas stations and fast-food bathrooms are frequently icky.

What to Pack

There are two magic words for traveling in Northern California: sunscreen and layers.

The first of these is always necessary, even where cool; high-altitude climates and overcast skies lull visitors into a false sense of security. The second is an absolute must: a day that is blisteringly hot in the Gold Country can be chilly in the Sierra and downright bone-chilling on the coast. This is particularly true in San Francisco, where the weather changes fast.

For outdoor vacations, bring broken-in shoes and your own camping equipment. Alternatively, outdoors gear can be purchased or often rented from outdoor stores. But remember that brand-new hiking shoes often result in blisters, and setting up a new tent in the dark ain't easy.

If you forget some critical piece of equipment, **Baby's Away** (www.babysaway.com) rents cribs, strollers, car seats, high chairs, backpacks, beach gear and more.

Before You Go

» Lonely Planet's *Travel with Children* is loaded with valuable tips and amusing anecdotes, especially for new parents and those with kids who haven't traveled before.

» **Lonelyplanet.com** (www.lonelyplanet.com) lets you ask questions and get advice from other travelers in the Thorn Tree's 'Kids to Go' and 'USA' forums.

» **California Travel & Tourism** (www.visitcalifornia.com), the state's official visitor website, lists family-friendly attractions, activities and more – just search for 'Family Fun' and 'Events'.

» **Family Travel Files** (www.thefamilytravelfiles.com/locations/california) is an info-packed site with vacation-planning articles, tips and discounts.

» **Parents Connect** (www.parentsconnect.com/family-travel) is a virtual encyclopedia of everything first-time family travelers need to know.

regions at a glance

A trip across Northern California is a chance to let your pulse quicken at the wonders of the west: dramatic mountains and epic coastal scenery, thriving cities and vibrant historic towns, road trips to visit some of the nation's top destinations for food and drink. The biggest thrills of the region – like Yosemite National Park, Lake Tahoe and the redwood-dotted North Coast – are only a half-day's drive from the multicultural mosaic of San Francisco.

But no matter where you go first, the brooding coastline, rugged mountain ranges and world-class vineyards are always an open invitation to more adventure.

San Francisco

Food ✓✓✓
Culture ✓✓✓
Museums ✓✓✓

California's 'Left Coast' reputation rests on SF, where DIY self-expression, sustainability and spontaneity are the highest virtues. Free thinkers, edgy neighborhoods, top-tier museums and ground-breaking arts scenes thrive here.

p52

Marin County & the Bay Area

Mountain-Biking ✓✓✓
Agrotourism ✓✓✓
Food ✓✓

Outdoors nuts adore Marin County, with its beaches, wildlife-watching, and hiking and mountain-biking trails. There's also a fertile garden of ecotourism experiences, including farms that inspire chefs all around the Bay Area.

p104

Napa & Sonoma Wine Country

Wineries ✓✓✓
Food ✓✓✓
Cycling & Canoeing ✓✓

Amid fruit orchards and ranch lands, these sunny valleys kissed by cool coastal fog have made Napa, Sonoma and the Russian River into California's premier wine-growing region – and also a showcase for farm-to-table cuisine.

p155

North Coast & Redwoods

Wildlife ✓✓✓
Hiking ✓✓✓
Beaches ✓✓

Primeval redwood forests are the prize along NorCal's foggy, rocky and wildly dramatic coastline. Let loose your inner hippie or Rastafarian in Humboldt County, or explore bootstrap fishing villages from Bodega Bay to Eureka.

p208

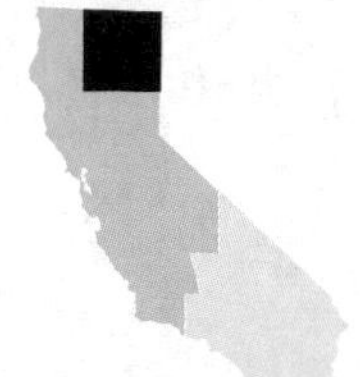

Northern Mountains

Mountains ✓✓✓
Lakes ✓✓✓
Scenic Drives ✓✓

Sacred Mt Shasta has brought together Native Americans, ice axe–wielding alpinists, poets and painters. Wilder places also await, from Lassen's volcanic Bumpass Hell and Lava Beds' subterranean caves to backcountry byways and lakes.

p262

Gold Country & Central Valley

History ✓✓✓
Museums ✓✓
Outdoor Activities ✓✓

The state capital is an unbeatable place to start digging up California's roots, then spread out across the river delta into the foothills to find a rich vein of Wild West history in gold-mining country.

p298

Lake Tahoe

Winter Sports ✓✓✓
Water Sports ✓✓
Cabins & Camping ✓✓

North America's largest alpine lake is a four-seasons outdoor-adventure land. Come for Olympic-worthy skiing in winter, or in summer when you can splash around by the beaches. Nevada's casinos are a bonus attraction.

p351

Yosemite & the Sierra Nevada

Scenery ✓✓✓
Wildlife ✓✓✓
Hiking ✓✓✓

Granite peaks, alpine meadows and lakes, North America's deepest canyon and shaggy forests of giant sequoias – the biggest trees on earth – grace California's iconic mountain range. Summer is prime time for all kinds of outdoor pursuits.

p393

Central Coast

Wildlife ✓✓✓
Beaches ✓✓✓
Scenic Drives ✓✓✓

Time to get outdoors! Hike Big Sur's redwood forests, where waterfalls spring to life; hop aboard a whale-watching boat in Monterey Bay; surf from Santa Cruz to Santa Barbara; or kayak the Channel Islands, California's Galapagos.

p449

Look out for these icons:

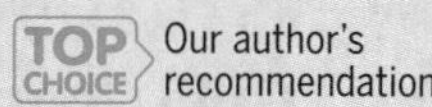 Our author's recommendation

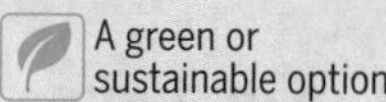 A green or sustainable option

 No payment required

See the Index for a full list of destinations covered in this book.

On the Road

San Francisco

Includes »

Best Places to Eat

» Coi (p83)
» Benu (p86)
» La Taquería (p86)
» Frances (p89)
» Aziza (p91)

Best Places to Stay

» Orchard Garden Hotel (p76)
» Hotel Vitale (p80)
» Hotel Bohème (p78)
» Inn San Fransisco (p80)
» Argonaut Hotel (p79)

Why Go?

Get to know the world capital of weird from the inside out, from mural-lined alleyways named after poets to clothing-optional beaches on a former military base. But don't be too quick to dismiss San Francisco's wild ideas. Biotech, gay rights, personal computers, cable cars and organic fine dining were once considered outlandish too, before San Francisco introduced these underground ideas into the mainstream decades ago. San Francisco's morning fog erases the boundaries between land and ocean, reality and infinite possibility.

Rules are never strictly followed here, but bliss is. Golden Gate Bridge and Alcatraz are entirely optional – San Franciscans mostly admire them from afar – leaving you free to pursue inspiration through Golden Gate Park, past flamboyantly painted Victorian homes and through Mission galleries. Just don't be late for your sensational, sustainable dinner: in San Francisco, you can find happiness and eat it too.

When to Go

San Francisco

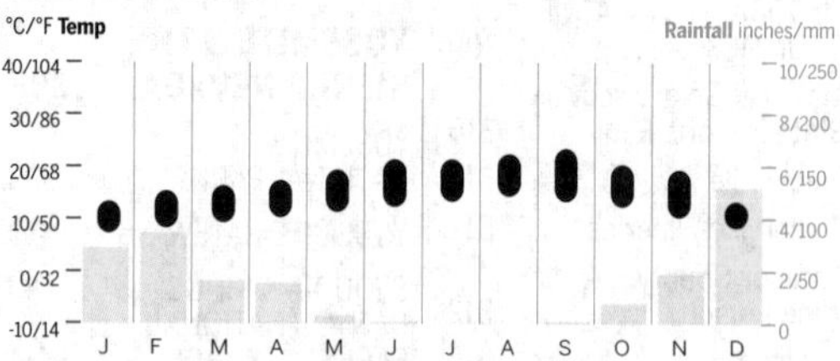

Jan–Mar Low-season rates, brisk but rarely cold days, and the colorful Lunar New Year parade.

May–Aug Farmers markets and festivals make up for high-season rates and chilly afternoon fog.

Sep–Nov Blue skies, free concerts, bargain hotel rates and flavor-bursting harvest cuisine.

Cable Cars

Groaning brakes and clanging brass bells only add to the thrills of San Francisco's cable cars, which have hardly changed since their introduction here in 1873. Cable cars still can't move in reverse, and require burly gripmen (and one buff gripwoman) to lean hard on hand-operated brakes to keep from careening downhill. The city receives many applicants for this job, but 80% fail the strenuous tests of upper-body strength and hand-eye coordination, and rarely try again. Today the cable car seems more like a steampunk carnival ride than modern transport, but it remains the killer app to conquer San Francisco's breakneck slopes. There are no seat belts, child seats or air bags on board – just jump onto the wooden sideboard, grab a strap, and enjoy the ride of your life.

DON'T MISS...

» **Saloons** The Barbary Coast is roaring back to life with historically researched whiskey cocktails and staggering absinthe concoctions in San Francisco's great Western saloon revival (p92).

» **Foraged fine dining** No SF tasting menu is complete without wild chanterelles, miner's lettuce from Berkeley hillsides or SF-backyard nasturtium flowers, from **Commonwealth** (p86) to **Coi** (p83).

» **Green everything** Recent reports rank San Francisco as the greenest city in North America, with its LEED-certified green hotels, pioneering citywide composting laws and America's biggest stretch of urban greenery: **Golden Gate Park** (p53).

» **Showtime** Bewigged satire, world premiere opera, year-round film festivals, Grammy-winning symphonies and legendary, jawdropping drag: no one puts on a show like San Francisco, and the cheering, back-talking local audiences demand encores in no uncertain terms.

SF's Best Free...

» **Music** Golden Gate Park (p53) hosts free concerts summer through fall, from opera to Hardly Strictly Bluegrass (p76).

» **Speech** City Lights Bookstore (p59) won a landmark free speech case over the publication of Allen Ginsberg's magnificent, incendiary *Howl;* take a seat in the designated Poet's Chair and celebrate your right to read freely.

» **Love** Pride (p75) fills San Francisco streets with free candy, free condoms, and over a million people freely smooching total strangers under rainbow flags.

» **Spirits** Anywhere within city limits, at any time – consider yourself warned.

DID YOU KNOW?

Despite slacker reputations cultivated at 30 medical marijuana clubs, San Franciscans hold more patents, read more books and earn more degrees per capita than residents of any other US city.

Fast Facts

» **Population** 805,235

» **Area** 7 square miles

» **Telephone area code** 415

Planning Your Trip

» **Three weeks before** Book Alcatraz trips and dinner at Coi or Frances.

» **Two weeks before** Build stamina for downtown hills, South of Market (SoMa) galleries and Mission bars.

» **One week before** Score tickets to San Francisco Symphony or Opera, and assemble your costume – SF throws parades whenever.

Resources

» **SF Bay Guardian** (www.sfbg.com) Hot tips on local entertainment, arts, politics.

» **SFGate** (www.sfgate.com) News and event listings.

San Francisco Highlights

1. Make yourself at home where the buffalo roam in **Golden Gate Park** (p53)
2. Reach new artistic heights at the **San Francisco Museum of Modern Art** (p64) rooftop sculpture garden
3. Watch fog dance atop the deco towers of the **Golden Gate Bridge** (p55)
4. Graze the **Ferry Building** (p55), SF's local, sustainable foodie destination
5. Plot your escape from **Alcatraz** (p75), SF's notorious island prison
6. Discover unlikely urban marine life along **Fisherman's Wharf** (p60): sea lions, sharks, and a WWII submarine
7. Unwind in Japanese baths and catch film screenings in **Japantown** (p61)
8. Get breathless from the climb, murals and panoramic views at **Coit Tower** (p61)
9. Wander through 150 years of California history in pagoda-topped **Chinatown** (p57)

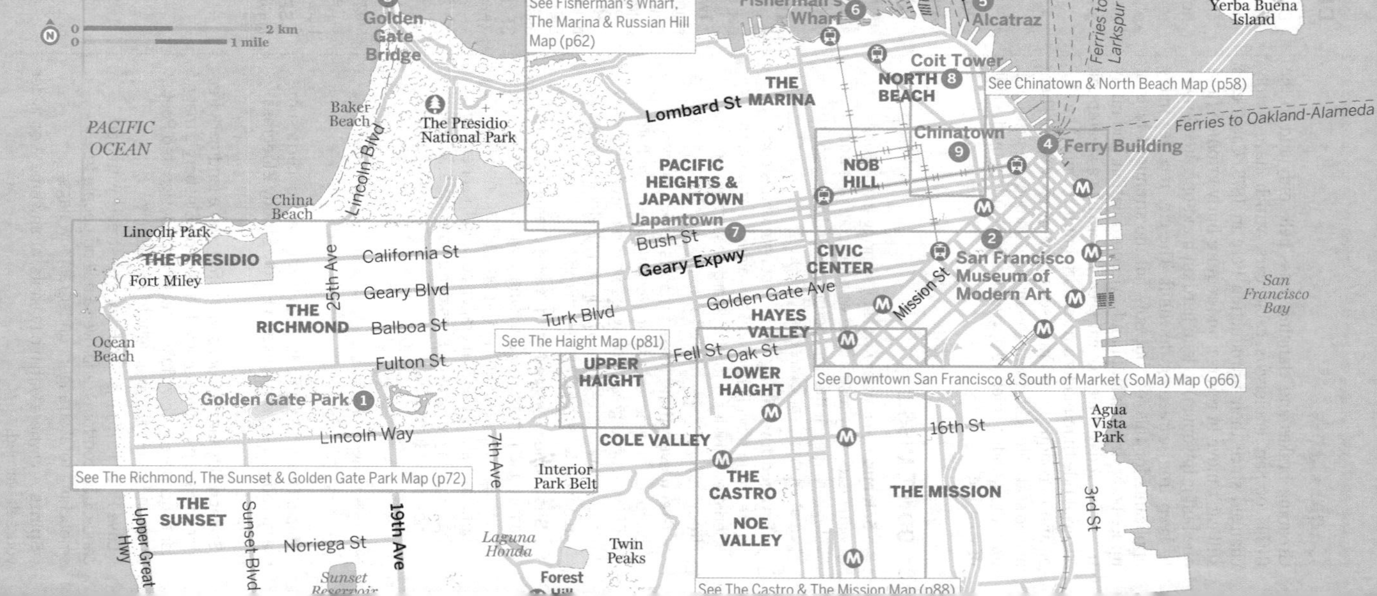

History

Oysters and acorn bread were prime dinner options in the Mexico-run Ohlone settlement of San Francisco circa 1848 – but a year and some gold nuggets later, Champagne and chow mein were served by the bucket. Gold found in the nearby Sierra Nevada foothills had turned a waterfront village of 800 into a port city of 100,000 prospectors, con artists, prostitutes and honest folk trying to make an honest living – good luck telling which was which. That friendly bartender might drug your drink, and you'd wake up a mile from shore, shanghaied into service on some ship bound for Argentina.

By 1850, California was nabbed from Mexico and fast-tracked for US statehood, and San Francisco attempted to introduce public order to 200 saloons and untold numbers of brothels and gambling dens. Panic struck when Australia glutted the market with gold in 1854, and ire turned irrationally on SF's Chinese community, who from 1877 to 1945 were restricted to living and working in Chinatown by anti-Chinese laws. The main way out of debt was dangerous work building railroads for the city's robber barons, who dynamited, mined and clear-cut their way across the Golden West, and built grand Nob Hill mansions above Chinatown.

The city's lofty ambitions and 20-plus theaters came crashing down in 1906, when earthquake and fire left 3000 dead, 100,000 homeless and much of the city reduced to rubble – including almost every mansion on Nob Hill. Theater troupes and opera divas performed for free amid smoldering ruins downtown, establishing SF's tradition of free public performances in parks.

Ambitious public works projects continued through the 1930s, when Diego Rivera, Frida Kahlo and federally funded muralists began the tradition of leftist politics in paint visible in some 400 Mission murals.

WWII brought seismic shifts to San Francisco's community as women and African Americans working in San Francisco shipyards created a new economic boom, and President Franklin Delano Roosevelt's Executive Order 9066 mandated the internment of the city's historic Japanese American community. A 40-year court battle ensued, ending in an unprecedented apology from the US government. San Francisco became a testing ground for civil rights and free speech, with Beat poet Lawrence Ferlinghetti and City Lights Bookstore winning a landmark 1957 ruling against book banning over the publication of Allen Ginsberg's splendid, incendiary *Howl and Other Poems*.

The Central Intelligence Agency (CIA) hoped an experimental drug called LSD might turn San Francisco test subject Ken Kesey into the ultimate fighting machine, but instead the author of *One Flew Over the Cuckoo's Nest* slipped some into Kool-Aid and kicked off the psychedelic '60s. The Summer of Love meant free food, love and music in The Haight until the '70s, when enterprising gay hippies founded an out-and-proud community in the Castro. San Francisco witnessed devastating losses from AIDS in the 1980s, but the city rallied to become a model for disease treatment and prevention.

Geeks and cyberpunks converged on SF in the mid-1990s, spawning the Web and dot-com boom – until the bubble popped in 2000. But risk-taking SF continues to float new ideas, and as recession hits elsewhere, social media, mobile apps and biotech are booming in San Francisco. Congratulations: you're just in time for San Francisco's next wild ride.

Sights

THE BAY & THE EMBARCADERO

TOP CHOICE **Golden Gate Bridge** BRIDGE

(Map p54; ☎415-921-5858; www.goldengate.org; Fort Point Lookout, Marine Dr; southbound car $6, carpools free) San Franciscans have passionate perspectives on every subject, but especially their signature landmark. Cinema buffs believe Hitchcock had it right: seen from below at **Fort Point**, the 1937 brige induces a thrilling case of *Vertigo*. Fog aficionados prefer the north-end lookout at Marin's **Vista Point**, to watch gusts billow through bridge cables like dry ice at a Kiss concert. Hard to believe the Navy almost nixed the soaring art deco design of architects Gertrude and Irving Murrow and engineer Joseph B Strauss in favor of a hulking concrete span painted with caution-yellow stripes.

To see both sides of the Golden Gate debate, hike or bike the 2-mile span. MUNI buses 28 and 29 run to the toll plaza, and pedestrians and cyclists can cross the bridge on the east side; Golden Gate Transit buses head back to SF from Marin.

Ferry Building HISTORIC BUILDING

(Map p66; www.ferrybuildingmarketplace.com; Embarcadero) Slackers have the right idea at the Ferry Building, the transport hub

NEIGHBORHOODS IN A NUTSHELL

North Beach & the Hills Poetry and parrots, top-of-the-world views, Italian gossip and opera on the jukebox.

Embarcadero & the Piers Gourmet treats, sea-lion antics, 19th-century video games, and getaways to and from Alcatraz.

Downtown & the Financial District The notorious Barbary Coast has gone legit with banks and boutiques, but reveals its wild side in provocative art galleries.

Chinatown Pagoda roofs, mahjong, and fortunes made and lost in historic alleyways.

Hayes Valley, Civic Center & the Tenderloin Grand buildings and great performances, dive bars and cable cars, foodie finds and local designs.

SoMa Where high technology meets higher art, and everyone gets down and dirty on the dance floor.

Mission A book in one hand, a burrito in the other, and murals all around.

Castro Out and proud with samba whistles, rainbow flags and policy platforms.

Haight Flashbacks and fashion-forwardness, free thinking, free music and pricey skateboards.

Japantown, the Fillmore & Pacific Heights Sushi in the fountains, John Coltrane over the altar, and rock at the Fillmore.

Marina & the Presidio Boutiques, organic dining, peace and public nudity at a former army base.

Golden Gate Park & the Avenues SF's mile-wide wild streak, surrounded by gourmet hangouts for hungry surfers.

turned gourmet emporium where no one's in a hurry to leave. Boat traffic tapered off after the grand hall and clock tower were built in 1898, and by the 1950s the building was literally overshadowed by a freeway overpass. But after the freeway collapsed in the 1989 Loma Prieta Earthquake, the city revived the Ferry Building as a tribute to San Francisco's monumental good taste. On weekends the **Ferry Building Farmers Market** (see the boxed text p84) fans out around the south end of the building like a fabulous garnish.

UNION SQUARE

Powell St Cable Car Turnaround CABLE CAR

(Map p66) Pause at Powell and Market to notice operators leap out of a century-old cable car, and slooowly turn it around on a revolving wooden platform by hand. As technology goes, this seems pretty iffy. Cable cars can't go in reverse, emit mechanical grunts on uphill climbs and require burly operators to lean hard on the handbrake to keep from careening down Nob Hill. For a city of risk-takers, this steampunk transport is the perfect joyride.

Folk Art International CULTURAL BUILDING

(Map p66; ☎415-392-9999; www.folkartintl.com; 140 Maiden Lane; ⏰10am-6pm Tue-Sat) Squeeze the Guggenheim into a brick box with a sunken Romanesque archway, and there you have Frank Lloyd Wright's 1949 Circle Gallery Building, which since 1979 has been the home of the **Xanadu Gallery**.

FINANCIAL DISTRICT

14, 49 and 77 Geary GALLERIES

(Map p66; www.sfada.com; ⏰most galleries 10:30am-5:30pm Tue-Fri, 11am-5pm Sat) Eccentric art collectors descend from hilltop mansions for First Thursday gallery openings of unpredictable art among outspoken crowds. Look for conceptual art at **Gallery Paule Anglim** at 14 Geary; four floors of contemporary art at 49 Geary, from installations by jailed Chinese artist Ai Weiwei at **Haines Gallery** to conceptual photography at **Fraenkel Gallery**; and at 77 Geary, Taravat Talepasand's Iranian-American superheroine portraits at **Marx & Zavattero Gallery** and Vik Muniz's collaged masterworks at **Rena Bransten Gallery**.

Transamerica Pyramid LANDMARK

(Map p66; 600 Montgomery St) Below the 1972 concrete rocketship that defines San Francisco's skyline, a half-acre redwood grove has taken root in the remains of old whaling ships. The building is off-limits to visitors, but the grove is open for daytime picnics on the site of a saloon frequented by Mark Twain and the newspaper office where Sun Yat-sen drafted his Proclamation of the Republic of China.

CIVIC CENTER & THE TENDERLOIN

TOP CHOICE **Asian Art Museum** MUSEUM

(Map p66; ☎415-581-3500; www.asianart.org; 200 Larkin St; adult/student $12/7; ⏲10am-5pm Tue, Wed, Fri-Sun, to 9pm Thu; 👪) Civic Center may be landlocked, but it has an unrivalled view of the Pacific thanks to this museum. Cover 6000 years and thousands of miles here in under an hour, from racy ancient Rajasthan miniatures to futuristic Japanese manga (graphic novels) via priceless Ming vases and even a Bhutan collection. The Asian has worked diplomatic wonders with a rotating collection of 17,000 treasures that bring Taiwan, China and Tibet together, unite Pakistan and India, and strike a harmonious balance among Japan, Korea and China. Stick around for outstanding educational events, from shadow-puppet shows and yoga for kids to First Thursday MATCHA nights from 5pm to 9pm, when soju cocktails flow, DJs spin Japanese hip-hop and guest acupuncturists assess visitors' tongues.

City Hall HISTORIC BUILDING

(Map p66; ☎415-554-4000, tour info 415-554-6023, art exhibit line 415-554-6080; www.ci.sf.ca.us/cityhall; 400 Van Ness Ave; ⏲8am-8pm Mon-Fri, tours 10am, noon & 2pm; 👪) From its Gilded Age dome to the avant-garde art in the basement, City Hall is quintessentially San Franciscan. Rising from the ashes of the 1906 earthquake, this Beaux Arts building has seen historic firsts under its splendid Tennessee pink marble and Colorado limestone rotunda: America's first sit-in on the grand staircase in 1960, protesting red-baiting McCarthy hearings; the 1977 election and 1978 assassination of openly gay Supervisor Harvey Milk; and 4037 same-sex marriages performed in 2004, until the state intervened. Intriguing art shows downstairs showcase local artists; weekly Board of Supervisors meetings are open to the public at 2pm on Tuesdays.

FREE **Luggage Store Gallery** GALLERY

(Map p66; ☎415-255-5971; www.luggagestoregallery.org; 1007 Market St; ⏲noon-5pm Wed-Sat) A dandelion pushing through cracks in the sidewalk, this plucky nonprofit gallery has brought signs of life to one of the toughest blocks in the Tenderloin for two decades. Streetwise art gets its due above an ex-luggage store in this second-floor gallery, which helped launch street satirists Barry McGee, Clare Rojas and Rigo. You'll recognize the place by its graffitied door and the rooftop mural by Brazilian duo Osgemeos of a defiant kid holding a lit firecracker. With such oddly touching works, poetry nights and monthly performing-arts events, this place puts the tender in the Tenderloin.

Glide Memorial United Methodist Church CHURCH

(Map p66; ☎415-674-6090; www.glide.org; 330 Ellis St; ⏲9am & 11am Sun) On Sundays, 1500 people add their voices to the electrifying gospel services at this GLBT-friendly (and just plain friendly) church. After the celebration ends in hearty handshakes and hugs, the radical Methodist congregation gets to work, providing one million free meals a year and homes for 52 formerly homeless families.

CHINATOWN

Chinese Historical Society of America Museum MUSEUM

(Map p58; ☎415-391-1188; www.chsa.org; 965 Clay St; adult/child $5/2, first Tue of month free; ⏲noon-5pm Tue-Fri, 11am-4pm Sat) Picture what it was like to be Chinese in America during the Gold Rush, the transcontinental railroad construction or in the Beat heyday at the nation's largest Chinese American historical institute. There are rotating exhibits across the courtyard in CHSA's graceful red-brick, green-tile-roofed landmark building, built as Chinatown's YWCA in 1932 by Julia Morgan, chief architect of Hearst Castle.

Chinese Culture Center CULTURAL CENTER

(Map p58; ☎415-986-1822; www.c-c-c.org; 3rd fl, Hilton Hotel, 750 Kearny St; gallery free, donation requested; ⏲10am-4pm Tue-Sat) You can see all the way to China on the 3rd floor of the Hilton inside this cultural center, which hosts exhibits of traditional Chinese arts; Xian Rui (Fresh & Sharp) cutting-edge art installations, such as Stella Zhang's discomfiting toothpick-studded pillows; and Art at Night, showcasing Chinese-inspired art, jazz, and food. Check the center's online

Chinatown & North Beach

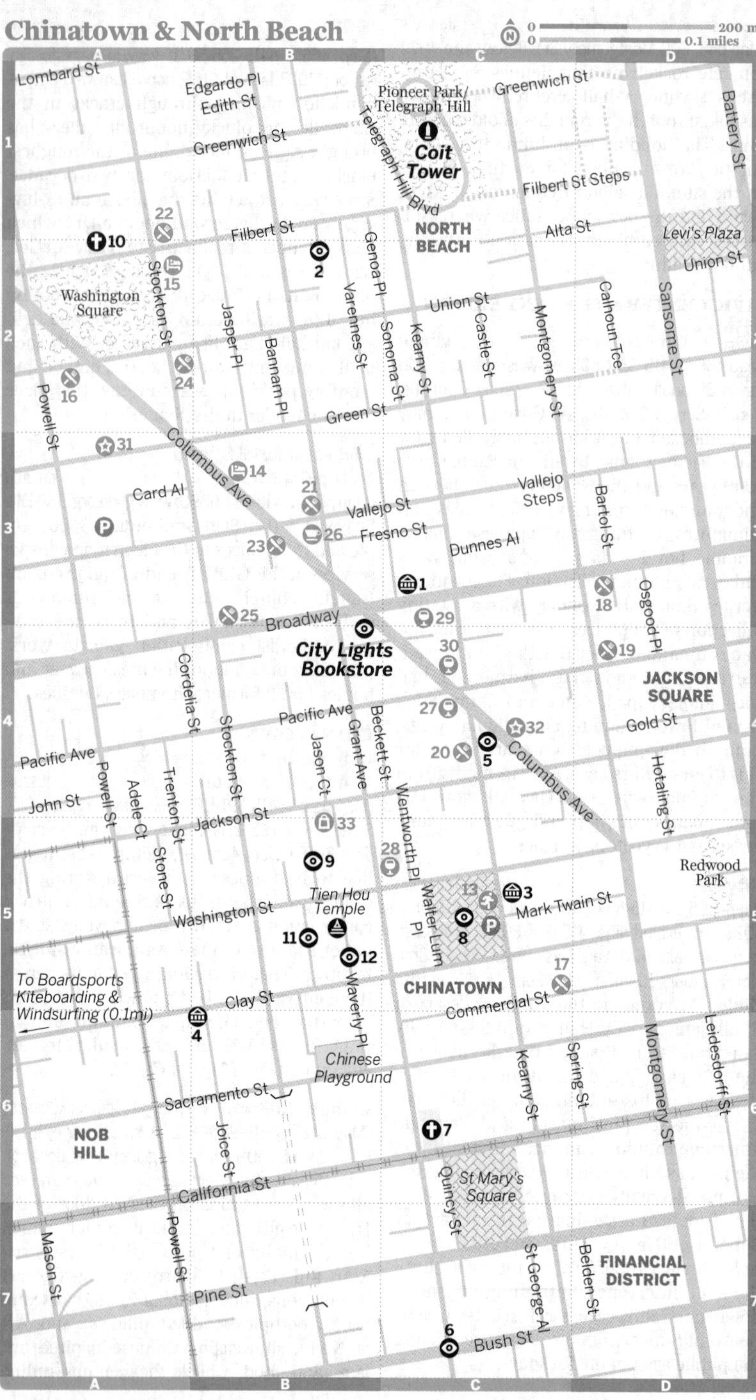

Chinatown & North Beach

Top Sights
- City Lights Bookstore ... B4
- Coit Tower ... C1

Sights
1 Beat Museum ... C3
2 Bob Kaufman Alley ... B2
3 Chinese Culture Center ... C5
4 Chinese Historical Society of America Museum ... B6
5 Columbus Tower ... C4
6 Dragon Gate ... C7
7 Old St Mary's Church ... C6
8 Portsmouth Square ... C5
9 Ross Alley ... B5
10 Saints Peter & Paul Church ... A2
11 Spofford Alley ... B5
12 Waverly Place ... B5

Activities, Courses & Tours
13 Chinatown Alleyways Tours ... C5

Sleeping
14 Hotel Bohème ... B3
15 Washington Square Inn ... A2

Eating
16 Cinecittà ... A2
17 City View ... C5
18 Coi ... D3
19 Cotogna ... D4
20 House of Nanking ... C4
21 Ideale ... B3
22 Liguria Bakery ... A1
23 Molinari ... B3
24 Tony's Coal-fired Pizza & Slice House ... A2
25 Yuet Lee ... B3

Drinking
26 Caffe Trieste ... B3
27 Comstock Saloon ... C4
28 Li Po ... C5
29 Specs' ... C3
30 Tosca Cafe ... C4

Entertainment
31 Beach Blanket Babylon ... A3
32 Purple Onion ... C4

Shopping
33 Golden Gate Fortune Cookie Company ... B5

schedule for concerts, hands-on arts workshops, Mandarin classes, genealogy services and Chinatown arts festivals.

Dragon Gate LANDMARK
(Map p58; at Bush St & Grant Ave) Enter the Dragon Gate donated by Taiwan in 1970, and you're on the once-notorious street known as Dupont in its red-light heyday. Forward-thinking Chinatown businessmen headed by Look Tin Ely pooled funds in the 1920s to reinvent the area as the tourist attraction you see today, hiring architects to create a signature 'Chinatown Deco' look with pagoda-style roofs and dragon lanterns lining Grant Ave.

Old St Mary's Church CHURCH
(Map p58; ☎415-288-3800; www.oldsaintmarys.org; 660 California St) For decades after its 1854 construction, the Catholic archdiocese valiantly tried to give this brothel district some religion. The 1906 fire destroyed one of the district's biggest bordellos directly across from the church, making room for St Mary's Sq, where skateboarders now ride handrails while Beniamino Bufano's 1929 **Sun Yat-sen statue** keeps a lookout.

Portsmouth Square SQUARE
(Map p58) Chinatown's outdoor living room is named after John B Montgomery's sloop that docked nearby in 1846, but the presiding deity at this people's park is the **Goddess of Democracy**, a bronze replica of the plaster statue made by Tiananmen Sq protesters in 1989. Historical markers dot the perimeter of the historic square, noting the site of San Francisco's first bookshop and newspaper, and the bawdy Jenny Lind Theater, which with a few modifications became San Francisco's first City Hall. A **night market** is held here from 6pm to 11pm each Saturday from July to October.

NORTH BEACH

TOP CHOICE City Lights Bookstore CULTURAL BUILDING
Map p58; www.citylights.com; 261 Columbus Ave; ⏲10am-midnight) Ever since manager Shigeyoshi Murao and founder and Beat poet Lawrence Ferlinghetti successfully defended their right to 'willfully and lewdly print' Allen Ginsberg's magnificent *Howl and Other Poems* in 1957, this bookstore has been a landmark. Celebrate your freedom to read freely in the designated Poet's Chair upstairs overlooking Jack Kerouac Alley, load up on 'zines on the mezzanine or entertain radical

THREE CHINATOWN ALLEYS THAT MADE HISTORY

» **Waverly Place** (Map p58) After the 1906 earthquake and fire devastated Chinatown, developers schemed to relocate Chinatown residents left homeless to less desirable real estate outside the city. But representatives from the Chinese consulate and several gun-toting merchants marched back to Waverly Place, holding temple services amid the rubble at still-smoldering altars. The alley is also the namesake for the main character in Amy Tan's bestselling *The Joy Luck Club*.

» **Spofford Alley** (Map p58) Sun Yat-sen plotted the overthrow of China's last emperor at No 36 and the 1920s brought bootleggers' gun battles to this alley, but Spofford has mellowed with age. In the evenings you'll hear the shuffling of mahjong tiles and an *erhu* (two-stringed Chinese fiddle) warming up at local senior centers.

» **Ross Alley** (Map p58) Alternately known as Manila, Spanish and Mexico St after the working girls who once worked this block, mural-lined Ross Alley is occasionally pimped out for Hollywood productions, including *Karate Kid II* and *Indiana Jones and the Temple of Doom*.

ideas downstairs in the Muckracking and Stolen Continents sections.

Beat Museum MUSEUM

(Map p58; ☎1-800-537-6822; www.thebeatmuseum.org; 540 Broadway; admission $5; ⏰10am-7pm Tue-Sun) For the complete Beat experience, stop by to check out City Lights' banned edition of Allen Ginsberg's *Howl,* Beat-era documentary footage in a makeshift theater, and tributes to authors who expanded the American outlook to include the margins – including a $10.18 check Jack Kerouac wrote for liquor.

Columbus Tower BUILDING

(Map p58; 916 Kearny St) Shady political boss Abe Ruef had only just finished this copper-clad building in 1905 when it was hit by the 1906 earthquake, and he restored it right before he was convicted of bribery and bankrupted in 1907. The Kingston Trio bought the building in the 1960s, and recorded reggae and the Grateful Dead in the basement. Since 1970 the building has belonged to filmmaker Francis Ford Coppola, who leases the top floors to fellow filmmakers Sean Penn and Wayne Wang and sells Italian fare and his own-label Napa wine at ground-level Café Niebaum-Coppola. Our advice: skip the pasta, take the cannoli.

Bob Kauffman Alley STREET

(Map p58; off Grant Ave near Filbert St) Enjoy a moment of profound silence courtesy of the Beat-bebop-jazz-poet-anarchist-voodoo-Jewish-biracial-African-all-American-streetcorner-prophet who refused to speak for 12 years after the assassination of John F Kennedy. The day the Vietnam War ended, he broke his silence by walking into a cafe and reciting his poem 'All Those Ships That Never Sailed'.

Saints Peter & Paul Church CHURCH

(Map p58; ☎415-421-0809; www.stspeterpaul.san-francisco.ca.us; 666 Filbert St; ⏰7:30am-4pm) Wedding-cake cravings are to be expected upon sight of this 1924 church, the frosting-white triple-decker cathedral where Joe Di Maggio and Marilyn Monroe famously posed for wedding photos (since they were both divorced, they were denied a church wedding here). The church overlooks Washington Sq, the North Beach park where nonagenarian *nonnas* (Italian grandmothers) feed wild parrots by the 1897 **Ben Franklin statue**.

FISHERMAN'S WHARF

Aquatic Park Bathhouse HISTORIC BUILDING

(Map p62; ☎415-447-5000; www.nps.gov/safr; 499 Jefferson at Hyde; adult/child $5/free; ⏰10am-4pm) A monumental hint to sailors in need of a scrub, this recently restored, ship-shape 1939 Streamline Moderne landmark is decked out with WPA art treasures: playful seal and frog sculptures by Beniamino Bufano, Hilaire Hiler's surreal underwater dreamscape murals and recently uncovered wood reliefs by Richard Ayer. Acclaimed African American artist Sargent Johnson created the stunning carved green slate marquee doorway and the veranda's mesmerizing aquatic mosaics, which he deliberately left unfinished on the east side to protest plans to include a private restaurant in this public facility. Johnson won: the east wing is now a maritime museum office.

FREE **Musée Mecanique** MUSEUM

(Map p62; ☎415-346-2000; www.museemecanique.org; Pier 45, Shed A; ⏲10am-7pm Mon-Fri, to 8pm Sat & Sun; 👪) A few quarters let you start bar brawls in coin-operated Wild West saloons, peep at belly-dancers through a vintage Mutoscope, save the world from Space Invaders and get your fortune told by an eerily lifelike wooden swami at this vintage arcade.

USS Pampanito HISTORIC SITE

(Map p62; ☎415-775-1943; www.maritime.org; Pier 45; adult/child $10/4; ⏲9am-5pm) Explore a restored WWII submarine that survived six tours of duty, while listening to submariners' tales of stealth mode and sudden attacks in a riveting audio tour ($2) that makes surfacing afterwards a relief (caution claustrophobes).

Pier 39 LANDMARK

(Map p62; ☎415-981-1280; www.pier39.com; Beach St & Embarcadero; 👪) Ever since they first hauled out here in 1990, 300 to 1300 sea lions have spent winter through summer bellyflopped on these yacht docks. While bulls jostle for prime sunning location on the piers, boardwalk B-boyers compete for street-dance supremacy and kids wage battles of the will with parents over souvenir teddy bears.

RUSSIAN HILL & NOB HILL

Grace Cathedral CHURCH

(Map p62; ☎415-749-6300; www.gracecathedral.org; 1100 California St; suggested donation adult/child $3/2; ⏲7am-6pm Mon-Fri, 8am-6pm Sat, 8am-7pm Sun, services with choir 8:30am & 11am Sun) Rebuilt three times since the Gold Rush, and still this progressive Episcopal church keeps pace with the times. Additions include the AIDS Interfaith Memorial Chapel, which features a bronze Keith Haring altarpiece; stained-glass 'Human Endeavor' windows that illuminate Albert Einstein in a swirl of nuclear particles; and pavement labyrinths offering guided meditation for restless souls.

San Francisco Art Institute GALLERY

(SFAI; Map p62; ☎415-771-7020; www.sfai.edu; 800 Chestnut St; ⏲9am-7:30pm) Founded during the 1870s, SFAI was the centre of the Bay Area's figurative art scene in the 1940s and '50s, turned to Bay Area Abstraction in the '60s and conceptual art in the '70s, and since the '90s has championed new media art in its **Walter and McBean Gallery** (⏲11am-6pm Mon-Sat). Also on campus, the **Diego Rivera Gallery** features Rivera's 1931 mural *The Making of a Fresco Showing a Building of a City,* a fresco within a fresco showing the back of the artist himself, as he pauses to admire the constant work in progress of San Francisco.

JAPANTOWN & PACIFIC HEIGHTS

Japan Center CULTURAL BUILDING

(off Map p62; www.sfjapantown.org; 1625 Post St; ⏲10am-midnight) Still looks much the way it did when it opened in 1968, with indoor wooden pedestrian bridges, *ikebana* (flower-arranging) displays and *maneki-neko* (waving cat) figurines beckoning from restaurant entryways.

Haas-Lilienthal House HISTORIC BUILDING

(Map p62; ☎415-441-3004; 2007 Franklin St; adult/child $8/5; ⏲noon-3pm Wed & Sat, 11am-4pm Sun) An 1882 Queen Anne with decor that looks

WORTH A TRIP

COIT TOWER

Adding an exclamation mark to San Francisco's landscape, **Coit Tower** (Map p58; ☎415-362-0808; Telegraph Hill; admission free, elevator rides $5; ⏲10am-6pm) offers views worth shouting about – especially after you climb the giddy, steep Filbert St or Greenwich St steps to the top of Telegraph Hill. This 210ft, peculiar projectile is a monument to San Francisco firefighters financed by eccentric heiress Lillie Hitchcock Coit. Lillie could drink, smoke and play cards as well as any off-duty firefighter, rarely missed a fire or a firefighter's funeral and even had the firehouse emblem embroidered on all her bedsheets.

When Lillie's totem was completed in 1934, the worker-glorifying, Diego Rivera–style WPA murals lining the lobby were denounced as Communist, as were the 25 artists who worked on them. Now protected as historic landmarks, the lobby murals broaden world-views just as surely as the 360-degree views of downtown from the tower-top viewing platform. To see more murals hidden inside Coit Tower's stairwell, take one of the free guided tours at 11am on Saturdays.

Fisherman's Wharf, The Marina & Russian Hill

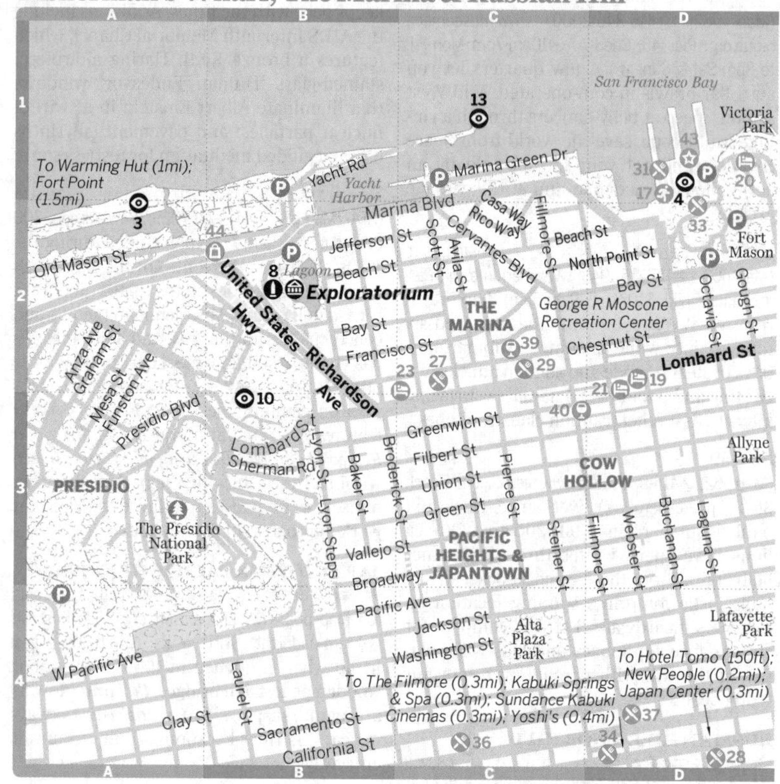

like a murder-mystery setting, including a dark-wood ballroom, red-velvet parlor and spooky stairways. One-hour tours are led by volunteers devoted to Victoriana.

Peace Pagoda MONUMENT

(off Map p66; Peace Plaza) San Francisco's sister city of Osaka in Japan gifted Yoshiro Taniguchi's striking minimalist concrete pagoda to the people of San Francisco in 1968.

THE MARINA

TOP CHOICE **Exploratorium** MUSEUM

(Map p62; ☎415-561-0360; www.exploratorium.edu; 3601 Lyon St; adult/child $15/10, incl. Tactile Dome $20; ⊙10am-5pm Tue-Sun; 👪) Budding Nobel Prize winners swarm this hands-on discovery museum that's been blowing minds since 1969, answering the questions you always wanted to ask in science class: does gravity apply to skateboarding, do robots have feelings and do toilets flush counterclockwise in Australia? One especially far-out exhibit is the **Tactile Dome**, a pitch-black space that you can crawl, climb and slide through (advance reservations required). It's moving to Piers 15 and 17 in 2013.

Palace of Fine Arts MONUMENT

(Map p62; www.lovethepalace.org; Palace Dr) When San Francisco's 1915 Panama-Pacific expo was over, SF couldn't bear to part with this Greco-Roman plaster palace. California Arts and Crafts architect Bernard Maybeck's artificial ruin was recast in concrete, so that future generations could gaze up at the rotunda relief to glimpse Art under attack by Materialists, with Idealists leaping to her rescue.

Wave Organ MONUMENT

(Map p62) Another intriguing Exploratorium project, this sound system of PVC tubes, concrete pipes and found marble from San Francisco's old cemetery was installed into the Marina Boat Harbor jetty by artist Peter

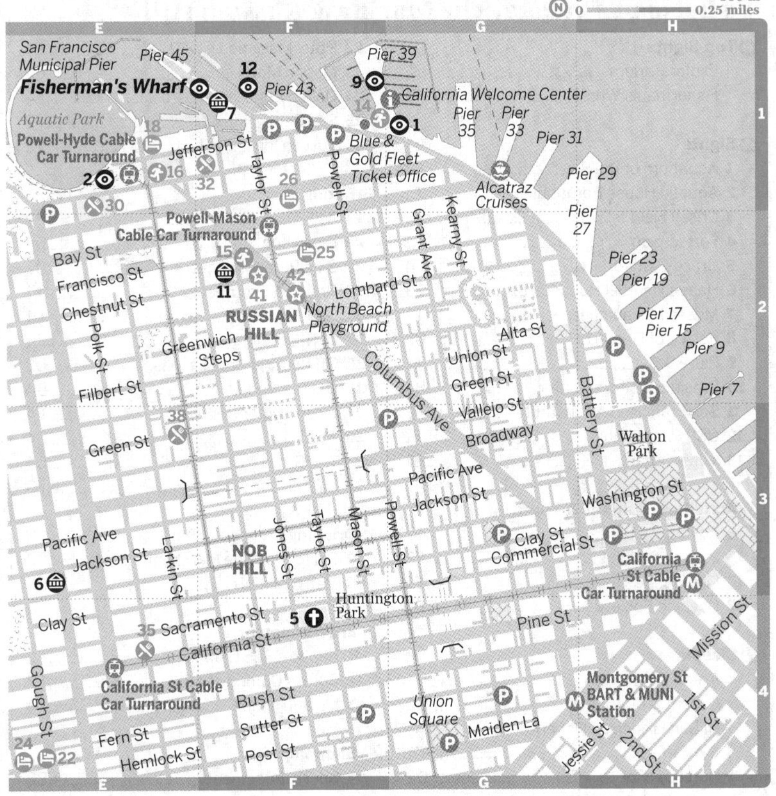

Richards in 1986. Depending on the waves, winds and tide, the tones emitted by the organ can sound like nervous humming, a gurgling baby or prank-call heavy breathing.

Fort Mason HISTORIC SITE

(Map p62; ☎415-345-7500; www.fortmason.org) Army sergeants would be scandalized by the frolicking at this former military outpost, including comedy improv workshops, vegetarian brunches at **Greens** (p85) and **Off the Grid** (p85), where gourmet trucks circle like pioneer wagons.

THE PRESIDIO

Presidio Visitors Center HISTORIC BUILDING

(Map p62; ☎415-561-4323; www.nps.gov/prsf; cnr Montgomery St & Lincoln Blvd; ⌚9am-5pm) San Francisco's official motto is still 'Oro in Paz, Fierro in Guerra' (Gold in Peace, Iron in War), but its main base hasn't seen much military action since it was built by conscripted Ohlone as a Spanish *presidio* (military post) in 1776. Jerry Garcia began and ended his ignominious military career here by going AWOL nine times in eight months and getting court-martialed twice before co-founding the Grateful Dead.

The Presidio's military role ended in 1994, when the 1480-acre plot became part of the Golden Gate National Recreation Area. The Visitors Center can direct you towards the **Pet Cemetery** off Crissy Field Ave, where handmade tombstones commemorate military hamsters who've completed their final tour of duty. Today the only wars waged around here are interstellar ones in George Lucas' screening room in the **Letterman Digital Arts Center**, right by the Yoda statue.

Crissy Field PARK

(Map p62; www.crissyfield.org; 603 Mason St; ⌚sunrise-sunset, Center 9am-5pm) War is now officially for the birds at this former military airstrip, restored as a tidal marsh and

Fisherman's Wharf, The Marina & Russian Hill

Top Sights
- Exploratorium B2
- Fisherman's Wharf F1

Sights
- 1 Aquarium of the Bay G1
- 2 Aquatic House Bathhouse E1
- 3 Crissy Field A2
- 4 Fort Mason D1
- 5 Grace Cathedral F4
- 6 Haas-Lilienthal House E3
- 7 Musée Mecanique F1
- 8 Palace of Fine Arts B2
- 9 Pier 39 ..... F1
- 10 Presidio Visitors Center B3
- 11 San Francisco Art Institute F2
- 12 USS Pampanito F1
- 13 Wave Organ C1

Activities, Courses & Tours
- 14 Adventure Cat F1
- 15 Blazing Saddles F2
- 16 Fire Engine Tours E1
- 17 Oceanic Society D1

Sleeping
- 18 Argonaut Hotel E1
- 19 Coventry Motor Inn D2
- 20 HI San Francisco Fisherman's Wharf D1
- 21 Hotel Del Sol D2
- 22 Hotel Majestic E4
- 23 Marina Motel C2
- 24 Queen Anne Hotel E4
- 25 San Remo Hotel F2
- 26 Tuscan Inn F1

Eating
- 27 A16 ..... C2
- 28 Benkyodo D4
- 29 Blue Barn Gourmet C2
- 30 Crown & Crumpet E1
- 31 Greens D1
- 32 In-N-Out Burger F1
- 33 Off the Grid D2
- 34 Out the Door D4
- 35 Swan Oyster Depot E4
- 36 Tataki C4
- 37 The Grove D4
- 38 Za E3

Drinking
- 39 California Wine Merchant C2
- 40 MatrixFillmore C3

Entertainment
- 41 Bimbo's 365 Club F2
- 42 Cobb's Comedy Club F2
- 43 Magic Theatre D1

Shopping
- 44 Sports Basement B2

reclaimed by knock-kneed coastal birds. On blustery days, bird-watch from the shelter of Crissy Field Center, which has a cafe counter facing the field with binoculars. Join joggers and puppies romping beachside trails that were once oil-stained asphalt, and on foggy days stop by the certified green **Warming Hut** (off Map p62; 983 Marine Dr; ⏰9am-5pm) to thaw out with Fair Trade coffee, browse field guides and sample honey made by Presidio honeybees.

Fort Point HISTORIC BUILDING
(off Map p62; ☎415-561-4395; www.nps.gov/fopo; Marine Dr; ⏰10am-5pm Thu-Mon) Despite its impressive guns, this Civil War fort saw no action – at least until Alfred Hitchcock shot scenes from *Vertigo* here, with stunning views of the Golden Gate Bridge from below.

Baker Beach BEACH
The city's best beach, with windswept pines uphill, craggy cliffs and a whole lot of exposed goosebumps on the breezy, clothing-optional north end.

SOUTH OF MARKET (SOMA)

TOP CHOICE **San Francisco Museum of Modern Art** MUSEUM
(SFMOMA; Map p66; ☎415-357-4000; www.sfmoma.org; 151 3rd St; adult/student/child $18/11/free, first Tue of month free; ⏰11am-6pm Fri-Tue, to 9pm Thu) Swiss architect Mario Botta's light-filled brick box leans full-tilt toward the horizon, with curators similarly inclined to take forward-thinking risks on Matthew Barney's poetic videos involving industrial quantities of Vaseline and Olafur Eliasson's outer-space light installations. SFMOMA has arguably the world's leading photography collection, with works by Ansel Adams, Daido Moriyama, Diane Arbus, Edward Weston, William Eggleston and Dorothea Lange, and since its 1995 grand reopening coincided with the tech boom, SFMOMA

became an early champion of new media art. Sculpture sprouts from the new rooftop garden, and a $480 million expansion is underway to accommodate 1100 major modern works donated by the Fisher family (local founders of Gap). Go Thursday nights after 6pm for half-price admission and the most artful flirting in town.

Contemporary Jewish Museum MUSEUM
(Map p66; ☎415-655-7800; www.jmsf.org; 736 Mission St; adult/student/child $10/8/free; ⏰11am-5:30pm Fri-Tue, 1-8:30pm Thu) In 2008, architect Daniel Liebskind reshaped San Francisco's 1881 power plant with a blue steel extension to form the Hebrew word *l'chaim* ('to life'). Inside this architectural statement are lively shows, ranging from a retrospective of modern art instigator and Bay Area native Gertrude Stein to Linda Ellia's *Our Struggle: Artists Respond to Mein Kampf,* for which 600 artists from 17 countries were invited to alter one page of Hitler's book.

Cartoon Art Museum MUSEUM
(Map p66; ☎415-227-8666; www.cartoonart.org; 655 Mission St; adult/student $7/5, 'pay what you wish' first Tue of month; ⏰11am-5pm Tue-Sun; 👪) Comics fans need no introduction to the museum founded on a grant from Bay Area cartoon legend Charles M Schultz (of *Peanuts* fame). International and noteworthy local talent includes longtime Haight resident R Crumb and East Bay graphic novelists Daniel Clowes *(Ghostworld),* Gene Yang *(American Born Chinese)* and Adrian Tomine *(Optic Nerve).* Lectures and openings are rare opportunities to mingle with comics legends, Pixar studio heads and obsessive collectors.

Museum of the African Diaspora MUSEUM
(MoAD; Map p66; ☎415-358-7200; www.moadsf.org; 685 Mission; adult/student $10/5; ⏰11am-6pm Wed-Sat, noon-5pm Sun; 👪) An international cast of characters tell the epic story of the diaspora, from Ethiopian painter Qes Adamu Tesfaw's three-faced icons to quilts by India's Siddi community, descended from 16th-century African slaves. Themed interactive displays vary in interest and depth, but don't miss the moving video of slave narratives voiced by Maya Angelou.

Museum of Craft and Folk Art MUSEUM
(Map p66; ☎415-227-4888; www.mocfa.org; 51 Yerba Buena Lane; adult/child $5/free; ⏰11am-5pm Tue-Sun) Intricate handiwork with fascinating personal backstories, from sublime Shaker women's woodworking to contemporary Korean *bojagi* (wrapping textiles).

FREE **Catharine Clark Gallery** GALLERY
(Map p66; ☎415-399-1439; www.cclarkgallery.com; 150 Minna St; ⏰11am-6pm Tue-Sat) No material is too political or risqué at San Francisco's most cutting-edge gallery: Masami Teraoka paints geishas and goddesses as superheroines fending off wayward priests, and Packard Jennings offers instructional pamphlets for converting cities into wildlife refuges.

THE MISSION

Mission Dolores CHURCH
(Map p88; ☎415-621-8203; www.missiondolores.org; cnr Dolores & 16th Sts; adult/child $5/3; ⏰9am-4pm) The city's oldest building and its namesake, the whitewashed adobe Misión San Francisco de Asis was founded in 1776 and rebuilt in 1782 with conscripted Ohlone and Miwok labor in exchange – note the ceiling patterned after Native baskets. In the cemetery beside the adobe mission, a replica Ohlone hut is a memorial to the 5000 Ohlone and Miwok who died in 1814 and 1826 measles epidemics. The mission is overshadowed by the adjoining ornate 1913 **basilica,** where stained-glass windows commemorate the 21 original California missions, from Santa Cruz to San Diego.

826 Valencia CULTURAL BUILDING
(Map p88; ☎415-642-5905; www.826valencia.com; 826 Valencia St; ⏰noon-6pm; 👪) A mural by comic-artist Chris Ware graces the storefront housing this nonprofit youth writing program and purveyor of essential pirate supplies: eye patches, tubs of lard and tall tales for long nights at sea. Stop by the Fish Theater to see pufferfish immersed in Method acting. He's no Sean Penn, but as it says on the sign: 'Please don't judge the fish.' Check the website for workshops for kids and adults on scripting video games and starting up magazines, taught by industry experts.

Creativity Explored GALLERY
(Map p88; ☎415-863-2108; www.creativityexplored.org; 3245 16th St; donations welcome; ⏰10am-3pm Mon-Fri, until 7pm Thu, 1-6pm Sat) Fresh perspectives on themes ranging from superheroes to architecture by critically acclaimed, developmentally disabled artists – don't miss joyous openings with the artists, their families and fans.

Downtown San Francisco & South of Market (SoMa)

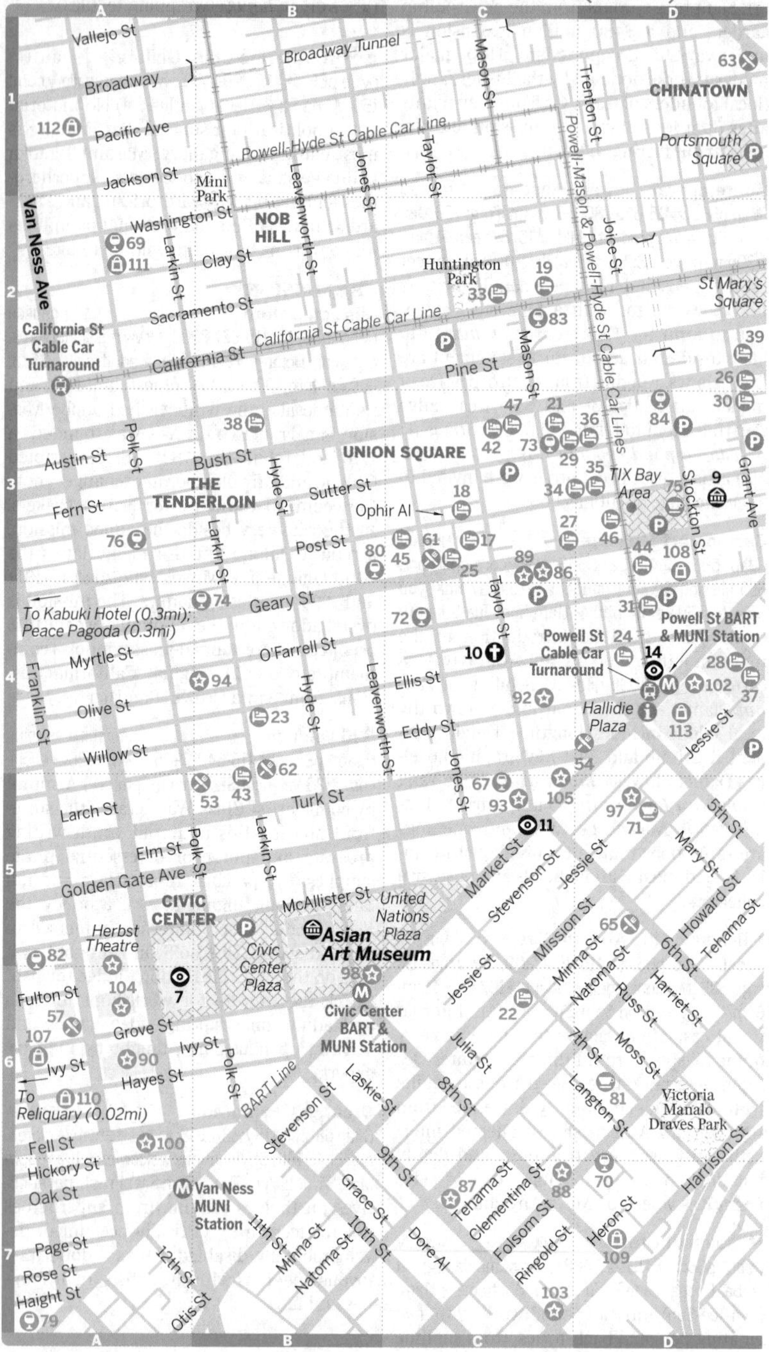

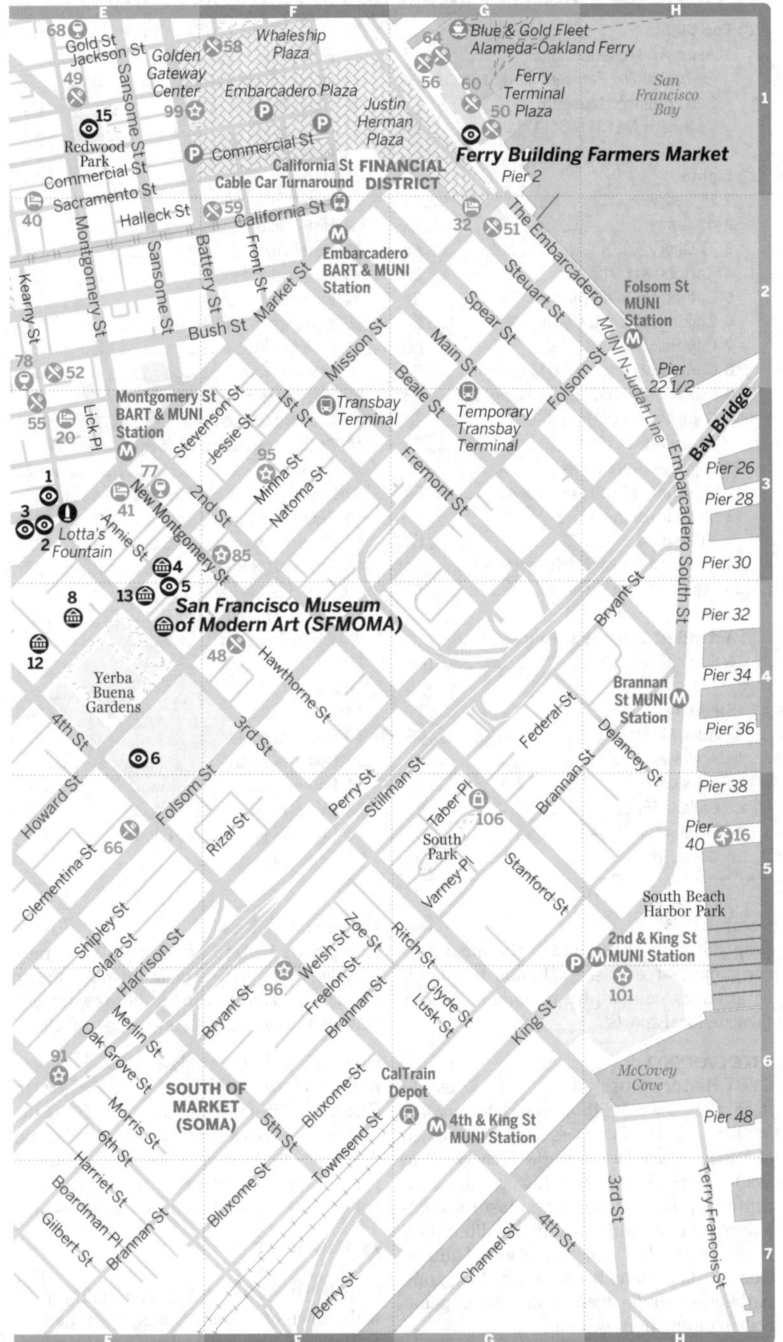

Blue & Gold Fleet
Alameda-Oakland Ferry
Ferry Terminal Plaza
San Francisco Bay
Whaleship Plaza
Golden Gateway Center
Embarcadero Plaza
Justin Herman Plaza
Ferry Building Farmers Market
Pier 2
Redwood Park
California St Cable Car Turnaround
FINANCIAL DISTRICT
Embarcadero BART & MUNI Station
Folsom St MUNI Station
Pier 22 1/2
Montgomery St BART & MUNI Station
Transbay Terminal
Temporary Transbay Terminal
Bay Bridge
Pier 26
Pier 28
Lotta's Fountain
Pier 30
San Francisco Museum of Modern Art (SFMOMA)
Pier 32
Yerba Buena Gardens
Pier 34
Brannan St MUNI Station
Pier 36
Pier 38
South Park
Pier 40
South Beach Harbor Park
2nd & King St MUNI Station
McCovey Cove
SOUTH OF MARKET (SOMA)
CalTrain Depot
4th & King St MUNI Station
Pier 48
SAN FRANCISCO

Downtown San Francisco & South of Market (SoMa)

Top Sights

Asian Art Museum ... B5
Ferry Building Farmers Market ... G1
San Francisco Museum of Modern Art (SFMOMA) ... E4

Sights

1 14 Geary ... E3
2 49 Geary ... E3
3 77 Geary ... E3
4 Cartoon Art Museum ... E3
5 Catharine Clark Gallery ... E4
6 Children's Creativity Center ... E4
7 City Hall ... A6
8 Contemporary Jewish Museum ... E4
9 Folk Art International Building ... D3
10 Glide Memorial United Methodist Church ... C4
11 Luggage Store Gallery ... C5
12 Museum of Craft and Folk Art ... E4
13 Museum of the African Diaspora ... E4
14 Powell St Cable Car Turnaround ... D4
15 Transamerica Pyramid ... E1

Activities, Courses & Tours

16 Spinnaker Sailing ... H5

Sleeping

17 Adelaide Hostel ... C3
18 Andrews Hotel ... C3
19 Fairmont ... C2
20 Galleria Park ... E3
21 Golden Gate Hotel ... C3
22 Good Hotel ... C6
23 HI San Francisco City Center ... B4
24 Hotel Abri ... D4
25 Hotel Adagio ... C3
26 Hotel Des Arts ... D2
27 Hotel Frank ... C3
28 Hotel Palomar ... D4
29 Hotel Rex ... C3
30 Hotel Triton ... D3
31 Hotel Union Square ... D4
32 Hotel Vitale ... G2
33 Huntington Hotel ... C2
34 Inn at Union Square ... C3
35 Kensington Park Hotel ... D3
36 Larkspur Hotel ... D3
37 Mosser Hotel ... D4
38 Nob Hill Hotel ... B3
39 Orchard Garden Hotel ... D2
40 Pacific Tradewinds Guest House ... E2
41 Palace Hotel ... E3
42 Petite Auberge ... C3
43 Phoenix Motel ... B5
44 Stratford Hotel ... D3
45 USA Hostels ... C3
46 Westin St Francis Hotel ... D3
47 White Swan Inn ... C3

Eating

48 Benu ... F4
49 Bocadillos ... E1
50 Boulette's Larder ... G1
51 Boulevard ... G2
52 Boxed Foods ... E2
53 Brenda's French Soul Food ... B5
54 farmerbrown ... D4

Dolores Park PARK
(Map p88; cnr Dolores & 18th Sts) The site of soccer games, street basketball, nonstop political protests, competitive tanning and other favorite local sports.

THE CASTRO

GLBT History Museum MUSEUM
(Map p88; ☎415-621-1107; www.glbthistory.org/museum; 4127 18th St; admission $5, free first Wed of month; ⌚11am-7pm Tue-Sat & noon-5pm Sun-Mon) America's first gay-history museum captures proud moments and historic challenges: Harvey Milk's campaign literature, interviews with trailblazing bisexual author Gore Vidal, matchbooks from long-gone bathhouses and pages of the 1950s penal code banning homosexuality.

Harvey Milk Plaza LANDMARK
(Map p88; cnr Market & Castro Sts) A giant rainbow flag greets arrivals on Muni to this Castro plaza, named for the camera store owner who became the nation's first openly gay official.

Human Rights Campaign Action Center HISTORIC SITE
(Map p88; ☎415-431-2200; www.hrc.org; 600 Castro St) Harvey Milk's former camera storefront is now home to the civil rights advocacy group, where supporters converge to sign petitions and score 'Equality' tees by Marc Jacobs.

THE HAIGHT

Alamo Square PARK
(Map p88; Hayes & Scott Sts) This hilltop park with downtown panoramas is framed by picturesque 'Painted Ladies' – the flamboy-

55	Gitane	E3
56	Hog Island Oyster Company	G1
57	Jardinière	A6
58	Kokkari	F1
59	Michael Mina	F2
60	Mijita	G1
61	Millennium	C3
62	Saigon Sandwich Shop	B4
63	Sentinel	D1
64	Slanted Door	G1
65	Split Pea Seduction	D5
66	Zero Zero	E5

Drinking

67	Aunt Charlie's Lounge	C5
68	Barrique	E1
69	Bigfoot Lodge	A2
70	Bloodhound	D7
71	Blue Bottle Coffee Company	D5
72	Bourbon & Branch	C4
73	Cantina	C3
74	Edinburgh Castle	B4
75	Emporio Rulli Caffè	D3
76	Hemlock Tavern	A3
77	House of Shields	E3
78	Irish Bank	E2
79	Rebel	A7
	Rickhouse	(see 52)
80	Rye	B3
81	Sightglass Coffee	D6
82	Smuggler's Cove	A5
83	Top of the Mark	C2
84	Tunnel Top Bar	D3

Entertainment

85	111 Minna	F3
86	American Conservatory Theater	C3
87	AsiaSF	C7
88	Cat Club	C7
89	Curran Theatre	C3
90	Davies Symphony Hall	A6
91	EndUp	E6
92	Exit Theatre	C4
93	Golden Gate Theatre	C5
94	Great American Music Hall	B4
95	Harlot	F3
96	Hotel Utah	F6
97	Mezzanine	D5
98	Orpheum Theatre	B6
99	Punch Line	E1
100	Rickshaw Stop	A6
101	San Francisco Giants	H6
102	Sisters of Perpetual Indulgence	D4
103	The Stud	C7
104	War Memorial Opera House	A6
105	Warfield	C5

Shopping

106	Jeremy's	G5
107	MAC	A6
108	Macy's	D3
109	Madame S & Mr S Leather	D7
110	Nancy Boy	A6
111	Studio	A2
112	Velvet da Vinci	A1
113	Westfield Shopping Center	D4

antly painted and outrageously ornamented Victorian homes that took San Franciscan liberties with the regal English style. The gingerbread-trimmed houses of Postcard Row facing the park along Steiner have been disappointingly repainted in innocuous neutrals, but stroll around the square between Steiner and Scott and you'll spot Painted Ladies with drag-diva color palettes.

Zen Center HISTORIC BUILDING
(Map p88; www.sfzc.org; 300 Page St) Find a moment of Zen at the largest Buddhist community outside Asia, headquartered in an elegant building designed by Julia Morgan.

THE RICHMOND

California Palace of the Legion of Honor MUSEUM
(Map p72; ☎415-750-3600; http://legionofhonor.famsf.org; 100 34th Ave; adult/child $10/6, $2 discount with Muni ticket, 1st Tue of month free; ⏲9:30am-5:15pm Tue-Sun) A nude sculptor's model who married well and collected art with a passion, 'Big Alma' de Bretteville Spreckels gifted this museum to San Francisco. Featured artworks range from Monet waterlilies to John Cage soundscapes, Iraqi ivories to R Crumb comics – part of the Legion's Achenbach Collection of 90,000 graphic artworks.

Cliff House HISTORIC BUILDING
(Map p72; www.cliffhouse.com; 1090 Point Lobos Ave) Built by populist millionaire Adolph Sutro in 1863 as a workingman's resort, Cliff House is now in its fourth incarnation as an upscale (overpriced) restaurant. Three of the resort's attractions remain: hiking trails around the splendid ruins of **Sutro Baths**, wintertime views of sea lions frolicking

MISSION MURALS

Inspired by visiting artist Diego Rivera and the WPA murals and outraged by US foreign policy in Central America, Mission *muralistas* set out in the 1970s to transform the political landscape, one alley at a time. Precita Eyes (p73) restores historic murals, commissions new ones, and offers muralist-led tours. Several of the most noteworthy Mission murals can be found in three locations:

» **Balmy Alley** (Map p88; www.balmyalley.com; off 24th St) Between Treat Ave and Harrison St, historic early works transform garage doors into artistic and political statements, from an early memorial for El Salvador activist Archbishop Òscar Romero to a homage to the golden age of Mexican cinema.

» **Clarion Alley** (Map p88; btwn 17th & 18th Sts, off Valencia St) Only the strongest street art survives in Clarion, where lesser works are peed on or painted over. Very few pieces have lasted years, such as Andrew Schoultz's mural of gentrifying elephants displacing scraggly birds, and topical murals like the new one honoring the Arab Spring usually go up on the west end.

» **Women's Building** (Map p88; ☎415-431-1180; www.womensbuilding.org; 3543 18th St) San Francisco's biggest mural is the 1994 *MaestraPeace*, a show of female strength painted by 90 *muralistas* that wraps around the Women's Building, with icons of female strength from Mayan and Chinese goddesses to modern trailblazers, including Nobel Peace Prize winner Rigoberta Menchu, poet Audre Lorde and former US Surgeon-General Dr Jocelyn Elders.

on **Seal Rock**, and the **Camera Obscura** (admission $2; ⌚11am-sunset), a Victorian invention projecting sea views inside a small building.

INSIDE GOLDEN GATE PARK

California Academy of Sciences AQUARIUM, WILDLIFE RESERVE
(Map p72; ☎415-321-8000; www.calacademy.org; 55 Concourse Dr; adult/child $30/25, $3 discount with Muni ticket, 6-10pm Thu over 21s $10; ⌚9:30am-5pm Mon-Sat, 11am-5pm Sun; 👪) Architect Renzo Piano's 2008 landmark LEED-certified green building houses 38,000 weird and wonderful animals in a four-story rainforest and split-level aquarium under a 'living roof' of California wildflowers. After the penguins nod off to sleep, the wild rumpus starts at kids'-only Academy Sleepovers and over-21 NightLife Thursdays, when rainforest-themed cocktails encourage strange mating rituals among shy Internet daters.

MH de Young Memorial Museum MUSEUM
(Map p72; ☎415-750-3600; www.famsf.org/deyoung; 50 Hagiwara Tea Garden Dr; adult/child $10/free, $2 discount with Muni ticket, 1st Tue of month free; ⌚9:30am-5:15pm Tue-Sun, until 8:45pm Fri) Follow sculptor Andy Goldsworthy's artificial fault-line in the sidewalk into Herzog & de Meuron's sleek, copper-clad building that's oxidizing to green, blending into the park. Don't be fooled by the de Young's camouflaged exterior: shows here boldly broaden artistic horizons from Oceanic ceremonial masks and Balenciaga gowns to sculptor Al Farrow's cathedrals built from bullets. Access to the tower viewing room is free, and worth the wait for the elevator.

Conservatory of Flowers GARDEN
(Map p72; ☎15-666-7001; www.conservatoryofflowers.org; Conservatory Dr West; adult/child $7/2; ⌚10am-4pm Tue-Sun) Flower power is alive inside the newly restored 1878 Victorian conservatory, where orchids sprawl out like Bohemian divas, lilies float contemplatively and carnivorous plants reek of insect belches.

Strybing Arboretum & Botanical Gardens GARDEN
(Map p72; ☎415-661-1316; www.strybing.org; 1199 9th Ave; admission $7; ⌚9am-6pm Apr-Oct, 10am-5pm Nov-Mar) There's always something blooming in these 70-acre gardens. The Garden of Fragrance is designed for the visually impaired, and the California native plant section explodes with color when the native wildflowers bloom in early spring, right off the redwood trail.

Japanese Tea Garden GARDEN
(Map p72; http://japaneseteagardensf.com; Hagiwara Tea Garden Dr; adult/child $7/5, Mon, Wed, Fri before 10am free; ⌚9am-6pm; 👪) Mellow out

in the Zen Garden, admire doll-sized trees that are pushing 100, and sip toasted-rice green tea under a pagoda in this picturesque 5-acre garden founded in 1894.

Stow Lake LAKE

(Map p72; http://sfrecpark.org/StowLake.aspx; paddleboats/canoes/rowboats/bikes per hr $24/20/19/8; ⊙rentals 10am-4pm) Huntington Falls tumble down 400ft Strawberry Hill into the lake, near a romantic Chinese pavilion and a 1946 boathouse offering boat and bike rentals.

Ocean Beach BEACH

(Map p72; ☎415-561-4323; www.parksconservancy.org; ⊙sunrise-sunset) The park ends at this blustery beach, too chilly for bikini-clad clambakes but ideal for wet-suited pro surfers braving rip tides (casual swimmers beware). Bonfires are permitted in designated fire-pits only; no alcohol allowed. One mile south of Ocean Beach, hang-gliders leap off 200ft cliffs and shorebirds nest in defunct Nike missile silos near the parking lot of **Fort Funston** (Skyline Blvd); follow the Great Hwy south, turn right onto Skyline Blvd and the entrance to the park is past Lake Merced on the right-hand side.

Activities

Cycling & Skating

Avenue Cyclery BICYCLE RENTAL

(Map p72; ☎415-387-3155; www.avenuecyclery.com; 756 Stanyan St; per hr/day $8/30; ⊙10am-6pm Mon-Sat, to 5pm Sun) Just outside Golden Gate Park in the Upper Haight; bike rental includes a helmet.

Blazing Saddles BICYCLE RENTAL

(Map p62; ☎415-202-8888; www.blazingsaddles.com; 2715 Hyde St; bikes per hr/day from $8/32; ⊙8am-7:30pm, weather permitting;) From this bike rental shop's Fisherman's Wharf outposts, cyclists can cross the Golden Gate Bridge and take the Sausalito ferry back to SF.

Golden Gate Park Bike & Skate CYCLING, SKATING

(Map p72; ☎415-668-1117; www.goldengateparkbikeandskate.com; 3038 Fulton St; per hr/day skates from $5/20, bikes from $3/15; ⊙10am-6pm;) To make the most of Golden Gate Park, rent wheels – especially Sundays and summer Saturdays, when JFK Dr is closed to vehicular traffic. Call ahead weekdays to make sure they're open if the weather's dismal.

Wheel Fun Rentals CYCLING, SKATING

(Map p72; ☎415-668-6699; www.wheelfunrentals.com; 50 Stow Lake Dr; per hr/day skates $6/20, bikes $8/25, tandems $12/40; ⊙9am-7pm) Glide around Golden Gate and dip into the Sunset on a reasonable rental. To cruise the waterfront, head to its second location in the Marina at Fort Mason.

Sailing, Kayaking, Windsurfing & Whale-Watching

Spinnaker Sailing SAILING

(Map p66; ☎415-543-7333; www.spinnaker-sailing.com; Pier 40; lessons $375; ⊙10am-5pm) Experienced sailors can captain a boat from Spinnaker and sail into the sunset, while landlubbers can charter a skippered vessel or take classes.

City Kayak KAYAKING

(☎415-357-1010; http://citykayak.com; South Beach Harbor; kayak rentals per hr $35-65, 3hr

DON'T MISS

GOLDEN GATE PARK

When San Franciscans refer to 'the park,' there's only one that gets the definite article. Everything that San Franciscans hold dear is in Golden Gate Park: free spirits, free music, redwoods, Frisbee, protests, fine art, bonsai and buffalo. An 1870 competition to design the park was won by 24-year-old William Hammond Hall, who spent the next two decades tenaciously fighting casino developers, theme-park boosters and slippery politicians to transform the 1017 acres of dunes into the world's largest developed park. Sporty and not-so-sporty types will appreciate the park's range of outdoor activities, with 7.5 miles of bicycle trails, 12 miles of equestrian trails, an archery range, baseball and softball diamonds, fly-casting pools, lawn bowling greens, four soccer fields and 21 tennis courts. There are places in and around the park to rent bicycles and skates.

Park information is available from **McLaren Lodge** (Map p72; ☎415-831-2700; cnr Fell & Stanyan Sts; ⊙8am-5pm Mon-Fri), and free park walking tours are organized by **Friends of Recreation & Parks** (☎415-263-0991).

The Richmond, The Sunset & Golden Gate Park

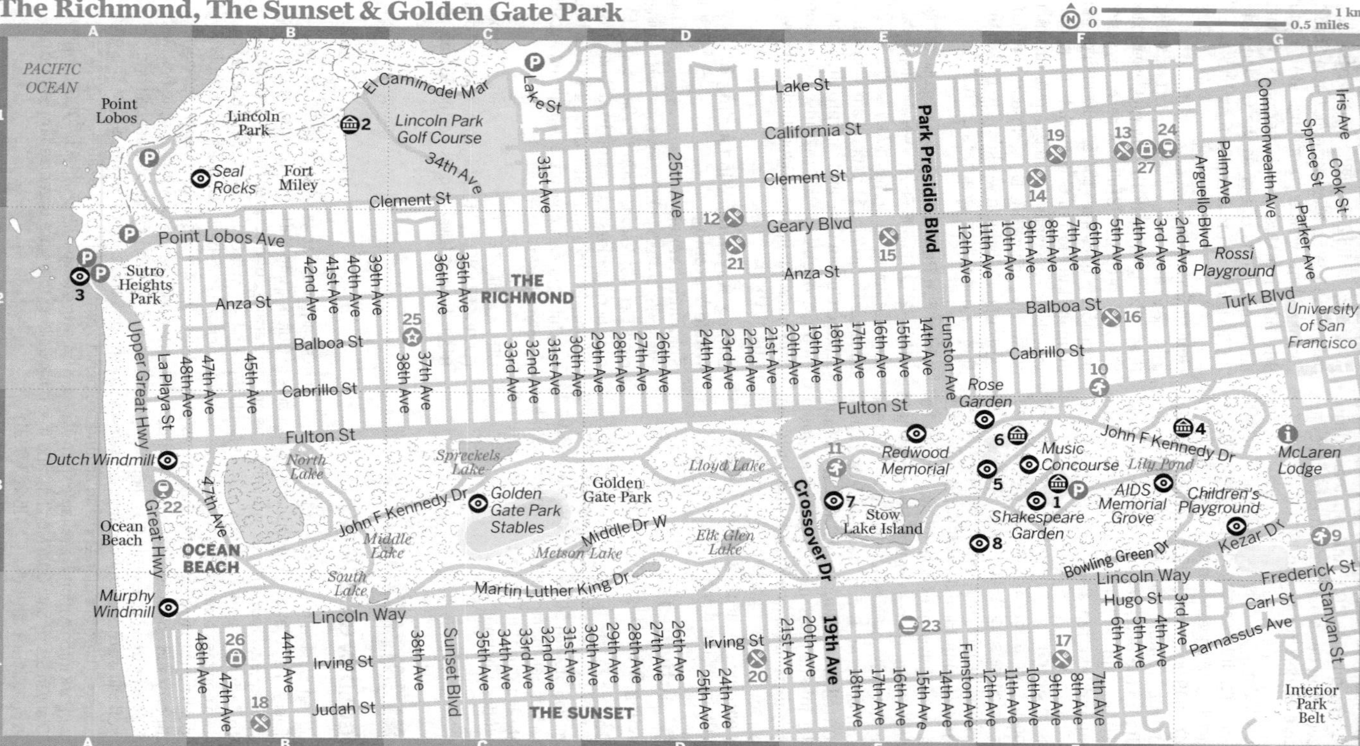

The Richmond, The Sunset & Golden Gate Park

Sights

1 California Academy of Sciences F3
2 California Palace of the Legion of Honor B1
3 Cliff House A2
4 Conservatory of Flowers G3
5 Japanese Tea Garden F3
6 MH de Young Memorial Museum F3
7 Stow Lake E3
8 Strybing Arboretum & Botanical Gardens F3

Activities, Courses & Tours

9 Avenue Cyclery G3
10 Golden Gate Park Bike & Skate F2
11 Wheel Fun Rentals E3

Eating

12 Aziza D2
13 Genki .... F
14 Halu .... F
15 Kabuto .... E
16 Namu F2
17 Nanking Road Bistro F4
18 Outerlands B4
19 Spices F1
20 Sunrise Deli D4
21 Ton Kiang D2

Drinking

22 Beach Chalet Brewery A3
23 Hollow E4
24 Plough & Stars F1

Entertainment

25 Balboa Theater C2

Shopping

26 Mollusk B4
27 Park Life F1

lesson & rental package $59, tours $65-75) Experienced paddlers hit the choppy waters beneath the Golden Gate Bridge or take a moonlit group tour, while newbies venture calm waters near the Bay Bridge.

Adventure Cat SAILING
(Map p62; ☎415-777-1630; www.adventurecat.com; Pier 39; adult/child $35/15, sunset cruise $50) Three daily catamaran cruises depart March-October; weekends only November-February.

Boardsports Kiteboarding & Windsurfing WINDSURFING
(off Map p58; ☎415-385-1224; www.boardsportsschool.com; 1200 Clay St; 1.5-2hr lessons $50-220; by appointment) Offers kiteboarding and windsurfing rentals and lessons; experienced windsurfers take on the bay at the beach off Crissy Field. Most beginner classes are held east across the bay in Alameda.

Oceanic Society WHALE-WATCHING
(Map p62; ☎415-474-3385; www.oceanic-society.org; per person $100-120; office 8:30am-5pm Mon-Fri, trips Sat & Sun) Whale sightings aren't a fluke on naturalist-led, ocean-going weekend boat trips during mid-October through December migrations. In the off-season, trips run to the Farallon Islands, 27 miles west of San Francisco.

Spas

Kabuki Springs & Spa SPA
(off Map p62; ☎415-922-6000; www.kabukisprings.com; 1750 Geary Blvd; admission $22-25; 10am-9:45pm) Soak muscles worked by SF's 43 hills in these Japanese baths for the ultimate cultural immersion experience. Men and women alternate days, and bathing suits are required on coed Tuesdays.

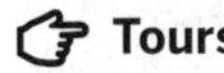

Tours

Precita Eyes Mural Tours WALKING
(Map p88; ☎415-285-2287; www.precitaeyes.org; 2981 24th St; adult/child $12-15/5; 11am, noon, 1:30pm Sat & Sun) Muralists lead two-hour tours on foot or bike covering 60 to 70 murals in a 6 to 10 block radius of mural-bedecked Balmy Alley; proceeds fund mural upkeep.

Chinatown Alleyways Tours WALKING
(Map p58; ☎415-984-1478; www.chinatownalleywaytours.org; adult/child $18/5/; 11am Sat & Sun) Neighborhood teens lead two-hour tours for up-close-and-personal peeks into Chinatown's past (weather permitting). Book five days ahead or pay double for Saturday walk-ins; cash only. Tour meeting points vary.

FREE **Public Library City Guides** WALKING
(www.sfcityguides.org) Volunteer local historians lead tours by neighborhood and theme: Art

Walking Tour

San Francisco Hilltops

Conquer San Francisco's three most famous hills – Telegraph, Russian and Nob – for views that are pure poetry.

Enter **1 Dragon Gate** and walk up dragon-lamp-lined Grant Ave to Sacramento St, where you'll turn left half a block up, then right onto **2 Waverly Place**, where prayer flags grace painted temple balconies. At Clay St, jog left and right again onto **3 Spofford Alley**, where Sun Yat-sen plotted revolution. At the end of the block on Washington, take a right and an immediate left onto **4 Ross Alley**, once San Francisco's bordello street.

Turn right down Jackson to Grant, then take the right-hand turnoff from Grant onto **5 Jack Kerouac Alley**, where the pavement echoes Kerouac's ode to San Francisco: 'The air was soft, the stars so fine, and the promise of every cobbled alley so great...' Ahead is literary landmark **6 City Lights**: head upstairs to Poetry, and read one poem.

Head left up Columbus to the corner of Vallejo and stop at **7 Molinari**, where you can get panini sandwiches for a picnic atop Telegraph Hill. Cross Columbus, veer right one block up Vallejo and fuel up with an espresso at **8 Caffe Trieste**, where Francis Ford Coppola drafted his script for *The Godfather*. Walk up Vallejo and scale the steps to Montgomery St. Go left three blocks, and turn left onto cottage-lined **9 Greenwich Street Steps** to summit Telegraph Hill. Inside **10 Coit Tower**, enjoy once-controversial murals downstairs and panoramic views of the bay up top.

Head downhill, past parrot-feeding *nonnas* (Italian grandmothers) at **11 Washington Square**. Turn left on Columbus, right on Vallejo, up three blocks and another picturesque stairway path to **12 Ina Coolbrith Park**. Any breath you have left will be taken away by sweeping views to Alcatraz. Summit your last hill of the day the easy way: catch the **13 Mason-Powell Cable Car** up Nob Hill.

WORTH A TRIP

ALCATRAZ

Almost 150 years before Guantanamo, a rocky island in the middle of San Francisco Bay became the nation's first military prison: **Alcatraz** (Map p54; ☎415-981-7625; www.alcatrazcruises.com, www.nps.gov/alcatraz; adult/child day $26/16, night $33/19.50; ⏰call center 8am-7pm, ferries depart Pier 33 every 30min 9am-3:55pm, plus 6:10pm & 6:45pm). Civil War deserters were kept in wooden pens along with Native American 'unfriendlies,' including 19 Hopis who refused to send their children to government boarding schools where Hopi religion and language were banned.

In 1934 the Federal Bureau of Prisons took over Alcatraz to make a public example of bootleggers and other gangsters. 'The Rock' only averaged 264 inmates, but its A-list criminals included Chicago crime boss Al Capone, Harlem poet-mafioso 'Bumpy' Johnson, and Morton Sobell, found guilty of Soviet espionage along with Julius and Ethel Rosenberg. Though Alcatraz was considered escape-proof, in 1962 the Anglin brothers and Frank Morris floated away on a makeshift raft and were never seen again.

Since importing guards and supplies cost more than putting up prisoners at the Ritz, the prison was closed in 1963. Native American leaders occupied the island from 1969–71 to protest US occupation of Native lands; their standoff with the FBI is commemorated in a dockside museum and 'This is Indian Land' water-tower graffiti.

Ferries depart for Alcatraz behind the Pier 33 ticket booth, but book tickets online at least two weeks ahead in summer. Day visits include captivating audio tours with prisoners and guards recalling cellhouse life, while popular, creepy twilight tours are led by park rangers.

Deco Marina, Gold Rush Downtown, Pacific Heights Victorians, North Beach by Night and more. See website for upcoming tours.

Haight-Ashbury Flower Power Walking Tour WALKING
(Map p81; ☎415-863-1621; www.haightashburytour.com; adult/under 9yr $20/free; ⏰9:30am Tue & Sat, 2pm Thu, 11am Fri) Take a long, strange trip through 12 blocks of hippie history, following in the steps of Jimi, Jerry and Janis – if you have to ask for last names, you really need this tour, man. Tours meet at the corner of Stanyan and Waller Sts and last about two hours; reservations required. Meeting points vary.

Victorian Home Walk WALKING
(Map p66; ☎415-252-9485; www.victorianwalk.com; Westin St Francis Hotel, cnr Powell & Post Sts; per person $25; ⏰11am) Learn to tell your Queen Annes from your Sticks with prime examples in Pacific Heights. Tours last about 2½ hours; meeting points vary.

Festivals & Events

February

Lunar New Year CULTURAL
(www.chineseparade.com) Firecrackers, legions of tiny-tot martial artists and a 200ft dancing dragon make this parade at the end of February the highlight of San Francisco winters.

April & May

Cherry Blossom Festival CULTURAL
(www.nccbf.org) Celebrate spring mid-April with scrumptious food-stall yakitori, raucous taiko drums and origami flower kits from the street crafts fair.

San Francisco International Film Festival FILM
(www.sffs.org) Pace yourself: the nation's longest-running film fest is a marathon event, with 325 films, 200 directors and sundry actors and producers over two weeks from late April.

Bay to Breakers QUIRKY
(www.baytobreakers.com; race registration $44-48) Run costumed or naked from Embarcadero to Ocean Beach the third Sunday in May, while joggers dressed as salmon run upstream.

Carnaval CULTURAL
(www.carnavalsf.com) Shake your tail feathers through the Mission on Memorial Day weekend in late May.

June

Other towns have a gay day, but SF goes all out for **Pride Month**, better known elsewhere as the month of June.

DEALS AND HIDDEN COSTS

San Francisco is the birthplace of the boutique hotel, offering stylish rooms for a price: $100 to $200 rooms midrange, plus 15.5% hotel tax (hostels exempt) and $35-50 for overnight parking. For vacancies and deals, check San Francisco Visitor Information Center's **reservation line** (800-637-5196, 415-391-2000; www.onlyinSanFrancisco.com), **Bed & Breakfast SF** (415-899-0060; www.bbsf.com) and **Lonely Planet** (http://hotels.lonelyplanet.com).

Gay and Lesbian Film Festival FILM
(www.frameline.org) Here, queer and ready for a premiere: the world's oldest, biggest GLBT film fest launches new talents from 30 countries, with 200 film screenings over the last half of June.

Dyke March & Pink Saturday PARADE
(www.dykemarch.org & www.sfpride.org) Around 50,000 lesbian, bisexual and transgender women converge in Dolores Park at 7:30pm and head to Castro St to show some coed Pride at the Pink Saturday street party on the last Saturday in June.

Lesbian, Gay, Bisexual and Transgender Pride Parade PARADE
(www.sfpride.org) No one does Pride like San Francisco on the last Sunday in June: 1.2 million people, seven stages, tons of glitter, ounces of bikinis and more queens for the day than anyone can count.

September

SF Shakespeare Fest CULTURAL
(www.sfshakes.org; 7:30pm Sat, 2:30pm Sun) The play's the thing in the Presidio, outdoors and free of charge on sunny September weekends.

Folsom Street Fair QUIRKY
(www.folsomstreetfair.com) Enjoy public spankings for local charities on the last Sunday in September. To answer the obvious question in advance: yes, people do actually get pierced there, but it's best not to stare unless you're prepared to strip down and compare.

October & November

Jazz Festival MUSIC
(www.sfjazz.org) Old schoolers and hot new talents jam around the city in late October.

Litquake CULTURAL
(www.litquake.org) Authors tell stories at the biggest lit fest in the West and spill trade secrets over drinks at the legendary Lit Crawl during the second week in October.

Hardly Strictly Bluegrass MUSIC
(www.strictlybluegrass.com) SF celebrates Western roots with three days of free Golden Gate Park concerts and headliners ranging from Elvis Costello to Gillian Welch in early October.

Diá de los Muertos CULTURAL
(Day of the Dead; www.dayofthedeadsf.org) Zombie brides, Aztec dancers and toddler Frida Kahlos with drawn-on unibrows lead the parade honoring the dead down 24th St on November 2.

Sleeping

UNION SQUARE

TOP CHOICE **Orchard Garden Hotel** BOUTIQUE HOTEL $$
(Map p66; 415-399-9807; www.theorchardgardenhotel.com; 466 Bush St; r $179-249;) SF's first all-green-practices hotel has soothingly quiet rooms with luxe touches, like Egyptian-cotton sheets, plus an organic rooftop garden.

Hotel Rex BOUTIQUE HOTEL $$
(Map p66; 415-433-4434; www.jdvhotels.com; 562 Sutter St; r $169-279;) Noir-novelist chic, with 1920s literary lounge and compact rooms with hand-painted lampshades, local art and sumptuous beds piled with down pillows.

Hotel Palomar BOUTIQUE HOTEL $$$
(Map p66; 415-348-1111, 866-373-4941; www.hotelpalomar-sf.com; 12 4th St; r $199-299;) The sexy Palomar is decked out with crocodile-print carpets, chocolate-brown wood and cheetah-print robes in the closet. Beds have feather-light down comforters and Frette linens, and there's floor space for in-room yoga (request mats and DVD at check-in). Smack downtown, but rooms have soundproof windows.

Hotel Triton BOUTIQUE HOTEL **$$**
(Map p66; ☎415-394-0500, 800-800-1299; www.hotel-tritonsf.com; 342 Grant Ave; r $169-239; ❄@📶) The lobby looks straight out of a comic book, and rooms are whimsically designed and ecofriendly; least-expensive rooms are tiny and celeb suites are named after Carlos Santana and Jerry Garcia. Don't miss tarot-card readings and chair massages during nightly happy hour.

Hotel Abri BOUTIQUE HOTEL **$$**
(Map p66; ☎415-392-8800, 866-823-4669; www.hotel-abri.com; 127 Ellis St; r $149-229; ❄@📶) Snazzy boutique hotel with bold black-and-tan motifs and ultra-mod cons: iPod docking stations, pillow-top beds, flat-screen TVs and rainfall showerheads.

Hotel des Arts QUIRKY **$$**
(Map p66; ☎415-956-3232; www.sfhoteldesarts.com; 447 Bush St; r $139-199, without bath $99-149; 📶) A budget hotel for art freaks, with specialty rooms painted by underground artists – it's like sleeping inside an art installation. Standard rooms are less exciting, but clean and good value; bring earplugs.

White Swan Inn BOUTIQUE HOTEL **$$**
(Map p66; ☎415-775-1755, 800-999-9570; www.jdvhotels.com; 845 Bush St; r $159-199; P@📶) An English country inn downtown, with cabbage-rose wallpaper, red-plaid flannel bedspreads and colonial-style furniture. Hipsters may find it stifling, but if you love Tudor style, you'll feel right at home. Every room has a gas fireplace.

Hotel Adagio BOUTIQUE HOTEL **$$**
(Map p66; ☎415-775-5000, 800-228-8830; www.thehoteladagio.com; 550 Geary St; r $159-249; ❄@📶) Huge rooms set the Adagio apart, along with the snappy style: chocolate-brown and off-white leather furnishings with bright-orange splashes. Sumptuous beds have Egyptian-cotton sheets and feather pillows; bathrooms are disappointing. Still, it's a hot address for a fair price – great bar, too.

Westin St Francis Hotel HISTORIC HOTEL **$$$**
(Map p66; ☎415-397-7000, 800-228-3000; www.westin.com; 335 Powell St; r $209-369; ❄@📶) One of the city's most famous hotels, the St Francis lords over Union Sq. Tower rooms have stellar views, but feel generic; we prefer the original building's old-fashioned charm, with its high ceilings and crown moldings. The Westin's beds set the industry standard for comfort.

Hotel Frank BOUTIQUE HOTEL **$$**
(Map p66; ☎415-986-2000, 800-553-1900; www.hotelfranksf.com; 386 Geary St; r $169-299; ❄📶) A block off Union Square, Frank has a snappy, swinging design aesthetic, with big black-and-white houndstooth rugs and faux-alligator headboards. The baths are tight, but extras like plasma-screen TVs compensate.

Larkspur Hotel BOUTIQUE HOTEL **$$**
(Map p66; ☎415-421-2865, 866-823-4669; www.larkspurhotelunionsquare.com; 524 Sutter St; r $169-199; @📶) Built in 1915 and overhauled in 2008, the understatedly fancy Larkspur has a monochromatic, earth-tone color scheme and simple, clean lines. Baths are tiny but have fab rainfall showerheads.

Golden Gate Hotel HOTEL **$$**
(Map p66; ☎415-392-3702, 800-835-1118; www.goldengatehotel.com; 775 Bush St; r $165, without bath $105; @📶) A homey Edwardian hotel with kindly owners, homemade cookies and a cuddly cat, safely uphill from the Tenderloin. Most rooms have private baths, some with clawfoot tubs.

Petite Auberge B&B **$$**
(Map p66; ☎415-928-6000, 800-365-3004; www.jdvhotels.com; 863 Bush St; r $169-219; 📶) French provincial charmer; some rooms have fireplaces.

Stratford Hotel HOTEL **$**
(Map p66; ☎415-397-7080; hotelstratford.com; 242 Powell St; r incl breakfast $89-149; @📶) Simple, smallish, clean rooms with rainfall showers; request rooms facing away from clanging Powell St cable cars.

Kensington Park Hotel BOUTIQUE HOTEL **$$$**
(Map p66; ☎415-788-6400; www.kensingtonparkhotel.com; 450 Post St; r $189-269; ❄@📶) Stellar location for shopping trips; great beds, stylish rooms.

Andrews Hotel HOTEL **$$**
(Map p66; ☎415-563-6877, 800-926-3739; www.andrewshotel.com; 624 Post St; r incl breakfast $109-199; 📶) Folksy character, great rates, good location.

Inn at Union Square HOTEL **$$$**
(Map p66; ☎415-397-3510, 800-288-4346; www.unionsquare.com; 440 Post St; r $229-289; ste

$309-359; ❄@📶) Quiet, conservative elegance steps from Union Sq.

Hotel Union Square HOTEL $$
(Map p66; ☎415-397-3000, 800-553-1900; www.hotelunionsquare.com; 114 Powell St; r $150-220; ❄@📶) Swank design touches such as concealed lighting, mirrored walls and plush fabrics complement the original brick walls, compensating for small, dark rooms. Convenient location near public transport; not all rooms have air-con.

Adelaide Hostel HOSTEL $
(Map p66; ☎415-359-1915, 877-359-1915; www.adelaidehostel.com; 5 Isadora Duncan Lane; dm $30-35, r $70-90, incl breakfast; @📶) The 22-room Adelaide sets the standard for SF hostels, with up-to-date furnishings, marble-tiled bathrooms and optional $5 dinners and group activities. Private rooms may be in the nearby Dakota or Fitzgerald Hotels; request the Fitzgerald.

USA Hostels HOSTEL $
(Map p66; ☎415-440-5600, 877-483-2950; www.usahostels.com; 711 Post St; dm $30-34, r $73-83; 📶) Built in 1909, this former hotel was recently converted into a spiffy hostel with great service. Private rooms sleep 3-4; onsite cafe serves inexpensive cafeteria-style dinners.

FINANCIAL DISTRICT

Palace Hotel HISTORIC HOTEL $$$
(Map p66; ☎415-512-1111, 800-325-3535; www.sfpalace.com; 2 New Montgomery St; r $199-329; ❄@📶🏊) The landmark Palace stands as a monument to turn-of-the-20th-century grandeur, aglow with century-old Austrian crystal chandeliers. Cushy (if staid) accommodations cater to expense-account travelers, but prices drop weekends. Even if you're not staying here, drop into the opulent Garden Court to sip tea.

Galleria Park BOUTIQUE HOTEL $$
(Map p66; ☎415-781-3060, 800-738-7477; www.jdvhotels.com; 191 Sutter St; r $189-229; ❄@📶) A restyled 1911 hotel with contemporary art, Frette linens, high-end bath amenities, free evening wine hour, and – most importantly – good service. Rooms on Sutter St are noisier, but get more light; interior rooms are quietest.

Pacific Tradewinds Guest House HOSTEL $
(Map p66; ☎415-433-7970, 888-734-6783; www.Sanfranciscohostel.org; 680 Sacramento St; dm $29.50; @📶) San Francisco's smartest-looking all-dorm hostel has a blue-and-white nautical theme, fully equipped kitchen and spotless glass-brick showers. The nearest BART station is Embarcadero, and you'll have to haul your bags up four flights – but service is terrific.

CIVIC CENTER & THE TENDERLOIN

Phoenix Motel MOTEL $$
(Map p66; ☎415-776-1380, 800-248-9466; www.jdvhospitality.com; 601 Eddy St; r $119-169 incl breakfast; P📶🏊) The city's rocker crash pad draws artists and hipsters to a vintage-1950s motor lodge with tropical décor in the gritty Tenderloin. Check out the shrine to actor Vincent Gallo, opposite Room 43, and happening lounge Chambers. Bring earplugs. Parking is free, as is weekday admission to Kabuki Springs & Spa (p73).

HI San Francisco City Center HOSTEL $
(Map p66; ☎415-474-5721; www.sfhostels.com; 685 Ellis St; dm incl breakfast $25-30, r $85-100; @📶) A converted seven-story 1920s apartment building, this hostel sports 262 beds and 11 private rooms, all with private baths. The neighborhood is grim, but cheap eats and good bars are nearby.

NORTH BEACH

TOP CHOICE **Hotel Bohème** BOUTIQUE HOTEL $$
(Map p58; ☎415-433-9111; www.hotelboheme.com; 444 Columbus Ave; r $174-194; @📶) Like a love letter to the jazz era, the Bohème has moody 1950s orange, black and sage-green color schemes. Inverted Chinese umbrellas hang from ceilings and photos from the Beat years decorate the walls. Rooms are smallish, and some front on noisy Columbus Ave, but the hotel is smack in the middle of North Beach's vibrant street scene.

San Remo Hotel HOTEL $
(Map p62; ☎415-776-8688, 800-352-7366; www.sanremohotel.com; 2237 Mason St; d $65-99; @📶) One of the city's best values, the 1906 San Remo has old-fashioned charm. Rooms are simply done with mismatched turn-of-the-century furnishings, and all share bathrooms. Note: least-expensive rooms have windows onto the corridor, not the outdoors; no elevator.

Washington Square Inn B&B $$$
(Map p58; ☎415-981-4220, 800-388-0220; www.wsisf.com; 1660 Stockton St; r $179-329 incl breakfast; @📶) On a leafy, sun-dappled park, this European-style inn has tasteful rooms and

a few choice antiques, including carved-wooden armoires; least-expensive rooms are tiny. Wine and cheese each evening, and breakfast in bed.

FISHERMAN'S WHARF

TOP CHOICE Argonaut Hotel HOTEL $$$
(Map p62; ☎415-563-0800, 866-415-0704; www.argonauthotel.com; 495 Jefferson St; r $205-325; P❄📶👪) Built as a cannery in 1908, the nautical-themed Argonaut has century-old wooden beams, exposed brick walls, and porthole-shaped mirrors. All rooms have ultra-comfy beds and CD players, but some are tiny and get limited sunlight; pay extra for mesmerizing bay views.

Tuscan Inn HOTEL $$
(Map p62; ☎415-561-1100, 800-648-4626; www.tuscaninn.com; 425 North Point St; r $169-229; P❄@📶👪) Way more character than the Wharf's other tourist hotels, with bold colors and mixed patterns – who says stripes and checks don't match? Managed by fashion-forward Kimpton Hotels, with character, spacious rooms, in-room Nintendo and wine hour for parents.

HI San Francisco Fisherman's Wharf HOSTEL $
(Map p62; ☎415-771-7277; www.sfhostels.com; Bldg 240, Fort Mason; dm $25-30, r $65-100; P@📶) Trade downtown convenience for a lush, green setting. Dorms range from four to 22 beds; some are coed. No curfew, and no heat on during the day in winter: bring warm clothes. Limited free parking.

NOB HILL

Huntington Hotel LUXURY HOTEL $$$
(Map p66; ☎415-474-5400, 800-227-4683; www.huntingtonhotel.com; 1075 California St; r from $325; ❄@📶🏊) The go-to address of society ladies who prefer the comfort of tradition over the garishness of style. Book a refurbished room and an appointment at on-site Nob Hill Spa, one of the city's best.

Fairmont HISTORIC HOTEL $$$
(Map p66; ☎415-772-5000, 800-441-1414; www.fairmont.com; 950 Mason St; r $219-339; ❄@📶) The historic lobby is decked out with crystal chandeliers and towering yellow-marble columns, and rooms are comfortably business-class; for maximum character, book a room in the original 1906 building. Tower rooms have stupendous views, but look generic.

HAVE YOUR SAY

Found a fantastic restaurant that you're longing to share with the world? Disagree with our recommendations? Or just want to talk about your most recent trip?

Whatever your reason, head to lonelyplanet.com, where you can post a review, ask or answer a question on the Thorntree forum, comment on a blog, or share your photos and tips on Groups. Or you can simply spend time chatting with like-minded travelers. So go on, have your say.

Nob Hill Hotel HOTEL $$
(Map p66; ☎415-673-6080; www.nobhillinn.com; 1000 Pine St; r $125-165, ste $195-275; 📶) A 1906 hotel dressed up in Victorian style, with brass beds and floral-print carpet. The look borders on grandma-lives-here, but it's definitely not cookie cutter. Rooms on Hyde St are loud; book in back. Friendly service. Wi-fi in lobby.

JAPANTOWN & PACIFIC HEIGHTS

Kabuki Hotel HOTEL $$
(off Map p66; ☎415-922-3200, 800-333-3333; www.radisson.com; 1625 Post St; r $189-249; ❄@📶) Shoji (rice-paper) screens, platform beds, deep Japanese soaking tubs and adjoining showers liven up boxy '60s architecture. Bonuses: bonsai garden and free weekday passes to Kabuki Springs & Spa (p73).

Hotel Tomo HOTEL $$
(of Map p62; ☎415-921-4000, 888-822-8666; www.jdvhotels.com/tomo; 1800 Sutter St; r $119-189; P❄@📶👪) Japanese pop culture makes a splash in minimalist, blond-wood rooms that look like cool college dorms, with *anime* murals and beanbags.

Hotel Majestic HOTEL $$
(Map p62; ☎415-441-1100, 800-869-8966; www.thehotelmajestic.com; 1500 Sutter St; r $100-175; @📶) Traditional elegance c 1902, with Chinese porcelain lamps beside triple-sheeted beds. Standard rooms are small and need updating, but good value; don't miss the clubby lobby bar.

Queen Anne Hotel B&B $$
(Map p62; ☎415-441-2828, 800-227-3970; www.queenanne.com; 1590 Sutter St; r incl breakfast

$123-169, ste $203-255; P@wifi) The Queen Anne Hotel occupies a lovely former Victorian girls' school, built in 1890, with frills galore. Comfortable (if sometimes tiny) rooms are antique-filled; some have wood-burning fireplaces.

THE MARINA & COW HOLLOW

Hotel Del Sol MOTEL $$

(Map p62; ☎415-921-5520; www.thehoteldelsol.com; 3100 Webster St; d $149-199; P❄@wifi pool family) A colorful, revamped 1950s motor lodge, with heated outdoor pool, board games, and family suites with bunk-beds.

Marina Motel MOTEL $

(Map p62; ☎415-928-1000; www.marinainn.com; 3110 Octavia Blvd; r $79-109; wifi) The Marina is a bougainvillea-bedecked 1939 motor court, offering some rooms with kitchens ($10 extra) and free parking. Request quiet rooms in back.

Coventry Motor Inn MOTEL $

(Map p62; ☎415-567-1200; www.coventrymotorinn.com; 1901 Lombard St; r $95-145; P❄wifi family) Of the motels lining Lombard St, the generic Coventry has the highest overall quality-to-value ratio, with spacious rooms and covered parking.

SOUTH OF MARKET (SOMA)

TOP CHOICE **Hotel Vitale** HOTEL $$$

(Map p66; ☎415-278-3700, 888-890-8688; www.hotelvitale.com; 8 Mission St; d $239-379; ❄@wifi) Behind that skyscraper exterior is a soothing spa-hotel, with silky-soft 450-thread-count sheets and rooftop hot tubs; upgrade to bay-view rooms.

Good Hotel MOTEL $$

(Map p66; ☎415-621-7001; www.thegoodhotel.com; 112 7th St; r $109-169; P@wifi pool) A revamped motor lodge that places a premium on green, with reclaimed wood headboards, light fixtures of repurposed bottles, and fleece bedspreads made of recycled soda bottles. The vibe is upbeat and there's a pool across the street and bikes for rent, but the neighborhood is sketchy.

Mosser Hotel HOTEL $$

(Map p66; ☎415-986-4400, 800-227-3804; www.themosser.com; 54 4th St; r $129-159, with shared bath $69-99; @wifi) Tiny rooms and tinier bathrooms, but with stylish details and central location.

THE MISSION

Inn San Francisco B&B $$

(Map p88; ☎415-641-0188; www.innsf.com; 943 S Van Ness Ave; r incl breakfast $175-285, with shared bath $120-145, cottage $335; P@wifi) Impeccably maintained and packed with antiques, this 1872 Italianate-Victorian mansion has a redwood hot tub in the English garden, genteel guestrooms with fresh-cut flowers and featherbeds and limited parking.

THE CASTRO

Parker Guest House B&B $$

(Map p88; ☎415-621-3222; www.parkerguesthouse.com; 520 Church St; r incl breakfast $149-229; P@wifi) SF's best gay B&B has cushy rooms with super-comfortable beds and down comforters in adjoining Edwardian mansions, plus a steam room and garden.

Belvedere House B&B $$

(off Map p88; ☎415-731-6654; www.belvederehouse.com; 598 Belvedere St; r incl breakfast $125-190; @wifi) Castro's romantic getaway on a leafy side street, with vintage chandeliers and eclectic art in six cozy rooms. Though primarily for gay guests, all are welcome – kids get child-sized bathrobes. No elevator.

Inn on Castro B&B $$

(Map p88; ☎415-861-0321; www.innoncastro.com; 321 Castro St; r $165-195, without bath $125-155, breakfast incl; self-catering apt $165-220; wifi) A portal to the Castro's disco heyday, this Edwardian townhouse is decked out with top-end '70s-mod furnishings, and the patio has a flower-festooned private deck. Breakfasts are exceptional – the owner is a chef. Also rents out nearby apartments.

Willows B&B $$

(Map p88; ☎415-431-4770; www.willowssf.com; 710 14th St; r $110-140; wifi) Homey comforts of a B&B, without the frills or fuss. None of the 12 rooms has a private bathroom; all have sinks. Shared kitchenette. Rooms on 14th St are sunnier and have good street views, but they're noisier. No elevator.

THE HAIGHT & HAYES VALLEY

The Parsonnage B&B $$$

(Map p88; ☎415-863-3699, 888-763-7722; www.theparsonage.com; 198 Haight St; r incl breakfast $200-250; @wifi) A 23-room Italiante-Victorian with original rose-brass chandeliers and Carrera-marble fireplaces, close to Market St. Spacious, airy rooms have oriental rugs and period antiques; some have wood-burning

The Haight

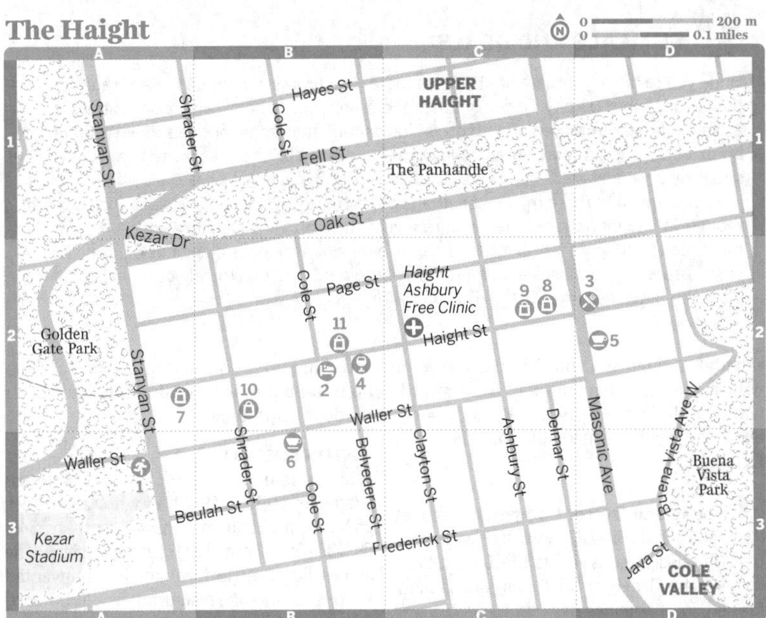

The Haight

Activities, Courses & Tours
1 Haight-Ashbury Flower Power Walking Tour A3

Sleeping
2 Red Victorian B2

Eating
3 Magnolia Brewpub D2

Drinking
4 Aub Zam Zam B2
5 Coffee to the People D2
6 Cole Valley Café B3

Shopping
7 Amoeba Records A2
8 Goorin Brothers Hats C2
9 Piedmont Boutique C2
10 SFO Snowboarding & FTC Skateboarding B2
11 Wasteland B2

fireplaces. Don't miss brandy and chocolates before bed.

Chateau Tivoli INN $$
(off Map p88; ☎415-776-5462, 800-228-1647; www.chateautivoli.com; 1057 Steiner St; r $140-200, r without bathroom $100-130, ste $250-290;) The glorious turreted chateau has faded since the days when Mark Twain and Isadora Duncan visited, and rooms are modest, but the place is full of soul, character and – rumor has it – the ghost of a Victorian opera diva. Wi-fi in lobby.

Red Victorian QUIRKY $$
(Map p81; ☎415-864-1978; www.redvic.net; 1665 Haight St; r $149-229, without bath $89-129, incl breakfast;) The '60s live on at the tripped-out Red Vic. The 18 rooms have themes such as Sunshine, Flower Children and the Summer of Love; only four have baths, but all come with breakfast in the organic cafe. Wi-fi in the lobby; no elevator.

Metro Hotel HOTEL $
(Map p88; ☎415-861-5364; www.metrohotelsf.com; 319 Divisadero St; r $76-120;) No-frills rooms in the center of The Haight, with good pizza and a garden downstairs and bars and shopping just outside. Rooms in back are quietest.

Eating

THE EMBARCADERO

Slanted Door VIETNAMESE, CALIFORNIAN $$
(Map p66; ☎415-861-8032; www.slanteddoor.com; 1 Ferry Bldg; lunch/dinner mains $13-24/$18-36; lunch & dinner) California ingredients, Con-

SF MEALS AND DEALS

Hope you're hungry – there are 10 times more restaurants per capita in San Francisco than in any other US city. Check out the recommendations below and foodie sites such as **www.chowhound.com** and **http://sf.eater.com**, then scan for deals at **www.blackboardeats.com** and **www.opentable.com** – and since SF's top restaurants are quite small, reserve now.

Prices are often more reasonable than you might expect for organic, sustainable fare, though you might notice some restaurants now tack on a 4% surcharge to cover city-mandated healthcare for SF food workers – a tacky way to pass along basic business costs, especially for upscale restaurants. Factor in 9.5% tax on top of your meal price, plus a tip ranging from 15% to 25%.

tinental influences and Vietnamese flair with a sparkling bay outlook, from award-winning chef/owner Charles Phan. Reserve ahead or picnic on takeout from the Open Door stall.

Hog Island Oyster Company SEAFOOD **$$**
(Map p66; ☎415-391-7117; www.hogislandoysters.com; 1 Ferry Bldg; oyster samplers $15-30; ⏰11:30am-8pm Mon-Fri, 11am-6pm Sat & Sun) Sustainably farmed, local Tomales Bay oysters served raw or cooked to perfection, with superb condiments and a glass of Sonoma bubbly. From 5pm to 7pm on Mondays and Thursdays, oysters are half-price and pints are $4.

Mijita MEXICAN **$**
(Map p66; ☎415-399-0814; www.mijitasf.com; No 44, 1 Ferry Bldg; small plates $2-9; ⏰10am-7pm Mon-Wed, to 8pm Thu-Sat, 10am-4pm Sun;) Sustainable fish tacos reign supreme and *agua fresca* (fruit punch) is made with fresh juice at chef Traci des Jardins' thoughtful tribute to her Mexican grandmother's cooking, with bay views to be savored from your leather stool.

Boulette's Larder CALIFORNIAN **$$**
(Map p66; ☎415-399-1155; www.bouletteslarder.com; 1 Ferry Bldg; breakfast $7.50-16.50, lunch $9-20, brunch $7-22; ⏰breakfast Mon-Fri, lunch Mon-Sat, brunch Sun) Dinner theater doesn't get better than brunch at Boulette's communal table, amid the swirl of chefs preparing for dinner service. Inspired by the truffled eggs and beignets? Get spices and mixes at the counter.

Il Cane Rosso CALIFORNIAN **$$**
(Map p66; ☎415-391-7599; http://canerossosf.com; 1 Ferry Bldg; mains $13; ⏰breakfast, lunch & dinner) Farm-fresh breakfasts and lunches and soul-satisfying three-course dinners for $25 from 5pm to 9pm in a Ferry Building hallway or outdoor bistro table.

UNION SQUARE

Michael Mina CALIFORNIAN **$$$**
(Map p66; ☎415-397-9222; www.michaelmina.net; 252 California St; lunch menus/dinner mains $49-59/$35-42; ⏰lunch Mon-Fri, dinner nightly) The James Beard Award winner has reinvented his posh namesake restaurant as a lighthearted take on French-Japanese cooking – there's still caviar and lobster, but also foie gras PB&J and lobster pot pie. Reservations essential, or grab bar bites and cocktails at the bar.

farmerbrown MODERN AMERICAN, ORGANIC **$$**
(Map p66; ☎415-409-3276; www.farmerbrownsf.com; 25 Mason St; mains $12-23; ⏰6-10:30pm Tue-Sun, weekend brunch 11am-2pm) A rebel from the wrong side of the block, dishing up seasonal watermelon margaritas with a cayenne-salt rim, ribs that stick to yours and coleslaw with kick. Chef-owner Jay Foster works with local organic and African American farmers to provide food with actual soul, in a shotgun-shack setting with live funk bands.

Millennium VEGETARIAN, VEGAN **$$$**
(Map p66; ☎415-345-3900; www.millenniumrestaurant.com; 580 Geary St; menus $39-72; ⏰dinner;) Three words you're not likely to hear together outside these doors sum up the menu: opulent vegan dining. GMO-free and proud of it, with wild mushrooms and organic produce in succulent seasonal concoctions. Book ahead for aphrodisiac dinners and vegetarian Thanksgiving.

FINANCIAL DISTRICT

Kokkari GREEK **$$$**
(Map p66; ☎415-981-0983; www.kokkari.com; 200 Jackson St; mains $21-35; ⏰lunch Mon-Fri,

dinner nightly;) This is one Greek restaurant where you'll want to lick your plate instead of break it, with starters such as grilled octopus with lemon-oregano zing, and a lamb and eggplant moussaka rich as the Pacific Stock Exchange. Reserve ahead, or make a meal of appetizers at the bar.

Bocadillos MEDITERRANEAN **$$**
(Map p66; 415-982-2622; www.bocasf.com; 710 Montgomery St; dishes $9-15; 7am-10pm Mon-Fri, 5-10:30pm Sat) Lunchtime fine dining that won't break the bank or pop buttons, with just-right Basque bites of lamb burger, snapper ceviche with Asian pears, Catalan sausages and wines by the glass.

Gitane MEDITERRANEAN **$$**
(Map p66; 415-788-6686; www.gitanerestaurant.com; 6 Claude Lane; mains $15-25; 5:30pm-midnight Tue-Sat, bar to 1am;) Slip out of the Financial District and into something more comfortable at this boudoir-styled bistro, featuring Basque- and Moroccan-inspired stuffed squash blossoms, silky pan-seared scallops, herb-spiked lamb tartare and craft cocktails.

Boxed Foods SANDWICHES **$**
(Map p66; www.boxedfoodscompany.com; 245 Kearny St; dishes $8-10; 8am-3pm Mon-Fri;) The SF salad standard is set here daily, with organic greens topped by tart goat cheese, smoked bacon, wild strawberries and other local treats. Grab hidden seating in back, or get yours to go to the Transamerica Pyramid redwood grove.

CIVIC CENTER & THE TENDERLOIN

TOP CHOICE **Jardinière** CALIFORNIAN **$$$**
(Map p66; 415-861-5555; www.jardiniere.com; 300 Grove St; mains $18-38; dinner) Opera arias can't compare to the high notes hit by James Beard Award winner, Iron Chef and Top Chef Master Traci des Jardins, who lavishes braised oxtail ravioli with summer truffles and stuffs crispy pork belly with salami and Mission figs. Go Mondays, when $45 scores three market-inspired, decadent courses with wine pairings, or enjoy post-SF Opera meals in the bar downstairs.

Brenda's French Soul Food CREOLE **$**
(Map p66; 415-345-8100; www.frenchsoulfood.com; 652 Polk St; mains $8-12; 8am-3pm Sun-Tue, 8am-10pm Wed-Sat) Chef-owner Brenda Buenviaje combines Creole cooking with French technique in hangover-curing Hangtown fry (omelette with cured pork and corn-breaded oysters), shrimp-stuffed po' boys, and fried chicken with collard greens and hot-pepper jelly – all worth inevitable waits on a sketchy stretch of sidewalk.

Saigon Sandwich Shop VIETNAMESE **$**
(Map p66; 415-475-5698; 560 Larkin St; sandwiches $3.50; 6:30am-5:30pm) Might as well order two of those roast-pork *banh mi* (Vietnamese sandwiches) with housemade pickled vegetables now, so you don't have to wait in line on this sketchy sidewalk again.

Bar Jules CALIFORNIAN **$$**
(Map p88; 415-621-5482; www.barjules.com; 609 Hayes St; mains $10-26; 6-10pm Tue, 11:30am-3pm & 6-10pm Wed-Sat, 11am-3pm Sun) Small and succulent is the credo at this dinky bistro, where the short daily menu packs a wallop of local flavor – think Sonoma duck breast with cherries, almonds and arugula, Napa wines and the dark, sinister 'chocolate nemesis.' Waits are a given, but so is unfussy, tasty food.

CHINATOWN

City View CHINESE **$**
(Map p58; 415-398-2838; 662 Commercial St; small plates $3-5; 11am-2:30pm Mon-Fri, 10am-2:30pm Sat & Sun) Take your seat in a sunny dining room and your pick from carts loaded with delicate shrimp and leek dumplings, tender black-bean asparagus and crisp Peking duck and other tantalizing, ultrafresh dim sum.

Yuet Lee CHINESE, SEAFOOD **$$**
(Map p58; 415-982-6020; 1300 Stockton St; 11am-3am Wed-Mon;) That brash fluorescent lighting isn't especially kind on dates, but if you're willing to share Yuet Lee's legendary crispy salt-and-pepper crab or smoky-sweet roast duck with your booth mate, it must be love.

House of Nanking CHINESE **$$**
(Map p58; 415-421-1429; 919 Kearny St; starters $5-8, mains $9-15; 11am-10pm Mon-Fri, noon-10pm Sat, noon-9pm Sun) Bossy service with bravura cooking. Supply the vaguest outlines for your dinner – maybe seafood, nothing deep-fried, perhaps some greens – and within minutes you'll be devouring pan-seared scallops, sautéed pea shoots and garlicky noodles.

NORTH BEACH

TOP CHOICE **Coi** CALIFORNIAN **$$$**
(Map p58; 415-393-9000; http://coirestaurant.com; 373 Broadway; set menu $145 per person;

TOP 5 SF FARMERS MARKETS

» **Fancy foods** **Ferry Building** (www.cuesa.org) showcases California-grown, organic produce, artisan meats and gourmet prepared foods at moderate-to-premium prices at markets held Tuesday, Thursday and Saturday mornings year-round.

» **Best value and selection** City-run **Alemany** (www.sfgov.org/site/alemany) has offered bargain prices on local and organic produce every Saturday year-round since 1943, plus stalls with ready-to-eat foods.

» **Most convenient** Sundays and Wednesdays from 7am to 5pm in UN Plaza, **Heart of the City** (www.hocfarmersmarket.org) offers local produce (some organics) at good prices and prepared-food stalls for downtown lunches at UN Plaza, which on other days is an obstacle course of skateboarders, Scientologists and raving self-talkers, plus a few crafts stalls.

» **Best for families** **Inner Sunset** (parking lot btwn 8th & 9th Ave, off Irving St; ⏲9am-1pm) has local and some organic produce and artisan foods at moderate prices, plus kids' programs on Sundays April–September.

» **Best evening market** **Castro farmers market** (Market St at Noe St; ⏲4-8pm Mar-Dec) has local and organic produce and artisan foods at moderate prices, cooking demos and live folk music.

⏲6-10pm Tue-Fri, 5:30-10pm Fri & Sat; ✎) Chef Daniel Patterson's wild tasting menu featuring foraged morels, wildflowers and Pacific seafood is like licking the California coastline. Black and green noodles are made from clams and Pacific seaweed, and purple ice-plant petals are strewn atop Sonoma duck's tongue, wild-caught abalone and just-picked arugula. Only-in-California flavors and intriguing wine pairings ($95; pours generous enough for two to share) will keep you California dreaming.

Cotogna ITALIAN $$

(Map p58; ☎415-775-8508; www.cotognasf.com; 470 Pacific Av; mains $14-24; ⏲noon-3pm & 7-10pm Mon-Sat; ✎) No wonder chef-owner Michael Tusk won the 2011 James Beard Award: his rustic Italian pastas and toothsome pizzas magically balance a few pristine, local flavors. Book ahead; the $24 prix-fixe is among SF's best dining deals.

Ideale ITALIAN $$

(Map p58; ☎415-391-4129; 1315 Grant Ave; ⏲5:30-10:30pm Mon-Sat, 5-10pm Sun) SF's most authentic Italian restaurant, with a Roman chef that grills a mean fish and whips up gorgeous truffled zucchini – but order anything with bacon or meat and Tuscan-staff-recommend wine, and everyone goes home happy.

Liguria Bakery ITALIAN, BAKERY $

(Map p58; ☎415-421-3786; 1700 Stockton St; focaccia $3; ⏲8am-1pm Mon-Fri, 7am-1pm Sat, 7am-noon Sun) Bleary-eyed art students and Italian grandmothers are in line by 8am for the cinnamon-raisin focaccia, leaving 9am dawdlers a choice of tomato or classic rosemary, and noontime arrivals out of luck.

Cinecittà PIZZA $

(Map p58; ☎415-291-8830; 663 Union St; ⏲noon-10pm Sun-Thu, to 11pm Fri & Sat; ✎👪) Squeeze in at the counter for your thin-crust pie and Anchor Steam on draft with a side order of sass from Roman owner Romina. Go with the two standouts: wild mushroom with sundried tomato for vegetarians, or the omnivore's delight with artichoke hearts, olives, prosciutto and egg.

Molinari ITALIAN, SANDWICHES $

(Map p58; ☎415-421-2337; 373 Columbus Ave; sandwiches $5-8; ⏲9am-5:30pm Mon-Fri, 7:30am-5:30pm Sat) Grab a number and wait your turn ogling Italian wines and cheeses, and by the time you're called, the scent of house-cured salami dangling from the rafters and Parma prosciutto will have made your choice for you.

Tony's Coal-Fired Pizza Slice House PIZZA, SANDWICHES $

(Map p58; ☎415-835-9888; www.tonyspizzanapoletana.com; 1556 Stockton St; ⏲noon-11pm Wed-Sun) Get a meatball sub or cheesy, thin-crust slice to go from nine-time world champ pizza-slinger Tony Gemignani, and take that slice to sunny Washington Square Park to savor amid wild parrots.

FISHERMAN'S WHARF

Crown & Crumpet DESSERTS, SANDWICHES $$

(Map p62; ☎415-771-4252; www.crownandcrumpet.com; 207 Ghirardelli Square; dishes $8-12; ⏰10am-9pm Mon-Fri, 9am-9pm Sat, 9am-6pm Sun; 👪) Designer style and rosy cheer usher teatime into the 21st century: dads and daughters clink teacups with crooked pinkies, Lolita Goth teens nibble cucumber sandwiches and girlfriends rehash dates over scones and champagne. Reservations recommended weekends.

In-N-Out Burger BURGERS $

(Map p62; ☎800-786-1000; www.in-n-out.com; 333 Jefferson St; burgers $3-6; ⏰10:30am-1am Sun-Thu, to 1:30am Fri & Sat; 👪) Serving burgers for 60 years the way California likes them: with prime chuck ground onsite, fries and shakes made with pronounceable ingredients, served by employees paid a living wage.

RUSSIAN HILL & NOB HILL

Swan Oyster Depot SEAFOOD $$

(Map p62; ☎415-673-1101; 1517 Polk St; dishes $10-20; ⏰8am-5:30pm Mon-Sat) Superior freshness without the superior attitude of most seafood restaurants. Order yours to go, browse nearby boutiques and breeze past the line to pick up your crab salad and oysters with mignonette (wine and shallot) picnic.

Za PIZZA $

(Map p62; ☎415-771-3100; www.zapizzasf.com; 1919 Hyde St; ⏰noon-10pm Sun-Wed, to 11pm Thu-Sat) Pizza lovers brave the uphill climb for cornmeal-dusted, thin-crust pizza by the slice piled with fresh ingredients, a pint of Anchor Steam and a cozy bar setting with highly flirtatious pizza-slingers – all for under 10 bucks.

JAPANTOWN & PACIFIC HEIGHTS

Tataki SUSHI $$

(Map p62; ☎415-931-1182; www.tatakisushibar.com; 2815 California St; dishes $12-20; ⏰11:30am-2pm & 5:30-10:30pm Mon-Fri, 5-11:30pm Sat, 5-9:30pm Sun) Rescue dinner dates and the oceans with sensational, sustainable sushi: silky arctic char drizzled with yuzu-citrus and capers replaces dubious farmed salmon, and the Golden State Roll is a local hero with spicy line-caught scallop, Pacific tuna, organic apple slivers and edible gold.

Out the Door VIETNAMESE $$

(Map p62; ☎415-923 9575; www.outthedoors.com; 2232 Bush St; lunch/dinner mains $12-18/$18-28; ⏰8am-4:30pm & 5:30pm-10pm Mon-Fri, 8am-3pm & 5:30pm-10pm Sat & Sun) Stellar French beignets and Vietnamese coffee, or salty-sweet dungeness-crab frittatas at this offshoot of famous Slanted Door (p81). Lunchtime's rice plates and noodles are replaced at dinner with savory clay-pot meats and fish.

Benkyodo JAPANESE, SANDWICHES $

(Map p62; ☎415-922-1244; www.benkyodocompany.com; 1747 Buchanan St; sandwiches $3-4; ⏰8am-5pm Mon-Sat) The perfect retro lunch counter cheerfully serves old-school egg salad and pastrami sandwiches, plus $1 chocolate-filled strawberry and green-tea mochi made in-house.

The Grove AMERICAN $

(Map p62; ☎415-474-1419; 2016 Fillmore St; dishes $8-12; ⏰7am-11pm; 📶👪) Rough-hewn recycled wood and a stone fireplace give this Fillmore St cafe ski-lodge coziness for made-to-order breakfasts, working lunches with salads, sandwiches and wi-fi, and chat sessions with warm-from-the-oven cookies and hot cocoa.

THE MARINA & COW HOLLOW

Off the Grid FOOD TRUCKS $

(Map p62; http://offthegridsf.com; Fort Mason parking lot; dishes under $10; ⏰5-10pm Fri; 🐾) Some 30 food trucks circle their wagons at SF's largest mobile-gourmet hootenanny (other nights/locations attract less than a dozen trucks; see website). Arrive before 6:30pm or expect 20-minute waits for Chairman Bao's clamshell buns stuffed with duck and mango, Roli Roti's free-range herbed roast chicken, or dessert from The Crème Brûlée Man. Cash only; take dinner to nearby docks for Golden Gate Bridge sunsets.

Blue Barn Gourmet SANDWICHES $

(Map p62; ☎415-441-3232; www.bluebarngourmet.com; salads & sandwiches $8-10; 2105 Chestnut St; ⏰11am-8:30pm Sun-Thu, to 7pm Fri & Sat; 🌶) Toss aside thoughts of ordinary salads with organic produce, heaped with fixings: artisan cheeses, caramelized onions, heirloom tomatoes, candied pecans, pomegranate seeds, even Meyer grilled sirloin. For something hot, try the toasted panini oozing with Manchego cheese, fig jam and salami.

Greens VEGETARIAN $$

(Map p62; ☎415-771-6222; www.greensrestaurant.com; Fort Mason Center, bldg A; mains $7-20; ⏰noon-2:30pm Tue-Sat, 5:30-9pm Mon-Sat, 9am-4pm Sun; 🌶) In a converted army barracks, enjoy Golden Gate views, smoky-rich black bean chili with pickled jalapeños and roasted eggplant panini. All Greens' dishes are meat-free and organic, mostly raised on a Zen farm in Marin – sure beats army rations.

A16 ITALIAN **$$**
(Map p62; ☎415-771-2216; www.a16sf.com; 2355 Chestnut St; pizza $12-18, mains $18-26; ⊙lunch Wed-Fri, dinner nightly) SF's James Beard Award–winning Neapolitan pizzeria requires reservations, then haughtily makes you wait in the foyer like a high-maintenance date. The housemade mozzarella burata and chewy-but-not-too-thick-crust pizza topped with kicky calamari makes it worth your while.

Warming Hut CAFE
(off Map p62; Crissy Field; pastries $2-4; ⊙9am-5pm) When the fog rolls into Crissy Field, head here for Fair Trade coffee, organic pastries and organic hot dogs within walls insulated with recycled denim; all purchases support Crissy Field conservation.

SOUTH OF MARKET (SOMA)

TOP CHOICE **Benu** CALIFORNIAN, FUSION **$$$**
(Map p66; ☎415-685-4860; www.benusf.com; 22 Hawthorne St; mains $25-40; ⊙5:30-10pm Tue-Sat) SF has refined fusion cuisine over 150 years, but no one rocks it quite like chef Corey Lee, who remixes local fine-dining staples and Pacific Rim flavors with a SoMa DJ's finesse. Velvety Sonoma foie gras with tangy, woodsy yuzu-sake glaze makes taste-buds bust wild moves, while Dungeness crab and black truffle custard bring such outsize flavor to faux-shark's fin soup, you'll swear there's Jaws in there. The tasting menu is steep ($160) and beverage pairings add $110, but you won't want to miss star-sommelier Yoon Ha's flights of fancy – including a rare 1968 Madeira with your soup.

Boulevard CALIFORNIAN **$$$**
(Map p66; ☎415-543-6084; www.boulevardrestaurant.com; 1 Mission St; lunch $17-25, dinner $29-39; ⊙lunch Mon-Fri, dinner daily) Belle epoque decor adds grace notes to this 1889 building that once housed the Coast Seamen's Union, but chef Nancy Oakes has kept the menu honest with juicy pork chops, enough soft-shell crab to satisfy a sailor and crowd-pleasing desserts.

Zero Zero PIZZA **$$**
(Map p66; ☎415-348-8800; www.zerozerosf.com; 826 Folsom St; pizzas $12-17; ⊙noon-2:30pm & 5:30-10pm Sun-Thu, to 11pm Fri & Sat) The name is a throw-down of Neapolitan pizza credentials – '00' flour is used exclusively for Naples' puffy-edged crust – and these pies deliver, with inspired SF-themed toppings. The Geary is piled with Manila clams, bacon and chillis, but the real crowd-pleaser is the Castro, turbo-loaded with house-made sausage.

Juhu Beach Club INDIAN **$**
(Map p88; ☎415-298-0471; www.facebook.com/JuhuBeachClub; 320 11th St; dishes $4-8 ⊙11:30am-2:30pm Mon-Fri) SoMa's gritty streets are looking positively upbeat ever since reinvented *chaat* (Indian street snacks) popped up inside Garage Café, serving lunchtime pork vindaloo buns, aromatic grilled Nahu chicken salad, and the aptly named, slow-cooked shredded steak 'holy cow' sandwich.

Sentinel SANDWICHES **$**
(Map p66; ☎415-284-9960; www.thesentinelsf.com; 37 New Montgomery St; sandwiches $8.50-9; ⊙7:30am-2:30pm Mon-Fri) Rebel SF chef Dennis Leary takes on the classics: tuna salad gets radical with chipotle mayo, and corned beef crosses borders with Swiss cheese and housemade Russian dressing. Menus change daily; come prepared for about a 10-minute wait, since sandwiches are made to order.

Split Pea Seduction SANDWICHES **$**
(Map p66; ☎415-551-2223; www.splitpeaseduction.com; 138 6th St; lunches $6-9.75; ⊙8am-5pm Mon-Fri; ✍) Right off Skid Row are unexpectedly healthy, homey soup-and-sandwich combos, including seasonal soups such as potato with housemade pesto and a signature *crostata* (open-faced sandwich), such as cambozola cheese and nectarine drizzled with honey.

THE MISSION

TOP CHOICE **La Taquería** MEXICAN **$**
(Map p88; ☎415-285-7117; 2889 Mission St; burritos $6-8; ⊙11am-9pm Mon-Sat, 11am-8pm Sun) No debatable tofu, saffron rice, spinach tortilla or mango salsa here: just classic tomatillo or mesquite salsa, marinated, grilled meats and flavorful beans inside a flour tortilla – optional housemade spicy pickles and sour cream highly recommended.

Commonwealth CALIFORNIAN **$$**
(Map p88; ☎415-355-1500; www.commonwealthsf.com; 2224 Mission St; small plates $5-16; ⊙5:30-10pm Tue-Thu & Sun, to 11pm Fri & Sat; ✍) Califor-

VEGETARIANS: TURNING THE TABLES IN SF

San Francisco offers far more than grilled cheese and veggie burgers for vegetarians and vegans.

» **Vegan** Three organic vegan options could convert even committed carnivores: **Millennium** (p82), **Greens** (p85) and **Samovar Tea Lounge** (p95).

» **Vegetarian prix-fixe** Multicourse options featuring local, seasonal produce are offered at fancy restaurants like **Michael Mina** (p82) and **Benu** (p86).

» **Ethnic vegetarian** Omnivores veer to the vegetarian side of the menu at ethnic specialty joints like Ethiopian **Axum Café** (p90), Mexican **Pancho Villa** (p87), and Indian **Udupi Palace** (p87).

» **Vegetarian power lunches** Organic soup/salad/sandwich joints downtown offer fresh perspectives on lunch: **Boxed Foods** (p83), **Split Pea Seduction** (p86)

nia's most imaginative farm-to-table dining isn't in some quaint barn, but the converted cinderblock Mission dive where chef Jason Fox serves crispy hen with toybox carrots cooked in hay (yes, hay), and sea urchin floating on a bed of farm egg and organic asparagus that looks like a tidepool and tastes like a dream. Savor the $65 prix-fixe knowing $10 is donated to charity.

Locanda ITALIAN **$$**

(Map p88; ☎415-863-6800; www.locandasf.com; 557 Valencia St; share plates $10-24; ⏰5:30pm-midnight) The vintage Duran Duran Rome concert poster in the bathroom is your first clue that Locanda is all about cheeky, streetwise Roman fare. Scrumptious tripe melting into rich tomato-mint sauce is a must, piazza bianco with figs and prosciutto creates obsessions, and Roman fried artichokes and sweetbreads mean authenticity minus the airfare.

Pizzeria Delfina PIZZA **$$**

(Map p88; ☎415-437-6800; www.delfinasf.com; 3611 18th St; pizzas $11-17; ⏰11:30am-10pm Tue-Thu, to 11pm Fri, noon-11pm Sat & Sun, 5:30-10pm Mon; 🖊) One bite explains why SF is obsessed with pizza lately: Delfina's thin crust supports the weight of fennel sausage and fresh mozzarella without drooping or cracking, while white pizzas let chefs freestyle with Cali-foodie ingredients like maitake mushrooms, broccoli rabe and artisan cheese. No reservations; sign up on the chalkboard and wait with wine at Delfina bar next door.

Range CALIFORNIAN **$$**

(Map p88; ☎415-282-8283; www.rangesf.com; 842 Valencia St; mains $20-28; ⏰5:30-10pm Sun-Thu, to 11pm Fri & Sat; 🖊) Inspired American dining is alive and well within Range. The menu is seasonal Californian, prices are reasonable and the style is repurposed industrial chic – think coffee-rubbed pork shoulder served with microbrewed beer from the blood-bank refrigerator.

Bi-Rite Creamery ICE CREAM **$$**

(Map p88; ☎415-626-5600; http://biritecreamery.com; 3692 18th St; ice cream $3.25-7; ⏰11am-10pm Sun-Thu, to 11pm Fri & Sat) Velvet ropes at clubs seem pretentious in laid-back San Francisco, but at organic Bi-Rite Creamery they make perfect sense: lines wrap around the corner for legendary salted-caramel ice cream with housemade hot fudge. For a quick fix, get balsamic strawberry soft serve at the soft-serve window (⏰1-9pm).

Pancho Villa MEXICAN **$**

(Map p88; ☎415-864-8840; www.sfpanchovilla.com; 3071 16th St; burritos $7-8.50; ⏰10am-noon; 🖊) The hero of the downtrodden and burrito-deprived, delivering tinfoil-wrapped meals the girth of your forearm and a worthy condiments bar. The line moves fast, and as you leave the door is held open for you and your Pancho's paunch.

Udupi Palace INDIAN **$**

(Map p88; ☎415-970-8000; www.udupipalaceca.com; 1007 Valencia St; mains $8-10; ⏰11am-10pm Mon-Thu, to 10:30pm Fri-Sun; 🖊) Tandoori in the Tenderloin is for novices – SF foodies swoon over the bright, clean flavors of South Indian *dosa,* a light, crispy pancake made with lentil flour dipped in mildly spicy vegetable *sambar* (soup) and coconut chutney.

Mission Chinese CALIFORNIAN, CHINESE **$$**

(Map p88; Lung Shan; ☎415-863-2800; www.missionchinesefood.com; 2234 Mission St; dishes

The Castro & The Mission

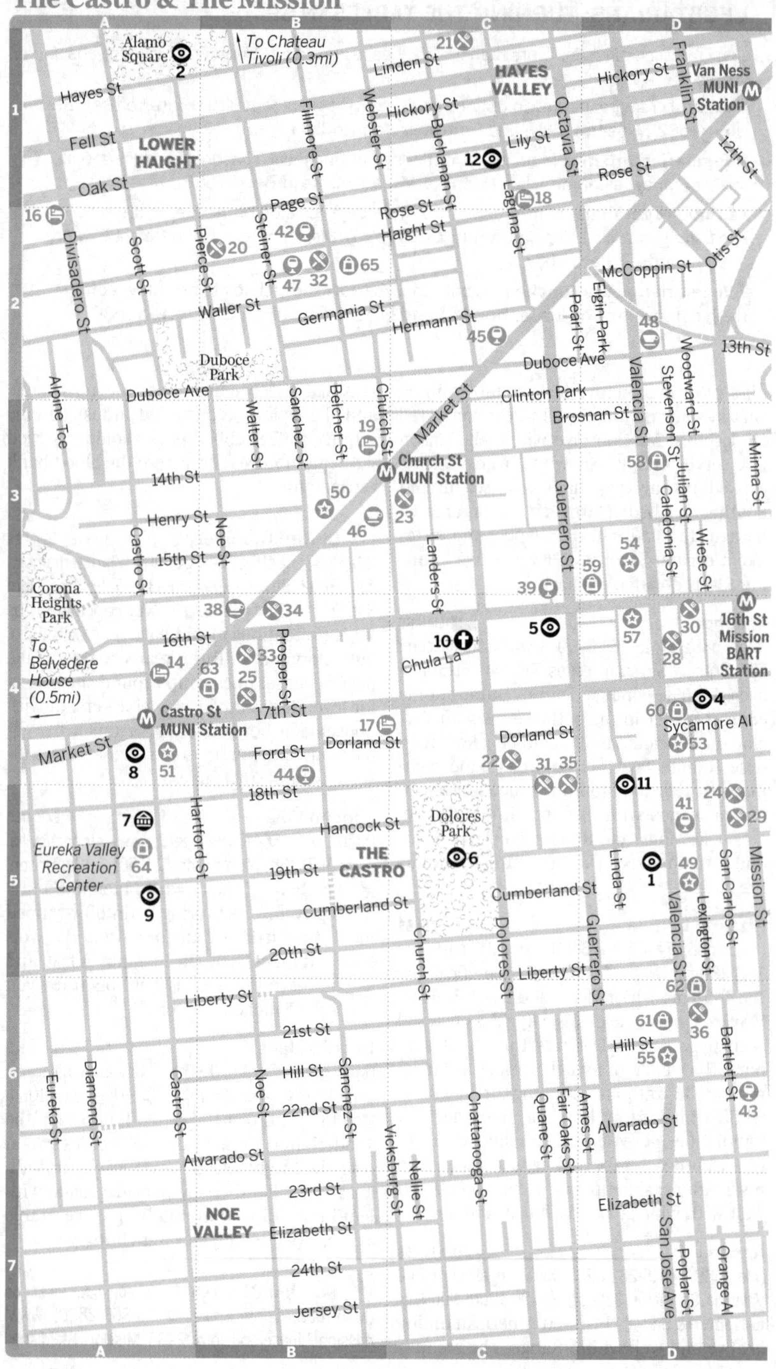

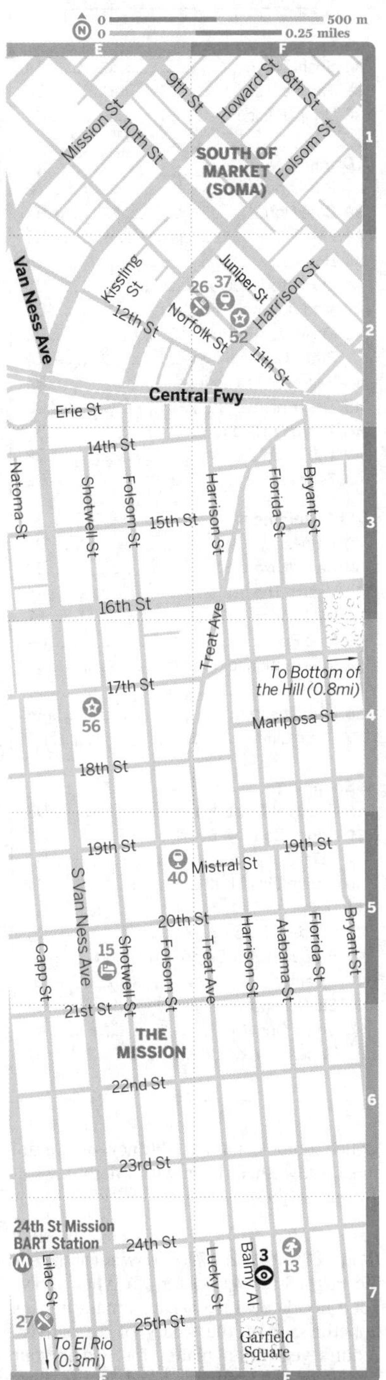

$9-16; ⏲11:30am-10:30pm Mon-Tue & Thu-Sun) Lovers of spicy food, Chinese takeout and sustainable meat converge on this gourmet dive. Creative, meaty mains such as tingly lamb noodles are big enough for two – if not for the salt-shy – and $0.75 from each main is donated to San Francisco Food Bank.

Tartine BAKERY **$**
(Map p88; ☎415-487-2600; www.tartinebakery.com; 600 Guerrero St; pastries $2-5; ⏲8am-7pm Mon-Wed, to 8pm Thu-Sat, 9am-8pm Sun) Lines out the door for pumpkin tea bread, Valrhona chocolate cookies and open-face *croques monsieurs* (toasted ham-and-cheese sandwiches) – all so loaded with butter that you feel fatter and happier just looking at them.

THE CASTRO

TOP CHOICE **Frances** CALIFORNIAN **$$**
(Map p88; ☎415-621-3870; www.frances-sf.com; 3870 17th St; mains $14-27; ⏲5-10.30pm Tue-Sun) Chef and owner Melissa Perello earned a Michelin star for fine dining, then ditched downtown to start this market-inspired neighborhood bistro. Daily menus showcase bright, seasonal flavors and luxurious textures: cloud-like sheep's milk ricotta gnocchi with crunchy breadcrumbs and broccolini, grilled calamari with preserved Meyer lemon, and artisan wine served by the ounce, directly from Wine Country.

Chilango MEXICAN **$$**
(Map p88; ☎415-552-5700; chilangorestaurantsf.com; 235 Church St; dishes $8-12; ⏲11am-10pm) Upgrade from to-go *taquerías* (Mexican fast-food restaurants) to organic *chilango* (Mexico City native) dishes worthy of a sit-down dinner, including grassfed filet mignon tacos, sustainable pork carnitas and sensational freerange chicken mole.

Starbelly CALIFORNIAN **$$**
(Map p88; ☎415-252-7500; www.starbellysf.com; 3583 16th St; dishes $6-19; ⏲11:30am-11pm, to midnight Fri & Sat) Reclaimed wood décor to match the food: market-fresh salads, scrumptious paté, roasted mussels with house-made sausage and juicy grassfed burgers. Reserve ahead to lounge amid flowering herbs on the heated patio, or join the communal table.

Sushi Time SUSHI **$**
(Map p88; ☎415-552-2280; www.sushitime-sf.com; 2275 Market St; rolls $4-10; ⏲dinner Mon-Sat) Devour sashimi and Barbie, GI Joe and Hello

The Castro & The Mission

Sights
1 826 Valencia ... D5
2 Alamo Square ... A1
3 Balmy Alley ... F7
Castro Theatre ... (see 51)
4 Clarion Alley ... D4
5 Creativity Explored ... C4
6 Dolores Park ... C5
7 GLBT History Museum ... A5
8 Harvey Milk Plaza ... A4
9 Human Rights Campaign Action Center ... A5
10 Mission Dolores Basilica ... C4
11 Women's Building ... D4
12 Zen Center ... C1

Activities, Courses & Tours
13 Precita Eyes ... F7

Sleeping
14 Inn on Castro ... A4
15 Inn San Francisco ... E5
16 Metro Hotel ... A2
17 Parker Guest House ... B4
18 The Parsonnage ... C1
19 Willows ... B3

Eating
20 Axum Café ... B2
21 Bar Jules ... C1
22 Bi-Rite Creamery ... C4
23 Chilango ... C3
24 Commonwealth ... D5
25 Frances ... B4
26 Juhu Beach Club ... F2
27 La Taquería ... E7
28 Locanda ... D4
29 Mission Chinese ... D5
30 Pancho Villa ... D4
31 Pizzeria Delfina ... C4
Range ... (see 1)
32 Rosamunde Sausage Grill ... B2
33 Starbelly ... B4
34 Sushi Time ... B4
35 Tartine ... C4
36 Udupi Palace ... D6

Drinking
37 Bar Agricole ... F2
38 Café Flore ... B4
39 Elixir ... C3
40 Homestead ... E5
41 Lexington Club ... D5
42 Mad Dog in the Fog ... B2
43 Make-Out Room ... D6
Ritual Coffee Roasters ... (see 55)
44 Samovar Tea Lounge ... B4
45 The Mint ... C2
46 Thorough Bread ... B3
47 Toronado ... B2
48 Zeitgeist ... D2

Entertainment
49 Amnesia ... D5
50 Cafe du Nord ... B3
51 Castro Theatre ... A4
52 DNA Lounge ... F2
53 Elbo Room ... D4
54 Intersection for the Arts ... D3
55 Marsh ... D6
56 ODC Theater ... E4
57 Roxie Cinema ... D4

Shopping
58 Accident & Artifact ... D3
59 Adobe Books & BackRoom Gallery ... D3
60 Community Thrift ... D4
61 Dema ... D6
62 Gravel & Gold ... D6
Human Rights Campaign Action Center ... (see 9)
63 Sui Generis ... B4
64 Under One Roof ... A5
65 Upper Playground ... B2

Kitty rolls in the tiny glassed-in patio like a shark in an aquarium. Happy-hour specials run from 5pm to 6:30pm.

THE HAIGHT & HAYES VALLEY

Rosamunde Sausage Grill SANDWICHES $
(Map p88; ☎415-437-6851; 545 Haight St; sausages $4-6; ⌚11:30am-10pm) Here's what they serve at baseball games in heaven: divine duck, spicy lamb or wild boar sausages, fully loaded with your choice of roasted peppers, grilled onions, mango chutney or wasabi mustard, washed down with microbrews at Toronado (p95).

Axum Café ETHIOPIAN $
(Map p88; ☎415-252-7912; www.axumcafe.com; 698 Haight St; $7-14; ⌚dinner; ✎) When you've got a hot date with a vegan, a marathoner's appetite and/or the salary of an activist, Axum's vegetarian platter for two is your saving grace: lip-tingling red lentils, fiery

mushrooms and mellow yellow chickpeas, scooped up with spongy *injera* bread.

Magnolia Brewpub CALIFORNIAN **$$**
(Map p81; 415-864-7468; www.magnoliapub.com; 1398 Haight St; mains $11-20; noon-midnight Mon-Thu, until 1am Fri, 10am-1am Sat, 10am-midnight Sun) Organic pub grub and homebrew samplers keep conversation flowing at communal tables, while grass-fed Prather Ranch burgers satisfy stoner appetites in side booths – it's like the Summer of Love is back, only with better food.

THE RICHMOND

TOP CHOICE **Aziza** CALIFORNIAN, NORTH AFRICAN **$$**
(Map p72; 415-752-2222; www.azizasf.com; 5800 Geary Blvd; mains $16-29; 5:30-10:30pm Wed-Mon;) Mourad Lahlou's inspiration is Moroccan and his produce organic Californian, but his flavors are out of this world: Sonoma duck confit melts into caramelized onion in flaky pastry *basteeya* (savory phyllo pastry), while sour cherries rouse slow-cooked local lamb shank from its barley bed.

Namu KOREAN, CALIFORNIAN **$$**
(Map p72; 415-386-8332; www.namusf.com; 439 Balboa St; small plates $8-16; 6-10:30pm Sun-Tue, 6pm-midnight Wed-Sat, 10:30am-3pm Sat & Sun) Organic ingredients, Silicon Valley inventiveness and Pacific Rim roots are showcased in Korean-inspired soul food, including housemade kimchee, umami-rich shitake mushroom dumplings and NorCal's definitive *bibimbap:* organic vegetables, grassfed steak and Sonoma farm egg served in a sizzling stone pot.

Ton Kiang DIM SUM **$**
(Map p72; 415-387-8273; www.tonkiang.net; 5821 Geary Blvd; dim sum $3-7; 10am-9pm Mon-Thu, 10am-9:30pm Fri, 9:30am-9:30pm Sat, 9am-9pm Sun;) Don't bother asking what's in those bamboo steamers: choose some on aroma alone and ask for the legendary *gao choy gat* (shrimp and chive dumplings), *dao miu gao* (pea tendril and shrimp dumplings) and *jin doy* (sesame balls) by name.

Kabuto CALIFORNIAN, SUSHI **$$**
(Map p72; 415-752-5652; www.kabutosushi.com; 5121 Geary Blvd; sushi $2-7, mains $9-13; dinner Tue-Sun) Innovative sushi served in a converted vintage hot-dog drive-in: nori-wrapped sushi rice with foie gras and ollalieberry reduction, *hamachi* (yellowtail) with pear and wasabi mustard, and – eureka! – the 49er oyster with sea urchin, caviar, a quail's egg and gold leaf, chased with rare sake.

Spices CHINESE **$**
(Map p72; 415-752-8884; http://spicesrestaurantonline.com; 294 8th Ave; mains $7-13; lunch & dinner) The menu reads like an oddly dubbed Hong Kong action flick, with dishes labeled 'explosive!!' and 'stinky!', but the chefs can call zesty pickled Napa cabbage, silky ma-po tofu and brain-curdling spicy chicken whatever they want – it's all worthy of exclamation. Cash only.

Halu JAPANESE **$**
(Map p 72; 415-221-9165; 312 8th Ave; yakitori $2.50-4, ramen $10-11; 5-10pm Tue-Sat) Dinner at this surreal, snug yakitori joint covered with Beatles memorabilia feels like stowing away on the Yellow Submarine. Small bites crammed onto sticks and barbecued, including bacon-wrapped scallops, quail eggs and mochi – and if you're up for offal, have a heart.

Genki DESSERT, SELF-CATERING **$**
(Map p72; 415-379-6414; www.genkicrepes.com; 330 Clement St; crepes $5; 2-10:30pm Mon, 10:30am-10:30pm Tue-Thu & Sun, 10am-11:30pm Fri & Sat) A teen mob scene for French crepes by way of Tokyo with green-tea ice cream and Nutella, and tropical fruit tapioca bubble tea. Stock up in the beauty supply and Pocky aisle to satisfy sudden snack or hair-dye whims.

THE SUNSET

TOP CHOICE **Outerlands** CALIFORNIAN **$**
(Map p72; 415-661-6140; http://outerlandssf.com; 4001 Judah St; sandwiches & small plates $8-9; 11am-3pm & 6-10pm Tue-Sat, 10am-2:30pm Sun) Drift into this beach-shack bistro for organic California comfort food: lunch means a $9 grilled artisan cheese combo with seasonal housemade soup, and dinner brings slow-cooked pork shoulder slouching into green-garlic risotto. Arrive early and sip wine outside until seats open up indoors.

Nanking Road Bistro CHINESE **$**
(Map p72; 415-753-2900; 1360 9th Ave; mains $7-12; 11:30am-10pm Mon-Fri, noon-10pm Sat & Sun;) Northern regional Chinese food is underrepresented in historically Cantonese SF, but the breakaway stars of Nanking Road's menu are clamshell *bao* (bun) folded over crispy Beijing duck and a definitive *kung*

pao chicken lunch special ($7), with the right ratio of chili to roast peanuts.

Sunrise Deli MIDDLE EASTERN $
(Map p72; ☎415-664-8210; 2115 Irving St; dishes $4-7; ⏰9am-9pm Mon-Sat, 10am-8pm Sun; ✍) A hidden gem in the fog belt, Sunrise dishes up what is arguably the city's best smoky baba ghanoush, *mujeddrah* (lentil-rice with crispy onions), garlicky *foul* (fava bean spread) and crispy falafel, either to go or to enjoy in the old-school cafe atmosphere.

Drinking

DOWNTOWN & SOUTH OF MARKET (SOMA)

Emporio Rulli Caffè CAFE
(Map p66; www.rulli.com; 333 Post St; ⏰7:30am-7pm) Ideal people-watching atop Union Sq, with excellent espresso and pastries to fuel up for shopping, plus wine by the glass afterward.

Bar Agricole BAR
(Map p88; www.baragricole.com; 355 11th St; 6-10pm Sun-Wed, til late Thu-Sat) Drink your way to a history degree with well-researched cocktails: Bellamy Scotch Sour with egg whites passes the test, but Tequila Fix with lime, pineapple gum, and hellfire bitters earns honors.

Sightglass Coffee CAFE
(Map p66; http://sightglasscoffee.com; 270 7th St; ⏰7am-6pm Mon-Sat, 8am-6pm Sun) San Francisco's newest cult coffee is roasted in a SoMa warehouse – follow the wafting aromas of Owl's Howl Espresso, and sample their family-grown, high-end 100% Bourbon-shrub coffee.

Bloodhound BAR
(Map p66; www.bloodhoundsf.com; 1145 Folsom St; ⏰4pm-2am) The murder of crows painted on the ceiling is definitely an omen: nights at Bloodhound assume mythic proportions with top-shelf booze served in Mason jars and pool marathons. SF's best food trucks often park out front; ask the barkeep to suggest a pairing.

House of Shields BAR
(Map p66; 39 New Montgomery St; ⏰2pm-2am Mon-Fri, from 7pm Sat) Flash back a hundred years at this recently restored mahogany bar, with original c 1908 chandeliers hanging from high ceilings and old-fashioned cocktails without the frippery.

Blue Bottle Coffee Company CAFE
(Map p66; www.bluebottlecoffee.net; 66 Mint St; ⏰7am-7pm Mon-Fri, 8am-6pm Sat, 8am-4pm Sun) The microroaster with the crazy-looking $20,000 coffee siphon for superior Fair Trade organic drip coffee is rivaled only by the bittersweet mochas and cappuccinos with ferns drawn in the foam. Expect a wait and $4 for your fix.

UNION SQUARE

Rickhouse BAR
(Map p66; www.rickhousebar.com; 246 Kearny St; ⏰Mon-Sat) Like a shotgun shack plunked downtown, Rickhouse is lined with repurposed whisky casks imported from Kentucky, and backbar shelving from an Ozark Mountains nunnery that once secretly brewed hooch. The emphasis is on bourbon, but authentic Pisco Punch (Peruvian-liquor citrus cocktail) is served in garage-sale punchbowls.

Barrique BAR
(Map p66; www.barriquesf.com; 461 Pacific Ave; ⏰3pm-10pm Tue-Sat) Roll out the barrel: get your glass of high-end small-batch vino straight from the cask, directly from the vineyard. Settle into white-leather sofas in back, near the casks, with artisan cheese and charcuterie plates.

Irish Bank PUB
(Map p66; www.theirishbank.com; 10 Mark Lane; ⏰11:30am-2am) Perfectly pulled pints, thick-cut fries with malt vinegar and juicy sausages served in a hidden alleyway or church pews indoors. Irish owner Ronin bought the place from his boss, and is now every working stiff's close and personal friend.

Tunnel Top Bar BAR
(Map p66; www.tunneltop.com; 601 Bush St; ⏰Mon-Sat) Chill two-story bar with exposed beams, beer-bottle chandelier, and a balcony where you can spy on the crowd below, grooving to hip-hop. Cash only.

Cantina BAR
(Map p66; www.cantinasf.com; 580 Sutter St; ⏰Mon-Sat) Latin-inspired cocktails made with fresh juice – there's not even a soda gun behind the bar – make this a go-to bar for off-duty bartenders; DJs spin weekends.

CIVIC CENTER & THE TENDERLOIN

Hemlock Tavern BAR
(Map p66; www.hemlocktavern.com; 1131 Polk St; ⏰4pm-2am) Cheap drinks at the oval bar,

pogo-worthy punk rock in the back room, a heated smoking area and free peanuts in the shell to eat and throw at literary events.

Edinburgh Castle BAR

(Map p66; www.castlenews.com; 950 Geary St; ⌚7pm-1am) Photos of bagpipers, the *Trainspotting* soundtrack on the jukebox, dart boards and a service delivering vinegary fish and chips in newspaper are all the Scottish authenticity you could ask for, short of haggis.

Rye BAR

(Map p66; www.ryesf.com; 688 Geary St; ⌚5:30pm-2am Mon-Fri, 7pm-2am Sat & Sun) Polished cocktails with herb-infused spirits and fresh-squeezed juice in a sleek darkwood setting. Come early, drink something challenging involving dark rum or juniper gin, and leave before the smoking cage overflows.

Bourbon & Branch BAR

(Map p66; ☎415-346-1735; www.bourbonandbranch.com; 501 Jones St; ⌚Wed-Sat by reservation) 'Don't even think of asking for a cosmo' reads one of many House Rules at this revived speakeasy, complete with secret exits from its Prohibition-era heyday. For top-shelf gin and bourbon cocktails in the Library, use the buzzer and the password 'books.'

CHINATOWN

Li Po BAR

(Map p58; 916 Grant Ave; ⌚2pm-2am) Enter the grotto doorway and get the once-over by the dusty Buddha as you slide into red vinyl booths beloved of Beats for beer or Chinese Mai Tai, made with *baiju* (rice liquor).

NORTH BEACH

TOP CHOICE **Caffe Trieste** CAFE

(Map p58; www.caffetrieste.com; 601 Vallejo St; ⌚6:30am-11pm Sun-Thu, 6:30am-midnight Fri & Sat; 📶) Look no further for inspiration: Francis Ford Coppola drafted *The Godfather* here under the mural of Sicily, and Poet Laureate Lawrence Ferlinghetti still swings by en route to City Lights. With opera on the jukebox and weekend accordion jam sessions, this is North Beach at its best since 1956.

Specs' BAR

(Map p58; 12 William Saroyan Pl; ⌚5pm-2am) A saloon that doubles as a museum of nautical memorabilia gives neighborhood characters license to drink like sailors, tell tall tales to gullible newcomers and plot mutinies against last call.

Comstock Saloon BAR

(Map p58; 155 Columbus Ave; ⌚11:30am-2am Mon-Fri, 2pm-2am Sat) A Victorian saloon with period-perfect Pisco Punch with real pineapple gum and Hop Toads with Jamaican rum, bitters and apricot brandy – plus beef shank and bone marrow pot pie and maple bourbon cake in the adjacent restaurant.

Tosca Cafe COCKTAIL BAR

(Map p58; http://toscacafesf.com; 242 Columbus Ave; ⌚5pm-2am Tue-Sun) Come early for your pick of opera on the jukebox and red circular booths, and stay late for Irish coffee nightcap crowds and chance sightings of Sean Penn, Bono or Robert De Niro.

NOB HILL

Bigfoot Lodge BAR

(Map p66; ☎415-440-2355; www.bigfootlodge.com; 1750 Polk St; ⌚3pm-2am) Cure cabin fever at this log-cabin bar with happy hours in the shadow of an 8ft Sasquatch, getting nicely toasted on Toasted Marshmallows – vanilla vodka, Bailey's and a flaming marshmallow.

Top of the Mark BAR

(Map p66; www.topofthemark.com; 999 California St; cover $5-15; ⌚5pm-midnight Sun-Thu, 4pm-1am Fri & Sat) Sashay across the dance floor and feel on top of the world overlooking SF. Cocktails will set you back $15 plus cover, but watch the sunset and then try to complain.

THE MARINA

California Wine Merchant WINE BAR

(Map p62; www.californiawinemerchant.com; 2113 Chestnut St; ⌚10am-midnight Mon-Wed, to 1:30am Thu-Sat, 11am-11pm Sun) Pair local wines by the glass with mild flirting in this wine cave, and be surprised by the subtleties of Central Coast pinots and playboys improving their game.

MatrixFillmore LOUNGE

(Map p62; 3138 Fillmore St; ⌚6pm-2am) The one bar in town where the presumption is that you're straight and interested. Modern and sleek, if a little sharp around the edges – and the same can be said of the crowd.

GAY/LESBIAN/BI/TRANS SAN FRANCISCO

Singling out the best places to be queer in San Francisco is almost redundant. Though the Castro is a gay hub and the Mission is a magnet for lesbians, the entire city is gay-friendly – hence the number of out elected representatives in City Hall at any given time. New York Marys may label SF the retirement home of the young – indeed, the sidewalks roll up early – but for sexual outlaws and underground weirdness, SF trounces New York. Dancing queens and slutty boys head South of Market (SoMa), the location of most thump-thump clubs. In the 1950s, bars euphemistically designated Sunday afternoons as 'tea dances,' appealing to gay crowds to make money at an otherwise slow time. The tradition now makes Sundays one of the busiest times for SF's gay bars. Top GLBT venues include:

The Stud (Map p66; ☎415-252-7883; www.studsf.com; 399 9th St; admission $5-8; ⏲5pm-3am) Rocking the gay scene since 1966, and branching out beyond leather daddies with rocker-grrrl Mondays, Tuesday drag variety shows, raunchy comedy/karaoke Wednesdays, Friday art-drag dance parties, and performance-art cabaret whenever hostess/DJ Anna Conda gets it together.

Lexington Club (Map p88; ☎415-863-2052; 3464 19th St; ⏲3pm-2am) Odds are eerily high you'll develop a crush on your ex-girlfriend's hot new girlfriend here over strong drink, pinball and tattoo comparisons – go on, live dangerously at SF's most famous/notorious full-time lesbian bar.

Rebel Bar (Map p66; ☎415-431-4202; 1760 Market St; admission varies; ⏲5pm-3am Mon-Thu, to 4am Fri, 11am-4am Sat & Sun) Funhouse southern biker disco, complete with antique mirrored walls, Hell's Angel cocktails (Bulleit bourbon, Chartreuse, OJ) and exposed pipes. The crowd is mostly 30-something, gay and tribally tattooed; on a good night, poles get thoroughly worked.

Aunt Charlie's (Map p66; ☎415-441-2922; www.auntcharlieslounge.com; 133 Turk St; ⏲9am-2am) Total dive, with the city's best classic drag show Fridays and Saturdays at 10pm. Thursday nights, art-school boys freak for bathhouse disco at Tubesteak ($5).

Endup (Map p66; ☎415-646-0999; www.theendup.com; 401 6th St; admission $5-20; ⏲10pm-4am Mon-Thu, 11pm-11am Fri, 10pm Sat to 4am Mon) Home of Sunday 'tea dances' (gay dance parties) since 1973, though technically the party starts Saturday – bring a change of clothes and EndUp watching the sunrise Monday over the freeway on-ramp.

Sisters of Perpetual Indulgence (Map p66; ☎415-820-9697; www.thesisters.org) For guerrilla antics and wild fundraisers, check in with the self-described 'leading-edge order of queer nuns,' a charitable organization and San Francisco institution.

THE MISSION

TOP CHOICE Zeitgeist BAR

(Map p88; www.zeitgeistsf.com; 199 Valencia St; ⏲9am-2am) When temperatures tip over 70°F (21°C), bikers and hipsters converge on Zeitgeist's huge outdoor beer garden (minus the garden) for 40 brews on tap pulled by SF's toughest lady barkeeps and late-night munchies courtesy of the Tamale Lady.

Elixir BAR

(Map p88; www.elixirsf.com; 3200 16th St; ⏲3pm-2am Mon-Fri, noon-2am Sat & Sun) Drinking is good for the environment at SF's first certified green bar, with your choice of organic, green and even biodynamic cocktails – *ayiyi,* those peach margaritas with ancho-chili-infused tequila. Mingle over darts and a killer jukebox.

Homestead BAR

(Map p88; 2301 Folsom St; ⏲5pm-1am) Your friendly Victorian corner dive c 1893, complete with carved-wood bar, roast peanuts in the shell, cheap draft beer and Victorian tin-stamped ceiling.

Make-Out Room BAR
(Map p88; www.makeoutroom.com; 3225 22nd St) Between the generous pours and Pabst beer specials, the Make-Out has convinced otherwise sane people to leap onstage and read from their teen journals for Mortified nights, sing along to punk-rock fiddle and flail to '80s one-hit-wonder DJ mashups.

Ritual Coffee Roasters CAFE
(Map p88; www.ritualroasters.com; 1026 Valencia St; ⏲6am-10pm Mon-Fri, 7am-10pm Sat, 7am-9pm Sun; wi-fi) Cults wish they inspired the same devotion as Ritual, where lines head out the door for house-roasted cappuccino with ferns in the foam and deliberately limited electrical outlets to encourage conversation.

THE CASTRO

Café Flore CAFE
(Map p88; 2298 Market St; ⏲7am-1am; wi-fi) The see-and-be-seen, glassed-in corner cafe at the center of the gay universe. Eavesdrop on blind dates with bracing cappuccino or knee-weakening absinthe.

Thorough Bread CAFE, BAKERY
(Map p88; www.thoroughbreadandpastry.com; 248 Church St; ⏲7am-7pm Tue-Sat, to 3pm Sun) Pedigreed pastries and excellent breads from San Francisco Baking Institute chefs, plus powerful drip coffee.

Samovar Tea Lounge TEAHOUSE
(Map p88; 498 Sanchez St; ⏲10am-11pm; wi-fi) Iron pots of tea with scintillating side dishes, from savory pumpkin dumplings to chocolate brownies with green-tea mousse.

The Mint THEME BAR
(Map p88; www.themint.net; 1942 Market St; ⏲4pm-2am) Show tunes are serious stuff at karaoke sessions starting at 9pm nightly, where it takes courage and a vodka gimlet to attempt Barbra Streisand. Prepare to be upstaged by a banker with a boa and a mean falsetto.

THE HAIGHT & HAYES VALLEY

Cole Valley Café CAFE
(Map p81; www.colevalleycafe.com; 701 Cole St; ⏲6:30am-8:30pm Mon-Fri, 6:30am-8pm Sat & Sun; wi-fi) Powerful coffee and chai, free wi-fi, and hot gourmet sandwiches that are a bargain at any price, let alone $6 for lip-smacking thyme-marinated chicken with lemony avocado spread or the smoky roasted eggplant with goat cheese and sundried tomatoes.

Coffee to the People CAFE
(Map p81; www.coffeetothepeople.squarespace.com; 1206 Masonic Ave; ⏲6am-8pm Mon-Fri, to 9pm Sat & Sun; wi-fi, vegetarian, family) The people, united, will never be decaffeinated at this utopian coffee shop with free wireless, 3% pledged to coffee-growers' nonprofits, a radical reading library and enough Fair Trade coffee to revive the Sandinista movement.

TOP CHOICE **Smuggler's Cove** THEME BAR
(Map p66; http://smugglerscovesf.com; 650 Gough St; ⏲5pm-2am) Yo-ho-ho and a bottle of rum…or make that 200 at this Barbary Coast shipwreck of a tiki bar. With tasting flights and 70 historic cocktail recipes gleaned from rum-running around the world, you won't be dry-docked for long.

TOP CHOICE **Toronado** BAR
(Map p88; www.toronado.com; 547 Haight St; ⏲6pm-1am) Bow before the chalkboard altar listing 50 microbrews and hundreds more bottled, including spectacular seasonal microbrews. Bring cash, come early and stay late, with a sausage from Rosamunde next door to accompany seasonal ales.

Aub Zam Zam LOUNGE
(Map p81; 1633 Haight St; ⏲3pm-2am) Arabesque arches, jazz on the jukebox and enough paisley to make Prince feel right at home pay homage to the purist Persian charm of dearly departed cocktail fascist Bruno, who'd throw you out for ordering a vodka martini.

THE RICHMOND

Beach Chalet Brewery BREWERY
(Map p72; www.beachchalet.com; 1000 Great Hwy; ⏲9am-10pm Sun-Thu, to 11pm Fri & Sat) Brews with views: sunsets over the Pacific, a backyard bar, and recently restored 1930s WPA frescoes downstairs showing a condensed history of San Francisco.

Plough & Stars PUB
(Map p72; www.theploughandstars.com; 116 Clement St; ⏲3pm-2am Mon-Thu, 2pm-2am Fri-Sun, showtime 9pm) The Emerald Isle by the Golden Gate. Jigs are to be expected after the first couple of rounds and rousing Irish fiddle tunes are played most nights by top Celtic talent.

THE SUNSET

Hollow CAFE
(Map p72; http://hollowsf.com; 1493 Irving St; ⏲8am-5pm Mon-Fri, 9am-5pm Sat & Sun) Between simple explanations and Golden Gate Park,

HOT TICKETS

Big events sell out fast in SF. Scan the free weeklies, the *San Francisco Bay Guardian* and the *SF Weekly*, and see what half-price and last-minute tickets you can find at **TIX Bay Area** (Map p66; ☎415-433-7827; Union Sq at 251 Stockton St; ⏲11am-6pm Tue-Thu, to 7pm Fri & Sat). Tickets are sold on the day of the performance for cash only. For tickets to theater shows and big-name concerts in advance, call **Ticketmaster** (☎415-421-8497) or **BASS** (☎415-478-2277).

there's Hollow: cultish Ritual coffee and Guiness cupcakes served amid art-installation displays of magnifying glasses, tin pails, and monster etchings.

★ Entertainment

Nightclubs

El Rio CLUB

(off Map p88; ☎415-282-3325; www.elriosf.com; 3158 Mission St; admission $3-8) Free-form funky grooves worked by regulars of every conceivable ethnicity and orientation. 'Salsa Sundays' are legendary – arrive at 3pm for lessons – and other nights feature oyster happy hours, eclectic music, and shameless flirting on the garden patio.

Cat Club CLUB

(Map p66; www.catclubsf.com; 1190 Folsom St; admission $5 after 10pm; ⏲Tue-Sun) Thursday's '1984' is a euphoric straight/gay/bi/whatever party scene from a lost John Hughes movie; other nights vary from Saturday power pop to Bondage-a-Go-Go.

AsiaSF CLUB

(Map p66; ☎415-255-2742; www.asiasf.com; 201 9th St; $35 minimum per person; ⏲Wed-Sun) Cocktails and Asian-inspired dishes are served with a tall order of sass and one little secret: your servers are drag stars. Your hostesses rock the bar/runway hourly – but once inspiration and drinks kick in, everyone mixes it up on the downstairs dance floor. The three-course 'Menage á Trois Menu' runs $39, cocktails around $10, and honey, those tips are well-earned.

DNA Lounge CLUB

(Map p88; www.dnalounge.com; 375 11th St; admission $3-25) SF's mega-club hosts live bands and big-name DJs. Second and fourth Saturdays bring Bootie, the kick-ass original mashup party; Monday's Goth Death Guild means shuffle-dancing and free tea service.

Harlot CLUB

(Map p66; www.harlotsf.com; 46 Minna St; admission $10-20, free 5-9pm Wed-Fri; ⏲Wed-Sat) Aptly named after 10pm, when the bordello-themed lounge cuts loose to house Thursdays, indie-rock Wednesdays, and women-only Fem Bar parties.

111 Minna CLUB

(Map p66; www.111minnagallery.com; 111 Minna St) Street-wise art gallery by day, after-work lounge and club after 9pm, when '90s and '80s dance parties take the back room by storm.

Live Music

TOP CHOICE **The Fillmore** LIVE MUSIC

(off Map p62; www.thefillmore.com; 1805 Geary Blvd; tickets from $20) Hendrix, Zeppelin, Janis – they all played the Fillmore. The legendary venue that launched the psychedelic era has the posters to prove it upstairs, and hosts arena acts in a 1250-seat venue where you can squeeze in next to the stage.

Slim's LIVE MUSIC

(www.slims-sf.com; 333 11th St; tickets $11-28) Guaranteed good times by Gogol Bordello, Tenacious D, and AC/DShe (the hard-rocking female tribute band) fill the bill at this mid-sized club, where Prince and Elvis Costello have shown up to play sets unannounced.

Yoshi's JAZZ

(off Map p62; www.yoshis.com; 1300 Fillmore St; tickets $12-50) San Francisco's definitive jazz club draws the world's top talent to the historic African and Japanese American Fillmore jazz district, and serves pretty good sushi besides.

Mezzanine LIVE MUSIC

(Map p66; www.mezzaninesf.com; 444 Jessie St; admission $10-40) The best sound system in SF bounces off the brick walls at breakthrough hiphop shows by Quest Love, Method Man, Nas and Snoop Dogg, plus throwback alt-classics like the Dandy Warhols and Psychedelic Furs.

Warfield LIVE MUSIC

(Map p66; www.thewarfieldtheatre.com; 982 Market St) Originally a vaudeville theater but now an obligatory stop for marquee acts from Beastie Boys and PJ Harvey to Furthur (formerly the Grateful Dead).

Great American Music Hall LIVE MUSIC

(Map p66; www.musichallsf.com; 859 O'Farrell St; admission $12-35) Previously a bordello and a dance hall, this ornate venue now hosts rock, country, jazz and world music artists. Arrive early to stake your claim to front-row balcony seats with a pint and a passable burger.

Bottom of the Hill LIVE MUSIC

(off Map p88; www.bottomofthehill.com; 1233 17th St; admission $5-12; ⏲Tue-Sat) Top of the list for breakthrough bands, from notable local alt-rockers like Deerhoof to newcomers worth checking out by name alone (Yesway, Stripmall Architecture, Excuses for Skipping) in *Rolling Stone*'s favorite SF venue; cash only.

Bimbo's 365 Club LIVE MUSIC

(Map p62; www.bimbos365club.com; 1025 Columbus Ave; tickets from $20) Anything goes behind these vintage-1931 speakeasy velvet curtains, lately including live shows by the likes of Cibo Matto, Ben Harper and Coldplay. Cash only, and bring something extra to tip the ladies' powder room attendant – this is a classy joint.

Hotel Utah LIVE MUSIC

(Map p66; www.thehotelutahsaloon.com; 500 4th St; bar admission free, shows $5-10) Whoopi Goldberg and Robin Williams broke in the stage of this historic Victorian hotel back in the '70s, and the thrill of finding SF's hidden talents draws crowds to singer-songwriter Open Mic Mondays, indie-label debuts and local favorites like Riot Earp, Saucy Monkey and The Dazzling Strangers.

Cafe du Nord LIVE MUSIC

(Map p88; www.cafedunord.com; 2170 Market St; admission $7-15) A 1930s downstairs speakeasy in the basement of the Swedish-American Hall serves 'em short and strong and glam-rocks, afrobeats, retro-rockabillies and indie-record-release parties almost nightly – plus pulled-on-stage performances by off-duty musicians and novelists.

Elbo Room LIVE MUSIC

(Map p88; www.elbo.com; 647 Valencia St; admission $5-8) Funny name, because there isn't much to speak of upstairs on show nights with crowd-favorite funk, dancehall dub, and offbeat indie bands like Uni and Her Ukelele.

Rickshaw Stop LIVE MUSIC

(Map p66; www.rickshawstop.com; 155 Fell St; admission $5-35) Noise-poppers, eccentric rockers and crafty DJs cross-pollinate hemispheres with something for everyone: badass banghra nights, Latin explosion bands, lesbian disco, and mainstay Thursday 18+ Popscene.

Amnesia LIVE MUSIC

(Map p88; www.amnesiathebar.com; 853 Valencia St) A teensy bar featuring nightly local music acts that may be playing in public for the first time, so show hardworking bands some love and buy that shy rapper a drink.

Theater

Musicals and Broadway spectaculars play at a number of downtown theaters. **SHN** (☎415-512-7770; www.shnsf.com) hosts touring Broadway shows at opulent **Orpheum Theatre** (Map p66; 1192 Market St), **Curran Theatre** (Map p66; 445 Geary St), and 1920s **Golden Gate Theatre** (Map p66; 1 Taylor St). But the pride of SF is its many indie theaters that host original, solo and experimental shows, including the following.

TOP CHOICE **American Conservatory Theater** THEATER

(Map p66; ACT; ☎415-749-2228; www.act-sf.org; 415 Geary St) San Francisco's most famous mainstream venue has put on original landmark productions of Tony Kushner's *Angels in America* and Robert Wilson's *Black Rider*, with a libretto by William S Burroughs and music by the Bay Area's own Tom Waits.

Beach Blanket Babylon COMEDY, CABARET

(Map p58; ☎415-421-4222; www.beachblanketbabylon.com; 678 Green St; seats $25-78) San Francisco's longest-running comedy cabaret keeps the belly laughs coming with giant hats, killer drag and social satire with bite. Spectators must be 21-plus, except at matinees.

Magic Theatre THEATER

(Map p62; ☎415-441-8822; www.magictheatre.org; Fort Mason, Bldg D) Risk-taking original productions from major playwrights, including Sam Shepard, Edna O'Brien and Terrence McNally, starring actors like Ed Harris and Sean Penn, plus staged works written by teenagers.

Cobb's Comedy Club COMEDY
(Map p62; ☎415-928-4320; www.cobbscomedyclub.com; 915 Columbus Ave; admission $13-33 plus 2-drink minimum) Bumper-to-bumper shared tables make for an intimate (and vulnerable) audience for stand-up acts, from new talent to HBO's Dave Chapelle and NBC's Tracy Morgan.

Exit Theater THEATER
(Map p66; ☎415-673-3847; http://theexit.org; 156 Eddy St; admission $15-20) Hosts the SF Fringe Festival and avant-garde productions year-round.

Intersection for the Arts LIVE MUSIC, THEATER
(Map p88; ☎415-626-2787; www.theintersection.org; 446 Valencia; admission $5-20) Ambidextrous nonprofit art space with famous playwrights-in-residence, a major jazz showcase and a provocative upstairs gallery program since 1965.

Marsh THEATER
(Map p88; ☎415-826-5750; www.themarsh.org; 1062 Valencia St; tickets $15-35) Choose your seat wisely: you'll spend the evening on the edge of it, with one-acts, monologues and works-in-progress that involve the audience.

Punch Line COMEDY
(Map p66; ☎415-397-4337; www.punchlinecomedyclub.com; 444 Battery St; admission $12-23, plus 2-drink minimum; ⊙Tue-Sun) Turns unknown comics into known names – Chris Rock, Ellen DeGeneres and David Cross, to name a few.

Purple Onion COMEDY
(Map p58; ☎415-956-1653; www.caffemacaroni.com; 140 Columbus Ave; admission $10-15) Woody Allen, Robin Williams and Phyllis Diller clawed their way up from underground at this grotto nightclub, and Zach Galifianakis shot an excruciatingly funny comedy special here.

Classical Music, Opera & Dance

TOP CHOICE **Davies Symphony Hall** CLASSICAL MUSIC
(Map p66; ☎415-864-6000; www.sfsymphony.org; 201 Van Ness Ave) Home of nine-time Grammy-winning SF Symphony, conducted with verve by Michael Tilson Thomas from September to May here – don't miss Beethoven.

War Memorial Opera House OPERA
(Map p66; ☎415-864-3330; www.sfopera.com; 301 Van Ness Ave) Rivaling City Hall's grandeur is the 1932 home to **San Francisco Opera** (www.sfopera.com) from June through December and the **San Francisco Ballet** (www.sfballet.org) from January through May. Student tickets and standing-room tickets go on sale two hours before performances.

TOP CHOICE **ODC Theater** DANCE
(Map p88; ☎415-863-9834; www.odctheater.org; 3153 17th St) For 40 years, redefining dance with risky, raw performances and the sheer joy of movement with performances September through December, and 200 dance classes a week.

Cinemas

TOP CHOICE **Castro Theatre** CINEMA
(Map p88; www.thecastrotheatre.com; 429 Castro St; adult/child $10/7.50) Showtunes on a Wurlitzer are the overture to independent cinema, silver-screen classics and unstoppable audience participation.

Sundance Kabuki Cinema CINEMA
(off Map p62; www.sundancecinemas.com/kabuki.html; 1881 Post St; adult/child $10-14) Trendsetting green multiplex with GMO-free popcorn, reserved seating in cushy recycled-fiber seats and the frankly brilliant Balcony Bar, where you can slurp seasonal cocktails during your movie.

Roxie Cinema CINEMA
(Map p88; www.roxie.com; 3117 16th St; adult/child $10/6.50) Independent gems, insightful documentaries and rare film noir you won't find elsewhere, in a landmark 1909 cinema recently upgraded with Dolby sound.

Balboa Theater CINEMA
(Map p72; www.balboamovies.com; 3630 Balboa St; double-features adult/child $10/7.50) Double-features perfect for foggy weather, including film fest contenders selected by the director of the Telluride Film Festival, in a renovated 1926 art deco cinema.

Sports

San Francisco Giants BASEBALL
(Map p66; http://Sanfrancisco.giants.mlb.com; AT&T Park; tickets $5-135; ⊙season Apr-Oct)

SAN FRANCISCO FOR CHILDREN

Imaginations come alive in this storybook city, with wild parrots squawking indignantly at passersby near **Coit Tower** (p61) on Telegraph Hill and sunning sea lions gleefully nudging one another off the docks at **Pier 39** (p61). For thrills, try rickety, seatbelt-free **cable cars** (p99), or pick up a dragon kite in Chinatown souvenir shops to fly at **Crissy Field** (p63) – just be sure to bundle up for the wind. Kids will find playmates in playgrounds at **Golden Gate Park** (p53) and **Portsmouth Square** (p59).

For organized activities, try these kid-friendly attractions:

» **Children's Creativity Museum** (Map p66; ☎415-820-3320; www.zeum.org; 221 4th St; admission $10; ⏲11am-5pm Tue-Sun; 👪) Technology that's too cool for school: robots, live-action video games, DIY music videos, and 3D animation workshops with Silicon Valley innovators. The vintage 1906 Loof Carousel out front operates until 6pm daily ($3 for two rides).

» **Aquarium of the Bay** (Map p62; www.aquariumofthebay.com; Pier 39; adult/child $17/8; ⏲9am-8pm summer, 10am-6pm winter; 👪) Glide through glass tubes underwater on conveyer belts as sharks circle and manta rays flutter overhead.

» **Fire Engine Tours** (Map p62; ☎415-333-7077; www.fireenginetours.com; Beach St at the Cannery; adult/child $50/30; ⏲tours depart 1pm; 👪) Hot stuff: a 75-minute, open-air vintage fire engine ride over Golden Gate Bridge.

See also: the **Exploratorium** (p62), **California Academy of Sciences** (p70), **Cartoon Art Museum** (p65), **Musée Mecanique** (p61) and **826 Valencia** (p65).

Watch and learn how the World Series is won – bushy beards, women's underwear and all. The city's National League baseball team draws crowds to AT&T Park and its solar-powered scoreboard; the Waterfront Promenade offers a free view of right field.

San Francisco 49ers FOOTBALL
(www.49ers.com; Candlestick Park; tickets from $59; ⏲season Aug-Dec) For NFL football, beer and garlic-fries, head to Candlestick Park. Lately they've been in a slump, but the '49ers are one of the most successful teams in National Football League history, with no fewer than five Super Bowl championships. Home games are played at cold and windy Candlestick Park, off Hwy 101 south of the city.

Shopping

San Francisco has big department stores and name-brand boutiques around Union Sq, including **Macy's** (Map p66; www.macys.com; 170 O'Farrell Street) and the sprawling new **Westfield Shopping Centre** (Map p66; www.westfield.com/SanFrancisco; 865 Market St; ⏲9:30am-9pm Mon-Sat, 10am-7pm Sun), but special, only-in-SF scores are found in the Haight, the Castro, the Mission and Hayes Valley (west of Civic Center).

TOP CHOICE **Adobe Books & BackRoom Gallery** BOOKS
(Map p88; http://adobebooksbackroomgallery.blogspot.com; 3166 16th St; ⏲11am-midnight) Come here for every book you never knew you needed used and cheap, plus 'zine launch parties, poetry readings, and BackRoom Gallery – but first you have to navigate the obstacle course of sofas, cats, art books and German philosophy.

TOP CHOICE **Under One Roof** GIFTS
(Map p88; www.underoneroof.org; 518a Castro St; ⏲10am-8pm Mon-Sat, 11am-7pm Sun) AIDS service organizations receive 100% of the proceeds from goods donated by local designers and retailers, so show volunteer salespeople some love for raising $11 million to date.

Reliquary CLOTHING, ACCESSORIES
(off Map p66; http://reliquarysf.com; 537 Octavia Blvd; ⏲11am-7pm Tue-Sat, noon-6pm Sun) Owner Leah Bershad was once a designer for Gap, but the folksy jet-set aesthetic here is the exact opposite of khaki-and-fleece global domination: Santa Fe woollen blankets, silver jewelry banged together by Humboldt hippies, Majestic tissue-tees and Clare Vivier pebble-leather clutches.

Piedmont Boutique ACCESSORIES
(Map p81; 1452 Haight St; ⏲11am-7pm) Glam up or get out at this supplier of drag fabulousness: pleather hot pants, airplane earrings and a wall of feather boas.

Amoeba Records MUSIC
(Map p81; www.amoeba.com; 1855 Haight St; ⏲10:30pm-10pm Mon-Sat, 11am-9pm Sun) Bowling-alley-turned-superstore of new and used records in all genres, plus free in-store concerts and Music We Like 'zine for great new finds.

MAC CLOTHING
(Map p66; http://modernappealingclothing.com; 387 Grove St; ⏲11am-7pm Mon-Sat, noon-6pm Sun) Impeccably structured looks for men from Belgian minimalist Dries Van Noten and Tsumori Chisato's Japanese luxe for the ladies; superb 40% to 75% off sales rack.

Velvet da Vinci JEWELRY
(Map p66; www.velvetdavinci.com; 2015 Polk St; ⏲11am-6pm Tue-Sat, to 4pm Sun) Ingenious jewelry by local and international artisans: Julia Turner's satellite-dish ring, Ben Neubauer's cage earrings, a drinking flask bracelet by William Clark.

Nancy Boy BEAUTY
(Map p66; www.nancyboy.com; 347 Hayes St; ⏲11am-7pm Mon-Fri, to 6pm Sat & Sun) Wear these highly effective moisturizers, pomades and sun balms with pride, all locally made with plant oils and tested on boyfriends, never animals.

New People CLOTHING, GIFTS
(off Map p62; www.newpeopleworld.com; 1746 Post St) An eye-popping three-story emporium devoted to Japanese art and pop culture, with contemporary art, Lolita fashions, traditional Japanese clothing with contemporary graphics, and *kawaii* (Japanese for all things cute).

Gravel & Gold HOUSEWARES, GIFTS
(Map p88; gravelandgold.com; 3266 21st St; ⏲noon-7pm Tue-Sat, noon-5pm Sun) A gallery/boutique celebrating the 1960s-1970s hippie homesteader movement, from stoneware teapots to hand-dyed smocked dresses – which you can try on among psychedelic murals behind a patched curtain.

Goorin Brothers Hats ACCESSORIES
(Map p81; www.goorin.com; 1446 Haight St; ⏲11am-7pm Sun-Fri, to 8pm Sat) Peacock feathers, high crowns and local-artist-designed embellishments make it easy to withstand the fog while standing out in a crowd in SF-designed fedoras, caps and cloches.

Accident & Artifact GIFTS, ACCESSORIES
(Map p88; www.accidentandartifact.com; 381 Valencia St; ⏲noon-6pm Thu-Sun) A most curious curiosity shop, even by Mission standards: decorative dried fungi, vintage Okinawan indigo textiles, artfully redrawn topographical maps and fur-covered televisions with antlers.

Dema CLOTHING
(Map p88; www.godemago.com; 1038 Valencia St; ⏲11am-7pm Mon-Fri, noon-6pm Sat & Sun) Wear-everywhere shifts in vintage-inspired prints by local designer Dema, plus clever cardigans and Orla Kiely tees.

Madame S & Mr S Leather CLOTHING
(Map p66; www.madame-s.com; 385 8th St; ⏲11am-7pm) S&M superstore, with such musts as leashes, dungeon furniture and for that special someone, a chrome-plated codpiece.

Wasteland VINTAGE, CLOTHING
(Map p81; www.thewasteland.com; 1660 Haight St; ⏲11am-8pm Mon-Sat, noon-7pm Sun) The catwalk of thrifting: psychedelic Pucci maxiskirts, barely worn Marc Jacobs smocks and a steady supply of go-go boots.

Jeremy's CLOTHING, ACCESSORIES
(Map p66; www.jeremys.com; 2 South Park St; ⏲11am-6pm Mon-Sat, to 5pm Sun) Window displays, photo shoot ensembles and department store customer returns translate to jaw-dropping bargains on major designers for men and women.

Park Life ARTWORK, BOOKS
(Map p72; www.parklifestore.com; 220 Clement St; ⏲11am-8pm) Design store, indie publisher and art gallery with gift options: tees with drawn-on pockets, Park Life's catalog of graffiti artist Andrew Schoultz, and Ian Johnson's portrait of Miles Davis radiating prismatic thought waves.

Sui Generis VINTAGE, CLOTHING
(Map p88; men's shop 2231 Market St, women's shop 2265 Market St; ⏲noon-7pm Tue-Thu, to 8pm Fri & Sat, to 4pm Sun) Straight-off-the-runway, lightly worn scores from Prada, Zegna, Armani & Co, some in the double-digit range.

Studio GIFTS
(Map p66; www.studiogallerysf.com; 1815 Polk St; ⏰11am-8pm Wed-Fri, to 6pm Sat & Sun) Winsome locally made arts and crafts at bargain prices, including Chiami Sekine's collages of boxing bears, SF architectural etchings by Alice Gibbons, and Monique Tse's fat-free glass cupcakes.

Golden Gate Fortune Cookie Company FOOD & DRINK
(Map p58; 56 Ross Alley; admission free; ⏰8am-7pm) Make a fortune in San Francisco at this bakery, where cookies are stamped out on old-fashioned presses and folded over your customized message (50c each). Cash only; 50c tip for photo requested.

Sports Basement OUTDOOR EQUIPMENT
(Map p62; www.sportsbasement.com; 610 Mason St; ⏰9am-8pm Mon-Fri, 8am-7pm Sat & Sun) There's 70,000 sq ft of sports and camping equipment housed in the Presidio's former US Army PX; free coffee and hot cider while you shop.

Community Thrift CLOTHING, HOUSEWARES
(Map p88; www.communitythriftsf.org; 623 Valencia St; ⏰10am-6:30pm) Vintage home furnishing scores and local retailer overstock, all sold to benefit local charities.

SFO Snowboarding & FTC Skateboarding OUTDOOR EQUIPMENT
(Map p81; 1630 Haight St; ⏰11am-7pm) State-of-the-art gear, snowboards and skateboards, some with designs by local artists.

Mollusk OUTDOOR EQUIPMENT
(Map p72; www.mollusksurfshop.com; 4500 Irving St; ⏰10am-6:30pm) For locally designed surf gear.

Information

Dangers & Annoyances

Keep your city smarts and wits about you, especially at night in SoMa, the Mission and the Haight. Unless you know where you're going, avoid the sketchy, depressing Tenderloin (bordered east–west by Powell and Polk Sts and north–south by O'Farrell and Market Sts), Skid Row (6th St between Market and Folsom Sts) and Bayview-Hunters Point. To cut through the Tenderloin, take Geary or Market Sts – still seedy, but tolerable. Panhandlers and homeless people are a fact of life in the city. People will probably ask you for spare change, but donations to local non-profits stretch further. For safety, don't engage with panhandlers at night or around ATMs. Otherwise, a simple 'I'm sorry,' is a polite response.

Emergency & Medical Services

San Francisco General Hospital (☎emergency room 415-206-8111, main 415-206-8000; www.sfdph.org; 1001 Potrero Ave) 24-hour care.

Walgreens (☎415-861-3136; www.walgreens.com 498 Castro St; ⏰24hr) Pharmacy and over-the-counter meds; dozens of locations citywide.

Internet Access

SF has free wi-fi hot spots citywide – locate one nearby with **www.openwifispots.com**. Connect for free in Union Sq and most cafes and hotel lobbies.

Apple Store (☎415-392-0202; www.apple.com/retail/SanFrancisco; 1 Stockton St; ⏰9am-9pm Mon-Sat, 10am-8pm Sun; 📶) Free wi-fi access and internet terminal usage.

Main Library (http://sfpl.org; 100 Larkin St; ⏰10am-6pm Mon & Sat, 9am-8pm Tue-Thu, noon-5pm Fri & Sun; 📶) Free 15-minute internet terminal usage; spotty wi-fi access.

Brain Wash (www.brainwash.com; 1122 Folsom St; per wash from $2; ⏰7am-10pm Mon-Thu, to 11pm Fri & Sat, 8am-10pm Sun; 📶) Come with laundry, stay for lunch, beer, live entertainment, pinball, free wi-fi and internet terminals ($3 per 20 minutes).

Money

Bank of America (www.bankamerica.com; One Market Plaza; ⏰9am-6pm Mon-Fri)

Post

Rincon Center post office (Map p66; www.usps.com; 180 Steuart St; ⏰8am-6pm Mon-Fri, 9am-2pm Sat) Postal services plus historic murals.

Union Square post office (Map p66; www.usps.com; 170 O'Farrell St; ⏰10am-5:30pm Mon-Sat, 11am-5pm Sun) In the basement of Macy's department store.

Tourist Information

California Welcome Center (Map p62; ☎415-981-1280; www.visitcwc.com; Pier 39, Bldg P, ste 241b; ⏰10am-5pm) Handy for travel information, brochures, maps and help booking accommodations.

San Francisco Visitors Information Center (Map p66; ☎415-391-2000; www.onlyinSanFrancisco.com; lower level, Hallidie Plaza; ⏰9am-5pm Mon-Fri, 9am-3pm Sat & Sun) Maps, guidebooks, brochures, accommodations help.

Websites

http://sfbay.craigslist.org Events, activities, partners, freebies and dates.

http://sf.eater.com SF food, nightlife and bars.

www.flavorpill.com Live music, lectures, art openings and movie premieres.

www.urbandaddy.com Bars, shops, restaurants and events.

Getting There & Away

Air

The Bay Area has three major airports: **San Francisco International Airport** (SFO; www.flysfo.com), 14 miles south of downtown SF, off Hwy 101; Oakland International Airport (see p132), a few miles across the bay; and San José International Airport (p132), at the southern end of the bay. The majority of international flights use SFO. Travelers from other US cities may find cheaper flights into Oakland on discount airlines such as JetBlue and Southwest.

Improvements over the last decade include a new international terminal, LEED-certified green Terminal 2 and a BART extension directly to the airport. All three SFO terminals have ATMs and information booths on the lower level, and **Travelers' Aid information booths** (⏰9am-9pm) on the upper level. The airport paging and information line is staffed 24 hours; call from any white courtesy phone.

Bus

Until the new terminal is complete in 2017, SF's intercity hub remains the **Temporary Transbay Terminal** (Map p66; Howard & Main Sts), where you can catch buses on **AC Transit** (www.actransit.org) to the East Bay, **Golden Gate Transit** (http://goldengatetransit.org) north to Marin and Sonoma Counties, and **SamTrans** (www.samtrans.com) south to Palo Alto and the Pacific coast. **Greyhound** (☎800-231-2222; www.greyhound.com) buses leave daily for Los Angeles ($56.50, eight to 12 hours), Truckee near Lake Tahoe ($33, 5½ hours), and other destinations.

Car & Motorcycle

All major car-rental operators (Alamo, Avis, Budget, Dollar, Hertz, Thrifty) are represented at the airports, and many have downtown offices.

Ferry

For Alcatraz Cruises, see p75.

Blue & Gold Fleet Ferries (Map p66; www.blueandgoldfleet.com) The Alameda-Oakland Ferry runs from the Ferry Building to Jack London Sq in Oakland ($6.25, 30 minutes). Ferries to Tiburon, Sausalito and Angel Island run from Pier 41 at Fisherman's Wharf.

Golden Gate Ferries (Map p66; ☎415-923-2000; www.goldengateferry.org; ⏰6am-10pm Mon-Fri, 10am-6pm Sat & Sun) Regular services run from the Ferry Building to Larkspur and Sausalito in Marin County. Transfers are available to MUNI bus services, and bicycles permitted.

Vallejo Ferries (Map p66; ☎415-773-1188; one way adult/child $15/7.50) Get to Napa car-free, with departures from Ferry Building docks about every hour from 6:30am through 7pm weekdays and every two hours from 11am through 7:30pm on weekends; bikes are permitted. From the Vallejo Ferry Terminal, take Napa Valley Vine bus 10 to downtown Napa, Yountville, St Helena or Calistoga. Also connects to Six Flags Marine World theme park in Vallejo.

Train

CalTrain (Map p66; www.caltrain.com; cnr 4th & King Sts) links San Francisco to the South Bay, including Palo Alto (Stanford University) and San Jose.

Amtrak (☎800-872-7245; www.amtrakcalifornia.com) offers low-emission, leisurely travel to and from San Francisco. *Coast Starlight*'s spectacular 35-hour run from Los Angeles to Seattle stops in Oakland, and the *California Zephyr* takes its sweet time (51 hours) traveling from Chicago through the Rockies to Oakland. Both have sleeping cars and dining/lounge cars with panoramic windows. Amtrak runs free shuttle buses to San Francisco's Ferry Building and CalTrain station.

Getting Around

For Bay Area transit options, departures and arrivals, check ☎511 or www.511.org.

To/From the Airport

» **BART** (Bay Area Rapid Transit; www.bart.gov; one-way $8.10) offers a fast, direct ride to downtown San Francisco.

» **SamTrans** (www.samtrans.com; one-way $5) express bus KX gets you to Temporary Transbay Terminal in about 30 minutes.

» **SuperShuttle** (☎800-258-3826; www.supershuttle.com; one-way $17) door-to-door vans depart from baggage-claim areas, taking 45 minutes to most SF locations.

» **Taxis** to downtown San Francisco cost $35-50.

Bicycle

San Francisco is cyclable, but traffic downtown can be dangerous; bicycling is best east of Van Ness Ave and across the bay. For bike shops and rentals, see p71. Bicycles can be carried on BART, but not in the commute direction during weekday rush hours.

Car & Motorcycle

If you can, avoid driving in San Francisco: street parking is harder to find than true love, and meter readers are ruthless. Convenient downtown parking lots are at Embarcadero Center, 5th and Mission Sts, Union Sq, and Sutter and Stockton Sts. National car-rental agencies have airport and downtown offices.

Before you set out to any bridge or other traffic choke-point, call ☎511 toll-free for a traffic update. Members of the **American Automobile Association** (AAA; ☎415-773-1900, 800-222-4357; www.aaa.com; 160 Sutter St; ⏰8:30am-5:30pm Mon-Fri) can call the 800 number any time for emergency road service and towing. AAA also provides travel insurance and free road maps of the region.

Parking authorities are quick to tow cars. If this should happen to you, you'll have to retrieve your car at **Autoreturn** (☎415-865-8200; www.autoreturn.com; 450 7th St; ⏰24hr). Besides at least $73 in fines for parking violations, you'll also have to fork out a towing and storage fee ($392.75 for the first four hours, $61.75 for the rest of the first day, $61.75 for every additional day, plus a $25.50 transfer fee if your car is moved to a long-term lot). Cars are usually stored at 415 7th St, corner of Harrison St.

Some of the cheaper downtown parking garages are **Sutter-Stockton Garage** (Map p66; ☎415-982-7275; cnr Sutter & Stockton Sts), **Ellis-O'Farrell Garage** (Map p66; ☎415-986-4800; 123 O'Farrell St) and **Fifth & Mission Garage** (Map p66; ☎415-982-8522; 833 Mission St), near Yerba Buena Gardens. The parking garage under Portsmouth Sq in Chinatown is reasonably priced for shorter stops; ditto for the **St Mary's Square Garage** (☎415-956-8106; California St), under the square, at Grant and Kearny Sts. Daily rates range between $20 and $35.

BART

Bay Area Rapid Transit (BART; ☎415-989-2278; www.bart.gov; ⏰4am-midnight Mon-Fri, 6am-midnight Sat, 8am-midnight Sun) is a subway system linking SFO, the Mission District, downtown, San Francisco and the East Bay. The fastest link between Downtown and the Mission District also offers transit to SF airport, Oakland ($3.20) and Berkeley ($3.75). Within SF, one-way fares start at $1.75.

MUNI

MUNI (Municipal Transit Agency; www.sfmuni.com) operates bus, streetcar and cable-car lines. Two cable-car lines leave from Powell and Market Sts; a third leaves from California and Markets Sts. A detailed *MUNI Street & Transit Map* is available free online and at the Powell MUNI kiosk ($3). Standard fare for buses or streetcars is $2, and tickets are good on buses or streetcars (not BART or cable cars) for 90 minutes; cable-car fare is $6 for a single ride.

Tickets are available on board, but you'll need exact change. Hang onto your ticket – if you're caught without one, you're subject to a $75 fine.

A **MUNI Passport** (one-/three-/seven-days $14/21/27) allows unlimited travel on all MUNI transport, including cable cars; it's sold at San Francisco's Visitor Information Center (p76) and at the TIX Bay Area kiosk at Union Sq and from a number of hotels. A seven-day **City Pass** (adult/child $69/39) covers Muni and admission to five attractions.

Key MUNI routes include:

» F Fisherman's Wharf and Embarcadero to Castro

» J Downtown to Mission/Castro/Noe Valley

» K, L, M Downtown to Castro

» N Caltrain and SBC Ballpark to Haight, Golden Gate Park and Ocean Beach

» T Embarcadero to Caltrain and Bayview

Taxi

Fares run about $2.25 per mile, plus 10% tip (starting at $1); meters start at $3.50. Major cab companies include:

Green Cab (☎415-626-4733; www.626green.com) Fuel-efficient hybrids; worker-owned collective.

DeSoto Cab (☎415-970-1300)

Luxor (☎415-282-4141)

Yellow Cab (☎415-333-3333)

Marin County & the Bay Area

Includes »

Best Places to Eat

- Chez Panisse (p139)
- Fish (p112)
- Bakesale Betty (p129)
- Duarte's Tavern (p152)
- Gather (p138)

Best Places to Stay

- Cavallo Point (p109)
- Mountain Home Inn (p116)
- Hotel Shattuck Plaza (p138)
- Pigeon Point Lighthouse Hostel (p152)
- East Brother Light Station (p143)

Why Go?

The region surrounding San Francisco encompasses a bonanza of natural vistas and wildlife. Cross the Golden Gate Bridge to Marin and visit wizened ancient redwoods body-blocking the sun and herds of elegant tule elk prancing along the bluffs of Tomales Bay. Gray whales show some fluke off the cape of wind-scoured Point Reyes, and hawks surf the skies in the pristine hills of the Marin Headlands.

On the cutting edge of intellectual thought, Stanford University and the University of California at Berkeley draw academics and students from around the world. The city of Berkeley sparked the locavore food movement and continues to be on the forefront of environmental and left-leaning political causes. South of San Francisco, Hwy 1 traces miles of undeveloped coastline and sandy pocket beaches.

When to Go

Berkeley

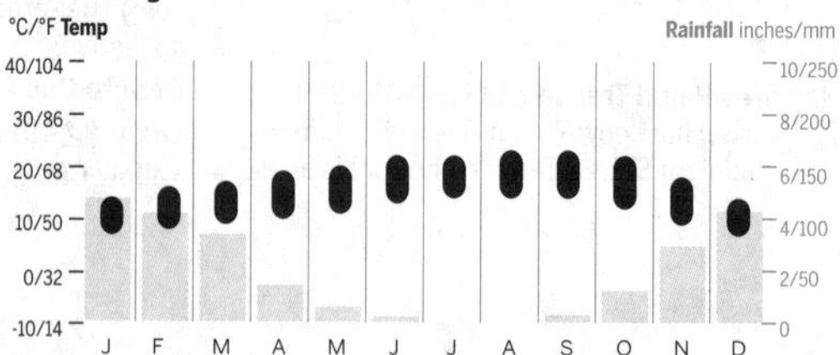

Dec–Mar Elephant seal pupping season and the peak of gray whale migrations.

Mar–Apr Wildflowers hit their peak on trails throughout the region.

Jun–Sep Farmers markets overflow with sweet seasonal fruit.

Getting Around

Visitors taking multiple forms of public transportation throughout the Bay Area should note that the regional **Clipper card** (www.clippercard.com) can be used on the Caltrain, BART, SamTrans, VTA, Golden Gate Transit and the Golden Gate Ferry systems. It can be a handy way to avoid buying multiple tickets, and offers some small discounts, plus almost 50% off on the Golden Gate Ferry system.

MARIN COUNTY

If there's a part of the Bay Area that consciously attempts to live up to the California dream, it's Marin County. Just across the Golden Gate Bridge from San Francisco, the region has a wealthy population that cultivates a seemingly laid-back lifestyle. Towns may look like idyllic rural hamlets, but the shops cater to cosmopolitan and expensive tastes. The 'common' folk here eat organic, vote Democrat and drive hybrids.

Geographically, Marin County is a near mirror image of San Francisco. It's a south-pointing peninsula that nearly touches the north-pointing tip of the city, and is surrounded by ocean and bay. But Marin is wilder, greener and more mountainous. Redwoods grow on the coast side of the hills, the surf crashes against cliffs, and hiking and cycling trails crisscross the blessed scenery of Point Reyes, Muir Woods and Mt Tamalpais. Nature is what makes Marin County such an excellent day trip or weekend escape from San Francisco.

Busy Hwy 101 heads north from the Golden Gate Bridge ($6 toll when heading back into San Francisco), spearing through Marin's middle; quiet Hwy 1 winds its way along the sparsely populated coast. In San Rafael, Sir Francis Drake Blvd cuts across west Marin from Hwy 101 to the ocean.

Hwy 580 comes in from the East Bay over the Richmond-San Rafael bridge ($5 toll for westbound traffic) to meet Hwy 101 at Larkspur.

Frequent **Marin Airporter** (415-461-4222; www.marinairporter.com; fare $20) buses connect from Marin stops to the San Francisco International Airport from 4am until about 10:30pm; SFO-Marin service departs every 30 minutes.

The **Marin Convention & Visitors Bureau** (415-925-2060, 866-925-2060; www.visitmarin.org; 1 Mitchell Blvd, San Rafael; 9am-5pm Mon-Fri) provides tourist information for the entire county.

Marin Headlands

The headlands rise majestically out of the water at the north end of the Golden Gate Bridge, their rugged beauty all the more striking given the fact that they're only a few miles from San Francisco's urban core. A few forts and bunkers are left over from a century of US military occupation – which is, ironically, the reason they are protected parklands today and free of development. It's no mystery why this is one of the Bay Area's most popular hiking and cycling destinations. As the trails wind through the headlands, they afford stunning views of the sea, the Golden Gate Bridge and San Francisco, leading to isolated beaches and secluded spots for picnics.

Sights

After crossing the Golden Gate Bridge, exit immediately at Alexander Ave, then dip left under the highway and head out west for the expansive views and hiking trailheads. Conzelman Rd snakes up into the hills, where it eventually forks. Conzelman Rd continues west, becoming a steep, one-lane road as it descends to Point Bonita. From here it continues to Rodeo Beach and Fort Barry. McCullough Rd heads inland, joining Bunker Rd toward Rodeo Beach.

Hawk Hill HILL

About 2 miles along Conzelman Rd is Hawk Hill, where thousands of migrating birds of prey soar along the cliffs from late summer to early fall.

Point Bonita Lighthouse LIGHTHOUSE

(www.nps.gov/goga/pobo.htm; 12:30-3:30pm Sat-Mon) At the end of Conzelman Rd, this light-

FAST FACTS

Population of Berkeley 112,500

Average temperature low/high in Berkeley Jan 43/56°F, Jul 54/70°F

Downtown Berkeley to Sacramento 80 miles, 1½ hours

San Jose to San Francisco 45 miles, one hour

San Francisco to Point Reyes Lighthouse 55 miles, 2½ hours

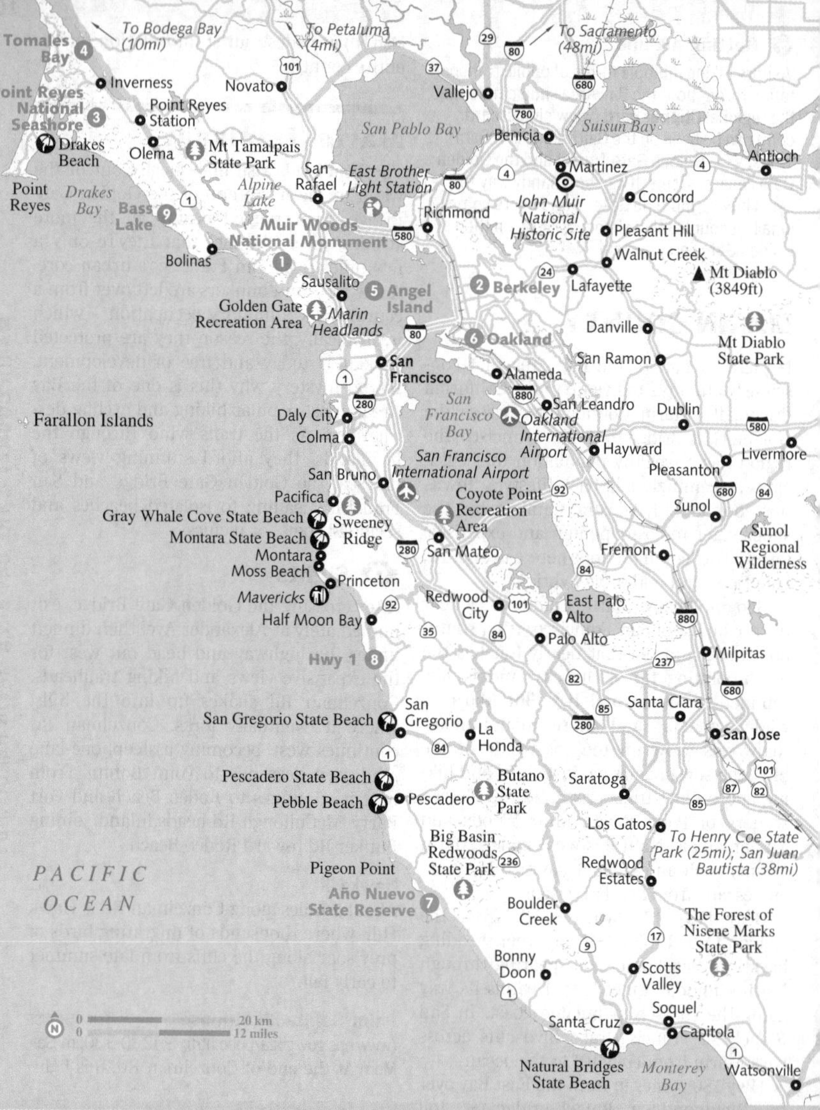

Marin County & the Bay Area Highlights

1. Gaze up at the majestic redwood canopy at **Muir Woods National Monument** (p119)
2. Feast your way through the delectable **Gourmet Ghetto** (p135) in Berkeley
3. Cavort with elk and gray whales at the **Point Reyes National Seashore** (p123)
4. Kayak **Tomales Bay** (p123) amid harbor seals and splendid shorelines
5. Hike or cycle the perimeter of panoramic **Angel Island** (p115)
6. Head to Oakland's **Chabot Space & Science Center** (p128) to marvel at the stars
7. Spy on the elephant seals at **Año Nuevo State Reserve** (p153)
8. Tour the beach cove coastline along **Hwy 1** (p150) from Pacifica to Santa Cruz
9. Cool off with a cannonball splash at blissful **Bass Lake** (p121)

house is a breathtaking half-mile walk from a small parking area. From the tip of Point Bonita, you can see the distant Golden Gate Bridge and beyond it the San Francisco skyline. It's an uncommon vantage point of the bay-centric city, and harbor seals haul out nearby in season. To reserve a spot on one of the free monthly full-moon tours of the promontory, call ☎415-331-1540.

FREE **Nike Missile Site SF-88** HISTORIC SITE
(☎415-331-1453; www.nps.gov/goga/nike-missile-site.htm; ⏲12:30-3:30pm Wed-Fri & 1st Sat of month) File past guard shacks with uniformed mannequins to witness the area's not-too-distant military history at this fascinating Cold War museum staffed by veterans. Watch them place a now-warhead-free missile into position, then ride a missile elevator to the cavernous underground silo to see the multikeyed launch controls that were thankfully never set in motion.

FREE **Marine Mammal Center** ANIMAL RESCUE CENTER
(☎415-289-7325; www.marinemammalcenter.org; ⏲10am-5pm; 👪) Set on the hill above Rodeo Lagoon, the newly expanded Marine Mammal Center rehabilitates injured, sick and orphaned sea mammals before returning them to the wild, and has educational exhibits about these animals and the dangers they face. During the spring pupping season the center can have up to several dozen orphaned seal pups on site and you can often see them before they're set free.

Headlands Center for the Arts ARTS CENTER
(☎415-331-2787; www.headlands.org) In Fort Barry, refurbished barracks converted into artist work spaces host open studios with its artists-in-residence, as well as talks, performances and other events.

Activities

Hiking

At the end of Bunker Rd sits Rodeo Beach, protected from wind by high cliffs. From here the **Coastal Trail** meanders 3.5 miles inland, past abandoned military bunkers, to the **Tennessee Valley Trail**. It then continues 6 miles along the blustery headlands all the way to Muir Beach.

All along the coastline you'll find cool old battery sites – abandoned concrete bunkers dug into the ground with fabulous views. Evocative **Battery Townsley**, a half-mile walk or bike ride up from the Fort Cronkite parking lot, opens for free subterranean tours from noon to 4pm on the first Sunday of the month.

Mountain-Biking

The Marin Headlands have some excellent mountain-biking routes, and it's an exhilarating ride across the Golden Gate Bridge to reach them (see the boxed text, p113).

For a good 12-mile dirt loop, choose the **Coastal Trail** west from the fork of Conzelman and McCullough Rds, bumping and winding down to Bunker Rd where it meets **Bobcat Trail**, which joins **Marincello Trail** and descends steeply into the Tennessee Valley parking area. The **Old Springs Trail** and the **Miwok Trail** take you back to Bunker Rd a bit more gently than the Bobcat Trail, though any attempt to avoid at least a couple of hefty climbs is futile.

Horseback Riding

For a ramble on all fours, **Miwok Livery Stables** (☎415-383-8048; www.miwokstables.com; 701 Tennessee Valley Rd; trail ride $75) offers hillside trail rides with stunning views of Mt Tam and the ocean.

Sleeping

There are four small campgrounds in the headlands, and two involve hiking (or cycling) in at least 1 mile from the nearest parking lot. **Hawk**, **Bicentennial** and **Haypress** campgrounds are inland, with free camping, but sites must be reserved through the Marin Headlands Visitors Center (p108).

Marin Headlands Hostel HOSTEL $
(☎415-331-2777; www.norcalhostels.org/marin; Bldg 941, Fort Barry, Marin Headlands; dm $22-26, r $72-92; @) Wake up to grazing deer and dew on the ground at this spartan 1907 military compound snuggled in the woods. It has comfortable beds and two well-stocked kitchens, and guests can gather round a fireplace in the common room, shoot pool or play ping-pong. Most importantly, the Hostelling International (HI) hostel is surrounded by hiking trails.

Kirby Cove Campground CAMPGROUND $
(☎877-444-6777; www.recreation.gov; tent sites $25; ⏲Apr-Oct) In a spectacular shady nook near the entrance to the bay, there's a small beach with the Golden Gate Bridge arching over the rocks nearby. At night you

WHY IS IT SO FOGGY?

When the summer sun's rays warm the air over the chilly Pacific, fog forms and hovers offshore; to grasp how it moves inland requires an understanding of California's geography. The vast agricultural region in the state's interior, the Central Valley, is ringed by mountains like a giant bathtub. The only substantial sea-level break in these mountains occurs at the Golden Gate, to the west, which happens to be the direction from which prevailing winds blow. As the inland valley heats up and the warm air rises, it creates a deficit of air at surface level, generating wind that gets sucked through the only opening it can find: the Golden Gate. It happens fast and it's unpredictable. Gusty wind is the only indication that the fog is about to roll in. But even this is inconsistent: there can be fog at the beaches south of the Golden Gate and sun a mile to the north. Hills block fog – especially at times of high atmospheric pressure, as often happens in summer. Because of this, weather forecasters speak of the Bay Area's 'microclimates.' In July it's not uncommon for inland areas to reach 100°F (38°C), while the mercury at the coast barely reaches 70°F (21°C).

can watch the phantom shadows of cargo ships passing by (and sometimes be lulled to sleep by the dirge of a fog horn). Reserve far ahead.

 Information

Information is available from the **Golden Gate National Recreation Area** (GGNRA; ☎415-561-4700; www.nps.gov/goga) and the **Marin Headlands Visitors Center** (☎415-331-1540; www.nps.gov/goga/marin-headlands.htm; ⌚9:30am-4:30pm), in an old chapel off Bunker Rd near Fort Barry.

 Getting There & Away

By car, take the Alexander Ave exit just after the Golden Gate Bridge and dip left under the freeway. Conzelman Rd, to the right, takes you up along the bluffs; you can also take Bunker Rd, which leads to the headlands through a one-way tunnel. It's also a snap to reach these roads from the bridge via bicycle.

Golden Gate Transit (☎415-455-2000, 511; www.goldengatetransit.org) bus 2 runs a limited weekday commuter service from the corner of Pine and Battery Sts in San Francisco's Financial District to Sausalito and the Headlands ($4.25). On Sunday and holidays **MUNI** (☎415-701-2311, 511; www.sfmta.com) bus 76 runs from the 4th St Caltrain depot in San Francisco to the Marin Headlands Visitors Center and Rodeo Beach.

Sausalito

Perfectly arranged on a secure little harbor on the bay, Sausalito is undeniably lovely. Named for the tiny willows that once populated the banks of its creeks, it's a small settlement of pretty houses that tumble neatly down a green hillside into a well-heeled downtown. Much of the town affords the visitor uninterrupted views of San Francisco and Angel Island, and due to the ridgeline at its back, fog generally skips past it.

Sausalito began as a 19,000-acre land grant to an army captain in 1838. When it became the terminus of the train line down the Pacific coast, it entered a new stage as a busy lumber port with a racy waterfront. Dramatic changes came in WWII when Sausalito became the site of Marinship, a huge shipbuilding yard. After the war a new bohemian period began, with a resident artists' colony living in 'arks' (houseboats moored along the bay). You'll still see dozens of these floating abodes.

Sausalito today is a major tourist haven, jam-packed with souvenir shops and costly boutiques. It's the first town you encounter after crossing the Golden Gate Bridge from San Francisco, so daytime crowds turn up in droves and make parking difficult. Ferrying over from San Francisco makes a more relaxing excursion.

Sights

Sausalito is actually on Richardson Bay, a smaller bay within San Francisco Bay. The commercial district is mainly one street, Bridgeway Blvd, on the waterfront.

FREE **Bay Model Visitor Center** MUSEUM
(☎415-332-3871; www.spn.usace.army.mil/bmvc; 2100 Bridgeway Blvd; ⌚9am-4pm Tue-Fri, plus 10am-5pm Sat & Sun in summer; 👪) One of the coolest things in town, fascinating to both

kids and adults, is the Army Corps of Engineers' visitor center. Housed in one of the old Marinship warehouses, it's a 1.5-acre hydraulic model of San Francisco Bay and the delta region. Self-guided tours take you over and around it as the water flows.

Bay Area Discovery Museum MUSEUM
(☎415-339-3900; www.baykidsmuseum.org; adult/child $10/8; ⌚9am-4pm Tue-Fri, 10am-5pm Sat & Sun;) Just under the north tower of the Golden Gate Bridge, at East Fort Baker, this excellent hands-on activity museum is specifically designed for children. Permanent (multilingual) exhibits include a wave workshop, a small underwater tunnel and a large outdoor play area with a shipwreck to romp around. A small cafe has healthy nibbles.

Plaza de Viña Del Mar PARK
Near the ferry terminal, the plaza has a fountain flanked by 14ft-tall elephant statues from the 1915 Panama–Pacific Exposition in San Francisco.

Activities

Sausalito is great for **bicycling**, whether for a leisurely ride around town, a trip across the Golden Gate Bridge or a longer-haul journey. From the ferry terminal, an easy option is to head south on Bridgeway Blvd, veering left onto East Rd toward the Bay Area Discovery Museum. Another nice route heads north along Bridgeway Blvd, then crosses under Hwy 101 to Mill Valley. At Blithedale Ave, you can veer east to Tiburon; a bike path parallels parts of Tiburon Blvd.

Sea Trek KAYAKING
(☎415-488-1000; www.seatrek.com; Schoonmaker Point Marina; single/double kayaks per hr $20/35) On a nice day, Richardson Bay is irresistible. Kayaks and stand-up paddleboards can be rented here, near the Bay Model Visitor Center. No experience is necessary, and lessons and group outings are also available.

Also on offer are guided kayaking excursions around Angel Island (see p115) from $75 per person, including overnight camping ($140). Tours include equipment and instructions. May through October is the best time to paddle.

Mike's Bikes BICYCLE RENTAL
(☎415-332-3200; 1 Gate 6 Rd; 24hr $40) At the north end of Bridgeway Blvd near Hwy 101, this shop rents out road and mountain bikes. Supplies are limited and reservations aren't accepted.

Sleeping

All of the lodgings below charge an additional $15 to $20 per night for parking.

Cavallo Point HOTEL $$$
(☎415-339-4700; www.cavallopoint.com; 601 Murray Circle, Fort Baker; r from $280;) Spread out over 45 acres of the Bay Area's most scenic parkland, Cavallo Point is a buzz-worthy lodge that flaunts a green focus, a full-service spa and easy access to outdoor activities. Choose from richly renovated rooms in the landmark Fort Baker officers' quarters or more contemporary solar-powered accommodations with exquisite bay views (including a turret of the Golden Gate Bridge).

Inn Above Tide INN $$$
(☎415-332-9535, 800-893-8433; www.innabovetide.com; 30 El Portal; r incl breakfast $320-595, ste $695-1100;) Next to the ferry terminal, ensconce yourself in one of the 29 modern and spacious rooms – most with private decks and wood-burning fireplaces – that practically levitate over the water. With envy-inducing bay views from your window, scan the horizon with the in-room binoculars. Free loaner bicycles available.

Gables Inn INN $$$
(☎415-289-1100; www.gablesinnsausalito.com; 62 Princess St; r incl breakfast $185-445;) Tranquil and inviting, this inn has nine guest rooms in a historic 1869 home, and six in a newer building. The more expensive rooms have Jacuzzi baths, fireplaces and balconies with spectacular views, but even the smaller, cheaper rooms are stylish and tranquil. Evening wine is included.

Hotel Sausalito HISTORIC HOTEL $$
(☎415-332-0700; www.hotelsausalito.com; 16 El Portal; r $155-195, ste $265-285;) Steps away from the ferry in the middle of downtown, this grand 1915 hotel has loads of period charm, paired with modern touches like MP3-player docking stations. Each guest room is decorated in Mediterranean hues, with sumptuous bathrooms and park or partial bay views.

Marin County

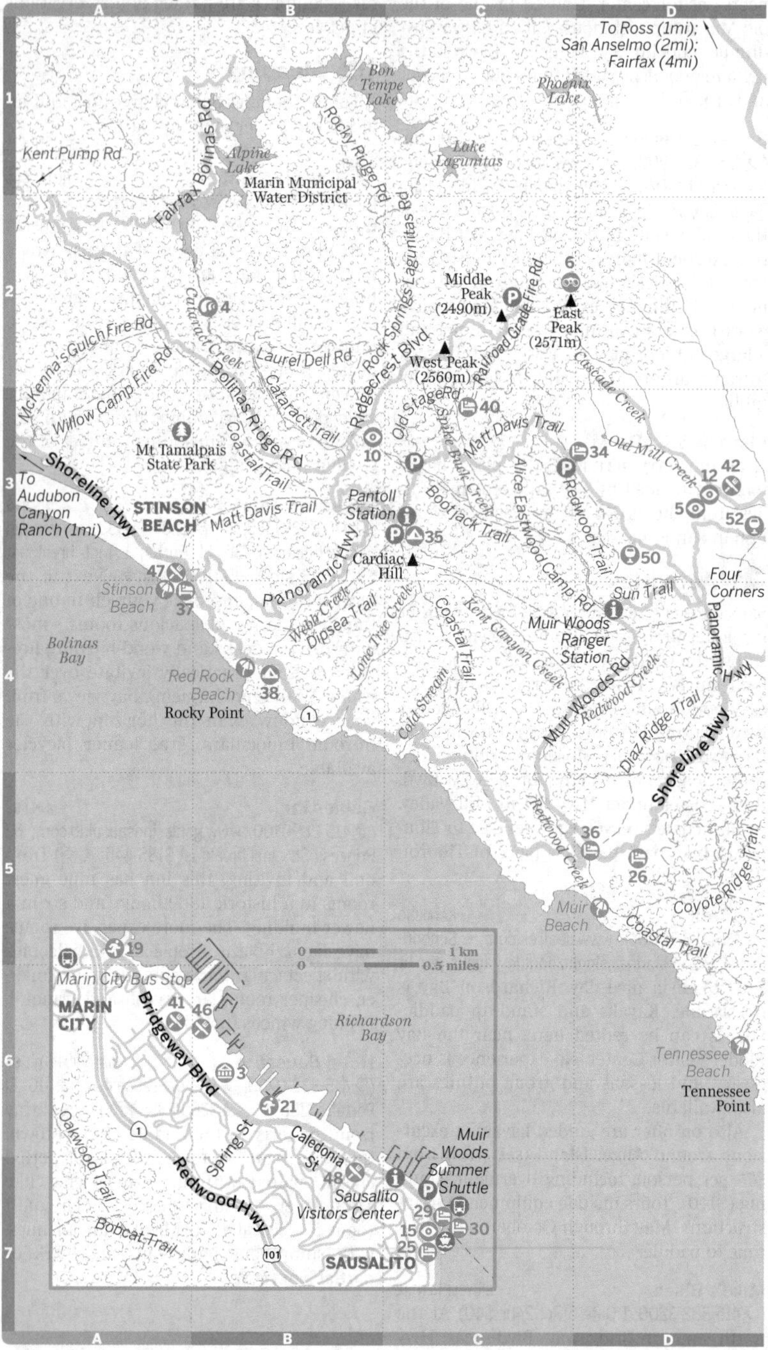

To Ross (1mi); San Anselmo (2mi); Fairfax (4mi)
Bon Tempe Lake
Phoenix Lake
Rocky Ridge Rd
Lake Lagunitas
Kent Pump Rd
Alpine Lake
Marin Municipal Water District
Fairfax Bolinas Rd
Rock Springs Lagunitas Rd
Railroad Grade Fire Rd
Middle Peak (2490m)
East Peak (2571m)
West Peak (2560m)
Cataract Creek
McKenna's Gulch Fire Rd
Willow Camp Fire Rd
Laurel Dell Rd
Ridgecrest Blvd
Bolinas Ridge Rd
Cataract Trail
Old Stage Rd
Spike Buck Creek
Matt Davis Trail
Cascade Creek
Old Mill Creek
Mt Tamalpais State Park
Coastal Trail
Shoreline Hwy
To Audubon Canyon Ranch (1mi)
STINSON BEACH
Pantoll Station
Bootjack Trail
Alice Eastwood Camp Rd
Redwood Trail
Cardiac Hill
Panoramic Hwy
Stinson Beach
Sun Trail
Four Corners
Webb Creek
Dipsea Trail
Lone Tree Creek
Kent Canyon Creek
Muir Woods Ranger Station
Bolinas Bay
Red Rock Beach
Rocky Point
Cold Stream
Muir Woods Rd
Redwood Creek
Diaz Ridge Trail
Coyote Ridge Trail
Muir Beach
Tennessee Beach
Tennessee Point
Marin City Bus Stop
MARIN CITY
Bridgeway Blvd
Richardson Bay
Oakwood Trail
Spring St
Caledonia St
Redwood Hwy
Bobcat Trail
Sausalito Visitors Center
Muir Woods Summer Shuttle
SAUSALITO
0 1 km
0 0.5 miles

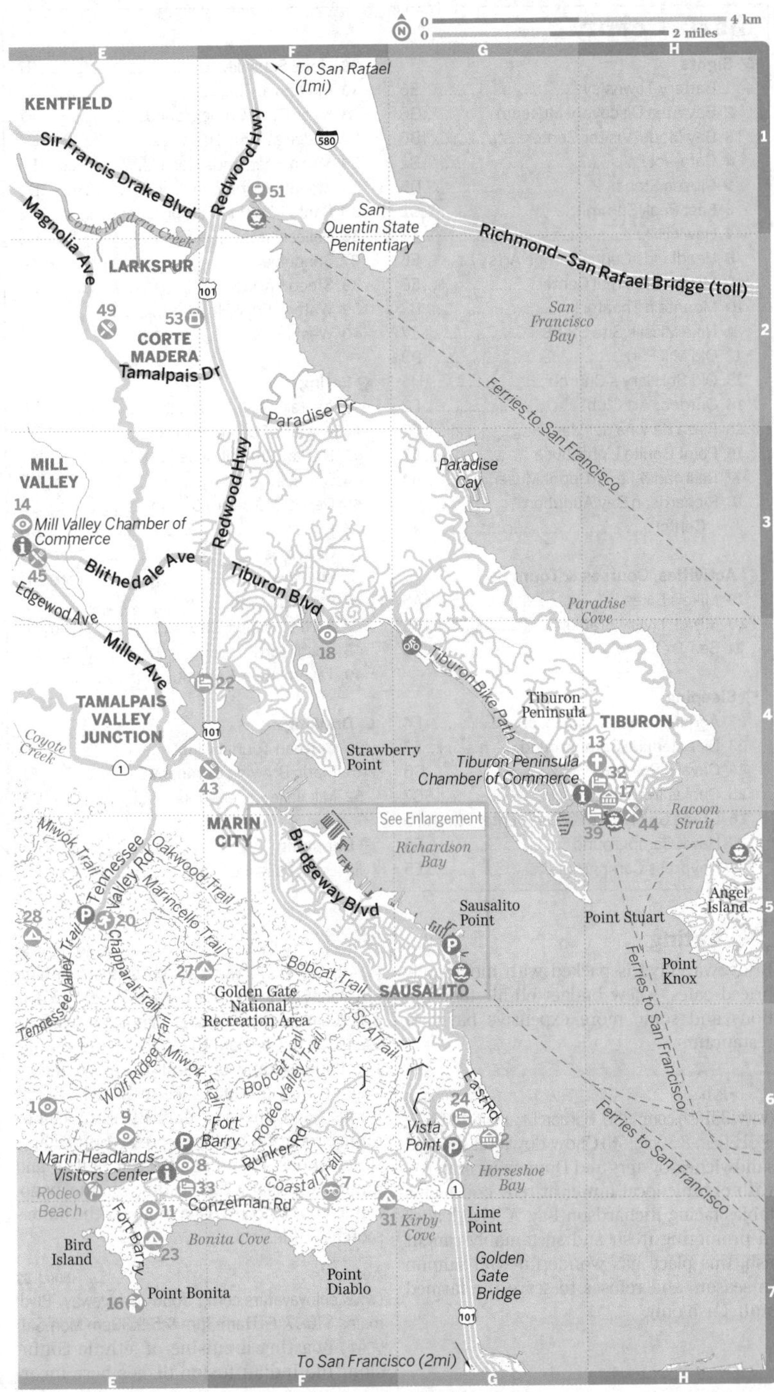
0
4 km
0
2 miles
To San Rafael (1mi)
KENTFIELD
Sir Francis Drake Blvd
Redwood Hwy
580
51
Magnolia Ave
Corte Madera Creek
San Quentin State Penitentiary
Richmond–San Rafael Bridge (toll)
LARKSPUR
101
49
53
CORTE MADERA
Tamalpais Dr
San Francisco Bay
Ferries to San Francisco
Paradise Dr
Redwood Hwy
Paradise Cay
MILL VALLEY
14
Mill Valley Chamber of Commerce
45
Blithedale Ave
Tiburon Blvd
Edgewod Ave
Paradise Cove
18
Tiburon Bike Path
Miller Ave
22
TAMALPAIS VALLEY JUNCTION
Tiburon Peninsula
TIBURON
101
Coyote Creek
1
Strawberry Point
13
32
Tiburon Peninsula Chamber of Commerce
17
43
See Enlargement
Racoon Strait
MARIN CITY
39
44
Richardson Bay
Miwok Trail
Tennessee Valley Rd
Oakwood Trail
Bridgeway Blvd
Angel Island
Marincello Trail
28
20
Sausalito Point
Point Stuart
Tennessee Valley Trail
Chapparal Trail
27
Bobcat Trail
Point Knox
Ferries to San Francisco
SAUSALITO
Golden Gate National Recreation Area
SCA Trail
Miwok Trail
Wolf Ridge Trail
Bobcat Trail
Rodeo Valley Trail
East Rd
24
1
9
Fort Barry
Bunker Rd
Vista Point
2
Ferries to San Francisco
Marin Headlands Visitors Center
8
33
Coastal Trail
7
Rodeo Beach
Horseshoe Bay
Fort Barry
11
Conzelman Rd
31
Kirby Cove
1
Lime Point
Bonita Cove
23
Bird Island
Golden Gate Bridge
Point Diablo
16
Point Bonita
101
To San Francisco (2mi)
E
F
G
H
1
2
3
4
5
6
7

Marin County

Sights

1 Battery Townsley E6
2 Bay Area Discovery Museum G6
3 Bay Model Visitor Center B6
4 Cataract Falls B2
5 Dipsea Steps D3
6 East Peak Summit C2
7 Hawk Hill F6
8 Headlands Center for the Arts E6
9 Marine Mammal Center E6
10 Mountain Theater B3
11 Nike Missile Site SF-88 .... E7
12 Old Mill Park D3
13 Old St Hilary's Church H4
14 Outdoor Art Club E3
15 Plaza de Viña del Mar C7
16 Point Bonita Lighthouse E7
17 Railroad & Ferry Depot Museum H4
18 Richardson Bay Audubon Center F4

Activities, Courses & Tours

19 Mike's Bikes A5
20 Miwok Livery Stables E5
21 Sea Trek B6

Sleeping

22 Acqua Hotel F4
23 Bicentennial Campground E7
24 Cavallo Point G6
25 Gables Inn C7
26 Green Gulch Farm & Zen Center D5
27 Hawk Campground E5
28 Haypress Campground E5
29 Hotel Sausalito C7
30 Inn Above Tide C7
31 Kirby Cove Campground F7
32 Lodge at Tiburon H4
33 Marin Headlands Hostel E6
34 Mountain Home Inn D3
35 Pantoll Station Campground C3
36 Pelican Inn D5
37 Sandpiper A4
38 Steep Ravine B4
39 Water's Edge Hotel H5
40 West Point Inn C3

Eating

41 Avatar's A6
42 Avatar's Punjabi Burritos D3
43 Buckeye Roadhouse F4
44 Caprice H5
45 Depot Bookstore & Cafe E3
46 Fish B6
Guaymas .... (see 39)
Murray Circle .... (see 24)
47 Parkside Cafe A3
Sam's Anchor Cafe .... (see 39)
48 Sushi Ran B7
49 Tavern at Lark Creek E2

Drinking

50 German Tourist Club D3
51 Marin Brewing Company F1
52 Mill Valley Beerworks D3

Shopping

53 Book Passage E2

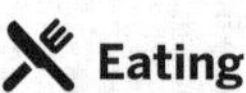

Eating

Bridgeway Blvd is packed with moderately priced cafes, a few budget ethnic food options and some more expensive bay-view restaurants.

Fish — SEAFOOD $$

(www.331fish.com; 350 Harbor Dr; mains $13-25; 11:30am-8:30pm;) Chow down on seafood sandwiches, oysters and Dungeness crab roll with organic local butter at redwood picnic tables facing Richardson Bay. A local leader in promoting fresh and sustainably caught fish, this place has wonderful wild salmon in season, and refuses to serve the farmed stuff. Cash only.

Murray Circle — AMERICAN $$

(415-339-4750; www.cavallopoint.com/dine.html; 601 Murray Circle, Fort Baker; mains $17-29; 7-11am & 11:30am-2pm Mon-Fri, to 2:30pm Sat & Sun, 5:30-10pm Sun-Thu, to 11pm Fri & Sat) At the Cavallo Point lodge, dine on locally sourced meats, seafood and produce, like grass-fed organic burgers or Dungeness crab BLT, in a clubby dining room topped by a pressed-tin ceiling. Reservations recommended for lunch and dinner, especially for seating on the panoramic-view balcony. Save room for the butterscotch soufflé.

Avatar's — INDIAN $$

(www.enjoyavatars.com; 2656 Bridgeway Blvd; mains $10-17; 11am-3pm & 5-9:30pm Mon-Sat;) Boasting a cuisine of 'ethnic confusion,' the Indian fusion dishes here incorporate Mexican, Italian and Caribbean ingredients and will bowl you over with their flavor and creativity. Think Punjabi enchilada with curried sweet potato or spinach and mushroom ravioli with mango and rose petal alfredo sauce. All diets (vegan, gluten-free, etc) are graciously accommodated.

Sushi Ran SUSHI **$$**
(☎415-332-3620; www.sushiran.com; 107 Caledonia St; sushi $4-19) Many Bay Area residents claim this place is the best sushi spot around. A wine and sake bar next door eases the pain of the long wait for a table.

Information

The **Sausalito Visitors Center** (☎415-332-0505; www.sausalito.org; 780 Bridgeway Blvd; ⏲11:30am-4pm Tue-Sun) has local information. There's also an information kiosk at the ferry terminal.

Getting There & Away

Driving to Sausalito from San Francisco, take the Alexander Ave exit (the first exit after the Golden Gate Bridge) and follow the signs into Sausalito. There are five municipal parking lots in town, and street parking is difficult to find.

Golden Gate Transit (☎415-455-2000; www.goldengatetransit.org) bus 10 runs daily to Sausalito from downtown San Francisco ($4.25).

The ferry is a fun and easy way to travel to Sausalito. **Golden Gate Ferry** (☎415-455-2000; www.goldengateferry.org; one-way $9.25) operates to and from the San Francisco Ferry Building six to nine times daily and takes 30 minutes. The **Blue & Gold Fleet** (☎415-705-8200; www.blueandgoldfleet.com; Pier 41, Fisherman's Wharf; one-way $10.50) sails to Sausalito four to five times daily from the Fisherman's Wharf area in San Francisco. Both ferries operate year-round and transport bicycles for free.

Tiburon

At the end of a small peninsula pointing out into the center of the bay, Tiburon is blessed with gorgeous views. The name comes from the Spanish *Punta de Tiburon* (Shark Point). Take the ferry from San Francisco, browse the shops on Main St, grab a bite to eat and you've seen Tiburon. The town is also a jumping-off point for nearby Angel Island (see p115).

Sights & Activities

The central part of town is comprised of Tiburon Blvd, with Juanita Lane and charming Main St arcing off. Main St, which is also known as Ark Row, is where the old houseboats have taken root on dry land and metamorphosed into classy shops and boutiques.

FREE **Railroad & Ferry Depot Museum** MUSEUM
(1920 Paradise Drive; www.landmarks-society.org; ⏲1-4pm Wed, Sat & Sun Mar-Oct) Formerly the terminus for a 3000-person ferry to San Francisco and a railroad that once reached north to Ukiah, this late 19th century building showcases a scale model of Tiburon's commercial hub, circa 1909. The restored

HIKING & CYCLING THE BRIDGE

Walking or cycling across the Golden Gate Bridge to Sausalito is a fun way to avoid traffic, get some great ocean views and bask in that refreshing Marin County air. It's a fairly easy journey, mostly flat or downhill when heading north from San Francisco (cycling back to the city involves one big climb out of Sausalito). You can also simply hop on a ferry back to SF (see p113).

The trip is about 4 miles from the south end of the bridge and takes less than an hour. Pedestrians have access to the bridge's east walkway between 5am and 9pm daily (until 6pm in winter). Cyclists generally use the west side, except on weekdays between 5am and 3:30pm, when they must share the east side with pedestrians (who have the right-of-way). After 9pm (6pm in winter), cyclists can still cross the bridge on the east side through a security gate. Check the bridge website (http://goldengatebridge.org/bikesbridge/bikes.php) for changes.

For more ambitious cyclists, the reopening of the Cal Park Hill Tunnel means a safe subterranean passage from Larkspur (another ferry terminus) to San Rafael.

More information and resources are available at the websites of the **San Francisco Bicycle Coalition** (www.sfbike.org) and the **Marin County Bicycle Coalition** (www.marinbike.org).

stationmaster's quarters can be visited upstairs.

Angel Island–Tiburon Ferry CRUISE
(☎415-435-2131; www.angelislandferry.com; adult/child $20/10) Runs sunset cruises on Friday and Saturday evenings from May through October. Reservations recommended.

Old St Hilary's Church CHURCH
(201 Esperanza; ⏲1-4pm Sun Apr-Oct) There are great views from the lovely hillside surrounding this fine 19th-century example of Carpenter Gothic.

Richardson Bay Audubon Center NATURE RESERVE
(☎415-388-2524; www.tiburonaudubon.org; 376 Greenwood Beach Rd; ⏲9am-5pm Mon-Sat) Off Tiburon Blvd, this center is home to a huge variety of water birds.

Sleeping

Water's Edge Hotel HOTEL $$
(☎415-789-5999; www.watersedgehotel.com; 25 Main St; r incl breakfast $169-499; ❄@🛜) This hotel, with its deck extending over the bay, is exemplary for its tasteful modernity. Rooms have an elegant minimalism that combines comfort and style, and all afford an immediate view of the bay. The rooms with rustic, high wood ceilings are quite romantic.

Lodge at Tiburon HOTEL $$
(☎415-435-3133; www.larkspurhotels.com/collection/tiburon; 1651 Tiburon Blvd; r from $135; ❄🏊@🛜🐾) Now a stylish and comfortable contemporary hotel with a grill restaurant, the concrete hallways and staircases testify to the more basic motel it once was. The best value in town, it's a short stroll to anywhere – including the ferry – and there's a pool, DVD library, free parking and a rooftop deck with fireplace and heady Mt Tamalpais views.

Eating

Sam's Anchor Cafe SEAFOOD $$
(www.samscafe.com; 27 Main St; mains $17-28; ⏲11am-10pm Mon-Fri, from 9:30am Sat & Sun) Sam's has been slinging seafood and burgers since 1920, and though the entrance looks like a shambling little shack, the area out back has unbeatable views. On a warm afternoon, you can't beat a cocktail or a tasty plate of sautéed prawns on the deck.

Caprice AMERICAN $$$
(☎415-435-3400; www.thecaprice.com; 2000 Paradise Dr; mains $18-49; ⏲5-10pm Tue-Sun, plus 11am-3pm Sun) Splurge-worthy and romantic, book a table here at sunset for riveting views of Angel Island, the Golden Gate Bridge and San Francisco. Caprice mostly features seafood, though other standouts include the artichoke bisque and the filet mignon. Take a peek at the fireplace downstairs – it's constructed into the coast bedrock. A three-course midweek dinner ($25) is easier on the wallet.

Guaymas MEXICAN $$
(www.guaymasrestaurant.com; 5 Main St; mains $15-25; ⏲11am-9pm Sun-Thu, 11am-10pm Fri & Sat) Steps from the ferry, noisy Guaymas packs in a fun, boisterous crowd. Margaritas energize the place, and solid Mexican seafood dishes help keep people upright.

Information

The **Tiburon Peninsula Chamber of Commerce** (☎415-435-5633; www.tiburonchamber.org; 96b Main St) can provide information about the area.

Getting There & Away

Golden Gate Transit (☎415-455-2000; www.goldengatetransit.org) commute bus 8 runs direct between San Francisco and Tiburon ($4.25) during the week.

On Hwy 101, look for the off-ramp for Tiburon Blvd, E Blithedale Ave and Hwy 131; driving east, it leads into town and intersects with Juanita Lane and Main St.

Blue & Gold Fleet (☎415-705-8200; one-way $10.50) sails daily from either Pier 41 or the Ferry Building in San Francisco to Tiburon; ferries dock right in front of the Guaymas restaurant on Main St. You can transport bicycles for free. From Tiburon, ferries also connect regularly to Angel Island.

Mill Valley

Nestled under the redwoods at the base of Mt Tamalpais, tiny Mill Valley is one of the Bay Area's most picturesque hamlets. Mill Valley was originally a logging town, its name stemming from an 1830s sawmill – the first in the Bay Area to provide lumber. Though the 1892 Mill Valley Lumber Company still greets motorists on Miller Ave, the town's a vastly different place today, packed with wildly expensive homes, fancy cars and pricey boutiques.

DON'T MISS

ANGEL ISLAND

Angel Island (☎415-435-5390; www.parks.ca.gov/?page_id=468), in San Francisco Bay, has a mild climate with fresh bay breezes, which make it pleasant for hiking and cycling. For a unique treat, picnic in a protected cove overlooking the close but distant urban surroundings. The island's varied history – it was a hunting and fishing ground for the Miwok people, served as a military base, an immigration station, a WWII Japanese internment camp and a Nike missile site – has left it with some evocative old forts and bunkers to poke around in. There are 12 miles of roads and trails around the island, including a hike to the summit of 781ft **Mt Livermore** (no bicycles) and a 5-mile perimeter trail.

The **Immigration Station**, which operated from 1910 to 1940, was the Ellis Island of the west coast. But this facility was primarily a screening and detention center for Chinese immigrants, who were at that time restricted from entering the US under the Chinese Exclusion Act. Many detainees were held here for long periods before ultimately being returned home, and one of the most unusual sights on the island is the sad and longing Chinese poetry etched into the barrack walls. A **visitor center** (www.aiisf.org/visit; ⏰usually 11am-3pm Wed-Sun) contains interpretive exhibits, and more extensive **tours** (☎415-435-3522, adult/child $7/5) can be reserved ahead or purchased at the cafe near the ferry dock.

Sea Trek (see p109) runs **kayaking** excursions around the island. You can rent **bicycles** at Ayala Cove (per hour/day $10/35), and there are **tram tours** ($13.50) around the island. Schedules vary seasonally; go to www.angelisland.com for more information.

You can camp on the island, and when the last ferry sails off for the night, the place is your own – except for the very persistent raccoons. The dozen hike-, bicycle- or kayak-in **campsites** (☎800-444-7275; www.reserveamerica.com; tent sites $30) are usually reserved months in advance. Near the ferry dock, there's a **cafe** that specializes in barbecued oysters.

From San Francisco, take a **Blue & Gold Fleet** (☎415-705-8200; www.blueandgoldfleet.com) ferry from Pier 41 or the Ferry Building. From May to September there are three ferries a day on weekends and two on weekdays; during the rest of the year the schedule is reduced. Round-trip tickets cost $16 for adults and $9 for children.

From Tiburon, take the **Angel Island–Tiburon Ferry** (☎415-435-2131; www.angelislandferry.com; round trip $13.50, plus $1 for bicycles).

Mill Valley also served as the starting point for the scenic railway that carried visitors up Mt Tamalpais (see p118). The tracks were removed in 1940, and today the Depot Bookstore & Cafe occupies the space of the former station.

Sights & Activities

Old Mill Park PARK

Several blocks west of downtown along Throckmorton Ave is Old Mill Park, perfect for a picnic. Here you'll also find a replica of the town's namesake sawmill. Just past the bridge at Old Mill Creek, the **Dipsea Steps** mark the start of the Dipsea Trail.

Mill Valley Film Festival FILM FESTIVAL

(www.mvff.com) Each October the Mill Valley Film Festival presents an innovative, internationally regarded program of independent films.

Tennessee Valley Trail HIKING

In the Marin Headlands, this trail offers beautiful views of the rugged coastline and is one of the most popular hikes in Marin (expect crowds on weekends), especially for families. It has easy, level access to the cove beach and ocean, and is a short 3.8-mile round trip. From Hwy 101, take the Mill Valley–Stinson Beach–Hwy 1 exit and turn left onto Tennessee Valley Rd from the Shoreline Hwy; follow it to the parking lot and trailhead.

TOP CHOICE **Dipsea Trail** HIKING

A beloved though more demanding hike is the 7-mile Dipsea Trail, which climbs over the coastal range and down to Stinson Beach, cutting through a corner of Muir Woods. This classic trail starts at Old Mill Park with a climb up 676 steps in three separate flights, and includes a few more ups and downs before reaching the ocean. **West Marin Stagecoach** (www.marintransit.org/stage.html) route 61 runs from Stinson Beach to Mill Valley, making it a doable one-way day hike.

Outdoor Art Club HISTORIC SITE
(www.outdoorartclub.org; cnr W Blithedale & Throckmorton Aves) Said to have been founded by 35 Mill Valley women determined to preserve the local environment, this private club is housed in a landmark 1904 building designed by prominent architect Bernard Maybeck.

Sleeping

Mountain Home Inn INN $$$
(415-381-9000; www.mtnhomeinn.com; 810 Panoramic Hwy; r incl breakfast $195-345;) Set amid redwood, spruce and pine trees on a ridge of Mt Tamalpais, this retreat is both modern and rustic. The larger (more expensive) rooms are rugged beauties, with unfinished timbers forming columns from floor to ceiling, as though the forest is shooting up through the floor. Smaller rooms are cozy dens for two. A lack of TVs and the positioning of a good local trail map on the dresser make it clear that it's a place to breathe and unwind.

Acqua Hotel BOUTIQUE HOTEL $$
(415-380-0400, 888-662-9555; www.marinhotels.com; 555 Redwood Hwy; r incl breakfast from $169;) With views of the bay and Mt Tamalpais, and a lobby with a soothing fireplace and fountain, the Acqua doesn't lack for pleasant eye candy. Contemporary rooms are sleekly designed with beautiful fabrics.

Eating & Drinking

Depot Bookstore & Cafe CAFE $
(www.depotbookstore.com; 87 Throckmorton Ave; meals under $10; 7am-7pm;) Smack in the town center, Depot serves cappuccinos, sandwiches and light meals. The bookstore sells lots of local publications, including trail guides.

Buckeye Roadhouse AMERICAN $$
(415-331-2600; www.buckeyeroadhouse.com; 15 Shoreline Hwy; mains $15-33; 11:30am-10:30pm Mon-Sat, 10:30am-10pm Sun) Originally opened as a roadside stop in 1932, the Buckeye is a Marin County gem, and its upscale American cuisine is in no danger of being compared to truck-stop fare. Stop off for chili-lime 'brick' chicken, baby back ribs or oysters Bingo and a devilish wedge of s'more pie before getting back on the highway.

Mill Valley Beerworks PUB
(www.millvalleybeerworks.com; 173 Throckmorton Ave; sandwiches & small plates $9-14; 11am-midnight) With 100 bottled varieties of brew and a few of its own on tap, beer lovers can giddily explore new frontiers while chewing on house-made pretzels. The setting is stark and stylish, with unfinished wood tables and a pressed-tin wall.

Avatar's Punjabi Burritos INDIAN $
(www.enjoyavatars.com; 15 Madrona St; mains $6.50-9; 11am-8pm Mon-Sat, to 7pm Sun;) For a quick bite, try a tasty burrito of lamb and curry or spicy veggies.

Information

Visitor information is available from the **Mill Valley Chamber of Commerce** (415-388-9700; www.millvalley.org; 85 Throckmorton Ave; 9am-5pm Mon-Fri).

Getting There & Away

From San Francisco or Sausalito, take Hwy 101 north to the Mill Valley–Stinson Beach–Hwy 1 exit. Follow Hwy 1 (also called the Shoreline Hwy) to Almonte Blvd (which becomes Miller Ave), then follow Miller Ave into downtown Mill Valley.

From the north, take the E Blithedale Ave exit from Hwy 101, then head west into downtown Mill Valley.

Golden Gate Transit (415-455-2000; www.goldengatetranist.org) bus 4 runs directly from San Francisco to Mill Valley ($4.25) on weekdays.

Sir Francis Drake Blvd & Around

The towns along and nearby the Sir Francis Drake Blvd corridor – including Larkspur, Corte Madera, Ross, San Anselmo and Fairfax – evoke charmed small-town life, even though things get busy around Hwy 101.

Starting from the eastern section in **Larkspur**, window-shop along Magnolia Ave or explore the redwoods in nearby Baltimore Canyon. On the east side of the freeway is the hulking mass of **San Quentin State Penitentiary**, California's oldest and most notorious prison, founded in 1852. Johnny Cash recorded an album here in 1969 after scoring a big hit with his live *Folsom Prison* album a few years earlier.

Take the bicycle and pedestrian bridge from the ferry terminal across the road to the **Marin Brewing Company** (www.marinbrewing.com; 1809 Larkspur Landing Cir, Marin Country Mart, Bldg 2, Larkspur; mains $10-15; ⌚11:30am-midnight Sun-Thu, to 1am Fri & Sat) brewpub, where you can see the glassed-in kettles behind the bar. The head brewer, Arne Johnson, has won many awards, and the Mt Tam Pale Ale complements the menu of pizza, burgers and hearty sandwiches.

The **Tavern at Lark Creek** (☎415-924-7766; 234 Magnolia Ave, Larkspur; mains $13-29; ⌚5:30-9:30pm Mon-Thu, to 10pm Fri & Sat, 10am-2pm & 5-9:30pm Sun; ✎) is in a lovely spot and offers a fine-dining experience. It's housed in an 1888 Victorian house tucked away in a redwood canyon, and the rotating farm-fresh American food (like the macaroni-and-cheese croquettes, pork loin chop and rainbow trout in brown butter) is gratifying.

Just south, **Corte Madera** is home to one of the Bay Area's best bookstores, **Book Passage** (☎415-927-0960; www.bookpassage.com; 51 Tamal Vista Blvd), in the Marketplace shopping center. It has a strong travel section, plus frequent author appearances.

Continuing west along Sir Francis Drake, **San Anselmo** has a cute, small downtown area along San Anselmo Ave, including several antique shops. The attractive center of neighboring **Fairfax** has ample dining and shopping options, and cyclists congregate at **Gestalt Haus Fairfax** (28 Bolinas Rd, Fairfax) for the indoor bicycle parking, board games, European draft beers and sausages of the meaty or vegan persuasion.

Arti (www.articafe.com; 7282 Sir Francis Drake Blvd, Lagunitas; mains $9-14; ⌚noon-9:30pm Tue-Sun; ✎), between Hwys 1 and 101 in the tiny hamlet of Lagunitas, is a tempting stop for organic Indian fare. There's a cozy casual dining room and an outdoor patio for warm days, and folks from miles around adore its sizzling chicken tikka platter.

Golden Gate Ferry (☎415-455-2000; www.goldengateferry.org) runs a daily ferry service ($8.75, 50 minutes) from the Ferry Building in San Francisco to Larkspur Landing on E Sir Francis Drake Blvd, directly east of Hwy 101. You can take bicycles on the ferry.

San Rafael

The oldest and largest town in Marin, San Rafael is slightly less upscale than most of its neighbors but doesn't lack atmosphere. It's a common stop for travelers on their way to Point Reyes. Just north of San Rafael, Lucas Valley Rd heads west to Point Reyes Station, passing George Lucas' Skywalker Ranch. Fourth St, San Rafael's main drag, is lined with cafes and shops. If you follow it west out of downtown San Rafael, it meets Sir Francis Drake Blvd and continues west to the coast.

Sights & Activities

Mission San Rafael Arcángel MISSION
(1104 5th Ave) The town began with this mission, founded in 1817, which served as a sanitarium for Native Americans suffering from European diseases. The present building is a replica dating from 1949.

China Camp State Park PARK
(☎415-456-0766; parking $5) About 4 miles east of San Rafael, this is a pleasant place to stop for a picnic or short hike. From Hwy 101, take the N San Pedro Rd exit and continue 3 miles east. A Chinese fishing village once stood here, and a small museum exhibits interesting artifacts from the settlement. At press time, the future of this state park was uncertain.

Rafael Film Center CINEMA
(☎415-454-1222; www.cafilm.org/rfc; 1118 4th St) A restored downtown cinema offering innovative art-house programming on three screens in state-of-the-art surroundings.

Sleeping & Eating

Panama Hotel B&B **$$**
(☎415-457-3993; www.panamahotel.com; 4 Bayview St; r $120-195; ❄📶) The 10 artsy rooms at this B&B, in a building dating from 1910, each have their own unique style and charming decor – like crazy quilts and vibrant accent walls. The hotel restaurant has an inviting courtyard patio.

TOP CHOICE **Sol Food Puerto Rican Cuisine** PUERTO RICAN **$$**
(☎415-451-4765; www.solfoodrestaurant.com; Lincoln Ave & 3rd St; mains $7.50-16; ⌚7am-midnight Mon-Thu, to 2am Fri, 8am-2am Sat, to midnight Sun) Lazy ceiling fans, a profusion of tropical plants and the pulse of Latin rhythms create a soothing atmosphere for delicious dishes like a *jíbaro* sandwich (thinly sliced steak served on green plantains) and other island-inspired meals concocted with *plátanos*, organic veggies and free range meats.

WORTH A TRIP

GERMAN TOURIST CLUB

A private club that occasionally shares its sudsy love, the **German Tourist Club** (415-388-9987; www.touristclubsf.org; 1-5pm 1st, 3rd & 4th weekends of the month), or Nature Friends (*Die Naturefreunde*), has a gorgeous beer garden patio overlooking Muir Woods and Mt Tamalpais that's a favored spot for parched Marin hikers. By car, turn onto Ridge Ave from Panoramic Hwy, park in the gravel driveway at the end of the road and start the 0.3-mile walk downhill. You can also hike in on the Sun Trail from Panoramic – a half-hour of mostly flat trail with views of the ocean and Muir Woods.

China Camp State Park CAMPGROUND $
(800-444-7275; www.reserveamerica.com; tent sites $35; ) The park has 30 walk-in campsites with pleasant shade.

Getting There & Away

Numerous **Golden Gate Transit** (415-455-2000; www.goldengatetransit.org) buses operate between San Francisco and the San Rafael Transit Center at 3rd and Hetherton Sts ($5.25, one hour).

Mt Tamalpais State Park

Standing guard over Marin County, majestic Mt Tamalpais (Mt Tam) has breathtaking 360-degree views of ocean, bay and hills rolling into the distance. The rich, natural beauty of the 2571ft mountain and its surrounding area is inspiring – especially considering it lies within an hour's drive from one of the state's largest metropolitan areas.

Mt Tamalpais State Park was formed in 1930, partly from land donated by congressman and naturalist William Kent (who also donated the land that became Muir Woods National Monument in 1907). Its 6300 acres are home to deer, foxes, bobcats and many miles of hiking and cycling trails.

Mt Tam was a sacred place to the coastal Miwok people for thousands of years before the arrival of European and American settlers. By the late 19th century, San Franciscans were escaping the bustle of the city with all-day outings on the mountain, and in 1896 the 'world's crookedest railroad' (281 turns) was completed from Mill Valley to the summit. Though the railroad was closed in 1930, Old Railroad Grade is today one of Mt Tam's most popular and scenic hiking and cycling paths.

Panoramic Hwy climbs from Mill Valley through the park to Stinson Beach. From Pantoll Station, it's 4.2 miles by car to **East Peak Summit**; take Pantoll Rd and then panoramic Ridgecrest Blvd to the top. Parking is $8 (good for the entire park) and a 10-minute hike leads to a fire lookout at the very top and awesome sea-to-bay views.

Mountain Theater THEATER
(415-383-1100; www.mountainplay.org) The park's natural-stone, 4000-seat theater hosts the annual 'Mountain Play' series on a half dozen weekend afternoons between mid-May and late June. Free shuttles are provided from Mill Valley. Free monthly **astronomy programs** (415-455-5370; www.mttam.net/astronomy.html; Apr-Oct) also take place here on Saturday nights around the new moon.

Activities

Hiking

The park map is a smart investment, as there are a dozen worthwhile hiking trails in the area. From Pantoll Station, the **Steep Ravine Trail** follows a wooded creek on to the coast (about 2.1 miles each way). For a longer hike, veer right (northwest) after 1.5 miles onto the **Dipsea Trail**, which meanders through trees for 1 mile before ending at Stinson Beach. Grab some lunch, then walk north through town and follow signs for the **Matt Davis Trail**, which leads 2.7 miles back to Pantoll Station, making a good loop. The Matt Davis Trail continues on beyond Pantoll Station, wrapping gently around the mountain with superb views.

Another worthy option is **Cataract Trail**, which runs along Cataract Creek from the end of Pantoll Rd; it's approximately 3 miles to Alpine Lake. The last mile is a spectacular rooty staircase as the trail descends alongside **Cataract Falls**.

Mountain-Biking

Cyclists must stay on the fire roads (and off the single-track trails) and keep to speeds under 15mph. Rangers are prickly about these rules, and a ticket can result in a steep fine.

The most popular ride is the **Old Railroad Grade**. For a sweaty, 6-mile, 2280ft climb, start in Mill Valley at the end of W Blithedale Ave and cycle up to East Peak. It takes about an hour to reach the West Point Inn (see below) from Mill Valley. For an easier start, begin partway up at the Mountain Home Inn (see p116) and follow the **Gravity Car Grade** to the Old Railroad Grade and the West Point Inn. From the Inn, it's an easy half-hour ride to the summit.

From just west of Pantoll Station, cyclists can either take the **Deer Park fire road**, which runs close to the Dipsea Trail, through giant redwoods to the main entrance of Muir Woods, or the southeastern extension of the **Coastal Trail**, which has breathtaking views of the coast before joining Hwy 1 about 2 miles north of Muir Beach. Either option requires a return to Mill Valley via Frank Valley/Muir Woods Rd, which climbs steadily (800ft) to Panoramic Hwy and then becomes Sequoia Valley Rd as it drops toward Mill Valley. A left turn on Wildomar and two right turns at Mill Creek Park lead to the center of Mill Valley.

For further information on bicycle routes and rules, contact the **Marin County Bicycle Coalition** (415-456-3469; www.marinbike.org), whose Marin Bicycle Map is the gold standard for local cycling.

Sleeping & Eating

TOP CHOICE **Steep Ravine** CABINS, CAMPGROUND $
(800-444-7275; www.reserveamerica.com; campsites/cabins $25/100; closed Oct) Just off Hwy 1, about 1 mile south of Stinson Beach, this jewel has seven beachfront campsites and nine rustic five-person cabins with wood stoves overlooking the ocean. Both options are booked out months in advance and reservations can be made up to seven months ahead.

West Point Inn INN $
(inn 415-388-9955, reservations 415-646-0702; www.westpointinn.com; per person r or cabin $50; closed Sun & Mon night) Load up your sleeping bag and hike in to this rustic 1904 hilltop hideaway built as a stopover for the Mill Valley and Mt Tamalpais Scenic Railway. Rates drop to $35 per person Tuesday through Thursday from mid-September until the end of May. It also hosts monthly pancake breakfasts ($10) on Sundays during the summer.

Pantoll Station Campground CAMPGROUND $
(415-388-2070; tent sites $25;) From the parking lot it's a 100yd walk or bicycle ride to the campground, with 16 first-come, first-served tent sites but no showers.

Information

Pantoll Station (415-388-2070; 801 Panoramic Hwy;) is the park headquarters. Detailed park maps are sold here. The **Mt Tamalpais Interpretative Association** (www.mttam.net; 11am-4pm Sat & Sun) staffs a small visitor center at East Peak.

Getting There & Away

To reach Pantoll Station by car, take Hwy 1 to the Panoramic Hwy and look for the Pantoll signs. **West Marin Stagecoach** (415-526-3239; www.marintransit.org/stage.html) route 61 runs daily minibuses ($2) from Marin City (via Mill Valley; plus weekend and holiday service from the Sausalito ferry) to both the Pantoll Station and Mountain Home Inn.

Muir Woods National Monument

Walking through an awesome stand of the world's tallest trees is an experience to be had only in Northern California and a small part of southern Oregon. The old-growth redwoods at **Muir Woods** (415-388-2595; www.nps.gov/muwo; adult/child under 16 $5/free; 8am-sunset), just 12 miles north of the Golden Gate Bridge, is the closest redwood stand to San Francisco. The trees were initially eyed by loggers, and Redwood Creek, as the area was known, seemed ideal for a dam. Those plans were halted when congressman and naturalist William Kent bought a section of Redwood Creek and, in 1907, donated 295 acres to the federal government. President Theodore Roosevelt made the site a national monument in 1908, the name honoring John Muir, naturalist and founder of environmental organization the Sierra Club.

Muir Woods can become quite crowded, especially on weekends. Try to come midweek, early in the morning or late in the afternoon, when tour buses are less of a problem. Even at busy times, a short hike will get you out of the densest crowds and onto trails with huge trees and stunning vistas. A lovely cafe serves local and organic goodies and hot drinks that hit the spot on foggy days.

Activities

The 1-mile **Main Trail Loop** is a gentle walk alongside Redwood Creek to the 1000-year-old trees at **Cathedral Grove**; it returns via **Bohemian Grove**, where the tallest tree in the park stands 254ft high. The **Dipsea Trail** is a good 2-mile hike up to the top of aptly named **Cardiac Hill**.

You can also walk down into Muir Woods by taking trails from the Panoramic Hwy, such as the **Bootjack Trail** from the Bootjack picnic area, or from Mt Tamalpais' Pantoll Station campground, along the **Ben Johnson Trail**.

Getting There & Away

The parking lot fills up during busy periods, so consider taking the summer shuttle operated by **Marin Transit** (www.marintransit.org; round trip adult/child $3/1; weekends & holidays late-May–Sep). The 40-minute shuttle connects with four Sausalito ferries arriving from San Francisco.

To get there by car, drive north on Hwy 101, exit at Hwy 1 and continue north along Hwy 1/ Shoreline Hwy to the Panoramic Hwy (a right-hand fork). Follow that for about 1 mile to Four Corners, where you turn left onto Muir Woods Rd (there are plenty of signs).

The Coast

MUIR BEACH

The turnoff to Muir Beach from Hwy 1 is marked by the longest row of mailboxes on the North Coast. Muir Beach is a quiet little town with a nice beach, but it has no direct bus service. Just north of Muir Beach there are superb views up and down the coast from the **Muir Beach Overlook**; during WWII, watch was kept from the surrounding concrete lookouts for invading Japanese ships.

Pelican Inn (415-383-6000; www.pelicaninn.com; 10 Pacific Way; r incl breakfast $190-265;) is the only commercial establishment in Muir Beach. The downstairs restaurant and pub (mains $9 to $34) is an Anglophile's dream and perfect for pre- or post-hike nourishment.

Green Gulch Farm & Zen Center (415-383-3134; www.sfzc.org; 1601 Shoreline Hwy; s $90-135, d $160-205, d cottage $300-350, all with 3 meals; @) is a Buddhist retreat in the hills above Muir Beach. The center's accommodations are elegant, restful and modern, and delicious buffet-style vegetarian meals are included. A hilltop retreat cottage is 25 minutes away by foot.

STINSON BEACH

Positively buzzing on warm weekends, Stinson Beach is 5 miles north of Muir Beach. The town flanks Hwy 1 for about three blocks and is densely packed with galleries, shops, eateries and B&Bs. The beach itself is often blanketed with fog, and when the sun's shining it's blanketed with surfers, families and gawkers. There are views of Point Reyes and San Francisco on clear days, and the beach is long enough for a vigorous stroll. From San Francisco it's nearly an hour's drive, though on weekends plan for toe-tapping traffic delays.

Three-mile-long **Stinson Beach** is a popular surf spot, but swimming is advised from late May to mid-September only; for updated weather and surf conditions call 415-868-1922. The beach is one block west of Hwy 1.

Around 1 mile south of Stinson Beach is **Red Rock Beach**. It's a clothing-optional beach that attracts smaller crowds, probably because it can only be accessed by a steep trail from Hwy 1.

TOP CHOICE **Audubon Canyon Ranch** (415-868-9244; www.egret.org; donations requested; 10am-4pm Sat, Sun & holidays mid-Mar–mid-Jul) is about 3.5 miles north of town on Hwy 1, in the hills above the Bolinas Lagoon. A major nesting ground for great blue herons and great egrets, viewing scopes are set up on hillside blinds where you can watch these magnificent birds congregate to nest and hatch their chicks in tall redwoods. At low tide, harbor seals often doze on sand bars in the lagoon.

Just off Hwy 1 and a quick stroll to the beach, the ten comfortable rooms of the **Sandpiper** (415-868-1632; www.sandpiperstinsonbeach.com; 1 Marine Wy; r $140-210;) have gas fireplaces and kitchenettes, and are ensconced in a lush garden and picnic area. Prices dip from November through March.

Parkside Cafe (415-868-1272; www.parksidecafe.com; 43 Arenal Ave; mains $9-25; 7:30am-9pm Mon-Fri, from 8am Sat & Sun) is famous for its hearty breakfasts and lunches, and noted far and wide for its excellent coastal cuisine. Reservations are recommended for dinner.

West Marin Stagecoach (415-526-3239; www.marintransit.org/stage.html) route 61 runs daily minibuses ($2) from Marin City, and weekend and holiday services to the Sausalito ferry; the 62 route runs three days a week from San Rafael.

BOLINAS

For a town that is so famously unexcited about tourism, Bolinas offers some fairly tempting attractions for the visitor. Known as Jugville during the Gold Rush days, the sleepy beachside community is home to writers, musicians and fisherfolk, and deliberately hard to find. The highway department used to put signs up at the turnoff from Hwy 1; locals kept taking them down, so the highway department finally gave up.

Sights & Activities

FREE Bolinas Museum MUSEUM
(☎415-868-0330; www.bolinasmuseum.org; 48 Wharf Rd; ⏱4-7pm Wed, 1-5pm Fri, noon-5pm Sat & Sun) This courtyard complex of five galleries exhibits local artists and showcases the region's history. Look for the weathered Bolinas highway sign affixed to the wall, since you certainly didn't see one on your way into town.

2 Mile Surf Shop SURFING
(☎415-868-0264; 22 Brighton Ave) Surfing's popular in these parts, and this shop behind the post office rents boards and wet suits and also gives lessons. Call ☎415-868-2412 for the surf report.

Agate Beach BEACH
There are tide pools along some 2 miles of coastline at Agate Beach, around the end of Duxbury Point.

PRBO Conservation Science BIRD-WATCHING
(☎415-868-0655; www.prbo.org) Off Mesa Rd west of downtown and formerly known as the Point Reyes Bird Observatory, the Palomarin Field Station of PRBO has bird-banding and netting demonstrations, a visitors center and nature trail. Banding demonstrations are held in the morning every Tuesday to Sunday from May to late November, and on Wednesday, Saturday and Sunday the rest of the year. Check its website for information on monthly bird walks held throughout the region.

HIKING

Beyond the observatory is the Palomarin parking lot and access to various **walking trails** in the southern part of the Point Reyes National Seashore (see p123), including the easy (and popular) 3-mile trail to lovely **Bass Lake**. A sweet inland spot buffered by tall trees, this small lake is perfect for a pastoral swim on a toasty day. You can dive in wearing your birthday suit (or not), bring an inner tube to float about, or do a long lap all the way across.

If you continue 1.5 miles northwest, you'll reach the unmaintained trail to **Alamere Falls**, a fantastic flume plunging 50ft off a cliff and down to the beach. But sketchy beach access makes it more enjoyable to walk another 1.5 miles to **Wildcat Beach** and then backtrack a mile on sand.

Sleeping & Eating

Smiley's Schooner Saloon & Hotel MOTEL $
(☎415-868-1311; www.smileyssaloon.com; 41 Wharf Rd; r $89-109; 📶) A crusty old place dating back to 1851, Smiley's has simple but decent rooms, and last-minute weekday rates can go down to $60. The bar, which serves some food, has live bands Thursday through Saturday and is frequented by plenty of salty dogs and grizzled deadheads.

Coast Café AMERICAN $$
(www.bolinascafe.com; 46 Wharf Rd; mains $10-22; ⏱11:30am-3pm & 5-8pm Tue & Wed, to 9pm Thu & Fri, 8am-3pm & 5-9pm Sat, to 8pm Sun; ✎👪🐾) The only 'real' restaurant in town, everyone jockeys for outdoor seats among the flowerboxes for fish and chips, barbecued oysters, or buttermilk pancakes with damn good coffee.

Bolinas People's Store MARKET $
(14 Wharf Rd; ⏱8:30am-6:30pm; ✎) An awesome little co-op grocery store hidden behind the community center, the People's Store serves Fair Trade coffee and sells organic produce, fresh soup and excellent tamales. Eat at the tables in the shady courtyard, and have a rummage through the Free Box, a shed full of clothes and other waiting-to-be-reused items.

Getting There & Away

Route 61 of the **West Marin Stagecoach** (☎415-526-3239; www.marintransit.org/stage.html) goes daily ($2) from the Marin City transit hub (weekend and holiday service from the Sausalito ferry) to downtown Bolinas; the 62 route runs three days a week from San Rafael. By car, follow Hwy 1 north from Stinson Beach and turn west (left) for Bolinas at the first road north of the lagoon. At the first stop sign, take another left onto Olema-Bolinas Rd and follow it 2 miles to town.

WORTH A TRIP

LOCAL AG ROADTRIP

Along the border of Marin and Sonoma County, make a detour for these two local favorites.

At **Marin French Cheese** (www.marinfrenchcheese.com; 7500 Red Hill Rd, Novato; ⌚8:30am-5pm), stop to picnic beside the languid pond of this 150-year-old cheese producer. Sample its soft cheeses, watch the cheesemaking process at one of its four daily tours, and savor the rolling green hills over a baguette with triple crème brie.

Continue north 9 miles on the Petaluma-Point Reyes Rd to Petaluma Blvd and turn left to the stately **Petaluma Seed Bank** (http://rareseeds.com/petaluma-seed-bank; 199 Petaluma Blvd N, Petaluma; ⌚9:30am-5:30pm Sun-Fri, shorter winter hrs). Formerly the Sonoma County National Bank, the soaring windows and carved ceiling of the 1925 building make it a stately place to peruse the 1200 varieties of heirloom seeds.

OLEMA & NICASIO

About 10 miles north of Stinson Beach near the junction of Hwy 1 and Sir Francis Drake Blvd, **Olema** was the main settlement in West Marin in the 1860s. Back then, there was a stagecoach service to San Rafael and there were *six* saloons. In 1875, when the railroad was built through Point Reyes Station instead of Olema, the town's importance began to fade. In 1906 it gained distinction once again as the epicenter of the Great Quake.

The **Bolinas Ridge Trail**, a 12-mile series of ups and downs for hikers or bikers, starts about 1 mile west of Olema, on Sir Francis Drake Blvd. It has great views.

About a 15-minute drive inland from Olema, at the geographic center of Marin County, is **Nicasio**, a tiny town with a low-key rural flavor and a cool saloon and music venue. It's at the west end of Lucas Valley Rd, 10 miles from Hwy 101.

Olema Inn & Restaurant (☎415-663-9559; www.theolemainn.com; cnr Sir Francis Drake Blvd & Hwy 1; r incl breakfast Mon-Thu $174-198, Fri & Sat $198-222; restaurant ⌚9am-9pm; 📶🐾) is a very stylish and peaceful country retreat. Its six rooms retain some of the building's antiquated charm, but are up to modern standards of comfort. The almost-entirely organic **restaurant** (mains $22-30) can set you up with Hog Island oysters, a small plate meal or something from the extensive list of smaller-scale California wineries.

Six miles east of Olema on Sir Francis Drake Blvd, **Samuel P Taylor State Park** (☎415-488-9897; www.reserveamerica.com; tent & RV sites $35; 📶🐾) has beautiful, secluded campsites in redwood groves. It's also located on the **Cross Marin bike path**, with miles of creekside landscape to explore along a former railroad grade. At press time, the future of this state park was uncertain and subject to closure or reduced services.

In the town center, **Rancho Nicasio** (☎415-662-2219; www.ranchonicasio.com; mains $17-23; ⌚11:30am-3pm & 5-9pm Mon-Thu, to 10pm Fri, 11am-3pm & 5-10pm Sat, to 9pm Sun) is the local fun spot. It's a rustic saloon that regularly attracts local and national blues, rock and country performers.

Route 68 of the **West Marin Stagecoach** (☎415-526-3239; www.marintransit.org/stage.html) runs daily to Olema and Samuel P Taylor State Park from the San Rafael Transit Center ($2).

POINT REYES STATION

Though the railroad stopped coming through in 1933 and the town is small, Point Reyes Station is nevertheless the hub of West Marin. Dominated by dairies and ranches, the region was invaded by artists in the 1960s. Today it's an interesting blend of art galleries and tourist shops. The town has a rowdy saloon and the occasional smell of cattle on the afternoon breeze.

Sleeping & Eating

Cute little cottages, cabins and B&Bs are plentiful in and around Point Reyes. The **West Marin Chamber of Commerce** (☎415-663-9232; www.pointreyes.org) has numerous listings, as does the **Point Reyes Lodging Association** (www.ptreyes.com).

Holly Tree Inn INN, COTTAGES **$$**
(☎415-663-1554, 800-286-4655; www.hollytreeinn.com; Silver Hills Rd; r incl breakfast $130-180, cottages $190-265) The Holly Tree Inn, off Bear Valley Rd, has four rooms and three private cottages in a beautiful country setting. The

Sea Star Cottage is a romantic refuge at the end of a small pier on Tomales Bay.

Bovine Bakery BAKERY $
(11315 Hwy 1; 6:30am-5pm Mon-Thu, 7am-5pm Sat & Sun) Don't leave town without sampling something buttery from possibly the best bakery in Marin. A bear claw (a large sweet pastry) and an organic coffee are a good way to kick off your morning.

Pine Cone Diner DINER $$
(www.pineconediner.com; 60 4th St; mains $9-13; 8am-2:30pm) The Pine Cone serves big breakfasts and lunches inside a cute retro dining room and at shaded al fresco picnic tables. Try the buttermilk biscuits, the chorizo or tofu scramble, or the fried oyster sandwich.

Osteria Stellina ITALIAN $$
(415-663-9988; www.osteriastellina.com; 11285 Hwy 1; mains $15-25; 11:30am-2:30pm & 5-9pm) This place specializes in rustic Italian cuisine, with pizza and pasta dishes and Niman Ranch meats. Head over Tuesday nights for lasagna and live music, and definitely make reservations for the weekend.

Tomales Bay Foods and Cowgirl Creamery MARKET $$
(415-663-9335; www.cowgirlcreamery.com; 80 4th St; 10am-6pm Wed-Sun) A local market in an old barn selling picnic items, including gourmet cheeses and organic produce. Reserve a spot in advance for the small-scale artisanal cheesemaker's demonstration and tasting ($5), where you can watch the curd-making and cutting, then sample a half dozen of the fresh and aged cheeses. All of the milk is local and organic, with vegetarian rennet in all its soft cheeses.

☆ Entertainment

The lively community center, **Dance Palace** (415-663-1075; www.dancepalace.org; 503 B St), has weekend events, movies and live music. The **Old Western Saloon** (415-663-1661; cnr Shoreline Hwy & 2nd St) is a rustic 1906 saloon with live bands and cool tables emblazoned with horseshoes. Prince Charles stopped in here for an impromptu pint during a local visit in 2006.

Getting There & Away

Hwy 1 becomes Main St in town, running right through the center. Route 68 of the **West Marin Stagecoach** (415-526-3239; www.marintransit.org/stage.html) runs here daily from the San Rafael Transit Center ($2), and the 62 route goes south to Bolinas and Stinson Beach on Tuesday, Thursday and Saturday.

INVERNESS

This tiny town, the last outpost on your journey westward, is spread along the west side of Tomales Bay. It's got good places to eat and, among the surrounding hills and picturesque shoreline, multiple rental cottages and quaint B&Bs. Several great beaches are only a short drive north.

Blue Waters Kayaking (415-669-2600; www.bwkayak.com; kayak rental 2/4hr $50/60), at the Tomales Bay Resort and across the bay in Marshall (on Hwy 1, eight miles north of Point Reyes Station), offers various Tomales Bay tours, or you can rent a kayak and paddle around secluded beaches and rocky crevices on your own; no experience necessary.

Formerly the Golden Hinde Inn, the bayside **Tomales Bay Resort** (415-669-1389; www.tomalesbayresort.com; 12938 Sir Francis Drake Blvd; r $120-225) has 36 recently renovated motel rooms, a pool (unheated) and a restaurant. When rates drop – Sunday through Thursday and in the winter – it's one of the best bargains around.

Inverness Valley Inn (415-669-7250, 800-416-0405; www.invernessvalleyinn.com; 13275 Sir Francis Drake Blvd; r $149-219) is a family-friendly place hidden away in the woods, just a mile from town. It offers clean, modern kitchenette rooms in A-frame structures, and has a tennis court, horseshoe pitches, barbecue pits and in-room DVD players. There's a large garden and a few farm animals on site, and guests receive free eggs from the inn's chickens. It's past the town, on the way down the Pt Reyes Peninsula.

From Hwy 1, Sir Francis Drake Blvd leads straight into Inverness. Route 68 of the **West Marin Stagecoach** (415-526-3239; www.marintransit.org/stage.html) makes daily stops here from San Rafael ($2).

POINT REYES NATIONAL SEASHORE

The windswept peninsula Point Reyes is a rough-hewn beauty that has always lured marine mammals and migratory birds as well as scores of shipwrecks. It was here in 1579 that Sir Francis Drake landed to repair his ship, the *Golden Hind*. During his five-week stay he mounted a brass plaque near the shore claiming this land for England. Historians believe this occurred at **Drakes Beach** and there is a marker there today. In

1595 the first of scores of ships lost in these waters, the *San Augustine,* went down. She was a Spanish treasure ship out of Manila laden with luxury goods, and to this day bits of her cargo wash up on shore. Despite modern navigation, the dangerous waters here continue to claim the odd boat.

Point Reyes National Seashore has 110 sq miles of pristine ocean beaches, and the peninsula offers excellent hiking and camping opportunities. Be sure to bring warm clothing, as even the sunniest days can quickly turn cold and foggy.

Sights & Activities

For an awe-inspiring view, follow the **Earthquake Trail** from the park headquarters at Bear Valley. The trail reaches a 16ft gap between the two halves of a once-connected fence line, a lasting testimonial to the power of the 1906 earthquake that was centered in this area. Another trail leads from the visitors center a short way to **Kule Loklo**, a reproduction of a Miwok village.

Limantour Rd, off Bear Valley Rd about 1 mile north of Bear Valley Visitor Center, leads to the Point Reyes Hostel (p124) and **Limantour Beach**, where a trail runs along Limantour Spit with Estero de Limantour on one side and Drakes Bay on the other. The **Inverness Ridge Trail** heads from Limantour Rd up to Mt Vision (1282ft), from where there are spectacular views of the entire national seashore. You can drive almost to the top of Mt Vision from the other side.

About 2 miles past Inverness, Pierce Point Rd splits off to the right from Sir Francis Drake Blvd. From here you can get to two nice swimming beaches on the bay: Marshall Beach requires a mile-long hike from the parking area, while Hearts Desire, in **Tomales Bay State Park** (whose future was uncertain at press time), is accessible by car.

Pierce Point Rd continues to the huge windswept sand dunes at **Abbotts Lagoon**, full of peeping killdeer and other shorebirds. At the end of the road is Pierce Point Ranch, the trailhead for the 3.5-mile **Tomales Point Trail** through the **Tule Elk Reserve**. The plentiful elk are an amazing sight, standing with their big horns against the backdrop of Tomales Point, with Bodega Bay to the north, Tomales Bay to the east and the Pacific Ocean to the west.

Five Brooks Stables HORSEBACK RIDING
(415-663-1570; www.fivebrooks.com; trail rides from $40;) Explore the landscape on horseback with a trail ride. Take a slow amble through a pasture or ascend over 1000ft to Inverness Ridge for views of the Olema Valley. If you can stay in the saddle for six hours, ride along the coastline to Alamere Falls (see p121) via Wildcat Beach.

TOP CHOICE **Point Reyes Lighthouse** LIGHTHOUSE
(415-669-1534; 10am-4:30pm Thu-Mon) At the very end of Sir Francis Drake Blvd, with wild terrain and ferocious winds, this spot feels like the ends of the earth and offers the best **whale-watching** along the coast. The lighthouse sits below the headlands; to reach it requires descending over 300 stairs. Nearby **Chimney Rock** is a fine short hike, especially in spring when the wildflowers are blossoming. A nearby viewing area allows you to spy on the park's **elephant seal colony**.

Keep back from the water's edge at the exposed North Beach and South Beach, as people have been dragged in and drowned by frequent rogue waves.

Sleeping & Eating

Wake up to deer nibbling under a blanket of fog at one of Point Reyes' four very popular hike-in **campgrounds** (415-663-8054; www.nps.gov/pore/planyourvisit/campgrounds.htm; tent sites $15), each with pit toilets, water and tables. Reservations accepted up to three months in advance, and weekends go fast. Reaching the campgrounds requires a 2- to 6-mile hike or bicycle ride, or you can try for a permit to kayak camp on the beach in Tomales Bay.

Point Reyes Hostel HOSTEL $
(415-663-8811; www.norcalhostels.org/reyes; dm/r $24/68; @) Just off Limantour Rd, this rustic HI property has bunkhouses with warm and cozy front rooms, big-view windows and outdoor areas with hill vistas, and a brand new LEED-certified building with four more private rooms in the works. It's in a beautiful secluded valley 2 miles from the ocean and surrounded by lovely hiking trails.

Drakes Bay Oyster Company SEAFOOD $$
(415-669-1149; www.drakesbayoyster.com; 17171 Sir Francis Drake Blvd, Inverness; 1 dozen oysters to go/on the half shell $15/24; 8:30am-4:30pm) Drakes Bay and nearby Tomales Bay are famous for excellent oysters. Stop by to do some on-the-spot shucking and slurping, or pick some up to grill later.

Information

The park headquarters, **Bear Valley Visitor Center** (☎415-464-5100; Bear Valley Rd; ⏰9am-5pm Mon-Fri, from 8am Sat & Sun), is near Olema and has information and maps. You can also get information at the Point Reyes Lighthouse and the **Ken Patrick Center** (☎415-669-1250; ⏰10am-5pm Sat, Sun & holidays) at Drakes Beach. All visitor centers have slightly longer hours in summer.

Getting There & Away

By car you can get to Point Reyes a few different ways. The curviest is along Hwy 1, through Stinson Beach and Olema. More direct is to exit Hwy 101 in San Rafael and follow Sir Francis Drake Blvd all the way to the tip of Point Reyes. For the latter route, take the Central San Rafael exit and head west on 4th St, which turns into Sir Francis Drake Blvd. By either route, it's about 1½ hours to Olema from San Francisco.

Just north of Olema, where Hwy 1 and Sir Francis Drake Blvd come together, is Bear Valley Rd; turn left to reach the Bear Valley Visitor Center. If you're heading to the further reaches of Point Reyes, follow Sir Francis Drake Blvd through Point Reyes Station and out onto the peninsula (about an hour's drive).

West Marin Stagecoach (☎415-526-3239; www.marintransit.org/stage.html) route 68 makes daily stops at the Bear Valley Visitor Center from San Rafael ($2).

EAST BAY

Berkeley and Oakland, collectively and affectionately called the 'five and dime,' after their 510 area code, are what most San Franciscans think of as the East Bay, though the area includes numerous other suburbs that swoop up from the bayside flats into exclusive enclaves in the hills. While many residents of the 'West Bay' would like to think they needn't ever cross the Bay Bridge or take a BART train under water, a wealth of museums, universities, excellent restaurants, woodsy parklands and better weather are just some of attractions that lure travelers from San Francisco.

Oakland

Named for the grand oak trees that once lined its streets, Oakland is to San Francisco what Brooklyn is to Manhattan. To some degree a less expensive alternative to the nearby city of hills, it's often where bohemian refugees have fled to escape pricey San Francisco housing costs. An ethnically diverse city, Oakland has a strong African American community and a long labor union history. Urban farmers raise chickens in their backyard or occupy abandoned lots to start community gardens, families find more room to stretch out, and self-satisfied residents thumb their noses at San Francisco's fog while basking in a sunnier Mediterranean climate.

POINT REYES SHUTTLE

On good-weather weekends and holidays from late December through mid-April, the road to Chimney Rock and the lighthouse is closed to private vehicles. Instead you must take a shuttle ($5, children under 17 free) from Drakes Beach.

Sights & Activities

Broadway is the backbone of downtown Oakland, running from Jack London Sq at the waterfront all the way north to Piedmont and Rockridge. Telegraph Ave branches off Broadway at 15th St and heads north straight to Berkeley via the Temescal neighborhood (located between 40th St and 51st St). San Pablo Ave also heads north from downtown into Berkeley. Running east from Broadway is Grand Ave, leading to the Lake Merritt commercial district.

Downtown BART stations are on Broadway at both 12th and 19th Sts; other stations are near Lake Merritt, Rockridge and Temescal (MacArthur station).

DOWNTOWN

Oakland's downtown is full of historic buildings and a growing number of colorful local businesses. With such easy access from San Francisco via BART and the ferry, it's worth spending part of a day exploring here – and nearby Chinatown and Jack London Sq – on foot or by bicycle.

The pedestrianized **City Center**, between Broadway and Clay St, 12th and 14th Sts, forms the heart of downtown Oakland. The twin towers of the **Ronald Dellums Federal Building** are on Clay St, just behind it. **City Hall**, at 14th & Clay Sts, is a beautifully refurbished 1914 beaux arts hall.

Continuing north of the City Center, the **Uptown** district contains many of the city's art deco beauties and a proliferating arts

Oakland

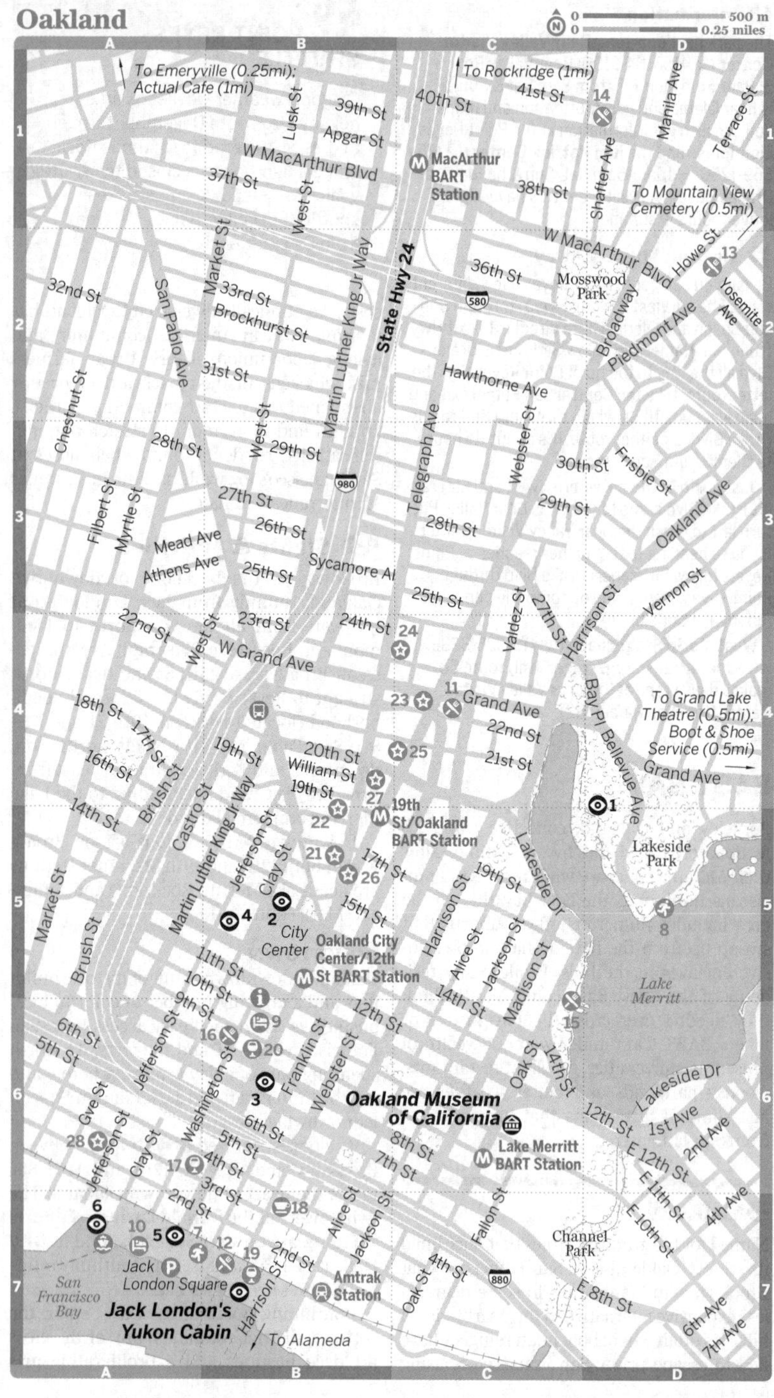
0 500 m
0 0.25 miles
To Emeryville (0.25mi); Actual Cafe (1mi)
To Rockridge (1mi)
To Mountain View Cemetery (0.5mi)
To Grand Lake Theatre (0.5mi); Boot & Shoe Service (0.5mi)
To Alameda
MacArthur BART Station
19th St/Oakland BART Station
Oakland City Center/12th St BART Station
Lake Merritt BART Station
Amtrak Station
Oakland Museum of California
Jack London's Yukon Cabin
Jack London Square
City Center
Mosswood Park
Lakeside Park
Lake Merritt
Channel Park
San Francisco Bay
State Hwy 24
W MacArthur Blvd
Martin Luther King Jr Way
Telegraph Ave
Broadway
Piedmont Ave
Grand Ave
Harrison St
Lakeside Dr
San Pablo Ave
Market St
E 12th St
E 8th St

and restaurant scene. The area stretches roughly between Telegraph and Broadway, bounded by Grand Ave to the north.

Old Oakland, along Washington St between 8th and 10th Sts, is lined with historic buildings dating from the 1860s to the 1880s. The buildings have been restored and the area has a lively restaurant and after-work scene. The area also hosts a lively **farmers market** every Friday morning.

East of Broadway and bustling with commerce, **Chinatown** centers on Franklin and Webster Sts, as it has since the 1870s. It's much smaller than the San Francisco version.

JACK LONDON SQUARE

The area where writer and adventurer Jack London once raised hell now bears his name, and recent spasms of redevelopment have added a new cinema complex, condo development, excellent restaurants and some eclectic watering holes. The pretty waterfront location is worth a stroll, especially when the Sunday **farmers market** (⌚10am-2pm) takes over, or get off your feet and kayak around the harbor. Catch a ferry from San Francisco – a worthwhile excursion in and of itself – and you'll land just paces away.

Jack London's Yukon Cabin LANDMARK

A replica of Jack London's Yukon cabin stands at the eastern end of the square. It's partially built from the timbers of a cabin London lived in during the Yukon gold rush. Oddly, people throw coins inside as if it's a fountain. Another interesting stop, adjacent to the tiny cabin, is Heinold's First & Last Chance Saloon (see p131).

USS Potomac HISTORIC SHIP

(☎510-627-1215; www.usspotomac.org; admission $10; ⌚11am-3pm Wed, Fri & Sun) Franklin D Roosevelt's 'floating White House,' the 165ft USS Potomac, is moored at Clay and Water Sts by the ferry dock, and is open for dockside tours. Two-hour history cruises (adult/child $45/25) are also held several times a month from May through October.

LAKE MERRITT

An urban respite, Lake Merritt is a popular place to stroll or go running (a 3.5-mile track circles the lake). The two main commercial streets skirting Lake Merritt are Lakeshore Ave on the eastern edge of the lake and Grand Ave, running along the north shore.

TOP CHOICE **Oakland Museum of California** MUSEUM

(☎510-238-2200; www.museumca.org; 1000 Oak St; adult/child 9-17/child under 9 $12/6/free, 1st Sun each month free; ⌚11am-5pm Wed-Sun, to 9pm Fri; 👪) Near the southern end of the lake and one block from the Lake Merritt BART sta-

Oakland

Top Sights
- Jack London's Yukon Cabin B7
- Oakland Museum of California C6

Sights
- 1 Children's Fairyland D4
- 2 City Hall B5
- 3 Friday farmers market B6
- 4 Ronald Dellums Federal Building B5
- 5 Sunday farmers market A7
- 6 USS Potomac A7

Activities, Courses & Tours
- 7 California Canoe & Kayak A7
- 8 Lake Merritt Boating Center D5

Sleeping
- 9 Washington Inn B6
- 10 Waterfront Hotel A7

Eating
- 11 Bakesale Betty C4
- 12 Bocanova B7
- 13 Commis D2
- 14 Homeroom D1
- 15 Lake Chalet C6
- Plum .... (see 11)
- 16 Ratto's B6

Drinking
- 17 Beer Revolution A6
- 18 Blue Bottle Coffee Company B7
- 19 Heinold's First & Last Chance Saloon B7
- Punchdown .... (see 11)
- 20 Trappist B6

Entertainment
- 21 Café Van Kleef B5
- 22 Fox Theater B5
- 23 Luka's Taproom & Lounge C4
- 24 Mama Buzz Café C4
- 25 Paramount Theatre C4
- 26 Rock Paper Scissors Collective B5
- 27 Uptown B4
- 28 Yoshi's A6

tion, this museum has rotating exhibitions on artistic and scientific themes, and excellent permanent galleries dedicated to the state's diverse ecology and history, as well as California art.

Children's Fairyland AMUSEMENT PARK
(☎510-238-6876; www.fairyland.org; admission $8; ⊙10am-4pm Mon-Fri, to 5pm Sat & Sun summer, 10am-4pm Wed-Sun spring & fall, Fri-Sun winter; 👪) Lakeside Park, at the northern end of the saltwater lake, includes this 10-acre attraction, which dates from 1950 and has charming fairy-tale-themed train, carousel and mini Ferris-wheel rides.

Lake Merritt Boating Center BOAT HIRE
(☎510-238-2196; ⊙Sat & Sun Nov-Feb, daily Mar-Oct; 👪) Rents canoes, rowboats, kayaks, pedal boats and sailboats for $10 to $18 per hour.

PIEDMONT AVE & ROCKRIDGE

North of downtown Oakland, Broadway becomes a lengthy strip of car dealerships called Broadway Auto Row. Just past that is **Piedmont Ave**, wall-to-wall with antique stores, coffeehouses, fine restaurants and an art cinema.

One of Oakland's most popular shopping areas is **Rockridge**, a lively, upscale neighborhood. It is centered on College Ave, which runs from Broadway all the way to the UC Berkeley Campus. College Ave is lined with clothing boutiques, good bookstores, a vintage record shop, several pubs and cafes, and quite a few upscale restaurants – maybe the largest concentration in the Bay Area. BART at the Rockridge station puts you in the thick of things.

Mountain View Cemetery CEMETERY
(www.mountainviewcemetery.org; 5000 Piedmont Ave) At the end of Piedmont Ave; perhaps the most serene and lovely artificial landscape in all the East Bay. Designed by Frederic Law Olmstead, the architect of New York City's Central Park, it's great for walking and the views are stupendous.

OAKLAND HILLS

The large parks of the Oakland Hills are ideal for day hiking and challenging cycling, and the **East Bay Regional Parks District** (www.ebparks.org) manages over 1200 miles of trails in 65 regional parks, preserves and recreation areas in the Alameda and Contra Costa counties.

Off Hwy 24, **Robert Sibley Volcanic Regional Preserve** is the northernmost of the Oakland Hills parks. It has great views of the Bay Area from its Round Top Peak (1761ft). From Sibley, Skyline Blvd runs south past **Redwood Regional Park** and adjacent **Joaquin Miller Park** to **Anthony Chabot Regional Park**. A hike or mountain-bike ride through the groves and along the hilltops of any of these sizable parks will make you forget you're in an urban area. At the southern end of Chabot Park is the enormous **Lake Chabot**, with an easy trail along its shore and canoes, kayaks and other boats for rent from the **Lake Chabot marina** (☎510-247-2526; www.norcalfishing.com/chabot).

Chabot Space & Science Center SCIENCE CENTER
(☎510-336-7300; www.chabotspace.org; 10000 Skyline Blvd, Oakland; adult/child $15/11; ⊙10am-5pm Wed & Thu, to 10pm Fri & Sat, 11am-5pm Sun, plus 10am-5pm Tue summer; 👪) Stargazers will go gaga over this science and technology center in the Oakland Hills with loads of exhibits on subjects such as space travel and eclipses, as well as cool planetarium shows. When the weather's good, check out the free Friday and Saturday evening viewings using a 20in refractor telescope.

Sleeping

If you like B&Bs, the **Berkeley and Oakland Bed & Breakfast Network** (www.bbonline.com/ca/berkeley-oakland) lists private homes that rent rooms, suites and cottages; prices start from $100 per night and many have a two-night-minimum stay. Reservations recommended.

Claremont Resort and Spa RESORT $$$
(☎510-843-3000, 800-551-7266; www.claremontresort.com; 41 Tunnel Rd; r $189-309; ❄🏊@📶) Oakland's classy crème de la crème, the Claremont is a glamorous white 1915 building with elegant restaurants, a fitness center, swimming pools, tennis courts and a full-service spa (room/spa packages are available). The bay view rooms are superb. It's located at the foot of the Oakland Hills, off Hwy 13 (Tunnel Rd) near Claremont Ave.

Waterfront Hotel BOUTIQUE HOTEL $$
(☎510-836-3800; www.waterfronthoteloakland.com; 10 Washington; r $149-269; ❄🏊@📶🐾) Paddle-printed wallpaper and lamps fashioned from faux lanterns round out the playful nautical theme of this bright and cheerful hotel at

harbor's edge. A huge brass-topped fireplace warms the foyer, and comfy rooms include MP3-player docking stations and coffeemakers, plus microwaves and fridges upon request. Unless you're an avid trainspotter, water-view rooms are preferred, as freight trains rattle by on the city side.

Washington Inn HISTORIC HOTEL **$$**
(510-452-1776; www.thewashingtoninn.com; 495 10th St; r incl breakfast $89-149;) Small and modern with a boutique feel, this historic downtown lodging offers updated comfort and character, with a lobby and guest rooms that project snazz and efficient sophistication. The carved lobby bar is perfect for a predinner cocktail, and you're spoiled for choice with several fine restaurants within a few block radius.

Anthony Chabot Regional Park CAMPGROUND **$**
(510-639-4751; www.ebparks.org/parks/anthony_chabot; tent sites $22, RV sites with hookups $22-28;) This 5000-acre park has 75 campsites open year-round and hot showers. Reservations ($8 service charge) at 888-327-2757 or www.reserveamerica.com.

Eating

Oakland has seen a restaurant renaissance, with scores of fun and sophisticated new eateries opening up all over town.

DOWNTOWN & JACK LONDON SQUARE

TOP CHOICE **Bakesale Betty** BAKERY **$**
(www.bakesalebetty.com; 2228 Broadway; pastries from $2, sandwiches $6.50-9; 11am-2pm Tue-Fri;) An Aussie expat and Chez Panisse alum, Betty Barakat (in signature blue wig) has patrons licking their lips and lining up out the door for her heavenly scones, strawberry shortcake and scrumptious fried chicken sandwiches. Rolling pins dangle from the ceiling, and blissed-out locals sit down at ironing-board sidewalk tables to savor buttery baked goods and seasonal specialties like sticky date pudding. Free cookie if there's a line!

Bocanova LATIN AMERICAN **$$**
(510-444-1233; www.bocanova.com; 55 Webster St; mains $12-28; 11:30am-10pm Mon-Thu, 11am-11pm Fri & Sat, to 10pm Sun) A new addition to Jack London Square, you can people-watch from the outdoor patio or eat in a chic industrial dining room lit by hanging glass lamps. The focus here is Pan-American cuisine, and standouts include the Dungeness crab deviled eggs, scallops in Brazilian curry sauce, and the sweet potato and chipotle gratin. Reservations recommended on Wednesday – when wine bottles are half-price – and weekends.

Ratto's DELI **$**
(www.rattos.com; 821 Washington St; sandwiches from $6; 9am-5:30pm Mon-Fri, 10am-3pm Sat;) If you want to eat outside on a sunny day, grab a sandwich from Ratto's, a vintage Oakland grocery (since 1897) with a deli counter that attracts a devoted lunch crowd.

Plum ORGANIC **$$**
(510-444-7586; www.plumoakland.com; 2214 Broadway; dishes $10-22; 11:30am-2pm & 5:30pm-1am Mon-Fri, 10am-2pm & 5pm-1am Sat & Sun;) Foodies and design fans pack the communal tables at this minimalist gallery-like space with bruise-black walls and sustainable entrees.

LAKE MERRITT

Lake Chalet SEAFOOD **$$**
(510-208-5253; www.thelakechalet.com; 1520 Lakeside Dr; mains $13-28; 11am-10pm Mon-Thu, to 11pm Fri, 10am-11pm Sat, to 10pm Sun) Whether you stop by the long pump house view bar for a martini and oysters during the buzzing happy hour (3pm to 6pm and 9pm to close), feast on a whole roasted crab by a window seat in the formal dining room, or cruise Lake Merritt on a Venetian-style **gondola** (www.gondolaservizio.com; per couple from $40), this 100-year-old former park office and boathouse is an enjoyable destination restaurant. Weekend reservations recommended.

Boot & Shoe Service PIZZERIA **$$**
(510-763-2668; www.bootandshoeservice.com; 3308 Grand Ave; pizza from $10; 5:30-10pm Tue-Thu, 5-10:30pm Fri & Sat, to 10pm Sun) The occasional old-timer comes in looking for the long-gone cobbler shop, but the current patrons pack this place for its wood-fired pizzas, original cocktails and creative antipasti made from sustainably sourced fresh ingredients. Seating is mostly at shared tables, under the watch of anthropomorphic footwear paintings.

Arizmendi BAKERY **$**
(http://lakeshore.arizmendi.coop; 3265 Lakeshore Ave; pizza slices $2.50; 7am-7pm Tue-Sat, to 6pm Sun, to 3pm Mon;) Great for breakfast or

lunch but beware – this bakery co-op is not for the weak-willed. The gourmet vegetarian pizza, yummy fresh breads and amazing scones are mouthwateringly addictive.

PIEDMONT AVE & ROCKRIDGE

Wood Tavern AMERICAN $$$
(☎510-654-6607; www.woodtavern.net; 6317 College Ave; lunch mains $10-19, dinner mains $19-32; ⊙11:30am-10pm Mon-Thu, to 10:30pm Fri & Sat, 5-9pm Sun) With a knock-out cheese board and charcuterie – the restaurant cures meats and makes its own salami – and a constantly changing menu of local and organic California cuisine featuring fish, pork and beef dishes with French and Italian influences, Wood Tavern has established itself as the local favorite for upscale food in a comfortable environment. The formal wood bar serves absinthe drinks and other elegant cocktails and the high-ceiling dining room is cozy enough that weekend dinner reservations are recommended.

À Côté MEDITERRANEAN $$
(☎510-655-6469; www.acoterestaurant.com; 5478 College Ave; dishes $8-18; ⊙5:30-10pm Sun-Tue, to 11pm Wed & Thu, to midnight Fri & Sat) This small plates eatery with individual and friendly communal tables is one of the best restaurants along College Ave. What the menu calls 'flatbread' is actually pizza for the gods. Mussels with Pernod is a signature dish.

Commis CALIFORNIAN $$$
(☎510-653-3902; www.commisrestaurant.com; 3859 Piedmont Ave; 5-course dinner $68; ⊙from 5:30pm Wed-Sat, from 5pm Sun; ☑) The only Michelin-starred restaurant in the East Bay, the signless and discreet dining room counts a minimalist decor and some coveted counter real estate (reservable by phone only) where patrons can watch chef James Syhabout and his team piece together creative and innovative dishes. Reservations highly recommended.

TEMESCAL & EMERYVILLE

Emeryville is a separate bite-sized city, wedged between Oakland and south Berkeley on I-80.

Homeroom AMERICAN $
(☎510-597-0400; www.homeroom510.com; 400 40th St; mains $7.50-10; ⊙11am-2pm Tue-Sat, plus 5-9pm Sun-Thu & 5-10pm Fri & Sat; ☑👪) Follow the instructions to fold your menu into a paper airplane at this quirky mac-n-cheese restaurant modeled after a school. A handy chalkboard caricature of California pinpoints the source of its regionally focused food, and the cheese choices – including cheddar, chêvre, vegan and firehouse jack – are more gourmet than anything Mom packed for your lunchbox.

Emeryville Public Market INTERNATIONAL $
(www.emerymarket.com; 5959 Shellmound St, Emeryville; mains under $10; ⊙7am-9pm Mon-Thu, from 9am Fri & Sat, 9am-8pm Sun) To satisfy a group of finicky eaters, cross the Amtrak tracks to the indoor and choose from dozens of ethnic food stalls dishing out a huge range of international cuisines.

Drinking

TOP CHOICE **Beer Revolution** BEER HALL
(www.beer-revolution.com; 464 3rd St) Go ahead and drool. With almost 50 beers on tap, and over 500 in the bottle, there's a lifetime of discovery ahead, so kick back on the sunny deck or park yourself at that barrel table embedded with bottle caps. Bonuses include no distracting TVs and a punk soundtrack played at conversation-friendly levels. Check the website for special events like the Wednesday night meet-the-brewer sessions and Sunday barbecues.

Actual Café CAFE
(www.actualcafe.com; 6334 San Pablo Ave; mains $4-7; ⊙7am-8pm Mon-Thu, to 10pm Fri, 8am-10pm Sat, to 8pm Sun; 📶) Known for its wi-fi-free weekends and inside bicycle parking, the Actual promotes sustainability and face-to-face community while keeping folks well fed with its housemade baked goods and sandwiches. Weekly movies (with free popcorn!) and live music promote mingling at its long wooden tables.

Blue Bottle Coffee Company CAFE
(www.bluebottlecoffee.net; 300 Webster St; pastries $2-3; ⊙7am-5pm Mon-Fri, from 8am Sat & Sun) The java gourmands queue up here for single-origin espressos and what some consider the best coffee in the country. The all-organic and very origin-specific beans are roasted on site, with compostable cups if you're taking your drink to go.

Trappist PUB
(www.thetrappist.com; 460 8th St) So popular that it busted out of its original brick-and-wood-paneled shoebox and expanded into a second storefront and back terrace, the

specialty here is Belgian ales. More than two dozen drafts rotate through the taps – with serving sizes varying based on alcohol content and special glasses for each brew – and tasty stews and sandwiches ($8 to $14) make it easy to linger.

Punchdown WINE BAR
(www.punchdownwine.com; 2212 Broadway; ⌚4-9pm Tue-Thu, to 10pm Fri, 5-1pm Sat) A super-new 'natural' wine bar, Punchdown seeks out organic, sustainably created and biodynamic producers. Playful flights include an 'adventurous orange' – whites with extended grape skin contact – and a blind flight that's free if you guess the three selections. There's an attractive outdoor area plus charcuterie and cheese board options.

Heinold's First & Last Chance Saloon BAR
(48 Webster St) An 1883 bar constructed from wood scavenged from an old whaling ship, you really have to hold on to your beer here. Keeled to a severe slant during the 1906 earthquake, the building's 20% grade might make you feel self-conscious about stumbling before you even order. Its big claim to fame is that author Jack London was a regular patron.

☆ Entertainment

Art

On the first Friday evening of the month, gallery-hop through downtown and Temescal as part of the **Oakland Art Murmur** (www.oaklandartmurmur.com; ⌚6-10pm). One fun place to check out is the crafty DIY art space of the **Rock Paper Scissors Collective** (www.rpscollective.com; 2278 Telegraph Ave).

Music

TOP CHOICE **Café Van Kleef** LIVE MUSIC, BAR
(www.cafevankleef.com; 1621 Telegraph Ave) Order a greyhound (with fresh-squeezed grapefruit juice) and take a gander at the profusion of antique musical instruments, fake taxidermy heads, sprawling formal chandeliers and bizarro ephemera clinging to every surface possible here. Quirky, kitschy and evocative even *before* you get lit, the decade-old Café Van Kleef features live blues, jazz and the occasional rock band from Thursday through Saturday ($5 cover).

Uptown LIVE MUSIC
(www.uptownnightclub.com; 1928 Telegraph Ave) For an eclectic calendar of indie, punk and experimental sounds, a weekly burlesque show and fun DJ dance parties, this club hits the spot. Come for a good mix of national acts and local talent, and the easy two-block walk to BART.

Yoshi's JAZZ
(☎510-238-9200; www.yoshis.com/oakland; 510 Embarcadero W; shows $12-40) Yoshi's has a solid jazz calendar, with talent from around the world passing through on a near-nightly basis. Often, touring artists will stop in for a stand of two or three nights. It's also a Japanese restaurant, so you might enjoy a sushi plate before the show.

Mama Buzz Café LIVE MUSIC
(www.mamabuzzcafe.com; 2318 Telegraph Ave; 📶🖊) This low-key hipster cafe and alternative arts space has an eclectic roster of free music shows most nights. It serves simple vegetarian fare as well as beer.

Luka's Taproom & Lounge DJ
(www.lukasoakland.com; 2221 Broadway) Go Uptown to get down. DJs spin nightly at this popular restaurant and lounge, with a soulful mix of hip-hop, reggae, funk and house. There's generally a $10 cover on Fridays and Saturdays after 11pm.

Theaters & Cinemas

The 2009 reopening of the Fox Theater has contributed to a groundswell of new restaurants and evening activity in the Uptown district.

Fox Theater THEATER
(www.thefoxoakland.com; 1807 Telegraph Ave) A phoenix arisen from the urban ashes, this 1928 art deco stunner was recently restored, adding dazzle to downtown and a corner-

PINBALL WIZARDS, UNITE!

Put down that video game console, cast aside your latest phone app, and return to the bygone days of pinball play. Lose yourself in bells and flashing lights at **Pacific Pinball Museum** (☎510-769-1349; www.pacificpinball.org; 1510 Webster St, Alameda; adult/child $15/7.50; ⌚2-9pm Tue-Thu, to midnight Fri, 11am-midnight Sat, to 9pm Sun; 👪), a pinball parlor with almost 100 games dating from the 1930s to the present, and vintage jukeboxes playing hits from the past. Take AC Transit bus 51A from downtown Oakland.

stone to the happening Uptown theater district. It's now a popular concert venue.

Paramount Theatre THEATER
(☎510-465-6400; www.paramounttheatre.com; 2025 Broadway) This massive 1931 art deco masterpiece shows classic films a few times each month and is also home to the Oakland East Bay Symphony (www.oebs.org) and Oakland Ballet (www.oaklandballet.org). It periodically books big-name concerts. Tours ($5) are given at 10am on the first and third Saturdays of the month.

Grand Lake Theatre CINEMA
(☎510-452-3556; www.renaissancerialto.com; 3200 Grand Ave) In Lake Merritt, this 1926 beauty lures you in with its huge corner marquee (which sometimes displays left-leaning political messages) and keeps you coming with a fun balcony and a Wurlitzer organ playing the pipes on weekends.

Sports

Sports teams play at **Overstock.com Coliseum** or the **Oracle Arena** off I-880 (Coliseum/Oakland Airport BART station). Cheer on the **Golden State Warriors**, the Bay Area's NBA basketball team, the **Oakland A's**, the Bay Area's American League baseball team, and the **Raiders**, Oakland's NFL team.

Information

Oakland's daily newspaper is the *Oakland Tribune*. The free weekly *East Bay Express* (www.eastbayexpress.com) has good Oakland and Berkeley listings.

Oakland Convention & Visitors Bureau (☎510-839-9000; www.visitoakland.org; 463 11th St; ⏲9am-5pm Mon-Fri) Between Broadway and Clay St.

Getting There & Away

Air

Oakland International Airport (www.flyoakland.com) is directly across the bay from San Francisco International Airport, and it's usually less crowded and less expensive to fly here. Southwest Airlines has a large presence.

BART

Within the Bay Area, the most convenient way to get to Oakland and back is by **BART** (☎510-465-2278, 511; www.bart.gov). Trains run on a set schedule from 4am to midnight on weekdays, 6am to midnight on Saturday and 8am to midnight on Sunday, and operate at 15- or 20-minute intervals on average.

To get to downtown Oakland, catch a Richmond or Pittsburg/Bay Point train. Fares to the 12th or 19th St stations from downtown San Francisco are $3.10. From San Francisco to Lake Merritt ($3.10) or the Oakland Coliseum/Airport station ($3.80), catch a BART train that is heading for Fremont or Dublin/Pleasanton. Rockridge ($3.50) is on the Pittsburg/Bay Point line. Between Oakland and downtown Berkeley you can catch a Fremont-Richmond train ($1.75).

For AC Transit connections, take a transfer from the white AC Transit machines in the BART station to save 25¢ off the bus fare.

Bus

Regional company **AC Transit** (☎510-817-1717, 511; www.actransit.org) runs convenient buses from San Francisco's Transbay Temporary Terminal at Howard and Main Streets to downtown Oakland and Berkeley, and between the two East Bay cities. Scores of buses go to Oakland from San Francisco during commute hours ($4.20), but only the 'O' line runs both ways all day and on weekends; you can catch the 'O' line at the corner of 5th and Washington Sts in downtown Oakland.

After BART trains stop, late-night transportation between San Francisco and Oakland is with the 800 line, which runs hourly from downtown Market St and the Transbay Temporary Terminal in San Francisco to the corner of 14th St and Broadway.

Between Berkeley and downtown Oakland ($2.10) on weekdays, take the fast and frequent 1R bus along Telegraph Ave between the two city centers. Alternatively, take bus 18 that runs via Martin Luther King Jr Way daily.

Greyhound (☎510-832-4730; www.greyhound.com; 2103 San Pablo Ave) operates direct buses from Oakland to Vallejo, San Jose, Santa Rosa and Sacramento. The station is pretty seedy.

Car & Motorcycle

From San Francisco by car, cross the Bay Bridge and enter Oakland via one of two ways: I-580, which leads to I-980 and drops you near the City Center; or I-880, which curves through West Oakland and lets you off near the south end of Broadway. I-880 then continues to the Coliseum, the Oakland International Airport and, eventually, San Jose.

Driving to San Francisco, the bridge toll is $4 to $6, depending on the time and day of the week.

Ferry

With splendid bay views, ferries are the most enjoyable way of traveling between San Francisco and Oakland, though also the slowest and most expensive. From San Francisco's Ferry Building, the **Alameda–Oakland ferry** (☎510-522-3300; www.eastbayferry.com) sails to Jack London Sq (one-way $6.25, 30 minutes, about 12 times a day on weekdays and six to nine times a day on weekends). Ferry tickets include a free transfer, which you can use on AC Transit buses from Jack London Sq.

Train

Oakland is a regular stop for Amtrak trains operating up and down the coast. From Oakland's **Amtrak station** (☎800-872-7245; www.amtrak.com; 245 2nd St) in Jack London Sq, you can catch AC Transit bus 72 to downtown Oakland (and on weekdays the free Broadway Shuttle), or take a ferry across the bay to San Francisco.

Amtrak passengers with reservations on to San Francisco need to disembark at the **Emeryville Amtrak station** (5885 Horton St), one stop away from Oakland. From there, an Amtrak bus shuttles you to San Francisco's Ferry Building stop. The free **Emery Go Round** (www.emerygoround.com) shuttle runs a circuit that includes the Emeryville Amtrak station and MacArthur BART.

Getting Around

To/From the Airport

BART is the cheapest and easiest transportation option. AirBART buses connect between the airport and the Coliseum/Oakland Airport BART station every 10 minutes until midnight. Tickets cost $3 with exact change or a BART ticket of that value.

SuperShuttle (☎800-258-3826; www.supershuttle.com) is one of many door-to-door shuttle services operating out of Oakland International Airport. One-way service to San Francisco destinations costs about $27 for the first person and $10 for the second. East Bay service destinations are also served. Reserve ahead.

A taxi from Oakland International Airport to downtown Oakland costs about $30; to downtown San Francisco about $60.

Bus

AC Transit (☎510-817-1717, 511; www.actransit.org) has a comprehensive bus network within Oakland. Fares are $2.10 and exact change is required.

On weekdays, the free new **Broadway Shuttle** (www.meetdowntownoak.com/shuttle.php; ⏲7am-7pm Mon-Fri) runs down Broadway between Jack London Square and Lake Merritt, stopping at Old Oakland/Chinatown, the downtown BART stations and the Uptown district. The lime-green buses arrive every 10 to 15 minutes.

Berkeley

As the birthplace of the Free Speech and disability rights movements, and the home of the hallowed halls of the University of California, Berkeley is no bashful wallflower. A national hotspot of (mostly left-of-center) intellectual discourse and one of the most vocal activist populations in the country, this infamous college town has an interesting mix of graying progressives and idealistic undergrads. It's easy to stereotype 'Beserkeley' for some of its recycle-or-else PC crankiness, but the city is often on the forefront of environmental and political issues that eventually go mainstream.

WATERSPORTS ON THE BAY

The San Francisco Bay makes a lovely postcard or snapshot, and there are myriad outfits to help you play in it.

California Canoe & Kayak (☎510-893-7833; www.calkayak.com; 409 Water St; rental per hr s/d kayak $15/25, canoe $25, stand-up paddleboard $15) Rents kayaks, canoes and stand-up paddleboards at Oakland's Jack London Square.

Cal Adventures (☎510-642-4000; www.recsports.berkeley.edu; 124 University Ave; 👪) Run by the UC Berkeley Aquatic Center and located at the Berkeley Marina, Cal offers sailing, surfing and sea kayaking classes and rentals for adults and youth.

Cal Sailing Club (www.cal-sailing.org) An affordable membership-based and volunteer-run nonprofit with sailing and windsurfing programs. Also based at the Berkeley Marina.

Boardsports School & Shop (http://boardsportsschool.com) Offers lessons and rentals for kiteboarding, windsurfing and stand-up paddleboarding from its three locations in San Francisco, Alameda (East Bay) and Coyote Point (p144).

Sea Trek (p109) Has kayaking and stand-up paddleboards, and a fabulous full moon paddle tour. Located in Sausalito.

Berkeley is also home to a large South Asian community, as evidenced by an abundance of sari shops on University Ave and a large number of excellent Indian restaurants.

Sights & Activities

Approximately 13 miles east of San Francisco, Berkeley is bordered by the bay to the west, the hills to the east and Oakland to the south. I-80 runs along the town's western edge, next to the marina; from here University Ave heads east to downtown and the campus.

Shattuck Ave crosses University Ave one block west of campus, forming the main crossroads of the downtown area. Immediately to the south is the downtown shopping strip and the downtown Berkeley BART station.

UNIVERSITY OF CALIFORNIA, BERKELEY

The Berkeley campus of the University of California (UCB, called 'Cal' by both students and locals) is the oldest university in the state. The decision to found the college was made in 1866, and the first students arrived in 1873. Today UCB has over 35,000 students, more than 1500 professors and more Nobel laureates than you could point a particle accelerator at.

From Telegraph Ave, enter the campus via Sproul Plaza and Sather Gate, a center for people-watching, soapbox oration and pseudotribal drumming. Or you can enter from Center St and Oxford Lane, near the downtown BART station.

UC Berkeley Art Museum MUSEUM

(☎510-642-0808; www.bampfa.berkeley.edu; 2626 Bancroft Way; adult/student $10/7, 1st Thu each month free; ⏰11am-5pm Wed-Sun) The museum has 11 galleries showcasing a huge range of works, from ancient Chinese to cutting-edge contemporary. The complex also houses a bookstore, cafe and sculpture garden. The museum and the much-loved Pacific Film Archive (see p140) are scheduled to move to a new home on Oxford St between Addison and Center Streets by 2014.

Campanile TOWER

(elevator rides $2; ⏰10am-4pm Mon-Fri, to 5pm Sat, to 1:30pm & 3-5pm Sun) Officially called Sather Tower, the Campanile was modeled on St Mark's Basilica in Venice. The 328ft spire offers fine views of the Bay Area, and at the top you can stare up into the carillon of 61 bells, ranging from the size of a cereal bowl to that of a Volkswagen. Recitals take place daily at 7:50am, noon and 6pm, with a longer piece performed at 2pm on Sunday.

FREE **Museum of Paleontology** MUSEUM

(☎510-642-1821; www.ucmp.berkeley.edu; ⏰8am-10pm Mon-Thu, to 5pm Fri, 10am-5pm Sat, 1-10pm Sun) Housed in the ornate Valley Life Sciences Building (and primarily a research facility that's closed to the public), you can see a number of fossil exhibits in the atrium, including a *Tyrannosaurus rex* skeleton.

Bancroft Library LIBRARY

(☎510-642-3781; http://bancroft.berkeley.edu; ⏰10am-5pm Mon-Fri) The Bancroft houses, among other gems, the papers of Mark Twain, a copy of Shakespeare's First Folio and the records of the Donner Party (see the boxed text, p378). Its small public exhibits of historical Californiana include the surprisingly small gold nugget that sparked the 1849 Gold Rush. You must register to use the library and, to do so, you need to be 18 years of age (or to have graduated from high school) and present two forms of identification (one with a photo). Stop by the registration desk on your way in.

FREE **Phoebe Hearst Museum of Anthropology** MUSEUM

(☎510-643-7649; http://hearstmuseum.berkeley.edu; ⏰10am-4:30pm Wed-Sat, noon-4pm Sun) South of the Campanile in Kroeber Hall, this museum includes exhibits from indigenous cultures around the world, including ancient Peruvian, Egyptian and African items. There's also a large collection highlighting native Californian cultures.

SOUTH OF CAMPUS

Telegraph Ave STREET

Telegraph Ave has traditionally been the throbbing heart of studentville in Berkeley, the sidewalks crowded with undergrads, postdocs and youthful shoppers squeezing their way past throngs of vendors, buskers and homeless people. Numerous cafes and budget food options cater to students, and most of them are very good.

The frenetic energy buzzing from the university's Sather Gate on any given day is a mixture of youthful posthippies reminiscing about days before their time and young hipsters and punk rockers who sneer at tie-dyed nostalgia. Panhandlers press you for change, and street stalls hawk everything from crystals to bumper stickers to self-published tracts.

People's Park PARK

This park, just east of Telegraph, between Haste St and Dwight Way, is a marker in local history as a political battleground between residents and the city and state government in the late 1960s. The park has since served mostly as a gathering spot for Berkeley's homeless. A publicly funded restoration spruced it up a bit, and occasional festivals do still happen here, but it's rather run-down.

Elmwood District DISTRICT

South along College Ave is the Elmwood District, a charming nook of shops and restaurants that offers a calming alternative to the frenetic buzz around Telegraph Ave. Continue further south and you'll be in Rockridge.

First Church of Christ Scientist CHURCH

(www.friendsoffirstchurch.org; 2619 Dwight Way; ⏲services Sun) Bernard Maybeck's impressive 1910 church uses concrete and wood in its blend of Arts and Crafts, Asian and Gothic influences. Maybeck was a professor of architecture at UC Berkeley and designed San Francisco's Palace of Fine Arts, plus many landmark homes in the Berkeley Hills. Free tours happen the first Sunday of every month at 12:15pm.

Julia Morgan Theatre THEATER

(☎510-845-8542; 2640 College Ave) To the southeast of People's Park is this beautifully understated, redwood-infused 1910 theater, a performance space (formerly a church) created by Bay Area architect Julia Morgan. She designed numerous Bay Area buildings and, most famously, the Hearst Castle (see p481).

DOWNTOWN

Berkeley's downtown, centered on Shattuck Ave between University Ave and Dwight Way, has far fewer traces of the city's tie-dyed reputation. The area has emerged as an exciting arts district with numerous shops and restaurants and restored public buildings. At the center are the acclaimed thespian stomping grounds of the Berkeley Repertory Theatre (see p140) and the Aurora Theatre Company (see p141) and live music at the Freight & Salvage Coffeehouse (see p140); a few good movie houses are also nearby.

NORTH BERKELEY

Not too far north of campus is a neighborhood filled with lovely garden-front homes, parks and some of the best restaurants in California. The popular **Gourmet Ghetto** stretches along Shattuck Ave north of University Ave for several blocks, anchored by Chez Panisse (see p139). Northwest of here, **Solano Ave**, which crosses from Berkeley into Albany, is lined with lots of funky shops and more good restaurants.

On Euclid Ave just south of Eunice St is the **Berkeley Rose Garden** and its eight terraces of colourful explosions. Here you'll find quiet benches and a plethora of almost perpetually blooming roses arranged by hue. Across the street is a picturesque park with a children's playground (including a very fun concrete slide, about 100ft long).

THE BERKELEY HILLS

Tilden Regional Park PARK

(www.ebparks.org/parks/tilden) This 2079-acre park, in the hills east of town, is Berkeley's crown jewel. It has more than 30 miles of trails of varying difficulty, from paved paths to hilly scrambles, including part of the magnificent Bay Area Ridge Trail. Other attractions include a miniature steam train ($2), a children's farm, a wonderfully wild-looking botanical garden, an 18-hole **golf course** (☎510-848-7373) and environmental education center. **Lake Anza** is a favorite area for picnics, and from spring through late fall you can swim here for $3.50. AC Transit bus 67 runs to the park on weekends and holidays from the downtown BART station, but only stops at the entrances on weekdays.

UC Botanical Garden GARDENS

(☎510-643-2755; http://botanicalgarden.berkeley.edu; 200 Centennial Dr; adult/child 13-17/child 5-12 $9/5/2, 1st Thu of month free; ⏲9am-5pm, closed 1st Tue of month) This is another great find in the hills, in Strawberry Canyon. With 34 acres and more than 12,000 species of plants, the garden is one of the most varied collections in the USA. It can be reached via the Bear Transit shuttle H line.

The nearby fire trail is a woodsy walking loop around Strawberry Canyon that has great views of town and the off-limits Lawrence Berkeley National Laboratory. Enter at the trailhead at the parking lot on Centennial Dr just southwest of the Botanical Garden; you'll emerge near the Lawrence Hall of Science.

Central Berkeley

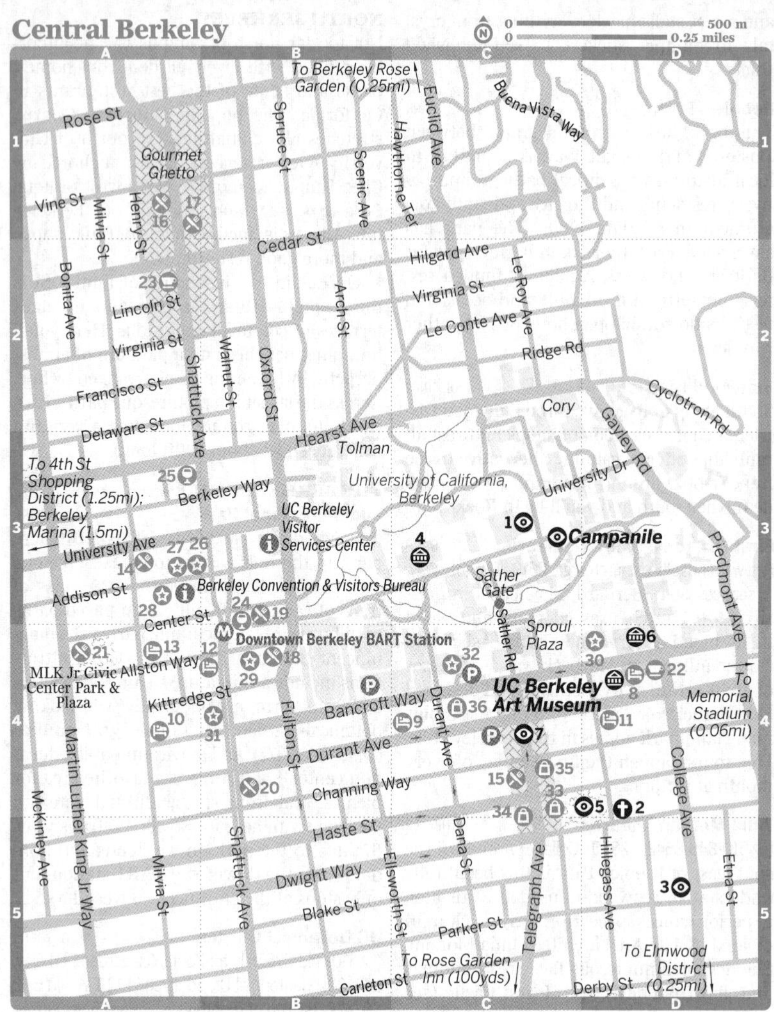

Lawrence Hall of Science SCIENCE CENTER
(☎510-642-5132; www.lawrencehallofscience.org; Centennial Dr; adult/senior & child 7-8/child 3-6 $12/9/6; ⊙10am-5pm daily; 👪) Near Grizzly Peak Blvd, the science hall is named after Ernest Lawrence, who won the Nobel Prize for his invention of the cyclotron particle accelerator. He was a key member of the WWII Manhattan Project, and he's also the name behind the Lawrence Berkeley and Lawrence Livermore laboratories. The Hall of Science has a huge collection of interactive exhibits for kids and adults on subjects ranging from earthquakes to nanotechnology, and outside there's a 60ft model of a DNA molecule. AC Transit bus 65 runs to the hall from the downtown BART station. You can also catch the university's Bear Transit shuttle (H line) from the Hearst Mining Circle.

WEST BERKELEY

San Pablo Ave STREET
Formerly US Rte 40, this was the main thoroughfare from the east before I-80 came along. The area north of University Ave is still lined with a few older motels, diners and atmospheric dive bars with neon signs. South of University Ave are pockets of trend-

Central Berkeley

Top Sights

Campanile ... C3
UC Berkeley Art Museum ... D4

Sights

1 Bancroft Library ... C3
2 First Church of Christ Scientist ... D4
3 Julia Morgan Theatre ... D5
4 Museum of Paleontology ... C3
5 People's Park ... D4
6 Phoebe Hearst Museum of Anthropology ... D4
7 Telegraph Avenue ... C4

Sleeping

8 Bancroft Hotel ... D4
9 Berkeley City Club ... C4
10 Downtown Berkeley Inn ... A4
11 Hotel Durant ... D4
12 Hotel Shattuck Plaza ... B4
13 YMCA ... A4

Eating

14 Au Coquelet Café ... A3
15 Café Intermezzo ... C4
16 Cheese Board Collective ... A1
17 Chez Panisse ... A1
18 Gather ... B4
19 Ippuku ... B3
20 La Note ... B4
21 Saturday Berkeley Farmers Market ... A4

Drinking

22 Caffe Strada ... D4
23 Guerilla Café ... A2
24 Jupiter ... B3
25 Triple Rock Brewery & Ale House ... A3

Entertainment

26 Aurora Theatre Company ... A3
27 Berkeley Repertory Theatre ... A3
28 Freight & Salvage Coffeehouse ... A3
29 Marsh ... B4
30 Pacific Film Archive ... D4
31 Shattuck Down Low ... B4
32 Zellerbach Hall ... C4

Shopping

33 Amoeba Music ... C4
34 Moe's ... C4
35 Rasputin ... C4
36 University Press Books ... C4

iness, such as the short stretch of gift shops and cafes around Dwight Way.

4th St Shopping District DISTRICT
Hidden within an industrial area near I-80 lies a three-block area offering shaded sidewalks for upscale shopping or just strolling, and a few good restaurants.

Berkeley Marina MARINA
At the west end of University Ave is the marina, frequented by squawking seagulls, silent types fishing from the pier, unleashed dogs and, especially on windy weekends, lots of colorful kites. Construction of the marina began in 1936, though the pier has much older origins. It was originally built in the 1870s, then replaced by a 3-mile-long ferry pier in 1920 (its length was dictated by the extreme shallowness of the bay). Part of the original pier is now rebuilt, affording visitors sweeping bay views.

Adventure Playground PLAYGROUND
(510-981-6720; www.cityofberkeley.info/marina; 11am-4pm Sat & Sun, closed last week of year;) At the marina is one of the coolest play spaces in the country – a free outdoor park encouraging creativity and cooperation where supervised kids of any age can help build and paint their own structures. Dress the tykes in play clothes, because they *will* get dirty.

FREE **Takara Sake** MUSEUM
(www.takarasake.com; 708 Addison St; noon-6pm) Stop in to see the traditional wooden tools used for making sake and a short video of the brewing process. Tours of the factory aren't offered, but you can view elements of modern production and bottling through a window. Flights ($5) are available in a spacious tasting room constructed with reclaimed wood and floor tiles fashioned from recycled glass.

Sleeping

Lodging rates spike during special university events like graduation (mid-May) and home football games. A number of older motels along University Ave can be handy during peak demand. For B&B options, see the Berkeley & Oakland Bed & Breakfast Network (p128).

TOP CHOICE **Hotel Shattuck Plaza** BOUTIQUE HOTEL $$$
(☎510-845-7300; www.hotelshattuckplaza.com; 2086 Allston Way; r $219-59; ❄@☎) Peace is quite posh following a $15 million renovation and greening of this 100-year-old downtown jewel. A foyer of red Italian glass lighting, flocked Victorian-style wallpaper – and yes, a peace sign tiled into the floor – leads to comfortable rooms with down comforters, and an airy and columned restaurant serving all meals. Accommodations off Shattuck are the quietest, and Cityscape rooms boast bay views.

Hotel Durant BOUTIQUE HOTEL $$
(☎510-845-8981; www.hoteldurant.com; 2600 Durant Ave; r from $134; @☎) Located a block from campus, this classic 1928 hotel has been cheekily renovated to highlight the connection to the university. The lobby is adorned with embarrassing yearbook photos and a ceiling mobile of exam books, and smallish rooms have dictionary-covered shower curtains and bongs repurposed into bedside lamps.

Berkeley City Club HISTORIC HOTEL $$
(☎510-848-7800; www.berkeleycityclub.com; 2315 Durant Ave; r/ste incl breakfast from $145/235; @☎) Designed by Julia Morgan, the architect of Hearst Castle (see p481), the 36 rooms and dazzling common areas of this refurbished 1929 historic landmark building (which is also a private club) feel like a glorious time warp into a more refined era. The hotel contains lush and serene Italianate courtyards, gardens and terraces, and a stunning indoor pool. Elegant Old-World rooms contain no TVs, and those with numbers ending in 4 and 8 have to-die-for views of the bay and the Golden Gate Bridge.

Bancroft Hotel HISTORIC HOTEL $$
(☎510-549-1000, 800-549-1002; www.bancrofthotel.com; 2680 Bancroft Way; r incl breakfast $129-149; @☎) A gorgeous 1928 Arts and Crafts building that was originally a women's club, the Bancroft is just across the street from campus and two blocks from Telegraph Ave. It has 22 comfortable, beautifully furnished rooms (number 302 boasts a lovely balcony) and a spectacular bay-view rooftop, though no elevator.

YMCA HOSTEL $
(☎510-848-6800; www.ymca-cba.org/downtown-berkeley; 2001 Allston Way; s/d $49/81; @☎) Recently remodeled with new bedding and carpet, the 100-year-old downtown Y building is still the best budget option in town. Rates for the austere private rooms (all with shared bathroom) include use of the sauna, pool and fitness center, and kitchen facilities, and wheelchair accessible rooms are available as well. Corner rooms 310 and 410 boast enviable bay views. Entrance on Milvia St.

Downtown Berkeley Inn MOTEL $
(☎510-843-4043; www.downtownberkeleyinn.com; 2001 Bancroft Way; r $89-109; ❄☎) A 27-room budget boutique-style motel with good-sized rooms and correspondingly ample flat-screen TVs.

Rose Garden Inn INN $$
(☎510-549-2145, 800-922-9005; www.rosegardeninn.com; 2740 Telegraph Ave; r incl breakfast $98-185; @☎) The decor flirting with flowery, this cute place is a few blocks south from the Telegraph Ave action and very peaceful, with two old houses surrounded by pretty gardens.

Eating

Telegraph Ave is packed with cafes, pizza counters and cheap restaurants, and Berkeley's Little India runs along the University Ave corridor. Many more restaurants can be found downtown along Shattuck Ave near the BART station. The section of Shattuck Ave north of University Ave is the 'Gourmet Ghetto,' home to lots of excellent eating establishments.

DOWNTOWN & AROUND CAMPUS

Gather AMERICAN $$
(☎510-809-0400; www.gatherrestaurant.com; 2200 Oxford St; lunch mains $10-17, dinner mains $14-19; ⊙11:30am-2pm Mon-Fri, 10am-2:30pm Sat & Sun, & 5-10pm daily; ☑) When vegan foodies and passionate farm-to-table types dine out together, they often end up here. Inside a salvaged wood interior punctuated by green vines streaking down over an open kitchen, patrons swoon over dishes created from locally sourced ingredients and sustainably raised meats. Reserve for dinner.

TOP CHOICE **Ippuku** JAPANESE $$
(☎510-665-1969; www.ippukuberkeley.com; 2130 Center St; small plates $5-18; ⊙5-11pm) Specializing in *shochu* (flights $12), a distilled alcohol made from rice, barley or sweet potato, Japanese expats gush that Ippuku reminds

them of *izakayas* (pub-style restaurants) back in Tokyo. Choose from a menu of skewered meats and settle in at one of the traditional wood platform tables (no shoes, please) or cozy booth perches. Reservations essential.

La Note FRENCH **$$**
(☎510-843-1535; www.lanoterestaurant.com; 2377 Shattuck Ave; mains $10-17; ⏰8am-2:30pm Mon-Fri, to 3pm Sat & Sun, & 6-10pm Thu-Sat) A rustic country-French bistro downtown, La Note serves excellent breakfasts. Wake up to a big bowl of café au lait, paired with oatmeal raspberry pancakes or lemon gingerbread pancakes with poached pears. Anticipate a wait on weekends.

Café Intermezzo CAFETERIA **$**
(2442 Telegraph Ave; sandwiches & salads $6.50) Mammoth salads draw a constant crowd, and we're not talking about delicate little rabbit food plates. Bring a friend, or you might drown while trying to polish off a Veggie Delight heaped with beans, hard-boiled egg and avocado.

Au Coquelet Café CAFE **$**
(www.aucoquelet.com; 2000 University Ave; mains $6-9; ⏰6am-1am Sun-Thu, to 1:30am Sat & Sun; 📶) Open till late, Au Coquelet is a popular stop for postmovie meals or late-night studying. The front section serves coffee and pastries while the skylit and spacious back room does a big range of omelets, pastas, sandwiches, burgers and salads.

Berkeley Farmers Market MARKET **$**
(⏰10am-3pm Sat) Pick up some organic produce or tasty prepared food at the downtown farmers market, operating year-round, at Center St and MLK Way, and sit down to munch at MLK Park across from city hall.

NORTH BERKELEY

TOP CHOICE **Chez Panisse** AMERICAN **$$$**
(☎restaurant 510-548-5525, cafe 510-548-5049; www.chezpanisse.com; 1517 Shattuck Ave; restaurant mains $60-95, cafe mains $18-29; ⏰restaurant dinner Mon-Sat, cafe lunch & dinner Mon-Sat) Foodies come to worship here at the church of Alice Waters, the inventor of California cuisine. The restaurant is as good and popular as it ever was, and despite its fame the place has retained a welcoming atmosphere. It's in a lovely Arts and Crafts house in the Gourmet Ghetto, and you can choose to pull all the stops with a prix-fixe meal downstairs, or go less expensive and a tad less formal in the cafe upstairs. Reserve weeks ahead.

Cheese Board Collective PIZZERIA **$**
(☎510-549-3183; www.cheeseboardcollective.coop; 1504 & 1512 Shattuck Ave; pizza slice $2.50; 🌿) Stop in to take stock of the over 300 cheeses available at this worker-owned business, and scoop up some fresh bread to make a picnic lunch. Or sit down for a slice of the fabulously crispy one-option-per-day veggie pizza just next door, where live music's often featured.

WEST BERKELEY

🌿 **Vik's Chaat Corner** INDIAN **$**
(www.vikschaatcorner.com; 2390 4th St; dishes $5-7; ⏰11am-6pm Mon-Thu, to 8pm Fri-Sun; 🌿) This longtime and very popular *chaat* house has moved to a larger space but still gets mobbed at lunchtime by regulars that include an equal number of hungry office workers and Indian families. Try a *cholle* (spicy garbanzo curry) or one of the many filling *dosas* (savory crepes) from the weekend menu. It's on the corner of Channing Way, one block east of the waterfront.

Bette's Oceanview Diner DINER **$**
(☎510-644-3230; www.bettesdiner.com; 1807 4th St; mains $7-11; ⏰6:30am-2:30pm Mon-Fri, to 4pm Sat & Sun) A buzzing breakfast spot, especially on the weekends, serving yummy baked soufflé pancakes and German-style potato pancakes with applesauce, plus eggs and sandwiches. Superfresh food and a nifty diner interior make it worth the wait. It's about a block north of University Ave.

Drinking

🌿 **Guerilla Café** CAFE
(☎510-845-2233; www.guerillacafe.com; 1620 Shattuck Ave) Exuding a 1970s flavor, this small and sparkling cafe has a creative political vibe, with polka-dot tiles on the counter handmade by one of the artist-owners, and order numbers spotlighting guerillas and liberation revolutionaries. Organic and Fair Trade ingredients feature in the breakfasts and panini sandwiches, and locally roasted Blue Bottle coffee is served. Occasional film screenings and pop-up cuisine nights pack the place.

Caffe Strada CAFE
(2300 College Ave; 📶) A popular, student-saturated hangout with an inviting shaded patio and strong espressos. Try the signature white chocolate mocha.

Jupiter PUB
(www.jupiterbeer.com; 2181 Shattuck Ave) This downtown pub has loads of regional microbrews, a beer garden, good pizza and live bands most nights. Sit upstairs for a bird's-eye view of bustling Shattuck Ave.

Casa Vino WINE BAR
(www.casavinobistro.com; 3136 Sacramento St) A few blocks west of Ashby BART, this unpretentious and somewhat nondescript wine bar serves an eyebrow-raising 95 wines by the glass. Relax on the outdoor patio during warm nights.

Albatross PUB
(www.albatrosspub.com; 1822 San Pablo Ave;) A block north of University Ave, Berkeley's oldest pub is one of the most inviting and friendly in the entire Bay Area. Some serious darts are played here, and boardgames will be going on around many of the worn-out tables. Sunday is Pub Quiz night.

Triple Rock Brewery & Ale House BREWERY
(1920 Shattuck Ave) Opened in 1986, Triple Rock was one of the country's first brewpubs. The house beers and pub grub are quite good, and the antique wooden bar and rooftop sun deck are delightful.

☆ Entertainment

The arts corridor on Addison St between Milvia and Shattuck Sts anchors a lively downtown entertainment scene.

Live Music

Berkeley has plenty of intimate live music venues. Cover charges range from $5 to $20, and a number of venues are all-ages or 18-and-over.

924 Gilman PUNK ROCK
(www.924gilman.org; 924 Gilman St; Fri-Sun) This volunteer-run and booze-free all-ages space is a West Coast punk rock institution. Take AC Transit bus 9 from Berkeley BART.

Freight & Salvage Coffeehouse FOLK, WORLD
(510-644-2020; www.thefreight.org; 2020 Addison St;) This legendary club has over 40 years of history and recently relocated to the downtown arts district. It still features great traditional folk and world music and welcomes all ages, with half price tickets for patrons under 21.

Shattuck Down Low CLUB
(510-548-1159; www.shattuckdownlow.com; 2284 Shattuck Ave) A fun multiethnic crowd fills this basement space that sometimes books big-name bands. Locals love the Tuesday karaoke nights and the smokin' all-levels-welcome salsa on Wednesdays.

La Peña Cultural Center WORLD
(510-849-2568; www.lapena.org; 3105 Shattuck Ave) A few blocks east of the Ashby BART station, this cultural center and Chilean cafe presents dynamic musical and visual arts programming with a peace and justice bent. Look for the vibrant mural on its facade.

Ashkenaz FOLK, WORLD
(510-525-5054; www.ashkenaz.com; 1317 San Pablo Ave;) Ashkenaz is a 'music and dance community center' attracting activists, hippies and fans of folk, swing and world music who love to dance (lessons offered).

Cinemas

Pacific Film Archive CINEMA
(510-642-1124; www.bampfa.berkeley.edu; 2575 Bancroft Way; adult/student & senior $9.50/6.50) A world-renowned film center with an ever-changing schedule of international and classic films, cineastes should seek this place out. The spacious theater has seats that are comfy enough for hours-long movie marathons.

Theater & Dance

Zellerbach Hall PERFORMING ARTS
(510-642-9988; http://tickets.berkeley.edu) On the south end of campus near Bancroft Way and Dana St, Zellerbach Hall features dance events, concerts and performances of all types by national and international artists. The onsite **Cal Performances Ticket Office** sells tickets without a handling fee.

Berkeley Repertory Theatre THEATER
(510-647-2949; www.berkeleyrep.org; 2025 Addison St) This highly respected company has produced bold versions of classical and modern plays since 1968.

California Shakespeare Theater THEATER
(510-548-9666; www.calshakes.org; box office 701 Heinz Ave) Headquartered in Berkeley, with a fantastic outdoor amphitheater further east in Orinda, 'Cal Shakes' is a warm-weather tradition of al fresco Shakespeare (and other classic) productions, with a season that lasts from about June through September.

Aurora Theatre Company THEATER
(☎510-843-4822; www.auroratheatre.org; 2081 Addison St) An intimate downtown theater, it performs contemporary and thought-provoking plays staged with a subtle chamber-theater aesthetic.

Marsh PERFORMING ARTS
(☎510-704-8291; www.themarsh.org; 2120 Allston Way) The 'breeding ground for new performance' now has a Berkeley toehold for eclectic solo and comedy acts.

Shotgun Players THEATER
(☎510-841-6500; www.shotgunplayers.org; 1901 Ashby Avenue) The country's first all-solar-powered theater company stages exciting and provocative work in an intimate space. Across from the Ashby BART station.

Sports

Memorial Stadium, which dates from 1923, is the university's 71,000-seat sporting venue, and the Hayward Fault runs just beneath it. On alternate years, it's the site of the famous football frenzy between the UC Berkeley and Stanford teams.

The **Cal Athletic Ticket Office** (☎800-462-3277; www.calbears.com) has ticket information on all UC Berkeley sports events. Keep in mind that some sell out weeks in advance.

Shopping

Branching off the UC campus, Telegraph Ave caters mostly to students, hawking a steady dose of urban hippie gear, handmade sidewalk-vendor jewelry and head-shop paraphernalia. Audiophiles will swoon over the music stores. Other shopping corridors include College Ave in the Elmwood District, 4th St (north of University Ave) and Solano Ave.

Amoeba Music MUSIC
(☎510-549-1125; 2455 Telegraph Ave) If you're a music junkie, you might plan on spending a few hours at the original Berkeley branch of Amoeba Music, packed with massive quantities of new and used CDs, DVDs, tapes and records (yes, lots of vinyl).

Moe's BOOKS
(☎510-849-2087; 2476 Telegraph Ave) A long-standing local favorite, Moe's offers four floors of new, used and remaindered books for hours of browsing.

University Press Books BOOKS
(☎510-548-0585; 2430 Bancroft Way) Across the street from campus, this academic and scholarly bookstore stocks works by UC Berkeley professors and other academic and museum publishers.

Down Home Music MUSIC
(☎510-525-2129; 10341 San Pablo Ave, El Cerrito) North of Berkeley in El Cerrito, this world-class store for roots, blues, folk, Latin and world music is affiliated with the Arhoolie record label, which has been issuing landmark recordings since the early 1960s.

Rasputin MUSIC
(☎800-350-8700; 2401 Telegraph Ave) Another large music store full of new and used releases.

Marmot Mountain Works OUTDOOR EQUIPMENT
(☎510-849-0735; 3049 Adeline St) Has climbing, ski and backpacking equipment for sale and for rent. Located one block north of Ashby BART station.

North Face Outlet OUTDOOR EQUIPMENT
(☎510-526-3530; cnr 5th & Gilman Sts) Discount store for the well-respected Bay Area-based brand of outdoor gear. It's a few blocks west of San Pablo Ave.

REI OUTDOOR EQUIPMENT
(☎510-527-4140; 1338 San Pablo Ave) This large and busy co-op lures in active folks for camping and mountaineering rentals, sports clothing and all kinds of nifty outdoor gear.

Information

Alta Bates Summit Medical Center (☎510-204-4444; 2450 Ashby Ave) 24-hour emergency services.

Berkeley Convention & Visitors Bureau (☎510-549-7040, 800-847-4823; www.visitberkeley.com; 2030 Addison St; ⏲9am-1pm & 2-5pm Mon-Fri) This helpful bureau has a free visitors guide.

UC Berkeley Visitor Services Center (☎510-642-5215; http://visitors.berkeley.edu; 101 Sproul Hall) Campus maps and information available. Free 90-minute campus tours are given at 10am Monday to Saturday and 1pm Sunday; reservations required.

Getting There & Away

BART

The easiest way to travel between San Francisco, Berkeley, Oakland and other East Bay points is on **BART** (☎510-465-2278, 511; www.bart.gov). Trains run approximately every 10 minutes

SHAKE, RATTLE & ROLL

Curious to find a few places where the earth shook? Visit these notorious spots in and around the Bay Area:

» **Earthquake Trail** (p124) at Point Reyes National Seashore shows the effects of the big one in 1906.

» Forty-two people died when the Cypress Freeway collapsed in West Oakland, one of the most horrifying and enduring images of the 1989 Loma Prieta quake. The **Cypress Freeway Memorial Park** at 14th St and Mandela Parkway commemorates those who perished and those who helped rescue survivors.

» Near Aptos in Santa Cruz County, a sign on the Aptos Creek Trail in the **Forest of Nisene Marks State Park** (☎831-763-7062; www.parks.ca.gov) marks the actual epicenter of the Loma Prieta quake, and on the Big Slide Trail a number of fissures can be spotted.

» The Hayward Fault runs just beneath **Memorial Stadium** (p141) at UC Berkeley.

from 4am to midnight on weekdays, with limited service from 6am on Saturday and from 8am on Sunday.

To get to Berkeley, catch a Richmond-bound train to one of three BART stations: Ashby (Adeline St and Ashby Ave), Downtown Berkeley (Shattuck Ave and Center St) or North Berkeley (Sacramento and Delaware Sts). The fare ranges from $3.50 to $3.85 between Berkeley and San Francisco; $1.75 between Berkeley and downtown Oakland. After 8pm on weekdays, 7pm on Saturday and all day Sunday, there is no direct service operating from San Francisco to Berkeley; instead, catch a Pittsburg/Bay Point train and transfer at 19th St station in Oakland.

A **BART-to-Bus** transfer ticket, available from white AC Transit machines near the BART turnstiles, reduces the connecting bus fare by 25¢.

Bus

The regional company **AC Transit** (☎510-817-1717, 511; www.actransit.org) operates a number of buses from San Francisco's **Transbay Temporary Terminal** (Howard & Main Sts) to the East Bay. The F line leaves from the Transbay Temporary Terminal to the corner of University and Shattuck Aves approximately every half-hour ($4.20, 30 minutes).

Between Berkeley and downtown Oakland ($2.10) on weekdays, take the fast and frequent 1R bus along Telegraph Ave between the two city centers, or bus 18 that runs daily via Martin Luther King Jr Way. Bus 51B travels along University Ave from Berkeley BART to the Berkeley Marina.

Car & Motorcycle

With your own wheels you can approach Berkeley from San Francisco by taking the Bay Bridge and then following either I-80 (for University Ave, downtown Berkeley and the UCB campus) or Hwy 24 (for College Ave and the Berkeley Hills).

Driving to San Francisco, the bridge toll is $4 to $6, depending on the time and day of the week.

Train

Amtrak does stop in Berkeley, but the shelter is not staffed and direct connections are few. More convenient is the nearby **Emeryville Amtrak station** (☎800-872-7245; www.amtrak.com; 5885 Horton St), a few miles south.

To reach the Emeryville station from downtown Berkeley, take a Transbay F bus or ride BART to the MacArthur station and then take the free Emery Go Round bus (Hollis route) to Amtrak.

ℹ Getting Around

Public transportation, cycling and walking are the best options for getting around central Berkeley.

BICYCLE Cycling is a popular means of transportation, and safe and well-marked 'bicycle boulevards' with signed distance information to landmarks make crosstown journeys very easy. Just north of Berkeley, **Solano Avenue Cyclery** (☎510-524-1094; 1554 Solano Ave, Albany; ⏰Mon-Sat) has 24-hour mountain- and road-bike rentals for $35 to $45.

BUS AC Transit operates public buses in and around Berkeley, and UC Berkeley's **Bear Transit** (http://pt.berkeley.edu/around/transit/routes) runs a shuttle from the downtown BART station to various points on campus ($1). From its stop at the Hearst Mining Circle, the H Line runs along Centennial Dr to the higher parts of the campus.

CAR & MOTORCYCLE Drivers should note that numerous barriers have been set up to prevent car traffic from traversing residential streets at high speeds, so zigzagging is necessary in some neighborhoods.

Mt Diablo State Park

Collecting a light dusting of snowflakes on the coldest days of winter, at 3849ft Mt Diablo is more than 1000ft higher than Mt Tamalpais in Marin County. On a clear day (early on a winter morning is a good bet) the views from Diablo's summit are vast and sweeping. To the west you can see over the bay and out to the Farallon Islands; to the east you can see over the Central Valley to the Sierra Nevada.

The **Mt Diablo State Park** (925-837-2525; www.mdia.org; per vehicle $6-10; 8am-sunset) has 50 miles of hiking trails, and can be reached from Walnut Creek, Danville or Clayton. You can also drive to the top, where there's a **visitors center** (10am-4pm). The park office is at the junction of the two entry roads. Of the three **campgrounds** (800-444-7275; www.reserveamerica.com; tent & RV sites $30), Juniper has showers, though all can be closed during high fire danger.

John Muir National Historic Site

Less than 15 miles north of Walnut Creek, the **John Muir residence** (925-228-8860; www.nps.gov/jomu; 4202 Alhambra Ave, Martinez; adult/child $3/free; 10am-5pm Wed-Sun) sits in a pastoral patch of farmland in bustling, modern Martinez. Though he wrote of sauntering the High Sierra with a sack of tea and bread, it may be a shock for those familiar with the iconic Sierra Club founder's ascetic weather-beaten appearance that the house (built by his father-in-law) is a model of Victorian Italianate refinement, with a tower cupola, a daintily upholstered parlor and splashes of fussy white lace. His 'scribble den' has been left as it was during his life, with crumbled papers overflowing from wire wastebaskets and dried bread balls – his preferred snack – resting on the mantelpiece. Acres of his fruit orchard still stand, and visitors can enjoy seasonal samples. The grounds include the 1849 **Martinez Adobe**, part of the rancho on which the house was built.

The park is just north of Hwy 4, and accessible by **County Connection** (http://cccta.org) buses from Amtrak and BART.

Vallejo

For one week in 1852 Vallejo was officially the California state capital – but the fickle legislature changed its mind. It tried Vallejo a second time in 1853, but after a month moved on again (to Benicia). That same year, Vallejo became the site of the first US naval installation on the West Coast (Mare Island Naval Shipyard, now closed). **Vallejo Naval & Historical Museum** (707-643-0077; www.vallejomuseum.org; 734 Marin St; admission $5; noon-4pm Tue-Sat) tells the story.

The town's biggest tourist draw, though, is **Six Flags Discovery Kingdom** (707-643-6722; www.sixflags.com/discoverykingdom; adult/child under 4ft $50/36; approx 10:30am-6pm Fri-Sun spring & fall, to 8pm or 9pm daily summer, variable weekend & holiday hr Dec), a modern wildlife and theme park offering mighty coasters and other rides alongside animal shows featuring sharks and a killer whale. Significant discounts are available on the park's website. Exit I-80 at Hwy 37 westbound, 5 miles north of downtown Vallejo. Parking is $15.

Operated by Blue & Gold Fleet, **Vallejo Baylink Ferry** (877-643-3779; www.baylinkferry.com; one way adult/child $13/6.50) runs ferries from San Francisco's Pier 41 at Fisherman's Wharf and the Ferry Building to Vallejo; the

WORTH A TRIP

EAST BROTHER LIGHT STATION

Most Bay Area residents have never heard of this speck of an island off the East Bay city of Richmond, and even fewer know that the **East Brother Light Station** (510-233-2385; www.ebls.org; d incl breakfast & dinner $355-415; Thu-Sun) is a extraordinary five-room Victorian B&B. Spend the night in the romantic lighthouse or fog signal building (the foghorn is used from October through March), where every window has stupendous bay views and harbor seals frolic in the frigid currents. Resident innkeepers serve afternoon hors d'oeuvres and champagne, and between gourmet meals you can stroll around the breezy one-acre islet and rummage through historical photos and artifacts journey takes one hour. Discount admission and transportation packages for Six Flags are available from San Francisco.

Vallejo is also somewhat of a gateway to the Wine Country. See p157 and p163.

THE PENINSULA

South of San Francisco, squeezed tightly between the bay and the coastal foothills, a vast swath of suburbia continues to San Jose and beyond. Dotted within this area are Palo Alto, Stanford University and Silicon Valley, the center of the Bay Area's immense tech industry. West of the foothills, Hwy 1 runs down the Pacific coast via Half Moon Bay and a string of beaches to Santa Cruz. Hwy 101 and I-280 both run to San Jose, where they connect with Hwy 17, the quickest route to Santa Cruz. Any of these routes can be combined into an interesting loop or extended to the Monterey Peninsula.

And don't bother looking for Silicon Valley on the map – you won't find it. Because silicon chips form the basis of modern microcomputers, and the Santa Clara Valley – stretching from Palo Alto down through Mountain View, Sunnyvale, Cupertino and Santa Clara to San Jose – is thought of as the birthplace of the microcomputer, it's been dubbed 'Silicon Valley.' The Santa Clara Valley is wide and flat, and its towns are essentially a string of shopping centers and industrial parks linked by a maze of freeways. It's hard to imagine that even after WWII this area was still a wide expanse of orchards and farms.

San Francisco to San Jose

South of the San Francisco peninsula, I-280 is the dividing line between the densely populated South Bay area and the rugged and lightly populated Pacific Coast. With sweeping views of hills and reservoirs, I-280 is a more scenic choice than crowded Hwy 101, which runs through miles of boring business parks. Unfortunately, these parallel north-south arteries are both clogged with traffic during commute times and often on weekends.

A historic site where European explorers first set eyes on San Francisco Bay, **Sweeney Ridge** (www.nps.gov/goga/planyourvisit/upload/sb-sweeney-2008.pdf), straddles a prime spot between Pacifica and San Bruno, and offers hikers unparalleled ocean and bay views. From I-280, exit at Sneath Lane and follow it 2 miles west until it dead ends at the trailhead.

Right on the bay at the northern edge of San Mateo, 4 miles south of San Francisco International Airport, is **Coyote Point Recreation Area** (per vehicle $5; 👪), a popular park and windsurfing destination. The main attraction – formerly known as the Coyote Point Museum – is **CuriOdyssey** (☎650-342-7755; www.curiodyssey.org; adult/child $8/4; ⏰10am-5pm Tue-Sat, noon-5pm Sun, free 1st Sun of month; 👪), with innovative exhibits for kids and adults concentrating on ecological and environmental issues. Exit Hwy 101 at Coyote Point Dr.

San Jose

Though culturally diverse and historic, San Jose has always been in San Francisco's shadow, awash in Silicon Valley's suburbia. Founded in 1777 as El Pueblo de San José de Guadalupe, San Jose is California's oldest Spanish civilian settlement. Its downtown is small and scarcely used for a city of its size, though it does bustle with 20-something clubgoers on the weekends. Industrial parks, high-tech computer firms and look-alike housing developments have sprawled across the city's landscape, taking over where farms, ranches and open spaces once spread between the bay and the surrounding hills.

Sights

Downtown San Jose is at the junction of Hwy 87 and I-280. Hwy 101 and I-880 complete the box. Running roughly north-south along the length of the city, from the old port town of Alviso on the San Francisco Bay all the way downtown, is 1st St; south of I-280, its name changes to Monterey Hwy.

San Jose State University is immediately east of downtown, and the SoFA district, with numerous nightclubs, restaurants and galleries, is on a stretch of S 1st St south of San Carlos St.

TOP CHOICE **History Park** PARK

(☎408-287-2290; www.historysanjose.org; cnr Senter Rd & Phelan Ave; ⏰11am-5pm Tue-Sun) Historic buildings from all over San Jose have been brought together in this open-air history museum, southeast of the city center in Kelley Park. The centerpiece is a dramatic half-scale

WORTH A TRIP

STANFORD UNIVERSITY

Sprawled over 8200 leafy acres in Palo Alto, **Stanford University** (www.stanford.edu) was founded by Leland Stanford, one of the Central Pacific Railroad's 'Big Four' founders and a former governor of California. When the Stanfords' only child died of typhoid during a European tour in 1884, they decided to build a university in his memory. Stanford University was opened in 1891, just two years before Leland Stanford's death, but the university grew to become a prestigious and wealthy institution. The campus was built on the site of the Stanfords' horse-breeding farm and, as a result, Stanford is still known as 'The Farm.'

Auguste Rodin's *Burghers of Calais* bronze sculpture marks the entrance to the **Main Quad**, an open plaza where the original 12 campus buildings, a mix of Romanesque and Mission revival styles, were joined by the **Memorial Church** (also called MemChu) in 1903. The church is noted for its beautiful mosaic-tiled frontage, stained-glass windows and four organs with over 8000 pipes.

A campus landmark at the east of the Main Quad, the 285ft-high **Hoover Tower** (adult/child $2/1; ⏲10am-4pm, closed during final exams, breaks btwn sessions & some holidays) offers superb views. The tower houses the university library, offices and part of the right-wing Hoover Institution on War, Revolution & Peace (where Donald Rumsfeld caused a university-wide stir by accepting a position after he resigned as Secretary of Defense).

The **Cantor Center for Visual Arts** (http://museum.stanford.edu; 328 Lomita Dr; admission free; ⏲11am-5pm Wed & Fri-Sun, to 8pm Thu) is a large museum originally dating from 1894. Its collection spans works from ancient civilizations to contemporary art, sculpture and photography, and rotating exhibits are eclectic in scope.

Immediately south is the open-air **Rodin Sculpture Garden**, which boasts the largest collection of bronze sculptures by Auguste Rodin outside of Paris, including reproductions of his towering *Gates of Hell*. More sculpture can be found around campus, including pieces by Andy Goldsworthy and Maya Lin.

The **Stanford Visitor Center** (www.stanford.edu/dept/visitorinfo; 295 Galvez St) offers free one-hour walking tours of the campus daily at 11am and 3:15pm, except during the winter break (mid-December through early January) and some holidays. Specialized tours are also available.

Stanford University's free public shuttle, **Marguerite** (http://transportation.stanford.edu/marguerite), provides service from Caltrain's Palo Alto and California Ave stations to the campus, and has bicycle racks. Parking on campus is expensive and trying.

replica of the 237ft-high 1881 **Electric Light Tower**. The original tower was a pioneering attempt at street lighting, intended to illuminate the entire town center. It was a complete failure but was left standing as a central landmark until it toppled over in 1915 because of rust and wind. Other buildings include an 1888 **Chinese temple** and the **Pacific Hotel**, which has rotating exhibits inside. The **Trolley Restoration Barn** restores historic trolley cars to operate on San Jose's light-rail line. Check the website for when you can ride a trolley along the park's own short line.

Tech Museum MUSEUM

(☎408-294-8324; www.thetech.org; 201 S Market St; museum & 1 IMAX theater admission $10; ⏲10am-5pm Mon-Wed, to 8pm Thu-Sun; 👪) This excellent technology museum, opposite Plaza de Cesar Chavez, examines subjects from robotics to space exploration to genetics. The museum also includes an IMAX dome theater, which screens different films throughout the day.

San Jose Museum of Art MUSEUM

(☎408-271-6840; www.sjmusart.org; 110 S Market St; adult/student & senior $8/5; ⏲11am-5pm Tue-Sun) With a strong permanent collection of 20th-century works and a variety of imaginative changing exhibits, the city's central art museum is one of the Bay Area's finest. The main building started life as the post office in 1892, was damaged by the 1906 earthquake and became an art gallery in 1933. A modern wing was added in 1991.

Rosicrucian Egyptian Museum MUSEUM
(☎408-947-3635; www.egyptianmuseum.org; 1342 Naglee Ave; adult/child/student $9/5/7; ⏲9am-5pm Wed-Fri, 10am-6pm Sat & Sun) West of downtown, this unusual and educational Egyptian Museum is one of San Jose's more interesting attractions, with an extensive collection that includes statues, household items and mummies. There's even a two-room, walk-through reproduction of an ancient subterranean tomb. The museum is the centerpiece of **Rosicrucian Park** (cnr Naglee & Park Aves), west of downtown San Jose.

FREE **MACLA** GALLERY
(Movimiento de Arte y Cultura Latino Americana; ☎408-998-2783; www.maclaarte.org; 510 S 1st St; ⏲noon-7pm Wed & Thu, noon-5pm Fri & Sat) A cutting-edge gallery highlighting themes by both established and emerging Latino artists, MACLA is one of the best community arts spaces in the Bay Area, with open-mic performances, hip-hop and other live music shows, experimental theater and well-curated and thought-provoking visual arts exhibits. It's also a hub for the popular **South First Fridays** (www.southfirstfridays.com) art walk and street fair.

Plaza de Cesar Chavez PLAZA
This leafy square in the center of downtown, which was part of the original plaza of El Pueblo de San José de Guadalupe, is the oldest public space in the city. It's named after Cesar Chavez – founder of the United Farm Workers, who lived part of his life in San Jose – and is surrounded by museums, theaters and hotels.

Cathedral Basilica of St Joseph CHURCH
(80 S Market St) At the top of the plaza, the pueblo's first church. Originally constructed of adobe brick in 1803, it was replaced three times due to earthquakes and fire; the present building dates from 1877.

Santana Row MARKET
(www.santanarow.com; Stevens Creek & Winchester Blvds) An upscale Main St-style mall, Santana Row is a mixed-use space west of downtown with shopping, dining and entertainment along with a boutique hotel, lofts and apartments. Restaurants spill out onto sidewalk terraces, and public spaces have been designed to invite loitering and promenading. On warm evenings, the Mediterranean-style area swarms with an energetic crowd.

San Jose for Children

Children's Discovery Museum MUSEUM
(☎408-298-5437; www.cdm.org; 180 Woz Way; admission $10; ⏲10am-5pm Tue-Sat, from noon Sun; 👪) Downtown, this science and creativity museum has hands-on displays incorporating art, technology and the environment, with plenty of toys, and very cool play-and-learn areas. The museum is on Woz Way, which is named after Steve Wozniak, the cofounder of Apple.

Great America AMUSEMENT PARK
(☎408-986-5886; www.cagreatamerica.com; adult/child under 48in $55/35; 4701 Great America Pkwy, Santa Clara; ⏲Apr-Oct; 👪) If you can handle the shameful product placements, kids love the roller coasters and other thrill rides. Note that online tickets cost much less than walk-up prices listed here; parking costs $12 but it's also accessible by public transportation.

Raging Waters AMUSEMENT PARK
(☎408-238-9900; www.rwsplash.com; 2333 South White Rd; adult/child under 48in $34/24, parking $6; ⏲May-Sep; 👪) A water park inside Lake Cunningham Regional Park, Raging Waters has fast water slides, a tidal pool and a nifty water fort.

Sleeping

Conventions and trade shows keep the downtown hotels busy year-round, and midweek rates are usually higher than weekends.

TOP CHOICE **Sainte Claire Hotel** HISTORIC HOTEL $$
(☎408-295-2000, 866-870-0726; www.thesainteclaire.com; 302 S Market St; r weekend/midweek from $95/169; ❄@📶🐾) Stretched leather ceilings top off the drop-dead beautiful lobby at this 1926 landmark hotel overlooking Plaza de Cesar Chavez. Guest rooms, while smallish, are modern and smartly designed, and bathrooms have hand-painted sky murals, dark wood vanities and restored tile floors.

Hotel De Anza HOTEL $$
(☎408-286-1000, 800-843-3700; www.hoteldeanza.com; 233 W Santa Clara St; r $149-229; ❄@📶🐾) This downtown hotel is a restored art deco beauty, although contemporary stylings overwhelm the place's history. Guest rooms offer plush comforts (the ones facing south are a tad larger) and full concierge service is available.

WHAT THE...?

An odd structure purposefully commissioned to be so by the heir to the Winchester rifle fortune, the **Winchester Mystery House** (☎408-247-2101; www.winchestermysteryhouse.com; 525 S Winchester Blvd; adult/senior/child 6-12 $30/27/20; ⏰9am-5pm Oct-Mar, 8am-7pm Apr-Sep) is a ridiculous Victorian mansion with 160 rooms of various sizes and little utility, with dead-end hallways and a staircase that runs up to a ceiling all jammed together like a toddler playing architect. Apparently, Sarah Winchester spent 38 years constructing this mammoth white elephant because the spirits of the people killed by Winchester rifles told her to. No expense was spared in the construction and the extreme results sprawl over 4 acres. Tours start every 30 minutes, and the standard hour-long guided mansion tour includes a self-guided romp through the gardens as well as entry to an exhibition of guns and rifles. It's west of central San Jose and just north of I-280, across the street from Santana Row.

Hotel Valencia BOUTIQUE HOTEL **$$$**
(☎408-551-0010, 866-842-0100; www.hotelvalencia-santanarow.com; 355 Santana Row; r incl breakfast $199-309; ❄@📶🏊) A burbly lobby fountain and deep-red corridor carpeting set the tone for this tranquil 212-room contemporary hotel in the Santana Row shopping complex. In-room minibars and bathrobes and an outdoor pool and hot tub create an oasis of luxury with European and Asian design accents.

Henry Coe State Park CAMPGROUND **$**
(☎408-779-2728, reservations 800-444-7275 or www.reserveamerica.com; www.coepark.org; sites $20) southeast of San Jose near Morgan Hill, this huge state park has 20 drive-in campsites at the top of an open ridge overlooking the hills and canyons of the park's backcountry. There are no showers. You can't make reservations less than two days in advance, though it rarely fills up except on spring and summer holidays and weekends.

Eating

Original Joe's ITALIAN **$$**
(www.originaljoes.com; 301 S 1st St; mains $14-34; ⏰11am-1am) Waiters in bow ties flit about this busy 1950s San Jose landmark, serving standard Italian dishes to locals and conventioneers. The dining room is a curious but tasteful hodgepodge of '50s brick, contemporary wood paneling and 5ft-tall Asian vases. Expect a wait.

Amber India INDIAN **$$**
(☎408-248-5400; www.amber-india.com; No 1140, 377 Santana Row; dinner mains $14-24) The cooking at this upscale Indian restaurant is superb, offering a full complement of kebabs, curries and tandooris. Presentation is highly styled, with artsy china and groovy paintings on the walls. Whet your whistle with an exotic cocktail as you feast on the delectable butter chicken.

Arcadia STEAKHOUSE **$$$**
(☎408-278-4555; www.michaelmina.net/restaurants; 100 W San Carlos St; lunch mains $11-16, dinner mains $24-42) This fine New American steakhouse restaurant in the Marriott Hotel is run by Chef Michael Mina, one of San Francisco's biggest celebrity chefs. It's not the daring, cutting-edge style Mina is known for, but it's slick, expensive and, of course, very good.

Tofoo Com Chay VEGETARIAN **$**
(www.tofoocomchay.com; 388 E Santa Clara St; mains $6.50; ⏰9am-9pm Mon-Fri, 10am-6pm Sat; 🌶) Conveniently located on the border of the San Jose State University campus, students and vegetarians queue up for the Vietnamese dishes like the fake-meat *pho* and the heaped combo plates.

Drinking

TOP CHOICE **singlebarrel** COCKTAIL BAR
(www.singlebarrelsj.com; 43 W San Salvador St; ⏰Tue-Sun) A new speakeasy-style lounge, where bartenders sheathed in tweed vests artfully mix custom cocktails ($10 to $11) tailored to customer's preferences, with some recipes dating back to before Prohibition. There's often a line out the door, but you'll be whisked downstairs as soon as they're ready to craft you a drink.

Caffe Trieste CAFE
(www.caffetrieste.com; 315 S 1st St; ⏰7am-10pm Mon-Thu, to midnight Fri, 8am-midnight Sat, to 9pm Sun; 📶) Photos of local theater folks line

PSYCHO DONUTS? QU'EST QUE C'EST?

Who knew that a sugary confection with a hole could induce such devious giggles and fiendish delight? Saunter on over to **Psycho Donuts** (www.psycho-donuts.com; 288 S 2nd St; ⏲7am-10pm Mon-Thu, to midnight Fri, 8am-11pm Sat, to 10pm Sun; ✎), where counter staff dressed in saucy medical garb hand out bubble wrap to pop as patrons choose from twisted flavors like Cereal Killer (topped with marshmallows and Cap'n Crunch breakfast cereal), Headbanger (death-metal visage oozing red jelly) and the too-true-to-life Hamburger (sesame seed donut with bacon strips).

the walls at this high-ceilinged outpost of San Francisco's North Beach treasure (p93). Linger over a cappuccino with a pastry or panini, and stop by for live music on Thursday, Friday and Saturday nights. Opera performances rattle the cups the first Friday of each month.

Trials Pub PUB
(www.trialspub.com; 265 N 1st St) If you seek a well-poured pint in a supremely comfortable atmosphere, Trials Pub, north of San Pedro Sq, has many excellent ales on tap (try a Fat Lip), all served in a warm and friendly room with no TVs. There's good pub food and a fireplace in the back room.

Hedley Club Lounge LOUNGE
(www.hoteldeanza.com/hedley_club.asp; 233 W Santa Clara St) Also downtown, inside the elegant 1931 Hotel De Anza, Hedley Club is a good place for a quiet drink in swanky art deco surroundings. Jazz combos play Thursday through Saturday night.

☆ Entertainment

Clubs

The biggest conglomeration of clubs is on S 1st St, aka SoFA, and around S 2nd at San Fernando. Raucous young clubgoers pack the streets on Friday and Saturday nights.

South First Billiards POOL HALL
(420 S 1st St; www.sofapool.com) It's a great place to shoot some stick, and a welcoming club to boot. Free rock shows on Friday and Saturday always draw a fun crowd.

Blank Club LIVE MUSIC
(44 S Almaden; www.theblankclub.com; ⏲Tue-Sat) A small club near the Greyhound station and off the main party streets. Live bands jam on a stage cascading with silver tinsel, and a glittering disco ball presides over fun retro dance parties.

Fahrenheit Ultra Lounge LOUNGE
(☎408-998-9998; www.fahrenheitsj.com; 99 E San Fernando St) Expect short party dresses, velvet ropes and clubbers enjoying bottle service and small-plates menu at this buzzing dance club. DJs play a mix and mash-ups of top 40, house and hip-hop, and bartenders pour drinks with flair.

Theaters

California Theatre THEATER
(☎408-792-4111; http://californiatheatre.sanjose.org; 345 S 1st St) The absolutely stunning Spanish interior of this landmark entertainment venue is cathedral-worthy. The theater is home to Opera San José, Symphony Silicon Valley, and is a venue for the city's annual film festival, **Cinequest** (www.cinequest.org), held in late February or early March.

San Jose Repertory Theatre THEATER
(☎408-367-7255; www.sjrep.com; 101 Paseo de San Antonio) Steaming ahead into its third decade, this company offers a full season of top-rated productions in a contemporary 525-seat venue downtown.

Sports

HP Pavilion STADIUM
(☎408-287-9200; www.hppsj.com; cnr Santa Clara & N Autumn Sts) The fanatically popular San Jose Sharks, the city's NHL (National Hockey League) team, plays at the HP Pavilion, a massive glass-and-metal stadium. The NHL season runs from September to April.

Buck Shaw Stadium STADIUM
(www.sjearthquakes.com; 500 El Camino Real, Santa Clara) Located at Santa Clara University, this is the home of the San Jose Earthquakes Major League Soccer team; games run from February through October.

Information

To find out what's happening and where, check out the free weekly *Metro* (www.metroactive.com) newspaper or the Friday 'eye' section of the daily *San Jose Mercury News* (www.mercurynews.com).

San Jose Convention & Visitors Bureau (☎408-295-9600, 800-726-5673; www.sanjose.org; 150 W San Carlos St; ⊙8am-5pm Mon-Fri) Inside the San Jose Convention Center.

Santa Clara Valley Medical Center (☎408-885-5000; 751 S Bascom Ave; ⊙24hr)

Getting There & Away

Air

Two miles north of downtown, between Hwy 101 and I-880, is **Mineta San José International Airport** (www.flysanjose.com). The airport has grown busier as the South Bay gets more crowded, with numerous domestic flights at two terminals and free wi-fi.

BART

To access the BART system in the East Bay, **VTA** (☎408-321-2300; www.vta.org) bus 181 runs daily between the Fremont BART station and downtown ($4).

Bus

Greyhound buses to San Francisco ($10, 90 minutes) and Los Angeles ($42 to $60, seven to 10 hours) leave from the **Greyhound station** (☎408-295-4151; www.greyhound.com; 70 Almaden Ave).

The VTA Hwy 17 Express bus (route 970) plies a handy daily route between Diridon Station and Santa Cruz ($5, one hour).

Car & Motorcycle

San Jose is right at the bottom end of the San Francisco Bay, about 40 miles from Oakland (via I-880) or San Francisco (via Hwy 101 or I-280). Expect lots of traffic at all times of the day on Hwy 101. Although I-280 is slightly longer, it's much prettier and usually less congested. Heading south, Hwy 17 leads over the hill to Santa Cruz.

Many downtown retailers offer two-hour parking validation, and on weekends until 6pm parking is free in city-owned lots and garages downtown. Check www.sjdowntownparking.com for details.

Train

A double-decker commuter rail service that operates up and down the Peninsula between San Jose and San Francisco, **Caltrain** (☎800-660-4287; www.caltrain.com) makes over three dozen trips daily (fewer on weekends); the 60-minute (on the Baby Bullet commuter trains) to 90-minute journey costs $8.50 each way and bicycles can be brought on designated cars. It's definitely your best bet, as traffic can be crazy any day of the week. San José's terminal, **Diridon Station** (off 65 Cahill St) is just south of the Alameda.

Diridon Station also serves as the terminal for **Amtrak** (☎408-287-7462; www.amtrak.com), serving Seattle, Los Angeles and Sacramento, and **Altamont Commuter Express** (ACE; www.acerail.com), which runs to Great America, Livermore and Stockton.

VTA runs a free weekday shuttle (known as the Downtown Area Shuttle or DASH) from the station to downtown.

Getting Around

VTA buses run all over Silicon Valley. From the airport, VTA Airport Flyer shuttles (route 10) run every 10 to 15 minutes to the Metro/Airport Light Rail station, where you can catch the San Jose light rail to downtown San Jose. The route also goes to the Santa Clara Caltrain station. Fares for buses (except express lines) and light-rail trains are $2 for a single ride and $6 for a day pass.

The main San Jose light-rail line runs 20 miles north-south from the city center. Heading south gets you as far as Almaden and Santa Teresa. The northern route runs to the Civic Center, the airport and Tasman, where it connects with another line that heads west past Great America to downtown Mountain View.

San Francisco to Half Moon Bay

One of the real surprises of the Bay Area is how fast the urban landscape disappears along the rugged and largely undeveloped coast. The 70-mile stretch of coastal Hwy 1 from San Francisco to Santa Cruz is one of the most beautiful motorways anywhere. For the most part a winding two-lane blacktop, it passes small farmstands and beach after beach, many of them little sandy coves hidden from the highway. Most beaches along Hwy 1 are buffeted by wild and unpredictable surf, making them more suitable for sunbathing (weather permitting) than swimming. The state beaches along the coast don't charge an access fee, but parking can cost a few dollars.

A cluster of isolated and supremely scenic HI hostels, at Point Montara (22 miles south of San Francisco) and Pigeon Point (36 miles), make this an interesting route for cyclists, though narrow Hwy 1 itself can be stressful, if not downright dangerous, for the inexperienced.

WORTH A TRIP

NERDS' NIRVANA

Now touted as the largest computer history exhibition in the world, a $19 million remodel has launched the **Computer History Museum** (650-810-1010; www.computerhistory.org; 1401 N Shoreline Blvd, Mountain View; adult/student & senior $15/12; 10am-5pm Wed-Sun) into a new league. Artifacts range from the abacus to the iPod, including Cray-1 supercomputers and the first Google server. Rotating exhibits draw from its 100,000-item collection and will keep you exploring this place for hours.

PACIFICA & DEVIL'S SLIDE

Pacifica and Point San Pedro, 15 miles from downtown San Francisco, signal the end of the urban sprawl. South of Pacifica is Devil's Slide, an unstable cliff area through which Hwy 1 winds and curves. Drive carefully, especially at night and when it is raining, as rock and mud slides are frequent. Heavy winter storms often lead to the road's temporary closure. A tunnel will soon bypass this dramatic stretch of the highway.

In Pacifica, collecting a suntan or catching a wave are the main attractions at **Rockaway Beach** and the more popular **Pacifica State Beach** (also known as Linda Mar Beach), where the nearby **Nor-Cal Surf Shop** (650-738-9283; 5460 Coast Hwy) rents surfboards ($18 per day) and wet suits ($16).

GRAY WHALE COVE TO MAVERICKS

One of the coast's popular 'clothing-optional' beaches is **Gray Whale Cove State Beach** (650-726-8819), just south of Point San Pedro. Park across the road and cross Hwy 1 to the beach *very* carefully. **Montara State Beach** is just a half-mile south. From the town of Montara, 22 miles from San Francisco, trails climb up from the Martini Creek parking lot into **McNee Ranch State Park**, which has hiking and cycling trails aplenty, including a strenuous ascent to the panoramic viewpoint of Montara Mountain.

Point Montara Lighthouse Hostel (650-728-7177; www.norcalhostels.org/montara; cnr Hwy 1 & 16th St; dm $29, r $78;) started life as a fog station in 1875. The hostel is adjacent to the current lighthouse, which dates from 1928. This very popular hostel has a living room, kitchen facilities and an international clientele. There are a few private rooms for couples or families. Reservations are a good idea anytime, but especially on weekends during summer. From Monday through Friday, SamTrans bus 294 will let you off at the hostel if you ask nicely; bus 17 runs daily and stops across the highway (a ten minute walk).

Montara has a few B&Bs, including the historic **Goose & Turrets B&B** (650-728-5451; www.gooseandturretsbandb.com; 835 George St; r $145-190;), with a lovely garden area, afternoon tea and bright red cannons out front to greet you.

TOP CHOICE **Fitzgerald Marine Reserve** (650-728-3584;), south of the lighthouse at Moss Beach, is an extensive area of natural tidal pools and a habitat for harbor seals. Walk out among the pools at low tide – wearing shoes that you can get wet – and explore the myriad crabs, sea stars, mollusks and rainbow-colored sea anemone. Note that it's illegal to remove any creatures, shells or even rocks from the marine reserve. From Hwy 1 in Moss Beach, turn west onto California Ave and drive to the end. SamTrans buses 294 and 17 stop along Hwy 1.

Moss Beach Distillery (650-728-5595; www.mossbeachdistillery.com; cnr Beach Way & Ocean Blvd; mains $15-33; noon-9pm Mon-Sat, from 11am Sun;) is a 1927 landmark overlooking the ocean. In fair weather the deck here is the best place for miles around to have a leisurely cocktail or glass of vino. Reservations recommended.

South of here is a hamlet named Princeton, with a stretch of coast called Pillar Point. Fishing boats bring in their catch at the Pillar Point Harbor, some of which gets cooked up in a bevy of seafront restaurants. In the harbor, **Half Moon Bay Kayak** (650-773-6101; www.hmbkayak.com) rents kayaks and offers guided trips of Pillar Point and the Fitzgerald Marine Reserve. **Half Moon Bay Brewing Company** (www.hmbbrewinco.com; 390 Capistrano Rd; mains $11-21; 11:30am-8:30pm, longer hr on weekends) serves seafood, burgers and a tantalizing menu of local brews from a sheltered and heated outdoor patio looking out over the bay, complemented by live music on the weekends.

At the western end of Pillar Point is **Mavericks**, a serious surf break that attracts the world's top big-wave riders to battle its huge, steep and very dangerous waves. The annual Mavericks surf contest, called on a few days' notice when the swells get huge, is usually held between December and March.

Half Moon Bay

Developed as a beach resort back in the Victorian era, Half Moon Bay is the main coastal town between San Francisco (28 miles north) and Santa Cruz (40 miles south). Its long stretches of beach still attract rambling weekenders and hearty surfers. Half Moon Bay spreads out along Hwy 1 (called Cabrillo Hwy in town), but despite the development it's still relatively small. The main drag is a five-block stretch called Main St lined with shops, cafes, restaurants and a few upscale B&Bs. Visitor information is available from the **Half Moon Bay Coastside Chamber of Commerce** (650-726-8380; www.halfmoonbaychamber.org; 235 Main St; 9am-5pm Mon-Fri).

Pumpkins are a major deal around Half Moon Bay, and the pre-Halloween harvest is celebrated in the annual **Art & Pumpkin Festival** (www.miramarevents.com/pumpkinfest). The mid-October event kicks off with the World Championship Pumpkin Weigh-Off, where the bulbous beasts can bust the scales at more than 1000lb.

Around 1 mile north of the Hwy 92 junction, **Sea Horse Ranch** (650-726-9903; www.seahorseranch.org) offers daily horseback rides along the beach. A two-hour ride is $75; an early-bird special leaves at 8am and cost just $50.

Sleeping & Eating

San Benito House HISTORIC HOTEL **$$$**
(650-726-3425; www.sanbenitohouse.com; 356 Main St; r incl breakfast with shared bath $80-100, r incl breakfast $130-200;) Supposedly a former bordello, this traditional Victorian inn has creaky wood floors and 11 neatly antiquated rooms without TVs. The saloon downstairs has live music a few nights a week, but doesn't stay open too late.

Pasta Moon ITALIAN **$$**
(650-726-5125; www.pastamoon.com; 315 Main St; mains $12-32; 11:30am-2:30pm & 5:30-9pm) If you're in the mood for romantic Italian, come here for yummy housemade pasta, organic produce, locally sourced ingredients and all-Italian wine list. Reservations recommended on weekends.

Getting There & Away

SamTrans (800-660-4287; www.samtrans.com) bus 294 operates from the Hillsdale Caltrain station to Half Moon Bay, and up the coast to Moss Beach and Pacifica, weekdays until about 7:30pm ($2).

Half Moon Bay to Santa Cruz

With its long coastline, mild weather and abundant fresh water, this area has always been prime real estate. When Spanish missionaries set up shop along the California coast in the late 1700s, it had been Ohlone

SCENIC DRIVE: HIGHWAY 84

Inland, large stretches of the hills are protected in a patchwork of parks that, just like the coast, remain remarkably untouched despite the huge urban populations only a short drive to the north and east. Heading east toward Palo Alto, Hwy 84 winds its way through thick stands of redwood trees and several local parks with mountain biking and hiking opportunities.

A mile in from San Gregorio State Beach on Hwy 1, kick off your shoes and stomp your feet to live bluegrass, Celtic and folk music on the weekends at the landmark **San Gregorio General Store** (www.sangregoriostore.com), and check out the wooden bar singed by area branding irons.

Eight miles east is the tiny township of **La Honda**, former home to *One Flew Over the Cuckoo's Nest* author Ken Kesey, and the launching spot for his 1964 psychedelic bus trip immortalized in Tom Wolfe's *The Electric Kool-Aid Acid Test*. Housed in an old blacksmith's shop, **Apple Jack's Inn** (650-747-0331) is a rustic, down-home bar offering live music on weekends and lots of local color.

Indian territory for thousands of years. Pescadero was formally established in 1856, when it was mostly a farming and dairy settlement, although its location along the stagecoach route – now called Stage Rd – transformed it into a popular vacation destination. The Pigeon Point promontory was an active whaling station until 1900, when Prohibition-era bootleggers favored the isolated regional beaches for smuggling booze.

PESCADERO

A foggy speck of coastside crossroads between the cities of San Francisco and Santa Cruz, 150-year-old Pescadero is a close-knit rural town of sugar-lending neighbors and community pancake breakfasts. But on weekends the tiny downtown strains its seams with long-distance cyclists panting for carbohydrates and day trippers dive-bombing in from the ocean-front highway. They're all drawn to the winter vistas of emerald-green hills parched to burlap brown in summer, the wild Pacific beaches populated by seals and pelicans, and the food at a revered destination restaurant. With its cornucopia of tide-pool coves and parks of sky-blotting redwood canopy, city dwellers come here to slow down and smell the sea breeze wafting over fields of bushy artichokes.

Sights & Activities

A number of pretty sand beaches speckle the coast, though one of the most interesting places to stop is **Pebble Beach**, a tide pool jewel a mile and a half south of Pescadero Creek Rd. As the name implies, the shore is awash in bite-sized eye candy of agate, jade and carnelians, and sandstone troughs are pockmarked by groovy honeycombed formations called tafoni. Bird-watchers enjoy **Pescadero Marsh Reserve**, across the highway from Pescadero State Beach, where numerous species feed year-round.

TOP CHOICE Pigeon Point Light Station LIGHTHOUSE
(☎650-879-2120; www.parks.ca.gov/?page_id=533) Five miles south along the coast, the 115ft Light Station is one of the tallest lighthouses on the West Coast. The 1872 landmark had to close access to the Fresnel lens when chunks of its cornice began to rain from the sky, but the beam still flashes brightly and the bluff is a prime though blustery spot to scan for breaching gray whales. The hostel here is one of the best in the state.

Butano State Park PARK
(☎650-879-2040; parking fee $10) About 5 miles south of Pescadero, bobcats and full-throated coyotes reside discreetly in a dense redwood canyon. The hiking is also excellent further down the coast at Big Basin Redwoods State Park (p459), with the easiest access from Santa Cruz. Camping ($35 per site) is available at both parks.

Sleeping & Eating

Pescadero Creek Inn B&B B&B $$
(☎888-307-1898; www.pescaderocreekinn.com; 393 Stage Rd; r $170-255;) Unwind in the private two-room cottage or one of the spotless Victorian rooms in a restored 100-year-old farmhouse. Afternoon wine and cheese features wine bottled by the owners, and organic ingredients from the creekside garden spice up a hot breakfast.

Pigeon Point Lighthouse Hostel HOSTEL $
(☎650-879-0633; www.norcalhostels.org/pigeon; dm $24-26, r $72-98; @) Not your workaday HI outpost, this highly coveted coastside hostel is all about location. Check in early to snag a spot in the outdoor hot tub, and contemplate roaring waves as the lighthouse beacon races through a starburst sky.

Costanoa Lodge RESORT $$
(☎650-879-1100, 877-262-7848; www.costanoa.com; 2001 Rossi Rd; tent cabin $89-145, cabin $189-199, lodge r $179-279;) Even though the resort includes a **campground** (☎800-562-9867; www.koa.com/campgrounds/santa-cruz-north; tent site $22-52, RV site from $65), no one can pull a straight face to declare they're actually roughing it here. Down bedding swaddles guests in cushy canvas tent cabins, and chill-averse tent campers can use communal 'comfort stations' with 24-hour dry saunas, fireside patio seating, heated floors and hot showers. Lodge rooms with private fireplaces and hot tub access fulfill the whims of those without such spartan delusions. There's a **restaurant** (dinner mains $15-27) and spa on site; bicycle rentals and horseback riding are available as well.

TOP CHOICE Duarte's Tavern AMERICAN $$
(☎650-879-0464; www.duartestavern.com; 202 Stage Rd; mains $11-40) You'll rub shoulders with fancy-pants foodies, spandex-swathed cyclists and dusty cowboys in spurs at this casual and surprisingly unpretentious

THE CULINARY COAST

Pescadero is renowned for Duarte's Tavern (see opposite page), but loads of other scrumptious tidbits are very close by.

Phipps Country Store (2700 Pescadero Creek Rd;) Peek inside the shop, known universally as 'the bean store,' to marvel at whitewashed bins overflowing with dried heirloom varieties with names like Eye of the Goat, Painted Lady and Desert Pebble.

Arcangeli Grocery/Norm's Market (287 Stage Rd; sandwiches $6-8.50) Create a picnic with made-to-order deli sandwiches, homemade artichoke salsa and a chilled bottle of California wine. And don't go breezing out the door without nabbing a crusty loaf of the famous artichoke garlic herb bread, fresh-baked almost hourly.

Harley Farms Cheese Shop (650-879-0480; www.harleyfarms.com; 250 North St;) Follow the cool wooden cut-outs of the goat and the Wellington-shod girl with the faraway eyes. Another local food treasure with creamy artisanal goat cheeses festooned with fruit, nuts and a rainbow of edible flowers. Weekend farm tours by reservation. Splurge for a seat at one of the monthly five-course farm dinners in the restored barn's airy hayloft.

Pie Ranch (www.pieranch.org; 2080 Cabrillo Hwy; noon-6pm Sat & Sun Mar-Oct;) Hit the brakes for this roadside farmstand in a wooden barn, and pick up fresh produce, eggs and coffee, plus amazing pies made with the fruit grown here. The historic pie-shaped farm is a nonprofit dedicated to leadership development and food education for urban youth. Check the website for details on its monthly farm tours and barn dances. Located 11 miles south of Pescadero Creek Rd.

Swanton Berry Farm (650-469-8804; www.swantonberryfarm.com; Coastways Ranch, 640 Cabrillo Hwy) To get a better appreciation of the rigors and rewards of farm life, smoosh up your shirtsleeves and harvest some fruit at this organic pick-your-own farm near Año Nuevo. It's a union outfit (operated by Cesar Chavez's United Farm Workers), with buckets of seasonal kiwis and olallieberries ripe for the plucking. Its farm stand and strawberry u-pick is 8.5 miles further south near Davenport.

fourth-generation family restaurant. Duarte's (pronounced DOO-arts) is the culinary magnet of Pescadero, and for many the town and eatery are synonymous. Feast on crab cioppino and a half-and-half split of the cream of artichoke and green chili soups, and bring it home with a wedge of olallieberry pie. Except for the unfortunate lull of Prohibition, the wood-paneled bar has been hosting the locals and their honored guests since 1894. Reservations recommended.

Getting There & Away

By car, the town is 3 miles east from Hwy 1 on Pescadero Creek Rd, south of San Gregorio State Beach. On weekdays, **SamTrans** bus 17 runs to/from Half Moon Bay twice a day.

AÑO NUEVO STATE RESERVE

More raucous than a full-moon beach rave, thousands of boisterous elephant seals party down year-round on the dunes of Año Nuevo point, their squeals and barks reaching fever pitch during the winter pupping season. The beach is 5 miles south of Pigeon Point and 27 miles north of Santa Cruz. Check out the park's live **SealCam** (www.parks.ca.gov/popup/main.asp).

Elephant seals were just as fearless two centuries ago as they are today, but unfortunately, club-toting seal trappers were not in the same seal-friendly category as camera-toting tourists. Between 1800 and 1850, the elephant seal was driven to the edge of extinction. Only a handful survived around the Guadalupe Islands off the Mexican state of Baja California. With the availability of substitutes for seal oil and the conservationist attitudes of more recent times, the elephant seal has made a comeback, reappearing on the Southern California coast from around 1920. In 1955 they returned to Año Nuevo Beach.

In the midwinter peak season, during the mating and birthing time from December 15 to the end of March, you must plan well ahead if you want to visit the reserve, because visitors are only permitted access through heavily booked guided tours. For the busiest period, mid-January to mid-February, it's recommended you book eight weeks ahead. If you haven't booked, bad weather can sometimes lead to last-minute cancellations.

The rest of the year, advance reservations aren't necessary, but visitor permits from the entrance station are required; arrive before 3pm from September through November and by 3:30pm from April through August.

Although the **park office** (☎650-879-2025, recorded information 650-879-0227; www.parks.ca.gov/?page_id=523) can answer general questions, high season tour bookings must be made at ☎800-444-4445 or http://anonuevo.reserveamerica.com. When required, these tours cost $7, and parking is $10 per car year-round. From the ranger station it's a 3- to 5-mile round-trip hike on sand, and a visit takes two to three hours. No dogs are allowed on-site, and visitors aren't permitted for the first two weeks of December.

There's another, more convenient viewing site further south in Piedras Blancas.

Napa & Sonoma Wine Country

Includes »

Best Places to Eat

» Zazu (p203)
» Oxbow Public Market (p167)
» Fremont Diner (p185)
» Madrona Manor (p206)

Best Places to Stay

» Beltane Ranch (p188)
» Cottages of Napa Valley (p166)
» Mountain Home Ranch (p174)
» El Bonita Motel (p171)
» Auberge du Soleil (p170)

Why Go?

America's premier viticulture region has earned its reputation among the world's best. Despite hype about Wine Country style, it's from the land that all Wine Country lore springs. Rolling hills, dotted with century-old oaks, turn the color of lion's fur under the summer sun and swaths of vineyards carpet hillsides as far as the eye can see. Where they end, lush redwood forests follow serpentine rivers to the sea.

There are over 600 wineries in Napa and Sonoma Counties, but it's quality, not quantity, that sets the region apart – especially in Napa, which competes with France and doubles as an outpost of San Francisco's top-end culinary scene. Sonoma prides itself on agricultural diversity, with goat-cheese farms, you-pick-em orchards and roadside fruit stands. Plan to get lost on back roads, and, as you picnic atop sun-dappled hillsides, grab a hunk of earth and know firsthand the thing of greatest meaning in Wine Country.

When to Go

Napa

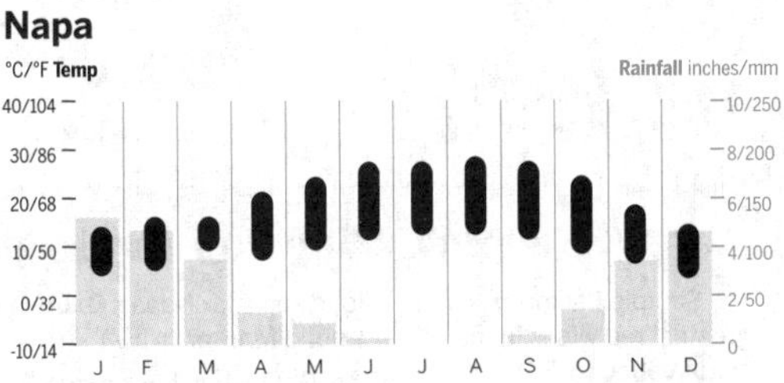

Jan Bright-yellow flowers carpet the valleys during the off-season; room rates plummet.

May Before summer holidays, the weather is perfect for touring, with long days and hot sun.

Sep–Oct 'Crush' time is peak season, when wine-making operations are in full force.

Wine Tasting

To help you discover the real Wine Country, we've mostly avoided factories and listed family-owned boutique houses (producing fewer than 20,000-annual cases) and midsized houses (20,000- to 60,000-annual cases). Why does it matter? Think of it. If you were to attend two dinner parties, one for 10 people, one for 1000, which would have the better food? Small wineries maintain tighter control. Also, you won't easily find these wines elsewhere.

Tastings are called 'flights' and include four-to-six different wines. Napa wineries charge $10 to $50. In Sonoma Valley, tastings cost $5 to $15, refundable with purchase. In Sonoma County, tastings are free or $5 to $10. You must be 21 to taste.

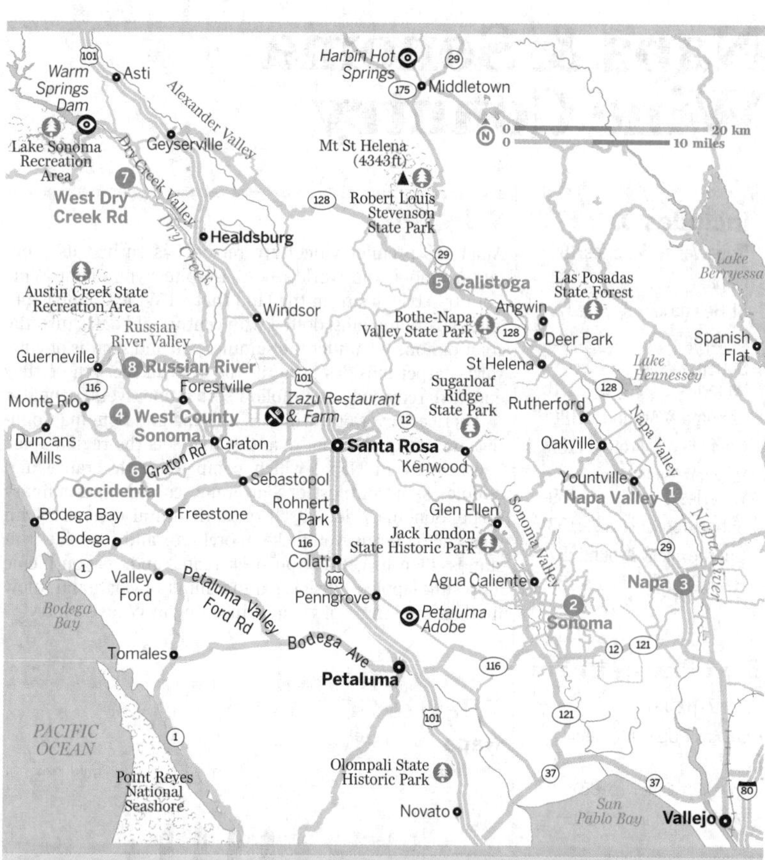

Napa & Sonoma Wine Country Highlights

1 Sample California's greatest red wines in the **Napa Valley** (p159)

2 Picnic in sun-dappled shade on the state's largest town square, **Sonoma Plaza** (p181)

3 Bite into the artisinal food scene at Napa's **Oxbow Public Market** (p167)

4 Get lost on back roads in **West County Sonoma** (p189)

5 Submerge yourself in a volcanic-ash mud bath in **Calistoga** (p173)

6 Chill with locals at the **Occidental Farmers Market** (p195)

7 Pedal between wineries along pastoral **West Dry Creek Rd** (p192)

8 Float in a canoe or kayak down the **Russian River** (p190)

Do not drink and drive. The curvy roads are dangerous, and police monitor traffic, especially on Napa's Hwy 29.

To avoid burnout, visit no more than three wineries per day. Most open daily from 10am or 11am to 4pm or 5pm, but call ahead if you've got your heart set, or absolutely want a tour, especially in Napa, where law requires that some wineries accept visitors only by appointment. If you're buying, ask if the winery has a wine club, which is often free to join and provides discounts, but you'll have to agree to buy a certain amount annually.

High Season vs Low

Many Wine Country restaurants and hotels diminish operations in wintertime. We list high-season hours and rates. Make reservations, especially in summer, or you may not eat. Hotel rates increase during September and October's grape-crushing season – the most popular time to come.

Getting There & Away

Napa and Sonoma counties each have an eponymous city and valley. So, the town of Sonoma is in Sonoma County, at the southern end of Sonoma Valley. The same goes for the city, county and valley of Napa.

From San Francisco, public transportation gets you to the valleys, but it's insufficient for vineyard-hopping. For public-transit information, dial ☎511 from Bay Area telephones, or look online at www.transit.511.org.

Both valleys are 90 minutes' drive from San Francisco. Napa, the farther inland, has over 400 wineries and attracts the most visitors (expect heavy traffic summer weekends). Sonoma County has 260 wineries, 40 in Sonoma Valley, which is less commercial and less congested than Napa. If you have time to visit only one, choose Sonoma for ease.

Bus

Evans Transportation (☎707-255-1559; www.evanstransportation.com) Shuttles ($29) to Napa from San Francisco and Oakland Airports.

Golden Gate Transit (☎415-923-2000; www.goldengate.org) Bus 70/80 from San Francisco to Petaluma ($9.25) and Santa Rosa ($10.25); board at 1st and Mission Sts. Connect with Sonoma County Transit buses (p157).

Greyhound (☎800-231-2222; www.greyhound.com) San Francisco to Santa Rosa ($22 to $30) and Vallejo ($17 to $23); transfer for local buses.

Napa Valley Vine (☎800-696-6443, 707-251-2800; www.nctpa.net) Operates bus 10 from the Vallejo Ferry Terminal and Vallejo Transit bus station, via Napa, to Calistoga ($2.90).

Sonoma County Airport Express (☎707-837-8700, 800-327-2024; www.airportexpressinc.com) Shuttles ($34) between Sonoma County Airport (Santa Rosa) and San Francisco and Oakland Airports.

Sonoma County Transit (☎707-576-7433, 800-345-7433; www.sctransit.com) Buses from Santa Rosa to Petaluma ($2.35, 70 minutes), Sonoma ($2.90, 1¼ hours) and western Sonoma County, including Russian River Valley towns ($2.90, 30 minutes).

Car

From San Francisco, take Hwy 101 north over the Golden Gate Bridge, then Hwy 37 east to Hwy 121 north; continue to the junction of Hwys 12/121. For Sonoma Valley, take Hwy 12 north; for Napa Valley, take Hwy 12/121 east. Plan 70 minutes in light traffic, two hours during weekday commute times.

Hwy 12/121 splits south of Napa: Hwy 121 turns north and joins with Hwy 29 (aka St Helena Hwy); Hwy 12 merges with southbound Hwy 29 toward Vallejo. Hwy 29 backs up weekdays 3pm to 7pm, slowing returns to San Francisco.

From the East Bay (or from downtown San Francisco), take I-80 east to Hwy 37 west (north of Vallejo), then northbound Hwy 29.

From Santa Rosa, take Hwy 12 east to access the northern end of Sonoma Valley. From Petaluma and Hwy 101, take Hwy 116 east.

Ferry

Baylink Ferry (☎877-643-3779; www.baylinkferry.com) Downtown San Francisco to Vallejo (adult/child $13/6.50, 60 minutes); connect with Napa Valley Vine Bus 10 (p157).

Trains

Amtrak (☎800-872-7245; www.amtrak.com) trains travel to Martinez (south of Vallejo), with connecting buses to Napa (45 minutes), Santa Rosa (1¼ hours) and Healdsburg (1¾ hours).

BART trains (☎415 989-2278; www.bart.gov) run from San Francisco to El Cerrito del Norte ($4.05, 30 minutes). Transfer to **Vallejo Transit** (☎707-648-4666; www.vallejotransit.com) for Vallejo ($5, 30 minutes), then take Napa Valley Vine buses to Napa and Calistoga.

Getting Around

You'll need a car to winery-hop. Alternatively visit tasting rooms in downtown Napa or downtown Sonoma.

Bicycle

Touring Wine Country by bicycle is unforgettable. Stick to back roads. We most love pastoral West Dry Creek Rd, northwest of Healdsburg, in

NAPA OR SONOMA?

Napa and Sonoma valleys run parallel, a few miles apart, separated by the narrow, imposing Mayacamas Mountains. The two couldn't be more different. It's easy to mock aggressively sophisticated Napa, its monuments to ego, trophy homes and trophy wives, $1000-a-night inns, $40+ tastings and wine-snob visitors, but Napa makes some of the world's best wines. Constrained by its geography, it stretches along a single valley, so it's easy to visit. Drawbacks are high prices and heavy traffic, but there are 400 nearly side-by-side wineries. And the valley is gorgeous.

Sonoma County is much more down-to-earth and politically left leaning. You'll see lots more rusted-out pick-ups. Though becoming gentrified, Sonoma lacks Napa's chic factor (Healdsburg notwithstanding), and locals like it that way. The wines are more approachable, but the county's 260 wineries are spread out (see boxed text p182). If you're here on a weekend, head to Sonoma (County or Valley), which gets less traffic, but on a weekday, see Napa, too. Ideally schedule two to four days: one for each valley, and one or two additional for western Sonoma County.

Spring and fall are the best times to visit. Summers are hot, dusty and crowded. Fall brings fine weather, harvest time and the 'crush,' the pressing of the grapes, but lodging prices skyrocket. For cost-saving tips on lodging in Napa, see p163.

Sonoma County. Through Sonoma Valley, take Arnold Dr instead of Hwy 12; through Napa Valley, take the Silverado Trail instead of Hwy 29.

Cycling between wineries isn't demanding – the valleys are mostly flat – but crossing between Napa and Sonoma Valleys is intense, particularly via steep Oakville Grade and Trinity Rd (between Oakville and Glen Ellen).

Bicycles, in boxes, can be checked on Greyhound buses for $30 to $40; bike boxes cost $10 (call ahead). You can transport bicycles on Golden Gate Transit buses, which usually have free racks available (first-come, first-served). For rentals, see Tours (this page).

Car

Napa Valley is 30-miles long and 5-miles wide at its widest point (the city of Napa), 1 mile at its narrowest (Calistoga). Two roads run north–south: Hwy 29 (St Helena Hwy) and the more scenic Silverado Trail, a mile east. Drive up one, down the other.

The American Automobile Association determined Napa Valley to be America's 8th most congested rural vacation destination. Summer and fall weekend traffic is unbearable, especially on Hwy 29 between Napa and St Helena. Plan accordingly.

Cross-valley roads that link Silverado Trail with Hwy 29 – including Yountville, Oakville and Rutherford crossroads – are bucolic and get less traffic. For scenery, the Oakville Grade and rural Trinity Rd (which leads southwest to Hwy 12 in Sonoma Valley) are narrow, curvy and beautiful – but treacherous in rainstorms. Mt Veeder Rd leads through pristine countryside west of Yountville.

Note: Police watch like hawks for traffic violators. *Don't drink and drive.*

Shortcuts between Napa and Sonoma Valleys: from Oakville, take Oakville Grade to Trinity Rd; from St Helena, take Spring Mountain Rd into Calistoga Rd; from Calistoga, take Petrified Forest Rd to Calistoga Rd.

Public Transportation

Napa Valley Vine (☎800-696-6443, 707-251-2800; www.nctpa.net) Bus 10 from downtown Napa to Calistoga ($2.15, 1¼ hours).

Sonoma County Transit (☎707-576-7433, 800-345-7433; www.sctransit.com) Buses from Santa Rosa to Petaluma ($2.35, 70 minutes), Sonoma ($2.90, 1¼ hours) and western Sonoma County, including Russian River Valley towns ($2.90, 30 minutes).

Train

A cushy, if touristy, way to see Wine Country, the **Napa Valley Wine Train** (☎707-253-2111, 800-427-4124; www.winetrain.com; adult/child from $89/55) offers three-hour daily trips in vintage Pullman dining cars, from Napa to St Helena and back, with an optional winery tour. Trains depart from McKinstry St near 1st St.

Tours

For balloons and airplane rides, see the boxed text, p169.

Bicycle

Guided tours start around $90 per day including bikes, tastings and lunch. Daily rentals cost $25 to $85; make reservations.

Backroads (☎800-462-2848; www.backroads.com) All-inclusive guided biking and walking.

Calistoga Bike Shop (☎707-942-9687, 866-942-2453; www.calistogabikeshop.com; 1318 Lincoln Ave, Calistoga) Wine-tour rental package ($80) includes wine pickup.

Getaway Adventures (☎707-568-3040, 800-499-2453; www.getawayadventures.com) Great guided tours, some combined with kayaking, of Napa, Sonoma, Calistoga, Healdsburg and Russian River. Single- and multi-day trips.

Good Time Touring (☎707-938-0453, 888-525-0453; www.goodtimetouring.com) Tours of Sonoma Valley, Dry Creek and West County Sonoma.

Napa River Vélo (☎707-258-8729; www.naparivervelo.com; 680 Main St, rear of Bldg, Napa) Daily rentals and weekend tours with wine pickup.

Napa Valley Adventure Tours (☎707-259-1833, 877-548-6877; www.napavalleyadventuretours.com; Oxbow Public Market, 610 1st St, Napa) Guides tours between wineries, off-road trips, hiking and kayaking. Daily rentals.

Napa Valley Bike Tours (☎707-944-2953, 800-707-2453; www.napavalleybiketours.com; 6488 Washington St, Yountville) Daily rentals; easy and moderately difficult tours.

Sonoma Valley Cyclery (Map p180; ☎707-935-3377; www.sonomacyclery.com; 20093 Broadway, Sonoma) Daily rentals; Sonoma Valley tours.

Spoke Folk Cyclery (☎707-433-7171; www.spokefolk.com; 201 Center St, Healdsburg) Daily rentals near Dry Creek Valley.

Jeeps

Wine Country Jeep Tours (☎707-546-1822, 800-539-5337; www.jeeptours.com; 3hr tour $75) Tour Wine Country's back roads and boutique wineries by Jeep, year-round at 10am and 1pm. Also operates tours of Sonoma Coast.

Limousine

Antique Tours Limousine (☎707-226-9227; www.antiquetours.net) Hit the road in style in a 1947 Packard convertible; tours cost $130 per hour (minimum five hours).

Beau Wine Tours (☎707-938-8001, 800-387-2328; www.beauwinetours.com) Winery tours in sedans and stretch limos; charges $60 to $95 per hour (3-hour minimum weekdays, 6 hours weekends).

Beyond the Label (☎707-363-4023; www.btlnv.com; per person $299) Personalized tours, including lunch at home with a vintner, guided by a Napa native.

Flying Horse Carriage Company (☎707-849-8989; www.flyinghorse.org; 4hr tours per person $145) Clippety-clop through Alexander Valley by horse-drawn carriage. Includes picnic.

Magnum Tours (☎707-753-0088; www.magnumwinetours.com) Sedans and specialty limousines from $65 to $125 per hour (four-hour minimum, five hours Saturdays). Exceptional service.

NAPA VALLEY

The birthplace of modern-day Wine Country is famous for regal cabernet sauvignons, château-like wineries and fabulous food. Napa Valley attracts more than four million visitors a year, each expecting to be wined, dined, soaked in hot-springs spas and tucked between crisp linens.

Just a few decades ago, this 5-by-35-mile strip of former stagecoach stops seemed forgotten by time. Grapes had grown here since the Gold Rush, but grape-sucking phylloxera bugs, Prohibition and the Great Depression reduced 140 wineries, in the 1890s, to around 25 by the 1960s.

In 1968, Napa was declared the 'Napa Valley Agricultural Preserve', effectively blocking future valley development for non-agricultural purposes. The law stipulated no subdivision of valley-floor land under 40 acres. This succeeded in preserving the valley's natural beauty, but when Napa wines earned top honors at a 1976 blind tasting in Paris, the wine-drinking world took note and land values shot through the roof. Only the very rich could afford to build. Hence, so many architecturally jaw-dropping wineries. Independent, family-owned wineries still exist – we highlight a number of them – but much of Napa Valley is now owned by global conglomerates.

The city of Napa anchors the valley, but the real work happens up-valley. Napa isn't as pretty as other towns, but has some noteworthy sights, among them Oxbow Public Market (p164). Scenic towns include St Helena, Yountville and Calistoga – the latter more famous for water than wine.

Napa Valley Wineries

Cab is king in Napa. No varietal captures imaginations like the fruit of the cabernet sauvignon vine – Bordeaux is the French equivalent – and no wine fetches a higher price. Napa farmers can't afford *not* to grow cabernet. Other heat-loving varietals, such as sangiovese and merlot, also thrive here.

Napa's wines merit their reputation among the world's finest – complex, with luxurious finishes. Napa wineries sell many 'buy-and-hold' wines, versus Sonoma's 'drink-now' wines.

Artesa Winery WINERY

(Map p160; ☎707-224-1668; www.artesawinery.com; 1345 Henry Rd; nonreserve/reserve tastings $10/15; ⊙10am-4:30pm) Begin or end the day with a glass of bubbly or pinot at Artesa, southwest of Napa. Built into a mountainside, the ultramodern Barcelona-style architecture is stunning, and you can't beat the top-of-the-world vistas over San Pablo Bay. Free tours leave 11am and 2pm. Bottles cost $20 to $60.

Vintners' Collective TASTING ROOM

(Map p165; ☎707-255-7150; www.vintnerscollective.com; 1245 Main St; Napa tasting $25; ⊙11am-6pm) Ditch the car and chill in downtown Napa at this super-cool tasting bar – inside a former 19th-century brothel – that represents 20 high-end boutique wineries too small to have their own tasting rooms.

Ceja WINERY

(Map p160; ☎707-226-6445; www.cejavineyards.com; 1248 First St; tasting $10; ⊙11am-6pm Sun-Wed, 11am-8pm Thu-Sat; 🐾) Ceja was founded by former vineyard workers, who now craft superb pinot noir and unusual blends, including a great pinot-syrah-cabernet for $20. The tasting room stays open late, and features interesting art, including Maceo Montoya's mural celebrating winemaking's roots. Bottles cost $20 to $50.

Twenty Rows WINERY

(off Map p165; ☎707-287-1063; www.vinoce.com; 880 Vallejo St, Napa; tasting $10; ⊙11am-5pm Tue-Sat) Downtown Napa's only working winery crafts light-on-the-palate cabernet sauvignon for a mere $20 a bottle. Taste in the barrel room – a chilly garage with plastic furniture – with fun dudes who know wine. Good sauvignon blanc, too.

Hess Collection WINERY

(Map p160; ☎707-255-1144; www.hesscollection.com; 4411 Redwood Rd; tastings $10; ⊙10am-4pm; 🐾) Art lovers: don't miss Hess Collection, whose galleries display mixed-media and large-canvas works, including pieces by Francis Bacon and Louis Soutter. In the cave-like tasting room, you can find well-known cabernet and chardonnay, but also try the viognier. Hess overlooks the valley, so be prepared to drive a winding road. (NB: Hess Collection is not be be confused

Napa Valley

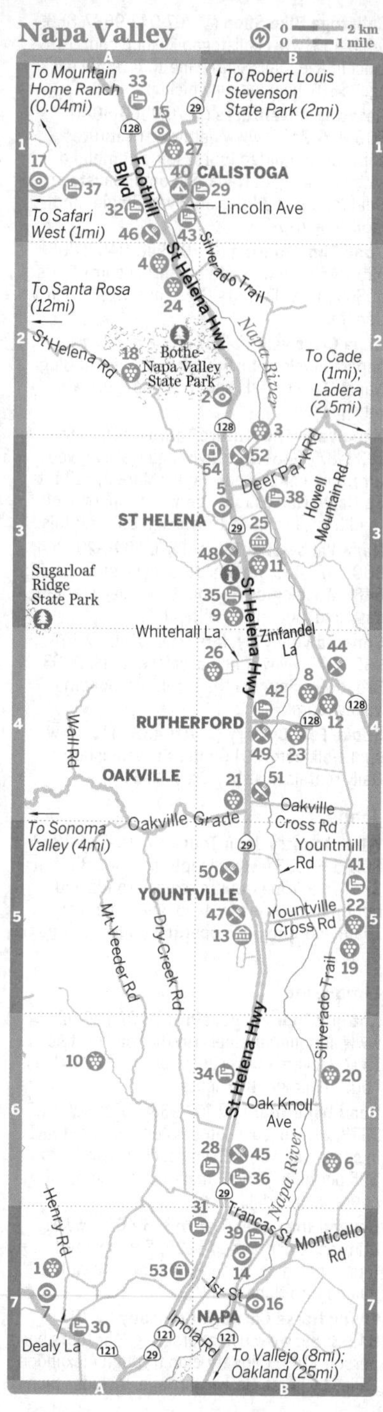

Napa Valley

Sights

1 Artesa Winery ... A7
2 Bale Grist Mill State Historic Park ... B2
3 Casa Nuestra ... B2
4 Castello di Amorosa ... A2
5 Culinary Institute of America at Greystone ... B3
6 Darioush ... B6
7 Di Rosa Preserve ... A7
Elizabeth Spencer ... (see 49)
8 Frog's Leap ... B4
9 Hall ... B3
10 Hess Collection ... A6
Lava Vine ... (see 43)
11 Long Meadow Ranch ... B3
12 Mumm Napa ... B4
13 Napa Valley Museum ... B5
14 Napa Valley Wine Train Depot ... B7
Oat Hill Mine MTB Trail ... (see 29)
15 Old Faithful Geyser ... A1
16 Oxbow Public Market ... B7
17 Petrified Forest ... A1
18 Pride Mountain ... A2
19 Quixote ... B5
20 Regusci ... B6
21 Robert Mondavi ... B4
22 Robert Sinskey ... B5
23 Round Pond ... B4
24 Schramsberg ... A2
25 Silverado Museum ... B3
26 Tres Sabores ... B4
27 Vincent Arroyo ... A1

Activities, Courses & Tours

Calistoga Spa Hot Springs ... (see 29)
Lavender Hill Spa ... (see 46)
Spa Solage ... (see 43)

Sleeping

Auberge de Soleil ... (see 44)
Aurora Park Cottage ... (see 32)
28 Best Western Ivy Hotel ... B6
29 Calistoga Spa Hot Springs ... B1
30 Carneros Inn ... A7
31 Chablis Inn ... B7
32 Chanric Inn ... A1
33 Chateau de Vie ... A1
34 Cottages of Napa Valley ... B6
35 El Bonita Motel ... B3
36 John Muir Inn ... B6
37 Meadowlark Country House ... A1
38 Meadowood ... B3
39 Milliken Creek Inn ... B7
40 Napa County Fairgrounds & RV Park ... A1
Napa Valley Redwood Inn ... (see 31)
41 Poetry Inn ... B5
42 Rancho Caymus ... B4
43 Solage ... A1
Wine Way Inn ... (see 46)

Eating

44 Auberge de Soleil ... B4
45 Bistro Don Giovanni ... B6
Boon Fly Café ... (see 30)
46 Buster's Southern BBQ ... A1
47 Étoile ... B5
Farmstead ... (see 11)
48 Gott's Roadside ... B3
49 La Luna Market & Taqueria ... B4
50 Mustards Grill ... B5
51 Oakville Grocery & Cafe ... B4
Oxbow Public Market ... (see 16)
Pica-Pica Maize Kitchen ... (see 16)
Restaurant at Meadowood ... (see 38)
52 Silverado Brewing Co. ... B3
Solbar ... (see 43)
Wine Spectator Restaurant at Greystone ... (see 5)

Entertainment

Lincoln Theater ... (see 13)

Shopping

53 Napa Premium Outlets ... A7
54 St Helena Marketplace ... B3

with Hess Select, the grocery-store brand.) Bottles cost $15 to $60. Reservations are recommended.

Darioush WINERY

(Map p160; ☎707-257-2345; www.darioush.com; 4240 Silverado Trail; tastings $18-35; ⌚10:30am-5pm) Like a modern-day Persian palace, Darioush ranks high on the fabulosity scale, with towering columns, Le Corbusier furniture, Persian rugs and travertine walls. Though known for cabernet, Darioush also bottles chardonnay, merlot and shiraz, all made with 100% of their respective varietals. Call about wine-and-cheese pairings. Bottles cost $40 to $80.

BOOKING APPOINTMENTS

Because of strict county zoning laws, many Napa wineries cannot legally receive drop-in visitors; unless you've come strictly to buy, you'll have to call ahead. This is *not* the case with all wineries. We recommend booking one appointment and planning your day around it.

Regusci WINERY
(Map p160; ☎707-254-0403; www.regusciwinery.com; 5584 Silverado Trail, Napa; tasting $15-25; ⏲10am-5pm; 🐾) One of Napa's oldest, unfussy Regusci dates to the late 1800s, with 173 acres of vineyards unfurling around a century-old stone winery that makes Bordeaux-style blends on the valley's quieter eastern side – good when traffic up-valley is bad. No appointment necessary; lovely oak-shaded picnic area. Bottles run $36 to $125.

Robert Sinskey WINERY
(Map p160; ☎707-944-9090; www.robertsinskey.com; 6320 Silverado Trail; tastings $25; ⏲10am-4:30pm) For hilltop views and food-friendly wines, visit chef-owned Robert Sinskey, whose discreetly dramatic tasting room of stone, redwood and teak resembles a small cathedral. The winery specializes in organically grown pinot, merlot and cabernet, great Alsatian varietals, *vin gris,* cabernet franc and dry rosé. Small bites accompany the vino. Tasting fees are discounted with a two-bottle purchase – a rarity in Napa. Call about special culinary tours. Bottles cost $22 to $95.

Quixote WINERY
(Map p160; ☎707-944-2659; www.quixotewinery.com; 6126 Silverado Trail; tastings $25; ⏲by appointment) Famed architect Friedensreich Hundertwasser (1928–2000) designed whimsical Quixote. The exterior is a riot of color, with the architect's signature gold-leaf onion dome crowning the building. No two windows are alike, no lines straight, no surfaces perfectly level. Tour it, by appointment only, on weekdays. Weekends, you can only glimpse it while sampling pretty-good, 100% organic petite sirah and cabernet. Bottles cost $40 to $60.

Robert Mondavi WINERY
(Map p160; ☎888-766-6328; www.robertmondavi.com; 7801 Hwy 29, Oakville; tour $25) This huge, corporate-owned winery draws oppressive crowds, but if you know nothing about wine, the worthwhile tours provide excellent insight into wine-making. Otherwise, skip it – unless you're here for one of the wonderful summer **concerts**, ranging from classical and jazz to R&B and Latin; call for schedules. Bottles run $19 to $150.

Tres Sabores WINERY
(Map p160; ☎707-967-8027; www.tressabores.com; 1620 South Whitehall Lane, St Helena; tour/tasting $20; ⏲by appointment; 🐾) At the valley's westernmost edge, where sloping vineyards meet wooded hillsides, Tres Sabores is a portal to old Napa – no fancy tasting room, no snobbery, just great wine in a spectacular setting. Bucking the cabernet custom, Tres Sabores crafts elegantly structured, Burgundian-style zinfandel, and spritely sauvignon blanc, which the *New York Times* dubbed a Top 10. Guinea fowl and sheep control pests on the 35-acre estate, while golden labs chase butterflies through gnarled old vines. Reservations essential, and include a tour. Afterward, linger at olive-shaded picnic tables and drink in gorgeous valley views. Bottles cost $22 to $80.

Mumm Napa WINERY
(Map p160; ☎800-686-6272; www.mummnapa.com; 8445 Silverado Trail, Rutherford; tasting $7-25; ⏲10am-4:45pm; 🐾) The valley views are spectacular at Mumm, which makes respectable sparkling wines that you can sample while seated on a vineyard-view terrace – ideal when you want to impress conservative parents-in-law. No appointment necessary; dodge crowds by paying $5 extra for the reserve-tasting terrace. Check website for discounted-tasting coupons.

Round Pond WINERY
(Map p160; ☎888-302-2575; www.roundpond.com; 875 Rutherford Rd, Rutherford; tastings $25; ⏲by appointment) Fantastic food pairings on a vineyard-view stone patio. We especially love the olive-oil and wine-vinegar tastings, included with guided tours of the olive mill ($25). Bottles $24 to $95.

TOP CHOICE **Frog's Leap** WINERY
(Map p160; ☎707-963-4704, 800-959-4704; www.frogsleap.com; 8815 Conn Creek Rd; tours & tastings $20, ⏲by appointment; 👪🐾) Meandering paths wind through magical gardens and fruit-bearing orchards – pick peaches in July – surrounding an 1884 barn and farmstead

with cats and chickens. But more than anything, it's the vibe that's wonderful: casual and down-to-earth, with a major emphasis on *fun*. Sauvignon blanc is its best-known wine, but the merlot merits attention. There's also a dry, restrained cabernet, atypical in Napa. All are organic. Appointments required. Bottles cost $18 to $42.

Hall WINERY

(Map p160; ☎707-967-2626; www.hallwines.com; 401 St Helena Hwy, St Helena; tastings $15-25; ⏰10am-5:30pm; 🐾) Owned by Clinton's former ambassador to Austria, Hall specializes in cabernet franc, sauvignon blanc, merlot and cabernet sauvignon. There's a cool abstract-sculpture garden, a lovely picnic area shaded by mulberry trees (with wines by the glass), and a LEED-gold-certified winery – California's first (tours $45, including barrel tastings). Bottles cost $22 to $80.

Elizabeth Spencer TASTING ROOM

(Map p160; ☎707-963-6067; www.elizabethspencerwines.com; 1165 Rutherford Rd, Rutherford; tastings $20; ⏰10am-6pm; 🐾) Taste inside an 1872 railroad depot or an outdoor garden. Small-lot wines include monster-sized pinot noir, and a well-priced grapefruity sauvignon blanc. Bottles $20 to $85.

Long Meadow Ranch TASTING ROOM

(Map p160; ☎707-963-4555; www.longmeadowranch.com; 738 Main St, St Helena; tastings $10-30; ⏰11am-6pm) Excellent olive-oil tastings (free) and fine cabernet and sauvignon blanc (bottles $19-35), served inside an 1874 farmhouse surrounded by lovely gardens.

Pride Mountain WINERY

(Map p160; ☎707-963-4949; www.pridewines.com; 4026 Spring Mountain Rd, St Helena; tastings $10; ⏰by appointment; 👪🐾) High atop Spring Mountain, cult-favorite Pride straddles the Napa-Sonoma border and bottles vintages under both appellations. The well-structured cabernet sauvignon and heavy-hitting merlot are the best-known wines, but there are also elegant viognier (perfect with oysters) and standout cab franc, available only at the winery. Picnicking here is spectacular (choose Viewpoint for drop-dead vistas, or Ghost Winery for shade and historic ruins of a 19th-century winery), but you *must* first reserve a tasting appointment. Bottles cost $37 to $85.

Cade WINERY

(Map p160; ☎707-965-2746; www.cadewinery.com; 360 Howell Mtn Rd, Angwin; tasting $20; ⏰by appointment) Ascend Mt Veeder for drop-dead vistas, 1800ft above the valley floor, at Napa's oh-so-swank, first-ever organically farmed, LEED gold-certified winery, owned in part by former San Francisco Mayor Gavin Newsom. Hawks ride thermals at eye level as you sample bright sauvignon blanc and luscious cabernet sauvignon that's more Bordelaise in style than Californian. Reservations required. Bring your camera.

Casa Nuestra WINERY

(Map p160; ☎707-963-5783; www.casanuestra.com; 3451 Silverado Trail, St Helena; tastings $10, refundable with purchase; ⏰by appointment; 👪🐾) A peace flag and a portrait of Elvis greet you in the tasting barn at this old-school, '70s-vintage, mom-and-pop winery, which produces unusual blends and interesting varietals (including good chenin blanc) and 100% cabernet franc. Vineyards are all-organic and the sun provides the power. Best of all, you can picnic free (call ahead and buy a bottle) beneath weeping willows, beside two happy goats. Bottles cost $20 to $55.

Ladera WINERY

(Map p160; ☎707-965-2445, 866-523-3728; www.laderavineyards.com; 150 White Cottage Rd S, Angwin; tastings $15; ⏰by appointment) High atop Howell Mountain, Ladera makes wonderful,

CUTTING COSTS IN NAPA

To avoid overspending on tasting fees, it's perfectly acceptable to pay for one tasting to share between two people. Ask in advance if fees are applicable to purchase (they usually aren't). Tour fees, by contrast, cannot be split. Ask at your hotel for free- or discounted-tasting coupons. If you can't afford the valley's hotels, try western Sonoma County, but if you want to be nearer Napa, try the suburban towns of Vallejo and American Canyon, about 20 minutes from downtown Napa. Both have motels for about $75 to $125 in high season. Also find chains 30 minutes away in Fairfield, off I-80 exits 41 (Pittman Rd) and 45 (Travis Blvd).

little-known, estate-grown cabernet sauvignon and sauvignon blanc. Make an appointment to visit this well-off-the-beaten-path 1886 stone-walled winery, one of Napa's oldest. Tasting fees refunded with two-bottle purchase. Bottles run $25 to $70.

Schramsberg WINERY

(Map p160; ☎707-942-4558; www.schramsberg.com; 1400 Schramsberg Rd; tastings $45; ⏲by appointment) Napa's second-oldest winery, Schramsberg makes some of California's best brut sparkling wines, and in 1972 was the first domestic wine served at the White House. Blanc de blancs is the signature. The appointment-only tasting and tour (book well ahead) is expensive, but you'll sample all the *tête de cuvées,* not just the low-end wines. Tours include a walk through the caves; bring a sweater. Located off Peterson Dr. Bottles cost $22 to $100.

Castello di Amorosa WINERY

(Map p160; ☎707-967-6272; www.castellodiamorosa.com; 4045 Hwy 29, Calistoga; tasting $10-15, tour adult/child $32/22; ⏲by appointment;) It took 14 years to build this perfectly replicated 12th-century Italian castle, complete with moat, hand-cut stone walls, ceiling frescoes by Italian artisans, Roman-style cross-vault brick catacombs, and a torture chamber with period equipment. You can taste without an appointment, but this is one tour worth taking. Oh, the wine? Some respectable Italian varietals, including a velvety Tuscan blend, and a merlot blend that goes great with pizza. Bottles cost $20 to $125.

Vincent Arroyo WINERY

(Map p160; ☎707-942-6995; www.vincentarroyo.com; 2361 Greenwood Ave, Calistoga; tastings free; ⏲by appointment;) The tasting room at Vincent Arroyo is a garage, where you may even meet Mr Arroyo, known for his all-estate-grown petite sirah and cabernet sauvignon. These wines are distributed nowhere else and are so consistently good that 75% of production is sold before it's bottled. Tastings are free, but appointments required. Bottles cost $22 to $45.

Lava Vine TASTING ROOM

(Map p160; ☎707-942-9500; www.lavavine.com; 965 Silverado Trail, Calistoga; tasting $10 waived with purchase; ⏲10am-5pm, appointment suggested;) Breaking ranks with Napa snobbery, the party kids at Lava Vine take a lighthearted approach to their seriously good wines, all paired with small bites, including some hot off the barbecue. Children and dogs play outside, while you let your guard down in the tiny tasting room and tap your toe to James Brown. Bring a picnic. Reservations recommended.

Napa

The valley's workaday hub was once a nothing-special city of storefronts, Victorian cottages and riverfront warehouses, but booming real-estate values caused an influx of new money that has transformed Napa into a growing city of arts and food.

Sights & Activities

Napa lies between Silverado Trail and St Helena Hwy/Hwy 29. For downtown, exit Hwy 29 at 1st St and drive east. Napa's main drag, 1st St, is lined with shops and restaurants.

Oxbow Public Market COVERED MARKET

(Map p165; ☎707-226-6529; www.oxbowpublicmarket.com; 610 1st St; ⏲9am-7pm Mon-Sat, to 8pm Tue, 10am-6pm Sun;) Showcasing all things culinary – from produce stalls to kitchen stores to fantastic edibles – Oxbow is foodie central, with an emphasis on seasonal-regional ingredients, grown sustainably. For more, see p167.

di Rosa Art & Nature Preserve GALLERY, NATURE RESERVE

(Map p160; ☎707-226-5991; www.dirosapreserve.org; 5200 Carneros Hwy 121; ⏲gallery 9:30am-3pm Wed-Fri, by appointment Sat) West of downtown, scrap-metal sheep graze Carneros vineyards at 217-acre di Rosa Preserve, a stunning collection of Northern California art, displayed indoors in galleries and outdoors in sculpture gardens. Reservations recommended for tours.

Sleeping

Summer demand exceeds supply. Weekend rates skyrocket. Also try Calistoga (p174).

TOP CHOICE **Carneros Inn** RESORT $$$

(Map p160; ☎707-299-4900; www.thecarnerosinn.com; 4048 Sonoma Hwy; r Mon-Fri $485-570, Sat & Sun $650-900;) Carneros Inn's snappy aesthetic and retro small-town agricultural theme shatters the predictable Wine Country mold. The semidetached, corrugated-metal cottages look like itinerant housing, but

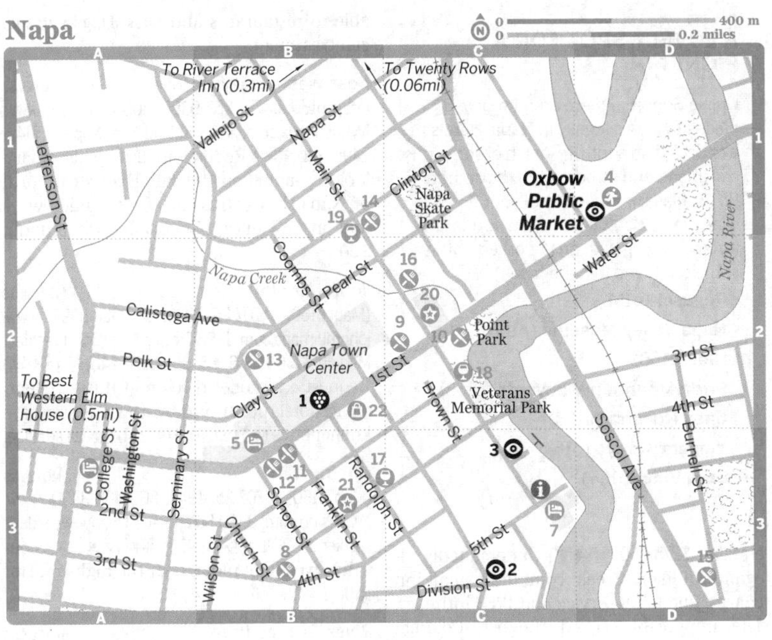

Napa

Top Sights

Oxbow Public Market D1

Sights

1 Ceja B2
2 Napa Library C3
3 Napa River Vélo C3

Activities, Courses & Tours

4 Napa Valley Adventure Tours D1

Sleeping

5 Avia Hotel B3
6 Blackbird Inn A3
7 Napa River Inn C3

Eating

8 Alexis Baking Co B3
9 Bistro Sabor C2
10 Bounty Hunter Wine Bar C2
11 Norman Rose Tavern B3
12 Oenotri B3
13 Pearl Bistro B2
14 Pizza Azzuro B1
15 Soscol Café D3
16 Ubuntu C2

Drinking

17 Billco's Billiards & Darts B3
18 Downtown Joe's C2
19 Vintners' Collective B1

Entertainment

20 Napa Valley Opera House C2
Salsa Saturdays at Bistro Sabor .... (see 9)
Silo's Jazz Club .... (see 7)
21 Uptown Theater B3

Shopping

22 Betty's Girl B2
Napa General Store .... (see 7)

inside they're snappy and chic, with cherry-wood floors, ultrasuede headboards, wood-burning fireplaces, heated-tile bathroom floors, giant tubs and indoor-outdoor showers. Splurge on a vineyard-view room. Linger by day at the hilltop swimming pool, and by night at the bar's outdoor fireplaces. Two excellent onsite restaurants.

Milliken Creek Inn INN $$$
(Map p160; ☎707-255-1197, 888-622-5775; www.millikencreekinn.com; 1815 Silverado Trail; r incl

A LOVELY SPOT FOR A PICNIC

Unlike Sonoma, there aren't many places to picnic legally in Napa. Here's a short list, in south-to-north order, but call ahead and remember to buy a bottle (or glass, if available) of your host's wine. If you don't finish it, California law forbids driving with an uncorked bottle in the car (keep it in the trunk).

» **Regusci** (p162)

» **Napa Valley Museum** (p168)

» **Hall** (p163)

» **Pride Mountain Vineyards** (p163)

» **Casa Nuestra** (p163)

» **Vincent Arroyo** (p164)

» **Lava Vine** (p164)

breakfast $275-650; ❄@☜) Understatedly elegant Milliken Creek combines small-inn charm, fine-hotel service and B&B intimacy. The impeccably styled, English Colonial rooms have top-flight amenities, fireplaces, ultrahigh-thread-count linens, and breakfast in bed. Book a river-view room.

Cottages of Napa Valley BUNGALOWS **$$$**
(Map p160; ☎707-252-7810; www.napacottages.com; 1012 Darns Lane; d $395-500, q $475-575; ❄☜) Originally constructed in the 1940s and rebuilt with top-end amenities in 2005, these eight cottages are ideal for a romantic hideaway, with extra-long soaking tubs, gas fireplaces, and outdoor fire pits beneath towering pines. Cottages 4 and 8 have private porches and swinging chairs. The only drawback is traffic noise, but interiors are silent.

Avia Hotel HOTEL **$$**
(Map p165; ☎707-224-3900; www.aviahotels.com; 1450 1st St, Napa; r $149-249; ❄@☜) Downtown Napa's newest hotel opened in 2009 and feels like a big-city hotel, with business-class-fancy rooms, styled in sexy retro-70s chic. Walkable to restaurants and bars.

Napa River Inn HOTEL **$$$**
(Map p165; ☎707-251-8500, 877-251-8500; www.napariverinn.com; 500 Main St; r include breakfast $229-349; ❄@☜🐾) Beside the river, in the 1884 Hatt Building, the inn has upper-midrange rooms in three satellite buildings, ranging from Victoriana to modern. Walkable to restaurants and bars. Dogs get special treatment.

Best Western Ivy Hotel HOTEL **$$**
(Map p160; ☎707-253-9300, 800-253-6272; www.ivyhotelnapa.com; 4195 Solano Ave, Napa; r $149-249; ❄@☜≋) Redone in 2011, this smart-looking motel, on the suburban strip north of Napa, has extras like fridge, microwave and onsite laundry. Good value when under $200.

John Muir Inn HOTEL **$$**
(Map p160; ☎707-257-7220, 800-522-8999; www.johnmuirnapa.com; 1998 Trower Ave; r incl breakfast Mon-Fri $130-155, Sat & Sun $170-240; ❄@☜≋) Request a remodeled room at this excellent-value hotel, north of downtown. Some have kitchenettes ($5 extra). Hot tub, great service.

Chablis Inn MOTEL **$$**
(Map p160; ☎707-257-1944, 800-443-3490; www.chablisinn.com; 3360 Solano Ave, Napa; r weekday/weekend $89-109/$159-179; ❄@☜≋) A good-value, well-kept motel near the highway. Hot tub.

River Terrace Inn HOTEL **$$$**
(☎7070-320-9000, 866-627-2386; www.riverterraceinn.com; 1600 Soscol Ave; r $189-289; ❄☜≋) An upmarket chain-style hotel, fronting on the Napa River. Heated outdoor pool.

Casita Bonita BUNGALOW **$$$**
(☎707-259-1980, 707-738-5587; www.lacasitabonita.com; q $375; ❄☜👪) Smartly decorated two-bedroom cottage with full kitchen and veggie garden – kids love the chickens. Perfect for two couples or a family.

Best Western Elm House INN **$$**
(off Map p165; ☎707-255-1831; www.bestwesternelmhouseinn.com; 800 California Blvd; r include breakfast $149-229; ❄@☜) Impeccably kept rooms with generic furnishings in soft pastels. Ideal for conservative travelers. Ten minute walk to downtown; easy highway access. Hot tub.

Blackbird Inn B&B **$$$**
(Map p165; ☎707-226-2450, 888-567-9811; www.blackbirdinnnapa.com; 1775 1st St; r incl breakfast $185-300; ❄☜) Gorgeous, eight-room Arts and Crafts–style B&B, but anticipate traffic noise.

Napa Valley Redwood Inn MOTEL **$$**
(☎707-257-6111, 877-872-6272; www.napavalleyredwoodinn.com; 3380 Solano Ave; r Mon-Fri $90-110,

Sat & Sun $140-150;) Generic freeway-side motel.

Eating

Make reservations when possible. July to mid-August, look for the peach stand at Deer Park Rd and Silverado Trail (across Deer Park Rd from Stewart's farmstand) for juicy-delicious heirloom varieties.

Oxbow Public Market COVERED MARKET $
(Map p165; www.oxbowpublicmarket.com; 610 & 644 First St, Napa; 9am-7pm Mon-Sat, 10am-5pm Sun;) Graze your way through this gourmet market and plug into the Northern California food scene. Look for Hog Island oysters (six for $15); comfort cooking at celeb-chef Todd Humphries' Kitchen Door (mains $13 to $20); Pica Pica's Venezuelan cornbread sandwiches ($8); standout Cal-Mexican at Casa (tacos $4 to $8); pastries at Ca'Momi ($1.50); and Three Twins certified-organic ice cream ($3.65 single cone). Tuesday is locals night, with many discounts. Tuesday and Saturday mornings, there's a farmers market. Friday nights bring live music. Some stalls remain open till 9pm, even on Sundays, but many close earlier.

Ubuntu VEGETARIAN $$
(Map p165; 707-251-5656; www.ubuntunapa.com; 1140 Main St, Napa; dishes $14-18; dinner nightly, lunch Sat & Sun;) The Michelin-starred, seasonal, vegetarian menu features artfully presented natural wonders from the biodynamic kitchen garden, satisfying hearty eaters with four-to-five inspired small plates, and eco-savvy drinkers with 100-plus sustainably produced wines.

Boon Fly Café AMERICAN $$
(Map p160; 707-299-4870; www.theboonflycafe.com; 4048 Sonoma Hwy; mains $10-20; 7am-9pm) For New American comfort food done well, make a beeline to Boon Fly – but avoid peak meal times unless you've made reservations. At breakfast, try homemade doughnuts or brioche French toast; at lunch and dinner, grilled Reubens, roasted chicken, and spinach salads. Save room for warm chocolate-chip cookies.

Pearl Restaurant NEW AMERICAN $$
(Map p165; 707-224-9161; www.therestaurantpearl.com; 1339 Pearl St; mains $14-19; Tue-Sat 5:30-9pm;) Meet locals at this dog-friendly bistro with red-painted concrete floors, pinewood tables and open-rafter ceilings. The winning down-to-earth cooking includes double-cut pork chops, chicken verde with polenta, steak tacos and the specialty, oysters.

Oenotri ITALIAN $$
(707-252-1022; www.oenotri.com; 1425 First St, Napa; mains $15-25; dinner, lunch hours vary) Housemade salumi and pastas, and wood-fired Naples-style pizzas are the stars at always-busy Oenotri, which draws bon vivants for its daily-changing lineup of locally sourced, rustic-Italian cooking, served in a cavernous brick-walled space.

Bistro Don Giovanni ITALIAN $$$
(Map p160; 707-224-3300; www.bistrodongiovanni.com; 4110 Howard Lane at Hwy 29; mains $19-26) This long-running favorite roadhouse cooks up modern-Italian pastas, crispy pizzas and wood-roasted meats. Reservations essential. Weekends get packed – and loud. Request a vineyard-view table (good luck).

Bounty Hunter Wine Bar AMERICAN $$
(Map p165; www.bountyhunterwine.com; 975 1st St; dishes $14-24; 11am-10pm;) Inside an 1888 grocery store, Bounty Hunter has an old West vibe and superb barbecue, made with house-smoked meats. The standout whole chicken is roasted over a can of Tecate. Ten local beers and 40 wines by the glass.

Bistro Sabor LATIN AMERICAN $
(Map p165; 707-252-0555; www.bistrosabor.com; 1126 1st St; dishes $8-11; 11:30am-11pm Tue-Thu, 11:30am-1:30am Fri & Sat;) Not your typical Mexican joint, this order-at-the-counter downtowner makes super-fresh Latin American street foods, including ceviches, papusas and chile rellenos. Save room for churros.

Alexis Baking Co CAFE $
(Map p165; 707-258-1827; www.alexisbakingcompany.com; 1517 3rd St; dishes $6-10; Mon-Fri 7:30am-3pm, Sat 7am-3pm, Sun 8am-2pm;) Our fave spot for scrambles, granola, focaccia sandwiches, big cups of joe and boxed lunches to go.

Pizza Azzuro PIZZERIA $$
(Map p165; 707-255-5552; www.azzurropizzeria.com; 1260 Main St; mains $12-16;) This Napa classic gets deafeningly loud, but the tender-crusted pizzas and salad-topped 'manciata'

bread make the noise worth bearing. Good Caesar salad and pastas.

Norman Rose Tavern PUB $$
(707-258-1516; normanrosenapa.com; 1401 1st St; mains $10-20; 11:30am-10pm) This happening gastropub, styled with reclaimed wood and tufted-leather banquettes, is good for a burger and beer. Great fries. Beer and wine only.

Soscol Café DINER $
(Map p165; 707-252-0651; 632 Soscol Av; dishes $6-9; 6am-2pm Mon-Sat, 7am-1pm Sun) The ultimate greasy-spoon diner, Soscol makes massive huevos rancheros, and chicken-fried steak and eggs. Not a high heel in sight.

Drinking & Entertainment

Silo's Jazz Club LIVE MUSIC
(Map p165; 707-251-5833; www.silosjazzclub.com; 530 Main St; cover varies; Wed-Thu 4-10pm, Fri & Sat to midnight) A cabaret-style wine-and-beer bar, Silo's hosts jazz and rock acts Friday and Saturday nights; Wednesday and Thursdays it's good for drinks. Reservations recommended weekends.

Salsa Saturdays at Bistro Sabor DANCE
(Map p165; www.bistrosabor.com; 1126 1st St; admission free; 10pm-1:30am Sat) DJs spin salsa and merengue at this happening Saturday-night restaurant dance party.

Billco's Billiards & Darts SPORTS BAR
(Map p165; www.billcos.com; 1234 3rd St; noon-1am) Dudes in khakis swill craft beers, shoot pool and throw darts.

Downtown Joe's SPORTS BAR, BREWERY
(Map p165; www.downtownjoes.com; 902 Main St at 2nd St;) Live music Thursday to Sunday, TV sports nightly. Often packed, sometimes messy.

Napa Valley Opera House THEATER
(Map p165; 707-226-7372; www.nvoh.org; 1030 Main St) Restored vintage-1880s opera house; straight plays, comedy and major acts.

Uptown Theatre THEATER
(Map p165; 707-259-0333; www.uptowntheatrenapa.com; 1350 3rd St) Big name acts play this restored 1937 theater.

Shopping

Betty's Girl WOMEN'S CLOTHING, VINTAGE
(707-254-7560; 1144 Main St) Hollywood costume designer Kim Northrup fits women with fabulous vintage cocktail dresses, altering and shipping for no additional charge.

Napa General Store GIFTS
(707-259-0762; www.napageneralstore.com; 540 Main St) Finally, clever Wine Country souvenirs that are reasonably priced. The on-site wine bar is convenient for non-shopping husbands.

Information

Napa Valley Welcome Center (707-260-0107; www.legendarynapavalley.com; 600 Main St; 9am-5pm) Spa deals, wine-tasting passes and comprehensive winery maps.

Napa Library (707-253-4241; www.countyofnapa.org/Library; 580 Coombs St; 10am-9pm Mon-Thu, 10am-6pm Fri & Sat; @) Email connections.

Queen of the Valley Medical Center (707-252-4411; 1000 Trancas St) Emergency medical.

Getting Around

Pedi cabs park outside downtown restaurants – especially at the foot of Main St, near the NV Welcome Center – in summertime.

Yountville

This onetime stagecoach stop, 9 miles north of Napa, is now a major foodie destination, with more Michelin stars per capita than any other American town. There are some good inns here, but it's deathly boring at night. You stay in Yountville to drink with dinner without having to drive afterward. St Helena and Calistoga make better bases. Most businesses are on Washington St.

Ma(i)sonry (707-944-0889; www.maisonry.com; 6711 Washington St; 9am-10pm) occupies a 1904 stone house, now transformed into a rustic-modern showplace for furniture, art and wine; the garden is a swank post-dinner fireside gathering spot for vino.

Yountville's modernist 40,000-sq-ft **Napa Valley Museum** (707-944-0500; www.napavalleymuseum.org; 55 Presidents Circle; adult/child $5/2.50; 10am-5pm Wed-Mon), off California Dr, chronicles cultural history and showcases local paintings. Good picnicking outside.

The only worthwhile shop at V Marketplace is TV-chef Michael Chiarello's **Napa Style** (www.napastyle.com; 6525 Washington St), but it's overpriced.

FLYING & BALLOONING

Wine Country is stunning from the air – a multihued tapestry of undulating hills, deep valleys and rambling vineyards. Make reservations.

The **Vintage Aircraft Company** (Map p180; ☎707-938-2444; www.vintageaircraft.com; 23982 Arnold Dr) flies over Sonoma in a vintage biplane with an awesome pilot who'll do loop-de-loops on request (add $50). Twenty-minute tours cost $175/270 for one/two adults.

Napa Valley's signature hot-air balloon flights leave early, around 6am or 7am, when the air is coolest; they usually include a champagne breakfast on landing. Adults pay about $200 to $250, and kids $130 to $150. Call **Balloons above the Valley** (☎707-253-2222, 800-464-6824; www.balloonrides.com) or **Napa Valley Balloons** (☎707-944-0228, 800-253-2224; www.napavalleyballoons.com), both in Yountville.

Sleeping

Bardessono LUXURY HOTEL $$$
(☎707-204-6000, 877-932-5333; www.bardessono.com; 6524 Yount St; r $600-800, ste from $800;) The outdoors flows indoors at California's first-ever LEED-platinum-certified green hotel, made of recycled everything, styled in Japanese-led austerity, with neutral tones and hard angles that feel exceptionally urban for farm country. Glam pool deck and onsite spa. Tops for a splurge.

Poetry Inn INN $$$
(☎707-944-0646; www.poetryinn.com; 6380 Silverado Trail; r incl breakfast $650-1400;) There's no better view of Napa Valley than from this understatedly chic, three-room inn, high on the hills east of Yountville. Rooms are decorated in Arts and Crafts-inspired style, and have private balconies, wood-burning fireplaces, 1000-thread-count linens and enormous baths with indoor-outdoor showers. Bring a ring.

Maison Fleurie B&B $$$
(☎707-944-2056, 800-788-0369; www.maisonfleurienapa.com; 6529 Yount St; r incl breakfast $145-295;) Rooms at this ivy-covered country inn are in a century-old home and carriage house, decorated in French-provincial style. There's a big breakfast, and afternoon wine and *hors d'oeuvres*. Hot tub.

Napa Valley Lodge HOTEL $$$
(☎707-944-2468, 888-944-3545; www.napavalleylodge.com; 2230 Madison St; r $300-455;) It looks like a condo complex, but rooms are spacious and modern, some with fireplaces. Hot tub, sauna and exercise room.

Petit Logis INN $$$
(☎707-944-2332, 877-944-2332; www.petitlogis.com; 6527 Yount St; r Mon-Fri $195-255, Sat & Sun $235-285;) This cedar-sided inn has five individually decorated rooms. Think white wicker furniture and dusty-rose fabric. Add $20 for breakfast for two.

Napa Valley Railway Inn THEME INN $$
(☎707-944-2000; www.napavalleyrailwayinn.com; 6523 Washington St, Yountville; r $125-260;) Sleep in a converted railroad car, part of two short trains parked at a central platform. They've little privacy, but are moderately priced. Bring earplugs.

Eating

Make reservations or you might not eat. **Yountville Park** (cnr Washington & Madison Sts) has picnic tables and barbecue grills, you'll find groceries across from the post office, and there's a great **taco truck** (6764 Washington St).

French Laundry CALIFORNIAN $$$
(☎707-944-2380; www.frenchlaundry.com; 6640 Washington St; prix fixe incl service charge $270; ⏱dinner, lunch Sat & Sun) The pinnacle of California dining, Thomas Keller's French Laundry is epic, a high-wattage culinary experience on par with the world's best. Book two months ahead at 10am sharp, or log onto OpenTable.com precisely at midnight. Avoid tables before 7pm; first-service seating moves faster than the second – sometimes too fast.

Bouchon FRENCH $$$
(☎707-944-8037; www.bouchonbistro.com; 6534 Washington St; mains $17-36; ⏱11:30am-12:30am) At celeb-chef Thomas Keller's French brasserie, everything from food to decor is so authentic, from zinc bar to white-aproned

waiters, you'd swear you were in Paris – even the Bermuda-shorts-clad Americans look out of place. On the menu: oysters, onion soup, roasted chicken, leg of lamb, trout with almonds, runny cheeses and profiteroles for dessert, impeccably prepared.

TOP CHOICE **Ad Hoc** NEW AMERICAN $$$
(☎707-944-2487; www.adhocrestaurant.com; 6476 Washington St, Yountville; menu $48; ⊙Wed-Mon dinner, Sun 10:30am-2pm) Another winning formula by Yountville's culinary oligarch, Thomas Keller, Ad Hoc serves the master's favorite American home cooking in four-course family-style menus, with no variations except for dietary restrictions. Monday is fried-chicken night, which you can also sample weekend lunchtime, take-out only, behind the restaurant at Keller's latest venture, **Addendum** (⊙11am-2pm Thu-Sat), which also serves barbecue; get the daily menu on Twitter at @AddendumatAdHoc.

Étoile CALIFORNIAN $$$
(Map p160; ☎707-944-8844; www.chandon.com; 1 California Dr; lunch/dinner mains $26-31/$32-36; ⊙11:30am-2:30pm & 6-9pm Thu-Mon) Within Chandon winery, Michelin-starred Étoile's is perfect for a lingering white-tablecloth lunch in the vines; ideal when you want to visit a winery and eat a good meal with minimal driving.

Bistro Jeanty FRENCH $$$
(☎707-944-0103; www.bistrojeanty.com; 6510 Washington St; mains $18-29) A true French bistro serves comfort food to weary travelers, and that's exactly what French-born chef-owner Philippe Jeanty does, with succulent cassoulet, coq au vin, *steak-frites,* braised pork with lentils, and scrumptious tomato soup.

Paninoteca Ottimo SANDWICHES, CAFE $
(☎707-945-1229; www.napastyleottimocafe.com; 6525 Washington St; dishes $8-10; ⊙10am-6pm Mon-Sat, 10am-5pm Sat) TV-chef Michael Chiarello's cafe makes stellar salads and delish paninos (try the slow-roasted pork) that pair well with his organically produced wines. Tops for picnic supplies.

Bouchon Bakery BAKERY $
(☎707-944-2253; www.bouchonbakery.com; 6528 Washington St; dishes $3-9; ⊙7am-7pm) Bouchon makes perfect French pastries and strong coffee. Order at the counter and sit outside, or pack a bag to go.

Mustards Grill CALIFORNIAN $$$
(Map p160; ☎707-944-2424; www.mustardsgrill.com; 7399 St Helena Hwy; mains $22-27;) The valley's original roadhouse whips up wood-fired California comfort food – roasted meats, lamb shanks, pork chops, hearty salads and sandwiches. Great crowd-pleaser.

Drinking & Entertainment

Pancha's DIVE BAR
(6764 Washington St) Swill tequila with vineyard workers early, restaurant waiters late.

Lincoln Theater THEATER
(Map p160; ☎707-944-1300, 866-944-9199; www.lincolntheater.org; 100 California Dr) Various artists play this 1200-seat theater, including the Napa Valley Symphony.

Oakville & Rutherford

But for its famous grocery, you'd drive through Oakville (pop 71) and never know you'd missed it. This is the middle of the grapes – vineyards sprawl in every direction. Rutherford (pop 164) is more conspicuous, but the wineries put these towns on the map.

Sleeping & Eating

There's no budget lodging here.

Auberge du Soleil LUXURY HOTEL $$$
(Map p160; ☎707-963-1211, 800-348-5406; www.aubergedusoleil.com; 180 Rutherford Hill Rd; r $650-975, ste $1400-2200;) The top splurge for a no-holds-barred romantic weekend, Auberge's hillside cottages are second to none. Less-expensive rooms feel comparatively cramped; book a suite. Excellent guests-only spa. Auberge's **dining room** (mains breakfast $16-19, lunch $29-42, 3-/4-/6-course prix-fixe dinner $98/115/140) showcases an expertly prepared Euro-Cal menu, among the valley's best. Come for a fancy breakfast, lazy lunch or will-you-wear-my-ring dinner. Valley views are mesmerizing from the terrace – *don't* sit inside. Make reservations; arrive before sunset.

Rancho Caymus HOTEL $$$
(☎707-963-1777, 800-845-1777; www.ranchocaymus.com; 1140 Rutherford Rd, Rutherford; r $175-285;) Styled after California's missions, this hacienda-style inn scores high marks for its tiled fountain courtyard, and rooms' kiva-style fireplaces, oak-beamed

ceilings and wood floors, but the furniture looks tired.

La Luna Market & Taqueria MARKET $
(Map p160; ☎707-963-3211; 1153 Rutherford Rd, Rutherford; dishes $4-6; ⊙9am-5pm May-Nov) Look no further for honest burritos with homemade hot sauce.

Rutherford Grill AMERICAN $$
(☎707-963-1792; www.hillstone.com; 1180 Rutherford Rd, Rutherford; mains $15-30) Yes, it's a chain (Houston's), but to rub shoulders with winemakers, snag a stool for lunch at the bar. The food is consistent – ribs, rotisserie chicken, outstanding grilled artichokes – and there's no corkage, so bring that bottle you just bought down the road.

Oakville Grocery & Cafe DELI $$
(Map p160; ☎707-944-8802; www.oakvillegrocery.com; 7856 Hwy 29, Oakville; ⊙8am-5:30pm) The once-definitive Wine Country deli has gotten ridiculously overpriced, with less variety than in previous years, but still carries excellent cheeses, charcuterie, bread, olives and wine. There are tables outside, but ask where to picnic nearby.

St Helena

You'll know you're arriving when traffic halts. St Helena (ha-*lee*-na) is the Rodeo Dr of Napa, with fancy boutiques lining Main St (Hwy 29). The historic downtown is good for a stroll, with great window-shopping, but parking is next-to-impossible summer weekends.

The **St Helena Welcome Center** (☎707-963-4456, 800-799-6456; www.sthelena.com; 657 Main St; ⊙9am-5pm Mon-Fri) has information and lodging assistance.

Sights & Activities

FREE **Silverado Museum** MUSEUM
(Map p160; ☎707-963-3757; www.silveradomuseum.org; 1490 Library Lane; ⊙noon-4pm Tue-Sat) Contains a fascinating collection of Robert Louis Stevenson memorabilia. In 1880, the author – then sick, penniless and unknown – stayed in an abandoned bunkhouse at the old Silverado Mine on Mt St Helena (p177) with his wife, Fanny Osbourne; his novel *The Silverado Squatters* is based on his time there. To reach Library Lane, turn east off Hwy 29 at the Adams St traffic light and cross the railroad tracks.

Culinary Institute of America at Greystone COOKING SCHOOL
(Map p160; ☎707-967-2320; www.ciachef.edu/california; 2555 Main St; mains $25-29, cooking demonstration $20; ⊙restaurant 11:30am-9pm, cooking demonstrations 1:30pm Sat & Sun) An 1889 stone chateau houses a gadget- and cookbook-filled **culinary shop**; fine **restaurant**; weekend **cooking demonstrations**; and **wine-tasting classes** by luminaries in the field, including Karen MacNeil, author of *The Wine Bible*.

Farmers market MARKET
(www.sthelenafarmersmkt.org; ⊙7:30am-noon Fri May-Oct) Meets at Crane Park, half a mile south of downtown.

Sleeping

Meadowood RESORT $$$
(Map p160; ☎707-963-3646, 800-458-8080; www.meadowood.com; 900 Meadowood Lane; r from $600;) Hidden in a wooded dell with towering pines and miles of hiking, Napa's grandest resort has cottages and rooms in satellite buildings surrounding a croquet lawn. We most like the hillside fireplace cottages; lawn-view rooms lack privacy but are good for families, with room to play outside. The vibe is country club, with white-clapboard buildings reminiscent of New England. Wear linen and play *Great Gatsby*. Kids love the mammoth pool.

Harvest Inn INN $$$
(☎707-963-9463, 800-950-8466; www.harvestinn.com; 1 Main St; r incl breakfast $329-549;) If you can't swing Meadowood, this former estate, with sprawling gardens and rooms in satellite buildings, is a lovely backup. The new building is generic; book the vineyard-view rooms, with their private hot tubs.

El Bonita Motel MOTEL $$
(Map p160; ☎707-963-3216, 800-541-3284; www.elbonita.com; 195 Main St, St Helena; $119-179; @) Book in advance to secure a room at this sought-after motel, with up-to-date rooms (quietest are in back), attractive grounds, hot tub and sauna.

Hotel St Helena HISTORIC HOTEL $$
(☎707-963-4388; www.hotelsthelena.net; 1309 Main St; r with/without bath $125-235/$105-165;) Decorated with period furnishings, this frayed-at-the-edges 1881 hotel sits right downtown. Rooms are tiny, but good value, especially those with shared bathroom. No elevator.

Eating

Make reservations where possible. If you're just after something quick, consider **Gillwood's Cafe** (www.gillwoodscafe.com; 1313 Main St; dishes $8-12; 7am-3pm) for an all-day breakfast; **Sunshine Foods** (www.sunshinefoodsmarket.com; 1115 Main St; 7:30am-8:30pm), the town's best grocery and deli; **Model Bakery** (www.themodelbakery.com; 1357 Main St; dishes $5-10; 7am-6pm Tue-Sun, 8am-4pm Sun) for great scones, muffins, salads, gelato, pizzas, sandwiches and strong coffee; or **Armadillo's** (1304 Main St; mains $8-12) for respectable and reasonable Mexican eats.

Gott's Roadside (Taylor's Auto Refresher) BURGERS $$

(707-963-3486; www.gottsroadside.com; 933 Main St; dishes $8-15; 10:30am-9pm;) Wiggle your toes in the grass and feast on all-natural burgers, Cobb salads and fried calamari at this classic roadside drive-in, whose original name, 'Taylor's Auto Refresher,' is still listed on the roadside sign. Avoid big weekend waits by calling in your order. There's another branch at **Oxbow Public Market** (p167).

Napa Valley Olive Oil Mfg Co MARKET $

(707-963-4173; www.oliveoilsainthelena.com; 835 Charter Oak St; 8am-5:30pm) Before the advent of fancy-food stores, this ramshackle Italian market introduced Napa to Italian delicacies – succulent prosciutto and salami, meaty olives, fresh bread, nutty cheeses and, of course, olive oil. Yellowed business cards from 50 years ago adorn the walls, and the owner knows everyone in town. He'll lend you a knife and a board to make a picnic at the rickety wooden tables outside in the grass. Cash only.

Cook CAL-ITALIAN $$

(707-963-7088; www.cooksthelena.com; 1310 Main St; lunch mains $12-21, dinner mains $17-25; 11:30am-10pm Mon-Sat, 5-10pm Sun) Locals crowd the counter at this tiny storefront bistro, much loved for its earthy cooking – homemade pasta, melt-off-the-bone ribs and simple-delicious burgers. Try the butter-braised Brussels sprouts – fantastic. Expect a wait, even with reservations.

Market NEW AMERICAN $$

(707-963-3799; www.marketsthelena.com; 1347 Main St; mains $13-24; 11:30am-9pm) We love the big portions of simple, fresh American cooking at Market. Maximizing the season's best produce, the chef creates enormous, inventive salads and soul-satisfying mains like buttermilk fried chicken. The stone-walled dining room dates to the 19th century, as does the ornate backbar, where cocktails are muddled to order.

Cindy's Backstreet Kitchen NEW AMERICAN $$

(707-963-1200; www.cindysbackstreetkitchen.com; 1327 Railroad Ave; mains $17-25) The inviting retro-homey decor complements the menu's Cal-American comfort food, like avocado-and-papaya salad, wood-fired duck, steak with French fries, and the simple grilled burger. The bar makes a mean mojito.

Farmstead NEW AMERICAN $$$

(707-963-9181; www.farmsteadnapa.com; 738 Main St; mains $16-26; 11:30am-9pm) A cavernous open-truss barn with big leather booths and rocking-chair porch, Farmstead grows many of its own ingredients – including grass-fed beef – for its earthy menu that highlights wood-fired cooking.

Terra CALIFORNIAN $$$

(707-963-8931; www.terrarestaurant.com; 1345 Railroad Ave; 3-/4-/5-/6-course menus $57/66/81/92; 6-9pm Wed-Sun) Inside an 1884 stone building, Terra wows diners with seamlessly blended Japanese, French and Italian culinary styles. The signature is broiled sake-marinated black cod with shrimp dumplings in shiso broth. Perfect. The bar serves small bites, but the dining room's the thing.

Restaurant at Meadowood CALIFORNIAN $$$

(Map p160; 707-967-1205; www.meadowood.com; 900 Meadowood Lane; 4-/9-course menu $125/225; 5:30-10pm Mon-Sat) If you couldn't score reservations at French Laundry, fear not: the clubby Restaurant at Meadowood – the valley's only other Michelin-three-star restaurant – has a more sensibly priced menu, elegant but unfussy forest-view dining room, and lavish haute cuisine that's never too esoteric. Auberge has better views, but Meadowood's food and service far surpass the former.

Silverado Brewing Co BREWPUB $$

(Map p160; 707-967-9876; www.silveradobrewingcompany.com; 3020 Hwy 29; mains $12-18; 11:30am-1am;) Silverados' microbrews measure up to Napa's wines – Brewmaster Ken Mee's Certifiable Blonde has organic ingredients and crazy-tasty malts, and competes for top choice with the hopped-up Amber Ale. Food is typical pub grub that keeps your buzz in check.

Shopping

Main St is lined with high-end boutiques (think $100 socks), but some mom-and-pop shops remain. Also see p178.

Woodhouse Chocolates FOOD
(www.woodhousechocolate.com; 1367 Main St) Woodhouse looks more like Tiffany & Co than a candy shop, with chocolates similarly priced, but they're made in town and their quality is beyond reproach.

Napa Soap Company BEAUTY
(www.napasoap.com; 651 Main St) Hand-crafted eco-friendly bath products, locally produced.

Lolo's Consignment VINTAGE
(www.lolosconsignment.com; 1120 Main St) Groovy dresses and cast-off cashmere.

Main Street Books BOOKS
(1315 Main St; ⏲Mon-Sat) Good used books.

Calistoga

The least gentrified town in Napa Valley feels refreshingly simple, with an old-fashioned main street lined with shops, not boutiques, and diverse characters wandering the sidewalks. Bad hair? No problem. Fancy-pants St Helena couldn't feel farther away. Most tourists don't make it this far north. You should.

Famed 19th-century author Robert Louis Stevenson said of Calistoga: 'the whole neighborhood of Mt St Helena is full of sulfur and boiling springs...Calistoga itself seems to repose on a mere film above a boiling, subterranean lake.'

Indeed, it does. Calistoga is synonymous with the mineral water bearing its name, bottled here since 1924. Its springs and geysers have earned it the nickname the 'hot springs of the West.' Plan to visit one of the town's spas, where you can indulge in the local specialty: a hot-mud bath, made of the volcanic ash from nearby volcanic Mt St Helena.

The town's odd name comes from Sam Brannan, who founded Calistoga in 1859, believing it would develop like the New York spa town of Saratoga. Apparently Sam liked his drink and at the founding ceremony tripped on his tongue, proclaiming it the 'Cali-stoga' of 'Sara-fornia.' The name stuck.

Sights

Hwys 128 and 29 run together from Rutherford through St Helena; in Calistoga, they split. Hwy 29 turns east and becomes Lincoln Ave, continuing across Silverado Trail, toward Clear Lake. Hwy 128 continues north as Foothill Blvd (not St Helena Hwy). Calistoga's shops and restaurants line Lincoln Ave.

Old Faithful Geyser GEYSER
(Map p160; ☎707-942-6463; www.oldfaithfulgeyser.com; 1299 Tubbs Lane; adult/child $10/free; ⏲9am-6pm summer, to 5pm winter; 👪) Calistoga's mini-version of Yellowstone's Old Faithful shoots boiling water 60ft to 100ft into the air, every 30 minutes. The vibe is pure roadside Americana, with folksy hand-painted interpretive exhibits, picnicking and a little petting zoo, where you can come nose-to-nose with llamas. It's 2 miles north of town, off Silverado Trail. Look for discount coupons around town.

Sharpsteen Museum MUSEUM
(☎707-942-5911; www.sharpsteen-museum.org; 1311 Washington St; adult/child $3/free; ⏲11am-4pm; 👪) Across from the picturesque 1902 City Hall (which was originally an opera house), the Sharpsteen Museum was created by an ex-Disney animator (whose Oscar is on display) and houses a fabulous diorama of the town in the 1860s, big Victorian dollhouse, full-size horse-drawn carriage, cool taxidermy and a restored cottage from Brannan's original resort. (The only Brannan cottage still at its

TOP KID-FRIENDLY WINERIES

» **Kaz** (p180) Play-Doh, playground and grape juice
» **Benziger** (p179) Open-air tram ride and peacocks
» **Frog's Leap** (p162) Cats, chickens and croquet.
» **Casa Nuestra** (p163) Playful goats.
» **Castello di Amorosa** (p164) Historical-imagination sparker.
» **Lava Vine** (p164) Mellow vibe, grassy play area.

original site is at 106 Wapoo Ave, near the Brannan Cottage Inn.)

Activities

Hardcore mountain bikers can tackle **Oat Hill Mine Trail**, one of Northern California's most technically challenging trails, just outside town. Find information and rentals at **Calistoga Bike Shop** (707-942-9687, 866-942-2453; www.calistogabikeshop.com; 1318 Lincoln Ave), which rents full-suspension mountain bikes (per day $75) and hybrids (per hour/day $10/35). Wine-touring packages (per day $80) include wine-rack baskets and free wine pickup.

SPAS

Calistoga is famous for hot-spring spas and mud-bath emporiums, where you're buried in hot mud and emerge feeling supple, detoxified and enlivened. (The mud is made with volcanic ash and peat; the higher the ash content, the better the bath.)

Packages take 60 to 90 minutes and cost $70 to $90. You start semi-submerged in hot mud, then soak in hot mineral water. A steam bath and blanket-wrap follow. The treatment can be extended with a massage, increasing the cost to $130 and up.

Baths can be taken solo or, at some spas, as couples. Variations include thin, painted-on clay-mud wraps (called 'fango' baths, good for those uncomfortable sitting in mud), herbal wraps, seaweed baths and various massage treatments. Discount coupons are sometimes available from the visitors center. Book ahead, especially on summer weekends. Reservations essential at all spas.

The following spas in downtown Calistoga offer one-day packages. Some also offer discounted spa-lodging packages.

TOP CHOICE Indian Springs SPA
(707-942-4913; www.indianspringscalistoga.com; 1712 Lincoln Ave; 8am-9pm) The longest continually operating spa and original Calistoga resort has concrete mud tubs and mines its own ash. Treatments include use of the huge, hot-spring-fed pool. Great cucumber body lotion.

Spa Solage SPA
(Map p160; 707-226-0825; www.solagecalistoga.com; 755 Silverado Trail; 8am-8pm) Chichi, austere, top-end spa, with couples' rooms and a fango-mud bar for DIY paint-on treatments. Also has zero-gravity chairs for blanket wraps, and a clothing-optional pool.

Dr Wilkinson's Hot Springs SPA
(707-942-4102; www.drwilkinson.com; 1507 Lincoln Ave; 8:30am-5:30pm) Fifty years running; 'the doc' uses more peat in its mud.

Mount View Spa SPA
(707-942-6877, 800-816-6877; www.mountviewhotel.com; 1457 Lincoln Ave; 9am-9pm) Traditional full-service, 12-room spa, good for clean-hands gals who prefer painted-on mud to submersion.

Lavender Hill Spa SPA
(Map p160; 707-942-4495; www.lavenderhillspa.com; 1015 Foothill Blvd; 10am-6pm, to 8pm Fri & Sat) Small, cute, two-room spa that uses much-lighter, less-icky lavender-infused mud; offers couples' treatments.

Golden Haven Hot Springs SPA
(707-942-8000; www.goldenhaven.com; 1713 Lake St; 8am-8pm) Old-school and unfussy; offers couples' mud baths and couples' massage.

Calistoga Spa Hot Springs SPA
(707-942-6269, 866-822-5772; www.calistogaspa.com; 1006 Washington St; appointments 8:30am-4:30pm Tue-Thu, to 9pm Fri-Mon;) Traditional mud baths and massage at a motel complex with two huge **swimming pools** (10am-9pm) where kids can play while you soak (pool passes $25).

Sleeping

Also see Safari West (p178).

TOP CHOICE Mountain Home Ranch LODGE, B&B **$$**
(off Map p160; 707-942-6616; www.mountainhomeranch.com; 3400 Mountain Home Ranch Rd; r $109-119, cabin with/without bath $119-144/$69;) In continuous operation since 1913, this 340-acre homestead ranch is a flashback to old California. Doubling as a retreat center, the ranch has simple lodge rooms and rustic freestanding cabins, some with kitchens and fireplaces, ideal for families, but you may be here during someone else's family reunion or spiritual quest. No matter. With miles of oak-woodland trails, a hilltop swimming pool, private lake with canoeing and fishing, and hike-to warm springs in a magical fault-line canyon, you may hardly notice – and you may never make it to a single winery. Breakfast included, but you'll have to drive 15 minutes to town for dinner. Pack hiking boots, not high heels.

Solage RESORT $$$

(Map p160; ☎707-226-0800, 866-942-7442; www.solagecalistoga.com; 755 Silverado Trail; r $510-625;) The latest addition to Calistoga's spa-hotels ups the style factor, with Cali-chic semidetached cottages and a glam palm-tree-lined pool. Rooms are austere, with vaulted ceilings, zillion-thread-count linens and pebble-floor showers. Cruiser bikes included.

Indian Springs Resort RESORT $$$

(☎707-942-4913; www.indianspringscalistoga.com; 1712 Lincoln Ave; motel r $229-299, bungalow $259-349, 2-bedroom bungalow $359-419;) The definitive old-school Calistoga resort, Indian Springs has bungalows facing a central lawn with palm trees, shuffleboard, bocce, hammocks and Weber grills – not unlike a vintage Florida resort. Some bungalows sleep six. There are also top-end motel-style rooms. Huge hot-springs-fed swimming pool.

Chateau De Vie B&B $$$

(Map p160; ☎707-942-6446, 877-558-2513; www.cdvnapavalley.com; 3250 Hwy 128; r incl breakfast $229-429;) Surrounded by vineyards, with gorgeous views of Mt St Helena, CDV has five modern B&B rooms with top-end amenities. The house is elegantly decorated, with zero froufrou. Charming owners serve wine every afternoon on the sun-dappled patio, then leave you alone. Hot tub, big pool. Gay-friendly.

Meadowlark Country House B&B $$$

(Map p160; ☎707-942-5651, 800-942-5651; www.meadowlarkinn.com; 601 Petrified Forest Rd; r incl breakfast $195-275, ste $285;) On 20 acres west of town, Meadowlark has luxury rooms decorated in contemporary style, most with decks and Jacuzzis. Outside there's a hot tub, sauna and clothing-optional pool. The truth-telling innkeeper lives in another house, offers helpful advice, then vanishes when you want privacy. There's a fabulous cottage for $450. Gay-friendly.

Mount View Hotel & Spa HISTORIC HOTEL $$$

(☎707-942-6877, 800-816-6877; www.mountviewhotel.com; 1457 Lincoln Ave; r $179-329;) Smack in the middle of town, this 1917 Mission Revival hotel was redone in 2009 in vaguely mod-Italian style, sometimes at odds with the vintage building, but clean and fresh-looking nonetheless. Gleaming bathrooms, on-site spa, year-round heated pool, but no elevator.

Eurospa Inn MOTEL $$

(☎707-942-6829; www.eurospa.com; 1202 Pine St, Calistoga; r $139-189;) Immaculate single-story motel on a quiet side street, with extras like gas-burning fireplaces, afternoon wine and small on-site spa. Wonderful service, but tiny pool.

Brannan Cottage Inn B&B $$$

(☎707-942-4200; www.brannancottageinn.com; 109 Wapoo Ave; r incl breakfast $195-230, ste $230-270;) Sam Brannan built this 1860 cottage, listed on the National Register of Historic Places. Long on folksy charm and friendly service, it's decorated with floral-print fabrics and simple country furnishings, but walls are thin and floors creak. Suites sleep four. Guests use the pool at Golden Haven motel.

Dr Wilkinson's Motel & Hideaway Cottages MOTEL, COTTAGES $$

(☎707-942-4102; www.drwilkinson.com; 1507 Lincoln Ave; r $149-255, cottages w/kitchens $165-270;) This good-value vintage-1950s motel has well-kept rooms facing a swimming-pool courtyard. No hot tub, but three pools (one indoors) and mud baths. Doc Wilkinson's also rents simple stand-alone cottages, with kitchens, at the affiliated Hideaway Cottages.

Chanric B&B $$$

(Map p160; ☎707-942-4535; www.thechanric.com; 1805 Foothill Blvd; r incl breakfast $229-349;) A converted Victorian close to the road, this B&B has smallish rooms with modern furnishings, but the affable owners compensate with a lavish three-course breakfast. Gay-friendly.

Aurora Park Cottages COTTAGES $$$

(Map p160; ☎707-942-6733, 877-942-7700; www.aurorapark.com; 1807 Foothill Blvd; cottages incl breakfast $259-289;) Six immaculately kept, sunny-yellow cottages – with polished-wood floors, featherbeds and sundeck – stand in a row beside flowering gardens, and though close to the road, they're quiet by night. The innkeeper couldn't be nicer.

Calistoga Spa Hot Springs MOTEL $$

(Map p160; ☎707-942-6269, 866-822-5772; www.calistogaspa.com; 1006 Washington St; r $132-252;) Great for families, who jam the place weekends, this motel-resort has slightly scuffed generic rooms, with kitchenettes, and fantastic pools – two full-size, a kiddie-pool with miniwaterfall and a huge adults-only Jacuzzi. Outside are barbecues and snack bar. Wi-fi in lobby.

Golden Haven Hot Springs MOTEL **$$**
(☎707-942-8000; www.goldenhaven.com; 1713 Lake St; r $149-219; ❄📶🏊) This motel-spa has mudbath-lodging packages and well-kept rooms; some have Jacuzzis.

Calistoga Inn & Brewery INN **$**
(☎707-942-4101; www.calistogainn.com; 1250 Lincoln Ave; r Mon-Fri/Sat & Sun $69/$119; 📶) For no-fuss bargain-hunters, this inn, upstairs from a busy bar, has 18 clean, basic rooms with shared bath. No TVs. Bring earplugs.

Bothe-Napa Valley State Park CAMPGROUND **$**
(☎707-942-4575, reservations 800-444-7275; www.reserveamerica.com; tent & RV sites $35; 🏊) Three miles south, Bothe has shady camping near redwoods, coin-operated showers, and gorgeous hiking, but call ahead to confirm it's open. Sites 28 to 36 are most secluded.

Napa County Fairgrounds & RV Park CAMPGROUND **$**
(Map p160; ☎707-942-5221; www.napacountyfair.org; 1435 Oak St; tent sites $20, RV sites w/hookups $33-36; 📶) A dusty RV park northwest of downtown.

Cottage Grove Inn BUNGALOWS **$$$**
(☎707-942-8400, 800-799-2284; www.cottagegrove.com; 1711 Lincoln Ave; cottages $250-425; ❄📶) Romantic cottages for over-40s, with wood-burning fireplaces, two-person tubs and rocking-chair front porches.

Chelsea Garden Inn B&B **$$$**
(☎707-942-0948; www.chelseagardeninn.com; 1443 2nd St; r incl breakfast $195-275; ❄📶🏊) On a quiet street, five floral-print rooms with private entrances. Pretty gardens, but the pool looked dingy at our last inspection.

Wine Way Inn B&B **$$**
(Map p160; ☎707-942-0680, 800-572-0679; www.winewayinn.com; 1019 Foothill Blvd; r $180-220; ❄📶) A small B&B, in a 1910-era house, close to the road; friendly owners.

Eating

Jolé CALIFORNIAN **$$**
(☎707-942-5938; www.jolerestaurant.com; 1457 Lincoln Ave, Calistoga; mains $15-20; ⏰5-9pm Sun-Thu, to 10pm Fri & Sat) The earthy and inventive farm-to-table small plates at chef-owned Jolé evolve seasonally, and may include such dishes as local sole with tangy miniature Napa grapes, caramelized Brussels sprouts with capers, and organic Baldwin apple strudel with burnt-caramel ice cream. Four courses cost $50. Reservations essential.

Solbar CALIFORNIAN **$$$**
(Map p160; ☎707-226-0850; www.solagecalistoga.com; 755 Silverado Trail; lunch/dinner mains $15-19/$30-37; ⏰7am-11am, 11:30am-3pm, 5:30-9pm) The ag-chic look at this superb restaurant is spare, with concrete floors, exposed-wood tables and soaring ceilings. Maximizing seasonal produce, each dish is elegantly composed, some with tongue-in-cheek playfulness. The menu is divided into light and hearty, so you can mind calories. Reservations essential.

All Seasons Bistro NEW AMERICAN **$$$**
(☎707-942-9111; www.allseasonsnapavalley.net; 1400 Lincoln Ave; lunch mains $10-15, dinner mains $16-22; ⏰noon-2pm & 5:30-8:30pm Tue-Sun) The dining room looks like a white-tablecloth soda fountain, but All Seasons makes some very fine meals, from simple steak-*frites* to composed dishes like cornmeal-crusted scallops with summer succotash. Good lobster bisque.

Buster's Southern BBQ BARBECUE **$**
(Map p160; ☎707-942-5605; www.busterssouthernbbq.com; 1207 Foothill Blvd; dishes $8-11; ⏰10am-7:30pm Mon-Sat, 10:30am-6:30pm Sun; 👪) The sheriff eats lunch at this indoor-outdoor barbecue joint, which serves smoky ribs, chicken, tri-tip steak and burgers, but closes early at dinnertime. Beer and wine.

Calistoga Inn & Brewery AMERICAN **$$**
(☎707-942-4101; www.calistogainn.com; 1250 Lincoln Ave; lunch/dinner mains $9-13/$14-26; ⏰11:30am-3pm & 5:30-9pm) Locals crowd the outdoor beer garden Sundays. Midweek we prefer the country dining room and its big oakwood tables, a homey spot for pot roast and other simple American dishes. There's live music summer weekends.

Drinking

Yo El Rey CAFE
(☎707-942-1180; www.yoelrey.com; 1217 Washington St; ⏰6:30am-8pm) Meet the hip kids at this micro-roastery cafe and living room, which brews superb small-batch fair-trade coffee.

Hydro Grill BAR
(☎707-942-9777; 1403 Lincoln Ave) Live music plays weekend evenings at this hoppin' corner bar-restaurant.

Solbar BAR
(Map p160; ☎707-226-0850; www.solagecalistoga.com; 755 Silverado Trail) Sip cocktails and wine on cane sofas beside outdoor fireplaces and a palm-lined pool. Wear white.

Brannan's Grill BAR
(☎707-942-2233; www.brannansgrill.com; 1374 Lincoln Ave) Calistoga's most handsome restaurant; the mahogany bar is great for martinis and microbrews, especially weekends, when jazz combos sometimes play.

Susie's Bar DIVE BAR
(☎707-942-6710; 1365 Lincoln Ave) Turn your baseball cap sideways, do shots and play pool while the juke box blares classic rock and country and western.

Shopping

Wine Garage WINE
(☎707-942-5332; www.winegarage.net; 1020 Foothill Blvd) Every bottle costs under $25 at this winning wine store, formerly a service station.

Mudd Hens BEAUTY
(☎707-942-0210; www.muddhens.com; 1348 Lincoln Ave) Recreate mud baths at home with mineral-rich Calistoga Mud ($27/pound) and volcanic-ash soap from this cute bath shop.

Calistoga Pottery CERAMICS
(☎707-942-0216; www.calistogapottery.com; 1001 Foothill Blvd) Winemakers aren't the only artisans in Napa. Watch potters throw vases, bowls and plates, all for sale.

Coperfield's Bookshop BOOKS
(☎707-942-1616; 1330 Lincoln Ave) Great indie bookshop, with local maps and guides.

Information

Chamber of Commerce & Visitors Center (☎707-942-6333, 866-306-5588; www.calistogavisitors.com; 1133 Washington St; ⏲9am-5pm)

Around Calistoga

Sights & Activities

Bale Grist Mill & Bothe-Napa Valley State Parks HISTORIC PARK $
There's good weekend picnicking at **Bale Grist Mill State Historic Park** (☎707-963-2236; adult/child $3/2; ⏲10am-5pm Sat & Sun 👪), which features a 36ft water-powered mill wheel dating from 1846 – the largest still operating in North America. Watch it grind corn and wheat into flour Saturdays and Sundays; call for times. In early October, look for the living-history festival, **Old Mill Days**.

A mile-long trail leads to adjacent **Bothe-Napa Valley State Park** (Map p160; ☎707-942-4575; parking $8; ⏲8am-sunset; 👪), where there's a **swimming pool** (adult/child $5/2; ⏲summer only) and lovely hiking through redwood groves.

Admission to one park includes the other. If you're more than three, go to Bothe first, and pay $8 instead of the per-head charge at Bale Grist Mill.

The mill and both parks are on Hwy 29/128, midway between St Helena and Calistoga.

FREE **Robert Louis Stevenson State Park** MOUNTAIN
(off Map p160; ☎707-942-4575; www.parks.ca.gov) The long-extinct volcanic cone of Mt St Helena marks the valley's end, 8 miles north of Calistoga. The undeveloped state park on Hwy 29 often gets snow in winter.

It's a strenuous 5-mile climb to the peak's 4343ft summit, but what a view – 200 miles on a clear winter's day. Check conditions before setting out. Also consider 2.2-mile one-way Table Rock Trail (go south from the summit parking area) for drop-dead valley views. Temperatures are best in wildflower season, February to May; fall is prettiest, when the vineyards change colors.

The park includes the site of the Silverado Mine where Stevenson and his wife honeymooned in 1880.

Petrified Forest FOREST
(Map p160; ☎707-942-6667; www.petrifiedforest.org; 4100 Petrified Forest Rd; adult/child $10/5; ⏲9am-7pm summer, to 5pm winter) Three million years ago, a volcanic eruption at nearby Mt St Helena blew down a stand of redwoods between Calistoga and Santa Rosa. The trees fell in the same direction, away from the blast, and were covered in ash and mud. Over the millennia, the mighty giants' trunks turned to stone; gradually the overlay eroded, exposing them. The first stumps were discovered in 1870. A monument marks Robert Louis Stevenson's 1880 visit. He describes it in *The Silverado Squatters*.

It's 5 miles northwest of town, off Hwy 128. Check online for 10%-off coupons.

OUTLET SHOPPING

Max out your credit cards on last season's close-outs.

Napa Premium Outlets (Map p160; ☎707-226-9876; www.premiumoutlets.com; 629 Factory Stores Dr, Napa) 50 stores

Petaluma Village Premium Outlets (☎707-778-9300; www.premiumoutlets.com; 2200 Petaluma Blvd North, Petaluma) 60 stores, Sonoma County

Vacaville Premium Outlets (☎707-447-5755; www.premiumoutlets.com/vacaville; 321 Nut Tree Rd, Vacaville) 120 stores, northeast of the Wine Country on I-80

Safari West WILDLIFE RESERVE

(off Map p160; ☎707-579-2551, 800-616-2695; www.safariwest.com; 3115 Porter Creek Rd; adult/child $68/30; 🚸) Giraffes in Wine Country? Whadya know! Safari West covers 400 acres and protects zebras, cheetahs and other exotic animals, which mostly roam free. See them on a guided three-hour safari in open-sided jeeps; reservations required. You'll also walk through an aviary and lemur condo. The reservations-only cafe serves lunch and dinner. If you're feeling adventurous, stay overnight in nifty canvas-sided **tent cabins** (cabins incl breakfast $200-295), right in the preserve.

SONOMA VALLEY

We have a soft spot for Sonoma's folksy ways. Unlike in fancy Napa, nobody cares if you drive a clunker and vote Green. Locals call it 'Slow-noma.' Anchoring the bucolic 17-mile-long Sonoma Valley, the town of Sonoma makes a great jumping-off point for exploring Wine Country – it's only an hour from San Francisco – and has a marvelous sense of place, with storied 19th-century historical sights surrounding the state's largest town square. Halfway up-valley, tiny Glen Ellen is right out of a Norman Rockwell painting, in stark contrast to the valley's northernmost town, Santa Rosa, the workaday urban center best known for its traffic. If you have more than a day, explore Sonoma's quiet, rustic side along the Russian River Valley (p190) and work your way to the sea.

Sonoma Hwy/Hwy 12 is lined with wineries and runs from Sonoma to Santa Rosa, then to western Sonoma County; Arnold Dr has less traffic (but few wineries) and runs parallel, up the valley's western side to Glen Ellen.

Sonoma Valley Wineries

Rolling grass-covered hills rise from 17-mile-long Sonoma Valley. Its 40 wineries get less attention than Napa's, but many are equally good. If you love zinfandel and syrah, you're in for a treat.

Picnicking is allowed at Sonoma wineries. Get maps and discount coupons in the town of Sonoma (p187) or, if you're approaching from the south, the **Sonoma Valley Visitors Bureau** (Map p180; ☎707-935-4747; www.sonomavalley.com; Cornerstone Gardens, 23570 Hwy 121; ⏲10am-4pm) at Cornerstone Gardens (p183).

Plan at least five hours to visit the valley from bottom to top. For other Sonoma County wineries, see the Russian River Valley section.

Homewood WINERY

(Map p180; ☎707-996-6353; www.homewoodwinery.com; 23120 Burndale Rd at Hwy 121/12; tastings free; ⏲10am-4pm; 🐾) A stripy rooster named Steve chases dogs in the parking lot of this down-home winery, where the tasting room is a garage, and the winemaker crafts standout ports and Rhône-style grenache, mourvèdre and syrah – 'Da redder, da better.' Ask about 'vertical tastings,' and sample wines from the same vineyards, but different years. Dogs welcome, but you've been warned. Bottles cost $18 to $32.

Nicholson Ranch WINERY

(☎707-938-8822; www.nicholsonranch.com; 4200 Napa Rd; tastings $10; ⏲10am-6pm) Unfiltered pinot noir and non-buttery chardonnay in a hilltop tasting room; lovely for picnicking.

Robledo WINERY

(Map p180; ☎707-939-6903; www.robledofamilywinery.com; 21901 Bonness Rd, of Hwy 116; tastings $5-10; ⏲by appointment only) Sonoma Valley's feel-good winery, Robledo was founded by a former grape-picker from Mexico who worked his way up to vineyard manager, then land owner, now vintner. His kids run the place. The wines – served at hand-carved Mexican furniture in a windowless tasting room – include a no-oak sauvignon blanc, jammy syrah, spicy cabernet, and bright-fruit pinot noir. Bottles cost $18 to $45.

Gundlach-Bundschu WINERY

(Map p180; ☎707-938-5277; www.gunbun.com; 2000 Denmark St; tastings $10; ⏲11am-4:30pm) One of Sonoma Valley's oldest and prettiest, Gundlach-Bundschu looks like a storybook castle. Founded in 1858 by Bavarian immigrant Jacob Gundlach, it's now at the cutting edge of sustainability. Signature wines are rieslings and gewürztraminers, but 'Gun-Bun' was the first American winery to produce 100% merlot. Tours of the 2000-barrel cave ($20) are available by reservation. Down a winding lane, it's a good bike-to winery, with picnicking, hiking and a small lake. Bottles cost $22 to $40.

Bartholomew Park Winery WINERY, MUSEUM

(Map p180; ☎707-939-3026; www.bartpark.com; 1000 Vineyard Lane; tasting $5-10, museum & park entry free; ⏲tasting room & museum 11am-4:30pm) Gundlach-Bundschu also runs nearby Bartholomew Park Winery (another good bike-to destination), a 400-acre preserve with vineyards originally cultivated in 1857 and now certified-organic, yielding citrusy sauvignon blanc and smoky merlot. Bottles cost $22 to $40.

Hawkes TASTING ROOM

(Map p184; ☎707-938-7620; www.hawkeswine.com; 383 1st St W; tasting $10, waived with purchase over $30; ⏲noon-6pm) When you're in downtown Sonoma and don't feel like fighting traffic, Hawke's refreshingly unfussy tasting room showcases meaty merlot and cabernet sauvignon, never blended with other grape varietals. Bottles cost $20 to $60.

Little Vineyards WINERY

(Map p180; ☎707-996-2750; www.littlevineyards.com; 15188 Sonoma Hwy, Glen Ellen; tastings $5; ⏲11am-4:30pm Thu-Mon; 👪) The name fits at this family-owned small-scale winery, long on atmosphere, with a lazy dog to greet you and a weathered, cigarette-burned tasting bar, which Jack London drank at (before it was moved here). The tiny tasting room is good for shy folks who dislike crowds. If you're new to wine, consider the $20 introductory class (call ahead). Good picnicking on the vineyard-view terrace. The big reds include syrah, petite sirah, zin, cab and several delish blends. Bottles cost $17 to $35. Also rents a cottage in the vines.

BR Cohn WINERY

(Map p180; ☎707-938-4064; www.brcohn.com; 15000 Sonoma Hwy, Glen Ellen; tasting $10, applicable to purchase; ⏲10am-5pm) Picnic like a rock star at always-busy BR Cohn, whose founder managed '70s superband the Doobie Brothers before moving on to make outstanding organic olive oils and fine wines – including excellent cabernet sauvignon, unusual in Sonoma. In autumn, he throws benefit concerts, amid the olives, by the likes of Skynyrd and the Doobies. Bottles cost $16 to $55.

Arrowood WINERY

(Map p180; ☎707-935-2600; www.arrowoodvineyards.com; 14347 Sonoma Hwy; tastings $5-10; ⏲10am-4:30pm) Excellent cabernet and chardonnay; stunning views.

Benziger WINERY

(Map p180; ☎888-490-2739; www.benziger.com; 1883 London Ranch Rd, Glen Ellen; tasting $10-20, tram tour adult incl tasting/child $15/5; ⏲10am-5pm; 👪) If you're new to wine, make Benziger your first stop for Sonoma's best crash course in wine-making. The worthwhile, non-reservable tour includes an open-air tram ride through biodynamic vineyards, and a four-wine tasting. Kids love the peacocks. The large-production wine's OK (head for the reserves); the tour's the thing. Bottles cost $15 to $80.

Imagery Estate WINERY

(Map p180; ☎877-550-4278; www.imagerywinery.com; 14355 Sonoma Hwy; tastings $10-15; ⏲10am-4:30pm) Obscure varietals, biodynamically grown, with artist-designed labels.

Loxton WINERY

(Map p180; ☎707-935-7221; www.loxtonwines.com; 11466 Dunbar Rd, Glen Ellen; tastings free) Say g'day to Chris, the Aussie winemaker, at Loxton, a no-frills winery with million-dollar views. The 'tasting room' is actually a small warehouse, where you can taste wonderful syrah and zinfandel; non-oaky, fruit-forward chardonnay; and good port. Bottles cost $15 to $25.

Wellington WINERY

(Map p180; ☎707-939-0708; www.wellingtonvineyards.com; 11600 Dunbar Rd, Glen Ellen; tastings $5) Known for port (including a white) and meaty reds, Wellington makes great zinfandel, one from vines planted in 1892 – wow, what color! The noir de noir is a cult favorite. Alas, servers have vineyard views, while you face the warehouse. Bottles cost $15 to $30.

Family Wineries TASTING ROOM
(Map p180; ☎707-433-0100; www.familywines.com; 9380 Sonoma Hwy at Laurel Ave; tastings $5-10; ⊙10:30am-5pm) Several labels under one roof. Standout: David Noyes pinot noir.

TOP CHOICE **Kaz** WINERY
(Map p180; ☎707-833-2536; www.kazwinery.com; 233 Adobe Canyon Rd, Kenwood; tastings $5; ⊙11am-5pm Fri-Mon;) Sonoma's cult favorite, supercool Kaz is about blends: whatever's in the organic vineyards goes into the wine – and they're blended at crush, not during fermentation. Expect lesser-known varietals like Alicante Bouchet and Lenoir, and a worthwhile cabernet-merlot blend. Kids can sample grape juice, then run around the playground out back, while you sift through LPs and pop your favorites onto the turntable. Crazy fun. Dogs welcome. Bottles cost $20 to $48.

Sonoma & Around

Fancy boutiques may lately be replacing hardware stores, but Sonoma still retains an old-fashioned charm, thanks to the plaza – California's largest town square – and its surrounding frozen-in-time historic buildings. You can legally drink on the plaza, a rarity in California parks.

Sonoma has rich history. In 1846 it was the site of a second American revolution, this time against Mexico, when General Mariano Guadalupe Vallejo deported all foreigners from California, prompting outraged American frontiersmen to occupy the Sonoma Presidio and declare independence. They dubbed California the Bear Flag Republic after the battle flag they'd fashioned.

The republic was short-lived. The Mexican-American War broke out a month later, and California was annexed by the US. The revolt gave California its flag, which remains emblazoned with the words 'California Republic' beneath a muscular brown bear. Vallejo was initially imprisoned, but ultimately returned to Sonoma and played a major role in the region's development.

Sights

Sonoma Hwy (Hwy 12) runs through town. Sonoma Plaza, laid out by General Vallejo

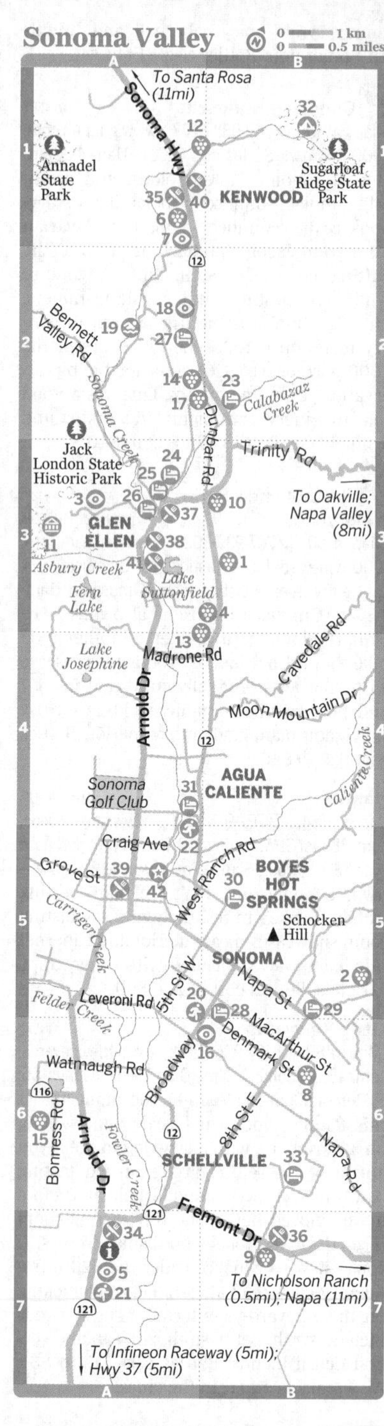

Sonoma Valley

Sights

1 Arrowood ... B3
2 Bartholomew Park & Winery ... B5
3 Benziger ... A3
4 BR Cohn ... B3
5 Cornerstone Gardens ... A7
6 Family Wineries ... A1
7 Figone's Olive Oil ... A1
8 Gundlach Bundschu ... B6
9 Homewood ... B7
10 Imagery Estate ... B3
11 Jack London Museum ... A3
12 Kaz ... A1
13 Little Vineyards ... A4
14 Loxton ... A2
15 Robledo ... A6
16 Traintown ... B6
17 Wellington ... A2
18 Wildwood Farm Nursery & Sculpture Garden ... A2
Wine Country Chocolates Tasting Bar ... (see 7)

Activities, Courses & Tours

19 Morton's Warm Springs Resort ... A2
20 Sonoma Valley Cyclery ... A5
21 Vintage Aircraft Company ... A7
22 Willow Stream Spa at Sonoma Mission Inn ... A5

Sleeping

23 Beltane Ranch ... B2
24 Gaige House ... A3
25 Glen Ellen Cottages ... A3
26 Jack London Lodge ... A3
27 Kenwood Inn & Spa ... A2
28 MacArthur Place ... B5
29 Les Petites Maisons ... B5
30 Sonoma Chalet ... B5
31 Sonoma Creek Inn ... A4
32 Sugarloaf Ridge State Park ... B1
33 Windhaven Cottage ... B6

Eating

34 Angelo's Wine Country Deli ... A7
35 Cafe Citti ... A1
Fig Café & Winebar ... (see 25)
36 Fremont Diner ... B7
37 Garden Court Cafe ... A3
Glen Ellen Inn ... (see 25)
38 Glen Ellen Village Market ... A3
39 Juanita Juanita ... A5
Mayo Winery Reserve Room ... (see 6)
Olive & Vine ... (see 7)
40 Vineyards Inn Bar & Grill ... A1
41 Yeti ... A3

Entertainment

42 Little Switzerland ... A5

Shopping

Kenwood Farmhouse ... (see 6)

in 1834, is the heart of downtown, lined with hotels, restaurants and shops. Pick up a walking-tour brochure from the visitors bureau. Immediately north along Hwy 12, expect a brief suburban landscape before the valley's pastoral gorgeousness begins, outside town.

SONOMA PLAZA & AROUND

Sonoma Plaza SQUARE

(Map p184) Smack in the center of the plaza, the Mission-revival-style **city hall**, built 1906–08, has identical facades on four sides, reportedly because plaza businesses all demanded City Hall face their direction. At the plaza's northeast corner, the **Bear Flag Monument** marks Sonoma's moment of revolutionary glory. The town shows up for the **farmers market** (5:30-8pm Tue, Apr-Oct), where you can sample Sonoma's exquisite produce.

Sonoma State Historic Park HISTORIC BUILDINGS

(707-938-1519; www.parks.ca.gov; adult/child $3/2; 10am-5pm Tue-Sun) The park is comprised of multiple sites. The **Mission San Francisco Solano de Sonoma** (Map p184; E Spain St), at the plaza's northeast corner, was built in 1823, in part to forestall the Russian coastal colony at Fort Ross from moving inland. The mission was the 21st and final California mission, and the only one built during the Mexican period (the rest were founded by the Spanish). It marks the northernmost point on El Camino Real. Five of the mission's original rooms remain. The not-to-be-missed chapel dates from 1841.

The adobe **Sonoma Barracks** (Map p184; E Spain St; daily) was built by Vallejo between 1836 and 1840 to house Mexican troops, but it became the capital of a rogue nation on June 14, 1846, when American settlers, of

A WINE COUNTRY PRIMER

When people talk about Sonoma, they're referring to the *whole* county, which unlike Napa is huge. It extends all the way from the coast, up the Russian River Valley, into Sonoma Valley and eastward to Napa Valley; in the south it stretches from San Pablo Bay (an extension of San Francisco Bay) to Healdsburg in the north. It's essential to break Sonoma down by district.

West County refers to everything west of Hwy 101 and includes the **Russian River Valley** and the coast. **Sonoma Valley** stretches north-south along Hwy 12. In northern Sonoma County, **Alexander Valley** lies east of Healdsburg, and **Dry Creek Valley** lies north of Healdsburg. In the south, **Carneros** straddles the Sonoma–Napa border, north of San Pablo Bay. Each region has its own particular wines; what grows where depends upon the weather.

Inland valleys get hot; coastal regions stay cool. In West County and Carneros, night-time fog blankets the vineyards. Burgundy-style wines do best, particularly pinot noir and chardonnay. Further inland, Alexander, Sonoma and much of Dry Creek Valleys (as well as Napa Valley) are fog-protected. Here, Bordeaux-style wines thrive, especially cabernet sauvignon, sauvignon blanc, merlot and other heat-loving varieties. For California's famous cabernets, head to Napa. Zinfandel and Rhône-style varieties, such as syrah and viognier, grow in both regions, warm and cool. In cooler climes, resultant wines are lighter, more elegant; in warmer areas they are heavier and more rustic.

For a handy-dandy reference on the road, pick up a copy of Karen MacNeil's *The Wine Bible* (2001, Workman Publishing) or Jancis Robinson's *Concise Wine Companion* (2001, Oxford University Press) to carry in the car.

varying sobriety, surprised the guards and declared an independent 'California Republc' [sic] with a homemade flag featuring a blotchy bear. The US took over the republic a month later, but abandoned the barracks during the Gold Rush, leaving Vallejo to turn then into (what else?) a winery in 1860. Today, displays describe life during the Mexican and American periods.

Next to the Sonoma Barracks, **Toscano Hotel** (Map p184; 20 E Spain St) opened as a store and library in the 1850s, then became a hotel in 1886. Peek into the lobby from 10am to 5pm; except for the traffic outside, you'd swear you'd stepped back in time. Free tours 1pm through 4pm, weekends and Mondays.

A half-mile northwest, the lovely **Vallejo Home** (Map p184; 363 3rd St W), otherwise known as Lachryma Montis (Latin for 'Tears of the Mountain'), was built 1851–52 for General Vallejo. It's named for the spring on the property; the Vallejo family later made a handy income piping water to town. The property remained in the family until 1933, when the state of California purchased it, retaining much of its original furnishings. A bike path leads to the house from downtown.

Admission here includes entry to the **Petaluma Adobe** (Map p156; ☎707-762-4871; www.petalumaadobe.com; 3325 Adobe Rd, Petaluma; ⊙10am-5pm Sat & Sun), a historic ranch 15 miles northwest in suburban Petaluma.

La Haye Art Center ARTS CENTER

(Map p184; ☎707-996-9665; www.lahayeartcenter.com; 148 E Napa St; ⊙11am-5pm) At this collective in a converted foundry, you can tour a storefront gallery and meet the artists – sculptor, potter and painters – in their garden studios. Beverly Prevost's asymmetrical ceramic dinnerware is featured next door at Café La Haye (p185).

Sonoma Valley Museum of Art MUSEUM

(Map p184; ☎707-939-7862; www.svma.org; 551 Broadway; adult/family $5/8; ⊙11am-5pm Wed-Sun) Though this 8000-sq-ft museum presents compelling work by local and international artists, such as David Hockney, the annual standout is October's Día de los Muertos exhibition.

BEYOND SONOMA PLAZA

FREE **Bartholomew Park** PARK

(Map p180; ☎707-935-9511; www.bartholomewparkwinery.com; 1000 Vineyard Lane) The top close-to-town outdoors destination is 375-acre Bartholomew Park, off Castle Rd, where you can picnic beneath giant oaks and hike three miles of trails, with hilltop vistas to San Francisco. There's also a good winery (p182) and small museum. The Palladian Villa, at the park's entrance, is a turn-of-the-20th-century replica of Count Haraszthy's original residence, open noon to 3pm, Saturdays and Sundays, operated by the **Bartholomew Foundation** (☎707-938-2244).

FREE **Cornerstone Gardens** GARDENS
(Map p180; ☎707-933-3010; www.cornerstongardens.com; 23570 Arnold Dr; ⊙10am-4pm; 👪) There's nothing traditional about Cornerstone Gardens, which showcase the work of 19 renowned avant-garde landscape designers. We especially love Pamela Burton's 'Earth Walk,' which descends into the ground; and Planet Horticulture's 'Rise,' which exaggerates space. Let the kids run around while you explore top-notch garden shops and gather information from the onsite **Sonoma Valley Visitors Bureau** (☎707-935-4747; www.sonomavalley.com; ⊙10am-4pm), then refuel at the on-site cafe. Look for the enormous blue chair at road's edge.

Traintown AMUSEMENT PARK
(Map p180; ☎707-938-3912; www.traintown.com; 20264 Broadway; ⊙10am-5pm daily summer, Fri-Sun only mid-Sep-late May) Little kids adore Traintown, one mile south of the plaza. A miniature steam engine makes 20-minute loops ($4.75), and there are vintage amusement-park rides ($2.75 per ride), including a carousel and a Ferris wheel.

Activities

Many local inns provide bicycles.

Sonoma Valley Cyclery BICYCLE RENTAL
(Map p180; ☎707-935-3377; www.sonomacyclery.com; 20091 Broadway/Hwy 12; bikes from $25 per day; ⊙10am-6pm Mon-Sat, to 4pm Sun; 👪) Sonoma is ideal for cycling – not too hilly – with multiple wineries near downtown. Book ahead weekends.

Willow Stream Spa at Sonoma Mission Inn SPA
(Map p180; ☎707-938-9000; www.fairmont.com/sonoma; 100 Boyes Blvd; ⊙7:30am-8pm) Few Wine Country spas compare with glitzy Sonoma Mission Inn, where two treatments – or $89 – allows use of three outdoor and two indoor mineral pools, gym, sauna, and herbal steam room at the Romanesque bathhouse. No children.

Triple Creek Horse Outfit HORSEBACK RIDING
(☎707-887-8700; www.triplecreekhorseoutfit.com; 1-/2hr rides $60/100; ⊙Wed-Mon) Hit the trail for stunning vistas of Sonoma Valley. Reservations required.

Courses

Ramekins Sonoma Valley Culinary School COOKING SCHOOL
(Map p184; ☎707-933-0450; www.ramekins.com; 450 W Spain St; 👪) Offers excellent demonstrations and hands-on classes for home chefs. Also runs weekend 'culinary camps' for both adults and kids.

Sleeping

Off-season rates plummet. Reserve ahead. Ask about parking; some historic inns have no lots. Also consider Glen Ellen (p188) and, if counting pennies, Santa Rosa (p202).

Sonoma Chalet B&B, COTTAGES $$
(Map p180; ☎707-938-3129; www.sonomachalet.com; 18935 5th St W; r without bath $125, r with bath $140-180, cottages $190-225; ❄) An old farmstead surrounded by rolling hills, Sonoma Chalet has rooms in a Swiss chalet-style house adorned with little balconies and country-style bric-a-brac. We love the free-standing cottages; Laura's has a wood-burning fireplace. Breakfast is served on a deck overlooking a nature preserve. No air-con in rooms with shared bath. No phones, no internet.

Sonoma Hotel HISTORIC HOTEL $$
(Map p184; ☎707-996-2996; www.sonomahotel.com; 110 W Spain St; r incl breakfast $170-200; ❄📶) Long on charm, this spiffy vintage-1880s hotel is decked with Spanish-colonial and American-country-crafts furnishings. No elevator or parking lot.

El Dorado Hotel HOTEL $$$
(Map p184; ☎707-996-3030, 800-289-3031; www.eldoradosonoma.com; 405 1st St W; r weekday/weekend $195/225; ❄📶🏊) Stylish touches like high-end linens make up for the rooms' compact size, as do private balconies overlooking the plaza or the rear courtyard (we prefer the plaza view, despite the noise). No elevator.

Swiss Hotel HISTORIC HOTEL $$
(Map p184; ☎707-938-2884; www.swisshotelsonoma.com; 18 W Spain St; r incl breakfast Mon-Fri $150-170, Sat & Sun $200-240; ❄📶) It opened in 1905, so you'll forgive the wavy floors. Think knotty pine and wicker. In the morning sip coffee on the shared plaza-view balcony. Downstairs there's a raucous bar and restaurant. No parking lot or elevator.

Sonoma

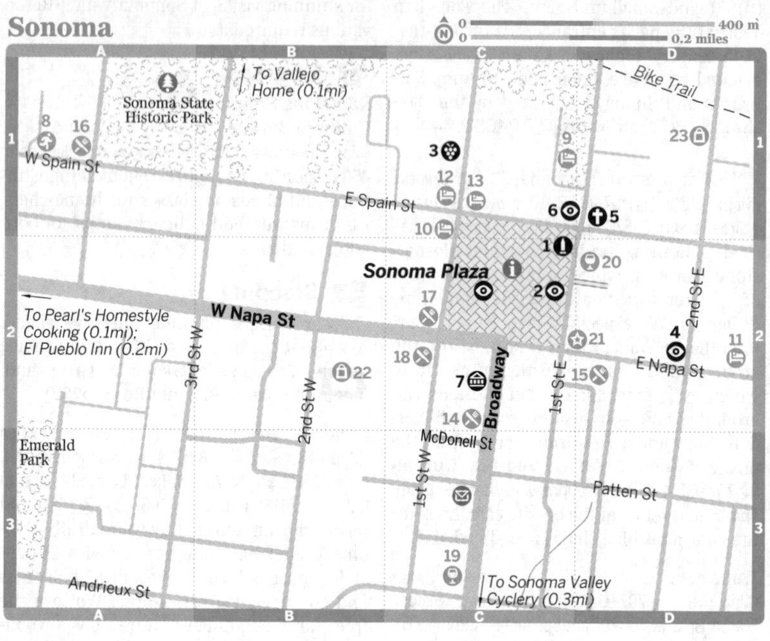

NAPA & SONOMA WINE COUNTRY SONOMA & AROUND

Sonoma

Top Sights

Sonoma Plaza C2

Sights

1 Bear Flag Monument C2
2 City Hall C2
3 Hawkes C1
4 La Haye Art Center D2
5 Mission San Francisco Solano de Sonoma D1
6 Sonoma Barracks C1
7 Sonoma Valley Museum of Art C2
Toscano Hotel .... (see 6)

Activities, Courses & Tours

8 Ramekins Sonoma Valley Culinary School A1

Sleeping

9 Bungalows 313 .... C1
10 El Dorado Hotel C1
11 Hidden Oak Inn D2
12 Sonoma Hotel C1
13 Swiss Hotel C1

Eating

14 599 Thai Cafe C2
Café la Haye .... (see 4)
15 Della Santina's D2
El Dorado Corner Cafe .... (see 10)
16 Estate A1
girl & the fig .... (see 12)
17 Harvest Moon Cafe C2
18 Red Grape C2
Taste of the Himalayas .... (see 20)

Drinking

Enoteca Della Santina .... (see 15)
19 Hopmonk Tavern C3
20 Murphy's Irish Pub D2
Steiner's .... (see 17)
Sunflower Caffé & Wine Bar .... (see 10)
Swiss Hotel .... (see 13)

Entertainment

21 Sebastiani Theater D2

Shopping

Chanticleer Books & Prints .... (see 4)
22 Chateau Sonoma B2
Readers' Books .... (see 4)
Sign of the Bear .... (see 17)
Tiddle E Winks .... (see 15)
23 Vella Cheese Co D1

El Pueblo Inn MOTEL $$
(Off Map p184; ☎707-996-3651, 800-900-8844; www.elpuebloinn.com; 896 W Napa St; r incl breakfast $169-289;) One mile west of downtown, family-owned El Pueblo has surprisingly cushy rooms with great beds. The big lawns and the heated pool are perfect for kids; parents appreciate the 24-hour hot tub.

Sonoma Creek Inn MOTEL $$
(Map p180; ☎707-939-9463, 888-712-1289; www.sonomacreekinn.com; 239 Boyes Blvd; r $139-199;) This cute-as-a-button motel has cheery, retro-Americana rooms, with primary colors and country quilts. It's not downtown; valley wineries are a short drive.

Les Petites Maisons COTTAGES $$$
(Map p180; ☎707-933-0340, 800-291-8962; www.lespetitesmaisons.com; 1190 E Napa St;cottages $165-295;) A mile east of the plaza, each of these four colorful, inviting cottages has a bedroom, living room, kitchen and barbecue, with comfy furniture, stereos, DVDs and bicycles.

Windhaven Cottage COTTAGE $$
(Map p180; ☎707-938-2175, 707-483-1856; www.windhavencottage.com; 21700 Pearson Ave; cottage $155-165;) Great-bargain Windhaven has two units: a hideaway cottage with vaulted wooden ceilings and a fireplace, and a handsome 800-sq-ft studio. We prefer the romantic cottage. Both have hot tubs. Tennis facilities, bicycles and barbecues sweeten the deal.

Bungalows 313 BUNGALOWS $$$
(Map p184; ☎707-996-8091; www.bungalows313.com; 313 1st St E; d $229-329, q $379-469;) Century-old brick farmhouse and bungalows with kitchens. Gorgeous gardens. Perfect for couples.

MacArthur Place INN $$$
(Map p180; ☎707-938-2929, 800-722-1866; www.macarthurplace.com; 29 E MacArthur St; r from $350, ste from $425;) Sonoma's top full-service inn; built on a former estate, with century-old gardens.

Hidden Oak Inn B&B $$$
(Map p180; ☎707-996-9863, 877-996-9863; www.hiddenoakinn.com; 214 E Napa St; r incl breakfast $195-245;) A B&B built c 1914.

Sugarloaf Ridge State Park CAMPGROUND $
(Map p180; ☎707-833-5712, reservations 800-444-7275; www.reserveamerica.com; 2605 Adobe Canyon Rd; sites $30) Sonoma's nearest camping is north of Kenwood at this lovely hilltop park, with 50 drive-in sites, clean coin-operated showers, and great hiking.

Eating

Also see Glen Ellen, p188. There's creek-side picnicking, with barbecue grills, up-valley at **Sugarloaf Ridge State Park** (2605 Adobe Canyon Rd; per car $8). Find late-night taco trucks on Hwy 12, between Boyes Blvd and Aqua Caliente.

Fremont Diner AMERICAN $
(Map p180; ☎707-938-7370; 2698 Fremont Dr/Hwy 121; mains $8-11; ⊗8am-3pm Mon-Fri, 7am-4pm Sat & Sun;) Lines snake out the door weekends at this order-at-the-counter, farm-to-table roadside diner. Snag a table indoors or out and feast on ricotta pancakes with real maple syrup, chicken and waffles, oyster po' boys and finger-licking barbecue. Arrive early to beat the line.

Café La Haye NEW AMERICAN $$$
(Map p184; ☎707-935-5994; www.cafelahaye.com; 140 E Napa St; mains $15-25; ⊗5:30-9pm Tue-Sat) One of Sonoma's top tables for earthy New American cooking, made with produce sourced from within 60 miles, La Haye's tiny dining room gets packed cheek-by-jowl and service can border on perfunctory, but the clean simplicity and flavor-packed cooking make it many foodies' first choice. Reserve well ahead.

Harvest Moon Cafe NEW AMERICAN $$
(Map p184; ☎707-933-8160; www.harvestmooncafesonoma.com; 487 1st St W; dinner/brunch mains $18-25/$10-15; ⊗5:30-9pm Wed-Mon, 10am-2pm Sun) Inside a cozy 1836 adobe, this casual bistro uses local ingredients in its changing menu, with simple soul-satisfying dishes like duck risotto with Bellwether Farms ricotta. Book a garden table.

Estate ITALIAN-CALIFORNIAN $$
(Map p184; ☎707-933-3633; www.estate-sonoma.com; 400 W Spain St; pizzas $10-14, dinner/brunch mains $21-24/$11-14; ⊗from 5pm nightly, 10am-3pm Sun) Sonoma's landmark mansion features earthy Cal-Italian cooking, on-site produce garden and lovely outdoor porch. Come before 6:30pm (6:15 Fri & Sat) for pizza and a glass of pinot noir for $15. Nightly four-course dinners cost $26. Great Sunday brunch. Make reservations.

girl & the fig FRENCH-CALIFORNIAN $$$
(Map p184; 707-938-3634; www.thegirlandthefig.com; 110 W Spain St; lunch mains $10-15, dinner mains $18-26) For a festive evening, book a garden table at this French-provincial bistro. We like the small plates ($11 to $14), especially the steamed mussels with matchstick fries, and duck confit with lentils. Weekday three-course prix-fixe costs $34; add $10 for wine. Stellar cheeses. Reservations essential.

Della Santina's ITALIAN $$
(Map p184; 707-935-0576; www.dellasantinas.com; 135 E Napa St; mains $11-17) The waiters have been here forever, and the 'specials' never change, but Della Santina's Italian-American cooking – linguini pesto, veal parmigiana, rotisserie chickens – is consistently good. The brick courtyard is charming on warm evenings.

El Dorado Corner Cafe CAFE $$
(Map p184; 707-996-3030; www.eldoradosonoma.com; 405 1st St W; dishes $9-15; 7am-10pm) Little sister to El Dorado Kitchen (whose chef had just left at the time of writing, hence the non-review of this noteworthy restaurant), the Corner Cafe has more affordable cooking – pizzas, sandwiches, and salads – all made with artisinal local produce and served continuously throughout the day. Save room for house-made ice cream.

Juanita Juanita MEXICAN $$
(Map p184; 707-935-3981; 19114 Arnold Dr; mains $8-15; Wed-Mon 11am-8pm;) Dig the crazy mural outside this drive-in Mexican, which makes winning tostadas, garlic-garlic burritos and fiery *chile verde* (green chili stew with pork or chicken). Dog-friendly patio. Beer and wine.

Red Grape PIZZA $$
(Map p184; 707-996-4103; www.theredgrape.com; 529 1st St W; mains $11-15; 11:30am-8:30pm;) A reliable spot for an easy meal, Red Grape serves good thin-crust pizzas and big salads in a cavernous, echoey space. Good for takeout, too.

Pearl's Homestyle Cooking DINER $
(Map p184; 707-996-1783; 561 5th St W; mains $7-10; 7am-2:30pm;) Across from Safeway's west-facing wall, Pearl's serves giant American breakfasts, including succulent bacon and waffles (the secret is melted vanilla ice cream in the batter).

Angelo's Wine Country Deli DELI $
(Map p180; 707-938-3688; 23400 Arnold Dr; sandwiches $6; 9am-5pm Tue-Sun) Look for the cow on the roof of this roadside deli, south of town, a fave for fat sandwiches and homemade jerky. In springtime, little lambs graze outside.

Taste of the Himalayas INDIAN, NEPALESE $$
(Map p184; 707-996-1161; 464 1st St E; mains $10-20; 11am-10pm) Spicy curries, luscious lentil soup and sizzle-platter meats – a refreshing break from the usual French-Italian Wine Country fare.

599 Thai Cafe THAI $
(Map p184; 707-938-8477; 599 Broadway; mains $7-10; 11am-9pm Mon-Sat;) Reliably good, tiny Thai cafe.

Sonoma Market DELI, MARKET $
(Map p184; 707-996-3411; www.sonoma-glenellenmkt.com; 500 W Napa St; sandwiches $7) Sonoma's best groceries and deli sandwiches.

Drinking

Murphy's Irish Pub PUB
(Map p184; 707-935-0660; www.sonomapub.com; 464 1st St E) Don't ask for Bud – only *real* brews here. Good hand-cut fries and shepherd's pie, too. Live music Thursday through Sunday evenings.

Swiss Hotel BAR
(Map p184; 18 W Spain St) Locals and tourists crowd the 1909 Swiss Hotel for afternoon cocktails. There's OK food, but the bar's the thing.

Hopmonk Tavern BREWERY
(Map p184; 707-935-9100; www.hopmonk.com; 691 Broadway; dishes $12-22; 11:30am-10pm) This happening gastro-pub and beer garden takes its brews seriously, with 16 on tap, served in type-appropriate glassware. Live music Friday through Sunday.

Enoteca Della Santina WINE BAR
(Map p184; www.enotecadellasantina.com; 127 E Napa St; 2-10pm Wed-Fri, noon-11pm Sat, 4-10pm Tue & Sun) Thirty global vintages by the glass let you compare what you're tasting in California with the rest of the world's wines.

Steiner's BAR
(Map p184; 456 1st St W) Sonoma's oldest bar gets crowded Sunday afternoons with cyclists and motorcyclists. Dig the taxidermy mountain lions.

Sunflower Caffé & Wine Bar CAFE $$
(707-996-6845; www.sonomasunflower.com; 421 1st St W; dishes $9-14; 7am-8pm;) The big back garden at this local hangout is a good spot for breakfast, a no-fuss lunch, or an afternoon glass of wine.

Entertainment

Free jazz concerts happen on the plaza every second Tuesday, June to September, 6pm to 8:30pm; arrive early and bring a picnic.

Little Switzerland BEER HALL
(Map p180; 707-938-9990; www.lilswiss.com; 401 Grove St; Wed-Sun) Long before Sonoma became 'Wine Country,' locals drank and shot pool at this old-fashioned beer garden and dance hall, open continuously since 1906 – dig the vintage 1936 murals of Switzerland. Latin bands play Friday evenings; Saturday it's jazz, swing or zydeco; Sundays the great tradition is polka parties (5-9pm), when you can bring kids. There's barbecue Friday through Sunday.

Sebastiani Theatre CINEMA
(Map p184; 707-996-2020; sebastianitheatre.com; 476 1st St E) The plaza's gorgeous 1934 Mission-revival cinema screens art house and revival films, and sometimes live theater.

Shopping

Vella Cheese Co FOOD
(Map p184; 707-928-3232; www.vellacheese.com; 315 2nd St E) Known for its dry-jack cheeses (made here since the 1930s), Vella also makes good Mezzo Secco with cocoa powder–dusted rind. Staff will vacuum-pack for shipping.

Tiddle E Winks TOYS
(Map p184; 7070-939-6993; www.tiddleewinks.com; 115 E Napa St;) Vintage five-and-dime, with classic, mid-20th-century toys.

Sign of the Bear HOMEWARES
(Map p184; 707-996-3722; 435 1st St W) Kitchen-gadget freaks: make a beeline to this indie cookware store.

Chateau Sonoma HOMEWARES, GIFTS
(Map p184; 707-935-8553; www.chateausonoma.com; 153 W Napa St) Provence meets Sonoma in a one-of-a-kind gifts and arty home decor.

Chanticleer Books & Prints BOOKS
(Map p184; 707-996-7613; chanticleerbooks.com; 127 E Napa St; Wed-Sun) Rare books, first editions and California history.

Readers' Books BOOKS
(Map p184; 707-939-1779; readers.indiebound.com; 130 E Napa St) Independent bookseller.

Information

Sonoma Post Office (800-275-8777; www.usps.com; 617 Broadway; Mon-Fri)
Sonoma Valley Hospital (707-935-5000; 347 Andrieux St)
Sonoma Valley Visitors Bureau (707-996-1090; www.sonomavalley.com; 453 1st St E; 9am-6pm Jul-Sep, to 5pm Oct-Jun) Arranges accommodations; has a good walking-tour pamphlet and information on events. There's another location at Cornerstone Gardens (p183).

Glen Ellen & Around

Sleepy Glen Ellen is a snapshot of old Sonoma, with white picket fences, tiny cottages and 19th-century brick buildings beside a poplar-lined creek. When downtown Sonoma is jammed, you can wander quiet Glen Ellen and feel far away. It's ideal for a leg-stretching stopover between wineries or a romantic overnight – the nighttime sky blazes with stars.

Arnold Dr is the main drag and the valley's back-way route. Kenwood is just north, along Hwy 12, but has no town center like Glen Ellen's. For services, drive 8 miles south to Sonoma.

Glen Ellen's biggest draws are Jack London State Historic Park (p189) and Benziger winery (p179); several interesting shops line Arnold Dr.

Two family-friendly alternatives to wine tasting: **Figone's Olive Oil** (Map p180; 707-282-9092; www.figoneoliveoil.com; 9580 Sonoma Hwy), in Kenwood, presses its own extra-virgin olive oil – including lovely Meyer lemon-infused oil – which you can taste; in Glen Ellen, compare chocolates of varying percentages of cacao at **Wine Country Chocolates Tasting Bar** (Map p180; 707-996-1010; www.winecountrychocolates.com; 14301 Arnold Dr).

Gardeners: don't miss **Wildwood Farm and Sculpture Garden** (Map p180; 707-833-1161, 888-833-4181; www.wildwoodmaples.com; 10300 Sonoma Hwy, Kenwood; 10am-4pm Wed-Sun, 10am-3pm Tue), where abstract outdoor sits between exotic plants and Japanese maples.

There's fantastic hiking (when it's not blazingly hot) at **Sugarloaf Ridge State Park** (Map p180; 707-833-5712; www.parks.ca.gov; 2605 Adobe Canyon Rd, Kenwood; per car

$8). On clear days, Bald Mountain has drop-dead views to the sea, while Bushy Peak Trail peers into Napa Valley. Both are moderately strenuous; plan four hours round-trip.

On hot days, families cool off in mineral-spring-fed swimming pools at **Morton's Warm Springs Resort** (Map p180; ☎707-833-5511; www.mortonswarmsprings.com; 1651 Warm Springs Rd; adult/child $8/7, reserved picnic & BBQ sites per person $11; ⏰10am-6pm Sat & Sun May & Sep, Tue-Sun Jun-Aug, closed Oct-Apr). From Sonoma Hwy in Kenwood, turn west on Warm Springs Rd.

For shopping, stop by **Kenwood Farmhouse** (Map p180; 9255 Sonoma Hwy, Kenwood; ⏰10:30am-7pm), a co-op of vendors selling artisinal crafts and gifts.

Sleeping

Jack London Lodge MOTEL $$
(Map p180; ☎707-938-8510; http://jacklondonlodge.com; 13740 Arnold Dr; r Mon-Fri/Sat & Sun $120/180) An old-fashioned wood-sided motel, with well-kept rooms decorated with a few antiques, this is a weekday bargain – and the manager will sometimes negotiate rates. Outside there's a hot tub; next door there's a saloon.

Beltane Ranch INN $$
(Map p180; ☎707-996-6501; www.beltaneranch.com; 11775 Hwy 12; r incl breakfast $150-240) Surrounded by horse pastures, Beltane is a throwback to 19th-century Sonoma. The cheerful, lemon-yellow 1890s ranch house occupies 100 acres and has double porches lined with swinging chairs and white wicker. Though technically a B&B, each unfussy, country-Americana-style room has a private entrance – nobody will make you pet the cat. Breakfast in bed. No phones or TVs mean zero distraction from pastoral bliss.

WHAT'S CRUSH?

Crush is harvest, the most atmospheric time of year, when the vine's leaves turn brilliant colors, and you can smell fermenting fruit on the breeze. Farmers throw big parties for the vineyard workers to celebrate their work. Everyone wants to be here. That's why room rates skyrocket. If you can afford it, come during autumn. To score party invitations, join your favorite winery's wine club.

Gaige House INN $$$
(Map p180; ☎707-935-0237, 800-935-0237; www.gaige.com; 13540 Arnold Dr, Glen Ellen; r $249-299, ste $299-599) Sonoma's chicest inn serves lavish breakfasts. An 1890 house contains five of the 22 rooms, decked out in Euro-Asian style. But best are the Japanese-style 'spa suites,' with requisite high-end bells and whistles, including freestanding tubs made from hollowed-out granite boulders. Fabulous.

Kenwood Inn & Spa INN $$$
(Map p180; ☎707-833-1293, 800-353-6966; www.kenwoodinn.com; 10400 Sonoma Hwy, Kenwood; r incl breakfast $425-850, ste $850-1375) Lush gardens surround ivy-covered bungalows at this gorgeous inn, which feels like a Mediterranean château. Two hot tubs (one with a waterfall) and an on-site spa make this ideal for lovers: leave the kids home. Book an upstairs balcony room.

Glen Ellen Cottages BUNGALOWS $$
(Map p180;☎707-996-1174; www.glenelleninn.com; 13670 Arnold Dr; cottage Mon-Fri/Sat & Sun $149/239) Hidden behind Glen Ellen Inn, these five creek-side cottages are designed for romance, with oversized jetted tubs, steam showers and gas fireplaces.

Eating

fig café & winebar CALIFORNIAN, FRENCH $$
(☎707-938-2130; www.thefigcafe.com; 13690 Arnold Dr, Glen Ellen; mains $15-20; ⏰5:30-9pm daily, 10am-2:30pm Sat & Sun) It's worth a trip to Glen Ellen for the fig's earthy California-Provençal comfort food, like flash-fried calamari with spicy-lemon aioli, duck confit and *moules-frites* (mussels and French fries). Good wine prices and weekend brunch give reason to return.

Vineyards Inn Bar & Grill SPANISH, TAPAS $$
(Map p180; ☎707-833-4500; www.vineyardsinn.com; 8445 Sonoma Hwy 12, Kenwood; mains $8-20; ⏰11:30am-9:30pm) Though nothing fancy, this roadside tavern's food is terrific – succulent organic burgers, line-caught seafood, paella, ceviche, and biodynamic produce from the chef's ranch. Full bar.

Cafe Citti ITALIAN $$
(☎707-833-2690; www.cafecitti.com; 9049 Sonoma Hwy; mains $8-15; ⏰11am-3:30pm, 5-9pm) Locals flock to this mom-and-pop Italian-

American deli-trattoria, where you order at the counter then snag a seat on the deck. Standouts include roasted chicken, homemade gnocchi and ravioli; at lunchtime, there's also pizza and housebaked focaccia-bread sandwiches.

Glen Ellen Village Market MARKET $
(Map p180; www.sonoma-glenellenmkt.com; 13751 Arnold Dr; ⏲6am-9pm) Fantastic market, perfect for picnics.

Olive & Vine NEW AMERICAN $$$
(Map p180; ☎707-996-9152; oliveandvinerestaurant.com; 14301 Arnold Dr; mains $17-28; ⏲5:30-9pm Wed-Sat) Part catering kitchen, part restaurant, with great seasonal flavors; make reservations.

Yeti INDIAN $$
(Map p180; ☎707-996-9930; www.yetirestaurant.com; 14301 Arnold Dr; mains $10-18; ⏲11:30am-2:30pm & 5-9pm) Indian on a creek-side patio. Great naan.

Glen Ellen Inn AMERICAN $$
(Map p180; ☎707-996-6409; www.glenelleninn.com; 13670 Arnold Dr; mains $13-23; ⏲11:30am-9pm) Oysters, martinis and grilled steaks. Lovely garden, full bar.

Garden Court Cafe CAFE $
(Map p180; ☎707-935-1565; www.gardencourtcafe.com; 13647 Arnold Dr; mains $9-12; ⏲7:30am-2pm Wed-Mon) Basic breakfasts, sandwiches and salads.

Mayo Winery Reserve Room WINERY $$
(Map p180; ☎707-833-5544; www.mayofamilywinery.com; 9200 Sonoma Hwy, Kenwood; 7-course menu $35; ⏲11am-5pm, by reservation) Snag a seven-course small-plates menu, paired with seven wines, for just $35 at this roadside wine-tasting room.

Jack London State Historic Park

Napa has Robert Louis Stevenson, but Sonoma's got Jack London. This 1400-acre **park** (Map p180; ☎707-938-5216; www.jacklondonpark.com; 2400 London Ranch Rd, Glen Ellen; parking $8; ⏲10am-5pm Thu-Mon; 👪) traces the last years of the author's life.

Changing occupations from Oakland fisherman to Alaska gold prospector to Pacific yachtsman – and novelist on the side – London (1876–1916) ultimately took up farming. He bought Beauty Ranch in 1905 and moved there in 1910. With his second wife, Charmian, he lived and wrote in a small cottage while his mansion, Wolf House, was under construction. On the eve of its completion in 1913, it burned down. The disaster devastated London, and although he toyed with rebuilding, he died before construction got underway. His widow, Charmian, built the House of Happy Walls, which has been preserved as a museum. It's a half-mile walk from there to the remains of Wolf House, passing London's grave along the way. Other paths wind around the farm to the cottage where he lived and worked. Miles of hiking trails (some open to mountain bikes) weave through oak-dotted woodlands, between 600ft and 2300ft elevation. Watch for poison oak. NB: State budget cuts may temporarily close this park; call ahead.

RUSSIAN RIVER AREA

Lesser-known West County Sonoma was formerly famous for its apple farms and vacation cottages. Lately vineyards are replacing the orchards, and the Russian River has now taken its place among California's important wine appellations for superb pinot noir.

'The River,' as locals call it, has long been a summertime weekend destination for Northern Californians, who come to canoe, wander country lanes, taste wine, hike redwood forests and live at a lazy pace. In winter the river floods, and nobody's here.

The Russian River begins in the mountains north of Ukiah, in Mendocino County, but the most famous sections lie southwest of Healdsburg, where it cuts a serpentine course toward the sea. Just north of Santa Rosa, River Rd, the lower valley's main artery, connects Hwy 101 with coastal Hwy 1 at Jenner. Hwy 116 heads northwest from Cotati through Sebastopol and on to Guerneville. Westside Rd connects Guerneville and Healdsburg. West County's winding roads get confusing; carry a map.

Russian River Area Wineries

Outside Sonoma Valley, Sonoma County's wine-growing regions encompass several diverse areas, each famous for different reasons (see A Wine Country Primer, p182). Pick up the free, useful *Russian River Wine*

Russian River Area

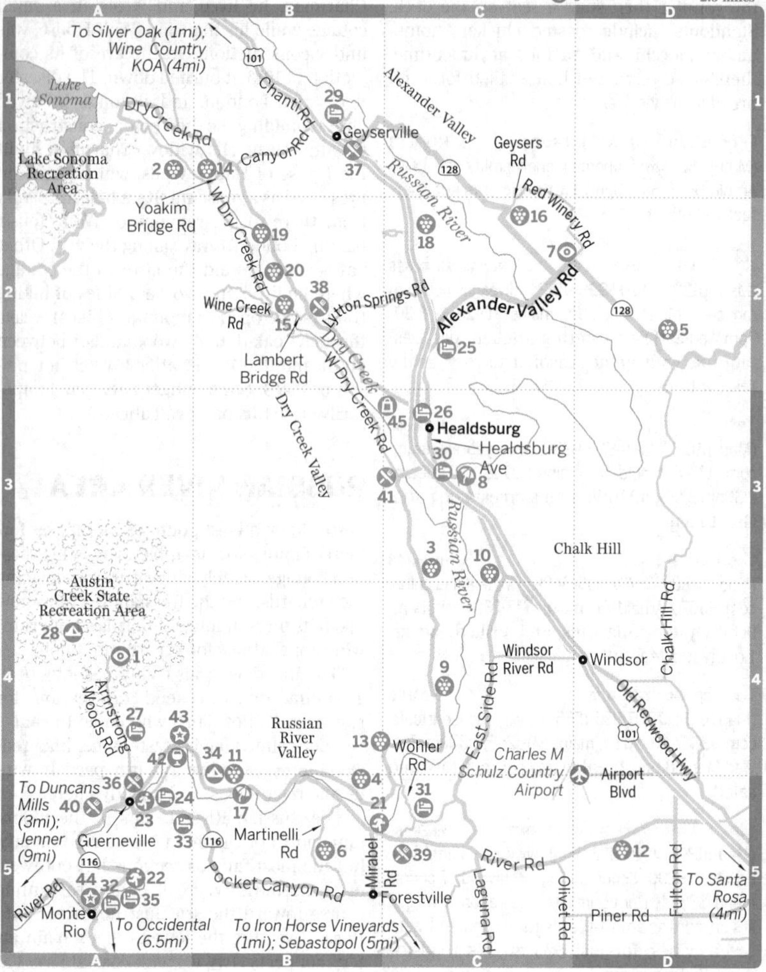

Road map (www.wineroad.com) in tourist-brochure racks.

RUSSIAN RIVER VALLEY

Nighttime coastal fog drifts up the Russian River Valley, then usually clears by midday. Pinot noir does beautifully here, as does chardonnay, which also grows in hotter regions, but prefers the longer 'hang time' of cooler climes. The highest concentration of wineries is along **Westside Rd**, between Guerneville and Healdsburg.

Hartford Family Winery WINERY

(Map p190; ☎707-887-8030; www.hartfordwines.com; 8075 Martinelli Rd, Forestville; tastings $5-15, applicable to purchase; ⏲10am-4:30pm; 🐾)

Surprisingly upscale for West County, Hartford sits in a pastoral valley surrounded by redwood-forested hills, on one of the area's prettiest back roads. It specializes in fine single-vineyard pinot (eight kinds), chardonnay and zinfandel, some from old-vine fruit. Umbrella-shaded picnic tables dot the garden. Bottles cost $35 to $70.

Russian River Area

Sights

1 Armstrong Redwoods State Reserve A4
2 Bella Vineyards A1
3 De la Montanya C3
4 Gary Farrell B5
5 Hanna D2
6 Hartford Family Winery B5
7 Hawkes C2
8 Healdsburg Veterans Memorial Beach C3
9 Hop Kiln Winery C4
10 J Winery C3
11 Korbel B4
Locals Tasting Room .... (see 37)
12 Martinelli D5
13 Porter Creek B4
14 Preston Vineyards B1
15 Quivira B2
Sophie's Cellars .... (see 32)
16 Stryker Sonoma C2
17 Sunset Beach B5
18 Trentadue C2
19 Truett-Hurst B2
20 Unti Vineyards B2

Activities, Courses & Tours

21 Burke's Canoe Trips B5
22 Northwood Golf Course A5
23 Pee Wee Golf & Arcade A5
River's Edge Kayak & Canoe Trips .... (see 8)
Russian River Adventures .... (see 8)

Sleeping

24 Applewood Inn A5
25 Belle de Jour Inn C2
26 Best Western Dry Creek Inn C3
27 Boon Hotel & Spa A4
28 Bullfrog Pond A4
Farmhouse Inn .... (see 39)
29 Geyserville Inn B1
Highland Dell .... (see 35)
30 L&M Motel C3
Madrona Manor .... (see 41)
31 Raford Inn C5
32 Rio Villa Beach Resort A5
33 Santa Nella House A5
34 Schoolhouse Canyon Campground B4
35 Village Inn A5

Eating

Applewood Inn Restaurant .... (see 24)
36 Coffee Bazaar A5
37 Diavola B1
Don's Dogs .... (see 44)
38 Dry Creek General Store B2
39 Farmhouse Inn C5
40 Garden Grill A5
Highland Dell .... (see 35)
Jimtown Store .... (see 7)
41 Madrona Manor C3
Village Inn .... (see 35)

Drinking

42 Stumptown Brewery A4

Entertainment

43 Rio Nido Roadhouse A4
44 Rio Theater A5

Shopping

45 Gardener C3

Sophie's Cellars WINE SHOP $

(Map p190; ☎707-865-1122; www.sophiescellars.com; 20293 Hwy 116; ⊙11am-7pm Thu-Tue) Stellar wine shop, with many hard-to-find local cult labels; the owner-connoisseur can help direct you to good wineries. Also stocks Sonoma cheeses, good for picnics. Find it across the road from Rio Villa Beach Resort.

Korbel WINERY

(Map p190; ☎707-824-7316, 707-824-7000; www.korbel.com; 13250 River Rd; tastings free; ⊙10am-5pm; 🐾) Gorgeous rose gardens (April to October) and stellar on-site deli make Korbel worth a stop, but the champagne's just OK.

Iron Horse Vineyards WINERY

(Map p156; ☎707-887-1507; www.ironhorsevineyards.com; 9786 Ross Station Rd, Sebastopol; tastings $10-20, refundable with purchase; ⊙10am-4:30pm; 🐾) Atop a hill with drop-dead views over the county, Iron Horse is known for pinot noir and sparkling wines, which the White House often pours. The outdoor tasting room is refreshingly unfussy; when you're done with your wine, pour it in the grass. Located off Hwy 116. Bottles cost $20 to $85.

Marimar WINERY

(Map p156; ☎707-823-4365; www.marimarestate.com; 11400 Graton Rd, Sebastopol; tastings $10;

11am-4pm;) Middle-of-nowhere Marimar specializes in all-organic pinot – seven different kinds – and chardonnay. The Spanish-style hilltop tasting room has a knockout vineyard-view terrace, lovely for picnics. Also consider tapas-and-wine pairings ($35). Bottles cost $29 to $52.

Gary Farrell WINERY

(Map p190; 707-473-2900; www.garyfarrellwines.com; 10701 Westside Rd; tastings $10-15; 10:30am-4:30pm;) High on a hilltop, overlooking the Russian River, Gary Farrell's tasting room sits perched among second-growth redwoods. The elegant chardonnay and long-finish pinot, made by a big-name winemaker, score high marks for consistency. Bottles cost $32 to $60.

Porter Creek WINERY

(Map p190; 707-433-6321; www.portercreekvineyards.com; 8735 Westside Rd; tastings free;) Inside a vintage 1920s garage, Porter Creek's tasting bar is a former bowling-alley lane, plunked atop barrels. Porter is old-school Northern California and an early pioneer in biodynamic farming. High-acid, food-friendly pinot noir and chardonnay are specialties, but there's silky zinfandel and other Burgundian- and Rhône-style wines, too. Check out the aviary and yurt. Bottles cost $24 to $65.

Hop Kiln Winery WINERY

(Map p190; 707-433-6491; www.hopkilnwinery.com; 6050 Westside Rd; tastings $5-7; 10am-5pm) Photogenic, historic landmark, with busy redwood tasting barn; the excellent artisinal vinegars make great $10 gifts.

De La Montanya WINERY

(Map p190; 707-433-3711; www.dlmwine.com; 2651 Westside Rd at Foreman Lane; tastings $5, refundable with purchase; Mon-Thu call ahead, Fri-Sun 11am-4:30pm;) On weekends, meet the practical-joker winemaker at this tiny winery, known for 17 small-batch varieties made with estate-grown fruit. Viognier, primitivo, pinot and cabernet are signatures; the 'summer white' and gewürztraminer are great back-porch wines. Apple-shaded picnic area and bocce ball, too. Bottles $20 to $60.

Martinelli WINERY

(Map p190; 707-525-0570; www.martinelliwinery.com; 3360 River Rd, Windsor; tastings $5-15; 10am-5pm;) Celeb winemaker Helen Turley makes the top-end pinot; there's also good syrah, sauvignon blanc and chardonnay in the gift shop-tasting barn.

J Winery WINERY

(Map p190; 707-431-3646; www.jwine.com; 11447 Old Redwood Hwy; tastings $20; 11am-5pm) Crafts crisp sparkling wines – some of Wine Country's best – but tastings are overpriced. Buy it in local shops.

DRY CREEK VALLEY

Hemmed in by 2000ft-high mountains, Dry Creek Valley is relatively warm, ideal for sauvignon blanc and zinfandel, and in some places cabernet sauvignon. It's west of Hwy 101, between Healdsburg and Lake Sonoma. Dry Creek Rd is the fast-moving main thoroughfare. Parallel-running West Dry Creek Rd is an undulating country lane with no center stripe – one of Sonoma's great back roads, ideal for cycling.

Bella Vineyards WINERY

(Map p190; 707-473-9171; www.bellawinery.com; 9711 W Dry Creek Rd; tasting $5-10; 11am-4:30pm;) Atop the valley's north end, always-fun Bella has caves built into the hillside. The estate-grown grapes include 110-year-old vines from the Alexander Valley. The focus is on big reds – zin and syrah – but there's terrific rosé (good for barbecues), and late-harvest zin (great with brownies). The wonderful vibe and dynamic staff make Bella special. Bottles cost $25 to $40.

Preston Vineyards WINERY

(Map p190; 707-433-3372; www.prestonvineyards.com; 9282 W Dry Creek Rd; tasting $10, refundable with purchase; 11am-4:30pm;) An early leader in organics, Lou Preston's 19th-century farm feels like old Sonoma County. Weathered picket fencing frames the 19th-century farmhouse-turned-tasting room, with candy-colored walls and tongue-in-groove ceilings setting a country mood. The signature is citrusy sauvignon blanc, but try the Rhône varietals and small-lot wines: mourvèdre, viognier, cinsault and cult-favorite barbera. Preston also bakes good bread; have a picnic in the shade of the walnut tree. Monday to Friday there's bocce ball. Bottles cost $24 to $38.

Truett-Hurst WINERY

(Map p190; 707-433-9545; www.truetthurst.com; 5610 Dry Creek Rd; tastings $5, refundable with purchase; 10am-5pm;) Pull up an Adirondack chair and picnic creekside at Truett-Hurst, Dry Creek's newest biodynamic winery.

Sample terrific old-vine zins, standout petite sirah and Russian River pinots at the handsome contemporary tasting room, then meander through fragrant butterfly gardens to the creek, where salmon spawn in autumn. Ever-fun weekends, with food-and-wine pairings and **live music** (1-5pm Sat & Sun).

Unti Vineyards WINERY

(Map p190; 707-433-5590; www.untivineyards.com; 4202 Dry Creek Rd; tastings $5, waived with purchase; by appointment 10am-4pm;) Inside a fluorescent-lit windowless garage, Unti makes all estate-grown reds – Châteauneuf-du-Pape–style grenache, compelling syrah, and superb sangiovese – favored by oenophiles for their structured tannins and concentrated fruit. If you love artisinal wines, don't miss Unti. Bottles cost $22 to $35.

Quivira WINERY

(Map p190; 707-431-8333; www.quivirawine.com; 4900 W Dry Creek Rd; tastings $5, waived with purchase; 11am-5pm;) Sunflowers, lavender and crowing roosters greet your arrival at this winery and biodynamic farm, with self-guided garden tours and picnic grove beside the vineyards. The kids can scan the grapes for the football-sized feral sow – the winery's mascot – while you sample Rhône varietals and unusual blends, including lip-smacking sauvignon blanc-gewürztraminer. Bottles cost $18 to $45.

ALEXANDER VALLEY

Bucolic Alexander Valley flanks the Mayacamas Mountains, with postcard-perfect vistas and wide-open vineyards. Summers are hot, ideal for cabernet sauvignon, merlot and warm-weather chardonnays, but there's also fine sauvignon blanc and zinfandel. For events info, visit www.alexandervalley.org.

Stryker Sonoma WINERY

(Map p190; 707-433-1944; www.strykersonoma.com; 5110 Hwy 128; tastings $10, refundable with purchase; 10:30am-5pm;) Wow, what a view from the hilltop concrete-and-glass tasting room at Stryker Sonoma. The standouts are fruit-forward zinfandel and sangiovese, which you can't buy anywhere else. Good picnicking. Bottles cost $20 to $50.

Hawkes TASTING ROOM

(Map p190; 707-433-4295; www.hawkeswine.com; 6734 Hwy 128; tastings $10, refundable with purchase; 10am-5pm;) Funky teapots grace the walls at friendly Hawkes', an easy roadside stopover while you're exploring the valley. The single-vineyard cab is damn good, as is the blend; there's also a clean-and-crisp, non-malolactic chardonnay. Bottles cost $20 to $70.

Hanna WINERY

(Map p190; 707-431-4310, 800-854-3987; http://hannawinery.com; 9280 Hwy 128; tastings $10; 10am-4pm;) Abutting oak-studded hills, Hanna's tasting room has lovely vineyard views and good picnicking. At the bar, find estate-grown merlot and cabernet, and big-fruit zins and syrah. Sit-down wine-and-cheese tastings available ($25). Bottles cost $15 to $48.

Silver Oak WINERY

(off Map p190; 800-273-8809; www.silveroak.com; 24625 Chianti Rd; tastings $20, partially applicable to purchase; 9am-4pm Mon-Sat) Sister to the legendary Napa winery; the Alexander Valley cabernet is similarly luxurious. Bottles start at $70.

Trentadue WINERY

(Map p190; 707-433-3104, 888-332-3032; www.trentadue.com; 19170 Geyserville Ave; port tastings $5; 10am-5pm) Specializes in ports (ruby, not tawny); the chocolate port makes a great gift.

Sebastopol

Grapes have replaced apples as the new cash crop, but Sebastopol's farm-town identity remains rooted in the apple – evidence the much-heralded summertime Gravenstein Apple Fair. The town center feels suburban because of traffic, but a hippie tinge gives it color. This is the refreshingly unfussy side of Wine Country, and makes a good-value home base for exploring the area.

Hwy 116 splits downtown; southbound traffic uses Main St, northbound traffic Petaluma Ave. North of town, it's called Gravenstein Hwy N and continues toward Guerneville; south of downtown, it's Gravenstein Hwy S, which heads toward Hwy 101 and Sonoma.

Sights & Activities

Around Sebastopol, look for family-friendly farms, gardens, animal sanctuaries and pick-your-own orchards. For a countywide list, check out the **Sonoma County Farm Trails Guide** (www.farmtrails.org).

Farmers market MARKET
(cnr Petaluma & McKinley Aves; ⏲10am-1:30pm Sun Apr–mid-Dec) Meets at the downtown plaza.

Sturgeon's Mill MILL
(www.sturgeonsmill.com; 2150 Green Hill Rd; 👪) A historic steam-powered sawmill, open for demonstrations several weekends a year; check the website.

Festivals & Events

Apple Blossom Festival CULTURAL
(www.sebastopol.org) April

Gravenstein Apple Fair FOOD
(www.farmtrails.org/gravenstein-apple-fair) August

Sleeping

Sebastopol is good for get-up-and-go travelers exploring Russian River Valley and the coast.

Sebastopol Inn MOTEL $$
(☎707-829-2500, 800-653-1082; www.sebastopolinn.com; 6751 Sebastopol Ave; r $119-179; ❄📶🏊👪) We like this independent, *non*-cookie-cutter motel for its quiet, off-street location, usually reasonable rates and good-looking if basic rooms. Outside are grassy areas for kids and a hot tub.

Vine Hill Inn B&B $$
(☎707-823-8832; www.vine-hill-inn.com; 3949 Vine Hill Rd; r incl breakfast $170; ❄📶🏊🐾) Mature landscaping surrounds this four-room 1897 Victorian farmhouse, with gorgeous vineyard views, just north of town off Hwy 116. Breakfast is made with eggs from the barn's chickens. Two rooms have Jacuzzis.

Raccoon Cottage COTTAGE $$
(☎707-545-5466; www.raccooncottage.com; 2685 Elizabeth Ct; cottage incl breakfast $130-150) A small B&B cottage, off Vine Hill Rd, amid oaks, fruit trees and gardens.

Fairfield Inn & Suites HOTEL $$
(☎707-829-6677, 800-465-4329; www.winecountryhi.com; 1101 Gravenstein Hwy S; r $129-209; ❄@📶🏊👪) Generic, but modern, with in-room refrigerators, coffee makers and hot tub.

Eating

Gourmet **food trucks** (⏲11:30am-2:30pm Thu) gather in the parking lot at **O'Reilly Media** (1050 Gravenstein Hwy N).

K&L Bistro FRENCH $$$
(☎707-823-6614; www.klbistro.com; 119 S Main St; lunch $14-20, dinner $19-29; ⏲11:30am-2:30pm & 5:30-9pm Mon-Sat) Sebastopol's top restaurant serves down-to-earth provincial Cal-French bistro cooking in a convivial – if loud – room, with classics like mussels and French fries, and grilled steaks with red-wine reduction. Tables are tight, but the crowd is friendly. Reservations essential.

Hopmonk Tavern PUB $$
(☎707-829-7300; www.hopmonk.com; 230 Petaluma Ave; mains $10-20; ⏲11:30am-9pm) Inside a converted 1903 railroad station, Hopmonk's competent cooking is designed to pair with beer – 76 varieties – served in type-specific glassware. Good burgers, fried calamari, charcuterie platters and salads.

East-West Cafe MEDITERRANEAN $
(☎707-829-2822; www.eastwestcafesebastopol.com; 128 N Main St; meals $9-12; ⏲8am-9pm Mon-Sat, 8am-8pm Sun; 🌱👪) This unfussy cafe serves everything from grass-fed burgers to macrobiotic wraps, stir-fries to *huevos rancheros* (corn tortilla with fried egg and chili-tomato sauce). Good blue-corn pancakes at breakfast.

Slice of Life VEGETARIAN $
(☎707-829-6627; www.thesliceoflife.com; 6970 McKinley St; mains under $10; ⏲11am-9pm Tue-Fri, 9am-9pm Sat & Sun; 🌱) This terrific vegan-vegetarian kitchen doubles as a pizzeria. Breakfast all day. Great smoothies and date shakes.

Mom's Apple Pie DESSERTS $
(☎707-823-8330; www.momsapplepieusa.com; 4550 Gravenstein Hwy N; whole pies $7-15; ⏲10am-6pm; 🌱👪) Pie's the thing here – and yum, that flaky crust. Apple is predictably good, especially in autumn, but the blueberry is our fave, made better with vanilla ice cream.

Viva Mexicana MEXICAN $
(☎707-823-5555, 707-829-5555; 841 Gravenstein Hwy S; mains $8-10; ⏲8am-8pm; 🌱) A tiny roadside *taquería* with outdoor tables and good vegetarian choices.

Fiesta Market MARKET $
(☎707-823-9735; fiestamkt.com; 550 Gravenstein Hwy N; ⏲8am-8pm) The town's best groceries and picnics.

Screamin' Mimi DESSERT $
(☎707-823-5902; www.screaminmimisicecream.com; 6902 Sebastopol Ave; ⏲11am-10pm) Delish homemade ice cream.

Drinking & Entertainment

Hardcore Espresso CAFE
(☎707-823-7588; 1798 Gravenstein Hwy S; ⏰6am-7pm; 📶) Meet local hippies and art freaks over coffee and smoothies at this classic Nor-Cal off-the-grid, indoor-outdoor coffeehouse that's essentially a corrugated-metal-roofed shack surrounded by umbrella tables. The organic coffee is the town's best.

Hopmonk Tavern PUB
(☎707-829-7300; www.hopmonk.com; 230 Petaluma Ave; ⏰11:30am-10pm, later weekends) Always-fun beer garden with 76 craft brews, several housemade. Live music most nights; Tuesday is open mic.

Aubergine After Dark CABARET
(☎707-861-9190; aubergineafterdark.com; 755 Petaluma Ave; ⏰4pm-midnight Sun-Thu, to 1am Sat & Sun) Various acts play weekends at this cool cafe with a bohemian bent, adjoining a vintage-thrift shop; full bar, snacks, and coffee drinks.

Jasper O'Farrell's BAR
(☎707-823-1389; 6957 Sebastopol Ave; ⏰Tue-Sun) Busy bar with billiards and live bands Wednesday nights; good drink specials.

Coffee Catz CAFE
(☎707-829-6600; www.coffeecatz.com; 6761 Sebastopol Ave; ⏰7am-10pm Fri & Sat, to 6pm Sun-Thu) Early-evening and afternoon acoustic music, Thursday to Sunday, at a cafe in an historic rail barn (Gravenstein Station).

Shopping

Antique shops line Gravenstein Hwy S toward Hwy 101.

Renga Arts ARTS & CRAFTS, GIFTS
(☎707-823-9407; www.rengaarts.com; ⏰11am-5pm Thu-Mon) Reduce, reuse, rejoice at Renga Arts, a functional-art shop, where every ingenious item is made with repurposed, reclaimed goods, from bottle-cap necklaces to birdhouses. Owner Joe is an excellent resource on all things West County Sonoma. Say hello.

Aubergine VINTAGE CLOTHING
(☎707-827-3460; www.aubergineafterdark.com; 755 Petaluma Ave, Sebastopol) Vast vintage emporium, specializing in cast-off European thrift-shop clothing.

Sumbody BEAUTY
(☎707-823-2053; www.sumbody.com; 118 N Main St; ⏰10am-7pm Mon-Sat, 10am-5pm Sun) Eco-friendly bath products made with all-natural ingredients. Also offers well-priced facials ($49) and massages ($75) at small on-site spa.

Toyworks TOYS
(☎707-829-2003; www.sonomatoyworks.com; 6940 Sebastopol Ave; 👪) Indie toy-seller with phenomenal selection of quality games for kids.

Antique Society ANTIQUES
(☎707-829-1733; www.antiquesociety.com; 2661 Gravenstein Hwy S) Antiques vendors, 125 of them, under one roof.

Beekind FOOD, HOMEWARES
(☎707-824-2905; www.beekind.com; 921 Gravenstein Hwy S) Local honey and beeswax candles.

Copperfield's Books BOOKS
(☎707-823-2618; www.copperfields.net; 138 N Main St) Indie bookshop with literary events.

Incredible Records MUSIC
(☎707-824-8099; 112 N Main St) A legendary record store.

Midgley's Country Flea Market MARKET
(☎707-823-7874; mfleamarket.com; 2200 Gravenstein Hwy S; ⏰6:30am-4:30pm Sat & Sun) The region's largest flea market.

Information

Sebastopol Area Chamber of Commerce & Visitors Center (☎707-823-3032, 877-828-4748; www.visitsebastopol.org; 265 S Main St; ⏰10am-4pm Mon-Fri) Maps, information and exhibits.

Occidental

Our favorite West County town is a haven of artists, back-to-the-landers and counterculturalists. Historic 19th-century buildings line a single main street, easy to explore in an hour; continue north by car and you'll hit the Russian River, in Monte Rio. Check out **Bohemian Connection** (www.bohemianconnection.com) for information. At Christmastime, Bay Area families flock to Occidental to buy trees. The town decorates to the nines, and there's weekend cookie-decorating and caroling at the Union Hotel's Bocce Ballroom.

Sights & Activities

Meet the whole community at the detour-worthy **farmers market** (www.occidentalfarmersmarket.com; 4pm-dusk Fridays, Jun-Oct), with musicians, craftspeople and – the star attraction – **Gerard's Paella** (www.gerardspaella.com) of TV-cooking-show fame.

Sonoma Canopy Tours ECOTOUR
(888-494-7868; www.sonomacanopytours.com; 6250 Bohemian Hwy; adult $79-89, child $49) North of town, fly through the redwood canopy on seven interconnected ziplines, ending with an 80ft-rappel descent; reservations required.

Osmosis Enzyme Bath & Massage BATH HOUSE
(707-823-8231; www.osmosis.com; 209 Bohemian Hwy; 9am-9pm) Three miles south in Freestone, tranquility prevails at this Japanese-inspired place, which indulges patrons with dry-enzyme baths of aromatic cedar fibers (bath-and-blanket wrap $85), lovely tea-and-meditation gardens, plus outdoor massages. Make reservations.

Sleeping

Inn at Occidental INN $$$
(707-874-1047, 800-522-6324; www.innatoccidental.com; 3657 Church St; r incl breakfast $229-339;) This beautifully restored 18-room Victorian inn – one of Sonoma's finest – is filled with collectible antiques; rooms have gas fireplaces and cozy feather beds.

Valley Ford Hotel INN $$
(707-876-1983; www.vfordhotel.com; r $115-165) Surrounded by pastureland in the nearby tiny town of Valley Ford, this 19th-century six-room inn has good beds, soft linens, and great rates. Downstairs there's a terrific roadhouse restaurant.

Occidental Hotel MOTEL $$
(707-874-3623, 877-867-6084; www.occidentalhotel.com; 3610 Bohemian Hwy; r $130-160, 2-bedroom q $180-200;) Fresh-looking motel rooms.

Eating

Bohemian Market (707-874-3312; 3633 Main St; 8am-9pm) has the best groceries. In Freestone, **Wild Flour Bakery** (707-874-3928; www.wildflourbread.coml 140 Bohemian Hwy; 8:30am-6pm Fri-Mon) makes hearty artisinal brick-oven breads, scones and coffee.

Bistro des Copains FRENCH-CALIFORNIAN $$$
(707-874-2436; www.bistrodescopains.com; 3728 Bohemian Hwy; mains $23-25, 3-course menu $38-42; 5-9pm Wed-Mon) Worth a special trip, this bistro draws bon vivants for its Cal-French country cooking, like steak-*frites* and roast duck. Great wines; $10 corkage for Sonoma vintages. Make reservations.

Howard Station Cafe CAFE $
(707-874-2838; www.howardstationcafe.com; 3811 Bohemian Hwy; mains $8-11; 7am-2:30pm;) Makes big plates of comfort cooking and fresh-squeezed juices.

Barley & Hops PUB $$
(707-874-9037; barleyandhopstavern.blogspot.com; 3688 Bohemian Hwy; mains $10-15; 4-9:30pm Mon-Fri, from 11am Sat & Sun;) Serves over 100 beers, sandwiches, giant salads and lamb stew.

Union Hotel ITALIAN $$
(707-874-3555; www.unionhoteloccidental.com; 3703 Bohemian Hwy; meals $15-25;) Occidental has two old-school American Italian restaurants that serve family-style meals. Of the two, the Union is slightly better than

SCENIC DRIVE: COLEMAN VALLEY ROAD

Wine Country's most scenic drive isn't through the grapes, but along these 10 miles of winding West County byway, from Occidental to the sea. It's best late morning, after the fog has cleared. Drive west, not east, with the sun behind you and the ocean ahead. First you'll pass through redwood forests and lush valleys where Douglas firs stand draped in sphagnum moss – an eerie sight in the fog. The real beauty shots lie further ahead, when the road ascends 1000ft hills, dotted with gnarled oaks and craggy rock formations, with the vast blue Pacific unfurling below. The road ends at coastal Hwy 1, where you can explore Sonoma Coast State Beach, then turn left and find your way to the tiny town of Bodega (not Bodega Bay) to see locales where Hitchcock shot his 1963 classic, *The Birds*.

WORTH A TRIP

VALLEY FORD

Valley Ford (population 147) is a tableau of rural California, with rolling hills dotted with grazing cows and manure lingering on the breeze – the forced sophistication of other Wine Country locales couldn't feel further away. It's ideal for an affordable one-nighter, or a lazy meal while exploring back roads.

West County Design (☎707-875-9140; 14390 Hwy 1; ⊗Thu-Sun) houses a stonemason's and custom furniture–builder's shops, giving a glimpse of contemporary California home-furnishings styles. 'Round back there's a man who builds birdhouses.

We love the flavor-rich cooking at **Rocker Oysterfeller's** (☎707-876-1983; www.rockeroysterfellers.com; 14415 Hwy 1; mains $14-22; ⊗Wed-Fri 4:30pm-8:30pm, 10am-8:30pm Sat & Sun), with its barbecued oysters, local crab cakes, steaks and fried chicken. Great wine bar, too. Or snag a picnic table at **Fish Bank** (☎707-876-3473; www.sonomacoastfishbank.com; 14435 Hwy 1; ⊗Wed-Sun 11:30am-6pm) for crab rolls, fish salads, chowder, cheese and bread – good picnic fixings if you're continuing to the coast. Stay the night at the Valley Ford Hotel (p196), with simple country B&B rooms.

Negri's (neither is great), and has a hard-to-beat lunch special in its 1869 saloon – whole pizza, salad and soda for $12. At dinner, sit in the fabulous Bocce Ballroom.

Negri's ITALIAN $$
(☎707-823-5301; www.negrisrestaurant.com; 3700 Bohemian Hwy; meals $15-25; 👪) Serves multi-course family-style dinners.

Shopping

Verdigris HOMEWARES
(☎707-874-9018; www.1lightartlamps.com; 72 Main St; ⊗Thu-Mon) Crafts gorgeous art lamps.

Hand Goods CERAMICS
(☎707-874-2161; www.handgoods.net; 3627 Main St) A collective of ceramicists and potters.

Guerneville & Around

The Russian River's biggest vacation-resort town, Guerneville gets busy summer weekends with party hardy gay boys, sun-worshipping lesbians and long-haired beer-drinking Harley riders, earning it the nickname 'Groin-ville.' The gay scene has died back since the unfortunate closure of Fife's, the world's first gay resort, but fun-seeking crowds still come to canoe, hike redwoods and hammer cocktails poolside.

Downriver, some areas are sketchy (due to drugs). The local chamber of commerce has chased most of the tweakers from Main St in Guerneville, but if some off-the-beaten-path areas feel creepy – especially campgrounds – they probably are.

Four miles downriver, tiny Monte Rio has a sign over Hwy 116 declaring it 'Vacation Wonderland' – an overstatement, but the dog-friendly beach is a hit with families. Further west, idyllic Duncans Mills is home to a few dozen souls, but has picture-ready historic buildings. Upriver, east of Guerneville, Forestville is where agricultural country resumes.

Sights & Activities

Look for sandy beaches and swimming holes along the river; there's good river access east of town at **Sunset Beach** (Map p190; www.sonoma-county.org/parks; 11403 River Rd, Forestville; per car $6). Fishing and watercraft outfitters operate mid-May to early October, after which winter rains dangerously swell the river. A **farmers market** meets downtown on Wednesdays June through September, from 4pm to 7pm. On summer Saturdays, there's also one at Monte Rio Beach, 11am to 2pm.

Armstrong Redwoods State Reserve NATURE RESERVE
(Map p190; www.parks.ca.gov; 17000 Armstrong Woods Rd; day use per vehicle $8) A magnificent redwood forest 2 miles north of Guerneville, the 805-acre Armstrong Redwoods State Reserve was set aside by a 19th-century lumber magnate. Walk or cycle in for free; you pay only to park. Short interpretive trails lead into magical forests; beyond lie 20 miles of backcountry trails, through oak woodlands, in adjoining **Austin Creek State Recreation Area**, one of Sonoma County's

few-remaining wilderness areas (although State budget cuts may temporarily close this park).

Burke's Canoe Trips CANOEING, KAYAKING
(Map p190; ☎707-887-1222; www.burkescanoetrips.com; 8600 River Rd, Forestville; canoes $60;) You can't beat Burke's for a day on the river. Self-guided canoe and kayak trips include shuttle back to your car. Make reservations; plan four hours. Camping in its riverside redwood grove costs $10 per person.

Pee Wee Golf & Arcade GOLF, BICYCLING
(Map p190; ☎707-869-9321; 16155 Drake Rd at Hwy 116; 18/36 holes $8/12; ⏲11am-10pm Memorial Day-Labor Day, Sat & Sun Sep;) Flashback to 1948 at this impeccably kept retro-kitsch 36-hole miniature golf course, just south of the Hwy 116 bridge, with brilliantly painted obstacles, including T Rex and Yogi Bear. Bring your own cocktails; also rents gas barbecue grills ($20) and bicycles ($30).

Armstrong Woods Pack Station HORSEBACK RIDING
(☎707-887-2939; www.redwoodhorses.com) Leads year-round 2½-hour trail rides ($80), full-day rides and overnight treks. Reservations required.

Johnson's Beach BOATING
(☎707-869-2022; www.johnsonsbeach.com; end of Church St, Guerneville) Canoe, paddleboat and watercraft rental (from $30).

King's Sport & Tackle FISHING, KAYAKING, CANOEING
(☎707-869-2156; www.kingsrussianriver.com; www.guernevillesport.com; 16258 Main St, Guerneville) *The* local source for fishing and river-condition information. Also rents kayaks ($35 to $55) and canoes ($55).

Northwood Golf Course GOLF
(Map p190; ☎707-865-1116; www.northwoodgolf.com; 19400 Hwy 116, Monte Rio) Vintage-1920s Alistair MacKenzie-designed, par-36, nine-hole course.

Festivals & Events

Monte Rio Variety Show MUSIC
(www.monterioshow.org) Members of the elite, secretive Bohemian Grove (Google it) perform publicly, sometimes showcasing unannounced celebrities; July.

Lazy Bear Weekend CULTURAL
(www.lazybearweekend.com) Read: heavy, furry gay men; August.

Russian River Jazz & Blues Festival MUSIC
(www.omegaevents.com/russianriver) September. A day of jazz, followed by a day of blues, with occasional luminaries like BB King.

Sleeping

Russian River has few budget sleeps, although prices drop midweek. On weekends and holidays, book ahead. Many places have no TVs. Because the river sometimes floods, some lodgings have cold linoleum floors, so pack slippers.

GUERNVILLE

The advantage of staying downtown is you can walk to dinner and bars. At this writing, the long-running gay hotel and disco, Russian River Resort (aka Triple R), had closed, but may re-open. Check with the chamber of commerce.

Applewood Inn INN $$$
(Map p190; ☎707-869-9093, 800-555-8509; www.applewoodinn.com; 13555 Hwy 116; r incl breakfast $195-345;) A former estate on a wooded hilltop south of town, cushy Applewood has marvelous Arts and Crafts-era detail, with dark wood and heavy furniture. Rooms sport Jacuzzis, couples' showers and top-end linens; some have fireplaces. Great hideaway. Small onsite spa.

Fern Grove Cottages CABINS $$
(☎707-869-8105; www.ferngrove.com; 16650 River Rd; cabins incl breakfast $159-219, with kitchen $199-269;) Downtown Guerneville's cheeriest resort, Fern Grove has vintage-1930s pine-paneled cabins, tucked beneath redwoods and surrounded by lush flowering gardens. Some have Jacuzzis and fireplaces. The pool uses salt, not chlorine; the lovely English innkeeper provides concierge service; and breakfast includes homemade scones.

Boon Hotel & Spa INN $$$
(Map p190; ☎707-869-2721; www.boonhotels.com; 14711 Armstrong Woods Rd; r $180-225;) Rooms surround a swimming-pool courtyard (with Jacuzzi) at this mid-century-modern, 14-room motel, gussied up in minimalist style. The look is austere but fresh, with organic-cotton linens and spacious rooms; most have wood-burning fireplaces. Drive to town, or ride the free bicycles.

Santa Nella House B&B $$
(Map p190; ☎707-869-9448; www.santanellahouse.com; 12130 Hwy 116; r incl breakfast $179-199; @📶) All four spotless rooms at this 1871 Victorian, south of town, have wood-burning fireplaces and frilly Victorian furnishings. Upstairs rooms are biggest. Outside there's a hot tub and sauna. Best for travelers who appreciate the B&B aesthetic.

Highlands Resort CABINS, CAMPGROUND $$
(☎707-869-0333; www.highlandsresort.com; 14000 Woodland Dr; tent sites $20-25; r with/without bathroom $90-100/70-80, cabins $120-205; 📶🏊) Guerneville's mellowest all-gay resort sits on a wooded hillside, walkable to town, and has simply furnished rooms and little cottages with porches. The large pool and hot tub are clothing-optional (weekday/weekend day use $5/10). There's camping, too.

Riverlane Resort CABINS $$
(☎707-869-2323, 800-201-2324; www.riverlaneresort.com; 16320 1st St; cabins $90-150; 📶🏊) Right downtown, Riverlane has cabins with kitchens, decorated with mismatched furniture, but they're very clean and all have decks with barbecues. Best for no-frills travelers or campers wanting an upgrade. Friendly service, heated pool, private beach and hot tub.

Johnson's Beach Resort CABINS, CAMPGROUND $
(☎707-869-2022; www.johnsonsbeach.com; 16241 1st St; tent sites $25, RV sites from $25-35, cabins $50, per week $300) On the river in Guerneville, Johnson's has rustic, but clean, thin-walled cabins on stilts; all have kitchens. Bring earplugs. There's camping, too, but it's loud. No credit cards.

Bullfrog Pond CAMPGROUND $
(Map p190; www.parks.ca.gov; tent sites $25) Reached via a steep road from Armstrong Redwoods, Bullfrog Pond has forested campsites, with cold water, and primitive hike-in and equestrian backcountry campsites. All are first-come, first-served. Budget cuts may limit operation to summer only.

Schoolhouse Canyon Campground CAMPGROUND $
(Map p190; ☎707-869-2311; www.schoolhousecanyon.com; 12600 River Rd; tent sites $30; 👪🐾) Two miles east of Guerneville, Schoolhouse's tent sites lie beneath tall trees, across the road from the river. Coin-operated hot showers, clean bathrooms, quiet location.

FORESTVILLE

Raford Inn B&B $$
(Map p190; ☎707-887-9573, 800-887-9503; www.rafordhouse.com; 10630 Wohler Rd, Healdsburg; r $160-260; ❄@📶) We love this 1880 Victorian B&B's secluded hilltop location, surrounded by tall palms and rambling vineyards. Rooms are big and airy, done with lace and antiques; some have fireplaces. And wow, those sunset views.

Farmhouse Inn INN $$$
(Map p190; ☎707-887-3300, 800-464-6642; www.farmhouseinn.com; 7871 River Rd; r $325-695; ❄@📶🏊) Think love nest. The area's premier inn has spacious rooms and cottages, styled with cushy amenities like saunas, steam-showers and wood-burning fireplaces. Small on-site spa and top-notch restaurant (p200). Check in early to maximize time.

MONTE RIO

Village Inn INN $$
(Map p190; ☎707-865-2304; www.villageinn-ca.com; 20822 River Blvd; r $145-235; @📶) A retired concierge owns this cute, old-fashioned 11-room inn, beneath towering trees, right on the river. Some rooms have river views; all have fridge and microwave.

Rio Villa Beach Resort INN $$
(Map p190; ☎707-865-1143, 877-746-8455; www.riovilla.com; 20292 Hwy 116; r with kitchen $149-209, r without kitchen $139-189; ❄📶🐾) Landscaping is lush at this small riverside resort with excellent sun exposure (you see redwoods, but you're not under them). Rooms are well kept but simple (request a quiet room, not by the road); the emphasis is on the outdoors, evident by the large riverside terrace, outdoor fireplace and barbecues.

Highland Dell INN $$
(Map p190; ☎707-865-2300; highlanddell.com; 21050 River Blvd; r $109-179; ❄📶) Built in 1906 in grand lodge style, redone in 2007, the inn fronts right on the river. Above the giant dining room are 12 bright, fresh-looking rooms (carpet stains notwithstanding) with comfy beds.

DUNCANS MILLS

Casini Ranch CAMPGROUND $
(☎707-865-2255, 800-451-8400; www.casiniranch.com; 22855 Moscow Rd, Duncans Mills; tent sites $38-45, RV sites partial/full hookups $40-51/46-49;

) In quiet Duncans Mills, beautifully set on riverfront ranchlands, Casini is an enormous, well-run campground. Amenities include kayaks and paddleboats (day use $3); bathrooms are spotless.

Eating

GUERNEVILLE

There's a good **taco truck** (16451 Main St), in the Safeway parking lot.

Boon Eat + Drink NEW AMERICAN **$$$**
(707-869-0780; www.eatatboon.com; 16248 Main St; lunch/dinner mains $10-12/$20-24; 11am-3pm & 5-9pm) Locally sourced ingredients inform the seasonal, Cali-smart cooking at this tiny, always-packed New American bistro, with cheek-by-jowl tables that fill every night. Make reservations or expect to wait.

Applewood Inn Restaurant CALIFORNIAN **$$$**
(Map p190; 707-869-9093, www.dineatapplewood.com; 13555 Hwy 116; mains $20-28; 5:30-8:30pm Wed-Sun) Cozy by the fire in the treetop-level dining room and sup on Michelin-starred Euro-Cal cooking that maximizes seasonal produce, with dishes like rack of lamb with minted *chimichuri* (garlic-parsley vinaigrette) and smoked trout with corn and crayfish. Reservations essential.

Coffee Bazaar CAFE **$**
(707-869-9706; www.mycoffeeb.com; 14045 Armstrong Woods Rd; dishes $5-9; 6am-8pm;) Happening cafe with salads, sandwiches and all-day breakfasts; adjoins a good used bookstore.

Garden Grill BARBECUE **$**
(707-869-3922; www.gardengrillbbq.com; 17132 Hwy 116, Guernewood Park; mains $6-12; 8am-8pm) The Garden Grill is a roadhouse barbecue joint, with a redwood-shaded patio, one mile west of Guerneville; good house-smoked meats, but the fries could be better. Breakfast till 3pm.

Andorno's Pizza PIZZERIA **$**
(707-869-0651; www.andornospizza.com; 16205 1st St; 11:30am-9pm;) Downtown pizzeria with river-view terrace.

Taqueria La Tapatia MEXICAN **$**
(707-869-1821; 16632 Main St; mains $7-14; 11am-9pm) Reasonable choice for traditional Mexican.

Big Bottom Market MARKET **$**
(707-604-7295; www.bigbottommarket.com; 16228 Main St) Gourmet deli and wine shop, with grab-and-go picnic supplies.

Food for Humans MARKET **$**
(707-869-3612; 16385 1st St; 9am-8pm;) Organic groceries; better alternative than neighboring Safeway, but no meat.

FORESTVILLE

Farmhouse Inn NEW AMERICAN **$$$**
(Map p190; 707-887-3300; www.farmhouseinn.com; 7871 River Rd; 3-/4-course dinner $69/89; dinner Thu-Sun) Special-occasion worthy, Michelin-starred Farmhouse changes its seasonal Euro-Cal menu daily, using locally raised, organic ingredients like Sonoma lamb, wild salmon and rabbit – the latter is the house specialty. Details are impeccable, from aperitifs in the garden to tableside cheese service. Make reservations.

MONTE RIO

Highland Dell GERMAN **$$**
(Map p190; 707-865-2300; http://highlanddell.com; 21050 River Blvd; lunch mains $9-15, dinner mains $16-26; 5-9pm Mon, Tue, Fri & Sat, 1-7pm Sun; closed Oct-May) A dramatic three-story-high chalet-style dining room with a river-view deck, Highland Dell makes pretty good German food – steaks, schnitzel, sauerbraten and sausage. Full bar.

Village Inn AMERICAN **$$$**
(Map p190; 707-865-2304; www.villageinn-ca.com; 20822 River Blvd; mains $19-26; 5-8:30pm Wed-Sun) The straightforward steaks-and-seafood menu is basic American and doesn't distract from the wonderful river views. Great local wine list, full bar.

Don's Dogs SNACK BAR **$**
(Map p190; 707-865-4190; cnr Bohemian Hwy & Hwy 116; 9am-5pm Wed-Sun) Gourmet hot dogs and coffee, behind the Rio Theater.

Drinking & Entertainment

Stumptown Brewery BREWERY
(Map p190; www.stumptown.com; 15045 River Rd; 11am-midnight Sun-Thu, 11-2am Fri & Sat) Guerneville's best straight bar is gay-friendly and has a foot-stompin' jukebox, billiards, riverside beer garden, and several homemade brews. Pretty good pub grub, including house-smoked barbecue.

Rio Theater CINEMA
(Map p190; ☎707-865-0913; www.riotheater.com; cnr Bohemian Hwy & Hwy 116, Monte Rio; adult/child $7/5; ⊙Fri-Sun) Dinner and a movie take on new meaning at this vintage-WWII Quonset hut converted to a cinema in 1950, with a concession stand serving gourmet hot dogs ($7). It's freezing inside on cool nights, but they supply blankets. Charming. Call to confirm showtimes, especially off-season.

Rainbow Cattle Company GAY
(www.queersteer.com; 16220 Main St) The stalwart gay watering hole.

Guerneville River Theater LIVE MUSIC, DJS
(www.rivertheater.biz; 16135 Main St; ⊙Wed, Fri & Sat) Former movie theater, now a honky-tonk club, with town's biggest dance floor. Live bands weekends, open mic Wednesdays. Very DIY feeling. Beer and wine only.

Rio Nido Roadhouse BAR, LIVE MUSIC
(www.rionidoroadhouse.com; 14540 Canyon Two, off River Rd) Raucous roadhouse bar with eclectic lineup of live bands. Shows start 6pm Saturdays and sometimes Fridays and Sundays, too; check website.

Main Street Station CABARET
(☎707-869-0501; www.mainststation.com; 16280 Main, Guerneville; cover $3-6) Live acoustic-only jazz, blues and cabaret nightly in summer, weekends in winter. Suggest reservations, but you can normally walk in. Also an Italian-American restaurant.

Kaya Organic Espresso CAFE
(16626 Main St, Guerneville; ⊙7am-2pm) Hippie kids strum guitars and play hackie sack outside this coffee shack.

Wine Tasting of Sonoma County WINE BAR $
(☎707-865-0565; winetastingofsonomacounty.com; 25179 Hwy 116, Duncans Mills; wine tastings $5; ⊙noon-5pm Fri-Mon) Local vino and cheeses alfresco.

Information

Get information and lodging referrals:

Russian River Chamber of Commerce & Visitor Center (☎707-869-9000, 877-644-9001; www.russianriver.com; 16209 1st St, Guerneville; ⊙10am-5pm Mon-Sat, to 4pm Sun)

Russian River Visitor Information Center (☎707-869-4096; ⊙10am-3:45pm) At Korbel Cellars.

Santa Rosa

Wine Country's biggest city, and the Sonoma County seat, Santa Rosa is known for traffic and suburban sprawl. It lacks small-town charm, but has reasonably priced accommodations and easy access to Sonoma County and Valley.

Santa Rosa claims two famous native sons – a world-renowned cartoonist and a celebrated horticulturalist – and you'll find enough museums, gardens and shopping for an afternoon. Otherwise, there ain't much to do, unless you're here in July during the **Sonoma County Fair** (www.sonomacountyfair.com), at the fairgrounds on Bennett Valley Rd.

Sights & Activities

The main shopping stretch is 4th St, which abruptly ends at Hwy 101 but reemerges on the other side at historic Railroad Sq. Downtown parking garages ($0.75/hour, $8 max) are cheaper than street parking. East of town, 4th St turns into Hwy 12 to Sonoma Valley.

FREE **Luther Burbank Home & Gardens** GARDENS
(☎707-524-5445; www.lutherburbank.org; ☎8am-dusk) Pioneering horticulturist Luther Burbank (1849–1926) developed many hybrid plant species at his 19th-century Greek-revival home, at Santa Rosa and Sonoma Aves, including the Shasta daisy. The extensive gardens are lovely. The house and adjacent **Carriage Museum** (guided tour adult/child $7/free, self-guided cell-phone tour free ⊙10am-3:30pm Tue-Sun Apr-Oct) have displays on Burbank's life and work. Across the street from Burbank's home, Julliard Park has a playground.

OLIVE-OIL TASTING

When you weary of wine tasting, pop in to one of the following olive-oil mills (all free except Round Pond) and dip some crusty bread. The harvest and pressing happen in November.

» **BR Cohn** (p201)
» **Long Meadow Ranch** (p163)
» **Round Pond** (p162) Ninety-minute mill tour and tasting $25.
» **Figone's Olive Oil** (p187)

Charles M Schulz Museum MUSEUM
(707-579-4452; www.schulzmuseum.org; 2301 Hardies Lane; adult/child $10/5; 11am-5pm Mon-Fri, 10am-5pm Sat & Sun, closed Tue Sep-May;) Charles Schulz, creator of *Peanuts* cartoons, was a long-term Santa Rosa resident. Born in 1922, he published his first drawing in 1937, introduced the world to Snoopy and Charlie Brown in 1950, and produced Peanuts cartoons until just before his death in 2000.

At the museum a glass wall overlooks a courtyard with a Snoopy labyrinth. Exhibits include Peanuts-related art and Schulz's actual studio. Skip Snoopy's Gallery gift shop; the museum has the good stuff.

Redwood Empire Ice Arena SKATING
(707-546-7147; www.snoopyshomeice.com; adult/child incl skates $12/10;) This skating rink was formerly owned and deeply loved by Schulz. It's open most afternoons (call for schedules). Bring a sweater.

Farmers Markets MARKET
Sonoma County's largest farmers market meets Wednesday, 5pm to 8:30pm, mid-May through August, at 4th and B Sts. A year-round market meets Saturdays at the Santa Rosa Veterans Building, 8:30am to 1pm, 1351 Maple Ave.

Sleeping

Look for hotels near Railroad Square. Nothing-special motels line Cleveland Ave, fronting Hwy 101's western side, between Steele Lane and Bicentennial Lane exits; skip the Motel 6. Also consider nearby Windsor, which has two chain hotels off Hwy 101 at the Central Windsor exit.

Hotel La Rose HISTORIC HOTEL $$
(707-579-3200; www.hotellarose.com; 308 Wilson St; r weekday/weekend $129-189/$199-219;) At Railroad Sq, this charming 1907 hotel has rooms with marble baths, sitting areas with thick carpeting and wing chairs, and supercomfy mattresses with feather beds. Great for a moderate splurge. Rooftop hot tub.

Vintners Inn INN $$$
(707-575-7350, 800-421-2584; www.vintnersinn.com; 4350 Barnes Rd; r $225-495;) Built in the 1980s, Vintners Inn sits on the rural outskirts of town (near River Rd) and appeals to the gated-community crowd. Rooms' amenities are business-class fancy. Jacuzzi, but no pool. Check for last-minute specials.

Flamingo Resort Hotel HOTEL $$
(707-545-8530, 800-848-8300; www.flamingoresort.com; 2777 4th St; r $99-219;) Sprawling over 11 acres, this mid-century modern hotel doubles as a conference center. Rooms are motel-generic, but what a gigantic pool – and it's 82 degrees year-round. Kids love it. On-site health-club and gym. Prices double summer weekends.

Hillside Inn MOTEL $
(707-546-9353; www.hillside-inn.com; 2901 4th St, Santa Rosa; s/d Nov-Mar $70/82, Apr-Oct $74/86;) One of Santa Rosa's best-kept motels, Hillside is close to Sonoma Valley; add $4 for kitchens. Furnishings are dated, but everything is scrupulously maintained. Adjoins an excellent breakfast cafe.

Best Western Garden Inn MOTEL $$
(707-546-4031, 888-256-8004; www.thegardeninn.com; 1500 Santa Rosa Ave; r $119-149;) Book a room in back for quiet, up front for privacy, at this well-kept cookie-cutter motel, south of downtown. The street gets seedy by night, but the hotel is secure, clean and comfortable.

Spring Lake Park CAMPGROUND $
(707-539-8092, reservations 707-565-2267; www.sonoma-county.org/parks; 5585 Newanga Ave; sites $28; daily May-Sep, weekends only Oct-Apr;) Lovely lakeside park, 4 miles from downtown; make reservations ($7 fee) 10am to 3pm weekdays. The park is open year-round, with **lake swimming** in summer; campground operates May to September, weekends October to April. Take 4th St eastbound, turn right on Farmer's Lane, pass the first Hoen St and turn left on the *second* Hoen St, then left on Newanga Ave.

Best Western Wine Country Inn & Suites HOTEL $$
(707-545-9000, 800-780-7234; www.winecountryhotel.com; 870 Hopper Ave; r weekday/weekends $120/170;) Generic chain hotel, off Cleveland Ave.

Sandman Hotel MOTEL $
(707-544-8570; www.sandmansantarosa.com; 3421 Cleveland Ave; $83-102) Cleveland Ave's reliable budget choice.

Eating

TOP CHOICE **Zazu** CALIFORNIAN, ITALIAN **$$**
(☎707-523-4814; 3535 Guerneville Rd, Santa Rosa; brunch mains $11-15, dinner mains $18-26; ⏰5:30-8:30pm Wed-Mon, 9am-2pm Sun) The cooking at Zazu is an expression of the land: if it's in the garden, it's on the plate. Husband-and-wife team Duske Estes and John Stewart use only local ingredients from within 30 miles of their little roadhouse restaurant, 10 miles west of downtown Santa Rosa. John raises heirloom pigs, which he transforms into gorgeous salumi. Duske fashions homemade pasta, using eggs from their own hens. Dishes skew Italian-country, using few ingredients that let the dynamic flavors sparkle. One of Sonoma's top tables for seasonal-regional cooking. Great brunch, too. Wednesday, Thursday and Sunday are pizza-and-pinot nights, with wine flights paired for pizza. For true farm-to-table cooking, don't miss Zazu.

Rosso Pizzeria & Wine Bar PIZZERIA **$$**
(☎707-544-3221; 53 Montgomery St, Creekside Shopping Centre; pizzas $12-15; ⏰11am-10pm; 👪) Crispy brick-oven pizzas – some of NorCal's best – along with inventive salads and a standout wine list make Rosso worth seeking out.

Jeffrey's Hillside Cafe AMERICAN **$**
(www.jeffreyshillsidecafe.com; 2901 4th St; dishes $8-12; ⏰7am-2pm; 👪) East of downtown, near the top of Sonoma Valley, chef-owned Jeffrey's is excellent for breakfast or brunch before wine tasting.

Taqueria Las Palmas MEXICAN **$**
(☎707-546-3091; 415 Santa Rosa Ave; dishes $4-7; ⏰9am-9pm; 🌶) For Mexican, this is the real deal, with standout *carnitas* (barbecued pork), homemade salsas and veggie burritos.

Pho Vietnam VIETNAMESE **$**
(☎707-571-7687; No 8, 711 Stony Point Rd; dishes $6-8; ⏰10am-8:30pm Mon-Sat, to 7:30pm Sun) Fantastic noodle bowls and rice plates at a hole-in-the-wall shopping-center restaurant, just off Hwy 12, west of downtown.

Willi's Wine Bar TAPAS **$$$**
(☎707-526-3096; www.williswinebar.net; dishes $10-15; ⏰11am-9:30pm Wed-Sat, 5-9pm Sun & Mon) Stellar small plates.

Traverso's Gourmet Foods DELI **$**
(☎707-542-2530; www.traversos.com; 2097 Stagecoach Rd; ⏰10am-6pm Mon-Sat) Excellent Italian deli and wine shop.

Mac's Delicatessen DELI **$**
(☎707-545-3785; 630 4th St; dishes under $10; ⏰7am-5pm Mon-Fri, 7am-4pm Sat) Downtown Kosher-style deli.

Drinking

Third Street Aleworks BREWERY
(thirdstreetaleworks.com; 610 3rd St; 📶) This giant brew pub gets packed weekends and game days. Great garlic fries and half-a-dozen pool tables.

Aroma Roasters CAFE
(www.aromaroasters.com; 95 5th St, Railroad Sq; 📶) Town's hippest café; serves no booze; acoustic music Friday and Saturday evenings.

Russian River Brewing Co BREWERY
(www.russianriverbrewing.com; 729 4th St) Locally crafted brews.

Information

Aroma Roasters (☎707-576-7765; 95 5th St, Railroad Sq; per 15min $1.50; ⏰6am-11pm Mon-Thu, 7am-midnight Fri & Sat, 7am-10pm Sun; @📶) Internet access. No electrical outlets for laptops.

California Welcome Center & Santa Rosa Visitors Bureau (☎707-577-8674, 800-404-7673; www.visitsantarosa.com; 9 4th St; ⏰9am-5pm Mon-Sat, 10am-5pm Sun) At Railroad Sq, west of Hwy 101; take the downtown Santa Rosa exit off Hwy 12 or Hwy 101.

Santa Rosa Memorial Hospital (☎707-935-5000; 347 Andrieux St)

Healdsburg

Once a sleepy ag town best known for its Future Farmers of America parade, Healdsburg has emerged as northern Sonoma County's culinary capital. Foodie-scenester restaurants and cafes, wine-tasting rooms and fancy boutiques line Healdsburg Plaza, the town's sun-dappled central square (bordered by Healdsburg Ave and Center, Matheson and Plaza Sts). Traffic grinds to a halt summer weekends, when second-home-owners and tourists jam downtown. Old-timers aren't happy with the Napa-style gentrification, but at least Healdsburg retains its historic look, if not its once-quiet summers. It's best visited weekdays – stroll tree-lined streets, sample locavore cooking and soak up the NorCal flavor.

Sights

Tasting rooms surround the plaza. Free summer concerts play Tuesday afternoons.

Healdsburg Museum MUSEUM
(☎707-431-3325; www.healdsburgmuseum.org; 221 Matheson St; donation requested; ⊙11am-4pm Thu-Sun) East of the plaza, worth a visit for a glimpse of Healdsburg's past. Exhibits include compelling installations on northern Sonoma County history. Pick up a walking-tour pamphlet.

Locals Tasting Room TASTING ROOM
(Map p190; ☎707-857-4900; www.tastelocalwines.com; tastings free; Geyserville Ave & Hwy 128; ⊙10am-6pm) Eight miles north, photo-ready one-block-long Geyserville is home to this indie tasting room, which represents ten small-production wineries.

Farmers Markets MARKET
(www.healdsburgfarmersmarket.org) Meet locals and discover the region's agricultural abundance at the **Tuesday market** (cnr Vine & North Sts; ⊙4-7pm Tue Jun-Oct) and **Saturday market** (one block west of the plaza; ⊙9am-noon Sat May-Nov).

Activities

The more active you are in Healdsburg, the more you can eat. After you've walked around the plaza, there isn't much to do in town. Go wine tasting in Dry Creek Valley (p192) or Russian River Valley (p190). Bicycling on winding West Dry Creek Rd is brilliant, as is paddling the Russian River, which runs through town. You can swim at **Healdsburg Veterans Memorial Beach** (Map p190; ☎707-433-1625; www.sonoma-county.org/parks; 13839 Healdsburg Ave; parking $7;); lifeguards are on duty daily in summer (call ahead). If you're squeamish, confirm current water quality online (www.sonoma-county.org/health/eh/russian_river.htm).

Russian River Adventures CANOEING
(Map p190; ☎707-433-5599; www.rradventures.info; 20 Healdsburg Ave; adult/child $50/25;) Paddle a secluded stretch of river, in quiet inflatable canoes, stopping for rope swings, swimming holes, gravel beaches, and bird-watching. This ecotourism outfit points you in the right direction and shuttles you back at day's end. Or they'll guide your kids downriver while you go wine-tasting (guides $120/day). Self-guided departures leave 10am sharp; reservations required.

Getaway Adventures CYCLING, KAYAKING
(☎707-763-3040, 800-499-2453; www.getawayadventures.com) Guides spectacular morning vineyard cycling in Dry Creek Valley, followed by lunch and optional kayaking on Russian River ($150 to $175).

River's Edge Kayak & Canoe Trips BOATING
(Map p190; ☎707-433-7247; www.riversedgekayakandcanoe.com; 13840 Healdsburg Ave) Rents hard-sided canoes ($70/85 per half/full day) and kayaks ($40/55). Self-guided rentals include shuttle. Guided trips – by reservation – originate upriver in Alexander Valley, and end in town.

Healdsburg Spoke Folk Cyclery BICYCLE RENTAL
(☎707-433-7171; www.spokefolk.com; 201 Center St) Rents touring, racing and tandem bicycles. Great service.

Relish Culinary Adventures COOKING COURSE
(☎707-431-9999, 877-759-1004; www.relishculinary.com; 14 Matheson St; ⊙by appointment) Plug into the locavore food scene with culinary day trips, demo-kitchen classes or winemaker dinners.

Festivals & Events

Russian River Wine Road Barrel Tasting WINE
(www.wineroad.com) March

Future Farmers Parade CULTURAL
(www.healdsburgfair.org) May

Wine & Food Affair FOOD
(www.wineroad.com/events) November

Sleeping

Healdsburg is expensive and demand exceeds supply. Rates drop winter to spring, but not by that much. Guerneville (p198) is much less expensive, and only 20 minutes away.

Most Healdsburg inns are within walking distance of the plaza; several B&Bs are in surrounding countryside. Two older motels lie south of the plaza, two to the north at Hwy 101's Dry Creek exit.

Hotel Healdsburg HOTEL $$$
(☎707-431-2800, 800-889-7188; www.hotelhealdsburg.com; 25 Matheson St; r incl breakfast $335-585;) Smack on the plaza, the chic

HH has a coolly minimalist style. Wear Armani and blend in. The ultracushy rooms, all hard angles and muted colors, have delicious beds and extra-deep tubs. Downstairs there's a full-service spa.

H2 Hotel HOTEL $$$
(707-431-2202, 707-922-5251; www.h2hotel.com; 219 Healdsburg Ave; r incl breakfast weekday $255-455, weekend $355-555;) Little sister to Hotel Healdsburg, H2 has the same angular concrete style, but was built LEED-gold-certified from the ground up, with a living roof, reclaimed everything, and fresh-looking rooms with cush organic linens. Tiny pool, free bikes.

Madrona Manor HISTORIC INN $$$
(Map p190; 707-433-4231, 800-258-4003; www.madronamanor.com; 1001 Westside Rd; r & ste $270-390;) The first choice of lovers of country inns and stately manor homes, the regal 1881 Madrona Manor exudes Victorian elegance. Surrounded by eight acres of woods and gorgeous century-old gardens, the hilltop mansion is decked out with many original furnishings. A mile west of downtown, it's convenient to Westside Rd wineries.

Belle de Jour Inn B&B $$$
(Map p190; 707-431-9777; www.belledejourinn.com; 16276 Healdsburg Ave; r $225-295, ste $355;) Belle de Jour's sunny, uncomplicated, lovely rooms have American-country furnishings, with extras like sun-dried sheets, hammocks and CD players. The manicured gardens are perfect for a moonlight tryst.

Healdsburg Inn on the Plaza INN $$$
(707-433-6991, 800-431-8663; www.healdsburginn.com; 110 Matheson St; r $295-375;) The spiffy, clean-lined rooms, conservatively styled in khaki and beige, feel bourgeois summer-house casual, with fine linens and gas fireplaces; some have jetted double tubs. The plaza-front location explains the price.

Best Western Dry Creek Inn MOTEL $$
(Map p190; 707-433-0300, 800-222-5784; www.drycreekinn.com; 198 Dry Creek Rd, Healdsburg; weekday/weekend r $59-129/199-259;) Town's top motel has good service and an outdoor hot tub. New rooms have jetted tubs and gas fireplaces. Check for weekday discounts.

Geyserville Inn MOTEL $$
(Map p190; 707-857-4343, 877-857-4343; www.geyservilleinn.com; 21714 Geyserville Ave, Geyserville; r weekday $119-169, weekend $189-249;) Eight miles north of Healdsburg, this immaculately kept upmarket motel is surrounded by vineyards. Rooms have unexpectedly smart furnishings, like overstuffed side chairs and fluffy feather pillows. Request a remodeled room. Hot tub.

Honor Mansion INN $$$
(707-433-4277, 800-554-4667; www.honormansion.com; 891 Grove St; r incl breakfast $300-550;) Victorian mansion c 1883; spectacular grounds.

Camellia Inn B&B $$$
(707-433-8182, 800-727-8182; www.camelliainn.com; 211 North St; r $139-329;) Italianate 1869 house; one room accommodates families.

George Alexander House B&B $$$
(707-433-1358, 800-310-1358; www.georgealexanderhouse.com; 423 Matheson St; r $180-350;) Queen Anne c 1905, with Victorian and Asian antiques; also a sauna.

Haydon Street Inn B&B $$$
(707-433-5228, 800-528-3703; www.haydon.com; 321 Haydon St; r $195-325, cottage $425;) Two-story Queen Anne with big front porch and cottage out back.

Piper Street Inn INN $$$
(707-433-8721, 877-703-0370; www.piperstreetinn.com; 402 Piper St; r $195-265;) Two rooms: homey bedroom, garden cottage.

L&M Motel MOTEL $$
(Map p190; 707-433-6528; www.landmmotel.com; 70 Healdsburg Ave, Healdsburg; r incl breakfast $100-140;) Simple, clean old-fashioned motel; big lawns and barbecue grills, great for families. Dry sauna and Jacuzzi.

Cloverdale Wine Country KOA CAMPGROUND $
(707-894-3337, 800-368-4558; www.winecountrykoa.com; 1166 Asti Ridge Rd, Cloverdale; tent/RV sites from $42/60, 1-/2-bedroom cabins $80/90;) Six miles from Central Cloverdale exit off Hwy 101; hot showers, pool, hot tub, laundry, paddleboats and bicycles.

Eating

Healdsburg is the gastronomic capital of Sonoma County. Your hardest decision will be choosing where to eat. Reservations essential.

Cyrus FRENCH-CALIFORNIAN $$$
(☎707-433-3311; www.cyrusrestaurant.com; 29 North St, Healdsburg; fixed-price menu $102-130; ⊙dinner Thu-Mon, lunch Sat) Napa's venerable French Laundry has stiff competition in swanky Cyrus, an ultrachic dining room in the great tradition of the French country auberge. The emphasis is on luxury foods, expertly prepared with a French sensibility and flavored with global spices, as in the signature Thai marinated lobster. The staff moves as if in a ballet, ever intuitive of your pace and tastes. From the caviar cart to the cheese course, Cyrus is a meal to remember.

TOP CHOICE **Madrona Manor** CALIFORNIAN $$$
(Map p190; ☎707-433-4231, 800-258-4003; www.madronamanor.com; 1001 Westside Rd; 4-/5-/6-course menu $73/82/91; ⊙6-9pm Wed-Sun) You'd be hard-pressed to find a lovelier place to pop the question than this retro-formal Victorian mansion's garden-view veranda – though there's nothing old-fashioned about the artful Californian haute cuisine: the kitchen churns its own butter, each course comes with a different variety of still-warm house-baked bread, lamb and cheese originate down the road, and deserts include ice cream flash-frozen tableside. Reserve a pre-sunset table.

Scopa ITALIAN $$
(☎707-433-5282; www.scopahealdsburg.com; 109-A Plaza St, Healdsburg; mains $12-26; ⊙5:30-10pm Tue-Sun) Space is tight inside this converted barbershop, but it's worth cramming in for perfect thin-crust pizza and rustic Italian home cooking, like Nonna's slow-braised chicken, with sautéed greens, melting into toasty polenta. A lively crowd and good wine prices create a convivial atmosphere.

Bovolo ITALIAN, CAFE $$
(☎707-431-2962; www.bovolorestaurant.com; 106 Matheson St, Healdsburg; dishes $6-14; [⊙9am-4pm Mon, Weds, Thu, 9am-8pm Tue, Fri, Sat, 9am-6pm Sun; 👪) Fast food gets a slow-food spin at this order-at-the-counter Cal-Ital bistro – little sister to Zazu (p203) – that serves farm-fresh egg breakfasts, just-picked salads, and hand-thrown pizzas topped with house-cured meats from heirloom pigs. Sit outside and save room for hand-turned gelato. Enter through the bookstore.

Healdsburg Bar & Grill PUB $$
(☎707-433-3333; www.healdsburgbarandgrill.com; 245 Healdsburg Ave; mains $9-15; ⊙11:30am-9pm) Great when you're famished but don't want to fuss, HBG does gastropub cooking right – mac-n-cheese, pulled-pork sandwiches, top-end burgers and truffle-parmesan fries. Sit in the garden, or watch the game at the bar.

Zin NEW AMERICAN $$
(☎707-473-0946; www.zinrestaurant.com; 344 Center St; lunch mains $10-20, dinner mains $76-27; ⊙11:30am-2:30pm Mon-Fri, dinner nightly; 👪) Reliable zin makes hearty Cal-American comfort food, designed to pair with zinfandel and other local varietals. Think pot roast and apple pie. Fun wine bar, good service.

Oakville Grocery DELI $$
(☎707-433-3200; www.oakvillegrocery.com; 124 Matheson St; sandwiches $10; ⊙8am-7pm) Luxurious smoked fish and caviar, fancy sandwiches and grab-and-go gourmet picnics. It's overpriced, but the plaza-view fireside terrace is ever-fun for scouting Botox blonds, while nibbling cheese and sipping vino.

Diavola ITALIAN $$
(Map p190;☎707-814-0111; www.diavolapizzera.com; 21021 Geyserville Ave, Geyserville; pizzas $12-15; ⊙11:30am-9pm Wed-Mon; 👪) Ideal for lunch while wine tasting in Alexander Valley, Diavola makes excellent salumi and thin-crust pizzas, served in an Old West brick-walled space, loud enough to drown out the kids.

Barndiva CALIFORNIAN $$$
(☎707-431-0100; www.barndiva.com; 231 Center St; brunch mains $16-22, dinner mains $25-34; ⊙noon-11pm Wed-Sun) Impeccable seasonal-regional cooking, happening bar, beautiful garden, but service sometimes misses.

Ravenous NEW AMERICAN $$
(☎707-431-1770; www.theravenous.com; 420 Center St; mains $13-17) Chalkboard-scrawled menu, with California comfort cooking and excellent burgers, served (s-l-o-w-l-y) inside a former cottage. Sit outside with Healdsburg's hipper half. $10 corkage.

Flaky Cream Coffee Shop DINER $
(☎707-433-3895; Healdsburg Shopping Center, 441 Center St; dishes $5-9; ⊙6am-2pm) Bacon-and-egg breakfasts, yummy doughnuts.

Self-Catering

Dry Creek General Store DELI $
(Map p190;☎707-433-4171; www.dcgstore.com; 3495 Dry Creek Rd; sandwiches $8-10; ⊙6am-6pm) Before wine tasting in Dry Creek Valley, make

a pit stop at this vintage general store, where locals and bicyclists gather for coffee on the creaky front porch. Perfect picnics supplies include Toscano-salami-and-manchego sandwiches on chewy-dense ciabatta.

Jimtown Store DELI $
(Map p190; ☎707-433-1212; www.jimtown.com; sandwiches $8-11; 6706 Hwy 128; ⏱7:30am-4pm) One of our favorite Alexander Valley stopovers, Jimtown is great for picnic supplies and sandwiches made with housemade condiment spreads.

Downtown Bakery & Creamery BAKERY $
(☎707-431-2719; www.downtownbakery.net; 308a Center St; ⏱7am-5:30pm) Healdsburg's finest bakery makes scrumptious pastries.

Costeaux French Bakery & Cafe BAKERY $
(☎707-433-1913; www.costeaux.com; 417 Healdsburg Ave; ⏱7am-4pm Mon-Sat, to 1pm Sun) Fresh bread and good boxed lunches.

Cheese Shop CHEESE $
(☎707-433-4998; www.doraliceimports.com; 423 Center St; ⏱Mon-Fri 11am-6pm, Sat 10am-6pm) Top-notch imported and local cheeses.

Shelton's Natural Foods MARKET, DELI $
(☎707-431-0530; www.sheltonsmarket.com; 428 Center S; ⏱8am-8pm) Indie alternative for groceries and picnic supplies more reasonably priced than Oakville Grocery.

Drinking & Entertainment

Flying Goat Coffee CAFE
(www.flyinggoatcoffee.com; 324 Center St; ⏱7am-6pm) See ya later, Starbucks. Flying Goat is what coffee should be – fair-trade and house-roasted – and locals line up for it every morning.

Bear Republic Brewing Company BREWERY
(www.bearrepublic.com; 345 Healdsburg Ave; ⏱11:30am-late) Bear Republic features handcrafted award-winning ales, non-award-winning pub grub and live music weekends.

Barndiva COCKTAIL BAR
(☎707-431-0100; www.barndiva.com; 231 Center St; ⏱noon-11pm Wed-Sun) Swanky seasonal cocktails, like blood-orange margaritas, with a pretty crowd.

Raven Theater & Film Center THEATER
(☎707-433-5448; www.raventheater.com; 115 N Main St) Hosts concerts, events and first-run art-house films.

Shopping

Arboretum CLOTHING
(☎707-433-7033; www.arboretumapparel.com; 332 Healdsburg Ave; ⏱Wed-Mon) Lending fresh meaning to 'fashion-conscious,' this eco-boutique features fair trade and US designers, with great finds like organic-cotton pants for men and ultra-soft bamboo-fiber cardigans for gals.

Jimtown Store GIFTS
(Map p190; ☎707-433-1212; www.jimtown.com; 6706 Hwy 128) Forage antique bric-a-brac, candles and Mexican oilcloths at this roadside deli and store in Alexander Valley.

Baksheesh GIFTS, HOMEWARES
(☎707-473-0880; www.baksheeshfairtrade.com; 106B Matheson St) Household goods with a global outlook: everything sourced from fair-trade collectives, from Alpaca shawls to Vietnamese trivets.

Gardener HOMEWARES
(Map p190; ☎707-431-1063; www.thegardener.com; 516 Dry Creek Rd) Garden-shop lovers: don't miss this rural beauty.

Studio Barndiva GIFTS, HOMEWARES
(☎707-431-7404; www.studiobarndiva; 237 Center St) Reclaimed ephemera never looked so chic: thousand-dollar *objets d'art.*

Copperfield's Books BOOKS
(☎707-433-9270; copperfieldsbooks.com; 104 Matheson St) Good general-interest books.

Levin & Company BOOKS, MUSIC
(☎707-433-1118; 306 Center St) Fiction and CDs; co-op art gallery.

Information

Healdsburg Chamber of Commerce & Visitors Bureau (☎707-433-6935, 800-648-9922; www.healdsburg.org; 217 Healdsburg Ave; ⏱9am-5pm Mon-Fri, to 3pm Sat, 10am-2pm Sun) A block south of the plaza. Has winery maps and information on hot-air ballooning, golf, tennis, spas and nearby farms (get the *Farm Trails* brochure); 24-hour walk-up booth.

Healdsburg Public Library (☎707-433-3772; www.sonoma.lib.ca.us; cnr Piper & Center Sts; ⏱10am-6pm Mon & Wed, to 8pm Tue & Thu-Sat; @ 📶) One-hour free internet access (bring ID). Wine Country's leading oenology-reference library.

North Coast & Redwoods

Includes »

Best Places to Eat

- Café Beaujolais (p223)
- Six Rivers Brewery (p252)
- Ravens (p223)
- Franny's Cup & Saucer (p218)
- Table 128 (p233)

Best Places to Stay

- Mar Vista (p216)
- Victorian Gardens (p218)
- Apple Farm (p232)
- Andiron (p221)
- Redwood National Park (p256)

Why Go?

The craggy cliffs, towering redwoods and windswept bluffs of the north have little in common with California's other coastline. This is no Beach Boys' song; there are no bikinis and few surfboards. The jagged edge of the continent is wild, scenic and even slightly foreboding, where spectral fog and outsider spirit have fostered the world's tallest trees, most potent weed and a string of idiosyncratic two-stoplight towns. Visitors explore hidden coves with a blanket and bottle of local wine, scan the horizon for migrating whales and retreat at night to fire-warmed Victorians. The further north you travel on the region's winding two-lane blacktop, the more dominant the landscape becomes, with valleys of redwood, wide rivers and mossy, overgrown forests. Befitting this dramatic clash of land and water are its unlikely mélange of residents: timber barons and tree huggers, pot farmers and political radicals of every stripe.

When to Go

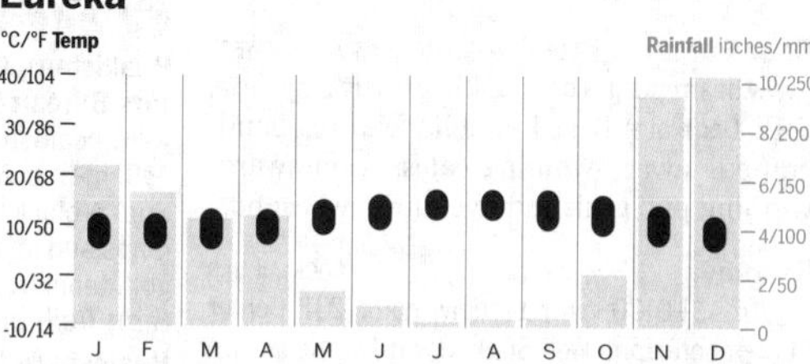

Jun–Jul The driest season in the Redwoods is spectacular for day hikes and big views.

Aug–Oct Warm weather and clear (or clearer) skies are the best for hiking the Lost Coast.

Dec–Apr Whales migrate off the coast. In early spring look for mothers and calves.

Getting Around

Although Hwy 1 is popular with cyclists and there are bus connections, you will almost certainly need a car to explore this region. Those headed to the far north and on a schedule should take Hwy 101, the faster, inland route and then cut over to the coast. Windy Hwy 1 hugs the coast, then cuts inland and ends at Leggett, where it joins Hwy 101. Neither Amtrak nor Greyhound serve cities on coastal Hwy 1.

Amtrak (☎800-872-7245; www.amtrakcalifornia.com) operates the *Coast Starlight* between Los Angeles and Seattle (see p569). From LA, buses connect to several North Coast towns including Leggett ($82, 11 hours, two daily) and Garberville ($84, 11½ hours, two daily).

Brave souls willing to piece together bus travel through the region will face a time-consuming headache, but connections are possible to almost every town in the region. **Greyhound** (☎800-231-2222; www.greyhound.com) runs buses from San Francisco to Santa Rosa ($22, 1¾ hours, one daily), Ukiah, ($40, three hours, one daily) Willits ($40, 3½ hours, one daily), Rio Dell (near Fortuna, $52.50, six hours, one daily), Eureka ($52.50, 6¾ hours, one daily) and Arcata ($52.20, seven hours, one daily). In Santa Rosa, **Golden Gate Transit** (☎707-541-2000; www.goldengatetransit.org) bus 80 serves San Rafael ($5.55, 1½ hours) and San Francisco ($8.80, 1¼ hours, 19 times daily), **Sonoma County Transit** (☎800-345-7433; www.sctransit.com) serves Sonoma County, and **Sonoma County Airport Express** (☎707-837-8700, 800-327-2024; www.airportexpressinc.com) operates buses to San Francisco ($32, 2¼ hours, 15 daily) and Oakland ($34, 2¼ hours, 10 daily) airports.

The **Mendocino Transit Authority** (MTA; ☎707-462-1422, 800-696-4682; www.4mta.org; fares $3.25-7.75) operates bus 65, which travels between Mendocino, Fort Bragg, Willits, Ukiah and Santa Rosa daily, with an afternoon return. Bus 95 runs between Point Arena and Santa Rosa, via Jenner, Bodega Bay and Sebastopol. Bus 54 connects Ukiah and Hopland on weekdays. Bus 75 heads north every weekday from Gualala to the Navarro River junction at Hwy 128, then runs inland through the Anderson Valley to Ukiah, returning in the afternoon. The North Coast route goes north from Navarro River junction to Albion, Little River, Mendocino and Fort Bragg, Monday to Friday. The best long distance option is a daily ride from Fort Bragg south to Santa Rosa via Willits and Ukiah ($21, three hours).

North of Mendocino County, the **Redwood Transit System** (☎707-443-0826; www.hta.org) operates buses ($2.75) Monday through Saturday between Scotia and Trinidad (2½ hours), stopping en route at Eureka (1¼ hours) and Arcata (1½ hours). **Redwood Coast Transit** (☎707-464-9314; www.redwoodcoasttransit.org) runs buses Monday to Saturday between Crescent City, Klamath ($1.50, one hour, five daily) and Arcata ($25, two hours, three time daily), with numerous stops along the way.

FAST FACTS

- **Population of Mendocino** 1000
- **Average temperature low/high in Mendocino** Jan 47/60°F, Jul 50/71°F
- **Mendocino to San Francisco** 155 miles, 3¼ hours
- **Mendocino to Los Angeles** 530 miles, nine hours
- **Mendocino to Eureka** 145 miles, three hours

COASTAL HIGHWAY 1

Down south it's called the 'PCH,' or Pacific Coast Hwy, but North Coast locals simply call it 'Hwy 1.' However you label it, get ready for a fabulous coastal drive, which cuts a winding course on isolated cliffs high above the crashing surf. Compared to the famous Big Sur coast, the serpentine stretch of Hwy 1 up the North Coast is more challenging, more remote and more *real*; passing farms, fishing towns and hidden beaches. Drivers use roadside pull-outs to scan the hazy Pacific horizon for migrating whales and explore a coastline dotted with rock formations that are relentlessly pounded by the surf. The drive between Bodega Bay and Fort Bragg takes four hours of daylight driving without stops. At night in the fog, it takes steely nerves and much, much longer. The most popular destination is the cliffside charmer of Mendocino.

Considering their proximity to the Bay Area, Sonoma and Mendocino counties remain unspoiled, and the austere coastal bluffs are some of the most spectacular in the country. But the trip north gets more rewarding and remote with every mile. By the time Hwy 1 cuts inland to join Hwy 101, the land along the Pacific – called the Lost Coast – the highway disappears and offers the state's best-preserved natural gifts.

Coastal accommodations (including campgrounds) can fill from Memorial Day to Labor Day and on fall weekends, and often require two-night stays, so reserve ahead. Try to visit

North Coast & Redwoods Highlights

1. Explore the largest stands of old growth redwood in **Humboldt Redwoods State Park** (p243)
2. Hike the remote and wild **Lost Coast** (p241)
3. Backpack under giants along **Redwood Creek** (p256)
4. Find a hidden cove on the **Sonoma Coast** (p213)
5. Get pampered at **Mendocino's B&Bs** (p221)
6. Drink the sampler at **Six Rivers Brewery** (p252), NorCal's best brewpub
7. Rent a canoe to float down the **Big River** (p221)
8. Visit immaculate botanical gardens in **Fort Bragg** (p225)
9. Tour the vineyards of the **Anderson Valley** (p232)
10. Stay at **Mar Vista** (p216), a plush and sustainable retreat

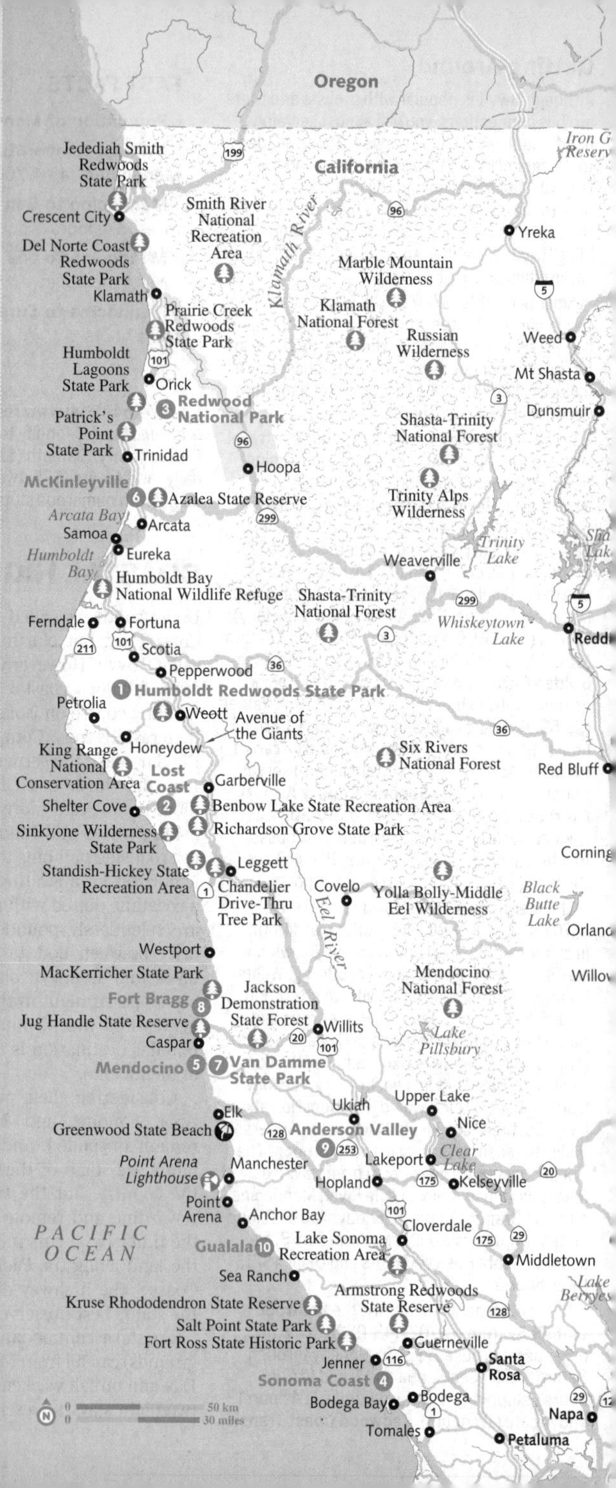

during spring or fall, especially in September and October; when the fog lifts, the ocean sparkles and most other visitors have gone home.

Bodega Bay

Bodega Bay is the first pearl in a string of sleepy fishing towns that line the North Coast and was the setting of Hitchcock's terrifying 1963 avian psycho-horror flick *The Birds*. The skies are free from bloodthirsty gulls today (though you best keep an eye on the picnic); it's Bay Area weekenders who descend en masse for extraordinary beaches, tide pools, whale-watching, fishing, surfing and seafood. Mostly a few restaurants, hotels and shops on both sides of Hwy 1, the downtown is not made for strolling, but it is a great base for exploring the endless nearby coves of the Sonoma Coast State Beach (p213).

Originally inhabited by the Pomo people, the bay takes its name from Juan Francisco de la Bodega y Quadra, captain of the Spanish sloop *Sonora,* which entered the bay in 1775. The area was then settled by Russians in the early 19th century, and farms were established to grow wheat for the Russian fur-trapping empire, which stretched from Alaska all the way down the coast to Fort Ross. The Russians pulled out in 1842, abandoning fort and farms, and American settlers moved in.

Hwy 1 runs through town and along the east side of Bodega Bay. On the west side, a peninsula resembling a crooked finger juts out to sea, forming the entrance to Bodega Harbor.

Sights & Activities

Surfing, beach combing and sportfishing are the main activities here – the latter requires advance booking. From December to April, the fishing boats host whale-watching trips, which are also good to book ahead. The excellent *Farm Trails* (www.farmtrails.org) guide at the Sonoma Coast Visitor Center has suggestions for tours of local ranches, orchards, farms and apiaries.

Bodega Head LOOKOUT
At the peninsula's tip, Bodega Head rises 265ft above sea level. To get there (and see the open ocean), head west from Hwy 1 onto Eastshore Rd, then turn right at the stop sign onto Bay Flat Rd. It's great for whale-watching. Landlubbers enjoy **hiking** above the surf, where several good trails include a 3.75-mile trek to Bodega Dunes Campground and a 2.2-mile walk to Salmon Creek Ranch. **Candy & Kites** (10am-5pm) is right along Hwy 1 in the middle of town – you can't miss it – selling kites to take advantage of all that wind.

Bodega Marine Laboratory & Reserve SCIENCE CENTER
(707-875-2211; www.bml.ucdavis.edu; 2099 Westside Rd; admission free; 2-4pm Fri) Run by University of California (UC) Davis, this spectacularly diverse teaching and research reserve surrounds the functioning research lab, which has studied Bodega Bay since the 1920s. The 263-acre reserve hosts many marine environments, including rocky intertidal coastal areas, mudflats and sandflats, salt marsh, sand dunes and freshwater wetlands. On most Friday afternoons docents give tours of the lab and its aquaria.

Ren Brown Collection Gallery GALLERY
(www.renbrown.com; 1781 Hwy 1; 10am-5pm Wed-Sun) The renowned collection of modern Japanese prints and California works at this small gallery is a tranquil escape from the elements.

Chanslor Riding Stables HORSEBACK RIDING
(707-875-3333; www.chanslor.com; 2660 Hwy 1, group rides $40-125) Just north of town, this friendly outfit leads horseback expeditions along the coastline and the rolling inland hills. Ron, the trip leader, is an amiable, sun-weathered cowboy straight from central casting; he recommends taking the Salmon Creek ride or calling ahead for weather-permitting moonlight rides. The 90-minute beach rides are donation based, and support a horse rescue program. Overnight trips in simple platform tents, which are excellent for families, can also be arranged. If you book a ride, you can park your RV at the ranch for free.

Bodega Bay Sportfishing Center FISHING, WHALE-WATCHING
(707-875-3344; www.bodegacharters.com; 1410 Bay Flat Rd) Beside the Sandpiper Cafe, this outfit organizes full-day fishing trips ($135) and whale-watching excursions (three hours adult/child $35/25). It also sells bait, tackle and fishing licenses. Call ahead to ask about recent sightings.

BLOODTHIRSTY BIRDS OF BODEGA BAY

Bodega Bay has the enduring claim to fame as the setting for Alfred Hitchcock's *The Birds*. Although special effects radically altered the actual layout of the town, you still get a good feel for the supposed site of the farm owned by Mitch Brenner (played by Rod Taylor). The once-cozy Tides Restaurant, where much avian-caused havoc occurs in the movie, is still there but since 1962 it has been transformed into a vast restaurant complex. Venture 5 miles inland to the tiny town of Bodega and you'll find two icons from the film: the schoolhouse and the church. Both stand just as they did in the movie – a crow overhead may make the hair rise on your neck.

Coincidentally, right after production of *The Birds* began, a real-life bird attack occurred in Capitola, the sleepy seaside town south of Santa Cruz. Thousands of seagulls ran amok, destroying property and attacking people.

Bodega Bay Surf Shack SURFING, KAYAKING
(www.bodegabaysurf.com; 1400 N Hwy 1; surfboards per day $15, kayaks per 4hr single/double $45/65 ⏲10am-6pm Mon-Fri, 9am-7pm Sat & Sun) If you want to get on the water, this easygoing one-stop shop has all kinds of rentals, lessons and good local information.

Festivals & Events

Bodega Seafood, Art & Wine Festival FOOD, WINE
(www.winecountryfestivals.com) In late August, this festival of food and drink brings together the best beer- and wine-makers of the area, tons of seafood and activities for kids.

Bodega Bay Fishermen's Festival CULTURAL
(www.bbfishfest.org) At the end of April, this festival culminates in a blessing of the fleet, a flamboyant parade of vessels, an arts-and-crafts fair, kite-flying and feasting.

Sleeping

There's a wide spread of options – RV and tent camping, quaint motels and fancy hotels. All fill up early during peak seasons. Campers should consider heading just north of town to the state-operated sites.

Bodega Bay Lodge & Spa LODGE $$$
(☎707-875-3525, 888-875-2250; www.bodegabaylodge.com; 103 Hwy 1; r $300-470; @🛜🏊) Bodega's plushest, this small oceanfront resort has indulgent accommodations and a price tag to match. There is an ocean-view swimming pool, a whirlpool and a state-of-the-art fitness club. In the evenings it hosts wine tastings. The more expensive rooms have commanding views, but all have balconies, high-thread-count sheets, feather pillows and the usual amenities of a full-service hotel. The other pluses on-site include a golf course, Bodega Bay's best spa and a fine-dining restaurant, the **Duck Club** (☎707-875-3525; mains $16-37; ⏲7:30-11am & 6-9pm), which is the fanciest dining in town.

Bodega Harbor Inn MOTEL $$
(☎707-875-3594; www.bodegaharborinn.com; 1345 Bodega Ave; r $90-155; 🛜🐾) Half a block inland from Hwy 1, surrounded by grassy lawns and furnished with both real and faux antiques, this modest blue-and-white shingled motel is the town's most economical option. Pets are allowed in some rooms for a fee of $15 plus a security deposit of $50. Freestanding cottages have BBQs.

Chanslor Guest Ranch RANCH $$
(☎707-875-2721; www.chanslorranch.com; 2660 Hwy 1; furnished tents & eco-cabins $75-125, r $350) A mile north of town, this working horse ranch has three rooms and options for upscale camping. Wildlife programs and guided horse tours make this one sweet place, with sweeping vistas across open grasslands to the sea. If you take a horse ride, you can negotiate a great deal for camping in your own tent.

Sonoma County Regional Parks CAMPGROUND $
(☎707-565-2267; www.sonoma-county.org/parks; tent 7 RV sites without hookups $30) There are a few walk-in sites at the **Doran Regional Park** (201 Doran Beach Rd), at the quiet Miwok Tent Campground, and **Westside Regional Park** (2400 Westshore Rd), which is best for RVs. It caters primarily to boaters and has windy exposures, beaches, hot showers, fishing and boat ramps. Both are heavily used. Excellent camping is also available at the Sonoma Coast State Beach (p213).

Eating & Drinking

For the old-fashioned thrill of seafood by the docks there are two options: **Tides Wharf & Restaurant** (835 Hwy 1; breakfast $6-12, lunch $12-22, dinner $15-25; 7:30am-9:30pm Mon-Thu, 7:30am-10pm Fri, 7am-10pm Sat, 7am-9:30pm Sun;) and **Lucas Wharf Restaurant & Bar** (595 Hwy 1; mains $14-25; 11:30am- 9pm Mon-Fri, 11am-10pm Sat;). Both have views and similar menus of clam chowder, fried fish and coleslaw and markets for picnic supplies. Tides boasts a great fish market, though Lucas Wharf feels less like a factory. Don't be surprised if a bus pulls up outside either of them.

Spud Point Crab Company SEAFOOD $
(www.spudpointcrab.com; 1860 Bay Flat Rd; mains $4-10; 9am-5pm Thu-Tue;) In the classic tradition of dockside crab shacks, Spud Point serves salty-sweet crab cocktails and *real* clam chowder, served at picnic tables overlooking the marina. Take Bay Flat Rd to get here.

Terrapin Creek Cafe & Restaurant CALIFORNIAN $$
(707-875-2700; www.terrapincreekcafe.com; 1580 Eastshore Dr; mains $18-20; 11am-2pm & 4:30-9pm Thu-Sun;) Bodega Bay's most exciting upscale restaurant is run by a husband-wife team who espouse the slow food movement and serve local dishes sourced from the surrounding area. Modest comfort-food offerings like the pulled pork sandwich are artfully executed, while the Dungeness crab salad is fresh, briny and perfect. Jazz and warm light complete the atmosphere.

Sandpiper Restaurant SEAFOOD $$
(www.sandpiperrestaurant.com; 1410 Bay Flat Rd; mains $13-26; 8am-8pm Sun-Thu, to 8:30pm Fri & Sat) Popular with the locals, Sandpiper serves breakfast, straightforward seafood and chowder that can be ordered in a formidable 'Viking Bowl' (downing two of these wins you a free t-shirt).

Dog House AMERICAN $
(573 Hwy 1; dishes $5-9; 11am-6pm) Load up on Vienna beef dogs, hand-cut fries and shakes made with hand-scooped ice cream. There's even a view.

Gourmet Au Bay WINE BAR $$
(11am-6pm Thu-Tue) The back deck of this wine bar offers a salty breeze with local zinfandel.

Information

Sonoma Coast Visitor Center (707-875-3866; www.bodegabay.com; 850 Hwy 1; 9am-5pm Mon-Thu & Sat, 9am-6pm Fri, 10am-5pm Sun) Opposite the Tides Wharf. The best reason to stop by is for a copy of the *North Coaster*, a small-press indie newspaper of essays and brilliant insight on local culture.

Sonoma Coast State Beach

Stretching 17 miles north from Bodega Head to Vista Trail, the glorious **Sonoma Coast State Beach** (707-875-3483) is actually a series of beaches separated by several beautiful rocky headlands. Some beaches are tiny, hidden in little coves, while others stretch far and wide. Most of the beaches are connected by vista-studded coastal hiking trails that wind along the bluffs. Exploring this area makes an excellent day-long adventure, so bring a picnic. Be advised however: the surf is often too treacherous to wade, so keep an eye on children. While this system of beaches and parks has some camping, you can't just pitch a tent anywhere; most are for day-use only.

Sights & Activities

Beaches

The following beaches are listed from south to north.

Salmon Creek Beach BEACH
Situated around a lagoon, this has 2 miles of hiking and good waves for surfing.

Portuguese Beach & Schoolhouse Beach BEACH
Both are very easy to access and have sheltered coves between rocky outcroppings.

Duncan's Landing BEACH
Small boats unload near this rocky headland in the morning. A good place to spot wild flowers in the spring.

Shell Beach BEACH
A boardwalk and trail leads out to a stretch perfect for tide-pooling and beachcombing.

Goat Rock BEACH
Famous for its colony of harbor seals, lazing in the sun at the mouth of the Russian River.

Sleeping

Bodega Dunes CAMPGROUND $
(800-444-7275; www.reserveamerica.com; 3095 Hwy 1, Bodega Bay; tent & RV sites $35, $8

day use) The largest campground in the Sonoma Coast State Beach system of parks, it is also closest to Bodega Bay. It gets a lot of use. Sites are in high dunes and have hot showers but be warned – the fog horn sounds all night.

Wright's Beach Campground CAMPGROUND $
(☎800-444-7275; www.reserveamerica.com; tent & RV sites $35, $8 day use) Of the few parks that allow camping along Sonoma Coast State Beach, this is the best, even though sites lack privacy. Sites can be booked six months in advance, and numbers 1–12 are right on the beach. There are BBQ pits for day use and it's a perfect launch for sea kayakers. Everyone else, stay out of the water; according to camp hosts the treacherous rip tides claim a life every season.

Willow Creek Environmental Campground CAMPGROUND $
(tent sites $20) The beautiful environmental campground is under a cathedral-like grove of second-growth redwoods on Willow Creek Rd, inland from Hwy 1 on the southern side of the Russian River Bridge. To reach the sites, walk the **Pomo Canyon trail** and emerge into wildflower-studded meadows with exquisite views of the Russian River and vistas that extend south as far as Pt Reyes on a clear day. Note that Willow Creek has no running water, though it is possible to filter water from the river. It is usually open April to November.

Jenner

Perched on the hills looking out to the Pacific and above the mouth of the Russian River, tiny Jenner offers access to the coast and the Russian River wine region (see p189). A **harbor-seal colony** sits at the river's mouth and pups are born here from March to August. There are restrictions about getting too close to the chubby, adorable pups – handling them can be dangerous and cause the pups to be abandoned by their mothers. Volunteers answer questions along the roped-off area where day trippers can look on at a distance. The best way to see them is by kayak and most of the year you will find a truck renting kayaks at the rivers edge. Heading north on Hwy 1 you will begin driving on one of the most beautiful, windy stretches of California highway. You'll also probably lose cell-phone service – possibly a blessing.

Sleeping & Eating

Jenner Inn & Cottages INN $$
(☎707-865-2377; www.jennerinn.com; 10400 Hwy 1; r incl breakfast creekside $118-178, ocean-view $178-278, cottages $228-278; @) It's difficult to sum up this collection of properties dispersed throughout Jenner – some are in fairly deluxe ocean-view cottages with kitchen and ready-to-light fireplaces, others are small upland near a creek. All have the furnishings of a stylish auntie from the early 1990s.

TOP CHOICE **River's End** CALIFORNIAN $$$
(☎707-865-2484; www.rivers-end.com; 11048 Hwy 1; lunch mains $13-26, dinner mains $25-39; ⊙noon-3pm & 5-8:30pm Thu-Mon; ✎) Unwind in style at this picture-perfect restaurant, perched on a cliff overlooking the river's mouth and the grand sweep of the Pacific Ocean. It serves world-class meals at world-class prices, but the real reward is the view. Its ocean-view **cottages** (r & cottages $120-200) are wood paneled and have no TVs, wi-fi or phones. Children under 12 are not recommended.

Café Aquatica CAFE $
(www.cafeaquatica.com; 11048 Hwy 1; sandwiches $10-13; ☎) This is the kind of North Coast coffee shop you've been dreaming of: fresh pastries, fog-lifting coffee and chatty locals. The expansive view of the Russian River from the patio and strangely appropriate new-age tunes are bonuses.

Fort Ross State Historic Park

A curious glimpse into Tsarist Russia's exploration of the California coast, the salt-washed buildings of Fort Ross State Historic Park offer a fascinating insight into the pre-American Wild West. It's a quiet, picturesque place with a riveting past.

In March 1812, a group of 25 Russians and 80 Alaskans (including members of the Kodiak and Aleutian tribes) built a wooden fort here, near a Kashaya Pomo village. The southernmost outpost of the 19th-century Russian fur trade on America's Pacific coast, Fort Ross was established as a base for sea-otter hunting operations and trade with Alta California, and for growing crops for Russian settlements in Alaska. The Russians dedicated the fort in August 1812 and occupied it until 1842, when it was abandoned because the sea otter population had been decimated and agricultural production had never taken off.

Fort Ross State Historic Park (☎707-847-3286; www.fortrossstatepark.org; 19005 Hwy 1; per car $8; ⏰10am-4:30pm), an accurate reconstruction of the fort, is 11 miles north of Jenner on a beautiful point. The original buildings were sold, dismantled and carried off to Sutter's Fort during the Gold Rush. The **visitor center** (☎707-847-3437) has a great museum with historical displays and an excellent bookshop on Californian and Russian history. Ask about hikes to the Russian cemetery.

On **Fort Ross Heritage Day**, the last Saturday in July, costumed volunteers bring the fort's history to life; check the website www.parks.ca.gov or call the visitor center for other special events.

Timber Cove Inn (☎707-847-3231, 800-987-8319; www.timbercoveinn.com; 21780 N Hwy 1; r from $155, ocean-view from $183) is a dramatic and quirky '60s-modern seaside inn that was once a top-of-the-line luxury lodge. Though the price remains high, it has slipped a bit. The rustic architectural shell is still stunning, though, and a duet of tinkling piano and crackling fire fills the lobby. The quirky rooms facing the ocean have a tree house feel, with rustic redwood details, balconies, fireplaces and lofted beds. Even those who don't bunk here should wander agape in the shadow of Benny Bufano's 93ft peace statue, a spectacular totem on the edge of the sea. The expensive restaurant on-site is nothing to write home about.

Stillwater Cove Regional Park (☎reservations 707-565-2267; www.sonoma-county.org/parks; 22455 N Hwy 1; tent & RV sites $28), 2 miles north of Timber Cove, has hot showers and hiking under Monterey pines. Sites 1, 2, 4, 6, 9 and 10 have ocean views.

Salt Point State Park

If you stop at only one park along the Sonoma Coast, make it 6000-acre **Salt Point State Park** (☎707-847-3221; per car $8), where sandstone cliffs drop dramatically into the kelp-strewn sea and hiking trails crisscross windswept prairies and wooded hills, connecting pygmy forests and coastal coves rich with tidepools. The 6-mile-wide park is bisected by the San Andreas Fault – the rock on the east side is vastly different from that on the west. Check out the eerily beautiful *tafonis,* honeycombed-sandstone formations, near Gerstle Cove. For a good roadside photo op, there's a pullout at mile-marker 45, with views of decaying redwood shacks, grazing goats and headlands jutting out to the sea.

Though many of the day use areas have been closed off due to budget cuts, trails lead off Hwy 1 pull-outs to views of the pristine coastline. The platform overlooking **Sentinel Rock** is just a short stroll from the Fisk Mill Cove parking lot at the park's north end. Further south, seals laze at **Gerstle Cove Marine Reserve**, one of California's first underwater parks. Tread lightly around tidepools and don't lift the rocks: even a glimpse of sunlight can kill some critters. If it's springtime, you *must* see **Kruse Rhododendron State Reserve**. Growing abundantly in the forest's filtered light, magnificent, pink rhododendrons reach heights of over 30ft, making them the tallest species in the world; turn east from Hwy 1 onto Kruse Ranch Rd and follow the signs.

Two campgrounds, **Woodside** and **Gerstle Cove** (☎800-444-7275; www.reserveamerica.com; tent & RV sites $35), both signposted off Hwy 1, have campsites with cold water. Inland Woodside is well protected by Monterey pines. Gerstle Cove's trees burned over a decade ago and have only grown halfway back, giving the gnarled, blackened trunks a ghostly look when the fog twirls between the branches.

Sea Ranch

Though not without its fans, the exclusive community of Sea Ranch might well be termed Stepford-by-the-Sea. The ritzy subdivision that sprawls 10 miles along the coast is connected with a well-watched network of private roads. Approved for construction prior to the existence of the watchdog Coastal Commission, the community was a precursor to the concept of 'slow growth,' with strict zoning laws requiring that houses be constructed of weathered wood only. According to *The Sea Ranch Design Manual:* 'This is not a place for the grand architectural statement; it's a place to explore the subtle nuances of fitting in...' Indeed. Though there are some lovely and recommended short-term rentals here, don't break any community rules – like throwing wild parties – or security will come knockin'. For supplies and gasoline, go to Gualala.

After years of litigation, public throughways onto private beaches have been legally mandated and are now well marked. Hiking trails lead from roadside parking lots to the sea and along the bluffs, but don't dare trespass on adjacent lands. **Stengel Beach** (Hwy 1 Mile 53.96) has a beach-access staircase, **Walk-On Beach** (Hwy 1 Mile 56.53) provides wheelchair access and **Shell Beach** (Hwy 1 Mile 55.24) also has beach-access stairs; parking at all three areas costs $6. For hiking details, including maps, contact the **Sea Ranch Association** (www.tsra.org).

Sea Ranch Lodge (☎707-785-2371, www.searanchlodge.com; 60 Sea Walk Dr; r incl breakfast from $212;), a marvel of '60s-modern California architecture, has spacious, luxurious, minimalist rooms, many with dramatic views to the ocean; some have hot tubs and fireplaces. For the past few years the entire lodge was slated for a decadent stem-to-stern renovation, but the last update was that they couldn't find a bank to float the loan. The fine contemporary **restaurant** (lunch mains $12-16, dinner mains $22-35; 8am-9pm) has a menu for discerning guests; expect everything from duck breast to local fish tacos. North of the lodge you'll see Sea Ranch's iconic nondenominational **chapel**; it's on the inland side of Hwy 1, mileage marker 55.66. For those short on time or on a budget, this is the best reason to pull over in Sea Ranch.

Depending on the season, it can be surprisingly affordable to rent a house in Sea Ranch; contact **Rams Head Realty** (www.ramshead-realty.com), **Sea Ranch Rentals** (www.searanchrentals.com), or **Sea Ranch Escape** (www.searanchescape.com).

Gualala & Anchor Bay

At just 2½ hours north of San Francisco, Gualala – pronounced by most locals as 'Wah-*la*-la' – is northern Sonoma coast's hub for a weekend getaway as it sits square in the middle of the 'Banana Belt,' a stretch of coast known for unusually sunny weather. Founded as a lumber town in the 1860s, the downtown stretches along Hwy 1 with a bustling commercial district that has a great grocery store and some cute, slightly upscale shops. Just north, quiet Anchor Bay has several inns, a tiny shopping center and, heading north, a string of secluded, hard-to-find beaches. Both are excellent jumping-off points for exploring the area.

Sights & Activities

Gualala Arts Center ARTS CENTER
(☎707-884-1138; www.gualalaarts.org; 9am-4pm Mon-Fri, noon-4pm Sat & Sun) Inland along Old State Rd, at the south end of town and beautifully built entirely by volunteers, this center hosts changing exhibitions, organizes the Art in the Redwoods Festival in late August and has loads of info on local art.

Adventure Rents CANOEING, KAYAKING
(☎707-884-4386, 888-881-4386; www.adventurerents.com) In the summer, a sand spit forms at the mouth of the river, cutting it off from the ocean and turning it into a warm-water lake. This outfit rents **canoes** (2 hours/half-day/full day $70/80/90) and **kayaks** (2 hours/half-day/full day $35/40/45) and provides instruction.

Seven miles north of Anchor Bay, pull off at mileage marker 11.41 for **Schooner Gulch**. A trail into the forest leads down cliffs to a sandy beach with tidepools. Bear right at the fork in the trail to reach iconic **Bowling Ball Beach**, where low tide reveals rows of big, round rocks resembling bowling balls. Consult tide tables for Arena Cove. The forecast low tide must be lower than +1.5ft on the tide chart for the rocks to be visible.

Sleeping & Eating

Of the two towns, Gualala has more services and is a more practical hub for exploring – there are a bunch of good motels and a pair of nice grocery stores. Get fresh veggies at the **farmers market** (Gualala Community Center; 10am-12:30pm Sat Jun-Oct) and organic supplies and local wine at the **Anchor Bay Village Market** (35513 S Hwy 1).

TOP CHOICE **Mar Vista Cottages** COTTAGES $$$
(☎707-884-3522, 877-855-3522; www.marvistamendocino.com; 35101 S Hwy 1, Anchor Bay; cottages from $155;) The elegantly renovated 1930s fishing cabins of Mar Vista is a simple, stylish seaside escape with a vanguard commitment to sustainability. The harmonious environment, situated in the sunny 'Banana Belt' of the North Coast, is the result of pitch perfect details: linens are line-dried over lavender, guests browse the organic vegetable garden to harvest their own dinner and chickens cluck around the grounds laying

the next morning's breakfast. It often requires two-night stays.

North Coast Country Inn B&B $$
(☎707-884-4537, 800-959-4537; www.northcoastcountryinn.com; 34591 S Hwy 1; r incl breakfast $195-225; @🐾) Perched on an inland hillside beneath towering trees, surrounded by lovely gardens, the perks of this place begin with the gregarious owner and a hot tub. The six spacious country-style rooms are decorated with lovely prints and boast exposed beams, fireplaces, board games and private entrances.

Gualala Point Regional Park CAMPGROUND $
(www.sonoma-county.org/parks; 42401 S Hwy 1, Gualala; tent & RV sites $28) Shaded by a stand of redwoods and fragrant California Bay Laurel trees, a short trail connects this creekside campground to the windswept beach. The quality of sites, including several secluded hike-in spots, makes it the best drive-in camping on this part of the coast.

St Orres Inn INN $$
(☎707-884-3303; www.saintorres.com; 36601 Hwy 1; B&B $95-135, cottages from $140; 🐾) Famous for its unusual Russian-inspired architecture: dramatic rough-hewn timbers and copper domes, there's no place quite like St Orres. On the property's 90 acres, hand-built cottages range from rustic to luxurious. The inn's fine **restaurant** (☎707-884-3335; dinner mains $40-50) serves inspired Californian cuisine in one of the coast's most romantic rooms. Decidedly spendy, sure, but the Andouille-stuffed pheasant with mushroom risotto is *so* worth it.

Gualala River Redwood Park COUNTY CAMPGROUND $
(☎707-884-3533; www.gualalapark.com; day use $6, tent & RV sites $22-42; ☎Memorial Day-Labor Day) Another excellent Sonoma County Park. Inland along Old State Rd, you can camp and do short hikes along the river.

Laura's Bakery & Taqueria MEXICAN $
(☎707-884-3175; 38411 Robinson Reef Rd at Hwy 1; mains $7-12; ☎7am-7pm Mon-Sat; ✍) Laura's is a refreshing, low-key break from Hwy 1 upscale dining. The menu's taqueria staples are fantastic (the Baja style fish tacos are a steal) but the fresh *mole* dishes and distant ocean view are the real surprises.

Bones Roadhouse BBQ $$
(www.bonesroadhouse.com; 39350 S Hwy 1, Gualala; mains $10-20; ⏲11:30am-9pm Sun-Thu, to 10pm Fri & Sat) Savory smoked meats make this Gualala's best lunch. On weekends, a codgerly blues outfit may be growling out 'Mustang Sally.'

ℹ Information

Redwood Coast Chamber of Commerce (www.redwoodcoastchamber.com) In Gualala; has local information.

Point Arena

This laid-back little town combines creature comforts with relaxed, eclectic California living and is the first town up the coast where the majority of residents don't seem to be retired Bay Area refugees. Sit by the docks a mile west of town at Arena Cove and watch surfers mingle with fishermen and hippies.

Point Arena Lighthouse LIGHTHOUSE
(www.pointarenalighthouse.com; adult/child $7.50/1; ☎10am-3:30pm winter, to 4:30pm summer) Two miles north of town, this 1908 lighthouse stands 10 stories high and is the only lighthouse in California you can ascend. Check in at the museum, then climb the 145 steps to the top and see the Fresnel lens and the jaw-dropping view. After $1.5-million renovations, the building and adjoining fog signal building are looking fantastic. True light house buffs should look into staying at the plain three-bedroom former **Coast Guard homes** (☎707-882-2777; houses $125-300) onsite. They're a quiet, wind-swept retreat.

Stornetta Public Lands NATURE AREA
For fabulous bird-watching, hiking on terraced rock past sea caves and access to hid-

TOP WHALE-WATCHING SPOTS

Watch for spouts, sounding and breaching whales and pods. Anywhere coastal will do, but the following are some of the north coast's best:

» Bodega Head (p211)
» Mendocino Headlands State Park (p221)
» Jug Handle State Reserve (p224)
» MacKerricher State Park (p228)
» Shelter Cove & The Lost Coast (p242)
» Trinidad Head Trail (p253)
» Klamath River Overlook (p257)

den coves, head 1 mile down Lighthouse Rd from Hwy 1 and look for the Bureau of Land Management (BLM) signs on the left indicating these 1132-acre public lands.

Sleeping & Eating

Wharf Master's Inn HOTEL $$$
(707-882-3171, 800-932-4031; www.wharfmasters.com; 785 Port Rd; r $105-255;) This is a cluster of small, modern rooms on a cliff overlooking fishing boats and a stilting pier. Tidy and very clean, rooms have the character of a chain hotel.

Coast Guard House Inn INN $$
(707-882-2442; www.coastguardhouse.com; 695 Arena Cove; r $105-225) Come here if you want to soak up old-world ocean side charm and are willing to deal with historic plumbing. It's a 1901 Cape Cod–style house and cottage, with water-view rooms.

TOP CHOICE **Franny's Cup & Saucer** PATISSERIE $
(707-882-2500; www.frannyscupandsaucer.com; 213 Main St; pastries $1-5; 8am-4pm Wed-Sat;) The cutest patisserie on this stretch of coast is run by Franny and her mother, Barbara (a veteran of Chez Panisse). The fresh berry tarts and rich chocolaty desserts seem too beautiful to eat, until you take the first bite and immediately want to order another. Several times a year they pull out all the stops for a Sunday garden brunch ($28).

Pizzas N Cream PIZZA $
(www.pizzasandcream.com; 790 Port Rd; pizzas $10-18; 11:30am-9pm;) In Arena Cove, this friendly place whips up exquisite pizzas and fresh salads, and serves beer and ice cream.

Arena Market ORGANIC DELI $
(www.arenaorganics.org; 183 Main St; 7:30am-7pm Mon-Sat, 8:30am-6pm Sun;) The deli in front of this fully stocked organic grocer makes excellent to-go veg options, often sourced from local farms.

Drinking & Entertainment

215 Main BAR
(www.facebook.com/215Main; 215 Main; 2pm-2am Tue-Sun) Head to this open, renovated historic building to drink local beer and wine. There's jazz on the weekends.

Arena Cinema CINEMA
(www.arenatheater.org; 214 Main St) shows mainstream, foreign and art films in a beautifully restored movie house. Sue, the ticket seller, has been in that booth for 40 years. Got a question about Point Arena? Ask Sue.

Information

Public library (707-882-3114; 225 Main St; noon-6pm Mon-Fri, to 3pm Sat) Free internet access.

Manchester

Follow Hwy 1 for about 7 miles north of Point Arena, through gorgeous rolling fields dropping down from the hills to the blue ocean, and a turnoff leads to **Manchester State Beach**, a long, wild stretch of sand. The area around here is remote and beautiful (only one grocery store), but it's a quick drive to Point Arena for more elaborate provisions.

Ross Ranch (707-877-1834; www.elkcoast.com/rossranch) at Irish Beach, another 5 miles to the north, arranges two-hour horseback beach ($60) and mountain ($50) rides; reservations recommended.

TOP CHOICE **Victorian Gardens** (707-882-3606; www.innatvictoriangardens.com; 14409 S Hwy 1; r $240-310) is wihout doubt the finest B&B on the coast. This lovingly restored 1904 farmhouse (smartly expanded by the owner, an architect) sits on 92 exquisitely situated acres just north of Manchester. Every detail here is picture perfect: the spacious gardens that provide fresh flowers and vegetables for gourmet meals, the rustic green house dining room which opens to the sea breeze and comfortable common spaces, decorated with a discerningly elegant mix of antique pieces and modern furniture. There's even a Picasso. For larger groups, the owners can prepare five-course authentic Italian dinners with carefully paired wines.

Mendocino Coast KOA (707-882-2375, www.manchesterbeachkoa.com; tent/RV sites from $35/50, cabins $68-78;) is an impressive private campground with tightly packed campsites beneath enormous Monterey pines, a cooking pavilion, hot showers, a hot tub and bicycles. The cabins are a great option for families who want to get the camping experience without roughing it.

A quarter-mile west, the sunny, exposed campground at **Manchester State Park** (tent & RV sites $25-35) has cold water and quiet right by the ocean. Sites are nonreservable. Budget cuts have all but eliminated ranger service.

Elk

Thirty minutes north of Point Arena, itty-bitty Elk is famous for its stunning cliff-top views of 'sea stacks,' towering rock formations jutting out of the water. There is *nothing* to do after dinner, so bring a book – and sleeping pills if you're a night owl. And you can forget about the cell phone, too; reception here is nonexistent. Elk's **visitor center** (5980 Hwy 1; ⏲11am-1pm Sat & Sun mid-Mar–Oct) has exhibits on the town's logging past. At the southern end of town, **Greenwood State Beach** sits where Greenwood Creek meets the sea. **Force 10** (☎707-877-3505; www.force10tours.com) guides ocean-kayaking tours ($115).

Tucked into a tiny clapboard house looking across the road to the ocean, the **Elk Studio Gallery & Artist's Collective** (www.artists-collective.net; 6031 S Hwy 1; ☎10am-5pm) is cluttered with tons of local art – everything from carvings and pottery to photography and jewelry.

Several upmarket B&Bs take advantage of the views. **Harbor House Inn** (☎707-877-3203, 800-720-7474; www.theharborhouseinn.com; 5600 S Hwy 1; r & cottages incl breakfast & dinner $360-490;), located in a 1915 Arts and Crafts–style mansion built by the town's lumber baron, has gorgeous cliff-top gardens and a private beach. The view from the Lookout, Oceansong and Shorepine rooms are the best. Rates include a superb four-course dinner for two in the ocean view room with a lauded wine list.

Griffin House (☎707-877-3422; www.griffinn.com; 5910 S Hwy 1; cottages $130-160, ocean-view cottages $145-325; @) is an unpretentious cluster of simple, powder-blue bluffside cottages with wood-burning stoves.

A new-agey feel pervades the Buddha-dotted grounds and ocean-view cottages at **Greenwood Pier Inn** (☎707-877-9997; www.greenwoodpierinn.com; 5928 S Hwy 1; d incl breakfast $185-335;). If you can look past the trippy art work, the rooms have fireplaces and private decks. Its cafe is open for lunch and dinner.

Everyone swears by excellent **Queenie's Roadhouse Cafe** (☎707-877-3285; 6061 S Hwy 1; dishes $6-10; ☎8am-3pm Thu-Mon;) for a creative range of breakfast (try the wild rice waffles) and lunch treats. Sweet, little **Bridget Dolan's** (☎707-877-1820; 5910 S Hwy 1; mains $10-15; ⏲4:30-8pm) serves straight-forward cookin' like pot pies, and bangers and mash.

Van Damme State Park

Three miles south of Mendocino, this gorgeous 1831-acre **park** (☎707-937-5804; www.parks.ca.gov; day use $6) draws divers, beachcombers and kayakers to its easy-access beach. It's also known for its **pygmy forest**, where the acidic soil and an impenetrable layer of hardpan just below the surface create a bonsai forest with decades-old trees growing only several feet high. A wheelchair-accessible boardwalk provides access to the forest. To get there, turn east off Hwy 1 onto Little River Airport Rd, a half-mile south of Van Damme State Park, and drive for 3 miles. Alternatively, hike or bike up from the campground on the 3.5-mile **Fern Canyon Scenic Trail**, which crosses back and forth over Little River.

The **visitor center** (☎707-937-4016; ⏲10am-3pm Fri-Sun) has nature exhibits, videos and programs; a half-hour marsh loop trail starts nearby.

Two pretty **campgrounds** (☎800-444-7275; www.reserveamerica.com; tent & RV sites $35;) are excellent for family car camping. They both have hot showers: one is just off Hwy 1, the other is in a highland meadow, which has lots of space for kids to run around. Nine **environmental campsites** (tent sites $25) lie just a 1¼-mile hike up Fern Canyon; there's untreated creek water.

For sea-cave kayaking tours ($50), contact **Lost Coast Kayaking** (☎707-937-2434; www.lostcoastkayaking.com).

Mendocino

Leading out to a gorgeous headland, Mendocino is the North Coast's salt-washed gem, with B&Bs surrounded by rose gardens, white-picket fences and New England–style redwood water towers. Bay Area weekenders walk along the headland among berry bramble and wildflowers, where cypress trees stand over dizzying cliffs. Nature's power is evident everywhere, from driftwood-littered fields and cave tunnels to the raging surf. The town itself is full of cute shops – no chains – and has earned the nickname 'Spendocino,' for its upscale goods. In summer, fragrant bursts of lavender and jasmine permeate the foggy wind, tempered by salt air from the churning surf, which is never out of earshot.

Built by transplanted New Englanders in the 1850s, Mendocino thrived late into the

Mendocino

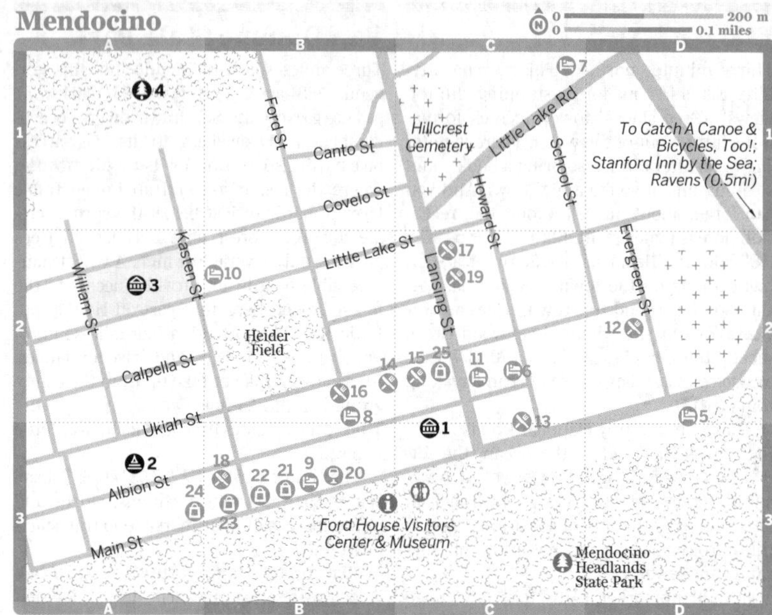

19th century, with ships transporting redwood timber from here to San Francisco. The mills shut down in the 1930s, and the town fell into disrepair until it was rediscovered in the 1950s by artists and bohemians. Today the culturally savvy, politically aware, well-traveled citizens welcome visitors, but eschew corporate interlopers – don't look for a Big Mac or try to use your cell phone. To avoid crowds, come midweek or in the low season, when the vibe is mellower – and prices more reasonable.

Sights

Mendocino is lined with all kinds of interesting galleries, which hold openings on the second Saturday of each month from 5pm to 8pm.

Mendocino Art Center GALLERY
(www.mendocinoartcenter.org; 45200 Little Lake St; ⊙10am-5pm Apr-Oct, to 4pm Tue-Sat Nov-Mar) Behind a yard of twisting iron sculpture, the city's art center takes up a whole tree-filled block, hosting exhibitions, the 81-seat Helen Schonei Theatre and nationally renowned art classes. This is also where to pick up the *Mendocino Arts Showcase* brochure, a quarterly publication listing all the happenings and festivals in town.

Kelley House Museum MUSEUM
(www.mendocinohistory.org; 45007 Albion St; admission $2; ⊙11am-3pm Thu-Tue Jun-Sep, Fri-Mon Oct-May) With a research library and changing exhibits on early California and Mendocino, the 1861 museum hosts seasonal, two-hour walking tours for $10; call for times.

Point Cabrillo Lighthouse LIGHTHOUSE
(www.pointcabrillo.org; Point Cabrillo Dr; admission free; ⊙11am-4pm Sat & Sun Jan & Feb, daily Mar-Oct, Fri-Mon Nov & Dec) Restored in 1909, this lighthouse stands on a 300-acre wildlife preserve north of town, between Russian Gulch and Caspar Beach. The head lighthouse keeper's home is now a simple lodging (p222). Guided walks of the preserve leave at 11am on Sundays from May to September.

Kwan Tai Temple TEMPLE
(www.kwantaitemple.org; 45160 Albion St) Peering in the window of this 1852 temple reveals an old altar dedicated to the Chinese god of war. Tours are available by appointment.

Activities

Wine tours, whale watching, shopping, hiking, cycling: there's more to do in the area than a thousand long weekends could accom-

Mendocino

Sights

1 Kelley House Museum C3
2 Kwan Tai Temple A3
3 Mendocino Art Center A2
4 Mendocino Headlands State Park A1

Sleeping

5 Alegria D2
6 Headlands Inn C2
7 Joshua Grindle Inn C1
8 MacCallum House Inn B2
9 Mendocino Hotel B3
10 Packard House B2
11 Sea Gull Inn C2

Eating

12 Café Beaujolais D2
13 Farmers Market C2
14 Garden Bakery B2
15 Lu's Kitchen C2
MacCallum House Restaurant .... (see 8)
Mendocino Cafe .... (see 11)
16 Mendocino Market B2
17 Mendosa's C2
18 Moosse Cafe B3
19 Patterson's Pub C2

Drinking

20 Dick's Place B3
Grey Whale Bar .... (see 8)
Mendocino Hotel .... (see 9)
Pattersons Pub .... (see 19)

Entertainment

Mendocino Theatre Company .... (see 3)

Shopping

21 Compass Rose Leather B3
22 Gallery Books B3
23 Out of This World B3
24 Twist A3
25 Village Toy Store C2

plish. For navigable river and ocean kayaking, launch from tiny Albion, which hugs the north side of the Albion River mouth, 5 miles south of Mendocino.

TOP CHOICE Catch A Canoe & Bicycles, Too! BICYCLE & CANOE RENTAL
(www.stanfordinn.com; Comptche-Ukiah Rd & Hwy 1; ☎9am-5pm) This friendly riverside outfit south of town rents bikes, kayaks and stable outrigger canoes for trips up the 8-mile Big River tidal estuary, the longest undeveloped estuary in Northern California. No highways or buildings, only beaches, forests, marshes, streams, abundant wildlife and historic logging sites. Bring a picnic and a camera to enjoy the ramshackle remnants of century-old train trestles and majestic blue herons.

Mendocino Headlands State Park COASTAL PARK
A spectacular park surrounds the village, with trails crisscrossing the bluffs and rocky coves. Ask at the visitor center about guided weekend walks, including spring wildflower walks and whale-watching.

Festivals & Events

For a complete list of Mendocino's many festivals, check with the visitor center or www.gomendo.com.

Mendocino Whale Festival WHALE-WATCHING
(www.mendowhale.com) Early March, with wine and chowder tastings, whale-watching and music.

Mendocino Music Festival MUSIC
(www.mendocinomusic.com) Mid-July, with orchestral and chamber music concerts on the headlands, children's matinees and open rehearsals.

Mendocino Wine & Mushroom Festival FOOD, WINE
(www.mendocino.com) Early November, guided mushroom tours and symposia.

Sleeping

Standards are high and so are prices; two-day minimums often crop up on weekends. Fort Bragg, 10 miles north, has cheaper lodgings (see p226). All B&B rates include breakfast; only a few places have TVs. For a range of cottages and B&Bs, contact **Mendocino Coast Reservations** (☎707-937-5033, 800-262-7801; www.mendocinovacations.com; 45084 Little Lake St; ☎9am-5pm).

TOP CHOICE Andiron COTTAGES $$
(☎800-955-6478; www.theandiorn.com; 6051 N Hwy 1, Mendocino; r $99-149;) Styled with hip vintage decor, this cluster of 1950s roadside cottages is a refreshingly playful option amid the stuffy cabbage-rose and

lace aesthetic of Mendocino. Each cabin houses two rooms with complementing themes: 'Read' has old books, comfy vintage chairs, and hip retro eyeglasses while the adjoining 'Write' features a huge chalkboard and ribbon typewriter. A favorite for travelers? 'Here' and 'There,' themed with old maps, 1960s airline paraphernalia and collectables from North Coast's yesteryear.

MacCallum House Inn B&B $$$
(☎707-937-0289, 800-609-0492; www.maccallumhouse.com; 45020 Albion St; r from $204; @🛜👪🐾) The finest B&B option in the center of town. When the weather is warm, the gardens surrounding the refurbished 1882 barn are a riot of color. There are bright and cheerful cottages, and a modern luxury home, but the most memorable space here is within one of Mendocino's iconic historic water towers – where living quarters fill the ground floor, a sauna is on the second and there's a view of the coast from the top. All accommodations have cushy extras like robes, DVD players, stereos and plush linens.

Stanford Inn by the Sea INN $$
(☎707-937-5615, 800-331-8884; www.stanfordinn.com; cnr Hwy 1 & Comptche-Ukiah Rd; r $195-305; @🛜🏊🐾) This masterpiece of a lodge standing on 10 lush acres has wood-burning fireplaces, original art, stereos and top-quality mattresses in every room. Figure in a stroll in the organic gardens, where they harvest food for the excellent on-site restaurant, the solarium-enclosed pool and the hot tub, and it's a sublime getaway.

Brewery Gulch Inn B&B $$$
(☎800-578-4454; www.brewerygulchinn.com; 9401 N Hwy 1, Mendocino; r $210-450; 🛜) Just south of Mendocino, this fresh place has 10 modern rooms (all with flat-screen televisions, iPod docs, gas fireplaces and spa bathtubs), and guests enjoy luxury touches like feather beds and leather reading chairs. The hosts pour heavily at the complimentary wine hour and leave out sweets for midnight snacking. Made-to-order breakfast is served in a small dining room overlooking the distant water.

Sea Gull Inn B&B $$
(☎707-937-5204, 888-937-5204; www.seagullbb.com; 44960 Albion St; r $130-165, barn $185; 👪🛜) With pristine white bedspreads, organic breakfasts and a flowering garden, this cute, converted motel is extremely comfortable, fairly priced, and right in the thick of the action.

Mendocino Hotel HISTORIC HOTEL $$
(☎707-937-0511, 800-548-0513; www.mendocinohotel.com; 45080 Main St; r with bath $135-295, without bath $95-125, ste $325-395; P🛜) Built in 1878 as the town's first hotel, this is like a piece of the Old West. The modern garden suites sit behind the main building and don't have a shade of old-school class, but are modern and serviceable. Some wheelchair accessible.

Packard House B&B $$$
(☎707-937-2677, 888-453-2677; www.packardhouse.com; 45170 Little Lake St; r $190-275) Decked out in contemporary style, this place is Mendocino's sleekest B&B choice – chic and elegant, with beautiful fabrics, colorful minimalist paintings and limestone bathrooms.

Alegria B&B $$
(☎707-937-5150, 800-780-7905; www.oceanfrontmagic.com; 44781 Main St; r $159-189, r with ocean view $239, cottages $179-269) Perfect for a romantic hideaway, rooms have ocean-view decks and wood-burning fireplaces; outside a gorgeous path leads to a private beach. Ever-so-friendly innkeepers rent simpler rooms in a 1900s Arts and Crafts place across the street.

Headlands Inn B&B $$$
(☎707-937-4431; www.headlandsinn.com; cnr Albion & Howard Sts; r $139-249) Homey saltbox with featherbeds and fireplaces. Quiet dorm rooms have sea views and staff will bring you the gourmet breakfast in bed.

Lighthouse Inn at Point Cabrillo HISTORIC B&B $$
(☎707-937-6124; 866-937-6124; www.pointcabrillo.org; Point Cabrillo Dr; r $152-279) On 300 acres, in the shadow of Point Cabrillo Lighthouse, the lightkeeper's house and several cottages have been turned into B&B rooms. Rates include a private night tour of the lighthouse and a five-course breakfast.

Joshua Grindle Inn B&B $$$
(☎707-937-4143, 800-474-6353; www.joshgrin.com; 44800 Little Lake Rd; r $189-299) Mendocino's oldest B&B has bright, airy, uncluttered rooms in an 1869 house, a weathered saltbox cottage and water tower. Enjoy goodies like fluffy muffins, warm hospitality and gorgeous gardens.

Glendeven B&B $$$
(☎707-937-0083; www.glendeven.com; 8205 N Hwy 1; r $135-320; 📶) Elegant estate 2 miles south of town with organic gardens.

Russian Gulch State Park CAMPGROUND $
(☎reservations 800-444-7275; www.reserveamerica.com; tent & RV sites $35) In a wooded canyon 2 miles north of town, with secluded drive-in sites, hot showers, a small waterfall and the Devil's Punch Bowl (a collapsed sea arch).

Eating

With quality to rival Napa Valley, the influx of Bay Area weekenders have fostered an excellent dining scene that enthusiastically espouses organic, sustainable principles. Make reservations. Gathering picnic supplies is easy at the central markets and the **farmers market** (Howard & Main St; ☎noon-2pm Fri May-Oct).

TOP CHOICE **Café Beaujolais** CALIFORNIAN, FUSION $$
(☎707-937-5614; www.cafebeaujolais.com; 961 Ukiah St; mains lunch $9-16, dinner $24-36; ⏰11:30am-2:30pm Wed-Sun, dinner from 5:30pm nightly) Mendocino's iconic, beloved country-Cal–French restaurant occupies an 1896 house restyled into a monochromatic urban-chic dining room, perfect for holding hands by candlelight. The refined, inspired cooking draws diners from San Francisco, who make this the centerpiece of their trip. The locally sourced menu changes with the seasons, but the Petaluma duck breast served with crispy skin is a gourmand's delight.

Ravens CALIFORNIAN $$$
(☎707-937-5615; www.ravensrestaurant.com; Stanford Inn, Comptche-Ukiah Rd; breakfast $11-15, mains $22-35; ⏰8-10:30am Mon-Sat, to noon Sun, dinner 5:30-10pm; ✎) Ravens brings haute-contemporary concepts to a completely vegetarian and vegan menu. Produce comes from the inn's own idyllic organic gardens, and the bold menu takes on everything from sea-palm strudel and portabella sliders to decadent (guilt-free) deserts.

MacCallum House Restaurant CALIFORNIAN $$$
(☎707-937-0289; www.maccallumhouse.com; 45020 Albion St; cafe dishes $12-16, mains $25-42; ⏰8:15-10am Mon-Fri, to 11am Sat & Sun, 5:30-9pm daily; ✎) Sit on the veranda or fireside for a romantic dinner of all-organic game, fish or risotto primavera. Chef Alan Kantor makes *everything* from scratch and his commitment to sustainability and organic ingredients is nearly as visionary as his menu. The cafe menu, served at the Grey Whale Bar, is one of Mendocino's few four-star bargains.

Garden Bakery BAKERY $
(☎707-937-0282; 10450 Lansing; baked goods $3-6; ⏰9am-4pm) Nearly every corner of Mendocino gets explored by hordes, but this little garden-side bakery still feels like a hidden gem. To describe the quality of the baked goods would invite hyperbole: they are *a-ma-zing*. The menu changes with the seasons and the baker's whim; one day, you're trying not to inhale the savory, cabbage-stuffed German pastry (a family recipe), on another you'll find apple cheddar croissants. If you show up early enough you'll get a taste of their renowned bear claw. If you don't find this place at first, keep looking: the bakery is located off the street, accessible by sidewalks that cut through the block.

Mendocino Cafe CALIFORNIAN, FUSION $$
(www.mendocinocafe.com; 10451 Lansing St; lunch mains $12-15, dinner mains $12-24; ⏰11:30am-8pm; ✎) One of Mendocino's few midpriced dinner spots also serves lovely alfresco lunches on its ocean-view deck surrounded by roses. Try the fish tacos or the Thai burrito. At dinner there's grilled steak and seafood.

Patterson's Pub PUB $$
(www.pattersonspub.com; 10485 Lansing St; mains $10-15 ⏰11am-11pm Mon-Fri, brunch 10am-2pm Sat & Sun) If you pull into town late and you're hungry, you'll thank your lucky stars for this place; it serves quality pub grub – fish and chips, huge burgers and dinner salads – with cold beer. The only spoiler to the traditional Irish pub ambience is the plethora of flat-screen TVs.

Moosse Cafe CALIFORNIAN $$
(☎707-937-4323; www.themoosse.com; 390 Kasten St; lunch mains $12-16, dinner mains $22-28; ⏰noon-2:30pm & 5:30-8:30pm; ✎) The blond woodwork and starched linen napkins set a relaxed yet elegant tone for top-notch Cal-French cooking. Try the cioppino in saffron-fennel-tomato broth at dinner; lunch is more casual. Note that it keeps variable hours in the winter and on slow weekdays.

Ledford House MEDITERRANEAN $$
(☎707-937-0282; www.ledfordhouse.com; 3000 N Hwy 1, Albion; mains $19-30; ⏰5-8pm Wed-Sun;

) Watch the water pound the rocks and the sun set out of the Mendocino hubbub (8 miles south) at this friendly Cal-Med bistro. Try the cassoulet or the gnocchi. It's a local hangout and gets hoppin' with live jazz most nights.

Mendosa's MARKET $
(www.harvestmarket.com; 10501 Lansing St; 8am-9pm) The town's biggest grocery store has legit organic credentials, an excellent cold food bar and great cheese and meat.

Mendocino Market DELI $
(45051 Ukiah St; sandwiches $6-9; 11am-5pm Mon-Fri, to 4pm Sat & Sun;) Pick up huge deli sandwiches and picnics here.

Lu's Kitchen INTERNATIONAL $
(707-937-4939; 45013 Ukiah St; mains $8-10; 11:30am-5:30pm;) Rustles up fab organic veggie burritos in a tiny shack; outdoor-only tables.

Drinking

Have cocktails at the **Mendocino Hotel** (45080 Main St) or the **Grey Whale Bar** (45020 Albion St)at the MacCallum House Inn.

Patterson's Pub PUB
(www.pattersonspub.com; 10485 Lansing St) This boisterous, inviting, Irish-style bar has a friendly staff and a good vibe.

Dick's Place DIVE BAR
(45080 Main St) A bit out of place among the fancy-pants shops downtown, but an excellent spot to check out the *other* Mendocino and do shots with rowdy locals.

Moody's Coffee Bar COFFEE SHOP
(10450 Lansing St; 6am-8pm;) Moody's covers the essentials: strong coffee, wi-fi and the *New York Times.*

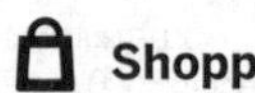

Shopping

Mendocino's walkable streets are great for shopping, and the ban on chain stores ensures unique, often upscale gifts. There are many small galleries in town where one-of-a-kind artwork is for sale.

Compass Rose Leather LEATHER GOODS
(45150 Main St) From hand-tooled belts and leather bound journals to purses and peg-secured storage boxes, the craftsmanship here is unquestionable.

Out Of This World OUTDOOR & SCIENCE SUPPLIES
(45100 Main St) Birders, astronomy buffs and science geeks head directly to this telescope, binocular and science-toy shop.

Village Toy Store TOYS
(10450 Lansing St) Get a kite to fly on Bodega head or browse the old-world selection of wooden toys and games that you won't find in the chains – hardly anything requires batteries.

Gallery Bookshop BOOKS
(www.gallerybookshop.com; 319 Kasten St) Stocks a great selection of books on local topics, titles from California's small presses and specialized outdoor guides.

Twist CLOTHING
(45140 Main St) Twist stocks ecofriendly, natural-fiber clothing and lots of locally made clothing and toys.

Moore Used Books SECONDHAND BOOKS
(990 Main St) An excellent bad weather hideout, the stacks here have over 10,000 used titles. The shop is in an old house at the far east end of Main Street.

Information

Ford House Visitor Center & Museum (707-937-5397; www.gomendo.com; 735 Main St; suggested donation $2; 11am-4pm) Maps, books, information and exhibits, including a scale model of 1890 Mendocino.

Mendocino Coast Clinics (707-964-1251; 205 South St; 9am-5pm Mon-Fri, to 8pm Wed, 9am-1pm Sat) Nonemergencies.

Jug Handle State Reserve

Between Mendocino and Fort Bragg, Jug Handle preserves an **ecological staircase** that you can view on a 5-mile (round-trip) self-guided nature trail. Five wave-cut terraces ascend in steps from the seashore, each 100ft and 100,000 years removed from the previous one, and each with its own distinct geology and vegetation. One of the terraces has a pygmy forest, similar to the better-known example at Van Damme State Park (p219). Pick up a printed guide detailing the area's geology, flora and fauna from the parking lot. The reserve is also a good spot to stroll the headlands, whale-watch or lounge on the beach. It's easy to miss the entrance; watch for the turnoff, just north of Caspar.

Jug Handle Creek Farm & Nature Center (☎707-964-4630; www.jughandlecreekfarm.com; tent sites $12, r & cabins adult $40-50, child $15, student $28-33; 🐾) is a nonprofit 39-acre farm with rustic cabins and hostel rooms in a 19th-century farmhouse. Call ahead about work-stay discounts. Drive 5 miles north of Mendocino to Caspar; the farm is on the east side of Hwy 1. Take the second driveway after Fern Creek Rd.

Fort Bragg

In the past, Fort Bragg was Mendocino's ugly stepsister, home to a lumber mill, a scrappy downtown and blue-collar locals who gave a cold welcome to outsiders. Since the mill closure in 2002, the town has started to reinvent itself, slowly warming to a tourism-based economy. What to do with the seaside mill site is the talk of the town, running the gamut from progressive ideas like a marine research center or university to disastrous ones like a condo development, a world-class golf course or (gasp!) another mill. Regardless, the effect on Fort Bragg is likely to be profound. Follow the progress at www.fortbraggmillsite.com.

In the meantime, Fort Bragg's downtown continues to develop as an unpretentious alternative to Mendocino, even if the southern end of town is hideous. Unlike the *entire* franchise-free 180-mile stretch of Coastal Hwy 1 between here and the Golden Gate, southern Fort Bragg is blighted by McDonalds, Starbucks and other Anywhere, USA chain stores polluting the coastal aesthetic. Put on blinkers and don't stop till you're downtown, where you'll find better hamburgers and coffee, old-school architecture and residents eager to show off their little town.

Twisting Hwy 20 provides the main access to Fort Bragg from the east, and most facilities are near Main St, a 2-mile stretch of Hwy 1. Franklin St runs parallel, one block east.

Sights & Activities

Fort Bragg has the same banner North Coast activities as Mendocino - beach combing, surfing, hiking - but basing yourself here is much cheaper and a little less quaint. The wharf lies at Noyo Harbor - the mouth of the Noyo River - south of downtown where you can find whale-watching cruises and deep-sea fishing trips.

NORTH COAST BEER TOUR

The craft breweries of the North Coast don't mess around – bold hop profiles, Belgium-style ales and smooth lagers are regional specialties, and they're produced with style. Some breweries are better than others, but the following tour makes for an excellent long weekend of beer tasting in the region.

- » Ukiah Brewing Company (p234), Ukiah
- » Anderson Valley Brewing Company (p232), Boonville.
- » North Coast Brewing Company (p227), Fort Bragg
- » Six Rivers Brewery (p252), McKinleyville
- » Eel River Brewing (p244), Fortuna

TOP CHOICE **Skunk Train** HISTORIC TRAIN
(☎707-964-6371, 866-866-1690; www.skunktrain.com; adult/child $49/24) Fort Bragg's pride and joy, the vintage train got its nickname in 1925 for its stinky gas-powered steam engines, but today the historic steam and diesel locomotives are odorless. Passing through redwood-forested mountains, along rivers, over bridges and through deep mountain tunnels, the trains run from both Fort Bragg and Willits (p236) to the midway point of Northspur, where they turn around (if you want to go to Willits, plan to spend the night). The depot is downtown at the foot of Laurel St, one block west of Main St.

Mendocino Coast Botanical Gardens GARDENS
(☎707-964-4352; www.gardenbythesea.org; 18220 N Hwy 1; adult/child/senior $14/5/10; ⏰9am-5pm Mar-Oct, to 4pm Nov-Feb; 🐾) This gem of Northern California displays native flora, rhododendrons and heritage roses. The succulent display alone is amazing and the organic garden is harvested by volunteers to feed area residents in need. The serpentine paths wander along 47 seafront acres south of town. Primary trails are wheelchair-accessible.

Glass Beach BEACH
Named for (what's left of) the sea-polished glass in the sand, remnants of its days as a city dump, this beach is now part of MacKerricher State Park where visitors comb

the sand for multicolored glass. Take the headlands trail from Elm St, off Main St, but leave the glass; as a part of the park system, visitors are not supposed to pocket souvenirs.

All-Aboard Adventures FISHING, WHALE-WATCHING
(☎707-964-1881; www.allaboardadventures.com; 32400 N Harbor Dr) Captain Tim leads crabbing and salmon fishing trips (five hours, $80) and whale watching during the whale migration (two hours, $35).

Northcoast Artists Gallery GALLERY
(www.northcoastartists.org; 362 N Main St; ⊙10am-6pm) An excellent local arts cooperative that has the useful *Fort Bragg Gallery & Exhibition Guide,* which directs you to other galleries around town. Openings are the first Fridays of the month. Antique and book stores line Franklin St, one block east.

FREE **Triangle Tattoo & Museum** MUSEUM
(www.triangletattoo.com; 356B N Main St; admission free; ☎noon-7pm) Shows multicultural, international tattoo art.

Guest House Museum MUSEUM
(☎707-964-4251; www.fortbragghistory.org; 343 N Main St; admission $2; ⊙1-3pm Mon, 11am-2pm Tue-Fri, 10am-4pm Sat-Sun May-Oct, 11am-2pm Thu-Sun) A majestic Victorian structure built in 1892, displays historical photos and relics of Fort Bragg's history. As hours vary, call ahead.

Pudding Creek Trestle BOARDWALK
The walk along the Pudding Creek Trestle, north of downtown, is fun for the whole family.

Festivals & Events

Fort Bragg Whale Festival WILDLIFE
(www.mendowhale.com) Held on the third weekend in March, with microbrew tastings, crafts fairs and whale-watching trips.

Paul Bunyan Days COMMUNITY FESTIVAL
(www.paulbunyandays.com) Held on Labor Day weekend in September, celebrate California's logging history with a logging show, square dancing, parade and fair.

Sleeping

Fort Bragg's lodging is cheaper than Mendocino's, but most of the motels along noisy Hwy 1 don't have air-conditioning, so you'll hear traffic through your windows. Most B&Bs do not have TVs and they all include breakfast. The usual chains abound.

Shoreline Cottages COTTAGES $$
(☎707-964-2977; www.shoreline-cottage.com; 18725 N Hwy 1; r $120-155;) Low-key and pet-friendly four-person rooms and cottages with kitchens surround a central tree-filled lawn. The family rooms are a good bargain, and suites feature modern art work and clean sight lines. All rooms have docks for your iPod, snacks and access to a library of DVDs.

Country Inn B&B $
(☎707-964-3737; www.beourguests.com; 18725 N Hwy 1; r $90-145;) This unpretentious bed & breakfast is right in the middle of town and is an excellent way to dodge the chain motels for a good value stay. The lovely family hosts are welcoming and easy going, and can offer good local tips. Breakfast can be delivered to your room and at night you can soak in a hot tub out back.

Weller House Inn B&B $$
(☎707-964-4415, 877-893-5537; www.wellerhouse.com; 524 Stewart St; r $130-195;) Rooms in this beautifully restored 1886 mansion have down comforters, good mattresses and fine linens. The water tower is the tallest structure in town – and it has a hot tub at the top! Breakfast is in the massive redwood ballroom.

Grey Whale Inn B&B $$
(☎707-964-0640, 800-382-7244; www.greywhaleinn.com; 615 N Main St; r $100-195;) Situated in a historic building on the north side of town, this comfortable, family-run inn has simple, straightforward rooms that are good value – especially for families.

California Department of Forestry CAMPING $
(☎707-964-5674; 802 N Main St; ⊙8am-4:30pm Mon, to noon Tue-Thu) Come here for maps, permits and camping information for the Jackson State Forest, east of Fort Bragg, where camping is free.

Eating

Similar to the lodging scene, the food in Fort Bragg is less spendy than Mendocino, and there are a number of good options. Self-caterers should try the **farmers market** (cnr Laurel & Franklin Sts; ⊙3:30-6pm Wed May-Oct) downtown or the **Harvest Market** (☎707-

964-7000; cnr Hwys 1 & 20; ⏱5am-11pm) for the best groceries.

TOP CHOICE **Piaci Pub & Pizzeria** PIZZA $
(www.piacipizza.com; 120 W Redwood Ave; pizza $8-12; ⏱11am-4pm Mon-Fri, 4-9pm Sun-Thu, 4-10pm Fri & Sat) Fort Bragg's must-visit pizzeria is the place to chat up locals while enjoying microbrews and a menu of fantastic wood-fired, brick-oven, 'adult' pizzas (a sight more sophisticated than your average Dominos pie). The 'Gustoso' – an immaculate selection with Chevre, pesto and seasonal pears – speaks to the carefully orchestrated thin-crust pies. It's tiny, loud and fun, but expect to wait at peak times.

Mendo Bistro AMERICAN $$
(☎707-964-4974; www.mendobistro.com; 301 N Main St; mains $14-25; ⏱5-9pm; 👪) This dining option gets packed with a young crowd on the weekend, offering a choose-your-own-adventure menu, where you select a meat, a preparation and an accompanying sauce from a litany of options. The loud, bustling 2nd-story room is big enough for kids to run around and nobody will notice.

Chapter & Moon AMERICAN $
(32150 N Harbor Dr; mains $8-18; ☎8am-8pm) Overlooking Noyo Harbor, this small cafe serves blue-plate American cooking: chicken and dumplings, meatloaf melts, and fish with yam chips. Save room for fruit cobbler.

North Coast Brewing Company BREWPUB $$
(www.northcoastbrewing.com; 444 N Main St; mains $8-25; ⏱7am-9:30pm Sun-Thu, to 10pm Fri & Sat) Though thick, rare slabs of steak and a list of specials demonstrate that they take the food as seriously as the bevvies, it's burgers and garlic fries that soak up the fantastic selection of handcrafted brews.

Headlands Coffeehouse DELI $
(www.headlandscoffeehouse.com; 120 E Laurel St; dishes $4-8; ⏱7am-10pm Mon-Sat, to 7pm Sun; 📶🌿) The town's best cafe is in the middle of the historic downtown, with high ceilings and lots of atmosphere. The menu gets raves for the Belgian waffles, homemade soups, veggie-friendly salads, panini and lasagna.

🌿 **Living Light Café** VEGAN, RAW $
(☎707-964-2420; 444 N Main St; mains $5-11; ⏱8am-5:30pm Mon-Sat, to 4pm Sun; 🌿) As an extension of the renowned Living Light Culinary Institute, one of the nation's leading raw food schools, this bright cafe serves a tasty to-go menu that's a sight better than bland crudités, like the Sicilian-style pizza on a spouted seed crust, raw desserts and tangy cold soups.

Eggheads BREAKFAST $
(www.eggheadsrestaurant.com; 326 N Main St; mains $8-13; ⏱7am-2pm) Enjoy the *Wizard of Oz* theme as you tuck into one of 50 varieties of omelet, crepe or burrito, some with local Dungeness crab.

La Playa MEXICAN $
(542 N Main St; mains $6-12; ⏱10am-9pm Mon-Sat) Down-home, no-frills Mexican cookin' right by the train tracks – try the *carne asada* (seasoned, roasted beef).

Cap'n Flint's SEAFOOD $$
(32250 N Harbor Dr; mains $11; ⏱11am-9pm) Skip the overpriced Wharf Restaurant (aka Silver's), and head next door to this unpretentious place to eat the same fried fish for less.

Drinking & Entertainment

Caspar Inn LIVE MUSIC
(www.casparinn.com; 14957 Caspar Rd; cover $3-25 Tue-Sat) Square in the middle of Mendocino and Fort Bragg, off Hwy 1, this jumpin' roadhouse rocks out the reggae, hip-hop, rockabilly, jam bands and international acts. The best live music venue on this stretch of the coast, it's worth checking out the calendar, which is posted on bulletin boards and public spaces throughout the area. Hours vary according to the events and the season.

North Coast Brewing Company BREWERY
(www.northcoastbrewing.com; 444 N Main St) Of all the many breweries up the coast, this might be the most *serious*, with an arsenal of handcrafted, bold brews. If you order the sampler, designate a driver.

Gloriana Opera Company THEATER COMPANY
(www.gloriana.org; 721 N Franklin St) Stages musical theater and operettas.

Shopping

There's plenty of window-shopping in Fort Bragg's compact downtown, including a string of antique shops along Franklin St.

Outdoor Store OUTDOOR EQUIPMENT
(www.mendooutdoors.com; 247 N Main St) If you're planning on camping on the coast or

exploring the Lost Coast, this is the best outfitter in the region, stocking detailed maps of the region's wilderness areas, fuel for stoves and high-quality gear.

Mendocino Vintage ANTIQUES
(www.mendocinovintage.com; 344 N Franklin St) Of the antique shops on Franklin, this is the hippest by a long shot, with a case full of vintage estate jewelry, antique glassware and old local oddities.

Information

Fort Bragg-Mendocino Coast Chamber of Commerce (www.fortbragg.com, www.mendocinocoast.com; 332 N Main St; per 15min $1; 9am-5pm Mon-Fri, to 3pm Sat) Internet access.

Mendocino Coast District Hospital (707-961-1234; 700 River Dr; 24hr) Emergency room.

Getting There & Around

Fort Bragg Cyclery (707-964-3509; www.fortbraggcyclery.com; 221a N Main St) Rents bicycles.

Mendocino Transit Authority (MTA; 707-462-1422, 800-696-4682; www.4mta.org) Runs local route 5 'BraggAbout' buses between Noyo Harbor and Elm St, north of downtown ($1). Service runs throughout the day.

Mackerricher State Park

Three miles north of Fort Bragg, the **MacKerricher State Park** (707-964-9112; www.parks.ca.gov) preserves 9 miles of pristine rocky headlands, sandy beaches, dunes and tidepools.

The **visitor center** (10am-4pm Mon-Fri & 9am-6pm Sat & Sun summer, 9am-3pm rest of year) sits next to the whale skeleton at the park entrance. Hike the **Coastal Trail** along dark-sand beaches and see rare and endangered plant species (tread lightly). **Lake Cleone** is a 30-acre freshwater lake stocked with trout and visited by over 90 species of birds. At nearby **Laguna Point** an interpretive disabled-accessible boardwalk overlooks harbor seals and, from December to April, migrating whales. **Ricochet Ridge Ranch** (707-964-7669; www.horse-vacation.com; 24201 N Hwy 1) offers horseback-riding trips through redwoods or along the beach ($45 for 90 minutes).

Popular **campgrounds** (800-444-2725; www.reserveamerica.com; tent & RV sites $35), nestled in pine forest, have hot showers and water; the first-choice reservable tent sites are numbers 21 to 59. Ten superb, secluded walk-in tent sites (numbers 1 to 10) are first-come, first-served.

Westport

If sleepy Westport feels like the peaceful edge of nowhere, that's because it is. The last hamlet before the Lost Coast, on a twisting 15-mile drive north of Fort Bragg, it is the last town before Hwy 1 veers inland on the 22-mile ascent to meet Hwy 101 in Leggett. For details on accessing the Lost Coast's southernmost reaches from Westport, see p242.

Head 1.5 miles north of town for the ruggedly beautiful **Westport-Union Landing State Beach** (707-937-5804; tent sites $25), which extends for 3 miles on coastal bluffs. A rough hiking trail leaves the primitive campground and passes by tidepools and streams, accessible at low tide. Bring your own water.

Simple accommodations in town include the blue-and-red, plastic-flower-festooned **Westport Inn** (707-964-5135; 37040 N Hwy 1; r incl breakfast from $77).

TOP CHOICE **Westport Hotel & Old Abalone Pub** (877-964-3688; www.westporthotel.us; Hwy 1; r $90-165, ste $125-200, cabins $140-195;) has been elegantly refashioned under new proprietors; the place is quiet enough to have a motto which brags 'You've finally found nowhere.' The rooms are bright and beautiful – feather duvets, hardwood furniture, simple patterns – and enjoy excellent views. The classy historic pub downstairs is the only option for dinner, so be thankful it's a delicious sampling of whimsical California fusions (like turduken sausage and buttermilk potatoes and rock shrimp mac and cheese) and hearty, expertly presented pub food.

Howard Creek Ranch (707-964-6725; www.howardcreekranch.com; 40501 N Hwy 1; r $90-165, ste $125-200, cabins $75-200;), sitting on 60 stunning acres of forest and farmland abutting the wilderness, has accommodations in an 1880s farmhouse or a carriage barn, whose way-cool redwood rooms have been expertly handcrafted by the owner. Rates include full breakfast. Bring hiking boots, not high heels.

ALONG HIGHWAY 101

To get into the most remote and wild parts of the North Coast on the quick, eschew winding Hwy 1 for inland Hwy 101, which runs north from San Francisco as a freeway, then as a two- or four-lane highway north of Sonoma County, occasionally pausing under the traffic lights of small towns.

Know that escaping the Bay Area at rush hour (weekdays between 4pm and 7pm) ain't easy. You might sit bumper-to-bumper through Santa Rosa or Willits, where trucks bound for the coast turn onto Hwy 20.

Although Hwy 101 may not look as enticing as the coastal route, it's faster and less winding, leaving you time along the way to detour into Sonoma and Mendocino counties' wine regions (Mendocino claims to be the greenest wine region in the country), explore pastoral Anderson Valley, splash about Clear Lake or soak at hot-springs resorts outside Ukiah – time well spent indeed!

Hopland

Cute Hopland is the gateway to Mendocino County's wine country. Hops were first grown here in 1866, but Prohibition brought the industry temporarily to a halt. Today, booze drives the local economy again with wine tasting as the primary draw.

Sights & Activities

For an excellent weekend trip, use Hopland as a base for exploring the regional wineries. More information about the constantly growing roster of wineries is available at www.destinationhopland.com. Find a map to the wine region at www.visitmendocino.com.

Real Goods Solar Living Center SOLAR ENERGY CENTER
(www.solarliving.org; 13771 S Hwy 101; ⌚9am-5pm; 👪) The progressive, futuristic 12-acre campus at the south end of town is largely responsible for the areas bold green initiates. There's no charge but the suggested donation is $3 to $5.

SIP! Mendocino TASTING ROOM
(www.sipmendocino.com; 13420 S Hwy 101; ⌚11am-6pm) In central Hopland, this is a friendly place to get your bearings, pick up a map to the region and taste several wines without navigating all the back roads. Amiable proprietors guide you through a tour of 18 wines with delectable appetizer pairings and a blossom-filled courtyard.

Saracina WINERY
(www.saracina.com; 11684 S Hwy 101; ⌚10am-5pm) The highlight of a tour here is the descent into the cool caves. Sensuous whites are all biodynamcially and sustainably farmed.

Fetzer Vineyards Organic Gardens WINERY
(www.fetzer.com; 13601 Eastside Rd; ⌚9am-5pm) Fetzer's sustainable practices have raised the bar, and their gardens are lovely. The wines are excellent value.

Brutocao Schoolhouse Plaza TASTING ROOM
(www.brutocaoschoolhouseplaza.com; 13500 S Hwy 101; ⌚11am-8pm) In central Hopland, this place has bocce courts and bold reds – a perfect combo.

Graziano Family of Wines WINERY
(www.grazianofamilyofwines.com; 13251 S Hwy 101; ⌚10am-5pm) Specializes in 'Cal-Ital' wines – nebbiolo, dolcetto, barbera and sangiovese – at some great prices.

Sleeping & Eating

Hopland Inn HISTORIC HOTEL $$
(☎707-744-1890, 800-266-1891; www.hoplandinn.com; 13401 S Hwy 101; r $180; ❄📶🐾) If you're spending the night in town, your only choice is a good one: the 1890 inn in the middle of town. Enjoy bevvies from the full bar downstairs in the cozy, wood-paneled library.

Bluebird Cafe AMERICAN $
(☎707-744-1633; 13340 S Hwy 101; breakfast & lunch $5-12, dinner $12-17; ⌚7am-2pm Mon-Thu, to 7pm Fri-Sun; 🖉) For conservative tastes, this classic American diner serves hearty breakfasts, giant burgers and homemade pie (the summer selection of peach-blueberry pie is dreamy). For a more exciting culinary adventure, try the wild game burgers, including boar with apple chutney and elk with a bite of horseradish.

Clear Lake

With over 100 miles of shoreline, Clear Lake is the largest naturally occurring freshwater lake in California (Tahoe is bigger, but crosses the Nevada state line). In summer the warm water thrives with algae, giving it a murky green appearance and creating a

TOP CLEAR LAKE WINERIES

From north to south, the following four wineries are the best; some offer tours by appointment.

» **Ceago Vinegarden** (www.ceago.com; 5115 E Hwy 20, Nice; ⏲10am-6pm) Ceago (cee-*ay*-go) occupies a spectacular spot on the north shore, and pours biodynamic, fruit-forward wines.

» **Wildhurst Vineyards** (www.wildhurst.com; 3855 Main St, Kelseyville; ⏲10am-5pm) The best wine on the lake, but lacks atmosphere. Try the sauvignon blanc.

» **Ployez Winery** (1171 S Hwy 29, Lower Lake; ⏲11am-5pm) Above-average *méthode champenoise* sparkling wines; surrounded by farmland.

» **Langtry Estate Vineyards** (21000 Butts Canyon Rd, Middletown; ⏲11am-5pm) The most beautiful vineyard. Try the port.

fabulous habitat for fish – especially bass – and tens of thousands of birds. Mt Konocti, a 4200ft-tall dormant volcano, lords over the scene. Alas, the human settlements don't always live up to the grandeur and thousands of acres near the lake remain scarred from wildfires in 2008.

Sights & Activities

Locals refer to the northwest portion as 'upper lake' and the southeast portion as 'lower lake.' **Lakeport** (population 5240) sits on the northwest shore, a 45-minute drive east of Hopland along Hwy 175 (off Hwy 101); **Kelseyville** (population 3000) is 7 miles south. **Clearlake**, off the southeastern shore, is the biggest (and ugliest) town.

Hwy 20 links the north-shore hamlets of **Nice** (the northernmost town) and **Lucerne**, 4 miles southeast. **Middletown**, a cute village, lies 20 miles south of Clearlake at the junction of Hwys 175 and 129, 40 minutes north of Calistoga.

Many outfits rent boats, including **On the Waterfront** (☎707-263-6789; 60 3rd St, Lakeport, six person boats per 3hr/day $185/350) and Konocti Harbor Resort & Spa in Kelseyville (p230).

Clear Lake State Park STATE PARK
(☎707-279-4293; 5300 Soda Bay Rd, Kelseyville; per car $8) Six miles from Lakeport, on the lake's west shore, the park is idyllic and gorgeous, with hiking trails, fishing, boating and camping. The **bird-watching** is extraordinary. The **visitor center** has geological and historical exhibits.

Redbud Audubon Society BIRD WATCHING
(www.redbudaudubon.org) In Lower Lake, this conservation group leads birding walks.

Sleeping & Eating

Make reservations on weekends and during summer, when people flock to the cool water.

LAKEPORT & KELSEYVILLE

There are a number of motels along the main drag in Keleysville and Lakeport, but if you want fresh air, Clear Lake State Park has four **campgrounds** (☎800-444-7275; www.reserveamerica.com; tent & RV sites $35) with showers. The weekly **farmers market** (Hwy 29 & Thomas Rd; ⏲8:30am-noon Sat May-Oct) is in Kelseyville.

TOP CHOICE **Lakeport English Inn** B&B $$
(☎707-263-4317; www.lakeportenglishinn.com; 675 N Main St, Lakeport; r $159-210, cottages $210; ❄📶) The finest B&B at Clear Lake is an 1875 Carpenter Gothic with 10 impeccably furnished rooms, styled with a nod to the English countryside. Weekends take high tea (public welcome by reservation) – with real Devonshire cream.

Konocti Harbor Resort & Spa RESORT $$
(☎707-279-4281, 800-660-5253; www.konoctiharbor.com; 8727 Soda Bay Rd, Konocti Bay; r $89-199, apt & beach cottages $199-349, ste $259-399; 📶🏊) On Konocti Bay, 4 miles from Kelseyville, this gargantuan resort, famous for huge concerts, includes four pools, a fitness center, tennis, golf, marina and spa. Rates spike on concert nights.

Mallard House MOTEL $
(☎707-262-1601; www.mallardhouse.com; 970 N Main St, Lakeport; r with kitchen $69-149, without $49-99; ❄📶) Waterfront motels with boat slips include this cottage-style place, which is a fantastic value during the week.

TOP CHOICE **Saw Shop Gallery Bistro** CALIFORNIAN $$$
(707-278-0129; www.sawshopbistro.com; 3825 Main St, Kelseyville; small plates $10-12, mains $18-30; dinner Tue-Sat) The best restaurant in Lake County serves a Californian-cuisine menu of wild salmon and rack of lamb, as well as a small plates menu of sushi, lobster tacos, Kobe-beef burgers and flatbread pizzas. Laid-back atmosphere, too.

Molly Brennan's PUB $
(www.mollybrennans.com; 175 Main St, Lakeport; mains $9-20; 11am-11pm Mon, Wed & Thu, to 2am Fri-Sun) Big mirrors and dark wood, pints of Guinness and bangers and mash make Molly Brennan's a quality pub. You'd be remiss to leave without trying the more ambitious menu items, like the lamb stew or pistachio-crusted salmon.

Bigg's 155 DINER $
(155 Park St, Lakeport; mains $5-12) It may look like a humble diner, but the menu is adventuresome (Shrimp Po' Boys?) and the ice cream treats are enormous.

NORTH SHORE

Tallman Hotel HISTORIC HOTEL $$
(707-274-0200, 888-880-5253; www.tallmanhotel.com; 4057 E Hwy 20, Nice; cottages $159-229;) The centerpiece may be the smartly renovated historic hotel – tile bathrooms, warm lighting, thick linens – but the rest of the property's lodging, including several modern, sustainably built cottages, are equally peaceful. The shaded garden, walled-in swimming pool, brick patios and big porches exude a timeless elegance. Garden rooms come with Japanese soaking tubs, all heated and cooled by an energy-efficient geothermal-solar system.

Featherbed Railroad Co HOTEL $$
(707-274-8378, 800-966-6322; www.featherbedrailroad.com; 2870 Lakeshore Blvd, Nice; cabooses incl breakfast $140-190;) A treat for train buffs and kids, Featherbed has 10 comfy, real cabooses on a grassy lawn. Some of the cabooses straddle the border between kitschy and tacky (the 'Easy Rider' has a Harley Davidson headboard and a mirrored ceiling), but they're great fun if you keep a sense of humor. There's a tiny beach across the road.

Sea Breeze Resort COTTAGES $$
(707-998-3327; www.seabreezeresort.net; 9595 Harbor Dr, Glenhaven; cottages with kitchen $130-150, without $100; Apr-Oct;) Just south of Lucerne on a small peninsula, gardens surround seven spotless lakeside cottages. All have barbecues.

MIDDLETOWN

Harbin Hot Springs SPA $$
(707-987-2377, 800-622-2477; www.harbin.org; Harbin Hot Springs Rd; tent & RV sites midweek/weekend $25/35, dm $35/50, s midweek $60-75, weekend $95-120, d midweek $90-190, weekend $140-260) Harbin is classic Northern California. Originally a 19th-century health spa and resort, it now has a retreat-center vibe and people come to unwind in silent, clothing-optional hot- and cold-spring pools. This is the birthplace of Watsu (floating massage) and there are wonderful body therapies as well as yoga, holistic-health workshops and 1160 acres of hiking. Accommodations are in Victorian buildings (which could use sprucing up) and share a common vegetarian-only kitchen. Food is available at the market, cafe and restaurant. Day-trippers are welcome; day rates are $25 and require one member of your group to purchase a membership (one month $10).

The springs are 3 miles off Hwy 175. From Middletown, take Barnes St, which becomes Big Canyon Rd, and head left at the fork.

Entertainment

Library Park, in Lakeport, has free lakeside Friday-evening **summer concerts**, with blues and rockabilly tunes to appeal to middle-aged roadtrippers. Harbin Hot Springs (p231) presents a surprising line-up of world music and dances. The Konocti Harbor Resort & Spa (p230) hosts national acts (recent guests include Los Lonely Boys and Lyle Lovett) in an outdoor amphitheater and indoor concert hall.

Information

Lake County Visitor Information Center (www.lakecounty.com; 6110 E Hwy 120, Lucerne; 9am-5pm Mon-Sat, noon-4pm Sun) Has complete information and an excellent website, which allows potential visitors to narrow their focus by interests.

Getting Around

Lake Transit (707-263-3334, 707-994-3334; www.laketransit.org) operates weekday routes between Middletown and Calistoga ($3.50, 35 minutes, three daily); on Thursday it connects through to Santa Rosa. Buses serve Ukiah ($3.50, two hours, four daily), from Clearlake via

TOP ANDERSON VALLEY WINERIES

The valley's cool nights yield high-acid, fruit-forward, food-friendly wines. Pinot noir, chardonnay and dry gewürztraminer flourish. Most **wineries** (www.avwines.com) sit outside Philo. Many are family-owned and offer tastings, some give tours. The following are particularly noteworthy.

» **Navarro** (www.navarrowine.com; 5601 Hwy 128; ⏲10am-6pm) The best option, and picnicking is encouraged.

» **Esterlina** (www.esterlinavineyards.com) For big reds, pack a picnic and head high up the rolling hills; call ahead.

» **Husch** (www.huschvineyards.com; 4400 Hwy 128; ⏲10am-5pm) Husch serves exquisite tastings inside a rose-covered cottage.

Lakeport ($2.25, 1¼ hours, seven daily). Since piecing together routes and times can be difficult, it's best to phone ahead.

Anderson Valley

Rolling hills surround pastoral Anderson Valley, famous for apple orchards, vineyards, pastures and quiet. Visitors come primarily to winery-hop, but there's good hiking and bicycling in the hills, and the chance to escape civilization. Traveling through the valley is the most common route to Mendocino from San Francisco.

Sights & Activities

Boonville (population 1370) and **Philo** (population 1000) are the valley's principal towns. From Ukiah, winding Hwy 253 heads 20 miles south to Boonville. Equally scenic Hwy 128 twists and turns 60 miles between Cloverdale on Hwy 101, south of Hopland, and Albion on coastal Hwy 1.

Apple Farm ORCHARD
(☎707-895-2333; www.philoapplefarm.com; 18501 Greenwood Rd, Philo; ⏲daylight) For the best fruit, skip the obvious roadside stands and head to this gorgeous farm for organic preserves, chutneys, heirloom apples and pears. It also hosts **cooking classes** with some of the Wine Country's best chefs. You can make a weekend out of it by staying in one of the orchard cottages (p232).

Anderson Valley Brewing Company BREWERY, FRISBEE GOLF
(☎707-895-2337; www.avbc.com; 17700 Hwy 253; tours $5; ⏲11am-6pm) East of the Hwy 128 crossroads, this solar-powered brewery crafts award-winning beers in a Bavarian-style brewhouse. You can also toss around a disc on the course while enjoying the brews, but, be warned, the sun can take its toll. Tours leave at 1:30pm and 3pm daily (only Tuesday and Wednesday in winter); call ahead.

Anderson Valley Historical Society Museum MUSEUM
(www.andersonvalleymuseum.org; 12340 Hwy 128; ⏲1-4pm Fri-Sun Feb-Nov) In a recently renovated little red schoolhouse west of Boonville, this museum displays historical artifacts.

Festivals & Events

Pinot Noir Festival WINE
(www.avwines.com) One of Anderson Valley's many wine celebrations.

Sierra Nevada World Music Festival MUSIC
(www.snwmf.com) In June, the sounds of reggae and roots fill the air, co-mingling with the scent of Mendocino county's *other* cash crop.

California Wool & Fiber Festival CRAFT
(www.fiberfestival.com) Events with names like 'Angora Rabbit Demonstration' bring out the natural-fiber fanatics from around the state.

Mendocino County Fair FAIR
(www.mendocountyfair.com) A county classic in mid-September.

Sleeping

Accommodations fill on weekends.

TOP CHOICE **Apple Farm** COTTAGES $$$
(☎707-895-2333; www.philoapplefarm.com; 18501 Greenwood Rd, Philo; r midweek/weekend $175/250) Set within the orchard, guests of Philo's bucolic Apple Farm choose from four exquisite cottages, each built with reclaimed materials. With bright, airy spaces, polished

plank floors, simple furnishings and views of the surrounding trees, each one is an absolute dream. Red Door cottage is a favorite because of the bathroom – you can soak in the slipper tub, or shower on the private deck under the open sky. The cottages often get booked with participants of the farm's **cooking classes**, so book well in advance. For a swim, the Navarro River is within walking distance.

Boonville Hotel BOUTIQUE HOTEL **$$**
(☎707-895-2210; www.boonvillehotel.com; 14040 Hwy 128; r $125-200, ste $225) Decked out in a contemporary American-country style with sea-grass flooring, pastel colors and fine linens that would make Martha Stewart proud, this historic hotel's rooms are safe for urbanites who refuse to abandon style just because they've gone to the country.

Hendy Woods State Park CAMPGROUND **$**
(☎707-937-5804, reservations 800-444-7275; www.reserveamerica.com; tent & RV sites $35, cabins $50) Bordered by the Navarro River on Hwy 128, west of Philo, the park has hiking, picnicking and a forested campground with hot showers.

Other Place COTTAGES **$$**
(☎707-895-3979; www.sheepdung.com; cottages $140-200;) Outside of town, 500 acres of ranch land surrounds private hilltop cottages.

Eating & Drinking

Boonville restaurants seem to open and close as they please, so expect variations in the hours listed below based on season and whimsy. There are several places along Hwy 128 which can supply a picnic with fancy local cheese and fresh bread.

Table 128 NEW AMERICAN **$$**
(☎707-895-2210; www.boonvillehotel.com; 14040 Hwy 128; 3-/4-course prixe fixe $40/50; 5-9pm Thu-Mon) Food-savvy travelers love the constantly changing New American menu here, featuring simple dishes done well, like roasted chicken, grilled local lamb and strawberry shortcake. The family-style service makes dinner here a freewheeling, elegant social affair, with big farm tables and soft lighting.

Paysenne ICE CREAM **$**
(14111 Hwy 128; ice cream cone $3; 10am-3pm Thu-Mon) Booneville's new ice-cream shop serves the innovative flavors of Three Twins Ice Cream, whose delightful flavors include Lemon Cookie and Strawberry Je Ne Sais Quoi (which has a hint of balsamic vinegar).

Boonville General Store DELI **$**
(17810 Farrer Lane; dishes $5-8; 7:30am-3pm Mon-Fri from 8:30am Sat & Sun, pizza night Fri 5:30-8pm) Opposite the Boonville Hotel, this deli is good to stock up for picnics, offering sandwiches on homemade bread, thin-crust pizzas and organic cheeses.

Lauren's AMERICAN **$$**
(www.laurensgoodfood.com; 14211 Hwy 128, Boonville; mains $8-14; 5-9pm Tue-Sat;) Locals pack Lauren's for eclectic homemade cookin' and a good wine list. Musicians sometimes jam on the stage by the front window.

Information

Anderson Valley Chamber of Commerce
(☎707-895-2379; www.andersonvalleychamber.com) Has tourist information and a complete schedule of annual events.

Ukiah

As the county seat and Mendocino's largest city, Ukiah is mostly a utilitarian stop for travelers to refuel the car and get a bite. But, if you have to stop here for the night, you could do much worse: the town is a friendly place, there are a plethora of cookie-cutter hotel chains, some cheaper midcentury motels and a handful of good dining options. The coolest attractions, a pair of thermal springs and a sprawling campus for Buddhist studies, lie outside the city limits.

BOONTLING

Boonville is famous for its unique language, 'Boontling,' which evolved about the turn of the 20th century when Boonville was very remote. Locals developed the language to *shark* (stump) outsiders and amuse themselves. You may hear *codgie kimmies* (old men) asking for a horn of *zeese* (a cup of coffee) or some *bahl gorms* (good food). If you are really lucky, you'll spot the tow truck called Boont Region De-arkin' Moshe (literally 'Anderson Valley Unwrecking Machine').

Sights

Grace Hudson Museum-Sun House MUSEUM
(www.gracehudsonmuseum.org; 431 S Main St; donation $2; ⏲10am-4:30pm Wed-Sat, from noon Sun) One block east of State St, the collection's mainstays are paintings by Grace Hudson (1865–1937). Her sensitive depictions of Pomo people complement the ethnological work and Native American baskets collected by her husband, John Hudson.

Festivals & Events

Redwood Empire Fair COUNTY FAIR
(www.redwoodempirefair.com) On the second weekend of August.

Ukiah Country PumpkinFest CULTURAL
(www.cityofukiah.com) In late October, with an arts-and-crafts fair, children's carnival and fiddle contest.

Sleeping

Every imaginable chain resort is here, just off the highway. For something with more personality, resorts and campgrounds cluster around Ukiah (see p235).

Sanford House B&B B&B $$
(☎707-462-1653; www.sanfordhouse.com; 306 S Pine St; s/d $95/175; ❄) This well-preserved Victorian is situated among a lovely garden. The rooms fit the standard of northern California's other Victorian B&Bs – lace curtains, wicker chairs, floral wallpaper and brass beds. The sweet owners offer an organic breakfast.

Sunrise Inn MOTEL $
(☎707-462-6601; www.sunriseinn.net; 650 S State St; r $58-78; ❄📶) Request one of the remodeled rooms at Ukiah's best budget motel. All have microwaves and refrigerators.

Discovery Inn Motel MOTEL $
(☎707-462-8873; www.discoveryinnukiahca.com; 1340 N State St; r $55-95; ❄📶🏊) Clean, but dated with a 75ft pool and several Jacuzzis.

Eating

It'd be a crime to eat the fast food junk located off the highway; Ukiah has a lot of affordable, excellent eateries.

TOP CHOICE **Oco Time** JAPANESE $$
(☎707-462-2422; www.ocotime.com; 111 W Church St; lunch mains $7-10, dinner mains $8-16; ⏲11:15am-2:30pm Tue-Fri, 5:30-8:30pm Mon-Sat; 🅥) Shoulder your way through the locals to get Ukiah's best sushi, noodle bowls and *oco* (a delicious mess of seaweed, grilled cabbage, egg and noodles). The 'Peace Café' has a great vibe, a friendly staff and interesting special rolls. Downside? The place gets mobbed, so reservations are a good idea.

Patrona NEW AMERICAN $$
(☎707-462-9181; www.patronarestaurant.com; 130 W Standley St; lunch mains $10-15, dinner mains $15-28; ⏲11am-3pm & 5-9pm Tue-Sat; 🅥) Foodies flock to excellent Patrona for earthy, flavor-packed, seasonal and regional organic cooking. The unfussy menu includes dishes like roasted chicken, brined-and-roasted pork chops, housemade pasta and local wines. Make reservations and ask about the prix fixe.

Ukiah Brewing Company BREWPUB $$
(www.ukiahbrewingco.com; 102 S State St, Ukiah; dinner mains $15-25; ⏲11:30am-9pm Sun-Thu, to 10pm Fri-Sat; 📶) The brews might outshine the food – barely – but there's no question that the dance floor is the most happening spot downtown. When it gets rowdy to live music on the weekend, this place is a blast. The menu has a strong organic and sustainable bent, with plenty of vegan and raw options.

Schat's Courthouse Bakery & Cafe CAFE $
(www.schats.com; 113 W Perkins St; lunch mains $3-7, dinner mains $8-14; ⏲5:30am-6pm Mon-Fri, to 5pm Sat) Founded by Dutch bakers, Schat's makes a dazzling array of chewy, dense breads, sandwiches, wraps, big salads, dee-lish hot mains and homemade pastries.

Kilkenny Kitchen CAFE $
(www.kilkennykitchen.com; 1093 S Dora St; lunch $7-10; ⏲10am-3pm Mon-Fri; 🅥) Tucked into a neighborhood south of downtown, county workers love this chipper yellow place for the fresh rotation of daily soups and sandwich specials (a recent visit on a blazing hot day found a heavenly, cold cucumber dill soup). The salads – like the pear, walnut and blue cheese – are also fantastic.

Himalayan Cafe HIMALAYAN $
(www.thehimalayancafe.com; 1639 S State St; mains lunch $9-13, dinner $10-17; 🅥) South of

downtown, find delicately spiced Nepalese cooking – tandoori breads and curries.

Ukiah farmers market MARKET
(cnr School & Clay Sts; 8:30am-noon Sat May-Oct, 3-6pm Tue Jun-Oct) The market offers farm-fresh produce, crafts and entertainment.

Drinking & Entertainment

Dive bars and scruffy cocktail lounges line State St. Ask at the chamber of commerce about cultural events, including Sunday summer concerts at Todd Grove Park, which have a delightfully festive atmosphere, and local square dances.

Ukiah Brewing Co BREWERY
(www.ukiahbrewingco.com; 102 S State St;) A great place to drink, this local brewpub makes organic beer and draws weekend crowds.

Coffee Critic COFFEE SHOP
(www.thecoffeecritic.com; 476 N State St;) Drop in for fair trade espresso, ice cream and occasional live music.

Shopping

Ukiah has a pleasant, walkable shopping district along School St near the courthouse.

Nomad's World JEWELRY, HOMEWARES
(www.nomads-world.com; 111 S School St; Mon-Sat) Step inside for cool jewelry and home furnishings.

Ruby Slippers VINTAGE
(110 N School St; Wed-Sat) Take turns trying on vintage drag.

Mendocino Book Co BOOKS
(www.mendocinobookcompany.com; 102 S School St; Mon-Sat) The best bookstore in town.

Information

Running north–south, west of Hwy 101, State St is Ukiah's main drag. School St, near Perkins St, is also good for strolling.

Bureau of Land Management (707-468-4000; 2550 N State St) Maps and information on backcountry camping, hiking and biking in wilderness areas.

Greater Ukiah Chamber of Commerce (707-462-4705; www.gomendo.com; 200 S School St; 9am-5pm Mon-Fri) One block west of State St; information on Ukiah, Hopland and Anderson Valley.

Around Ukiah

UKIAH WINERIES

You'll notice the acres of grapes stretching out in every direction on your way into town. Winemakers around Ukiah enjoy much of the same climatic conditions that made Napa so famous. Pick up a wineries map from the Ukiah chamber of commerce (p235).

Parducci Wine Cellars WINERY
(www.parducci.com; 501 Parducci Rd, Ukiah; 10am-5pm) Sustainably grown, harvested and produced, 'America's Greenest Winery' produces affordable, bold, earthy reds. The tasting room, lined in brick and soft light, is a perfect little cave-like environment to get out of the summer heat, sip wine and chat about sustainability practices.

Fife WINERY
(707-485-0323; www.fifevineyards.com; 3621 Ricetti Lane, Redwood Valley; 10am-5pm) Fruit-forward reds include a peppery zinfandel and petite sirah, both affordable and food-friendly. And oh, the hilltop views! Bring a picnic.

Germain-Robin DISTILLERY
(707-462-0314; Unit 35, 3001 S State St; by appointment) Makes some of the world's best brandy, which is handcrafted by a fifth-generation brandy-maker from the Cognac region of France. It's just a freeway-side warehouse, but if you're into cognac, you gotta come.

VICHY HOT SPRINGS RESORT

Opened in 1854, Vichy is the oldest continuously operating mineral-springs spa in California. The water's composition perfectly matches that of its famous namesake in Vichy, France. A century ago, Mark Twain, Jack London and Robert Louis Stevenson traveled here for the water's restorative properties, which ameliorate everything from arthritis to poison oak.

Today, the beautifully maintained historic **resort** (707-462-9515; www.vichysprings.com; 2605 Vichy Springs Rd, Ukiah; lodge s/d $135/195, creekside r $195/245, cottages from $280;) has the only warm-water, naturally carbonated mineral baths in North America. Unlike others, Vichy requires swimsuits (rentals $2). Day use costs $30 for two hours, $50 for a full day.

Facilities include a swimming pool, outdoor mineral hot tub, 10 indoor and outdoor tubs with natural 100°F waters, and a grotto for sipping the effervescent waters. Massages and facials are available. Entry includes use of the 700-acre grounds, abutting Bureau of Land Management (BLM) lands; hiking trails lead to a 40ft waterfall, an old cinnabar mine and 1100ft peaks – great for sunset views.

The resort's suite and two cottages, built in 1854, are Mendocino County's three oldest structures. The cozy rooms have wooden floors, top-quality beds, breakfast and spa privileges, and no TVs.

From Hwy 101, exit at Vichy Springs Rd and follow the state-landmark signs east for 3 miles. Ukiah is five minutes, but a world, away.

ORR HOT SPRINGS

A clothing-optional resort that's beloved by locals, back-to-the-land hipsters, backpackers and liberal-minded tourists, **springs** (☎707-462-6277; tent sites $45-50, d $140-160, cottages $195-230; ⏲10am-10pm;) has private tubs, a sauna, spring-fed rock-bottomed swimming pool, steam, massage and magical gardens. Day use costs $25, $20 on Mondays.

Accommodation includes use of the spa and communal kitchen; some cottages have kitchens. Reservations are essential.

To get there from Hwy 101, take N State St exit, go north a quarter of a mile to Orr Springs Rd, then 9 miles west. The steep, winding mountain road takes 30 minutes to drive.

MONTGOMERY WOODS STATE RESERVE

Two miles west of Orr, this 1140-acre **reserve** (Orr Springs Rd) protects five old-growth redwood groves, and some of the best groves within a day's drive from San Francisco. A 2-mile loop trail crosses the creek, winding through the serene groves, starting near the picnic tables and toilets. It's out of the way, so visitors are likely to have it mostly to themselves. Day use only; no camping.

LAKE MENDOCINO

Amid rolling hills, 5 miles northeast of Ukiah, this tranquil 1822-acre artificial lake fills a valley, once the ancestral home of the Pomo people. On the lake's north side, **Pomo Visitor Center** (☎707-467-4200) is modeled after a Pomo roundhouse, with exhibits on tribal culture and the dam. The center was closed indefinitely for upgrades at the time of update, but was still offering information via phone about camping.

Coyote Dam, 3500ft long and 160ft high, marks the lake's southwest corner; the lake's eastern part is a 689-acre protected wildlife habitat. The **Army Corps of Engineers** (www.spn.usace.army.mil/mendocino; 1160 Lake Mendocino Dr; ⏲8am-4pm Mon-Fri) built the dam, manages the lake and provides recreation information. Its office is inconveniently located on the lower lake.

There are 300 **tent and RV sites** (☎877-444-6777; www.reserveusa.com; $20-22), most with hot showers and primitive boat-in sites ($8).

CITY OF TEN THOUSAND BUDDHAS

Three miles east of Ukiah, via Talmage Rd, the **site** (☎707-462-0939; www.cttbusa.org; 2001 Talmage Rd; ⏲8am-6pm) used to be a state mental hospital. Since 1976 it has been a lush, quiet 488-acre Chinese-Buddhist community. Don't miss the temple hall, which really does have 10,000 Buddhas. As this is a place of worship, please be respectful of those who use the grounds for meditating. Stay for lunch in the vegetarian Chinese **restaurant** (4951 Bodhi Way; mains $10; ⏲noon-3pm;).

Willits

Twenty miles north of Ukiah, Willits mixes NorCal dropouts with loggers and ranchers (the high school has a bull-riding team). Lamp posts of the main drag are decorated with bucking broncos and cowboys, but the heart of the place is just as boho. Though ranching, timber and manufacturing may be its mainstays, tie-dye is de rigueur. For visitors, Willits' greatest claim to fame is as the eastern terminus of the Skunk Train. Fort Bragg is 35 miles away on the coast; allow an hour to navigate twisty Hwy 20.

Sights & Activities

Ten miles north of Willits, **Hwy 162/Covelo Rd** makes for a superb drive following the route of the Northwestern Pacific Railroad along the Eel River and through the Mendocino National Forest. The trip is only about 30 miles, but plan on taking at least an hour on the winding road, passing exquisite river canyons and rolling hills. Eventually, you'll reach **Covelo**, known for its unusual round valley.

Skunk Train HISTORIC TRAIN
(☎707-964-6371, 866-866-1690; www.skunktrain.com; adult/child $49/24) The depot is on E Commercial St, three blocks east of Hwy 101. Trains run between Willits and Fort Bragg (p225).

Mendocino County Museum MUSEUM
(www.mendocinomuseum.org; 400 E Commercial St; adult/child $4/1; ⊙10am-4:30pm Wed-Sun) Among the best community museum's in the northern half of the state, this puts the lives of early settlers in excellent historical context – much drawn from old letters – and there's an entire 1920s soda fountain and barber shop inside. You could spend an hour perusing Pomo and Yuki basketry and artifacts, or reading about local scandals and countercultural movements. Outside, the **Roots of Motive Power** (www.rootsofmotivepower.com) exhibit occasionally demonstrates steam logging and machinery.

Ridgewood Ranch RANCH
(☎reservations 707-459-7910; www.seabiscuitheritage.com; 16200 N Hwy 101; tours $15-25) Willits' most famous resident was the horse Seabiscuit, which grew up here. Ninety-minute tours operate on Monday, Wednesday and Friday (June to September); once a month on Saturday there's a three-hour tour by reservation.

Jackson Demonstration State Forest HIKING
Fifteen miles west of Willits on Hwy 20, the forest offers day-use recreational activities, including educational hiking trails and mountain-biking. You can also camp here (see p237).

Festivals & Events

Willits Frontier Days & Rodeo RODEO
(www.willitsfrontierdays.com) Dating from 1926, Willits has the oldest continuous rodeo in California, occurring the first week in July.

Willits Renaissance Faire CULTURAL
(www.willitsfaire.com) Held in August, featuring Highland Scottish games, food, music, jugglers, arts and crafts.

Sleeping

Some of the in-town motels – and there seems to be about a hundred of them – are dumps, so absolutely check out the room before checking in. Ask about Skunk Train packages. There are a couple crowded, loud RV parks on the edges of town for only the most desperate campers.

Baechtel Creek Inn & Spa BOUTIQUE HOTEL $$
(☎707-459-9063, 800-459-9911; www.baechtelcreekinn.com; 101 Gregory Lane; d incl breakfast $100-130; ❄@≋) As Willits' only upscale option, this place draws an interesting mix: Japanese bus tours, business travelers and wine trippers. The standard rooms are nothing too flashy, but they have top knotch linens, iPod docks and tasteful art. Custom rooms come with local wine and more space. The immaculate pool and lovely egg breakfast on the patio are perks.

Best Value Inn Holiday Lodge MOTEL $
(☎707-459-5361, 800-835-3972; www.bestvalueinn.com; 1540 S Main St; d from $63; ❄📶≋) It's a bit of a draw between the 1950s motels that line Willits' main drag, but this is our favorite because of the kind staff and relatively quiet rooms.

Jackson Demonstration State Forest CAMPGROUND $
(☎707-964-5674; sites free) Campsites have barbecue pits and pit toilets, but no water. Get a permit from the on-site host, or from a self-registration kiosk.

Eating

TOP CHOICE **Zaza's Bakery, Bistro & Gallery** BAKERY, CAFE $
(35 E Commercial St; pastries $2-4, sandwiches $8; ⊙9am-2pm) So far, little Zaza's is the only bakery in California to sell a bagel that could be mistaken for one baked in New York. And that's only where the delightful surprises begin: a delicious, delicate soup menu that changes every day (last visit it was red snapper, corn and coconut chowder), a bright atmosphere completed by good artwork, jazz on the radio and hearty sandwiches on nutty, multigrain bread.

Purple Thistle FUSION $$
(☎707-459-4750; 50 S Main St; mains $13-25; ⊙5-9pm) Willits' best fine dining; cooks up Cajun- and Japanese-inspired 'Mendonesian' cuisine, using fresh organic ingredients. Make reservations, and expect it to be a bit crowded.

Loose Caboose Cafe SANDWICHES $
(10 Woods St; sandwiches $7-10; ⊙7:30am-3pm) People tend to get a bit flushed when talking about the sandwiches at the Loose Caboose,

which gets jammed at lunch. The Reuben and Sante Fe Chicken sandwiches are two savory delights.

Burrito Exquisito MEXICAN $
(42 S Hain St; mains $7; ⌚11am-7pm) A cute hippie burrito shop dishes out big burritos, which you can eat in the back garden.

Ardella's Kitchen DINER $$
(35 E Commercial St; mains $5-11; ⌚6am-noon Tue-Sat) For quick eats, this tiny place is tops for breakfast – and is *the* place for gossip.

Mariposa Market GROCERIES $
(600 S Main St) Willits natural food outlet.

Drinking & Entertainment

Shanachie Pub BAR
(50B S Main St; ⌚Mon-Sat) Sharing the garden with Burrito Exquisito, this is a friendly little dive with tons on tap.

Willits Community Theatre THEATER
(www.willitstheatre.org; 212 S Main St) Stages award-winning plays, poetry readings and comedy.

Shopping

JD Redhouse & Co CLOTHING, HOMEWARES
(212 S Main St; ⌚10am-6pm) Family-owned and operated, this central mercantile is a good reflection of Willits itself, balancing cowboy essentials – boots and grain, tools and denim – with treats for the weekend tourist. The ice cream counter is a good place to cool off when the heat on the sidewalk gets intense.

Book Juggler BOOKS
(50B S Main St; ⌚10am-7pm Mon-Thu, to 8pm Fri, 10am-6pm Sat, noon-5pm Sun) Has dense rows of new and used books, music books and local papers (pick up the weird, locally printed *Anderson Valley Advertiser* here).

SOUTHERN REDWOOD COAST

There's some real magic in the loamy soil and misty air 'beyond the redwood curtain'; it yields the tallest trees and most potent herb on the planet. North of Fort Bragg, Bay Area weekenders and antique-stuffed B&Bs give way to lumber wars, pot farmers and an army of carved bears. The 'growing' culture here is palpable and the huge profit it brings to the region has evident cultural side effects – an omnipresent population of transients who work the harvests, a chilling respect for 'No Trespassing' signs and a political culture that is an uneasy balance between gun-toting libertarians, ultra-left progressives and typical college-town chaos. Nevertheless, the reason to visit is to soak in the magnificent landscape, which runs through a number of pristine, ancient redwood forests.

Information

Redwood Coast Heritage Trails (www.redwoods.info) Gives a nuanced slant on the region with itineraries based around lighthouses, Native American culture, the timber and rail industries, and maritime life.

Leggett

Leggett marks the redwood country's beginning and Hwy 1's end. There ain't much but an expensive gas station, pizza joint and two markets.

Visit 1000-acre **Standish-Hickey State Recreation Area** (69350 Hwy 101; day use $8), 1.5 miles to the north, for picnicking, swimming and fishing in the Eel River and hiking trails among virgin and second-growth redwoods. Year-round **campgrounds** (☎800-444-7275; www.reserveamerica.com; tent & RV sites $35) with hot showers book up in summer. Avoid highway-side sites.

Chandelier Drive-Thru Tree Park (www.drivethrutree.com; Drive-Thru Tree Rd; per car $5; ⌚8am-dusk) has 200 private acres of virgin redwoods with picnicking and nature walks. And yes, there's a redwood with a square hole carved out, which cars can drive through. Only in America.

The 1949 tourist trap of **Confusion Hill** (www.confusionhill.com; 75001 N Hwy 101; adult/child Gravity House $5/4, train rides $8.50/6.50; ⌚9am-6pm May-Sep, 10am-5pm Oct-Apr; 👪) is an enduring curiosity and the most elaborate of the old-fashioned stops that line the route north. The Gravity House challenges queasy visitors to keep their balance while standing at a 40-degree angle (a rad photo op). Kids and fans of kitsch go nuts for the playhouse quality of the space and the narrow-gauge train rides are exciting for toddlers.

For basic supplies, visit **Price's Peg House** (☎707-925-6444; 69501 Hwy 101; ⌚8am-9pm).

Richardson Grove State Park

Fifteen miles to the north, and bisected by the Eel River, serene **Richardson Grove** (Hwy 101; per car $8) occupies 1400 acres of virgin forest. Many trees are over 1000 years old and 300ft tall, but there aren't many hiking trails. In winter, there's good fishing for silver and king salmon. At the time of research, CalTrans was considering widening the road through Richardson Grove, which sparked an intense protest.

The **visitor center** (☎707-247-3318; ⏰9am-2pm) sells books inside a 1930s lodge, which often has a fire going during cool weather. The park is primarily a **campground** (☎reservations 800-444-7275; www.reserveamerica.com; tent & RV sites $35) with three separate areas with hot showers; some remain open year-round. Summer-only Oak Flat on the east side of the river is shady and has a sandy beach.

Benbow Lake

On the Eel River, 2 miles south of Garberville, the 1200-acre **Benbow Lake State Recreation Area** (☎summer 707-923-3238, winter 707-923-3318; per car $8) exists when a seasonal dam forms the 26-acre Benbow Lake, mid-June to mid-September. In mid-August, avoid swimming in the lake or river until two weeks after the Reggae on the River festival (p240), when 25,000 people use the river as a bathtub. The water is cleanest in early summer. The year-round riverside **campground** (☎reservations 800-444- 7275; www.reserveamerica.com; tent & RV sites $35) is subject to wintertime bridge closures due to flooding. This part of the Eel has wide banks and is also excellent for swimming and sunbathing. You can avoid the day use fee by parking near the bridge and walking down to the river. According to a ranger, you can float from here all the way through the redwood groves along the Avenue of the Giants.

Benbow Inn (☎707-923-2124, 800-355-3301; www.benbowinn.com; 445 Lake Benbow Dr; r $90-305, cottage $395-595; ❄📶🚭) is a monument to 1920s rustic elegance; the Redwood Empire's first luxury resort is a national historic landmark. Hollywood's elite once frolicked in the Tudor-style resort's lobby, where you can play chess by the crackling fire, and enjoy complimentary afternoon tea and evening hors d'oeuvres. Rooms have top-quality beds and antique furniture. The window-lined dining room (br eakfast and lunch $10 to $15, dinner mains $22 to $32) serves excellent meals and the rib eye earns raves.

Garberville

The main supply center for southern Humboldt County is the primary jumping-off point for both the Lost Coast, to the west, and the Avenue of the Giants, to the north. There's an uneasy relationship between the old-guard loggers and the hippies, many of whom came in the 1970s to grow sinsemilla (potent, seedless marijuana) after the feds chased them out of Santa Cruz. At last count, the hippies were winning the culture wars, but it rages on: a sign on the door of a local bar reads simply: 'Absolutely NO patchouli oil!!!' Two miles west, Garberville's ragtag sister, Redway, has fewer services. Garberville is about four hours north of San Francisco, one hour south of Eureka.

Festivals & Events

The **Mateel Community Center** (www.mateel.org), in Redway, is the nerve center for many of the area's long-running annual festivals, which celebrate everything from hemp to miming.

Reggae on the River/Reggae Rising MUSIC
(www.reggaeontheriver.com) In mid-July, drawing huge crowds for reggae, world music, arts and craft fairs, camping and swimming in the river.

Avenue of the Giants Marathon MARATHON
(www.theave.org) Among the nation's most picturesque marathons, held in May.

Harley-Davidson Redwood Run MOTORCYCLE RALLY
(www.redwoodrun.com) The redwoods rumble with the sound of hundreds of shiny bikes in June.

Sleeping

Garberville is lined with motels, and many of them are serviceable, if uninspiring. South of town, Benbow Inn (p239) blows away the competition. For cheaper lodging, there are two satisfactory motels. First try **Sherwood Forest** (707-923-2721; www.sherwoodforestmotel.com; 814 Redwood Dr; r $66-84;), then **Humboldt Redwoods Inn** (707-923-2451; www.humboldtredwoodsinn.com; 987 Redwood Dr; r $59-95;), though the desk clerks are hardly ever there, so call ahead.

Eating & Drinking

Woodrose Café BREAKFAST $
(www.woodrosecafe.com; 911 Redwood Dr; meals $7-11; 7am-1pm;) Garberville's beloved cafe serves organic omelettes, veggie scrambles and buckwheat pancakes with *real* maple syrup in a cozy room. Lunch brings crunchy salads, sandwiches with all-natural meats and good burritos. No credit cards.

Cecil's New Orleans Bistro CAJUN $$$
(www.cecilsrestaurant.com; 733 Redwood Dr; dinner mains $20-26; 6-10pm Thu-Mon) This 2nd story eatery overlooks Main St and serves ambitious dishes that may have minted the California-Cajun style. Start with fried green tomatoes before launching into the smoked boar gumbo.

Mateel Café AMERICAN $$
(3342-3344 Redwood Dr, Redway; mains lunch $8-12, dinner $20-26; 11:30am-9pm Mon-Sat) The big, diverse menu of this Redway joint includes a rack of lamb, stone-baked pizzas and terrific salads. There's pleasant patio seating out back.

Chautauqua Natural Foods HEALTH FOOD $
(436 Church St; sandwiches & lunch plates $5-10; 10am-6pm Mon-Sat) Sells natural groceries. It has a small dining area and a great bulletin board.

Nacho Mama MEXICAN $
(375 Sprowel Creek Rd; meals under $6; 11am-7pm Mon-Sat) A tiny shack on the corner of Redwood Dr with organic fast-food Mexican.

Calico's Deli & Pasta ITALIAN $
(808 Redwood Dr; dishes $6-13; 11am-9pm;) Calico's has house-made pasta and sandwiches, and is good for kids.

Branding Iron Saloon BAR $
(744 Redwood Dr) Craft beer, nice locals and a hopping pool table. We'll forgive the stripper pole in the middle of the room.

Information

Garberville-Redway Area Chamber of Commerce (www.garberville.org; 784 Redwood Dr; 10am-4pm May-Aug, Mon-Fri Sep-Apr) Inside the Redwood Dr Center.

KMUD FM91 (www.kmud.org) Find out what's really happening by tuning in to community radio.

Lost Coast

The North Coast's superlative backpacking destination is a rugged, mystifying stretch of coast where narrow dirt trails ascend rugged coastal peaks and volcanic beaches of black sand and ethereal mist hovers above the roaring surf as majestic Roosevelt elk graze the forests. Here, the rugged King Range boldly rises 4000ft within 3 miles of the coast between where Hwy 1 cuts inland north of Westport to just south of Ferndale. The coast became 'lost' when the state's highway system deemed the region impassable in the early 20th century.

The best hiking and camping is within the King Range National Conservation Area and the Sinkyone Wilderness State Park, which make up the central and southern stretch of the region. The area north of the King Range is more accessible, if less dramatic.

In autumn, the weather is clear and cool. Wildflowers bloom from April through May and gray whales migrate from December through April. The warmest, driest months are June to August, but days are foggy. Note that the weather can quickly change.

Hiking

The best way to see the Lost Coast is to hike, and the best hiking is through the southern regions within the Sinkyone and Kings Range Wilderness areas. Some of the best trails start from Mattole Campground, just south Petrolia, which is on the northern border of the Kings Range. It's at the ocean end of Lighthouse Rd, 4 miles from Mattole Rd (sometimes marked as Hwy 211), southeast of Petrolia.

The **Lost Coast Trail** follows 24.7 miles of coastline from Mattole Campground in the north to Black Sands Beach at Shelter Cove in the south. The prevailing northerly winds make it best to hike from north to south; plan for three or four days. In October and November, and April and May, the weather is iffy and winds can blow south to north, depending on whether there's a low-pressure system overhead. The best times to come are summer weekdays in early June, at the end of August, September and October. The trail will often have hikers; busiest times are Memorial Day, Labor Day and summer weekends. Only two shuttles have permits to transport backpackers through the area, **Lost Coast Trail Transport Services** (☎707-986-9909; www.lostcoasttrail.com) or the more reliable **Lost Coast Shuttle** (☎707-223-1547; www.lostcoastshuttle.com). Neither is cheap; prices for the ride between Mattole and Black Sands Beach start at $100 per person with a two-person minimum.

Highlights include an abandoned lighthouse at Punta Gorda, remnants of early shipwrecks, tidepools and abundant wildlife including sea lions, seals and some 300 bird species. The trail is mostly level, passing beaches and crossing over rocky outcrops. Along the Lost Coast Trail, **Big Flat** is the most popular backcountry destination. Carry a tide table, lest you get trapped: from Buck Creek to Miller Creek, you can only hike during an outgoing tide.

A good **day hike** starts at the Mattole Campground trailhead and travels 3 miles south along the coast to the Punta Gorda lighthouse (return against the wind).

People have discovered the Lost Coast Trail. To ditch the crowds, take any of the (strenuous) upland trails off the beach toward the ridgeline. For a satisfying, hard 21-mile-long hike originating at the Lost Coast Trail, take Buck Creek Trail to King Crest Trail to Rattlesnake Ridge Trail. The 360 degree views from **King Peak** are stupendous, particularly with a full moon or during a meteor shower. Note that if you hike up, it can be hellishly hot on the ridges, though the coast remains cool and foggy; wear removable layers. Carry a topographical map and a compass: signage is limited.

Both Wailaki and Nadelos have developed **campgrounds** (tent sites $8) with toilets and water. There are another four developed campgrounds around the range, with toilets but no water (except Honeydew, which has purifiable creek water). There are multiple primitive walk-in sites. You'll need a bear canister and backcountry permit, both available from BLM offices.

ℹ Information

Aside from a few one-horse villages, Shelter Cove, the isolated unincorporated town 25 long miles west of Garberville, is the option for services. Get supplies in Garberville, Fort Bragg, Eureka or Arcata. The area is a patchwork of government-owned land and private property; visit the Bureau of Land Management office (p253) for information, permits and maps. There are few circuitous routes for hikers, and rangers can advise on reliable (if expensive) shuttle services in the area. A few words of caution: lots of weed is grown around here and it's wise to stay on trail to and respect no trespassing signs, lest you find yourself at the business end of someone's right to bear arms. And pot farmers don't pose the only threat: you'll want to check for ticks (Lyme disease is common) and keep food in bear-proof containers, which are required for camping.

SINKYONE WILDERNESS STATE PARK

Named for the Sinkyone people who once lived here, this 7367-acre wilderness extends south of Shelter Cove along pristine coastline. The **Lost Coast Trail** continues here for another 22 miles, from Whale Gulch south to Usal Beach Campground, taking at least three days to walk as it meanders along high ridges, providing bird's-eye views down to deserted beaches and the crashing surf (side trails descend to water level). Near the park's northern end, the (haunted!) **Needle Rock Ranch** (☎707-986-7711; tent sites $35) serves as a remote visitor center. Register here for the adjacent campsites ($25 to $35). This is the only source of potable water. For information on when the ranch is closed (most of the time), call **Richardson Grove State Park** (☎707-247-3318).

To get to Sinkyone, drive west from Garberville and Redway on Briceland-Thorn Rd, 21 miles through Whitethorn to Four Corners. Turn left (south) and continue for 3.5 miles down a very rugged road to the ranch house; it takes 1½ hours.

There's access to the **Usal Beach Campground** (tent sites $25) at the south end of the park from Hwy 1 (you can't make reservations). North of Westport, take the unpaved County Rd 431 beginning from Hwy 1's Mile 90.88 and travel 6 miles up the coast to the campground. The road is graded yearly in late spring and is passable in summer via two-wheel-drive vehicles. Most sites are past the message board by the beach. Use bear canisters or keep food in your trunk. Look for giant elk feeding on the tall grass – they live behind sites No 1 and 2 – and osprey by the creek's mouth.

North of the campground, Usal Rd (County Rd 431) is much rougher and recommended only if you have a high-clearance 4WD and a chainsaw. Seriously.

KING RANGE NATIONAL CONSERVATION AREA

Stretching over 35 miles of virgin coastline, with ridge after ridge of mountainous terrain plunging to the surf, the 60,000-acre area tops out at namesake King's Peak (4087ft). The wettest spot in California, the range receives over 120 inches – and sometimes as much as 240 inches – of annual rainfall, causing frequent landslides; in winter, snow falls on the ridges. (By contrast, nearby sea-level Shelter Cove gets only 69 inches of rain and no snow.) Two-thirds of the area is awaiting wilderness designation.

Nine miles east of Shelter Cove, the **Bureau of Land Management** (BLM; ☎707-986-5400, 707-825-2300; 768 Shelter Cove Rd; ⌚8am-4:30pm Mon-Sat Memorial Day-Labor Day, 8am-4:30pm Mon-Fri May-Sep) has maps and directions for trails and campsites; they're posted outside after hours. For overnight hikes, you'll need a backcountry-use permit. Don't turn left onto Briceland-Thorn Rd to try to find the 'town' of Whitethorn; it doesn't exist. Whitethorn is the BLM's name for the *general* area. To reach the BLM office from Garberville/Redway, follow signs to Shelter Cove; look for the roadside information panel, 0.25 miles past the post office. Information and permits are also available from the BLM in Arcata (p253).

Fire restrictions begin July 1 and last until the first soaking rain, usually in November. During this time, there are no campfires allowed outside developed campgrounds.

NORTH OF THE KING RANGE

Though it's less of an adventure, you can reach the Lost Coast's northern section year-round via paved, narrow Mattole Rd. Plan three hours to navigate the sinuous 68 miles from Ferndale in the north to the coast at Cape Mendocino, then inland to Humboldt Redwoods State Park and Hwy 101. Don't expect redwoods; the vegetation is grassland and pasture. It's beautiful in spots – lined sweeping vistas and wildflowers that are prettiest in spring.

You'll pass two tiny settlements, both 19th-century stage-coach stops. **Petrolia** has an all-in-one **store** (☎707-629-3455; ⌚9am-5pm) which rents bear canisters and sells supplies for the trail, good beer and gasoline. **Honeydew** also has a **general store**. The drive is enjoyable, but the Lost Coast's wild, spectacular scenery lies further south in the more remote regions.

SHELTER COVE

The only sizable community on the Lost Coast, Shelter Cove is surrounded by the King Range National Conservation Area and abuts a large south-facing cove. It's a tiny

DRIVE-THRU TREES

Three carved-out (but living) redwoods await along Hwy 101, a bizarre holdover from a yesteryear road trip.

Chandelier Drive-Thru Tree Fold in your mirrors and inch forward, then cool off in the uberkitschy gift shop; in Leggett.

Shrine Drive-Thru Tree Look up to the sky as you roll through, on the Ave of the Giants in Myers Flat. The least impressive of the three.

Tour Thru Tree Take exit 769 in Klamath, squeeze through a tree and check out an emu.

seaside subdivision with an airstrip in the middle – indeed, many visitors are private pilots. Fifty years ago, Southern California swindlers subdivided the land, built the airstrip and flew in potential investors, fast-talking them into buying seaside land for retirement. But they didn't tell buyers that a steep, winding, one-lane dirt road provided the *only* access and that the seaside plots were eroding into the sea.

Today, there's still only one route, but now it's paved. Cell phones don't work here: this is a good place to disappear. The town is a mild disappointment, with not much to do, but stunning **Black Sands Beach** stretches for miles northward.

Sleeping

Shelter Cove has some plain motels and decent inns, but camping is far and away the best way to spend the night here.

TOP CHOICE **Tides Inn** INN $$
(707-986-7900, 888-998-4377; www.sheltercovetidesinn.com; 59 Surf Point Rd; r from $155;) Perched above tidepools teeming with starfish and sea urchins, this is the top-choice indoor sleeping in Shelter Cove. The squeaky clean rooms offer excellent views (go for the mini suites on the 3rd floor). The suite options are good for families, and kids are greeted warmly by the innkeeper with an activity kit.

Inn of the Lost Coast INN $$
(707-986-7521, 888-570-9676; www.innofthelostcoast.com; 205 Wave Dr; r $160-250;) After a big overhaul, this renovated inn has breathtaking ocean views and clean, fireplace rooms. Downstairs there's a serviceable take-out pizza place and Shelter Cove's only breakfast joint, an espresso stand named Fish Tanks.

Oceanfront Inn & Lighthouse INN $$
(707-986-7002; www.sheltercoveoceanfrontinn.com; 10 Seal Court; r $135-165, ste $195) The tidy, modern rooms here have microwaves, refrigerators and balconies overlooking the sea. The decor is spartan so as not to detract from the view. Splurge on a kitchen suite; the best is upstairs, with its peaked ceiling and giant windows.

Shelter Cove RV Park, Campground & Deli CAMPGROUND $
(707-986-7474; 492 Machi Rd; tent/RV sites $33/43) The services may be basic, but the fresh gusts of ocean air can't be beat – the deli has good fish and chips.

Eating

The first-choice place to eat, **Cove Restaurant** (707-986-1197; 10 Seal Court; mains $6-19; 5-9pm Thu-Sun), has everything from veggie stir-fries to New York steaks. For those who are self-catering, **Shelter Cove General Store** (707-986-7733; 7272 Shelter Cove Rd) is 2 miles beyond town. Get groceries and gasoline here.

Humboldt Redwoods State Park & Avenue of the Giants

Don't miss this magical drive through California's largest redwood park, **Humboldt Redwoods State Park** (www.humboldtredwoods.org), which covers 53,000 acres – 17,000 of which are old-growth – and contains some of the world's most magnificent trees. It also boasts three-quarters of the world's tallest 100 trees. Tree huggers take note: these groves rival (and many say surpass) those in Redwood National Park, which is a long drive further north.

Exit Hwy 101 when you see the 'Avenue of the Giants' sign, take this smaller alternative to the interstate; it's an incredible, 32-mile, two-lane stretch. You'll find free driving guides at roadside signboards at both the avenue's southern entrance, 6 miles north of Garberville, near Phillipsville, and at the northern entrance, south of Scotia, at Pepperwood; there are access points off Hwy 101.

South of Weott, a volunteer-staffed **visitor center** (☎707-946-2263; ☎9am-5pm May-Sep, 10am-4pm Oct-Apr) shows videos and sells maps.

Three miles north, the **California Federation of Women's Clubs Grove** is home to an interesting four-sided hearth designed by renowned San Franciscan architect Julia Morgan in 1931 to commemorate 'the untouched nature of the forest.'

Primeval **Rockefeller Forest**, 4.5 miles west of the avenue via Mattole Rd, appears as it did a century ago. You quickly walk out of sight of cars and feel like you have fallen into the time of dinosaurs. It's the world's largest contiguous old-growth redwood forest, and contains about 20% of all such remaining trees. Check out the subtly variegated rings (count one for each year) on the cross sections of some of the downed giants that are left to mulch back into the earth over the next few hundred years.

In **Founders Grove**, north of the visitor center, the **Dyerville Giant** was knocked over in 1991 by another falling tree. A walk along its gargantuan 370ft length, with its wide trunk towering above, helps you appreciate how huge these ancient trees are.

The park has over 100 miles of trails for hiking, mountain-biking and horseback riding. Easy walks include short nature trails in Founders Grove and Rockefeller Forest and **Drury-Chaney Loop Trail** (with berry picking in summer). Challenging treks include popular **Grasshopper Peak Trail**, south of the visitor center, which climbs to the 3379ft fire lookout.

Sleeping & Eating

If you want to stay along the avenue, several towns have simple lodgings of varying calibers and levels of hospitality, but camping at Humboldt Redwoods is by far the best option.

Humboldt Redwoods State Park Campgrounds CAMPGROUND $
(☎reservations 800-444-7275; www.reserveamerica.com; tent & RV sites $20-35) The park runs three campgrounds, with hot showers, two environmental camps, five trail camps, a hike/bike camp and an equestrian camp. Of the developed spots, **Burlington Campground** is open year-round beside the visitor center and near a number of trailheads. **Hidden Springs Campground**, 5 miles south, and **Albee Creek Campground**, on Mattole Rd past Rockefeller Forest, are open mid-May to early fall.

Miranda Gardens Resort RESORT $$
(☎707-943-3011; www.mirandagardens.com; 6766 Ave of the Giants, Miranda; cottages with kitchen $165-275, without $115-175;) The best indoor stay along the avenue. The cozy, slightly rustic cottages have redwood paneling, some with fireplaces, and are spotlessly clean. The grounds – replete with outdoor ping pong and a play area for kids and swaying redwoods – have wholesome appeal for families.

Riverbend Cellars TASTING ROOM $$
(www.riverbendcellars.com; 12990 Ave of the Giants, Myers Flat; 11am-5pm) For something a bit more posh, pull over here. The El Centauro red – named for Pancho Villa – is an excellent estate-grown blend.

Groves NEW AMERICAN $$
(13065 Ave of the Giants, Myers Flat; 5-9pm) This is the most refined eating option within miles, despite an aloof staff. The menu turns out simple, brick oven pizzas, but spicy prawns and fresh salads are all artfully plated.

Chimney Tree AMERICAN $
(1111 Ave of the Giants, Phillipsville; burgers $7-11; 10am-7pm May-Sep) If you're just passing through and want something quick, come here. It raises its own grass-fed beef. Alas, the fries are frozen, but those burgers... mmm-mmm!

Scotia

For years, Scotia was California's last 'company town,' entirely owned and operated by the Pacific Lumber Company, which built cookie-cut houses and had an open contempt for long-haired outsiders who liked to get between their saws and the big trees. The company recently went belly up, sold the mill to another redwood company and, though the town still has a creepy *Twilight Zone* vibe, you no longer have to operate by the company's posted 'Code of Conduct.' A history of the town awaits at the **Scotia Museum & Visitor Center** (www.townofscotia.com; cnr Main & Bridge Sts; 8am-4:30pm Mon-Fri Jun-Sep), at the town's south end. The museum's **fisheries center** (admission free) is remarkably informative – ironic, considering that logging destroys fish habitats – and houses the largest freshwater aquarium on the North Coast.

There are dingy motels and diners in **Rio Dell** (aka 'Real Dull'), across the river. Back in the day, this is where the debauchery happened: because it wasn't a company town, Rio Dell had bars and hookers. In 1969, the freeway bypassed the town and it withered.

As you drive along Hwy 101 and see what appears to be a never-ending redwood forest, understand that this 'forest' sometimes consists of trees only a few rows deep – called a 'beauty strip' – a carefully crafted illusion for tourists. Most old-growth trees have been cut. **Bay Area Coalition for Headwaters Forest** (www.headwaterspreserve.org) helped preserve over 7000 acres of land with public funds through provisions in a long-negotiated agreement between the Pacific Lumber Company and state and federal agencies.

Up Hwy 101 there's a great pit stop at **Eel River Brewing** (www.eelriverbrewing.com; 1777 Alamar Way, Fortuna; ⏲11am-11pm Mon-Sun), where a breezy beer garden and excellent burgers accompany all-organic brews.

Ferndale

The North Coast's most charming town is stuffed with impeccable Victorians – known locally as 'butterfat palaces' because of the dairy wealth that built them. There are so many, in fact, that the entire place is a state and federal historical landmark. Dairy farmers built the town in the 19th century and it's still run by the 'milk mafia': you're not a local till you've lived here 40 years. A stroll down Main St offers galleries, old-world emporiums and soda fountains. Although Ferndale relies on tourism, it has avoided becoming a tourist trap – and has no chain stores. Though a lovely place to spend a summer night, it's dead as a doornail in winter.

Sights & Activities

Half a mile from downtown via Bluff St, enjoy short tramps through fields of wildflowers, beside ponds, past redwood groves and eucalyptus trees at 110-acre **Russ Park**. The **cemetery**, also on Bluff St, is amazingly cool with graves dating to the 1800s and expansive views to the ocean. Five miles down Centerville Rd, **Centerville Beach** is one of the few off-leash dog beaches in Humboldt County.

FREE **Kinetic Sculpture Museum** MUSEUM, GALLERY

(580 Main St; ⏲10am-5pm Mon-Sat, noon-4pm Sun; 👪) This warehouse holds the fanciful, astounding, human-powered contraptions used in the town's annual Kinetic Grand Championship. Shaped like giant fish and UFOs, these colorful piles of junk propel racers over roads, water and marsh in the May event.

Fern Cottage HISTORIC BUILDING

(☎707-786-4835; www.ferncottage.org; Centerville Rd; group tours $10 per person; ⏲by appointment) This 1866 Carpenter Gothic grew to a 32-room mansion. Only one family ever lived here, so the interior is completely preserved.

Gingerbread Mansion HISTORIC BUILDING

(400 Berding St) An 1898 Queen Anne-Eastlake, this is the town's most photographed building. It held guests as a B&B for years, but has recently closed.

Festivals & Events

This wee town has a packed social calendar, especially in the summer. If you're planning a visit, check the events page at www.victorianferndale.com.

Tour of the Unknown Coast BICYCLE RACE

(www.tuccycle.org) A challenging event in May, in which participants of the 100 mile race climb nearly 10,000 feet.

Humboldt County Fair FAIR

(www.humboldtcountyfair.org) Held in mid-August, the longest running county fair in California.

Sleeping

Shaw House B&B $$

(☎707-786-9958, 800-557-7429; www.shawhouse.com; 703 Main St; r $145-175, ste $225-275; 📶) Shaw House, an emblematic 'butterfat palace,' was the first permanent structure in Ferndale, completed by founding father Seth Shaw in 1866. Today, it's California's oldest B&B, set back on extensive grounds. Original details remain, including painted wooden ceilings. Most of the rooms have private entrances, and three have private balconies over a large garden.

Francis Creek Inn MOTEL $

(☎707-786-9611; www.franciscreekinn.com; 577 Main St; r from $85; 📶) White picket balconies stand in front of this sweet little downtown motel, which is family owned and operated (you check in at the Red Front convenience store, right around the corner). Spartan rooms are basic, clean and furnished simply, and the value is outstanding.

Hotel Ivanhoe HISTORIC HOTEL $$
(☎707-786-9000; www.ivanhoe-hotel.com; 315 Main St; r $95-145) Ferndale's oldest hostelry opened in 1875. It has four antique-laden rooms and an Old West–style 2nd-floor gallery, perfect for morning coffee. The adjoining saloon, with dark wood and lots of brass, is an atmospheric place for a nightcap.

Victorian Inn HISTORIC HOTEL $$
(☎707-786-4949, 888-589-1808; www.victorianvillageinn.com; 400 Ocean Ave; r $105-225; 📶) The bright, sunny rooms inside this venerable 1890 two-story, former bank building, are comfortably furnished with thick carpeting, good linens and antiques.

Humboldt County Fairgrounds CAMPGROUND $
(☎707-786-9511; www.humboldtcountyfair.org; 1250 5th St; tent/RV sites $10/20) Turn west onto Van Ness St and go a few blocks for lawn camping with showers.

Eating

A **farmers market** (400 Ocean Ave; ⏰10:30am-2pm Sat May-Oct) has locally grown veggies and locally produced dairy – including the freshest cheese you'll find anywhere. Main St has lots of cafe options for eating, as well as white table cloth spots in both historic hotels.

Lotus Asian Bistro & Tea Room PAN-ASIAN $
(www.lotusasianbistro.com; 619 Main St; mains $7-14; ⏰11:30am-9pm Sat, Sun & Tue, 4-9pm Mon & Fri) Cherry glazed beef, crispy scallion pancakes with pulled duck and udon bowls spiced with a ginger broth – the menu at this excellent Asian fusion bistro offers welcome diversity to Ferndale's lunch and dinner options.

No Brand Burger Stand BURGERS $
(989 Milton St; burgers $7; ⏰11am-5pm) Sitting near the entrance to town, this hole-in-the-wall turns out a juicy jalpeño double cheese burger that ranks easily as the North Coast's best burger. The shakes – so thick your cheeks hurt from pulling on the straw – are about the only other thing on the menu.

Poppa Joe's AMERICAN $
(409 Main St; mains $5-7; ⏰11am-8:30pm Mon-Fri, 6am-noon Sat & Sun) You can't beat the atmosphere at this diner, where trophy heads hang from the wall, the floors slant at a precarious angle and old men play poker all day. The American-style breakfasts are good, too – especially the pancakes.

Sweetness & Light CANDY $
(554 Main St; confections $2-3) The house-made, gooey Moo bars are this antique candy shop's flagship. It also serves great ice cream and espresso.

☆ Entertainment

Ferndale Repertory Theatre THEATER
(☎707-786-5483; www.ferndale-rep.org; 447 Main St) This top-shelf community company produces excellent contemporary theatre in the historic Hart Theatre Building.

Shopping

Blacksmith Shop & Gallery METAL GOODS
(☎707-786-4216; www.ferndaleblacksmith.com; 455 & 491 Main St) From wrought-iron art to hand-forged furniture, this is the largest collection of contemporary blacksmithing in America.

Abraxas Jewelry & Leather Goods JEWELRY
(505 Main St) The pieces of locally forged jewelry here are extremely cool and moderately priced. The back room is filled with tons of hats.

Farmer's Daughter CLOTHING
(358 Main; ⏰11am-5pm Tue-Sat, noon-4pm Sun) An actual dairy farmer's daughter owns this cute Western boutique.

Humboldt Bay National Wildlife Refuge

This pristine **wildlife refuge** (☎707-733-5406; ⏰sunrise-sunset) protects wetland habitats for more than 200 species of birds migrating annually along the Pacific Flyway. Between the fall and early spring, when Aleutian geese descend en masse to the area, more than 25,000 geese might be seen in a cackling gaggle outside the visitor center.

The peak season for waterbirds and raptors runs September to March; for black brant geese and migratory shorebirds mid-March to late April. Gulls, terns, cormorants, pelicans, egrets and herons come year-round. Look for harbor seals offshore; bring binoculars. If it's open, drive out South Jetty Rd to the mouth of Humboldt Bay for a stunning perspective.

Pick up a map from the **visitor center** (1020 Ranch Rd; ⏲8am-5pm). Exit Hwy 101 at Hookton Rd, 11 miles south of Eureka, turn north along the frontage road, on the freeway's west side. In April, look for the **Godwit Days** festival.

Eureka

One hour north of Garberville, on the edge of the giant Humboldt Bay, lies Eureka, the largest bay north of San Francisco. With strip-mall sprawl surrounding a lovely historic downtown, it wears its role as the county seat a bit clumsily. Despite a diverse and interesting community of artists, writers, pagans and other free-thinkers, Eureka's wild side slips out only occasionally – the **Redwood Coast Dixieland Jazz Festival** (www.redwoodcoastmusicfestivals.org) is a rollicking festival with events all over town, and summer concerts rock out the F Street Pier – but mostly, it goes to bed early. Make for Old Town, a small district with colorful Victorians, good shopping and a revitalized waterfront. For night life, head to Eureka's trippy sister up the road, Arcata.

Sights

The free *Eureka Visitors Map,* available at tourist offices, details walking tours and scenic drives, focusing on architecture and history. **Old Town**, along 2nd and 3rd Sts from C St to M St, was once down-and-out, but has been refurbished into a buzzing pedestrian district. The F Street Plaza and Boardwalk run along the waterfront at the foot of F St. Gallery openings fall on the first Saturday of every month.

Blue Ox Millworks & Historic Park MILL
(www.blueoxmill.com; adult/child 6-12yr $7.50/3.50; ⏲9am-4pm Mon-Sat; 👪) One of only seven of its kind in America, antique tools and mills are used to produce authentic gingerbread trim for Victorian buildings; one-hour self-guided tours take you through the mill and historical buildings, including a blacksmith shop and 19th-century skid camp. Kids love the oxen.

Romano Gabriel Wooden Sculpture Garden ART INSTALLATION
(315 2nd St) The coolest thing to gawk at downtown is this collection of whimsical outsider art that's enclosed by glass. For 30 years, wooden characters in Gabriel's front yard delighted locals. After he died in 1977, the city moved the collection here.

Clarke Historical Museum MUSEUM
(www.clarkemuseum.org; 240 E St; admission $1; ⏲11am-4pm Wed-Sat) The best community historical museum on this stretch of the coast houses a set of typically musty relics – needlework hankies and paintings of the area's history-making notables (in this case Ulysses Grant, who was once dismissed from his post at Fort Humboldt for drunkenness). Its best collection is that of intricately woven baskets from local tribes. One look at the scenes of animals and warriors that unfold in the weave and you'll quickly understand the Pomo saying that 'every basket tells a story.'

Carson Mansion HISTORIC BUILDING
(134 M St) Of Eureka's fine Victorian buildings the most famous is the ornate 1880s home of lumber baron William Carson. It took 100 men a full year to build. Today it's a private men's club. The **pink house** opposite, at 202 M St, is an 1884 Queen Anne Victorian designed by the same architects and built as a wedding gift for Carson's son.

Sequoia Park PARK
(www.sequoiaparkzoo.net; 3414 W St; park free, zoo adult/child $5.50/3.50; ⏲zoo 10am-5pm May-Sep, Tue-Sun Oct-Apr; 👪) A 77-acre old-growth redwood grove is a surprising green gem in the middle of a residential neighborhood. It has biking and hiking trails, a children's playground and picnic areas, and a small zoo.

Morris Graves Museum of Art MUSEUM
(www.humboldtarts.org; 636 F St; suggested donation $4; ⏲noon-5pm Thu-Sun) Across Hwy 101, the excellent museum shows rotating Californian artists and hosts performances inside the 1904 Carnegie library, the state's first public library.

Discovery Museum MUSEUM
(www.discovery-museum.org; 517 3rd St; admission $4; ☎10am-4pm Tue-Sat, from noon Sun; 👪) A hands-on kids' museum.

Activities

Harbor Cruise HARBOR CRUISE
(www.humboldtbaymaritimemuseum.com; 75-minute narrated cruise adult/child $18/10, 1-hour cocktail cruise $10) Board the 1910 *Madaket,* America's oldest continuously operating passenger vessel, and learn the history of Humboldt Bay. Located at the foot of C St, it originally ferried

mill workers and passengers until the Samoa Bridge was built in 1972. The $10 sunset cocktail cruise serves from the smallest licensed bar in the state.

Hum-Boats Sail, Canoe & Kayak Center BOAT RENTAL
(www.humboats.com; Startare Dr; ☎9am-5pm Mon-Fri, 9am-6pm Sat & Sun Apr-Oct, 9am-2:30pm Nov-Mar) At Woodley Island Marina, this outfit rents kayaks and sailboats, offering lessons, tours, charters, sunset sails and full-moon paddles.

Sleeping

Every brand of chain hotel is along Hwy 101. Room rates run high midsummer; you can sometimes find cheaper in Arcata, to the north, or Fortuna, to the south. There are also a handful of motels which cost from $60 to $100 and have no air-conditioning; choose places set back from the road. The cheapest are south of downtown on the suburban strip.

Hotel Carter & Carter House Victorians HOTEL, B&B $$$
(☎707-444-8067, 800-404-1390; www.carterhouse.com; 301 L St; r incl breakfast $159-225, ste incl breakfast $304-385;) For those with a few extra bucks, the Hotel Carter and its associated Victorian rentals bear the standard for North Coast luxury. Recently constructed in period style, the hotel is a Victorian look-alike, holding rooms with top-quality linens and modern amenities; suites have in-room whirlpools and marble fireplaces. The same owners operate three sumptuously decorated houses: a single-level 1900 house, a honeymoon-hideaway cottage and a replica of an 1880s San Francisco mansion, which the owner built himself, entirely by hand. Unlike elsewhere, you won't see the innkeeper unless you want to. Guests have an in-room breakfast or can eat at the understated, elegant restaurant.

Eagle House Inn HISTORIC INN $$
(☎707-444-3344; www.eaglehouseinn.com; 139 2nd St; r $105-205;) This hulking Victorian hotel in Old Town has 24 rooms above a turn-of-the-century ballroom perfect for hide-and-seek. Rooms aren't overly stuffed with precious period furniture – carved headboards, floral-print carpeting and antique armoires – but some have bizarre touches (like the bright red spa tub that would fit in on an '80s adult film set). The coolest rooms are in the corner and have sitting areas in turrets looking over the street.

Abigail's Elegant Victorian Mansion B&B $$
(☎707-444-3144; www.eureka-california.com; 1406 C St; r $145-215) Inside this National Historic Landmark that's practically a living-history museum, the sweet-as-could-be innkeepers lavish guests with warm hospitality.

Daly Inn B&B $$
(☎707-445-3638, 800-321-9656; www.dalyinn.com; 1125 H St; r with bathroom $170-185, without bathroom $130) This impeccably maintained 1905 Colonial Revival mansion has individually decorated rooms with turn-of-the-20th-century European and American antiques. Guest parlors are trimmed with rare woods; outside are century-old flowering trees.

Bayview Motel MOTEL $
(☎707-442-1673, 866-725-6813; www.bayviewmotel.com; 2844 Fairfield St; r $109;) Spotless rooms are of the chain motel standard; some have patios overlooking Humboldt Bay.

Eureka Inn HISTORIC HOTEL $
(☎707-497-6903, 877-552-3985; www.eurekainn.com; cnr 7th & F St; r $65-90, ste $85-130;) This enormous historic hotel, long dormant, has found a new owner. While rooms are bland, they're cheap and the structure itself is magnificent.

Ship's Inn B&B $$
(☎707-443-7583, 877-443-7583; www.shipsinn.net; 821 D St; r $130-175, cottages $160;) Warmly modern furnishings with nautical themes, kind hosts and a full breakfast make this three-room inn a favorite for return guests.

Eating

Eureka is blessed with two excellent natural food grocery stores – **Eureka Co-op** (cnr 5th & L Sts) and **Eureka Natural Foods** (1626 Broadway) – and two weekly farmers markets – at the corner of **2nd & F Sts** (⊙10am-1pm Tue Jun-Oct) and the **Henderson Center** (☎10am-1pm Thu Jun-Oct). The vibrant dining scene is focused in the Old Town district.

Kyoto JAPANESE $$
(☎707-443-7777; 320 F St; sushi $4-6, mains $15-25; ⊙5:30-9:30pm Wed-Sat) New owners have had big shoes to fill by taking over a place renowned as the best sushi in Humboldt County, but the quality has not slipped and the atmosphere – in a tiny, packed room,

where conversation with the neighboring table is inevitable – is as fun as ever. A menu of sushi and sashimi is rounded out by grilled scallops and fern tip salad. North coast travelers who absolutely need sushi should phone ahead for a reservation.

Hurricane Kate's TAPAS **$$**
(www.hurricanekates.com; 511 2nd St; lunch mains $9-15, dinner mains $16-26; ⊙11am-2:30pm & 5-9pm;) The favorite spot of local *bon vivants*, Kate's open kitchen pumps out pretty good, eclectic, tapas-style dishes and roast meats, but the wood-fired pizzas are the standout option. There is a full bar.

Restaurant 301 CALIFORNIAN **$$$**
(☎707-444-8062; www.carterhouse.com; 301 L St; breakfast $11, dinner mains $20-35, 4-course menu $62; ⊙7:30-10am & 6-9pm) Eureka's top table, romantic, sophisticated 301 serves a contemporary Californian menu, using produce from its organic gardens (tours available). Mains are pricey, but the prix-fixe menu is a good way to taste local food in its finest presentation. The eight-course Chef's Grand Menu ($92) is only worthy of *really* special occasions.

Waterfront Café Oyster Bar SEAFOOD **$$**
(102 F St; mains lunch $8-13, dinner $13-20; ⊙9am-9pm) With a nice bay view and baskets of steamed clams, fish and chips, oysters and chowder, this is a solid bay-side lunch. A top spot for Sunday brunch, with jazz and Ramos fizzes.

La Chapala MEXICAN **$**
(201 2nd St; mains $6-14; ⊙11am-8pm) For Mexican, family-owned La Chapala makes strong margaritas and homemade flan.

Ramone's BAKERY, DELI **$**
(2223 Harrison St; mains $6-10; ⊙7am-6pm Mon-Sat, 8am-4pm Sun) For grab-and-go sandwiches, fresh soups and wraps.

Drinking

Lost Coast Brewery BREWERY
(☎707-445-4480; 617 4th St;) The roster of the regular brews at Eureka's colorful brewery might not knock the socks off a serious beer snob (and can't hold a candle to some of the others on the coast), but highlights include the Downtown Brown Ale, Great White and Lost Coast Pale Ale. After downing a few pints, the fried pub grub starts to look pretty tasty.

Shanty DIVE BAR
(213 2nd St; ⊙noon-2am;) The coolest spot in town is grungy and fun. Play pool, Donkey Kong, Ms Pac Man or Ping Pong, or kick it on the back patio with local 20- and 30-something hipsters.

321 Coffee COFFEE SHOP
(321 3rd St; ⊙8am-9pm;) Students sip French-press coffee and play chess at this living-room-like coffeehouse. Good soup.

Shopping

Eureka's streets lie on a grid; numbered streets cross lettered streets. For the best window-shopping, head to the 300, 400 and 500 blocks of 2nd St, between D and G Sts. The town's low rents and cool old spaces harbor lots of indie boutiques.

Shipwreck VINTAGE
(430 3rd St) The quality of vintage goods here – *genuinely* distressed jeans and leather jackets, 1940s housedresses and hats – is complimented by hand-made local jewelry and paper products.

Going Places TRAVELGOODS, BOOKS
(www.goingplacesworld.com; 1328 2nd St) Guidebooks, travel gear and international goods are certain to give a thrill to any vagabond. It's one of three excellent book shops in Old Town.

Entertainment

Morris Graves Museum of Art PERFORMANCE SPACE
(www.humboldtarts.org; 636 F St; suggested donation $4; ⊙noon-5pm Thu-Sun) Hosts performing-arts events between September and May, usually on Saturday evenings and Sunday afternoons.

Arkley Center for the Performing Arts ARTS CENTER
(www.arkleycenter.com; 412 G St) Home to the Eureka Symphony and North Coast Dance, and stages musicals and plays.

Club Triangle at The Alibi CLUB
(535 5th St) On Sunday nights this place becomes the North Coast's gay dance club. For gay events, log onto www.queerhumboldt.com.

Information

Eureka Chamber of Commerce (☎707-442-3738, 800-356-6381, www.eurekachamber.com; 2112 Broadway; ⊙8:30am-5pm Mon-Fri)

The main visitor information center is on Hwy 101.

Pride Enterprises Tours (☎707-445-2117, 800-400-1849) Local historian Ray Hillman leads outstanding history tours. He's also licensed to guide in the national parks.

Six Rivers National Forest Headquarters (☎707-442-1721; 1330 Bayshore Way; ⏰8am-4:30pm Mon-Fri) Maps and information.

Getting There & Around

The Arcata/Eureka airport (ACV) is a small, expensive airport which connects regionally. See p253 for more information. The Greyhound station is in Arcata; see p253.

Eureka Transit Service (☎707-443-0826; www.eurekatransit.org) operates local buses ($1.30), Monday to Saturday.

Samoa Peninsula

Grassy dunes and windswept beaches extend along the half-mile-wide, 7-mile long Samoa Peninsula, Humboldt Bay's western boundary. Stretches of it are spectacular, particularly the dunes, which are part of a 34-mile-long dune system – the largest in Northern California – and the wildlife viewing is excellent. The shoreline road (Hwy 255) is a backdoor route between Arcata and Eureka.

At the peninsula's south end, **Samoa Dunes Recreation Area** (⏰sunrise-sunset) is good for picnicking and fishing. For wildlife, head to **Mad River Slough & Dunes**; from Arcata, take Samoa Blvd west for 3 miles, then turn right at Young St, the Manila turnoff. Park at the community center lot, from where a trail passes mudflats, salt marsh and tidal channels. There are over 200 species of birds: migrating waterfowl in spring and fall, songbirds in spring and summer, shorebirds in fall and winter, and waders year-round.

These undisturbed dunes reach heights of over 80ft. Because of the environment's fragility, access is by guided tour only. **Friends of the Dunes** (www.friendsofthedunes.org) leads free guided walks; register via email through the website. Check online for departure locations and information.

The lunch place on the peninsula is the **Samoa Cookhouse** (☎707-442-1659; www.samoacookhouse.net; off Samoa Blvd; breakfast/lunch/dinner $12/13/16; 👪), the last surviving lumber camp cookhouse in the West, where you can shovel down all-you-can-eat family meals at long red-checkered tables. Kids eat for half-price. The cookhouse is five minutes northwest of Eureka, across the Samoa Bridge; follow the signs. From Arcata, take Samoa Blvd (Hwy 255).

Arcata

The North Coast's most progressive town, Arcata surrounds a tidy central square that fills with college students, campers, transients and tourists. Sure, it occasionally reeks of patchouli and its politics lean far left (in 2003, the city outlawed voluntary compliance with the USA Patriot Act, in 2006 it spearheaded a coalition of cities to impeach conservative president George W Bush), but its earnest embrace of sustainability has fostered some of the most progressive civic action in America. Here, garbage trucks run on biodiesel, recycling gets picked up by tandem bicycle, wastewater gets filtered clean in marshlands and almost every street has a bike lane.

Founded in 1850 as a base for lumber camps, today Arcata is defined as a magnate for 20-somethings looking to expand their minds: either at Humboldt State University (HSU), and/or on the highly potent marijuana which grows around here like, um, weeds. After a 1996 state proposition legalized marijuana for medical purposes, Arcata became what one *New Yorker* article referred to as the 'heartland of high grade marijuana.' The economy of the regions has become inexorably tied to the crop since.

Roads run on a grid, with numbered streets traveling east–west and lettered streets going north–south. G and H Sts run north and south (respectively) to HSU and Hwy 101. The plaza is bordered by G and H and 8th and 9th Sts.

Sights

Around **Arcata Plaza** are two National Historic Landmarks: the 1857 **Jacoby's Storehouse** (cnr H & 8th Sts) and the 1915 **Hotel Arcata** (cnr G & 9th Sts). Another great historic building is the 1914 **Minor Theatre** (1013 10th St), which some local historians claim is the oldest theater in the US built specifically for showing film.

Humboldt State University UNIVERSITY
(HSU; www.humboldt.edu) The University on the northeastern side of town holds the Campus Center for Appropriate Technology (CCAT), a

world leader in developing sustainable technologies; on Fridays at 2pm you can take a self-guided tour of the **CCAT House**, a converted residence that uses only 4% of the energy of a comparably sized dwelling.

Arcata Marsh & Wildlife Sanctuary WILDLIFE SANCTUARY
On the shores of Humboldt Bay, this has 5 miles of walking trails and outstanding birding. The **Redwood Region Audubon Society** (www.rras.org; donation welcome) offers guided walks Saturdays at 8:30am, rain or shine, from the parking lot at I St's south end. Friends of Arcata Marsh offer guided tours Saturdays at 2pm from the **Arcata Marsh Interpretive Center** (707-826-2359; 569 South G St; tours free; 9am-5pm).

Activities

TOP CHOICE **Finnish Country Sauna & Tubs** HOT TUBS, SAUNA
(707-822-2228, www.cafemokkaarcata.com; cnr 5th & J Sts; noon-11pm Sun-Thu, to 1am Fri & Sat) Like some kind of Euro-crunchy bohemian dream, these private, open-air redwood hot tubs (half-hour/hour $9/17) and sauna are situated around a small frog pond, perfect for the sore legs of hikers or weary travelers up Hwy 101. The rates are reasonable, the staff is easygoing, and the facility is relaxing, simple and clean. Reserve ahead, especially on weekends.

HSU Center Activities OUTDOOR ACTIVITIES
(www.humboldt.edu/centeractivities) An office on the 2nd floor of the University Center, beside the campus clock tower, sponsors myriad workshops, outings and sporting-gear rentals; nonstudents welcome.

Arcata Community Pool SWIMMING
(ww.arcatapool.com; 1150 16th St; adult/child $7/5.25; 5:30am-9pm Mon-Fri, 9am-6pm Sat, 1-4pm Sun;) Has a coed hot tub, sauna and exercise room.

Adventure's Edge OUTDOOR GEAR RENTAL
(www.adventuresedge.com; 650 10th St; 9am-6pm Mon-Sat, 10am-5pm Sun) Rents, sells and services outdoor equipment.

Festivals & Events

Kinetic Grand Championship RACE
(www.kineticgrandchampionship.com) Arcata's most famous event is held Memorial Day weekend: people on amazing self-propelled contraptions travel 38 miles from Arcata to Ferndale.

Arcata Bay Oyster Festival FOOD FESTIVAL
(www.oysterfestival.net) A magical celebration of oysters and beer happens in June.

North Country Fair FAIR
(www.sameoldpeopl.org) A fun September street fair, where bands with names like The Fickle Hillbillies jam.

Sleeping

Arcata has affordable but limited lodgings. A cluster of hotels – Comfort Inn, Hampton Inn, etc – is just north of town, off Hwy 101's Giuntoli Lane. There's cheap camping further north at Clam Beach (p254).

Hotel Arcata HISTORIC HOTEL $$
(707-826-0217, 800-344-1221; www.hotelarcata.com; 708 9th St; r $96-156;) Anchoring the plaza, the renovated 1915 brick landmark has friendly staff, high ceilings and comfortable, old-world rooms of mixed quality. The rooms in front are an excellent perch for people-watching on the square, but the quietest face the back.

Lady Anne Inn B&B $$
(707-822-2797; www.ladyanneinn.com; 902 14th St; r $125-140) Roses line the walkway to this 1888 mansion full of Victorian bric-a-brac. The frilly rooms are pretty, but there's no breakfast.

Arcata Stay VACATION RENTALS $$
(707-822-0935, 877-822-0935; www.arcatastay.com; apt from $165) A network of excellent

MONEY TREES: ECONOMICS OF HUMBOLDT HERB

» Estimated percentage of Humboldt residents (18–65) with income partially tied to cultivating marijuana: 50

» Estimated wholesale value of one pound of 'Humboldt Kush': $3000

» Number of plants allowed per Proposition 215 card holder: 99

» Number of pounds produced by one high-yield plant: 1

» Estimated cost of production, one ounce: $100–180

» Estimated street value, one ounce: $300–600

apartment and cottage rentals. There is a two-night minimum.

Fairwinds Motel MOTEL $
(☎707-822-4824; www.fairwindsmotelarcata.com; 1674 G St; s $70-75, d $80-90;) Serviceable rooms in this standard-issue motel, with some noise from Hwy 101.

Eating

Great food abounds in restaurants throughout Arcata, almost all casual.

There are fantastic **farmers markets**, at the **Arcata Plaza** (9am-2pm Sat Apr-Nov) and in the parking lot of **Wildberries Market** (3:30-6:30pm Tue Jun-Oct). Even at other times, **Wildberries Marketplace** (www.wildberries.com; 747 13th St; 7am-11pm), has a deli counter and a great selection of natural foods. The gigantic **North Coast Co-op** (cnr 8th & I Sts; 6am-9pm) carries organic foods and is a community staple; check the kiosk out front. Just a few blocks north of downtown, there is a cluster of the town's best restaurants on G St.

Folie Douce NEW AMERICAN $$$
(☎707-822-1042; www.holyfolie.com; 1551 G St; dinner mains $27-36; 5:30-9pm Tue-Thu, to 10pm Fri-Sat;) Just a slip of a place, but with an enormous reputation. The short but inventive menu features seasonally inspired bistro cooking, from Asian to Mediterranean, with an emphasis on local organics. Wood-fired pizzas ($14 to $19) are renowned. Sunday brunch, too. Reservations essential.

Jambalaya LATIN AMERICAN FUSION $$
(915 H St; mains lunch $7-9, dinner $15-20; 5pm-2am Mon-Tue & Thu-Fri, from 9pm Wed, from 10am Sat-Sun) Probably the most vibrant dining option on the square, Jambalaya serves a mishmash of Caribbean-influenced dishes – at lunch Cuban sandwiches, at dinner wild salmon and (of course) jambalaya. The drink menu also shines, with fresh fruit cocktails and a great beer selection. As if this wasn't fun enough, it also hosts Arcata's best live music scene.

3 Foods Cafe FUSION $$
(www.cafeattheendoftheuniverse.com; 835 J St; mains brunch $8-14, dinner $10-30; 5:30am-10pm Tue-Thu, to 11pm Fri & Sat, to 9pm Sun;) A perfect fit with the Arcata dining scene: whimsical, creative, worldly dishes (think Korean beef in a spicy chili sauce) at moderate prices (a prix fixe is sometimes available for $20). The lavender-infused cocktails start things off on the right foot. The mac and cheese is the crowd favorite.

Wildflower Cafe & Bakery CAFE $$
(☎707-822-0360; 1604 G St; breakfast & lunch $5-8, dinner mains $15-16; 8am-8pm Sun-Wed;) Tops for vegetarians, this tiny storefront serves fab frittatas, pancakes and curries, and big crunchy salads.

Japhy's Soup & Noodles NOODLES $
(1563 G St; mains $5-8; 11:30am-8pm Mon-Fri) Big salads, tasty coconut curry, cold noodle salads and homemade soups – and cheap!

Stars Hamburgers BURGERS $
(1535 G St; burgers $3-5; 11am-8pm Mon-Thu, to 9pm Fri, to 7pm Sat, noon-6pm Sun;) Uses grass-fed beef to make fantastic burgers.

Don's Donuts FAST FOOD $
(933 HSt; donuts $0.80-1.35, sandwiches from $6; 24hr) Get a southeast-Asian sandwich.

Drinking

Dive bars and cocktail lounges line the plaza's northern side. Arcata is awash in coffeehouses.

TOP CHOICE **Six Rivers Brewery** BREWPUB
(www.sixriversbrewery.com; 1300 Central Ave, McKinleyville; mains $11-18; 11:30am-midnight Tue-Sun, from 4pm Mon) One of the first female-owned breweries in California, the 'brew with a view' kills it in every category: great beer, amazing community vibe, occasional live music and delicious hot wings. The spicy chili pepper ale is amazing. At first glance the menu might seem like ho-hum pub grub, but the batter crusted halibut is a golden treat and the salads are fresh and huge. They also make a helluva pizza.

Humboldt Brews BAR
(www.humbrews.com; 856 10th St; pub grub $5-10) This popular beer house has been elegantly remodeled and has a huge selection of carefully selected beer taps, fish tacos and buffalo wings. Live music nightly.

Cafe Mokka COFFEE SHOP
(www.cafemokkaarcata.com; cnr 5th & J Sts; snacks $4) Bohos head to this cafe at Finnish Country Sauna & Tubs (p251) for a mellow, old-world vibe, good coffee drinks and homemade cookies.

Entertainment

Arcata Theatre CINEMA
(www.arcatatheater.com; 1036 G St) An exquisite remodeling has revived this classic movie house, which shows art films, rock documentaries, silent films and more. Plus, it serves beer.

Center Arts ARTS CENTER
(tickets 707-826-3928; www.humboldt.edu/centerarts/) Hosts events on campus and you'd be amazed at who shows up: from Diana Krall and Dave Brubeck to Lou Reed and Ani Difranco. The place to buy tickets is at the University Ticket Office in the HSY Bookstore on the 3rd floor of the University Center.

Information

Arcata Eye (www.arcataeye.com) Free newspaper listing local events; the 'Police Log' column is hysterical.

Bureau of Land Management (BLM; 707-825-2300; 1695 Heindon Rd) Has information on the Lost Coast.

California Welcome Center (707-822-3619; www.arcatachamber.com; 1635 Heindon Rd; 9am-5pm) Two miles north of town, off Giuntoli Lane, Hwy 101's west side. Operated by the Arcata Chamber of Commerce. Provides local and statewide information. Get the free *Official Map Guide to Arcata*.

Tin Can Mailman (www.tincanbooks.com; 1000 HSt) Used volumes on two floors; excellent for hard-to-find books.

Getting There & Around

Horizon Air (www.alaskaair.com) and **United** (www.united.com) make regional connections (which are predictably expensive) to the Arcata/Eureka airport.

Greyhound (www.greyhound.com) serves Arcata; from San Francisco budget $53 and seven hours. **Redwood Transit buses** (www.hta.org) serve Arcata and Eureka on the Trinidad–Scotia routes ($2.50, 2½ hours), which don't run on Sunday.

Arcata city buses (707-822-3775; Mon-Sat) stop at the **Arcata Transit Center** (707-825-8934; 925 E St at 9th St). For shared rides, read the bulletin board at the North Coast Co-op (p252).

Revolution Bicycle (www.revolutionbicycle.com; 1360 G St) and **Life Cycle Bike Shop** (www.lifecyclearcata.com; 1593 G St; Mon-Sat) rent, service and sell bicycles.

Only in Arcata: borrow a bike from **Library Bike** (www.arcata.com/greenbikes; 865 8th St) for a $20 deposit, which gets refunded when you return the bike – up to six months later! They're beaters, but they ride.

Though hitchhiking is still fairly rare and safety concerns should be taken seriously, a culture of hippies of all ages and transient marijuana harvesters makes this the easiest region in California to thumb a ride.

NORTHERN REDWOOD COAST

Congratulations, traveler, you've reached the middle of nowhere, or at least the top of the middle of nowhere. Here, the trees are so large that the tiny towns along the road seem even smaller. The scenery is pure drama: cliffs and rocks, native lore, legendary salmon runs, mammoth trees, redneck towns and RVing retirees. It's certainly the *weirdest* part of the California Coast. Leave time to dawdle and bask in the haunting grandeur of it all and, even though there are scores of mid-century motels, you simply must make an effort to sleep outdoors if possible.

Trinidad

Cheery Trinidad perches prettily on the side of the ocean, combining upscale homes with a mellow surfer vibe. Somehow it feels a bit off-the-beaten-path even though tourism augments fishing to keep the economy going. Trinidad gained its name when Spanish sea captains arrived on Trinity Sunday in 1775 and named the area La Santisima Trinidad (the Holy Trinity). It didn't boom, though, until the 1850s, when it became an important port for miners.

Sights & Activities

Trinidad is small: approach via Hwy 101 or from the north via Patrick's Point Dr (which becomes Scenic Dr further south). To reach town, take Main St.

The free town map at the information kiosk shows several fantastic hiking trails, most notably the **Trinidad Head Trail** with superb coastal views; excellent for whale-watching (December to April). Stroll along an exceptionally beautiful cove at **Trinidad State Beach**; take Main St and bear right at Stagecoach, then take the second turn left (the first is a picnic area) into the small lot.

Scenic Dr twists south along coastal bluffs, passing tiny coves with views back

toward the bay. It peters out before reaching the broad expanses of **Luffenholtz Beach** (accessible via the staircase) and serene white-sand **Moonstone Beach**. Exit Hwy 101 at 6th Ave/Westhaven to get there. Further south Moonstone becomes **Clam Beach County Park**.

Surfing is good year-round, but potentially dangerous: unless you know how to judge conditions and get yourself out of trouble – there are no lifeguards here – surf in better-protected Crescent City.

FREE **HSU Telonicher Marine Laboratory** SCIENCE CENTER

(☎707-826-3671; www.humboldt.edu/marinelab; Ewing St; 9am-4:30pm Mon-Fri, noon-4pm Sat Sep–mid-May;) Near Edwards St, has a touch tank, several aquariums (look for the giant Pacific octopus), an enormous whale jaw and a cool three-dimensional map of the ocean floor. You can also join a naturalist on tide pooling expeditions (90 minutes, $3); call ahead to ask about conditions.

Sleeping

Many of the inns line Patrick's Point Dr, north of town. **Trinidad Retreats** (www.trinidadretreats.com) and **Redwood Coast Vacation Rentals** (www.enjoytrinidad.com) handle local property rentals.

TOP CHOICE **Trinidad Bay B&B** B&B **$$$**

(☎707-677-0840; www.trinidadbaybnb.com; 560 Edwards St; r incl breakfast from $200;) Opposite the lighthouse, this gorgeous light-filled Cape Cod overlooks the harbor and Trinidad Head. Breakfast is delivered to your uniquely styled room and in the afternoon the house fills with the scent of freshly baked cookies. Each room also comes with a loaner iPad to use, loaded up with apps focused on local events and activities.

Clam Beach CAMPGROUND **$**

(tent sites per vehicle $10) South of town off Hwy 101, has excellent camping, but can get very crowded. Pitch your tent in the dunes (look for natural windbreaks). Facilities include pit toilets, cold water, picnic tables and fire rings.

View Crest Lodge LODGE **$$**

(☎707-677-3393; www.viewcrestlodge.com; 3415 Patrick's Point Dr; sites $32, 1-bedroom cottages $95-170;) On a hill above the ocean on the inland side, some of the well-maintained, modern cottages have views and Jacuzzis;

most have kitchens. Also a good campground.

Trinidad Inn INN $
(707-677-3349; www.trinidadinn.com; 1170 Patrick's Point Dr; r $75-115;) Sparklingly clean and attractively decorated rooms (many with kitchens) fill this upmarket, gray-shingled motel under tall trees.

Bishop Pine Lodge LODGE $$
(707-677-3314; www.bishoppinelodge.com; 1481 Patrick's Point Dr; cottages with/without kitchen from $150/110;) It feels like summer camp: rent free-standing redwood cottages in a grassy meadow. Expect woodsy charm and unintentionally retro-funky furniture.

Lost Whale Inn B&B $$$
(707-677-3425; www.lostwhaleinn.com; 3452 Patrick's Point Dr; r all incl breakfast $200-285, ste all incl breakfast $375;) Perched atop a grassy cliff, high above crashing waves and braying sea lions, this spacious, modern, light-filled B&B has jaw-dropping views out to the sea. The lovely gardens have a 24-hour hot tub.

Eating & Drinking

TOP CHOICE **Larrupin Cafe** CALIFORNIAN $$$
(707-677-0230; www.larrupin.com; 1658 Patrick's Point Dr; mains $20-30; 5-9pm Thu-Tue) Everybody loves Larrupin, where Moroccan rugs, chocolate brown walls, gravity-defying floral arrangements and deep-burgundy Oriental carpets create a moody atmosphere perfect for a lovers' tryst. On the menu, expect consistently good mesquite-grilled seafood and meats. In the summer, book a table on the garden patio. No credit cards.

Kahish's Catch Café FAST FOOD $
(707-677-0390; 355 Main St; mains $6-9; 11am-7pm Tue-Sun;) Across from the Chevron, this fun little hippie joint makes good food fast, using mostly organic ingredients – from pizzettas and grass-fed burgers to brown rice and veggies. Order at the counter and then sit outside.

Moonstone Grill SEAFOOD $$$
(Moonstone Beach; mains $20-32; 5:30-8:30pm Wed-Sun) Enjoy drop-dead sunset views over a picture-perfect beach while supping on the likes of oysters on the half-shell, Pacific wild king salmon or spice-rubbed rib eye. If the high price tag is a bit out-of-budget, drop in for a glass of wine.

Katy's Smokehouse & Fishmarket SEAFOOD $
(www.katyssmokehouse.com; 740 Edwards St; 9am-6pm) Makes its own chemical-free smoked and canned fish, using line-caught sushi-grade seafood.

Beachcomber Café CAFE $
(707-677-0106; 363 Trinity St; 7am-4pm Mon-Fri, 9am-4pm Sat & Sun) Head here for the best homemade cookies and to meet locals. Friday rocks live music.

Information

Beachcomber Cafe (707-677-0106; 363 Trinity St; per hr $5; 7am-4pm Mon-Thu, to 9pm Fri, 9am-4pm Sat & Sun) Internet access.

Information kiosk (cnr Patrick's Point Dr & Main St) Just west of the freeway. The pamphlet *Discover Trinidad* has an excellent map.

Trinidad Chamber of Commerce (707-667-1610; www.trinidadcalif.com) Information on the web, but no visitor center.

Patrick's Point State Park

Coastal bluffs jut out to sea at 640-acre **Patrick's Point** (707-677-3570; 4150 Patrick's Point Dr; day use $8;), where sandy beaches abut rocky headlands. Five miles north of Trinidad, with supereasy access to dramatic coastal bluffs, it's a best-bet for families. Stroll scenic overlooks, climb giant rock formations, watch whales breach, gaze into tidepools, or listen to barking sea lions and singing birds from this manicured park.

Sumêg is an authentic reproduction of a Yurok village, with hand-hewn redwood buildings where Native Americans gather for traditional ceremonies. In the native plant garden you'll find species for making traditional baskets and medicines.

On **Agate Beach** look for stray bits of jade and sea-polished agate. Follow the signs to tidepools, but tread lightly and obey regulations. The 2-mile **Rim Trail**, a former Yurok trail around the bluffs, circles the point with access to huge rocky outcroppings. Don't miss **Wedding Rock**, one of the park's most romantic spots. Other trails lead around unusual formations like **Ceremonial Rock** and **Lookout Rock**.

The park's three well-tended **campgrounds** (reservations 800-444-7275; www.reserveamerica.com; tent & RV sites $35) have coin-operated hot showers and very clean bathrooms. Penn Creek and Abalone campgrounds are more sheltered than Agate Beach.

Humboldt Lagoons State Park

Stretching out for miles along the coast, **Humboldt Lagoons** has long, sandy beaches and a string of coastal lagoons. **Big Lagoon** and the even prettier **Stone Lagoon** are both excellent for kayaking and bird-watching. Sunsets are spectacular, with no manmade structures in sight. Picnic at Stone Lagoon's north end. The Stone Lagoon Visitor Center, on Hwy 101, has closed due to staffing shortages, but there's a toilet and a bulletin board displaying information.

A mile north, **Freshwater Lagoon** is also great for birding. South of Stone Lagoon, tiny **Dry Lagoon** (a freshwater marsh) has a fantastic day hike. Park at Dry Lagoon's picnic area and hike north on the unmarked trail to Stone Lagoon; the trail skirts the southwestern shore and ends up at the ocean, passing through woods and marshland rich with wildlife. Mostly flat, it's about 2.5 miles one way – and nobody takes it because it's unmarked.

All campsites are first-come, first-served. The park runs two **environmental campgrounds** (tent sites $20; ⌚Apr-Oct); bring water. Stone Lagoon has six boat-in environmental campsites; Dry Lagoon has six walk-in campsites. Check in at Patrick's Point State Park, at least 30 minutes before sunset.

Humboldt County Parks (☎707-445-7651; tent sites $20) operates a lovely cypress-grove picnic area and campground beside Big Lagoon, a mile off Hwy 101, with flush toilets and cold water, but no showers.

Redwood National & State Parks

A patchwork of public lands jointly administered by the state and federal governments, the **Redwood National & State Parks** include Redwood National Park, Prairie Creek Redwoods State Park (p257), Del Norte Coast Redwoods State Park (p258) and Jedediah Smith Redwoods State Park (p261). A smattering of small towns break up the forested area, making it a bit confusing to get a sense of the parks as a whole. Prairie Creek and Jedediah Smith parks were originally land slated for clear-cutting, but in the '60s activists successfully protected them and today all these parks are an International Biosphere Reserve and World Heritage Site. At one time the national park was to absorb at least two of the state parks, but that did not happen, and so the cooperative structure remains.

Little-visited compared to their southern brethren, the world's tallest living trees have been standing here for time immemorial, predating the Roman Empire by over 500 years. Prepare to be impressed.

The small town of **Orick** (population 650), at the southern tip of the park, in a lush valley, is barely more than a few storefronts and a vast conglomeration of woodcarving.

Sights & Activities

Just north of the southern visitor center, turn east onto Bald Hills Rd and travel 2 miles to **Lady Bird Johnson Grove**, one of the park's most spectacular groves, accessible via a gentle 1-mile loop trail. Continue for another 5 miles up Bald Hills to **Redwood Creek Overlook**. On the top of the ridgeline at 2100ft get views over the forest and the entire watershed – provided it's not foggy. Just past the overlook lies the gated turnoff for **Tall Trees Grove**, the location of several of the world's tallest trees. Rangers issue only 50 vehicle permits per day, but they rarely run out. Pick one up, along with the gate-lock combination, from the visitor centers. Allow four hours for the round-trip, which includes a 6-mile drive down a rough dirt road (speed limit 15mph) and a steep 1.3-mile one-way hike, which descends 800ft to the grove.

Several longer trails include the awe-inspiring **Redwood Creek Trail**, which also reaches Tall Trees Grove. You'll need a free backcountry permit to hike and camp (highly recommended, as the best backcountry camping in on the North Coast), but the area is most accessible from Memorial Day to Labor Day, when summer footbridges are up. Otherwise, getting across the creek can be perilous or impossible.

Information

Unlike most national parks, there are no fees and no highway entrance stations at Redwood National Park, so it's imperative to pick up the free map at the park headquarters (p260) in Crescent City or at the **Redwood Information Center** (Kuchel Visitor Center;

(☎707-464-6101; www.nps.gov/redw; Hwy 101; ⊙9am-6pm June-Aug, to 5pm Sept-Oct & March-May, to 4pm Nov-Feb) in Orick. Rangers here issue permits to visit Tall Trees Grove and loan bear-proof containers for backpackers. For in-depth redwood ecology, buy the excellent official park handbook. The **Redwood Parks Association** (www.redwoodparksassociation.org) provides good information on its website, including detailed descriptions of all the parks hikes.

Prairie Creek Redwoods State Park

Famous for virgin redwood and unspoiled coastline, this 14,000-acre section of Redwood National & State Parks has spectacular scenic drives and 70 miles of hiking trails, many of which are excellent for children. Pick up maps and information and sit by the river-rock fireplace at **Prairie Creek Visitor Center** (☎707-464-6101; ⊙9am-5pm Mar-Oct, 10am-4pm Nov-Feb; 👪). Kids will love the taxidermy dioramas with push-button, light-up displays. Outside, elk roam grassy flats.

Sights & Activities

Newton B Drury Scenic Parkway SCENIC DRIVE

Just north of Orick is the turn off for the 8-mile parkway, which runs parallel to Hwy 101 through untouched ancient redwood forests. It's worth the short detour off the freeway to view the magnificence of these trees. Numerous trails branch off from roadside pullouts, including family- and ADA (American Disabilities Act) -friendly trails including Big Tree and Revelation Trail.

Hiking & Mountain-Biking

There are 28 mountain-biking and hiking trails through the park, from simple to strenuous. Only a few of these will appeal to hard core hikers, who should take on the Del Norte Coast Redwoods. Those tight on time or with mobility impairments should stop at **Big Tree**, an easy 100yd walk from the car park. Several other easy nature trails start near the visitor center, including **Revelation Trail** and **Elk Prairie Trail**. Stroll the recently reforested logging road on the **Ah-Pah Interpretive Trail** at the park's north end. The most challenging hike in this corner of the park is the truly spectacular 11.5-mile **Coastal Trail** which goes through primordial redwoods.

Just past the **Gold Bluffs Beach Campground** the road dead ends at **Fern Canyon**, where 60ft fern-covered sheer-rock walls can be seen from Steven Spielberg's *Jurassic Park 2: The Lost World*. This is one of the most photographed spots on the North Coast – damp and lush, all emerald green – and *totally* worth getting your toes wet to see.

Sleeping

Welcome to the great outdoors: without any motels or cabins, the only choice here is to pitch a tent in the campgrounds at the southern end of the park.

Gold Bluffs Beach CAMPGROUND $

(no reservations; tent sites $35) This campground sits between 100ft cliffs and wide-open ocean, but there are some windbreaks and solar-heated showers. Look for sites up the cliff under the trees.

Elk Prairie Campground CAMPGROUND $

(☎reservations 800-444-7275; www.reserveamerica.com; tent & RV sites $35) Elk roam this popular campground, where you can sleep under redwoods or at the prairie's edge. There are hot showers, some hike-in sites and a shallow creek to splash in. Sites 1–7 and 69–76 are on grassy prairies and get full sun; sites 8–68 are wooded. To camp in a mixed redwood forest, book sites 20–27.

Klamath

Giant metal-cast golden bears stand sentry at the bridge across the Klamath River, announcing Klamath, one of the tiny settlements that break up Redwood National & State Parks. With a gas station/market, a great diner and a casino, Klamath is basically a wide spot in the road. The Yurok Tribal Headquarters is here and the entire town and much of the surrounding area is the tribe's ancestral land. Klamath is roughly an hour north of Eureka.

Sights & Activities

The mouth of the **Klamath River** is a dramatic sight. Marine, riparian, forest and meadow ecological zones all converge and the birding is exceptional. For the best views, head north of town to Requa Rd and the **Klamath River Overlook** and picnic on high bluffs above driftwood-strewn beaches. On a clear day, this is one of the most spectacular viewpoints on the North Coast, and one of the best whale-watching spots in California. For a good hike, head north along the Coastal Trail. You'll have the sand to yourself at **Hidden Beach**; access the trail at the northern end of Motel Trees.

Just south of the river, on Hwy 101, follow signs for the scenic **Coastal Drive**, a narrow, winding country road (unsuitable for RVs and trailers) atop extremely high cliffs over the ocean. Come when it's not foggy, and mind your driving. Though technically in Redwood National Park, it's much closer to Klamath.

Klamath Jet Boat Tours BOAT TOURS
(www.jetboattours.com; 2hr tours adult/child $42/22) Book jet-boat excursions and fishing trips.

Sleeping & Eating

Woodsy Klamath is cheaper than Crescent City, but there aren't as many places to eat or buy groceries, and there's nothing to do at night but play cards. There are ample private RV parks in the area.

TOP CHOICE **Historic Requa Inn** HISTORIC HOTEL $
(707-482-1425; www.requainn.com; 451 Requa Rd, Klamath; r $85-155;) A woodsy country lodge on bluffs overlooking the mouth of the Klamath, the 1914 Requa Inn is one of our North Coast favorites and – a cherry on top – it's a carbon neutral facility. Many of the charming country-style rooms have mesmerizing views over the misty river, as does the dining room, where guests have breakfast.

Ravenwood Motel MOTEL $$
(707-482-5911, 866-520-9875; www.ravenwoodmotel.com; 131 Klamath Blvd; r/ste with kitchen $75/115) The spotlessly clean rooms are better than anything in Crescent City and individually decorated with furnishings and flair you'd expect in a city hotel, not a small-town motel.

FREE **Flint Ridge Campground** CAMPGROUND
(707-464-6101) Four miles from the Klamath River Bridge via Coastal Dr, this tent-only, hike-in campground sits among a wild, overgrown meadow of ghostly, overgrown ferns and moss. It's a 10-minute walk east, uphill from the dirt parking area. There's no water, plenty of bear sightings (bear boxes on site) and you have to pack out trash. But, hey, it's free.

Klamath River Cafe AMERICAN $
(707-482-1000;mains $8-12; 7:30am-2pm) With excellent homemade baked goods, a daily pie special and excellent breakfast food, this shiny new place is the best diner food within miles. The breakfasts are killer. Seasonal hours vary, so call ahead. If you arrive around dinner time, cross your fingers – it's open sporadically for dinner.

WHAT THE...?

It's hard to miss the giant statues of Paul Bunyan and Babe the Blue Ox towering over the parking lot at **Trees of Mystery** (707-482-2251; www.treesofmystery.net; 15500 Hwy 101; adult/child & senior $14/7; 8am-7pm Jun-Aug, 9am-4pm Sep-May;), a shameless tourist trap with a gondola running through the redwood canopy. The **End of the Trail Museum** located behind the Trees of Mystery gift shop has an outstanding collection of Native American arts and artifacts, and it's *free*.

Del Norte Coast Redwoods State Park

Marked by steep canyons and dense woods, half the 6400 acres of this **park** (vehicle day-use $8) are virgin redwood forest, crisscrossed by 15 miles of hiking trails. Even the most cynical of redwood-watchers can't help but be moved.

Pick up maps and inquire about guided walks at the Redwood National & State Parks Headquarters (p260) in Crescent City or the Redwood Information Center in Orick (p256).

Hwy 1 winds in from the coast at rugged, dramatic **Wilson Beach**, and traverses the dense forest, with groves stretching off as far as you can see.

Picnic on the sand at **False Klamath Cove**. Heading north, tall trees cling precipitously to canyon walls that drop to the rocky, timber-strewn coastline, and it's almost impossible to get to the water, except via gorgeous but steep **Damnation Creek Trail** or **Footsteps Rock Trail**.

Between these two, serious hikers will be most greatly rewarded by the Damnation Creek Trail. It's only 4 miles long, but the 1100-foot elevation change and cliff-side redwood makes it the park's best hike. The

WORTH A TRIP

SMITH RIVER NATIONAL RECREATION AREA

West of Jedediah Smith Redwoods, the Smith River, the state's last remaining undammed waterway, runs right beside Hwy 199. Originating high in the Siskiyou Mountains, its serpentine course cuts through deep canyons beneath thick forests. Chinook salmon and steelhead trout annually migrate up its clear waters. Camp, hike, raft and kayak here, but check regulations if you want to fish. Stop by the **Six Rivers National Forest Headquarters** (707-457-3131; www.fs.fed.us/r5/sixrivers; 10600 Hwy 199, Gasquet; 8am-4:30pm daily May-Sep, 8am-4:30pm Mon-Fri Oct-Apr) to get your bearings. Pick up pamphlets for the **Darlingtonia Trail** and **Myrtle Creek Botanical Area**, both easy jaunts into the woods, where you can see rare plants and learn about the area's geology.

unmarked trailhead starts from a parking area off Hwy 101 at mile mark 16.

Crescent Beach Overlook and picnic area has superb wintertime whale-watching. At the park's north end, watch the surf pound at **Crescent Beach**, just south of Crescent City via Enderts Beach Rd.

Mill Creek Campground (800-444-7275; www.reserveamerica.com; tent & RV sites $35) has hot showers and 145 sites in a redwood grove, 2 miles east of Hwy 101 and 7 miles south of Crescent City. Sites 1-74 are woodsier; sites 75-145 sunnier. Hike-in sites are prettiest.

Crescent City

Though Crescent City was founded as a thriving 1853 seaport and supply center for inland gold mines, the town's history was quite literally washed away in 1964, when half the town was swallowed by a tsunami. Of course, it was rebuilt (though mostly with the utilitarian ugliness of ticky-tacky buildings), but its marina was devastated by the 2011 Japan earthquake and tsunami, when the city was evacuated. Crescent City remains California's last big town north of Arcata, though the constant fog (and sounding fog horn) and damp, '60s sprawl makes it about as charming as a wet bag of dirty laundry. The economy depends heavily on shrimp and crab fishing, hotel tax and on Pelican Bay maximum-security prison, just north of town, which adds tension to the air and lots of cops on the streets.

Sights & Activities

Hwy 101 splits into two parallel one-way streets, with the southbound traffic on L St, northbound on M St. To see the major sights, turn west on Front St toward the lighthouse. Downtown is centered along 3rd St.

If you're in town in August, the **Del Norte County Fair** features a rodeo, and lots of characters.

North Coast Marine Mammal Center SCIENCE CENTER
(707-465-6265; www.northcoastmmc.org; 424 Howe Dr; by donation; 10am-5pm;) Just east of Battery Point, this is the ecologically minded foil to the garish Ocean World: the clinic treats injured seals, sea lions and dolphins and releases them back into the wild (donation requested).

Battery Point Lighthouse LIGHTHOUSE
(www.delnortehistory.org/lighthouse) The 1856 lighthouse, at the south end of A St, still operates on a tiny, rocky island that you can easily reach at low tide. From April to September, tour the **museum** (adult/child $3/1; 10am-4pm Mon-Sat May-Sep); hours vary with tides and weather.

Beachfront Park PARK
(Howe Dr;) Between B and H Sts, this park has a harborside beach with no large waves, making it perfect for little ones. Further east on Howe Dr, near J St, you'll come to **Kidtown**, with slides and swings and a make-believe castle.

Sleeping

Most people stop here for one night while traveling; motels are overpriced, but you'll pass a slew of hotels on the main arteries leading into and out of town. The county operates two excellent reservable **campgrounds** (707-464-7230; tent & RV sites $10) just outside of town. **Florence Keller Park** (3400 Cunningham Lane) has 50 sites in a beautiful grove of young redwoods (take Hwy 101 north to Elk Valley Cross Rd and follow the signs). **Ruby Van Deventer Park** (4705 N Bank Rd) has 18 sites along the Smith River, off Hwy 197. Both of these are an excellent bargain.

TOP CHOICE **Curly Redwood Lodge** MOTEL $
(707-464-2137; www.curlyredwoodlodge.com; 701 Hwy 101 S; r $68-73;) The Redwood Lodge is a marvel: it's entirely built and paneled from a single curly redwood tree which measured over 18-in thick in diameter. Progressively restored and polished into a gem of mid-century kitsch, the inn is a delight for retro junkies. Rooms are clean, large and comfortable (request one away from the road). For truly modern accommodations, look elsewhere.

Bay View Inn HOTEL $
(800-742-8439; www.bayviewinn.net; 2844 Fairfield; r $74-89;) Bright, modern, updated rooms with microwaves and refrigerators fill this centrally located independent hotel. It may seem a bit like better-than-average highway exit chain, but colorful bead spreads and warm hosts add necessary homespun appeal. The rooms upstairs in the back have views of the lighthouse and the harbor.

Crescent Beach Motel MOTEL $
(707-464-5436; www.crescentbeachmotel.com; 1455 Hwy 101 S; r $70-100;) Just south of town, this basic, old-fashioned motel is the only place in town to stay right on the beach, offering views that distract you from the somewhat plain indoor environs. Try here first, but skip rooms without a view.

Anchor Beach Inn HOTEL $
(707-464-2600; www.anchorbeachinn.com; 880 Hwy 101 S; r $85-105;) Microwave, DSL, soundproof walls and personality-free.

Eating & Drinking

Beacon Burger BURGERS $
(160 Anchor Way; burgers $6-10; 11:30am-8:30pm Mon-Sat) This scrappy little one-room burger joint has been here forever, square in the middle of a parking lot overlooking the South Bay. It looks like it might invite a health inspector's scorn, but you'll quickly forgive it after ordering a burger – perfectly greasy and mysteriously wonderful. They come sided with potato gems and a menu of thick shakes.

Wing Wah Restaurant CHINESE $
(383 M St; mains $7-11; 11:30am-9pm Sun-Thu, to 9:30 Fri & Sat) Tucked into a shopping center, Wing Wah serves Crescent City's best Chinese food; savory pork and beef dishes are fresh and come quickly to the table.

Good Harvest Café AMERICAN $
(575 Hwy 101 S; mains $7-10; 7am-9pm Mon-Sat, from 8am Sun;) This popular local cafe recently moved into a spacious new location across from the harbor. It also added a dinner menu on par with the quality salads, smoothies and sandwiches that made it so popular in the first place. Good beers, a crackling fire and loads of vegetarian options make this the best dining spot in town.

Chart Room SEAFOOD $
(130 Anchor Way; dinner mains $9-23; 6:30am-7pm Sun-Thu, to 8pm Fri & Sat;) At the tip of the South Harbor pier, this joint is renowned far and wide for its fish and chips: batter-caked golden beauties which deliver on their reputation. It's often a hive of families, retirees, Harley riders and local businessmen, so grab a beer at the small bar and wait for a table.

Tomasini's CAFE $
(960 3rd St; mains $4-8; 7:30am-2pm;) Stop in for salads, sandwiches or jazz on weekend nights. Hands down the most happening place downtown.

Information

Crescent City-Del Norte Chamber of Commerce (707-464-3174, 800-343-8300; www.northerncalifornia.net; 1001 Front St; 9am-5pm May-Aug, 9am-5pm Mon-Fri Sep-Apr) Local information.

Redwood National & State Parks Headquarters (707-464-6101; 1111 2nd St; 9am-5pm Oct-May, to 6pm Jun-Sep) On the corner of K St; rangers and information about all four parks under its jurisdiction.

Getting There & Around

United Express (800-241-6522) flies into tiny **Crescent City Airport** (CEC), north of town. **Redwood Coast Transit** (www.redwoodcoasttransit.org) serves Crescent City with local buses ($1), and runs buses Monday to Saturday to Klamath ($1.50, one hour, two daily) and Arcata ($20, two hours, two daily) with stops in between.

Tolowa Dunes State Park & Lake Earl Wildlife Area

Two miles north of Crescent City, this **state park and wildlife area** (707-464-6101, ext 5112; sunrise-sunset) encompasses 10,000 acres of wetlands, dunes, meadows and two lakes, **Lake Earl** and **Lake Tolowa**. This major stopover on the Pacific Flyway route brings over 250 species of birds. Listen for the whistling, warbling chorus. On land, look for coyotes and deer, Angle for trout, or hike or ride 20 miles of trails; at sea, spot whales, seals and sea lions.

The park and wildlife area is a patchwork of lands administered by California State Parks and the Department of Fish and Game (DFG). The DFG focuses on single-species management, hunting and fishing; the State Parks' focus is on ecodiversity and recreation. You might be hiking a vast expanse of pristine dunes, then suddenly hear a shotgun or a whining 4WD. Strict regulations limit where and when you can hunt and drive; trails are clearly marked.

Register for two primitive, nonreservable **campgrounds** (tent sites $20) at Jedediah Smith or Del Norte Coast Redwoods State Park campgrounds. The mosquitoes are plentiful in the spring and early summer.

Jedediah Smith Redwoods State Park

The northern-most park in the system of Redwood National & State Parks, the dense stands at **Jedediah Smith** (day use $8) are 10 miles northeast of Crescent City (via Hwy 101 east to Hwy 197). The redwood stands are so thick that few trails penetrate the park, but the outstanding 11-mile **Howland Hill scenic drive** cuts through otherwise inaccessible areas (take Hwy 199 to South Fork Rd; turn right after crossing two bridges). It's a rough road, impassable for RVs, but if you can't hike, it's the best way to see the forest.

Stop for a stroll under enormous trees in **Simpson-Reed Grove**. If it's foggy at the coast it may be sunny here. There's a **swimming hole** and picnic area near the park entrance. An easy half-mile trail, departing from the far side of the campground, crosses the **Smith River** via a summer-only footbridge, leading to **Stout Grove**, the park's most famous grove. The **visitor center** (☎707-464-6101; ⏲10am-4pm daily Jun-Aug, 10am-4pm Sat & Sun Sep-Oct & Apr-May) sells hiking maps and nature guides. If you wade in the river, be careful in the spring when currents are swift and the water cold.

The popular **campground** (☎reservations 800-444-7275; www.reserveamerica.com; tent & RV sites $35) has gorgeous sites tucked through the redwoods beside the Smith River.

If you don't camp, try the renovated **Hiouchi Motel** (☎707-458-3041, 888-881-0819; www.hiouchimotel.com; 2097 Hwy 199; s $50, d $65-70; @📶) offering clean, straightforward motel rooms.

Pelican Beach State Park

Never-crowded **Pelican State Beach** (☎707-464-6101, ext 5151) occupies five coastal acres on the Oregon border. There are no facilities, but it's great for kite flying; pick one up at the shop just over the border in Oregon.

The best reason to visit is to stay at secluded, charming **Casa Rubio** (☎707-487-4313; www.casarubio.com; 17285 Crissey Rd; r $108-168; @📶🐾), where three of the four ocean-view rooms have kitchens.

Pitch a tent by the ocean (no windbreaks) at **Clifford Kamph Memorial Park** (☎707-464-7230; 15100 Hwy 101; tent sites $10); no RVs. It's a steal for the beachside location and, even though sites are exposed in a grassy area and there isn't much privacy, all have BBQs.

Northern Mountains

Includes »

Best Places to Eat

- Jack's Grill (p265)
- Red Onion Grill (p273)
- Café Le Coq (p277)
- Trinity Café (p283)
- Vivify (p283)

Best Places to Stay

- McCloud River Mercantile Hotel (p288)
- Houseboat on Shasta Lake (p268)
- Bidwell House B&B (p273)
- Feather Bed B&B (p276)
- Feather River Canyon Campgrounds (p276)

Why Go?

The northeast corner is the remote, rugged, refreshingly pristine backyard of a state better known for sunny cities, sandy beaches and foggy groves of redwoods. This is California's wild frontier, where vast expanses of wilderness – some 24,000 protected acres – are divided by rivers and streams, dotted with cobalt lakes, horse ranches and alpine peaks. Much of it doesn't even look the way people envision California – the topography more resembles the older mountains of the Rockies than the relatively young granite Goliaths in Yosemite. Don't come here for the company (the towns are hospitable but tiny, with virtually no urban comforts); come to get lost in vast remoteness. Even the two principal attractions, Mt Shasta and Lassen Volcanic National Park, remain uncrowded (and sometimes snow-covered) at the peak of the summer.

When to Go

Lassen National Park

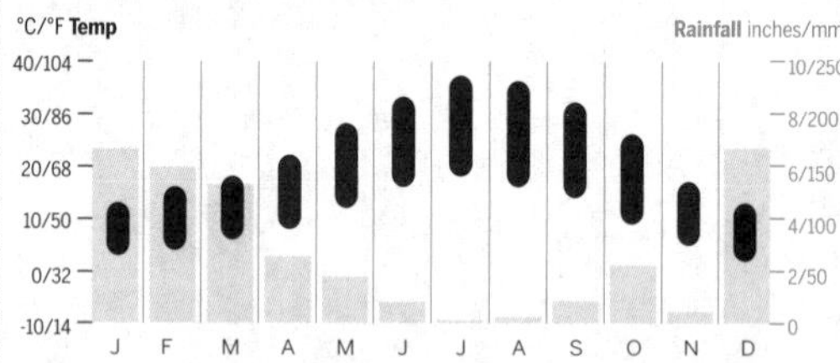

Jul–Sep Warm weather and snow-free passes are ideal for backcountry camping.

Oct–Nov & Apr–May Shoulder seasons; scattered showers and snow at the high elevations.

Nov–Jan Skiing Mt Shasta is the main draw. Prices drop outside of ski areas.

REDDING & AROUND

North of Red Bluff the dusty central corridor along I-5 starts to give way to panoramic mountain ranges on either side. Redding is the last major outpost before the small towns of the far north, and the surrounding lakes make for easy day trips or overnight camps. If you get off the highway – way off – this can be an exceptionally rewarding area of the state to explore.

FAST FACTS

» **Population of Redding** 90,050

» **Average temperature low/high in Redding** Jan 35/55°F, Jul 64/98°F

» **Redding to San Francisco** 215 miles, 3½ hours

» **Redding to Los Angeles** 545 miles, 8¼ hours

» **Redding to Eureka** 150 miles, three hours

Redding

Originally called Poverty Flats during the Gold Rush for its lack of wealth, Redding today has a whole lot of tasteless new money – malls, big-box stores and large housing developments surround its core. A tourist destination it is not, though it is the major gateway city to the northeast corner of the state and a useful spot for restocking before long jaunts into the wilderness. Recent constructions like the Sundial Bridge and Turtle Bay Exploration Park are enticing lures and worth a visit…but not a long one. Downtown is bordered by the Sacramento River to the north and east. Major thoroughfares are Pine and Market Sts.

Sights & Activities

Sundial Bridge BRIDGE

Resembling a beached cruise ship, the shimmering-white 2004 Sundial Bridge spans the river and is one of Redding's marquee attractions, providing an excellent photo op. The glass-deck pedestrian overpass connects the Turtle Bay Exploration Park to the north bank of the Sacramento River and was designed by renowned Spanish architect Santiago Calatrava. The bridge/sundial attracts visitors from around the world, who come to marvel at this unique feat of engineering artistry. It is accessed from the park and connects to the Sacramento River Trail system.

Turtle Bay Exploration Park SCIENCE CENTER

(www.turtlebay.org; 840 Auditorium Dr; adult/child 4-12yr $14/10; 9am-5pm May-Sep, 9am-4pm Wed-Sat & 10am-4pm Sun Oct-Apr;) Situated on 300 meandering acres, this is an artistic, cultural and scientific center for visitors of all ages, with an emphasis on the Sacramento River watershed. The complex houses art and natural science museums, fun interactive exhibits for kids (a recent show was 'Grossology', a study of the human body's less-delicate biology). There are also extensive arboretum gardens, a butterfly house and a 22,000-gallon, walk-through river aquarium full of regional aquatic life (yes, including turtles). The on-site **Café at Turtle Bay** (meals $12) serves excellent gourmet coffee and great light meals.

Redding Aquatic Center WATER PARK

(www.reddingaquaticcenter.com; adult/child $5/3; 1-5pm summer, with seasonal variations) Further west in Caldwell Park, this hugely popular center contains an Olympic-size pool, another vast recreation pool and a 160ft-long water slide. Also in Caldwell Park, you can pick up the **Sacramento River Trail** (www.reddingtrails.com), a paved walking and cycling path that meanders along the river for miles.

Cascade Theatre HISTORIC BUILDING

(www.cascadetheatre.org; 1733 Market St) Try to catch some live music downtown at this refurbished 1935 art deco theater. Usually it hosts second-tier national acts but, if nothing else, take a peek inside; this is a neon-lit gem.

Sleeping

Redding's many motels and hotels huddle around noisy thoroughfares, though a few rooms can be found on less busy N Market St. A couple of motel rows lie close to I-5 at the southern end of town: just west of the freeway close to the Cypress Ave exit on Bechelli Lane, and on the east side of the freeway on Hilltop Dr. The chain hotels – and there are plenty of them – are all off I-5 and you can get great last-minute deals on the internet. The best tent camping is just up the road at Whiskeytown Lake (p267) or Shasta Lake (p267).

Northern Mountains Highlights

1. Stand agape at geothermal spectacles in **Lassen Volcanic National Park** (p269)
2. Wander the cute mountainside community of **Mt Shasta City** (p280)
3. Explore the many caves of **Lava Beds National Monument** (p289)
4. Look overhead at the bird superhighway at **Tule Lake** (p290)
5. Get lost in **Modoc** (p291), California's most remote national forest
6. Hide out and wade in the trout-filled water near **Weaverville** (p292)
7. Camp along the shores of gorgeous **Eagle Lake** (p275)
8. Hit the dramatic slopes of **Shasta** (p279)
9. Float with a dozen pals on a **Shasta Lake houseboat** (p268)
10. Kick up your heels at **McCloud's famous dance hall** (p288)

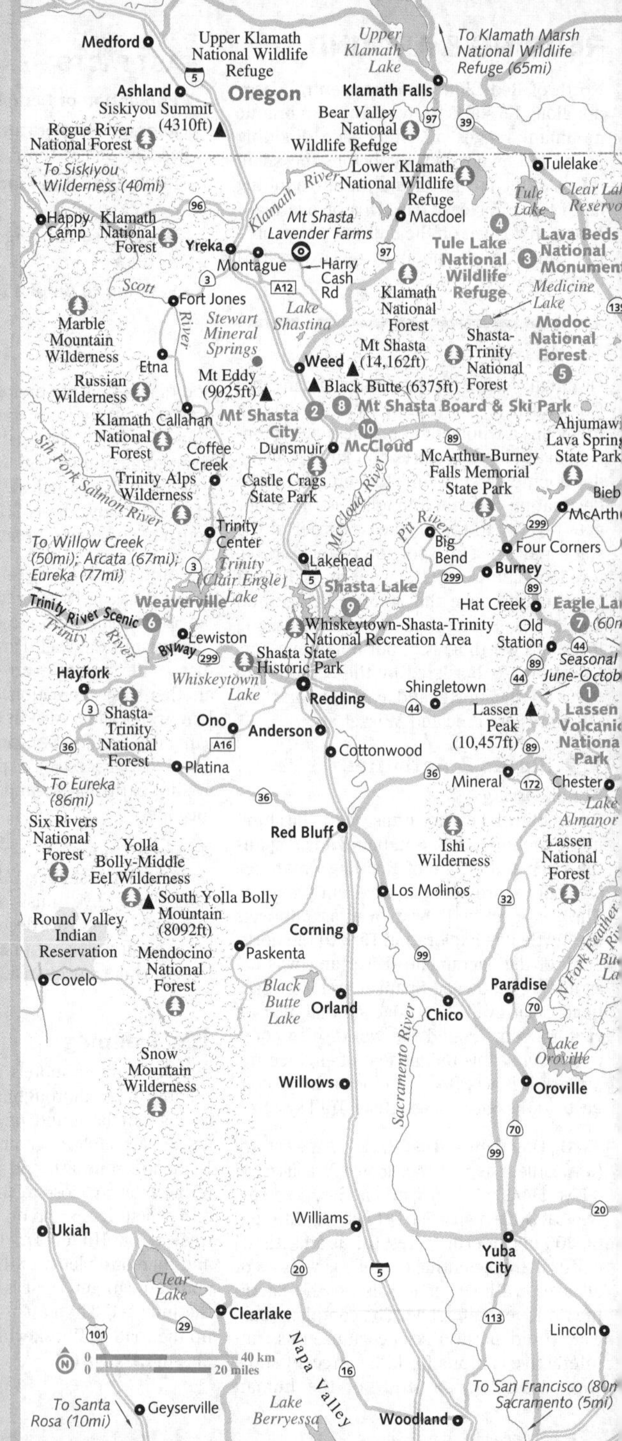

Apples' Riverhouse B&B B&B $$
(☎530-243-8440; www.applesriverhouse.com; 201 Mora Ct; r $95-110) Just steps from the Sacramento River Trail, this modern, ranch-style home has three comfortable upstairs rooms, two with decks. It's a bit suburban, but it's the best independent stay in Redding. In the evening the sociable hosts invite you for cheese and wine. Bikes are yours to borrow and the proximity to the trail is inviting.

Tiffany House B&B Inn B&B $$
(☎530-244-3225; www.tiffanyhousebb.com; 1510 Barbara Rd; r $110-120, cottage $170;) In a quiet cul-de-sac, a mile north of the river, this Victorian cottage has an expansive garden with sweeping views. Cozy rooms are packed with antiques, rosebuds and ruffles. Affable hosts make a big yummy to-do over breakfast.

Eating & Drinking

If you want Redding's best food, it's essential that you get off the highway and into the downtown area.

Carnegie's CALIFORNIAN $$
(1600 Oregon St; meals $12; 10am-3pm Mon & Tue, to 11pm Wed-Fri;) This hip and homey, split-level cafe serves up healthy food – big fresh salads, garlicky prawns and pasta and homemade tomato soup. There's a good selection of beer and wine, too. Friday nights get a little rowdy, and there can be a wait.

Jack's Grill STEAKHOUSE $$$
(www.jacksgrillredding.com; 1743 California St; mains $15-31; 5-11pm, bar from 4pm Mon-Sat) This funky little old-time place doesn't look so inviting – the windows are blacked out and it's dark as a crypt inside – but the popularity with locals starts with its stubborn ain't-broke-don't-fix-it ethos and ends with its steak – a big, thick, charbroiled decadence. Regulars start lining up for dinner at 4pm, when cocktail hour begins. There are no reservations, so it easily takes an hour to get a seat.

Grilla Bites SANDWICHES $
(www.grillabites.com; 1427 Market St; meals $5-10; 11am-8pm Mon-Thu, to 9pm Fri & Sat, to 4pm Sun;) It doesn't get much simpler than this menu of grilled sandwiches and pay-by-the-pound salad bar but, to Grilla's credit, the food is fresh, locally sourced and the sandwiches are punched up with fresh herbs and global fusions. The grilled Italian Veggie sandwich is a savory melt of pesto and cheese, and the Thai Tuna is a local favorite.

DETOUR AROUND THE I-5 DOLDRUMS

A good alternative for travelers heading north and south on I-5 is to drive along Hwy 3 through the Scott Valley, which rewards with world-class views of the Trinity Alps. Compared to rushing along the dull highway, this scenic detour will add an additional half a day of driving.

Thai Cafe THAI $$
(www.thaicafeofredding.com; 820 Butte St; mains $10-15; 11am-9pm Mon-Sat) To mix it up after days of camp-stove cooking on the trail, hit this excellent Thai place with an extensive menu. The seafood mains (so far from the sea) are surprisingly fresh, and the tom yum soup – with lemongrass, cilantro and the right amount of sourness – is spot on.

Gironda's Chicago Style Italian Restaurant ITALIAN $$
(www.2girondas.com; 1100 Center St; mains $10-20; 11:30am-9pm Mon-Thu, to 10pm Sat;) It's a little pricey and finding the place is a bit of a chore (it hides near the Eureka Way rail overpass, just off downtown), but the plates of Chicago-style deep dish, fresh pastas and relaxed family vibe are a nice break from the highway-side chains. Start with the crispy calamari.

Buz's Crab SEAFOOD $
(www.buzscrab.com; 2159 East St; meals $5-12; 11am-9pm) There's zero pretension to Buz's; it's just a low-slung crab shack along the busy central district of Redding. The menu has fish and chips alongside healthier choices like grilled trout and salmon. It comes sided with garlic bread on 'almost famous' sourdough and slaw. The attached market has lobster and good advice about what to grill for a picnic.

Alehouse Pub BAR
(www.reddingalehouse.com; 2181 Hilltop Dr; 3pm-midnight Mon-Thu, to 1:30am Fri & Sat) Too bad for fans of the cheap stuff, this local pub keeps a selection of highly hopped beers on tap and sells T-shirts emblazoned with 'No Crap on Tap.' It's a fun local place that gets packed after Redding's young professionals get out of work.

Breaking New Grounds CAFE
(☎530-246-4563; 1320 Yuba St; 6am-7pm Mon-Thu, to 10pm Fri, 7am-4pm Sat;) With a sort

Redding

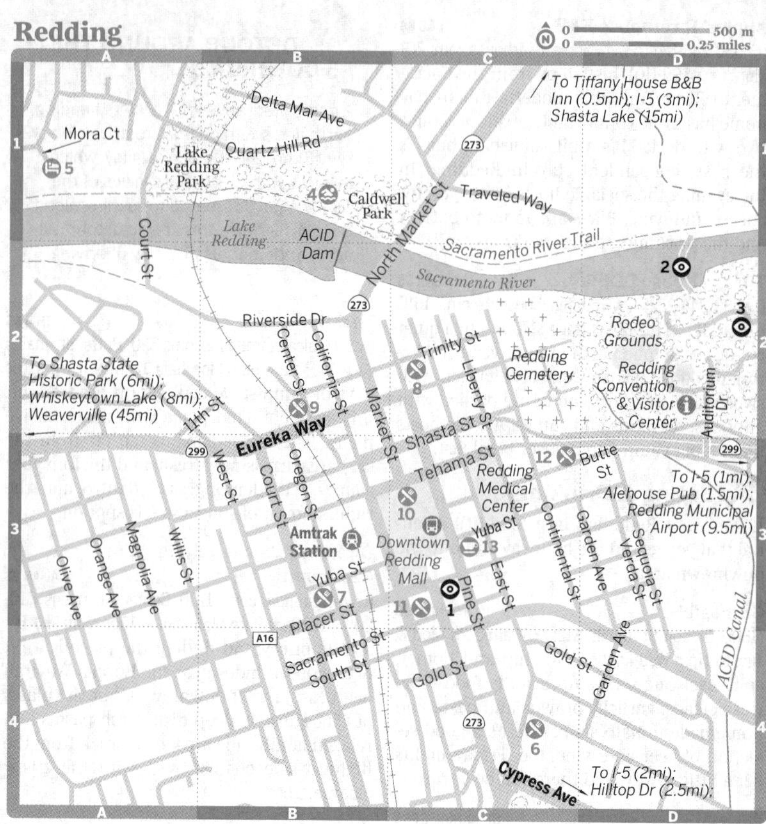

of relaxed living-room feel, this wi-fi cafe attracts a cross section of local folks. Live acoustic music is featured on Friday nights.

Information

California Welcome Center (☎530-365-1180; www.shastacascade.org; 1699 Hwy 273, Anderson; ⊙9am-6pm Mon-Sat, from 10am Sun) About 10 miles south of Redding, in Anderson's Prime Outlets Mall. It's an easy stop for northbound travelers who are likely to pass it on the I-5 approach. It stocks maps for hiking and guides to outdoor activities, and the website has an excellent trip planning section for the region.

Redding Convention & Visitor Center (☎530-225-4100; www.visitredding.com; 777 Auditorium Dr; ⊙9am-6pm Mon-Fri, 10am-5pm Sat) Near Turtle Bay Exploration Park.

Shasta-Trinity National Forest Headquarters (☎530-226-2500; 3644 Avtech Pkwy; ⊙8am-4:30pm Mon-Fri) South of town, in the USDA Service Center near the airport. Has maps and free camping permits for all seven national forests in Northern California.

Getting There & Around

Redding Municipal Airport (RDD; www.ci.redding.ca.us; 6751 Woodrum Circle,) is 9.5 miles southeast of the city, just off Airport Rd. United Express flies to San Francisco.

The **Amtrak station** (www.amtrak.com; 1620 Yuba St), one block west of the Downtown Redding Mall, is not staffed. For the *Coast Starlight* service, make advance reservations by phone or via the website, then pay the conductor when you board the train. Amtrak travels once daily to Oakland ($62, six hours), Sacramento ($47, four hours) and Dunsmuir ($22, 1¾ hours).

The **Greyhound bus station** (1321 Butte St), adjacent to the Downtown Redding Mall, never closes. Destinations include San Francisco ($41, 8½ hours, four daily) and Weed ($24.50, 1½ hours, three daily). The **Redding Area Bus Authority** (RABA; www.rabaride.com) has a dozen city routes operating until around 6pm

Redding

Sights

1 Cascade Theatre....C3
2 Sundial Bridge....D2
3 Turtle Bay Exploration Park....D2

Activities, Courses & Tours

4 Redding Aquatic Center....B1

Sleeping

5 Apples' Riverhouse B&B....A1

Eating

6 Buz's Crab....C4
7 Carnegie's....B3
8 Chu's Too....C2
9 Gironda's Chicago Style Italian Restaurant....B2
10 Grilla Bites....C3
11 Jack's Grill....C3
12 Thai Cafe....C3

Drinking

13 Breaking New Grounds....C3

Monday to Saturday. Fares start at $1.50 (exact change only).

Around Redding

SHASTA STATE HISTORIC PARK

On Hwy 299, 6 miles west of Redding, this **state historic park** (sunrise-sunset) preserves the ruins of an 1850s Gold Rush mining town called Shasta – not to be confused with Mt Shasta City (p280). When the Gold Rush was at its heady height, everything and everyone passed through this Shasta. But when the railroad bypassed it to set up in Poverty Flats (present-day Redding), poor Shasta lost its raison d'être. Shopkeepers packed up shingle and moved to Redding – literally. They moved many of Shasta's businesses brick by brick.

An 1861 courthouse contains the excellent **museum** (530-243-8194; admission $2; 10am-5pm Wed-Sun;), the best in this part of the state. With its amazing gun collection, spooky holograms in the basement and a gallows out back, it's a thrill ride. There's also a fantastic collection of art. Pick up walking-tour pamphlets from the information desk and follow trails to the Catholic cemetery, brewery ruins and many other historic sites. At the time of writing, the future of this state park was uncertain and it was subject to closure.

WHISKEYTOWN LAKE

Two miles further west on Hwy 299, sparkling **Whiskeytown Lake** (530-242-3400; www.nps.gov/whis; day use per vehicle $5) takes its name from an old mining camp. When the lake was created in the 1960s by the construction of a 263ft dam, designed for power generation and Central Valley irrigation, the few remaining buildings of old Whiskeytown were moved and the camp was submerged. John F Kennedy was present at the dedication ceremony, less than two months before his assassination. Today folks descend on the lake's serene 36 miles of forested shoreline to camp, swim, sail, mountain bike and pan for gold.

The **visitors center** (530-246-1225; 9am-6pm May-Sep, 10am-4pm Oct-Apr), on the northeast point of the lake, just off Hwy 299, provides free maps and information on Whiskeytown and Whiskeytown-Shasta-Trinity National Recreation Area from knowledgeable and agreeable staff. Look for ranger-led interpretive programs and guided walks. The hike from the visitors center to roaring **Whiskeytown Falls** (3.4 miles round trip) follows a former logging road and is a good quick trip.

On the southern shore of the lake, **Brandy Creek** is ideal for swimming. Just off Hwy 299, on the northern edge of the lake, **Oak Bottom Marina** (530-359-2269) rents boats. On the western side of the lake, the **Tower House Historic District** contains the El Dorado mine ruins and the pioneer Camden House, open for summer tours. In winter, when the trees are bare, it's an atmospheric, quiet place to explore.

Oak Bottom Campground (800-365-2267; tent/RV sites $20/22) is a privately run place with RV and tent camping. It's a bit tight, but nicer than most private campgrounds, with lots of manzanita shade. Most attractive are the walk-in sites right on the shore. **Primitive campsites** (summer/winter $10/5) surround the lake. The most accessible of these is the one at **Crystal Creek** – which doesn't have water, but has nice views.

Shasta Lake

About 15 minutes north of Redding, the largest reservoir in California, **Shasta Lake** (www.shastalake.com), is home to the state's biggest population of nesting bald eagles. Surrounded by hiking trails and campgrounds, the lake gets packed in summer. The lake is also home to more than 20 different kinds of fish, including rainbow trout.

The **ranger station** (☎530-275-1589; 14250 Holiday Rd; ⏰8am-4:30pm daily May-Sep, Mon-Fri Oct-Apr) offers free maps and information about fishing, boating and hiking. To get here take the Mountaingate Wonderland Blvd exit off I-5, about 9 miles north of Redding, and turn right.

Sights & Activities

Shasta Dam
DAM

On scale with the enormous natural features of the area, this colossal, 15-million-ton dam is second only in size to Hoover Dam in Nevada. It's at the south end of the lake on Shasta Dam Blvd (Hwy 151). Built between 1938 and 1945, its 487ft spillway is as high as a 60-story building – three times higher than Niagara Falls. Woody Guthrie wrote 'This Land is Your Land' while he was here working on the dam. The **Shasta Dam visitors center** (☎530-275-4463; ⏰8:30am-4:30pm) offers fascinating free guided tours of the structure's rumbling interior.

Lake Shasta Caverns
CAVE TOUR

(www.lakeshastacaverns.com; adult/child 3-11yr $22/13; ⏰tours 9am-4pm; 👪) High in the limestone megaliths at the north end of the lake hide these prehistoric caves. Tours of the crystalline caves operate daily and include a boat ride across Lake Shasta, and the office has a spacious play area for kids. The Cathedral Room is particularly stunning. Bring a sweater for the tours, as the temperature inside is 58°F (14°C) year-round. To get there take the Shasta Caverns Rd exit from I-5, about 15 miles north of Redding, and follow the signs for 1.5 miles.

Sleeping & Eating

Hike-in camping and RV parks are sprinkled around the shores of the lake and houseboats are a wildly popular option. Most houseboats require a two-night minimum stay. Make reservations as far in advance as possible, especially in the summer months. Boats usually sleep 10 to 16 adults and cost around $1400 to $8400 per week. The RV parks are often crowded and lack shade, but they have on-site restaurants. If you want to explore the area on a day trip, stay in Redding (p263).

US Forest Service (USFS) campgrounds
CAMPGROUNDS $

(☎877-444-6777; www.reserveusa.com; tent sites $6-26) About half of the USFS campgrounds around the lake are open year-round. The lake's many fingers have a huge range of camping, with lake and mountain views, and some of them are very remote. Free boat-in sites are first-come, first-served. Camping outside organized campgrounds requires a campfire permit from May to October, available free from any USFS office.

Holiday Harbor Resort
HOUSEBOATS & CAMPGROUND $

(☎530-238-2383; www.lakeshasta.com; Holiday Harbor Rd; tent & RV sites $36, houseboats for 2 nights from $920; 📶👪) Primarily an RV campground, it also rents houseboats and the busy marina offers parasailing and fishing-boat rentals. A little **cafe** (⏰8am-3pm) sits lakefront. It's off Shasta Caverns Rd, next to the lake.

Antlers RV Park & Campground
CAMPGROUND & CABINS $

(☎530-238-2322; www.shastalakevacations.com; 20679 Antlers Rd; tent & RV sites $17-35, cabins from $179; 🏊👪) East of I-5 in Lakehead, at the north end of the lake, this family-oriented campground has cabins, a country store and a marina renting watercraft and houseboats.

Lakeshore Inn & RV
CAMPGROUND $

(☎530-238-2003; www.shastacamping.com; 20483 Lakeshore Dr; RV sites $20-33, cabins from $95; 📶🏊👪) On the western side of I-5, this lakeside vacation park has a restaurant and tavern, horseshoes and basic cabins.

MT LASSEN & AROUND

The dramatic crags, volcanic formations and alpine lakes of Lassen Volcanic National Park seem surprisingly untrammeled when you consider they are only a few hours from the Bay Area. Snowed in through most of winter, the park blossoms in late spring. While it is only 50 miles from Redding, and thus close enough to be enjoyed on a day trip, to really do it justice you'll want to invest a few days exploring the area along its scenic, winding roads. From Lassen Volcanic National Park you can take one of two very picturesque routes: Hwy 36, which heads east past Chester, Lake Almanor and historic Susanville; or Hwy 89, which leads southeast to the cozy mountain town of Quincy.

Lassen Volcanic National Park

The dry, smoldering, treeless terrain within this 106,000-acre national park stands in stunning contrast to the cool, green conifer forest that surrounds it. That's the summer; in winter tons of snow ensures you won't get too far inside its borders. Still, entering the park from the southwest entrance is to suddenly step into another world. The lavascape offers a fascinating glimpse into the earth's fiery core. In a fuming display the terrain is marked by roiling hot springs, steamy mud pots, noxious sulfur vents, fumaroles, lava flows, cinder cones, craters and crater lakes.

In earlier times the region was a summer encampment and meeting point for Native American tribes – namely the Atsugewi, Yana, Yahi and Maidu. They hunted deer and gathered plants for basket-making here. Some indigenous people still live nearby and work closely with the park to help educate visitors on their ancient history and contemporary culture.

KNOW ABOUT THE SNOW

Rangers tell rueful stories about people who drive across the country in their RVs to find the roads of Lassen Volcanic National Park impassable; don't let it happen to you. The road through the park is usually only open from June to October, though it has been closed due to snow (as much as 40ft of it) well into July at times. Travelers need to call ahead or check the park website (www.nps.gov/lavo; click 'Current Conditions') to get weather conditions before considering a visit during all but a couple of months of the year – the only safe bets are August and September. A slow melt or freak storm can close major parts of the park at any other time of year.

Sights & Activities

Lassen Peak, the world's largest plug-dome volcano, rises 2000ft over the surrounding landscape to 10,457ft above sea level. Classified as an active volcano, its most recent eruption was in 1917, when it spewed a giant cloud of smoke, steam and ash 7 miles into the atmosphere. The national park was created the following year to protect the newly formed landscape. Some areas destroyed by the blast, including the aptly named **Devastated Area** northeast of the peak, are recovering impressively. You can hike the **Lassen Peak Trail**, which has been under renovation for some time; check in with rangers before attempting to get to the top. An easy 1.3 mile hike partway up, to the Grandview viewpoint, is suitable for families. The 360-degree view from the top is stunning, even if the weather is a bit hazy.

Hwy 89, the road through the park, wraps around Lassen Peak on three sides and provides access to dramatic geothermal formations, pure lakes, gorgeous picnic areas and remote hiking trails.

In total, the park has 150 miles of **hiking trails**, including a 17-mile section of the Pacific Crest Trail. Experienced hikers can attack the Lassen Peak Trail; it takes at least 4½ hours to make the 5-mile round trip. Early in the season you'll need snow and ice-climbing equipment to reach the summit. Near the Kom Yah-mah-nee visitor facility, a gentler 2.3-mile trail leads through meadows and forest to **Mill Creek Falls**. Further north on Hwy 89 you'll recognize the roadside **sulfur works** by its bubbling mud pots, hissing steam vent, fountains and fumaroles. At **Bumpass Hell** a moderate 1.5-mile trail and boardwalk lead to an active geothermal area, with bizarrely colored pools and billowing clouds of steam.

The road and trails wind through cinder cones, lava and lush alpine glades, with views of Juniper Lake, Snag Lake and the plains beyond. Most of the lakes at higher elevations remain partially and beautifully frozen in summer. Leave time to fish, swim or boat on **Manzanita Lake**, a slightly lower emerald gem near the northern entrance.

Sleeping & Eating

If you're coming to Lassen Volcanic National Park from the north on Hwy 89, you won't see many gas/food/lodgings signs after Mt Shasta City and your best option is to stock up en route and camp.

The park has eight developed **campgrounds** (☎877-444-6777; www.recreation.gov; tent & RV sites $10-18), and there are many more in the surrounding Lassen National Forest. Campgrounds in the park are open from late May to late October, depending on snow conditions. Manzanita Lake is the only one with hot showers, but the two Summit Lake campgrounds, in the middle of the park, are also

Lassen Volcanic National Park

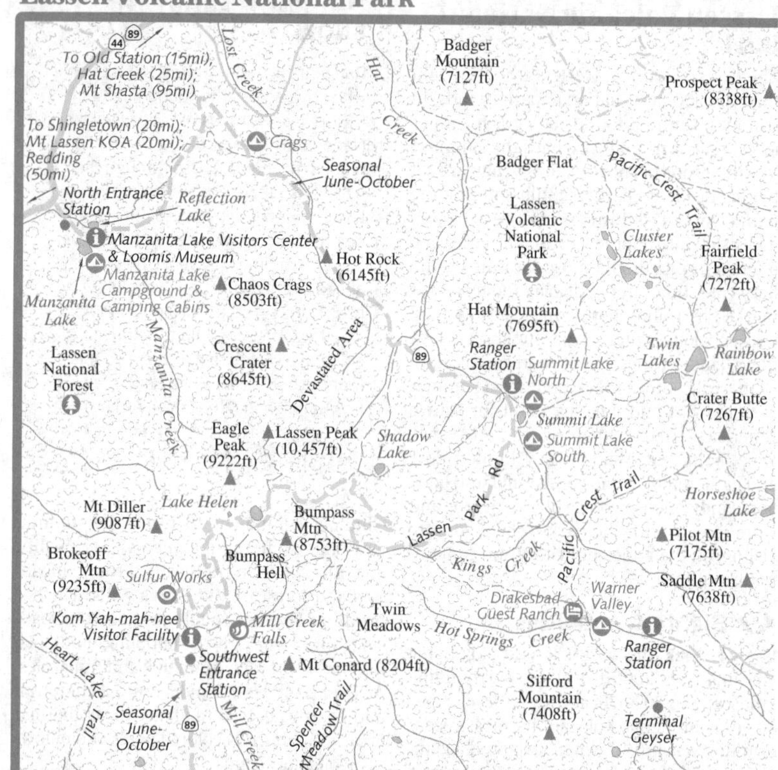

popular. Reservations are permitted at Butte Lake in the northeast corner of the park, Manzanita Lake in the northwest, Summit Lake North and Summit Lake South.

If you don't want to camp, the nearest place to stay is Chester (p272), which accesses the south entrance of the park. There are some basic services near the split of Hwy 88 and Hwy 44, in the north.

NORTH ENTRANCE OF THE PARK

Manzanita Lake Camping Cabins CABINS & CAMPGROUND **$**

(☎winter 530-200-4578, summer 530-335-7557; www.lassenrecreation.com; Hwy 89, near Manzanita Lake; tent & RV sites $18, r $57-81;) These freshly built log cabins enjoy a lovely position on one of Lassen's lakes and they come in one- and two-bedroom options and slightly more basic bunk configurations, which are a bargain for groups. They all have bear boxes and fire rings. Those who want to get a small taste of Lassen's more rustic comforts can call ahead to arrange a 'Camper Package,' which includes basic supplies for a night under the stars (starting at $100, it includes a s'mores kit).

Hat Creek Resort & RV Park CABINS, CAMPGROUND **$**

(☎800-568-0109; www.hatcreekresortrv.com; 12533 Hwy 44/89; ten & RV sites without/with hookups $22/39, r $90-180;) Outside the park Old Station makes a decent stop before entering and is a good second choice after Manzanita Lake Camping Cabins, sitting along a fast-moving, trout-stocked creek. Some simple motel rooms and cabins have full kitchens. Stock up at the convenience store and deli, then eat on a picnic table by the river.

SOUTH ENTRANCE OF THE PARK

Drakesbad Guest Ranch RANCH **$$$**

(☎530-529-1512, ext 120; www.drakesbad.com; Warner Valley Rd; r per person $176-190; ⊙Jun-early Oct;) Seventeen miles northwest of Ches-

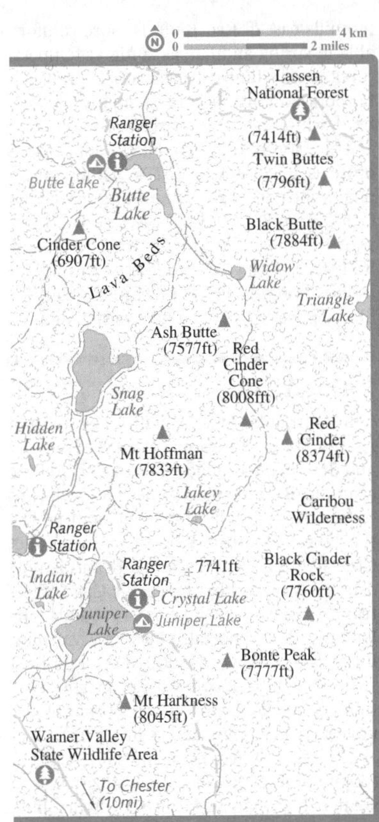

ter, this fabulously secluded place lies inside the park's southern boundary. Guests, many of whom are faithful repeat visitors, use the hot-springs-fed swimming pool or go horseback riding. Except in the main lodge, there's no electricity here (the kerosene lamps and campfires give things a lovely glow). Rates include country-style meals (vegetarian options available) and campfire barbecues every Wednesday. This is one of the few places in the region to book up solidly, so make advance reservations as soon as possible.

Childs Meadow Resort CABINS **$$**
(☎530-595-3383; www.childsmeadowresort.com; 41500 E Hwy 36, Mill Creek; d $60-70, cabins $75-150;) Rustic cabins – some of them more like permanently parked RV trailers – sit at the edge of a spectacularly lush mountain meadow 9 miles outside the park's southwest entrance. Don't expect the Ritz; it's an old-fashioned, very rustic, mountain resort experience, but it's very close to the park.

Mt Lassen KOA CAMPGROUND **$**
(☎530-474-3133; www.koa.com; 7749 KOA Rd; tent sites $28, RV sites from $40, cabins $57-140; mid-Mar–Nov;) Enjoy all the standard KOA amenities: a playground, a deli and laundry facilities. It's off Hwy 44 in Shingletown, about 20 miles west of the park.

Information

Whether you enter at the north or southwest entrance, you'll be given a free map with general information.

Kom Yah-mah-nee visitor facility (☎530-595-4480; 9am-6pm Jun-Sep, hr vary Oct-May) About half a mile north of the park's southwest entrance, this handsome new center is certified at the highest standard by the US Green Building Council. Inside there are educational exhibits (including a cool topographical volcano), a bookstore, an auditorium, a gift shop and a restaurant. Visitor information and maps available.

Manzanita Lake Visitors Center & Loomis Museum (☎530-595-4480; 9am-5pm Jun-Sep) Just past the entrance-fee station at the park's northern boundary, you can see exhibits and an orientation video inside this museum. During summer, rangers and volunteers lead programs on geology, wildlife, astronomy and local culture. Visitor information and maps available.

Park headquarters (☎530-595-4444; www.nps.gov/lavo; 38050 Hwy 36; 8am-4:30pm daily Jun-Sep, 8am-4:30pm Mon-Fri Oct-May) About a mile west of the tiny town of Mineral, it's the nearest stop for refueling and supplies.

Getting There & Away

There's virtually no way to visit this park without a car, though all the two-lane roads around the park and the ample free national forest camping options make for excellent, if fairly serious, cycle touring.

The park has two entrances. The northern entrance, at Manzanita Lake, is 50 miles east of Redding via Hwy 44. The southwest entrance is on Hwy 89, about 5 miles north of the junction with Hwy 36. From this junction it is 5 miles west on Hwy 36 to Mineral and 44 miles west to Red Bluff. Heading east on Hwy 36, Chester is 25 miles away and Susanville about 60 miles. Quincy is 65 miles southeast from the junction on Hwy 89.

Mt Lassen Transit (☎530-529-2722; www.mtlassentransit.com) buses between Red Bluff and Susanville ($25) run via Mineral ($15), which is the stop closest to the park. There's no public transportation within the park or on the 5 miles between Hwy 36 and the park entrance. Call ahead to arrange pick-up.

WORTH A TRIP

WILD HORSE SANCTUARY

Since 1978 the **Wild Horse Sanctuary** (☎530-335-2241; www.wildhorsesanctuary.com; Shingletown; admission free; ⏲9am-4pm Wed & Sat) has been sheltering horses and burros that would otherwise have been destroyed. You can visit its humble visitors center on Wednesdays and Saturdays to see these lovely animals or even volunteer for a day, with advance arrangement. To see them on the open plains, take a two- to three-day weekend pack trip in spring or summer (from $435 per person). Shingletown lies 20 miles to the west of Lassen Volcanic National Park.

Lassen National Forest

The vast **Lassen National Forest** (www.fs.fed.us/r5/lassen) surrounding Lassen Peak and Lassen Volcanic National Park, is so big that it's hard to comprehend: it covers 1.2 million acres (1875 sq miles) of wilderness in an area called the Crossroads, where the granite Sierra, volcanic Cascades, Modoc Plateau and Central Valley meet. It's largely unspoiled land, though if you wander too far off the byways surrounding the park, you'll certainly see evidence of logging and mining operations that still happen within its borders.

The forest has some serious hikes, with 460 miles of **trails**, ranging from the brutally challenging (120 miles of the Pacific Crest Trail), to ambitious day hikes (the 12-mile Spencer Meadows National Recreation Trail), to just-want-to-stretch-the-legs-a-little trails (the 3.5-mile Heart Lake National Recreation Trail). Near the intersection of Hwys 44 and 89, visitors to the area will find one of the most spectacular features of the forest, the pitch-black 600yd **Subway Cave** lava tube. Other points of interest include the 1.5-mile volcanic **Spattercone Crest Trail**, **Willow Lake** and **Crater Lake**, 7684ft **Antelope Peak**, and the 900ft-high, 14-mile-long **Hat Creek Rim** escarpment.

For those seeking to get far off the beaten trail, the forest has three wilderness areas. Two high-elevation wilderness areas are the **Caribou Wilderness** and **Thousand Lakes Wilderness**, best visited from mid-June to mid-October. The **Ishi Wilderness**, at a much lower elevation in the Central Valley foothills east of Red Bluff, is more comfortable in spring and fall, as summer temperatures often climb to over 100°F (37°C). It harbors California's largest migratory deer herd, which can be upwards of 20,000 head.

The Lassen National Forest supervisor's office is in Susanville (p274). Other ranger offices include **Eagle Lake Ranger District** (☎530-257-4188; 477-050 Eagle Lake Rd, Susanville), **Hat Creek Ranger District** (☎530-336-5521; 43225 E Hwy 299, Fall River Mills) and **Almanor Ranger District** (☎530-258-2141; 900 E Hwy 36, Chester), about a mile west of Chester.

Lake Almanor Area

Calm, turquoise Lake Almanor lies south of Lassen Volcanic National Park via Hwys 89 and 36. This man-made lake is a crystalline example of California's sometimes awkward conservation and land-management policy: the lake was created by the now-defunct Great Western Power Company and is now ostensibly owned by the Pacific Gas & Electric Company. The lake is surrounded by lush meadows and tall pines and was once little-visited. Now, a 3000-acre ski resort sits on the hills above, with properties continually being developed near its shore and power boats zipping across its surface.

The main town near the lake, Chester (population 2500, elevation 4528ft), is a sight better than some of the dreary little towns of the area. Though you could whiz right by and dismiss it as a few blocks of nondescript roadside storefronts, don't – it's not. This robust little community has a fledgling art scene, decent restaurants and some comfy places to stay.

Sleeping & Eating

The best sleeping options for campers are in the surrounding national forest.

CHESTER

Along Chester's main drag you'll find a scattering of '50s-style inns, some chain motels and a few chain lodgings (the nicest of which is the fairly overpriced Best Western Rose Quartz Inn). Many of these places keep seasonal hours and, when you live in a place where it can snow in mid-June, the season is short.

St Bernard Lodge B&B $
(☎530-258-3382; www.stbernardlodge.com; 44801 E Hwy 36, Mill Creek; d with shared bath $99; 📶) Located 10 miles west of Chester, at Mill Creek,

this old-world charmer has seven B&B rooms with views to the mountains and forest. All have knotty-pine paneling and quilted bedspreads. There are stables on site where those travelling with a horse can board them and have access to the nearby network of Lassen's trails. The tavern is good too – serving meaty American lunches and dinner.

Bidwell House B&B B&B $$
(☎530-258-3338; www.bidwellhouse.com; 1 Main St; r with shared bath $85, r with private bath $115-165, cottage $175;) Set back from the street, this historic summer home of pioneers John and Annie Bidwell, is packed with antiques. The classic accommodations come with all the modern amenities (including a spa in some rooms) – no roughing it here. Enjoy goodies like a three-course breakfast, home-baked cookies and afternoon sherry.

Cinnamon Teal Inn VACATION RENTAL $$
(☎530-258-3993; www.cinnamontealinn.net; 227 Feather River Dr; r from $140) You can rent out just one room or the entire large home, a half-block back from Main St. There's a more intimate option on the property – perfect for three people – with the small nearby cottage. All have river access from the gardens. Fluffy feather beds dominate each wood-paneled room. The cottage has a full kitchen.

TOP CHOICE **Red Onion Grill** NEW AMERICAN $$$
(www.redoniongrill.com; 384 Main St; meals $10-25; 11am-9pm) Hand's-down the finest dining that Chester has on offer, the upscale New American cuisine has generous Italian influences (like the simply prepared rock shrimp and crab Alfredo) and bar food that's executed with real panache. The setting is casual and fun – wall lanterns and a crackling fire – made all the more warm by the best wine list in town.

Knotbumper Restaurant AMERICAN $
(274 Main St; meals $8-10; 11am-8pm Tue-Sat) The Knotbumper is unlikely to dish up your most memorable meal, but it has a generous deli menu, including tamale pies, shrimp salad sandwiches and other eclectic selections. On summer days, eat on the lively front porch and watch the trucks rumble by. This place virtually closes down in the winter.

AROUND THE LAKE

Book ahead for lakefront lodgings in summer. There are restaurants at the resorts.

Federal campgrounds CAMPGROUNDS $
(☎reservations 877-444-6777; www.reserveusa.com; tent sites $12-20) These campgrounds lie within the surrounding Lassen and Plumas National Forests on the lake's southwest shore. Sites tend to be more tranquil than the RV-centric private campgrounds that are right on the water. A favorite for tents and RVs, **Rocky Point Campground** is right on the lake, with some sites basically on the beach. For something more remote, try the **Cool Springs Campground** at the Butt Reservoir (try to say that with a straight face!). It's at the south end of the lake, at the end of Prattville Butt Reservoir Rd.

SCENIC DRIVE: LASSEN SCENIC BYWAY

Even in the peak of summer, you'll have the uncrowded byways of the Lassen Scenic Byway mostly to yourself. The long loop though Northern California wilderness skirts the edge of Lassen Volcanic National Park (p269) and circles Lassen Peak (p269) one of the largest dormant volcanoes on the planet. It mostly covers the big green patches on the map: expansive areas perfect for hiking, fishing, camping or just getting lost. This is a place where few people venture, and those who do come back with stories.

The launching point for this big loop could be either Redding (p263) or Sacramento (p322), but there are few comforts for travelers along this course. The only cities in this neck of the woods – little places like Chester (p272) and Susanville (p274) – aren't all that exciting on their own; they're mostly just places to gas up, buy some beef jerky and enjoy the week's only hot meal. But the banner attractions are visible in every direction – the ominous, dormant volcanic peak of Lassen, the wind-swept high plains and the seemingly endless wilderness of the Lassen and Plumas National Forests.

This loop is formed by Hwy 36, Hwy 44 and Hwy 89. (You can see the map and some of the highlights at www.byways.org/explore/byways/2195.) Its best to do the drive between late June through mid-October. Other times of the year some of these roads close due to snow.

North Shore Campground CABINS, CAMPGROUND $
(☎530-258-3376; www.northshorecampground.com; tent sites $35, RV sites $39-51, cabins $150-230; 📶) Two miles east of Chester on Hwy 36, these expansive, forested grounds stretch for a mile along the water, but they get filled up with mostly RVs. Ranch-style cabins have full kitchens and are a good option for families. This place is fine if you want to spend all your time waterskiing on the lake, but those seeking the solitude of nature should look elsewhere.

Knotty Pine Resort & Marina CABINS $$
(☎530-596-3348; www.knottypine.net; 430 Peninsula Dr; weekly RV sites $175, 2-bedroom cabins with kitchen $155, r $195; 🏊) This full-service lakeside alternative, 7 miles east of Chester, has simple cabins and rents boats, kayaks and canoes.

Information

Rent boats and water-sports equipment at many places around the lake.

Bodfish Bicycles & Quiet Mountain Sports (☎530-258-2338; www.bodfishbicycles.com; 152 Main St, Chester) This outfit rents bicycles ($40 per day), cross-country skis and snowshoes, and sells canoes and kayaks. It's a great source of mountain-biking and bicycle-touring advice. If you want just a taste of the lovely rides possible in this part of the state, make this a priority stop.

Chester & Lake Almanor Chamber of Commerce (☎530-258-2426; www.chester-lakealmanor.com; 529 Main St, Chester; ⌚9am-4pm Mon-Fri) Get information about lodging and recreation around the lake, in Lassen National Forest and in Lassen Volcanic National Park.

Lassen National Forest Almanor ranger station (☎530-258-2141; 900 E Hwy 36; ⌚8am-4:30pm Mon-Fri) About a mile west of Chester, with similar information to the chamber of commerce.

Susanville

Though it sits on a lovely high desert plateau, the Lassen County seat (population 17,974) isn't so much of a charmer; it's a resupply post with a Wal-Mart, a few stop lights and two prisons. Not a tourist destination in itself, it does provide basic services for travelers passing through. It lies 35 miles east of Lake Almanor and 85 miles northwest of Reno – and is home to a couple of modest historic sites. Despite the fact that it recently ranked 29th as a place for hunters and fishermen to live in *Outdoor Life* magazine, chances are this will be a place to stop on the way to somewhere else. The best event in town is the **Lassen County Fair** (☎530-251-8900; www.lassencountyfair.org), which swings into gear in July.

For local information about the town visit the **Lassen County Chamber of Commerce** (☎530-257-4323; www.lassencountychamber.org; 84 N Lassen St; ⌚9am-4pm Mon-Fri), while the **Lassen National Forest supervisor's office** (☎530-257-2151; 2550 Riverside Dr; ⌚8am-4:30pm Mon-Fri) has maps and recreation information for getting into the surrounding wilds.

The restored **Susanville Railroad Depot**, south of Main St, off Weatherlow St, sits beside the terminus of the Bizz Johnson Trail (see the boxed text, p275). The **visitors center** (☎530-257-3252; 601 Richmond Rd; ⌚10am-4pm May-Oct) rents bicycles and has brochures on mountain-biking trails in the area.

The town's oldest building, **Roop's Fort** (1853), is named after Susanville's founder, Isaac Roop. The fort was a trading post on the Nobles Trail, a California emigrant route. The town itself was named after Roop's daughter, Susan. Beside the fort is the freshly built **Lassen Historical Museum** (75 N Weatherlow St; admission by donation; ⌚10am-4pm Mon-Fri May-Oct), which has well-presented displays of clothing and memorabilia from the area that's worth a 20-minute visit.

Motels along Main St, none of them exceptional, average $50 to $75 per night. Try **Roseberry House B&B** (☎530-257-5675; www.roseberryhouse.com; 609 North St; r/ste $110/135; 👪) for more character. This sweet 1902 Victorian house is two blocks north of Main St. Striking dark-wood antique headboards and armoires combine with rosebuds and frill. There are nice little touches, like bath salts and candy dishes. In the morning, expect homemade muffins and jam as part of the full breakfast turned out by Richard, a culinary-school grad.

For simple, quick lunches and dinners, the best bet is the standout **Happy Garden** (1960 Main St; mains $6-13; ⌚11am-7pm), which serves steaming plates of noodles and a big lunch combo that comes with soup, an egg roll and rice for $7. The serviceable Chinese food is served in a light-filled, centrally located former diner.

The other option for food is the historic **Pioneer Café** (724 Main St), the oldest surviving watering hole on Main St. One saloon or another has been operating on this site since 1862 and today it's a combination bar, billiards room and inexpensive eatery. At the time of research it was closed.

Mt Lassen Transit (530-529-2722) buses leave Red Bluff at 8:30am Monday to Saturday ($25, 4½ hours) and return from Susanville at 2pm. **Susanville City Buses** (530-252-7433) make a circuit around town (fare $1).

Eagle Lake

Those who have the time to get all the way out to Eagle Lake, California's second-largest natural lake, are rewarded with one of the most striking sites in the region: a stunningly blue jewel on the high plateau. From late spring until fall this lovely lake, about 15 miles northwest of Susanville, attracts a smattering of visitors who come to cool off, swim, fish, boat and camp. On the south shore, you'll find a pristine 5-mile **recreational trail** and several busy **campgrounds** (reservations 877-444-6777; www.recreation.gov; tent sites $20, RV sites $29-33) administered by Lassen National Forest and the **Bureau of Land Management** (BLM; 530-257-5381). Campgrounds for tent camping include Merrill, Aspen, Christie and Eagle. Most of them are fairly scrubby, considering how lovely the lake is, though there are some highly sought-after lakeside sites in Merrill. Merrill and Eagle also have RV sites. Nearby **Eagle Lake Marina** (www.eaglelakerecreationarea.com) offers hot showers, laundry and boat rentals. It also can help you get out onto the lake with a fishing license.

Eagle Lake RV Park (530-825-3133; www.eaglelakeandrv.com; 687-125 Palmetto Way; tent/RV sites $25/37, cabins $115-170;), on the western shore, and **Mariners Resort** (530-825-3333; Stones Landing; RV sites $37-40, cabins $115-185), on the quieter northern shore, both rent boats.

Quincy

Idyllic Quincy (population 1738) is one of the Northern Mountains three mountain communities, which teeter on the edge of becoming an incorporated town (the other two are Burney, in Shasta County, and Weaverville). It's no metropolis, but it does have a large grocery store and two of the three fast-food franchises in the entirety of Plumas County. Nestled in a high valley in the northern Sierra, southeast of both Lassen Volcanic National Park and Lake Almanor via Hwy 89, it is a lovely little place, endowed with just enough edge by the student population of the local Feather River College. Nearby Feather River, Plumas National Forest, Tahoe National Forest and their oodles of open space make Quincy an excellent base from which to explore.

Once in town Hwy 70/89 splits into two one-way streets, with traffic on Main St heading east, and traffic on Lawrence St heading west. Jackson St runs parallel to Main St, one block south, and is another main artery. Just about everything you need is on, near or between these three streets, making up Quincy's low-key commercial district.

WORTH A TRIP

WESTWOOD & THE BIZZ JOHNSON TRAIL

A few miles east of Chester is Westwood, a tiny speck of a town that marks the beginning of the **Bizz Johnson Trail**, an extremely picturesque route that runs the remote 25.5 miles from Westwood to Susanville. Once part of the old Southern Pacific right-of-way, the wooden bridges and serenely crossing-free trail are traversable by foot, mountain bike, horseback or cross-country skis (no motorized vehicles allowed!). Do the trail in the Westwood–Susanville direction, as it's mostly downhill that way. Get trail guides at the chamber of commerce in Chester (p274) or at the Susanville Railroad Depot (p274).

Sights & Activities

Pick up free walking and driving tour pamphlets from the visitors center to guide you through the gorgeous surrounding **American Valley**. The Feather River Scenic Byway (Hwy 70) leads into the Sierra. In summer the icy waters of county namesake **Feather River** (*plumas* is Spanish for feathers) are excellent for swimming, kayaking, fishing and floating in old inner tubes. The area is also a wonderland of winter activities, especially at Bucks Lake (p277).

Plumas County Museum MUSEUM
(www.plumasmuseum.org; 500 Jackson St, at Coburn St; adult/child $2/1; 9am-4:30pm Tue-Sat;) In the block behind the courthouse, this excellent multifloor county museum has

flowering gardens, as well as hundreds of historical photos and relics from the county's pioneer and Maidu days, its early mining and timber industries, and construction of the Western Pacific Railroad. Unlike most other Northern Mountains community museums, it's not easy to see this all within an hour.

Plumas County Courthouse HISTORIC BUILDING
(Main St) Pop into the 1921 Plumas County Courthouse, at the west end of Main St, to see enormous interior marble posts and staircases, and a 1-ton bronze-and-glass chandelier in the lobby.

Sierra Mountain Sports OUTDOORS
(www.sierramountainsports.net; 501 W Main St) Across from the courthouse, rent cross-country ski gear and snowshoes here.

Big Daddy's Guide Service FISHING TRIPS
(www.bigdaddyfishing.com) Captain Bryan Roccucci is Big Daddy, the only fishing guide in Northeast California. He knows the lakes well and leads trips for all levels (starting at $150 per person).

Festivals & Events

TOP CHOICE **High Sierra Music Festival** MUSIC
(www.highsierramusic.com) On the first weekend in July, quiet Quincy is host to this blowout festival, renowned statewide. The four-day extravaganza brings a five-stage smorgasbord of art and music from a spectrum of cultural corners (indie rock, classic blues, folk and jazz). Local national acts include My Morning Jacket, Gillian Welch, former James Brown saxophonist Maceo Parker and Neko Case. Sure, a curmudgeonly local might call it the Hippie Fest, but it's pretty tame in comparison to some of Northern California's true fringe festivals. If you plan to attend, reserve a room or campsite a couple of months in advance. For those who don't want to camp in nearby national forest land, Susanville (p274), one hour away, will have the largest number of rooms.

Sleeping

TOP CHOICE **Quincy Courtyard Suites** VACATION RENTAL $$
(☎530-283-1401; www.quincycourtyardsuites.com; 436 Main St; apt $129-159;) Staying in this beautifully renovated 1908 Clinch building, overlooking the small main drag of Quincy's downtown, feels just right, like renting the village's cutest apartment. The warmly decorated rooms are modern – no fussy clutter – and apartments have spacious, modern kitchens, claw-foot tubs and gas fireplaces.

Feather Bed B&B B&B $$
(☎530-283-0102; www.featherbed-inn.com; 542 Jackson St, at Court St; d from $150, cottages $179-190;) Just behind the courthouse, this frilly pink 1893 Queen Anne home is all antiques and cuteness – a teddy bear adorns every quilted bed (just one reason this is a family-friendly B&B). The buildings share space on a block of wide lawns and big old trees. Gracious hosts make afternoon tea with cookies, killer breakfasts (fresh fruit smoothies, eggs and sausage) and guests can borrow bikes. The cottage is accessible for travelers with disabilities.

Feather River Canyon Campgrounds CAMPGROUNDS $
(☎reservations 877-444-6777; www.recreation.gov; tent & RV sites $15-20) Area campgrounds are administered through the Mt Hough Ranger District Office. They are in a cluster along the north fork of the Feather River west of Quincy – five are no-fee, but also have no piped water.

Ada's Place B&B $$
(☎530-283-1954; www.adasplace.com; 562 Jackson St; cottages $100-145;) Even though it has the feel of a B&B, it's a bit of a misnomer. Without breakfast, Ada's is just an excelent B. No problem, as each of the three brightly painted garden units has a full kitchen. Ada's Cottage is worth the slight extra charge, as its skylights offer an open feel. It's very quiet and private, with a DSL internet connection.

Pine Hill Motel MOTEL $
(☎530-283-1670; www.pinehillmotel.com; 42075 Hwy 70; s/d/cabin from $69/75/150;) A mile west of downtown Quincy, this little hotel is protected by an army of statues and surrounded by a big lawn. The units are nothing fancy, but they're clean and in a constant state of renovation. Each is equipped with a microwave, coffeemaker and refrigerator; some cabins have full kitchens.

Greenhorn Guest Ranch RANCH $$$
(☎800-334-6939; www.greenhornranch.com; 2116 Greenhorn Ranch Rd; per person per day incl trail rides from $290; May-Oct;) Not a 'dude' ranch but rather a 'guest' ranch: instead of shoveling stalls, guests are pampered with mountain trail rides, riding lessons, even rodeo practice. Or you can just fish, hike,

square dance and attend evening bonfires, cookouts and frog races – think of it like a cowboy version of the getaway resort in *Dirty Dancing*. Before you raise an eyebrow at the price, note that meals and riding are all included.

Eating & Drinking

Quincy is a good supply point for those headed into or out of the wilderness. There are some good restaurants, a big grocery store, and a sprawling **farmers market** (cnr Church & Main Sts; 5-8pm Thu mid-Jul–mid-Sep).

Café Le Coq FRENCH $$
(530-283-0114; www.cafelecoq.biz; 189 Main St; prix fixe menu lunch/dinner $17/32; 11:30am-1:30pm Mon-Wed & 5-8pm Tue-Sat) The French chef/owner, Michel LeCoq, flutters about this cute little Victorian; on a leisurely (perfectly French) lunch, he'll amble out to explain the specials (the $10 prix fixe lunch is a steal), help guide you in the right direction, cook them and check in when it's done. Delicious gourmet French meals, including house-cured meats, are served in a homey dining area or on the wraparound porch in summer.

Pangaea Café & Pub CAFE $
(www.pangaeapub.com; 461 W Main St; mains $8-12; 11am-9pm Mon-Thu, to 10pm Fri) Like a stranger you feel you've met before, this earthy spot feels warmly familiar, all the more lovable when you consider its commitment to serving produce from local farmers. The specialty is panini, which come in flavorful, mostly veggie combinations. The beer list has lots of interesting choices, too. The little nook in the back has a computer and it has live music most weekends.

Morning Thunder Café BREAKFAST $$
(557 Lawrence St; meals $9-15; 7am-2pm) Homey and hip, this is the best place in town for breakfast and the vine-shaded patio is a lovely way to start the day. The menu is mainly, though not exclusively, vegetarian. Try the vegetaters: roasted veg and potatoes smothered in cheese, the chicken avocado 'thunder melt,' or the 'drunken pig,' which brilliant balances savory pork and pineapple.

Moon's ITALIAN $$
(530-283-0765; 497 Lawrence St; mains $11-24; 5-8:30pm Tue-Sun) Follow the aroma of garlic to this welcoming little chalet with a charming ambience. Dig into choice steaks and Italian-American classics, including excellent pizza and rich lasagna.

Sweet Lorraine's CALIFORNIAN $$
(384 Main St; meals $12-22; lunch Mon-Fri, dinner Mon-Sat) On a warm day – or, better yet, evening – the patio here is especially sweet. The menu features light Californian cuisine (fish, poultry, soups and salads), but it's also known for its award-winning St Louis ribs. Finish things off with the whiskey bread pudding.

Drunk Brush WINE BAR
(www.facebook.com/TheDrunkBrush; 438 Main St) A sweet little courtyard wine bar pours 25 wines and a few beers. Sample delicious appetizer pairings in a welcoming, arty atmosphere.

Information

Mt Hough Ranger District Office (530-283-0555; 39696 Hwy 70; 8am-4:30pm Mon-Fri) Five miles west of town. Has maps and outdoors information.

Plumas County visitors center (530-283-6345; www.plumascounty.org; 550 Crescent St; 8am-5pm Mon-Sat) Half a mile west of town.

Plumas National Forest headquarters (530-283-2050; 159 Lawrence St; 8am-4:30pm Mon-Fri) For maps and outdoors information.

Bucks Lake

This clear mountain lake is cherished by locals in the know. Surrounded by pine forests, it's excellent for swimming, fishing and boating. It's about 17 miles southwest of Quincy, via the white-knuckle roads of Bucks Lake Rd (Hwy 119). The region is lined with beautiful **hiking trails**, including the Pacific Crest Trail, which passes through the adjoining 21,000-acre Bucks Lake Wilderness in the northwestern part of Plumas National Forest. In winter, the last 3 miles of Bucks Lake Rd are closed by snow, making it ideal for cross-country skiers.

Bucks Lake Lodge (530-283-2262; www.buckslakelodge.com; 16525 Bucks Lake Rd; d & cabins $109-119) rents boats and fishing tackle in summer and cross-country skis in winter. The **restaurant** (mains $7-16) is popular with locals. **Haskins Valley Inn** (530-283-9667; www.haskinsvalleyinn.com; 1305 Haskins Circle; r from $149) is actually a lakefront B&B with cozily overstuffed furnishings, woodsy paintings, Jacuzzis, fireplaces and a deck. The bold southwestern rugs and heavy rough timber bed post of the Cowboy Room is a favorite.

Five first-come, first-served **campgrounds** (sites $20-25) are open from June to September. Get a map at the Plumas National Forest Headquarters or the ranger station, both in Quincy (see p277).

MT SHASTA & AROUND

'Lonely as God, and white as a winter moon, Mount Shasta starts up sudden and solitary from the heart of the great black forests of Northern California,' wrote poet Joaquin Miller on the sight of this lovely mountain. A sight of it is so awe-inspiring that the new age prattle about its power as an 'energy vortex' begins to sound plausible after a few days in its shadow. There are a million ways to explore the mountain and surrounding Shasta-Trinity National Forest, depending on the season – you can take scenic drives or get out and hike, mountain-bike, raft, ski or snowshoe. At Mt Shasta's base sit three excellent little towns: Dunsmuir, Mt Shasta City and McCloud. Each community has a distinct personality but all share a wild-mountain sensibility and first-rate restaurants and places to stay. In the same dramatic vicinity rise the snaggle-toothed peaks of Castle Crags, just 6 miles west of Dunsmuir.

Northeast of Mt Shasta, a long drive and a world away, is remote, eerily beautiful Lava Beds National Monument, a blistered badland of petrified fire. The contrasting cool wetlands of Klamath Basin National Wildlife Refuges are just west of Lava Beds.

Further east, high desert plateaus give way to the mountains of the northern Sierra. Folks in this remote area are genuinely happy to greet a traveler, even if they're a bit uncertain why you've come.

Mt Shasta

'When I first caught sight of it I was 50 miles away and afoot, alone and weary. Yet all my blood turned to wine, and I have not been weary since,' wrote naturalist John Muir of Mt Shasta in 1874. Mt Shasta's beauty is intoxicating, and the closer you get to her the headier you begin to feel. Dominating the landscape, the mountain is visible for more than 100 miles from many parts of Northern California and southern Oregon. Though not California's highest peak (at 14,162ft it ranks fifth), Mt Shasta is especially magnificent because it rises alone on the horizon, unrivaled by other mountains.

Mt Shasta is part of the vast volcanic Cascade chain that includes Lassen Peak to the south and Mt St Helens and Mt Rainier to the north in Washington state. The presence of thermal hot springs indicates that Mt Shasta is dormant, not extinct. Smoke was seen puffing out of the crater on the summit in the 1850s, though the last eruption was about 200 years ago. The mountain has two cones: the main cone has a crater about 200yd across; the younger, shorter cone on the western flank, called Shastina, has a crater about half a mile wide.

The mountain and surrounding **Shasta-Trinity National Forest** (www.fs.fed.us/r5/shastatrinity) are crisscrossed by trails and dotted with alpine lakes. It's easy to spend days or weeks here, camping, hiking, river rafting, skiing, mountain-biking and boating.

The story of the first settlers here is a sadly familiar one: European fur trappers arrived in the area in the 1820s, encountering several Native American tribes, including the Shasta, Karuk, Klamath, Modoc, Wintu and Pit River people. By 1851, hordes of Gold Rush miners had arrived and steamrolled the place, destroying the tribes' traditional life and nearly causing their extinction. Later the newly completed railroad began to import workers and export timber for the booming lumber industry. And since Mt Shasta City (called Sisson at the time) was the only non-dry town around, it became *the* bawdy, good-time hangout for lumberjacks.

The lumberjacks have now been replaced by middle-aged mystics and outdoor sports enthusiasts. While the slopes have immediate appeal for explorers, spiritual seekers are attracted to the peak's reported cosmic properties. In 1987, about 5000 believers from around the world convened here for the Harmonic Convergence, a communal meditation for peace. Reverence for the mountain is nothing new; for centuries Native Americans have honored the mountain as sacred, considering it to be no less than the Great Spirit's wigwam.

Many use Redding (p263) as a base since there are plenty of chain options along the highway, but Mt Shasta City (p281) is the best balance of convenience, value and personality. For food, there are satisfying restaurants at all the mountain towns, though consider having snacks on hand in the car as the winding drives from the woods to the lunch counter are time-consuming.

Sights & Activities

THE MOUNTAIN

You can drive almost the whole way up the mountain via the Everitt Memorial Hwy (Hwy A10) and see exquisite views at any time of year. Simply head east on Lake St from downtown Mt Shasta City, then turn left onto Washington Dr and keep going. **Bunny Flat** (6860ft), which has a trailhead for Horse Camp and the Avalanche Gulch summit route, is a busy place with parking spaces, information signboards and a toilet. The section of highway beyond Bunny Flat is only open from about mid-June to October, depending on snow, but if it's clear, it's worth the trouble. This road leads to **Lower Panther Meadow**, where trails connect the campground to a Wintu sacred spring, in the upper meadows near the **Old Ski Bowl** (7800ft) parking area. Shortly thereafter is the highlight of the drive, **Everitt Vista Point** (7900ft), where a short interpretive walk from the parking lot leads to a stone-walled outcrop affording exceptional views of Lassen Peak to the south, the Mt Eddy and Marble Mountains to the west and the whole Strawberry Valley below.

Climbing the summit is best done between May and September, preferably in spring and early summer, when there's still enough soft snow on the southern flank to make footholds easier on the nontechnical route. Although the elements are occasionally volatile and the winds are incredibly strong, the round trip could conceivably be done in one day with 12 or more hours of solid hiking. A more enjoyable trip takes at least two days with one night on the mountain. How long it actually takes depends on the route selected, the physical condition of the climbers and weather conditions (for weather information call the recorded message of the Forest Service Mt Shasta climbing advisory on ☎530-926-9613).

The hike to the summit from Bunny Flat follows the **Avalanche Gulch Route**. Although it is only about 7 miles, the vertical climb is more than 7000ft, so acclimatizing to the elevation is important – even hearty hikers will be short of breath. Additionally this route requires crampons, an ice ax and a helmet, all of which can be rented locally. Rock slides, while rare, are also a hazard. If

Mt Shasta Area

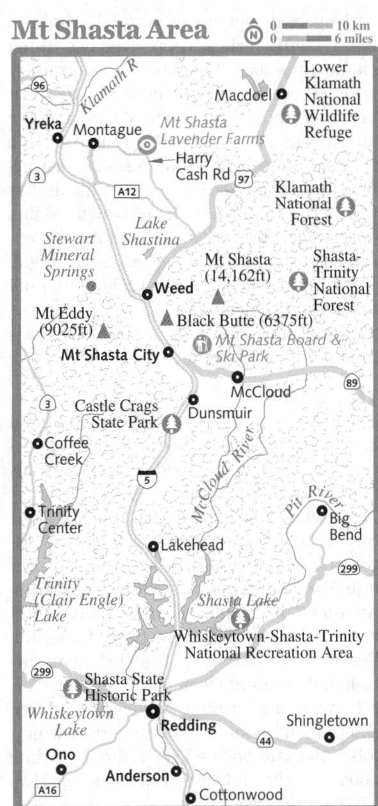

you want to make the climb without gear, the only option is the **Clear Creek Route** to the top, which leaves from the east side of the mountain. In late summer, this route is usually manageable in hiking boots, though there's still loose scree, and it should be done as an overnight hike. Novices should contact the Mt Shasta ranger station for a list of available guides.

There's a charge to climb beyond 10,000ft: a three-day summit pass costs $20; an annual pass is $30. Contact the ranger station for details. You must obtain a free wilderness permit any time you go into the wilderness, whether on the mountain or in the surrounding area.

Mt Shasta Board & Ski Park SNOW SPORTS
(☎snow reports 530-926-8686; www.skipark.com; full-day lift tickets adult/child $39/20; ⏰9am-9pm Thu-Sat, to 4pm Sun-Tue) On the south slope of Mt Shasta, off Hwy 89 heading toward McCloud, this winter skiing and snowboarding

park opens depending on snowfall. The park has a 1390ft vertical drop, over two dozen alpine runs and 18 miles of cross-country trails. These are all exceptionally good for beginner and intermediate skiers, and the area makes a less-crowded alternative to the slopes around Lake Tahoe. Rentals, instruction and weekly specials are available. It's Northern California's largest night-skiing operation. There are lots of inexpensive options for skiing half a day or just at night, when hitting the slopes and taking in a full moon can be enchanting.

In summer, the park occasionally hosts mountain-biking events.

THE LAKES

There are a number of pristine mountain lakes near Mt Shasta. Some of them are accessible only by dirt roads or hiking trails and are great for getting away from it all.

The closest lake to Mt Shasta City is **Lake Siskiyou** (also the largest), 2.5 miles southwest on Old Stage Rd, where you can peer into **Box Canyon Dam**, a 200ft-deep chasm. Another 7 miles up in the mountains, southwest of Lake Siskiyou on Castle Lake Rd, lies **Castle Lake**, an unspoiled gem surrounded by granite formations and pine forest. Swimming, fishing, picnicking and free camping are popular in summer; in winter folks ice-skate on the lake. **Lake Shastina**, about 15 miles northwest of town, off Hwy 97, is another beauty.

Information

Peak tourist season is from Memorial Day through Labor Day and weekends during ski season (late November to mid-April). The ranger station and visitors center are in Mt Shasta City (p284).

Mt Shasta City

No town, no matter how lovely – and Mt Shasta City (population 3394) is lovely – could compete with the surrounding natural beauty here. Understandably most visitors don't make a pilgrimage here to visit the fish hatchery, they come to meet the mountain. Still, downtown itself is charming; you can spend hours poking around bookstores, galleries and boutiques. Orienting yourself is easy with Mt Shasta looming over the east side of town. The downtown area is a few blocks east of I-5. Take the Central Mt Shasta exit, then drive east on Lake St past the visitors center, up to the town's main intersection at Mt Shasta Blvd, the principal drag.

Sights & Activities

To head out hiking on your own, first stop by the ranger station or the visitors center for excellent free trail guides, including several access points along the **Pacific Crest Trail**. Gorgeous **Black Butte**, a striking, treeless, black volcanic cone, rises almost 3000ft. The 2.5-mile trail to the top takes at least 2½ hours for the round trip. It's steep and rocky in many places, and there is no shade or water, so don't hike on a hot summer day. Wear good, thick-soled shoes or hiking boots and bring plenty of water. If you want an easier amble, try the 10-mile **Sisson-Callahan National Recreation Trail**, a partially paved trail that affords great views of Mt Shasta and the jagged Castle Crags, following a historic route established in the mid-1800s by prospectors, trappers and cattle ranchers to connect the mining town of Callahan with the town of Sisson, now called Mt Shasta City.

Mt Shasta City Park & Sacramento River Headwaters PARK

(Nixon Rd) Off Mt Shasta Blvd, about a mile north of downtown, the headwaters of the Sacramento River gurgle up from the ground in a large, cool spring. It's about as pure as water can get – so bring a bottle and have a drink. The park also has walking trails, picnic spots, sports fields and courts and a children's playground.

Sisson Museum MUSEUM

(www.mountshastasissonmuseum.org; 1 Old Stage Rd; admission $1; ⏲10am-4pm Mon-Sat, 1-4pm Sun Jun-Sep, 1-4pm Fri-Sun Oct-Dec, 1-4pm daily Apr & May) A half-mile west of the freeway, this former hatchery headquarters is full of curious mountaineering artifacts and old pictures. The changing exhibitions highlight history – geological and human – but also occasionally showcase local artists. Next door, the oldest operating hatchery in the West maintains outdoor ponds teeming with thousands of rainbow trout that will eventually be released into lakes and rivers.

Shastice Park SKATING

(www.msrec.org; adult/child $10/5; cnr Rockfellow & Adams Drs; ⏲10am-5pm Mon-Thu, to 9pm Fri & Sat, 1:30-5pm Sun) East of downtown the immense outdoor skating rink is open to ice-skaters in winter and in-line skaters on summer weekends.

River Dancers Rafting & Kayaking RAFTING
(☎530-926-3517; www.riverdancers.com; 302 Terry Lynn Ave) Excellent outfit run by active environmentalists who guide one- to five-day whitewater rafting excursions down the area's rivers: the Klamath, Sacramento, Salmon, Trinity and Scott. Prices start with a half-day on the nearby Sacramento River for $75.

Shasta Mountain Guides CLIMBING
(www.shastaguides.com) Offers two-day guided climbs of Mt Shasta between April and September, with all gear and meals included, for around $500. The experienced mountaineers have operated in Shasta for 30 years.

Shasta Valley Balloons BALLOONING
(☎530-926-3612; 316 Pony Trail; rides $200) Live a dream by seeing the area from a hot-air balloon.

Courses

Osprey Outdoors Kayak School MOUNTAINEERING
(www.ospreykayak.com; 2925 Cantara Loop Rd) Owner and instructor Michael Kirwin has a reputation for quality classes on high mountain lakes and rivers. Expect to pay around $80 to $100 per adult per day.

Mt Shasta Mountaineering School CLIMBING
(www.swsmtns.com; 210a E Lake St) Conducts clinics and courses for serious climbers, or those looking to get serious. A two-day summit climb of Mt Shasta costs $450.

Tours

Note that hiking Mt Shasta doesn't require an operator, but those wanting one have plenty of options. For information on summiting the mountain on your own, see p279.

Shasta Vortex Adventures SPIRITUAL
(www.shastavortex.com; 400 Chestnut St) For a uniquely Mt Shasta outdoor experience, Shasta Vortex offers low-impact trips accented with the spiritual quest as much as the physical journey. The focus of the trips includes guided meditation and an exploration of the mountain's metaphysical power. Full-day tours for two people cost $456; larger groups get a slight discount.

Sleeping

Shasta really has it all – from free rustic camping to plush boutique B&Bs. If you are intent on staying at the upper end of the spectrum you should make reservations well in advance, especially on weekends and holidays and during ski season.

Camping & Cabins

Camping in the area is excellent and the visitors center has details on over two dozen campgrounds around Mt Shasta. Check with the Mt Shasta and McCloud ranger stations about USFS campgrounds in the area. As long as you set up camp at least 200ft from the water and get a free campfire permit from a ranger station, you can camp near many mountain lakes. Castle Lake (6450ft) and Gumboot Lake (6000ft) have free tent camping (purify your own drinking water) but are closed in winter. Lovely Toad Lake (7060ft), 18 miles from Mt Shasta City, isn't a designated camping area, but you may camp there if you follow the regulations. To get there go down the 11-mile gravel road (4WD advised) and walk the last quarter-mile.

TOP CHOICE **Historic Lookout & Cabin Rentals** CABIN $
(☎530-994-2184; www.fs.fed.us/r5/shastatrinity; up to 4 people from $35) What better way to rough it in style than to bunk down in a restored fire lookout on the slopes of Little Mt Hoffman or Girard Ridge? Built from the 1920s to '40s, they come with cots, tables and chairs, have panoramic views and can accommodate four people. You can find a listing of them on the national forest website.

Panther Meadows CAMPGROUND $
(tent sites free) Ten walk-in tent sites (no drinking water) sit at the timberline, right at the base of the mountain. They're a few miles up the mountain from other options, but are still easily accessible from Everitt Memorial Hwy. No reservations; arrive early to secure a site.

McBride Springs CAMPGROUND $
(tent sites $10) Easily accessible from Everitt Memorial Hwy, this campground has running water and pit toilets, but no showers. It's near mile-marker 4, at an elevation of 5000ft. It's no beauty – a recent root disease killed many of the white fir trees that shaded the sites – but it's convenient. Arrive early in the morning to secure a spot (no reservations).

Horse Camp ALPINE HUT $
(per person without/with tent $3/5) This 1923 alpine lodge run by the Sierra Club is a 2-mile hike uphill from Bunny Flat, at 8000ft. The stone construction and natural setting are lovely. Caretakers staff the hut from May to September only.

WORTH A TRIP

WEED & STEWART MINERAL SPRINGS

Just outside of Weed, **Stewart Mineral Springs** (☎530-938-2222; www.stewartmineralsprings.com; 4617 Stewart Springs Rd; mineral baths $28, sauna $18; ⊙10am-6pm Sun-Wed, to 7pm Thu-Sat) is a popular alternative (read clothing-optional) hangout on the banks of a clear mountain stream. Locals come for the day and visitors from afar come for weeks. Henry Stewart founded these springs in 1875 after Native Americans revived him from a near-death experience. He attributed his recovery to the healthful properties of the mineral waters, said to draw toxins out of the body.

Today you can soak in a private claw-foot tub or steam in the dry-wood sauna. Other perks include massage, body wraps, meditation, a Native American sweat lodge and a riverside sunbathing deck. You'll want to call ahead to be sure there is space in the steam and soaking rooms, especially on busy weekends. Dining and **accommodations** (tent & RV sites $35, tipis $45, r $65-85) are available. To reach the springs, go 10 miles north of Mt Shasta City on I-5, past Weed to the Edgewood exit, then turn left at Stewart Springs Rd and follow the signs.

While in the area, tickle your other senses at the **Mt Shasta Lavender Farms** (www.mtshastalavenderfarms.com), 16 miles northwest of Weed, off Hwy A12, on Harry Cash Rd. You can harvest your own sweet French lavender in the June and July blooming season. Or drink up the tasty porter at the **Weed Mt Shasta Brewing Company** (www.weedales.com; 360 College Ave, Weed). The rich, amber-colored Mountain High IPA is delicious, but watch out – at 7% ABV it has real kick.

Lake Siskiyou Camp-Resort RV PARK $
(☎530-926-2618; www.lakesis.com; 4239 WA Barr Rd; tent/RV sites from $20/29, cabins $100-145; 🐾) Tucked away on the shore of Lake Siskiyou, this sprawling campus has a summer-camp feel (there's an arcade and ice-cream stand). Hardly rustic, it has a swimming beach, and kayak, canoe, fishing boat and paddle boat rentals. Lots of amenities make it a good option for families on an RV trip.

Bed & Breakfasts, Hotels & Motels

Many modest motels stretch along S Mt Shasta Blvd. All have hot tubs, wi-fi and rooms cost between $60 and $140 in peak season. As many of them were built in the '50s, the cost difference is basically based on how recently they were remodeled. Many motels offer discount ski packages in winter and lower midweek rates year-round.

TOP CHOICE **Shasta MountInn** B&B $$
(☎530-926-1810; www.shastamountinn.com; 203 Birch St; r without/with fireplace $130/175; @ 📶) Only antique on the outside, inside this bright Victorian farmhouse is all relaxed minimalism, bold colors and graceful decor. Each airy room has a designer mattress and exquisite views of the luminous mountain. Enjoy the expansive garden, wraparound deck and outdoor sauna. Not relaxed enough yet? There are also a couple of perfectly placed porch swings and on-site massage.

Dream Inn B&B $$
(☎530-926-1536; www.dreaminnmtshastacity.com; 326 Chestnut St; r with shared bath $80-110, ste $120-160; @ 📶) Made up of two houses in the center of town: one is a meticulously kept Victorian cottage stuffed with fussy knickknacks; the other a Spanish-style two-story with chunky, raw-wood furniture and no clutter. A rose garden with a koi pond joins the two properties. A hefty breakfast is included.

Finlandia Motel MOTEL $$
(☎530-926-5596; www.finlandiamotel.com; 1612 S Mt Shasta Blvd; r $60-120, with kitchen $89-150) An excellent deal, the standard rooms are… standard – clean and simple. The suites get a little chalet flair with vaulted pine-wood ceilings and mountain views. There's an outdoor hot tub and the Finnish sauna is available by appointment.

Woodsman Cabins & Lodge MOTEL $
(☎530-926-3411; 1121 S Mt Shasta Blvd; r $89-139; ❄ 📶) Owned by the same folks who have the Strawberry Valley Inn across the street, the cluster of renovated mid-century buildings that make up the Woodsman is the mannish alternative. Taxidermy looks over the reception area, where a fire keeps things warm in

the winter. At the time of writing there was a plan to open a causal restaurant on site.

Strawberry Valley Inn B&B **$$**
(☎530-926-2052; 1142 S Mt Shasta Blvd; d from $139;) The understated rooms surround a garden courtyard, allowing you to enjoy the intimate feel of a B&B without the pressure of having to chat with the darling newlyweds around the breakfast table. A full vegetarian breakfast is included. In the evenings there's complimentary wine.

Mt Shasta Resort RESORT **$$**
(☎530-926-3030; www.mountshastaresort.com; 1000 Siskiyou Lake Blvd; r from $90, 1-/2-bedroom chalets from $154/193) Divinely situated away from town, this upscale golf resort and spa has Arts and Crafts–style chalets nestled in the woods around the shores of Lake Siskiyou. They're a bit soulless, but immaculate, and each has a kitchen and gas fireplace. Basic lodge rooms are near the golf course, which boasts some challenging greens and offers amazing views of the mountain. The restaurant has excellent views as well and serves Californian cuisine with a large selection of steaks.

Evergreen Lodge MOTEL **$**
(☎530-926-2143; www.evergreenlodgemtshasta.com; 1312 S Mt Shasta Blvd; r $70;) The economy rooms up front are a bit rundown, but the rooms in back are newer with high ceilings and good light. The small fee for the sauna? Worth it.

Swiss Holiday Lodge MOTEL **$**
(☎530-926-3446; www.swissholidaylodge.com; 2400 S Mt Shasta Blvd; d $60;) Don't think of the furnishings as old…they're vintage.

Eating

Trendy restaurants and cafes here come and go with the snowmelt. Most of the following are tried and true, favored by locals and visitors alike. A **farmers market** (3:30-6pm Mon) sets up on Mt Shasta Blvd during summer.

TOP CHOICE **Trinity Café** CALIFORNIAN **$$**
(☎530-926-6200; 622 N Mt Shasta Blvd; mains $17-28; 5-9pm Tue-Sat) Trinity has long rivaled the Bay Area's best. The owners, who hail from Napa, infuse the bistro with a Wine Country feel and an extensive, excellent wine selection. The organic menu ranges from delectable, perfectly cooked steaks, savory roast game hen to creamy-on-the-inside, crispy-on-the-outside polenta. The warm, mellow mood makes for an overall delicious experience.

Mount Shasta Pastry BAKERY **$**
(610 S Mt Shasta Blvd; mains $17-28; 6am-2:30pm Mon-Sat, 7am-1pm Sun) Walk in hungry and you'll be plagued with an existential breakfast crisis: the potato and egg frittata topped with red peppers, ham and melted cheese, or the smoky breakfast burrito? The flaky croissants or peach cobbler? It also serves terrific sandwiches and gourmet pizza.

Vivify JAPANESE **$$**
(☎530-926-1345; www.vivifyshasta.com; 531 Chestnut St; meals $9-18; 5:30-10pm Wed-Mon) Bowls of udon and ramen accompany a long list of rolls at Shasta's reigning sushi place. But the food goes a lot deeper than Japanese basics, with hearty savory dishes (a roast rack of local lamb quinoa and curry) and light raw and wheat-free options. Be warned, it's popular and the dining room gets crowded.

Poncho & Lefkowitz FOOD CART **$**
(401 S Mt Shasta Blvd; meals $4-10; 11am-4pm Tue-Sat;) Surrounded by picnic tables, this classy, wood-sided food cart – sort of a cafe on wheels – turns out juicy Polish sausage, big plates of nachos and veggie burritos. It's a good bet for food on the go.

Lily's BREAKFAST **$$**
(www.lilysrestaurant.com; 1013 S Mt Shasta Blvd; breakfast & lunch mains $9-15, dinner mains $15-22; 8am-4pm Mon-Fri, 4-10pm Sat & Sun;) Enjoy quality Californian cuisine – Asian- and Mediterranean-touched salads, fresh sandwiches and all kinds of veg options – in a cute, white, clapboard house. Outdoor tables overhung by flowering trellises are almost always full, especially for breakfast.

Berryvale Grocery & Deli MARKET **$**
(www.berryvale.com; 305 S Mt Shasta Blvd; mains $9; 8:30am-7pm Mon-Sat, 10am-6pm Sun;) This market sells groceries and organic produce to the health conscious. The excellent deli cafe serves good coffee and an array of tasty – mostly veggie – salads, sandwiches and burritos.

Andaman Healthy Thai Cuisine THAI **$**
(313 N Shasta Blvd; mains $8; 11am-9pm Mon, Tue, Thu & Fri, from 4pm Sat & Sun) The food is great, but the kitchen and the staff can't keep up with the crowds. If it's full, look elsewhere.

Black Bear Diner DINER $
(401 W Lake St; mains $8; ⊙breakfast, lunch & dinner) Part of a cute bear-themed chain; it's right off the highway and enjoys a nice view.

Drinking & Entertainment

The Goats Tavern BAR
(www.thegoatmountshasta.com; 107 Chestnut St; ⊙7am-6pm;) Come here first to drink – it has 12 taps rotating some of the best microbrewed beer in the country – and then tuck into a 'wino burger,' which comes topped with peppered goat cheese, thick sliced bacon and a red-wine reduction sauce. It's a friendly place with an affable staff, surly regulars and a great summer patio.

Stage Door Coffeehouse & Cabaret LIVE MUSIC
(www.stagedoorcabaret.com; 414 N Mt Shasta Blvd; ⊙7am-6pm, longer during performances;) The menu at this popular cafe-bar and theater features espresso, microbrews, wine and lots of veggie dishes. On Wednesday nights there are indie films; on weekends, live music – anything from Celtic punk to bluegrass.

Has Beans Coffeehouse COFFEE
(www.hasbeans.com; 1011 S Mt Shasta Blvd; ⊙5:30am-7pm; @) This snug little hangout serves organic, locally roasted coffee. One computer is tucked away in the back corner (internet $3 per hour). There's live acoustic music some evenings.

Shopping

Looking for an imported African hand drum, some prayer flags or a nice crystal? You've come to the right place. The downtown shopping district has a handful of cute little boutiques to indulge a little shopping for the spiritual seeker. Both **Village Books** (320 N Mt Shasta Blvd) and **Golden Bough Books** (219 N Mt Shasta Blvd) carry fascinating volumes about Mt Shasta, on topics from geology and hiking to folklore and mysticism, as does the Sisson Museum shop (p280).

A favorite outdoor store in Shasta, **Fifth Season Sports** (www.thefifthseason.com; 300 N Mt Shasta Blvd, at Lake St) rents camping, mountain-climbing and backpacking gear and has staff familiar with the mountain (a three-day rental of crampons and an ice ax to summit Shasta costs $24). It also rents skis, snowshoes and snowboards.

Information

Mt Shasta ranger station (☎530-926-4511; 204 W Alma St; ⊙8am-4:30pm) One block west of Mt Shasta Blvd. Issues wilderness and mountain-climbing permits, good advice, weather reports and all you need for exploring the area. It also sells topographic maps.

Mt Shasta visitors center (☎530-926-4865; www.mtshastachamber.com; 300 Pine St; ⊙9am-5:30pm Mon-Sat, to 4:30pm Sun summer, 10am-4pm daily winter) Detailed information on recreation and lodging across Siskiyou County.

Getting There & Around

Greyhound (www.greyhound.com) buses heading north and south on I-5 stop opposite the Vet's Club (406 N Mt Shasta Blvd) and at the **depot** (628 S Weed Blvd) in Weed, 8 miles north on I-5. Services include Redding ($27.50, one hour and 20 minutes, three daily), Sacramento ($63, 5½ hours, three daily) and San Francisco ($80.50, 10½ hours, two or three times daily).

The **STAGE bus** (☎530-842-8295; www.co.siskiyou.ca.us) includes Mt Shasta City in its local I-5 corridor route (fares $1.50 to $8, depending on distance), which also serves McCloud, Dunsmuir, Weed and Yreka several times each weekday. Other buses connect at Yreka (see p297).

The **California Highway Patrol** (CHP; ☎530-842-4438) recorded report gives weather and road conditions for Siskiyou County.

Dunsmuir

Built by Central Pacific Railroad, Dunsmuir (population 1650) was originally named Pusher, for the auxiliary 'pusher' engines that muscled the heavy steam engines up the steep mountain grade. In 1886 Canadian coal baron Alexander Dunsmuir came to Pusher and was so enchanted that he promised the people a fountain if they would name the town after him. The fountain stands in the park today. Stop there to quench your thirst; it could easily be – as locals claim – 'the best water on earth.'

Dunsmuir might have aptly been named Phoenix. Rising from the ashes, this town has survived one cataclysmic disaster after another – avalanche, fire, flood, even a toxic railroad spill in 1991. Long since cleaned up, the river has been restored to pristine levels and the community has a notably plucky spirit, though today a number of empty storefronts attest to the community's greatest challenge: the Global Economic Crisis.

Still, it's home to a spirited set of artists, naturalists, urban refugees and native Dunsmuirians who are rightly proud of the pristine rivers around their little community. Its downtown streets – once a bawdy Gold Rush district of five saloons and three brothels – hold cafes, restaurants and galleries, and the town's reputation is still inseparable from the trains.

Sights & Activities

The chamber of commerce stocks maps of **cycling trails** and **swimming holes** on the Upper Sacramento River.

Ruddle Cottage GALLERY
(www.ruddlecottage.net; 5815 Sacramento Ave; 10am-4pm May-Oct, 11am-4pm Nov-Apr) Behind a shaded garden, cluttered with eclectic sculptures, Jayne Bruck-Fryer's colorful gallery feels a bit like something from a fairy tale. Fryer makes each and every ingenious creation – from sculptures to jewelry – from recycled materials. The pretty fish hanging in the window? Dryer lint!

California Theater HISTORIC BUILDING
(5741 Dunsmuir Ave) At downtown's north end stands what was once the town's pride. In a grassroots community effort, this long-defunct, once-glamorous venue is being carefully restored to its original glory. First opened in 1926 the theater hosted stars such as Clark Gable, Carole Lombard and the Marx Brothers. Today the lineup includes films, musical performances, theater groups and comedians.

Dunsmuir City Park & Botanical Gardens PARK
(www.dunsmuirparks.org; admission free; dawn to dusk) As you follow winding Dunsmuir Ave north over the freeway, look for this park with its local native gardens and a **vintage steam engine** in front. A forest path from the riverside gardens leads to a small waterfall, but **Mossbrae Falls** are the larger and more spectacular of Dunsmuir's waterfalls. To get there from Dunsmuir Ave, turn west onto Scarlett Way, passing under an archway marked 'Shasta Retreat.' Park by the railroad tracks (there's no sign), then walk north along the right-hand side of the tracks for a half-hour until you reach a railroad bridge built in 1901. Backtracking slightly from the bridge, you'll find a little path going down through the trees to the river and the falls. Be *extremely careful* of trains as you walk by the tracks – the river's sound can make it impossible to hear them coming.

Sleeping

Railroad Park Resort BOUTIQUE HOTEL $$
(530-235-4440; www.rrpark.com; 100 Railroad Park Rd; tent/RV sites $27/35, caboose & boxcar ste $115-120;) About a mile south of town, off I-5, visitors can spend the night inside vintage railroad cars and cabooses that have been refitted from a number of the area's historic operators. The grounds are fun for kids, who can run around the iron engines and plunge in a centrally situated pool. The deluxe boxcars are furnished with antiques and claw-foot tubs, although the cabooses are simpler and a bit less expensive. You get tremendous views of Castle Crags, a peaceful creekside setting and tall pines shading the adjoining campground.

Dunsmuir Lodge MOTEL $
(530-235-2884; www.dunsmuirlodge.net; 6604 Dunsmuir Ave; r $79-153;) Toward the south entrance of town, the simple but tastefully renovated rooms have hardwood floors, big chunky blond-wood bed frames and tiled baths. A grassy communal picnic area overlooks the canyon slope. It's a peaceful little place and very good value.

Cave Springs Resort MOTEL $
(530-235-2721; www.cavesprings.com; 4727 Dunsmuir Ave; r $56-76;) These creek-side cabins seem unchanged since the 1950s, and they are rustic – *very* rustic – but their location is sublime. Nestled on a piney crag above the Sacramento River, the river is right outside the backdoor and ideal for anglers. Though mostly frequented by anglers, the place has romantic appeal if you can handle the cobwebs: at night there's nothing but the sound of rushing water and the haunting whistle of trains. The motel rooms are bland, but they're up to modern standards and have more amenities.

Dunsmuir Inn & Suites MOTEL $
(530-235-4395; www.dunsmuirinn.com; 5400 Dunsmuir Ave; r $69-159;) Straightforward, immaculately clean motel rooms make a good, no-fuss option.

Eating & Drinking

TOP CHOICE **Café Maddalena** MEDITERRANEAN $$$
(530-235-2725; 5801 Sacramento Ave; mains $17-25; 5-10pm Thu-Sun) Simple and elegant, this cafe put Dunsmuir on the foodie map.

NORTHERN BITES

Northern California was propelled into culinary stardom by the Bay Area and Wine Country's fine restaurants, not by the mountain region's greasy spoons. Still, the area doesn't suffer from foodie famine. Don't expect concentrations of fine bistros here, but enjoy the sprinkling (like a fine dusting of cocoa powder over tiramisu) of exceptional restaurants you do find.

Try the area's top recommended spots:

Café Maddalena (p285) Dunsmuir

Trinity Café (p283) Mt Shasta City

La Grange Café (p293) Weaverville

Vivify (p283) Mt Shasta City

The menu was designed by chef Bret LaMott (of Trinity Café fame, p283) and changes weekly to feature dishes from southern Europe and north Africa. Some highlights include seared scallops with orange glaze, or fresh angel hair with heirloom tomatoes. The wine bar is stocked with rare Mediterranean labels, including a great selection of Spanish varietals.

Dunsmuir Brewery Works BREWPUB $$
(☎530-235-1900; www.dunsmuirbreweryworks.info; 5701 Dunsmuir Ave; mains $11-20; ⏲11am-9pm Tue-Sun; 📶) It's hard to describe this little microbrew pub without veering into hyperbole. Start with the beer: the crisp ales and chocolate porter are perfectly balanced and the IPA is apparently pretty good too, because patrons are always drinking it dry. Soak it up with the short menu of awesome bar food – a warm potato salad, bratwurst or a thick Angus burger. The atmosphere, with a buzzing patio and aw-shucks staff, completes a perfect picture.

Sengthongs Restaurant & Blue Sky Room ASIAN $$
(☎530-235-4770; www.sengthongs.com; 5843 Dunsmuir Ave; mains $11-20; ⏲11am-8pm Mon-Fri, with seasonal variations) This funky joint serves up sizzling Thai, Lao and Vietnamese food and books first-rate jazz, reggae, salsa or blues most nights. Many dishes are simply heaping bowls of noodles, though the meat dishes – flavored with ginger, scallions and spices – are more complex and uniformly delicious.

Cornerstone Bakery & Café CAFE $
(5759 Dunsmuir Ave; mains $8-9; ⏲8am-2pm Thu-Mon; 🖉) Smack in the middle of town, it serves smooth, strong coffee, espresso and chai. All the baked goods – including thick, gooey cinnamon rolls – are warm from the oven. Creative omelets include cactus. The wine list is extensive, as is the dessert selection.

Brown Trout Café & Gallery CAFE $$
(☎530-235-0754; 5841 Sacramento Ave; mains $10; ⏲7am-5pm Mon-Sat, from 8am Sun; 📶🖉) This casual, high-ceilinged, brick-walled hangout (formerly the town mercantile) serves strong fair-trade coffee and light snacks. There's also a short wine and microbrew list.

Railroad Park Dinner House CALIFORNIAN $$
(☎530-235-4440; Railroad Park Resort, 100 Railroad Park Rd; mains $15-25; ⏲5-9pm Fri & Sat Apr-Nov) Set inside a vintage railroad car, this popular restaurant-bar offers trainloads of dining-car ambience and Californian cuisine.

Information

The **Dunsmuir Chamber of Commerce** (☎530-235-2177; www.dunsmuir.com; Suite 100, 5915 Dunsmuir Ave; ⏲10am-3:30pm Tue-Sat) has free maps, walking-guide pamphlets and excellent information on outdoor activities.

Getting There & Away

Dunsmuir's **Amtrak station** (www.amtrak.com; 5750 Sacramento Ave) is the only train stop in Siskiyou County and it is not staffed. Buy tickets for the north–south *Coast Starlight* on board the train, but only after making reservations by phone or via the website. The *Coast Starlight* runs once daily to Redding ($22, 1¾ hours), Sacramento ($60, 5¾ hours) and Oakland ($79, eight hours).

The **STAGE bus** (☎530-842-8295) includes Dunsmuir in its local I-5 corridor route, which also serves Mt Shasta City ($2, 20 minutes), Weed ($3.50, 30 minutes) and Yreka ($5, 1¼ hours) several times each weekday. The bus runs on Dunsmuir Ave.

Castle Crags State Park

The stars of this glorious state park alongside Castle Crags Wilderness Area are its soaring spires of ancient granite formed some 225 million years ago, with elevations ranging from 2000ft along the Sacramento River to more than 6500ft at the peaks. The crags are similar to the granite formations of the eastern Sierra, and Castle Dome resembles Yosemite's famous Half Dome.

Rangers at the **park entrance station** (☎530-235-2684; day use per vehicle $8) have information and maps covering nearly 28 miles of **hiking trails**. There's also **fishing** in the Sacramento River at the picnic area on the opposite side of I-5.

If you drive past the campground you'll reach **Vista Point**, near the start of the strenuous 2.7-mile **Crags Trail**, which rises through the forest past the Indian Springs spur trail, then clambers up to the base of **Castle Dome**. You're rewarded with unsurpassed views of Mt Shasta, especially if you scramble the last 100yd or so up into the rocky saddle gap. The park also has gentle **nature trails** and 8 miles of the **Pacific Crest Trail**, which passes through the park at the base of the crags.

The **campground** (☎reservations 800-444-7275; www.reserveamerica.com; sites $35) is one of the nicer public campgrounds in this area, and very easily accessible from the highway. It has running water, hot showers, and three spots that can accommodate RVs but have no hookups. Sites are shady, but suffer from traffic noise. You can camp anywhere in the Shasta-Trinity National Forest surrounding the park if you get a free campfire permit, issued at park offices. At the time of writing the future of this state park was uncertain because of budget issues.

McCloud

This tiny, historic mill town (population 1101) sits at the foot of the south slope of Mt Shasta, and is an alternative to staying in Mt Shasta City. Quiet streets retain a simple, easygoing charm, centered around the enormous McCloud Mercantile, which has enjoyed a vibrant revitalization and hosts the town's best hotel, a cute store and a couple of good places to eat. It's the closest settlement to Mt Shasta Board & Ski Park (p279) and is surrounded by abundant natural beauty. Hidden in the woods upriver are woodsy getaways for the Western aristocracy, including mansions owned by the Hearst and Levi Strauss estates.

The town made some press during a recent battle against the Nestlé corporation, which announced a plan for a water bottling facility on the site of the defunct mill. Fearing the damage to the local watershed, a cadre of residents organized to oppose the factory. By 2009 they succeeded in sufficiently entangling the multinational giant in red tape and bad publicity, and Nestlé scuttled the project. Still, for a little town hungry for job creation, the situation brought neighbor-against-neighbor politics to a fever pitch. Things have settled down, and curious visitors can wander around the eerily quiet site of the McCloud lumber mill, which would have been home to the plant. The mill's main building is as big as an airplane hangar, and completely empty.

Sights & Activities

The **McCloud River Loop**, a gorgeous, 6-mile, partially paved road along the Upper McCloud River, begins at Fowlers Camp, 5.5 miles east of town on Hwy 89, and re-emerges about 11 miles east of McCloud. Along the loop, turn off at **Three Falls** for a pretty trail that passes…yep, three lovely falls and a riparian habitat for bird-watching in the Bigelow Meadow. The loop can easily be done by car, bicycle or on foot, and has five first-come, first-served campgrounds.

Other good hiking trails include the **Squaw Valley Creek Trail** (not to be confused with the ski area near Lake Tahoe), an easy 5-mile loop trail south of town, with options for swimming, fishing and picnicking. Also south of town, **Ah-Di-Na** is the remains of a Native American settlement and historic homestead once owned by the William Randolph Hearst family. Sections of the **Pacific Crest Trail** are accessible from Ah-Di-Na Campground, off Squaw Valley Rd, and also up near Bartle Gap, offering head-spinning views.

Fishing and swimming are popular on remote **Lake McCloud** reservoir, 9 miles south of town on Squaw Valley Rd, which is signposted in town as Southern. You can also go fishing on the Upper McCloud River (stocked with trout) and at the Squaw Valley Creek.

The huge **McCloud Mercantile** (www.mccloudmercantile.com; ⏲8am-6pm) anchors the downtown. There's a hotel upstairs and it hosts a couple of restaurants (p288) that warrant a longer stay, but those just passing though can get a bag of licorice at the old-world candy counter or browse the main floor. The collection of dry goods is very woodsy and very NorCal: Woolrich blankets, handmade soap and interesting gifts for the gardener, outdoors person or chef.

A tiny **historical museum** (admission free; ⏲11am-3pm Mon-Sat, 1-3pm Sun) sits opposite the depot and could use a bit of organization – it has the feel of a cluttered, messy thrift store – but tucked in the nooks and crannies are plenty of worthwhile curiosities from the town's past.

Sleeping

Lodging in McCloud is taken seriously – all are excellent and reservations are recommended. For camping go to the McCloud ranger district office for information on the half-dozen campgrounds nearby. Fowlers Camp is the most popular. The campgrounds have a range of facilities, from primitive (no running water and no fee) to developed (hot showers and fees of up to $20 per site). Ask about nearby fire-lookout cabins for rent – they give amazing, remote views of the area.

TOP CHOICE McCloud River Mercantile Hotel BOUTIQUE HOTEL $$
(530-964-2330; www.mccloudmercantile.com; 241 Main St; r $129-250;) Stoll up the stairs to the 2nd floor of McCloud's central Mercantile and try not to fall in love; it's all high ceilings, exposed brick and a perfect marriage of preservationist class and modern panache. The rooms with antique furnishings are situated within open floor plans. Guests are greeted with fresh flowers and can drift to sleep on feather beds after soaking in claw-foot tubs. Certainly the best hotel in the Northern Mountains.

McCloud Hotel HISTORIC HOTEL $$
(530-964-2822; www.mccloudhotel.com; 408 Main St; r $100-235;) Regal, butter-yellow and a whole block long, the grand hotel opposite the depot first opened in 1916 and has been a destination for Shasta's visitors ever since. The elegant historic landmark has been restored to a luxurious standard, and the included breakfast has gourmet flair. Many rooms have Jacuzzi tubs; one room is accessible for travelers with disabilities.

Stoney Brook Inn HOTEL $
(530-964-2300; www.stoneybrookinn.com; 309 W Colombero Dr; s & d with shared bath $79, with private bath $94, ste with kitchen $99-156) Smack in the middle of town, under a stand of pines, this alternative B&B also sponsors group retreats. Creature comforts include an outdoor hot tub, a sauna, a Native American sweat lodge and massage by appointment. Downstairs rooms are nicest. Vegetarian breakfast available.

McCloud River Lodge LODGE $
(530-964-2700; www.mccloudlodge.com; 140 Squaw Valley Rd; d $89-113,) Tidy, new log cabins surround a lush central grassy area. Simple rooms have homey, plush, quilted beds and many have fireplaces and Jacuzzis. Accessible rooms for travelers with disabilities are available.

McCloud River Inn B&B $$
(530-964-2130; www.mccloudriverinn.com; 325 Lawndale Ct; r $115-199;) Rooms in this rambling, quaint Victorian are fabulously big – the bathrooms alone could sleep two. In the morning look out for the frittatas; in the evening enjoy a couple of glasses of wine in the cute downstairs wine bar. The relaxed and familial atmosphere guarantees that it books up quickly.

McCloud Dance Country RV Park CAMPGROUND $
(530-964-2252; www.mccloudrvpark.com; 480 Hwy 89, at Southern Ave; tent sites $14-24, RV sites $21-37, cabins $85-120;) Chock-full of RVs, with sites under the trees and a small creek, this is a good option for families. The view of the mountain is breathtaking and there's a large, grassy picnic ground. Cabins are basic but clean.

Eating

McCloud's eating options are few. For more variety, make the 10-mile trip over to Mt Shasta City.

Mountain Star Cafe VEGETARIAN $
(241 Main St; mains $7-9; 8am-3pm) Deep within the creaking Mercantile, this sweet lunch counter is a surprise, serving vegetarian specials made from locally sourced, organic produce. Some options on the menu during a recent visit included the morale biscuits and gravy, a garlicky tempeh Ruben, roast vegetable salad and a homemade oat and veggie burger.

White Mountain Fountain Cafe AMERICAN $
(241 Main St; mains $8; 8am-4pm) In the window-lined corner of the Mercantile, this old-fashioned little soda fountain serves burgers and shakes. The one coyly called 'Not the Dolly Varden' is an excellent vegetarian sandwich with roasted zucchini, red peppers and garlic aioli.

Entertainment

McCloud Dance Country DANCEHALL
(www.mcclouddancecountry.com; cnr Broadway & Pine Sts; per couple $20; 7pm Fri & Sat) Dust it up on the 5000-sq-ft maple dance floor in the

1906 Broadway Ballroom. Square dancing, round dancing, ballroom dancing – they do it all. Starting at $289 per couple, multiday packages include lessons and evening dances. It's a worthwhile centerpiece to a weekend getaway. Visit the website to see what's on and whether you need a reservation for the event.

Information

McCloud Chamber of Commerce (☎530-964-3113; www.mccloudchamber.com; 205 Quincy St; ⏰10am-4pm Mon-Fri)

McCloud ranger district office (☎530-964-2184; Hwy 89; ⏰8am-4:30pm Mon-Sat summer, 8am-4:30pm Mon-Fri rest of year) A quarter-mile east of town. Detailed information on camping, hiking and recreation.

McArthur-Burney Falls Memorial State Park

This beautiful state park (☎530-335-2777; www.parks.ca.gov; day use per vehicle $8) lies southeast of McCloud, near the crossroads of Hwys 89 and 299 from Redding. The 129ft falls cascade with the same volume of water – 100 million gallons per day – and at the same temperature – 42°F (5°C) – year-round. Clear, lava-filtered water surges over the top and also from springs in the waterfall's face. Teddy Roosevelt loved this place; he called it the 'Eighth Wonder of the World.'

A lookout point beside the parking lot also has trails going up and down the creek from the falls. (Be careful of your footing here; in 2011 there was a fatality in the park when someone slipped on the rocks.) The nature trail heading downstream leads to Lake Britton; other hiking trails include a portion of the Pacific Crest Trail. The scenes in the film *Stand By Me* (1986) where the boys dodge the train were shot on the Lake Britton Bridge trestle in the park.

The park's **campgrounds** (☎530-335-2777, summer reservations 800-444-7275; www.reserveamerica.com; day use $8, sites $35) have hot showers and are open year-round.

About 10 miles northeast of McArthur-Burney Falls, the 6000-acre **Ahjumawi Lava Springs State Park** is known for its abundant springs, aquamarine bays, islets, and jagged flows of black basalt lava. It can only be reached by boats that are launched from Rat Farm, 3 miles north of the town of McArthur along a graded dirt road. Arrangements for primitive camping can be made by calling McArthur-Burney Falls Memorial State Park.

Lava Beds National Monument

A wild landscape of charred volcanic rock and rolling hills, this remote **national monument** (☎530-667-8100; www.nps.gov/labe; 7-day entry per vehicle/hiker/cyclist $10/5/5, cash only) is reason enough to visit the region. Off Hwy 139, immediately south of Tule Lake National Wildlife Refuge, it's a truly remarkable 72-sq-mile landscape of volcanic features – lava flows, craters, cinder cones, spatter cones, shield volcanoes and amazing lava tubes.

Lava tubes are formed when hot, spreading lava cools and hardens when the surfaces get exposed to the cold air. The lava inside is thus insulated and stays molten, flowing away to leave an empty tube of solidified lava. Nearly 400 such tubular caves have been found in the monument, and many more are expected to be discovered. About two dozen or so are currently open for exploration by visitors.

On the south side of the park, the **visitors center** (☎530-667-2282, ext 230; ⏰8am-6pm, shorter hrs in winter) has free maps, activity books for kids and information about the monument and its volcanic features and history. Rangers loan flashlights, rent helmets and kneepads for cave exploration and lead summer interpretive programs, including campfire talks and guided cave walks. To explore the caves it's essential you use a high-powered flashlight, wear good shoes and long sleeves (lava is sharp), and do not go alone.

Near the visitors center, a short, one-way **Cave Loop** drive provides access to many lava-tube caves. **Mushpot Cave**, the one nearest the visitors center, has lighting and information signs and is a good introductory hike. There are a number of caves that are a bit more challenging, including Labyrinth, Hercules Leg, Golden Dome and Blue Grotto. Each one of these caves has an interesting history – visitors used to ice-skate by lantern light in the bottom of Merrill Cave, and when Ovls Cave was discovered, it was littered with bighorn sheep skulls. There are good brochures with details about each cave available from the visitors center. Rangers are stern with their warnings for new cavers though, so be sure to check in with the visitors center before exploring to avoid harming the fragile geological and biological resources in the park.

The tall black cone of **Schonchin Butte** (5253ft) has a magnificent outlook accessed via a steep 1-mile hiking trail. Once you reach the top, you can visit the fire-lookout staff between June and September. **Mammoth Crater** is the source of most of the area's lava flows.

The weathered Modoc **petroglyphs** at the base of a high cliff at the far northeastern end of the monument, called Petroglyph Point, are thousands of years old. At the visitors center, be sure to take the leaflet explaining the origin of the petroglyphs and their probable meaning. Look for the hundreds of nests in holes high up in the cliff face, which provide shelter for birds that sojourn at the wildlife refuges nearby.

Also at the north end of the monument, be sure to go to the labyrinthine landscape of **Captain Jack's Stronghold**. A brochure will guide you through the breathtaking Stronghold Trail.

Indian Well Campground (tent & RV sites $10), near the visitors center at the south end of the park, has water and flush toilets, but no showers. The campsites are lovely and have broad views of the surrounding valleys. The nearest place to buy food and camping supplies is on Hwy 139 in the nearby town of Tulelake, but the place is pretty rugged – just a couple of bars, a bunch of boarded-up buildings and a pair of gas stations.

Klamath Basin National Wildlife Refuges

Of the six stunning national wildlife refuges in this group, Tule Lake and Clear Lake refuges are wholly within California, Lower Klamath refuge straddles the California–Oregon border, and the Upper Klamath, Klamath Marsh and Bear Valley refuges are across the border in Oregon. Bear Valley and Clear Lake (not to be confused with the Clear Lake just east of Ukiah) are closed to the public to protect their delicate habitats, but the rest are open during daylight hours.

These refuges provide habitats for a stunning array of birds migrating along the Pacific Flyway (see the boxed text, p291). Some stop over only briefly; others stay longer to mate, make nests and raise their young. The refuges are always packed with birds, but during the spring and fall migrations, populations can rise into the hundreds of thousands.

The **Klamath Basin National Wildlife Refuges visitors center** (☎530-667-2231; http://klamathbasinrefuges.fws.gov; 4009 Hill Rd, Tulelake; ⏰8am-4:30pm Mon-Fri, 10am-4pm Sat & Sun) sits on the west side of the Tule Lake refuge, about 5 miles west of Hwy 139, near the town of Tulelake. Follow the signs from Hwy 139 or from Lava Beds National Monument. The center has a bookstore and interesting video program, as well as maps, information on recent bird sightings and updates on road conditions. It rents photo blinds. Be sure to pick up the excellent, free *Klamath Basin Birding Trail* brochure for detailed lookouts, maps, color photos and a species checklist.

The spring migration peaks during March, and in some years more than a million birds fill the skies. In April and May the songbirds, waterfowl and shorebirds arrive, some to stay and nest, others to build up their energy before they continue north. In summer ducks, Canada geese and many other waterbirds are raised here. The fall migration peaks in early November. In cold weather the area hosts the largest wintering concentration of bald eagles in the lower 48 states, with 1000 in residence at times from December to February. The Tule Lake and Lower Klamath refuges are the best places to see eagles and other raptors.

The Lower Klamath and Tule Lake refuges attract the largest numbers of birds year-round, and **auto trails** (driving routes) have been set up; a free pamphlet from the visitors center shows the routes. Self-guided **canoe trails** have been established in three of the refuges. Those in the Tule Lake and Klamath Marsh refuges are usually open from July 1 to September 30; no canoe rentals are available. Canoe trails in the Upper Klamath refuge are open year-round. Here, canoes can be rented at **Rocky Point Resort** (☎541-356-2287; 28121 Rocky Point Rd, Klamath Falls, OR; canoe, kayak & paddle boat rental per hr/half-day/day $15/30/40), on the west side of Upper Klamath Lake.

Camp at nearby Lava Beds National Monument (p289). A couple of RV parks and budget motels cluster along Hwy 139 near the tiny town of Tulelake (4035ft), including the friendly **Ellis Motel** (☎530-667-5242; 2238 Hwy 139; d without/with kitchen $75/95). Comfortable **Fe's B&B** (☎877-478-0184; www.fesbandb.com; 660 Main St; s/d with shared bath $60/70) has four simple rooms, with a big breakfast included.

THE AVIAN SUPERHIGHWAY

California is on the Pacific Flyway, a migratory route for hundreds of species of birds heading south in winter and north in summer. There are birds to see year-round, but the best viewing opportunities are during the spring and fall migrations. Flyway regulars include everything from tiny finches, hummingbirds, swallows and woodpeckers to eagles, hawks, swans, geese, ducks, cranes and herons. Much of the flyway route corresponds with I-5 (or Fly-5 in the birds' case), so a drive up the interstate in spring or fall is a show: great Vs of geese undulate in the sky and noble hawks stare from roadside perches.

In Northern California, established wildlife refuges safeguard wetlands used by migrating waterfowl. The Klamath Basin National Wildlife Refuges (p290) offer extraordinary year-round bird-watching.

Modoc National Forest

It's nearly impossible to get your head around this enormous **national forest** (www.fs.usda.gov/modoc) – it covers almost two million spectacular, remote acres of California's northeastern corner. Travelers through the remote northeast of the state will be passing in and out of its borders constantly. Fourteen miles south of Lava Beds National Monument, on the western edge of the forest, **Medicine Lake** is a stunning crater lake in a caldera (collapsed volcano) surrounded by pine forest, volcanic formations and campgrounds. The enormous volcano that formed the lake is the largest in area in California. When it erupted it ejected pumice followed by flows of obsidian, as can be seen at **Little Glass Mountain**, east of the lake.

Pick up the *Medicine Lake Highlands: Self-Guided Roadside Geology Tour* pamphlet from the McCloud ranger district office (p289) to find and learn about the glass flows, pumice deposits, lava tubes and cinder cones throughout the area. Roads are closed by snow from around mid-November to mid-June, but the area is still popular for winter sports, and accessible by cross-country skiing and snowshoeing.

Congratulations are in order for travelers who make it all the way to the **Warner Mountains**. This spur of the Cascade Range in the east of the Modoc National Forest is probably the least visited range in California. With extremely changeable weather, it's also not so hospitable; there have been snowstorms here in every season of the year. The range divides into the North Warners and South Warners at **Cedar Pass** (elevation 6305ft), east of Alturas. Remote **Cedar Pass Snow Park** (530-233-3323; all day T-bar adult/child under 6yr/6-18yr $15/5/12, all-day rope tow $5; 10am-4pm Sat, Sun & holidays during ski season) offers downhill and cross-country skiing. The majestic **South Warner Wilderness** contains 77 miles of hiking and riding trails. The best time to use them is from July to mid-October.

Maps, campfire permits and information are all available at the **Modoc National Forest supervisor's headquarters** (530-233-5811; 800 W 12th St; 8am-5pm Mon-Fri) in Alturas.

If you are heading east into Nevada from the forest, you'll pass through **Alturas**, the fairly uninspiring seat of Modoc County. The town was founded by the Dorris family in 1874 as a supply point for travelers, and it serves the same function today, providing basic services, motels and family-style restaurants. If you are looking for supplies yourself, seek out the **Four Corners Market** (1077 N Main St), a bright and friendly grocery with a handful of specialty items and surprisingly fresh produce.

WEST OF I-5

The wilderness west of I-5 is right in the sweet spot: here are some of the most rugged towns and seductive wilderness areas in the entire state of California – just difficult enough to reach to discourage big crowds.

The **Trinity River Scenic Byway** (Hwy 299) winds spectacularly along the Trinity River and beneath towering cliffs as it makes its way from the plains of Redding to the coastal redwood forests around Arcata. It provides a chance to cut through some of the Northern Mountains' most pristine wilderness and passes through the vibrant Gold Rush town of Weaverville.

Heavenly Hwy 3 (a highly recommended – although slower and windier – alternative

WHAT THE...?

Pop over to the **Willow Creek China Flat Museum** (☎530-629-2653; www.bigfootcountry.net; Hwy 299, Willow Creek; admission free, donations accepted; ⏰10am-4pm Wed-Sun May-Sep, 11am-4pm Fri & Sat, noon-4pm Sun Oct-Apr) to take in its persuasive Bigfoot collection. Footprints, handprints, hair...it has all kinds of goodies to substantiate the ole boy's existence. In fact, namesake Bigfoot Scenic Byway (Hwy 96) starts here and heads north, winding through breathtaking mountain and river country.

route to I-5) heads north from Weaverville. This mountain byway transports you through the Trinity Alps – a stunning granite range dotted with azure alpine lakes – past the shores of Lewiston and Trinity Lakes, over the Scott Mountains and finally into emerald, mountain-rimmed Scott Valley. Rough-and-ready Yreka awaits you at the end of the line.

Weaverville

In 1941 a reporter interviewed James Hilton, the British author of *Lost Horizon*. 'In all your wanderings,' the journalist asked, 'what's the closest you've found to a real-life Shangri-La?' Hilton's response? 'A little town in northern California. A little town called Weaverville.'

Cute as a button, Weaverville's streets are lined with flower boxes in the summer and banks of snow in the winter. The seat of Trinity County, it sits amid an endless tract of mountain and forest area that's 75% federally owned. With its almost 3300 sq miles, the county is roughly the size of Delaware and Rhode Island together, yet has a total population of only 13,700 and not one traffic light, freeway or parking meter.

Weaverville (population 3600) is a small gem of a town on the National Register of Historic Places and has a laid-back, gentle bohemian feel (thanks in part to the young back-to-landers and marijuana-growing subculture). You can easily spend a day here just strolling around the quaint storefronts and visiting art galleries, museums and historic structures.

Sights & Activities

TOP CHOICE **Joss House State Historic Park** TEMPLE
(☎530-623-5284; cnr Hwy 299 & Oregon St; admission $3; ⏰10am-5pm Sat winter, 10am-5pm Wed-Sun rest of year) Of all California's historic parks, these are the walls that actually talk – they're papered inside with 150-year-old donation ledgers from the once-thriving Chinese community, a testament to the rich culture of immigrants who built Northern California's infrastructure, a culture that has all but disappeared. It's an unexpected surprise that the oldest continuously used Chinese temple in California, dating to the 1870s, is in little Weaverville. The rich blue-and-gold Taoist shrine contains an ornate altar, more than 3000 years old, which was brought here from China. The adjoining schoolhouse was the first to teach Chinese students in California. Tours depart from 10am until 4pm, on the hour. Sadly, state budget issues have made the future of this park uncertain.

JJ Jackson Memorial Museum & Trinity County Historical Park MUSEUM
(www.trinitymuseum.org; 508 Main St; donation requested; ⏰10am-5pm daily May-Oct, noon-4pm daily Apr & Nov-Dec 24, noon-4pm Tue & Sat Dec 26-Mar) Next door to the Joss House you'll find gold-mining and cultural exhibits, plus vintage machinery, memorabilia, an old miner's cabin and a blacksmith shop.

Highland Art Center GALLERY
(www.highlandartcenter.org; 691 Main St; ⏰10am-5pm Mon-Sat, 11am-4pm Sun) Stroll through galleries showcasing local artists.

Coffee Creek Ranch OUTFITTER
(☎530-266-3343; www.coffeecreekranch.com) In Trinity Center, these guys lead fishing and fully outfitted pack trips into the Trinity Alps Wilderness and week-long fishing excursions.

Sleeping

The ranger station has information on many USFS campgrounds in the area, especially around Trinity Lake. Commercial RV parks, some with tent sites, dot Hwy 299.

TOP CHOICE **Weaverville Hotel** HISTORIC HOTEL $$
(☎800-750-8957; www.weavervillehotel.com; 203 Main St; r $100-260; ❄📶) Play like you're in the Old West at this upscale hotel and historic landmark, refurbished in grand Victorian style. It's luxurious but not stuffy, and

the very gracious owners take great care in looking after you. Guests may use the local gym, and breakfast at a neighboring cafe is on the house.

Red Hill Motel & Cabins MOTEL $
(☎530-623-4331; 116 Red Hill Rd; d $42, cabins without/with kitchen $48/59) This very quiet and simple motel is tucked under ponderosa pines at the west end of town, just off Main St, next to the library. It's a set of red wooden cabins built in the 1940s and the kitchenettes and mini refrigerators make it a good option for people who are on a longer stay. It's nothing fancy, but the rooms are simple, clean and very good value.

Whitmore Inn HISTORIC INN $$
(☎530-623-2509; www.whitmoreinn.com; 761 Main St; r $100-165;) Settle into plush, cozy rooms in this downtown Victorian with a wraparound deck and abundant gardens. One room is accessible for travelers with disabilities.

Eating

Downtown Weaverville is ready to feed hungry hikers – in the summer the main drag has many cheap, filling options. There's also a fantastic **farmers market** (4:30-7:30pm Wed May-Oct), which takes over Main St in the warmer months. In winter the tourist season dries up and opening hours get very short.

TOP CHOICE **La Grange Café** CALIFORNIAN $$
(☎530-623-5325; 315 N Main St; mains $15-30; 11:30am-9pm Mon-Thu, to 10pm Fri-Sun, with seasonal variations) Spacious yet intimate, this celebrated multistar restaurant serves exceptional light, fresh and satisfying fare. Chef and owner Sharon Heryford knows how to do dining without a whiff of pretention: apple-stuffed red cabbage in the fall, and brightly flavored chicken enchiladas in the summer, plus game dishes and seasonal vegetables. Exposed brick and open sight lines complement the exceedingly friendly atmosphere. A seat at the bar is great when the tables are full, which they often are. The all-you-can-eat soup and salad is a stroke of genius.

Trinideli DELI $
(201 Trinity Lakes Blvd, at Center St; sandwiches $5-7; 6am-4pm Mon-Fri) Cheerful staff prepare decadent sandwiches stuffed with fresh goodness. The 'Peasant's Pleasure' with Braunschweiger, horseradish and pickles is satisfying for brave palates, and simple turkey and ham standards explode with fresh veggies and tons of flavor. The suite of breakfast burritos are perfect for a quick pre-hike fill up.

Noelle's Garden Café CAFE $
(☎530-623-2058; 252 Main St; mains $9; breakfast & lunch;) *The* best place for breakfast. Sit inside the cheery white clapboard house, or out on the adjoining vine-trellised deck when the weather is fair. Lunch on soups, sandwiches and salads – with lots of veggie options.

Johnny's Pizza PIZZA $$
(227 Main St; pizzas $10-15; 11am-8pm) A small-town pizza joint with a good vibe, rock and roll on the stereo and friendly staff.

La Casita MEXICAN $
(570 Main St; mains $9; 11am-7pm) Tucked next door to Noelle's, low-ceilinged little La Casita serves passable Mexican classics.

Mountain Marketplace MARKET $
(222 S Main St; 9am-6pm Mon-Fri, 10am-5pm Sat;) Stock up on natural foods or hit its juice bar and vegetarian deli.

Drinking & Entertainment

Mamma Llama COFFEE SHOP
(www.mammallama.com; 208 N Main St; 6am-6pm Mon-Fri, 7am-6pm Sat, 7am-3pm Sun;) A local institution, this coffeehouse is a roomy and relaxed chill spot under the white arcade. The espresso is well made, there's a selection of books and CDs, and there are couches for lounging. The small menu does wraps and sandwiches. Live folk music (often including a hand drum) takes over occasionally.

Red House COFFEE SHOP
(www.vivalaredhouse.com; 218 S Miner St; 6:30am-5:30pm Mon-Fri, 7:30am-1pm Sun) This airy, light and bamboo-bedecked spot serves a wide selection of teas, light snacks and organic, fair-trade, shade-grown coffee. The daily food specials include a delicious chicken-and-rice soup on Mondays. If you're in a hurry (rare in Weaverville) there's a drive-through window.

Trinity Theatre CINEMA
(310 Main St) Plays first-run movies.

Information

Trinity County Chamber of Commerce (☎530-623-6101; www.trinitycounty.com; 215 Main St; 10am-4pm) Knowledgeable staff with lots of useful information.

Weaverville ranger station (☎530-623-2121; 210 N Main St; ⏲8am-4:30pm Mon-Fri) Maps, information and permits for all lakes, national forests and wilderness areas in and near Trinity County.

Getting There & Away

A local **Trinity Transit** (☎530-623-5438; www.trinitytransportation.org; fares 50¢) bus makes a Weaverville–Lewiston loop via Hwy 299 and Hwy 3 from Monday to Friday. Another one runs between Weaverville and Hayfork, a small town about 30 miles to the southwest on Hwy 3.

Lewiston Lake

Pleasant little **Lewiston** (www.lewistonca.com) is little more than a collection of buildings beside a crossroad, 26 miles west of Redding, around 5 miles off Hwy 299 on Trinity Dam Blvd and a few miles south of Lewiston Lake. It's right beside the Trinity River, and the locals here are in tune with the environment – they know fishing spots on the rivers and lakes, where to hike and how to get around.

The lake is about 1.5 miles north of town and is a serene alternative to the other area lakes because of its 10mph boat speedlimit. The water is kept at a constant level, providing a nurturing habitat for fish and waterfowl. Migrating bird species sojourn here – early in the evening you may see ospreys and bald eagles diving for fish. The **Trinity River Fish Hatchery** (⏲sunrise-sunset) traps juvenile salmon and steelhead and holds them until they are ready to be released into the river. The only marina on the lake, **Pine Cove Marina** (www.pine-cove-marina.com; 9435 Trinity Dam Blvd), has free information about the lake and its wildlife, boat and canoe rentals, potluck dinners and guided off-road tours.

If you're just passing through town, make a stop at the **Country Peddler** (4 Deadwood Rd), a drafty old barn that sits behind a field of red poppies and is filled with cool antiques, rusting road signs and antique collectibles that seem like they were pulled out of some long-lost uncle's hunting cabin. The owners, avid outdoor enthusiasts, know the area like the back of their hand.

Sleeping & Eating

Several commercial campgrounds dot the rim of the lake. For information on USFS campgrounds, contact the ranger station in Weaverville (p294). Two of these are right on the lake: the wooded **Mary Smith**, which is more private; and the sunny **Ackerman** (sites $11), which has more grassy space for families. If there's no host, both have self-registration options. There are all kinds of RV parks, cabins for rent and motels in Lewiston.

Lewiston Hotel HISTORIC HOTEL **$**
(☎530-778-3823; www.lewistonhotel.net; 125 Deadwood Rd; r $69-89; 📶) Squarely in the center of town, this 1862 hotel was recently reopened to guests and the rooms – with quilts, historic photos and river views – have tons of character. The pizza place on-site, **Trinity Dam Good Pizza** (mains $8-10; ⏲11am-7pm, with seasonal variations), serves a helluva tuna melt, gooey pizza and stiff drinks. This is also the best place to hang out after dark. If you're lucky, there may be live music and dancing.

Old Lewiston Inn B&B B&B **$$**
(☎530-778-3385; www.theoldlewistoninn.com; Deadwood Rd; r $110-125; ❄) In town, beside the river, this B&B is in an 1875 house and serves country-style breakfasts. Enjoy the hot tub, or ask about all-inclusive fly-fishing packages.

Lewiston Valley Motel MOTEL **$**
(☎530-778-3942; www.lewistonvalleymotel.com; 4789 Trinity Dam Blvd; RV sites $20, r $60; 🏊🐾) This simple, plain-Jane motel has an RV park and sits next to a gas station and convenience store.

Old Lewiston Bridge RV Resort RV PARK **$**
(☎530-778-3894; www.lewistonbridgerv.com; 8460 Rush Creek Rd, at Turnpike Rd; tent/RV sites $15/28) A pleasant place to park the RV, with campsites beside the river bridge.

Lakeview Terrace Resort CABINS, RV PARK **$**
(☎530-778-3803; www.lakeviewterraceresort.com; RV sites $30, cabins $80-135; ❄🏊) Five miles north of Lewiston, this is a woodsy Club Med, which rents boats.

Trinity (Clair Engle) Lake

Placid Trinity Lake, California's third-largest reservoir, sits beneath dramatic snowcapped alps north of Lewiston Lake. In the off season it is serenely quiet, but it attracts multitudes in the summer, who come for swimming, fishing and other water sports. Most of the campgrounds, RV parks, motels, boat rentals and restaurants line the west side of the lake.

The **Pinewood Cove Resort** (☎530-286-2201; www.pinewoodcove.com; 45110 Hwy 3; tent/RV sites $28/40, cabins $126-147; ❄), on the waterfront, is a popular place to stay, but doesn't provide bed linens.

The east side of the lake is quieter, with more secluded campgrounds, some accessible only by boat. The Weaverville ranger station (p294) has information on USFS campgrounds.

Klamath & Siskiyou Mountains

A dense conglomeration of rugged coastal mountains gives this region the nickname 'the Klamath Knot.' Wet, coastal, temperate rain forest gives way to moist inland forest, creating an immense diversity of habitats for many species, some found nowhere else in the world. Around 3500 native plants live here. Local fauna includes the northern spotted owl, the bald eagle, the tailed frog, several species of Pacific salmon and carnivores like the wolverine and the mountain lion. One theory for the extraordinary biodiversity of this area is that it escaped extensive glaciation during recent ice ages. This may have given species refuge and longer stretches of relatively favorable conditions during which to adapt.

The region also includes the largest concentration of wild and scenic rivers in the US: the Salmon, Smith, Trinity, Eel and Klamath, to name a few. The fall color change is magnificent.

Five main wilderness areas dot the Klamath Knot. The **Marble Mountain Wilderness** in the north is marked by high rugged mountains, valleys and lakes, all sprinkled with colorful geological formations of marble and granite, and a huge array of flora. The **Russian Wilderness** is 8000 acres of high peaks and isolated, beautiful mountain lakes. The **Trinity Alps Wilderness**, west of Hwy 3, is one of the area's most lovely regions for hiking and backcountry camping, and has more than 600 miles of trails that cross passes over its granite peaks and head along its deep alpine lakes. The **Yolla Bolly-Middle Eel Wilderness** in the south is little-visited, despite its proximity to the Bay Area, and so affords spectacular, secluded backcountry experiences. The **Siskiyou Wilderness**, closest to the coast, rises to heights of 7300ft, from where you can see the ocean. An extensive trail system crisscrosses the wilderness, but it is difficult to make loops.

WORTH A TRIP

ALPEN CELLARS

Jaunt over to little-known, utterly picturesque **Alpen Cellars** (☎530-266-9513; www.alpencellars.com; ⏰10am-4pm summer, by appointment Oct-May). Specializing in riesling, gewürztraminer, chardonnay and pinot noir, the vineyard is open for tours, tastings and picnicking on idyllic riverside grounds. To get there from Weaverville, take Hwy 3 for about 35 miles to the north end of Trinity Lake (5 miles past Trinity Center), then turn right on East Side Rd; 8 miles further, head left on East Fork Rd and continue for 2 miles.

The Trinity River Scenic Byway (Hwy 299) follows the rushing **Trinity River** to the Pacific coast and is dotted with lodges, RV parks and blink-and-you'll-miss-'em burgs. There's river rafting at Willow Creek, 55 miles west of Weaverville. **Bigfoot Rafting Company** (☎530-629-2263; www.bigfootrafting.com) leads guided trips (from $79) and also rents rafts and kayaks (from $38 per day).

Scott Valley

North of Trinity Lake, Hwy 3 climbs along the gorgeous eastern flank of the Trinity Alps Wilderness to Scott Mountain Summit (5401ft) and then drops gracefully down into verdant Scott Valley, a bucolic agricultural area nestled between towering mountains. There are good opportunities for hiking, cycling and mountain-biking, or taking horse trips to mountain lakes. For a bit of history, pick up the *Trinity Heritage Scenic Byway* brochure from the Weaverville ranger station (p294) before taking this world-class drive.

Etna (population 737), toward the north end of the valley, is known by its residents as 'California's Last Great Place' and they might be right. It hosts a fantastic **Bluegrass Festival** at the end of July and the tiny **Etna Brewing Company** (www.etnabrew.net; 131 Callahan St; brewery tours free; ⏰pub 11am-4pm Tue, to 8pm Wed & Thu, to 9pm Fri & Sat, to 7pm Sun, tours by appointment) offers delicious beers and pub grub. If you're sticking around try the immaculate 10-room **Motel Etna** (☎530-467-5338; 317 Collier Way; d $55). **Scott Valley Drug** (www.scottvalleydrug.com; 511 Main St; ⏰Mon-Sat) serves up old-fashioned ice-cream sodas.

THE STATE OF JEFFERSON

Welcome to the **State of Jefferson** (www.jeffersonstate.com). When you first notice the billboards and bumper stickers ('Jefferson: A State of Mind') endorsing the proposed 51st state it might seem like a joke, but as you travel the two-lane blacktop in Northern California and Southern Oregon, the cultural differences of the states' border region start to make more sense. The State of Jefferson was originally proposed in 1941 by a band of well-armed locals, who were exceptionally pissed off about the terrible conditions of local roads. Jefferson's original draft included a good chunk of Northern California – including Del Norte, Siskiyou, Modoc, Humboldt, Trinity, Shasta and Lassen Counties – and several more in Southern Oregon. But just as the movement was gaining momentum, the Japanese bombing of Pearl Harbor brought a swell of US nationalism, and plans for the 51st state were scuttled. Today Jefferson feels alive and well in the libertarian spirit of the locals, and you can tune into news of the area by listening to **Jefferson Public Radio** (www.ijpr.org), transmitting on KNCA 89.7 FM from Redding and KNSQ 88.1 FM from Mt Shasta.

Beyond Etna **Fort Jones** (population 839) is just 18 miles from Yreka. The **visitors center** (☎530-468-5442; 11943 Main St; ⊙10am-5pm Tue-Sat, noon-4pm Sun) sits at the back of the Guild Shop mercantile. Down the street, a small **museum** (www.fortjonesmuseum.com; 11913 Main St; donation requested; ⊙Mon-Sat Memorial Day-Labor Day) houses Native American artifacts.

Yreka

Inland California's northernmost town, Yreka (wy-*ree*-kah; population 7400) was once a booming Gold Rush settlement. Most travelers only pass through en route to Oregon. Yreka, especially the quaint historic downtown, makes a good spot to stretch, eat and refuel before heading out into the hinterlands of the Scott Valley or the northeastern California wilderness.

Sights & Activities

About 25 miles north of Yreka, on I-5, just across the Oregon border, Siskiyou Summit (elevation 4310ft) often closes in winter – even when the weather is just fine on either side. Call ☎530-842-4438 to check.

Siskiyou County Museum MUSEUM
(www.siskiyoucountyhistoricalsociety.org; 910 S Main St; admission $3; ⊙9am-3pm Tue-Thu, 10am-4pm Sat) Several blocks south of the downtown grid, this exceptionally well-curated museum brings together pioneer and Native American history. An outdoor section contains historic buildings brought from around the county.

Siskiyou County Courthouse HISTORIC BUILDING
(311 4th St) This hulking downtown building was built in 1857 and has a collection of gold nuggets, flakes and dust in the foyer.

Yreka Creek Greenway WALKING, CYCLING
(www.yrekagreenway.org) Behind the museum, the Yreka Creek Greenway has walking and cycling paths winding through the trees.

Blue Goose Steam Excursion Train TRAIN RIDE
(www.yrekawesternrr.com; adult/child 2-12yr $20/12) This train hisses and chugs along a 100-year-old track. The schedule is sporadic; look at the website for current information. It's one of the last remaining railroads of California's quickly vanishing historic rail network.

Sleeping & Eating

Motels, motels and more motels: budget travelers can do lots of comparison shopping along Yreka's Main St. There are mid-century motels galore. Many chains hotels are set up along the highway to help catch travelers rushing along I-5; there's a cluster off exit 773 south of town. Klamath National Forest runs several campgrounds; the supervisor's office (p297) has information. RV parks cluster on the edge of town.

Third Street Inn B&B $$
(☎530-841-1120; www.yrekabedandbreakfast.com; 326 Third St; d $105-120) The cute little cottage is the best deal for privacy, but the other three rooms in this family-run Victorian B&B are immaculate and exude homespun charm.

Klamath Motor Lodge MOTEL $
(530-842-2751; www.klamathmotorlodge.net; 1111 S Main St; d $70;) Folks at this motor court are especially friendly, the rooms are clean and – bonus for those headed in from the wilderness – it has an on-site laundry. Of all the motels in Yreka, this is tops.

The Audacity & Cafe CAFE & WINE BAR $
(http://theaudacitycafe.wordpress.com; 200 W Miner St; sandwiches $7-10; 9am-5pm Mon-Thu, to 10pm Sat;) This mother-daughter venture is Yreka's most-happening place on a Saturday night, when the little stage comes alive with local folk and rock acts and people sip wine and sit back on the comfortable couches. The food is simple – wraps and fresh salads, smoothies and sandwiches.

Klander's Deli DELI $
(211 S Oregon St; sandwiches $6; 8am-2pm Mon-Fri) Local to the core, the long list of yummy sandwiches is named after regulars. Bob is a favorite, named for the first owner and stacked with ham, turkey, roast beef and Swiss.

Nature's Kitchen NATURAL FOODS $
(530-842-1136; 412 S Main St; dishes $7; 8am-5pm Mon-Sat;) Friendly natural-foods store and bakery, serving healthy and tasty vegetarian dishes, fresh juices and good espresso. The adjoining store has all kinds of fairies, herbal supplements and new-agey trinkets.

Grandma's House AMERICAN $
(123 E Center St; mains $8-15; 7am-8pm) Home-style platters include a killer open-faced turkey sandwich and rib-sticking breakfast dishes. Look for the cutesy gingerbread house east of downtown between Main St and I-5.

Information

Klamath National Forest supervisor's office (530-842-6131; 1312 Fairlane Rd, at Oberlin Rd; 8am-4:30pm Mon-Fri) At the south edge of town, with the lowdown on recreation and camping. This place is enormous; you can see it from the highway.

Yreka Chamber of Commerce (530-842-1649; www.yrekachamber.com; 117 W Miner St; 9am-5pm, with seasonal variations;)

Getting There & Away

STAGE (530-842-8295; fares from $1.75) buses run throughout the region from a few different stops in Yreka. There are several daily services on weekdays along the I-5 corridor to Weed, Mt Shasta, McCloud and Dunsmuir. Other buses depart daily for Fort Jones (25 minutes), Greenview (35 minutes) and Etna (45 minutes) in the Scott Valley. On Monday and Friday only, buses go out to Klamath River (40 minutes) and Happy Camp (two hours).

Gold Country & Central Valley

Includes »

Why Go?

Gold Country is where it all began – the drowsy hill towns and oak-lined byways of today's quiet road trip belie the wild chaos of California's founding. Shortly after a sparkle caught James Marshall's eye in 1848, the rush for gold brought a stampede of 300,000 '49ers to the Sierra foothills. Today, fading historical markers tell tales of bloodlust and banditry, while the surviving boom towns survive on antiques, ice cream, wine and gold-rush ephemera. This 400-mile-long green strip of the Central Valley, in the center of the state, is the most agriculturally productive region in America. Many travelers hardly hit the brakes while rushing between California's coasts and mountains, or cities of the south and the Bay Area, but those who slow down long enough are rewarded with fresh farm stands, twangy country music traditions and, naturally, wine.

Best Places to Eat

» Noriega Hotel (p348)

» Dusty Buns Bistro Bus (p344)

» Treats (p305)

» V Restaurant (p318)

» Mulvaney's Building and Loan (p328)

Best Places to Stay

» Padre Hotel (p347)

» Citizen Hotel (p326)

» Outside Inn (p304)

» Lure Resort (p307)

» Camino Hotel (p313)

When to Go

Sacramento

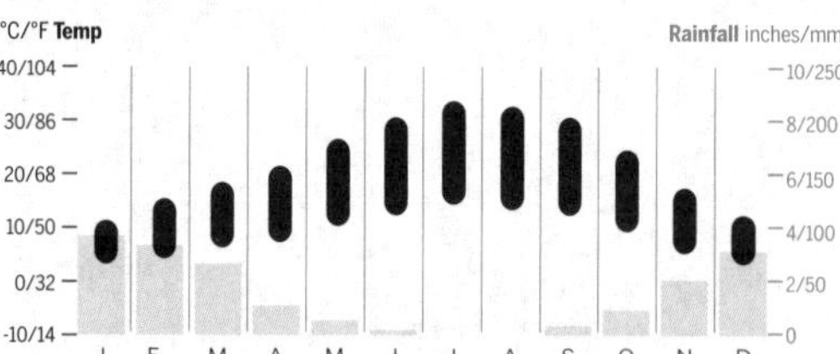

Jul When temperatures are scorching, plunge into a Gold Country swimming hole.

Oct & Nov The trees explode with color and fall fairs happen throughout the region.

Apr–Jun The Central Valley's spring crops bring food festivals galore.

NEVADA COUNTY & NORTHERN GOLD COUNTRY

The '49ers hit it big in Nevada County – the richest score of the mother lode – and the wealth built one of the most picturesque and well-preserved boomtowns, Nevada City. Get out of town and you'll find lovely, remote wilderness areas, a clutch of historic parks and rusting relics of the long-gone miners. This is also a magnet for adrenaline junkies looking to fly down single-track mountain-bike lanes or plunge into icy swimming holes that are remote enough for skinny-dipping.

FAST FACTS

» **Population of Sacramento** 407,000

» **Average temperature low/high in Sacramento** Jan 37/52°F, Jul 55/87°F

» **San Francisco to Nevada City** 148 miles, 2½ hours

» **Sacramento to Bakersfield** 277 miles, 4½ hours

» **Bakersfield to Los Angeles** 112 miles, two hours

Auburn

Look for the big man: a 45-ton effigy of pioneer gold panner Claude announces the visitor's arrival in Gold Country. The hallmarks of Gold Country – ice-cream shops, strollable historic districts, antiques, curious historical sites – are all here. A major stop on the Central Pacific's transcontinental route, Auburn is busy with trains on the Union Pacific's main line to the east and a popular stop for those rushing along I-80 between the Bay Area and Lake Tahoe. You'll have to venture along Hwy 49 for a deeper taste of Gold Country, but those who want just a sample will be rewarded in this accessible town.

Sights & Activities

The fact that Auburn has minted itself the 'Endurance Sport Capital of the World' will give you a sense of how good the area is for cycling, trail running and other gut-busting athletics. See www.auburnendurancecapital.com for a complete list of events.

FREE **Placer County Museum** MUSEUM
(101 Maple St; admission free; ⏲10am-4pm) The 1st floor of the monumental 1898 **Placer County Courthouse** (⏲8am-5pm) has Native American artifacts and displays of Auburn's transportation heritage. It's the easiest museum to visit and gives a good overview of area history; there's also the impressive bling of the museum's gold collection.

Bernhard Museum Complex MUSEUM
(☎530-888-6891; 291 Auburn-Folsom Rd; donation requested; ⏲11am-4pm Tue-Sun) At the south end of High St, this museum was built in 1851 as the Traveler's Rest Hotel. The museum has displays depicting the typical life of a 19th-century farm family, and at times volunteers in period garb ham it up.

FREE **Gold Country Museum** MUSEUM
(1273 High St; admission free; ⏲11am-4pm Tue-Sun) Those with a taste for exploring history should hit this museum, which is toward the back of the fairgrounds, where you can walk through a reproduced mining tunnel and try panning for gold for a small fee.

Sleeping & Eating

Upper Lincoln Way toward the Chamber of Commerce has several restaurants popular with locals, but there's plenty of sunny outdoor eating right off the highway. For a place to sleep look to the highway exits where there's every brand of chain hotel.

Auburn Ale House BREWPUB $
(www.auburnalehouse.com; 289 Washington; mains $7-17; ⏲11am-10pm Sun-Thu, to 11pm weekends) One of those rare brewpubs that offers excellent craft beer *and* excellent food; patrons dig into burgers, sweet potato fries, 'adult mac and cheese' and sweet-and-savory salads (the walnut gorgonzola is delicious). The beer sampler is a great deal, and a must for beer fans, as Auburn brings home tons of festival medals for their spread of ales and pilsners. Hand over the keys before trying too many of the PU240 Imperial IPAs, its flavor profile sporting a 'weapons grade hop bomb.'

Ikedas BURGERS, GROCERY $
(www.ikedas.com; 13500 Lincoln Way; burgers $9-12; ⏲8am-7pm, to 8pm weekends) If you're cruising this part of the state without time to explore, the best pit stop is off I-80 at exit 121. This place feeds Tahoe-bound travelers

Gold Country & Central Valley Highlights

1 Touring Amador County's unpretentious vineyards in the hills around **Plymouth** (p313)

2 Discovering the birthplace of California at **Marshall Gold Discovery Park** (p310)

3 Rumbling down California's best single-track trails at **Downieville** (p307)

4 Wandering the historic streets of Gold Country's gem, **Nevada City** (p304)

5 Honkytonking with **Bakersfield's** (p346) twanging musical icons

6 Uncorking **Lodi's** (p339) emerging wine scene

7 Tubing through the icy rivers of **Chico** (p334)

8 Running the white-water of the **American River** (p301)

9 Hunting for antiques and ice cream on **Highway 49**

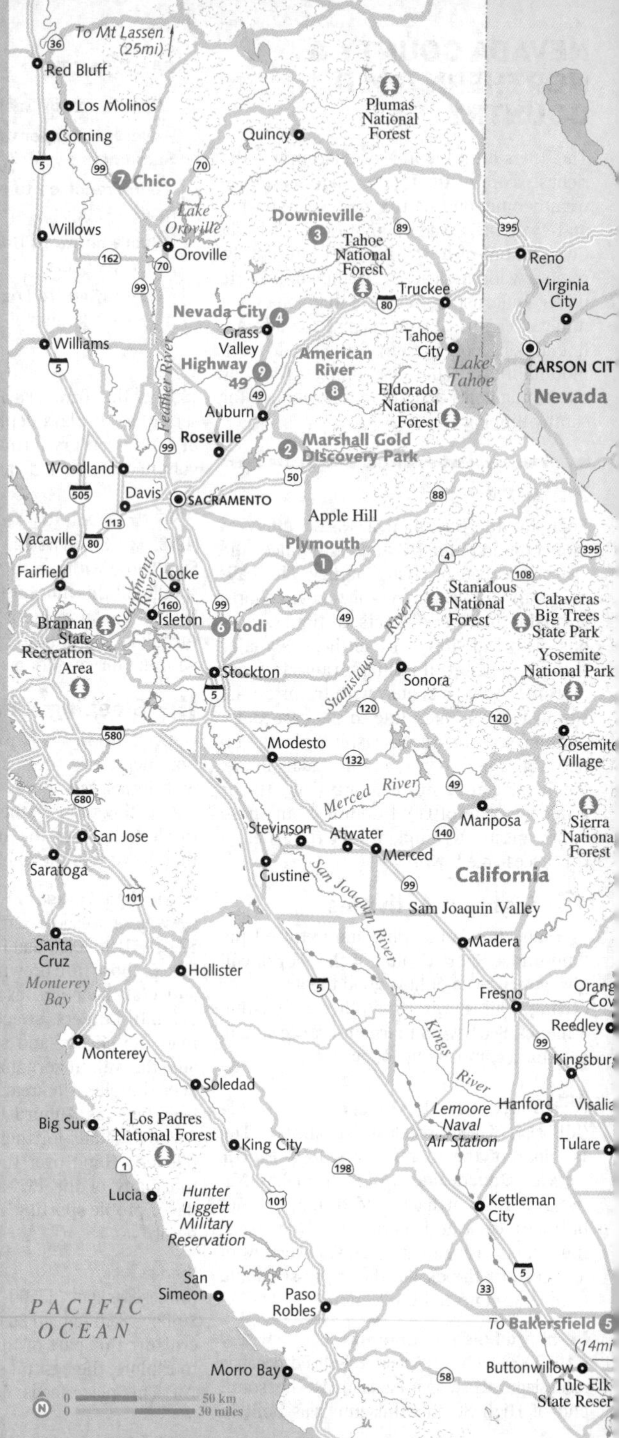

thick, grass-fed burgers, homemade pies and snacks. The seasonal fresh peach shake is deliriously good.

Awful Annie's AMERICAN $
(www.awfulannies.com; 321 Spring St; mains $9-15; 8am-3pm) Huge breakfast scrambles and a sunny patio keep Annie's packed. Worth the wait.

Katrina's BREAKFAST $
(www.katrinascafe.com; 456 Grass Valley Hwy; mains $10-15; 7am-2:30pm Wed-Sat, to 1:30pm Sun) Lemon pancakes, Tuscan scrambles and a homey atmosphere; this place is legit.

Tsuda's Old Town Eatery DELI $
(www.tsudas.com; 103 Sacramento; mains $8; 7am-6pm Mon-Thu, to 9pm Fri & Sat, 8am-6pm Sun;) An organic deli with something for every dietary consideration (gluten-free, veg, etc), an excellent kid's menu (with organic fruit leather) and a brick patio welcoming to dogs.

Information

Auburn Area Chamber of Commerce (530-885-5616; www.auburnchamber.net; 601 Lincoln Way; 9am-5pm Mon-Fri) Housed in the old Southern Pacific railroad depot at the north end of Lincoln Way, it has lots of useful local info. There's a nearby monument to the first transcontinental railroad.

California Welcome Center (530-887-2111; www.visitplacer.com; 13411 Lincoln Way; 9am-4:30pm Mon-Sat, 11am-4pm Sun) Right off I-80 at the Foresthill exit; there is oodles of information for those entering the state from the east.

Getting There & Away

BUS **Amtrak** (800-872-7245; www.amtrak.com) runs several buses a day linking Auburn with Sacramento ($15, one hour) where you can connect to Bay Area and Central Valley trains. There are usually two buses daily east to Reno (2½ hours).

The **Gold Country Stage** (www.goldcountrystage.com) links Auburn with Grass Valley and Nevada City several times a day. Weekends have a slightly more limited schedule. Adult fare between the cities is $3 and the trip takes about 50 minutes.

TRAIN Amtrak's *California Zephyr* stops in Auburn on its daily runs between the Bay Area and Chicago via Reno and Denver. The trip between Auburn and San Francisco takes just over three hours and costs $32.

Auburn State Recreation Area

The deep gorges of this popular **park** (530-885-4527; www.parks.ca.gov, day use fee for some areas $10) were cut by the rushing waters of the North and Middle Forks of the **American River**, which converge below a bridge on Hwy 49, about 4 miles south of Auburn. In the early spring, when waters are high, this is immensely popular for white-water rafting, as the rivers offer a range of difficulty levels. Later in the summer the waters get a bit quieter, perfect for sunning and swimming. Numerous trails in the area are shared by hikers, mountain-bikers and horses.

The best tour of the area is offered by **All-Outdoors California Whitewater Rafting** (800-247-2387; www.aorafting.com), a family-run outfit that was the first on the remote Middle Fork. It is one of the few to lead adventuresome two-day wilderness ventures that break up the trip with waterfall-lined hikes and historically significant sightseeing on the canyon. On the two-day trips they haul your camping gear and feed you. The burrito lunch might be worth the trip alone. All-Outdoors also operates excellent tours on other rivers throughout the area.

One of the most popular trails is the **Western States Trail**, which connects Auburn State Recreation Area to Folsom Lake State Recreation Area and Folsom Lake. It's the site of the **Western States 100 Mile Endurance Run** (www.ws100.com). For more information check the website.

The **Quarry Trail** takes a level path from Hwy 49, just south of the bridge, along the Middle Fork of the American. Several side trails go down to the river.

WHAT THE...?

Floating along any of the rivers in Gold Country, you're bound to pass someone still trying to get rich on the gold of the Sierras using a suction dredge – a floating contraption that sucks up rocks from the river bed and sorts the gold. Even though the dredging season is short and tightly regulated by the state, prospecting pays off – locals claim to average around $50,000 a year.

Gold Country

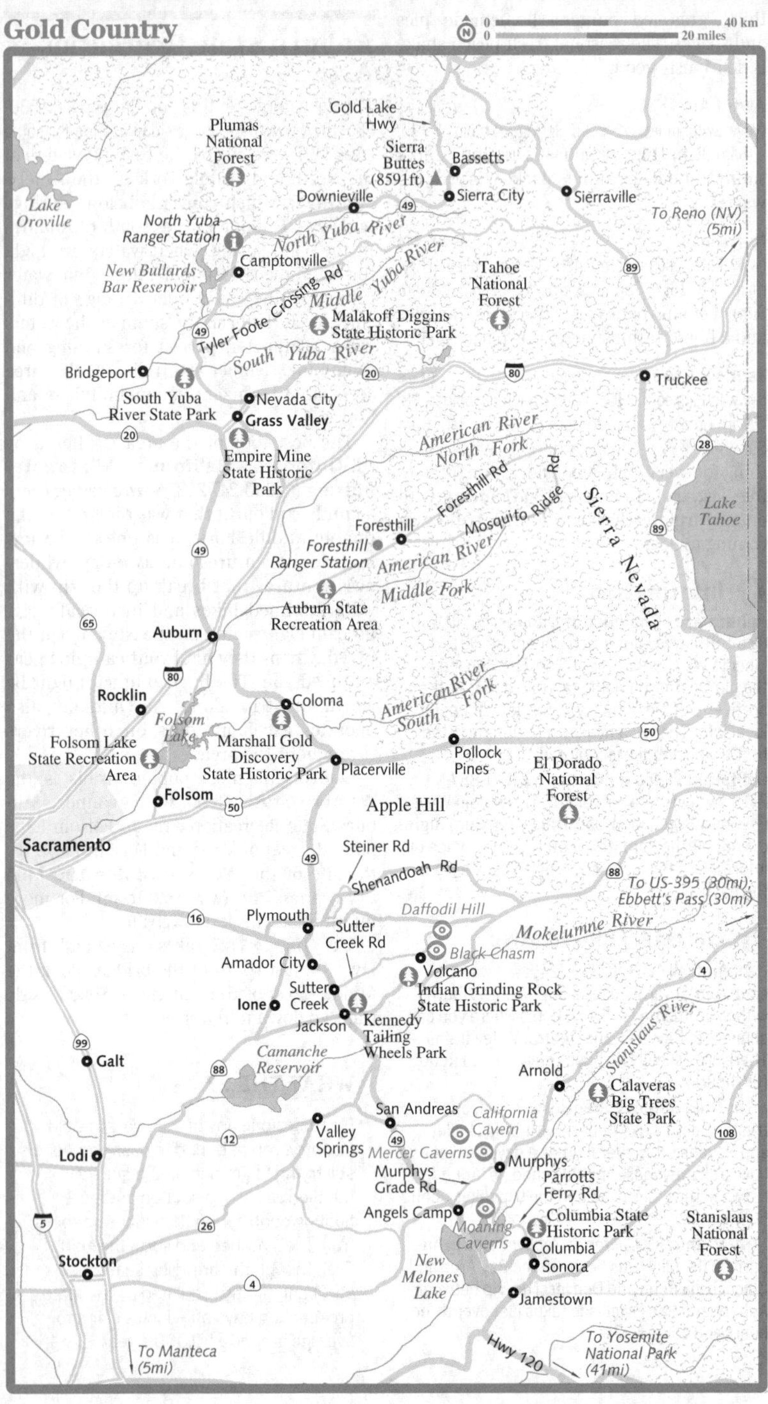

For camping, there are some basic sites on a sweeping bend of the Middle Fork at the blackberry-dotted **Ford's Bar**. It's accessible only by a 2-mile hike or half-day raft. A hike begins at the end of Ruck-A-Chucky Rd. Permits to this and other government-operated camping areas are available from **Foresthill Ranger Station** (☎530-367-2224; www.fs.fed.us; 22830 Foresthill Rd, Foresthill) for $25 to $35.

Grass Valley

From the margins, Grass Valley, with its Anywhere, USA, chain stores, is the ugly utilitarian sister to Nevada City – where people come to buy groceries, get oil changes and groom their pets. But if you get under the surface by driving to the historic business district, the little gem at the center of the sprawl is another rich Gold Country downtown.

The mines in Grass Valley – some of the first shaft mines in the state – were hugely profitable, and the first to flaunt the benefits of lode-mining techniques. Nearly 400 miles of shaft made up the Empire Mine, now a state park.

Grass Valley's main thoroughfares of Mill St and W Main St are the heart of the historic district, which boasts an old-time movie theater, cafes and bars. E Main St goes north to shopping centers and mini-malls, continuing north into Nevada City, while S Auburn St divides E and W Main St.

On Thursday nights in July and August, Mill St is closed to car traffic with farmstead food, arts and crafts and music.

Sights & Activities

Empire Mine State Historic Park PARK
(www.empiremine.org; 10791 E Empire St; adult/child $7/3; ⏲10am-5pm) Situated atop miles of mine shafts is Gold Country's best-preserved gold quartz-mining operation – worth a solid half-day's exploration. From 1850 to 1956 the mines produced six million ounces of gold (about four billion modern dollars' worth). The mine yard is littered with massive mining equipment and buildings constructed from waste rock. There are docent-led tours and sunny hiking. There are plans to open the main mine shaft, next to the largest head frame (a structure that held the pulleys, which once hoisted the plunder up from underground) in the yard, for subterranean tours.

Around the side of the visitors center you'll find stately buildings that belonged to the Bourne family, who ran the mine. They did it in style too, apparent in the elegant country club, English manor home, gardener's house and rose garden. Take a guided tour; check the visitors center for schedules.

Hiking trails begin near the old stamp mill in the mine yard and pass abandoned mines and equipment. A trail map is available at the visitors center. The park is 2 miles east of Grass Valley via the Empire St exit off Hwy 49.

Sleeping & Eating

The quality of food here is proportional to how much you hunt for it: there are several good eateries and bars around downtown, and every imaginable chain lurks among the strip malls by the highway.

Holbrooke Hotel HISTORIC HOTEL **$$**
(☎530-273-1353; www.holbrooke.com; 212 W Main St; r $119-239; ❄@📶) The register in this 1862 hotel boasts the signatures of Mark Twain and Ulysses Grant and well-appointed rooms are named after other presidents who slept there. The bistro (mains $10 to $20) serves casual fare in the ornate dining room or on the shaded patio. The bar has tables overlooking the Main St action.

Cousin Jack Pasties PASTIES **$**
(100 S Auburn St; meals $4-10; ⏲11am-7pm) Cousin Jack and his kin have been serving flaky pasties – a meat-and-potato- stuffed pastry beloved by Cornish miners – for five generations. The pies – pesto lamb, steak and ale and several vegetarian options – are all made from local meat and vegetables.

Tofanelli's ITALIAN **$$**
(www.tofanellis.com; 302 W Main St; meals $13-26) Hugely popular with those locals in the know, this creative restaurant has everything from salads to hearty steaks with seasonal accents like summer squash ravioli. Portions are burly, prices are small and the patio is a treat.

Dorado Chocolates SWEETS **$**
(104 E Main St; snacks $3; ⏲10am-5pm Tue-Sat) Ken Kossoudji's handmade chocolates are made to savor slowly, and when the snow falls the hot chocolate is divine.

Information

Grass Valley/Nevada County Chamber of Commerce (☎530-272-8315; www.grassvalleychamber.com; 248 Mill St; ⊙9am-5pm Mon-Fri) In the former Mill St home of enchantress Lola Montez. It has some very good maps and brochures. Be sure to pick up a copy of the historic walking-tour brochure.

Getting There & Away

Gold Country Stage bus service (www.goldcountrystage.com) Links Nevada City with Grass Valley (adult $1.50, adult one-day pass $4.50, 30 minutes) at least hourly from 7am to 5pm. It also offers information about using the bus for sightseeing in gold country on its website and day passes to all points between Auburn and Nevada City for $7.50.

Nevada City

Maybe it's all those prayer flags, or new-agey Zen goodies that clutter the sandalwood-scented gift shops, but, like a yogi in the lotus position, Nevada City is all about *balance*. The city has the requisite Victorian Gold Rush tourist attractions – an elegantly restored town center, an informative local history museum, girlishly decorated bed-and-breakfasts by the dozen – and a proud contemporary identity, with a small but thriving independent arts and culture scene. Perch on a bar stool in any of the area watering holes and the person next to you might just as easily be a crusty old-timer, a sun-pink tourist or a mystical folk artist.

Spending a couple days here, you'll soak up distinctly rural NorCal culture – with theater companies, alternative film houses, bookstores and live music performances almost every night. Nevada City's streets, best navigated on foot, are jammed with pedestrians by day, especially in the summer. Broad St is the main drag, reached by the Broad St exit off Hwy 49/20. Just north of town on Hwy 49, look for dusty pull-outs at the trailheads to icy swimming holes. In December the blankets of snow and twinkling lights are something out of a storybook.

Sights & Activities

The main attraction is the town itself – its restored buildings, all brick and wrought-iron trimmings, wear their history proudly. There are curious (if pricey) boutiques, galleries and places for food and drink everywhere, all with exhaustive information about the town's history.

Firehouse Museum MUSEUM
(www.nevadacountyhistory.org; 214 Main St; admission by donation; ⊙1-4pm Tue-Sun, varies seasonally) History buffs flock to this museum. Run by the Nevada Country Historical Society, the museum's shady interior smells of old wood and features an impressive collection from Chinese laborers who often built but seldom profited from the mines.

Nevada City Winery WINERY
(☎530-265-9463; 321 Spring St; ⊙11am-5pm Mon-Sat, noon-5pm Sun) This popular winery bottles two regional varietals, syrah and zinfandel, which you can savor while overlooking the production facility. It's a good place to get information on touring the surrounding wine region.

Sleeping

During weekends, Nevada City fills up with urban refugees who inevitably weigh themselves down with real-estate brochures. There are frilly B&Bs everywhere, but the cheapest options are the National Forest campgrounds, just outside of town in any direction.

TOP CHOICE **Broad Street Inn** B&B $$
(☎530-265-2239; www.broadstreetinn.com; 517 E Broad St, Nevada City; r $110-120; ❄📶) It seems as if there are a million bed-and-breakfasts in town, but this six-room inn is a favorite because it keeps it simple. (No weird old dolls, no yellowing lace doilies.) The rooms are modern, brightly furnished and elegant. The delicious breakfast adds to the amazing value.

Outside Inn MOTEL $
(☎530-265-2233; www.outsideinn.com; 575 E Broad St, Nevada City; r $75-150; ❄📶🏊👪) The best option for active explorers, this is an exceptionally friendly and fun motel, with 14 individually named and decorated rooms and a staff that loves the outdoors. Some rooms have a patio overlooking a small creek; all of them have nice quilts, access to BBQ grills and excellent information about hiking in the area. It's a 10-minute walk from downtown.

Red Castle Historic Lodgings B&B $$
(☎530-265-5135; www.redcastleinn.com; 109 Prospect St; r $120-185; ❄🏊) In a city chock-

full of B&Bs this is the granddaddy of them all – the first in Nevada City and one of the oldest in the state. The historic red-brick building combines a Gothic Revival exterior with a well-appointed Victorian interior. Every detail is faithful to 19th century Victorian – even the selection of breakfast foods, and elevated beds. It sits atop a hill a short walk from town and is surrounded by shady walking paths. The Garden Room is the most private.

Northern Queen Inn MOTEL, CABINS $$
(530-265-3720; www.northernqueeninn.com; 400 Railroad Ave; r $99-154;) With a wide range of options – from basic queen rooms to two-story chalets – this hotel might be a bit dated, but the cabins, with small kitchens, are a good deal for small groups and families.

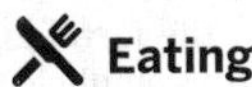

Eating

TOP CHOICE **Treats** ICE CREAM $
(www.treatsnevadacity.com; 110 York St; meals $7-21; noon-8pm Sun-Thu, to 10pm Fri & Sat) It's a crowded contest for Gold Country's best ice-cream shop, but this cute little place – the brilliant second career of avuncular scooper Bob Wright – wins in a walk. The organic flavors are sourced from ripe local fruit: highlights are the rhubarb strawberry, rose and salt caramel but the natural mint and dark chocolate chip is like reinventing the wheel.

Sopa Thai THAI $$
(www.sopathai.net; 312 Commercial St; meals $7-21; 11am-3pm & 5-9:30pm Mon-Fri) Mango red curry, steamed mussels and springs rolls are all excellent at Nevada City's best and most popular Thai restaurant. The interior is furnished with lovely imported carvings and silk, and the patio seating in back is a busy scene midday. The $10 lunch special is a great value.

Café Mekka CAFE $
(237 Commercial St; meals $5-15; 7am-10pm Mon-Thu, to midnight Fri, 8am-midnight Sat, to 10pm Sun) Decorated in a style best described as 'whorehouse baroque,' this charmer serves coffee and beer through the day, along with sandwiches, pizzas and famous desserts. Listen for live folk music on some nights.

Ike's Quarter Cafe CAJUN, BREAKFAST $$
(www.ikesquartercafe.com; 401 Commercial St; meals $8-19; 8am-8pm Wed-Mon) Ike's serves splendid Cajun fare with a sassy charm that leaves the blue hairs pink-cheeked. The creative menu features banana and pecan pancakes, jambalaya and more. It's an excellent place to get the 'Hangtown Fry' – a cornmeal crusted mess of oysters, bacon, caramelized onions and spinach. This is right out of the Garden District in New Orleans.

New Moon Café CALIFORNIAN $$
(www.thenewmooncafe.com; 230 York St; mains $13-20; 11:30-2pm Tue-Fri & 5-8:30pm Tue-Sun) Pure elegance, Peter Selaya's regularly changing menu keeps an organic, local bent. If you visit during the peak of the summer keep to the aquatic theme by trying the wild, line-caught fish or seared duck, prepared with a French-Asian fusion.

Entertainment

There's always something going on in Nevada City – this little village has a vibrant scene for the arts. The Arts section of the *Union* newspaper comes out on Thursday, with a listing of what's going on around the area.

Nevada Theater THEATRE, CINEMA
(www.nevadatheatre.com; 401 Broad St) This brick fortress is one of California's first theaters (1865) and has welcomed the likes of Jack London and Mark Twain to its stage. Now it's used for productions of the top-notch **Foothill Theater Company** (530-265-8587; www.foothillstheatre.com), as well as off-beat movie screenings.

Magic Theatre CINEMA
(www.themagictheatrenc.com; 107 Argall Way) This fantastic theater screens a matchless line-up of unusual films and is about a mile south of downtown Nevada City. Enjoy bowls of fresh popcorn, coffee in real mugs and hot brownies at intermission.

Information

Nevada City Chamber of Commerce (530-265-2692, 800-655-6569; www.nevadacitychamber.com; 132 Main St; 9am-5pm Mon-Sat, 11am-4pm Sun) Ideally located at the east end of Commercial St, this has two welcome comforts for the traveler – an immaculate public toilet and expert local advice.

Tahoe National Forest USFS Headquarters (530-265-4531; 631 Coyote St; 8am-5pm Mon-Sat) A useful and friendly resource for trail and campground information, covering the area from here to Lake Tahoe. It sells topographical maps.

Getting There & Away

Gold Country Stage bus service (530-477-0103; www.goldcountrystage.com) Links Nevada City with Grass Valley at least hourly from 7am to 5pm. Serves the Amtrak station in Auburn several times a day ($1.50).

South Yuba River State Park

Icy swimming holes are fed by rushing rapids in this 11,000-acre plot along the South Yuba River, a combination of state land and acres of federal jurisdiction. This area has a growing network of trails, including the wheelchair-accessible **Independence Trail**, which starts from the south side of the South Yuba River bridge on Hwy 49 and continues for a couple miles with canyon overlooks. June is the best time, when the rivers are rushing and the wildflowers are out.

The longest, single-span, wood-truss **covered bridge** in the USA, all 251ft of it, crosses the South Yuba River at Bridgeport (not to be confused with the Eastern Sierra town of the same name). It's easy to spend a whole day hiking and swimming in this wild area, where crowds can be left behind with little effort. The **Buttermilk Bend Trail** skirts the South Yuba for 1.4 miles, offering river access and wonderful wildflower-viewing around April.

Maps and park information are available from the **state park headquarters** (530-432-2546; 11am-4pm) in Bridgeport, or from the Tahoe National Forest USFS (United States Forest Service) Headquarters in Nevada City. At press time, the future of this state park was uncertain due to budget cuts, though it is under the watchful protection the **South Yuba Citizen's league** (www.yubariver.org), a great source for information.

Malakoff Diggins State Historic Park

A bizarre testament to the mechanical determination of the gold hunt, **Malakoff Diggins** (admission per car $8; sunrise-sunset) is a place to get lost on fern-lined trails and take in the surprising beauty of the recovering landscape. The red stratified cliffs and small mountains of tailings are curiously beautiful, and all part of the deeply scarred landscape left behind from hydraulic mining.

Water cannons designed specifically for hydraulic mining cut a 200ft canyon through ancient bedrock during the 1850s to reach gold veins. Rubble washed down into the Yuba River and this often-toxic waste was filled with heavy metals, many of which remain in the Sacramento Valley floor. By the 1860s, 20ft mud glaciers blocked rivers and caused severe flooding during the snowmelt. After a year of heated courtroom (and bar-room) debate between farmers and miners, the 1884 court case (known as the Sawyer Decision) makes a profoundly timely statement today: a destructive, profitable industry can be stopped for public good. No longer able to reap profits from blasting down the hills with hydraulic cannons, the fortune-hunting game was over. North Bloomfield, the mining community at the center of Malakoff's operation, packed up the shingle shortly after, and what remains is an eerily quiet ghost town within the park's limits.

The **Park Headquarters and Museum** (530-265-2740; admission per vehicle $6; 9am-5pm) offers tours at 1:30pm daily and the chance to see some impressive gold nuggets. The one-mile **Digging Loop Trail** is the quick way to get a glimpse of the scarred moonscape.

You can reach Tyler Foote Crossing Rd, the turnoff for the park, 10 miles northwest of Nevada City on Hwy 49. At press time the future of the park was uncertain due to budget issues.

North Yuba River

The northernmost segment of Hwy 49 follows the North Yuba River through some stunning, remote parts of the Sierra Nevada, known for a tough, short season of white water and great fly-fishing. An entire lifetime could hardly cover the trails that are crossed every season by hikers, mountain-bikers and skiers. Even in summer, snow is likely at the highest elevations and many places have roaring fireplaces year-round.

The best source of trail and camping information is the **North Yuba Ranger Station** (530-288-3231; 15924 Hwy 49; 8am-4:30pm Mon-Fri) in Camptonville.

DOWNIEVILLE

Downieville is the biggest town in the remote Sierra County, located at the junction of the North Yuba and Downie Rivers. With a reputation that quietly rivals Moab, Utah (before it got big), the town is the premiere place for mountain-bike riding in the state, and a staging area for true wilderness adventures.

Like most Gold Rush survivors it wasn't always fun and games: its first justice of the peace was the local barkeep, and the only woman to ever hang in California did so from Downieville's gallows in what was an allegedly racially motivated punishment. (It's a town that seems to have a grisly affection for frontier justice; a reconstructed gallows is across the river, by the civic building.)

Sights & Activities

Brave souls bomb down the **Downieville Downhill**, a molar-rattling 5000ft vertical descent, which is rated among the best mountain-bike routes in the USA. It hosts the annual Downieville Classic, drawing world-class athletes. Slightly more casual riders get shuttled to the top, which can be arranged from outfitters in town.

Yuba Expeditions (☎530-289-3010; www.yubaexpeditions.com; 105 Commercial St; bike rentals $65-85; ⏲9am-5pm Thu-Mon) is a center of the summer trail-bike scene. The other option for a bike rental and shuttle is **Downieville Outfitters** (☎530-289-3010; www.downievilleoutfitters.com; 114 Main St; bike rentals from $65, shuttles $20; ⏲shuttles 10am, 2pm weekdays, every 2hr weekends).

Favorite hikes in the area include the **Chimney Rock Trail** and **Empire Creek Trail**. Both are a bit tricky to reach, so pick up a trail guide at the North Yuba Ranger Station or the USFS Headquarters in Nevada City.

Sleeping

Downtown Downieville has several places to stay where the rustle of the rapids lull weary bikers to sleep. The town's charming streets boast several vintage bars and eateries, some with river views.

Lure Resort CABINS, CAMPGROUND $$
(☎800-671-4084; www.lureresort.com; camping cabins $75, housekeeping cabins $135-260;) The best option if you want to come with biking buddies or a family, this tidy place has modern log cabins along a sublime stretch of river, and big green lawns where kids can play games and adults can lounge in the sun. The spare camping cabins, which have campfire rings instead of a kitchen and a shared bathroom, are a basic, affordable option.

Riverside Inn INN $
(☎530-289-1000; www.downieville.us; 206 Commercial St; r $97-120;) Has 11 stove-warmed rooms that are the first choice in Downieville. Some rooms have balconies that overlook the river and all have a secluded, rustic charm, with warm comforters and a homey breakfast area. Riverside rooms are best; you can open the screen door and listen to the water run by. They also have excellent information about hiking and biking in the area, and in winter they lend snowshoes.

Tahoe National Forest campgrounds CAMPGROUND $
(☎530-993-1410; tent sites $21) Just west of town Hwy 49 has a number of beautiful sites at this campground. Most have vault toilets, running water and unreserved sites along the Yuba River. Of these, the prettiest is **Fiddlecreek**, which has tent-only sites right on the river.

Carriage House Inn INN $
(☎530-289-3573; www.downievillecarriagehouse.com; 110 Commercial St; r $55-100;) This homelike inn has country-style charms, which include rockers and river views. Some have private baths and TVs.

Sierra Shangri-La CABINS, HOTEL $$
(☎530-289-3455; www.sierrashangrila.com; r $115, cabins $160-260) Near Lure and also a secluded option, this is 3 miles east of Downieville on Hwy 49. In July and August the cabins are usually booked with standing reservations, but rooms – each with a balcony overlooking the river – are often available.

SIERRA CITY & THE LAKES BASIN

Sierra City is the primary supply station for people headed to the **Sierra Buttes**, a rugged, rocky shock of mountains that are probably the closest thing to the Alps you'll find in California without hoisting a backpack. It's also the last supply point for people headed into the remote and lovely fishing paradise of the Lakes Basin. There's information about lodging and area activities at www.sierracity.com.

Sights & Activities

There's a vast network of trails, including access to the famous **Pacific Crest Trail**, which is ideal for backpacking and casual hikes. The **Sierra Country Store** (☎530-862-1181; Hwy 49; ⏰9am-7pm; 📶) is about the only consistently open place in town, and it welcomes Pacific Crest Trail refugees with its laundromat and deli.

To reach the Buttes, and many lakes and streams nearby, take Gold Lake Hwy north from Hwy 49 at Bassetts, 9 miles northeast of Sierra City. An excellent hiking trail leads 1.5 miles to **Haskell Peak** (8107ft), where you can see from the Sierra Buttes right to Mt Shasta and beyond. To reach the trailhead, turn right from Gold Lake Hwy at Haskell Peak Rd (Forest Rd 9) and follow it for 8.5 miles.

Sleeping

One of several USFS campgrounds recommended for camping north of Hwy 49 is **Salmon Creek campground** (☎530-993-1410; tent & RV sites without hook-ups $21), 2 miles north of Bassetts on Gold Lake Hwy. It has vault toilets, running water and first-come, first-served sites for RVs and tents, but no hook-ups. This site has the most dramatic view of the Sierra Buttes. Sites 16 and 20 are separated from the rest by a creek.

Going east from Sierra City along Hwy 49 are Wild Plum, Sierra, Chapman Creek and Yuba Pass **USFS campgrounds** (☎530-993-1410; tent sites $21). They have vault toilets and running water (Sierra has river water only), and first-come, first-served sites. Wild Plum (47 sites) is the most scenic.

In the heart of Sierra City, the small **Buttes Resort** (☎530-862-1170, 800-991-1170; www.sierracity.com; 230 Main St; cabins $75-145) occupies a lovely spot overlooking the river and is a favorite with hikers looking to recharge. Most cabins have a private deck and barbecue, some have full kitchens. You can borrow bikes and games from the kind owners.

Eating

Red Moose Cafe CAFE $
(☎530-862-1502; 224 Main St; mains $6-12; ⏰breakfast & lunch Tue-Sun) A local institution that's been serving rib-sticking fare since 1940. Anything with 'Red Moose' in

GOING FOR THE GOLD

California's Gold Rush started in 1848 when James Marshall was inspecting the fatefully sited lumber mill he was building for John Sutter near present-day Coloma. He saw a sparkle in the mill's tailrace water and pulled out a nugget 'roughly half the size of a pea.' Marshall hightailed it to Sacramento and consulted Sutter, who tested the gold by methods described in an encyclopedia. But Sutter wanted to finish his mill so made a deal with his laborers, allowing them to keep gold they found in their spare time if they kept working. Before long, word of the find leaked out.

Sam Brannan, for example, went to Coloma to investigate the rumors just a few months after Marshall's find. After finding 6oz of gold in one afternoon, he returned to San Francisco and paraded through the streets proclaiming, 'There's gold in the Sierra foothills!' Convinced there was money to be made, he bought every piece of mining equipment in the area – from handkerchiefs to shovels. When gold seekers needed equipment for their adventure, Brannan sold them goods at a 100% markup and was a rich man by the time the first folks hit the foothills.

By the time the mill's construction was finished in the spring of 1848, gold seekers had begun to arrive, the first wave coming from San Francisco. Only a few months later, San Francisco was almost depleted of able-bodied men, while towns near the 'diggins,' as the mines were called, swelled with thousands of people. News of the Gold Rush spread around the world, and by 1849 more than 60,000 people (who became widely known as '49ers) rushed to California. They were looking for the mother lode: the mythical big deposit that miners believed was the source of all the gold found in the streams and riverbeds.

Most prospectors didn't stick around after the initial diggings petered out; gold-extraction processes became increasingly complex and invasive. It culminated in the practice of hydraulic mining, by which miners drained lakes and rivers to power their water cannons and blast away entire hillsides (see Malakoff Diggins State Historic Park, p306). People downstream who were inundated by the muck sued, and eventually the environmental cost was too great to justify staying in business.

the name comes with chili, be it omelet or burger. The scent of their fresh cinnamon wafts down Main St every morning.

Big Springs Gardens BRUNCH $$$
(530-862-1333; www.bigspringsgardens.com; 32163 Hwy 49; mains incl price of admission $37-39; buffet meals at noon & 6pm Fri, 1pm Sat, 10:30pm Sun, reservations required) Offers the perfect brunch of berries from the surrounding hills and trout fresh from the pond, served in an open-air dining area. The hiking trails pass the 'Wild Garden,' a waterfall-laced natural area with views well worth the heart-pumping hike.

EL DORADO & AMADOR COUNTIES

In the heart of the pine- and oak-covered Sierra foothills, this is where gold was first discovered – Spanish-speaking settlers appropriately named El Dorado County after a mythical city of riches. Today, SUVs en route to South Lake Tahoe pull off Hwy 50 to find a rolling hillside dotted with the historic towns, sun-soaked terraces and rocky soil of one of California's underdog wine regions. If you make the stop, don't leave without toasting a glass of regional zinfandel, which, like the locals, is packed with earthy attitude and regional character. It's also worth the detour to pause a few minutes at the shore where a glint of gold caught James Marshall's eye and gave birth to the Golden State.

Traveling through much of the central part of Gold Country requires a car, as the public transportation is unreliable between the towns. The good news? This stretch of Hwy 49 makes an excellent road trip.

Coloma

Coloma is the nearest town to Sutter's Mill (the site of California's first gold discovery) and Marshall Gold Discovery State Historic Park (p310). There's little here – just a ramshackle strip of wooden historic buildings and an obligatory blacksmith shop – but it is also a great launching pad for **rafting** operations. The **South Fork of the American River** gets the most traffic, since it features exciting rapids, but is still manageable for beginners. Adrenaline junkies who have never rafted before should try the Middle Fork (p301).

Half-day rafting trips usually begin at the Chile Bar and end close to the state park. Full-day trips put in at the Coloma Bridge and take out at Salmon Falls, near Folsom Lake. The half-day options start in Class III rapids and are action-packed (full-day trips start out slowly, then build up to Class III as a climax). Full-day trips include a lavish lunch. The season usually runs from May to mid-October, depending on snow melts. Prices are generally lower on weekdays.

Whitewater Connection (530-622-6446, 800-336-7238; www.whitewaterconnection.com; half-day trips $89-109, full-day trips $109-129) is typical of the area's operators, with knowledgeable guides and excellent food.

Don't want to get wet? Watch people navigate the **Trouble Maker Rapids**, upstream from the bridge next to Sutter's Mill in the state park.

Sleeping & Eating

If you're looking for a basic hotel and don't mind the blandness of a highway motel, Auburn is a better bet.

Coloma Country Inn B&B $$
(530-622-6919; www.colomacountryinn.com; 345 High St; r $125-195;) The four-room B&B is situated in a historic farmhouse and the hosts offer good advice about area rafting. The rooms are bright and lovely, as are the hosts. If you're not in a rush, try the quiet cottage suite, where you can spend an afternoon floating on the pond.

American River Resort CAMPGROUND, CABINS $
(530-622-6700; www.americanriverresort.com; 6019 New River Rd; tent & RV sites $30-35, cabins $170-280;) Only a quarter mile off Hwy 49, just south of the state park. The site is more cushy than most other area campgrounds: there's a restaurant and bar, a playground, a pond and farm animals. The sites are basic, but some are right on the river. The most spacious and pretty oak-shaded sites are 14 to 29.

Coloma Resort CAMPGROUND, CABINS $
(530-621-2267; www.colomaresort.com; 6921 Mt Murphy Rd; tent & RV sites $45-49, tent cabins & on-site RV rentals $125-165;) Another long-established riverside campground, this is better for RVs. It comes with a full range of activities, playgrounds and wireless internet. With lots of family activities, this has the feel of a summer camp.

Coloma Club Cafe & Saloon BAR & GRILL $
(530-626-6390; 7171 Hwy 49; restaurant 6:30am-9pm, bar 10am-2am) North of Marshall SHP, the patio at this rowdy hangout comes alive with guides and river rats when the water is high.

Marshall Gold Discovery State Historic Park

Compared to the stampede of gun-toting, hill-blasting, hell-raising settlers that populate tall tales along Hwy 49, the **Marshall Gold Discovery State Historic Park** (admission per car $5; 8am-7pm;) is a place of bucolic tranquillity, with two tragic heroes in John Sutter and James Marshall. Sutter, who had a fort in Sacramento, partnered with Marshall to build a sawmill on a swift stretch of the American River in 1847. It was Marshall who discovered gold here on January 24, 1848, and though the men tried to keep their findings secret, it eventually brought a chaotic rush of prospectors from around the world. In one of the great tragic ironies of the Gold Rush, the men who made this discovery died nearly penniless.

If there aren't a million school kids squealing around, the pastoral park is quietly befitting of this legacy, with a grassy area bordered on the east by the river. Follow a simple dirt path to the place along the bank where Marshall found gold and started the revolutionary birth of the 'Golden State.'

The park's quiet charms are mostly experienced outdoors, strolling past the carefully reconstructed mill and taking in the grounds. There's also a humble **Visitor Information Center & Museum** (530-622-3470; Bridge St; 10am-4pm Tue-Sun) with a tidy shop where you can buy kitsch from the frontier days.

On a hill overlooking the park is the **James Marshall Monument**, where he was buried in 1885, a ward of the state. You can drive a circuit but it's much better to meander the many trails around the park, past old mining artifacts and pioneer cemeteries.

Panning for gold is popular – you can pay $7 for a quick training session and 45 minutes of gold panning, or pan for free if you have your own.

Placerville

Placerville has always been a travelers' town: it was originally a destination for fortune hunters who reached California by following the South Fork of the American River. In 1857 the first stagecoach to cross the Sierra Nevada linked Placerville to Nevada's Carson Valley, which eventually became part of the nation's first transcontinental stagecoach route. Today, Placerville is a place to gas up, stretch your legs and get a bite while traveling between Sacramento and Tahoe on Hwy 50. It has a thriving and well-preserved downtown with antique shops and bars, where local wags cherish the wild reputation of 'Hangtown' – a name earned when a handful of men swung from the gallows in the mid-1800s. Among the many other awesome local legends is 'Snowshoe' John A Thompson, a postal carrier who carried some 80lbs of mail on skis from Placerville over the Sierra to Carson Valley during the winter.

Sights & Activities

Main St is the heart of downtown Placerville and runs parallel to Hwy 50 between Canal St and Cedar Ravine Rd. Hwy 49 meets Main St at the west edge of downtown. Looking like a movie set, most buildings along Main St are false fronts and sturdy brick structures from the 1850s, dominated by the spindly **Bell Tower**, a relic from 1856 that once rallied volunteer firemen.

Gold Bug Park HISTORIC SITE
(www.goldbugpark.org; 10am-4pm Apr-Oct, noon-4pm Sat & Sun Nov-Mar) The best museum in Placerville, about 1 mile north of town on Bedford Ave. The park stands over the site of four mining claims that yielded gold from 1849 to 1888; you can descend into the self-guided Gold Bug Mine, do some gold panning ($2) and explore the grounds and picnic area for free.

FREE **El Dorado County Historical Museum** MUSEUM
(530-621-5865; 104 Placerville Dr; admission free; 10am-4pm Wed-Sat, noon-4pm Sun) On the El Dorado County Fairgrounds west of downtown (exit north on Placerville Dr from Hwy 50), is an extensive complex of restored buildings, mining equipment and re-created businesses.

Sleeping & Eating

Chain motels and fast-food places can be found at either end of the historic center of Placerville along Hwy 50.

Cary House Hotel HISTORIC HOTEL $$
(☎530-622-4271; www.caryhouse.com; 300 Main St; r from $114; ❄@🛜) This historic hotel is centrally located in the middle of downtown Placerville and has a large, comfortable lobby with back-lit stained glass depicting scenes from the region's history. Once a bordello, it's said to be haunted, though modern rooms (some with kitchenettes) with tasteful period decor and drop ceilings in the hallways belie its rich history. Ask for a room at the back of the hotel overlooking the courtyard to avoid street noise, or for room 212, which is rumored to be a supernatural hangout.

National 9 Inn MOTEL $
(☎530-622-3884, 1500 Broadway; r $50-89; ❄🛜) This mid-century motel, recently renovated by a young couple, is the best bargain in Placerville, even if it lies at the lonely north end of town. The building's exterior is ho-hum, but the rooms are sparkling, bathrooms are remodeled and all come with refrigerators and microwaves. It's a great option for travelers who want a clean, no-frills stay and to support independent business.

Albert Shafsky House B&B B&B $$
(☎530-642-2776; www.shafsky.com; 2942 Coloma St; r $145-185; ❄🛜) Of all the Victorian bed-and-breakfast options in Placerville, Albert's proximity to downtown, ornate period furnishings and luxurious bedding make this cozy three-room option a favorite.

Heyday Café CAFE $
(www.heydaycafe.com; 325 Main St; mains $9-24; ⊙11am-8pm Tue-Sun) Fresh, and well-executed, the menu here leans toward simple Italian comfort food, made all the more comfortable by the wood-and-brick interior. The wine list is long on area vineyards and locals rave about its lunch menu.

Z-Pie AMERICAN $
(www.z-pie.com; 3182 Center St; mains $5-6; ⊙11am-9pm) With its whimsical take on the all-American comfort food staple, this casual stop across from City Hall stuffs flaky, butter-crusted pot pies with a gourmet flourish (steak cabernet! Thai chicken! black bean chili and tofu!). California beers are on tap and the four-beer sampler ($9) is ideal for the undecided.

Sweetie Pie's BREAKFAST $
(www.sweetiepies.biz; 577 Main St; mains $5-12; ⊙breakfast & lunch Tue-Sun) Ski bunnies and bums fill this diner and bakery counter on the weekends en route to Tahoe slopes, filling up with egg dishes and top-notch homemade baked goods. Breakfast is its specialty, but it also does a capable lunch, with sandwiches and salads. The cinnamon rolls alone are worth a stop.

Cozmic Cafe CAFE $
(www.ourcoz.com; 594 Main St; meals $6-10; ⊙breakfast, lunch & dinner; ✎) In the historic Placerville Soda Works building, the menu is organic and boasts vegetarian and healthy fare backed by fresh smoothies. There's a good selection of microbrews and live music on weekends, when it is often open late.

Drinking

The wines of El Dorado County are rising in profile, and several tasting rooms dot the main street offering earthy, elegant zins of the region (see p312 for more on wineries). Placerville's bars, on the other hand, are akin to the neighborhood watering holes in the Midwest: they open around 6am, get an annual cleaning at Christmas and are great for people who want to chew the fat with a colorful cast of locals.

Liars' Bench BAR
(☎530-622-0494; 255 Main St) With the closure of the shady Hangman's Tree dive bar, the Liar's Bench survives at the town's classic watering hole under a neon martini sign that beckons after dark.

Shopping

TOP CHOICE **Gothic Rose Antiques** ANTIQUES, CURIOSITIES
(www.gothicroseantiques.com; 484 Main St) This artfully designed curiosity shop likely frightens the wigs off the other antique dealers in town, with its collection of haute gothic house wares, antique occult goods and flawlessly macabre sensibility. Browsing the antique medical instruments, taxidermy, 19th-century photos of corpses and – just for fun – a few garments of latex and lace, is titillating. The most interesting

antique store in Gold Country? It's a dead ringer.

Placerville Hardware HARDWARE
(www.placervillehardware.com; 441 Main St) The 1852 building, an anchor of Placerville's main drag, is the oldest continuously operating hardware store west of the Mississippi and one of many places along Main St to pick up a brochure for a self-guided tour of the town. The store has a smattering of Gold Country bric-a-brac but most of the goods that clutter the place are bona fide dry goods, like hammers and buckets, all unusually curious within the tight aisles.

Placerville Antiques ANTIQUES
(448 Main St) Of Placerville's many antique shops, the collection of dealers in this brightly lit space is a favorite. Reasonably priced mid-century dishware is a particular strength.

Bookery BOOKS
(326 Main St; ⏲10am-5:30pm Mon-Thu, to 7pm Fri & Sat, to 4pm Sun) A great used-book store to stock up on vacation pulp.

Information

El Dorado County Chamber of Commerce (www.eldoradocounty.org; 542 Main St; ⏲9am-5pm Mon-Fri) Has decent maps and local information.

Placerville News Co (www.pvillenews.com; 409 Main St; ⏲8am-6:30pm Mon-Thu, to 7pm Fri & Sat, to 5:30pm Sun) This plank-floored shop has a wealth of excellent maps, history and local interest books.

Getting There & Away

Amtrak (☎800-872-7245; www.capitolcorridor.org) Runs several buses daily to Sacramento ($15, one hour 20 minutes), though some require train connections to points further along the Capital Corridor route.

El Dorado Transit (www.eldoradotransit.com) Operates weekday commuter buses to Sacramento ($5, one hour 30 minutes) out of the **Placerville Transit Station** (2984 Mosquito Rd), a charming covered bus stop with benches and restrooms. It's about half a mile from downtown, on the north side of Hwy 50.

Placerville Wineries

The region's high heat and rocky soil produces excellent wines, which frequently appear on California menus. Oenophiles could spend a long afternoon rambling through the welcoming vineyards of El Dorado Country alone (though a full weekend of tasting could be had if it was coupled with adjoining Amador County). Details can be found at the **El Dorado Winery Association** (☎800-306-3956; www.eldoradowines.org) or **Wine Smith** (www.thewinesmith.com; 346 Main St; ⏲11am-8pm), a local shop with just about everything grown in the area.

Some noteworthy wineries, all north of Hwy 50, include **Lava Cap Winery** (www.lavacap.com; 2221 Fruitridge Rd; ⏲11am-5pm), which has an on-hand deli for picnic supplies and **Boeger Winery** (www.boegerwinery.com; 1709 Carson Rd; ⏲10am-5pm). Both have free tastings.

Amador County Wine Region

Amador County might be something of an underdog among California's winemaking regions, but a thriving circuit of family wineries, Gold Rush history and local characters make for excellent wine touring without a whiff of pretension. The region lays claim to the oldest zinfandel vines in the United States and the surrounding country has a lot in common with this celebrated variety – bold and richly colored, earthy and constantly surprising.

The region has two tiny towns, Plymouth and Amador City, which offer a range of services aimed at those on the wine circuit. To begin the circuit of Amador wineries, leave Hwy 49 in Plymouth and follow Shenandoah Rd, which takes you through rows of vines basking in the heat. You'll see hill after rolling hill covered with rocky rows of neatly pruned vines, soaking up gallons of too-bright sun. Tastings at the family-operated wineries around the county have little in common with those in the Napa Valley – most hosts are welcoming and helpful, offering free tastes and information about their operations.

Maps are available at the wineries, and from the **Amador Vintners Association** (www.amadorwine.com).

Drytown Cellars WINERY
(www.drytowncellars.com; 16030 Hwy 49; ⏲11am-5pm Fri-Sun) This is the most fun tasting room in Amador County, thanks to Allan, a gregarious host and an array of stunning reds.

Deaver Vineyards WINERY
(www.deavervineyard.com; 12455 Steiner Rd; ⏲10:30am-4pm) A true family affair where

nearly everyone's last name seems to match the one on the bottles.

Sobon Estate WINERY
(www.sobonwine.com; 14430 Shenandoah Rd; ⏲10am-5pm) Founded in 1856, it's home to the Shenandoah Valley Museum featuring wine-related memorabilia.

Wildrotter WINERY
(www.wildrottervineyard.com; 19890 Shenandoah School Rd; ⏲10am-5pm Fri-Sun, 11am-4pm Mon & Thu) This winery brought home prestigious honors for California's best red at a recent State Fair.

PLYMOUTH & AMADOR CITY

Two small, sunny villages make equally decent bases for exploring Amador County's wine region. The first, Plymouth, is where the region's Gold Rush history is evident in its original name, Pokerville. Few card sharks haunt the slumbering town today; it wakes late when the tiny main street fills with the smell of barbecue, a few strolling tourists and the odd rumble of a motorcycle posse. Amador City was once home to the Keystone Mine – one of the most prolific gold producers in California – but the town lay deserted from 1942 (when the mine closed) until the 1950s, when a family from Sacramento bought the dilapidated buildings and converted them into antique shops.

FREE **Amador Whitney Museum** (www.amador-city.com; Main St, Amador City; admission free; ⏲noon-4pm Fri-Sun) is the only sight of any note. It has a covered wagon and a replica school house scene and mineshaft. It's worth the 15-minute stop.

TOP CHOICE **Imperial Hotel** (☎209-267-9172; www.imperialamador.com; 14202 Main St, Amador City; r $120-145; ❄📶) is the nicest place to stay. Built in 1879, it's one of the area's most inventive updates to the typical antique-cluttered hotels, with sleek deco touches accenting the usual gingerbread flourish, a genteel bar and an excellent seasonally minded restaurant (dinner $20 to $30). On weekends during the summer, expect a two-night minimum.

Book a table at **Taste** (☎209-245-3463; 9402 Main St, Plymouth; mains $31-50; ⏲5-9pm Thu-Mon & 11:30-2pm Sat), where excellent Amador wines are paired with a four-star menu of California fusions. Pull on the oversized fork-shaped door handle to be greeted by smells of fresh, seasonally changing dishes, all artfully presented.

Tired of wine? Hit the **Drytown Club** (www.drytownclub.com; 15950 Hwy 49), the kind of rowdy roadhouse where people start drinking a little too early and soak it up with weekend BBQ. The bands on the weekend are bluesy, boozy and sometimes brilliant. The dance floor of this place has seen the death of many visitors' inhibitions.

Sutter Creek

Perch on the balcony of one of the gracefully restored buildings on Main St and view Sutter Creek, a gem of a Gold Country town with raised, arcaded sidewalks and high-balconied buildings with false fronts that are perfect examples of California's 19th-century architecture. This is an excellent place to stay

WORTH A TRIP

APPLE HILL

In 1860, a miner planted a Rhode Island Greening apple tree on a hill just up the way from Placerville and with it the foundation for bountiful Apple Hill, a 20-sq-mile area east of Placerville and north of Hwy 50 where there are more than 60 orchards. Apple growers sell directly to the public, usually from August to December, and some let you pick your own. Other fruits are available during different seasons.

A decent map of Apple Hill is available at the **Apple Hill Visitors Center** (☎530-644-7692; www.applehill.com) in the Camino Hotel, near the Camino exit off Hwy 50. If you'd rather do it yourself, there's a good map of 'El Dorado County Farm Trails' at www.visit-eldorado.com.

The **Camino Hotel** (☎530-644-1800; www.caminohotel.com; r incl breakfast $75-125; 👪) is a former lumberjack bunkhouse – every bit as creaky and crooked as you'd hope – with rooms that have been recently redone. The rates are a steal (as low as $50 on weekdays) and room 4 is perfect for families with two rooms adjoined by a central sitting room. The breakfast is made to order. A great spot to hunker down while touring Apple Hill's farms.

when visiting Amador and El Dorado County wineries.

Begin the visit at volunteer-operated **Sutter Creek Visitor Center** (☎209-267-1344; www.suttercreek.org; 25 Eureka St; ⊙hours vary) to collect a walking-tour map of town or an excellent, free driving-tour guide to local gold mines. The website has seasonal suggestions for day trippers.

Sights & Activities

FREE Monteverde General Store
HISTORIC BUILDING

(☎209-267-0493; admission free; ⊙by appointment) Next door to the visitor center, this building goes back in time to when the general store was the center of the town's social and economic life, represented by the chairs that circle the potbelly stove and the detailed historic scale. Senior docents lead fun tours by appointment.

Knight Foundry
MINE

(www.knightfoundry.org; 81 Eureka St) In its prime, Sutter Creek was Gold Country's main supply center. Three foundries operating in 1873 made pans and rock crushers. This foundry operated until 1996 as the last water-powered foundry and machine shop in the US. You can still see the workings of the foundry, and on some days volunteers can explain how everything worked while they toil to put the foundry back into production.

Sutter Creek Theatre
PERFORMING ARTS

(www.suttercreektheater.com; 44 Main St) One of several excellent Gold Country arts groups, it has nearly a 100-year-long history of presenting live drama, films and other cultural events.

Sleeping & Eating

Eureka Street Inn
B&B $$

(☎209-267-5500; www.eurekastreetinn.com; 55 Eureka St; r $145; ❄📶) Each of the four rooms in this 1914 Arts-and-Crafts–style home has unique decor and gas fireplaces. Once the home of a wealthy stagecoach operator, the inn is on a quiet street close to everything and serves a delicious breakfast with strong coffee and fresh fruit.

Sutter Creek Inn
B&B $$

(☎209-267-5606; www.suttercreekinn.com; 75 Main St; r $90-195; ❄) The 17 rooms and cottages here vary in decor and amenities (antiques, fireplaces, sunny patios) but all have private bathrooms. Guests can snooze in the hammock by the gardens or sprawl out on the large lawn, which is dotted with comfy chairs for curling up in with a book. Of course it's jammed with knickknacks, including a spectacular collection of cow-shaped coffee creamers.

Sutter Creek Ice Cream Emporium
SWEETS $

(51 Main St; ⊙11am-6pm Thu-Sun) The sugared environment of this shop of sweets gets downright enchanted when Stevens Price, the man behind the counter, takes to the 1919 Milton Piano and plays ragtime. Price also organizes the Sutter Creek Ragtime Festival each August.

Pizza Plus
PIZZA $

(20 Eureka St; pizzas $14; ⊙11am-9pm; 👪) Crisp, chewy thin-crust pizza and pitchers of beer make this a favorite; it's the perfect place to hang out and chat up the locals. Special topping combinations like the BBQ pizza put it over the top.

Thomi's Coffee & Eatery
AMERICAN $

(40 Hanford St; meals $7-12; ⊙8am-3pm Fri-Wed; 📶) A real star in a galaxy of them, Thomi serves classic griddle breakfasts, huge salads to prime rib dinners. The brick dining room is welcoming in winter; in summer there's a sunny little patio.

Sutter Creek Cheese
MARKET $

(www.suttercreekcheese.com; 33 Main St; ⊙11am-5pm) A stop for cheese from California and Europe.

Volcano

One of the many fading plaques in Volcano accurately calls it a place of 'quiet history,' and even though the little L-shaped village on the bank of Sutter Creek yielded tons of gold and a Civil War battle, today it slumbers away in remote solitude. Now only a scattering of greening bronze monuments attest to Volcano's lively past.

Large sandstone rocks line Sutter Creek, which skirts the center of town. The rocks, now flanked by picnic tables, were blasted from surrounding hills by a hydraulic process before being scraped clean of gold-bearing dirt. The process had dire environmental consequences, but at its peak miners made nearly $100 a day.

The winding 12-mile drive from Sutter Creek is along lovely Sutter Creek Rd.

Sights & Activities

Daffodil Hill FLOWER FARM
(donations accepted; daily mid-Mar–mid-Apr) This hilltop farm, 2 miles northeast of Volcano, is blanketed with more than 300,000 daffodils. The McLaughlin and Ryan families have operated the farm since 1887 and keep hyacinths, tulips, violets, lilacs and the occasional peacock among the daffodils.

Black Chasm CAVE TOUR
(888-762-2837; www.caverntours.com; 15701 Pioneer Volcano Rd; adult/child $14.75/7.50; 9am-5pm) A quarter of a mile east of Volcano, this has the whiff of a tourist trap, but one look at the helictite crystals – rare, sparkling white formations that look like enlarged snowflakes – makes the crowd more sufferable. The tour guides are all experienced cavers.

Indian Grinding Rock State Historic Park HISTORIC SITE
(209-296-7488; Pine Grove-Volcano Rd; admission per vehicle $8) Two miles southwest of Volcano is a sacred area for the local Miwok people. There's a limestone outcrop that's covered with petroglyphs – 363 originals and a few modern additions – and over 1000 mortar holes called *chaw'ses* used for grinding acorns into meal.

Volcano Theatre Company PERFORMING ARTS
(209-223-4663; www.volcanotheatre.org; adult/child $16/11) On weekends between April and November, this highly regarded company produces live dramas in the restored Cobblestone Theater.

Sleeping & Eating

Volcano Union Inn HISTORIC HOTEL $$
(209-296-4458; www.volcanounion.com; 16104 Main St, Volcano; r incl breakfast $109-129;) The preferred of two historic hotels in Volcano, there are four lovingly updated rooms with crooked floors: two have street-facing balconies. Flat-screen TVs and modern touches are a bit incongruous with the old building, but it's a comfortable place to stay and the on-site Union Pub has a superb menu and will host the occasional old-time fiddler.

St George Hotel HISTORIC HOTEL $$
(209-296-4458; www.stgeorgehotel.com; 16104 Main St; r $80-190) Up the crooked stairs of this charming, creaky hotel are 20 rooms which vary in size and amenity and are free of clutter. The restaurant (open for dinner Thursday to Sunday, brunch Sunday) has a menu anchored by steak, but the best place to hang out is in the accompanying bar, where the local concoction of 'Moose Milk' (a whisky-and-dairy–based inebriant) is worthy of the bartender's playful warning.

Indian Grinding Rock State Historic Park CAMPGROUND $
(www.reserveamerica.com; tent and RV sites $25) The beautiful campground at Indian Grinding Rock State Historic Park has fresh water, plumbing and 23 unreserved sites set among the trees, with tent sites and hookups for RVs.

Jackson

Jackson has some historic buildings and a small downtown, but it ain't much to look at; standing at the junction of Hwy 49 and Hwy 88 it's probably the least attractive Gold Rush hub. Hwy 88 turns east from Hwy 49 here and heads over the Sierra near the Kirkwood ski resort (see p354).

Sights

Kennedy Tailing Wheels Park HISTORIC SIGHT
One mile from downtown Jackson via North Main St, Kennedy Tailing Wheels Park doesn't look like much at first glance, but the four iron and wood wheels, 58ft in diameter (which look like fallen carnival rides), transported tailings from the Eureka Mine over two low hills and are marvelous examples of engineering and craftsmanship. Be sure to climb to the top of the hill behind the wheels to see the impounding dam.

Mokelumne Hill HISTORIC AREA
Somewhat undiscovered Mokelumne Hill, which lies 7 miles south of Jackson just off Hwy 49, was settled by French trappers in the early 1840s. It's a good place to see historic buildings without the common glut of antique stores and gift shops.

Sleeping & Eating

National Hotel HISTORIC HOTEL $
(209-223-0500; www.national-hotel.com; 2 Water St; r $75-195) This is Jackson's historic hotel, though the rooms, decorated with themed flair from pop icons, don't jibe with the historic facade. The rooms are worn, and there's plenty of sound from the nearby highway and locals who gather on the bar's balcony

below, so light sleepers should look elsewhere.

Mel's and Faye's Diner AMERICAN **$$**
(www.melandfayesdiner.com; 205 N Hwy 49; meals $5-12; ⏲4am-10pm Mon-Thu, to 11pm Fri-Sun) A local institution near Hwy 88. It serves up excellent diner fare that includes breakfasts that could feed a small family, classic burgers (try the chili-soaked 'Miner') and – to balance the divine grease binge – a decent salad bar.

Information

Amador County Chamber of Commerce (☎209-223-0350, www.amadorcountychamber.com; 125 Peek St; ⏲9am-4pm Mon-Fri) On the corner of Hwys 49 and 88. Has enough brochures to fill several recycling bins.

Getting There & Away

The only way to reliably travel through this area is with your own wheels. Placer Country runs its (fairly pathetic) bus system out of Jackson, but good luck catching it – the buses are few and far between. **Amador Transit** (209-267-9395; www.amadortransit.com) is a bit better. It makes two daily connections to Sacramento ($1, one hour) and, if you have enough patience, you can connect to Calaveras County and southern Gold Country. By car, Jackson is 2½ hours from San Francisco and just over one hour to the ski resorts of S Lake Tahoe.

CALAVERAS COUNTY & SOUTH GOLD COUNTRY

The southern region of Gold Country is hot as blazes in the summer so cruising through its historic Gold Rush hubs will demand more than one stop for ice cream. The tall tales of yesteryear come alive here through the region's infamous former residents: author Mark Twain, who got his start writing about a jumping frog contest in Calaveras County, and Joaquin Murrieta, a Robin Hood figure who somehow seems to have frequented every old bar and hotel in the area.

Angels Camp

On the southern stretch of Hwy 49 one figure looms over all others: literary giant Mark Twain, who got his first big break with the story of *The Celebrated Jumping Frog of Calaveras County*, written and set in Angels Camp. There are differing claims as to when or where Twain heard this tale, but Angels Camp makes the most of it. There are gentlemanly Twain impersonators, statues and dozens of bronze frogs embedded in the sidewalk of Main St celebrating amphibious champions of the past 80 years. Look for the plaque of Rosie the Riveter, who set an impressive 21ft record in 1986. Today the town is an attractive mix of buildings from the Gold Rush to art deco periods.

Calaveras County Visitors Bureau (☎209-736-0049; www.gocalaveras.com; 1192 S Main St; ⏲9am-5pm Mon-Sat, 11am-3pm Sun; 📶) has a walking and driving tour of Angels Camp, history books and lots more information for your trip.

Sights & Activities

Angels Camp makes the most of the Twain connection; hosting the **Jumping Frog Jubilee** the third weekend in May (in conjunction with the county fair and something of a Harley rally) and **Mark Twain Days** over the Fourth of July weekend.

Moaning Cavern CAVE TOURS
(☎209-736-2708; www.caverntours.com; adult/child $14.75/7.50; ⏲10am-5pm) Though nearby California Cavern offers roomier digs with more impressive natural formations this cave has more thrills by allowing visitors to rappel down the 165ft shaft to the bottom ($65). They also have an above-ground zip line and self-guided nature walk. A pile of bones found at the bottom were some of the oldest human remains ever found in the United States. In winter, they host caroling (amazing considering the cave's acoustics) and a rappelling Santa Claus.

Eating

Strung out along Hwy 49 are a number of motels, fast-food joints and places to fill up the gas tank.

Sidewinders CAL-MEX **$**
(1251 S Main St; mains $8-12; ⏲11am-8pm Tue-Sat; 👪) The guacamole-dressed white panko fish tacos are excellent. When the sun pounds down on Angels Camp, the cool stone walls and pints of regional California beer are soothing.

Crusco's ITALIAN **$$**
(www.cruscos.com; 1240 S Main St; mains $14-26; ⏲11am-3pm & 5-9pm Thu-Mon) The class act in downtown Angels Camp puts out a serious,

WORTH A TRIP

CALAVERAS BIG TREES STATE PARK

From Angels Camp, Hwy 4 ascends into the High Sierra, eventually cresting at Ebbetts Pass (8730ft) and then descending to junctions with Hwys 89 and 395. Along the way the road passes through the workmanlike town of Arnold, which has a few cafes and motels strung along the roadside. But the real reason for taking Hwy 4 is 2 miles east of Arnold and 20 miles east of Murphys: a chance to commune with the largest living things on the planet.

Calaveras Big Trees State Park (209-795-2334; admission per vehicle $6) is home to giant sequoia redwood trees. Reaching as high as 325ft and with trunk diameters up to 33ft, these leftovers from the Mesozoic era are thought to weigh upwards of 3000 tons, or close to 20 blue whales.

The redwood giants are distributed in two large groves, one of which is easily seen from the **North Grove Big Trees Trail**, a 1.5-mile self-guided loop, near the entrance, where the air is fresh with pine and rich soil. A 4-mile trail that branches off from the self-guided loop climbs out of the North Grove, crosses a ridge and descends 1500ft to the Stanislaus River.

It's possible to find giant trees throughout the park's 6000 acres, though the largest are in fairly remote locations. The **visitor center** (9am-4pm) can offer maps and lots of good advice on the miles of trails. It also has good exhibits about the trees and how a few dedicated individuals fought for decades to save them from becoming so many thousands of picnic tables.

Camping is popular and **reservations** (800-444-7275; www.parks.ca.gov; tent & RV sites $35) are essential. North Grove Campground is near the park entrance; less crowded is Oak Hollow Campground, 4 miles further on the park's main road. Most atmospheric are the hike-in environmental sites.

authentic northern Italian menu. Each year the owners travel to Italy in search of new recipes and bring home treats like polenta Castellana (creamy corn meal with garlic and parsley).

Getting There & Away

Calaveras Transit (209-754-4450; www.calaverastransit.com) operates the most reliable public transportation system in the region from the **Government Center** (891 Mountain Ranch Rd) in downtown San Andreas. You can use it to connect to Angels Camp ($2, 30 minutes, several times daily) and other surrounding towns. To connect via public transportation to the rest of California is tough – you have to take Route 1 to the Mokelumne Hill and transfer to Amador County Transit.

Murphys

With its white picket fences and old world charm, Murphys is one of the most picturesque towns along the southern stretch of Gold Country, befitting its nickname as 'Queen of the Sierra.' It lies 8 miles east of Hwy 49 on Murphys Grade Rd, and is named for Daniel and John Murphy, who founded a trading post and mining operation on Murphy Creek in 1848, in conjunction with the local Maidu people. John was apparently very friendly with the tribe and eventually married the chief's daughter. The town's Main St is refined with tons of wine-tasting rooms, boutiques, galleries and good strolling. For information and a town overview, look to www.visitmurphys.com.

Sights & Activities

Even more than frogs, wine touring is a consistent draw in Calaveras County, and Murphys is the hub of it – a couple new tasting rooms seem to pop up downtown every summer.

California Cavern CAVE TOURS
(209-736-2708; www.caverntours.com; adult/child $14.75/7.50; 10am-5pm Apr-Oct;) In Cave City, 12 winding miles north of Muphys (take Main St to Sheep Ranch Rd to Cave City Rd), is another natural cavern, which John Muir described as 'graceful flowing folds deeply placketed like stiff silken drapery.' Regular tours take 60 to 90 minutes. For $148 you can try a Middle Earth Expedition, which lasts five hours and includes

CAVES AT A GLANCE

» **California Cavern** Large variety of tours, lengthy adventure trips.

» **Moaning Cavern** Allows rapelling down the tallest public shaft in California, above ground zip line.

» **Black Chasm** Quiet self-guided Zen Garden walk above ground, rare helictite crystals.

» **Lake Shasta Caverns** Sublime natural setting, tours include boat ride.

» **Lava Beds National Monument** Very remote and stunning natural area, no touristy vibe.

» **Crystal Cave** In Sequoia National Park, with large marble rooms, only 3 miles from giant sequoias.

serious spelunking (note that these happen in the dry summer season only). The lakes walking tour, available only in the wet season, is magical.

Ironstone Vineyards WINERY
(www.ironstonevineyards.com; 1894 Six Mile Rd; ⏲10am-5pm; 👪) We love everything *but* the wine at Ironstone – there's a natural spring waterfall, a mechanical pipe organ, frequent exhibits by local artists, and blossoming grounds. The large winery is particularly distinct for its family-friendly atmosphere, a deli and a museum which displays the world's largest crystalline gold leaf specimen (it weighs 44lb and was found in Jamestown in 1992). While crowds are frequent, the wine-tasting room is spacious. Ironstone is 1 mile south of town via Six Mile Rd, and other wineries cluster nearby.

Murphys Old Timers Museum MUSEUM
(☎209-728-1160; donation requested; ⏲11am-4pm Fri-Sun) The name is a good hint that this place approaches history with a whimsical touch. Housed in an 1856 building, it holds a photograph of so-called Mexican Robin Hood, Joaquin Murrieta (p320), and the excellent 'Wall of Relative Ovation.' Guided tours leave from the museum every Saturday at 10am.

Sleeping

Most accommodations in Murphys are top-end B&Bs. Check nearby Angels Camp or Arnold for cheaper alternatives.

TOP CHOICE Victoria Inn B&B $$
(☎209-728-8933; www.victoriainn-murphys.com; 402 Main St; r $125-350; 📶) This newly built B&B is thankfully free of dusty antique clutter. Its elegantly furnished rooms and well-appointed common spaces have a chic country-modern appeal with claw foot slipper tubs, sleigh beds and balconies. (Opi's Cabin – with its iron bed and exposed beams – is the most interesting of the basic rooms.) There's a long veranda where you can enjoy good tapas and wines from the long list at the **bar** (mains $6-12; ⏲noon-10pm Wed-Sun).

Murphys Historic Hotel & Lodge B&B $$
(☎209-728-3444, 800-532-7684; www.murphyshotel.com; 457 Main St; r $89-125) Dating back to either 1855 or 1856 (you have your pick of plaques out front), Murphys anchors Main St. A must-stop on the Twain tour of the area (he was a guest here, as was the bandit Black Bart), the original structure is a little rough around the edges, but has a bar that blends locals and 1850s decor. The adjoining building has bland, if modern rooms. The dining room's menu (mains $8 to $35) goes deep into game dishes like elk, duck and wild boar.

Murphys Inn Motel MOTEL $$
(☎209-728-1818, 888-796-1800; www.centralsierralodging.com; 76 Main St; r $129-149; ❄@📶🏊) Just off Hwy 4, half a mile from the center of town, this option has clean and modern motel rooms with a small pool. Not much by way of personality, but a solid choice.

Eating

TOP CHOICE V Restaurant MEDITERRANEAN $$
(☎209-728-0107; 402 Main St; mains $10-25; ⏲11:30am-9pm Thu-Sun, from 5pm Wed) Attached to the Victoria Inn, Murphys' most elegant dinner spot offers Mediterranean small and large plates and a creative cocktail list. Options start with excellent tapas (deep-fried anchovy-stuffed olives!) and end with a commanding rib eye – rubbed in cumin and served with scientific perfection. The room fills up on weekends with wine tourists, so call ahead for a reservation.

Fire Wood PIZZA $
(www.firewoodeats.com; 420 Main St; meals $9-15; ⏲11am-9pm) A rarity in a town with so much historical frill, Fire Wood's exposed concrete walls and corrugated metal offers the feel of a minimalist urban loft. When the weather's

nice and the front wall is opened onto the street, the space has a casual al fresco atmosphere. There are wines by the glass, half a dozen beers on tap and basic pub fare, but the wood-fired pizzas are their hallmark.

Grounds BISTRO $
(209-728-8663; www.groundsrestaurant.com; 402 Main St; meals $8-24; 7am-3pm, from 8am Sun, to 9pm Wed-Sun;) Casual and refined, Grounds does everything competently – expert breakfast foods, a roster of light lunch mains and weekend dinners of steaks and fresh fish. The herbal ice tea and fresh vegetarian options are key when the temperatures rise.

Alchemy Market & Café MARKET $
(www.alchemymarket.com; 191 Main St; meals $7-15; 11am-7pm with seasonal variations) For fancy picnic supplies. The adjoining cafe has a small fusion menu to enjoy on the patio.

Columbia State Historic Park

More than any other place in Gold Country, Columbia blurs the lines between present and past with a carefully preserved Gold Rush town – complete with volunteers in authentic dress – at the center of a modern community. In 1850 Columbia was founded over the 'Gem of the Southern Mines,' and the center of the town (which was taken over by the state parks system) looks almost exactly as it did then. The authenticity of the old Main St is only shaken a bit by the sugared fragrance of the fudge and the occasional play-acting '49er who forgets to remove his digital watch. On the fringe of these blocks are homes and businesses that blend in so well that it becomes hard to tell what's park and what's not.

The blacksmith's shop, theater, old hotels and authentic bar are a carefully framed window into history, completed by gold panning and breezy picnic spots.

Looking rather like dinosaur bones, limestone and granite boulders are noticeable around town. These were washed out of the surrounding hills by hydraulic mining and scraped clean by prospectors. There's a fascinating explanation of this technique at the renovated **Columbia Museum** (209-532-4301; cnr Main & State Sts; admission free; 10am-4:30pm). For information and snacks, stop at the friendly **Columbia Mercantile** (209-532-7511; cnr Main & Jackson Sts; 9am-6pm), which also has a wide variety of groceries.

After most shops and attractions close around 5pm, you can have the atmospheric town to yourself, which makes staying here an attractive option.

Among the many elegant hotel restorations in the area, the **City Hotel** (209-532-1479; www.cityhotel.com; r $126-148;) is the most thoughtful, and rooms overlook a shady stretch of street and open on lovely sitting rooms. The acclaimed **restaurant** (meals $14-30) is frequented by a Twain impersonator and the adjoining What Cheer Saloon is one of those atmospheric Gold Country saloons with oil paintings of lusty ladies and stripped wallpaper.

Fallon Hotel (209-532-1470; www.cityhotel.com; cnr Washington St & Broadway; r $90-148;) is just as refined and has wider options. It also hosts the most professional theater troupe in the region, the **Sierra Repertory Theatre** (209-532-3120; www.sierrarep.org), who mix chestnuts of the stage *(Romeo & Juliet, South Pacific)* with popular reviews.

Sonora & Jamestown

Settled in 1848 by miners from Sonora, Mexico, this area was once a cosmopolitan center of commerce and culture with parks, elaborate saloons and the Southern Mines' largest concentration of gamblers, drunkards and gold. Racial unrest drove the Mexican settlers out and their European immigrant replacements got rich on the Big Bonanza Mine, where Sonora High School now stands. That mine yielded 12 tons of gold in two years (including a 28lb nugget).

Today, people en route to Yosemite National Park use Sonora as a staging area, wandering though its pubs for refreshment or grabbing quick eats at the chain restaurants and stores that have cropped up on its periphery. Fortunately, the historic center is well preserved (so much so that it's a frequent backdrop in films, including *Unforgiven* and *Back to The Future III*).

Little Jamestown is 3 miles south of Sonora, just south of the Hwy 49/108 junction. Founded around the time of Tuolumne County's first gold strike in 1848 it has suffered the ups and downs of the region's roller-coaster development, and today it limps along on

JOAQUIN MURRIETA: AVENGER OR TERRORIST?

In a land where tall tales tower, none casts a darker shadow than Joaquin Murrieta, the rakish immigrant miner long celebrated as the Robin Hood of the Gold Rush, whose inscrutable portrait gazes out from a tin type (an early method of photography) at the Murphys Old Timers Museum (p318). Stories of the bloodthirsty Murrieta are as ubiquitous as they are incongruous: he was born in either Sonora, Mexico or Quillota, Chile and, after immigrating to California seeking gold in 1850, he became either a treacherous villain or a folk avenger for brutally persecuted Mexicans in Gold Country. In the soft focus of historical hindsight, the fiery wrath of Joaquin Murrieta – real or not – has forged Gold Country's most intriguing antihero.

Consolidating 'Once upon a time' stories goes like this: Murrieta and his brother had a claim near Hangtown (now known, somewhat blandly, as Placerville). They had some luck, but refused to pay a newly established 'foreign miners tax' levied by the state in response to the overwhelming success of experienced Mexican and Chileno prospectors. To force Murrieta off his claim, a mob of jealous Anglo miners whipped Murrieta and raped his wife. With no recourse in the justice system, Murrieta formed a posse to kill his assaulters and began a life of banditry that left a trail of slashed throats and purloined gold. His band of highwaymen, known as the Five Joaquins, terrorized the countryside between 1850 and 1853.

Governor John Bigler put a large price on Murrieta's head, and in July of 1853 a Texas bounty hunter named Harry Love produced a jar containing the severed head of a man he claimed was Murrieta. Love toured cities of Northern California charging audiences $1 to see his trophy but, even in death, Murrieta's legend grew: a woman claiming to be his sister disputed the kill and sightings of the bandit continued long after his supposed death. Joaquin Murrieta was celebrated as a peoples' hero by many Latin Americans who were enraged by the oppressive, racist laws of the Gold Rush, which are largely unmentioned today, and his legend is a centerpiece of Gold Rush folklore.

tourism and antiques. It has its charm, but is only a few blocks long.

Sights & Activities

Two highways cross the Sierra Nevada east of Sonora and connect with Hwy 395 in the Eastern Sierra: Hwy 108 via Sonora Pass and Hwy 120 via Tioga Pass. Note that the section of Hwy 120 traveling through Yosemite National Park is only open in summer (see the boxed text, p399).

The center of downtown Sonora is the T-shaped intersection of Washington and Stockton Sts, with Washington as the main thoroughfare. There are boutiques, shops, cafes, bars and more. If you're looking to get out of town, try a short hike through the oaks on the newly developed **Dragoon Gulch Trail**, which can be found just northwest of the main drag on Alpine Lane.

Sonora is also a base for white-water rafting: the Tuolumne River is known for Class IV rapids and its population of golden eagles and red-tailed hawks, while the Stanislaus River is more accessible and better for novices. **Sierra Mac River Trips** (☎209-532-1327; www.sierramac.com; trips from $225) and **All-Outdoors** (☎800-247-2387; www.aorafting.com) both have good reputations and run trips of one day or more.

TOP CHOICE **Railtown 1897 State Historic Park** HISTORIC RAILYARD
(☎209-984-3953; www.railtown1897.org; 5th Ave, Jamestown; admission $5, train ride $8; ⏰9:30am-4:30pm; 👪) Five blocks south of Jamestown's Main St, this 26-acre collection of trains and railroad equipment is the little sister to the huge rail museum in Sacramento, though the surrounding hills have made it the backdrop for countless films and TV shows including *High Noon* and *Back to the Future*. There's a lyrical romance to the place, where an explosion of orange poppies grow among the rusting shells of steel goliaths. On some weekends and holidays you can ride the narrow-gauge railroad that once transported ore, lumber and miners, though today it has been shortened to a quick 3-mile circuit. Still, it's the best train ride in Gold Country, with the air spiced with creosote, campfire and pine, and green views. The state-operated park is staffed by

passionate volunteers and includes a restored station, engine house and bookstore.

Gold Prospecting Adventures GOLD PANNING (www.goldprospecting.com; 18170 Main St, Jamestown) Gold-finding outings involving pans and sluices start at $30. It even offers a three-day college-accredited gold-prospecting course ($595). Look for the (disturbing!) hanging dummy on Jamestown's main drag.

FREE **Tuolumne County Museum** HISTORY MUSEUM (www.tchistory.org; 158 W Bradford St, Sonora; admission free; 10am-4pm) In the former 1857 Tuolumne County Jail, two blocks west of Washington St is this interesting museum with a fortune's worth of gold on display.

Sleeping & Eating

Gunn House Hotel HISTORIC HOTEL $ (209-532-3421; www.gunnhousehotel.com; 286 S Washington St, Sonora; r $79-115;) For a lovable alternative to Gold Country's cookie-cut chains, this historic hotel hits the sweet spot. Rooms feature period decor and guests take to rocking chairs on the wide porches in the evening. Stuffed bears, a nice pool and a big breakfast also make it a hit with families.

Bradford Place Inn B&B $$ (209-532-2400; www.bradfordplaceinn.com; 56 W Bradford St, Sonora; r $130-245;) Gorgeous gardens and inviting porch seats surround this four-room B&B, which emphasizes green living. With a two-person claw-foot tub, the Bradford Suite is the definitive, romantic B&B experience.

TOP CHOICE **Lighthouse Deli & Ice Cream Shop** CAJUN DELI $ (www.thelighthousedeli.com; 28 S Washington, Sonora; mains $7-9; 10am-4pm Mon-Fri, 11am-3pm Sat, with seasonal variations) The flavors of 'N'Awlins' make this unassuming deli an unexpected delight. The muffeletta – a toasted piece of Cajun paradise that's stacked with ham, salami, cheese and olive tapenade – is the best sandwich within 100 miles.

Diamondback Grill MEDITERRANEAN $$ (www.thediamondbackgrill.com; 93 S Washington St, Sonora; meals $6-10; 11am-9pm) With exposed brick and modern fixtures, the fresh menu and contemporary details at this cafe are a reprieve from occasionally overbearing Victorian frill. Sandwiches dominate the menu (the salmon and mozzarella eggplant are both excellent) and everything is homemade, but for the freshest fare try one of the six (count 'em – six!) daily specials scrawled on the chalkboard.

Entertainment

The free and widely available weekend supplement of the *Union Democrat* comes out on Friday and lists movies, music, performance art and events for Tuolumne County.

Iron Horse Lounge BAR (209-532-4482; 97 S Washington St, Sonora) The most elaborate of the traditional old taverns in the center; bottles glitter like gold on the backlit bar.

Sierra Repertory Theatre PERFORMING ARTS (209-532-3120; www.sierrarep.com; 13891 Hwy 108, Sonora; tickets $18-32) In East Sonora, close to the Junction Shopping Center, is the same critically acclaimed company that performs in the Fallon Hotel in Columbia.

Information

Mi-Wuk Ranger District Office (209-586-3234; 24695 State Hwy 108; 8am-4:30pm Mon-Fri) For information and permits for the Stanislaus National Forest.

Sierra Nevada Adventure Company (www.snacattack.com; 173 S Washington St, Sonora; 9am-6pm Sun-Thu, to 7pm Fri & Sat) For maps, equipment rental and sales and friendly advice from guides with a passionate knowledge of the area.

Tuolumne County Visitors Bureau (209-533-4420; www.tcvb.com; 542 Stockton St, Sonora; 9am-6pm Jun-Sep, 9am-6pm Mon-Sat Oct-May) More so than many other brochure-jammed chamber of commerce joints, the staff here offers helpful trip planning throughout Gold Country. It also covers Yosemite National Park and Stanislaus National Forest up in the Sierras on Hwy 108.

Getting There & Away

Like elsewhere in Southern Gold Country, you're in for trouble if you try to navigate this region on public transportation. Bus service to Sonora, the major town in the region, ended in 2005. Hwy 108 is the main access road and it links up with I-5, 55 miles west near Stockton. An entrance to Yosemite National Park is 60 scenic miles south on Hwy 120. Many Yosemite visitors stay in the Sonora area. There is a new **Historic Trolley Service** (www.historic49trolleyservice.com) which offers free rides between Sonora and Jamestown on weekends through Labor Day.

SACRAMENTO VALLEY

The labyrinth of waterways that makes up the Sacramento–San Joaquin River Delta feeds the San Francisco Bay and divides the Central Valley in half, with the Sacramento Valley in the north and the San Joaquin Valley in the south. The Sacramento River, California's largest, rushes out of the northern mountains from Shasta Lake before hitting the valley basin above Red Bluff. Then, it snakes south across grassy plains and orchards before lazily skirting the state capital, fanning across the delta and draining into the San Francisco Bay. Lined with fruit and nut orchards and huge tracts of grazing land, the valley is a subtle beauty, particularly in spring when orchards are in full blossom. In the summer, it's a place of wide horizons and punishing, relentless sunshine; the skies go gray in fall, when they are decorated with the Vs of migratory birds.

Travelers going through the valley are often on their way to or from some other destination – the Bay Area, Gold Country or Lake Tahoe being the popular neighbors – but the shady streets, gardens and stately marble buildings of Sacramento and the inviting college town of Davis warrant exploring.

Sacramento

Sacramento has become a city of head-scratching anomalies. It's a former cow town that gets choked with rush-hour traffic, with the polished sedans of state legislators idling next to muddy half-ton pickup trucks. It claims stunning racial diversity, yet its neighborhoods are homogenous pockets of single ethnicities. Square in the middle of the sweltering valley, Sacramento's downtown is couched by the confluence of two cool rivers – the American and the Sacramento – and its

Metropolitan Sacramento

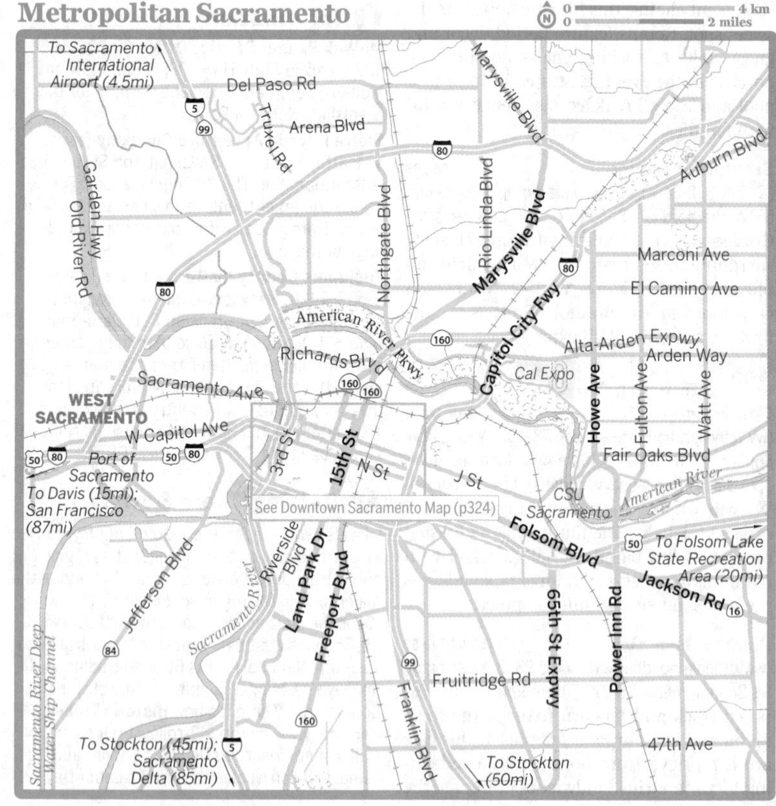

streets are shushed by the leaves of huge oaks. Its sprawling suburbanization has recently turned around, placing lofts and upscale eateries next to abandoned mid-century shops in Midtown – an area called 'the Grid' for its uniformly square streets.

If you find yourself jammed on the roads that bypass Sacramento, jump off the highway for scoops at one of the city's vintage ice-cream parlors, or spend the evening in one of its elegantly preserved movie houses or friendly dive bars, where newcomers are welcomed with cheap drinks and sent off with slaps on the back.

The people of 'Sac' are an unpretentious lot, and have fostered small but thriving arts and nightlife scenes. They beam with pride about Second Saturday, the monthly Midtown gallery crawl that is emblematic of the city's cultural awakening. The summer is best: fat-tired cruisers meander around the Grid, people crack cold ones and chat with neighbors on the porches of high-water Victorians (built to resist the flooding rivers in the years before they were levied), and farmers markets dot the downtown parks every day of the week.

Remember not to bruise feelings of locals by comparing Sacramento to the Bay Area – their perspective on the bigger, prettier kid-sister city is colored with an underdog's dismissiveness. After you spend a few hours here, the Bay Area's bustle might start to seem jarring.

History

If you ask local historians, modern California was born here. Paleo-era peoples fished the rivers and lived in the area for generations before a hot-headed Swiss immigrant named John Sutter showed up. Realizing the strategic importance of the rivers, he built an outpost here, which quickly became a safe haven for traders. Sutter raised a militia of Native Americans and extended his operations to the surrounding area and it was at his lumber mill near Coloma that gold was discovered in 1848. Gold rushers flowed through the trading post, which was eventually handed over to Sutter's son, who christened the newly sprung town 'Sacramento.' Though plagued by fires and relentless flooding, the riverfront settlement prospered and became the state capital in 1850.

The transcontinental railroad was conceived in Sacramento by a quartet of local merchants known as the 'Big Four' – Leland Stanford, Mark Hopkins, Collis P Huntington and Charles Crocker – who are pictured in a fresco inside the Amtrak station. They founded the Central Pacific Railroad, which began construction in Sacramento in 1863 and connected with the Union Pacific in Promontory, Utah, in 1869.

Sights

At the confluence of the Sacramento and American Rivers, Sacramento is roughly halfway between San Francisco and Lake Tahoe. The city is boxed in by four main highways: Hwy 99, which is the best route through the Central Valley, and I-5, which runs along its west side; I-80 skirts downtown on the city's northern edge, heading west to the Bay Area and east to Reno; and Hwy 50 runs along downtown's southern edge (where it's also called Business Route 80) before heading east to Lake Tahoe.

Downtown, numbered streets run from north to south and lettered streets run east to west (Capitol Ave replaces M St). One-way J St is a main drag east from Downtown to Midtown. The Tower District is south of downtown at the corner of Broadway and 16th St.

Cal Expo (Map p322), the site of the California State Fair every August, is east of I-80 from the Cal Expo exit.

THE GRID

Finding sights along the grid is easy – every road is in a straight line – but they are spread out.

TOP CHOICE **California Museum** MUSEUM

(Map p324; www.californiamuseum.org; 1020 O St; adult/child 6-13yr $8.50/7; 10am-5pm Mon-Sat, noon-5pm Sun;) A few blocks away from the brilliantly white capitol dome is the attractive, modern California Museum, home to the California Hall Of Fame – perhaps the only place to simultaneously encounter Cesar Chavez, Mark Zuckerburg and Amelia Earhart. Nary a dusty 19th-century relic lies in slumber among graceful modern exhibits, which tell an even-handed story of California's youth, by giving attention to typically underrepresented stories from the margins of history books. Perfect example: the newly opened exhibit *California Indians: Making A Difference* is the state's best view of the traditions and culture of California's first residents, past and present.

Downtown Sacramento

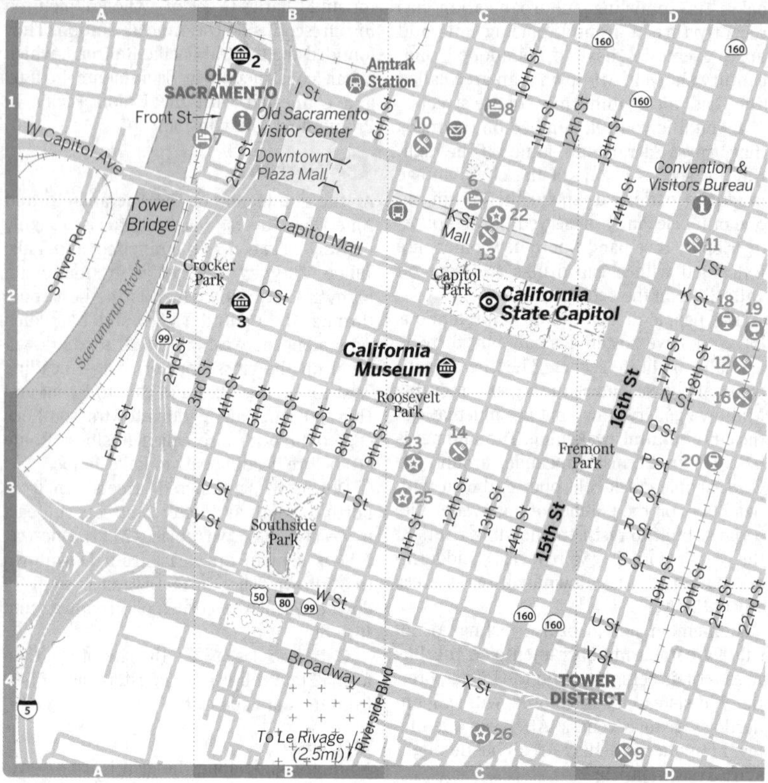

FREE **California State Capitol** HISTORIC BUILDING

(Map p324; ☎916-324-0333; cnr 10th & L Sts; ⏰9am-5pm) The California State Capitol is Sacramento's most recognizable structure. Built in the late 19th century, it underwent major reconstruction in the 1970s, and its marble halls offer a cool place for a stroll. There's a **bookstore** (⏰9:30am-4pm) in the basement, but the real attraction is in the west wing, where there is a painting of a Hollywood action hero posing as a governor. (Oh, wait a minute...) It could be argued that the 40 acres of garden surrounding the dome, **Capitol Park**, are better than the building itself. There are exotic trees from around the world, stern-looking statues of missionaries and a powerful Vietnam War Memorial. A quieter war commemoration is the Civil War Memorial Grove, which was planted in 1897 with saplings from famous battlefields.

Sutter's Fort State Historic Park HISTORIC SITE

(Map p324; www.parks.ca.gov/suttersfort; cnr 27th & L Sts; adult/child $5/3; ⏰10am-5pm) Originally built by John Sutter, the park was once the only trace of white settlement for hundreds of miles – hard to tell by the housing developments that surround the park today. California history buffs should carve out a couple hours to stroll within its walls, where original furniture, equipment and a working ironsmith are straight out of the 1850s.

California State Indian Museum MUSEUM

(Map p324; ☎916-324-0971; 2618 K St; adult/child $3/2; ⏰10am-2pm) It's with some irony that the humble structure of the State Indian Museum sits across the park in the shadow of the turrets of Sutter's Fort. The fascinating pieces of Native American handicrafts – including immaculate weaving that once thrived in the area – were all but lost during the Gold Rush.

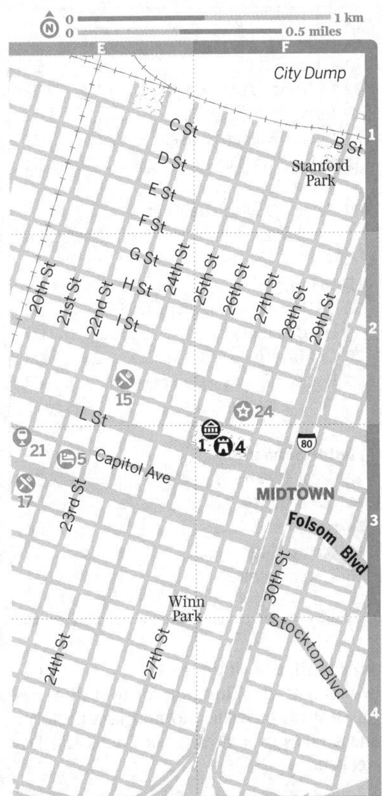

OLD SACRAMENTO

Though the art and culture of Midtown have challenged the conventional perception of Sacramento's visitors attractions as lackluster, this historic river port, adjacent to downtown, is the city's stalwart tourist draw. The pervasive scent of salt-water taffy and the somewhat garish restoration give Sacramento the vibe of a second-rate Frontierland, but it's good for a stroll on summer evenings, when boomers rumble though the brick streets on Harleys, and tourists and dolled-up legislative aides stroll the elevated sidewalks. It has California's largest concentration of buildings on the National Register of Historic Places (most of which now peddle Gold Rush trinkets and fudge) and a couple of quality attractions. Unfortunately, the restaurant scene is a bust – to eat and drink, head to Midtown.

California State Railroad Museum MUSEUM
(Map p324; www.californiastaterailroadmuseum.org; 125 I St; adult/child 6-17yr $9/4; 10am-5pm) At Old Sac's north end is this excellent museum, the largest of its kind in the US. It has an impressive collection of railcars, locomotives, toy models and memorabilia, and a fully outfitted Pullman sleeper and vintage diner cars to induce joy in railroad enthusiasts. Tickets include entrance to the restored **Central Pacific Passenger Depot**, across the plaza from the museum entrance. On weekends from April to September, you can board a steam-powered passenger train from the depot (adult/child $10/5) for a 40-minute jaunt along the riverfront.

Crocker Art Museum ART MUSEUM
(Map p324; www.crockerartmuseum.org; 216 O St; adult/student $10/5, 3rd Sun of each month by donation; 10am-5pm Tue-Sun, to 9pm Thu) Housed in a pair of side-by-side Victorians, the Crocker Art Museum is stunning as much for its outrageous stairways and beautiful tile floors as it is for its fine collection. There are some fine early California paintings and stellar drawings by European masters. The curatorial passion really comes through in its enthusiastic presentation of modern art.

Discovery Museum CHILDREN'S MUSEUM
(Map p324; www.thediscovery.org; 101 I St; adult/child $5/3; 10am-5pm Jun-Aug, Tue-Sun Sep-May;) Next door to the railroad museum, this place has hands-on exhibits and Gold Rush displays for the kids. A major expansion is in the works.

TOWER DISTRICT

South of Midtown, Tower District is dominated by Tower Theatre, a beautiful 1938 art deco movie palace (see p329), which you'll probably spot on the way into town. From the theater, head east on Broadway to pass a stretch of the city's most eclectic and affordable ethnic eateries – including an excellent pair of side-by-side Thai restaurants. The **Tower Records** chain started here, and the original neon sign survives, though the retailer itself closed its doors in 2006, a casualty of the digital music revolution.

Activities

The **American River Parkway** (Map p322), a 23-mile river system on the north bank of the American River, is surely Sacramento's

Downtown Sacramento

Top Sights

California Museum C2
California State Capitol C2

Sights

1 California State Indian Museum F3
2 California State Railroad Museum B1
3 Crocker Art Museum B2
Discovery Museum .... (see 2)
4 Sutter's Fort State Historic Park F3

Sleeping

5 Amber House E3
6 Citizen Hotel C1
7 Delta King B1
8 Sacramento HI Hostel C1

Eating

9 Andy Nguyen's D4
10 La Bonne Soupe Café C1
11 Lucca D2
12 Mulvaney's Building And Loan D2
13 Pizza Rock C2
14 Shoki II Ramen House C3
15 Sugar Plum Vegan E2
16 Water Boy D3
17 Zelda's Original Gourmet Pizza E3

Drinking

18 58 Degrees and Holding Co. D2
19 Head Hunters D2
20 Old Tavern Bar & Grill D3
21 Rubicon Brewing Company E3
Temple Coffee House .... (see 6)

Entertainment

22 Crest Theatre C2
23 Fox & Goose C3
24 Harlow's F2
25 Old Ironsides C3
26 Tower Theatre C4

most appealing geographic feature. It's one of the most extensive riparian habitats in the continental US, lined by a network of well-marked and maintained trails and picnic areas. It's accessible from Old Sacramento by taking Front St north until it becomes Jiboom St and crosses the river, or by taking the Jiboom St exit off I-5/Hwy 99. The parkway includes a lovely bicycle and jogging path called the **Jedediah Smith National Recreation Trail**, which stretches over 30 miles from Old Sac to Folsom.

Festivals & Events

In the summer, when the Central Valley's harvest is in full swing, Sacramento has an excellent farmers market nearly every day. Check www.california-grown.com for listings.

Second Saturday STREET
(www.2nd-sat.com) Every second Saturday the galleries and shops in midtown draw people of all ages to the streets, where open-air music and culture events abound. It has rightly become a major point of civic pride and helped revitalize Sacramento's once-fading Midtown grid.

Jazz Festival & Jubilee MUSIC
(www.sacjazz.com) Running for over 30 years, this festival of Dixieland and jazz performances takes over the city on Memorial Day weekend.

Gold Rush Days HISTORICAL
(www.sacramentogoldrushdays.com; 👪) Horse races and historical costumes, music and kids' events make Old Sacramento particularly festive each Labor Day weekend.

Sleeping

The capital is a magnet for business travelers, so Sacramento doesn't suffer a lack of hotels – many of which sport good deals during the legislative break. Unless you're in town for the California State Fair or something else at Cal Expo, stay Downtown or in Midtown, where there's plenty to do within walking distance. If you're into cheap and kitschy motor lodges of the 1950s, cross the river into West Sac and look for 'Motel Row' on Rte 40.

TOP CHOICE **Citizen Hotel** BOUTIQUE HOTEL **$$**
(Map p324; ☎916-492-4460; 926 J St; r $159, ste from $215; 📶) With an elegant, ultra-hip upgrade by the Joie de Vivre group, the long-vacant Citizen has suddenly become one

of the coolest stays in this part of the state. Rooms are lovely with luxurious linen, bold patterned fabrics and stations for your iPod. The little touches make a big impression too: vintage political cartoons adorning the walls, loaner bikes and a nightly wine reception. There's an upscale farm-to-table restaurant on the ground floor (a daily menu of seasonal mains starts around $25).

Sacramento HI Hostel HOSTEL **$**
(Map p324; ☎916-443-1691, www.norcalhostels.org/sac; 925 H St; dm $28, r $56; P@) In a grand Victorian mansion, this hostel offers impressive trimmings at rock-bottom prices. It's within walking distance of the capitol, Old Sac and the train station and has a piano in the parlor and large dining room. It attracts an international crowd and is a useful place to find rides to San Francisco and Lake Tahoe.

Amber House B&B **$$**
(Map p324; ☎916-444-8085, 800-755-6526; www.amberhouse.com; 1315 22nd St; r $149-259; @) This Dutch Colonial home in Midtown has been transformed into an elegant bed and breakfast, where rooms named for composers and writers come with Jacuzzi baths and fireplaces. Breakfast is served in the rooms – this is best enjoyed in Mozart, which boasts a private balcony.

Le Rivage BOUTIQUE HOTEL **$$$**
(off Map p324; ☎916-443-8400; www.lerivagehotel.com; 4800 Riverside Blvd; from r $199; @) From the outside, this hotel has a lot in common with much of Sacramento architecture: enormous, new, with vaguely pre-fab Mediterranean touches. Inside, the rich linens and lovely views are a different story. Add a riverfront location and lovely spa, and this independent luxury option is excellent for the speedboat set.

Delta King RIVERBOAT **$$**
(Map p324; ☎916-444-5464, 800-825-5464; www.deltaking.com; 100 Front St; r $113-163; @) If you stay near Old Town, you can't beat the experience of sleeping aboard the *Delta King,* a docked 1927 paddlewheeler that lights up like a Christmas tree at night.

Folsom Lake State Recreation Area CAMPGROUND **$**
(off Map p322; ☎916-988-0205; www.parks.ca.gov; 7806 Folsom-Auburn Rd; tent & RV sites without/with hookups $25/55; office 6am-10pm summer, 7am-7pm winter) Sacramento is a good staging area before going into the Sierras, and this campground, while hardly picturesque, is the best option for testing out your gear before heading into the mountains. It's not ideal – the rangers can be overbearing, the sites rocky and the lake overrun by powerboats, but the only other nearby camping is a KOA west of town on I-80.

Eating

Skip the overpriced fare in Old Sacramento or near the capitol and go to Midtown or the Tower District for higher-quality food at a

GETTING AROUND THE CENTRAL VALLEY

Although the Central Valley's main artery is connected with bus and Amtrak, much of the region is most easily traveled by car. The main routes through this part of California are Hwy 99 and I-5. I-80 meets Hwy 99 in Sacramento, and I-5 meets Hwy 99 south of Bakersfield. Amtrak also intersects the state with two lines – the *San Joaquin* route through the Central Valley and the *Pacific Surfliner* between the Central Coast and San Diego (see p569 for more information). The *San Joaquin* service stops in just about every town covered here. **Greyhound** (☎800-229-9424) stops in all of the Central Valley towns and cities covered in this chapter. Trips between Sacramento and Bakersfield take about 6½ hours and cost around $50.

The Central Valley has lots of long, straight byways for those making the trip on bikes, and the **American River Parkway** (p325) is a veritable human-powered expressway for commuters between Downtown Sacramento and Auburn.

Still, the transportation talk in the Central Valley these days is all about high speed rail. California voters gave a green light to start work on a network of super fast trains that would eventually connect San Francisco to Los Angeles at speeds of up to 220 miles per hour (it would make the trip just over 2 ½ hours). The total price tag is estimated at a whopping $50 billion, but the beginning is comically humble; the first stage will connect two tiny farm towns in the Central Valley, Borden and Concordion.

lower price. A cruise up J St or Broadway will pass a number of hip, affordable restaurants where tables sprawl out onto the sidewalks in the summer.

TOP CHOICE La Bonne Soupe Cafe SANDWICHES $
(Map p324; www.labonnesoupe.com; 920 8th St; $8-10; ⏲11am-3pm Mon-Fri) Chef Daniel Pont assembles his divine sandwiches with such loving, affectionate care that the line of downtown lunchers snakes out the door. If you're in a hurry, skip it; Pont's humble lunch counter is focused on quality that predates drive-through haste. If you do have time, consider yourself lucky and ponder: smoky duck breast or apples and brie? Braised pork or smoked salmon? And the creamy soups made from scratch prove the restaurant's name is a painful understatement.

Andy Nguyen's VEGETARIAN, THAI $$
(Map p324; www.andynguyenvegetarianrestaurant.com; 2007 Broadway; meals $8-16; ⏲11:30am-9pm Sun-Mon, to 9:30pm Tue-Thu, to 10pm Fri & Sat; ✎) The best vegetarian fare in all of California might be at this tranquil Buddhist Thai diner. Try the steaming curries and artful fake meat dishes (the 'chicken' leg has a little wooden bone).

Shoki II Ramen House JAPANESE $$
(☎916-441-0011; 1201 R St; meals $8-16; ⏲11am-10pm Mon-Fri, from noon Sat, 11am-8pm Sun) In their old location, Shoki would get cheek-to-jowl with noodle-slurping dinner guests, but their new Midtown location has more space and the same amazing handmade noodles. The methodical technique, evident in walls covered in notes about the broths and the strict ban on to-go orders, are the work of noodle masters.

Mulvaney's Building and Loan MODERN AMERICAN $$$
(Map p324; ☎916-443-1189; 2726 Capitol Ave; mains $20-40; ⏲dinner Wed-Sun) With an obsessive flourish for seasonality, the menu here changes every single day. Patrick Mulvaney flutters between the kitchen and the dining room, offering delicate pasta dishes and buttery braised meats.

Zelda's Original Gourmet Pizza PIZZA $$
(Map p324; www.zeldasgourmetpizza.com; 1415 21st St; mains $10-20; ⏲lunch Mon-Fri, dinner daily) Zelda's roughshod windowless exterior doesn't look like much, but through the doors of this Nixon-era pizza dive, a troupe of gruff veteran waitresses sling a magical, messy variation of doughy Chicago deep-dish. It can take a while to come out of the kitchen, so occupy yourself with cheap little glasses of Bud at the bar. And no, you can't get the dressing on the side.

Sugar Plum Vegan VEGAN $
(Map p324; www.sugarplumvegan.com; 2315 K St; $8-11; ⏲10am-9pm Wed-Sun; ✎) This is an excellent vegan option in a restored Victorian with a back garden and creaking floors. The vegan tacos are good, but the baked goods – including a dark chocolate cup cake with almond paste – are simply decadent.

Pizza Rock PIZZA $
(Map p324; www.pizzarocksacramento.com; 1020 K St; meals $8-18; ⏲11am-10pm Sun-Tue, to midnight Wed, to 3am Thu-Sat) An anchor of the newly renovated K Street Mall area, this loud, enormous pizza joint has fun, kitschy rock 'n roll themes, DJs and a staff who are cheerful and absolutely covered in tattoos. Pizza Chef Tony Gemignani scored an underdog win in the 2007 Pizza Cup in Naples, Italy for his dead-simple Margherita.

Water Boy CALIFORNIAN $$
(Map p324; ☎916-498-9891; www.waterboyrestaurant.com; 2000 Capitol Ave; mains $15-40; ⏲11:30am-9pm Thu-Mon, to 10pm Fri & Sat) The wicker and palms in the windowed dining room reflect the French colonial spin of the menu's California fusions. The seasonal menu soars from the briny oyster starter through the crispy skin of the poultry and smoky fresh catches. If it's too steep, look across the street for comfort food at Jack's Urban Eats.

Kitchen Restaurant CALIFORNIAN $$
(☎916-568-7171; www.thekitchenrestaurant.com; No 101, 2225 Hurley Way; prix-fixe dinner $125; ⏲5-10pm Wed-Sun) The cozy dining room of husband-and-wife team Randall Selland and Nancy Zimmer is the pinnacle of Sacramento's foodie world. Their demonstration dinners focus on local, organic foods, immaculately prepared before your eyes. Book well in advance, and brace yourself. Reservations are absolutely essential. Just when you thought it was perfect, consider the location: it's in the northeast suburbs. To get here, take I-80 east and exit at Exposition Blvd Exit. Take a left on Howe Ave and a right on Hurley Way.

Lucca ITALIAN $$

(Map p324; ☎916-669-5300; 1615 J St; meals $8-18; ⌚11:30am-10pm Mon-Thu, to 11pm Fri, noon-11pm Sat, 4-9pm Sun) Within a stroll of the convention center is this quality Italian eatery. The escargot – wrapped in a buttery, flaky dough crust – is the way to start.

Gunther's ICE CREAM $

(www.gunthersicecream.com; 2801 Franklin Blvd; shakes $4; ⌚10am-10pm) A beautiful vintage soda fountain that makes its own excellent ice cream. South of Broadway and Hwy 50.

Drinking

Sacramento has a split personality when it comes to drinking – sleek upscale joints that serve a fruity rainbow of vodka drinks to dressed-up weekenders from the 'burbs, and sans-bullshit dive bars with vintage neons and menus that begin and end with a-shot-ana-beer. Both options dot the Midtown grid.

Rubicon Brewing Company BREWPUB

(Map p324; www.rubiconbrewing.com; 2004 Capitol Ave; 📶) These people take their hops *seriously*. Their heady selection is brewed onsite and crowned by Monkey Knife Fight Pale Ale, ideal to wash back platters of liptingling wings ($10 for one dozen).

Temple Coffee House COFFEE SHOP

(Map p324; www.templecoffee.com; 1014 10th St; ⌚6am-11pm; 📶) The warm environs of this Downtown coffee shop still imbibe the comfy feel of the bookstore that used to be in this space. Hip young patrons nurse organic free-trade coffee and chai while tapping at their wi-fi connected laptops.

58 Degrees and Holding Co WINE BAR

(Map p324; www.58degrees.com; 1217 18th St) A huge selection of California reds and a refined bistro menu make this a favorite for young professional singles on the prowl.

Old Tavern Bar & Grill BAR

(Map p324; 1510 20th St) This friendly dive is a standout among Sacramento's many excellent workaday joints for their huge beer selection, tall pours and rowdy mix of tattooed bar hounds.

Head Hunters CLUB

(Map p324; www.headhuntersonk.com; 1930 K St) Though wilder bars are within sight, start here before partying around the two-block radius of gay bars and clubs that locals coyly call 'Lavender Heights.' You might be back at the end of the night; the kitchen stays open into the wee hours.

DON'T MISS

CALIFORNIA STATE FAIR

For the last two weeks in August, the **California State Fair** (☎916-263-3000; 1600 Exposition Blvd, Sacramento; adult/child $10/6) fills the Cal Expo with a small city of cows, candied apples and carnival rides. It's likely the only place on earth where you can plant a redwood tree, watch a pig give birth, ride a roller coaster, catch some barrel racing, taste exquisite Napa vintages and eat a deep-fried Snickers bar within an (admittedly exhausting) afternoon. Put on some comfy sneakers and pencil in two whole days, making time to see some of the auctions ($500 for a dozen eggs!) and the interactive exhibits run by the University of California, Davis. Try to book a room at the hotels near Cal Expo, which run regular shuttles to the event.

Entertainment

Pick up a copy of the free weekly *Sacramento News & Review* (www.newsandreview.com) for a list of current happenings around town.

Harlow's LIVE MUSIC

(Map p324; www.harlows.com; 2708 J St) A classy joint that's a solid bet for quality jazz, R&B and the occasional salsa or indie act...if you don't get lost on the potent martinis.

Old Ironsides LIVE MUSIC

(Map p324; www.theoldironsides.com; 1901 10th St; cover $3-10) The tiny back room of this cool, somewhat crusty, venue hosts some of the best indie bands that come through town.

California Musical Theatre PERFORMING ARTS

(www.calmt.com) A top-notch company holds court at a few venues around town, including the Music Circus and the Cosmopolitan Caberet.

Tower Theatre CINEMA

(Map p324; ☎916-442-4700; www.thetowertheatre.com; 2508 Landpark Dr) Classic, foreign and indie films screen at this historic movie house. Call to check if your film is showing on the main screen, rather than in a smaller side room.

Crest Theatre CINEMA
(Map p324; www.thecrest.com; 1013 K St) Another classic old movie house that's been lovingly restored to its 1949 splendor, hosting indie and foreign films and the annual Trash Film Orgy.

Fox & Goose Pub LIVE MUSIC
(Map p324; www.foxandgoose.com; 1001 R St) This spacious, fern-filled warehouse-pub has good beer on tap and a jovial open-mic scene.

Information

Convention & Visitors Bureau (Map p324; 916-264-7777; www.discovergold.org; 1608 I St; 8am-5pm Mon-Fri) Local information, including event and bus schedules.

Old Sacramento Visitor Center (Map p324; www.oldsacramento.com; 1002 2nd St; 10am-5pm) Also has local information, including event and bus schedules.

Getting There & Away

Amtrak Station (Map p324; cnr 5th & I Sts) Between downtown and Old Sac. This station is a major hub for connecting trains to all points east and west, as well as regional bus lines serving the Central Valley.

Greyhound (Map p324; 916-444-6858; cnr 7th & L Sts) Stops near the Capitol. Greyhound service between Sacramento and Colfax, in Gold Country, cost $20 and takes 1½ hours.

Sacramento International Airport (off Map p322; 916-929-5411; www.sacairports.org) This small but busy airport 15 miles north of Downtown off I-5 is serviced by all major airlines and offers some indirect flights to Europe. Flights in and out of here can be an amazingly good value, especially considering the easy rail connection to the Bay Area.

Getting Around

The regional **Yolobus** (916-371-2877; www.yolobus.com) route 42A costs $2 and runs hourly between the airport and Downtown (take the counter-clockwise loop) and also goes to West Sacramento, Woodland and Davis. Local **Sacramento Regional Transit** (RT; 916-321-2877; www.sacrt.com) buses cost $2.50 per ticket or $6 for a day pass. RT also runs a trolley between Old Sacramento and Downtown, as well as Sacramento's light-rail system, which is mostly used for commuting from outlying communities. Sacramento is also a fantastic city to cruise around on a bike. The best place to rent is **City Bicycle Works** (www.citybicycleworks.com; 2419 K St; 10am-7pm Mon-Fri, to 6pm Sat, to 5pm Sun), which charges by the hour (from $5) or by the day (from $20).

Sacramento River Delta

The Sacramento Delta is a sprawling web of waterways and one-stoplight towns that feel plucked out of the 1930s – popular for locals who like to gun powerboats on glassy waterways and cruise winding levy roads. Its marshy area encompasses a huge patch of the state map – from the San Francisco Bay to Sacramento, and all the way south to Stockton. Travelers often zoom by on I-80 and I-5 without stopping to smell the mossy Delta breeze blowing off the conflux of the Sacramento and San Joaquin Rivers, which drain into the San Francisco Bay. If you have the time to take the unhurried route between San Francisco and Sacramento, travel across the rusting iron bridges and gracefully winding roads of Hwy 160, which lazily makes its way through a region of lush wetlands, vast orchards and little towns with long histories.

In the 1930s the Bureau of Reclamation issued an aggressive water-redirection program – the Central Valley and California State Water Projects – that dammed California's major rivers and directed 75% of their supply through the Central Valley (for agricultural use) and Southern California. The siphoning has affected the Sacramento Delta, its wetlands and estuaries, and has been a source of environmental, ecological and political debate ever since. No one knows about this more than the folks at the Hartland Nursery, home of **Delta Ecotours** (916-775-4545; www.hartlandnursery.com; 13737 Grand Island Rd, Walnut Grove; admission free, tours adult/child $45/20; Sat by appointment). Led by Jeff Hart, the tours are ideal for land lubbers wanting to travel the channels and learn about the area's unique agricultural, environmental and historical concerns. The nursery is filled with regional plants and is a worthy stop even if the tours aren't happening

Locke (www.locketown.com) is the delta's most fascinating town, built by Chinese farmers after a fire wiped out Walnut Grove's Chinatown in 1912. In its time, Locke was the only free-standing Chinatown in the US and its unincorporated status kept it free of pesky lawmen, encouraging gambling houses and bootleg gin joints. Tucked below the highway and the levee, Locke's main street still has the feel of a Western ghost town, with weather-beaten buildings leaning into each other over the town's single street, all protected by the National Register of Historic Places. The handful of shops and galleries, worn by age and proximity to the water, are worth a stroll.

Keeping the town's heritage alive is the dusty but worthwhile **Dai Loy Museum** (www.locketown.com/museum; admission $1.25; ⏲noon-4pm Sat & Sun), an old gambling hall filled with photos and relics of gaming operations, including betting tables and the antique safe.

Locke's unlikely centerpiece is **Al the Wop's** (meals $8-20), a wooden bar that's been pouring since 1934. The draw isn't the food – the special is a peanut-butter-slathered Texas toast – as much as it is the ambience. Below are creaking floorboards; above, the ceiling's covered in crusty dollar bills and more than one pair of erstwhile undies.

Hwy 160 passes through **Isleton**, so-called Crawdad Town USA, whose main street is lined with shops, restaurants, bars and buildings hinting at the region's Chinese heritage. Isleton's **Crawdad Festival**, at the end of June, draws folks from all over the state, but you can slurp down the fresh little crayfish all year long at **Isleton Joe's** (www.isletonjoes.com; mains $6-16; ⏲8am-9pm).

Further west on Hwy 160 you'll see signs for the **Delta Loop**, a drive that passes boater bars and marinas where you can rent something to take on the water. At the end, you come to the **Brannan State Recreation Area** (⏲Fri-Mon) a tidy state-run facility with boat-in, drive-in and walk-in **campsites** (⏲Fri & Sat, sites $30-40) and picnic facilities galore.

Davis

Davis, home to a University of California school, is a sunny college town where bikes outnumber cars two-to-one (it boasts more bikes per capita than any other American city). With students comprising about half of the population, it's a progressive outpost amid the conservative farm towns of Sacramento Valley. Its vibrant cafe, pub and arts scene comes alive during the school year.

Dodging the bikes on a walk through downtown Davis you will pass a number of cute small businesses (the progressive city council has forbidden any store over 50,000 sq ft – sorry, Wal-Mart).

I-80 skirts the south edge of town, and you can reach downtown via the Richards Blvd exit. University of California, Davis (UCD) is southwest of downtown, bordered by A St, 1st St and Russell Blvd. The campus' main entrances are accessed from I-80 via Old Davis Rd or from downtown via 3rd St. East of the campus, Hwy 113 heads north 10 miles to Woodland, where it intersects with I-5; another 28 miles north it connects with Hwy 99.

Sights & Activities

Bicycling is popular here, probably because the only hill around is the bridge that crosses over the freeway. **Lake Berryessa**, around 30 miles west, is a favorite destination. See p333 for bike-rental information.

Pence Gallery GALLERY

(www.pencegallery.org; 212 D St; ⏲11:30am-5pm Tue-Sun) The impressive, purpose-built gallery exhibits contemporary California art and hosts lectures and art films.

UC Davis Arboretum PARK

(http://arboretum.ucdavis.edu) For a short hike, there is a paved 2-mile trail through the peaceful arboretum.

Sleeping

Davis isn't a great town for hotels. Like most university towns, the rates are stable until graduation or special campus events, when they rise high and sell out fast. Worse, the trains that roll though the middle of town will infuriate a light sleeper. For a utilitarian (if bland) stay, look for chains along the highway.

University Park Inn & Suites HOTEL $$

(☎530-756-0910; www.universityparkinn.com; 111 Richards Blvd; r $110-140; P❄@📶) Right off the highway and a short walk from campus and downtown, this independently operated hotel is not the Ritz, but is clean and has spacious suites.

Aggie Inn HOTEL $$

(☎530-756-0352; www.aggieinn.com; 245 1st St; r from $129; ❄📶) Across from UCD's east entrance, the Aggie is neat, modern and unassuming. The hotel has a Jacuzzi and offers free coffee and pastries.

TULE FOG

Radiation or tule (*too*-lee) fog causes dozens of collisions each year on Central Valley roads, including Hwy 99 and I-5. As thick as the proverbial pea soup, the fog limits visibility to about 10ft, making driving nearly impossible. The fog is thickest from November to February, when cold mountain air settles on the warm valley floor and condenses into fog as the ground cools at night. The fog often lifts for a few hours during the afternoon, just long enough for the ground to warm back up and thus perpetuate the cycle.

If you end up on a fog-covered road, drive with your low beams on, keep a good distance from the car in front of you, stay at a constant speed, avoid sudden stops and never try to pass other cars.

Eating

College students love to eat and drink cheap, and downtown has no short supply of lively ethnic eateries gunning for the student dollar. The **Davis farmers market** (www.davisfarmersmarket.org; cnr 4th & C Sts; ⌚8am-noon Sat, 2-8.30pm Wed) features food vendors, street performers and live bands. There are a number of good options for self-catering.

Davis Noodle City ASIAN $
(129 E St; mains $5-10; ⌚11am-9pm Mon-Sat, to 8:30pm Sun) Situated in the back of a courtyard behind Sophia's Thai Kitchen, the menu here has dishes from all over Asia, with homemade noodles and superb scallion pancakes. The pork-chop noodle soup – with thick noodles and slices of tender pork rubbed with Chinese five spice – is the best thing on the menu.

Delta of Venus Coffeehouse & Pub CAFE $
(www.deltaofvenus.org; 122b St; meals $5-10; ⌚7:30am-10pm; 🖉) This converted Arts and Crafts bungalow has a very social shaded front patio. The chalkboard menu has breakfast items, salads, soups and sandwiches, including vegetarian and vegan options. At dinner time you can order jerk-seasoned Caribbean dishes and wash them down with a beer or wine. It comes alive with a hip folk scene at night.

Woodstocks PIZZA $
(www.woodstocksdavis.com; 219 G St; slice $2.50, pizzas $15-20; ⌚lunch & dinner) Woodstocks has Davis' most popular pizza, which is also sold by the slice for lunch. In addition to cheap and meaty favorites, the menu gets a touch more sophisticated with a variety of veggie and gourmet pies that come with a chewy wheat crust. Open until 2am Thursday to Saturday when school is in session.

Redrum BURGERS $
(☎530-756-2142; 978 Olive Dr; meals $5-10; ⌚10am-11pm Mon-Thu, to midnight Fri & Sat) Formerly known as Murder Burger, Redrum is popular with students and travelers for fresh, made-to-order beef, turkey and ostrich burgers, thick espresso shakes and crispy curly fries. The ZOOM – a gnarled, deep-fried pile of zucchini, onion rings and mushrooms – is the menu must.

Entertainment

Major theater, music, dance and other performances take place at **Mondavi Center for the Performing Arts** (www.mondaviarts.org; 1 Shields Ave), a state-of-the-art venue on the UCD campus. **Varsity Theatre** (☎530-759-8724; 616 2nd St) also stages performances. For tickets and information on shows at either the Varsity or the Mondavi Center, you can also call the **UC Davis Ticket Office** (☎530-752-1915, 866-823-2787).

Just up the road in Winters, **Palm's Playhouse** (www.palmsplayhouse.com) books lots of rhythm 'n' blues, cover bands and blues.

Information

Davis Conference and Visitor Bureau (☎530-297-1900; www.davisvisitor.com; Suite 300, 105 E St; ⌚8:30am-4:30pm Mon-Fri) Has free maps and brochures. The exhaustive www.daviswiki.org is useful to peruse.

Getting There & Away

Amtrak (☎530-758-4220; 840 2nd St) Davis' station is on the southern edge of downtown. There are trains bound for Sacramento or San Francisco throughout the day. The fare to San Francisco is $25 and the trip takes about two hours.

Yolobus (☎530-666-2877; ⌚5am-11pm) Route 42A ($2) loops between Davis and the Sacramento airport. The route also connects Davis with Woodland and Downtown Sacramento.

Getting Around

When driving around – especially when you pull out from a parking space – be aware of bike traffic: it's the primary mode of transportation here.

Ken's Bike & Ski (www.kensbikeski.com; 650 G St) Rents basic bikes (from $19 per day) as well as serious road and mountain bikes.

Unitrans (530-752-2877; http://unitrans.ucdavis.edu; one-way fare $1) If you're not biking, this student-run outfit shuttles people around town and campus. Many buses are red double-deckers.

Oroville

Oroville has seen quite a reversal: the lust for gold initially attracted white settlers to the area, who displaced native tribes. Today, crowds flock to the thriving tribal casinos on the periphery of the town seeking riches. Aside from the slots, the economy leans on the plastic-bag factory on the outskirts of town and the tourists who mill though the throng of antique stores. Oroville's population boomed in recent years, with families fleeing the high-priced housing of the Bay Area, but the housing bubble's burst has hit these suburbs hard. Oroville's most enduring attraction, aside from the nearby lake, is an excellent museum left behind by a long-gone Chinese community.

Gold was discovered near here in 1848 by John Bidwell, and the booming little town took the name Ophir (Gold) City. Oroville was where Ishi, the last surviving member of the local Yahi tribe, was 'found' back in 1911 (p334).

Sights & Activities

Chinese Temple TEMPLE

(1500 Broderick St; adult/child $3/free; noon-4pm) A relatively quiet monument to the 10,000 Chinese people who once lived here, the temple is a compelling draw that exceeds expectations. The temple seved a Chinese community who worked to rebuild the area levees after a devastating 1907 flood wiped out Chinatown. During the 19th century, theater troupes from China toured a circuit of Chinatowns in California and Oroville was the end of the line. The troupes often left their sets, costumes and puppets here before returning to China, which has left the temple with an unrivaled collection of 19th-century Chinese stage finery. The temple itself is a beautifully preserved building bursting with religious shrines, festival tapestries, ancient lion masks and furniture. To keep everything in context, take advantage of docent-led tours, which can take an hour.

Sacramento National Wildlife Refuge BIRD-WATCHING

Serious bird-watchers should head to the Sacramento National Wildlife Refuge during winter, where the migratory waterfowl are a spectacular sight. The **visitor center** (530-934-2801; www.fws.gov/sacramentovalleyrefuges; 752 County Rd, Willows; 7:30am-4pm Mon-Fri) is off I-5 near Willows; a 6-mile driving trail ($3) and walking trails are open daily. The peak season to see birds is between October and late February, with large populations of geese in December and January.

Lake Oroville (www.lakeoroville.net), a popular summertime destination, sits 9 miles northeast of town behind **Oroville Dam**, the largest earthen dam in the US. The surrounding Lake Oroville State Recreation Area attracts boaters, campers, swimmers, bicyclists, hikers and fishing folk. Oroville is also a gateway to the gorgeous Feather River Canyon and the rugged northern reaches of the Sierra Nevada. The lake's **visitor center** (530-538-2219; 917 Kelly Ridge Rd; 9am-5pm) has exhibits on the California State Water Project and local Native American history, plus a viewing tower and loads of recreational information.

The area surrounding Lake Oroville is full of hiking trails, and a favorite is the 7-mile round-trip walk to 640ft **Feather Falls**, which takes about four hours. The **Freeman Bicycle Trail** is a 41-mile off-road loop that takes cyclists to the top of 770ft Oroville Dam, then follows the Feather River back to the Thermalito Forebay and Afterbay storage reservoirs, east of Hwy 70. The ride is mostly flat, but the dam ascent is steep. Get a free map of the ride from the chamber of commerce. The **Forebay Aquatic Center** (www.aschico.com/forebayaquaticcenter; Garden Dr) rents watercraft to get out on the water.

Hwys 162 and 70 head northeast from Oroville into the mountains and on to Quincy. Hwy 70 snakes along the magnificent **Feather River Canyon**, an especially captivating drive during the fall.

Sleeping & Eating

A launching pad for outdoorsy trips, there's plenty of camping in the area, which you can arrange through the chamber of com-

LONE YAHI FOUND IN OROVILLE

At daybreak on August 29, 1911, frantic dogs woke the butchers sleeping inside a slaughterhouse outside Oroville. When they came out, they found their dogs holding a man at bay – a Native American clad only in a loincloth, starving, exhausted and unable to speak English.

The stories of the discovery of a 'wild man' spread through California papers, eventually attracting Berkeley anthropologists Alfred L Kroeber and Thomas Talbot Waterman. They traveled to Oroville and, with scraps of nearly lost vocabulary from vanished native languages, eventually discovered the man belonged to the Yahi, the southernmost tribe of the Yana, who were believed to be extinct.

Waterman took 'Ishi,' meaning 'man' in the Yahi language, to the museum at the university, where he was cared for and brought back to health. Ishi spent his remaining years there, telling the anthropologists his life story and teaching them his tribal language, lore and ways.

Ishi's tribe had been virtually exterminated by settlers before he was born. In 1870, when he was a child, there were only 12 or 15 Yahi people left, hiding in remote areas in the foothills east of Red Bluff. By 1908 Ishi, his mother, sister and an old man were all who were left of the Yahi tribe. In that year the others died and Ishi was left alone. On March 25, 1916, Ishi died of tuberculosis at the university hospital and the Yahi disappeared forever.

The site where Ishi was found is east of Oroville along Oro-Quincy Hwy at Oak Ave, marked by a small monument. Part of the Lassen National Forest where Ishi and the Yahi people lived, is now called the Ishi Wilderness.

merce, the USFS office or the Lake Oroville visitor center. A strip of decent budget motels – mostly chains and some humble mid-century cheapies – are clustered on Feather River Blvd, between Hwy 162 to the south and Montgomery St to the north. There's not much of a chance that you'll be thrilled about the dining options in town, but aside from fast-food joints by the major eateries, there are some passable places in the small downtown offering plates of Mexican and pub grub.

Lake Oroville State Recreation Area CAMPGROUND **$**
(☎530-538-2219; www.parks.ca.gov; 917 Kelly Ridge Rd; tent/RV sites $20/40; wi-fi) The wi-fi might be the first clue that this isn't the most rustic choice, but there are a variety of sites. There are good primitive sites if you're willing to hike, and – perhaps the coolest feature of the park – floating campsites on platforms that are accessible only by boat.

Information

The office of the USFS **Feather River Ranger District** (☎530-534-6500; 875 Mitchell Ave; 8am-4:30pm Mon-Fri) has maps and brochures. For road conditions, phone ☎800-427-7623.

Getting There & Away

Although Greyhound buses stop at **Tom's Sierra Chevron** (☎530-533-1333; cnr 5th Ave & Oro Dam Blvd), a few blocks east of Hwy 70, a car is far and away the simplest and most cost effective way to reach the area. There are two buses daily between Oroville and Sacramento. The trip takes 1½ hours and costs $37.

Chico

With its huge population of students, Chico has the devil-may-care energy of a college kegger during the school year, and a lazy, lethargic hangover during the summertime. Its oak-shaded downtown and university attractions makes it one of Sacramento Valley's more attractive social and cultural hubs, where easygoing folks mingle late in the restaurants and bars, which open onto patios in the balmy summer evenings.

And though Chico wilts in the heat of the summer, the swimming holes in Bidwell Park take the edge off during the day, as does a tubing trip down the gentle Sacramento River. The fine pale ales produced at the Sierra Nevada Brewing Company, near downtown, are another of Chico's refreshing blessings.

There's a bit of irony in the fact a town so widely celebrated for its brews was founded by John Bidwell, the illustrious California pioneer who made a bid for US president with the Prohibitionist party. In 1868, Bidwell and his wife, Annie Ellicott Kennedy, moved to the new mansion he had built, now the Bidwell Mansion State Historic Park. After John died in 1900, Annie continued as a philanthropist until her death in 1918.

Sights

Downtown is west of Hwy 99, easily reached via Hwy 32 (8th St). Main St and Broadway are the central downtown streets; from there, Park Ave stretches southward and the tree-lined Esplanade heads north.

Sierra Nevada Brewing Company BREWERY
(www.sierranevada.com; 1075 E 20th St) Though too big to officially qualify as a 'microbrewery,' this hotspot draws hordes of beer snobs to the birthplace of their nationally distributed Sierra Nevada Pale Ale and Schwarber, a Chico-only black ale. Also for sale are the **'Beer Camp' brews** (www.sierrabeercamp.com), which are short-run boutique beers brewed by ultra beer nerds at invitation-only three-day summer seminars. The brewery is on the very cutting edge of sustainable business practices – their rooftop solar fields are among the largest privately owned solar fields in the US and they extended a spur of local railroad to increase transportation efficiency. Excellent tours are given at 2:30pm daily, and continuously from noon to 5pm on Saturdays. There's also a pub and restaurant (see p336).

Chico Creek Nature Center NATURE CENTER
(www.bidwellpark.org; 1968 East 8th St; suggested donation $1; 11am-4pm Tue-Sun;) If you plan on spending the afternoon in Bidwell Park, first stop at this sparkling new nature center, with great displays on local plants and animals and excellent hands-on science programs for families.

Chico State University UNIVERSITY
Ask for a free map of the Chico State University campus, or ask about campus events and tours, at the **CSU Information Center** (530-898-4636; www.csuchico.edu; cnr Chestnut & W 2nd Sts), on the main floor of Bell Memorial Union. The attractive campus is infused with sweet floral fragrances in spring, and there's a rose garden at its center.

Honey Run Covered Bridge HISTORIC SITE
The historic 1894 bridge is straight out of *The Legend of Sleepy Hollow* – and an unusual type of bridge in this part of the country. Take the Skyway exit off Hwy 99 on the southern outskirts of Chico, head east and go left on Honey Run-Humbug Rd; the bridge is 5 miles along, in a small park.

Bidwell Mansion State Historic Park HISTORIC BUILDING
(530-895-6144; 525 Esplanade; adult/child $6/3; noon-5pm Wed-Fri, 11am-5pm Sat & Sun) Chico's most prominent landmark, the opulent Victorian home built for Chico's founders John and Annie Bidwell. The 26-room mansion was built between 1865 and 1868 and hosted many US presidents. Tours start every hour on the hour. Due to budget difficulty, this park was slated for closure in 2012.

Activities

Growing out of downtown, the 3670-acre **Bidwell Park** (www.bidwellpark.org) is the nation's third-largest municipal park. It stretches 10 miles northwest along Chico Creek with lush groves and miles of trails. The upper part of the park is fairly untamed, which is surprising to find smack dab in the middle of the city. Several classic movies have been shot here, including *The Adventures of Robin Hood* and parts of *Gone with the Wind*.

The park is full of hiking and mountain-biking trails and swimming spots, and has a nature center. You'll find pools at One-Mile and Five-Mile recreation areas and swimming holes (including Bear Hole, Salmon Hole and Brown Hole) in Upper Bidwell Park, north of Manzanita Ave. Don't be surprised if locals opt for birthday suits, not swimsuits.

In summer you'll want to cool off from the hike by **tubing** the Sacramento. Inner tubes can be rented at grocery stores and other shops along Nord Ave (Hwy 32) for around $6. Tubers enter at the Irvine Finch Launch Ramp on Hwy 32, a few miles west of Chico, and come out at the Washout, off River Rd.

Festivals & Events

With the students out of town, family-friendly outdoor events take over the town each summer. The **Thursday Night Market** fills several blocks of Broadway every Thursday evening from April to September. At City Plaza you'll find free **Friday Night Concerts** starting in

May. **Shakespeare in the Park** (☎530-891-1382; www.ensembletheatreofchico.com; admission free), at Cedar Grove in lower Bidwell Park, runs from mid-July to the end of August.

Sleeping

There's an abundance of well-kept independent motels with sparkling swimming pools, some of them along the shaded Esplanade north of downtown. Beware that Chico State's graduation and homecoming mania (in May and October, respectively) send prices through the roof.

TOP CHOICE Hotel Diamond HISTORIC HOTEL **$$$**
(☎866-993-3100; www.hoteldiamondchico.com; 220 W 4th St; r from $189; ❄@📶) This whitewashed 1904 building is the most luxurious place to lay your head in Chico, with high-thread-count linens, valet laundry and room service of comfort foods in California-fusion style like prawn-dressed macaroni and cheese. The Diamond Suite, with its balcony, original furnishings and spacious top-floor balcony is a-*maz*-ing.

Matador Motel MOTEL **$**
(☎530-342-7543; 1934 Esplanade; r $47-51; ❄≋) This pleasant courtyard motel not far from downtown has simple rooms done up with old-fashioned Mission-style details. The buildings wrap around a beautiful tiled swimming pool shaded by palms.

The Grateful Bed B&B **$$**
(☎530-342-2464; www.thegratefulbed.net; 1462 Arcadian Ave; r $105-160; ❄@) Well, obviously you're a bedhead if you stay here. Tucked in a residential neighborhood near downtown, it's a stately 1905 Victorian home with four sweetly decorated rooms with warm hosts. Breakfast is included.

Woodson Bridge State Recreation Area CAMPGROUND **$**
(☎530-839-2112; tent sites $25) This shaded campground, adjacent to a huge native riparian preserve, has 46 tent sites on the banks of the Sacramento River. It's about 25 miles north of Chico on Hwy 99, then west toward Corning.

Eating

Downtown Chico is packed with fun places to eat, many of them catering to a student budget. The outdoor **farmers market** (cnr Wall & E 2nd Sts; ⊙7:30am-1pm Sat) draws from the plentiful surrounding valley.

Café Coda BREAKFAST, BRUNCH **$**
(www.cafecoda.com; 265 Humboldt Ave; mains $6-10; ⊙7am-2pm Tue-Sun; 📶) Café Coda is Chico's best breakfast for its expert Southwestern-influenced scrambles, sweet selections (like lemon poppyseed pancakes with mint butter) and thrifty Champagne brunch (all you can drink for only $4.50). Served by a chipper staff, all breakfasts come in half-portions upon request. Appropriate to their name, they host live music on some evenings.

Nobby's BURGERS **$**
(1444 Park Ave; burgers $5-7; ⊙10:30am-9pm Tue-Sun) Simply put, the Nobby Burger, topped with a large fried disc of cheese and crispy, thick bacon, is a heart attack. Worth it? Probably. Note that the place is tiny and you'll likely have to stand. Cash only.

Sierra Nevada Taproom & Restaurant BREWPUB **$$**
(www.sierranevada.com; 1075 E 20th St; meals $8-15; ⊙11am-9pm Sun-Thu, to 10pm Fri & Sat) The apple-malt pork loin is a standout at the Sierra Nevada Brewery's on-site restaurant, a genuine Chico destination. It's great to soak up the brews, but lacks ambience – the huge, loud dining room feels a bit like a factory cafeteria (which it kind of is). Still, it has better-than-average pub food, superb fresh ales and lagers on tap, some not available anywhere else.

5th Street Steakhouse AMERICAN **$$$**
(☎530-899-8075; www.5thstreetsteakhouse.com; 345 W 5th Street; mains $16-37; ⊙from 4:30pm) This is the joint where college students take their visiting parents, featuring steaks tender enough to cut with a reproachful look, and occasional live jazz. The interior is stately, with exposed brick and crisp white tablecloths.

Red Tavern FUSION **$$$**
(☎530-894-3463; www.redtavern.com; 1250 Esplanade; mains $15-29; ⊙from 4:30pm Mon-Sat) Slightly swanky, the Red Tavern is one of Chico's favorite fine-dining experiences, with a sophisticated menu that balances discriminatingly between Europe and Asia and uses local, seasonal organic food.

Celestino's Live from New York Pizza PIZZA **$**
(101 Salem St; mains $3-7; ⊙10:30am-10pm Mon-Thu, to 11pm Fri & Sat) One of the best imitations of 'real' New York pizza in Northern California, they serve slices with a thin,

chewy crust and playfully themed variations like the meaty Godfather. The slice-n-a-soda lunch special for $4 is a good deal.

Sins of Cortez CAFE $
(www.sinofcortez.com; 101 Salem St; mains $6-16; ⌚7am-9pm) The service won't win awards for speed, but this local favorite draws a mob for its burly breakfast plates. Order anything with the homemade chorizo.

Shubert's Ice Cream & Candy ICE CREAM $
(178 E 7th St; ⌚9:30am-10pm Mon-Fri, 11am-10pm Sat & Sun) Having produced delicious homemade ice cream and chocolates for more than 60 years, this is a beloved Chico landmark.

El Pasia Taco Truck MEXICAN $
(cnr 8th & Pine Sts; mains $1.50-5; ⌚11am-8pm) Debate about which of Chico's taco trucks is the best can quickly lead to fisticuffs – but the smoky *carnitas* (braised pork) tacos here are a broke college student's dream.

Drinking

As you might have guessed from Chico's party-school rep, you're unlikely to go thirsty. There's a strip of bars on Main St if you want to go hopping.

Madison Bear Garden BAR
(www.madisonbeargarden.com; 316 W 2nd St; ⌚noon-2am; wifi) This whimsically decorated student hangout is housed in a spacious brick building. It's the place to chat to students over thick burgers and cool beers. Toward the end of the night, the ramshackle disorder of the decor is a perfect match with the boozy, high-fiving co-eds in the big beer garden. They serve burgers to soak up the beers.

Panama Bar & Cafe BAR
(128 Broadway; ⌚11am-10pm) The house specializes in variations of Long Island iced tea (most of which are priced around $3), so brace yourself. For a wild night out in Chico, the only way to consume more liquor would be with an IV drip.

Naked Lounge COFFEE SHOP
(118 2nd St; ⌚10am-9pm Sun-Thu, to midnight Fri & Sat; wifi) With its dark-red, enveloping interior and expertly drawn espresso drinks, this is Chico's best place to get caffeinated.

Entertainment

For entertainment options, pick up the free weekly *Chico News & Review* (www.newsandreview.com), available in newspaper boxes and businesses downtown. For theater, films, concerts, art exhibits and other cultural events at the CSU campus, contact the **CSU Box Office** (☎530-898-6333) or the **CSU Information Center** (☎530-898-4636) in the Bell Memorial Union.

LaSalle's CLUB
(www.lasallesbar.com; 229 Broadway) This venue is open nightly for hip-hop, Top 40 and retro dance nights and live bands that play anything to pack people in – from reggae to hard rock.

Pageant Theatre CINEMA
(www.pageantchico.com; 351 E 6th St) Screens international and alternative films. Monday is bargain night, with all seats just $3.

Chico Caberet CABERET
(☎530-895-0245; www.chicocabaret.com; tickets $16) All fishnets and sass, this local theater troupe brings racy annual shows to Butte County theaters.

Information

Chico Chamber of Commerce & Visitor Center (☎530-891-5559; www.chicochamber.com; 300 Salem St; ⌚9am-5pm Mon-Fri, 10am-3pm Sat) Offers local information.

Getting There & Around

Greyhound (www.greyhound.com) buses stop at the **Amtrak station** (cnr W 5th & Orange Sts). The train station is unattended so purchase tickets in advance from travel agents or on board from the conductor. Trips between Chico and Sacramento on the *Coast Starlight* line are $26 (2½ hours, once daily). Amtrak also operates buses from the station multiple times daily for a similar fare.

B-Line (☎530-342-0221, www.blinetransit.com) handles all buses throughout Butte County, and can get you around Chico and down to Oroville (tickets $2, four times daily).

Bicycles can be rented from **Campus Bicycles** (www.campusbicycles.com; 330 Main St; mountain bikes half/full day $20/35).

Red Bluff

The smoldering streets of Red Bluff – one of California's hottest towns due to the hot air trap of the Shasta Cascades – are of marginal interest unto themselves, but looking to the mountain-dominated horizon offers a clue to the outdoor activities that bring most travelers through town. The agreeable tree-lined neighborhoods are full of restored

19th-century Victorian mansions and there are some historic storefronts in the business district filled with antiques and Western wear.

Peter Lassen laid out the town site in 1847 and it grew into a key port along the Sacramento River. Now it's more of a pit stop on the way to the national park that bears his name and other points along on I-5.

Cowboy culture is alive and well here. Catch it in action the third weekend of April at the **Red Bluff Round-Up** (www.redbluffroundup.com; tickets $10-20), a major rodeo event dating back to 1921, or in any of the dive bars where the jukeboxes are stocked with Nashville, and plenty of big-buckled cowboys belly up to the bar.

Sights & Activities

Red Bluff Lake Recreation Area PARK

A good break from the highway, the Red Bluff Lake Recreation Area, on the east bank of the Sacramento River, is a spacious park full of trees, birds and meadows. It offers numerous picnicking, swimming, hiking and camping opportunities and has interpretive trails, bicycle paths, boat ramps, a wildlife-viewing area with excellent bird-watching, a fish ladder (in operation between May and September) and a 2-acre native-plant garden.

William B Ide Adobe State Historic Park HISTORIC SITE

(☎530-529-8599; 21659 Adobe Rd; ⊙sunrise-sunset) Set on a beautiful, shaded piece of land overlooking a languorous section of the Sacramento River, the park preserves the original adobe home and grounds of pioneer William B Ide, who 'fought' in the 1846 Bear Flag Revolt at Sonoma and was named president of the short-lived California Republic (though, even with the blacksmith shop and the gift shop, these are humble digs for a president). To get to the park, head about a mile north on Main St, turn east onto Adobe Rd and go another mile, following the signs. At press time, the future of this state park was uncertain and subject to closure.

Sacramento River Discovery Center SCIENCE CENTER

(1000 Sale Lane; ⊙11am-4pm Tue-Sat; 👪) The center has kid-friendly displays about the river, fairly subjective information about the benefits of cattle grazing and resources about the Diversion Dam just outside its doors. From mid-May to mid-September, the dam diverts water into irrigation canals and in the process creates Red Bluff Lake, which is a popular swimming destination.

Sleeping & Eating

Over a dozen motels are found beside I-5 and south of town along Main St, and the historic residential neighborhood has some bed-and-breakfasts. The restaurant scene isn't thrilling – a lot of cheap take-out Chinese, pizza and stick-to-the-ribs grub that's straight from a can.

Sycamore Grove Camping Area CAMPGROUND $

(☎530-824-5196; www.recreation.gov; undeveloped/developed sites $16/$25) Beside the river in the Red Bluff Lake Recreation Area is this quiet, attractive USFS campground. Campsites for tents and RVs are on a first-come, first-served basis. It also has a large group campground, Camp Discovery, where cabins are available (reservations required).

Los Mariachis MEXICAN $

(☎530-529-1217; 248 S Main St; mains $5-14 ⊙9am-9pm; 👪) This bright, friendly, family-run Mexican dinner spot is lined with windows looking over the central junction of Red Bluff, and is a perfect stop for families. They have great salsa and *molcajetes* (meat or seafood stew, served in a stone bowl) big enough to satisfy hungry campers – big enough to share otherwise. To get a feel for the locals, saddle up to the bright yellow bar (facing a taxidermy rattle snake) and order a couple cold ones, served in frosty mugs.

New Thai House THAI $

(www.newthaihouse.com; 248 S Main St; mains $5-14; ⊙11am-9pm Mon-Fri, from noon Sat, 🌶) This is a remarkably good Thai restaurant, with excellent curries and tom yum soup.

Hal's Eat 'Em Up DRIVE-IN $

(158 Main St) If the heat is raging, grab a root-beer float from Hal's, a great small-town drive-in just south of downtown.

Information

Red Bluff Chamber of Commerce (☎530-527-6220, www.redbluffchamber.com; 100 Main St; ⊙8:30am-4pm Mon, to 5pm Tue-Thu, to 4:30pm Fri) To get your bearings and a stack of brochures, go south of downtown to this small place.

Getting There & Away

Most visitors come to Red Bluff to take a break from the busy I-5. By the highway, the town is three hours north of San Francisco and 15 minutes north of Sacramento. **Greyhound** (www.greyhound.com) and **Amtrak** (www.amtrak.com) connect it with other California cities via bus. The station is east of town at the corner of Hwy 36 E.

SAN JOAQUIN VALLEY

The southern half of California's Central Valley – named for the San Joaquin River – sprawls from Stockton to the turbine-covered Tehachapi Mountains, southeast of Bakersfield. Everything stretches to the horizon in straight lines – railroad tracks, two-lane blacktop and long irrigation channels. Through the elaborate politics and machinery of water management, this once-arid region ranks among the most agriculturally productive places in the world, though the profits often go to agribusiness shareholders, not the increasingly displaced family farmer. While some of the tiny towns scattering the region, such as Gustine and Reedley, retain a classic Main Street Americana feel, many have adapted to the influx of Latino culture brought by enormous immigrant force that harvests these fields in unaccounted numbers. Many other towns are paved over with housing developments that are populated by families escaping the onerous housing prices of the Bay Area.

Today the San Joaquin Valley is beguiling for both travelers and locals, where intense heat and dubious reminders of history and the valley's development are evident through tract houses and rusting tractors, scrawling spray-painted gang signs and the arching spray of irrigation systems.

It's also a place of seismic, often contentious, development. High housing prices in the coastal cities have resulted in unchecked eastward sprawl – some half a million acres have been paved over in the last decade. Where there once were cattle ranches and vineyards there are now the nostalgically named developments of American anyplace: a big-box shopping complex named Indian Ranch, a tidy row of McMansions named Vineyard Estates.

To sink your teeth into the region, skip I-5 and travel on Hwy 99 – a road with nearly as long a history as the famous Route 66. It'll be hot – very hot – so put the windows down and crank up the twangy traditional country or the booming traditional *norteño* (an accordion-driven genre of folk music imported from Mexico). If you have the time, exit often for bushels of the freshest produce on earth and brushes with California's nearly forgotten past.

Many of the following towns are excellent launching points for Yosemite National Park, and Hwy 99 is lined with classic, affordable motor lodges and hotel chains.

Lodi

Although Lodi used to be the 'Watermelon capital of the world,' today, wine rules this patch of the valley. Breezes from the Sacramento River Delta soothe the area's hot vineyards, where more zinfandel grapes are grown than anywhere else in the world. Some particularly old vines have been tended by the same families for over a century. Lodi's diverse soil is sometimes rocky, sometimes a fine sandy loam, giving its zins a range of distinctive characteristics.

Get your first taste of Lodi's powerful, sun-soaked zins at the **Lodi Wine & Visitor Center** (209-365-0621; www.lodiwine.com; 2545 W Turner Rd; tastings $5; 10am-5pm), where 100 local vintages are sold by the glass at the solid-wood tasting bar. They'll provide maps to wineries of the region. Another stop to sip the region's boutique wines and experimental labels by more famous names is the Italian-style **Vino Piazza** (209-727-3270; 12470 Locke Rd, Lockeford) where you can park the car, order a bistro lunch and amble between tasting rooms. It is just east of town. Follow the signs from Hwy 12.

Given Lodi's love of the tipple, it's no surprise that they have a slew of festivals dedicated to wine, including the **Grape & Harvest Festival** in September and **Zinfest** in May.

Lodi's **Micke Grove Regional Park and Zoo** (209-953-8840; www.mgzoo.com; admission $2; 2545 W Turner Rd; 10am-5pm;) is a good stop for the seriously underage, with a water play area, hissing cockroaches and some barking sea lions. There's also a small children's amusement park, where rides cost a nominal extra fee.

Sleeping & Eating

Along Hwy 99, Lodi hosts a string of budget chain hotels. Though the rooms are bland, the competition ensures that they are all very clean; they can be a real bargain.

TOP LODI WINERIES

Low key and constantly improving, Lodi's vineyards make an easy escape from the Bay Area, and the quality of grapes will delight Napa veterans. It's also an incredibly easy wine area to navigate, as the roads are well marked. For a map, try the **Lodi Wine & Visitor Center** (www.lodiwine.com). Opinions on Lodi's best wineries tend to be as entangled as the vines, but these are some favorites. The region is easily accessed from I-5 or Hwy 99.

Jesse's Grove (www.jessiesgrovewinery.com; 1973 W Turner Rd; ⌚noon-5pm) With its 'Groovin' in the Grove' summer concert series and long family tradition of estate grown wines, this is an anchor of Lodi wine producers. The tasting room has a terrific collection of historic photos of Lodi. During events you can sometimes camp here.

Michael David (www.michaeldavidwinery.com; 4580 W Hwy 12; ⌚10am-5pm) With a cafe that serves platters of fresh food (count yourself lucky if you get here on taco Tuesday) and an old-fashioned dry goods store, Michael David produces a renowned zinfandel, 7 Deadly Zins.

Harney Lane (www.harneylane.com; 9010 E Harney Lane; ⌚noon-5pm Thu-Sun) A sweet family outfit that's been around Lodi forever, their tempranillo is an overachiever in wine competitions.

d'Art (www.dartwines.com; 13299 N Curry Ave; ⌚noon-5pm Thu-Sun) Helen and Dave Dart bring artisanal passion to their bold Cab. The tasting room is comfortable and fun.

Jeremy Wine Co (www.jeremywineco.com; 6 W Pine St; ⌚1-5pm Wed-Sun) For those who don't have time for a countryside tour, Jeremy's brass- and wood-fitted tasting room in central Lodi offers a good taste of the region's promise. The bright fruit-forward sangiovese is their best.

Wine & Roses BOUTIQUE HOTEL $$$
(☎209-334-6988; www.winerose.com; 2505 W Turner Rd; r $169-269, ste from $325) Surrounded by a giant rose garden and deep green lawns, Wine & Roses is a surprisingly luxurious offering to spring up amid the blistering heat of Lodi's vineyards. Tasteful, modern and romantic, the rooms have slate bathrooms and high quality bath products, luxurious sheets and large sitting areas. Naturally each one has a pair of wine glasses too. The suites? Even more over-the-top; some open to private terraces. There's also an acclaimed spa and on-site restaurant.

Crush Kitchen & Bar ITALIAN $$
(www.crushkitchen.com; 115 S School St; mains $17-23; ⌚11:30am-9:30pm Sun, Mon, Thu, to 11:30pm Fri & Sat, 5-9pm Wed) With an excellent, extremely long wine list and a menu that leans heavily Italian, Crush is several notches of sophistication ahead of anything else in town. The plates are expert, simple and rustic cooking: fresh tomato salad, gnocchi with a touch of truffle oil and duck confit. If you don't have time to sit, the accompanying market has all kinds of cured meat, artisanal cheese and local honey for a perfect picnic.

Cheese Central MARKET $
(www.cheesecentrallodi.com; 11 N School St; ⌚10am-6pm Mon-Sat) Ask Cindy, the owner of this shop, for thoughtful pairings with Lodi's wine. If there's just two of you, check the 'mouse trap,' a cute little cheese board where excellent imported selections are offered in modest portions. If you want to make a weekend out of Lodi's wine region, the cooking classes here get rave reviews.

Stockton

Little Stockton looked down and out for a while there. What remained of its proud past as a major inland port was blighted by crime-ridden streets and crumbling facades. This not-so-distant past is evident in the city's outskirts, which are lined with slouching, sun-bleached houses, old doughnut shops, liquor stores and taco trucks – a sad fate for a major supply point for Gold Rushers, which was hit hard by a decline in its shipbuilding and commercial transportation industries. But the downtown and waterfront redevelopment is one of the valley's more promising turnarounds, warranting a short detour.

You'll know you've reached the good part of town when you see the modern white edifice of the **Weber Point Events Center** (221 Center St), standing in the middle of a grassy park looking rather like a pile of sailboats. The events center is where much of the action is, with the huge **Asparagus Festival** in April, a series of open-air concerts, and fountains where squealing children cool off during summer break. Nearby is the beautiful new **Banner Island Ballpark** (www.stocktonports.com; 404 W Freemont St), where the minor-league Stockton Seals play baseball (April to September). Also near is the **Haggin Museum** (www.hagginmuseum.org; 1201 N Pershing Ave; tickets $5; ⌚1:30am-5pm Wed-Fri, noon-5pm Sat & Sun), which has an excellent collection of American landscape paintings and an Egyptian mummy.

Just across the channel is the Greater Stockton Chamber of Commerce's **Department of Tourism** (☎209-547-2770; www.visitstockton.org; Suite 220, 445 W Weber Ave; ⌚9am-5pm Mon-Fri), with complete information about the goings-on in town.

Get lunch a few blocks north at **Manny's California Fresh Café** (☎209-463-6415; 1612 Pacific Ave; mains $6-15; ⌚10am-9:45pm), where rotisserie meats and fried-chicken sandwiches burst with flavor. It's at the edge of the **Miracle Mile** district (a developing shopping stretch on Pacific Ave, north of downtown).

If you're spending the night here after a ball game, the best bet is the **University Plaza Waterfront Hotel** (☎209-944-1140; www.universityplazawaterfronthotel.com; 110 W Fremont St; r $99-109; 📶), a place where work travelers mingle with students (the upper floors have student lofts). The very modern building overlooking the harbor and historic park, unlike the highway side chains, is walkable from other locations at the city center.

Modesto

Cruising was banned in Modesto in 1993, but the town still touts itself as the 'cruising capital of the world.' That notoriety stems mostly from hometown boy George Lucas' 1973 film *American Graffiti*. You'll still see hot rods and flashy wheels around town, but they won't be clogging thoroughfares on Friday night. The Ernest & Julio Gallo Winery, makers of America's best-selling jug wines, is among the town's biggest businesses. Old oaks arch over the city's attractive streets and you can eat well in the compact downtown. This is a good spot for getting off the dusty highway.

Downtown sits just east of Hwy 99 (avoid the area west of the freeway), centering on 10th and J Sts. From downtown, Yosemite Blvd (Hwy 132) runs east toward Yosemite National Park.

Many historic buildings have survived revitalization, including the 1934 **State Theatre** (www.thestate.org; 1307 J St), which hosts films and live music, and the old **SP depot**, a Mission-style beauty. The famous **Modesto Arch**, on the corner of 9th and I Sts, erected in 1912, stands at what was once the city's main entry point (see boxed text, p301). Classic car shows are held in **Graffiti Month** (June); for details, call the **chamber of commerce** (☎209-577-5757; 1114 J St; ⌚8:30am-5pm Mon-Fri).

Amid all the '50s charm of Modesto, **Brighter Side** (www.brighter-side.com; cnr 13th & K Sts; mains $4-6, ⌚11am-3:30pm Mon-Fri) is an earthy little sandwich shop that seems about a decade late to the party; housed in a wood-shingled former gas station, they make amazing sandwiches. The sandwiches all have personalized names, like the flavorful Larry (polish sausage, mushrooms, green onions on rye) or the crisp Christine, enjoyed on the sunny patio by a crowd of Modesto's downtown office workers.

Papachino's Greco-Roman Restaurant (www.mypapachinos.com; 1212t J St; mains

DON'T MISS

STOCKTON ASPARAGUS FESTIVAL

Of all the Central Valley food celebrations, none pay such creative respect to the main ingredient as the **Stockton Asparagus Festival** (www.asparagusfest.com), which brings together more than 500 vendors who serve the little green stalks in every presentation imaginable – more than 10 tons of it! – along 'Asparagus Alley.' It all unfolds along the lovely waterfront at the end of April.

WHAT THE...?

The old arch that made Modesto famous tells a traveler what the four main tenets of the town are. The slogan, 'Water, Wealth, Contentment, Health,' resulted from a local contest held prior to the construction of the arch. It is a pithy little poem and is as true today as when the arch went up in 1912. Interestingly, the slogan gracing the arch didn't actually win the contest. Judges chose the folksy, if less eloquent, slogan 'Nobody's Got Modesto's Goat' but were overruled by the city government.

$9-13, 11am-8pm Mon-Sat;) is another quick, quality meal in an equally eclectic setting – don't be put off by the trippy murals. The gyro plate is savory, garlicky and dressed in a brightly flavored dill sauce and the lamb is a favorite. The yogurt is homemade and there are lots of options for vegetarians. Lunches are served with a simple white bean soup.

A&W Drive-In (cnr 14th & G Sts; mains $3-9, 10am-10pm) is a vintage burger stand (part of a chain founded in nearby Lodi) filled with poodle-skirt corniness, though roller-skating carhops, classic cars and ties to *American Graffiti* move a lot of root beer. (George Lucas supposedly cruised here as a youth.)

Merced

You can jog over to Yosemite from many of the small towns in this part of the valley, but this is the most convenient staging area, right on Hwy 140. The machine of progress has not been kind to Merced, as it suffers more than its share of strip malls, but at its core there are tree-lined streets, historic Victorian homes and a magnificent 1875 courthouse. The downtown business district is a work-in-progress, with 1930s movie theaters, antique stores and a few casual eateries undergoing constant renovation.

Merced is right in the midst of a population makeover, thanks to the newest University of California campus, opened in 2005. UC Merced's first freshman class numbered just 1000 students, but the school continues to grow with a diverse student body, which has begun to dramatically shape the city.

Downtown Merced is east of Hwy 99 along Main St, between R St and Martin Luther King Jr Way. The **California Welcome Center** (209-384-2791; 710 W 16th St), adjacent to the bus depot, has local maps and information on Merced and Yosemite.

The big attraction is the **Castle Air Museum** (209-723-2178; 5050 Santa Fe Dr; adult/child $10/5; 9am-5pm) in Atwater, about 6 miles northwest of Merced. A squadron of restored military aircrafts from WWII, the Korean War and the Vietnam War sit eerily dormant across from a large hangar. Even the most conscientious of objectors stand agape at these streamlined killing machines.

In a grand old Colonial-style mansion, **Hooper House Bear Creek Inn** (209-723-3991; www.hooperhouse.com; 575 W North Bear Creek Dr; r $129-159;) is a leisurely retreat. Rooms are large and beautifully furnished with hardwood furniture, soft beds and tiled bathrooms. A full breakfast is included, which you can have sent to your room.

The six-bed, family-style **HI Merced Home Hostel** (209-725-0407; dm $15-18; reception 5:30-10pm) is in the home of longtime Merced residents. The place is like staying at the home of long-lost aunt and uncle (think collectable spoons) who sit around the kitchen table at night to help lend sage advice for excursions into Yosemite. The hostel fills quickly, especially during summer weekends. Beds must be reserved in advance; call between 5:30pm and 10pm. The hostel is in a quiet residential neighborhood and doesn't give out its address, but it will pick up and drop off guests at the bus and train stations.

The **Branding Iron** (www.thebrandingiron-merced.com; 640 W 16th St; lunch mains $9-11, dinner mains $10-25; 11am-9pm Mon-Fri, from 5pm Sat & Sun) roadhouse, a favorite of ranchers in the area, has been spruced up a bit for the tour buses, but folks dig the hearty steak platters and Western atmosphere. Presiding over the dining room is 'Old Blue,' a massive stuffed bull's head from a local dairy farm.

Yarts (209-388-9589, www.yarts.com) buses depart four times daily for Yosemite Valley from several Merced locations, including the **Merced Transpo Center** (cnr 16th & N Sts) and the **Amtrak station** (cnr 24th &

K Sts). The trip takes about 2½ hours and stops include Mariposa, Midpines and the Yosemite Bug Lodge & Hostel. Round-trip adult/child tickets cost $25/18 and include the park entrance fee (quite a bargain!). There's also space on the Yarts buses for bicycles, but space is limited, so show up early.

Greyhound (710 W 16th St) also operates from the Transpo Center.

Fresno

Bulging like a blister in the arid center of the state, Fresno is the biggest city in the San Joaquin Valley by far. The old brick warehouses lining the Santa Fe railroad tracks are an impressive sight, as are the many historic downtown buildings, such as the 1894 Fresno Water Tower and the 1928 Pantages (Warnors) Theatre. These compete for attention with newer structures, including the sprawling Convention Center and the modern ballpark, Chukchansi Park, for Fresno's Triple-A baseball team, the Grizzlies.

The biggest interest for a traveler is the Tower District, which boasts the only active alternative-culture neighborhood between Sacramento and Los Angeles. North of downtown, the Tower District has book and record stores, music clubs and a handful of stylish restaurants.

Like many valley towns, Fresno's huge diversity comes from Mexican, Basque and Chinese communities, which have been here for decades. More recently thousands of Hmong people have put down roots in the area. The longstanding Armenian community is most famously represented by author and playwright William Saroyan, who was born, lived and died in this city he loved dearly.

Sights & Activities

Downtown lies between Divisadero St, Hwy 41 and Hwy 99. Two miles north, the Tower District sits around the corner of E Olive Ave and N Fulton Ave.

Forestiere Underground Gardens BOTANICAL GARDENS

(☎559-271-0734; www.undergroundgardens.info; 5021 W Shaw Ave; adult/child $12/7; ⊙tours 11am-2pm hourly Thu-Fri, 10am, 11am, noon, 1:30pm & 2:30pm Sat & Sun) If you see only one thing in Fresno, make it this, two blocks east of Hwy 99. The gardens are the singular result of Sicilian immigrant Baldasare Forestiere, who dug out some 70 acres beneath the hardpan soil to plant citrus trees, starting in 1906. With a unique skylight system, he created a beautiful subterranean space for commercial crops and his own living quarters. Some fruit trees grow to full maturity with the sun only from the skylights. The tunnel system includes bedrooms, a library, patios, grottos and a fish pond, and is now a historic landmark. This utterly fantastical accomplishment took Forestiere some 40 years to complete and when he died in 1946 he left behind one of the Central Valley's most intriguing attractions.

Tower Theatre HISTORIC BUILDING

(☎559-485-9050; www.towertheaterfresno.com; 815 E Olive Ave) Fresno's **Tower District** began as a shopping mecca during the 1920s, gaining its name from the Tower Theatre, a beautiful art deco movie house that opened in 1939. The theater is now used as a center for the performing arts. Surrounding it are bookstores, shops, high-end restaurants and coffeehouses, which cater to Fresno's gay and alternative communities. This is the city's best neighborhood for browsing and kicking back with an iced latte – even if the hipster quotient is tiny by comparison to that of, say, San Francisco's Mission District.

Fresno Art Museum ART MUSEUM

(☎559-441-4221; www.fresnoartmuseum.org; 2233 N 1st St; adult/student $4/2, Tue admission free; ⊙11am-5pm Fri-Wed, to 8pm Thu) In Radio Park, this museum has rotating exhibits of contemporary art – including work by local artists – that are among the most intriguing in the valley.

HOMEWORK ON CALIFORNIA'S HEARTLAND

» *Where I Was From* (2003) – Joan Didion

» *The Grapes of Wrath* (1939) – John Steinbeck

» *The Other California* (1990) – Gerald Haslam

» *Proud to Be an Okie: Cultural Politics, Country Music, and Migration to Southern California* (2007) – Peter La Chapelle

» *Cadillac Desert* (1986) – Marc Reisner

Fresno Metropolitan Museum of Art & Science SCIENCE MUSEUM
(☎559-441-1444; www.fresnomet.org; 1515 Van Ness Ave; adult/child under 2yr/child 3-12yr/students & seniors $9/free/5/7; ⏲10am-6pm Fri-Wed, to 8pm Thu;) A favorite with children, the recently renovated museum has hands-on science exhibits, Native American crafts, a large collection of antique puzzles and a William Saroyan gallery. The museum's holdings also include a large collection of Ansel Adams photographs. After major renovations, hours and fees are in flux, so be sure to confirm via phone before visiting.

Roeding Park PARK
(per vehicle $3) On Olive Ave just east of Hwy 99, this large and shady park is home to the small **Chaffee Zoological Gardens** (☎559-498-2671; www.fresnochaffeezoo.com; adult/child $7/3.50; ⏲9am-4pm;). Adjacent to it are **Storyland** (☎559-264-2235; adult/child $4/3; ⏲10am-5:30pm Sat & Sun, with seasonal variations;), a kitschy children's fairytale world dating from 1962, and **Playland** (adult/child $5/3.50;), which has kiddie rides and games.

Sleeping & Eating

Fresno has room to grow when it comes to world-class accommodations, but those using it as a launch pad for visiting Sequoia and Kings Canyon National Parks have plenty of options, either in slightly weathered midcentury structures on Hwy 99, a cluster of chains near the airport or a couple of high-rise offerings downtown. For food, the best stuff is found in the Tower District, though there's a strip of places catering to college students (read: insane beer and chicken-wing specials).

Piccadilly Inn Shaw HOTEL $$
(☎559-226-3850; www.picadillyinn.com; 2305 W Shaw Ave; r $119-179;) This is Fresno's nicest option, with a lovely pool, big rooms and tons of amenities. Ask for a room with a fireplace to cuddle by in winter. If they are full, try one of their other properties in town: Piccadilly Inn University, the Piccadilly Inn Express and the Piccadilly Inn Airport.

TOP CHOICE **Dusty Buns Bistro Bus** FOOD TRUCK $
(www.dustybuns.com, http://twitter.com/dustybunsbistro; mains $7; ⏲lunch Wed-Sun hours vary) This brightly painted bus dishes out organic, seasonal sandwiches which have single handedly actualized Fresno's would-be foodie culture. The young couple in the drivers' seat has made the business as exciting as their signature Dusty Bun (a brilliant little number of chipotle roast chicken and sesame cucumber summer slaw on a bun) by announcing the hours, location and menu via

BLOODLESS BULLFIGHTS

Bullfighting has been illegal in the USA since 1957, but there are exceptions to the rule. When Portuguese communities in the Central Valley have *festas* (religious festivals) they are permitted to stage bloodless bullfights. The *festas* are huge events, attracting as many as 25,000 Portuguese Americans, and the bullfights are generally the climax of several days of parades, food, music and beauty contests.

Portuguese fishermen and farmers, mostly from the Azores, began settling in California during the late 19th century. The communities grew, especially in the Central Valley, with steady immigration continuing until very recently. Many people in the valley still speak Portuguese fluently and attend the *festas* that are held up and down the state.

Festas are largely cultural events, typically to honor religious icons such as St Anthony or Our Lady of Fátima. Candlelight processions, folk dancing, blessing of the cows, performances of *pezinho* songs (sad melodies with a lilting violin accompaniment) and eating until you feel like a plump sausage are all part of the experience. The *festa* queen contests are taken very seriously by the contestants.

Festas are held throughout the summer, with major events in Hanford, Gustine (along Hwy 33, north of the junction of I-5 and Hwy 152) and Stevinson (east of Gustine). They're not well publicized and the relevant websites that go up are often temporary. The only reliable thing to do is search 'festas california' and see what comes up in English.

their Twitter feed. Seem like a highbrow lark doomed to wither in little ol' Fresno? There's plenty of time to ponder that question while waiting in the lines that stretch around the block.

Loving Hut THAI $
(www.lovinghut.us; 1495 N Van Ness Ave; mains $7; 11am-2pm & 5-8pm Wed-Sat;) The star of this excellent vegan place, situated just off the Tower District in an old Craftsman house, is the 'Heavenly Rhelms,' a savory plate of BBQ fake-chicken drumsticks. The 'Ocean of Love' ain't half bad either, it's a vegan dish cooked in black pepper sauce, sided with rice and steamed veggies. Amid the valley's cow country, this place is a vegetarian's dream come true.

Grand Marie's Chicken Pie Shop AMERICAN $
(559-237-5042; 2861 E Olive Ave; mains $5-12; breakfast & lunch daily, dinner Mon-Sat) With a ladle of gravy and a flaky crust, the beautiful chicken-stuffed pies at this chipper Tower District stalwart bear no resemblance to the frozen, soggy mess of your childhood. Breakfast is also supreme thanks to buttery biscuits.

Sam's Italian Deli & Market DELI $
(2415 N First St; mains $5-9; 8:30am-6pm Mon-Sat) This Italian market and deli is the real deal, stacking up the 'New Yorker' pastrami and some mean prosciutto and mozzarella.

Entertainment

Tower Theatre for the Performing Arts PERFORMING ARTS
(www.towertheatrefresno.com; 815 E Olive Ave) In the center of Fresno's hippest neighborhood, it's hard to miss the neon phallus, a stunning deco palace that opens its stage to touring rock and jazz acts and ballet, and seasonal cultural events.

Information

Fresno Convention & Visitors Bureau (559-237-0988, 800-788-0836; www.fresnocvb.org; cnr Fresno & O Sts; 10am-4pm Mon-Fri, 11am-3pm Sat) Inside the Fresno Water Tower.

Getting There & Around

Fresno Yosemite International Airport Just east of the center of town is this dreary if serviceable two-runway strip surrounded by chain hotels. The 'Yosemite' and 'International' elements of the name are generous – it's a two-hour drive to the interior of the park and the only air service outside the States is to Mexico City.

Fresno Area Express (FAX; 559-488-1122; one-way fare $1.25) The local service that has daily bus services to the Tower District (bus 22 or 26) and Forestiere Underground Gardens (bus 20, transfer to bus 9) from the downtown transit center at Van Ness Ave and Fresno St.

Greyhound (559-268-1829; 1033 Broadway) Stops downtown near the new ballpark. One-way trips to or from Los Angeles are $39. One way between Fresno and San Francisco is $29.50 (five hours, five daily).

Visalia

Its agricultural prosperity and well-maintained downtown make Visalia one of the valley's most charming places to stay en route to Sequoia and Kings Canyon National Parks or the Sierra Peaks. Bypassed a century ago by the railroad, the city is 5 miles east of Hwy 99, along Hwy 198. Its downtown has great old buildings and makes for a nice stroll.

Sights & Activities

The original Victorian and Arts-and-Crafts-style homes in Visalia are architectural gems worth viewing on foot. Get information about a self-guided walking tour from the **Visalia Chamber of Commerce & Visitor Center** (www.visaliatourism.com; 720 W Mineral King Ave; 8:30am-5pm Mon-Fri). The tour leads north of Main St on both N Willis and Encina Sts.

Kaweah Oak Preserve NATURE PRESERVE
About 7 miles east of Visalia is Kaweah Oak Preserve, home to 324 acres of valley oak trees, which once stretched from the Sierras to (long-gone) Tulare Lake in the valley. Nice for a short hike, it's a rare glimpse into the valley's past before orchards and vineyards took over. From Hwy 198, turn north onto Rd 182; the park is about a half-mile along on your left.

Cellar Door LIVE MUSIC
(www.cellardoorvisalia.com; cnr W Main & Court Sts) Visalia is blessed with this great small venue, which snags touring indie acts from well beyond the Central Valley. They also have a big wine list and host open mic nights.

SCENIC DRIVE: THE BLOSSOM TRAIL

When the Central Valley's trees blossom, the roads surrounding Visalia make for a stunning, leisurely afternoon drive past citrus and vineyards. The 62-mile **Blossom Trail** (www.gofresnocounty.com) is an excellent scenic drive between February and March, when everything is flowering (those with allergies beware). You a get a map of the route at the Fresno City & County Convention and Visitors Bureau, but a DIY trip can be just as pretty. Pull out a roadmap and start navigating back roads between Reedley, Orange Cove, Selma and Kingsburg.

The last of these is another Central Valley town with a striking ethnic heritage – the town was founded by Swedish farmers and its Main St is decked out with bright red and yellow Dala Horses, Swedish gift shops and buttery bakeries.

Fox Theatre LIVE MUSIC
(☎box office 559-625-1369; www.foxvisalia.org; cnr W Main & Encina Sts) The gloriously restored 1930 theater hosts concerts, classic films and special events.

Sleeping & Eating

There are tons of dining options, including a spread of ethnic food, in the middle of town. If you want to follow your nose just wander down Main St between Floral and Bridge Sts.

Spalding House B&B $
(☎559-739-7877; www.thespaldinghouse.com; 631 N Encina St; r $95; ❄) This B&B has three classy suites, each with an antique bed, a sitting room and a modern bathroom. The full-on breakfasts will get you going in the morning, and you can tickle the keys of the 1923 Steinway piano in the parlor all evening.

TOP CHOICE **Brewbaker's Brewing Company** BREWPUB $
(www.brewbakersbrewingco.com; 219 E Main St; mains $6-12; ⏰11:30am-10pm; 📶) A wait is normal on busy weekends at Brewbaker's, but the microbrews are worth it, particularly the smooth flagship Sequoia Red or chocolatey Possum Porter. The atmosphere is downright classy – brightly polished copper tanks and Tiffany-style stained-glass fixtures – which is befitting of the well-executed pub food.

The Vintage Press CALIFORNIAN $$$
(☎559-733-3033; www.thevintagepress.com; 216 N Willits; mains $12-29; ⏰11:30am-2pm & 5:30pm-10pm Mon-Sat, 10am-9pm Sun) Red leather booths, stained glass and dark woods suggest the fairly buttoned-up Continental fare at this long-running Central Valley fine-dining destination. It hasn't gotten hip to the local eating trend – the menu includes an Australian lobster, New Zealand lamb rack and Hawaiian fish – but it's grilled and sautéed to the delight of the moneyed ranchers who come here to celebrate anniversaries.

Getting There & Away

Amtrak (www.amtrak.com) Shuttles connect with the station in Hanford by reservation only. From Hanford, riders can connect to all other Amtrak routes in the state, including the *San Joaquin*, which travels north to Sacramento ($31, four hours, two direct services daily) or south to Bakersfield ($16, 1½ hours, six trains daily).

Bakersfield

Nearing Bakersfield, the landscape is dotted with evidence of California's *other* gold rush: rusting rigs alongside the route burrow into Southern California's vast oil fields. Oil was discovered here in the late 1800s, and Kern County, the southernmost county on Hwy 99, still pumps more than some OPEC countries. (This is the setting of Upton Sinclair's *Oil!*, which was adapted into the 2007 Academy Award–winning film, *There Will Be Blood*.) In the 1930s the oil attracted a stream of 'Okies' – farmers who migrated out of the dusty Great Plains – to work the derricks (see boxed text, p348). The children of these tough-as-nails roughnecks minted the 'Bakersfield Sound' in the mid-1950s, with heroes Buck Owens and Merle Haggard waving a defiant middle finger to the silky Nashville establishment (see boxed text, p347 for a Bakersfield roadtrip soundtrack).

As Bakersfield tries to become all sophisticated like some of its valley neighbors, it has an uneasy relationship with the rhinestone-studded country pluckers of its past. Much of the twangy Bakersfield sound went to the grave with Buck Owens, who passed away in 2006.

Though some parts of town are rather shabby, downtown holds some real surprises in its upbeat mix of restored buildings, county offices, restaurants and antique shops, such as the **Five and Dime** (cnr 19th & K Sts; ⊙10am-5pm Mon-Sat, noon-5pm Sun) inside an original Woolworth's building. The 1930 **Fox Theater** hosts regular performances; Merle Haggard was on the marquee during a recent visit.

Sights

The Kern River flows along Bakersfield's northern edge, separating it from its blue-collar neighbor, Oildale, and a host of oil fields. Truxtun and Chester Aves are the main downtown thoroughfares. Though currently suffering from a bit of neglect, Old Town Kern, located east of downtown around Baker and Sumner Sts, was once a bustling centre. It certainly makes for an interesting view into the region's decaying past. The **Bakersfield Historic Preservation Commission** (www.bakersfieldcity.us/edcd/historic/) has downloadable maps of walking tours covering Old Town Kern and Bakersfield's historic downtown.

Kern County Museum & Lori Brock Children's Discovery Center MUSEUM
(www.kcmuseum.org; 3801 Chester Ave; adult/student $10/9; ⊙10am-5pm Wed-Sun,) This museum has a pioneer village with more than 50 restored and replicated buildings. The musty main structure has a large (and fairly disturbing) display of the area's taxidermied wildlife. On the 2nd floor waits a collection of pristine memorabilia from Bakersfield's musical heyday.

California Living Museum ZOO
(www.calmzoo.org; 10500 Alfred Harrell Hwy; adult/child $9/5; ⊙9am-5pm;) A half-hour northeast of town, the zoo and botanical gardens have a menagerie of native animals, including black bear and bald eagles. Kids will squirm in the rattlesnake house, which has every type of rattler in the state. It's about a 20-minute drive from downtown Bakersfield.

Sleeping & Eating

Chain motels line the highways near Bakersfield like weeds. Old-school budget motels, starting from about $35, line Union Ave heading south from Hwy 178, though some are pretty shady. Bakersfield is blessed with a clutch of traditional Basque restaurants, where food is served family-style in a series of courses including soup, salad, beans and thin slices of tangy beef tongue. All this comes *before* the main course, so arrive hungry.

TOP CHOICE **Padre Hotel** BOUTIQUE HOTEL $$
(☎661-427-4900; www.thepadrehotel.com; 1702 8th St; r $89-199, ste from $500;) After standing vacant for years, this historic tower found long-sought investors and opened with a blindingly stylish facelift, including an upscale restaurant and pair of bars that instantly became *the* place for cocktails in Bakersfield. The standard rooms have lush details: foam beds, thick sheets and designer furniture. The two themed suites – the 'Oil Baron' and 'Farmer's Daughter' – are *way* over the top, with velvet wallpaper, leather couches and showers for two. Did

KINGS OF BAKERSFIELD SOUND

Driving down Hwy 99 requires getting on a first-name basis with Bakersfield's two drawling titans: Merle and Buck. Masters of twanging Telecasters and hayseed heartbreak, they're country kings of the Central Valley.

» 'I'm Gonna Break Every Heart I Can' – Merle Haggard
» 'I've Got A Tiger by the Tail' – Buck Owens
» 'Okie from Muskogee' – Merle Haggard
» 'Second Fiddle' – Buck Owens
» 'The Bottle Let Me Down' – Merle Haggard
» 'Under Your Spell Again' – Buck Owens
» 'Swinging Doors' – Merle Haggard
» 'The Streets of Bakersfield' – Buck Owens and Dwight Yoakam

we mention the suite with the 'stripper pole' in the shower?

TOP CHOICE **Noriega Hotel** BASQUE $$
(☎661-322-8419; www.noriegahotel.com; 525 Sumner St; lunch $14, dinner $20; ⊙Tue-Sun) Surly Basque gentlemen pat their ample stomachs, joke in several languages and pass around the communal bottles of zinfandel at Bakersfield's last remaining family-style Basque institution. Join diners at a long communal table for a rotating offering of silky oxtail stew, pork chops and veal. The ambience is simply magic – long tables and checkered floors, black-and-white photos of the multigenerational owners – all of which likely helped them to win a prestigious James Beard award. Note that dining hours are strict (breakfast 7am to 9am, lunch at noon, dinner at 7pm).

Dewar's Candy Shop ICE CREAM $
(www.dewarscandy.com; 1120 Eye St; ice cream $3-10; ⊙11am-9pm Mon-Thu, to 10pm Fri & Sat) Perched on the pastel stools at the counter, families dig into homemade ice cream with ingredients sourced from surrounding farms. Dreamy flavors like lemon flake and cotton candy change seasonally.

Luigi's ITALIAN $
(www.shopluigis.com; 725 E 19th St; mains $6-12; ⊙lunch Tue-Sat) Lined with black-and-white photos of sporting legends, this amazing lunch spot has been around over 100 years. The stuffed chicken melts in your mouth and the excellent bakery turns out soft, buttery rolls and an amazingly rich Butterfinger Pie. Vegetarian options include a mushroom ravioli in sage butter sauce.

Jake's Original Tex Mex Cafe SOUTHWESTERN $
(www.jakestexmex.com; 1710 Oak E St; mains $7-14; ⊙lunch & dinner Mon-Sat) More Tex than Mex, this excellent cafeteria packs in city workers for smoky slow-roasted pit beef. The chili fries are a messy delight, and Herb's Belcher Spuds are as decadent as the name suggests.

Wool Growers BASQUE $
(☎661-327-9584; www.woolgrowers.net; 620 E 19th St; mains $7-20; ⊙lunch & dinner Mon-Sat) Another simple Basque eating hall loaded with character. A fried chicken dinner will leave you full for a week.

☆ Entertainment

TOP CHOICE **Buck Owens' Crystal Palace** LIVE MUSIC
(☎661-328-7560; www.buckowens.com; 2800 Buck Owens Blvd) For fans of the city's plucky musical heritage, this is the first stop – hard to miss thanks to the huge neon sign in the shape of Buck's famous red, white and blue guitar. Part music museum, part honkytonk, part steakhouse, the Palace has a top-drawer country act on stage every night, and locals in meticulous snap-button shirts, shiny boots and pressed jeans tear up the dance floor.

Trout's & the Blackboard Stage HONKY-TONK
(www.troutsblackboard.com; 805 N Chester Ave at Decatur St) The legendary Trout's, in neigh-

WORTH A TRIP

WEEDPATCH LABOR CAMP

In the years following the Depression, Kern County boasted California's highest proportion of poor white farm laborers from the South and the Great Plains. Called 'Okies' (whether they came from Oklahoma or not), they came with dreams of a new life in the fields the Golden State. The majority, though, found only migrant labor jobs and continued hardship.

Dating from 1935, this Farm Security Administration labor camp (the model for 'Weedpatch Camp' in *The Grapes of Wrath*) was one of about 16 in the US set up at the time to aid migrant workers – and it's the only one with any original buildings left. After some recent restoration, the camp sparkles with a surreal sheen, but it remains a fascinating vision into the past – and a wake-up call to the continuing dichotomy between corporate agribusiness and its strife with the migrant workforce. From Bakersfield, take Hwy 58 east to Weedpatch Hwy; head south for about 7 miles, past Lamont; then turn left on Sunset Blvd, driving another mile. The buildings (the sign reads 'Arvin Farm Labor Center') are on your right. **Dust Bowl Days** (www.weedpatchcamp.com) is a celebration of Okie history held here each October.

boring Oildale, is the only remaining honky-tonk in these parts, hobbling along after half a century as a testament to the hell-raisin' days gone by. Expect no Crystal Palace – the parking lot glistens only in broken glass and the bartender is one salty princess – but the live music comes from Bakersfield legends and their disciples. Monday is a memorable 'Seniors Night.'

Information

Greater Bakersfield Convention & Visitors Bureau (661-325-5051; www.bakersfieldcvb.org; 515 Truxtun Ave; 8:30am-5pm Mon-Fri) Carries maps and brochures.

Getting There & Around

Airport Bus of Bakersfield (805-395-0635; 2530 F St) Runs a shuttle seven times daily between Bakersfield and LAX ($32, 2½ hours).

Amtrak station (661-395-3175; 601 Truxtun Ave at S St) Trains head north from here to Sacramento ($43 to $77, five hours, two direct trains). Buses head to LA ($16 to $33), though only available in combination with a train ticket.

Golden Empire Transit (GET; www.getbus.org; basic fare 90¢) The local bus system. Route 2 runs north on Chester Ave to the Kern County Museum and Oildale.

Greyhound (661-327-5617; 1820 18th St) Depot is downtown near the Padre Hotel.

Kern River Area

A half-century ago the Kern River originated on the slopes of Mt Whitney and journeyed close to 170 miles before finally settling into Buena Vista Lake in the Central Valley. Now, after its wild ride from the high country – where the river drops an incredible 60ft per mile – it's dammed in several places and almost entirely tapped for agricultural use after hitting the valley floor. Its upper reaches, declared wild and scenic by the Secretary of the Interior, is nicknamed the 'Killer Kern' for its occasionally lethal force, but there's no denying it provides some of the best rafting in the Western US.

Hwy 178 follows the dramatic **Kern River Canyon**, making for a stunning drive through the lower reaches of Sequoia National Forest. East of the lake, Hwy 178 winds another 50 miles through a picturesque mixture of pine and Joshua trees before reaching Hwy 395.

There are two **USFS Ranger Stations** in the area; one in Kernville (760-376-3781; 105 Whitney Rd; 8am-4:30pm Mon-Fri) and another in Lake Isabella (760-379-5646; 4875 Ponderosa Dr; 8am-4:30pm). Both have hiking and camping information, maps and wilderness permits.

Sights & Activities

This part of the state is all about the white water, and rafting is the banner attraction for visitors. The town of **Lake Isabella** is a dreary strip of local businesses on the south end of the lake, but Hwy 155 runs north, around the west side to **Kernville**, a cute little town straddling the Kern River. The town is *the* hub for rafting in the area. While the lake is popular for cooling off, note that the river's deceptively strong currents can be extremely dangerous.

The Upper Kern and Forks of the Kern (both sections of the river north of Kernville) yield Class IV and V rapids during spring runoff and offer some of the most awe-inspiring white-water trips in the country. You'll need experience before tackling these sections, though there are plenty more opportunities for novices. Below Lake Isabella, the Kern is tamer and steadier.

Currently five rafting companies are licensed to operate out of Kernville; all offer competitive prices and run trips from May to August, depending on conditions. Excursions include popular one-hour runs ($30), day-long Lower Kern trips ($150 to $190) and multiday Forks of the Kern wilderness experiences ($600 to $920). Walk-ups are welcome and experience is not necessary. Kids aged six and up can usually participate too.

Mountain & River Adventures RAFTING, OUTDOOR OUTFITTERS
(800-861-6553, 760-376-6553; www.mtnriver.com; 11113 Kernville Rd) Offers rafting trips, guided climbing and camping excursions.

Sierra South RAFTING
(760-376-3745, 800-457-2082; www.sierrasouth.com; 11300 Kernville Rd)

Whitewater Voyages RAFTING
(800-400-7238, 660-376-8806; www.whitewatervoyages.com)

Sleeping

Lake Isabella has motels, but Kernville is a nicer location with more reasonable rates.

Many of Kernville's motels have two-day minimum stays on weekends.

USFS campgrounds CAMPGROUND $
(☎877-444-6777; developed/undeveloped sites $12/16) These campgrounds line the 10-mile stretch between Lake Isabella and Kernville, and several more lie north of Kernville on Mtn 99. Rangers recommend the Fairview and Limestone sites for their seclusion. Any campground without running water and electricity is free.

Whispering Pines Lodge B&B $$$
(☎760-376-3733; www.kernvalley.com/whisperingpines; 13745 Sierra Way; r $219-299; ☒) This secluded B&B, blending rustic character with luxurious comfort, is just north of town.

Lake Tahoe

Includes »

Best Places to Eat

» Moody's Bistro & Lounge (p380)
» Café Fiore (p367)
» Wild Goose (p382)
» Fire Sign Café (p373)
» Dockside 700 Wine Bar & Grill (p375)

Best Places to Stay

» Cedar House Sport Hotel (p379)
» Plumpjack Squaw Valley Inn (p376)
» Tahoma Meadows Bed & Breakfast Cottages (p372)
» Deerfield Lodge at Heavenly (p365)
» Clair Tappaan Lodge (p379)

Why Go?

Shimmering in myriad shades of blue and green, Lake Tahoe is the USA's second-deepest lake and, at 6255ft high, it's also one of the highest-elevation lakes in the country. Generally speaking, the north shore is quiet and upscale; the west shore, rugged and old-timey; the east shore, undeveloped; and the south shore, busy and tacky, with aging motels and flashy casinos. Driving around the lake's spellbinding 72-mile scenic shoreline will give you quite a workout behind the wheel.

The horned peaks surrounding the lake, which straddles the California–Nevada state line, are year-round destinations. The sun shines on Tahoe three out of four days in the year. Swimming, boating, kayaking, windsurfing, stand-up paddle boarding and other water sports take over in summer, as do hiking, camping and wilderness backpacking adventures. Winter brings bundles of snow, perfect for those of all ages to hit the slopes at Tahoe's top-tier ski and snowboard resorts.

When to Go

South Lake Tahoe

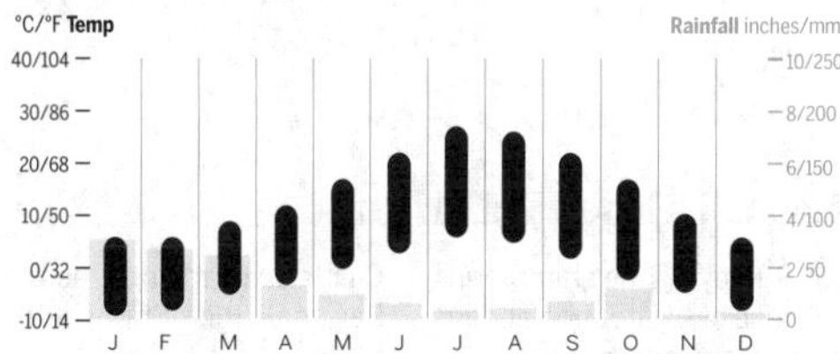

Jul–Aug Beach season; wildflowers bloom, and hiking and mountain-biking trails open.

Sep–Oct Cooler temperatures, colorful foliage and fewer tourists after Labor Day.

Dec–Mar Snow sports galore at resorts; storms bring hazardous roads.

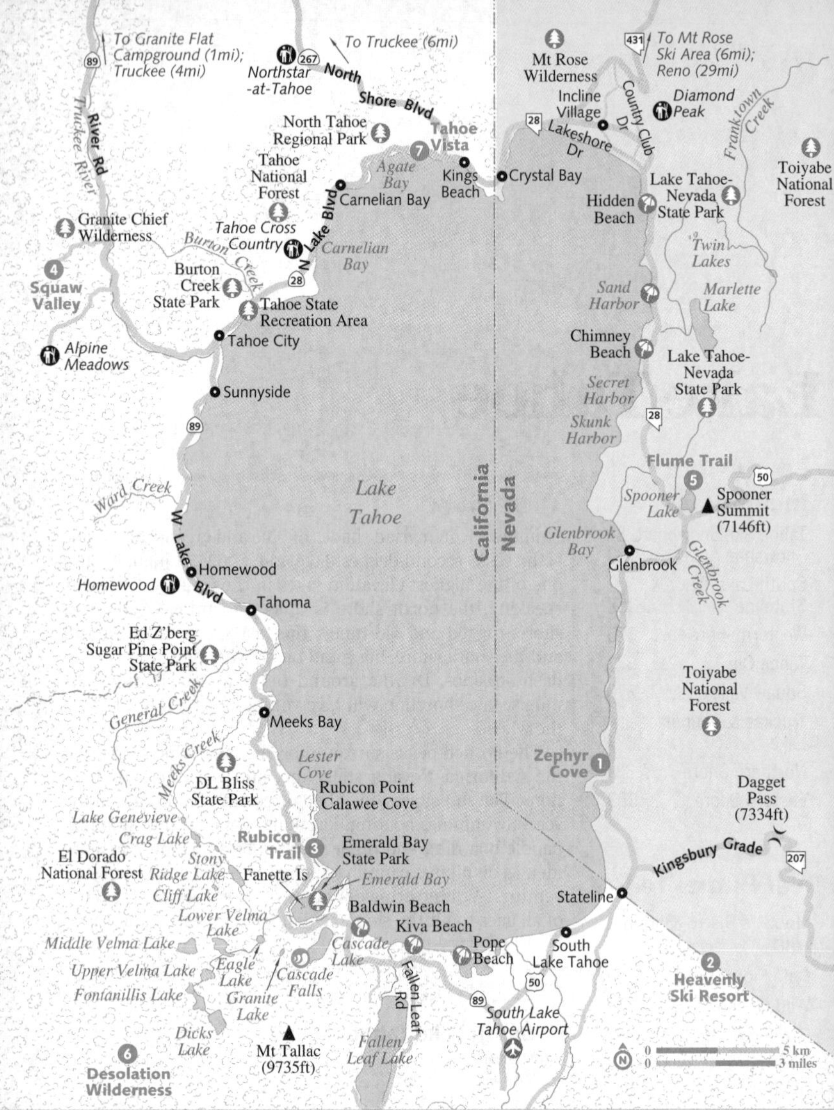

Lake Tahoe Highlights

1. Surveying the shimmering expanse of Lake Tahoe aboard a kayak or from the sandy beach at **Zephyr Cove** (p361)
2. Swooshing down the vertiginous double-black-diamond runs of **Heavenly ski resort** (p354)
3. Trekking the **Rubicon Trail** (p371) from Vikingsholm Castle on sparkling Emerald Bay, to DL Bliss State Park
4. Swimming in an outdoor lagoon, or ice-skating above 8000ft atop the cable-car line in **Squaw Valley** (p376)
5. Thundering down the **Flume Trail** (p384) on a mountain bike to tranquil Spooner Lake.
6. Escaping summer crowds with an overnight backpack to alpine lakes and high-country meadows in the **Desolation Wilderness** (p362)
7. Cozying up with your family around a lakefront beach firepit or inside a cozy cabin at **Tahoe Vista** (p381) on the no-fuss northern shore

Tahoe Ski, Snowboard & Snowshoe Areas

Lake Tahoe has phenomenal skiing, with thousands of acres of the white stuff beckoning at more than a dozen resorts. Winter-sports complexes range from the giant, jet-set slopes of Squaw Valley, Heavenly and Northstar-at-Tahoe, to the no less enticing insider playgrounds like Sugar Bowl and Homewood. Tahoe's simply got a hill for everybody, from kids to kamikazes.

Ski season generally runs November to April, although it can start as early as October, and last until the last storm whips through in May or even June. All resorts have ski schools, equipment rental and other facilities; check their websites for snow conditions, weather reports and ski-season shuttle buses from area lodgings.

Downhill Skiing & Snowboarding

Tahoe's downhill resorts are usually open every day from December through April, weather permitting. All of these resorts rent equipment and have places to warm up slopeside and grab a quick bite or après-ski beer. Most offer group ski and snowboard lessons for adults and children (a surcharge applies, but usually no reservations are required).

TRUCKEE & DONNER PASS

Northstar-at-Tahoe SKIING, SNOWBOARDING

(☎530-562-1010, 800-466-6784; www.northstarattahoe.com; 5001 Northstar Dr, off Hwy 267, Truckee; adult/child 5-12yr/youth 13-22yr $92/41/80; ⏰8:30am-4pm; 👪) An easy 7 miles south of I-80, this hugely popular resort has great intermediate terrain. Northstar's relatively sheltered location makes it the second-best choice after Homewood when it's snowing, and the seven terrain parks and pipes are top-ranked. Advanced and expert skiers can look for tree-skiing challenges on the back of the mountain, reached via a new high-speed lift. Recent additions to Northstar's 'Village' are making it look a lot more like amenity-rich Squaw. Weekends get superbusy. Stats: 19 lifts, 2280 vertical feet, 93 runs.

Sugar Bowl SKIING, SNOWBOARDING

(☎530-426-9000; www.sugarbowl.com; 629 Sugar Bowl Rd, off Donner Pass Rd, Truckee; adult/child 6-12yr/youth 13-22yr $71/23/59; ⏰9am-4pm; 👪) Cofounded by Walt Disney in 1939, this is one of the Sierra's oldest ski resorts and a miniature Squaw Valley in terms of variety of terrain, including plenty of exhilarating gullies and chutes. Views are stellar on sunny days, but conditions go downhill pretty quickly, so to speak, during stormy weather. It's 4 miles southeast of I-80 (exit Soda Springs/Norden). Stats: 13 lifts, 1500 vertical feet, 95 runs.

Boreal SKIING, SNOWBOARDING

(☎530-426-3666; www.borealski.com; 19659 Boreal Ridge Rd, off I-80 exit Castle Peak/Boreal Ridge Rd, Truckee; adult/child 5-12yr/teen 13-19yr $49/15/39, night-skiing adult/child 5-12yr $25/12; ⏰9am-9pm; 👪) Fun for newbies and intermediate skiers, Boreal is traditionally the first resort to open each year in the Tahoe area. For boarders, there are four terrain parks including a competition-level 450ft superpipe. Boreal is the only North Tahoe downhill resort besides Squaw that offers night skiing. Stats: nine lifts, 500 vertical feet, 41 runs.

Soda Springs SKIING, SNOWBOARDING

(☎530-426-3901; www.skisodasprings.com; 10244 Soda Springs Rd, off I-80 exit Soda Springs/Norden, Soda Springs; adult/child under 18yr $35/25, snowmobiling $10, tubing $25; ⏰9am-4pm Thu-Mon, daily during holidays; 👪) This cute little resort is a winner with kids, who can snow-tube, ride around in pint-sized snowmobiles, or learn to ski and snowboard. Stats: two lifts, 650 vertical feet, 16 runs.

Donner Ski Ranch SKIING, SNOWBOARDING

(☎530-426-3635; www.donnerskiranch.com; 19320 Donner Pass Rd, Norden; adult/child 7-12yr/teen 13-19yr $42/13/34; ⏰9am-4pm; 👪) Generations of skiers have enjoyed this itty-bitty family-owned resort. It's a great place to

FAST FACTS

» **Population of South Lake Tahoe** 21,403

» **Average temperature low/high in South Lake Tahoe** Jan 15/41°F, Jul 40/79°F

» **Reno, NV to Truckee** 35 miles, 40 to 60 minutes

» **Tahoe City to South Lake Tahoe/Stateline, NV** 30 miles, 1 to 1½ hours

» **Truckee to San Francisco** 190 miles, 3½ to five hours

Tahoe Ski & Snowboard Areas

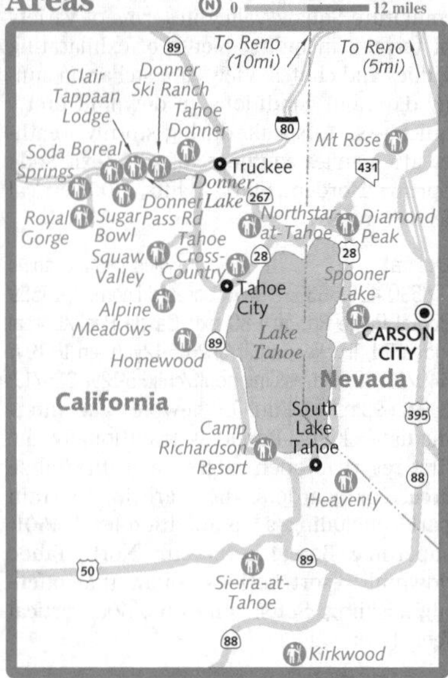

teach your kids how to ski, or for beginners to build skills. Prices drop after 12:30pm. It's 3.5 miles southeast of I-80, exit Soda Springs/Norden. Stats: six lifts, 750 vertical feet, 52 runs.

Tahoe Donner SKIING, SNOWBOARDING

(☎530-587-9444; www.skitahoedonner.com; 11603 Snowpeak Way, off I-80 exit Donner Pass Rd, Truckee; adult/child 7-12yr $39/19; ⏲9am-4pm; 👪) Small, low-key and low-tech, Tahoe Donner is a darling resort with family-friendly beginner and intermediate runs only. Stats: four lifts, 600 vertical feet, 14 runs.

TAHOE CITY & AROUND

TOP CHOICE **Squaw Valley** SKIING, SNOWBOARDING

(☎530-583-6985, 800-403-0206; www.squaw.com; 1960 Squaw Valley Rd, off Hwy 89, Olympic Valley; adult/child under 13yr/teen 13-19yr $88/10/64; ⏲9am-7pm Mon-Thu, to 9pm Fri-Sun) Few ski hounds can resist the siren call of this mega-sized, world-class, see-and-be-seen resort that hosted the 1960 Winter Olympic Games. Hardcore skiers thrill to white-knuckle cornices, chutes and bowls, while beginners practice their turns in a separate area on the upper mountain. Coming attractions: upgraded terrain parks, including a gnarly superpipe. The valley turn-off is 5 miles northwest of Tahoe City. Stats: 34 lifts, 2850 vertical feet, over 170 runs.

Alpine Meadows SKIING, SNOWBOARDING

(☎530-583-4232, 800-441-4423; www.skialpine.com; 2600 Alpine Meadows Rd, off Hwy 89, Tahoe City; adult/child 5-12yr/teen 13-19yr $69/15/54; ⏲9am-4pm) Alpine is a no-nonsense resort without the fancy village, attitude or crowds. It gets more snow than neighboring Squaw and its open-boundary policy makes it the most backcountry-friendly around. Boarders jib down the mountain in a terrain park designed by Eric Rosenwald. Also look for the adorable – and supersmart – ski patrol dogs. The turn-off is 4 miles northwest of Tahoe City. Stats: 13 lifts, 1800 vertical feet, 100 runs.

Homewood SKIING, SNOWBOARDING

(☎530-525-2992; www.skihomewood.com; 5145 Westlake Blvd, off Hwy 89; adult/child 5-12yr/teen 13-19yr Fri-Sun $61/15/42; ⏲9am-4pm; 👪) Larger than it looks from the road, this gem, 6 miles south of Tahoe City, proves that bigger isn't always better. Locals and in-the-know visitors cherish the awesome lake views, laid-back ambience, smaller crowds, tree-lined slopes, open bowls (including the excellent but expert 'Quail Face') and a high-speed quad that gets things moving. Families love the wide, gentle slopes. It's also the best place to ski during stormy weather. Stats: seven lifts, 1650 vertical feet, 60 runs.

SOUTH LAKE TAHOE

Heavenly SKIING, SNOWBOARDING

(☎775-586-7000, 800-432-8365; www.skiheavenly.com; 3860 Saddle Rd, South Lake Tahoe; adult/child 5-12yr/teen 13-19yr $90/50/78; ⏲9am-4pm Mon-Fri, 8:30am-4pm Sat, Sun & holidays) The 'mother' of all Tahoe mountains boasts the most acreage, the longest run (5.5 miles) and the biggest vertical drop around. Follow the sun by skiing on the Nevada side in the morning, moving to the California side in the afternoon. Views of the lake and the high desert are heavenly indeed. Five terrain parks won't strand snowboarders of any skill level, with the High Roller for experts only. Stats: 30 lifts, 3500 vertical feet, 94 runs.

Kirkwood SKIING, SNOWBOARDING

(☎209-258-6000; www.kirkwood.com; 1501 Kirkwood Meadows Dr, off Hwy 88, Kirkwood; adult/child 6-12yr/teen 13-19yr $79/20/62; ⏲9am-4pm) Off-the-beaten-path Kirkwood, set in a high-elevation valley, gets great snow and holds it longer than almost any other Tahoe resort. It has stellar tree-skiing, gullies, chutes and terrain parks, and is the only Tahoe resort with backcountry runs accessible by snowcats. Novice out-of-bounds skiers should sign up in advance for backcountry safety-skills clinics. It's 35 miles southwest of South Lake Tahoe via Hwy 89; ski-season shuttles are available (from $15). Stats: 14 lifts, 2000 vertical feet, 72 runs.

Sierra-at-Tahoe SNOWBOARDING, SKIING
(☎530-659-7453; www.sierraattahoe.com; 1111 Sierra-at-Tahoe-Rd, off Hwy 50, Twin Bridges; adult/child 5-12yr/youth 13-22yr $75/18/65; ⏲9am-4pm Mon-Fri, 8:30am-4pm Sat, Sun & holidays; 👪) About 18 miles southwest of South Lake Tahoe, this is snowboarding central, with five raging terrain parks and a 17ft-high superpipe. A great beginners' run meanders gently for 2.5 miles from the summit, but there are also gnarly steeps and chutes for speed demons. Kids get four 'adventure zones' while adults-only Huckleberry Gates tempts with steep-and-deep backcountry terrain for experts. Stats: 14 lifts, 2200 vertical feet, 46 runs.

NEVADA

Mt Rose SKIING, SNOWBOARDING
☎775-849-0704, 800-754-7673; www.mtrose.com; 22222 Mt Rose Hwy/Hwy 431, Reno; adult/child 6-12yr/teen 13-19yr $69/19/55; ⏲9am-4pm) Conveniently the closest ski resort to Reno, Mt Rose has Tahoe's highest base elevation (8260ft) and offers four terrain parks and good snow conditions well into spring. 'The Chutes' expert terrain delivers some screamers along its north-facing steeps. Crowds aren't too bad, but the mountain's exposure means it gets hammered in a storm and avalanche control may intermittently close runs. Stats: eight lifts, 1800 vertical feet, 60 runs.

Diamond Peak SKIING, SNOWBOARDING
(☎775-832-1177, 877-468-4397; www.diamondpeak.com; 1210 Ski Way, off Tahoe Blvd/Hwy 28, Incline Village; adult/child 7-14yr/youth 15-17yr $49/18/39; ⏲9am-4pm; 👪) This midsize mountain is a good place to learn, and boarders can romp around the terrain park, but experts get bored quickly. From the top you'll have a 360-degree panorama of desert, peaks and the lake. Free ski-season shuttle from Incline Village and Crystal Bay. Stats: six lifts, 1840 vertical feet, 30 runs.

Cross-Country Skiing & Snowshoeing

Tahoe's cross-country ski resorts are usually open daily from December through March, and sometimes into April. Most rent equipment and offer lessons; reservations typically aren't taken for either, so show up early in the morning for the best availability.

TRUCKEE & DONNER PASS

TOP CHOICE **Royal Gorge** SKIING, SNOWSHOEING
(☎530-426-3871; www.royalgorge.com; 9411 Hillside Dr, off I-80 exit Soda Springs/Norden, Soda Springs; adult/child Sat & Sun $29/18, Mon-Fri $25/16; ⏲9am-5pm Mon-Fri, 8:30am-5pm Sat & Sun; 👪) Nordic skiing aficionados won't want to pass up a spin around North America's largest cross-country resort with its mind-boggling 205 miles of groomed track crisscrossing 9000 acres of terrain on 90 trails. It has great skating lanes and diagonal stride tracks and also welcomes telemark skiers and snowshoers. Group lessons are offered a few times daily, with ski camps for kids ages 6 to 12 (reservations recommended). Consider overnighting at one of the resort's two cozy lodges.

Tahoe Donner SKIING, SNOWSHOEING
(☎530-587-9484; www.tdxc.com; 15275 Alder Creek Rd, off I-80 exit Donner Pass Rd, Truckee;

WINTER DRIVING AROUND LAKE TAHOE

From late fall through early spring, always pack snow chains in case a storm rolls in. Chains can also be purchased and installed in towns along I-80 and Hwy 50. Also stash some emergency supplies (eg blankets, water, flashlights) in the trunk, just in case your car breaks down, traffic gets tied up or roads close completely due to snowfall or avalanche danger.

Before hopping in the car and driving up to Tahoe, check road closures and conditions with:

California Department of Transportation (Caltrans; ☎800-427-7623; www.dot.ca.gov)

Nevada Department of Transportation (NDOT; ☎877-687-6237, 511 within Nevada; www.safetravelusa.com/nv)

Lake Tahoe

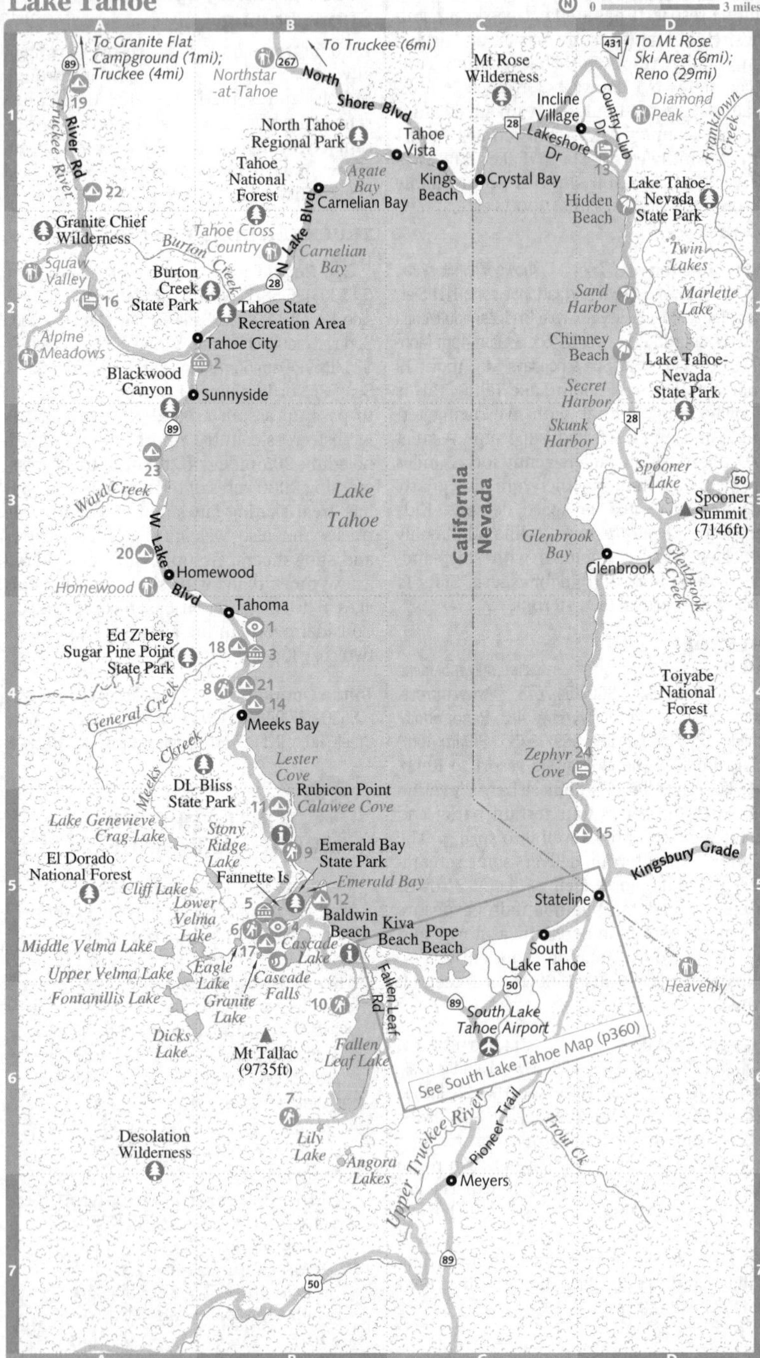
0 5 km
0 3 miles
To Granite Flat Campground (1mi); Truckee (4mi)
To Truckee (6mi)
Northstar-at-Tahoe
North Shore Blvd
Mt Rose Wilderness
To Mt Rose Ski Area (6mi); Reno (29mi)
Incline Village
Country Club Dr
Lakeshore Dr
Diamond Peak
Franktown Creek
North Tahoe Regional Park
Tahoe Vista
Kings Beach
Crystal Bay
Truckee River
River Rd
Tahoe National Forest
Agate Bay
Carnelian Bay
Lake Tahoe-Nevada State Park
Hidden Beach
Granite Chief Wilderness
Tahoe Cross Country
N Lake Blvd
Carnelian Bay
Burton Creek
Twin Lakes
Squaw Valley
Burton Creek State Park
Sand Harbor
Marlette Lake
Tahoe State Recreation Area
Tahoe City
Alpine Meadows
Chimney Beach
Lake Tahoe-Nevada State Park
Blackwood Canyon
Sunnyside
Secret Harbor
Skunk Harbor
Spooner Lake
Ward Creek
Lake Tahoe
California
Nevada
Spooner Summit (7146ft)
W Lake Blvd
Glenbrook Bay
Glenbrook
Glenbrook Creek
Homewood
Homewood
Tahoma
Ed Z'berg Sugar Pine Point State Park
Toiyabe National Forest
General Creek
Meeks Bay
Meeks Ckreek
Lester Cove
Zephyr Cove
DL Bliss State Park
Rubicon Point
Calawee Cove
Lake Genevieve
Crag Lake
Stony Ridge Lake
Emerald Bay State Park
Kingsbury Grade
El Dorado National Forest
Fannette Is
Emerald Bay
Cliff Lake
Stateline
Lower Velma Lake
Baldwin Beach
Kiva Beach
Pope Beach
Middle Velma Lake
Cascade Lake
South Lake Tahoe
Upper Velma Lake
Eagle Lake
Cascade Falls
Heavenly
Fontanillis Lake
Granite Lake
Fallen Leaf Rd
South Lake Tahoe Airport
Dicks Lake
Mt Tallac (9735ft)
Fallen Leaf Lake
See South Lake Tahoe Map (p360)
Upper Truckee River
Pioneer Trail
Trout Ck
Desolation Wilderness
Lily Lake
Angora Lakes
Meyers

Lake Tahoe

Sights

1 Cabin of William Phipps B4
2 Gatekeeper's Museum & Marion Steinbach Indian Basket Museum B2
3 Hellman-Ehrman Mansion B4
4 Inspiration Point B5
MS Dixie II .... (see 24)
5 Vikingsholm Castle B5

Activities, Courses & Tours

Bayview Trailhead .... (see 17)
6 Eagle Falls Trailhead B5
7 Glen Alpine Trailhead B6
8 Meeks Bay Trailhead B4
9 Rubicon Trailhead B5
10 Tallac Trailhead B6

Sleeping

11 DL Bliss State Park Campground B5
12 Eagle Point Campground B5
13 Hyatt Regency Lake Tahoe D1
14 Meeks Bay Campground B4
15 Nevada Beach Campground D5
16 River Ranch Lodge A2
17 USFS Bayview Campground B5
18 USFS General Creek Campground B4
19 USFS Goose Meadow Campground A1
20 USFS Kaspian Campground A3
21 USFS Meeks Bay Resort B4
22 USFS Silver Creek Campground A1
23 USFS William Kent Campground A3
24 Zephyr Cove Resort & Marina D4

adult/child under 13yr $24/free; ⌚8:30am-5pm, night skiing 5-7pm Wed; 👪) Occupying 4800 acres of thick forest north of Truckee, Tahoe Donner has lovely and varied terrain with over 62 miles of groomed tracks that cover three track systems and 51 trails. The most beautiful spot is secluded Euer Valley, where a warm hut serves food on weekends. A 1.5-mile loop stays open for night skiing, usually on Wednesdays. Group lessons for beginners and 'Tiny Tracks,' a supervised kids' ski and snow-play camp, are available; reserve ahead for intermediate skills clinics.

Northstar-at-Tahoe SKIING, SNOWSHOEING
☎530-562-3270, 800-466-6784; www.northstarattahoe.com; 5001 Northstar Dr, off Hwy 267, Truckee; adult/child 5-12yr $25/13; ⌚9am-3pm Mon-Thu, 8:30am-4pm Fri-Sun & holidays; 👪) Seven miles southeast of I-80, this mega ski resort has a highly regarded Nordic and telemark school, making it a great choice for novices. A package, which includes the trail fee, ski rental and a group lesson, costs $65. Afterwards you can explore the nearly 40km of groomed trails. Moonlight snowshoe tours and open-range biathlon-race and clinic days take place monthly.

Clair Tappaan Lodge SKIING, SNOWSHOEING
(☎530-426-3632; www.sierraclub.org/outings/lodges/ctl; 19940 Donner Pass Rd, off I-80 exit Soda Springs/Norden, Norden; adult/child under 12yr $7/3.50; ⌚9am-5pm; 👪) You can ski right out the door if you're staying at this rustic mountain lodge (see p379) near Donner Summit. Its 12km of groomed and tracked trails are great for beginners and intermediate skiers, and connect to miles of backcountry skiing (for overnight hut reservations, call ☎800-679-6775). Stop by the lodge for ski and snowshoe rentals, and value-priced ski lessons at all skill levels (sign-up starts at 9am daily).

TAHOE CITY & AROUND

Tahoe Cross Country SKIING, SNOWSHOEING
(☎530-583-5475; www.tahoexc.org; 925 Country Club Dr, off N Lake Blvd/Hwy 28, Tahoe City; adult/child under 10yr/youth 10-17yr $22/free/18; ⌚8:30am-5pm; 👪🐾) Run by the nonprofit Tahoe Cross Country Ski Education Association, this center, about 3 miles north of Tahoe City, has 65km of groomed tracks (19 trails) that wind through lovely forest, suitable for all skill levels. Dogs are allowed on two trails. Group lessons come with good-value equipment-rental packages; half-day and twilight trail-pass discounts are also available. Ask about free skate clinics and beginners' cross-country mid-week lessons.

Squaw Valley SKIING, SNOWSHOEING
(☎530-583-6300, 800-403-0206; www.squaw.com; 1960 Squaw Valley Rd, off Hwy 89, Olympic Valley; adult/child under 13yr/youth 13-19yr $88/10/64; ⌚9am-5pm) Although downhill skiers rule the roost at this ex-Olympic resort, 11 miles of groomed track winding around an alpine meadow will keep beginner-level Nordic skiers busy too. Book ahead

TOP WAYS TO SKI TAHOE FOR LESS MONEY

Midweek and half-day afternoon discounts on lift tickets are usually available, but expect higher prices on weekends and holidays. Lift-ticket rates go up incrementally almost every year, too. Parents should ask about interchangeable 'Parent Predicament' lift tickets offered by some resorts, which let one parent ski while the other one babysits the kids, then switch off later.

The **Bay Area Ski Bus** (925-680-4386; www.bayareaskibus.com) allows you to leave the headache of driving I-80 to others. Round-trips start at $109 including lift tickets, with various add-on packages available. Pick-up locations include San Francisco and Sacramento.

Handy money-saving websites include:

» **Ski Lake Tahoe** (www.skilaketahoe.com) Portal for the seven biggest Tahoe resorts, with deals covering all.

» **Sliding on the Cheap** (www.slidingonthecheap.com) Homegrown website listing discounts and deals on lift tickets.

for monthly moonlight snowshoe tours high atop the mountain. To reach the trailheads at the Resort at Squaw Creek, which supplies cross-country ski, snowshoe and sled rentals, grab a free shuttle from the main downhill ski-area parking lot.

SOUTH LAKE TAHOE

Kirkwood SKIING, SNOWSHOEING
(209-258-7248; www.kirkwood.com; 1501 Kirkwood Meadows Dr, off Hwy 88, Kirkwood; adult/child under 10yr/child 11-12yr/youth 13-19yr $22/free/8/17; 9am-4pm;) Definitely not a jogging trail, this cross-country network has sections that are very challenging and where you can actually gain some elevation. Groomed track stretches for 80km with separate skating lanes and three trailside warming huts; the views from the higher slopes are phenomenal. Dogs are welcome on one ridgeline loop. Rentals, lessons and tours all available. It's at least an hour's drive south of Lake Tahoe.

Camp Richardson Resort SKIING, SNOWSHOEING
(530-542-6584; www.camprichardson.com; 1900 Jameson Beach Rd, off Emerald Bay Rd/Hwy 89, South Lake Tahoe; adult/child under 13yr/teen 13-19yr $20/free/14) At this woodsy resort with 21 miles of groomed track, you can ski lakeside or head for the solitude of the Desolation Wilderness. Locals turn out in droves for full-moon ski and snowshoe parties, which kick off at the resort's Beacon Bar & Grill.

NEVADA

Spooner Lake SKIING, SNOWSHOEING
(775-749-5349; www.spoonerlake.com; 3709 Hwy 28, Glenbrook, NV; adult/child under 13yr/youth 13-19yr $21/free/10; 9am-5pm;) This nature preserve, near the junction of Hwys 28 and 50 in Nevada, offers pretty trails - some around petite Spooner Lake, some through aspen and pine forest, and some through high country - with fabulous views. Altogether there are 50 miles of groomed trails for all levels of expertise and fitness. Equipment rentals, including snowshoes or sleds for kids, and group lessons are available, with midweek discounts and half-day and twilight trail passes. Make reservations for overnight stays in wilderness backcountry ski-in cabins.

South Lake Tahoe & Stateline

Highly congested and arguably overdeveloped, South Lake Tahoe is a chock-a-block commercial strip bordering the lake and framed by picture-perfect alpine mountains. At the foot of the world-class Heavenly mountain resort and buzzing from the gambling tables in the casinos just across the border in Stateline, Nevada, Lake Tahoe's south shore draws visitors with a cornucopia of activities and lodging and restaurant options, especially for summer beach access and tons of powdery winter snow.

Sights

FREE **Tallac Historic Site** HISTORIC SITE
(530-541-5227; www.fs.usda.gov; Tallac Rd, off Hwy 89/Emerald Bay Rd; tours adult/child 6-12yr $5/3; usually 10am-4:30pm mid-Jun–Sep, Fri

& Sat only late May–mid-Jun;) Sheltered by a pine grove and bordering a wide, sandy beach, this national historic site sits on the archaeologically excavated grounds of the former Tallac Resort, a swish vacation retreat for San Francisco's high society around the turn of the 20th century.

Inside the 1921 Baldwin Estate, the **Tallac Museum** (donation requested; 11am-4pm late May–mid-Jun & early Sep–mid-Sep, 10:30am-4:30pm mid-Jun–early Sep) has exhibits on the history of the resort and its founder, Elias 'Lucky' Baldwin, who made a bundle off Nevada's Comstock Lode. Nearby is the 1894 **Pope Estate**, now used for art exhibits and open for guided tours (daily except Wednesday). The boathouse of the **Valhalla Estate** functions as a theater venue – for tickets and schedules, call 530-541-4795. The 1923 Grand Hall contains an art gallery and gift shop.

Feel free to just amble or cycle around the breezy forested grounds, today transformed into a community arts hub, where leashed dogs are allowed. In summer, concerts, plays and other cultural events happen here, most notably the three-decade-old **Valhalla Festival of Arts, Music & Film** (www.valhallatahoe.com; July-Sep).

The parking lot is about 3 miles north of the 'Y' junction of Hwys 89 and 50.

FREE **Lake Tahoe Historical Society Museum** MUSEUM

(www.laketahoemuseum.org; 3058 Lake Tahoe Blvd; 11am-3pm Thu-Mon late May-early Sep) A small but interesting museum displays artifacts from Tahoe's pioneer past, including Washoe tribal baskets, vintage black-and-white films, hoary mining memorabilia and a model of a classic Lake Tahoe steamship. On summer Saturday afternoons, join a volunteer-led tour of the restored 1930s cabin out back.

Activities

For downhill skiing and snowboarding around South Lake Tahoe, see p354; for cross-country skiing and snowshoeing, see p358.

Heavenly Gondola GONDOLA, ZIP LINE

(www.skiheavenly.com; Heavenly Village; adult/child 5-12yr/teen 13-19yr from $32/20/26; 10am-5pm Jun-Aug, reduced off-season hr;) Soar to the top of the world as you ride this gondola, which sweeps you from Heavenly Village to some 2.4 miles up the mountain in just 12 minutes. From the observation deck at 9123ft, get gobstopping panoramic views of the entire Tahoe Basin, the Desolation Wilderness and Carson Valley. Then jump on the Tamarack Express chair lift to get all the way to the mountain summit, where the longest zip line in the continental US, **Heavenly Flyer** (per trip $40; 11am-4pm), lets you speed through the air for a heady 3100ft.

Hiking

Many miles of summer hiking trails start from the top of the **Heavenly Gondola** (see p359), many with mesmerizing lake views. On the Nevada side of the state line, **Lam Watah Nature Trail** meanders for just over a mile each way across USFS land, winding underneath pine trees and beside meadows and ponds, on its way between Hwy 50 and Nevada Beach, starting from the community park off Kahle Dr.

Several easy kid- and dog-friendly hikes begin near the USFS Taylor Creek Visitor Center off Hwy 89. The mile-long, mostly flat **Rainbow Trail** loops around a creekside meadow, with educational panels about ecology and wildlife all along the way. On the opposite side of Hwy 89, the gentle, rolling one-mile **Moraine Trail** follows the shoreline of Fallen Leaf Lake; free trailhead parking is available near campsite No 75. Up at cooler elevations, the mile-long round-trip to **Angora Lakes** is another popular trek with kids, especially because it ends by a sandy swimming beach and a summer snack bar selling ice-cream treats. You'll find the trailhead on Angora Ridge Rd, off Tahoe Mountain Rd, accessed from Hwy 89.

For longer and more strenuous day hikes to alpine lakes and meadows, several major trailheads provide easy access to the evocatively named **Desolation Wilderness** (see p362): **Echo Lakes** (south of town); **Glen Alpine** (near Lily Lake, south of Fallen Leaf Lake), to visit a historic tourist resort and waterfall; and **Tallac** (opposite the entrance to Baldwin Beach). The latter two trailheads also lead to the peak of Mt Tallac (9735ft), a strenuous 10- to 12-mile day hike. Self-serve wilderness permits for day hikers only are freely available at trailheads; for overnight backpacking permits, which are subject to quotas, see the boxed text, p362.

South Lake Tahoe

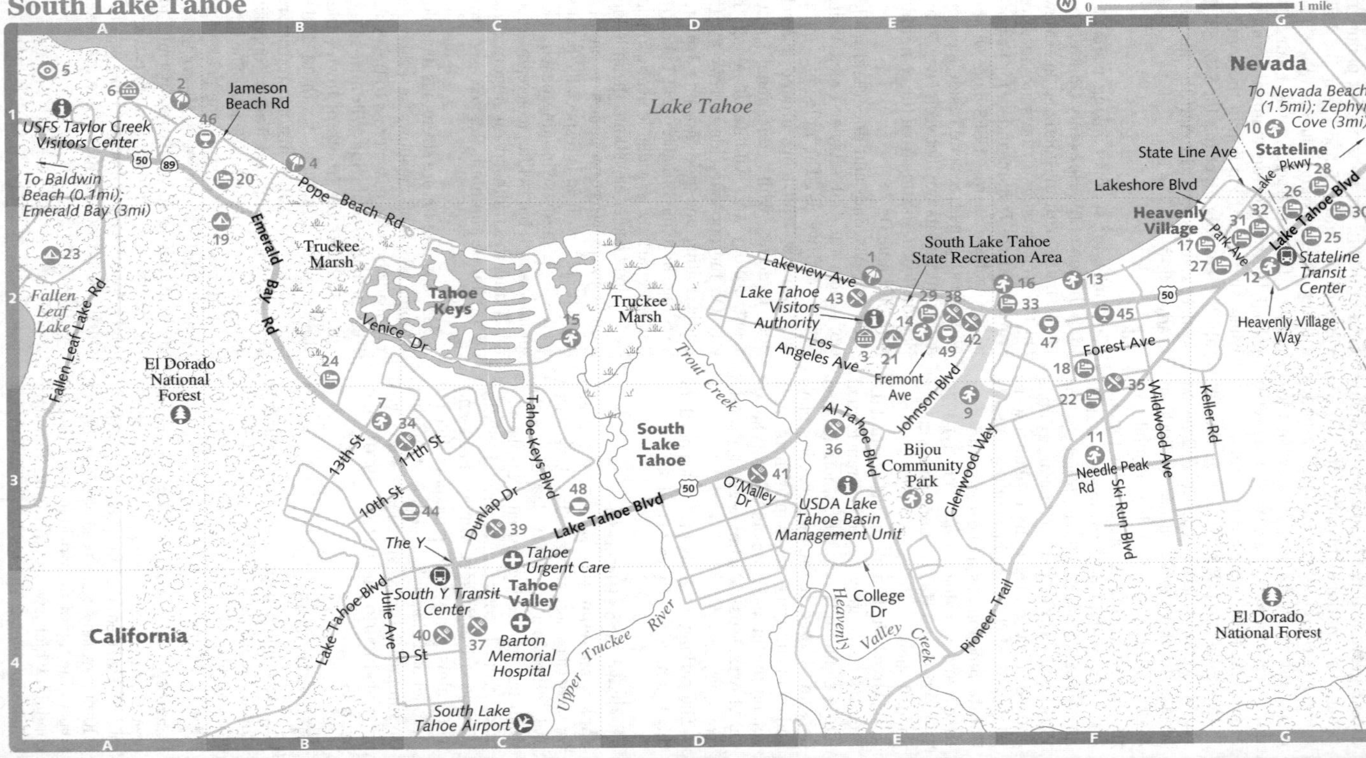

South Lake Tahoe

Sights

1 El Dorado Beach ... E1
2 Kiva Beach ... A1
3 Lake Tahoe Historical Society Museum ... E2
4 Pope Beach ... B1
5 Stream Profile Chamber ... A1
6 Tallac Historic Site ... A1

Activities, Courses & Tours

Action Watersports ... (see 16)
7 Anderson's Bike Rental ... B3
8 Bijou Community Park Disc Golf Course ... E3
9 Bijou Golf Course ... E3
Camp Richardson Corral & Pack Station ... (see 20)
Camp Richardson Resort Marina (see 46)
10 Edgewood Tahoe Golf Course ... G1
11 Hansen's Resort ... F3
12 Heavenly Gondola ... G2
Lake Tahoe Balloons ... (see 15)
Lake Tahoe Cruises (Tahoe Queen) ... (see 13)
Scuba Mood ... (see 15)
Shops at Heavenly Village ... (see 12)
Ski Run Boat Company ... (see 13)
13 Ski Run Marina ... F2
14 Tahoe Bowl ... E3
Tahoe Keys Boat & Charter Rentals ... (see 15)
15 Tahoe Keys Marina ... C2
16 Timber Cove Marina ... F2

Sleeping

17 968 Park Hotel ... G2
18 Alder Inn ... F2
Avalon Lodge ... (see 32)
19 Camp Richardson Campground ... B2
20 Camp Richardson Resort ... B1
21 Campground by the Lake ... E2
22 Deerfield Lodge at Heavenly ... F3
23 Fallen Leaf Campground ... A2
24 Fireside Lodge ... B2
25 Harrah's ... G2
26 Harvey's ... G2
27 Highland Inn ... G2
28 Horizon ... G1
29 Inn by the Lake ... E2
30 MontBleu ... G2
31 Paradice Inn ... G2
32 Seven Seas Inn ... G2
Spruce Grove Cabins ... (see 22)
33 Tahoe Lakeshore Lodge & Spa ... F2
Timber Lodge ... (see 12)

Eating

Blue Angel Cafe ... (see 22)
34 Burger Lounge ... C3
35 Café Fiore ... F3
36 Cork & More ... E3
37 Ernie's Coffee Shop ... C4
38 Freshie's ... E2
39 Grass Roots Natural Foods ... C3
40 Lake Tahoe Pizza Company ... C4
41 Off the Hook Sushi ... D3
42 Safeway ... E2
43 Sprouts ... E2
Sugar Pine Bakery ... (see 47)

Drinking

44 Alpina Coffee Café ... C3
45 Après Wine Company ... F2
46 Beacon Bar & Grill ... B1
47 Brewery at Lake Tahoe ... F2
Fresh Ketch ... (see 15)
Improv ... (see 26)
48 Keys Café ... C3
49 Macduffs Pub ... E2
Mt Tallac Brewing Company ... (see 39)
Opal Ultra Lounge ... (see 30)
Stateline Brewery ... (see 12)

Beaches & Swimming

On the California side, the nicest strands are **Pope Beach** (www.fs.usda.gov/tahoe; per car $7; 🚻), **Kiva Beach** (🐾) and **Baldwin Beach** (www.fs.usda.gov/tahoe; per car $7; 🚻), each with picnic tables and barbecue grills; Kiva beach offers free parking and allows leashed dogs, too. They're all found along Emerald Bay Rd (Hwy 89), running west and east of Tallac Historic Site. Nearby, **Fallen Leaf Lake**, where scenes from the Hollywood flicks *The Bodyguard* and *City of Angels* were filmed, is also good for summer swims. **El Dorado Beach** is a free public beach in town, just off Lake Tahoe Blvd.

Many folks prefer to head over to Stateline and keep driving north 2 miles to pretty **Nevada Beach** (www.fs.usda.gov/tahoe; per car $7), where the wind really picks up in the afternoons, or always-busy **Zephyr Cove** (www.zephyrcove.com; per car $8; 🚻), which has rustic resort and marina facilities along its sandy mile-long shoreline.

DON'T MISS

HIKING & BACKPACKING THE DESOLATION WILDERNESS

Sculpted by powerful glaciers eons ago, this relatively compact **wilderness area** (www.fs.fed.us/r5/eldorado/recreation/wild/deso/) spreads south and west of Lake Tahoe and is the most popular in the Sierra Nevada. It's a 100-sq-mile wonderland of polished granite peaks, deep-blue alpine lakes, glacier-carved valleys and pine forests that thin quickly at the higher elevations. In summer, wildflowers nudge out from between the rocks.

All this splendor makes for some exquisite backcountry exploration. Six major trailheads provide access from the Lake Tahoe side: Glen Alpine, Tallac, Echo Lakes (the southernmost trailhead), Bayview, Eagle Falls and Meeks Bay. Tallac and Eagle Falls get the most traffic, but solitude comes quickly once you've scampered past the day hikers.

Wilderness permits are required year-round for both day and overnight explorations. Day hikers can self-register at the trailheads, but overnight permits must be either reserved online (fee $6) at www.recreation.gov and printed at home, or picked up in person at the USFS Taylor Creek Visitor Center or USDA Lake Tahoe Basin Management Unit, both in South Lake Tahoe (see p369). Permits cost $5 per person for one night or $10 per person for two or more nights.

Quotas are in effect from late May through the end of September. Half of the permits for the entire season may be reserved online usually starting in late March or April; the other half are available on a first-arrival basis on the day of entry only.

Bearproof canisters are strongly advised in all wilderness areas (hanging your food in trees will not work – these bears are too smart!). Borrow canisters for free from the USFS Taylor Creek Visitors Center. Bring bug repellent as the mosquitoes can be merciless. Wood fires are a no-no, but portable stoves are OK. Dogs must be leashed at *all* times.

Boating & Water Sports

Ski Run Boat Company (☎530-544-0200; www.tahoesports.com; 900 Ski Run Blvd), at the Ski Run Marina, and **Tahoe Keys Boat & Charter Rentals** (☎530-544-8888; www.tahoesports.com; 2435 Venice Dr), at the Tahoe Keys Marina, both rent motorized powerboats, pontoons, sailboats and jet skis (rentals per hour $95 to $200), as well as human-powered kayaks, canoes, hydro bikes, paddleboats and paddleboard sets (per hour $15 to $35). If you want to go parasailing up to 1200ft above Lake Tahoe's waves, the Ski Run Marina branch can hook you up (rides $50 to $75). For summer boat dives, book ahead with **Scuba Mood** (☎916-420-9820; www.scubamood.com; Tahoe Keys Marina, 2435 Venice Dr East).

Kayak Tahoe KAYAKING
(☎530-544-2011; www.kayaktahoe.com; rental kayaks $15-60, lessons & tours from $30; ⊙usually 9am-5:30pm Jul & Aug, shorter hr Jun & Sep) Rent a kayak, take a lesson or sign up for a guided tour, including sunset cove paddles, trips to Emerald Bay and explorations of the Upper Truckee River estuary and the eastern shore. Four seasonal locations at Timber Cove Marina and Baldwin, Pope and Nevada Beaches.

Zephyr Cove Resort & Marina MARINA
(Map p356; ☎775-589-4901; www.zephyrcove.com; 760 Hwy 50, NV; ⊙9am-5pm) Rents powerboats, pedal boats, waverunners, jet skis, canoes, kayaks and stand-up paddleboards (SUP); also offers single and tandem parasailing flights ($59 to $129).

Camp Richardson Resort Marina MARINA
(☎530-542-6570; www.camprichardson.com; 1900 Jameson Beach Rd) Rents powerboats, paddleboats, water skis, kayaks and SUP gear.

Mountain-Biking

For expert mountain-bikers, the classic **Mr Toad's Wild Ride**, with its steep downhill sections and banked turns reminiscent of a Disneyland theme-park ride, should prove sufficiently challenging. Usually open from June until October, the one-way trail along Saxon Creek starts off Hwy 89 south of town near Grass Lake and Luther Pass.

Intermediate mountain-bikers should steer towards the mostly single-track **Pow-**

erline Trail, which traverses ravines and creeks. You can pick up the trail off Ski Run Blvd near the Heavenly resort, from the western end of Saddle Rd. For a more leisurely outing over mostly level terrain, you can pedal around scenic Fallen Leaf Lake. Anyone with good lungs might try the **Angora Lakes Trail**, which is steep but technically easy and rewards you with sweeping views of Mt Tallac and Fallen Leaf Lake. It starts further east, off Angora Ridge and Tahoe Mountain Ridge Rds.

For shuttle service and mountain-bike rentals for Mr Toad's Wild Ride, the Tahoe Rim Trail and other downhill adventures, as well as family-friendly tours, talk to **Wanna Ride** (775-588-5800; www.wannaridetahoe.com). For mountain-biking trail conditions, race schedules, volunteer days and other special events, contact the **Tahoe Area Mountain Biking Association** (http://mountainbiketahoe.org).

Cycling

The **South Lake Tahoe Bike Path** is a level, leisurely ride suitable for anyone. It heads west from El Dorado Beach, eventually connecting with the **Pope-Baldwin Bike Path** past Camp Richardson, Tallac Historic Site and the USFS Taylor Creek Visitor Center. Visitors centers carry the excellent Lake Tahoe bike route map, available online from the **Lake Tahoe Bicycle Coalition** (www.tahoebike.org), which has an info-packed website for cycling enthusiasts. **Anderson's Bike Rental** (530-541-0500, 877-720-2121; www.laketahoebikerental.com; 645 Emerald Bay Rd/Hwy 89; per hr $9;), about 1.5 miles north of the 'Y,' rents hybrid bikes with helmets.

Golf

Edgewood Tahoe Golf Course GOLF
(775-588-2787; www.edgewood-tahoe.com; 100 Lake Pkwy, Stateline; green fee $110-240) Stunning lakeside scenery is a major distraction at this challenging championship 18-hole course designed by George Fazio, a favorite for celebrity golf tournaments. Tee-time reservations are required; cart and club rentals available.

Bijou Golf Course GOLF
(530-542-6097; www.cityofslt.us; 3464 Fairway Ave; green fee $19-37, club/cart rental $15/5; call for hr) So you don't know your putter from your 9-iron? That's OK at this laid-back, no-reservations municipal course with views of Heavenly Mountain. Built in the 1920s, it's got just 9 holes, which you can play twice around.

FREE **Kirkwood Disc-Wood** DISC GOLF
(209-258-7210; www.kirkwood.com; 1501 Kirkwood Meadows Dr, Kirkwood) Crazy terrain, tons of distance and high-elevation Sierra Nevada views from an epic 18 holes. Call ahead for directions and to check opening hours before making the hour-long drive southwest of South Lake Tahoe.

FREE **Zephyr Cove Park** DISC GOLF
(Hwy 50 at Warrior Way, north of Stateline, NV) PDGA-approved 18-hole course is scenically set on the eastern shore, with kick-ass uphill and downhill shoots.

FREE **Bijou Community Park** DISC GOLF
(Bijou Community Park, 1201 Al Tahoe Blvd) In town, these 27 holes will taunt even experts with loooong greens on a mostly flat, forested course (ahoy, trees!).

Horseback Riding

Both **Camp Richardson Corral & Pack Station** (530-541-3113, 877-541-3113; www.camprichardsoncorral.com; Emerald Bay Rd/Hwy 89; trail rides $40-90;) and **Zephyr Cove Stables** (775-588-5664; www.zephyrcovestable.com; Hwy 50, NV; trail rides $40-70;), about 4 miles north of Stateline casinos, offer daily horseback rides in summer, varying from one-hour kid-friendly trips through the forest, to extended treks with meadow and lake views (reservations required).

South Lake Tahoe for Children

FREE **Stream Profile Chamber** HIKING
(530-543-2674; trailhead at USFS Taylor Creek Visitor Center, off Hwy 89; 8am-4:30pm late May–mid-Jun & Oct, to 5:30pm mid-Jun–Sep) Along a family-friendly hiking trail, this submerged glass structure in a teeming creek lets you check out what plants and fish live below the waterline. The best time to visit is in October during the Kokanee salmon run, when the brilliant red beauties arrive to spawn.

Tahoe Bowl BOWLING
(530-544-3700; http://tahoebowl.com; 1030 Fremont Ave; game per person $4.50, shoe rental $4.50; schedules vary;) For yucky-weather days or to tire out the tots by bedtime, this is a fun indoor haunt with 16

SLEDDING, TUBING & SNOW PLAY FOR KIDS

Major ski resorts such as Heavenly and Kirkwood around South Lake Tahoe, and Squaw Valley and Northstar-at-Tahoe near Truckee, offer sledding hills for the kiddos, some with tubing rentals and thrilling rope tows. Smaller ski mountains including Sierra-at-Tahoe outside South Lake Tahoe, and Boreal, Soda Springs and Tahoe Donner, all near Truckee, also offer child-friendly slopes.

To avoid the crowds, bring your own sleds to designated local snow-play areas at North Tahoe Regional Park in Tahoe Vista on the north shore, or to Nevada's Incline Village, Tahoe Meadows off the Mt Rose Hwy (Hwy 431) or Spooner Summit on Hwy 50, all along the east shore. Back in California, free DIY **Sno-Parks** (☎916-324-1222; www.parks.ca.gov/?page_id=1233) are found along Hwy 89 at Blackwood Canyon, 3 miles south of Tahoe City on the west shore, and Taylor Creek, just north of Camp Richardson at South Lake Tahoe. Coming from Sacramento or the San Francisco Bay Area, two Sno-Parks are along I-80 at Yuba Gap (exit 161) and Donner Summit (exit 176 Castle Peak/Boreal Ridge Rd); their parking lots often fill by 11am on winter weekends.

For private groomed sledding and tubing hills, swing by **Hansen's Resort** (Map p360; ☎530-577-4352; www.hansensresort.com; 1360 Ski Run Blvd; per person incl rental per hr $10; ⊙9am-5pm) in South Lake Tahoe or **Adventure Mountain** (☎530-577-4352; www.adventuremountaintahoe.com; 21200 Hwy 50; per car $15, rentals available; ⊙10am-4:30pm Mon-Fri, 9am-5pm Sat, Sun & holidays), south of town at Echo Summit.

bowling lanes and a pocket-sized pizza parlor and video arcade. Call ahead for open-play schedules.

Shops at Heavenly Village MINI-GOLF, SKATING
(☎530-542-1215; www.theshopsatheavenly.com; 1001 Heavenly Way; ⊙seasonal hr vary; 👪) If you don't feel like wandering far, this downtown outdoor mall sets up a little putt-putt golf course in summer, and opens an outdoor ice-skating rink in winter. Call for current schedules and prices.

Tours

Lake Tahoe Cruises CRUISES
(☎800-238-2463; www.zephyrcove.com; 2hr cruise adult/child from $45/15; 👪) Two paddle wheelers ply Lake Tahoe's 'big blue' year-round with a variety of sightseeing, drinking, dining and dancing cruises, including a narrated two-hour daytime trip to Emerald Bay. The *Tahoe Queen* leaves from Ski Run Marina in town, while the MS *Dixie II* is based at Zephyr Cove Marina on the eastern shore in Nevada.

Woodwind Cruises CRUISES
(☎775-588-1881; www.sailwoodwind.com; Zephyr Cove Marina, 760 Hwy 50, NV; 1hr cruise adult/child 2-12yr from $34/15) Sunset champagne and happy-hour floats aboard this sailing catamaran are the perfect way to chill after a sunny afternoon lazing on the beach. Five daily departures during summer; reservations recommended.

Action Watersports SPEEDBOAT TOURS
(☎530-544-5387; www.action-watersports.com; Timber Cove Marina, 3411 Lake Tahoe Blvd; adult/child under 13yr $60/30) In a hurry to get to Emerald Cove? Wanna avoid those near-constant traffic jams on Hwy 89? Jump on board the *Tahoe Thunder* speedboat, which zips across the lake – watch out, though, you'll get wet!

Lake Tahoe Balloons BALLOONING
(☎530-544-1221, 800-872-9294; www.laketahoeballoons.com; per person $250) From May through October (weather permitting), you can cruise on a catamaran launched from Tahoe Keys Marina, then clamber aboard a hot-air balloon launched right from the boat's upper deck. The lake and Sierra Nevada mountain views may take away what little breath you have left up at 10,000ft high.

Sleeping

SOUTH LAKE TAHOE

South Lake Tahoe has a bazillion choices for all budgets. Lodging options line Lake Tahoe Blvd (Hwy 50) between Stateline and Ski Run Blvd. Further west, closer to the 'Y,' at the intersection of Hwys 50 and 89 is a string of mostly budget motels ranging from barely adequate to inexcusable. Prices listed here are for peak season (generally winter ski season from December to March and summer from June to August). Some properties may impose minimum stays, especially on weekends and holidays. For more ski condos and hotel rooms near the slopes, contact **Heavenly** (775-586-7000, 800-432-8365; www.skiheavenly.com).

TOP CHOICE Deerfield Lodge at Heavenly BOUTIQUE HOTEL **$$$**
(530-544-3337, 888-757-3337; http://tahoedeerfieldlodge.com; 1200 Ski Run Blvd; r/ste incl breakfast from $219/259;) A small boutique hotel close to Heavenly ski resort, Deerfield has a dozen intimate rooms and spacious suites that each have a patio or balcony facing the green courtyard, along with a whirlpool tub, flickering gas fireplace and amusing coat racks crafted from skis and snowboards. Happy-hour party snacks and drinks are complimentary, and barbecue grills appear in summer. Pet fee $25.

Timber Lodge HOTEL **$$**
(530-542-6600, 800-845-5279; www.marriott.com; 4100 Lake Tahoe Blvd; r $179-219, ste $219-299;) Don't let the Marriott chain-gang brand put you off this modern ski lodge with an enviable position, where you can watch the Heavenly gondola whoosh by outside your window. Cookie-cutter hotel rooms have kitchenettes, while apartment-style 'vacation villa' suites come with full kitchens, gas fireplaces and deep soaking tubs for après-ski warm-ups.

968 Park Hotel BOUTIQUE MOTEL **$$**
(530-544-0968, 877-544-0968; www.968parkhotel.com; 968 Park Ave; r $109-309;) Critics cry 'Lipstick on a pig!', but this refashioned motel has serious hipster edge. Recycled, rescued and re-envisioned building materials have made this LEED-certified property an ecohaven near the lake, within walking distance of the Stateline border scene. In summer, unwind in a cabana by the sunny pool or in the zen garden, then sink into your dreamy Sterling bed.

Alder Inn B&B **$$**
(530-544-4485; www.thealderinn.com; 1072 Ski Run Blvd; r $99-209;) Even better than staying at your best friend's house by the lake, this hospitable inn on the Heavenly ski-shuttle route charms with color schemes that really pop, pillow-top mattresses, organic bath goodies, mini-fridges, microwaves and flat-screen TVs. Dip your toes in the kidney-shaped pool in summer.

Fireside Lodge INN **$$**
(530-544-5515; www.tahoefiresidelodge.com; 515 Emerald Bay Rd/Hwy 89; d incl breakfast $119-255;) This woodsy cabin B&B wholeheartedly welcomes families, with free bikes and kayaks to borrow and evening s'mores. Kitchenette rooms and suites have river-rock gas fireplaces, cozy patchwork quilts and pioneer-themed touches like wagon wheels or vintage skis. Pet fee $20.

Paradice Inn MOTEL **$$**
(530-544-6800; www.paradicemoteltahoe.com; 953 Park Ave; r $120-210;) Harried travelers will appreciate the hospitality at this small two-story motel property. Step outside your minimalist room bordered by flower boxes that overflow with geraniums, then stroll across the street to the Heavenly gondola. Families should ask about two-bedroom suites.

Tahoe Lakeshore Lodge & Spa HOTEL **$$$**
(530-541-2180, 800-448-4577; www.tahoelakeshorelodge.com; 930 Bal Bijou Rd; d $169-319;) It's all about the lakefront views at this centrally located conference hotel. Renovated rooms in the main lodge all share the same log-cabin decor, while nearby condos with full kitchens vary depending on the whims of their individual owners.

Inn by the Lake HOTEL **$$$**
(530-542-0330, 800-877-1466; www.innbythelake.com; 3300 Lake Tahoe Blvd; r $170-270;) Rooms here are disappointingly nondescript, although a bilevel outdoor hot tub, spa suites with kitchens, and bicycles and snowshoes to borrow are nifty. Rooms out back are cheaper and quieter, but then you'll miss the lake views.

Highland Inn MOTEL **$$**
(530-544-4161, 800-798-7311; www.highlandlaketahoe.com; 3979 Lake Tahoe Blvd; r $59-159;) Budget-conscious stylemongers will enjoy this older, two-story remodeled motel. Artsy prints, light wood floors and new plasma TVs make it an altogether fairly pleasant, if thin-walled place to bunk down. Pet fee $20.

Avalon Lodge MOTEL **$$**
(530-544-2285, 888-544-7829; http://avalonlodge.com; 4075 Manzanita Ave; r $115-220;

) A quiet, roomy two-story motor lodge off the main drag; pet fee $20.

Seven Seas Inn MOTEL $
(530-544-7031, 800-800-7327; www.sevenseastahoe.com; 4145 Manzanita Ave; r $50-100;) Friendly, tidy, bargain-basement motel with a hot tub; pet fee $10.

Camping & Cabins

Spruce Grove Cabins CABINS $$
(530-544-0549, 800-777-0914; http://sprucegrovetahoe.com; 3599-3605 Spruce Ave; d $159-205;) Away from the Heavenly hubbub, these tidy, private cabins are fenced off on a quiet residential street. The vintage look of these kitchen-equipped cabins, from knotty pine walls to the stone-bordered gas fireplaces, will make you feel like you're staying lakeside. Let your dogs cavort in the yard while you swing in the hammock or soak in outdoor hot tubs. Cleaning fee $30; refundable pet deposit $100.

Camp Richardson Resort CABINS, CAMPGROUND $
(530-541-1801, 800-544-1801; www.camprichardson.com; 1900 Jameson Beach Rd; tent sites from $35, RV sites with partial/full hookups from $40/45, r $95-180, cabins $100-265;) Removed from downtown's strip-mall aesthetic, this sprawling family camp is a hectic place offering seasonal camping (expect marauding bears all night long!), forested cabins rented by the week in summer, and so-so beachside hotel rooms. Sports gear and bicycle rentals available. Wi-fi in lobby only.

Fallen Leaf Campground CABINS, CAMPGROUND $
(info 530-544-0426, reservations 877-444-6777; www.recreation.gov; Fallen Leaf Lake Rd; tent & RV sites $30, yurts $85; mid-May–mid-Oct;) Near the north shore of stunning Fallen Leaf Lake, this is one of the biggest and most popular campgrounds on the south shore, with 180 wooded sites and newly built canvas-sided yurts that can sleep a family of five (bring your own sleeping bags).

Campground by the Lake CAMPGROUND $
(530-542-6096; www.cityofslt.us; 1150 Rufus Allen Blvd; tent & RV sites without/with electric hookups from $29/40, cabins $51-69; Apr-Oct;) Highway noise can be an around-the-clock irritant, though proximity to the city pool and ice rink make this wooded in-town campground with an RV dump station a decent choice. Basic sleeping-platform cabins are available between Memorial Day (late May) and Labor Day (early September).

STATELINE, NV

At Nevada's high-rise casino complexes, prices rise and fall like your luck at the slot machines. Season, day of the week and type of room are key. In winter ask about special ski-and-stay packages.

Harrah's CASINO HOTEL $$$
(775-588-6611, 800-223-7277; www.harrahslaketahoe.com; 15 Hwy 50, Stateline; r $139-449;) Clad in an oddly tasteful forest-green facade, this buzzing casino hotel is Stateline's top contender. Let yourself be swallowed up by even standard 'luxury' rooms, which each have two bathrooms with their own mini TVs and telephones, or spring for a luxury suite with panoramic lake-vista windows. For more eye-popping views, snag a window table at one of Harrah's upper-floor restaurants.

MontBleu CASINO HOTEL $$
(775-588-3515, 888-829-7630; www.montbleuresort.com; 55 Hwy 50, Stateline; r $70-280;) The public areas may sport über-cool modern boutique decor, but rooms still have that classic, tacky casino hotel look (some of the marble-accented bathrooms come with hedonistic whirlpool tubs, however). Unwind instead in the lavish indoor pool lagoon, accented by a rockscape and mini waterfalls.

Harvey's CASINO HOTEL $$
(775-588-2411, 800-223-7277; www.harveystahoe.com; 18 Hwy 50, Stateline; r $79-559;) Harvey's was South Lake Tahoe's first casino, and with 740 rooms, is also its biggest. Lake Tower rooms have fancy marble bathrooms and oodles of space, but renovated Mountain Tower rooms are more chic and design-savvy. The heated outdoor pool is open year-round, for beach and snow bunnies alike. Pet fee $40.

Horizon CASINO HOTEL $$
(775-588-6211, 800-648-3322; www.horizoncasino.com; 50 Hwy 50, Stateline; r $70-290;) Diehard Elvis fans can stay in the special suite where the star himself once boozed and snoozed at this otherwise generic property, formerly the Sahara. Family-friendly touches include Tahoe's largest outdoor summer pool, a huge game arcade and a multiplex movie theater.

Camping & Cabins

Zephyr Cove Resort & Marina CABIN, CAMPGROUND $$$

(Map p356; ☎800-238-2463; www.zephyrcove.com; 760 Hwy 50, NV; tent & RV sites without/with hookups from $27/43, cabins $169-339; ⏲cabins year-round, camping May-Sep;) On the Nevada side, about 4 miles north of Stateline, this family-oriented lakeside resort on USFS land has historic cabins scattered among the pines and similar campground facilities to Camp Richardson, including hot showers, coin-op laundry, barbecue grills and fire rings. Take your pick of 93 paved RV or 10 drive-in tent sites (a few dozen with lake views), or 47 walk-in tent sites tucked deeper into the shady forest. Leashed dogs allowed, except on the main beach.

Nevada Beach Campground CAMPGROUND $

(Map p356; ☎info 775-588-5562, reservations 877-444-6777; www.recreation.gov; off Hwy 50, NV; tent & RV sites $28-34; ⏲mid-May–mid-Oct;) Bed down on a carpet of pine needles at this tidy lakeside campground, about 3 miles north of Stateline, where 48 sites are nestled amid pines. Leashed dogs allowed at campsites, but not the beach.

Eating

For late-night cravings, each of the big casinos in Stateline has a 24-hour coffee shop for hangover-helper and night-owl breakfasts. If you're just looking for filling pub grub or après-ski appetizers and cocktails, most bars and cafes also serve just-OK food, some with waterfront views and live music too.

TOP CHOICE **Café Fiore** ITALIAN $$$

(☎530-541-2908; www.cafefiore.com; 1169 Ski Run Blvd; mains $16-31; ⏲5:30-9pm Sun-Thu, to 9:30pm Fri & Sat) Upscale Italian without pretension, this tiny romantic eatery pairs succulent pasta, seafood and meats with an award-winning 300-vintage wine list. Swoon over the rack of lamb, homemade white-chocolate ice cream and near-perfect garlic bread. With only seven tables (a baker's dozen in summer when the candle-lit outdoor patio opens), reservations are essential.

Freshie's ECLECTIC $$

(☎530-542-3630; www.freshiestahoe.com; 3330 Lake Tahoe Blvd; mains $14-27; ⏲11:30am-9pm) From vegans to seafood lovers, nobody should have a problem finding a favorite on the extensive menu at this Hawaiian fusion joint with sunset upper-deck views. Most of the produce is local and organic, and the blackened fish tacos are South Lake Tahoe's best. Service, although full of aloha, is slooow. Make reservations for dinner.

Blue Angel Cafe CALIFORNIAN $$

(☎530-544-6544; www.theblueangelcafe.com; 1132 Ski Run Blvd; lunch $10-14, dinner $12-26; ⏲11am-9pm Sun-Thu, to 10pm Fri & Sat;) Inside a cute wooden house on the way uphill to ski at Heavenly, this modern American kitchen churns out crispy kettle chips, club sandwiches, elaborate salads and flank steaks to stuff your belly. Turn up for happy hour or the blue-plate lunch and dinner specials.

Off the Hook Sushi FUSION $$

(www.offthehooksushi.com; 2660 Lake Tahoe Blvd; mains $14-23; ⏲5-10pm) Sushi, so far from the ocean? Yup. Locals keep on coming back to this dynamite little sushi shack, where you can feast on bento boxes and *nigiri* combos, or big steaming bowls of floury udon noodles and pan-fried halibut steaks off the Japanese, Hawaiian and Californian menu.

Latin Soul LATIN AMERICAN $$

(www.lakesideinn.com; 168 Hwy 50, Stateline; mains $8-24; ⏲8am-10pm) For something completely different, steal away to this little casino kitchen with a big, bold menu of spicy south-of-the-border flavors: Argentinean churrasco-grilled steak, Veracruz shrimp ceviche, goat *bírria* (stew) and outrageously mixed mojitos.

Getaway Cafe COMFORT FOOD $$

(www.getawaycafe.com; 3140 Hwy 50; mains breakfast & lunch $8-12, dinner $10-22; ⏲7am-2pm Mon & Tue, 7am-9pm Wed-Sun Jun-Aug, reduced off-season hr;) On the outskirts of town, south of the airport, this place really lives up to its name: avoid the weekend crowds here. Friendly waitresses sling heaped-up buffalo chicken salads, barbecue burgers, chorizo quesadillas, coconut-crusted French toast and more.

Burger Lounge AMERICAN $

(www.tahoeburgerlounge.com; 717 Emerald Bay Rd/Hwy 89; dishes $3-6; ⏲11am-8pm, to 9pm Jun-Aug;) You can't miss that giant beer mug standing outside a shingled cabin. Step inside for the south shore's tastiest burgers, including the crazy 'Just a Jiffy' (with peanut butter, bacon and cheddar cheese) or the zingy pesto fries.

Sprouts VEGETARIAN $
(3123 Harrison Ave; mains $6-9; 8am-9pm;) Cheerful chatter greets you at this energetic, mostly organic cafe that gets extra kudos for its smoothies. A healthy menu will have you noshing happily on satisfying soups, rice bowls, sandwiches, burrito wraps, tempeh burgers and fresh salads.

Ernie's Coffee Shop DINER $
(www.erniescoffeeshop.com; 1207 Emerald Bay Rd/Hwy 89; mains $7-11; 6am-2pm;) A sun-filled local institution, Ernie's dishes out filling four-egg omelets, hearty biscuits with gravy, fruity and nutty waffles, mix-your-own salads and bottomless cups of locally roasted coffee. Toddlers can happily munch the ears off the Mickey Mouse pancake.

Lake Tahoe Pizza Co PIZZERIA $$
(www.laketahoepizzaco.com; 1168 Emerald Bay Rd/Hwy 89; pizzas $11-22; 4-9:30pm, to 10pm Jun-Aug;) Since the '70s, this classic pizza parlor has been hand rolling its house-made dough (cornmeal or whole wheat, anyone?), then piling the pizzas with crafty combos such as the meaty 'Barnyard Massacre' or vegan 'Green Giant.'

Self-caterers can stock up at:

Cork & More DELI $
(http://thecorkandmore.com; 1032 Al Tahoe Blvd; 10am-7pm) Specialty foods, gourmet deli (sandwiches, soups, salads) and picnic baskets to go.

Sugar Pine Bakery BAKERY $
(3564 Lake Tahoe Blvd; 8am-6pm Tue-Sat, 8am-4pm Sun) Crunchy baguettes, ooey-gooey cinnamon rolls, fruit tarts and choco-chunk cookies.

Grass Roots Natural Foods GROCERY
(2040 Dunlap Dr; 9am-7pm Mon-Sat, 10am-6pm Sun;) Organic produce and home-baked muffins, sandwiches and fresh pizzas.

Safeway GROCERY
(www.safeway.com; 1020 Johnson Blvd; 9am-8pm Mon-Fri, 9am-5pm Sat & Sun) Standard supermarket fare, with an in-house deli and bakery.

Drinking & Entertainment

The siren song of blackjack and slot machines calls the masses over to Stateline. It's no Vegas, but there are plenty of ways to help you part with a bankroll. Each of the major casinos has live entertainment and several bars and lounges for you to while away the night. Published on Thursdays, the free alt-weekly newspaper **Reno News & Review** (www.newsreview.com) has comprehensive Stateline entertainment and events listings. For what's going on around South Lake Tahoe, pick up a copy of the free weekly *Lake Tahoe Action,* published by the **Tahoe Daily Tribune** (www.tahoedailytribune.com).

Beacon Bar & Grill BAR
(www.camprichardson.com; Camp Richardson Resort, 1900 Jameson Beach Rd; 11am-10pm) Imagine all of Lake Tahoe is your very own front yard when you and your buddies sprawl across this big wraparound wooden deck. If you want to get schnockered, order the signature Rum Runner cocktail. Bands rock here in summer.

Brewery at Lake Tahoe BREWPUB
(www.brewerylaketahoe.com; 3542 Lake Tahoe Blvd; opens at 11am daily, closing time varies) Crazy-popular brewpub pumps its signature Bad Ass Ale into grateful local patrons, who may sniff at bright-eyed out-of-towners. The barbecue is dynamite and a roadside patio opens in summer. Don't leave without a bumper sticker!

Macduffs Pub PUB
(www.macduffspub.com; 1041 Fremont Ave; 11:30am-2am) With Boddingtons on tap, fish-and-chips and full-on Scottish breakfasts on the menu, as well as a dart board on the wall, this dark and bustling pub wouldn't look out of place in Edinburgh. Sports fans and spirit drinkers, step right up.

Opal Ultra Lounge NIGHTCLUB
(775-586-2000; www.montbleuresort.com; MontBleu, 55 Hwy 50, Stateline; cover free-$10; 10pm-3am Wed-Sat) With DJ booths and go-go dancers, this Top 40 and electro dance club draws a young party crowd that enjoys getting their bodies painted in-house. Ladies might get in free before midnight. On summer Sunday nights, hit up the casino's poolside DJ parties. Dress to impress.

Stateline Brewery BREWPUB
(www.statelinebrewery.com; 4118 Lake Tahoe Blvd; 11am-9pm Sun-Thu, to 10pm Fri & Sat) Seat yourself by the shiny industrial brewing vats at this subterranean spot. German, Scotch and American-style ales taste mighty good after a day of sunning yourself on the lakeshore or skiing Heavenly (the gondola swings nearby).

Fresh Ketch BAR
(http://thefreshketch.com; Tahoe Keys Marina, 2345 Venice Dr; ⏲11:30am-10pm) We know all you're really looking for is sunset drinks on the waterfront with blissful lake views, right? Kick back on the outdoor waterfront patio, or inside at the bar, where live blues, jazz and acoustic guitarists groove several nights a week.

Improv COMEDY CLUB
(www.harveystahoe.com; 18 Hwy 50, Stateline; tickets $25-30; ⏲usually 9pm Wed & Fri-Sun, 8 & 10pm Sat) Catch up-and-coming stand-up comedians doing their funny shtick at the intimate cabaret theater inside Harvey's old-school casino.

Mt Tallac Brewing Company MICROBREWERY
(2060 Eloise Ave; ⏲usually 5-7pm) Tiny mom-and-pop joint is so jammed with locals, it's practically standing-room only (and brrrr, cold in winter). Pints are cheap, the company chill and the brews – well, they're serious beer-geek heaven.

Après Wine Company WINE BAR
(http://apreswineco.com; Ski Run Center, 3668 Lake Tahoe Blvd; ⏲11am-10pm Mon-Sat, 2-9pm Sun) Tucked away, this teensy wine shop lures oenophiles with happy hours, sipper specials, tapas-sized bites and DIY enomatic wine dispensers.

For a jolt of java, tea or free wi-fi:

Alpina Coffee Café COFFEE SHOP
(822 Emerald Bay Rd/Hwy 89; ⏲6am-5pm; @📶) Internet-connected laptops, plus locally roasted brews, toasted bagels and a summer garden patio.

Keys Café COFFEE SHOP
(www.tahoekeyscafe.com; 2279 Lake Tahoe Blvd; ⏲7am-4pm; 📶) Butter-yellow roadside cabin for single-origin coffees, espresso, organic teas and fresh smoothies.

ℹ Information

Barton Memorial Hospital (☎530-541-3420; www.bartonhealth.org; 2170 South Ave; ⏲24hr) Around-the-clock emergency room. Barton's urgent-care clinic is inside the Stateline Medical Center at 155 Hwy 50, Stateline, NV.

Explore Tahoe (☎530-542-2908; www.cityofslt.us; Heavenly Village Transit Center, 4114 Lake Tahoe Blvd; ⏲9am-5pm) Interpretive exhibits and recreational and transportation information at a multipurpose 'urban trailhead.'

Lake Tahoe Visitors Authority (☎800-288-2463; http://tahoesouth.com); Stateline (☎775-588-5900; 169 Hwy 50, Stateline, NV; ⏲9am-5pm Mon-Fri); South Lake Tahoe (☎530-544-5050; 3066 Lake Tahoe Blvd; ⏲9am-5pm) Tourist information, maps, brochures and money-saving coupons.

South Lake Tahoe Library (☎530-573-3185; www.eldoradolibrary.org/tahoe.htm; 1000 Rufus Allen Blvd; ⏲10am-8pm Tue-Wed, 10am-5pm Thu-Sat; @) First-come, first-served free internet terminals.

Tahoe Urgent Care (☎530-541-3277; 2130 Lake Tahoe Blvd; ⏲8am-6pm) Walk-in medical clinic for nonemergencies.

USDA Lake Tahoe Basin Management Unit (☎530-543-2600; www.fs.usda.gov/ltbmu; 35 College Dr; ⏲8am-4:30pm Mon-Fri) Wilderness permits and camping and outdoor recreation information.

USFS Taylor Creek Visitor Center (☎530-543-2674; Hwy 89; ⏲8am-4:30pm late May–mid-Jun & Oct, to 5:30pm mid-Jun–Sep) Outdoor information, wilderness permits and daily ranger-led walks and talks during July and August.

ℹ Getting There & Away

From Reno-Tahoe International Airport (see p448), **South Tahoe Express** (☎866-898-2463; www.southtahoeexpress.com; adult/child 4-12yr one-way $27/15, round-trip $48/27) operates several daily shuttle buses to Stateline casinos; the journey takes 75 minutes up to two hours.

Amtrak (☎800-872-7245; www.amtrak.com) has a daily Thruway bus service between Sacramento and South Lake Tahoe ($34, 2½ hours), stopping at the South Y Transit Center.

ℹ Getting Around

South Lake Tahoe's main transportation hubs are the **South Y Transit Center** (1000 Emerald Bay Rd/Hwy 89), just south of the 'Y' intersection of Hwys 50 and 89; and the more central **Heavenly Village Transit Center** (4114 Lake Tahoe Blvd).

BlueGO (☎530-541-7149; www.bluego.org; single-ride/day pass $2/5) local buses operate year-round from 6am to 11pm daily, stopping all along Hwy 50 between the two transit centers. BlueGO also operates a reservable on-demand shuttle anywhere within South Lake Tahoe ($4 to $6).

In summer, BlueGO's **Nifty Fifty Trolley** (single-ride/day pass $2/5; ⏲hourly from 9am or 10am to 5pm or 6pm daily Jul-early Sep, Sat & Sun only Jun & mid-Sep–early Oct) heads north from the South Y Transit Center along the western shore to Tahoma. During winter ski season, BlueGO provides free and frequent

NAVIGATING SOUTH LAKE TAHOE TRAFFIC

South Lake Tahoe's main east–west thoroughfare is a 5-mile stretch of Hwy 50 called Lake Tahoe Blvd. Most hotels and businesses hover around the California–Nevada state line and Heavenly Village. Casinos are located in Stateline, which is officially a separate city.

West of town, Hwy 50 runs into Hwy 89 at the 'Y' junction. Heavy snowfall sometimes closes Hwy 89 north of the Tallac Historic Site. The section of Hwy 89 between South Lake Tahoe and Emerald Bay is also known as Emerald Bay Rd.

Traffic all along Hwy 50 between the 'Y' junction and Heavenly Village gets jammed around lunchtime and again by 5pm Monday to Friday in both summer and winter, but Sunday afternoons when skiers head back down the mountain are the worst.

An alternate, less-crowded route through town is Pioneer Trail, which branches east off the Hwy 89/50 junction (south of the 'Y') and reconnects with Hwy 50 at Stateline.

shuttle service from Stateline and South Lake Tahoe to all Heavenly base operations every 30 minutes from stops along Hwy 50, Ski Run Blvd and Pioneer Trail.

Western Shore

Lake Tahoe's densely forested western shore, between Emerald Bay and Tahoe City, is idyllic. Hwy 89 sinuously wends past gorgeous state parks with swimming beaches, hiking trails, pine-shaded campgrounds and historic mansions. Several trailheads also access the rugged splendor of the Desolation Wilderness (see the boxed text, p362).

All campgrounds and many businesses shut down between November and May. Hwy 89 often closes after snowfall for plowing or due to imminent avalanche danger. Once you drive its torturous slopeside curves, you'll understand why. The further south you go, the more of a roller coaster it is, no matter the season – so grip that steering wheel!

EMERALD BAY STATE PARK

Sheer granite cliffs and a jagged shoreline hem in glacier-carved **Emerald Bay** (☎530-541-3030; www.parks.ca.gov; per car $8; ⏰late May-Sep), a teardrop cove that will have you digging for your camera. Its most captivating aspect is the water, which changes from cloverleaf green to light jade depending on the angle of the sun.

Sights

You'll spy panoramic pullouts all along Hwy 89, including at **Inspiration Point**, opposite Bayview Campground. Just south, the road shoulder evaporates on both sides of a steep drop-off, revealing a postcard-perfect view of Emerald Bay to the north and Cascade Lake to the south.

The mesmerizing blue-green waters of the bay frame **Fannette Island**. This uninhabited granite speck, Lake Tahoe's only island, holds the vandalized remains of a tiny 1920s teahouse belonging to heiress Lora Knight, who would occasionally motorboat guests to the island from **Vikingsholm Castle** (tours adult/child 6-13yr $8/5; ⏰10am-4pm late May-Sep), her Scandinavian-style mansion on the bay. The focal point of the state park, Vikingsholm Castle is a rare example of ancient Scandinavian-style architecture. Completed in 1929, it has trippy design elements aplenty, including sod-covered roofs that sprout wildflowers in late spring. The mansion is reached by a steep 1-mile trail, which also leads to a visitors center.

Activities & Tours

HIKING

Vikingsholm Castle is the southern terminus of the famous Rubicon Trail (see p371).

Two popular trailheads lead into the Desolation Wilderness (see the boxed text, p362). From the Eagle Falls parking lot ($5), the **Eagle Falls Trail** travels one steep mile to Eagle Lake, crossing by Eagle Falls along the way. This scenic short hike often gets choked with visitors, but crowds disappear quickly as the trail continues up to the Tahoe Rim Trail and Velma, Dicks and Fontanillis Lakes (up to 10 miles round-trip).

From the back of Bayview Campground, it's a steep 1-mile climb to glacial Granite Lake or a moderate 1.5-mile round-trip to Cascade Falls, which rushes with snowmelt in early summer.

BOATING

Fannette Island is accessible by boat, except during Canada goose nesting season (typically February to mid-June). Rent boats at Meeks Bay or South Lake Tahoe; from the latter, you can also catch narrated bay cruises or speedboat tours.

Sleeping

Eagle Point Campground CAMPGROUND $
(info 530-525-7277, reservations 800-444-7275; www.reserveamerica.com; Hwy 89; tent & RV sites $35; mid-Jun–early Sep;) With over 90 sites perched on the tip of Eagle Point, this state-park campground provides flush toilets, hot pay showers, beach access and bay views. Another 20 scattered sites are reserved for boat-in campers.

USFS Bayview Campground CAMPGROUND $
(Hwy 89; tent & RV sites $15; Jun-Sep) This rustic, nay, primitive forest-service campground has 13 no-reservation sites and vault toilets, but its potable water supplies are often exhausted sometime in July. It's opposite Inspiration Point.

DL BLISS STATE PARK

Emerald Bay State Park spills over into **DL Bliss State Park** (530-525-7277; www.parks.ca.gov; per car $8; late May-late Sep), which has the western shore's most alluring beaches at Lester Cove and Calawee Cove. A half-mile round-trip nature trail leads to **Balancing Rock**, a 130-ton chunk of granite perched on a natural pedestal. Pick up an interpretive trail guide to park ecology and wildlife from the **visitor center** (8am-5pm) near the entrance.

Near Calawee Cove is the northern terminus of the scenic one-way **Rubicon Trail**, which ribbons along the lakeshore for 4.5 mostly gentle miles from Vikingsholm Castle (add one mile for the downhill walk to the castle from Hwy 89) in Emerald Bay State Park. It leads past small coves perfect for taking a cooling dip, and treats you to great views along the way. Add an extra mile to loop around and visit the restored historic lighthouse, a square wood-enclosed beacon constructed by the Coast Guard in 1916. Poised above 6800ft, it's the USA's highest-elevation lighthouse.

The park's **campground** (800-444-7275; www.reserveamerica.com; tent & RV sites $35-45, hike-and-bike sites $7; mid-May–Sep;) has 145 sites, including some coveted spots near the beach, along with flush toilets, hot pay showers, picnic tables, fire rings and an RV dump station.

The small visitor parking lot at Calawee Cove usually fills up by 10am, in which case it's a 2-mile walk from the park entrance to the beach. Alternatively, ask park staff at the entrance station about closer access points to the Rubicon Trail.

MEEKS BAY

With a wide sweep of shoreline, sleek and shallow **Meeks Bay** has warm water by Tahoe standards and is fringed by a beautiful, but busy, sandy beach. On the west side of the highway, a few hundred feet north of the fire station, is another **trailhead** for the Desolation Wilderness (see the boxed text, p362). A moderate, mostly level and nicely shaded path parallels Meeks Creek before kicking off more steeply uphill through the forest to **Lake Genevieve** (9 miles round-trip), **Crag Lake** (10 miles round-trip) and other backcountry ponds, all surrounded by scenic Sierra peaks.

Sleeping & Eating

Meeks Bay Resort CABIN, CAMPGROUND $$
(530-525-6946, 877-326-3357; www.meeksbayresort.com; 7941 Emerald Bay Rd/Hwy 89; tent & RV sites without/with full hookups $25/45, cabins $125-400; May-Oct;) The Washoe tribe offers various lodging options (cabins require minimum stays) plus kayak, canoe and paddleboat rentals. If you're hungry, swing by the fast-food snack bar or small market, which stocks limited groceries and

DON'T MISS

TAHOE RIM TRAIL

Partly paralleling the Pacific Crest Trail, the 165-mile **Tahoe Rim Trail** (www.tahoerimtrail.org) wraps around the lofty ridges and mountaintops of the Lake Tahoe Basin. Hikers, equestrians and – in some sections – mountain-bikers can enjoy inspirational views of the lake and the snowcapped Sierra Nevada while tracing the footsteps of early pioneers, Basque shepherds and Washoe tribespeople. Dozens of marked trailheads all around the lakeshore provide easy access points for hikers, bikers and horseback riders. The drone of car traffic can be an occasional nuisance, however.

DON'T MISS

SNOWSHOEING UNDER THE STARS

A crisp quiet night with a blazing glow across the lake. What could be more magical than a full-moon snowshoe tour? Reserve ahead, as ramblings at these places are very popular:

- Ed Z'Berg Sugar Pine Point State Park (p372)
- Squaw Valley (p357)
- Camp Richardson Resort (p358)
- Northstar-at-Tahoe (p357)
- Kirkwood (p358)

camping, fishing and beach gear, as well as Native American crafts and cultural books.

USFS Meeks Bay Campground CAMPGROUND $
(☎info 530-525-4733, reservations 877-444-6777; www.recreation.gov; tent & RV sites $23-25; ⊙mid-May–mid-Oct; 🐾) This developed campground offers 36 reservable sites along the beach, and flush toilets, picnic tables and fire rings. For pay showers, head to Meeks Bay Resort next door.

ED Z'BERG SUGAR PINE POINT STATE PARK

About 10 miles south of Tahoe City, this woodsy **state park** (☎530-525-7982; www.parks.ca.gov; per car $8) occupies a promontory blanketed by a fragrant mix of pine, juniper, aspen and fir. It has a swimming beach, over a dozen miles of hiking trails and abundant fishing in General Creek. A paved cycling path travels north to Tahoe City. In winter, 12 miles of groomed cross-country trails await inside the park; book ahead for ranger-guided full-moon **snowshoe tours** (☎530-525-9920; adult/child under 13yr incl snowshoe rental $15/free).

Historic sights include the modest 1872 **cabin** of William 'General' Phipps, an early Tahoe settler, and the considerably grander 1903 Queen Anne–style **Hellman-Ehrman Mansion** (tours adult/child under 13yr $5/3; ⊙usually 10am-3pm mid-Jun–Sep), an elegant lakefront house also known as Pine Lodge. Guided tours take in the richly detailed interior, including marble fireplaces, leaded-glass windows and period furnishings.

The park's secluded **USFS General Creek Campground** (☎800-444-7275; www.reserveamerica.com; tent & RV sites $20-25; ⊙late May–mid-Sep; 👪🐾) has 110 fairly spacious, pine-shaded sites, plus flush toilets and hot pay showers.

TAHOMA

Another blink-and-you'll-miss-it lakeside outpost, Tahoma has a post office and a handful of places to stay and eat.

Cute but not too kitschy, the red cabins of **Tahoma Meadows Bed & Breakfast Cottages** (☎530-525-1553, 866-525-1533; www.tahomameadows.com; 6821 W Lake Blvd; cottages incl breakfast $109-199, with kitchen $159-395; 📶👪🐾) dot a pine grove. Each has classy country decor, thick down comforters, a small TV, and bathrooms with clawfoot tubs. Pick up the in-room journal to record your impressions while you're toasting your feet by the gas-burning fireplace. Pet fee $20.

Nearby, the **PDQ Market** (6890 W Lake Blvd; ⊙6:30am-10pm) has groceries and a deli. Laying claim to being Tahoe's oldest bar, lakeside **Chamber's Landing** (☎530-525-9190; 6400 W Lake Blvd; ⊙usually noon-8pm Jun-Sep) sees the biggest crowds descend for drinks and appetizers in the all-day bar, especially during happy hour. Do yourself a favor and skip the 'Chamber's Punch,' though.

HOMEWOOD

This quiet hamlet is popular with summertime boaters and, in winter, skiers and snowboarders (see p354). **West Shore Sports** (☎530-525-9920; www.westshoresports.com; 5395 W Lake Blvd; ⊙8am-5pm Sun-Fri, 7:30am-5:30pm Sat) rents bicycles, kayaks, stand-up paddle boarding (SUP) gear and snow-sports equipment (eg skis, snowboards, snowshoes).

Sleeping & Eating

West Shore Inn INN $$$
(☎530-525-5200; www.skihomewood.com/westshorecafe/lodging; 5160 W Lake Blvd; r/ste incl breakfast from $249/349; ❄📶) Oriental rugs and Arts & Crafts decor give this luxurious six-room inn a classic, aged feel, and the lake's so close you feel like you could dive in. It's an upscale mountain lodge where crisp, modern suites feel decadent, and each has a fireplace and lake-view balcony. Rates include complimentary use of bicycles, kayaks and stand-up paddleboards.

USFS Kaspian Campground CAMPGROUND $
(☎877-444-6777; www.recreation.gov; tent sites $17-19; ⊙mid-May–mid-Oct), The closest campground is this nine-site, tent-only spot set

among ponderosa and fir trees; amenities include flush toilets, picnic tables and fire rings.

West Shore Café CALIFORNIAN $$$
(☎530-525-5200; www.skihomewood.com/westshorecafe; 5160 W Lake Blvd; mains $12-33; ⊙11:30am-9:30pm late Jun-Sep, 5-9:30pm Oct–mid-Jun) At the inn's cozy restaurant, chef Rusty Johns whips up California cuisine using artisanal cheeses, fresh produce and ranched meats, from juicy burgers to buffalo rib-eye steaks accompanied by tender broccoli rabe. Dinner reservations recommended.

SUNNYSIDE

Sunnyside is yet another lakeshore hamlet that may be just a dot on the map, but has a couple of detour-worthy restaurants worth stopping for. To work off all that dang good eating, rent a bicycle from **Cyclepaths** (☎530-581-1171; www.cyclepaths.net; 1785 W Lake Blvd), where you can get the scoop on all sorts of local outdoor information. You can pedal all the way north to Tahoe City along the paved bike path, or rent a stand-up paddle boarding (SUP) set and hit the popular local beaches.

Sleeping & Eating

USFS William Kent Campground CAMPGROUND $
(☎877-444-6777; www.recreation.gov; Hwy 89; tent & RV sites $23-25; ⊙mid-May–mid-Oct) About 2 miles south of Tahoe City, this roadside campground offers over 85 nicely shaded, but cramped, sites that often fill up. Amenities include flush toilets, picnic tables and fire rings, along with swimming beach access.

Sunnyside Restaurant & Lodge INN, CALIFORNIAN $$
(☎530-583-7200; www.sunnysidetahoe.com; 1850 W Lake Blvd; d incl breakfast $135-380, mains lunch $11-17, dinner $15-35; 📶) Classic and innovative contemporary takes on steak and seafood – think porterhouse pork with cherry chutney, or roasted chicken with braised fennel – pervade the lakeside dining room. In summer you'll probably have more fun doing lunch – or drinks with the signature zucchini sticks – on the huge lakefront deck. Two dozen noisy roadside lodge rooms and suites spell Old Tahoe; some have river-rock gas fireplaces and lake views.

TOP CHOICE **Fire Sign Café** DINER $
(☎530-583-0871; 1785 W Lake Blvd; mains $6-12; ⊙7am-3pm; 👪) For breakfast, everyone heads to the friendly Fire Sign for down-home omelets, blueberry pancakes, eggs Benedict with smoked salmon, fresh made-from-scratch pastries and other carbo-loading bombs, plus organic coffee. In summer, hit the outdoor patio. Lines are usually very long, so get there early.

Getting There & Around

In summer, BlueGO's **Nifty Fifty Trolley** (☎530-541-7149; www.bluego.org; single/day pass $2/5; ⊙9:15am-5:15pm daily Jul-early Sep, Sat & Sun only Jun & mid-Sep–early Oct) rolls along the western shore every hour, from South Lake Tahoe's South Y Transit Center north to Tahoma, stopping at Emerald Bay State Park (including Inspiration Point and Vikingsholm Castle parking lot), DL Bliss State Park, Ed Z'berg Sugar Pine Point State Park and Meeks Bay. From Tahoma, **Tahoe Area Rapid Transit** (TART; ☎530-550-1212, 800-736-6365; www.laketahoetransit.com; single/day pass $2/4; ⊙10am-6pm) buses continue north every hour to Tahoe City, stopping at Homewood and Sunnyside; between June and September, TART also stops at Ed Z'berg Sugar Pine Point State Park.

Tahoe City

The north shore's commercial hub, Tahoe City straddles the junction of Hwys 89 and 28, making it almost inevitable that you'll find yourself breezing through here at least once during your 'round-the-lake sojourn. The town is handy for grabbing food and supplies and renting sports gear. It's also the closest lake town to Squaw Valley (p354). The main drag, N Lake Blvd, is chockablock with outdoor outfitters, touristy shops and cafes.

Sights

Gatekeeper's Museum & Marion Steinbach Indian Basket Museum MUSEUM
(☎530-583-1762; 130 W Lake Blvd/Hwy 89; adult/child under 13yr $3/1; ⊙usually 10am-5pm Wed-Mon May-Sep, 11am-3pm Sat & Sun Oct-Apr) In a reconstructed log cabin close to town, this museum has a small but fascinating collection of Tahoe memorabilia, including Olympics history and relics from the early steamboat era and tourism explosion around the lake. In the museum's newer wing, uncover an exquisite array of Native

American baskets collected from over 85 indigenous California tribes.

Fanny Bridge LANDMARK

Just south of the always-jammed Hwy 89/28 traffic stoplight junction, the Truckee River flows through dam floodgates and passes beneath this bridge, cutely named for the most prominent feature of people leaning over the railings to look at fish (in American slang, 'fanny' means your rear end).

Watson Cabin MUSEUM

(530-583-8717; 560 N Lake Tahoe Blvd; admission by donation; noon-4pm Wed-Mon mid-Jun–early Sep) A few blocks east, this well-preserved 1908 settlers' cabin is one of the town's oldest buildings, built overlooking the beach.

Activities

Beaches & River Rafting

Though not an outstanding swimming area, **Commons Beach** is a small, attractive park with sandy and grassy areas, picnic tables, barbecue grills, a climbing rock and playground for kids, as well as free summer concerts and outdoor movie nights. Leashed dogs welcome.

The Truckee River itself is gentle and wide as it flows northwest from the lake – perfect for novice paddlers. **Truckee River Raft Rentals** (530-583-0123; www.truckeeriverraft.com; 185 River Rd; adult/child 6-12yr $30/25; 8:30am-3:30pm Jun-Sep;) rents rafts for the 5-mile float from Tahoe City to the River Ranch Lodge, including transportation back to town. Reservations strongly advised.

Hiking

Explore the fabulous trails of the **Granite Chief Wilderness** north and west of Tahoe City. For maps and trailhead directions, stop by the visitors center. Recommended day hikes include the moderately strenuous **Five Lakes Trail** (over 4 miles round-trip), which starts from Alpine Meadows Rd off Hwy 89 heading toward Squaw Valley, and the easy trek to **Paige Meadows**, leading onto the Tahoe Rim Trail. Paige Meadows is also good terrain for novice mountain-bikers and for snowshoeing. Wilderness permits are not required, even for overnight trips, but free campfire permits are needed, even for gas stoves. Leashed dogs are allowed on these trails.

Cycling

The paved 4-mile **Truckee River Bike Trail** runs from Tahoe City toward Squaw Valley, while the multi-use **West Shore Bike Path** heads 9 miles south to Ed Z'berg Sugar Pine Point State Park, including highway shoulder and residential street sections. Both are fairly easy rides, but expect crowds on summer weekends. The whole family can rent bicycles from any of several shops along N Lake Blvd.

Winter Sports

Tahoe City is within easy reach of a half dozen downhill and cross-country skiing and snowboarding resorts (see p354). For winter sports equipment rentals, drop by:

Tahoe Dave's OUTDOOR OUTFITTER

(530-583-6415/0400, 800-398-8915; www.tahoedaves.com; 590 N Lake Tahoe Blvd) Additional branches at Squaw Valley, Kings Beach and Truckee (rentals can be returned to any shop); reservations accepted.

Porters Tahoe OUTDOOR OUTFITTER

(530-583-2314; www.porterstahoe.com; 501 N Lake Blvd; 10am-6pm) First-come, first-served rentals only.

Sleeping

If you show up without reservations, dingy, last-resort budget motels are along N Lake Blvd. For camping, head north to USFS campgrounds off Hwy 89 (see p380) or south along Hwy 89 to state parks and small towns along the lake's western shore.

Mother Nature's Inn INN $$

(530-581-4278, 800-558-4278; www.mothernaturesinn.com; 551 N Lake Blvd; r $60-135;) Right in town behind Cabin Fever knickknack boutique, this good-value option offers quiet motel-style rooms with a tidy country look, fridges, eclectic furniture and comfy pillow-top mattresses. It's within walking distance of Commons Beach. Pet fee $5.

Pepper Tree Inn MOTEL $$

(530-583-3711, 800-624-8590; www.peppertreetahoe.com; 645 N Lake Blvd; r incl breakfast $90-199;) The tallest building in town, this somberly painted establishment redeems itself with some birds-eye lake views. Fairly comfortable modern rooms with that familiar log-cabin decor each have a microwave and mini fridge. Top-floor rooms with hot tubs are most in demand.

Granlibakken LODGE $$

(☎530-583-4242, 800-543-3221; www.granlibakken.com; 725 Granlibakken Rd, off Hwy 89; r/ste from $130/230, 1/2/3 br townhome from $330/380/430;) Sleep seriously old-school at this cross-country ski area and kitschy wedding and conference venue. Basic lodge rooms are spacious, but timeshare townhomes with kitchens, fireplaces and lofts can be a decent deal for families and groups.

River Ranch Lodge INN $$

(☎530-583-4264, 866-991-9912; www.riverranchlodge.com; Hwy 89 at Alpine Meadows Rd; r incl breakfast $115-195;) If it weren't for noise from traffic outside and the bar downstairs, you'd be drifting off to dreamland as the Truckee River tumbles below your window here. Rooms bulge with lodgepole-pine furniture; those upstairs have wistful balconies. Pet-friendly rooms available in summer only.

Eating & Drinking

TOP CHOICE Dockside 700 Wine Bar & Grill AMERICAN $$

(☎530-581-0303; www.dockside700.com; 700 N Lake Blvd; breakfast & lunch $5-10, dinner $13-29; 9am-9pm Mon-Fri, 8am-9pm Sat & Sun;) On a lazy summer afternoon, grab a table on the back deck that overlooks the boats bobbing at Tahoe City Marina. On weekends, barbecue chicken, ribs and steak light a fire under dinner (reservations advised), alongside seafood pastas and pizzas. Caramelized praline French toast and build-your-own sandwiches show up earlier in the day.

River Ranch Lodge NEW AMERICAN $$$

(☎530-583-4264; www.riverranchlodge.com; Hwy 89 at Alpine Meadows Rd; mains patio & cafe $8-15, restaurant $18-31; lunch Jun-Sep, dinner year-round, call for seasonal hr) This riverside dining room is a popular stop, drawing rafters and bikers to its patio for summer barbecue lunches. Dinner is a meat-heavy affair, with filet mignon and roasted duck. However, the bar's eclectic cafe menu – anything from Hawaii-style ahi *poke* (marinated raw fish) to pulled-pork sliders – will leave you feeling less like you overpaid.

Fat Cat CALIFORNIAN $$

(www.fatcattahoe.com; 599 N Tahoe Blvd; mains $10-15; 11am-9pm, bar till 2am;) Hitting that happy Goldilocks median – not too expensive, but not too cheap – this casual, family-run restaurant with local art splashed on the walls does it all: from-scratch soups, heaped salads, sandwiches, pasta bowls and plenty of fried munchies for friends to share. Look for live indie music on Friday and Saturday nights.

Rosie's Cafe DINER $$

(www.rosiescafe.com; 571 N Lake Blvd; breakfast & lunch $7-14, dinner $14-20; 7:30am-9:30pm Mon-Thu, 7:30am-10pm Fri, 7am-10pm Sat & Sun;) With antique skis, shiny bikes and lots of pointy antlers belonging to stuffed wildlife mounted on the walls, this quirky place serves breakfast until 2:30pm. The all-American hodge-podge menu is all right, but the convivial atmosphere is a winner.

Tahoe House Bakery BAKERY, TAKEOUT $

(www.tahoe-house.com; 625 W Lake Blvd; items $2-10; 6am-6pm, closing at 4pm Sun-Thu Oct-May) Before you take off down the western shore for a bike ride or hike, drop by this mom-and-pop shop that opened in the 1970s. Their motto: 'While you sleep, we loaf.' Sweet cookies, European pastries, fresh-baked deli sandwiches and homemade salads and soups will keep you going all afternoon on the trail.

Spoon AMERICAN, TAKEOUT $$

(☎530-581-5400; www.spoontakeout.com; 1785 W Lake Blvd; mains $9-14; 3-9pm, closed Tue & Wed Oct-May;) Call ahead for takeout, or squeeze yourselves into the cozy upstairs dining room at this little slat-sided cabin by the side of the highway. Barbecue tri-tip beef sandwiches, roasted veggies, baked pastas and chicken enchiladas are the comfort-food staples, with brownies and ice cream for dessert.

New Moon Natural Foods GROCERY, TAKEOUT $

(505 W Lake Blvd; dishes $6-10; 9am-7pm Mon-Sat, 10am-6pm Sun;) Tucked away in a tiny but well-stocked natural-foods store, this gem of a deli concocts scrumptious ethnic food to go, all packaged in biodegradable and compostable containers. Try the Thai salad with organic greens and spicy peanut sauce.

Dam Café CAFE $

(55 W Lake Blvd; items $2-8; 7am-3:30pm) Right by the Truckee River dam and the Fanny Bridge, stash your bikes in the racks outside this cute cottage and walk inside for a breakfast burrito, ice-cream fruit smoothie or pick-me-up espresso.

Syd's Bagelry and Espresso CAFE $
(550 N Lake Blvd; items $2-10; ⏲6am-4pm; 📶) A handy spot on the main drag serves bagels and locally roasted coffee, plus smoothies and fresh homemade soups (often vegan) made with organic produce.

Bridgetender Tavern BAR, GRILL $$
(www.tahoebridgetender.com; 65 W Lake Blvd; mains $8-12; ⏲11am-11pm, to midnight Fri & Sat) Après-ski crowds gather for beer, burgers and chili-cheese or garlic waffle fries at this woodsy bar. In summer, grab a seat on the open-air patio.

Information

Tahoe City Downtown Association (www.visittahoecity.org) Free tourist information and online events calendar.

Tahoe City Library (☎530-583-3382; Boatworks Mall, 740 N Lake Blvd; ⏲10am-5pm Tue & Thu-Fri, noon-7pm Wed, 10am-2pm Sun; @📶) Free wi-fi and walk-in internet terminals.

Tahoe City Visitors Information Center (☎530-581-6900, 888-434-1262; www.gotahoenorth.com; 380 N Lake Blvd; ⏲9am-5pm) North of the fire station.

Truckee Tahoe Medical Group (☎530-581-8864 ext 3; www.ttmg.net; Trading Post Center, 925 N Lake Blvd; ⏲9am-6pm Mon-Sat year-round, also 10am-5pm Sun early Jul-early Sep) Walk-in clinic for nonemergencies.

Getting There & Around

With a saucy acronym and reliable service, **Tahoe Area Rapid Transit** (TART; ☎530-550-1212, 800-736-6365; www.laketahoetransit.com; single/day pass $2/4) runs buses along the north shore as far as Incline Village, down the western shore to Tahoma (continuing south to Ed Z'berg Sugar Pine Point State Park between June and September only), and north to Squaw Valley and Truckee via Hwy 89. The main routes typically run every 30 to 60 minutes from 6am or 7am until 5pm or 6pm daily.

Between June and September, TART also operates a night-time **Tahoe Trolley**, a free local bus service connecting Squaw Valley, Tahoe City, Carnelian Bay, Tahoe Vista, Kings Beach, Crystal Bay and Incline Village hourly from 7pm until 10pm, 11pm or midnight. Two more free nighttime summer-only trolley routes loop between Tahoe City and Tahoma via Sunnyside and Homewood, and between Northstar-at-Tahoe, Kings Beach and Crystal Bay, every hour from 6pm until 10:30pm daily.

Squaw Valley

The nirvana of the north shore, Squaw Valley played host to the 1960 Olympic Winter Games and still ranks among the world's top ski resorts (also see p354). The stunning setting amid granite peaks, though, makes it a superb destination in any season, and this deluxe family-friendly resort stays almost as busy in summer as in winter.

Sights & Activities

Much of the summertime action centers on 8200ft **High Camp** (☎800-403-0206; www.squaw.com; cable-car adult/child under 13/youth 13-18yr $29/10/22, all-access pass $63/57/57; 🐾), reached by a dizzying cable car (leashed dogs OK). At the top you'll find a heated seasonal outdoor swimming lagoon (adult/child $14/7), 18-hole disc-golf course (free), two high-altitude tennis courts (racquet rentals and ball purchase available), a kids-only zip line ($12) and a roller-skating rink (adult/child $10/5) that doubles as an ice-skating rink in winter. Cable-car tickets include admission to the **Olympic Museum**, which relives those magic moments from 1960.

Several hiking trails radiate out from High Camp, or try the lovely, moderate **Shirley Lake Trail** (round-trip 5 miles), which follows a sprightly creek to waterfalls, granite boulders and abundant wildflowers. It starts at the mountain base, near the end of Squaw Peak Rd, behind the cable-car building. Leashed dogs are allowed.

Other fun activities down below include a ropes course, a climbing wall, mini golf and a Sky Jump (bungee trampoline), all operated by the **Squaw Valley Adventure Center** (☎530-583-7673; www.squawadventure.com). Golfers tee up at the 18-hole, par 71, Scottish-style links **Resort at Squaw Creek Golf Course** (☎530-581-6637; www.squawcreek.com; green fee incl cart $50-95); rental clubs are available.

Sleeping & Eating

For more resort hotel and condo lodging options, including ski-vacation packages, contact **Squaw Valley** (☎800-403-0206; www.squaw.com).

TOP CHOICE **PlumpJack Squaw Valley Inn** BOUTIQUE HOTEL $$$
(☎530-583-1576, 800-323-7666; www.plumpjacksquawvalleyinn.com; 1920 Squaw Valley Rd, Olym-

pic Valley; r incl breakfast $169-349;) Bed down at this artsy boutique hotel in the village, where every room has mountain views and extra-comfort factors like plush terry-cloth robes and slippers. Ski-in, ski-out access doesn't hurt either, but a $150 pet fee will. The chic **PlumpJack Cafe** (mains $23-31; 6pm-9pm, bar 11:30am-10pm), with its crisp linens and plush banquettes, serves seasonally inspired California cuisine with ace wines.

Le Chamois & Loft Bar PIZZERIA, PUB **$$**
(www.squawchamois.com; 1970 Squaw Valley Rd; mains $8-16; 11am-6pm Mon-Fri, to 8pm Sat & Sun, bar open to 9pm or 10pm;) For a social bite after shedding your bindings, this slope-side favorite is handily positioned between the cable-car building and the rental shop. Slide on over to devour a hot sammy or pizza and a beer with eye-pleasing mountain views.

Wildflour Baking Company BAKERY, TAKEOUT **$**
(http://wildfloursquaw.com; items $2-10; 7am-7pm or later;) Fresh-baked bread sandwiches and bagels make great breakfasts or afternoon snacks at this to-go counter in the cable-car building. Baristas whip up Scharffenberger hot chocolate and brew Peet's coffee and teas.

Getting There & Away

The village at Squaw Valley, at the base of the mountain cable-car, is about a 20-minute drive from Tahoe City or Truckee via Hwy 89 (turn off at Squaw Valley Rd).

Tahoe Area Rapid Transit (TART; 530-550-1212, 800-736-6365; www.laketahoetransit.com; single/day pass $2/4) buses between Truckee and Tahoe City, Kings Beach and Crystal Bay stop at Squaw Valley every hour or so between 7am and 5pm daily, with a free morning ski shuttle from December to April.

Truckee & Donner Lake

Cradled by mountains and the Tahoe National Forest, Truckee is a thriving town steeped in Old West history. It was put on the map by the railroad, grew rich on logging and ice harvesting, and even had its brush with Hollywood during the 1924 filming of Charlie Chaplin's *The Gold Rush*. Today tourism fills much of the city's coffers, thanks to a well-preserved historical downtown and its proximity to Lake Tahoe and no fewer than six downhill and four cross-country ski resorts (see p353).

Sights

The aura of the Old West still lingers over Truckee's teensy one-horse downtown, where railroad workers and lumberjacks once milled about in raucous saloons, bawdy brothels and shady gambling halls. Most of the late-19th-century buildings now contain restaurants and upscale boutiques. Donner Memorial State Park and three-mile-long Donner Lake, a busy recreational hub, are another 3 miles further west.

Donner Memorial State Park PARK
(530-582-7892; www.parks.ca.gov; per car $8; seasonal park hr vary, museum 9am-4pm year-round) At the eastern end of Donner Lake, this state-run park occupies one of the sites where the doomed Donner Party got trapped during the fateful winter of 1846–47 (see the boxed text, p378). Though its history is gruesome, the park is gorgeous and has a sandy beach, picnic tables hiking trails and wintertime cross-country skiing and snowshoeing.

The entry fee includes admission to the excellent **Emigrant Trail Museum**, which has fascinating, if admittedly macabre historical exhibits and a 25-minute film re-enacting the Donner Party's horrific plight. (In future years, it will be replaced by a newer, bigger and more multicultural High Sierra Crossing Museum.) Outside, the **Pioneer Monument** has a 22ft pedestal – the exact depth of the snow piles that horrendous winter. A short trail leads to a memorial at one family's cabin site.

Old Jail HISTORIC BUILDING
(http://truckeehistory.org; 10142 Jiboom St, cnr Spring St; suggested donation $2; 11am-4pm Sat & Sun late May & mid-Jun–mid-Sep) Continuously in use until the 1960s, this 1875 red-brick building is filled with relics from the wild days of yore. George 'Machine Gun' Kelly was reportedly once held here for shoplifting at a local variety store, and 'Baby Face' Nelson and 'Ma' Spinelli and her gang did time too.

Activities

For outdoor-sports equipment rentals and in-the-know local advice, try:

THE DOOMED DONNER PARTY

In the 19th century, tens of thousands of people migrated west along the Overland Trail with dreams of a better life in California. Among them was the ill-fated Donner Party.

When the families of George and Jacob Donner and their friend James Reed departed Springfield, Illinois, in April 1846 with six wagons and a herd of livestock, they intended to make the arduous journey as comfortable as possible. But the going was slow and, when other pioneers told them about a cutoff that would save 200 miles, they jumped at the chance.

However, there was no road for the wagons in the Wasatch Mountains, and most of the livestock succumbed under the merciless heat of the Great Salt Lake Desert. Arguments and fights broke out. James Reed killed a man, was kicked out of the group and left to trundle off to California alone. By the time the party reached the eastern foot of the Sierra Nevada, near present-day Reno, morale and food supplies ran dangerously low.

To restore their livestock's energy and reprovision, the emigrants decided to rest here for a few days. But an exceptionally fierce winter came early, quickly rendering what later came to be called Donner Pass impassable and forcing the pioneers to build basic shelter near today's Donner Lake. They had food to last a month and the fervent hope that the weather would clear by then. It didn't.

Snow fell for weeks, reaching a depth of 22ft. Hunting and fishing became impossible. In mid-December a small group of people made a desperate attempt to cross the pass. They quickly became disoriented and had to ride out a three-day storm that killed some of them. One month later, less than half of the original 15 staggered into Sutter's Fort near Sacramento, having survived on one deer and their dead friends.

By the time the first rescue party arrived at Donner Lake in late February, the trapped pioneers were still surviving – barely – on boiled ox hides. But when the second rescue party, led by the banished James Reed, made it through in March, evidence of cannibalism was everywhere. Journals and reports tell of 'half-crazed people living in absolute filth, with naked, half-eaten bodies strewn about the cabins.' Many were too weak to travel.

When the last rescue party arrived in mid-April, only a sole survivor, Lewis Keseberg, was there to greet them. The rescuers found George Donner's body cleansed and wrapped in a sheet, but no sign of Tasmen Donner, George's wife. Keseberg admitted to surviving on the flesh of the dead, but denied charges that he had killed Tasmen for fresh meat. He spent the rest of his life trying to clear his name.

In the end, only 47 of the 89 members of the Donner Party survived. They settled in California, their lives forever changed by the harrowing winter at Donner Lake.

Back Country OUTDOOR OUTFITTER
(☎530-582-0909; www.thebackcountry.com; 11400 Donner Pass Rd; ⏰8:30am-6pm, call ahead in winter & spring) Rents bicycles and snowshoes, and rents and sells new and used climbing gear, as well as backcountry ski gear.

Porters Tahoe OUTDOOR OUTFITTER
(☎530-587-1500; www.porterstahoe.com; 11391 Deerfield Dr; ⏰10am-6pm; 👪) In the Crossroads Center strip mall, Porters rents skis, snowboards and snowshoes on a first-come, first-served basis.

Truckee Sports Exchange OUTDOOR OUTFITTER
(☎530-582-4510; www.truckeesportsexchange.com; 10095 W River St; ⏰call for seasonal hr) Big indoor climbing gym (day pass $5, shoe rental $5); rents kayaks and SUP gear.

Beaches & Water Sports

Warmer than Lake Tahoe, tree-lined **Donner Lake** is great for swimming, boating, fishing (license required), waterskiing and windsurfing. **West End Beach** (adult/child 1-17yr $4/3; 👪) is a favorite of families for its roped-off swimming area, snack stand, volleyball nets and kayak, paddleboat and stand-up paddle boarding (SUP) rentals.

Tributary Whitewater Tours RIVER RUNNING
(☎530-346-6812, 800-672-3846; www.whitewatertours.com; half-day trip per adult/child 7-17yr $69/62; 👪) From roughly mid-May through September, this long-running outfitter operates a 7-mile, half-day rafting run on the Truckee River over Class III+ rapids that

will thrill kids and their nervous parents alike.

Hiking & Climbing

Truckee is a great base for treks in the Tahoe National Forest, especially around Donner Summit. One popular 5-mile hike reaches the summit of 8243ft **Mt Judah** for awesome views of Donner Lake and the surrounding peaks. A longer, more strenuous ridge-crest hike links **Donner Pass** to **Squaw Valley** (15 miles each way) skirting the base of prominent peaks, but you'll need two cars for this shuttle hike.

Donner Summit is also a major rock-climbing mecca, with over 300 traditional and sport climbing routes. To learn the ropes, so to speak, take a class with **Alpine Skills International** (☎530-582-9170; www.alpineskills.com; 11400 Donner Pass Rd).

Tours

Tahoe Adventure Company OUTDOOR SPORTS
(☎530-913-9212, 866-830-6125; http://tahoeadventurecompany.com; tours per person from $50) A great option for guided high-Sierra adventures. Staff know the backcountry inside out and can customize any outing to your interest and skill level, from kayaking, hiking, mountain-biking and rock climbing to any combination thereof. They also offer full-moon snowshoe tours, and SUP lessons and guided lake paddles.

Sleeping

A few dependable midrange chain motels and hotels are also found off I-80 exits.

TOP CHOICE **Cedar House Sport Hotel** BOUTIQUE HOTEL $$$
(☎530-582-5655, 866-582-5655; www.cedarhousesporthotel.com; 10918 Brockway Rd; r incl breakfast $170-270;) This chic, environmentally conscious contemporary lodge aims at getting folks out into nature. It boasts countertops made from recycled paper, 'rain chains' that redistribute water from the green roof garden, low-flow plumbing and in-room recycling. However, it doesn't skimp on plush robes, sexy platform beds with pillow-top mattresses, flat-screen TVs or the outdoor hot tub. Guided tours and multisport outdoor adventures can be arranged in-house. Pet fee $50 to $100.

Clair Tappaan Lodge HOSTEL $
(☎530-426-3632, 800-629-6775; www.sierraclub.org/outings/lodges/ctl; 19940 Donner Pass Rd; dm incl family-style meals per adult $50-60, child under 14yr $25-32;) About a mile west of Sugar Bowl, this cozy Sierra Club–owned rustic mountain lodge puts you near major ski resorts and sleeps up to 140 people in dorms and family rooms. Rates include family-style meals, but you're expected to do small chores and bring your own sleeping bag, towel and swimsuit (for the hot tub!). In winter, go cross-country skiing or snowshoeing (see p357), or careen down the sledding hill out back.

Larkspur Hotel Truckee-Tahoe HOTEL $$$
(☎530-587-4525, 800-824-6385; www.larkspurhotels.com; 11331 Brockway Rd; r incl breakfast $159-249;) Forget about retro ski-lodge kitsch as you cozy up inside these crisp, earth-toned and down-to-earth hotel rooms that abound in sunny, natural woods. Sink back onto the feather-topped mattresses, refresh yourself with spa-quality bath amenities or hit the seasonal outdoor heated pool by the hot tub and cedar dry sauna. Continental breakfast buffet included. Pet fee $25 to $75.

Truckee Donner Lodge HOTEL $$
(☎530-582-9999, 877-878-2533; www.truckeedonnerlodge.com; 10527 Cold Stream Rd, off I-80 exit Donner Pass Rd; r incl breakfast $84-204;) Just west of Hwy 89, this ex-Holiday Inn property gives you easy driving access to area ski resorts, shaving time off your morning commute to the slopes. No-nonsense, spacious hotel rooms come with microwaves and mini-fridges, and some have gas fireplaces. The hot-and-cold continental breakfast bar is complimentary.

Truckee Hotel HISTORIC HOTEL $$
(☎530-587-4444, 800-659-6921; www.truckeehotel.com; 10007 Bridge St; r with shared bath $49-169, with private bath $99-169, all incl breakfast;) Tucked behind an atmospheric red-brick street front arcade, Truckee's most historic abode has welcomed weary travelers since 1873. It's fully restored but still gives you that total Victorian immersion. Expect simply furnished rooms with drab, mismatched antiques and some train noise. Parking is inconvenient – ask first to avoid being towed.

River Street Inn B&B $$
(☎530-550-9290; http://riverstreetinntruckee.com; 10009 E River St; r incl breakfast $115-195) On the far side of the tracks, this sweet 1885 Victorian in Truckee's historic downtown

has 11 rooms that blend nostalgic touches like clawfoot tubs with down comforters, but have few amenities other than TVs. Mingle with other guests over breakfast in the lounge. Bring earplugs to dull the occasional train noise.

Donner Memorial State Park Campground CAMPGROUND $
(☎info 530-582-7894, reservations 800-444-7275; www.reserveamerica.com; tent & RV sites $35, hike-and-bike sites $7; ⊙late May-late Sep;) Near Donner Lake, this family-oriented campground has 138 campsites with flush toilets and hot pay showers.

USFS Campgrounds CAMPGROUND $
(☎877-444-6777; www.recreation.gov; tent & RV sites $17-38; ⊙mid-May–mid-Oct;) Conveniently located along Hwy 89 are three minimally developed riverside camping areas: Granite Flat, Goose Meadow and Silver Creek. All have potable water and vault toilets.

Eating & Drinking

TOP CHOICE **Moody's Bistro & Lounge** CALIFORNIAN $$$
(☎530-587-8688; www.moodysbistro.com; 10007 Bridge St; lunch $12-16, dinner $20-34; ⊙11:30am-9:30pm Mon-Thu, 11:30am-10pm Fri, 11am-10pm Sat & 11am-9:30pm Sun) With its sophisticated supper-club looks and live jazz (Thursday to Saturday evenings), this gourmet restaurant in the Truckee Hotel oozes urbane flair. Only the freshest, organic and locally grown ingredients make it into the chef's perfectly pitched concoctions like pork lion with peach barbecue sauce, roasted beets with shaved fennel, or tempura-fried mozzarella with herbs.

Stella ECLECTIC $$$
(☎530-582-5665; www.cedarhousesporthotel.com; 10918 Brockway Rd; mains $18-31; ⊙usually 5:30-8:30pm Wed-Sun) Housed at the trendy Cedar House Sport Hotel, this modern mountain-lodge dining room elevates Truckee's dining scene with Californian flair, harmonizing Asian and Mediterranean influences on its seasonal menu of housemade pastas, grilled meats and pan-roasted seafood. Bonuses: veggies grown on-site, housemade artisan bread and a killer wine list.

Squeeze In DINER $$
(☎530-587-9814; www.squeezein.com; 10060 Donner Pass Rd; mains $8-13; ⊙7am-2pm;) Across from the Amtrak station, this snug locals' favorite dishes up breakfasts big enough to feed a lumberjack. Over 60 varieties of humungous omelets – along with burgers, burritos and big salads – are dished up in this funky place crammed with silly tchotchkes and colorful handwritten notes plastered on the walls.

Burger Me AMERICAN $$
(http://burgermetruckee.com; 10418 Donner Pass Rd; items $2-14; ⊙11am-9pm;) Getting two thumbs up from Food Network punk Guy Fieri may have gone to these guys' heads, but this fresh take on a burger shop still stocks all-natural meats and farm-fresh vegetables in the kitchen. Try the 'Truckee Trainwreck' – a beef patty topped with cheddar cheese, onion rings, turkey chili and a fried egg – if you dare.

Coffeebar CAFE $
(www.coffeebartruckee.com; 10120 Jiboom St; items $2-8; ⊙6am-8pm;) Acid-orange molded chairs and electro tunes set the backdrop for this beatnik, bare-bones industrial coffee shop. Go for tantalizing breakfast crepes and overstuffed panini on herbed focaccia bread, or go for a jolt of organic espresso or an inspired specialty nectar like Vanilla Earl Cambric.

Fifty Fifty Brewing Co BREWPUB $$
(www.fiftyfiftybrewing.com; 11197 Brockway Rd; mains $10-27; ⊙11:30am-2am, kitchen closes earlier) Inhale the aroma of toasting grains at this brewpub south of downtown, near the Hwy 267 intersection. Sip the popular Donner Party Porter or Eclipse barrel-aged imperial stout while noshing a huge plate of nachos, but skip the other so-so pub grub. Cozy Avec wine-tasting bar is nearby.

Information

Tahoe Forest Hospital (☎530-587-6011; www.tfhd.com; 10121 Pine Ave, cnr Donner Pass Rd; ⊙24hr) Emergency room, specializing in sports injuries.

Truckee Donner Chamber of Commerce (☎530-587-2757, 866-443-2027; www.truckee.com; 10065 Donner Pass Rd; internet access per 15min $3; ⊙9am-6pm; @) Inside the Amtrak train depot; free walking-tour maps and wi-fi.

USFS Truckee District Ranger Station (☎530-587-3558; 10811 Stockrest Springs Rd, off I-80 exit 188; ⊙8am-5pm Mon-Sat) Keeps shorter winter hours.

Getting There & Around

Truckee straddles the I-80 and is connected to the lakeshore via Hwy 89 to Tahoe City or Hwy 267 to Kings Beach. The main drag through downtown Truckee is Donner Pass Rd, where you'll find the Amtrak train depot and metered on-street parking. Brockway Rd begins south of the river, connecting over to Hwy 267.

Though the Truckee Tahoe Airport has no commercial air service, **North Lake Tahoe Express** (☎866-216-5222; www.northlaketahoeexpress.com; one-way/round-trip per person $40/75) shuttles to the closest airport at Reno (see p448). Buses make several runs daily from 3:30am to midnight, serving multiple northern and western shore towns and Northstar-at-Tahoe and Squaw Valley ski resorts. Make reservations in advance.

Greyhound (☎800-231-2222; www.greyhound.com) has twice-daily buses to Reno ($18, one hour), Sacramento ($36, 2½ hours) and San Francisco ($34, 5½ to six hours). Greyhound buses stop at the train depot, as do **Amtrak** (☎800-872-7245; www.amtrak.com) Thruway buses and the daily *California Zephyr* train to Reno ($18, 1½ hours), Sacramento ($37, 4½ hours) and Emeryville/San Francisco ($41, 6½ hours).

The **Truckee Trolley** (☎530-587-7451; www.laketahoetransit.com; single/day pass $2/4) links the Amtrak train depot with Donner Lake hourly from 9am to 5pm daily. For Tahoe City and other towns on the lake's north, west or east shores, hop on the TART bus (p376) at the train depot. Single-ride TART tickets cost $2 (day pass $4). During ski season, additional buses run to many area ski resorts.

Northern Shore

Northeast of Tahoe City, Hwy 28 cruises through a string of cute, low-key towns, many fronting superb sandy beaches, with reasonably priced roadside motels and hotels all crowded together along the lakeshore. Oozing old-fashioned charm, the north shore is a blissful escape from the teeming crowds of South Lake Tahoe, Tahoe City and Truckee, but still puts you within easy reach of winter ski resorts and snow parks, summertime swimming, kayaking, hiking trails and more.

The **North Lake Tahoe Visitors' Bureaus** (☎800-824-0348; www.gotahoenorth.com) can help get you oriented, although their closest walk-in office is at Incline Village, Nevada (see p383).

TAHOE VISTA

Pretty little Tahoe Vista has more **public beaches** (http://northtahoeparks.com) than any other lakeshore town. Sandy strands along Hwy 28 include small but popular **Moon Dunes Beach**, with picnic tables and firepits opposite the Rustic Cottages; **Tahoe Vista Recreation Area** (7010 N Lake Blvd), a locals' favorite with a small grassy area and marina; and **North Tahoe Beach** (7860 N Lake Blvd), near the Hwy 267 intersection, with picnic facilities, barbecue grills, beach volleyball courts and the **Tahoe Adventure Company** (☎530-913-9212, 866-830-6125; http://tahoeadventurecompany.com) for rental kayaks and SUP gear ($15 to $80).

Away from all the maddening crowds, **North Tahoe Regional Park** (http://northtahoeparks.com; 6600 Donner Rd; per car $3; 👪) offers forested hiking and mountain-biking trails, an 18-hole disc-golf course, a children's playground and tennis courts lit-up for night play. In winter, a sledding hill and ungroomed cross-country ski and snowshoe tracks beckon. To find this hidden park, drive almost a mile uphill from Hwy 28 on National Ave, then go left on Donner Rd and follow the signs.

Sleeping

Rustic Cottages COTTAGE $$
(☎530-546-3523, 888-778-7842; www.rusticcottages.com; 7449 N Lake Blvd; cottages incl breakfast $75-229; 📶🐾) These cottages consist of a cluster of about 20 little storybook houses in the pines, with nametags fashioned from hand saws. They sport beautiful wrought-iron beds and a bevy of amenities. Most cabins have full kitchens, and some have gas or real wood-burning fireplaces to warm your heart's cockles. Other perks: waffles and homemade muffins at breakfast, and free sleds and snowshoes to borrow in winter.

Franciscan Lakeside Lodge CABIN, COTTAGE $$
(☎530-546-6300, 800-564-6754; http://franciscanlodge.com; 6944 N Lake Blvd; cabins, cottages & ste $85-345; 📶🏊👪) Spend the day on a private sandy beach or in the outdoor pool, then light the barbecue grill after sunset – ah, now that's relaxation. All of the simple cabins, cottages and suites have kitchenettes. Lakeside lodgings have better beach access and views, but roomier cabins near the back of the complex tend to be quieter and will appeal to families with younger kids in tow.

Cedar Glen Lodge INN $$
(☎530-546-4281; www.tahoecedarglen.com; 6589 N Lake Blvd; r, ste & cottages incl breakfast $89-199;) Kids go nuts over all the freebies, from ping-pong tables, horseshoe pit, volleyball and croquet courts to an outdoor swimming pool and toasty firepit. Opposite the beach, some of these woodsy suites and cottages have kitchenettes and air-con, though standard-issue rooms look bland. Morning waffles and Bananas Foster on weekends help sleepyheads rise and shine. Pet fee $30.

Eating & Drinking

TOP CHOICE **Wild Goose** CALIFORNIAN $$$
(☎530-546-3640; www.wildgoosetahoe.com; 7320 N Lake Blvd; mains $20-36; ⏲5:30-9pm Wed-Mon, bar from 2pm Wed-Thu & Sun-Mon, from 4pm Fri & Sat) Inhabiting a rehabbed ecofriendly lakefront building with inspirational panoramic windows, this New American bistro claims a globally inspired chef and a cellar that gets the nod from *Wine Spectator*. Leek and goat-cheese ravioli, oven-roasted chicken with fried artichoke and filet mignon with melted Maytag blue-cheese butter share a menu with Valhrona dark-chocolate fondue. Reservations are essential, but waterfront tables on the open-air deck are still first-come, first-served.

Gar Woods Grill & Pier AMERICAN $$$
(☎530-546-3366; www.garwoods.com; 5000 N Lake Blvd; mains lunch $12-18, dinner $18-37; ⏲noon-9:30pm Mon-Thu, noon-10pm Fri, 11:30am-10pm Sat, 11:30am-9:30pm Sun, bar till 11:30pm Sun-Thu, midnight Fri & Sat) A shoreline hot spot judging by the rowdy crowds, Gar Woods pays tribute to the era of classic wooden boats. Don't show up for the lackadaisical grill fare, but instead to slurp a Wet Woody cocktail while watching sunset over the lake. Be prepared to duke it out for a table on the no-reservations side of the beachfront deck out back.

Old Post Office Cafe DINER $
(5245 N Lake Blvd; mains $6-12; ⏲6:30am-2pm) Head west of town toward Carnelian Bay, where this always-packed, cheery wooden shack serves scrumptious breakfasts – buttery potatoes, crab-cake eggs Benedict, biscuits with gravy, fluffy omelettes with lotsa fillings and fresh-fruit smoothies. Waits for a table get long on summer and winter weekends, so roll up early.

El Sancho's MEXICAN, TAKEOUT $
(7019 N Lake Blvd; items $4-10; ⏲9am-9pm) Grab a big fat burrito or an order of *huaraches* – fried *masa* (cornmeal dough) topped with sauce, cheese and fried meat or beans – and a Mexican cane-sugar soda pop from this roadside *taqueria*.

KINGS BEACH

The utilitarian character of fetchingly picturesque Kings Beach lies in its smattering of back-to-basics retro motels all lined up along the highway. But in summer all eyes are on **Kings Beach State Recreation Area** (www.parks.ca.gov;), a seductive 700ft-long beach that often gets deluged with sun-seekers and leashed dogs. At the beach, you'll find picnic tables, barbecue grills and a fun kids' play structure, while nearby concessionaires rent kayaks, jet skis, paddleboats, SUP gear and more. **Adrift Tahoe** (☎530-546-1112, 888-676-7702; www.standuppaddletahoe.com; 8338 N Lake Blvd; ⏲call for seasonal hr) is one of several local outfitters offering kayak, outrigger canoe and SUP rentals, private lessons and tours, as well as yoga classes on the beach. Further inland, the nostalgic 1920s **Old Brockway Golf Course** (☎530-546-9909; www.oldbrockway.com; 7900 N Lake Blvd; green fee $25-40, club/cart rental from $18/20) is a quick par-36, nine-hole diversion with peekaboo lake views from along pine tree-lined fairways where Hollywood celebs hobnobbed back in the day.

Eating & Drinking

Log Cabin Café DINER $$
(☎530-546-7109; www.logcabinbreakfast.com; 8692 N Lake Blvd; mains $8-15; ⏲7am-2pm) Come early (especially on weekends) to join the queue for the North Shore's best breakfast. Eggs Benedict, whole-wheat pancakes with hot fresh fruit and cranberry-orange waffles are just a few highlights from the huge menu. Tip: call ahead to put your name on the waitlist if you'd rather not wait an hour for a table.

Lanza's ITALIAN $$
(www.lanzastahoe.com; 7739 N Lake Blvd; mains $12-22; ⏲5-10pm, bar from 4:30pm) Next to the Safeway supermarket stands this beloved Italian trattoria where a tantalizing aroma of garlic, rosemary and 'secret' spices perfumes the air. Dinners, though undoubtedly not the tastiest you've ever had, are hugely filling and include salad and bread. Look for

the owner's sepia-colored family photos in the entranceway.

Jason's Beachside Grille BAR & GRILL $$
(www.jasonsbeachsidegrille.com; 8338 N Lake Blvd; mains lunch $8-13, dinner $13-25; ⏲11am-10pm) Looking for the party around sundown? Hit this waterfront deck with a schooner of microbrew. Never mind the unexciting American fare, like smoked chicken pasta, alongside an overflowing salad bar. On colder days, red-velvet sofas orbiting a sunken fireplace are the coziest, but in summer it's all about sunset views.

Char-Pit AMERICAN $
(www.charpit.com; 8732 N Lake Blvd; items $2-8; ⏲11am-9pm; 👪) No gimmicks at this 1960s fast-food stand, which grills juicy burgers and St Louis–style baby back ribs, and also fries up crispy onion rings and breaded mozzarella sticks. Somebody call an ambulance!

Grid Bar & Grill PUB $
(www.thegridbarandgrill.com; 8545 N Lake Blvd; items $4-11; ⏲11am-2pm) This locals' dive bar looks rough round the edges, but happy hours are super-cheap and you can catch live music, from bluegrass to punk, DJs, dancing or karaoke, or trivia nights.

ℹ Getting There & Around

Tahoe Area Rapid Transit (TART; ☎530-550-1212, 800-736-6365; www.laketahoetransit.com; single/day pass $2/4) buses between Tahoe City and Incline Village make stops in Tahoe Vista, Kings Beach and Crystal Bay every 30 minutes from approximately 6am until 6pm daily. Another TART route connects Crystal Bay and Kings Beach with the Northstar-at-Tahoe resort every hour or so from 8am until 5pm daily; in winter, this bus continues to Truckee (between May and November, you'll have to detour via Tahoe City first).

Eastern Shore

Lake Tahoe's eastern shore lies entirely within Nevada. Much of it is relatively undeveloped thanks to George Whittell Jr, an eccentric San Franciscan playboy who once owned a lot of this land, including 27 miles of shoreline. Upon his death in 1969, it was sold off to a private investor, who later wheeled and dealed most of it to the US Forest Service and Nevada State Parks. And lucky it was, because today the eastern shore offers some of Tahoe's best scenery and outdoor diversion. Hwy 28 rolls into Nevada at Crystal Bay and runs past Incline Village, heading along the eastern shore to intersect with Hwy 50, which rolls south to Zephyr Cove and Stateline casinos.

CRYSTAL BAY

Crossing into Nevada, the neon starts to flash and old-school gambling palaces pant after your hard-earned cash. The historic **Cal-Neva Resort** (☎info 800-233-5551, reservations 800-225-6382; www.calnevaresort.com; 2 Stateline Rd; r $79-209; ❄📶🏊🐾) literally straddles the California–Nevada border and has a colorful history involving ghosts, mobsters and Frank Sinatra, who once owned the joint. Shabby hotel rooms don't invite overnight stays (pet fee $50), but ask about the guided secret tunnel tours.

Also on the main drag, the **Tahoe Biltmore Lodge & Casino** (☎800-245-8667; www.tahoebiltmore.com; 5 Hwy 28; r $34-99; 📶🏊), plays up its longevity with classic Tahoe photographs in the divey hotel rooms, though radiators give away the building's age. For greasy-spoon grill fare, duck under the mirrored ceilings into the artificial forest of the chintzy **Café Biltmore** (mains $8-15; ⏲7am-10pm Sun-Thu, to midnight Fri & Sat). Then catch a live-music show across the street at the **Crystal Bay Club Casino** (☎775-831-0512; www.crystalbaycasino.com; 14 Hwy 28).

For a breath of pine-scented air, flee the smoky casinos for the steep one-mile hike up paved Forest Service Rd 1601 to **Stateline Lookout**. Sunset views over Lake Tahoe and the snowy mountains are all around. A nature trail loops around the site of the former fire lookout tower – nowadays there's a split-level stone observation platform. To find the trailhead, drive up Reservoir Rd, just east of the Tahoe Biltmore parking lot, then take a quick right onto Lakeview Ave and follow it uphill just over a half-mile to the (usually locked) iron gate on your left.

INCLINE VILLAGE

One of Lake Tahoe's ritziest communities, Incline Village is the gateway to Diamond Peak and Mt Rose ski resorts (see p355). The latter is a 12-mile drive northeast via Hwy 431 (Mt Rose Hwy). During summer, the nearby **Mt Rose Wilderness** offers miles of unspoiled terrain, including a strenuous 10-mile round-trip to the summit of majestic **Mt Rose** (10,776ft). The trail starts from the deceptively named Mt Rose Summit parking lot, 9 miles uphill from Incline Village. For a more mellow meadow stroll that even young kids can handle, pull over a mile or so earlier at wildflower-strewn **Tahoe Meadows**. Stay on the nature loop trails to avoid trampling the fragile meadows; leashed dogs are allowed.

In summer, you can also visit George Whittell's mansion, **Thunderbird Lodge** (800-468-2463; www.thunderbirdlodge.org; adult/child 6-12yr $39/19; usually Tue-Sat Jun-Sep, reservations required), where he spent summers with his pet lion, Bill. Tours include a trip down a 600ft tunnel to the card house where George used to play poker with Howard Hughes and other famous recluses. The only way to get to the lodge is by shuttle bus, leaving from the helpful in-town **Incline Village/Crystal Bay Visitors Bureau** (775-832-1606, 800-468-2463; www.gotahoenorth.com; 696 Tahoe Blvd; 8am-5pm Mon-Fri, 10am-4pm Sat & Sun;), or on a boat cruise or kayak tour ($110 to $135).

Sleeping

Hyatt Regency Lake Tahoe HOTEL $$$

(775-832-1234, 800-633-7313; http://laketahoe.hyatt.com; 111 Country Club Dr; r from $305;) Decorated like an Arts & Crafts–style mountain lodge, every room and lakeside cottage looks lavish, and the spa is even bigger than the casino. In summer you can sprawl on a private lakefront beach, or in winter let the heated outdoor swimming lagoon warm you up after a day on the slopes.

Eating & Drinking

Bite CALIFORNIAN $$

(775-831-1000; www.bitetahoe.com; shared plates $5-18; 5-10pm Sun-Wed, to 11pm Thu-Sat;) Don't let the strip-mall location stop you from rocking this creative, eclectic tapas and wine bar. Mix light, seasonal, veggie-friendly dishes with modern takes on rib-sticking comfort food like honeyed baby back ribs or green-chili mac 'n' cheese. An après-ski crowd turns up for happy hour.

Austin's AMERICAN $$

(www.austinstahoe.com; 120 Country Club Dr; mains $7-22; 11am-9pm, from 5pm Sat & Sun Sep-Jun;) A hearty welcome for the whole family is what you'll find at this wood-cabin diner with an outdoor deck. Buttermilk fries with jalapeño dipping sauce, chicken-fried steak, classic meatloaf, burgers, huge salad bowls and sandwiches will fill you up – and so will mountain-sized martinis.

Lone Eagle Grille BAR

(http://laketahoe.hyatt.com; 111 Country Club Dr; 11:30am-10pm Sun-Thu, to 11pm Fri & Sat) At the Hyatt's many-hearthed cocktail lounge, sip a divine orange-flavored margarita, then head outside for sunset and to flirt by the beach fire pit.

LAKE TAHOE-NEVADA STATE PARK

Back on the lake, heading south, is **Lake Tahoe-Nevada State Park** (775-831-0494; http://parks.nv.gov/lt.htm; Hwy 50; per car $7-12), which has beaches, lakes and miles of trails. Just 3 miles south of Incline Village is beautiful **Sand Harbor**, where two sand spits have formed a shallow bay with brilliant, warm turquoise water and white, boulder-strewn beaches. It gets very busy here, especially during July and August, when the **Lake Tahoe Shakespeare Festival** (800-747-4697; www.tahoebard.com) is underway.

At the park's southern end, just north of the Hwy 50/Hwy 28 junction, **Spooner Lake** is popular for catch-and-release fishing, picnicking, nature walks and cross-country skiing (p358). Spooner Lake is also the start of the famous 13-mile **Flume Trail**, a holy grail for experienced mountain-bikers. From the trail's end near Incline Village you can either backtrack 10 miles along the narrow, twisting shoulder of Hwy 28 or board a shuttle bus. Arrange shuttles and rent bikes by the trailhead inside the park at **Flume Trail Mountain Bikes** (775-749-5349; www.theflumetrail.com; mountain-bike rental per day $45-65, shuttle $10-15; 8:30am-6pm Jun-Nov).

A Taste of Northern California

Mango, strawberry, mint and ice-cream dessert, Sonoma County

JERRY ALEXANDER/LONELY PLANET IMAGES ©

Regional Specialties

Northern California is a place of heavenly sights, revolutionary instincts, exceptional natural bounty and extraordinary culture. But maybe we should talk about something other than lunch...

The City

Let's face it: your best meals will likely be in the cities of Northern California, which are blessed with fresh ingredients, a thriving (and cutthroat) scene of ethnic restaurants, and lots of attention.

Take San Francisco: between 1849 and 1850 it ballooned from a sleepy cove of 800 to a Gold Rush boomtown of 25,000. Since men outnumbered women roughly 100 to 1 (and 19th-century men didn't often take Home Ec), someone had to cook. From Chinese noodle shops to fancy French dining, San Francisco became an instant culinary capital. There's still one restaurant for every 28 San Franciscans – 10 times more than any other North American city – and San Francisco has more award-winning chefs per capita than any other US city (sorry, New York). Today the hottest trend is gourmet food trucks and 'pop-up restaurants,' which serve haute food for low overhead, adhere to lenient regulation and appeal to rebellious culinary innovators. Could anything be more emblematic of Northern California?

The Valley

From above, the Central Valley – America's most agriculturally rich region – looks like a green garden. As it should; it accounts for a sizable percentage of domestic produce. Hot, sunny, and watered with Sierra snowmelt, this area grows anything that isn't tropical, and produces millions of pounds of tomatoes, grapes, stone fruit, almonds and asparagus. Even though much valley turf is controlled by huge

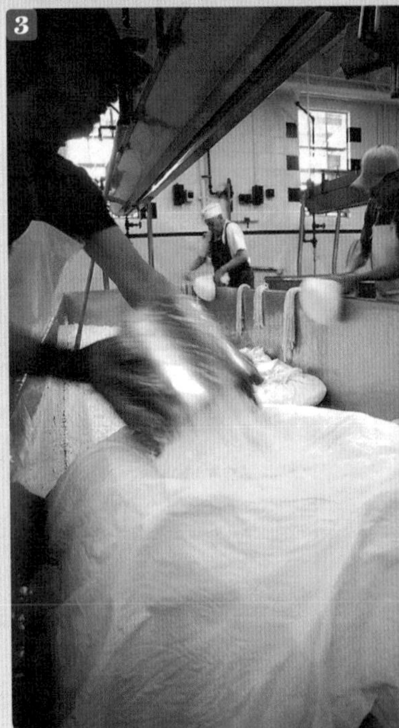

Clockwise from top left

1. Burrito, corn chips and salsa **2.** Preparing crabs at Fisherman's Wharf (p60), San Francisco **3.** Making cheese at Vella Cheese Co (p187), Sonoma

JERRY ALEXANDER/LONELY PLANET IMAGES ©

LEE FOSTER/LONELY PLANET IMAGES ©

ibusiness conglomerates, it also hosts rowing number of farms dedicated organic vegetables, dairy products l meat, whose goods often end up discerning restaurants in Northern ifornia. You'll be hard pressed to find sher food – organic or not – than at the n stands of the Central Valley.

ne Coast

housand miles of Pacific coastline and res of rushing rivers mean that the fruits he waters are a staple of the California t. In the winter, travelers tie on bibs rab feeds on the coast; from spring ough fall, local salmon is on the menu; l tourists obsess about clam chowder in ourdough bowl year-round. Though most he indigenous oysters are gone, you still shuck fresh, briny ones at oyster ns in Drakes Bay near Point Reyes. But nember to eat responsibly. Monterey Bay uarium (www.montereybayaquarium.org) olishes a 'Seafood Watch: West Coast' wnloadable pocket guide that lists good, tainably harvested seafood.

The Mountains

Nature smiles on the mountains, which are both rugged and lush, yielding mountain honey, wild blackberries, chanterelle mushrooms and other wild-crafted delicacies. At roadside inns, restaurants and saloons, the cuisine has a historical precedent to cater equally to rugged appetites and downright lushes. Lacking the patience for agriculture or families for consolation, miners wanted fast food, faster women and strong drink. Breweries and bordellos flourished; public health did not. But there were competing culinary forces at work in seasonal, local, wild-crafted Ohlone and Miwok cuisine. In addition to fishing, hunting game, and gathering wild mushrooms and berries, these indigenous Californians tended orchards and cultivated foods. Some of these traditions are still around today, even though mountain menus often are geared to hikers who are ready to indulge carnivorous inclinations.

From Farm to Table

Calculate the distance between your tomato's origin and your fork: chances are it's shorter than usual. Northern Californian 'locavores' fancy themselves on the sustainable-food vanguard, and they might be right.

Seeds of Revolt

The long-simmering reaction to the previous generation's rapid industrialization of food found particularly assertive expression in Northern California. Measured against the rest of the country, Californians are picky eaters indeed.

This spirit is most evident in the region's abundant farmers markets, which have affected the food economy by connecting families directly to farmers. The Bay Area hosts nearly 200 farmers markets, many of which fill public spaces on weekends.

In addition to the standard veggies, markets offer sustainable meats, rare and heirloom varieties of vegetables, and foods picked at peak ripeness – often too delicate for conventional packing and shipping. And the difference is apparent from the first bite.

Sustainable Dining

You don't have to have a kitchen to enjoy the fruits of Northern California. The region's delicious strengths are equally evident when you sit down to order at a restaurant. Restaurants in Northern California are more dedicated to sustainable, organic, local ingredients than any other region of the US.

The connection between the rich soil and waters of Northern California and its elegant houses of fine dining is unavoidable. Organic, local produce is almost a given; you'll also find rare treats like sustainably farmed abalone (the prized dish of Native Americans), a winter harvest of wild mushrooms and line-caught trout.

Clockwise from top left
1. Harvesting fresh blueberries 2. Kitchen at French Laundry restaurant (p169), Yountville 3. Organic vegetables at the Occidental farmers market (p196)

THE QUEEN OF CALIFORNIA CUISINE: ALICE WATERS

Some revolutions start with a manifesto. But Alice Waters – chef, author and proprietor of now-famous Berkeley restaurant Chez Panisse – changed American diets with a menu. Back in 1971, diners at Chez Panisse lacked the terminology to describe the food they tasted. It would be years until terms like 'California cuisine,' 'certified organic,' and 'locavore' (one who eats food grown locally) were coined.

Waters' programs outside her restaurant – like the Edible Schoolyard program, which encourages healthy food in public schools, and the Chez Panisse Foundation, which partnered with First Lady Michelle Obama's 'Let's Move!' campaign against childhood obesity – have made lasting impacts. Waters even helped plant a garden at the White House.

ED YOUNG/AGSTOCK IMAGES/CORBIS ©

2

JERRY ALEXANDER/LONELY PLANET IMAGES ©

3

JUDY BELLAH/LONELY PLANET IMAGES ©

Wine

California's wine producers are the best in America and among the best in the world. Far beyond Napa Valley, the wines of Northern California are well worth a day-long detour.

America's Vineyard

California might still be a Mexican province guzzling Australian wines but for one drunken night in Sonoma in 1846. Under the influence of local wine, a group of frontier rabble-rousers decided to seize the state government from Mexican authorities. California history and Sonoma's reputation for drink were made. One hundred and thirty years later, neighboring Napa Valley kicked off another revolution at the 1976 Paris Tasting, aka the 'World Cup of Wine,' when a Stag's Leap cabernet sauvignon and a Chateau Montelena chardonnay beat home-*terroir* French favorites.

Napa, Sonoma, Santa Cruz and Mendocino counties continue to produce the state's most illustrious vintages. With an exceptional combination of coastal fog, sunny valleys, rocky hillsides and volcanic soils, Napa and Sonoma Valleys together mimic wine-growing regions across France and Italy. Precious bottom-land sells for up to $20,000 an acre in skinny, 30-mile-long Napa, where many wineries understandably stick to established, marketable chardonnay and cabernet sauvignon. Neighboring Sonoma and Mendocino have complex microclimates, with morning fog cover to protect the thin-skinned, prized pinot noir grape.

But California's risk-taking attitude prevails even on prestigious Napa, Sonoma and Mendocino turf, with unconventional red blends and freak-factor pinots with 'forest floor' flavors claiming top honors in industry mags and the Super Bowl of US wine competitions, the San Francisco Chronicle Wine Competition.

Clockwise from top left
1. Wine-tasting at Iron Horse Vineyards (p191), Sebastopol 2. Vineyard, Napa Valley (p159) 3. Browsing wine racks at the Oakville Grocery store (p206)

OTHER NORCAL WINE REGIONS

Although a tour through Napa is the Holy Grail of American oenophiles, younger wine regions turn out wines of notable quality for a fraction of the attitude. These are some of our favorites.

» **Amador & El Dorado Counties** With intense, earthy zinfandels and zero pretense, Gold Country's wineries (p312) are the best for budget-conscious wine lovers.

» **Paso Robles** One of the largest wine regions in the south, this area (p492) has all of the accolades of Napa's wineries, and easier access to the Pacific Ocean.

» **Lodi** A quick trip from the Bay Area and the perfect detour on the way to LA, the country roads surrounding Lodi (p339) turn out excellent zins, big cabs and jammy merlot.

» **Santa Ynez & Santa Maria Valleys** North of Santa Barbara, pinot grapes thrive on the rolling hills (p504) made famous in the film *Sideways*.

JUDY BELLAH/LONELY PLANET IMAGES ©

2

JERRY ALEXANDER/LONELY PLANET IMAGES ©

3

JERRY ALEXANDER/LONELY PLANET IMAGES ©

Beer & Beyond

Don't be surprised if ordering a Budweiser earns you a scornful look in these parts. Alongside excellent beer scenes in Colorado and Oregon, Northern California's craft breweries are a point of locals' hubris...especially after they've had a couple.

Some of the most famous labels are found in the region, but excellent, largely unknown microbreweries are also found in many small towns.

Like most of the small breweries of the western US, these breweries specialize in bold, hoppy India Pale Ales (IPAs) and creative Belgium-inspired fusions. Both of these have high alcohol content, so remember to take it slow.

NORCAL'S BEST MICROBREW

» **Six Rivers Brewery** (p252) Women-owned brewery with excellent beer and a great view.

» **North Coast Brewing Co** (p227) Red Seal amber ale and aged Belgian-style brews.

» **Anderson Valley Brewing** (p232) Play disc golf with amber ale or oatmeal stout in hand at this solar-powered Bavarian brewhouse.

» **Dunsmuir Brewery Works** (p286) The IPA at this small-town gem is so good it frequently sells out.

Below
Taproom at the Firestone Walker Brewing Co (p494), Paso Robles

Yosemite & the Sierra Nevada

Includes »

Best Places to Eat

» Mountain Room Restaurant (p407)

» Lakefront Restaurant (p436)

» Yosemite Bug Rustic Mountain Resort (p413)

» Convict Lake Resort (p438)

» Narrow Gauge Inn (p411)

Best Places to Stay

» Yosemite High Sierra Camps (p409)

» Ahwahnee Hotel (p405)

» Sierra Sky Ranch (p411)

Why Go?

An outdoor adventurer's wonderland, the Sierra Nevada is a year-round pageant of snow sports, white-water rafting, hiking, cycling and rock climbing. Skiers and snowboarders blaze through hushed pine-tree slopes, and wilderness seekers come to escape the stresses of modern civilization.

With fierce granite mountains standing watch over high-altitude lakes, the eastern spine of California is a formidable but exquisite topographical barrier enclosing magnificent natural landscapes. And interspersed between its river canyons and 14,000ft peaks are the decomposing ghost towns left behind by California's early white settlers, bubbling natural hot springs and Native American tribes that still call it home.

In the majestic national parks of Yosemite and Sequoia & Kings Canyon, visitors will be humbled by the groves of solemn giant sequoias, ancient rock formations and valleys, and the ever-present opportunity to see bears and other wildlife.

When to Go

Yosemite National Park

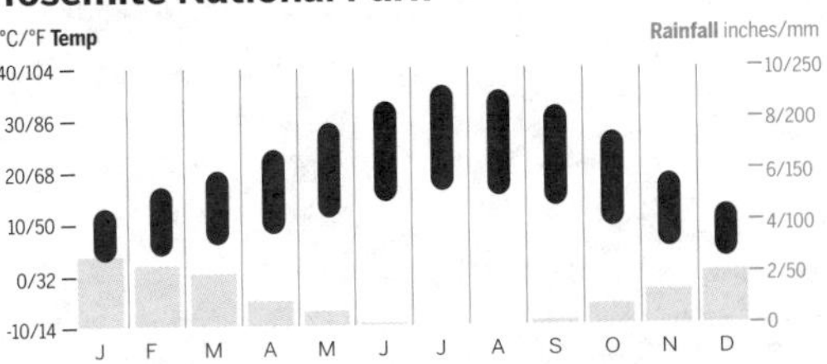

May & Jun The Yosemite waterfalls are gushing and spectacular in spring.

Jul & Aug Head for the mountains for wilderness adventures and glorious sunshine.

Dec–Mar Take a wintertime romp through snowy forests.

Yosemite & the Sierra Nevada Highlights

1 Marvel at the waterfall gush in spring at **Yosemite National Park** (p396)

2 Whoosh down the wintertime heights of snow-draped **Mammoth Mountain** (p432)

3 Gaze heavenward through the celestial sequoia canopies of **Sequoia & Kings Canyon National Parks** (p414)

4 Kayak the rapids at **Truckee River Whitewater Park** (p445) in Reno, Nevada

5 Amble around the evocative ghost town of **Bodie** (p428)

6 Canoe or kayak **Mono Lake** (p430) amid its haunting tufa

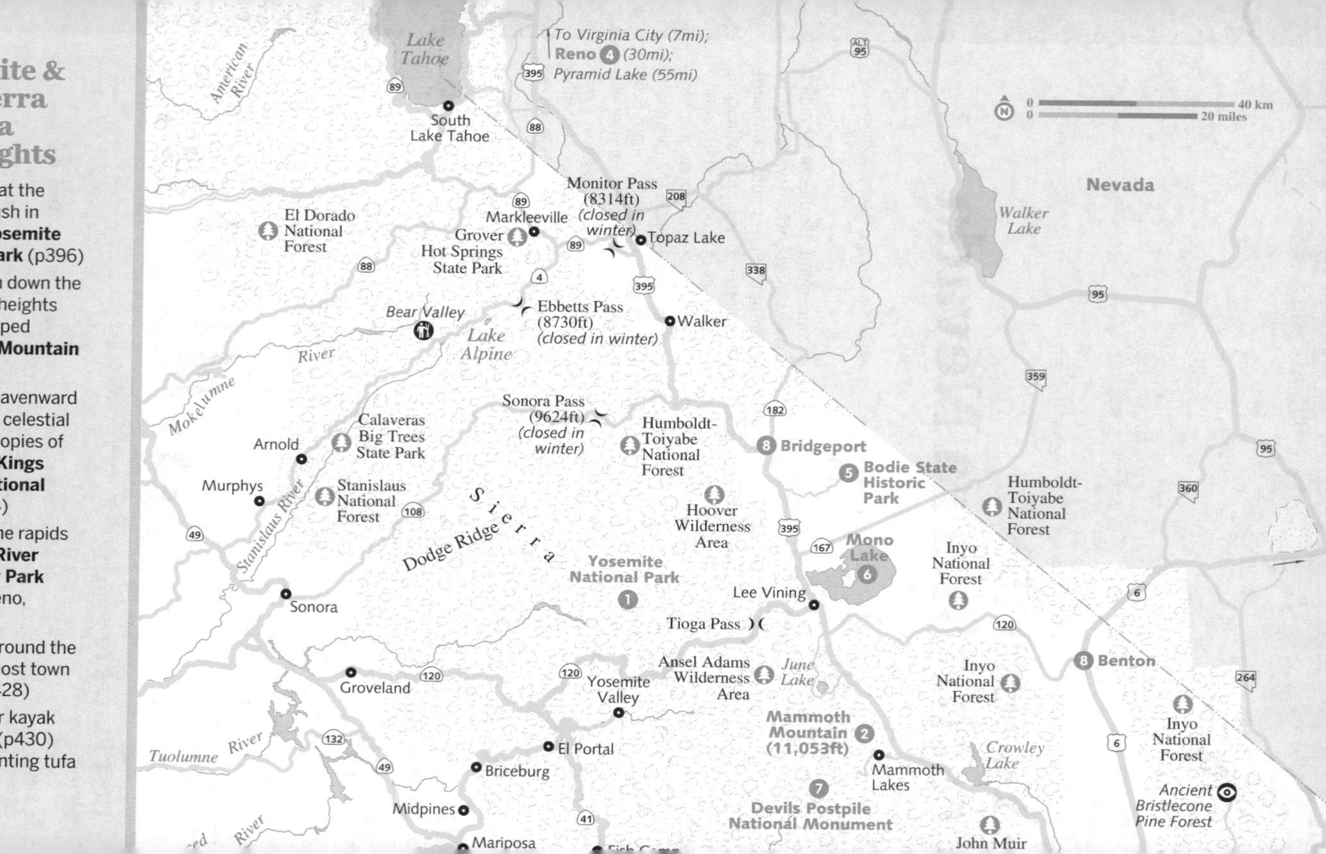

7 View the bizarre volcanic formation of **Devils Postpile** (p437)

8 Soak your troubles away at **hot spring pools** in Bridgeport (p425) and Benton (p439)

9 Visit the **Manzanar National Historic Site** (p442) where one of the darkest events in US history is memorialized

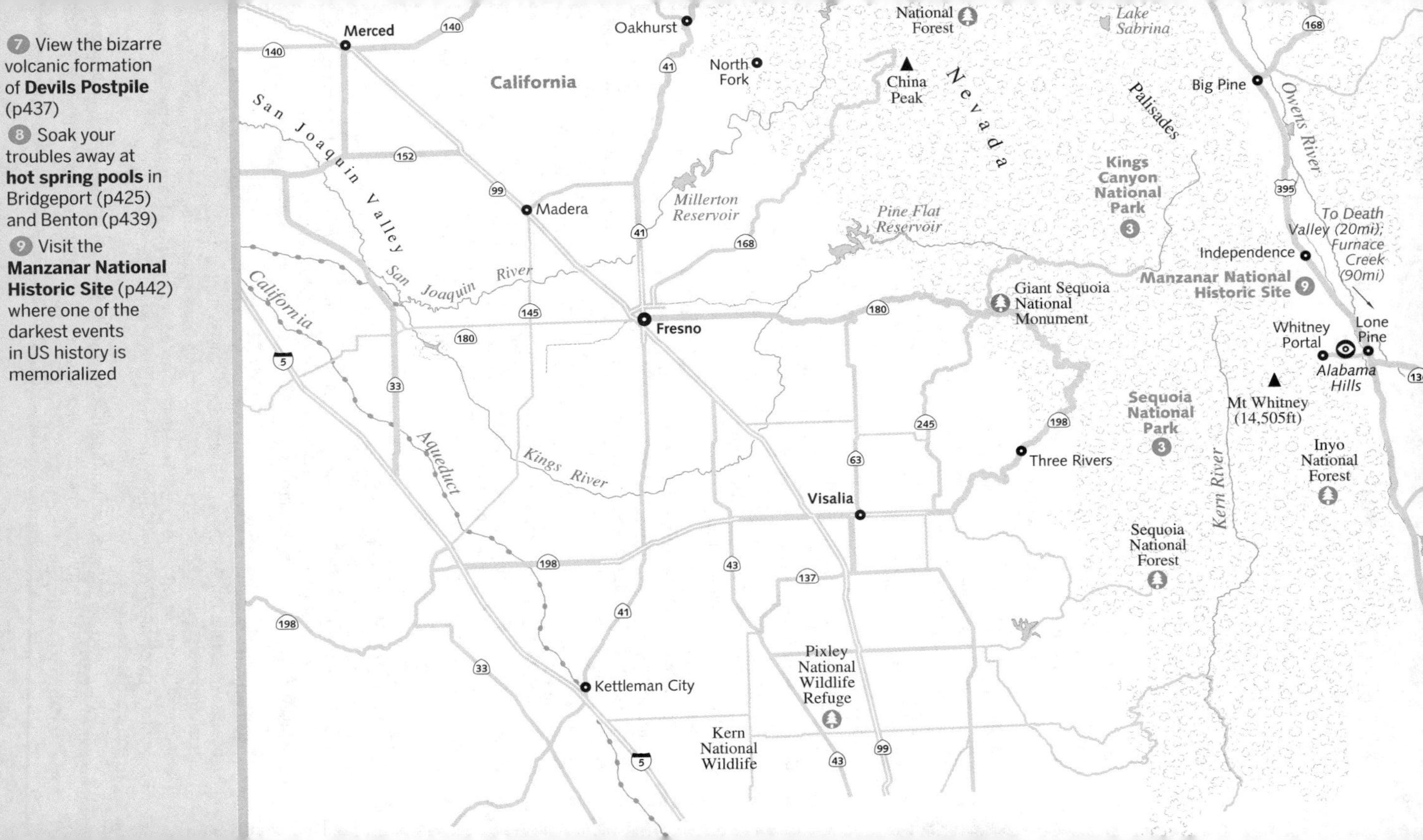

YOSEMITE NATIONAL PARK

The jaw-dropping head-turner of America's national parks, and a Unesco World Heritage site, Yosemite (yo-*sem*-it-ee) garners the devotion of all who enter. From the waterfall-striped granite walls buttressing emerald-green Yosemite Valley to the skyscraping giant sequoias catapulting into the air at Mariposa Grove, the place inspires a sense of awe and reverence – four million visitors wend their way to the country's third-oldest national park annually. But lift your eyes above the crowds and you'll feel your heart instantly moved by unrivalled splendors: the haughty profile of Half Dome, the hulking presence of El Capitan, the drenching mists of Yosemite Falls, the gemstone lakes of the high country's subalpine wilderness and Hetch Hetchy's pristine pathways.

History

The Ahwahneechee, a group of Miwok and Paiute peoples, lived in the Yosemite area for around 4000 years before a group of pioneers, most likely led by legendary explorer Joseph Rutherford Walker, came through in 1833. During the Gold Rush era, conflict between the miners and native tribes escalated to the point where a military expedition (the Mariposa Battalion) was dispatched in 1851 to punish the Ahwahneechee, eventually forcing the capitulation of Chief Tenaya and his tribe.

Tales of thunderous waterfalls and towering stone columns followed the Mariposa Battalion out of Yosemite and soon spread into the public's awareness. In 1855 San Francisco entrepreneur James Hutchings organized the first tourist party to the valley. Published accounts of his trip, in which he extolled the area's untarnished beauty, prompted others to follow, and it wasn't long before inns and roads began springing up. Alarmed by this development, conservationists petitioned Congress to protect the area – with success. In 1864 President Abraham Lincoln signed the Yosemite Grant, which eventually ceded Yosemite Valley and the Mariposa Grove of Giant Sequoias to California as a state park. This landmark decision paved the way for a national park system, of which Yosemite became a part in 1890, thanks to efforts led by pioneering conservationist John Muir.

Yosemite's popularity as a tourist destination continued to soar throughout the 20th century and, by the mid-1970s, traffic and congestion draped the valley in a smoggy haze. The General Management Plan (GMP), developed in 1980 to alleviate this and other problems, ran into numerous challenges and delays. Despite many improvements, and the need to preserve the natural beauty that draws visitors to Yosemite in the first place, the plan still hasn't been fully implemented.

Sights

There are four main entrances to the park: South Entrance (Hwy 41), Arch Rock (Hwy 140), Big Oak Flat (Hwy 120 W) and Tioga Pass (Hwy 120 E). Hwy 120 traverses the park as Tioga Rd, connecting Yosemite Valley with the Eastern Sierra.

Visitor activity is concentrated in Yosemite Valley, especially in Yosemite Village, which has the main visitors center, a post office, a museum, eateries and other

VISITING YOSEMITE

From late June to September, the entire park is accessible – all visitor facilities are open and everything from backcountry campgrounds to ice-cream stands are at maximum capacity. This is also when it's hardest – though not impossible – to evade the crush of humanity.

Crowds are smallest in winter but road closures (most notably of Tioga Rd, see p399, but also of Glacier Point Rd beyond Badger Pass Ski Area) mean that activity is concentrated in the valley and on Badger Pass. Visitor facilities are scaled down to a bare minimum and most campgrounds are closed and other lodging options limited. Note that 'winter' in Yosemite starts with the first heavy snowfall, which can be as early as October, and often lasts until May.

Spring, when the waterfalls are at their best, is a particularly excellent time to visit. Fall brings fewer people, an enchanting rainbow of foliage and crisp, clear weather (although waterfalls have usually dried to a trickle by then).

services. Curry Village is another hub. Notably less busy, Tuolumne (too-*ahl*-uh-*mee*) Meadows, toward the eastern end of Tioga Rd, primarily draws hikers, backpackers and climbers. Wawona, the park's southern focal point, also has good infrastructure. In the northwestern corner, Hetch Hetchy, which has no services at all, receives the smallest number of visitors.

YOSEMITE VALLEY

The park's crown jewel, spectacular meadow-carpeted Yosemite Valley stretches 7 miles long, bisected by the rippling Merced River and hemmed in by some of the most majestic chunks of granite anywhere on earth. The most famous are, of course, the monumental 7569ft **El Capitan** (El Cap; Map p400), one of the world's largest monoliths and a magnet for rock climbers, and 8842ft **Half Dome** (Map p400), the park's spiritual centerpiece – its rounded granite pate forms an unmistakable silhouette. You'll have great views of both from **Valley View** (Map p400) on the valley floor, but for the classic photo op head up Hwy 41 to **Tunnel View** (Map p400), which boasts a new viewing area. With a little sweat you'll have even better postcard panoramas – sans the crowds – from **Inspiration Point** (Map p400). The trail (2.6-mile round-trip) starts at the tunnel.

Yosemite's waterfalls mesmerize even the most jaded traveler, especially when the spring runoff turns them into thunderous cataracts. **Yosemite Falls** (Map p400) is considered the tallest in North America, dropping 2425ft in three tiers. A slick wheelchair-accessible trail leads to the bottom of this cascade or, if you prefer solitude and different perspectives, you can also clamber up the **Yosemite Falls Trail** (Map p404), which puts you atop the falls after a grueling 3.4 miles. No less impressive is nearby **Bridalveil Fall** (Map p400) and others scattered throughout the valley.

Any aspiring Ansel Adams should lug their camera gear along the 1-mile paved trail to **Mirror Lake** (off Map p404) early or late in the day to catch the ever-shifting reflection of Half Dome in the still waters. The lake all but dries up by late summer.

South of here, where the Merced River courses around two small islands, lies **Happy Isles**, a popular area for picnics, swimming and strolls. It also marks the start of the **John Muir Trail** (Map p404) and **Mist Trail** to several waterfalls and Half Dome.

FAST FACTS

- **Population of Reno** 225,000
- **Wilderness Area** approximately 4 million acres
- **San Francisco to Yosemite Valley** 190 miles, 3½ to four hours
- **Los Angeles to Mammoth Lakes** 325 miles, six hours

FREE **Yosemite Museum** MUSEUM
(Map p404; 9am-4:30pm or 5pm, closed for lunch) This museum has Miwok and Paiute artifacts, including woven baskets, beaded buckskin dresses and dance capes made from feathers. There's also an **art gallery** with paintings and photographs from the museum's permanent collection. Behind the museum, a self-guided interpretive trail winds past a reconstructed c 1870 **Indian village** with pounding stones, an acorn granary, a ceremonial roundhouse and a conical bark house.

Ahwahnee Hotel HISTORIC BUILDING
(Map p404) About a quarter-mile east of Yosemite Village, the Ahwahnee Hotel is a graceful blend of rustic mountain retreat and elegant mansion dating back to 1927. You don't need to be a guest to have a gawk and a wander. Built from local granite, pine and cedar, the building is splendidly decorated with leaded glass, sculpted tiles, Native American rugs and Turkish kilims. You can enjoy a meal in the baronial dining room or a casual drink in the piano bar. Around Christmas, the Ahwahnee hosts the **Bracebridge Dinner** (801-559-5000; www.bracebridgedinners.com; per person $425), sort of a combination banquet and Renaissance *faire*. Book early.

FREE **Nature Center at Happy Isles** MUSEUM
(Map p404; 9:30am-4pm May-Sep;) A great hands-on nature museum, the Nature Center displays explain the differences between the park's various pinecones, rocks, animal tracks and (everyone's favorite subject) scat. Out back, don't miss an exhibit on the 1996 rock fall, when an 80,000-ton rock slab plunged 2000ft to the nearby valley floor, killing a man and felling about 1000 trees.

GLACIER POINT

A lofty 3200ft above the valley floor, 7214ft **Glacier Point** (Map p404) presents one of

MANDATORY HALF DOME PERMITS

To stem lengthy lines (and increasingly dangerous conditions) on the vertiginous cables of Half Dome, the park now requires that all-day hikers obtain an advance **permit** (☎877-444-6777; www.recreation.gov; per person $1.50) to climb the cables. Permits go on sale four months in advance, and the 300 available per day sell out almost immediately. Backpackers can obtain permits when they pick up wilderness permits, without having to reserve in advance. The process is still in development, so check www.nps.gov/yose/planyourvisit/hdpermits.htm for the latest information.

the park's most eye-popping vistas and practically puts you at eye level with Half Dome. To the left of Half Dome lies U-shaped, glacially carved Tenaya Canyon, while below you'll see Vernal and Nevada Falls. Glacier Point is about an hour's drive from Yosemite Valley via Glacier Point Rd off Hwy 41. Along the road, hiking trails lead to other spectacular viewpoints, such as **Dewey Point** (Map p400) and **Sentinel Dome** (Map p404). You can also hike up from the valley floor to Glacier Point via the thigh-burning **Four Mile Trail** (see p399). If you've driven up to Glacier Point and want to get away from the madding crowd, hiking down the Four Mile Trail for a bit will net you comparative solitude and more breathtaking views. Another way to get here is on the Glacier Point Hikers' Bus (p410). Many hikers take the bus one way and hike the other. Drivers should go in the morning to avoid the afternoon backup from the parking lot.

TIOGA ROAD & TUOLUMNE MEADOWS

Tioga Rd (or Hwy 120 E), the only road through the park, travels through 56 miles of superb high country at elevations ranging from 6200ft at Crane Flat to 9945ft at Tioga Pass. Heavy snowfall keeps it closed from about November until May. Beautiful views await after many a bend in the road, the most impressive being **Olmsted Point** (Map p400), where you can gawp all the way down Tenaya Canyon to Half Dome. Above the canyon's east side looms the aptly named 9926ft **Clouds Rest** (Map p400). Continuing east on Tioga Rd soon drops you at **Tenaya Lake** (Map p400), a placid blue basin framed by pines and granite cliffs.

Beyond here, about 55 miles from Yosemite Valley, 8600ft **Tuolumne Meadows** (Map p400) is the largest subalpine meadow in the Sierra. It provides a dazzling contrast to the valley, with its lush open fields, clear blue lakes, ragged granite peaks and domes, and cooler temperatures. If you come during July or August, you'll find a painter's palette of wildflowers decorating the shaggy meadows.

Tuolumne is far less crowded than the valley, though the area around the campground, lodge store and visitors center does get busy, especially on weekends. Some hiking trails, such as the one to **Dog Lake** (Map p400), are also well traveled. Remember that the altitude makes breathing a lot harder than in the valley, and nights can get nippy, so pack warm clothes.

The main meadow is about 2.5 miles long and lies on the north side of Tioga Rd between **Lembert Dome** (Map p400) and **Pothole Dome** (Map p400). The 200ft scramble to the top of the latter – preferably at sunset – gives you great views of the meadow. An interpretive trail leads from the stables to muddy **Soda Springs** (Map p400), where carbonated water bubbles up in red-tinted pools. The nearby **Parsons Memorial Lodge** (Map p400) has a few displays.

Hikers and climbers will find a paradise of options around Tuolumne Meadows, which is also the gateway to the High Sierra Camps (p409).

The Tuolumne Meadows Tour & Hikers' Bus (p410) makes the trip along Tioga Rd once daily in each direction, and can be used for one-way hikes. There's also a free Tuolumne Meadows Shuttle (p410), which travels between the Tuolumne Meadows Lodge and Olmsted Point, including a stop at Tenaya Lake.

WAWONA

Wawona, about 27 miles south of Yosemite Valley, is the park's historical center, home to the park's first headquarters (supervised by Captain AE Wood on the site of the Wawona Campground) and its first tourist facilities.

Mariposa Grove FOREST

(Map p400) The main lure in this area of the park is the biggest and most impressive cluster of giant sequoias in Yosemite. The star of the show – and what everyone comes to see – is the **Grizzly Giant**, a behemoth that sprang to life some 2700 years ago, or about the time the ancient Greeks held the first Olympic Games. You can't miss it – it's a half-mile walk along a well-worn path starting near the parking lot. Beyond here, crowds begin to thin out a bit, although for more solitude you should arrive early in the morning or after 6pm. Also nearby is the walk-through **California Tunnel Tree**, which continues to survive despite having its heart hacked out in 1895.

In the upper grove you'll find the **Fallen Wawona Tunnel Tree**, the famous drive-through tree that toppled over in 1969. For scenic views, take a 1-mile (round-trip) amble from the fallen tree to **Wawona Point**.

Also in the upper grove, the **Mariposa Grove Museum** (admission free; ⌚10am-4pm May-Sep) has displays about sequoia ecology. The full hike from the parking lot to the upper grove is about 2.5 miles.

Parking can be very limited, so come early or late, or take the free shuttle bus from the Wawona Store or the park entrance. The grove can also be explored on a one-hour **guided tour** (☎209-375-1621; adult/child $25/18; ⌚May-Sep) aboard a noisy open-air tram leaving from the parking lot.

FREE Pioneer Yosemite History Center MUSEUM

(Map p400; ⌚24hr) In Wawona itself, about 6 miles north of the grove, take in the manicured grounds of the elegant Wawona Hotel (p407) and cross a covered bridge to this rustic center, where some of the park's oldest buildings were relocated. It also features stagecoaches that brought early tourists to Yosemite, and offers short **rides** (adult/child $4/3; ⌚Wed-Sun Jun-Sep).

HETCH HETCHY

In the park's northwestern corner, Hetch Hetchy, which is Miwok for 'place of tall grass,' gets the least amount of traffic yet sports waterfalls and granite cliffs that rival its famous counterparts in Yosemite Valley. The main difference is that Hetch Hetchy Valley is now filled with water, following a long political and environmental battle in the early 20th century. It's a lovely, quiet spot and well worth the 40-mile drive from Yosemite Valley, especially if you're tired of the avalanche of humanity rolling through that area.

The 8-mile long **Hetch Hetchy Reservoir** (Map p400), its placid surface reflecting clouds and cliffs, stretches behind O'Shaughnessy Dam, site of a parking lot and trailheads. An easy 5.4-mile (round-trip) trail leads to the spectacular **Tueeulala** (*twee*-lala) and **Wapama Falls** (Map p400), which each plummet more than 1000ft over fractured granite walls on the north shore of the reservoir. **Hetch Hetchy Dome** (Map p400) rises up in the distance. This hike is best in spring, when temperatures are moderate and wildflowers poke out everywhere. Keep an eye out for rattlesnakes and the occasional bear, especially in summer.

There are no visitor services at Hetch Hetchy. The road is only open during daylight hours; specifics are posted at the Evergreen Rd turnoff.

Activities

Hiking

Over 800 miles of hiking trails cater to hikers of all abilities. Take an easy half-mile stroll on the valley floor; venture out all day on a quest for viewpoints, waterfalls and lakes; or go camping in the remote outer reaches of the backcountry.

IMPASSABLE TIOGA PASS

Hwy 120, the main route into Yosemite National Park from the Eastern Sierra, climbs through Tioga Pass, the highest pass in the Sierra at 9945ft. On most maps of California, you'll find a parenthetical remark – 'closed in winter' – printed on the map. While true, this statement is also misleading. Tioga Rd is usually closed from the first heavy snowfall in October to May, June or even July! If you're planning a trip through Tioga Pass in spring, you're likely to be out of luck. According to official park policy, the earliest date the road will be plowed is 15 April, yet the pass has been open in April only once since 1980. Other mountain roads further north, such as Hwys 108, 4 and 88/89, may also be closed due to heavy snow, albeit only temporarily. Call ☎800-427-7623 for road and weather conditions.

Yosemite National Park

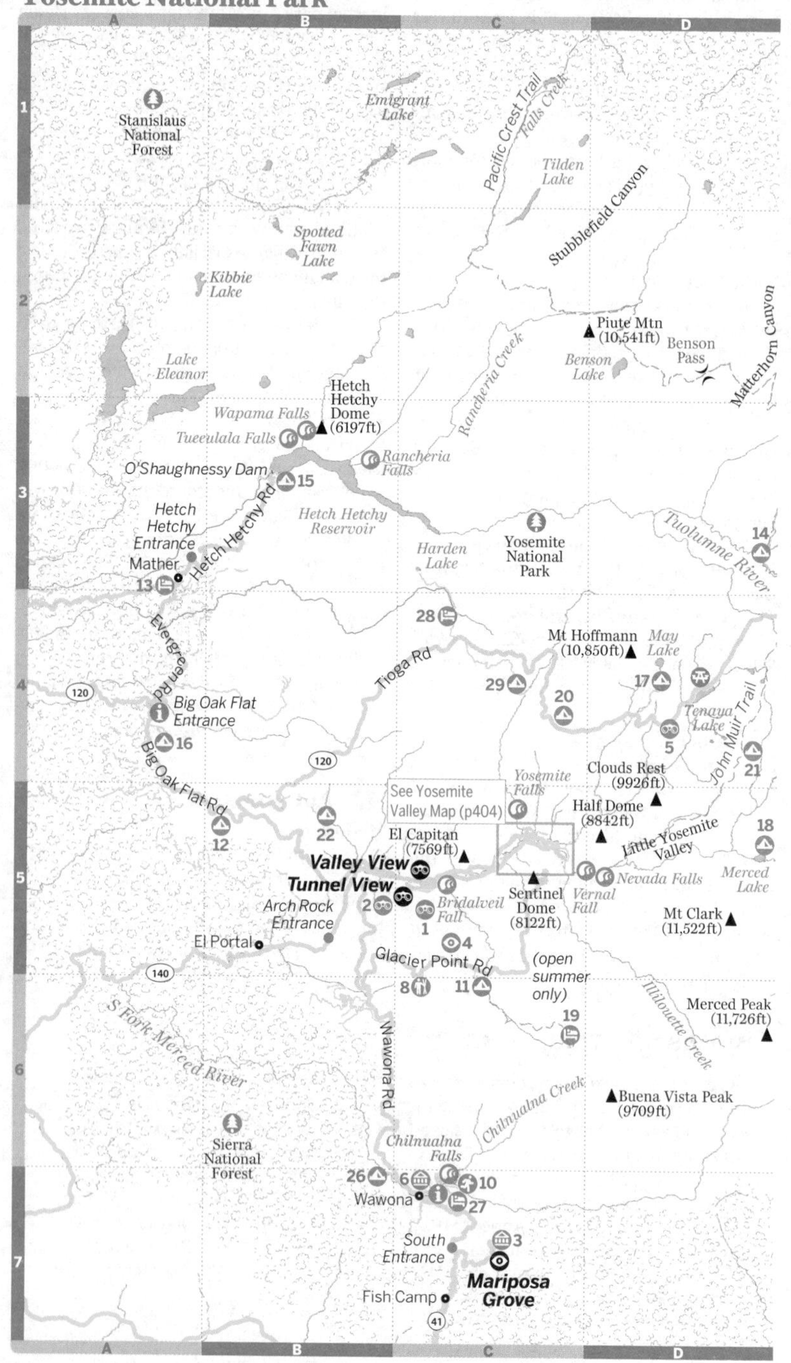

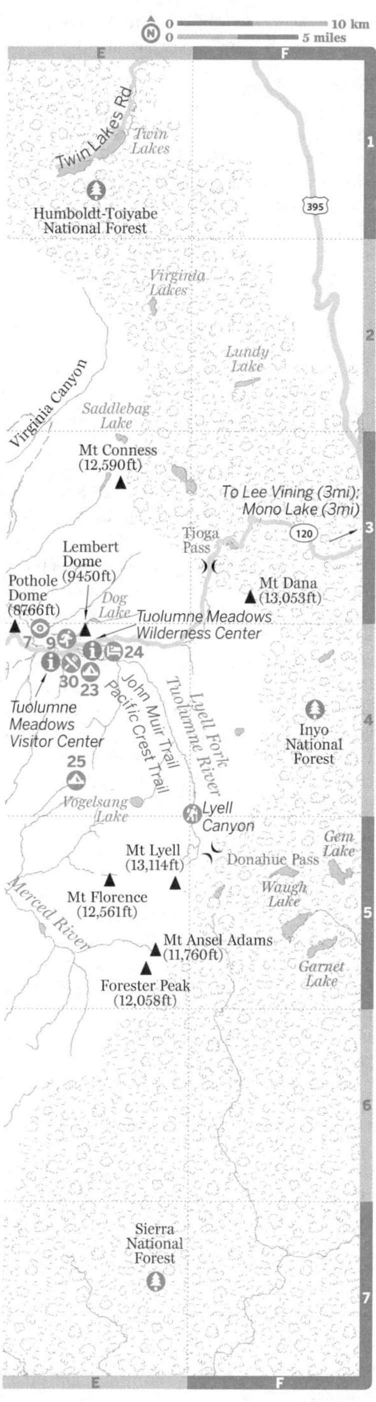

Some of the park's most popular hikes start right in Yosemite Valley, including to the top of Half Dome (17-mile round-trip), the most famous of all. It follows a section of the John Muir Trail and is strenuous, difficult and best tackled in two days with an overnight in Little Yosemite Valley. Reaching the top can only be done after rangers have installed fixed cables. Depending on snow conditions, this may occur as early as late May or as late as July, and the cables usually come down in mid-October. To whittle down the cables' notorious human logjams, the park now requires permits for day hikers (see the boxed text p398), but the route is still nerve-wracking as hikers must 'share the road.' The less ambitious or physically fit will still have a ball following the same trail as far as **Vernal Fall** (Map p400; 2.6-mile round-trip), the top of **Nevada Fall** (Map p400; 6.5-mile round-trip) or idyllic **Little Yosemite Valley** (Map p400; 8-mile round-trip). The **Four Mile Trail** (Map p404; 9.2-mile round-trip) to Glacier Point is a strenuous but satisfying climb to a glorious viewpoint (also see p397).

If you've got the kids in tow, nice and easy destinations include **Mirror Lake** (off Map p404; 2-mile round-trip, 4.5 miles via the Tenaya Canyon Loop) in the valley, the **McGurk Meadow** (Map p400; 1.6-mile round-trip) trail on Glacier Point Rd, which has a historic log cabin to romp around in, and the trails meandering beneath the big trees of the Mariposa Grove (p398) in Wawona.

Also in the Wawona area is one of the park's prettiest (and often overlooked) hikes to **Chilnualna Falls** (Map p400; 8.6-mile round-trip). Best done between April and June, it follows a cascading creek to the top of the dramatic overlook falls, starting gently, then hitting you with some grinding switchbacks before sort of leveling out again.

The highest concentration of hikes lies in the high country of Tuolumne Meadows, which is only accessible in summer. A popular choice here is the hike to **Dog Lake** (Map p400; 2.8-mile round-trip), but it gets busy. You can also hike along a relatively flat part of the John Muir Trail into lovely **Lyell Canyon** (Map p400; 17.6-mile round-trip), following the Lyell Fork of the Tuolumne River.

Backpacks, tents and other equipment can be rented from the **Yosemite Mountaineering School** (Map p404; ☎209-372-

Yosemite National Park

Top Sights

	Mariposa Grove	C7
	Tunnel View	C5
	Valley View	C5

Sights

1	Dewey Pt Lookout	C5
2	Inspiration Pt	B5
3	Mariposa Grove Museum	C7
4	McGurk Meadow	C5
5	Olmsted Pt	D4
	Parsons Memorial Lodge	(see 7)
6	Pioneer Yosemite History Center	C7
7	Soda Springs	E4

Activities, Courses & Tours

8	Badger Pass Ski Area	C6
9	Tuolumne Meadows Stables	E4
10	Wawona Stables	C7
	Yosemite Ski School	(see 8)

Sleeping

11	Bridalveil Creek Campground	C6
12	Crane Flat Campground	B5
13	Evergreen Lodge	A3
14	Glen Aulin High Sierra Camp	D3
15	Hetch Hetchy Campground	B3
16	Hodgdon Meadow Campground	A4
17	May Lake High Sierra Camp	D4
18	Merced Lake High Sierra Camp	D5
19	Ostrander Ski Hut	C6
20	Porcupine Flat Campground	C4
21	Sunrise High Sierra Camp	D4
22	Tamarack Flat Campground	B5
23	Tuolumne Meadows Campground	E4
24	Tuolumne Meadows Lodge	E4
25	Vogelsang High Sierra Camp	E4
26	Wawona Campground	B7
27	Wawona Hotel	C7
	White Wolf Campground	(see 28)
28	White Wolf Lodge	C4
29	Yosemite Creek Campground	C4

Eating

30	Tuolumne Meadows Grill	E4
	Wawona Hotel Dining Room	(see 27)

8344; www.yosemitemountaineering.com; Curry Village Mountain Shop). The school also offers two-day Learn to Backpack trips for novices and all-inclusive three- and four-day guided backpacking trips ($300 to $400 per person), which are great for inexperienced and solo travelers. In summer, the school operates a branch from Tuolumne Meadows.

Rock Climbing

With its sheer spires, polished domes and soaring monoliths, Yosemite is rock-climbing nirvana. The main climbing season runs from April to October. Most climbers, including some legendary stars, stay at Camp 4 (p405) near El Capitan, especially in spring and fall. In summer, another base camp springs up at Tuolumne Meadows Campground (p406). Climbers looking for partners post notices on bulletin boards at either campground.

Yosemite Mountaineering School (p401) offers top-flight instruction for novice to advanced rock hounds, plus guided climbs and equipment rental. All-day group classes for beginners are $148 per person.

The meadow across from El Capitan and the northeastern end of Tenaya Lake (off Tioga Rd) are good for watching climbers dangle from granite (you need binoculars for a really good view). Look for the haul bags first – they're bigger, more colorful and move around more than the climbers, making them easier to spot. The **Yosemite Climbing Association** (www.yosemiteclimbing.org) began an 'Ask-a-Climber' program in 2011, where it sets up a telescope at El Capitan Bridge for a few hours a day (mid-May through mid-October) and answers visitors' questions.

Cycling

Mountain-biking isn't permitted within the park, but cycling along the 12 miles of paved trails is a popular and environmentally friendly way of exploring the valley. It's also the fastest way to get around when Valley traffic is at a standstill. Many families bring bicycles, and you'll often find kids doing laps through the campgrounds. See p410 for rental information.

Swimming

On a hot summer day, nothing beats a dip in the gentle Merced River, though if chilly water doesn't float your boat, you can always pay to play in the scenic outdoor swimming pools at Curry Village and Yosemite Lodge at the Falls (p409; adult/child $5/4). With a sandy beach, Tenaya Lake is a frigid but interesting option, though White Wolf's Harden Lake warms up to a balmy temperature by mid-summer.

Horseback Riding

Yosemite Stables (trips 2hr/half-/full day $64/85/128) runs guided trips to such scenic locales as Mirror Lake, Chilnualna Falls and the Tuolumne River from three bases: **Tuolumne Meadows** (Map p400; ☎209-372-8427), **Wawona** (Map p400; ☎209-375-6502) and **Yosemite Valley** (Map p404; ☎209-372-8348). The season runs from May to October, although this varies slightly by location. No experience is needed for the two-hour and half-day rides, but reservations are advised, especially at the Yosemite Valley stables. Some mounts are horses, but most likely you'll be riding a sure-footed mule.

Rafting

From around late May to July, floating the Merced River from Stoneman Meadow, near Curry Village, to Sentinel Bridge is a leisurely way to soak up Yosemite Valley views. Four-person **raft rentals** (☎209-372-4386; per adult/child over 50lbs $26/16) for the 3-mile trip are available from the concessionaire in Curry Village and include equipment and a shuttle ride back to the rental kiosk. Or bring your own and pay $5 to shuttle back.

River rats are also attracted to the fierce **Tuolumne River** (Map p400), a classic Class IV run that plunges and thunders through boulder gardens and cascades. See p412 for outfitters.

Winter Sports

The white coat of winter opens up a different set of things to do, as the valley becomes a quiet, frosty world of snow-draped evergreens, ice-coated lakes and vivid vistas of gleaming white mountains sparkling against blue skies. Winter tends to arrive in full force by mid-November and peter out in early April.

Cross-country skiers can explore 350 miles of skiable trails and roads, including 90 miles of marked trails and 25 miles of machine-groomed track near Badger Pass. The scenic but grueling trail to Glacier Point (21-mile round-trip) also starts from here. More trails are at Crane Flat and the Mariposa Grove. The nongroomed trails can also be explored with snowshoes.

A free shuttle bus connects the Valley and Badger Pass. Roads in the Valley are plowed, and Hwys 41, 120 and 140 are usually kept open, conditions permitting. The Tioga Rd (Hwy 120 E), however, closes with the first snowfall (see boxed text, p399). Be sure to bring snow chains with you, as prices for them double once you hit the foothills.

Badger Pass Ski Area SKIING, SNOWBOARDING
(Map p400; ☎209-372-8430; www.badgerpass.com; lift ticket adult/child $42/23; 👪) Most of the action converges on one of California's oldest ski resorts. The gentle slopes are perfect for families and beginner skiers and snowboarders. It's about 22 miles from the valley on Glacier Point Rd. There are five chairlifts, 800 vertical feet and 10 runs, a full-service lodge, equipment rental ($23 to $35 for a full set of gear) and the excellent **Yosemite Ski School**, where generations of novices have learned how to get down a hill safely (group lessons from $35).

Badger Pass Cross-Country Center & Ski School SKIING
(Map p400; ☎209-372-8444) Located in the Badger Pass Ski Area, this school offers beginners' lesson and rental packages ($46), equipment rentals ($23) and guided tours. The center also runs overnight trips to **Glacier Point Ski Hut** (Map p404), a rustic stone-and-log cabin. Rates, including meals, are $350/120 guided/self-guided for one night or $550/240 for two nights.

Ostrander Ski Hut SKIING
(Map p400; www.yosemiteconservancy.org) More experienced skiers can trek 10 miles out to the popular hut on Ostrander Lake, operated by Yosemite Conservancy. The hut is staffed all winter and open to backcountry skiers and snowshoers for $32 to $52

TOP FIVE THINGS TO DO IN WINTER

- Snowshoeing among the giants of Mariposa Grove (p398)
- Ice-skating at Curry Village (p404)
- Taking an overnight cross-country skiing trip to Glacier Point Ski Hut (p403)
- Toasting s'mores in the Mountain Room Lounge (p408)
- Feasting like royalty at the Bracebridge Dinner (p397) in the Ahwahnee Hotel

Yosemite Valley

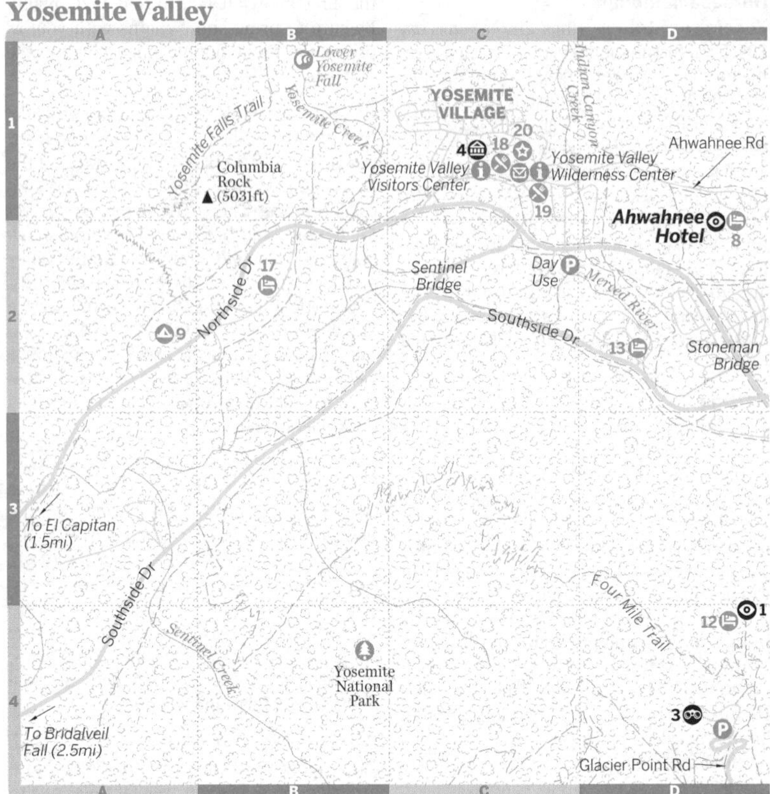

per person, per night. See the website for details.

Curry Village Ice Rink SKATING

(Map p404; per session adult/child $8/6, rental skates $3; ⏲Nov-Mar) A delightful winter activity is taking a spin on the outdoor rink, where you'll be skating under the watchful eye of Half Dome.

Tours

The Yosemite Bug (see p413) runs handy tours to Yosemite year-round from San Francisco.

The nonprofit **Yosemite Conservancy** (yosemiteconservancy.org) has scheduled tours of all kinds, plus custom trips available.

First-timers often appreciate the two-hour **Valley Floor Tour** (per adult/child $25/13; ⏲year-round) run by DNC Parks & Resorts, which covers the valley highlights.

For other tour options stop at the tour and activity desks at Yosemite Lodge at the Falls (see p409), Curry Village or Yosemite Village, call ☎209-372-4386 or check www.yosemitepark.com.

Sleeping

Competition for campsites is fierce from May to September, when arriving without a reservation and hoping for the best is tantamount to getting someone to lug your Barcalounger up Half Dome. Even first-come, first-served campgrounds tend to fill by noon, especially on weekends and around holidays. Campsites can be reserved up to five months in advance. **Reservations** (☎877-444-6777, 518-885-3639; www.recreation.gov) become available from 7am PST on the 15th of every month in one-month blocks, and often sell out within minutes.

Without a booking, your only chance is to hightail it to an open first-come, first-

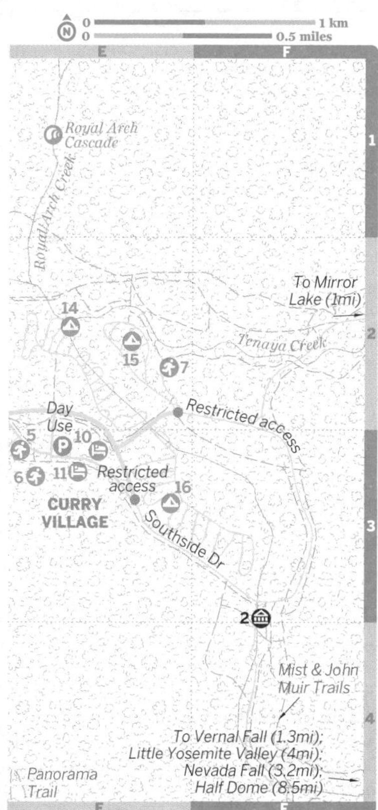

served campground or proceed to one of four campground reservation offices in Yosemite Valley, Wawona, Big Oak Flat and Tuolumne Meadows (the latter three are only open seasonally). Try to get there before 8am (when they open), put your name on a waiting list and then hope for a cancellation or early departure. Return when the ranger tells you to (usually 3pm) and if you hear your name, consider yourself very lucky indeed.

All campgrounds have flush toilets, except for Tamarack Flat, Yosemite Creek and Porcupine Flat, which have vault toilets and no potable water. Those at higher elevations get chilly at night, even in summer, so pack accordingly. The Yosemite Mountaineering School (p401) rents camping gear.

If you hold a wilderness permit, you may spend the nights before and after your trip in the backpacker campgrounds at Tuolumne Meadows, Hetch Hetchy, White Wolf and behind North Pines in Yosemite Valley. The cost is $5 per person, per night and reservations aren't necessary.

Opening dates for seasonal campgrounds vary according to the weather.

All noncamping reservations within the park are handled by **DNC Parks & Resorts** (☎801-559-4884; www.yosemitepark.com) and can be made up to 366 days in advance; reservations are absolutely critical from May to early September. Rates – and demand – drop from October to April.

YOSEMITE VALLEY

TOP CHOICE **Ahwahnee Hotel** HISTORIC HOTEL **$$$**
(Map p404; r from $449;) The crème de la crème of Yosemite's lodging, this sumptuous historic property dazzles with soaring ceilings, Turkish kilims lining the hallways and atmospheric lounges with mammoth stone fireplaces. It's the gold standard for upscale lodges, though if you're not blessed with bullion, you can still soak up the ambience during afternoon tea, a drink in the bar or a gourmet meal.

North Pines CAMPGROUND **$**
(Map p404; Yosemite Valley; tent & RV sites $20; Apr-Sep;) A bit off the beaten path (4000ft) with 81 sites near Mirror Lake; reservations required.

Upper Pines CAMPGROUND **$**
(Map p404; Yosemite Valley; tent & RV sites $20; year-round;) Busy, busy, busy – and big (238 sites, 4000ft); reservations required mid-March through November.

Lower Pines CAMPGROUND **$**
(Map p404; tent & RV sites $20; Mar-Oct;) Crammed and noisy with 60 sites at 4000ft; reservations required.

Camp 4 CAMPGROUND **$**
(Map p404; per person $5; year-round) Walk-in campground at 4000ft, popular with climbers; sites are shared.

Housekeeping Camp CABIN **$**
(Map p404; 4-person tent cabin $93; Apr-Oct) This cluster of 266 cabins, each walled in by concrete on three sides and lidded by a canvas roof, is crammed and noisy, but the setting along the Merced River has its merits. Each unit can sleep up to six and has electricity, light, a table and chairs, and a covered patio with picnic tables.

Yosemite Valley

Top Sights

	Ahwahnee Hotel	D2

Sights

	Art Gallery	(see 4)
1	Glacier Point	D4
	Indian Village	(see 4)
2	Nature Center at Happy Isles	F3
3	Sentinel Dome Lookout	D4
4	Yosemite Museum	C1

Activities, Courses & Tours

5	Curry Village Ice Rink	E3
6	Yosemite Mountaineering School	E3
7	Yosemite Valley Stables	E2

Sleeping

8	Ahwahnee Hotel	D2
9	Camp 4	A2
10	Campground Reservation Office	E3
11	Curry Village	E3
12	Glacier Point Ski Hut	D4
13	Housekeeping Camp	D2
14	Lower Pines Campground	E2
15	North Pines Campground	E2
16	Upper Pines Campground	E3
17	Yosemite Lodge at the Falls	B2

Eating

	Ahwahnee Dining Room	(see 8)
	Curry Village Coffee Corner	(see 6)
	Curry Village Dining Pavilion	(see 6)
	Curry Village Pizza Patio	(see 6)
	Curry Village Taqueria	(see 6)
	Degnan's Deli	(see 18)
18	Degnan's Loft	C1
	Mountain Room Restaurant	(see 17)
	Village Grill	(see 19)
19	Village Store	C1
	Yosemite Lodge Food Court	(see 17)

Drinking

	Ahwahnee Bar	(see 8)
	Mountain Room Lounge	(see 17)

Entertainment

20	Yosemite Theater	C1

Yosemite Lodge at the Falls MOTEL **$$**
(Map p404; r $191-218; @) Situated a short walk from Yosemite Falls, this multibuilding complex gets a thumbs up for its centrality, wide range of eateries, lively bar, big pool and other handy amenities. Rooms are fairly generic; the nicest are the upstairs units with beamed ceilings and Native American touches. All have cable TV, a telephone and, mostly, great panoramas unfolding from your patio or balcony.

Curry Village CABINS, TENT CABINS **$$**
(Map p404; tent cabins $112-120, cabins with/without bath $168/127;) Founded in 1899 as a summer camp, Curry has hundreds of units squished tightly together beneath towering evergreens. The canvas cabins are basically glorified tents, so for more comfort, quiet and privacy get one of the cozy wood cabins, which have bedspreads, drapes and vintage posters. There are also 18 attractive motel-style rooms in the **Stoneman House** (r $191), including a loft suite sleeping up to six.

TIOGA ROAD

Tuolumne Meadows campers should note that the closest pay showers are located at Mono Vista RV Park (p430).

Tuolumne Meadows CAMPGROUND **$**
(Map p400; tent & RV sites $20; Jul-Sep;) Biggest campground in the park (8600ft) with 304 fairly well-spaced sites; half of these can be reserved.

Porcupine Flat CAMPGROUND **$**
(Map p400; tent & RV sites $10; Jul-Sep) Primitive 52-site area, at 8100ft; some sites near the road.

Tamarack Flat CAMPGROUND **$**
(Map p400; tent sites $10; Jul-Sep) Quiet, secluded, primitive at 6315ft; the 52 tent sites are a rough 3-mile drive off Tioga Rd.

White Wolf CAMPGROUND **$**
(Map p400; tent & RV sites $14; Jul-early Sep;) Attractive setting at 8000ft, but the 74 sites are fairly boxed in.

Yosemite Creek CAMPGROUND **$**
(Map p400; tent sites $10; Jul–mid-Sep;) The most secluded and quiet campground (7659ft) in the park, reached via a rough 4.5-mile road. There are 75 primitive sites.

Tuolumne Meadows Lodge TENT CABINS **$$**
(Map p400; tent cabins $107; mid-Jun–mid-Sep) In the high country, about 55 miles from the valley, this option attracts hikers to its 69

canvas tent cabins with four beds, a wood-burning stove and candles (no electricity). Breakfast and dinner are available.

White Wolf Lodge CABINS, TENT CABINS **$$**
(Map p400; tent cabins $99, cabins with bath $120; ⌚Jul–mid-Sep) This complex enjoys its own little world a mile up a spur road, away from the hubbub and traffic of Hwy 120 and the Valley. There are 24 spartan four-bedded tent cabins without electricity and four very-in-demand hard-walled cabins that feel like rustic motel rooms. The generator cuts out at 11pm, so you'll need a flashlight until early morning. There's also a dining room and a tiny counter-service store.

HETCH HETCHY & BIG OAK FLAT RD

TOP CHOICE **Evergreen Lodge** RESORT **$$**
(Map p400; ☎209-379-2606, 800-935-6343; www.evergreenlodge.com; 33160 Evergreen Rd; tents $75-110, cabins $175-350; @) Outside the park near the entrance to Hetch Hetchy, this classic 90-year-old resort lets roughing-it guests cheat with comfy, prefurnished tents and rustic to deluxe mountain cabins with private porches but no phone or TV. Outdoor recreational activities abound, many of them family-oriented, with equipment rentals available. There's a **general store**, **tavern** with a pool table and a **restaurant** (dinner mains $18-28) serving three hearty meals every day.

Crane Flat CAMPGROUND **$**
(Map p400; Big Oak Flat Rd; tent & RV sites $20; ⌚Jun-Sep;) Large family campground at 6192ft, with 166 sites.

Hodgdon Meadow CAMPGROUND **$**
(Map p400; Big Oak Flat Rd; tent & RV sites $14-20; ⌚year-round;) Utilitarian and crowded 105-site campground at 4872ft; reservations required mid-April to mid-October.

WAWONA & GLACIER POINT RD

Bridalveil Creek CAMPGROUND **$**
(Map p400; Glacier Point Rd; tent & RV sites $14; ⌚Jul-early Sep;) Quieter than the Valley campgrounds, with 110 sites at 7200ft.

Wawona CAMPGROUND **$**
(Map p400; Wawona; tent & RV sites $14-20; ⌚year-round;) Idyllic riverside setting at 4000ft with 93 well-spaced sites; reservations required April to September.

Wawona Hotel HISTORIC HOTEL **$$**
(Map p400; Wawona; r with/without bath incl breakfast $217/147; ⌚mid-Mar–Dec;) This National Historic Landmark, dating from 1879, is a collection of six graceful, whitewashed New England–style buildings flanked by wide porches. The 104 rooms – with no phone or TV – come with Victorian-style furniture and other period items, and about half the rooms share bathrooms, with nice robes provided for the walk there. The grounds are lovely, with a spacious lawn dotted with Adirondack chairs.

Eating

You can find food options for all budgets and palates within the park, from greasy slabs of fast food to swanky cuts of top-notch steak.

Bringing in or buying your own food saves money but remember that you *must* remove it all from your car (or backpack or bicycle) and store it overnight in a bear box or canister. The **Village Store** (Map p404) in Yosemite Village has the best selection (including toiletries, health-food items and some organic produce), while stores at Curry Village, Wawona, Tuolumne Meadows, Housekeeping Camp and the Yosemite Lodge are more limited.

TOP CHOICE **Mountain Room Restaurant** STEAKHOUSE **$$**
(Map p404; ☎209-372-1281; Yosemite Lodge; mains $17-35; ⌚5:30-9:30pm, shorter winter hours;) With a killer view of Yosemite Falls, the window tables at this casual and elegant contemporary steakhouse are a hot commodity. The chefs at the lodge whip up the best meals in the park, with flat-iron steak and locally caught mountain trout wooing diners under a rotating display of nature photographs. Reservations accepted only for groups larger than eight, and casual dress is okay.

Ahwahnee Dining Room CALIFORNIAN **$$$**
(Map p404; ☎209-372-1489; Ahwahnee Hotel; mains breakfast $7-16, lunch $16-23, dinner $26-46; ⌚7-10:30am, 11:30am-3pm & 5:30-9pm) The formal ambience (mind your manners) may not be for everybody, but few would not be awed by the sumptuous decor, soaring beamed ceiling and palatial chandeliers. The menu is constantly in flux, but most dishes have perfect pitch and are beautifully presented. There's a dress code at dinner,

but otherwise shorts and sneakers are okay. Sunday brunch ($39.50; 7am to 3pm) is amazing. Reservations highly recommended for brunch and dinner.

Wawona Hotel Dining Room AMERICAN $$
(Map p400; Wawona Hotel; mains breakfast & lunch $11-15, dinner $19-30; 7:30-10am, 11:30am-1:30pm & 5:30-9pm Easter-Dec;) Beautiful sequoia-painted lamps light this old-fashioned white-tablecloth dining room, and the Victorian detail makes it an enchanting place to have an upscale (though somewhat overpriced) meal. 'Tasteful, casual attire' is the rule for dinner dress, and there's a barbecue on the lawn every Saturday during summer. The Wawona's wide, white porch makes a snazzy destination for evening cocktails, and listen for veteran pianist Tom Bopp in the lobby.

Yosemite Lodge Food Court CAFETERIA $
(Map p404; Yosemite Lodge; mains $7-12; 6:30am-8:30pm Sun-Thu, to 9pm Fri & Sat;) This self-service restaurant has several tummy-filling stations serving pastas, burgers, pizza and sandwiches, either made to order or served from beneath heat lamps. Proceed to the cashier and find a table inside or on the patio.

Curry Village Pizza Patio PIZZERIA $
(Map p404; Curry Village; pizzas from $8; noon-10pm, shorter winter hours) Enjoy tasty pizza at this buzzing eatery that becomes a chatty après-hike hangout in the late afternoon.

Degnan's Loft PIZZERIA $
(Map p404; Yosemite Village; mains $8-10; 5-9pm Mon-Fri Nov-Mar, daily Apr-Oct) Head upstairs to this convivial place with high-beamed ceilings and a many-sided fireplace, and kick back under the dangling lift chair for decent salads, veggie lasagna and pizza.

Curry Village Dining Pavilion CAFETERIA $$
(Map p404; Curry Village; mains breakfast adult/child $11.50/7.75, dinner adult/child $15.25/8.25; 7-10am & 5:30-8pm Apr-Nov) Although the cafeteria-style setting has all the charm of a train-station waiting room, the mediocre all-you-can-eat breakfast and dinner buffets are great for families, gluttons and the undecided.

Degnan's Deli DELI $
(Map p404; Yosemite Village; sandwiches $6-8; 7am-5pm) Excellent made-to-order sandwiches, breakfast items and snack foods.

Curry Village Coffee Corner CAFE $
(Map p404; Curry Village; pastries $2-4; 6am-10pm, shorter winter hours) For a coffee jolt or sugar fix.

Curry Village Taqueria MEXICAN $
(Map p404; Curry Village; mains $4.50-10; 11am-5pm spring-fall) Tacos and big burritos on a deck near the parking area.

Tuolumne Meadows Grill FAST FOOD $
(Map p400; Tuolumne Meadows; mains under $10; 8am-5pm Jul–mid-Sep) Scarf down burgers and grill items at the outdoor picnic tables.

Village Grill FAST FOOD $
(Map p404; Yosemite Village; items $5-7; Apr-Oct) Fight the chipmunks for burgers and tasty fries alfresco.

Drinking

No one will mistake Yosemite for nightlife central, but there are some nice spots to relax with a cabernet, cocktail or cold beer. Outside the park, the Yosemite Bug Rustic Mountain Resort (p413) and the Evergreen Lodge (p407) both have lively lounges.

Mountain Room Lounge BAR
(Map p404; Yosemite Lodge, Yosemite Valley) Catch up on the latest sports news while knocking back draft brews at this large bar that buzzes in wintertime. Order a s'mores kit (graham crackers, chocolate squares and marshmallows) to roast in the open-pit fireplace. Kids welcome until 9pm.

Ahwahnee Bar BAR
(Map p404; Ahwahnee Hotel, Yosemite Valley) The perfect way to experience the Ahwahnee without dipping too deep into your pockets; settle in for a drink at this cozy bar, complete with pianist. Appetizers and light meals ($9.50 to $23) provide sustenance.

Entertainment

At the **Yosemite Theater** (Map p404; Yosemite Village; adult/child $8/4) take your pick from a rotating cast of performers, including Wawona Hotel pianist Tom Bopp, actor Lee Stetson, who portrays the fascinating life and philosophy of John Muir, and Park Ranger Shelton Johnson, who re-creates the experiences of a Buffalo Soldier (see the boxed text, p414). There are also special children's shows.

Other activities scheduled year-round include campfire programs, children's photo walks, twilight strolls, night-sky watching,

HIGH SIERRA CAMPS

In the backcountry near Tuolumne Meadows, the exceptionally popular **High Sierra Camps** (Map p400) provide shelter and sustenance to hikers who'd rather not carry food or a tent. The camps – called **Vogelsang**, **Merced Lake**, **Sunrise**, **May Lake** and **Glen Aulin** – are set 6 to 10 miles apart along a loop trail. They consist of dormitory-style canvas tent cabins with beds, blankets or comforters, plus showers (at May Lake, Sunrise and Merced Lake – subject to water availability) and a central dining tent. Guests bring their own sheets and towels. The rate is $151 per adult ($91 for children seven to twelve) per night, including breakfast and dinner. Organized hiking or saddle trips led by ranger naturalists are also available (from $901).

A short season (roughly late June to September) and high demand mean that there's a lottery for reservations. **Applications** (☎801-559-4909; www.yosemitepark.com) are currently accepted in September and October only. If you don't have a reservation, call from February to check for cancellations. Dates vary year to year, so watch the website for updates.

ranger talks and slide shows, while the tavern at the Evergreen Lodge (p407) has live bands some weekends. Scan the *Yosemite Guide* for full details.

Information

Yosemite's entrance fee is $20 per vehicle or $10 for those on bicycle or foot and is valid for seven consecutive days. Upon entering the park, you'll receive an NPS map, an illustrated booklet and, most importantly, a copy of the seasonal *Yosemite Guide* newspaper, which includes an activity schedule and current opening hours of all facilities.

For recorded park information, campground availability, and road and weather conditions, call ☎209-372-0200.

Dangers & Annoyances

Yosemite is prime black bear habitat. To find out how to protect the bears and yourself from each other, see p560. Mosquitoes can be pesky in summer, so bug spray's not a bad idea. And please don't feed those squirrels. They may look cute but they've got a nasty bite.

Internet Access

Curry Village Lounge (Curry Village, behind registration office) Free wi-fi.

Degnan's Cafe (Yosemite Village; per min 25¢) Pay terminals in this cafe adjacent to Degnan's Deli.

Mariposa County Public Library Yosemite Valley (Girls Club Bldg, 58 Cedar Ct, Yosemite Valley; ⌚8:30-11:30am Mon, 2-5pm Tue, 8:30am-12:30pm Wed, 4-7pm Thu); Bassett Memorial Library (Chilnualna Falls Rd, Wawona; ⌚1-6pm Mon-Fri, 10am-3pm Sat, shorter hours fall-spring) Free internet terminals available.

Yosemite Lodge at the Falls (Yosemite Valley; per min 25¢) Pay terminals are in the lobby. Wi-fi costs $6 per day for nonguests.

Internet Resources

Yosemite Conservancy (www.yosemiteconservancy.org) Information and educational programs offered by the nonprofit park support organization.

Yosemite National Park (www.nps.gov/yose) Official Yosemite National Park Service site with the most comprehensive and current information.

Yosemite Park (www.yosemitepark.com) Online home of DNC Parks & Resorts, Yosemite's main concessionaire. Has lots of practical information and a lodging reservations function.

Medical Services

Yosemite Medical Clinic (☎209-372-4637; Ahwahnee Dr, Yosemite Valley; ⌚approx 9am-5pm) Twenty-four hour emergency service available. A **dental clinic** (☎209-372-4200) is also available next door.

Money

Stores in Yosemite Village, Curry Village and Wawona all have ATMs, as does the Yosemite Lodge at the Falls.

Post

The main post office is in Yosemite Village, but Wawona and Yosemite Lodge also have year-round services. A seasonal branch operates in Tuolumne Meadows.

Telephone

There are pay phones at every developed location throughout the park. Cell-phone reception is sketchy, depending on your location; AT&T, Verizon and Sprint have the best coverage.

Tourist Information

Extended summer hours may apply.

Big Oak Flat Information Station (Map p400; ☎209-379-1899; ⏲8am-5pm May-Sep) Also has a wilderness permit desk.

Tuolumne Meadows Visitor Center (Map p400; ☎209-372-0263; ⏲9am-6pm late spring-early fall)

Tuolumne Meadows Wilderness Center (Map p400; ☎209-372-0309; ⏲approx 8am-4:30pm spring & fall, 7:30am-5pm Jul & Aug) Issues wilderness permits.

Valley Wilderness Center (Map p404; ☎209-372-0745; Yosemite Village; ⏲7:30am-5pm May-Sep) Wilderness permits, maps and backcountry advice.

Wawona Information Station (Map p400; ☎209-375-9531; ⏲8:30am-5pm May-Sep) Issues wilderness permits.

Yosemite Valley Visitor Center (Map p404; ☎209-372-0299; Yosemite Village; ⏲9am-7:30pm summer, shorter hours year-round) The main office, with exhibits and free film screenings of *Spirit of Yosemite.*

Getting There & Away

Car

Yosemite is accessible year-round from the west (via Hwys 120 W and 140) and south (Hwy 41), and in summer also from the east (via Hwy 120 E). Roads are plowed in winter, but snow chains may be required at any time. In 2006 a mammoth rockslide buried part of Hwy 140, 6 miles west of the park; traffic there is restricted to vehicles under 45ft.

Gas up year-round at Wawona and Crane Flat inside the park or at El Portal on Hwy 140 just outside its boundaries. In summer, gas is also sold at Tuolumne Meadows. You'll pay dearly.

Public Transportation

Yosemite is one of the few national parks that can be easily reached by public transportation. **Greyhound** buses and **Amtrak** trains serve Merced, west of the park, where they are met by buses operated by **Yosemite Area Regional Transportation System** (YARTS; ☎209-388-9589, 877-989-2787; www.yarts.com), and you can buy Amtrak tickets that include the YARTS segment all the way into the park. Buses travel to Yosemite Valley along Hwy 140 several times daily year-round, stopping along the way.

In summer, another YARTS route runs from Mammoth Lakes along Hwy 395 to Yosemite Valley via Hwy 120. One-way tickets to Yosemite Valley are $13 ($9 child and senior, three hours) from Merced and $15 ($10 child and senior, 3½ hours) from Mammoth Lakes, less if boarding in between.

YARTS fares include the park entrance fee, making them a super bargain.

Getting Around

Bicycle

Bicycling is an ideal way to take in Yosemite Valley. You can rent a wide-handled cruiser (per hour/day $10/28) or a bike with an attached child trailer (per hour/day $16.50/54) at the Yosemite Lodge at the Falls or Curry Village.

Car

Roadside signs with red bears mark the many spots where bears have been hit by motorists, so think before you hit the accelerator. Glacier Point and Tioga Rds are closed in winter.

Public Transportation

The free, air-conditioned **Yosemite Valley Shuttle Bus** is a comfortable and efficient way of traveling around the park. Buses operate year-round at frequent intervals and stop at 21 numbered locations, including parking lots, campgrounds, trailheads and lodges. For a route map, see the *Yosemite Guide*.

Free buses also operate between Wawona and the Mariposa Grove (spring to fall), and Yosemite Valley and Badger Pass (winter only). The **Tuolumne Meadows Shuttle** runs between Tuolumne Lodge and Olmsted Point in Tuolumne Meadows (usually mid-June to early September), and the **El Capitan Shuttle** runs a summertime valley loop from Yosemite Village to El Capitan.

Two fee-based hikers' buses also travel from Yosemite Valley. For trailheads along Tioga Rd, catch the **Tuolumne Meadows Tour & Hikers' Bus** (☎209-372-4386; ⏲Jul-early Sep), which runs once daily in each direction. Fares depend on distance traveled; the trip to Tuolumne Meadows costs $14.50/23 one way/round-trip. The **Glacier Point Hikers' Bus** (☎209-372-4386; one way/return $25/41; ⏲mid-May–Oct) is good for hikers as well as for people reluctant to drive up the long, windy road themselves. Reservations are required.

YOSEMITE GATEWAYS

Fish Camp

Fish Camp, just south of the park on Hwy 41, is more of a bend in the road, but it does have some good lodging options as well as the ever-popular **Sugar Pine Railroad** (☎559-683-7273; www.yosemitesteamtrains.com; rides adult/child $18/9; ⏲Mar-Oct; 👪), a historic steam train that chugs through the woods on a 4-mile loop.

Sleeping & Eating

TOP CHOICE **Narrow Gauge Inn** INN $$

(☎559-683-7720, 888-644-9050; www.narrowgaugeinn.com; 48571 Hwy 41; r incl breakfast Nov-Mar $79-109, Apr-Oct $120-220;) Next door to the railroad, this friendly, beautiful and supremely comfortable 26-room inn counts a hot tub, small bar, and the finest **restaurant** (mains $19-37, ⏲5:30-9pm Wed-Sun Apr-Oct) in the area. Each tastefully appointed room features unique decor and a pleasant deck facing the trees and mountains, and all have flat-screen TVs.

White Chief Mountain Lodge MOTEL $$

(☎559-683-5444; www.whitechiefmountainlodge.com; 7776 White Chief Mountain Rd; r $125-190; ⏲Apr-Oct) The cheapest and most basic option in town is this 1950s-era motel with simple kitchenette rooms. It's located a few hundred yards east of Hwy 41; watch for the sign and go up the wooded country road.

Summerdale Campground CAMPGROUND $

(☎877-444-6677; www.recreation.gov; tent & RV sites $21; ⏲May-Sep;) Has 28 well-dispersed United States Forest Service (USFS) sites along Big Creek.

Oakhurst

At the junction of Hwys 41 and 49, about 15 miles south of the park entrance, Oakhurst functions primarily as a service town. This is your last chance to stock up on reasonably priced groceries, gasoline and camping supplies.

Sleeping & Eating

TOP CHOICE **Sierra Sky Ranch** LODGE $$

(☎559-683-8040; www.sierraskyranch.com; 50552 Rd 632; r incl breakfast $145-225;) This former ranch dates back to 1875 and has numerous outdoor activities available on 14 attractive acres. The homespun rooms are phone-free and pet-friendly, with oversized wooden headboards and double doors that open onto shady verandas. The rambling and beautiful old lodge features a **restaurant** (dinner mains $12-41) and a rustic saloon, and has loads of comfortable lounging areas. With a storied history including previous uses as a TB hospital and a bordello, its past guests include Marilyn Monroe and John Wayne. Many swear that it's cheerfully haunted by former residents.

WILDERNESS PERMITS FOR OVERNIGHT CAMPING

Shedding the high-season crowds is easiest when you set foot into Yosemite's backcountry wilderness. Start by identifying a route that matches your schedule, skill and fitness level. Then secure a **wilderness permit** (☎209-372-0740; fax 209-372-0739; www.nps.gov/yose/planyourvisit/wpres.htm; advance reservation fee $5, plus $5 per person, free for walk-ins; ⏲8:30am-4:30pm Mon-Fri late Nov-Oct), which is mandatory for overnight trips. To prevent tent cities sprouting in the woods, a quota system limits the number of people leaving from each trailhead each day. For trips between mid-May and September, 60% of the quota may be reserved by fax, phone, or mail from 24 weeks to two days before your trip. Faxes received between 5pm (the previous day) and 7:30am (the first morning you can reserve) get first priority.

The remainder are distributed by the office closest to the trailhead on a first-come, first-served basis (beginning at 11am one day before your planned hike) at Yosemite Valley Wilderness Center (p410), Tuolumne Meadows Wilderness Center (p410), the information stations at Wawona (Map p400) and Big Oak Flat (Map p400), and the Hetch Hetchy Entrance Station (Map p400). Hikers who turn up at the wilderness center nearest the trailhead get priority over those at another wilderness center. For example, if a person who's been waiting for hours in the valley wants the last permit left for Lyell Canyon, the Yosemite Valley Wilderness Center calls the Tuolumne Meadows Wilderness Center to see if any hikers in Tuolumne want it. If a hiker waltzing into the Tuolumne office says 'yes!', they get priority over the person in the Valley.

Reservations are not available from October to April, but you'll still need to get a permit.

At night you must be sure to store all scented items in bear-resistant containers, which may be rented for $5 per week at the wilderness and visitors centers. For locations and details, check www.nps.gov/yose/planyourvisit/bearcanrentals.htm.

SCENIC DRIVE: SIERRA VISTA NATIONAL SCENIC BYWAY

Set entirely within Sierra National Forest, this scenic route (www.sierravistascenicbyway.org) follows USFS roads in an 83-mile loop that takes you from 3000ft to nearly 7000ft. Along the way are dramatic vistas, excellent fishing, and camping almost anywhere you like (dispersed camping is allowed in most areas). It's a great way for car campers – and curious day trippers – to lose themselves within the mountains.

From its start in **North Fork**, the route takes a half-day to complete, emerging on Hwy 41 a few miles north of **Oakhurst**. Open from June to November, the road is paved most of the way, but narrow and laced with curves. See www.byways.org/explore/byways/2300 for a map and information on sights and the best overlooks.

Château du Sureau BOUTIQUE HOTEL **$$$**
(☎559-683-6860; www.chateaudusureau.com; r incl breakfast $385-585, 2-bedroom villa $2950; ❄@📶🏊) Never in a billion years would you expect to find this in Oakhurst. A luxe and discreet full-service European-style hotel and world-class spa, this serene destination property boasts an exceptional level of service. With wall tapestries, oil paintings and ornate chandeliers, its **restaurant** (prix fixe dinner $95) could be a countryside castle.

Hounds Tooth Inn B&B **$$**
(☎559-642-6600; www.houndstoothinn.com; 42071 Hwy 41; r incl breakfast $95-179; ❄📶) A few miles north of Oakhurst, this gorgeous garden B&B is swimming in rosebushes and Victorian-esque charm. Its 12 airy rooms, some with spas and fireplaces, feel a bit like an English manor house. Complimentary wine and hot drinks are available in the afternoon.

Oakhurst Lodge MOTEL **$$**
(☎559-683-4417, 800-655-6343; www.oakhurstlodge.com; 40302 Hwy 41; r $145-160; ❄📶🏊🐾) Right in the center of town, this 58-unit motel presents a fine no-frills budget option, with quiet, clean rooms, some with kitchenettes.

Merced River Canyon

The approach to Yosemite via Hwy 140 is one of the most scenic, especially the section that meanders through Merced River Canyon. The springtime runoff makes this a spectacular spot for **river rafting**, with many miles of class III and IV rapids. Age minimums vary with water levels.

Outfitters include **Zephyr Whitewater Expeditions** (☎209-532-6249, 800-431-3636; www.zrafting.com; half-day/1-day trips per person from $105/125), a large, reputable outfitter with a seasonal office in El Portal, and **OARS** (☎209-736-4677, 800-346-6277; www.oars.com; 1-day trips per person $144-170), a worldwide rafting operator with a solid reputation.

Mariposa

About halfway between Merced and Yosemite Valley, Mariposa (Spanish for 'butterfly') is the largest and most interesting town near the park. Established as a mining and railroad town during the Gold Rush, it has the oldest courthouse in continuous use (since 1854) west of the Mississippi and a friendly feel.

Rock hounds should drive to the **Mariposa County Fairgrounds**, 2 miles south of town on Hwy 49, to see the 13-pound 'Fricot Nugget' – the largest crystallized gold specimen from the California Gold Rush era – and other gems and machinery at the **California State Mining & Mineral Museum** (☎209-742-7625; www.parks.ca.gov/?page_id=588; admission $4; ⏲10am-5pm Thu-Sun May-Sep, to 4pm Oct-Apr). An exhibit on glow-in-the-dark minerals is also very cool.

At the junction of Hwy 49s and 140 is the info-laden **Mariposa County Visitor Center** (☎209-966-7081, 866-425-3366; www.homeofyosemite.com; ⏲8am-8pm mid-May–mid-Oct, to 5pm mid-Oct–mid-May), which has friendly staff and racks of brochures.

YARTS (☎209-388-9589, 877-989-2787; www.yarts.com) buses run year-round along Hwy 140 into Yosemite Valley (adult/child $12/8 round-trip, 1¾ hours one way) stopping at the Mariposa visitor center. Tickets include park admission.

Sleeping & Eating

TOP CHOICE **River Rock Inn** MOTEL **$$**
(☎209-966-5793; www.riverrockncafe.com; 4993 7th St; r incl breakfast $109-159; ❄📶🐾) A bold splash of psychedelic purple and dusty or-

ange paint spruces up what claims to be the oldest motel in town. Rooms done up in artsy earth tones have TVs but no phones, and calming ceiling fans resemble lily pads. A block removed from Hwy 140 on a quiet side street, it features a small courtyard deck and deli cafe serving beer and wine, with live acoustic music some summer evenings.

Mariposa Lodge MOTEL $$
(209-966-3607, 800-966-8819; www.mariposalodge.com; 5052 Hwy 140; r $119-159;) More of a generic motel, the simple, well-kept Mariposa sports clean, quiet rooms (with TVs and phones) and friendly staff. It earns pluses for the good-sized rooms and for the blooming flowers that border the grounds.

Happy Burger DINER $
(www.happyburgerdiner.com; Hwy 140 at 12th St; mains $6-10; 5:30am-9pm;) Boasting the largest menu in the Sierra, this buzzing roadside joint decorated with old LP album covers serves the cheapest meals in Mariposa. Its all-American cuisine means burgers, sandwiches, Mexican food and a ton of sinful ice-cream desserts.

Savoury's NEW AMERICAN $$
(209-966-7677; www.savouryrestaurant.com; 5034 Hwy 140; mains $15-30; 5-9pm Thu-Tue;) Now in a roomier location, upscale yet casual Savoury's is still the best restaurant in town. Black lacquered tables and contemporary art create a tranquil window dressing for dishes like apricot- and miso-glazed pork chops, hearty pastas and Steak Diane.

Midpines

The highlight of this almost nonexistent town is the folksy **Yosemite Bug Rustic Mountain Resort** (209-966-6666, 866-826-7108; www.yosemitebug.com; dm $25, tent cabins $45-75, r $75-155, cabins without bath $65-100; @), tucked away on a forested hillside about 25 miles from Yosemite National Park. It's more like a convivial mountain retreat than a hostel: at night, friendly folks of all ages and backgrounds share stories, music and delicious freshly prepared meals in the woodsy **cafe** (mains $8.50-18; 7am-9pm;) before retreating to their beds. Dorm dwellers have access to a communal kitchen, and the resort has a spa with a hot tub; yoga lessons and massages are also available.

The YARTS bus stops a quarter mile up the driveway, and the resort's **Bug Bus tours** offer a range of hiking trips (including overnights) to Yosemite year-round. A two-night package including transportation, lodging, meals and a park tour starts at $245. See details at www.yosemitebugbus.com.

Briceburg

Some 20 miles outside the park, right where the Merced River meets Hwy 140, the town of Briceburg consists of a **visitors center** (209-379-9414; www.blm.gov/ca/st/en/fo/folsom/mercedriverrec.html; 1-5pm Fri, from 9am Sat & Sun late Apr-early Sep) and three primitive **Bureau of Land Management (BLM)**

SCENIC DRIVE: EBBETTS PASS SCENIC BYWAY

For outdoor fanatics, a scenic 61-mile section of Hwys 4 and 89 called the **Ebbetts Pass Scenic Byway** (www.scenic4.org) is a road trip through paradise. Heading northeast from Arnold, gaze up at the giant sequoias of **Calaveras Big Trees State Park** (www.parks.ca.gov/?page_id=551; per vehicle $8), and in winter stop at the family-friendly ski resort of **Bear Valley** (209-753-2301; www.bearvalley.com; lift tickets adult/child $62/15;). Continuing east, the stunningly beautiful **Lake Alpine** is skirted by slabs of granite, several great beaches and a handful of campgrounds, and boasts excellent watersports, fishing and hiking.

The next stretch is the most dramatic, when the narrow highway continues past picturesque **Mosquito Lake** and the **Pacific Grade Summit** (8060ft) before slaloming through historic Hermit Valley and finally winding up and over the 8730ft summit of **Ebbetts Pass**. North on Hwy 89 and just west of **Markleeville**, visit the two developed pools and seasonal campground at **Grover Hot Springs State Park** (530-694-2249; www.parks.ca.gov/?page_id=508; parking $8, pool admission adult/child $5/3, tent & RV sites $35; variable hours year-round).

From San Francisco, it's a three-hour drive north to Arnold, via Hwy 108 and Hwy 49. Ebbetts Pass closes after the first major snowfall and doesn't reopen until June, but Hwy 4 is usually plowed from the west as far as Bear Valley.

THE BUFFALO SOLDIERS

After the creation of the national parks in 1890, the US Army was called in to safeguard these natural resources. In the summer of 1903, troops from the 9th Cavalry – one of four well-respected (though segregated) African American regiments, known as the 'Buffalo Soldiers' – were sent to patrol here and in Yosemite. In Sequoia and what was then General Grant National Park, the troops had an impressively productive summer – building roads, creating a trail system and setting a high standard as stewards of the land.

The troops were commanded by Captain (later Colonel) Charles Young. At the time, Young was the only African American captain in the Army; his post as Acting Superintendent made him the first African American superintendent of a national park.

campgrounds (tent & RV sites $10) with a to-die-for location right on the river. To reach them, you cross a beautiful 1920s wooden suspension bridge, so long trailers and large RVs are not recommended.

El Portal

Right outside the Arch Rock entrance, and primarily inhabited by park employees, El Portal makes a convenient Yosemite base. YARTS buses run to Yosemite Valley (adult/child round-trip $7/5, one hour).

Primarily an inexpensive private campground, **Indian Flat RV Park** (209-379-2339, www.indianflatrvpark.com; 9988 Hwy 140; tent sites $25, RV sites $37-42, tent cabins $59, cottages $109; year-round) also has a number of interesting housing options, including two pretty stone cabin cottages with air-conditioning. Guests can use the pool and wi-fi at its sister property next door, and nonguests can pay to shower.

Less than 2 miles from the park entrance, **Yosemite View Lodge** (209-379-2681, 888-742-4371; www.stayyosemiteviewlodge.com; 11136 Hwy 140; r $164-254, ste $304-714) is a big, modern complex with hot tubs, two restaurants and four pools. All the 336 rooms feature kitchenettes, some have gas fireplaces and views of the Merced River, and the ground-floor rooms have big patios. The souped-up 'majestic suites' are massive, with opulent bathrooms featuring waterfall showers and plasma-TV entertainment centers.

Groveland

From the Big Oak Flat entrance, it's 22 miles to Groveland, an adorable town with restored Gold Rush–era buildings.

A friendly 10-room 1918 confection with beds adorned in patchwork quilts, the **Hotel Charlotte** (209-962-6455; www.hotelcharlotte.com; 18736 Main St; r incl breakfast $129-225) keeps the vintage flair alive. The cute **restaurant** (mains $12-20) serves a creative international menu.

Across the street from the Hotel Charlotte, the historic **Groveland Hotel** (209-962-4000, 800-273-3314; www.groveland.com; 18767 Main St; r incl breakfast $135-349) dates from 1850 and now houses a small **bar**, an upscale **restaurant** (mains $14-21) and 17 bright, lovingly decorated rooms with wraparound verandas and resident teddy bears.

SEQUOIA & KINGS CANYON NATIONAL PARKS

The twin parks of Sequoia & Kings Canyon dazzle with superlatives, though they're often overshadowed by Yosemite, their smaller neighbor to the north (a three-hour drive away). With towering forests of giant sequoias containing some of the largest trees in the world, and the mighty Kings River careening through the depths of Kings Canyon, one of the deepest chasms in the country, the parks are lesser-visited jewels where it's easier to find quiet and solitude. Throw in opportunities for cave spelunking, rock climbing and backcountry hiking through granite-carved Sierra landscapes, and backdoor access to Mt Whitney – the tallest peak in the lower 48 states – and you have all the ingredients for two of the best parks in the country.

The two parks, though distinct, are operated as one unit with a single admission (valid for seven consecutive days) of $20 per carload. For 24-hour recorded information, including road conditions, call 559-565-3341 or visit www.nps.gov/seki, the parks' comprehensive website. At either entrance station (Big Stump or Ash Mountain), you'll receive an NPS map and a copy of the parks' *The Guide* newspaper, with information on seasonal activities, camping and special programs, including those in the surrounding national forests and the Giant Sequoia National Monument.

Cell-phone coverage is nonexistent except for limited reception at Grant Grove, and gas is available at Hume Lake and Stony Creek Lodge, both on USFS land.

History

In 1890 Sequoia became the second national park in the USA (after Yellowstone). A few days later, the 4 sq miles around Grant Grove were declared General Grant National Park and, in 1940, absorbed into the newly created Kings Canyon National Park. In 2000, to protect additional sequoia groves, vast tracts of land in the surrounding national forest became the Giant Sequoia National Monument.

Dangers & Annoyances

Air pollution wafting up from the Sequoia Central Valley and Kings Canyon often thwarts long-range visibility, and people with respiratory problems should check with a visitors center about current pollution levels. Black bears are common and proper food storage is always required. Heed park instructions on wildlife procedures and see p560 for more information.

Kings Canyon National Park

With a dramatic cleft deeper than the Grand Canyon, Kings Canyon offers true adventure to those who crave seemingly endless trails, rushing streams and gargantuan rock formations. The camping, backcountry exploring and climbing here are all superb.

Sights & Activities

Kings Canyon National Park has two developed areas with markets, lodging, showers and visitor information. Grant Grove Village is only 4 miles past the Big Stump entrance (in the park's west), while Cedar Grove Village is 31 miles east at the bottom of the canyon. The two are separated by the Giant Sequoia National Monument and are linked by Kings Canyon Scenic Byway/Hwy 180.

GRANT GROVE

General Grant Grove FOREST

This sequoia grove is nothing short of magnificent. The paved half-mile **General Grant Tree Trail** is an interpretive walk that visits a number of mature sequoias, including the 27-story **General Grant Tree**. This giant

SCENIC DRIVE: KINGS CANYON SCENIC BYWAY (HIGHWAY 180)

The 31-mile rollercoaster road connecting Grant Grove and Cedar Grove ranks among the most dazzling in all of California. It winds past the **Converse Basin Grove**, which once contained the world's largest grove of mature sequoias until loggers turned it into a sequoia cemetery in the 1880s. A half-mile loop trail leads to the 20ft-high **Chicago Stump**, the remains of the 3200-year-old tree that was cut down, sectioned and reassembled for the 1893 World Columbian Exposition in Chicago. North of here, a second side road goes to **Stump Meadow**, where stumps and fallen logs make good picnic platforms, and to the **Boole Tree Trail**, a 2.5-mile loop to the only 'monarch' left to live.

The road then begins its jaw-dropping descent into the canyon, snaking past chiseled rock walls, some tinged by green moss and red iron minerals, others decorated by waterfalls. Turnouts provide superb views, especially at **Junction View**.

Eventually the road runs parallel with the gushing Kings River, its thunderous roar ricocheting off granite cliffs soaring as high as 8000ft, making Kings Canyon even deeper than the Grand Canyon. Stop at **Boyden Cavern** (888-965-8243; www.boydencavern.com; tours adult/child from $13/8; 10am-5pm late May-Sep, 11am-4pm late Apr-late May & Oct–mid-Nov) for a tour of its whimsical formations. While beautiful, they are smaller and less impressive than those in Crystal Cave (p421) in Sequoia National Park, but no advance tickets are required. About 5 miles further east, **Grizzly Falls** can be torrential or drizzly, depending on the time of year.

On your return trip, consider a detour via **Hume Lake**, created in 1908 as a dam for logging operations and now offering boating, swimming and fishing. Facilities include a small market and a gas station.

Sequoia & Kings Canyon National Parks

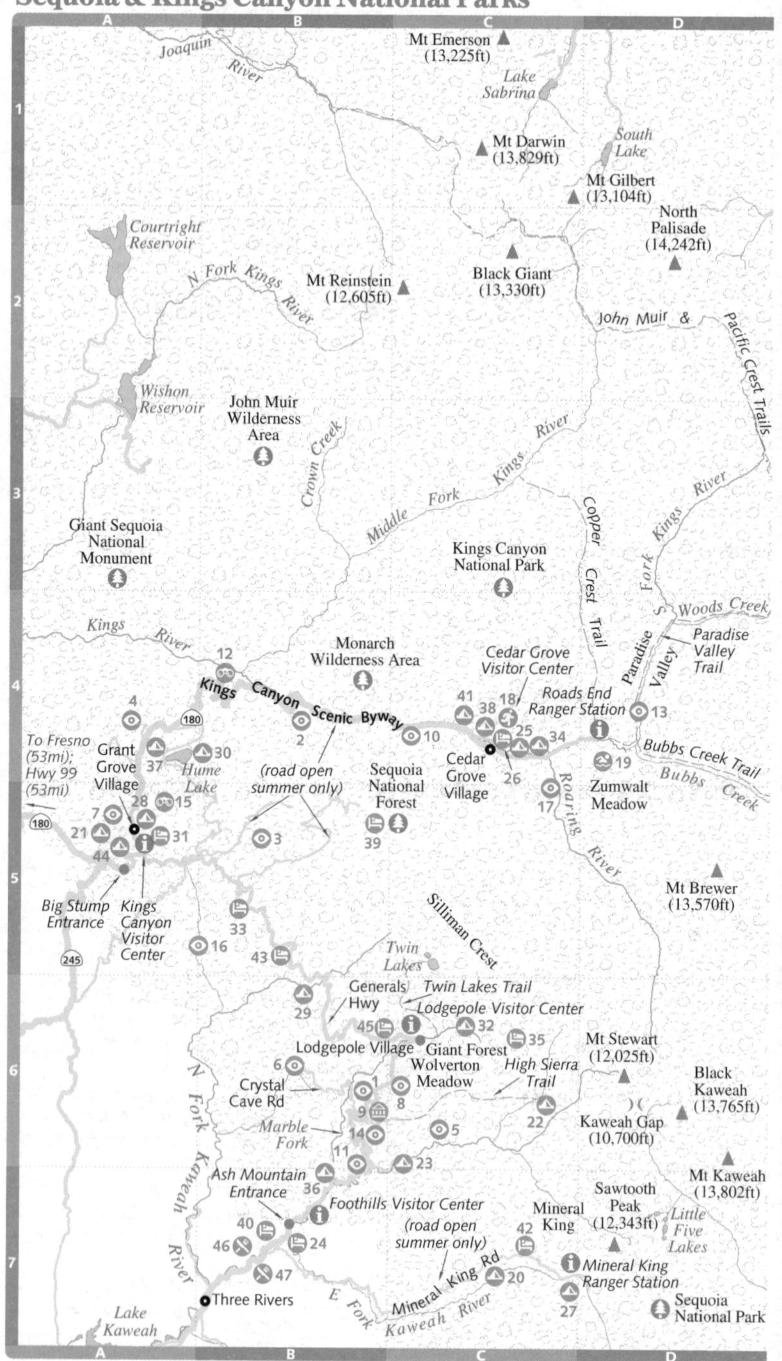

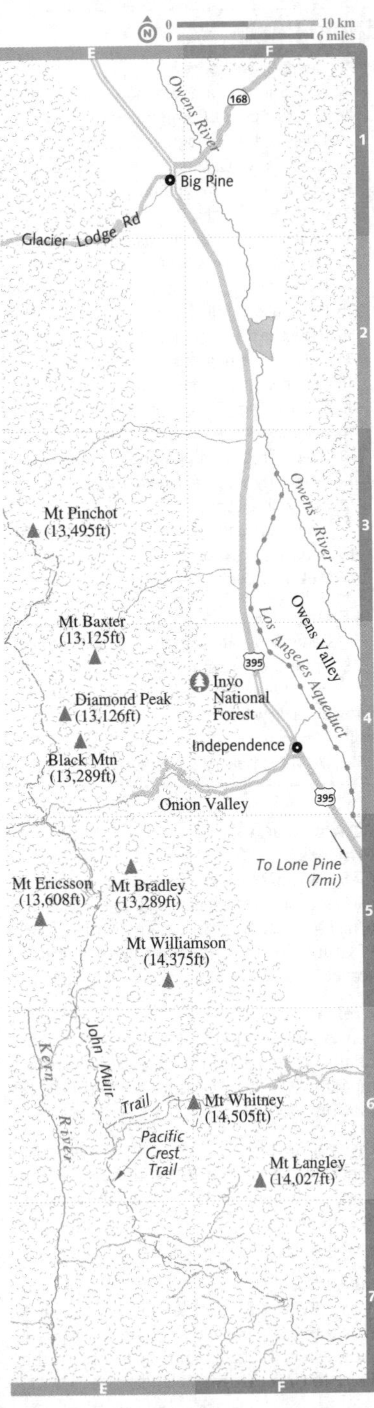

holds triple honors as the world's third-largest living tree, a memorial to US soldiers killed in war, and as the nation's Christmas tree. The nearby **Fallen Monarch**, a massive, fire-hollowed trunk that you can walk through, has been a cabin, hotel, saloon and stables for US Cavalry horses.

Panoramic Point LOOKOUT

For a breathtaking view of Kings Canyon, head 2.3 miles up narrow, steep and winding Panoramic Point Rd (trailers and RVs aren't recommended), which branches off Hwy 180. Follow a short paved trail uphill from the parking lot to the viewpoint, where precipitous canyons and the snowcapped peaks of the Great Western Divide unfold below you. Snow closes the road to vehicles during winter, when it becomes a cross-country ski and snowshoe route.

Redwood Canyon CANYON

South of Grant Grove Village, more than 15,000 sequoias cluster in this secluded and pristine corner of the park, making it the world's largest such grove. Relatively inaccessible, this area lets you enjoy the majesty of the giants away from the crowds on several moderate-to-strenuous trails. The trailhead is at the end of an unsigned, 2-mile bumpy dirt road across from the Hume Lake/Quail Flat sign on Generals Hwy, about 6 miles south of the village.

CEDAR GROVE & ROADS END

At Cedar Grove Village, a simple lodge and snack bar provide the last outpost of civilization before the rugged grandeur of the backcountry takes over. Pretty spots around here include **Roaring River Falls**, where water whips down a sculpted rock channel before tumbling into a churning pool, and the 1.5-mile **Zumwalt Meadow Loop**, an easy nature trail around a verdant green meadow bordered by river and granite canyon. A short walk from Roads End, **Muir Rock** is a large flat river boulder where John Muir often gave talks during Sierra Club field trips. The rock now bears his name, and the lazy river abounds with gleeful swimmers in summer.

The trail to **Mist Falls** (8-mile round-trip) is an easy to moderate hike to one of the park's larger waterfalls. The first 2 miles are fairly exposed, so start early to avoid the midday heat. Continuing past Mist Falls, the trail eventually connects with the John Muir/Pacific Crest Trail to form the 42-mile **Rae Lakes Loop**, the most popular long-dis-

Sequoia & Kings Canyon National Parks

Sights

1 Beetle Rock Education Center B6
2 Boyden Cavern B4
3 Buck Rock Lookout B5
4 Converse Basin Grove A4
5 Crescent Meadow C6
6 Crystal Cave B6
7 General Grant Grove A5
8 General Sherman Tree C6
9 Giant Forest Museum B6
10 Grizzly Falls C4
11 Hospital Rock B6
12 Junction View B4
13 Mist Falls D4
14 Moro Rock B6
15 Panoramic Pt A5
16 Redwood Canyon B5
17 Roaring River Falls C5

Activities, Courses & Tours

18 Cedar Grove Pack Station C4
19 Muir Rock D4

Sleeping

20 Atwell Mill Campground C7
21 Azalea Campground A5
22 Bearpaw High Sierra Camp C6
23 Buckeye Flat Campground C6
24 Buckeye Tree Lodge B7
25 Canyon View Campground C4
26 Cedar Grove Lodge C4
27 Cold Springs Campground C7
28 Crystal Springs Campground A5
29 Dorst Creek Campground B6
Grant Grove Cabins .... (see 31)
30 Hume Lake Campground B4
31 John Muir Lodge A5
32 Lodgepole Campground C6
33 Montecito Lake Resort B5
34 Moraine Campground C4
35 Pear Lake Ski Hut C6
36 Potwisha Campground B7
37 Princess Campground A4
38 Sentinel Campground C4
39 Sequoia High Sierra Camp B5
40 Sequoia Village Inn B7
41 Sheep Creek Campground C4
42 Silver City Mountain Resort C7
43 Stony Creek Lodge & Campground B5
44 Sunset Campground A5
45 Wuksachi Lodge B6

Eating

Cedar Grove Restaurant .... (see 26)
Grant Grove Restaurant .... (see 31)
Pizza Parlor .... (see 31)
46 River View Restaurant & Lounge B7
47 We Three Bakery & Restaurant B7

tance hike in Kings Canyon National Park (a wilderness permit is required, see p422).

For guided horse trips, both day and overnight, check with **Cedar Grove Pack Station** (559-565-3464).

Sleeping & Eating

Unless noted, all campsites are first-come, first-served. Showers are available at Grant Grove Village and Cedar Grove Village.

Potential campers should also keep in mind that there are great free uncrowded and undeveloped campgrounds off Big Meadows Rd in the Sequoia National Forest. They're some of the only empty campsites in the Sierra Nevada during peak summer season. Free roadside camping is also allowed in the forest, but no campfires without a permit (available from the Grant Grove Visitor Center).

Markets in Grant Grove Village and Cedar Grove Village have a limited selection of groceries.

GRANT GROVE

Princess CAMPGROUND $

(877-444-6777; www.recreation.gov; Giant Sequoia National Monument; tent & RV sites $18; mid-May–late Sep;) About 6 miles north of Grant Grove, with vault toilets and 90 reservable sites.

Azalea CAMPGROUND $

(tent & RV sites $10-18; year-round;) Flush toilets, 110 sites; the nicest sites border a meadow. Close to Grant Grove Village (elevation 6500ft).

Crystal Springs CAMPGROUND $

(tent & RV sites $18; mid-May–mid-Sep;) Fifty wooded, well-spaced sites with flush toilets; the smallest campground in the Grant Grove area and generally very quiet.

Sunset CAMPGROUND $

(tent & RV sites $18; late May-early Sep;) Flush toilets, 157 sites, some overlooking the western foothills and the Central Valley. Close to Grant Grove Village.

Hume Lake CAMPGROUND $
(☎877-444-6777; www.recreation.gov; Hume Lake Rd, Giant Sequoia National Monument; tent & RV sites $20; ⊙late May-early Sep;) Flush toilets, 74 reservable and uncrowded shady campsites, a handful with lake views; on the lake's northern shore about 10 miles northeast of Grant Grove.

John Muir Lodge LODGE $$$
(☎559-335-5500, 866-522-6966; www.sequoia-kingscanyon.com; Grant Grove Village, off Generals Hwy; r $69-190) An atmospheric wooden building hung with historical black-and-white photographs, this year-round hotel is a place to lay your head and still feel like you're in the forest. Wide porches have wooden rocking chairs, and homespun, if thin-walled, rooms contain rough-hewn wood furniture and patchwork bedspreads (no TVs). Cozy up to the big stone fireplace on chilly nights with a board game.

Grant Grove Cabins CABINS $$
(☎559-335-5500, 866-522-6966; www.sequoia-kingscanyon.com; Grant Grove Village, off Generals Hwy; cabins $65-140) Set amid towering sugar pines, around 50 cabins range from decrepit tent-top shacks (open from early June until early September) to rustic but comfortable heated duplexes (a few are wheelchair-accessible) with electricity, private bathrooms and double beds. For lovebirds, number 9 is the lone hard-sided, free-standing 'Honeymoon Cabin' with a queen bed, and can book up to a year in advance.

Grant Grove Restaurant AMERICAN $$
(Grant Grove Village, off Generals Hwy; mains $7-16; ⊙7-10:30am, 11am-4pm & 5-9pm late May-early Sep, reduced hours early Sep-late May;) More of a diner, this is where most visitors to Grant Grove Village chow down, and there can be a wait at times. There's a breakfast buffet, lunch sandwiches and filling full dinners.

Pizza Parlor PIZZERIA $$
(pizza $12-22; ⊙2-9pm 9pm late May-early Sep, variable hours otherwise;) Excellent crisp-crust pizzeria hidden off the back porch of the Grant Grove Restaurant; shows movies.

CEDAR GROVE

Cedar Grove's **Sentinel** campground, next to the village area, is open whenever Hwy 180 is open; **Sheep Creek**, **Canyon View** (tent only) and **Moraine** are opened as overflow when needed. These campgrounds are usually the last to fill up on busy summer weekends and are also good bets early and late in the season thanks to their comparatively low elevation (4600ft). All have flush toilets and $18 sites. Other facilities in the village don't start operating until mid-May.

Cedar Grove Lodge LODGE $$
(☎559-335-5500, 866-522-6966; www.sequoia-kingscanyon.com; Cedar Grove Village, Hwy 180; r $119-135; ⊙mid-May–mid-Oct;) The only indoor sleeping option in the canyon, the riverside lodge offers 21 motel-style rooms, some with air-con. Hallways tend toward dingy, bathrooms are cramped and the bedspreads scream frumpy. But the three ground-floor rooms with shady furnished patios have spiffy river views and kitchenettes. All rooms have phones but no TVs.

Cedar Grove Restaurant FAST FOOD $
(Cedar Grove Village; mains under $10; ⊙7-10:30am, 11am-2pm & 5-8pm mid-May–mid-Oct;) A basic grill with hot and greasy fare.

Information

ATMs exist at Grant Grove Village and Cedar Grove Village. There's free wi-fi near the lodging check-in desk inside the Grant Grove Restaurant building in Grant Grove Village.

Cedar Grove Visitor Center (☎559-565-3793; ⊙9am-5pm late May-early Sep) Small visitor center in Cedar Grove Village. The Roads End Ranger Station, which dispenses wilderness permits and rents bear canisters, is 6 miles further east.

Kings Canyon Visitor Center (☎559-565-4307; ⊙8am-7pm early Jul-late Aug, variable hours otherwise) In Grant Grove Village. Has exhibits, maps and wilderness permits.

Getting There & Around

From the west, Kings Canyon Scenic Byway (Hwy 180) travels 53 miles east from Fresno to the Big Stump entrance. Coming from the south, you're in for a long 46-mile drive through Sequoia National Park along sinuous Generals Hwy. Budget about two hours' driving time from the Ash Mountain entrance to Grant Grove Village. The road to Cedar Grove Village is only open from around April or May until the first snowfall.

Sequoia National Park

Picture unzipping your tent flap and crawling out into a 'front yard' of trees as high as a 20-story building and as old as the Bible. Brew some coffee as you plan your day in this extraordinary park with its soul-sustain-ing forests and gigantic peaks soaring above 12,000ft.

Sights & Activities

Nearly all of the park's star attractions are conveniently lined up along the Generals Hwy, which starts at the Ash Mountain entrance and continues north into Kings Canyon. Tourist activity concentrates in the Giant Forest area and in Lodgepole Village, which has the most facilities, including a visitors center and market. The road to remote Mineral King veers off Hwy 198 in the town of Three Rivers, just south of the park's Ash Mountain entrance.

GIANT FOREST

Named by John Muir in 1875, this area is the top destination in the parks, and about 2 miles south of Lodgepole Village. By volume the largest living tree on earth, the massive **General Sherman Tree** rockets 275ft to the sky. Pay your respects via a short descent from the Wolverton Rd parking lot, or join the **Congress Trail**, a paved 2-mile pathway that takes in General Sherman and other notable named trees, including the **Washington Tree**, the world's second biggest sequoia, and the see-through **Telescope Tree**. To lose the crowds, set off on the 5-mile **Trail of the Sequoias**, which puts you into the heart of the forest.

Open in the warmer months, Crescent Meadow Rd heads east from the Giant Forest Museum for 3 miles to **Crescent Meadow**, a relaxing picnic spot, especially in spring when it's ablaze with wildflowers. Several short hikes start from here, including the 1-mile trail to **Tharp's Log**, where the area's first white settler spent summers in a fallen tree. The road also passes **Moro Rock**, a landmark granite dome whose top can be reached via a quarter-mile carved staircase for breathtaking views of the Great Western Divide, a chain of mountains running north to south through the center of Sequoia National Park.

FREE **Giant Forest Museum** MUSEUM
(☎559-565-4480; ⏰9am-7pm summer, to 5 or 6pm spring & fall, to 4pm winter) For a primer on the intriguing ecology, fire cycle and history of the 'big trees,' drop in at this excellent museum, then follow up your visit with a spin around the paved (and wheelchair-accessible) 1.2-mile interpretive **Big Trees Trail**, which starts from the museum parking lot.

FREE **Beetle Rock Education Center** EDUCATION CENTER
(☎559-565-4480; ⏰1-4pm late Jun–mid-Aug; 👪) Bugs, bones and artificial animal scat are just some of the cool things children get to play with at this bright and cheerful cabin with activity stations galore. Here inquisitive kiddos can scan bugs with digital microscopes, touch a taxidermied bobcat, put on a puppet show and paint ecology posters. Tents are set up for inside play, and binoculars lure youngsters outside to spot animals.

FOOTHILLS

From the Ash Mountain entrance in Three Rivers, the Generals Hwy ascends steeply through this southern section of Sequoia National Park. With an average elevation of about 2000ft, the Foothills are much drier and warmer than the rest of the park. Hiking here is best in spring when the air is still cool and wildflowers put on a colorful show. Summers are buggy and muggy, but fall again brings moderate temperatures and lush foliage.

The Potwisha people lived in this area until the early 1900s, relying primarily on acorn meal. Pictographs and grinding holes still grace the **Hospital Rock** picnic

GIANT SEQUOIAS: KINGS OF THE FOREST

In California you can stand under the world's oldest trees and its tallest, but the record for biggest in terms of volume belongs to the giant sequoias *(Sequoiadendron giganteum)*. They grow only on the Sierra's western slope and are most abundant in Sequoia & Kings Canyon and Yosemite National Parks. John Muir called them 'nature's forest masterpiece' and anyone who's ever craned their neck to take in their soaring vastness has done so with the awe usually reserved for Gothic cathedrals. Trees can grow to 300ft tall and over 100ft in circumference, with bark over 2ft thick. The Giant Forest Museum (p420) in Sequoia National Park has excellent exhibits about their fascinating history and ecology.

DON'T MISS

CRYSTAL CAVE

Discovered in 1918 by two fishermen, **Crystal Cave** (☎559-565-3759; www.sequoiahistory.org; Crystal Cave Rd; adult/child/senior $13/7/12; ⏱tours 10:30am-4:30pm mid-May–late Oct) was carved by an underground river and has formations estimated to be 10,000 years old. Stalactites hang like daggers from the ceiling, and milky white marble formations take the shape of ethereal curtains, domes, columns and shields. The cave is also a unique biodiverse habitat for spiders, bats and tiny aquatic insects that are found nowhere else on earth. The 45-minute tour covers a half-mile of chambers, though adults can also sign up for more in-depth lantern-lit cave explorations and full-day spelunking adventures.

Tickets are *only* sold at the Lodgepole and Foothills visitors centers (see p423) and *not* at the cave. Allow about one hour to get to the cave entrance, which is a half-mile walk from the parking lot at the end of a twisty 7-mile road; the turnoff is about 3 miles south of the Giant Forest. Bring a sweater or light jacket, as it's a huddle-for-warmth 48°F inside.

area, once a Potwisha village site. **Swimming holes** abound along the Marble Fork of the Kaweah River, especially near Potwisha Campground. Be careful, though – the currents can be deadly, especially when the river is swollen from the spring runoff.

MINERAL KING

A scenic, subalpine valley at 7500ft, Mineral King is Sequoia's backpacking mecca and a good place to find solitude. Gorgeous and gigantic, its glacially sculpted valley is ringed by massive mountains, including the jagged 12,343ft **Sawtooth Peak**. The area is reached via Mineral King Rd – a slinky, steep and narrow 25-mile road, not suitable for RVs or speed demons; the road is usually open from late May through October. Plan on spending the night unless you don't mind driving three hours round-trip.

Hiking anywhere from here involves a steep climb out of the valley along strenuous trails, so be aware of the altitude, even on short hikes. Enjoyable day hikes go to **Crystal**, **Monarch**, **Mosquito** and **Eagle Lakes**. For long trips, locals recommend the **Little Five Lakes** and, further along the High Sierra Trail, **Kaweah Gap**, surrounded by **Black Kaweah**, **Mt Stewart** and **Eagle Scout Peak**– all above 12,000ft.

In spring and early summer, hordes of hungry marmots terrorize parked cars at Mineral King, chewing on radiator hoses, belts and wiring of vehicles to get the salt they crave after their winter hibernation. If you're thinking of going hiking during that time, you'd be a fool not to protect your car by wrapping the underside with chicken wire or a diaper-like tarp.

From the 1860s to 1890s, Mineral King witnessed heavy silver mining and lumber activity. There are remnants of old shafts and stamp mills, though it takes some exploring to find them. A proposal by the Walt Disney Corporation to develop the area into a massive ski resort was thwarted when Congress annexed it to the national park in 1978. The website of the **Mineral King Preservation Society** (www.mineralking.org) has all kinds of info on the area, including its rustic and still-occupied historic mining cabins.

Sleeping & Eating

The **market** at Lodgepole Village is the best stocked in either park, but basic supplies are also available at the small **store** in Stony Creek Lodge (closed in winter).

GENERALS HIGHWAY

A handful of campgrounds line the highway and rarely fill up, although space may get tight on holiday weekends. Those in the Foothills area are best in spring and fall when the higher elevations are still chilly, but they get hot and buggy in summer. Unless noted, sites are available on a first-come, first-served basis. Free dispersed camping is possible in the Giant Sequoia National Monument. Stop by a visitors center or ranger station for details or a fire permit. Lodgepole Village and Stony Creek Lodge have pay showers.

Stony Creek CAMPGROUND $
(☎877-444-6777; www.recreation.gov; tent & RV sites $20; ⏱mid-May–late Sep; 🐾) USFS-operated with 49 comfortable wooded sites, including some right on the creek, and flush

BACKPACKING IN SEQUOIA & KINGS CANYON NATIONAL PARKS

With over 850 miles of marked trails, the parks are a backpacker's dream. **Cedar Grove** and **Mineral King** offer the best backcountry access. Trails are usually open by mid to late May.

For overnight backcountry trips you'll need a **wilderness permit** (per group $15), which is subject to a quota system in summer; permits are free and available by self-registration outside the quota season. About 75% of spaces can be reserved, while the rest are available in person on a first-come, first-served basis. Reservations can be made from March 1 until two weeks before your trip. For details see www.nps.gov/seki/planyourvisit/wilderness_permits.htm. There's also a dedicated wilderness desk at the Lodgepole Visitor Center (see p423).

All ranger stations and visitors centers carry topo maps and hiking guides. Note that you need to store your food in park-approved bearproof canisters, which can be rented at markets and visitors centers (from $5 per trip).

toilets. Smaller, primitive **Upper Stony Creek campground** is across the street but not reservable.

Lodgepole CAMPGROUND $

(☎877-444-6777; www.recreation.gov; tent & RV sites $10-20; ⏰year-round; 👪🐾) Closest to the Giant Forest area with over 200 closely packed sites and flush toilets; this place fills quickly because of proximity to Lodgepole Village amenities.

Buckeye Flat CAMPGROUND $

(tent sites $18; ⏰Apr-Sep; 🐾) This campground is in the Foothills area, in an open stand of oaks about 6 miles north of the Ash Mountain entrance. There are 28 tent-only sites and flush toilets. Can be somewhat rowdy.

Potwisha CAMPGROUND $

(tent & RV sites $18; ⏰year-round; 🐾) Also in the Foothills, and blazing in summertime, this campground has decent shade and swimming spots on the Kaweah River. It's 3 miles north of the Ash Mountain entrance, with 42 sites and flush toilets.

Dorst Creek CAMPGROUND $

(☎877-444-6777; www.recreation.gov; tent & RV sites $20; ⏰late Jun-early Sep; 🐾) Big and busy campground with 204 sites and flush toilets; quieter back sites are tent-only.

Stony Creek Lodge LODGE $$

(☎559-335-5500, 866-522-6966; www.sequoia-kingscanyon.com; 65569 Generals Hwy; r $109-189; ⏰mid-May–mid-Oct; 📶👪) About halfway between Grant Grove Village and Giant Forest, this lodge has a big river-rock fireplace in its lobby and 11 aging but folksy motel rooms with telephone but no TV.

Wuksachi Lodge HOTEL $$$

(☎559-565-4070, 866-807-3598; www.visitsequoia.com; 64740 Wuksachi Way, off Generals Hwy; r $90-335; 📶) Built in 1999, the Wuksachi Lodge is the most upscale lodging and dining option in the park. But don't get too excited – the wood-paneled atrium lobby has an inviting stone fireplace and forest views, but charmless motel-style rooms with oak furniture and thin walls have an institutional feel. The lodge's location, however, just north of Lodgepole Village, can't be beat.

Sequoia High Sierra Camp CABINS $$$

(☎877-591-8982; www.sequoiahighsierracamp.com; r without bath incl all meals per adult/child $250/100; ⏰mid-Jun–early Oct) Accessed via a 1-mile hike deep into the Sequoia National Forest, off General's Hwy, this off-the-grid, all-inclusive resort is nirvana for active, sociable people who don't think 'luxury camping' is an oxymoron. Canvas cabins are spiffed up by pillow-top mattresses, down pillows and cozy wool rugs, with shared restrooms and a shower house. Reservations are required.

Lodgepole Village MARKET $

(Generals Hwy; mains $6-10; ⏰market & snack bar 9am-6pm mid-Apr–late May & early Sep–mid-Oct, 8am-8pm late May-early Sep, deli 11am-6pm mid-Apr–mid-Oct; 👪) The park's most extensive market sells all kinds of groceries, camping supplies and snacks. Inside, a fast-food snack bar slings burgers and grilled sandwiches and dishes up breakfast. The adjacent deli is a tad more upscale and healthy, with focaccia sandwiches, veggie wraps and picnic salads.

BACKCOUNTRY

Bearpaw High Sierra Camp CABINS $$$
(☎reservations 801-559-4930, 866-807-3598; www.visitsequoia.com; tent cabin per person $175; ⊙mid-Jun–mid-Sep) About 11.5 miles east of Giant Forest on the High Sierra Trail, this tent hotel is ideal for exploring the backcountry without lugging your own camping gear. Rates include showers, dinner and breakfast, as well as bedding and towels. Bookings start at 7am every January 2 and sell out almost immediately, though you should always check for cancellations.

MINERAL KING

Mineral King's two pretty campgrounds, **Atwell Mill** (tent sites $12; ⊙late May-Oct; 🐾) and **Cold Springs** (tent sites $12; ⊙late May-Oct; 🐾), often fill up on summer weekends. Pay showers available at the Silver City Mountain Resort.

Silver City Mountain Resort CABINS $$
(☎559-561-3223; www.silvercityresort.com; Mineral King Rd; cabins with/without bathroom $195/120, chalets $250-395; ⊙late May-late Oct; 📶👪) The only food and lodging option anywhere near these parts, this rustic, old-fashioned and family-friendly place rents everything from cute and cozy 1950s-era cabins to modern chalets (one is wheelchair-accessible) that sleep up to eight. There's a ping-pong table, outdoor swings, and nearby ponds to splash around in. All guests must bring their own sheets and towels. Most cabins don't have electricity, and the property's generator usually shuts off around 10pm. Its **restaurant** (mains $6 to $10; ⊙8am-8pm Thu-Mon, pie & coffee only 8am-5pm Tue-Wed) serves delicious homemade pies and simple fare on wooden picnic tables under the trees. It's located 3.5 miles west of the ranger station.

THREE RIVERS

Named for the nearby convergence of three Kaweah River forks, Three Rivers is a friendly small town populated mostly by retirees and artsy newcomers. The town's main drag, Sierra Dr (Hwy 198), is sparsely lined with motels, eateries and shops.

Sequoia Village Inn CABINS, COTTAGES $$
(☎559-561-3652; www.sequoiavillageinn.com; 45971 Sierra Dr; d $120-235; ❄📶🏊👪🐾) These 10 pretty modern cottages, cabins and chalets (many with kitchens), border the park and are great for families or groups. Most have outdoor woodsy decks and BBQs, and the largest can sleep 12.

Buckeye Tree Lodge MOTEL $$
(☎559-561-5900; www.buckeyetreelodge.com; 46000 Sierra Dr; d incl breakfast $125-150; ❄📶🏊🐾) Sit out on your grassy back patio or perch on the balcony and watch the river ease through a maze of boulders. Modern white-brick motel rooms, some with kitchenettes, feel airy and bright.

We Three Bakery & Restaurant CAFE $
(43368 Sierra Dr; mains $6-11; ⊙7am-4pm; 📶) Cinnamon French toast, biscuits with gravy and diner-style coffee lure in the breakfast crowd, while hot and cold sandwiches on blindingly bright Fiesta-ware make it a delish lunch spot. Chow down on the outdoor patio under a shady oak.

River View Restaurant & Lounge AMERICAN $$
(42323 Sierra Dr; mains lunch $6-12, dinner $12-26; ⊙6:30am-9pm, to 10pm Fri & Sat, bar open late) Colorful honky-tonk with great back patio; live music Fridays and Saturdays.

ℹ Information

Lodgepole Village has an ATM, and there's free wi-fi at Wuksachi Lodge.

Foothills Visitor Center (☎559-565-3135; ⊙8am-4:30pm, to 6pm late May-early Sep) One mile north of the Ash Mountain entrance.

Lodgepole Visitor Center (☎559-565-4436; ⊙9am-4:30pm mid-Apr–mid-May, from 8am mid-May–late Jun & early Sep–mid-Oct, 7am-

DON'T MISS

BUCK ROCK LOOKOUT

Built in 1923, this active **fire lookout** (www.buckrock.org; ⊙9:30am-6pm Jul-Oct) is one of the finest restored watchtowers you could ever hope to visit. Staffed in fire season, its 172 stairs lead to a dollhouse-sized wooden cab on a dramatic 8500ft granite rise with panoramic forest views. To reach it from General Hwy, go about 1 mile north of the Montecito Lake Resort and then east onto Big Meadows Rd (FS road 14S11). At approximately 2.5 miles, turn north on the signed dirt road (FS road 13S04) and follow signs another 3 miles to the lookout parking area.

WINTER FUN

In winter, a thick blanket of snow drapes over trees and meadows, the pace of activity slows and a hush falls over the roads and trails. Note that snow often closes Generals Hwy between Grant Grove and Giant Forest and that tire chains may be required at any time. These can usually be rented near the parks' entrances, although you're not supposed to put them on rental cars. For up-to-date road conditions call ☎559-565-3341 or check www.nps.gov/seki.

Snowshoeing and cross-country skiing are both hugely popular activities, with 50 miles of marked but ungroomed trails crisscrossing the Grant Grove and Giant Forest areas. Winter road closures also make for excellent cross-country skiing and snowshoeing on Sequoia's Moro Rock–Crescent Meadow Rd, Kings Canyons' Panoramic Point Rd and the Sequoia National Forest's Big Meadows Rd. Trail maps are available at the visitors centers, and park rangers lead free snowshoe tours (equipment included). Tree-marked trails connect with those in the Giant Sequoia National Monument and the 30 miles of groomed terrain maintained by the private **Montecito Lake Resort** (☎559-565-3388, 800-227-9900; www.montecitosequoia.com; 8000 Generals Hwy). Equipment rentals are available at Grant Grove Village, the Wuksachi Lodge and the Montecito Lake Resort. There are also snow-play areas near Columbine and Big Stump in the Grant Grove region and at Wolverton Meadow in Sequoia.

In winter, cross-country skiers with reservations can sleep in one of the 10 bunks at **Pear Lake Ski Hut** (☎559-565-3759; www.sequoiahistory.org; dm $40; ⏲mid-Dec–late Apr), a 1940-era pine-and-granite building run by the Sequoia Natural History Association. You'll be glad to see it after the strenuous 6-mile cross-country ski or snowshoe trek from Wolverton Meadow. Reservations are assigned by lottery in November. Call or check the website for details.

6pm late Jun-early Sep) Maps, information, exhibits, Crystal Cave tickets and wilderness permits.

Mineral King Ranger Station (☎559-565-3768; ⏲8am-4pm late May-early Sep) Twenty-four miles east of Generals Hwy; wilderness permits and campground availability info.

ℹ Getting There & Around

Coming from the south, Hwy 198 runs north from Visalia through Three Rivers past Mineral King Rd to the Ash Mountain entrance. Beyond here the road continues as the Generals Hwy, a narrow and windy road snaking all the way into Kings Canyon National Park, where it joins the Kings Canyon Scenic Byway (Hwy 180) near the western Big Stump entrance. Vehicles over 22ft long may have trouble negotiating the steep road with its many hairpin curves. Budget about one hour to drive from the entrance to the Giant Forest/Lodgepole area and another hour from there to Grant Grove Village in Kings Canyon.

Sequoia Shuttle (☎877-287-4453; www.sequoiashuttle.com; one way/round-trip $7.50/15; ⏲late May-late Sep) buses run five times daily between Visalia and the Giant Forest Museum (2½ hours) via Three Rivers; reservations required.

Shuttle buses run every 15 minutes from the Giant Forest Museum to Moro Rock and Crescent Meadow or to the General Sherman Tree parking areas and Lodgepole Village. Another route links Lodgepole, Wuksachi Lodge and Dorst Creek Campground every 30 minutes. All routes are free and currently operate from late May to late September.

EASTERN SIERRA

Cloud-dappled hills and sun-streaked mountaintops dabbed with snow typify the landscape of the Eastern Sierra, where slashing peaks – many over 14,000ft – rush abruptly upward from the arid expanses of the Great Basin and Mojave deserts. It's a dramatic juxtaposition that makes for a potent cocktail of scenery. Pine forests, lush meadows, ice-blue lakes, simmering hot springs and glacier-gouged canyons are only some of the beautiful sights you'll find in this region.

The Eastern Sierra Scenic Byway, officially known as Hwy 395, runs the entire length of the range. Turnoffs dead-ending at the foot of the mountains deliver you to pristine wilderness and countless trails, including the famous Pacific Crest Trail, John Muir Trail and main Mt Whitney Trail. The most important portals are the towns of Bridgeport, Mammoth Lakes, Bishop and Lone Pine. Note that in winter, when traffic thins, many facilities are closed.

Locally produced and available throughout the region, Sierra Maps' *Eastern Sierra: Bridgeport to Lone Pine* recreation and road map shows hot springs, ghost towns, hiking trails and climbing areas. Check out www.thesierraweb.com for area events and links to local visitor information.

Getting There & Around

The Eastern Sierra is easiest to explore under your own steam, although it's possible to access the area by public transportation. Buses operated by **Eastern Sierra Transit Authority** (760-872-1901, 800-922-1930; www.easternsierrattransitauthority.com) make round-trips between Lone Pine and Reno ($54, six hours) on Monday, Tuesday, Thursday and Friday, stopping at all Hwy 395 towns in between. Fares depend on distance, and reservations are recommended. There's also an express bus between Mammoth and Bishop ($6.50, one hour, three times daily) that operates Monday through Friday.

In the summer, connect to Yosemite via YARTS bus (see p410) in Mammoth Lakes or Lee Vining.

Mono Lake Area

BRIDGEPORT

Barely three blocks long, set amid open high valley and in view of the peaks of Sawtooth Ridge, Bridgeport flaunts classic western flair with charming old storefronts and a homey ambience. Most everything shuts down or cuts back hours for the brutal winters, but the rest of the year the town is a magnet for anglers, hikers, climbers and hot-spring devotees. Stop by the **Bridgeport Ranger Station & Visitor Center** (760-932-7070; www.fs.usda.gov/htnf; Hwy 395; 8am-4:30pm daily Jul & Aug, 8am-4:30pm Mon-Fri Sep-Jun) for maps, information and Hoover Wilderness permits.

Sights & Activities

Mono County Courthouse HISTORIC BUILDING

(9am-5pm Mon-Fri) The gavel has been dropped since 1880 at the courthouse, an all-white Italianate dreamboat surrounded by a gracious lawn and a wrought-iron fence. On the street behind it, look for the Old County Jail, a spartan facility fashioned with iron latticework doors and stone walls 2ft thick. Unlucky inmates overnighted in its six cells from 1883 until 1964.

Mono County Museum MUSEUM

(760-932-5281; www.monocomuseum.org; Emigrant St; adult/child $2/1; 9am-4pm Tue-Sat Jun-Sep) Two blocks away from the courthouse, in a schoolhouse of the same age, this museum has mining artifacts on display from all the local ghost towns, plus a room of fine Paiute baskets.

Travertine Hot Spring HOT SPRING

A bit south of town, head here to watch a panoramic Sierra sunset from three hot pools set amid impressive rock formations. To get there, turn east on Jack Sawyer Rd just before the ranger station, then follow the dirt road uphill for about 1 mile.

If you're trolling for trout, try the **Bridgeport Reservoir** and the **East Walker River**. For information and fishing gear, stop by **Ken's Sporting Goods** (760-932-7707; www.kenssport.com; 258 Main St; 7am-8pm Mon-Thu, to 9pm Fri & Sat mid-Apr–mid-Nov, 9am-4pm Tue-Sat mid-Nov–mid-Apr).

Sleeping & Eating

Redwood Motel MOTEL $

(760-932-7060, 888-932-3292; www.redwoodmotel.net; 425 Main St; d from $59-89; Apr-Nov;) A bucking bronco, an ox in a Ha-

TIRED OF TAHOE?

To throw a few snowballs without blowing your family's budget or plodding along in weekend traffic, aim for some of California's 19 maintained **sno-parks** (http://ohv.parks.ca.gov/?page_id=1233; day pass/season permit per vehicle $5/25). Clustered along Sierra highways, these inexpensive winter activity parks offer opportunities for raucous sledding, serene cross-country ski touring or unhurried snowperson construction.

Or consider some of the smaller ski resorts. In addition to cheaper lift tickets, **Bear Valley** (Map p394; www.bearvalley.com; Hwy 4) has its own snow play area, **Dodge Ridge** (Map p394; www.dodgeridge.com; Hwy 108) has extensive get-to-know-the-snow lessons for kids, and **China Peak** (Map p394; www.skichinapeak.com; Hwy 168) gets sparse crowds and is nowhere near the congested Tahoe-bound freeways.

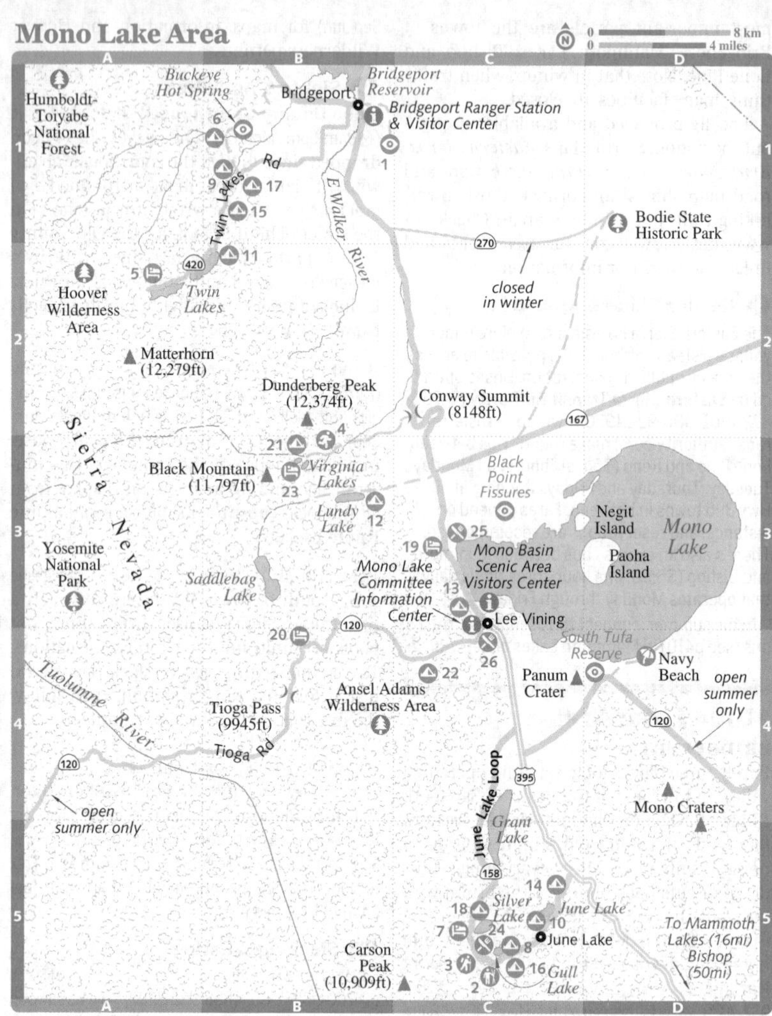

waiian shirt and other wacky farm animal sculptures provide a cheerful welcome to this little motel. Rooms are spotless and your dog-friendly host is super helpful in dispensing local area tips.

Bodie Victorian Hotel HISTORIC HOTEL **$**
(☎760-932-7020; www.bodievictorianhotel.com; 85 Main St; r $50-90; ⊙May-Oct) Go back to the 1800s in this curious building transplanted from Bodie (p428) that's completely furnished with antiques and rumored to be haunted. The bold Victorian wallpaper and striking bordello accoutrements more than make up for the slightly run-down feel. If no one's there, poke your head inside the Sportsmens Bar & Grill next door to rustle up an employee.

Rhino's Bar & Grille AMERICAN **$**
(247 Main St; mains $9-20; ⊙10am-9pm Sun-Thu, to 10pm Fri & Sat May-Oct, 11am-8pm Nov-Dec & Mar-Apr) Folks seek out Rhino's freshly ground burgers and its smoldering chicken wings in nitro sauce. A local favorite decorated with license plates and beer taps suspended from the ceiling, it has good prices and a big selection of sandwiches, salads, steaks and pizzas (dinner only). Also has a bar and pool table.

Mono Lake Area

Sights
Mono Basin Historical Society Museum ...(see 26)
1 Travertine Hot Spring ... B1

Activities, Courses & Tours
2 June Mountain Ski Area ... C5
3 Rush Creek Trailhead ... C5
4 Virginia Lakes Pack Station ... B3

Sleeping
5 Annett's Mono Village ... A2
6 Buckeye Campground ... B1
Crags Campground ... (see 11)
7 Double Eagle Resort & Spa ... C5
8 Gull Lake Campground ... C5
9 Honeymoon Flat Campground ... B1
10 June Lake Campground ... C5
June Lake Motel ... (see 10)
11 Lower Twin Lakes Campground ... B2
12 Lundy Canyon Campground ... B3
13 Mono Vista RV Park ... C3
14 Oh! Ridge Campground ... C5
15 Paha Campground ... B1
16 Reversed Creek Campground ... C5
17 Robinson Creek Campground ... B1
18 Silver Lake Campground ... C5
19 Tioga Lodge ... C3
20 Tioga Pass Resort ... B4
21 Trumbull Lake Campground ... B3
22 USFS Campgrounds ... C4
23 Virginia Lakes Resort ... B3

Eating
24 Carson Peak Inn ... C5
25 Historic Mono Inn ... C3
Tiger Bar ... (see 10)
26 Whoa Nellie Deli ... C4

Hays Street Cafe AMERICAN $
(www.haysstreetcafe.com; 21 Hays St; mains under $10; ⏲6am-2pm May-Oct, 7am-1pm Nov-Apr) On the south end of town, this country-style place prides itself on its many homemade items, including its biscuits and gravy, and cinnamon rolls as big as bricks.

Pop's Galley AMERICAN $
(www.popsgalley.com; 247 Main St; mains $6-10; ⏲7am-9pm late May-early Sep, otherwise variable hours) Finger-lickin' fish and chips.

TWIN LAKES

Eager anglers line the shoreline of Twin Lakes, a gorgeous duo of basins cradled by the fittingly named Sawtooth Ridge. The area's famous for its fishing – especially since some lucky guy bagged the state's largest ever brown trout here in 1987 (it weighed in at a hefty 26lb). Lower Twin is quieter, while Upper Twin allows boating and waterskiing. Other activities include mountain-biking and, of course, hiking in the Hoover Wilderness Area and on into the eastern, lake-riddled reaches of Yosemite National Park. The main trailhead is at the end of Twin Lakes Rd just past Annett's Mono Village; weekly overnight parking is $10 per vehicle.

Twin Lakes Rd (Rte 420) runs through pastures and foothills for about 10 miles before reaching Lower Twin Lake. The road is a satisfying route for moderately fit cyclists, with mostly level terrain and heavenly scenery.

A stroll down a loose hillside brings you to out-of-the-way **Buckeye Hot Spring**, though it can get crowded. The water emerges piping hot from a steep hillside and cools as it trickles down into several rock pools right by the side of lively Buckeye Creek, which is handy for taking a cooling dip. One pool is partially tucked into a small cave made from a rock overhang. Clothing is optional.

To get there, turn right at Doc & Al's Resort (7 miles from Hwy 395), driving 3 miles on a (momentarily paved and then) graded dirt road. Cross the bridge at Buckeye Creek (at 2.5 miles), and bear right at the Y-junction, following signs to the hot spring. Go uphill a half mile until you see a flattish parking area on your right. Follow a trail down to the pools.

If you go left at the signed Y-junction instead, a road goes 2 miles to **Buckeye Campground** (tent & RV sites $17; ⏲May–mid-Oct), with tables, fire grates, potable water and toilets. You can also camp for free in undeveloped spots along Buckeye Creek on both sides of the creek bridge.

Honeymoon Flat, Robinson Creek, Paha, Crags and Lower Twin Lakes are all **USFS campgrounds** (☎800-444-7275; www.recreation.gov; tent & RV sites $17-20; ⏲mid-May–Sep) set among Jeffrey pine and sagebrush along Robinson Creek and Lower Twin Lake. All have flush toilets except for Honeymoon Flat, which has vault toilets.

WILDERNESS PERMITS: EASTERN SIERRA

Free wilderness permits for overnight camping are required year-round in the Ansel Adams, John Muir, Golden Trout and Hoover Wilderness areas. For the first three, trailhead quotas are in effect from May through October and about 60% of the quota may be reserved for a $5 fee (per person) from the **Inyo National Forest Wilderness Permit Office** (☎760-873-2483). From November to April, you can pick up permits at any ranger station mentioned in this section. If you find the station closed, look for self-issue permits outside the office. Permits are expected to be available online by the time you read this, so call or check www.fs.fed.us/r5/inyo for the latest.

Permits for the **Hoover Wilderness** (part of both the Inyo and the Humboldt-Toiyabe National Forests) can also be obtained at the Tuolumne Meadows Wilderness Center (p410) and the Bridgeport Ranger Station and Visitor Center (p425).

Twin Lakes Rd dead-ends at **Annett's Mono Village** (☎760-932-7071; www.monovillage.com; tent sites $18, RV sites with hookups $29, r $68, cabin $80-185; ⊙late Apr-Oct; 📶), a huge and rather chaotic tumbledown resort on Upper Twin Lake. It has cheap but cramped lodging, and a kitschy low-ceilinged **cafe** (mains $8-16) studded with taxidermied fish. Pay showers available.

BODIE STATE HISTORIC PARK

For a time warp back to the Gold Rush era, swing by **Bodie** (☎760-647-6445; www.parks.ca.gov/?page_id=509; Hwy 270; adult/child $7/5; ⊙9am-6pm Jun-Aug, to 3pm Sep-May), one of the West's most authentic and best-preserved ghost towns. Gold was first discovered here in 1859, and within 20 years the place grew from a rough mining camp to an even rougher boomtown with a population of 10,000 and a reputation for unbridled lawlessness. Fights and murders took place almost daily, the violence no doubt fueled by liquor dispensed in the town's 65 saloons, some of which did double duty as brothels, gambling halls or opium dens. The hills disgorged some $35 million worth of gold and silver in the 1870s and '80s, but when production plummeted, so did the population, and eventually the town was abandoned to the elements.

About 200 weather-beaten buildings still sit frozen in time in this cold, barren and windswept valley heaped with tailing piles. Peering through dusty windows you'll see stocked stores, furnished homes, a schoolhouse with desks and books, and workshops filled with tools. The jail is still there, as are the fire station, churches, a bank vault and many other buildings. The former Miners' Union Hall now houses a **museum** and **visitors center** (⊙9am to one hour before park closes). Rangers conduct free general tours. In summertime, they also offer tours of the landscape and the cemetery; call for details. The second Saturday of August is **Friends of Bodie Day** (www.bodiefoundation.org), with stagecoach rides, history presentations and lots of devotees in period costumes.

Bodie is about 13 miles east of Hwy 395 via Rte 270; the last 3 miles are unpaved. Although the park is open year-round, the road is usually closed in winter and early spring, so you'd have to don snowshoes or cross-country skis to get there.

VIRGINIA LAKES

South of Bridgeport, Hwy 395 gradually arrives at its highest point, **Conway Summit** (8148ft), where you'll be whipping out your camera to capture the awe-inspiring panorama of Mono Lake, backed by the Mono Craters, and June and Mammoth Mountains.

Also at the top is the turnout for Virginia Lakes Rd, which parallels Virginia Creek for about 6 miles to a cluster of lakes flanked by **Dunderberg Peak** (12,374ft) and **Black Mountain** (11,797ft). A trailhead at the end of the road gives access to the Hoover Wilderness Area and the **Pacific Crest Trail**. The trail continues down Cold Canyon through to Yosemite National Park. Check with the folks at the **Virginia Lakes Resort** (☎760-647-6484; www.virginialakesresort.com; cabins from $107; ⊙mid-May–mid-Oct; 🐾), opened in 1923, for maps and tips about specific trails. The resort itself has snug cabins, a **cafe** and a **general store**. Cabins sleep two to 12 people, and usually have a minimum stay.

There's also the option of camping at **Trumbull Lake Campground** (☎800-444-7275; www.recreation.gov; tent & RV sites $17; ⊙mid-Jun–mid-Oct). The shady sites here are located among lodgepole pines.

Nearby, **Virginia Lakes Pack Station** (☎760-937-0326; www.virginialakes.com) offers horseback riding trips.

LUNDY LAKE

After Conway Summit, Hwy 395 twists down steeply into the Mono Basin. Before reaching Mono Lake, Lundy Lake Rd meanders west of the highway for about 5 miles to Lundy Lake. This is a gorgeous spot, especially in spring when wildflowers carpet the canyon along Mill Creek, or in fall when it is brightened by colorful foliage. Before reaching the lake, the road skirts first-come, first-served **Lundy Canyon Campground** (tent & RV sites $12; ⏰mid-April–mid-Nov), with vault toilets but no water. At the end of the lake, there's a ramshackle resort on the site of an 1880s mining town, plus a small store and boat rentals.

Past the resort, a dirt road leads into **Lundy Canyon** where, in 2 miles, it dead-ends at the trailhead for the Hoover Wilderness Area. A moderate 1.5-mile hike follows Mill Creek to the 200ft-high **Lundy Falls**. Ambitious types can continue on via Lundy Pass to Saddlebag Lake.

LEE VINING

Hwy 395 skirts the western bank of Mono Lake, rolling into the gateway town of Lee Vining where you can eat, sleep, gas up (for a pretty penny) and catch Hwy 120 to Yosemite National Park when the road's open. A superb base for exploring Mono Lake, Lee Vining is only 12 miles (about a 30-minute drive) from Yosemite's Tioga Pass entrance. **Lee Vining Canyon** is a popular location for **ice climbing**.

In town, take a quick look at the **Upside-Down House**, a kooky tourist attraction created by silent film actress Nellie Bly O'Bryan. Originally situated along Tioga Rd, it now resides in a park in front of the tiny **Mono Basin Historical Society Museum** (www.monobasinhs.org; donation $2; ⏰10am-4pm Thu-Mon, from noon Sun mid-May–early Oct). To find it, turn east on 1st St and go one block to Mattley Ave.

Sleeping & Eating

Lodging rates drop when Tioga Pass is closed.

TOP CHOICE **Whoa Nellie Deli** DELI $$
(www.whoanelliedeli.com; near junction of Hwys 120 & 395; mains $8-19; ⏰7am-9pm mid-Apr–Oct) Great food in a gas station? Come on… No, really, you gotta try this amazing kitchen where chef Matt 'Tioga' Toomey feeds delicious fish tacos, wild buffalo meatloaf and other tasty morsels to locals and clued-in passersby.

El Mono Motel MOTEL $
(☎760-647-6310; www.elmonomotel.com; 51 Hwy 395; r $69-99; ⏰May-Oct; 📶) Grab a board game or soak up some mountain sunshine in this friendly flower-ringed place attached to an excellent cafe. In operation since 1927, and often booked solid, each of its 11 simple rooms (a few share bathrooms) is unique, decorated with vibrant and colorful art and fabrics.

Historic Mono Inn CALIFORNIAN $$$
(☎760-647-6581; www.monoinn.com; 55620 Hwy 395; dinner mains $8-25; ⏰11am-9pm May-Dec) A restored 1922 lodge owned by the family of photographer Ansel Adams, this is now an elegant lakefront restaurant with outstanding California comfort food, fabulous wine and views to match. Browse the 1000-volume cookbook collection upstairs, and stop in for music on the creekside terrace. It's located about 5 miles north of Lee Vining. Reservations recommended.

Tioga Lodge CABINS $$
(☎760-647-6423; www.tiogalodgeatmonolake.com; cabin $129-159; ⏰mid-May–mid-Oct; @📶) About 2 miles north of Lee Vining, this cluster of cheery cabins has verandas overlooking Mono Lake. The **restaurant** (dinner mains $13-25) and registration buildings were moved here from Bodie in 1897.

Tioga Pass Resort CABINS $$
(tiogapassresortllc@gmail.com; Hwy 120; r $125, cabin $160-240; ⏰May–mid-Oct) Founded in 1914 and located 2 miles east of Tioga Pass, this resort attracts a fiercely loyal clientele to its basic and cozy cabins beside Lee Vining Creek. The thimble-sized **cafe** (mains lunch $8-9, dinner $15) serves excellent fare all day at a few tables and a broken horseshoe counter, with a house pastry chef concocting dozens of freshly made desserts. Reserve lodging via email.

USFS campgrounds CAMPGROUNDS $
(www.fs.usda.gov/inyo; tent & RV sites $15-19) Towards Yosemite, there are a handful of first-come, first-served campgrounds along Tioga Rd (Hwy 120) and Lee Vining Creek, most with vault toilets and about half with potable water.

Mono Vista RV Park CAMPGROUND $
(☎760-647-6401; Hwy 395; showers $2.50; ⏰9am-6pm Apr-Oct) This campground has the closest pay showers to Tuolumne Meadows.

MONO LAKE

North America's second-oldest lake is a quiet and mysterious expanse of deep blue water, whose glassy surface reflects jagged Sierra peaks, young volcanic cones and the unearthly tufa (*too*-fah) towers that make the lake so distinctive. Jutting from the water like drip sand castles, tufas form when calcium bubbles up from subterranean springs and combines with carbonate in the alkaline lake waters.

In *Roughing It,* Mark Twain described Mono Lake as California's 'dead sea.' Hardly. The brackish water teems with buzzing alkali flies and brine shrimp, both considered delicacies by dozens of migratory bird species that return here year after year. So do about 85% of the state's nesting population of California gulls, which takes over the lake's volcanic islands from April to August. Mono Lake has also been at the heart of an environmental controversy (see boxed text, p431).

Sights & Activities

South Tufa Reserve NATURE RESERVE
(☎office 760-647-6331; adult/child $3/free) Tufa spires ring the lake, but the biggest grove is on the south rim with a mile-long interpretive trail. Ask about ranger-led tours at the Mono Basin Scenic Area Visitors Center (p430). To get to the reserve, head south from Lee Vining on Hwy 395 for 6 miles, then east on Hwy 120 for 5 miles to the dirt road leading to a parking lot.

Navy Beach BEACH
The best place for swimming is at Navy Beach, just east of the reserve. It's also the best place to put in canoes or kayaks. From late June to early September, the **Mono Lake Committee** (☎760-647-6595; www.monolake.org/visit/canoe; tours $25; ⏰8am, 9:30am & 11am Sat & Sun) operates one-hour canoe tours around the tufas. Half-day kayak tours along the shore or out to Paoha Island are also offered by **Caldera Kayaks** (☎760-934-1691; www.calderakayak.com; tours $75; ⏰mid-May–mid-Oct). Both require reservations.

Panum Crater NATURAL FEATURE
Rising above the south shore, Panum Crater is the youngest (about 640 years old), smallest and most accessible of the craters that string south toward Mammoth Mountain. A panoramic trail circles the crater rim (about 30 to 45 minutes), and a short but steep 'plug trail' puts you at the crater's core. A dirt road leads to the trailhead from Hwy 120, about 3 miles east of the junction with Hwy 395.

Black Point Fissures NATURAL FEATURE
On the north shore of the lake are the Black Point Fissures, narrow crags that opened when lava mass cooled and contracted about 13,000 years ago. Access is from three places: east of Mono Lake County Park, from the west shore off Hwy 395, or south off Hwy 167. Check at the Mono Basin Scenic Area Visitors Center (p430) for specific directions.

Information

Mono Basin Scenic Area Visitors Center
(☎760-647-3044; www.fs.usda.gov/inyo; Hwy 395, ⏰8am-5pm mid-Apr–Nov) Half a mile north of Lee Vining, this center has maps, interpretive displays, wilderness permits, bear-canister rentals, a bookstore and a 20-minute movie about Mono Lake.

Mono Lake Committee Information Center
(☎760-647-6595; www.monolake.org; cnr Hwy 395 & 3rd St; ⏰9am-5pm late Oct–mid-Jun, 8am-9pm mid-Jun–Sep) Internet access ($2 per 15 minutes), maps, books, free 30-minute video about Mono Lake and passionate, preservation-minded staff. Public restroom too.

JUNE LAKE LOOP

Under the shadow of massive Carson Peak (10,909ft), the stunning 14-mile June Lake Loop (Hwy 158) meanders through a picture-perfect horseshoe canyon, past the relaxed resort town of June Lake and four sparkling, fish-rich lakes: Grant, Silver, Gull and June. It's especially scenic in fall when the basin is ablaze with golden aspens. Catch the loop a few miles south of Lee Vining.

Activities

June Lake is backed by the Ansel Adams Wilderness area, which runs into Yosemite National Park. **Rush Creek Trailhead** has a day-use parking lot, posted maps and self-registration permits. Gem and Agnew Lakes make spectacular day hikes, while Thousand Island and Emerald Lake (both on the Pacific Crest/John Muir Trail) are stunning overnight destinations.

Boat and tackle rentals, as well as fishing licenses, are available at five marinas.

June Mountain Ski Area SKIING
(☎24hr snow info 760-934-2224, 888-586-3686; www.junemountain.com; lift tickets adult/child

WATER FOR A THIRSTY GIANT: A TALE OF TWO LAKES

Los Angeles may be 250 miles away, but its history and fate are closely linked with that of the Eastern Sierra. When LA's population surged around the turn of the 20th century, it became clear that groundwater levels would soon be inadequate to meet the city's needs, let alone sustain future growth. Water had to be imported, and Fred Eaton, a former LA mayor, and William Mulholland, head of the LA Department of Water & Power (LADWP), knew just how and where to get it: by aqueduct from the Owens Valley, which receives enormous runoff from the Sierra Nevada.

The fact that the Owens Valley itself was settled by farmers who needed the water for irrigation didn't bother either of the two men. Nor did it cause qualms in the least with the federal government, which actively supported the city's less-than-ethical maneuvering in acquiring land and securing water rights in the valley area. Voters gave Mulholland the $24.5 million he needed to build the aqueduct and work began in 1908. An amazing feat of engineering – crossing barren desert as well as rugged mountain terrain – the aqueduct opened to great fanfare on November 5, 1913. The Owens Valley, though, would never be the same.

With most of its inflows diverted, Owens Lake, which had once been 30ft deep and an important stopover for migrating waterfowl, quickly shriveled up. A bitter feud between local farmers and ranchers and the city grew violent when some of the opponents tried to sabotage the aqueduct by blowing up a section of it. All to no avail. By 1928 LA owned 90% of the water in Owens Valley and agriculture was effectively dead. These early water wars formed the basis for the 1974 movie *Chinatown*.

But as LA kept burgeoning, its water needs also grew. In the 1930s, the LADWP bought up water rights in the Mono Basin and extended the aqueduct by 105 miles, diverting four of the five streams feeding into Mono Lake. Not surprisingly, the volume of water in the lake dropped significantly, doubling the salinity and posing a major threat to its ecological balance.

In 1976 environmentalist David Gaines began to study the concerns surrounding the lake's depletion and found that, if left untouched, it would totally dry up within about 20 years. To avert this certain disaster, he formed the Mono Lake Committee in 1978 and enlisted the help of the National Audubon Society. Years of lobbying and legal action followed, but eventually the committee succeeded. In 1994 the California State Water Resources Control Board mandated the LADWP to substantially reduce its diversions and allow the lake level to rise by 20ft. In July 2011 its surface stood at 6383ft, still about 8ft short of the goal.

The Owens Lake, meanwhile, was not as lucky. It remains a mostly barren lakebed and the site of alkali dust storms, which are especially harmful to people with respiratory problems. A plan finalized in 1999, however, saw 30 sq miles of the lake (out of 100) shallow flooded, and by 2006 this had largely cleared the dust storms and re-created an important habitat for waterfowl.

Though conditions and habitat have improved, the **Owens Valley Committee** (www.ovcweb.org) and Sierra Club continue to closely monitor the LADWP, bringing the department to court regularly to force its compliance on mitigation agreements.

$69/35) Winter fun concentrates in this area, which is smaller and less crowded than nearby Mammoth Mountain and perfect for beginner and intermediate skiers. Some 35 trails crisscross 500 acres of terrain served by seven lifts, including two high-speed quads. Boarders can get their adrenaline flowing at three terrain parks with a kick-ass superpipe.

Ernie's Tackle & Ski Shop OUTDOOR EQUIPMENT
(☎760-648-7756; www.erniestackleandski.com; 2604 Hwy 158) One of the most established outfitters in June Lake village.

Sleeping & Eating

Double Eagle Resort & Spa RESORT **$$$**
(☎760-648-7004; www.doubleeagleresort.com; 5587 Hwy 158; r incl breakfast $199, cabins $349;) A swanky spot for these parts. The sleek two-bedroom log cabins and balconied

hotel rooms lack no comfort, while worries disappear at the elegant spa. Its **restaurant** (dinner mains $15-30; ⌚8am-9pm) exudes rustic elegance, with cozy booths, a high ceiling and a huge fireplace.

June Lake Motel MOTEL **$$**
(☎760-648-7547, www.junelakemotel.com; 2716 Hwy 158; r with/without kitchen $115/105; @📶) Enormous rooms – most with full kitchens – catch delicious mountain breezes and sport attractive light-wood furniture. There's a fish-cleaning sink and BBQs, plus a book library and a friendly resident Newfoundland dog.

USFS Campgrounds CAMPGROUNDS **$**
(☎800-444-7275; www.recreation.gov; tent & RV sites $20; ⌚mid-Apr–Oct) These include: June Lake, Oh! Ridge, Silver Lake, Gull Lake and Reversed Creek. The first three accept reservations; Silver Lake has gorgeous mountain views.

Carson Peak Inn AMERICAN **$$**
(☎760-648-7575; Hwy 158 btwn Gull & Silver Lakes; meals $19-34; ⌚5-10pm, shorter winter hours) Inside a cozy house with a fireplace, this restaurant is much beloved for its tasty old-time indulgences, such as beef brochette, pan-fried trout and chopped sirloin steak. Portion sizes can be ordered for regular or 'hearty' appetites.

Tiger Bar AMERICAN **$$**
(www.thetigerbarcafe.com; 2620 Hwy 158; mains $8-17; ⌚8am-10pm) After a day on slopes or trails, people gather at the long bar or around the pool table of this no-nonsense, no-attitude place. The kitchen feeds all appetites, with burgers, salads, tacos and other tasty grub, including homemade fries.

eastsierra.net CAFE **$**
(2775 Hwy 158; ⌚6am-5pm; 📶) Internet cafe with organic coffees and teas.

Mammoth Lakes

This is a small mountain resort town endowed with larger-than-life scenery – active outdoorsy folks worship at the base of its dizzying 11,053ft Mammoth Mountain. Everlasting powder clings to these slopes, and when the snow finally fades, the area's an outdoor wonderland of mountain-bike trails, excellent fishing, endless alpine hiking and blissful hidden spots for hot-spring soaking. The Eastern Sierra's commercial hub and a four-season resort, outdoorsy Mammoth is backed by a ridgeline of jutting peaks, ringed by clusters of crystalline alpine lakes and enshrouded by the dense Inyo National Forest.

Sights

TOP CHOICE **Earthquake Fault** NATURAL FEATURE
(Map p433) On Minaret Rd, about 1 mile west of the Mammoth Scenic Loop, detour to gape at Earthquake Fault, a sinuous fissure half a mile long gouging a crevice up to 20ft deep into the earth. Ice and snow often linger at the bottom until late summer, and Native Americans and early settlers used it to store perishable food.

Mammoth Museum MUSEUM
(Map p434; ☎760-934-6918; 5489 Sherwin Creek Rd; suggested donation $3; ⌚10am-6pm mid-May–Sep) For a walk down memory lane, stop by this little museum inside a historic log cabin.

Activities

Skiing & Snowboarding

There's free cross-country skiing along the 19 miles of nongroomed trails of the **Blue Diamond Trails System**, which winds through several patches of scenic forest around town. Pick up a map at the Mammoth Lakes Welcome Center (p437) or check out www.mammothnordic.com.

Mammoth Mountain SKIING
(Map p433; ☎760-934-2571, 800-626-6684, 24hr snow report 888-766-9778; www.mammothmountain.com; lift tickets adult/senior & child $92/46) This is a skiers' and snowboarders' dream resort, where sunny skies, a reliably long season (usually from November to June) and over 3500 acres of fantastic tree-line and open-bowl skiing are a potent cocktail. At the top you'll be dealing with some gnarly, nearly vertical chutes. The other stats are just as impressive: 3100 vertical feet, 150 trails, 29 lifts (including 10 quads). Boarders, meanwhile, will find world-class challenges in nine terrain parks with three intense superpipes and urban-style jibs.

There are five hubs at the base of the mountain: **Main Lodge** (Map p433), **Canyon Lodge** (Map p434), **Eagle Lodge** (Map p434), the **Mill Cafe** (Map p433) and the **Mountain Center** (Map p434), each with ticket offices and parking lots. Free ski shuttles pick up throughout town. Alternatively, hop on the **Village Gondola** (Map p434),

Mammoth Lakes Area

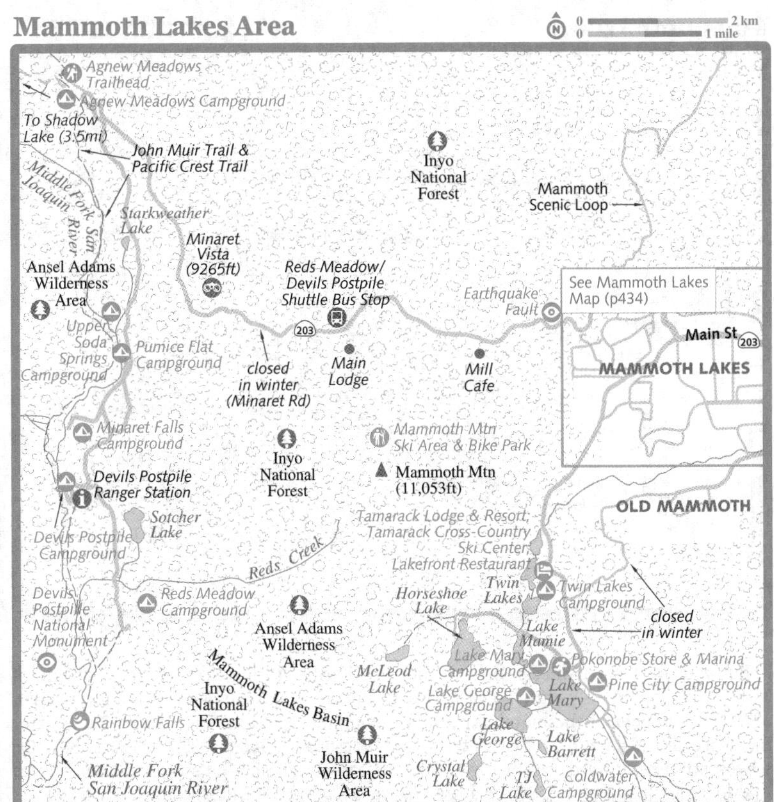

which whisks you up to Canyon Lodge – the base of several chair lifts – in six minutes.

Tamarack Cross-Country Ski Center SKIING
(Map p433; ☎760-934-2442; Lake Mary Rd; all-day trail pass adult/child/senior $27/15/21; ⏰8:30am-5pm) Let the town shuttle take you to the Tamarack Lodge, which has almost 20 miles of meticulously groomed track around Twin Lakes and the lakes basin. The terrain is also great for snowshoeing. Rentals and lessons are available.

Cycling & Mountain-Biking

Stop at the Mammoth Lakes Welcome Center (p437) for a free map with area route descriptions and updated trail conditions.

Lakes Basin Path CYCLING
(Map p434; www.mammothtrails.org) A local recreational umbrella group has been developing a fantastic new system of bicycle paths. One completed segment is the 5.3-mile Lakes Basin Path, which begins at the southwest corner of Lake Mary and Minaret Rds and heads uphill (at a 5% to 10% grade) to Horseshoe Lake, skirting lovely lakes and accessing open mountain views. For a one-way ride, use the free Lakes Basin Trolley, which tows a 12-bicycle trailer.

Mammoth Mountain Bike Park MOUNTAIN-BIKING
(Map p433; ☎800-626-6684; www.mammothmountain.com; day pass adult/child $43/22; ⏰9am-4:30pm Jun-Sep) Come summer, Mammoth Mountain morphs into the massive Mammoth Mountain Bike Park, with more than 80 miles of well-kept single-track trails. Several other trails traverse the surrounding forest. In general, Mammoth-style riding translates into plenty of hills and soft, sandy shoulders, which are best navigated with big knobby tires.

Mammoth Lakes

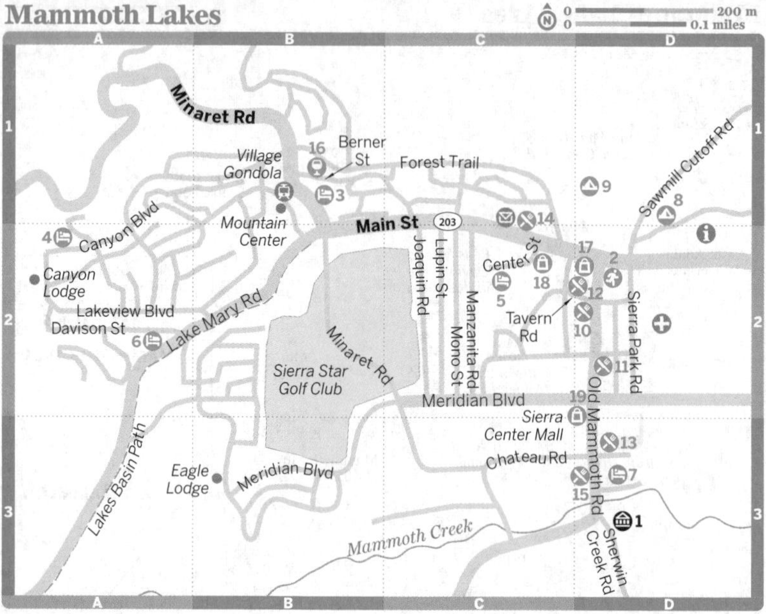

But you don't need wheels (or a medic) to ride the vertiginous **gondola** (adult/senior $23/12) to the apex of the mountain, where there's a cafe and an interpretive center with scopes pointing toward the nearby peaks. And for kids 13 and under, there's a fun **zip line** (1 zip $12, additional $7, ⌚summer) behind the Adventure Center.

When the park's open, it runs a free **mountain-bike shuttle** (⌚9am-5:30pm) from the Village area to the Main Lodge. Shuttles depart every 30 minutes, and mountain-bikers with paid mountain passes get priority over pedestrians.

Hiking

Mammoth Lakes rubs up against the **Ansel Adams Wilderness** and **John Muir Wilderness** areas, both laced with fabulous trails leading to shimmering lakes, rugged peaks and hidden canyons. Major trailheads leave from the Mammoth Lakes Basin, Reds Meadow and Agnew Meadows; the latter two are accessible only by shuttle (see p437). **Shadow Lake** (off Map p433) is a stunning 7-mile day hike from Agnew Meadows.

Fishing & Boating

From the last Saturday in April, the dozens of lakes that give the town its name lure in fly and trout fishers from near and far. California fishing licenses are available at sporting goods stores throughout town. For equipment and advice, head to **Troutfitter** (Map p434; ☎760-934-2517; cnr Main St & Old Mammoth Rd) or **Rick's Sports Center** (Map p434; ☎760-934-3416; cnr Main & Center Sts).

The **Pokonobe Store and Marina** (Map p433; ☎760-934-2437; www.pokonoberesort.com), on the north end of Lake Mary, rents motor boats ($20 per hour), rowboats ($10), canoes ($16) and kayaks ($16 to $20). **Caldera Kayaks** (☎760-935-1691; www.calderakayak.com) has single ($30 for a half-day) and double kayaks ($50) for use on Crowley Lake.

Sleeping

Mammoth B&Bs and inns rarely sell out midweek, when rates tend to be lower. During ski season, reservations are a good idea on weekends and essential during holidays. Many properties offer ski-and-stay packages. Condo rentals often work out cheaper for groups.

Stop by the Mammoth Lakes Welcome Center (p437) or check its website for a full list of campgrounds, dispersed free camping locations (don't forget to pick up a free but mandatory fire permit) and public showers.

Mammoth Lakes

Mammoth Creek Inn INN $$
(Map p434; ☎760-934-6162, 800-466-7000; www.mammothcreekinn.com; 663 Old Mammoth Rd; r $190-235, with kitchen $277-356; @📶) It's amenities galore at this pretty inn at the end of a commercial strip, with down comforters and fluffy terry robes, as well as a sauna, a hot tub and a fun pool table loft. The best rooms overlook the majestic Sherwin Mountains, and some have full kitchens and can sleep up to six.

TOP CHOICE Tamarack Lodge & Resort RESORT $$
(Map p433; ☎760-934-2442, 800-626-6684; www.tamaracklodge.com; lodge r $99-169, cabins $169-599; @📶🐾) Kind people run this charming year-round resort on the shore of Lower Twin Lake. In business since 1924, the cozy lodge includes a fireplace, bar, excellent restaurant, 11 rustic rooms and 35 cabins. The cabins range from very simple to simply deluxe, and come with full kitchen, private bathroom, porch and wood-burning stove. Some can sleep up to 10 people.

Cinnamon Bear Inn B&B $$
(Map p434; ☎760-934-2873, 800-845-2873; www.cinnamonbearinn.com; 133 Center St; r incl breakfast $79-179; @📶) At this down-to-earth inn you'll sleep like a log in four-poster beds, and most rooms have cozy gas fireplaces. Swap stories about the day's adventures with other guests over homemade refreshments in the afternoon, or soak away soreness in the small outdoor Jacuzzi.

Austria Hof Lodge LODGE $$
(Map p434; ☎760-934-2764; www.austriahof.com; 924 Canyon Blvd; r incl breakfast $130-215; 📶) Close to Canyon Lodge, rooms here have modern knotty pine furniture, thick down duvets and DVD players. Ski lockers and a sundeck hot tub make winter stays here even sweeter. The lodge **restaurant** (dinner mains $24-37) serves meaty gourmet German fare in an evocative stained-glass dining room.

Alpenhof Lodge HOTEL $$
(Map p434; ☎760-934-6330, 800-828-0371; www.alpenhof-lodge.com; 6080 Minaret Rd; r $159-239; @📶🏊) This Euro-flavored inn is a snowball's toss away from the Village and has fairly nondescript yet comfortable lodge rooms, plus more luxurious accommodations with gas fireplaces or kitchens.

Davison Street Guest House HOSTEL $
(Map p434; ☎760-924-2188, reservations 858-755-8648; www.mammoth-guest.com; 19 Davison St; dm $35-49, d $75-120; 📶) A cute, five-room A-frame chalet hostel on a quiet residential street, this place has a stocked kitchen, plus mountain views from the living room with fireplace or sun deck. There's self-registration when the manager isn't around.

USFS campgrounds CAMPGROUNDS $
(Maps p433 & p434; ☎877-444-6777; www.recreation.gov; tent & RV sites $20-21; 🐾; ⌚approx mid-Jun–mid-Sep) About 15 USFS campgrounds (see 'Recreation' at www.fs.usda.gov/inyo) are scattered in and around Mammoth

Lakes, all with flush toilets but no showers. Many sites are available on a first-come, first-served basis, and some are reservable. Note that nights get chilly at these elevations, even in July. Campgrounds include: New Shady Rest, Old Shady Rest, Twin Lakes, Lake Mary, Pine City, Coldwater, Lake George, Reds Meadow, Pumice Flat, Minaret Falls, Upper Soda Springs and Agnew Meadows.

Eating & Drinking

Lakefront Restaurant CALIFORNIAN, FRENCH $$$
(Map p433; ☎760-934-3534; www.tamaracklodge.com/lakefront-restaurant; Lakes Loop Rd, Twin Lakes; mains $28-38; ⏲5-9:30pm year-round, plus 11am-2pm summer, closed Tue & Wed in fall & spring) The Tamarack Lodge has an intimate and romantic dining room overlooking Twin Lakes. The chef crafts French–Californian specialties like elk medallions au poivre and heirloom tomatoes with Basque cheese, and the staff are superbly friendly. Reservations recommended.

TOP CHOICE **Skadi** EUROPEAN $$$
(Map p434; ☎760-934-3902; www.skadirestaurant.com; 587 Old Mammoth Rd; mains $24-32; ⏲5:30-9:30pm Wed-Sun) Upstairs in a nondescript office complex, Skadi's 'alpine cuisine' includes dishes like roasted salmon and sausage made from its own ranch-raised venison. Sample its excellent European and California wines and gaze out at the dreamy Sherwin Range vistas. Reservations recommended.

Petra's Bistro & Wine Bar CALIFORNIAN, FRENCH $$$
(Map p434; ☎760-934-3500; www.petrasbistro.com; 6080 Minaret Rd; mains $19-34; ⏲5-9:30pm Tue-Sun) Settle in here for seasonal cuisine and wines recommended by the three staff sommeliers. In wintertime, the best seats in the house are the cozy fireside couches. Start the evening with a cheese course and choose from 28 wines available by the glass or 250 vintages by the bottle. Reservations recommended.

Good Life Cafe CALIFORNIAN $
(Map p434; www.mammothgoodlifecafe.com; Mammoth Mall, 126 Old Mammoth Rd; mains $8-10; ⏲6:30am-3pm;) Healthy food, generously filled veggie wraps and big bowls of salad make this a perennially popular place. The front patio is blissful for a long brunch on a warm day.

Stellar Brew CAFE $
(Map p434; www.stellarbrewnaturalcafe.com; 3280 B Main St; salads & sandwiches $5.50; ⏲5:30am-8pm;) Proudly locavore and mostly organic, settle into a comfy sofa here for your daily dose of locally roasted coffee, homemade granola and scrumptious vegan (and some gluten-free) pastries.

Roberto's Cafe MEXICAN $$
(Map p434; www.robertoscafe.com; 271 Old Mammoth Rd; mains $7-15; ⏲11am-8pm, to 10pm winter & summer) Serving Mammoth's hands-down best Mexican food and a selection of more than 30 brands of tequila, this fun restaurant is usually bustling. Locals pack the outdoor deck to look out on a beautiful wildflower garden, or quaff margaritas in the tropical-themed upstairs cantina.

Stove CAFE $
(Map p434; www.thestoverestaurant.com; 644 Old Mammoth Rd; breakfast mains $6-10; ⏲6:30am-2pm & 5-9pm) Great coffee and carbs; try the cinnamon-bread French toast.

Sierra Sundance Whole Foods HEALTH FOOD $
(Map p434; 26 Old Mammoth Rd;) Self-catering vegetarians can stock up on organic produce, bulk foods and tofu at this handy store and deli.

Clocktower Cellar PUB
(Map p434; www.clocktowercellar.com; 6080 Minaret Rd) In the winter especially, locals throng this half-hidden basement of the Alpenhof Lodge. The ceiling is tiled with a swirl of bottle caps, and the bar stocks 31 beers on tap (in particular German brews) and about 50 bottled varieties.

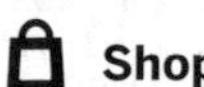

FREE **Mammoth Brewing Company Tasting Room** BREWERY
(Map p434; ☎760-934-7141; www.mammothbrewingco.com; 94 Berner St; ⏲10am-6pm) Free samples anyone? Try some of the dozen brews on tap, then buy some IPA 395 or Double Nut Brown to go.

Shopping

For outdoor equipment sales and rentals, in-town shops are usually cheaper than at Mammoth Mountain.

Footloose OUTDOOR EQUIPMENT
(Map p434; ☎760-934-2400; www.footloosesports.com; cnr Main St & Old Mammoth Rd) Full range

DON'T MISS

DEVILS POSTPILE

The most fascinating attraction in Reds Meadow is the surreal volcanic formation of **Devils Postpile National Monument** (Map p433). The 60ft curtains of near-vertical, six-sided basalt columns formed when rivers of molten lava slowed, cooled and cracked with perplexing symmetry. This honeycomb design is best appreciated from atop the columns, reached by a short trail. The columns are an easy, half-mile hike from the **Devils Postpile Ranger Station** (Map p433; ☎760-934-2289; www.nps.gov/depo; ⏰9am-5pm summer).

From the monument, a 2.5-mile hike passing through fire-scarred forest leads to the spectacular **Rainbow Falls** (Map p433), where the San Joaquin River gushes over a 101ft basalt cliff. Chances of actually seeing a rainbow forming in the billowing mist are greatest at midday. The falls can also be reached via an easy 1.5-mile walk from the Reds Meadow area, which also has a cafe, store, the **Reds Meadow campground** (Map p433) and a pack station.

of footwear and seasonal equipment; local biking info.

Mammoth Mountaineering Supply OUTDOOR EQUIPMENT
(Map p434; ☎760-934-4191; www.mammothgear.com; 3189 Main St) Offers friendly advice, topo maps and all-season equipment rentals.

Mammoth Sporting Goods OUTDOOR EQUIPMENT
(Map p434; ☎760-934-3239; www.mammothsportinggoods.com; Sierra Center Mall, Old Mammoth Rd) Bikes, boards and skis; across from Von's supermarket.

ℹ Information

The **Mammoth Lakes Welcome Center** (☎760-934-2712, 888-466-2666; www.visitmammoth.com; ⏰8am-5pm) and the **Mammoth Lakes Ranger Station** (☎760-924-5500; www.fs.fed.us/r5/inyo; ⏰8am-5pm) share a building on the north side of Hwy 203. This one-stop information center issues wilderness permits, helps find accommodations and campgrounds, and provides road and trail condition updates. From May through October, when trail quotas are in effect, walk-in wilderness permits are released at 11am the day before; permits are self-issue the rest of the year.

Mammoth Hospital (☎760-934-3311; 85 Sierra Park Rd; ⏰24hr) Emergency room.

Mammoth Times (www.mammothtimes.com) Free weekly tabloid.

ℹ Getting There & Away

Mammoth's updated airport **Mammoth Yosemite** (MMH) has a daily nonstop flight to San Francisco, operating winter through to spring on **United** (www.united.com). **Alaska Airlines** (www.alaskaair.com) runs a similar seasonal (and cheaper) San Jose flight and year-round service to Los Angeles. All flights are about an hour. Taxis meet incoming flights, and some lodgings provide free transfers. **Mammoth Taxi** (☎760-934-8294; www.mammoth-taxi.com) does airport runs as well as hiker shuttles throughout the Sierra.

Mammoth is a snap to navigate by public transportation year-round. In the summertime, **YARTS** (☎877-989-2787; www.yarts.com) runs buses to and from Yosemite Valley, and the **Eastern Sierra Transit Authority** (☎800-922-1930; www.easternsierratransitauthority.com) has year-round service along Hwy 395, north to Reno and south to Lone Pine. See p425 for details.

Within Mammoth, a year-round system of free and frequent **bus shuttles** connects the whole town with the Mammoth Mountain lodges; in summer, routes with bicycle trailers service the Lakes Basin and Mammoth Mountain Bike Park.

Around Mammoth Lakes

REDS MEADOW

One of the beautiful and varied landscapes near Mammoth is the Reds Meadow Valley, west of Mammoth Mountain. Drive on Hwy 203 as far as **Minaret Vista** (Map p433) for eye-popping views (best at sunset) of the Ritter Range, the serrated Minarets and the remote reaches of Yosemite National Park.

The road to Reds Meadow is only accessible from about June until September, weather permitting. To minimize impact when it's open, the road is closed to private vehicles beyond Minaret Vista unless you are camping, have lodge reservations or are disabled, in which case you must pay a $10 per car fee. Otherwise you must use a mandatory

shuttle bus (Map p433; per adult/child $7/4). It leaves from a lot in front of the Adventure Center approximately every 30 minutes between 7:30am and 7pm (last bus out leaves Reds Meadow at 7:45pm), and you must buy tickets inside before joining the queue. There are also a half dozen direct departures from the Village (on Canyon Blvd, under the gondola) in the morning. The bus stops at trailheads, viewpoints and campgrounds before completing the one-way trip to Reds Meadow (45 minutes to an hour).

The valley road provides access to six campgrounds along the San Joaquin River. Tranquil willow-shaded **Minaret Falls Campground** (Map p433; tent & RV sites $20; 🐾) is a popular fishing spot where the best riverside sites have views of its namesake cascade.

HOT CREEK GEOLOGICAL SITE

For a graphic view of the area's geothermal power, journey a few miles south of Mammoth to where chilly Mammoth Creek blends with hot springs and continues its journey as Hot Creek. It eventually enters a small gorge and forms a series of steaming, bubbling cauldrons, with water shimmering in shades of blue and green reminiscent of the tropics. Until recently, soakers reveled in the blissful but somewhat scary temperate zones where the hot springs mixed with frigid creek water. But in 2006 a significant increase in geothermal activity began sending violent geysers of boiling water into the air, and the site is off-limits for swimming until the danger has subsided.

To reach the site, turn off Hwy 395 about 5 miles south of town and follow signs to the Hot Creek Fish Hatchery. From here, it's another 2 miles on gravel road to the parking area, and a short hike down into the canyon and creek.

For a soak that *won't* cook your goose, take Hwy 395 about 9 miles south of Mammoth to Benton Crossing Rd, which accesses a trove of primitive **hot spring pools**. Locals call this 'Green Church Rd,' because of the road's unmistakable marker. For detailed directions and maps, pick up the bible – Matt Bischoff's excellent *Touring California and Nevada Hot Springs*. And keep in mind these three golden rules: no glass, no additives to the water and, if you can, no bathing suit.

CONVICT LAKE

Located just southeast of Mammoth, Convict Lake is one of the area's prettiest lakes, with emerald water embraced by massive peaks. A hike along the gentle trail skirting the lake, through aspen and cottonwood trees, is great if you're still adjusting to the altitude. A trailhead on the southeastern shore gives access to Genevieve, Edith, Dorothy and Mildred Lakes in the John Muir Wilderness. To reach the lake, turn south from Hwy 395 on Convict Lake Rd (across from the Mammoth airport) and go 2 miles.

In 1871 Convict Lake was the site of a bloody shoot-out between a band of escaped convicts and a posse that had given chase. Posse leader, Sheriff Robert Morrison, was killed during the gunfight and the taller peak, Mt Morrison (12,268ft), was later named in his honor. The bad guys got away only to be apprehended later near Bishop.

The **campground** (☎877-444-6777; www.recreation.gov; tent & RV sites $20; ⊙mid-Apr–Oct) has flush toilets and nicely terraced sites. Otherwise your only option is **Convict Lake Resort** (☎760-934-3800, 800-992-2260; www.convictlake.com; cabins from $189; 📶🐾), whose three houses and 27 cabins with kitchens sleep from two to 34 and range from rustic to ritzy. Foodies with deep pockets flock to the elegant **restaurant** (☎760-934-3803, mains lunch $8-15, dinner $23-42; ⊙5:30-9pm daily, plus 11am-2:30pm Jul & Aug), which many consider the best within a 100-mile radius.

Bishop

The second-largest town in the Eastern Sierra, Bishop is about two hours from Yosemite's Tioga Pass entrance. A major recreation hub, Bishop offers access to excellent fishing in nearby lakes, climbing in the Buttermilks just west of town, and hiking in the John Muir Wilderness via Bishop Creek Canyon and the Rock Creek drainage. The area is especially lovely in fall when dropping temperatures cloak aspen, willow and cottonwood in myriad glowing shades.

The earliest inhabitants of the Owens Valley were Paiute and Shoshone Native Americans, who today live on four reservations. White settlers came on the scene in the 1860s and began raising cattle to sell to nearby mining settlements.

⊙ Sights

TOP CHOICE **Laws Railroad Museum** MUSEUM
(☎760-873-5950; www.lawsmuseum.org; requested donation $5; ⊙10am-4pm; 👪) Railroad

WORTH A TRIP

BENTON HOT SPRINGS

Soak in your own hot springs tub and snooze beneath the moonlight at **Benton Hot Springs** (760-933-2287; www.historicbentonhotsprings.com; Hwy 120, Benton; tent & RV sites for 2 people $40-50, d with/without bath incl breakfast $129/109;), a small historic resort in a 150-year-old former silver mining town nestled along the White Mountains. Choose from nine well-spaced campsites with private tubs or one of the themed antique-filled B&B rooms with semi-private tubs. Daytime dips ($10 hourly per person) are also available, and reservations are essential for all visits.

It's reachable from Mono Lake via Hwy 120 (in summer), Mammoth Lakes by way of Benton Crossing Rd, or Hwy 6 from Bishop; the first two options are undulating drives with sweeping red-rock vistas that glow at sunset, and all take approximately one hour. An **Eastern Sierra Transit Authority bus** (800-922-1930; www.easternsierratransitauthority.com) connects Bishop and Benton ($5, one hour) on Tuesday and Friday, stopping right at the resort.

If you have time, ask for directions to the **Volcanic Tablelands petroglyphs** off Hwy 6, where ancient drawings decorate scenic rock walls.

and Old West aficionados should make the 6-mile detour north on Hwy 6 to this museum. It re-creates the village of Laws, an important stop on the route of the *Slim Princess,* a narrow-gauge train that hauled freight and passengers across the Owens Valley for nearly 80 years. The original 1883 train depot is here, as are a post office, a schoolhouse and other rickety old buildings. Many contain funky and eclectic displays (dolls, bottles, fire equipment, antique stoves etc) from the pioneer days.

FREE **Owens Valley Paiute Shoshone Cultural Center** CULTURAL BUILDING
(760-873-3584; www.bishoppaiutetribe.com/culturalcenter.html; 2300 W Line St; 9am-5pm) A mile west of Hwy 395, this tribal cultural center is fronted by a native plant garden and includes exhibits on local basketry and the use of medical herbs.

FREE **Mountain Light Gallery** GALLERY
(760-873-7700; 106 S Main St; 10am-6pm) To see the Sierra on display in all its majesty, pop into this gallery, which features the stunning outdoor images of the late Galen Rowell. His work bursts with color, and the High Sierra photographs are some of the best in existence.

Activities

Bishop is prime **bouldering** and **rock climbing** territory, with terrain to match any level of fitness, experience and climbing style. The main areas are the granite Buttermilk Country, west of town on Buttermilk Rd, and the stark Volcanic Tablelands and Owens River Valley to the north. For details, consult with the staff at **Wilson's Eastside Sports** (760-873-7520; 224 N Main St), which rents equipment and sells maps and guidebooks. Another excellent resource is **Mammoth Mountaineering Supply** (760-873-4300; 298 N Main St), which also sells used gear, including shoes. The tablelands are also a wellspring of Native American petroglyphs – tread lightly.

Hikers will want to head to the high country by following Line St (Hwy 168) west along Bishop Creek Canyon, past Buttermilk Country and on to several lakes, including Lake Sabrina and South Lake. Trailheads lead into the John Muir Wilderness and on into Kings Canyon National Park. Check with the White Mountain Ranger Station (p440) for suggestions, maps and wilderness permits for overnight stays.

Fishing is good in all lakes but North Lake is the least crowded.

For hot springs, try **Keough's Hot Springs** (760-872-4670; www.keoughshotsprings.com; 800 Keough Hot Springs Rd; adult/conc $8/6; 11am-7pm Wed-Fri & Mon, 9am-8pm Sat & Sun, longer summer hours). About 8 miles south of Bishop, this historic institutional-green outdoor pool (dating from 1919) is filled with bathwater-warm water from local mineral springs and doused with spray at one end. A smaller and sheltered 104°F soaking pool sits beside it. Camping and tent cabins also available.

Sleeping

For a scenic night, stretch out your sleeping bag beneath the stars. The closest **USFS campgrounds** (tent & RV sites $21; ⌚May-Sep), all but one first-come, first-served, are between 9 miles and 15 miles west of town on Bishop Creek along Hwy 168, at elevations between 7500ft and 9000ft.

Joseph House Inn Bed & Breakfast B&B $$
(☎760-872-3389; www.josephhouseinn.com; 376 W Yaney St; r incl breakfast $143-178; ❄📶🐾) A beautiful restored ranch-style home, this place has a patio overlooking a tranquil 3-acre garden, and six nicely furnished rooms, some with fireplaces, all with TV and VCR. Guests enjoy a complimentary gourmet breakfast and afternoon wine and snacks.

Chalfant House B&B $$
(☎760-872-1790, 800-641-2996; www.chalfanthouse.com; 213 Academy; d incl breakfast $80-110; ❄📶🐾) Lace curtains and Victorian accents swirl through the six rooms of this restored historic home. Originally built by the editor and publisher of Owens Valley's first newspaper, some of the rooms are named after Chalfant family members.

Eating & Drinking

Raymond's Deli DELI $
(www.raymondsdeli.com; 206 N Main St; sandwiches $7-9; ⌚10am-6pm; 🍸) A sassy den of kitsch, pinball and Pac-man, Rayond's serves heaping sandwiches with names like 'When Pigs Fly,' 'Flaming Farm' and 'Soy U Like Tofu.' Kick back with a Lobotomy Bock and watch your food order get flung to the cook along a mini zip line.

Looney Bean CAFE $
(399 N Main St; pastries $3; ⌚6am-7pm; 📶) The combination of really fine coffee, a comfortable modern space and free wi-fi guarantee the popularity of this central cafe. It carries some organic brews, and lots of tasty scones and pastries for snacking.

Erick Schat's Bakkerÿ BAKERY $
(www.erickschatsbakery.com; 763 N Main St; sandwiches $5-8.50; ⌚6am-6pm Sun-Thu, to 8pm Fri) A much-hyped tourist mecca filled to the rafters with racks of fresh bread, it has been making its signature shepherd bread and other baked goodies since 1938. The bakery also features a popular sandwich bar.

Whiskey Creek AMERICAN $$
(www.whiskeycreekbishop.com; 524 N Main St; mains $11-29; ⌚11am-9pm, to 10:30pm Fri & Sat) This country dining room has comfort food like meatloaf and chicken pot pie, and a smattering of seafood and pastas.

Information

Public showers are available in town at **Wash Tub** (☎760-873-6627; 236 Warren St; ⌚approx 5pm & 8-10pm), and near South Lake at **Bishop Creek Lodge** (☎760-873-4484; www.bishopcreekresort.com; 2100 South Lake Rd; ⌚May-Oct) and **Parchers Resort** (☎760-873-4177; www.parchersresort.net; 5001 South Lake Rd; ⌚late May–mid-Oct).

Bishop Area Visitors Bureau (☎760-873-8405; www.bishopvisitor.com; 690 N Main St; ⌚10am-5pm Mon-Fri, to 4pm Sat & Sun)

Inyo County Free Library (☎760-873-5115; 210 Academy) Free internet access.

Spellbinder Books (☎760-873-4511; 124 S Main St; 📶) Great indie bookstore with attached cafe and wi-fi.

White Mountain Ranger Station (☎760-873-2500; www.fs.usda.gov/inyo; 798 N Main St; ⌚8am-5pm daily May-Oct, Mon-Fri rest of year) Wilderness permits, trail and campground information for the entire area.

Big Pine

This blink-and-you-missed-it town has a few motels and basic eateries. It mainly functions as a launch pad for the Ancient Bristlecone Pine Forest (see the boxed text, p441) and to the granite **Palisades** in the John Muir Wilderness, a rugged cluster of peaks including six above 14,000ft. Stretching beneath the pinnacles is **Palisades Glacier**, the southernmost in the USA and the largest in the Sierra.

To get to the trailhead, turn onto Glacier Lodge Rd (Crocker Ave in town), which follows trout-rich Big Pine Creek up Big Pine Canyon, 10 miles west into a bowl-shaped valley. The strenuous 9-mile hike to Palisades Glacier via the North Fork Trail skirts several lakes – turned a milky turquoise color by glacial runoff – and a stone cabin built by horror-film actor Lon Chaney in 1925.

An ear-popping ascent up Glacier Lodge Rd passes by a trio of **USFS campgrounds** (☎877-444-6777; www.recreation.gov; tent & RV sites $20; ⌚May–mid-Oct) – Big Pine Creek, Sage Flat and Upper Sage Flat. Showers are available for $5 at **Glacier Lodge** (☎760-

DON'T MISS

ANCIENT BRISTLECONE PINE FOREST

For encounters with some of the earth's oldest living things, plan at least a half-day trip to the Ancient Bristlecone Pine Forest. These gnarled, otherworldly looking trees thrive above 10,000ft on the slopes of the seemingly inhospitable White Mountains, a parched and stark range that once stood even higher than the Sierra. The oldest tree – called Methuselah – is estimated to be over 4700 years old, beating even the Great Sphinx of Giza by about two centuries.

To reach the groves, take Hwy 168 east 12 miles from Big Pine to White Mountain Rd, then turn left (north) and climb the curvy road 10 miles to **Schulman Grove**, named for the scientist who first discovered the trees' biblical age in the 1950s. The entire trip takes about one hour. There's access to self-guided trails, and a new solar-powered **visitors center** (760-873-2500; www.fs.usda.gov/inyo; admission $5 per vehicle; late May-Oct) is scheduled to open in summer 2012. White Mountain Rd is usually closed from November to April. It's nicest in August when wildflowers sneak out through the rough soil.

A second grove, the **Patriarch Grove**, is dramatically set within an open bowl and reached via a 12-mile graded dirt road. Four miles further on you'll find a locked gate, which is the departure point for day hikes to the **White Mountain Peak** – at 14,246ft it's the third-highest mountain in California. The round-trip is about 14 miles via an abandoned road, soon passing through the **Barcroft High Altitude Research Station**. Some ride the route on mountain bikes: the nontechnical and marmot-laden road winds above the tree line, though naturally, high elevation makes the going tough. Allow plenty of time, bring at least two quarts of water per person. For maps and details, stop at the White Mountain Ranger Station (p440) in Bishop.

For altitude adjustment or some good star gazing, spend a night at the **Grandview Campground** (donation $5) at 8600ft. It has awesome views, tables and vault toilets, but no water.

938-2837; www.jewelofthesierra.com; tent & RV sites $35, cabins $125; mid-Apr–mid-Nov;), a bunch of rustic cabins with kitchens, as well as a campground, with a two-night minimum stay; it was one of the earliest Sierra getaways when built in 1917.

Independence

This sleepy highway town has been a county seat since 1866 and is home to the **Eastern California Museum** (760-878-0364; www.inyocounty.us/ecmuseum; 155 N Grant St; donation requested; 10am-5pm). It contains one of the most complete collections of Paiute and Shoshone baskets in the country, as well as artifacts from the Manzanar relocation camp (see the boxed text, p443) and historic photographs of primitively equipped local rock climbers scaling Sierra peaks, including Mt Whitney.

Fans of **Mary Austin** (1868–1934), renowned author of *The Land of Little Rain* and vocal foe of the desertification of the Owens Valley, can follow signs leading to her former house at 253 Market St.

West of town via Onion Valley Rd (Market St in town), pretty **Onion Valley** harbors the trailhead for the **Kearsarge Pass** (9.4 miles round-trip), an old Paiute trade route. This is also the quickest eastside access to the Pacific Crest Trail and Kings Canyon National Park.

In addition to a few small motels in town, Onion Valley has a couple of **campgrounds** (877-444-6777; www.recreation.gov; tent & RV sites $16; May-Sep) along Independence Creek.

Inexplicably located in a town otherwise inhabited by greasy spoon diners, **Still Life Cafe** (760-878-2555; 135 S Edward St; mains lunch $10-16, dinner $20-25; 11am-3pm & 6-9:30pm Wed-Mon), a French gourmet bistro, pops out like an orchid in a salt flat. Escargot, duck-liver mousse, steak au poivre and other French delectables are served with Gallic charm in this bright, artistic dining room.

Next to the courthouse, bustling **Jenny's Cafe** (246 N Edwards St; mains lunch $7-9, dinner $12-22; 6am-9pm Thu-Tue) serves rib-sticking fare like burgers, sandwiches and steaks in a country kitchen setting of rooster-print curtains and old teapots.

Manzanar National Historic Site

A stark wooden guard tower alerts drivers to one of the darkest chapters in US history, which unfolded on a barren and windy sweep of land some 5 miles south of Independence. Little remains of the infamous war concentration camp, a dusty square mile where more than 10,000 people of Japanese ancestry were corralled during WWII following the attack on Pearl Harbor (see the boxed text, p443). The camp's lone remaining building, the former high-school auditorium, houses a superb **interpretive center** (☎760-878-2194; www.nps.gov/manz; ⊙9am-4:30pm Nov-Mar, to 5:30pm Apr-Oct). A visit here is one of the historical highlights of the state and should not be missed.

Watch the 20-minute documentary, then explore the thought-provoking exhibits chronicling the stories of the families that languished here yet built a vibrant community. Afterwards, take a self-guided 3.2-mile driving tour around the grounds, which includes a re-created mess hall and barracks, vestiges of buildings and gardens, as well as the haunting camp cemetery.

Lone Pine

A tiny town, Lone Pine is the gateway to big things, most notably Mt Whitney (14,505ft), the loftiest peak in the contiguous USA, and Hollywood. In the 1920s cinematographers discovered that nearby Alabama Hills were a picture-perfect movie set for Westerns, and stars from Gary Cooper to Gregory Peck could often be spotted swaggering about town.

Sights & Activities

A few basic motels, a supermarket, restaurants and stores (including gear and equipment shops) flank Hwy 395 (Main St in town). Whitney Portal Rd heads west at the lone stoplight, while Hwy 136 to Death Valley veers away about 2 miles south of town.

Mt Whitney MOUNTAIN

West of Lone Pine, the jagged incisors of the Sierra surge skyward in all their raw and fierce glory. Cradled by scores of smaller pinnacles, Mt Whitney is a bit hard to pick out from Hwy 395, so for the best views, take a drive along Whitney Portal Rd through the Alabama Hills. As you get a fix on this majestic megalith, remember that the country's lowest point is only 80 miles (as the crow flies) east of here: Badwater in Death Valley. Climbing to Mt Whitney's summit is among the most popular hikes in the entire country (see the boxed text p444).

TOP CHOICE **Alabama Hills** NATURAL FEATURE

Located on Whitney Portal Rd, the warm colors and rounded contours of the Alabama Hills stand in contrast to the jagged snowy Sierras just behind. The setting for countless ride-'em-out movies and the popular *Lone Ranger* TV series, the stunning orange rock formations are a beautiful place to experience sunrise or sunset. You can drive, walk or mountain-bike along dirt roads rambling through the boulders, and along Tuttle and Lone Pine creeks. A number of graceful rock arches are within easy hiking distance of the roads. Head west on Whitney Portal Rd and either turn left at Tuttle Creek Rd, after a half-mile, or north on Movie Rd, after about 3 miles. The websites of the Lone Pine Chamber of Commerce (p443) and the Museum of Lone Pine Film History have excellent movie location maps.

Museum of Lone Pine Film History MUSEUM

(☎760-876-9909; www.lonepinefilmhistorymuseum.org; 701 S Main St; admission $5; ⊙10am-6pm Mon-Wed, to 7pm Thu-Sat, to 4pm Sun) Over 450 movies have been shot in the area, and this museum contains exhibits of paraphernalia from locally set films. Don't miss the 7pm screenings in its theater every Thursday and Friday or the tricked-out Cadillac convertible in its foyer.

Sleeping & Eating

Dow Hotel & Dow Villa Motel MOTEL, HOTEL $$

(☎760-876-5521, 800-824-9317; www.dowvillamotel.com; 310 S Main St; hotel r with/without bath $70/54, motel r $104-140; ❄📶🏊🐾) John Wayne and Errol Flynn are among the stars who have stayed at this venerable hotel. Built in 1922, the place has been restored but retains much of its rustic charm. The rooms in the newer motel section are more comfortable and bright, but also more generic.

Whitney Portal Hostel HOSTEL $

(☎760-876-0030; www.whitneyportalstore.com; 238 S Main St; dm $20, q $60; ❄@📶🐾) A popu-

CAMP OF INFAMY

On December 7, 1941 – a day that, according to President Roosevelt, would forever live in infamy – Japanese war planes bombed Pearl Harbor. The attack plunged the US into WWII and fanned the flames of racial prejudice that had been fomenting against Japanese Americans for decades. Amid fears of sabotage and espionage, bigotry grew into full-blown hysteria, prompting Roosevelt to sign Executive Order 9066 in February 1942; another day that now lives in infamy. The act stated that all West Coast Japanese – most of them American-born citizens – were to be rounded up and moved to relocation camps.

Manzanar was the first of 10 such camps, built among pear and apple orchards in the dusty Owens Valley near Independence. Between 1942 and 1945, up to 10,000 men, women and children lived crammed into makeshift barracks pounded by fierce winds and the blistering desert sun, enclosed by barbed wire patrolled by military police.

After the war the camp was leveled and its dark history remained buried beneath the dust for decades. Recognition remained elusive until 1973, when the site was given landmark status; in 1992 it was designated a national historic site, and in 2004 a long-awaited interpretive center opened. On the last Saturday of every April, former internees and their descendants make a **pilgrimage** (www.manzanarcommittee.org) to honor family members who died here, keeping alive the memory of this national tragedy. For a vivid and haunting account of what life was like at the camp, read Jean Wakatsuki Houston's classic *Farewell to Manzanar*.

lar launching pad for Whitney trips and for post-hike wash-ups (public showers available), the carpeted bunk-bed rooms have towels and TVs to reacclimatize the weary, plus there's free coffee in the communal kitchenette (no stove). Reserve two months ahead for July and August.

Lone Pine Campground CAMPGROUND **$**
(☎518-885-3639, 877-444-6777; www.recreation.gov; Whitney Portal Rd; tent & RV sites $15-17; ⏲mid-Apr–Oct) About midway between Lone Pine and Whitney Portal, this popular creekside USFS campground (elevation 6000ft) offers flush toilets and potable water.

Alabama Hills Cafe DINER **$**
(111 W Post St; mains $8-12; ⏲6am-2pm Mon-Fri, from 7am Sat & Sun; ✎) Everyone's favorite breakfast joint, the portions here are big, the bread fresh-baked, and the hearty soups and scratch-made fruit pies make lunch an attractive option too.

Seasons NEW AMERICAN **$$**
(☎760-876-8927; 206 N Main St; mains $17-29; ⏲5-10pm daily Apr-Oct, to 9pm Mon-Sat Nov-Mar) Seasons has everything you fantasized about the last time you choked down freeze-dried rations. Sauteed trout, roasted duck, filet mignon and plates of carb-replenishing pasta will revitalize your appetite, and nice and naughty desserts will leave you purring.

ℹ Information

Eastern Sierra InterAgency Visitor Center (☎760-876-6222; www.fs.fed.us/r5/inyo; ⏲8am-5pm, extended summer hours) USFS information central for the Sierra, Death Valley and Mt Whitney; about 1.5 miles south of town at the junction of Hwys 395 and 136.

Lone Pine Chamber of Commerce (☎760-876-4444; www.lonepinechamber.org; 120 S Main St; ⏲8:30am-4:30pm Mon-Fri)

RENO (NEVADA)

A soothingly schizophrenic city of big-time gambling and top-notch outdoor adventures, Reno resists pigeonholing. 'The Biggest Little City in the World' has something to raise the pulse of adrenaline junkies, hardcore gamblers and city people craving easy access to wide open spaces.

Sights

National Automobile Museum MUSEUM
(☎775-333-9300; www.automuseum.org; 10 S Lake St; adult/child/senior $10/4/8; ⏲9:30am-5:30pm Mon-Sat, 10am-4pm Sun; 👪) Stylized street scenes illustrate a century's worth of automobile history at this engaging car

HIKING MT WHITNEY

The mystique of Mt Whitney captures the imagination, and conquering its hulking bulk becomes a sort of obsession for many. The main **Mt Whitney Trail** (the easiest and busiest one) leaves from Whitney Portal, about 13 miles west of Lone Pine via the Whitney Portal Rd (closed in winter), and climbs about 6000ft over 11 miles. It's a super strenuous, really, *really* long walk that'll wear out even experienced mountaineers, but doesn't require technical skills if attempted in summer or early fall. Earlier or later in the season, you'll likely need an ice axe and crampons.

Many people in good physical condition make it to the top, although only superbly conditioned, previously acclimatized hikers should attempt this as a day hike. Breathing becomes difficult at these elevations and altitude sickness is a common problem. Rangers recommend spending a night or two camping at the trailhead and another at one of the two camps along the route: **Outpost Camp** at 3.5 miles or **Trail Camp** at 6 miles up the trail.

When considering an ascent, do your homework. One recommended book is *Mt Whitney: The Complete Trailhead-to-Summit Hiking Guide* by Paul Richins Jr. When you pick up your permit and pack-out kits (hikers must pack out their poop) at the Eastern Sierra Interagency Visitor Center in Lone Pine, get the latest info on weather and trail conditions.

Near the trailhead, the **Whitney Portal Store** (www.whitneyportalstore.com; ⏲May-Oct) sells groceries and snacks. It also has public showers ($3) and a **cafe** with enormous burgers and pancakes. Its excellent website is a comprehensive starting point for Whitney research.

The biggest obstacle in getting to the peak may be to obtain a **wilderness permit** (per person $15), which is required for all overnight trips and for day hikes past Lone Pine Lake (about 2.8 miles from the trailhead). A quota system limits daily access to 60 overnight and 100 day hikers from May through October. Because of the huge demand, permits are distributed via the **Mt Whitney lottery**. Historically, lottery applications have been accepted only by mail in February (and mixed up by a leaf blower in the stairwell!), but may be migrating online. Check www.fs.fed.us/r5/inyo for current procedures.

Want to avoid the hassle of getting a permit for the main Mt Whitney Trail? Consider ascending this popular pinnacle from the west, using the backdoor route from Sequoia & Kings Canyon National Parks. It takes about six days from Crescent Meadow via the High Sierra Trail to the John Muir Trail – with no Whitney Zone permit required – and wilderness permits are much easier to secure. See p422 for park permit information.

museum. The collection is enormous and impressive, with one-of-a-kind vehicles – including James Dean's 1949 Mercury from *Rebel Without a Cause,* a 1938 Phantom Corsair and a 24-karat gold-plated DeLorean – and rotating exhibits bringing in all kinds of souped-up or fabulously retro rides.

Nevada Museum of Art MUSEUM
(☎775-329-3333; www.nevadaart.org; 160 W Liberty St; adult/child $10/1; ⏲10am-5pm Wed-Sun, to 8pm Thu) In a sparkling building inspired by the geological formations of the Black Rock Desert, north of town, a floating staircase leads to galleries showcasing temporary exhibits and images related to the American West. Great **cafe** for postcultural refueling.

FREE **Fleischmann Planetarium & Science Center** SCIENCE CENTER
(☎775-784-4811; http://planetarium.unr.nevada.edu; 1650 N Virginia St; ⏲noon-5pm Mon & Tue, to 9pm Fri, 10am-9pm Sat, to 5pm Sun) Pop into this flying saucer–shaped building, at the University of Nevada, for a window on the universe during star shows and feature presentations (adult/child $6/4).

Nevada Historical Society Museum MUSEUM
(☎775-688-1190; www.museums.nevadaculture.org; 1650 N Virginia St; adult/child $4/free;

⏲10am-5pm Wed-Sat) Near the science center, this museum includes permanent exhibits on neon signs, local Native American culture and the presence of the federal government.

Activities

Reno is a 30- to 60-minute drive from Lake Tahoe ski resorts, and many hotels and casinos offer special stay-and-ski packages.

For extensive information on regional hiking and mountain-biking trails, including the Mt Rose summit trail and the Tahoe-Pyramid Bikeway, download the **Truckee Meadows Trails guide** (www.reno.gov/Index.aspx?page=291).

Mere steps from the casinos, the Class II and III rapids at the **Truckee River Whitewater Park** are gentle enough for kids riding inner tubes, yet sufficiently challenging for professional freestyle kayakers. Two courses wrap around Wingfield Park, a small river island that hosts free concerts in summertime. **Tahoe Whitewater Tours** (☎775-787-5000; www.gowhitewater.com) and **Wild Sierra Adventures** (☎866-323-8928; www.wildsierra.com) offer kayak trips and lessons.

The **Historic Reno Preservation Society** (☎775-747-4478; www.historicreno.org; tours $10) will help you dig deeper with a walking or cycling tour of the city, highlighting subjects including architecture, politics and literary history.

Festivals & Events

Reno River Festival SPORTS
(www.renoriverfestival.com) The world's top freestyle kayakers compete in a mad paddling dash through Whitewater Park in mid-May. Free music concerts as well.

Tour de Nez SPORTS
(www.tourdenez.com) Called the 'coolest bike race in America,' the Tour de Nez brings together pros and amateurs for five days of races and partying in July.

Hot August Nights CULTURAL
(www.hotaugustnights.net) Catch the *American Graffiti* vibe during this seven-day celebration of hot rods and rock 'n' roll in early August. Hotel rates skyrocket to their peak.

Sleeping

Lodging rates vary widely depending on the day of the week and local events. Sunday through Thursday are generally the least expensive; Friday is somewhat more expensive and Saturday can be as much as triple the midweek rate.

Peppermill CASINO HOTEL $$
(☎775-826-2121, 866-821-9996; www.peppermillreno.com; 2707 S Virginia St; r Sun-Thu $50-140, Fri & Sat $70-200; ❄@📶🏊) Now awash in Vegas-style opulence, the popular Peppermill boasts Tuscan-themed rooms in its newest 600-room tower, and has almost completed a plush remodel of its older rooms. The three sparkling pools (one indoor) are dreamy, with a full spa on hand. Geothermal energy powers the resort's hot water and heat.

Sands Regency CASINO HOTEL $
(☎775-348-2200, 866-386-7829; www.sandsregency.com; 345 N Arlington Ave; r Sun-Thu, Fri & Sat from $29/89; ❄📶🏊🐾) With some of the largest standard digs in town, rooms here are decked out in a cheerful tropical palette of upbeat blues, reds and greens – a visual relief from standard-issue motel decor. The 17th-floor gym and Jacuzzi are perfectly positioned to capture your eyes with drop-dead panoramic mountain views. Empress Tower rooms are best.

Wildflower Village MOTEL $
(☎775-747-8848; www.wildflowervillage.com; 4395 W 4th St; r $50-75, B&B $100-125; ❄@📶) Perhaps more of a state of mind than a motel, this artists colony on the west edge of town has a tumbledown yet creative vibe. Individual murals decorate the facade of each room, and you can hear the freight trains rumble on by.

GREAT BALLS OF FIRE!

For one week at the end of August, **Burning Man** (www.burningman.com; admission $210-320) explodes onto the sunbaked Black Rock Desert, and Nevada sprouts a third major population center – Black Rock City. An experiential art party (and alternative universe) that climaxes in the immolation of a towering stick figure, Burning Man is a whirlwind of outlandish theme camps, dust-caked bicycles, bizarre bartering, costume-enhanced nudity and a general relinquishment of inhibitions.

WORTH A TRIP

VIRGINIA CITY

Virginia City, about 23 miles south of Reno, was the site of the legendary Comstock Lode, a massive silver bonanza that began in 1859 and stands as one of the world's richest strikes. Some of the silver barons went on to become major players in California history, among them Leland Stanford of university fame and Bank of California founder William Ralston. Much of San Francisco was built with the treasure dug up from the soil beneath the town.

At its peak, Virginia City had over 30,000 residents and, as befits a mining town, was a wild and raucous place. A young local newspaper writer captured the shenanigans in a book called *Roughing It*, published under his pen name Mark Twain. A National Historic Landmark since 1961, Virginia City draws big crowds in search of Old West icons and lore. Though it sometimes has the feel of a frontier theme park, it's still a fun place to while away a few hours.

On the main drag, C street, you'll find the **visitors center** (www.virginiacity-nv.org; 86 South C St; ⏲10am-4pm), vintage buildings restored into wacky saloons, cheesy souvenir shops and small museums ranging from hokey to intriguing. To see how the mining elite lived, stop by the **Mackay Mansion** (D St) and the **Castle** (B St).

Drink like an old-time miner at one of the many Victorian-era watering holes that line C street. The longtime family-run **Bucket of Blood Saloon** (www.bucketofbloodsaloonvc.com; 1 South C St; ⏲2-7pm) serves up beer and 'bar rules' ('If the bartender doesn't laugh, you are not funny') at its antique wooden bar, and the **Palace Restaurant & Saloon** (www.palacerestaurant1875.com; 1 South C St; mains $6-10; ⏲hours vary) is full of town memorabilia and has tasty breakfasts and lunches.

The drive to Virginia City from Reno offers great views of the mountain. Take Hwy 395 south for about 10 miles, then Hwy 341 east for 13 miles.

Mt Rose CAMPGROUND **$**
(☎877-444-6777; www.recreation.gov; Hwy 431; RV & tent sites $16) In the summer months, there's gorgeous high altitude camping here.

Eating & Drinking

Reno's dining scene goes far beyond the casino buffets.

TOP CHOICE **Old Granite Street Eatery** AMERICAN **$$**
(☎775-622-3222; www.oldgranitestreeteatery.com; 243 S Sierra St; dishes $9-24; ⏲11am-10pm Mon-Thu, variable hours otherwise) A lovely well-lit place for organic and local comfort food, old-school artisanal cocktails and seasonal craft beers, this antique-strewn hotspot enchants diners with its stately wooden bar, water served in old liquor bottles and lengthy seasonal menu. Forgot to make a reservation? Check out the iconic rooster and pig murals and wait for seats at a community table fashioned from a barn door.

Pneumatic Diner VEGETARIAN **$**
(2nd fl, 501 W 1st St; dishes $6-9; ⏲noon-10pm Mon, 11am-11pm Tue-Sat, 8am-10pm Sun; 🖉) Consume a garden of vegetarian delights under salvaged neon lights. This groovy little place near the river has meatless and vegan comfort food and desserts to tickle your inner two-year-old, like the ice-cream laden Cookie Bomb. It's attached to the Truckee River Terrace apartment complex; use the Ralston St entrance.

Silver Peak Restaurant & Brewery PUB **$$**
(www.silverpeakbrewery.com; 124 Wonder St; mains lunch $8-10, dinner $9-21; ⏲11am-midnight) Casual and pretense-free, this place hums with the chatter of happy locals settling in for a night of microbrews and great eats, from pizza with roasted chicken to shrimp pasta and filet mignon.

Peg's Glorified Ham & Eggs DINER **$**
(www.pegsglorifiedhamneggs.com; 420 S Sierra St; dishes $7-10; ⏲6:30am-2pm; 👪) Locally regarded as the best breakfast in town, Peg's offers tasty grill food that's not too greasy.

Jungle Java & Jungle Vino CAFE, WINE BAR
(www.javajunglevino.com; 246 W 1st St; ⏲6am-midnight; 📶) A side-by-side coffee shop and wine bar with a cool mosaic floor and an internet cafe all rolled into one. The wine bar has

weekly tastings, while the cafe serves breakfast bagels and lunchtime sandwiches ($8) and puts on diverse music shows.

Imperial Bar & Lounge BAR
(www.imperialbarandlounge.com; 150 N Arlington Ave; ⏲11am-2am Thu-Sat, to midnight Sun-Wed) A classy bar inhabiting a relic of the past – this building was once an old bank, and in the middle of the wood floor you can see cement where the vault once stood. Sandwiches and pizzas go with 16 beers on tap and a buzzing weekend scene.

St James Infirmary BAR
(445 California Ave) With an eclectic menu of 120 bottled varieties and 18 on tap, beer aficionados will short circuit with delight. Red lights blush over black-and-white retro banquettes and a wall of movie and music stills. The bar hosts sporadic events, including jazz and bluegrass performances.

☆ Entertainment

The free weekly *Reno News & Review* (www.newsreview.com) is your best source for listings.

Wedged between the I-80 and the Truckee River, downtown's N Virginia St is casino central. South of the river it continues as S Virginia St. All of the hotel casinos listed are open 24 hours.

Edge CLUB
(www.edgeofreno.com; Peppermill, 2707 S Virginia St; admission $10-20; ⏲Thu-Sun) The Peppermill reels in the nighthounds with a big glitzy dance club, where go-go dancers, smoke machines and laser lights may cause sensory overload. If so, step outside to the lounge patio and relax in front of cozy fire pits.

Knitting Factory LIVE MUSIC
(☎775-323-5648; http://re.knittingfactory.com; 211 N Virginia St) This midsized venue opened in 2010, filling a gap in Reno's music scene with mainstream and indie favorites.

Circus Circus CASINO
(www.circusreno.com; 500 N Sierra St; 👪) The most family-friendly of the bunch, Circus Circus has free circus acts to entertain kids beneath a giant, candy-striped big top, which also harbors a gazillion carnival and video games that look awfully similar to slot machines.

Silver Legacy CASINO
(www.silverlegacyreno.com; 407 N Virginia St) A Victorian-themed place, the Silver Legacy is easily recognized by its white landmark dome, where a giant mock mining rig periodically erupts into a fairly tame sound-and-light spectacle.

Eldorado CASINO
(www.eldoradoreno.com; 345 N Virginia St) The Eldorado has a kitschy Fountain of Fortune that probably has Italian sculptor Bernini spinning in his grave.

Harrah's CASINO
(www.harrahsreno.com; 219 N Center St) Founded by Nevada gambling pioneer William Harrah in 1946, this is still one of the biggest and most popular casinos in town.

Peppermill CASINO
(www.peppermillreno.com; 2707 S Virginia St) Dazzles with a 17-story Tuscan-style tower. About 2 miles south of downtown.

Atlantis CASINO
(www.atlantiscasino.com; 3800 S Virginia St) Now more classy than zany, with an extensive spa, the remodeled casino retains a few tropical flourishes like indoor waterfalls and palm trees.

ℹ Information

An information center sits near the baggage claim at **Reno-Tahoe International Airport**, which also has free wi-fi.

Java Jungle (246 W 1st St; per hr $2; ⏲6am-midnight; 📶) Great riverfront cafe with a few computers and free wi-fi.

Reno-Sparks Convention & Visitors Authority (☎800-367-7366; www.visitrenotahoe.com; 2nd

WORTH A TRIP

PYRAMID LAKE

A piercingly blue expanse in an otherwise barren landscape, 25 miles north of Reno on the Paiute Indian Reservation, Pyramid Lake is popular for recreation. Permits for **camping** (primitive campsites per vehicle per night $9) and **fishing** (per person $9) are available at outdoor suppliers and CVS drugstore locations in Reno, and at the **ranger station** (☎775-476-1155; www.pyramidlake.us; ⏲8am-6pm) on SR 445 in Sutcliffe.

fl, Reno Town Mall, 4001 S Virginia St; ⏲8am-5pm Mon-Fri)

Getting There & Away

About 5 miles southeast of downtown, the **Reno-Tahoe International Airport** (RNO; www.renoairport.com;) is served by most major airlines.

The **North Lake Tahoe Express** (☎866-216-5222; www.northlaketahoeexpress.com) operates a shuttle ($40, six to eight daily, 3:30am to midnight) to and from the airport to multiple North Shore Lake Tahoe locations including Truckee, Squaw Valley and Incline Village. Reserve in advance.

The **South Tahoe Express** (☎866-898-2463; www.southtahoeexpress.com; adult/child one way $27/15, round-trip $48/27) operates several daily shuttle buses from the airport to Stateline casinos; the journey takes 75 minutes up to two hours.

To reach South Lake Tahoe (weekdays only), take the wi-fi-equipped **RTC Intercity bus** (www.rtcwashoe.com) to the Nevada DOT stop in Carson City ($4, one hour, five daily Monday to Friday) and then the **BlueGo** (www.bluego.org) 21X bus ($2 with RTC Intercity transfer, one hour, seven to eight daily) to the Stateline Transit Center.

Greyhound (☎775-322-2970; www.greyhound.com; 155 Stevenson St) buses run daily service to Truckee, Sacramento and San Francisco ($34, five to seven hours), as does the once-daily westbound *California Zephyr* route operated by **Amtrak** (☎775-329-8638, 800-872-7245; 280 N Center St). The train is slower and more expensive, but also more scenic and comfortable, with a bus connection from Emeryville for passengers to San Francisco ($46, 7½ hours).

Getting Around

Casino hotels offer frequent free airport shuttles for their guests (and don't ask to see reservations).

The local **RTC Ride buses** (☎775-348-7433; www.rtcwashoe.com; per ride/all day $2/4) blanket the city, and most routes converge at the RTC 4th St station downtown. Useful routes include the RTC Rapid line for S Virginia St, 11 for Sparks and 19 for the airport.

The free **Sierra Spirit bus** loops around all major downtown landmarks – including the casinos and the university – every 15 minutes from 7am to 7pm.

Central Coast

Includes »

Best Places to Eat

- Passionfish (p470)
- Cracked Crab (p503)
- Cass House Restaurant (p485)
- San Luis Obispo Farmers Market (p495)
- Bouchon (p515)

Best Places to Stay

- Post Ranch Inn (p478)
- Inn of the Spanish Garden (p514)
- Cass House Inn (p484)
- El Capitan Canyon (p514)
- Dream Inn (p453)

Why Go?

Too often forgotten or dismissed as 'flyover' country between San Francisco and LA, this fairytale stretch of California coast is packed with wild Pacific beaches, misty redwood forests where hot springs hide, and rolling golden hills of fertile vineyards and farm fields.

Here Hwy 1 pulls out all the stops, scenery-wise. Flower-power Santa Cruz and the historic port town of Monterey are gateways to the rugged wild lands of the bohemian Big Sur coast. It's an epic journey snaking down to vainglorious Hearst Castle, past lighthouses and cliffs over which condors soar.

Or get acquainted with California's agricultural heartland along inland Hwy 101, called El Camino Real (the King's Highway) by Spanish conquistadors and Franciscan friars. Then soothe your nature-loving soul between laid-back San Luis Obispo and idyllic seaside Santa Barbara, just a short hop from the Channel Islands.

When to Go

Santa Barbara

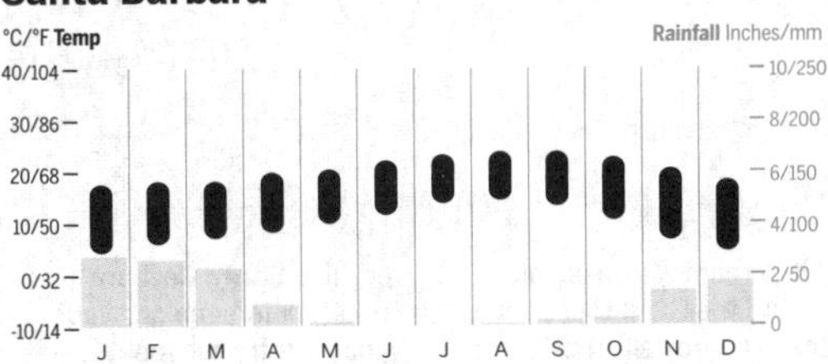

Apr Balmy temperatures and fewer tourists than summer. Wildflowers bloom.

Jul Summer vacation and beach season kick off; SoCal ocean waters warm up.

Oct Sunny blue skies, yet smaller crowds. Wine country harvests celebrated.

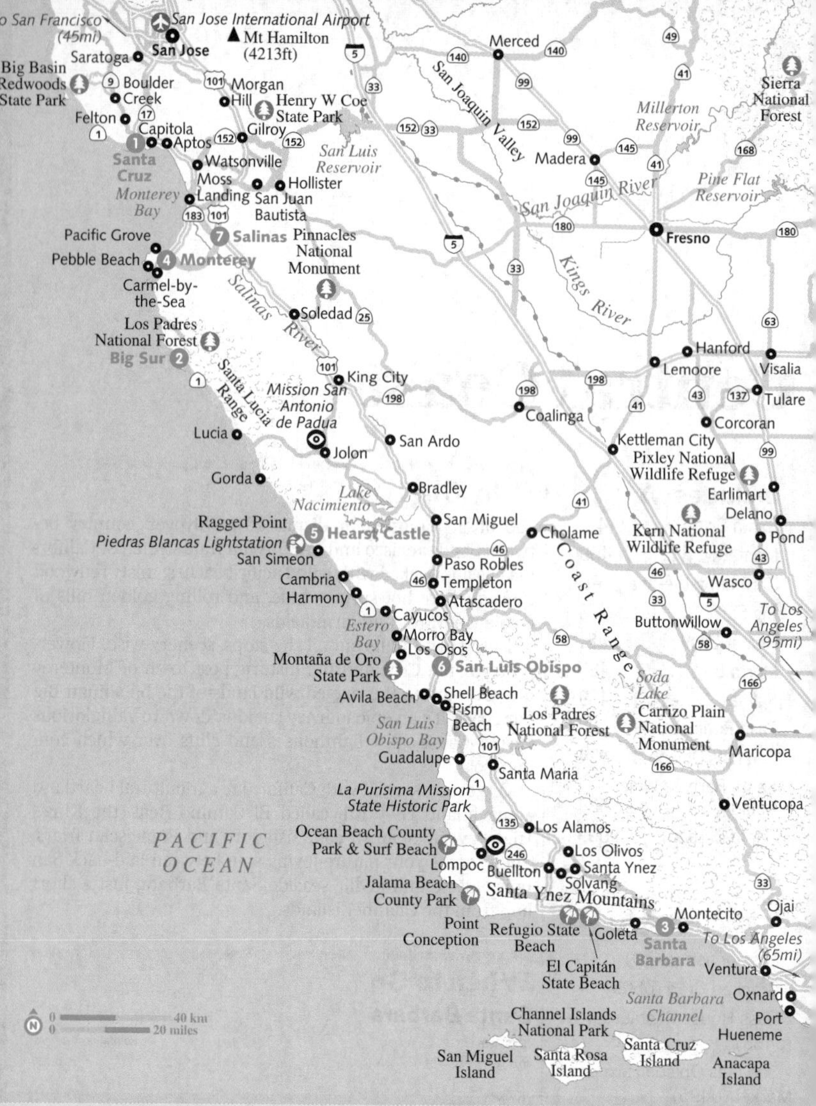

Central Coast Highlights

1. Scream your head off aboard the Giant Dipper on the beach boardwalk, then learn to surf in **Santa Cruz** (p451)
2. Cruise Hwy 1, where the sky touches the sea, along the rocky coastline of fairytale **Big Sur** (p473)
3. Soak up the chic atmosphere of whitewashed, red-tiled **Santa Barbara** (p509) before making your wine-country escape
4. Brings the kids to gawk at the aquatic denizens of the 'indoor ocean' at the **Monterey Bay Aquarium** (p460)
5. Marvel in disbelief at the grandiosity of **Hearst Castle** (p481) after meeting the neighbors: ginormous elephant seals
6. Hang loose in college-town **San Luis Obispo** (p494), surrounded by bodacious beaches and parklands
7. Explore down-to-earth novelist John Steinbeck's blue-collar world in the agricultural valley town of **Salinas** (p489)

ALONG HIGHWAY 1

Teeming with richly varied marine life, lined with often deserted beaches, and home to towns full of character and idiosyncratic charm all along its half-moon shore, Monterey Bay is anchored by Santa Cruz to the north. On the 125-mile stretch south of the Monterey Peninsula, you'll snake along an unbelievably picturesque coast until Hwy 1 joins with Hwy 101 at San Luis Obispo.

Santa Cruz

Santa Cruz has marched to its own beat since long before the Beat Generation. It's counterculture central, a touchy-feely, new-agey city famous for its leftie-liberal politics and live-and-let-live ideology – except when it comes to dogs (rarely allowed off-leash), parking (meters run seven days a week) and Republicans (allegedly shot on sight). It's still cool to be a hippie or a stoner here (or better yet, both), although some far-out–looking freaks are just slumming Silicon Valley millionaires and trust-fund babies underneath.

Santa Cruz is a city of madcap fun, with a vibrant but chaotic downtown. On the waterfront is the famous beach boardwalk, and in the hills redwood groves embrace the University of California, Santa Cruz (UCSC) campus. Plan to spend at least half a day here, but to appreciate the aesthetic of jangly skirts, crystal pendants and Rastafarian dreadlocks, stay longer and plunge headlong into the rich local brew of surfers, students, punks and eccentric characters.

Sights

One of the best things to do in Santa Cruz is simply stroll, shop and people-watch along **Pacific Ave** downtown. A 15-minute walk away is the beach and the **Municipal Wharf**, where seafood restaurants, gift shops and barking sea lions compete for attention. Ocean-view **West Cliff Dr** follows the waterfront southwest of the wharf, paralleled by a paved recreational path.

Santa Cruz Beach Boardwalk AMUSEMENT PARK

(Map p454; ☎831-423-5590; www.beachboardwalk.com; 400 Beach St; per ride $3-5, all-day pass $30; ⏰from 10am or 11am daily May-Sep; 👪) The West Coast's oldest beachfront amusement park, this 1907 boardwalk has a glorious old-school Americana vibe, with the smell of cotton candy mixing with the salt air, punctuated by the squeals of kids hanging upside down on carnival rides. Famous thrills include the Giant Dipper, a 1924 wooden roller coaster, and the 1911 Looff carousel, both National Historic Landmarks. On summer Friday nights, catch free concerts by rock veterans you may have thought were already dead. For kid-friendly train rides up into the redwoods, see p459. Closing times and off-season hours vary.

Seymour Marine Discovery Center MUSEUM

(Map p458; www2.ucsc.edu/seymourcenter; end of Delaware Ave; adult/child 4-16yr $6/4; ⏰10am-5pm Tue-Sat, noon-5pm Sun, also 10am-5pm Mon Jul & Aug; 👪) Near Natural Bridges State Beach, this kids' educational center is part of UCSC's Long Marine Laboratory. Interactive natural-science exhibits include tidal touch pools and aquariums, while outside you can gawk at the world's largest blue-whale skeleton. Guided tours are usually given at 1pm, 2pm and 3pm daily; sign up in person an hour in advance (no reservations).

Santa Cruz Surfing Museum MUSEUM

(Map p458; www.santacruzsurfingmuseum.org; 701 W Cliff Dr; admission by donation; ⏰noon-4pm Thu-Mon Sep-Jun, 10am-5pm Wed-Mon Jul & Aug) A mile south of the wharf along the coast, the old lighthouse is packed with memorabilia, including vintage redwood surfboards. Fittingly, Lighthouse Point overlooks two popular surf breaks.

University of California, Santa Cruz UNIVERSITY

(UCSC; Map p458; www.ucsc.edu) Check it: the school mascot is a banana slug! Established

FAST FACTS

- **Population of Santa Barbara** 88,410
- **Average temperature low/high in Santa Barbara** Jan 42/65°F, Jul 57/77°F
- **Los Angeles to Santa Barbara** 95 miles, 1¾ to 2½ hours
- **Monterey to San Luis Obispo** 140 miles, 2½ to three hours
- **San Francisco to Santa Cruz** 75 miles, 1½ to two hours

MYSTERY SPOT

A kitschy, old-fashioned tourist trap, Santa Cruz's **Mystery Spot** (☎831-423-8897; www.mysteryspot.com; 465 Mystery Spot Rd; admission $5, parking $5; ⏰10am-6pm Sun-Thu & 9am-7pm Fri & Sat late May-early Sep, 10am-4pm Sun-Thu & 10am-5pm Fri & Sat early Sep-late May; 👪) has scarcely changed since it opened in 1940. On a steeply sloping hillside, compasses seem to point crazily, mysterious forces push you around and buildings lean at odd angles. Make reservations, or risk being stuck waiting for a tour. It's 3 miles north of downtown: take Water St to Market St, turn left and continue on Branciforte Dr into the hills.

in 1965 in the hills above town, this youthful university is known for its creative, liberal bent. The rural campus has fine stands of redwoods and architecturally interesting buildings – some made with recycled materials – designed to blend in with rolling pastureland. Peruse two top-notch art galleries, a peaceful **arboretum** (http://arboretum.ucsc.edu/; 1156 High St; adult/child 6-17yr $5/2, free 1st Tue of the month; ⏰9am-5pm) and picturesquely decaying 19th-century structures from Cowell Ranch, upon which the campus was built.

Santa Cruz Museum of Natural History MUSEUM
(Map p458; www.santacruzmuseums.org; 1305 E Cliff Dr; adult/child under 18yr $4/free; ⏰10am-5pm Wed-Sun late May-early Sep, 10am-5pm Tue-Sat early Sep-late May; 👪) The collections at this pint-sized museum include cultural artifacts from Ohlone tribespeople and a touch-friendly tidepool that shows off sea critters living along the beach right across the street.

Museum of Art & History MUSEUM
(Map p454; www.santacruzmah.org; McPherson Center, 705 Front St; adult/child 12-17yr $5/2; ⏰11am-5pm Tue-Sun, to 9pm 1st Fri of the month) Downtown, this smart little museum is worth a look for its rotating displays by contemporary California artists and exhibits exploring offbeat local history.

Beaches

Sun-kissed Santa Cruz has warmer beaches than often-foggy Monterey. *Baywatch* it isn't, but 29 miles of coastline reveal a few Hawaii-worthy beaches, craggy coves, some primo surf spots and big sandy stretches where your kids will have a blast. Too bad fog ruins many a summer morning; it often burns off by the afternoon.

West Cliff Dr is lined with scramble-down-to coves and plentiful parking. If you don't want sand in your shoes, park yourself on a bench and watch enormous pelicans dive for fish. You'll find bathrooms and showers at the lighthouse parking lot.

Locals favor less-trampled **East Cliff Dr** beaches, which are bigger and more protected from the wind, meaning calmer waters. Except at a small metered lot at 26th Ave, parking is by permit only on weekends (buy a $7 per day permit at 9th Ave).

Less crowded **state beaches** (www.parks.ca.gov; per car $10; ⏰8am-sunset) await off Hwy 1 southbound. In Aptos, **Seacliff State Beach** (☎831-685-6442) harbors a 'cement boat,' a quixotic freighter built of concrete that floated OK, but ended up here as a coastal fishing pier. Further south near Watsonville, the La Selva Beach exit off Hwy 1 leads to **Manresa State Beach** (☎831-761-1975) and **Sunset State Beach** (☎831-763-7062), for miles of sand and surf practically all to yourself.

Activities

Surfing

Year-round, water temperatures average less than 60°F, meaning that without a wetsuit, body parts quickly turn blue. Surfing is incredibly popular, especially at experts-only **Steamer Lane** and beginners' **Cowell's**, both off West Cliff Dr. Other favorite surf spots include **Pleasure Point Beach**, on East Cliff Dr toward Capitola, and South County's **Manresa State Beach** off Hwy 1.

Santa Cruz Surf School SURFING
(Map p454; ☎831-426-7072; www.santacruzsurfschool.com; 322 Pacific Ave; 2hr lesson incl equipment rental $80-90) Wanna learn to surf? Near the wharf, friendly male and female instructors will have you standing and surfing on your first day out.

O'Neill Surf Shop SURFING
(Map p458; ☎831-475-4151; www.oneill.com; 1115 41st Ave; wetsuit/surfboard rental from $10/20; ⏰9am-8pm Mon-Fri, 8am-8pm Sat & Sun) Head east to Capitola to worship at this internationally renowned surfboard maker's flagship store. Also on the beach boardwalk and downtown.

Cowell's Beach Surf Shop SURFING
(Map p454; ☎831-427-2355; 30 Front St; 2hr lesson $80; ⊗8am-6pm;) Rent surfboards, boogie boards, wetsuits and other beach gear near the wharf, where veteran staff offer heaps of local tips and teach surfing too.

Kayaking

Kayaking lets you discover the craggy coastline and kelp beds where sea otters float.

Venture Quest KAYAKING
(Map p454; ☎831-427-2267; www.kayaksantacruz.com; Municipal Wharf; kayak rentals $30-100, tours $30-70;) Convenient rentals on the wharf, with whale-watching and sea-cave tours, including moonlight paddles.

Kayak Connection KAYAKING
(Map p458; ☎831-479-1121; www.kayakconnection.com; Santa Cruz Harbor, 413 Lake Ave; kayak rentals $35-50, tours & lessons $50-100;) Rents kayaks and offers lessons and tours, including sunrise, sunset and full-moon trips on Monterey Bay.

Whale-Watching & Fishing

Winter whale-watching trips run from December to April, though there's plenty of marine life to see on a summer bay cruise, too. Many fishing trips depart from the wharf, where a few shops rent fishing tackle and poles, if you're keen to join locals waiting patiently for a bite.

Stagnaro's CRUISES, TOURS
(☎800-979-3370; www.stagnaros.com) This longstanding tour operator offers scenic and sunset cruises around Monterey Bay (adult/child under 14 years from $20/13), whale-watching tours (adult/child under 14 years $45/31) and fishing trips (adult/child under 16 years from $50/40).

Festivals & Events

Woodies on the Wharf CULTURAL
(www.santacruzwoodies.com) A classic car show featuring vintage surf-style station wagons in late June.

Shakespeare Santa Cruz THEATER
(www.shakespearesantacruz.org) Damn good productions of the Bard at UCSC and in a redwood grove during July, August and September.

Open Studio Art Tour CULTURAL
(www.ccscc.org) Explore local artists' creative workshops over three weekends in October.

Sleeping

Santa Cruz does not have not enough beds to satisfy demand: expect outrageous prices at peak times for nothing-special rooms. Places near the boardwalk run the gamut from friendly to frightening. If you're looking for a straightforward motel, check out Ocean St further inland or Mission St (Hwy 1) near the UCSC campus.

TOP CHOICE **Dream Inn** BOUTIQUE HOTEL $$$
(Map p454; ☎831-426-4330, 866-774-7735; www.dreaminnsantacruz.com; 175 W Cliff Dr; r $200-380;) Overlooking the wharf from a spectacular hillside perch, this retro-chic boutique-on-the-cheap hotel is as stylish as Santa Cruz gets. Rooms have all mod cons, while the beach is just steps away. Don't miss happy hour at Aquarius restaurant's ocean-view bar.

DON'T MISS

TOP SANTA CRUZ BEACHES

» **Main Beach** *The* scene, with a huge sandy stretch, volleyball courts and swarms of people. Park on East Cliff Dr and walk across the *Lost Boys* trestle to the boardwalk.

» **Its Beach** The only official off-leash beach for dogs (before 10am and after 4pm) is just west of the lighthouse. The field across the street is another good romping ground.

» **Natural Bridges State Beach** Best for sunsets, this family favorite has lots of sand, tidepools and monarch butterflies from mid-October through late February. It's at the far end of West Cliff Dr; parking costs $10.

» **Twin Lakes State Beach** Big beach with bonfire pits and a lagoon, good for kids and often fairly empty. It's off East Cliff Dr around 7th Ave.

» **Moran Lake County Park** With a good surf break and bathrooms, this pretty all-around sandy spot is further east at 26th Ave off East Cliff Dr.

Santa Cruz

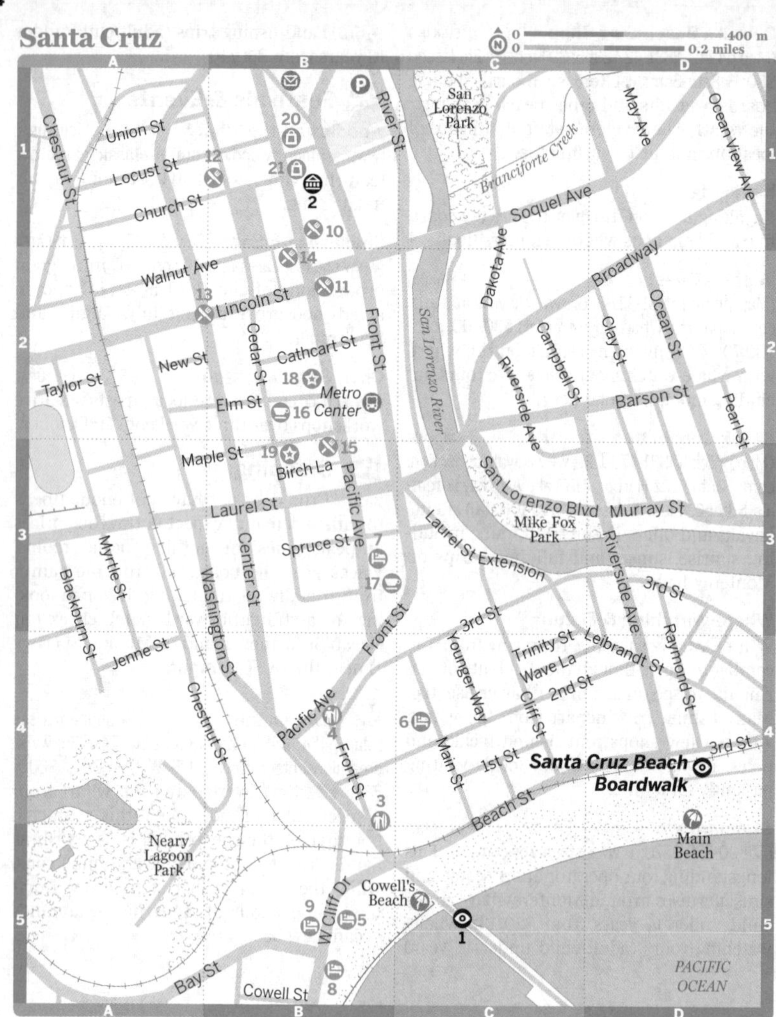

Adobe on Green B&B B&B $$
(Map p458; ☎831-469-9866; www.adobeongreen.com; 103 Green St; r incl breakfast $149-199; 📶) Peace and quiet are the mantras at this place, a short walk from Pacific Ave. The hosts are practically invisible, but their thoughtful touches are everywhere, from boutique-hotel amenities in spacious, stylish and solar-powered rooms to breakfast spreads from their organic gardens.

Pleasure Point Inn INN $$$
(Map p458; ☎831-475-4657; www.pleasurepointinn.com; 23665 E Cliff Dr; r incl breakfast $225-295; 📶) Live out your fantasy of California beachfront living in four clean-lined, contemporary rooms with hardwood floors, tiled bathrooms with Jacuzzi tubs, kitchenettes and private patios. Climb to the rooftop hot-tub deck for drop-dead ocean views.

Pacific Blue Inn B&B $$
(Map p454; ☎831-600-8880; http://pacificblueinn.com; 636 Pacific Ave; r incl breakfast $170-240; 📶) This downtown courtyard B&B is an eco-conscious gem, with water-saving fixtures and both renewable and recycled building materials. Refreshingly sleek rooms have

Santa Cruz

Top Sights
Santa Cruz Beach Boardwalk D4

Sights
1 Municipal Wharf C5
2 Museum of Art & History B1

Activities, Courses & Tours
3 Cowell's Beach Surf Shop B4
4 Santa Cruz Surf School B4
Venture Quest .... (see 1)

Sleeping
5 Dream Inn B5
6 HI Santa Cruz Hostel C4
7 Pacific Blue Inn B3
8 Sea & Sand Inn B5
9 West Cliff Inn B5

Eating
Bagelry .... (see 19)
10 El Palomar B1
11 New Leaf Community Market B2
12 Penny Ice Creamery B1
13 Santa Cruz Farmers Market A2
14 Soif B2
15 Zachary's B3

Drinking
16 Caffe Pergolesi B2
17 Firefly Coffee House B3
Surf City Billiards & Cafe .... (see 15)
Vino Prima .... (see 1)

Entertainment
18 Catalyst B2
19 Kuumbwa Jazz Center B3

Shopping
Annieglass .... (see 21)
20 Bookshop Santa Cruz B1
21 O'Neill Surf Shop B1

pillowtop beds, fireplaces and flat-screen TVs with DVD players. Free loaner bikes.

West Cliff Inn INN $$$
(Map p454; ☎831-457-2200; www.westcliffinn.com; 174 W Cliff Dr; r incl breakfast $175-400; 📶) In a classy Victorian house west of the wharf, this boutique inn's quaint rooms mix sea-grass wicker, dark wood and jaunty striped curtains. The most romantic suites have gas fireplaces and let you spy on the breaking surf.

Sea & Sand Inn MOTEL $$$
(Map p454; ☎831-427-3400; www.santacruzmotels.com; 201 W Cliff Dr; r $109-429; 📶) With a grassy lawn at the cliff's edge, this spiffy, if overpriced motel overlooks Main Beach and the wharf. Fall asleep to braying sea lions! Rooms are smallish, but ocean views can be stellar.

Pelican Point Inn INN $$
(Map p458; ☎831-475-3381; www.pelicanpointinn-santacruz.com; 21345 E Cliff Dr; ste $99-199; 👪) Ideal for families, these roomy apartments near a kid-friendly beach are equipped with everything you'll need for a lazy vacation, from kitchenettes to high-speed internet. Weekly rates available.

Sunny Cove Motel MOTEL $$
(Map p458; ☎831-475-1741; www.sunnycovemotel.com; 21610 E Cliff Dr; r $90-200; 🏊🐾) It's nothing fancy, but this tidy little hideaway east of downtown is a staunch budget fave. The long-time Santa Cruzian owner rents retro beach-house rooms and kitchenette suites.

HI Santa Cruz Hostel HOSTEL $
(Map p454; ☎831-423-8304; www.hi-santacruz.org; 321 Main St; dm $25-28, r $55-105, all with shared bath; ⏲check-in 5-10pm; @) Budget overnighters dig this cute hostel at the century-old Carmelita Cottages surrounded by flowering gardens, just two blocks from the beach. Cons: 11pm curfew, three-night maximum stay. Reservations essential.

State Park Campgrounds CAMPGROUND $
(☎reservations 800-444-7275; www.reserveamerica.com; tent & RV sites $35-50) Book well ahead to camp by the beaches and in the cool Santa Cruz Mountains. Terrific spots include Henry Cowell Redwoods and Big Basin Redwoods State Parks, in the redwood forests off Hwy 9 (see p459); New Brighton State Beach, near Capitola; and Manresa and Sunset State Beaches farther south off Hwy 1 (see p512).

Best Western Plus Capitola By-the-Sea Inn & Suites MOTEL $$
(Map p458; ☎831-477-0607; www.bestwesterncapitola.com; 1435 41st Ave; r incl breakfast $90-240; ❄@📶🏊👪) Dependable motel away from the beach. Impeccably clean rooms, spacious enough for families.

Mission Inn MOTEL $$
(Map p458; ☎831-425-5455, 800-895-5455; www.mission-inn.com; 2250 Mission St (Hwy 1); r incl breakfast $80-140;) Serviceable motel with a sauna and garden courtyard, near UCSC. Away from the beach.

Eating

Alas, Santa Cruz's food scene lacks luster. Downtown is chockablock with just-okay cafes. If you're looking for seafood, wander among the wharf's takeout counter joints. Mission St near UCSC and neighboring Capitola offer cheap, casual eats.

Soif BISTRO $$$
(Map p454; ☎831-423-2020; www.soifwine.com; 105 Walnut Ave; small plates $5-17, mains $19-28; ⊙5-10pm Sun-Thu, to 11pm Fri & Sat) Downtown is where bon vivants flock for a heady selection of 50 international wines by the glass, paired with a sophisticated, seasonally driven Euro-Cal menu. Expect tastebud-ticklers like wild arugula salad with roasted apricot and curry-honey vinaigrette or baby back ribs with coffee-barbecue sauce. Live music some nights.

Cellar Door CALIFORNIAN $$$
(Map p458; ☎831-425-6771; www.bonnydoonvineyard.com; 328 Ingalls St; small plates $5-22, prix-fixe dinner $25-40; ⊙noon-2pm Sat & Sun, 5:30-9pm Thu-Sun, community dinner 6:30pm Wed) At Bonny Doon Vineyard's tasting room, this hideaway cafe packs organic, biodynamic and seasonal farm-to-table goodness into tidy tapas plates and hosts barrel-tasting winemakers' dinners. Linger over a glass of whimsically named *Le Cigare Volant*, a wicked Rhone blend.

Engfer Pizza Works PIZZERIA $$
(Map p458; www.engferpizzaworks.com; 537 Seabright Ave; pizzas $8-23; ⊙4-9:30pm Tue-Sun;) Detour to find this old factory, where wood-fired oven pizzas are made from scratch with love – the no-name specialty is like a giant salad on roasted bread. Play ping-pong and down draft microbrews while you wait.

El Palomar MEXICAN $$
(Map p454; ☎831-425-7575; 1336 Pacific Ave; mains $7-27; ⊙11am-11pm;) Always packed and consistently good (if not great), El Palomar serves tasty Mexican staples – try the seafood *ceviches* – and fruity margaritas. Tortillas are made fresh by charming women in the covered courtyard.

Zachary's AMERICAN $
(Map p454; 819 Pacific Ave; mains $6-11; ⊙7am-2:30pm Tue-Sun) At the scruffy brunch spot that locals don't want you to know about, huge portions of sourdough pancakes and blueberry cream-cheese coffee cake will keep you going all day. 'Mike's Mess' is the kitchen-sink standout.

Tacos Moreno MEXICAN $
(Map p458; www.tacosmoreno.com; 1053 Water St; dishes $2-6; ⊙11am-8pm) Who cares how long the line is at lunchtime when every hungry surfer in town is here? Aficionados find taquería heaven, from marinated pork, chicken and beef soft tacos and quesadillas to supremely stuffed burritos.

Buttery BAKERY $
(Map p458; http://butterybakery.com; 702 Soquel Ave; snacks $4-8; ⊙7am-7pm;) For more than two decades, this bustling bakery has been baking such old-world confections as chocolate croissants and fruit tarts. Squeeze yourself into the corner cafe for deli sandwiches and soups.

Bagelry DELI $
(Map p454; 320a Cedar St; items $3-6; ⊙6:30am-5:30pm Mon-Fri, 7:30am-4:30pm Sat, 6:30am-4pm Sun;) The bagels here are twice-cooked (boiled, then baked), and come with fantastic crunchy spreads, like hummus and egg salad. Check out the bulletin board for community goings-on.

Penny Ice Creamery ICE CREAM $
(Map p454; http://thepennyicecreamery.com; 913 Cedar St; ice cream $2-4; ⊙noon-9pm Sun-Wed, to 11pm Thu-Sat) With a cult following, this artisan ice-cream shop makes its zany flavors, like avocado, cherry-balsamic or roasted barley, from scratch using local, organic and even wild ingredients.

Donnelly Fine Chocolates CANDY $
(Map p458; www.donnellychocolates.com; 1509 Mission St; candy $2-5; ⊙10:30am-6pm Tue-Fri, noon-6pm Sat & Sun) The Willy Wonka of Santa Cruz makes stratospherically priced chocolates on par with the big city. This guy is an alchemist! Try the cardamom truffles.

New Leaf Community Market GROCERIES $
(Map p454; www.newleaf.com; 1134 Pacific Ave; ⊙9am-9pm) Organic local produce, natural-foods groceries and deli take-out downtown.

Santa Cruz Farmers Market MARKET $

(Map p454; www.santacruzfarmersmarket.org; cnr Lincoln & Center Sts; 2:30-6:30pm Wed) For organic produce and an authentic taste of the local vibe.

Drinking

Downtown overflows with bars, hookah lounges and coffee shops.

Caffe Pergolesi CAFE

(Map p454; www.theperg.com; 418 Cedar St; 7am-11pm;) Discuss conspiracy theories over stalwart coffee, tea or beer at this way-popular landmark cafe in a Victorian house with a big ol' tree-shaded veranda overlooking the street. Local art hangs on the walls, with live musicians some evenings.

Santa Cruz Mountain Brewing BREWPUB

(Map p458; www.santacruzmountainbrewing.com; Swift Street Courtyard, 402 Ingalls St; noon-10pm) Bold organic brews are poured at this tiny brewpub, squeezed between Santa Cruz Mountains wine-tasting rooms just west of town off Mission St (Hwy 1). Oddest flavor? Olallieberry cream ale.

Vino Prima WINE BAR

(Map p454; www.vinoprimawines.com; Municipal Wharf; 2-8pm Mon-Tue, 2-10pm Wed-Fri, noon-10pm Sat, noon-8pm Sun) Near the far end of the wharf, with dreamy ocean views, this spot pours California boutique wines, including hard-to-find bottles from Santa Cruz and Monterey Counties.

Surf City Billiards & Cafe BAR

(Map p454; www.surfcitybilliards.com; 931 Pacific Ave; 4-11pm Mon-Thu, 4pm-1am Fri & Sat, 10am-11pm Sun) A relief from downtown's dive bars, this upstairs pool hall has Brunswick Gold Crown tables for shooting stick, pro dartboards, big-screen TVs and pretty good pub grub.

Verve Coffee Roasters CAFE

(Map p458; www.vervecoffeeroasters.com; 816 41st Ave; 6am-7:30pm Mon-Fri, 7am-8:30pm Sat, 7am-7:30pm Sun;) To sip freshly roasted artisan espresso, join the surfers and internet hipsters at this industrial-zen cafe. Single-origin brews and house-made blends rule.

Firefly Coffee House CAFE

(Map p454; 131 Front St; 5:30am-6pm Mon-Sat, 7am-2pm Sun;) Bohemian indoor/outdoor people's coffeeshop brews organic, fair-trade java and delish chai flavored with orange zest and an Indian bazaar's worth of spices.

Entertainment

Free weeklies *Metro Santa Cruz* (www.metrosantacruz.com) and *Good Times* (www.gtweekly.com) cover the music, arts and nightlife scenes.

Catalyst LIVE MUSIC

(Map p454; 831-423-1336; www.catalystclub.com; 1011 Pacific Ave) Over the years, this venue for local bands has seen big-time national acts perform, from Queens of the Stone Age to Snoop Dogg. When there's no music, hang in the upstairs bar and pool room.

Moe's Alley LIVE MUSIC

(Map p458; 831-479-1854; www.moesalley.com; 1535 Commercial Way; Tue-Sun) Hidden in an industrial wasteland, this casual place puts on live sounds almost every night, from jazz and blues to reggae, roots, salsa and acoustic world-music jams.

Kuumbwa Jazz Center LIVE MUSIC

(Map p454; 831-427-2227; www.kuumbwajazz.org; 320 Cedar St) Hosting jazz luminaries since 1975, this nonprofit theater is for serious jazz cats who come for the famous-name performers in an electrically intimate room.

Shopping

Wander Pacific Ave and downtown's side streets to find one-of-a-kind, locally owned boutiques (not just head shops, we promise).

Annieglass ART

(Map p454; www.annieglass.com; 110 Cooper St; 11am-6pm Mon-Sat, to 5pm Sun) Handcrafted sculptural glassware sold in ultrachic New York department stores and displayed in the Smithsonian American Art Museum are made right here in wackadoodle Santa Cruz. Go figure.

O'Neill Surf Shop SURFBOARDS, CLOTHING

(Map p454; www.oneills.com; 110 Cooper St; 10am-6pm) For Santa Cruz' own internationally popular brand of surf wear and gear, from hoodies to board shorts. Also on the beach boardwalk and in Capitola.

Bookshop Santa Cruz BOOKS

(Map p454; www.bookshopsantacruz.com; 1520 Pacific Ave; 9am-10pm Sun-Thu, to 11pm Fri & Sat) Vast selection of new books, a few used ones, and popular and unusual magazines. Buy 'Keep Santa Cruz Weird' bumper stickers here.

Around Santa Cruz

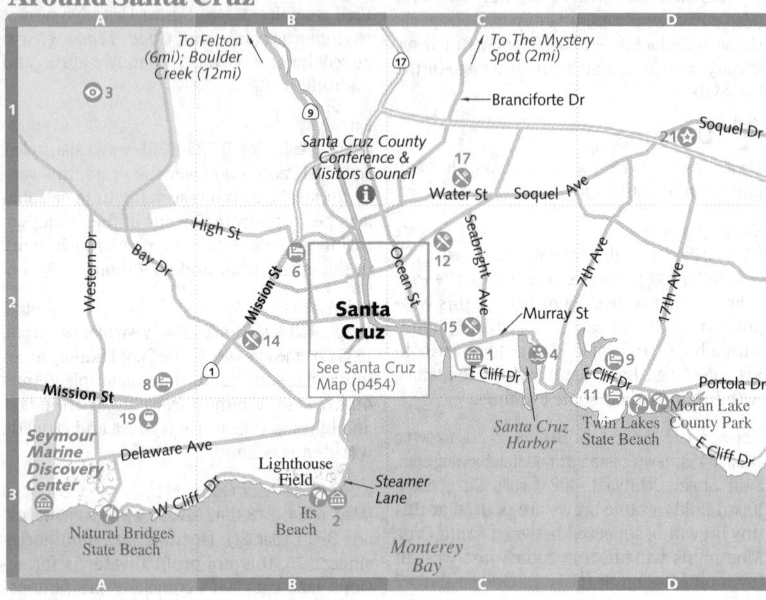

Around Santa Cruz

Top Sights
Seymour Marine Discovery Center....... A3

Sights
1 Santa Cruz Museum of Natural History C2
2 Santa Cruz Surfing Museum B3
3 University of California, Santa Cruz..... A1

Activities, Courses & Tours
4 Kayak Connection C2
5 O'Neill Surf Shop E2

Sleeping
6 Adobe on Green B&B B2
7 Best Western Plus Capitola By-the-Sea Inn & Suites E2
8 Mission Inn A2
9 Pelican Point Inn D2
10 Pleasure Point Inn E3
11 Sunny Cove Motel D2

Eating
12 Buttery C2
13 Dharma's E2
14 Donnelly Fine Chocolate B2
15 Engfer Pizza Works C2
16 Gayle's Bakery & Rosticceria E2
17 Tacos Moreno C1

Drinking
18 Mr Toots Coffeehouse E2
19 Santa Cruz Mountain Brewing A3
20 Verve Coffee Roasters E2

Entertainment
Cellar Door .... (see 19)
21 Moe's Alley D1

Information

FedEx Office (Map p454; 712 Front St; per min 20-30¢; ⏲24hr Mon-Thu, midnight-11pm Fri, 9am-9pm Sat, 9am-midnight Sun; @📶) Pay-as-you-go internet workstations and free wi-fi.

KPIG 107.5FM Plays the classic Santa Cruz soundtrack (think Bob Marley, Janis Joplin and Willie Nelson).

Post office (Map p454; www.usps.com; 850 Front St; ⏲9am-5pm Mon-Fri)

Public library (Map p454; www.santacruzpl.org; 224 Church St; ⏲10am-7pm Mon-Thu, 10am-5pm Sat, 1-5pm Sun; @📶) Free wi-fi and public internet terminals.

Santa Cruz County Conference & Visitors Council (Map p458; ☎831-425-1234; www.

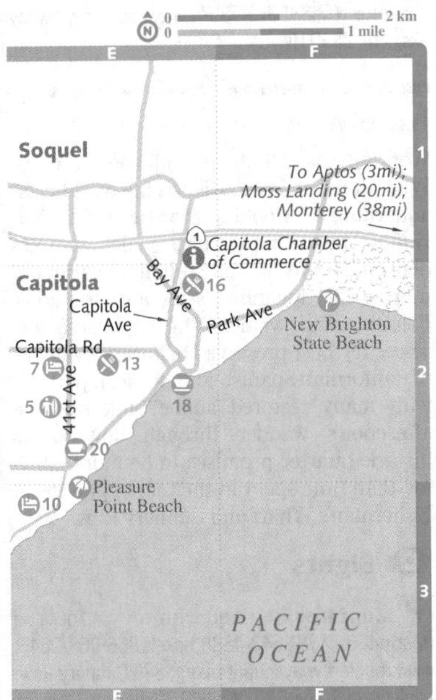

santacruzca.org; 1211 Ocean St; ⏲9am-5pm Mon-Fri, 10am-4pm Sat & Sun; @) Free brochures, maps and internet-terminal access.

Getting There & Around

Santa Cruz is 75 miles south of San Francisco via Hwy 17, a nail-bitingly narrow, winding mountain road. Monterey is about an hour's drive further south via Hwy 1.

Greyhound (www.greyhound.com; Metro Center, 920 Pacific St) has a few daily buses to San Francisco ($16, three hours), Salinas ($14, 65 minutes), Santa Barbara ($50, six hours) and Los Angeles ($57, nine hours).

Santa Cruz Metro (☎831-425-8600; www.scmtd.com; single-ride/day pass $1.50/4.50) operates local and countywide bus routes that converge on downtown's **Metro Center** (Map p454; 920 Pacific Ave). Frequent Hwy 17 express buses link Santa Cruz with San Jose's Amtrak/CalTrain station ($5, 50 minutes).

Santa Cruz Airport Shuttles (☎831-421-9883; http://santacruzshuttles.com) runs shared shuttles to/from the airports at San Jose ($45), San Francisco ($75) and Oakland ($75); prices are the same for one or two passengers (credit-card surcharge $5).

Around Santa Cruz

SANTA CRUZ MOUNTAINS

Winding between Santa Cruz and Silicon Valley, Hwy 9 is a 40-mile backwoods byway through the Santa Cruz Mountains, passing tiny towns, towering redwood forests and fog-kissed vineyards (estate-bottled pinot noir is a specialty). Many wineries are only open on 'Passport Days' on the third Saturday of January, April, July and November. The **Santa Cruz Mountains Winegrowers Association** (www.scmwa.com) publishes a free winery map, available at tasting rooms, including those that have relocated to Santa Cruz itself, west of downtown off Hwy 1.

Heading north from Santa Cruz, it's 7 miles to Felton, passing **Henry Cowell Redwoods State Park** (☎831-335-4598; www.parks.ca.gov; 101 N Big Trees Park Rd; per car $10; ⏲sunrise-sunset), which has miles of hiking trails through old-growth redwood groves and camping along the San Lorenzo River. In Felton, **Roaring Camp Railroads** (☎831-335-4484; www.roaringcamp.com; 5401 Graham Hill Rd; tours adult/child 2-12yr from $24/17, parking $8; ⏲call for schedules) operates narrow-gauge steam trains up into the redwoods and a standard-gauge train down to the Santa Cruz Beach Boardwalk (p451).

Seven miles further north on Hwy 9, you'll drive through the pretty town of **Boulder Creek**, a good place to grab a bite. Roadside **Boulder Creek Brewery & Cafe Company** (www.bouldercreekbrewery.net; 13040 Hwy 9; mains $7-15; ⏲11:30am-10pm Sun-Thu, to 10:30pm Fri & Sat) is a local institution.

Follow Hwy 236 northwest for nine twisting miles to **Big Basin Redwoods State Park** (☎831-338-8860; www.bigbasin.org, www.parks.ca.gov; 21600 Big Basin Way; per car $10), where nature trails loop past giant old-growth redwoods. A 12.5-mile one-way section of the exhilarating **Skyline to the Sea Trail** ends at Waddell Beach on the coast, almost 20 miles northwest of Santa Cruz. On weekends, if you check Santa Cruz Metro schedules carefully, you may be able to ride up to Big Basin on bus 35A in the morning and get picked up by bus 40 at the beach in the afternoon.

CAPITOLA

Six miles east of Santa Cruz, the little seaside town of Capitola, nestled quaintly between ocean bluffs, attracts affluent crowds and families. Downtown is laid out for strolling, with arty shops and touristy restaurants inside seaside houses. Show up for mid-September's **Capitola Art & Wine Festival**, or the famous **Begonia Festival**, held over Labor Day weekend, with a flotilla of floral floats along Soquel Creek.

Catch an organic, shade-grown and fairly traded caffeine buzz at **Mr Toots Coffeehouse** (Map p458; http://tootscoffee.com; 2nd fl, 231 Esplanade; 7am-10pm;), which has an art gallery and live music. Head inland to **Gayle's Bakery & Rosticceria** (Map p458; www.gaylesbakery.com; 504 Bay Ave; 6:30am-8:30pm;), with its fresh deli where you can assemble beach picnics, or **Dharma's** (Map p458; www.dharmaland.com; 4250 Capitola Rd; mains $7-14; 8am-9pm;), a global-fusion fast-food vegetarian and vegan restaurant.

The **Capitola Chamber of Commerce** (Map p458; 800-474-6522; www.capitolachamber.com; 716g Capitola Ave; 10am-4pm) offers travel tips. Driving downtown can be a nightmare in summer and on weekends; try the parking lot behind City Hall, off Capitola Ave by Riverview Dr.

MOSS LANDING & ELKHORN SLOUGH

Hwy 1 swings back toward the coast at Moss Landing, just south of the Santa Cruz County line, and almost 20 miles north of Monterey. From the working fishing harbor, **Sanctuary Cruises** (831-917-1042; www.sanctuarycruises.com; tours adult/child under 3yr/child 3-12yr $48/10/38) operates year-round whale-watching and dolphin-spotting cruises aboard biodiesel-fueled boats (reservations essential). Devour dock-fresh seafood down at warehouse-sized **Phil's Fish Market** (www.philsfishmarket.com; 7600 Sandholdt Rd; mains $10-20; 10am-8pm Sun-Thu, to 9pm Fri & Sat) or, after browsing the antiques shops, lunch at the **Haute Enchilada** (www.hauteenchilada.com; 7902 Moss Landing Rd; mains $11-26; 10am-8pm), an inspired Mexican restaurant inside a Frida Kahlo–esque art gallery.

Just east, **Elkhorn Slough National Estuarine Research Reserve** (831-728-2822; www.elkhornslough.org; 1700 Elkhorn Rd; adult/child under 16yr $2.50/free; 1700 Elkhorn Rd, Watsonville; 9am-5pm Wed-Sun) is popular with bird-watchers and hikers. Docent-led tours are typically offered at 10am and 1pm on Saturday and Sunday. Kayaking is a fantastic way to see the slough, though not on a windy day or when the tide is against you. Reserve ahead for kayak rentals ($35 to $70) or guided tours ($30 to $120) with **Kayak Connection** (831-724-5692; www.kayakconnection.com; 2370 Hwy 1) or **Monterey Bay Kayaks** (831-373-5357; www.montereybaykayaks.com; 2390 Hwy 1).

Monterey

Working-class Monterey is all about the sea. What draws many tourists is the world-class aquarium, overlooking **Monterey Bay National Marine Sanctuary**, which protects dense kelp forests and a sublime variety of marine life, including seals and sea lions, dolphins and whales. The city itself possesses the best-preserved historical evidence of California's Spanish and Mexican periods, with many restored adobe buildings. An afternoon's wander through downtown's historic quarter promises to be more edifying than time spent in the tourist ghettos of Fisherman's Wharf and Cannery Row.

Sights

Monterey Bay Aquarium AQUARIUM
(Map p466; 831-648-4888, tickets 866-963-9645; www.montereybayaquarium.org; 886 Cannery Row; adult/child 3-12yr $30/20; 9:30am-6pm Mon-Fri, 9:30am-8pm Sat & Sun Jun-Aug, 10am-5pm or 6pm daily Sep-May;) Monterey's most mesmerizing experience is its enormous aquarium, built on the former site of the city's largest sardine cannery. All kinds of aquatic creatures are on proud display, from kid-tolerant sea stars and slimy sea slugs to animated sea otters and surprisingly nimble 800lb tuna. The aquarium is much more than an impressive collection of glass tanks – thoughtful placards underscore the bay's cultural and historical contexts.

Every minute, upwards of 2000 gallons of seawater is pumped into the three-story **kelp forest**, re-creating as closely as possible the natural conditions you see out the windows to the east. The large fish of prey are at their charismatic best during mealtimes; divers hand-feed at 11:30am and 4pm. More entertaining are the sea otters, which may be seen basking in the **Great Tide Pool** outside the aquarium, where they are readied for reintroduction to the wild.

Even new-agey music and the occasional infinity-mirror illusion don't detract from the astounding beauty of jellyfish in the **Jellies Gallery**. To see fish – including hammerhead sharks and green sea turtles – that outweigh kids many times over, ponder the awesome **Open Sea** tank. Upstairs and downstairs you'll find **touch pools**, where you can get close to sea cucumbers, bat rays and tidepool creatures. Younger kids will love the interactive, bilingual **Splash Zone**, with penguin feedings at 10:30am and 3pm.

A visit can easily become a full-day affair, so get your hand stamped and break for lunch. To avoid long lines in summer and on weekends and holidays, buy tickets in advance. Metered on-street parking is limited, but parking lots and garages offering daily rates are plentiful uphill from Cannery Row.

Cannery Row HISTORIC SITE

(Map p466) John Steinbeck's novel *Cannery Row* immortalized the sardine-canning business that was Monterey's lifeblood for the first half of the 20th century. Back in Steinbeck's day, it was a stinky, hardscrabble, working-class melting pot, which the novelist described as 'a poem, a stink, a grating noise, a quality of light, a tone, a habit, a nostalgia, a dream.' Sadly, there's precious little evidence of that era now. Overfishing and climatic changes caused the industry's collapse in the 1950s.

A bronze **bust** of the Pulitzer Prize–winning writer sits at the bottom of Prescott Ave, just steps from the unabashedly commercial experience his row has devolved into, chockablock with chain restaurants and souvenir shops hawking saltwater taffy. Check out the **Cannery Workers Shacks** at the base of flowery Bruce Ariss Way, which have sobering explanations of the hard lives led by the Filipino, Japanese, Spanish and other immigrant laborers.

Monterey State Historic Park HISTORIC SITE

(☎cellphone audiotour 831-998-9458; www.parks.ca.gov) Old Monterey is home to an extraordinary assemblage of 19th-century brick and adobe buildings, administered as Monterey State Historic Park, all found along a 2-mile self-guided walking tour portentously called the Path of History. You can inspect dozens of buildings, many with charming gardens; expect some to be open while others aren't, according to a capricious schedule dictated by severe state-park budget cutbacks.

Pacific House Museum

(Map p466; ☎831-649-7118; 20 Custom House Plaza; donations welcome; ⏲10am-4:30pm) Grab a free map, find out what's currently open and buy guided tour tickets for individual historic houses inside this 1847 adobe building, which has in-depth exhibits covering the state's multinational history. Nearby are a few more of the park's highlights, including an **old whaling station**, California's first **theater** and a short walk further afield, the **old Monterey jail** featured in John Steinbeck's novel *Tortilla Flat*.

Custom House

(Map p466; Custom House Plaza; ⏲10am-4pm Sat & Sun) In 1822 newly independent Mexico ended the Spanish trade monopoly and stipulated that any traders bringing goods to Alta California must first unload their cargoes here for duty to be assessed. In 1846 when the US flag was raised over the Custom House, *voilà!* California was formally annexed from Mexico. Restored to its 1840s appearance, today the house displays an exotic selection of goods that traders brought to exchange for California cowhides.

Casa Soberanes

(Map p466; 336 Pacific St) A beautiful garden with meandering walkways paved with abalone shells, bottle glass and even whalebones fronts, this adobe house was built in the 1840s during the late Mexican period. The interior is adorned with an eclectic mix of New England antiques, 19th-century goods imported on Chinese trading ships and modern Mexican folk art. Opening hours vary.

Across Pacific St, the large and colorful **Monterey Mural**, a contemporary mosaic on the exterior of the Monterey Conference Center, illustrates the city's history.

Stevenson House

(Map p466; 530 Houston St; ⏲1-4pm Sat) Scottish writer Robert Louis Stevenson came to Monterey in 1879 to court his wife-to-be, Fanny Osbourne. This building, then the French Hotel, was where he stayed while reputedly devising his novel *Treasure Island*. The boarding-house rooms were primitive and Stevenson was still a penniless unknown. Today the house displays a superb collection of the writer's memorabilia.

Cooper-Molera Adobe

(Map p466; 525 Polk St; ⏲store 10am-4pm daily, to 5pm May-Sep, tour schedules vary) In 1827, this stately adobe home was built by John Rogers Cooper, a New England sea captain, and three generations of his family resided here until 1968. Over time, the adobe buildings were partitioned and expanded, gardens were added, and it was later willed to the National Trust. Worth a browse, the bookshop also sells nostalgic toys and household goods.

Monterey Peninsula

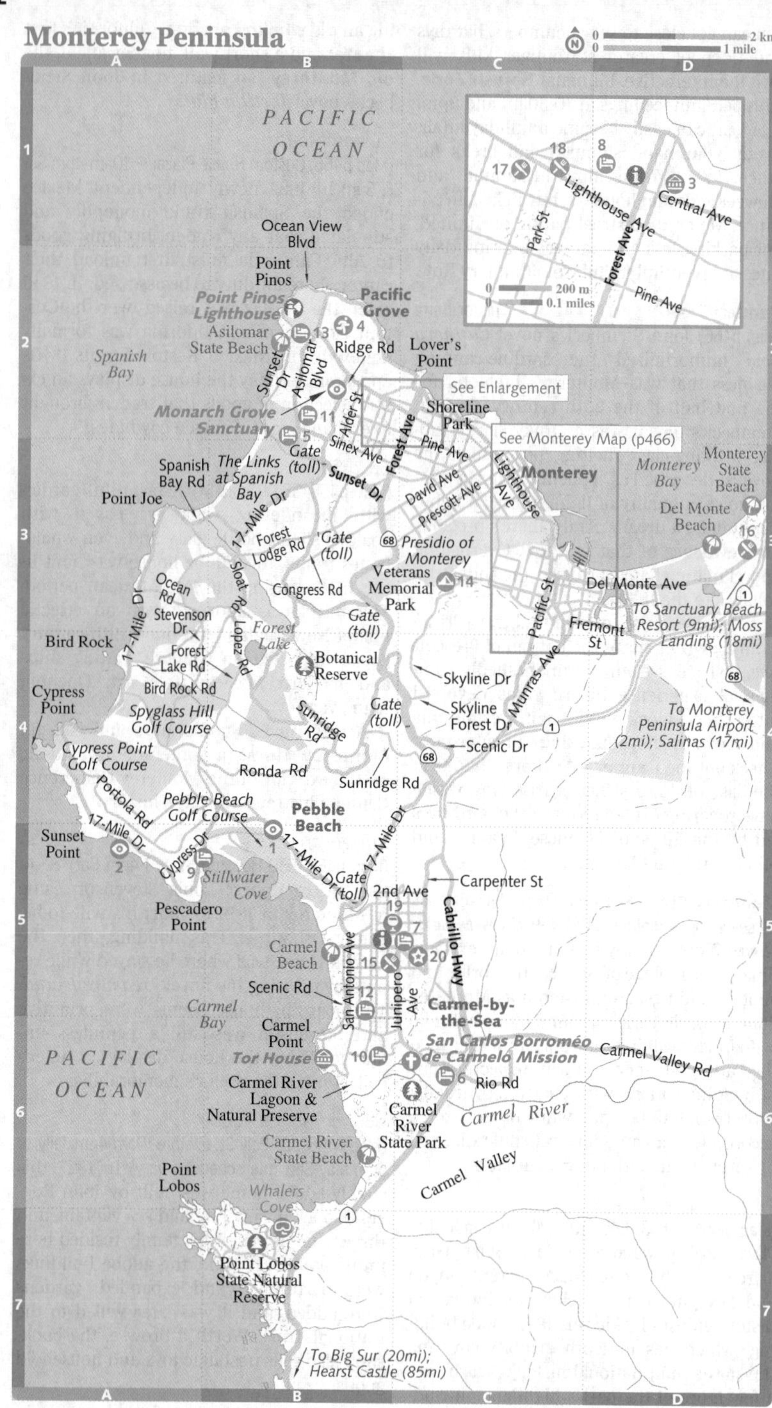

Monterey Peninsula

Top Sights

Monarch Grove Sanctuary	B2
Point Pinos Lighthouse	B2
San Carlos Borroméo de Carmelo Mission	C6
Tor House	B6

Sights

1 17-Mile Drive	B5
2 Lone Cypress	A5
3 Museum of Natural History	D1

Activities, Courses & Tours

4 Pacific Grove Golf Links	B2

Sleeping

5 Asilomar Conference Grounds	B2
6 Carmel River Inn	C6
7 Carmel Village Inn	C5
8 Centrella Inn	D1
9 Lodge at Pebble Beach	A5
10 Mission Ranch	B6
11 Pacific Gardens Inn	B2
12 Sea View Inn	B5
13 Sunset Inn Hotel	B2
14 Veterans Memorial Park Campground	C3

Eating

Bruno's Market & Deli	(see 7)
Carmel Belle	(see 15)
15 La Bicyclette	B5
16 Monterey's Fish House	D3
Mundaka	(see 15)
17 Passionfish	C1
18 Red House Cafe	C1

Drinking

19 Jack London's	B5

Entertainment

20 Forest Theater	C5

Monterey History & Maritime Museum MUSEUM
(Map p466; ☎831-372-2608; http://montereyhistory.org; 5 Custom House Plaza; admission $5, free after 3pm on 1st Tue of the month; ⏲10am-5pm Tue-Sun) Near the waterfront, this voluminous modern exhibition hall illuminates Monterey's salty past, from early Spanish explorers to the roller-coaster–like rise and fall of the local sardine industry that brought Cannery Row to life in the mid-20th century. Highlights include a ship-in-a-bottle collection and the historic Fresnel lens from Point Sur Lightstation.

Monterey Museum of Art MUSEUM
(MMA; www.montereyart.org; adult/child under 13 $10/free; ⏲11am-5pm Wed-Sat & 1-4pm Sun) Downtown, **MMA Pacific Street** (Map p466; ☎831-372-5477; 559 Pacific St) is particularly strong in California contemporary art and modern landscape painters and photographers, including Ansel Adams and Edward Weston. Temporary exhibits fill **MMA La Mirada** (Map p466; ☎831-372-3689; 720 Via Mirada), a silent-film-star's villa, whose humble adobe origins are exquisitely concealed. Visit both locations on the same ticket.

Royal Presidio Chapel CHURCH
(Map p466; www.sancarloscathedral.net; San Carlos Cathedral, 500 Church St; admission by donation; ⏲10am-noon Wed, 10am-3pm Fri, 10am-2pm Sat, 1-3pm Sun, also 10am-noon & 1:15-3:15pm 2nd & 4th Mon of the month) Built of sandstone in 1794, this graceful chapel is California's oldest continuously functioning church. The original 1770 mission church stood here before being moved to Carmel. As Monterey expanded under Mexican rule in the 1820s, older buildings were gradually destroyed, leaving behind this National Historic Landmark as the strongest reminder of the defeated Spanish colonial presence.

FREE **Presidio of Monterey Museum** MUSEUM
(Map p466; www.monterey.org; Bldg 113, Corporal Ewing Rd; ⏲10am-1pm Mon, 10am-4pm Thu-Sat, 1-4pm Sun) On the grounds of the original Spanish fort, this minor museum treats Monterey's history from a military perspective, looking at the Native American, Mexican and American periods.

Activities

Like its larger namesake in San Francisco, **Fisherman's Wharf** is a tacky tourist trap at heart, and a jumping-off point for deep-sea fishing trips. On the flip side, the authentic **Municipal Wharf II** is a short walk east. There fishing boats bob and sway, painters work on their canvases and seafood purveyors hawk fresh catches.

FREE **Dennis the Menace Park** PLAYGROUND
(Map p466; 777 Pearl St; ⌚10am-dusk, closed Tue Sep-May;) A must for fans of kick-ass playgrounds, this park was the brainchild of Hank Ketcham, the creator of the classic comic strip. This ain't your standard dumbed-down playground, suffocated by Big Brother's safety regulations. With lightning-fast slides, a hedge maze and towering climbing walls, even some adults can't resist playing here.

Cycling & Mountain-Biking

Along a former railway line, the **Monterey Peninsula Recreational Trail** travels 18 car-free miles along the waterfront, passing Cannery Row en route to Lovers Point in Pacific Grove. Road-cycling enthusiasts with nerves of steel can make the round trip to Carmel along the **17-Mile Drive** (see the boxed text, p471). Mountain-bikers head to **Fort Ord** for 50 miles of single-track and fire roads; the **Sea Otter Classic** (www.seaotterclassic.com) races there in mid-April.

Adventures by the Sea CYCLING
(Map p466; ☎831-372-1807; www.adventuresbythesea.com; 299 Cannery Row; rental per hr/day $7/25) Beach cruiser and hybrid mountain-bike rentals on Cannery Row and **downtown** (210 Alvarado St).

Bay Bikes CYCLING
(Map p466; ☎831-655-2453; www.baybikes.com; 585 Cannery Row; per hr/day from $8/32) Cruiser, tandem, hybrid and mountain bike rentals near the aquarium.

Whale-Watching

You can spot whales off the coast of Monterey Bay year-round. The season for blue and humpback whales runs from late April to early December, while gray whales pass by from mid-December to mid-April. Tour boats depart from downtown's Fisherman's Wharf and also Moss Landing (see p460). Reserve trips at least a day in advance; be prepared for a bumpy, cold ride.

Monterey Whale Watching BOAT TOURS
(Map p466; ☎831-372-2203, tickets 800-979-3370; www.montereywhalewatching.com; 96 Fisherman's Wharf; 2½hr tour adult/child 3-12yr $40/30) Several daily departures.

Monterey Bay Whale Watch BOAT TOURS
(Map p466; ☎831-375-4658; www.montereybaywhalewatch.com; 84 Fisherman's Wharf; 2½hr tour adult/child 4-12yr from $38/27) Morning and afternoon departures.

Diving & Snorkeling

Monterey Bay offers world-renowned diving and snorkeling, including off **Lovers Point** in Pacific Grove and at **Point Lobos State Natural Reserve** near Carmel-by-the-Sea. You'll want a wetsuit year-round. In summer upwelling currents carry cold water from the deep canyon below the bay, sending a rich supply of nutrients up toward the surface level to feed the bay's diverse marine life. These frigid currents also account for the bay's chilly water temperatures and summer fog that blankets the peninsula.

Monterey Bay Dive Charters SCUBA DIVING
(☎831-383-9276; www.mbdcscuba.com; scuba rental per day $79-89, shore/boat dive from $49/199) Rent a full scuba kit with wetsuit, arrange small-group shore or boat dives or take a virgin undersea plunge by booking a three-hour beginners' dive experience ($159, no PADI certification required).

Kayaking & Surfing

Monterey Bay Kayaks KAYAKING
(Map p466; ☎800-649-5357; www.montereybaykayaks.com; 693 Del Monte Ave; rental per day $30-50, tours adult/child from $50/40;) Rents kayaks and stand-up paddle boarding (SUP) equipment and leads kayaking lessons and guided tours of Monterey Bay, including full-moon, sunrise and sunset trips, and family adventures.

Sunshine Freestyle Surf SURFING
(Map p466; ☎831-375-5015; http://sunshinefreestyle.com; 443 Lighthouse Ave; rental per half/full day surfboard $20/30, wetsuit $10/15, boogie board $7/10) Monterey's oldest surf shop rents and sells all the gear you'll need. Staff grudgingly dole out tips.

Festivals & Events

AT&T Pebble Beach National Pro-Am GOLF
(www.attpbgolf.com) Famous golf tournament mixes pros with celebrities; in early February.

Castroville Artichoke Festival FOOD
(www.artichoke-festival.org) North of Monterey, features 3D 'agro art' sculptures, cooking demos, a farmers market and field tours; in mid-May.

Strawberry Festival at Monterey Bay FOOD

(www.mbsf.com) Berry-licious pie-eating contests and live bands in Watsonville, north of Monterey, in early August.

Concours d'Elegance STREET

(www.pebblebeachconcours.net) Classic cars roll onto the fairways at Pebble Beach in mid-August.

Monterey County Fair CULTURE

(www.montereycountyfair.com) Old-fashioned fun, carnival rides, horse-riding and livestock competitions, wine tasting and live music in late August and early September.

TOP CHOICE **Monterey Jazz Festival** MUSIC

(www.montereyjazzfestival.org) One of the world's longest-running jazz festivals (since 1958), held in mid-September.

Sleeping

Book ahead for special events and summer visits. To avoid the tourist congestion and jacked-up prices of Cannery Row, consider staying in Pacific Grove (p470). Cheaper chain and indie motels line Munras Ave, south of downtown, and N Fremont St, east of Hwy 1.

InterContinental–The Clement HOTEL $$$

(Map p466; ☎831-375-4500, 888-424-6835; www.intercontinental.com; 750 Cannery Row; r $200-455; ❄@📶🏊👪) Like an upscale version of a New England millionaire's seaside compound, this all-encompassing resort presides over Cannery Row. For the utmost luxury and romance, book an ocean-view suite with a balcony and private fireplace, then breakfast in bayfront C Restaurant downstairs. Parking $18.

Sanctuary Beach Resort HOTEL $$$

(☎831-883-9478, 877-944-3863; www.thesanctuarybeachresort.com; 3295 Dunes Dr, Marina; r $179-329; ❄@📶🏊👪) Be lulled to sleep by the surf at this low-lying retreat hidden in the sand dunes north of Monterey. Townhouses harbor petite rooms with gas fireplaces and binoculars to borrow for whale-watching. The beach is an off-limits nature preserve, but there are plenty of other beaches and walking trails nearby.

Jabberwock B&B $$$

(Map p466; ☎831-372-4777, 888-428-7253; www.jabberwockinn.com; 598 Laine St; r incl breakfast $169-309; @📶) High atop a hill and barely visible through a shroud of foliage, this 1911 Arts and Crafts house hums a playful *Alice in Wonderland* tune through its seven immaculate rooms. Over afternoon tea and cookies or evening wine and hors d'oeuvres, ask the genial hosts about the house's many salvaged architectural elements.

Casa Munras BOUTIQUE HOTEL $$

(Map p466; ☎831-375-2411; www.hotelcasamunras.com; 700 Munras Ave; r $185-279; @📶🏊🐾) Built around an adobe hacienda once owned by a 19th-century Spanish colonial don, chic modern rooms come with lofty beds and some gas fireplaces, all inside two-story motel-esque buildings. Splash in a heated outdoor pool, unwind at the tapas bar or take a sea-salt scrub in the tiny spa. Pet fee $50.

Hotel Abrego BOUTIQUE HOTEL $$

(Map p466; ☎831-372-7551; www.hotelabrego.com; 755 Abrego St; r $140-270; 📶🏊🐾) Another downtown boutique hotel, albeit with slightly fewer amenities, where most of the spacious, clean-lined contemporary rooms have gas fireplaces and chaise longues. Take a dip in the outdoor pool or warm up in the hot tub. Pet fee $30.

Monterey Hotel HISTORIC HOTEL $$

(Map p466; ☎831-375-3184, 800-966-6490; www.montereyhotel.com; 406 Alvarado St; r $70-310; 📶) In the heart of downtown and a short walk from Fisherman's Wharf, this 1904 edifice harbors five dozen small, somewhat noisy, but freshly renovated rooms with Victorian-styled furniture and plantation shutters. No elevator. Parking $17.

Colton Inn MOTEL $$

(Map p466; ☎831-649-6500; www.coltoninn.com; 707 Pacific St; r $109-199; ❄📶) Downtown, this champ of a motel prides itself on cleanliness and friendliness. There's no pool and zero view, but staff loan out DVDs, some rooms have real log-burning fireplaces, hot tubs or kitchenettes, and there's even a dry sauna for guests.

HI Monterey Hostel HOSTEL $

(Map p466; ☎831-649-0375; www.montereyhostel.org; 778 Hawthorne St; dm $25-28, r $59-75, all with shared bath; ⊙check-in 4-10pm; @) Four blocks from Cannery Row and the aquarium, this simple, clean hostel lets budget backpackers stuff themselves silly with make-your-own waffle breakfasts. Reservations strongly

Monterey

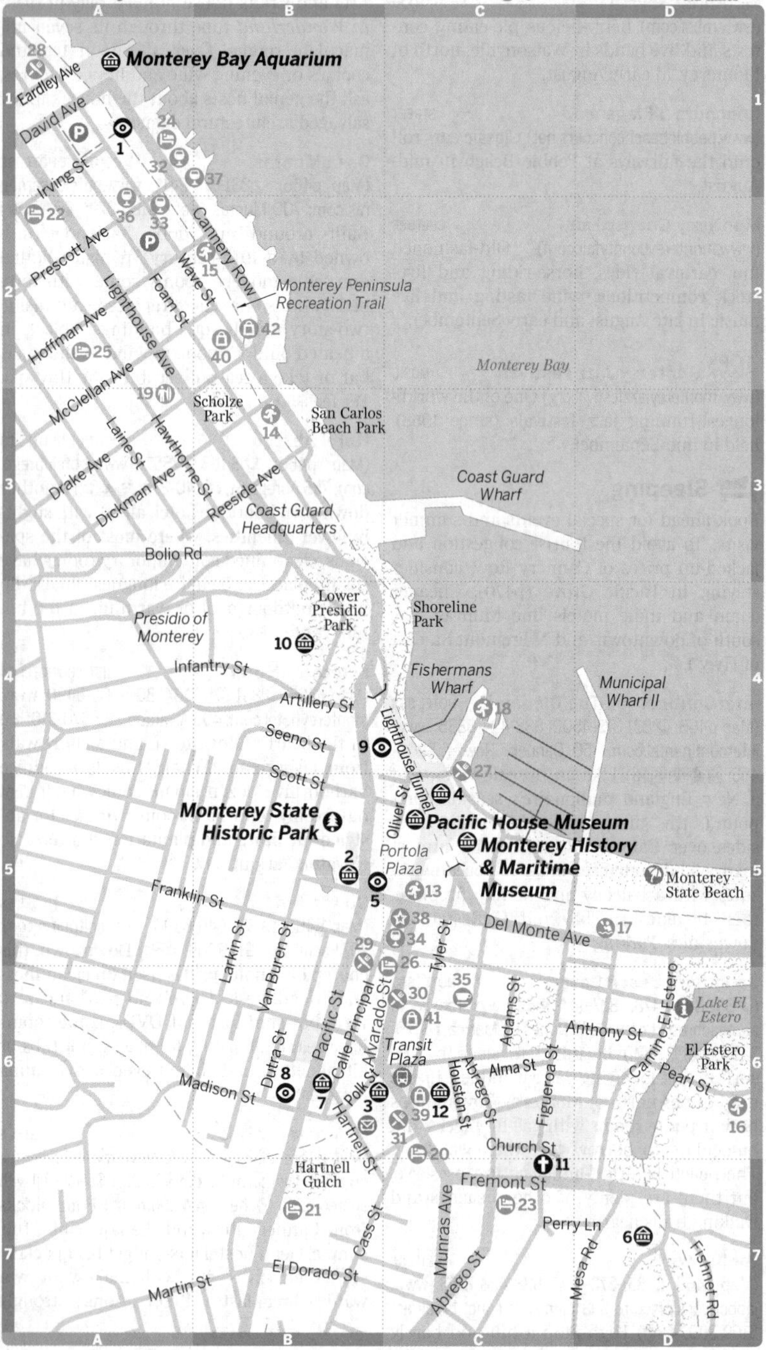

0 400 m
0 0.2 miles

A B C D
1 2 3 4 5 6 7

Monterey Bay Aquarium
28
Eardley Ave
David Ave
1
24
32
37
Irving St
22
36
33
Prescott Ave
Cannery Row
15
Wave St
Foam St
Lighthouse Ave
Monterey Peninsula Recreation Trail
Hoffman Ave
25
42
40
McClellan Ave
19
Scholze Park
San Carlos Beach Park
14
Monterey Bay
Laine St
Hawthorne St
Drake Ave
Dickman Ave
Reeside Ave
Coast Guard Wharf
Coast Guard Headquarters
Bolio Rd
Lower Presidio Park
Shoreline Park
Presidio of Monterey
10
Infantry St
Fishermans Wharf
Municipal Wharf II
18
Artillery St
Lighthouse Tunnel
Seeno St
9
27
Scott St
4
Oliver St
Monterey State Historic Park
Pacific House Museum
Monterey History & Maritime Museum
Portola Plaza
2
5
13
Monterey State Beach
Franklin St
38
Del Monte Ave
17
34
Larkin St
Van Buren St
29
26
Tyler St
35
30
Adams St
Camino El Estero
Lake El Estero
Pacific St
Calle Principal
Alvarado St
41
Anthony St
Transit Plaza
Dutra St
El Estero Park
8
7
Polk St
3
Houston St
Abrego St
Alma St
Figueroa St
Pearl St
Madison St
39
12
16
Hartnell St
31
Church St
20
11
Hartnell Gulch
Fremont St
21
23
Cass St
Munras Ave
Perry Ln
6
Mesa Rd
Fishnet Rd
El Dorado St
Abrego St
Martin St

Monterey

Top Sights
Monterey Bay Aquarium........................A1
Monterey History & Maritime Museum...........C5
Monterey State Historic Park.................B5
Pacific House Museum.........................C5

Sights
1 Cannery Row Workers' Shacks.................A1
2 Casa Soberanes..............................B5
3 Cooper-Molera Adobe.........................B6
4 Custom House................................C5
5 Monterey Conference Center..................B5
Monterey Mural..........................(see 5)
6 Monterey Museum of Art (MMA) La Mirada......D7
7 Monterey Museum of Art (MMA) Pacific Street.B6
8 Old Monterey Jail...........................B6
9 Old Whaling Station.........................B4
10 Presidio of Monterey Museum................B4
11 Royal Presidio Chapel......................C7
12 Stevenson House............................C6

Activities, Courses & Tours
13 Adventures by the Sea......................C5
14 Adventures by the Sea......................B3
15 Bay Bikes..................................B2
16 Dennis the Menace Park.....................D6
17 Monterey Bay Kayaks........................D5
Monterey Bay Whale Watch...............(see 18)
18 Monterey Whale Watching....................C4
19 Sunshine Freestyle Surf....................A3

Sleeping
20 Casa Munras................................C6
21 Colton Inn.................................B7
22 HI Monterey Hostel.........................A2
23 Hotel Abrego...............................C7
24 InterContinental - The Clement.............A1
25 Jabberwock.................................A2
26 Monterey Hotel.............................C5

Eating
27 Crêpes of Brittany.........................C4
28 First Awakenings...........................A1
29 Montrio Bistro.............................B5
30 Old Monterey Marketplace...................C6
31 RG Burgers.................................C6

Drinking
32 A Taste of Monterey........................A1
33 Cannery Row Brewing Co....................A2
34 Crown & Anchor.............................C5
35 East Village Coffee Lounge.................C6
36 Sardine Factory............................A2
37 Sly McFly's Fueling Station................B1

Entertainment
38 Osio Cinemas...............................C5

Shopping
39 Book Haven.................................C6
40 Cannery Row Antique Mall...................B2
41 Luna Blu...................................C6
42 Monterey Peninsula Art Foundation Gallery..B2

recommended. Take MST bus 1 from downtown's Transit Plaza.

Veterans Memorial Park CAMPGROUND $
(Map p462; ☎831-646-3865; www.monterey.org; Veterans Memorial Park, off Skyline Dr; tent & RV sites $25-30) Tucked into the forest, this municipal campground has 40 well-kept, grassy, nonreservable sites near nature-preserve hiking trails. Amenities include coin-op hot showers, flush toilets, drinking water, firepits and BBQ picnic areas. Three-night maximum stay.

Eating

Uphill from Cannery Row, Lighthouse Ave is lined with budget-friendly, multiethnic eateries, from Japanese sushi to Hawaiian barbecue to Middle Eastern kebabs. Alternatively, keep going west to Pacific Grove (p470).

First Awakenings BRUNCH $
(Map p466; www.firstawakenings.net; American Tin Cannery Mall, 125 Oceanview Blvd; mains $5-12; 7am-2pm Mon-Fri, to 2:30pm Sat & Sun;) Sweet and savory, all-American breakfasts and lunches and bottomless pitchers of coffee merrily weigh down outdoor tables at this hideaway cafe. Order creative dishes like 'bluegerm' pancakes or the spicy 'Viva Carnita' egg scramble.

Monterey's Fish House SEAFOOD $$$
(Map p462; ☎831-373-4647; 2114 Del Monte Ave; mains $12-35; 11:30am-2:30pm Mon-Fri, 5-9:30pm daily) Watched over by photos of Sicilian fishermen, dig into dock-fresh seafood with an occasional Asian twist. Reservations are essential (it's *so* crowded), but the vibe is island-casual: Hawaiian shirts seem to be de rigueur for men. Try the barbecued oysters

or, for those stout of heart, the Mexican squid steak.

Montrio Bistro CALIFORNIAN $$$
(Map p466; ☎831-648-8880; www.montrio.com; 414 Calle Principal; mains $14-29; ⏲5-10pm Sun-Thu, to 11pm Fri & Sat;) Inside a 1910 firehouse, Montrio looks dolled up with leather walls and iron trellises, but the tables have butcher paper and crayons for kids. The seasonal New American menu mixes local, organic fare with California flair, including tapas-style small bites.

RG Burgers DINER $
(Map p466; www.rgburgers.com; 570 Munras Ave; items $4-12; ⏲11am-8:30pm Sun-Thu, to 9pm Fri & Sat) Next to Trader Joe's supermarket, where you can stock up on trail mix and take-out salads, this locally owned burger shop slings beef, bison, turkey, chicken and veggie patties, sweet tater fries and thick milkshakes.

Old Monterey Marketplace FARMERS MARKET $
(Map p466; www.oldmonterey.org; Alvarado St, btwn Del Monte Ave & Pearl St; ⏲4-7pm Tue Sep-May, to 8pm Jun-Aug) Rain or shine, head downtown for farm-fresh fruit and veggies, artisan cheeses and baked goods, and multiethnic takeout.

Crêpes of Brittany SNACKS $
(Map p466; www.vivalecrepemonterey.com; 6 Old Fisherman's Wharf; snacks $4-9; ⏲8:30am-7pm Sun-Thu, 8:30am-8pm Sun) Find authentic savory and sweet crepes swirled by a French expat – the homemade caramel is a treat. Expect long lines on weekends. Hours are reduced in winter.

Drinking & Entertainment

Prowl downtown's Alvarado St, touristy Cannery Row and locals-only Lighthouse Ave for more watering holes. For comprehensive entertainment and nightlife listings, check the free tabloid *Monterey County Weekly* (www.montereycountyweekly.com).

A Taste of Monterey WINE BAR
(Map p466; www.atasteofmonterey.com; 700 Cannery Row; tasting fee $5-20; ⏲11am-6pm) Sample medal-winning Monterey County wines from as far away as the Santa Lucia Highlands while soaking up dreamy sea views, then peruse thoughtful exhibits on barrel-making and cork production.

East Village Coffee Lounge CAFE
(Map p466; www.eastvillagecoffeelounge.com; 498 Washington St; ⏲6am-late Mon-Fri, 7am-late Sat & Sun) Sleek coffeehouse on a busy downtown corner brews fair-trade, organic beans. At night, it pulls off a big-city lounge vibe with film, open-mic, live-music and DJ nights and an all-important booze license.

Cannery Row Brewing Co BREWPUB
(Map p466; www.canneryrowbrewingcompany.com; 95 Prescott Ave; ⏲11:30am-midnight Sun-Thu, to 2am Fri & Sat) Brews from around the world bring crowds to Cannery Row's microbrew bar, as does the enticing outdoor deck with roaring firepits. Decent brewpub menu of burgers, fries, salads, BBQ and more.

Crown & Anchor PUB
(Map p466; www.crownandanchor.net; 150 W Franklin St; ⏲11am-2am) Descend into the basement of this British pub and the first thing you'll notice is the red plaid carpeting. At least these blokes know their way around a bar, with plentiful draft beers and single-malt scotch, not to mention damn fine fish and chips.

Sly McFly's Fueling Station LIVE MUSIC
(Map p466; www.slymcflys.net; 700 Cannery Row; ⏲11:30am-2am) Rubbing shoulders with billiards halls, comedy shops and touristy restaurants, this waterfront dive shows live blues, jazz and rock bands nightly. Skip the food, though.

Sardine Factory LOUNGE
(Map p466; www.sardinefactory.com; 701 Wave St; ⏲5pm-midnight) The legendary restaurant's fireplace cocktail lounge pours wines by the glass, delivers filling appetizers to your table and features live piano some nights.

Osio Cinemas CINEMA
(Map p466; ☎831-644-8171; www.osiocinemas.com; 350 Alvarado St) Downtown cinema screens indie dramas, cutting-edge documentaries and offbeat Hollywood films. Drop by Cafe Lumiere for decadent cheesecakes and loose-leaf or bubble teas.

Shopping

Cannery Row is jammed with touristy shops, while downtown side streets hide one-of-a-kind finds.

Monterey Peninsula Art Foundation Gallery ART
(Map p466; www.mpaf.org; 425 Cannery Row; ⏲11am-5pm) Inside a cozy sea-view house, over two dozen local artists sell their plein-

air paintings and sketches, plus contemporary works in all media.

Cannery Row Antique Mall ANTIQUES
(Map p466; http://canneryrowantiquemall.com; 471 Wave St; ⌚10am-5:30pm) Inside a historic 1920s canning company building, two floors are stacked high with beguiling flotsam and jetsam from decades past.

Book Haven BOOKS
(Map p466; 559 Tyler St; ⌚10am-6pm Mon-Sat) Tall shelves of new and used books, including rare first editions and John Steinbeck titles.

Luna Blu CLOTHING
(Map p466; 176 Bonifacio Pl; ⌚11am-7pm Tue-Sat, to 5pm Sun & Mon) Vintage and name-brand consignment clothing, bags, and jaunty hats for women and men.

Information

Doctors on Duty (Map p466; ☎831-649-0770; http://doctorsonduty.com; 501 Lighthouse Ave; ⌚8am-8pm Mon-Sat, 8am-6pm Sun) Walk-in, nonemergency medical clinic.

FedEx Office (Map p466; www.fedex.com; 799 Lighthouse Ave; per min 20-30¢; ⌚7am-11pm Mon-Fri, 9am-9pm Sat & Sun; @📶) Pay-as-you-go internet workstations and free wi-fi.

Monterey County Convention & Visitors Bureau (Map p466; ☎831-657-6400, 877-666-8373; www.seemonterey.com; 401 Camino El Estero; ⌚9am-6pm Mon-Sat, to 5pm Sun) Ask for a free *Monterey County Film & Literary Map*. Closes one hour earlier November to March.

Post office (Map p466; www.usps.com; 565 Hartnell St; ⌚8:30am-5pm Mon-Fri, 10am-2pm Sat)

Public library (Map p466; www.monterey.org; 625 Pacific St; ⌚noon-8pm Mon-Wed, 10am-6pm Thu-Sat; @📶) Free wi-fi and public internet terminals.

Getting There & Around

A few miles east of downtown off Hwy 68, **Monterey Peninsula Airport** (MRY; www.montereyairport.com; 200 Fred Kane Dr, off Olmsted Rd) has flights with United (LA, San Francisco and Denver), American (LA), Allegiant Air (Las Vegas) and US Airways (Phoenix).

Monterey Airbus (☎831-373-7777; www.montereyairbus.com) links Monterey with airports in San Jose ($35, 90 minutes) and San Francisco ($45, 2¼ hours) almost a dozen times daily.

If you don't fly or drive to Monterey, first take a Greyhound bus or Amtrak train to Salinas, then catch a local Monterey-Salinas Transit bus (for details, see p490).

Monterey-Salinas Transit (☎888-678-2871; www.mst.org) operates local and regional buses; one-way fares cost $1 to $3 (day pass $8). Routes converge on downtown's **Transit Plaza** (Map p466; cnr Pearl & Alvarado Sts).

From late May until early September, MST's free **trolley** loops around downtown, Fisherman's Wharf and Cannery Row from 10am to 7pm daily.

Pacific Grove

Founded as a tranquil Methodist summer retreat in 1875, PG maintained a quaint, holier-than-thou attitude well into the 20th century – the selling of liquor was illegal up until 1969, making it California's last 'dry' town. Today, leafy streets are lined by stately Victorian homes. The charming, compact downtown orbits Lighthouse Ave.

Sights & Activities

Aptly named **Ocean View Blvd** affords views from Lover's Point west to Point Pinos, where it becomes **Sunset Dr**, offering tempting turnouts where you can stroll by pounding surf, rocky outcrops and teeming tidepools. This seaside route is great for cycling too. Some say it even rivals the famous 17-Mile Drive for beauty, and it's free.

Point Pinos Lighthouse LIGHTHOUSE
(Map p462; www.ci.pg.ca.us/lighthouse; off Asilomar Ave; adult/child $2/1; ⌚1-4pm Thu-Mon) On the tip of the Monterey Peninsula, the West Coast's oldest continuously operating lighthouse has been warning ships off this hazardous point since 1855. Inside are modest exhibits on the lighthouse's history and, alas, its failures – local shipwrecks.

FREE **Monarch Grove Sanctuary** PARK
(Map p462; www.ci.pg.ca.us/monarchs; off Ridge Rd, Pacific Grove; ⌚dawn-dusk) Between October and February, over 25,000 migratory monarch butterflies cluster in this thicket of tall eucalyptus trees, secreted inland from Lighthouse Ave. Volunteers are on hand to answer all of your questions.

Museum of Natural History MUSEUM
(Map p462; www.pgmuseum.org; 165 Forest Ave; suggested donation per person/family $3/5; ⌚10am-5pm Tue-Sat; 👪) With a gray whale sculpture out front, this small kids' museum has old-fashioned exhibits about sea otters,

coastal bird life, butterflies, the Big Sur coast and Native American tribes.

Pacific Grove Golf Links GOLF
(Map p462; ☎831-648-5775; www.pggolflinks.com; 77 Asilomar Blvd; greens fees $42-65) Can't afford to play at famous Pebble Beach? This historic 18-hole municipal course, where black-tailed deer freely range, has impressive sea views, and it's a lot easier (not to mention cheaper) to book a tee time.

Sleeping

B&Bs have taken over many stately Victorian homes around downtown and by the beach. Motels cluster at the peninsula's western end, off Lighthouse and Asilomar Aves.

TOP CHOICE **Asilomar Conference Grounds** LODGE $$
(Map p462; ☎831-372-8016, 888-635-5310; www.visitasilomar.com; 800 Asilomar Ave, Pacific Grove; r incl breakfast $115-175;) Sprawling over more than 100 acres of sand dunes and pine forests, this state-park lodge is a find. Skip ho-hum motel rooms for historic houses designed by early-20th-century architect Julia Morgan (of Hearst Castle fame) – the thin-walled, hardwood-floored rooms may be small, but share a sociable fireplace lounge. The lobby rec room has ping-pong and pool tables, and wi-fi. Bike rentals available.

Centrella Inn B&B $$$
(Map p462; ☎831-372-3372, 800-233-3372; www.centrellainn.com; 612 Central Ave; d incl breakfast $119-399; @) For a romantic night inside a Victorian seaside mansion, this turreted National Historic Landmark beckons with enchanting gardens and a player piano. Some of the stately rooms have fireplaces, clawfoot tubs and kitchenettes, while private cottages welcome honeymooners and families. Rates include afternoon fresh-baked cookies and evening wine and hors d'oeuvres.

Sunset Inn Hotel MOTEL $$$
(Map p462; ☎831-375-3529; www.gosunsetinn.com; 133 Asilomar Blvd; r $139-400;) At this small motor lodge near the golf course and the beach, attentive staff check you into crisply redesigned rooms that have hardwood floors, king-sized beds with cheery floral-print comforters and some hot tubs and fireplaces. Ask about guest access to the top-notch Spa at Pebble Beach.

Pacific Gardens Inn MOTEL $$
(Map p462; ☎831-646-9414, 800-262-1566; www.pacificgardensinn.com; 701 Asilomar Blvd; d $105-225; @) A hospitable owner and a communal lobby make all the difference at this welcoming, wood-shingled motor lodge sheltered among tall oak trees. For chilly nights, some comfy rooms have wood-burning fireplaces. It's an easy stroll over to the beach.

Eating

Make reservations for these popular downtown eateries.

TOP CHOICE **Passionfish** SEAFOOD $$$
(Map p462; ☎831-655-3311; www.passionfish.net; 701 Lighthouse Ave; mains $16-28; 5-10pm) Fresh, sustainable seafood is artfully presented in any number of inventive ways, and the seasonally inspired menu also carries slow-cooked meats and vegetarian dishes. The earth-tone decor is spare, with tables squeezed a tad too close together. But an ambitious world-ranging wine list is priced near retail, and there are twice as many Chinese teas as wines by the glass.

Red House Cafe CAFE $$
(Map p462; ☎831-643-1060; www.redhousecafe.com; 662 Lighthouse Ave; mains $5-16; 8-11am Sat & Sun, 11am-2:30pm & 5-9pm Tue-Sun;) Crowded with locals, this 1895 shingled house dishes up comfort food with delightful haute touches, from cinnamon-brioche French toast for breakfast to blue-cheese soufflés and roast chicken at dinner. Haute French tea list. Cash only.

Information

Pacific Grove Chamber of Commerce (Map p462; ☎831-373-3304, 800-656-6650; www.pacificgrove.org; 584 Central Ave; 9:30am-5pm Mon-Fri, 10am-3pm Sat) Tourist information.

Getting There & Around

MST (☎888-678-2871; www.mst.org) bus 1 connects downtown Monterey, Cannery Row and Pacific Grove every half hour from 6:15am to 10:45pm daily.

Carmel-by-the-Sea

With borderline fanatical devotion to its canine citizens, quaint Carmel-by-the-Sea has the well-manicured feel of a country club. Simply plop down in any cafe and watch

SCENIC DRIVE: 17-MILE DRIVE

What to See

Pacific Grove and Carmel are linked by the spectacularly scenic, if overhyped 17-Mile Drive (Map p462), which meanders through Pebble Beach, a wealthy private resort. It's no chore staying within the 25mph limit – every curve in the road reveals another postcard vista, especially when wildflowers bloom. Cycling the drive is enormously popular, but try to do it during the week, when traffic isn't as heavy, and ride with the flow of traffic, from north to south.

Using the self-guided touring map provided upon entry, you can easily pick out landmarks such as **Spanish Bay**, where explorer Gaspar de Portolá dropped anchor in 1769; treacherously rocky **Point Joe**, which in the past was often mistaken for the entrance to Monterey Bay and thus became the site of several shipwrecks; and **Bird Rock**, also a haven for harbor seals and sea lions. The ostensible pièce de résistance is the trademark **Lone Cypress**, which has perched on a seaward rock for more than 250 years.

Besides the coastal scenery, star attractions at Pebble Beach include world-famous **golf courses**, where a celebrity and pro tournament happens every February – just imagine Tiger Woods driving down the spectacular 18th-hole fairway for a victory. The luxurious **Lodge at Pebble Beach** (☎831-624-3811, 800-654-9300; www.pebblebeach.com; 1700 17-Mile Drive; r $715-995;) embraces a spa and designer shops where the most demanding of tastes are catered to. Even if you're not a trust-fund baby, you can still soak up the rich atmosphere in the resort's art-filled public spaces or at the cocktail bar.

The Route

Operated as a toll road by the **Pebble Beach Company** (www.pebblebeach.com; per vehicle/bicycle $9.50/free), 17-Mile Drive is open from sunrise to sunset. The toll can be refunded later as a discount on a $25 minimum food purchase at Pebble Beach restaurants.

Time & Mileage

There are five separate gates for the 17-Mile Drive; how far you drive and how long you take is up to you. For the most scenery, enter at Pacific Grove (off Sunset Dr) and exit at Carmel.

the parade of behatted ladies toting fancy-label shopping bags to lunch and dapper gents driving top-down convertibles along Ocean Ave, the village's slow-mo main drag. Fairy-tale Comstock cottages, with their characteristic stone chimneys and pitched gable roofs, dot the town. Even payphones, garbage cans and newspaper vending boxes are shingled, and local bylaws forbid neon signs and billboards.

Founded as a seaside resort in the 1880s – fairly odd, given that its beach is often blanketed in fog – Carmel quickly attracted famous artists and writers, such as Sinclair Lewis and Jack London, and their hangers-on. An artistic flavor survives in the more than 100 galleries that line the town's immaculate streets, but sky-high property values have long obliterated any salt-of-the-earth bohemia.

Sights

Escape downtown's harried shopping streets and stroll tree-lined neighborhoods on the lookout for domiciles charming and peculiar. The Hansel and Gretel houses on Torres St, between 5th and 6th Avenues, are just how you'd imagine them. Another wicked cool house in the shape of a ship, made from stone and salvaged ship parts, is near 6th Ave and Guadalupe St, about three blocks east of Torres St.

San Carlos Borroméo de Carmelo Mission CHURCH

(Map p462; www.carmelmission.org; 3080 Rio Rd; adult/child $6.50/2; ⌚9:30am-5pm Mon-Sat, 10:30am-5pm Sun) The original Monterey mission was established by Spanish priest Junípero Serra in 1770, but poor soil and the corrupting influence of Spanish soldiers forced the move to Carmel two years later. Today this is one of the most strikingly beautiful missions in California, an oasis of solemnity bathed in flowering gardens.

The mission's adobe (formerly wooden) chapel was later replaced with an arched basilica made of stone quarried in the Santa Lucia Mountains. Museum exhibits are scattered throughout the meditative complex. The spartan cell attributed to Serra looks like something out of *The Good, the Bad and the Ugly*, while a separate chapel houses his memorial tomb. Don't overlook the gravestone of 'Old Gabriel,' a Native American convert whom Serra baptized, and whose dates put him at 151 years old when he died. People say he smoked like a chimney and outlived seven wives. There's a lesson in there somewhere.

Tor House HISTORIC BUILDING

(Map p462; ☎831-624-1813; www.torhouse.org; 26304 Ocean View Ave; tour adult/child 12-17yr $10/5; ⏰10am-3pm Fri & Sat) Even if you've never heard of 20th-century poet Robinson Jeffers, a pilgrimage to this house, which was built with his own hands, offers fascinating insights into both the man and the bohemian ethos of Old Carmel. A porthole in the Celtic-inspired **Hawk Tower** reputedly came from the wrecked ship that carried Napoleon from Elba. The only way to visit the property is to reserve space on a tour (children under 12 not allowed), although the tower can be glimpsed from the street.

Activities

Not always sunny, **Carmel Beach** is a gorgeous white-sand crescent, where pampered pups excitedly run off-leash.

TOP CHOICE **Point Lobos State Natural Reserve** PARK

(Map p462; www.parks.ca.gov, www.pointlobos.org; per car $10; ⏰8am-30min after sunset; 👪) They bark, they bathe and they're fun to watch – sea lions are the stars here at Punta de los Lobos Marinos (Point of the Sea Wolves), 4 miles south of Carmel, where a dramatically rocky coastline offers excellent tide-pooling.

The full perimeter hike is 6 miles, but shorter walks take in wild scenery too, including **Bird Island**, shady **Piney Woods**, the historic **Whaler's Cabin** and **Devil's Cauldron**, a whirlpool that gets splashy at high tide. The kelp forest at **Whalers Cove** is popular with snorkelers and divers; reservations for **scuba-diving permits** (☎831-624-8413; per two-person team $10) are required.

Arrive early on weekends; parking is limited. Don't skip paying the entry fee by parking along Hwy 1; California's state parks are chronically underfunded, and need your help!

Festivals & Events

Carmel Art Festival CULTURE

(www.carmelartfestival.org) Meet plein-air painters and local sculptors in Devendorf Park over a long weekend in mid-May.

Carmel Bach Festival MUSIC

(www.bachfestival.org) In July, classical and chamber-music performances and open rehearsals take place around town.

Harvest Farm-to-Table FOOD, WINE

(www.harvestcarmel.com) Chefs' cooking demos, gardening and BBQ workshops, and wine and artisan-cheese tasting in the neighboring Carmel Valley in late September.

Sleeping

Seriously overpriced boutique hotels, inns and B&Bs fill up quickly, especially in summer; expect a two-night minimum on weekends. Ask at the chamber of commerce about last-minute lodging deals. For better-value lodgings, head north to Monterey.

Mission Ranch INN $$$

(Map p462; ☎831-624-6436, 800-538-8221; www.missionranchcarmel.com; 26270 Dolores St; r incl breakfast $135-285; 📶) If woolly sheep grazing on green fields within view of the Pacific don't convince you to stay here, perhaps knowing that actor and director Clint Eastwood restored this historic ranch will. Accommodations range from shabby-chic rooms inside a converted barn to a family-sized 1850s farmhouse.

Sea View Inn B&B $$

(Map p462; ☎831-624-8778; www.seaviewinncarmel.com; Camino Real btwn 11th & 12th Aves; r incl breakfast $135-265; 📶) At the Sea View – an intimate retreat away from downtown's hustle – fireside nooks are tailor-made for reading or taking afternoon tea. The cheapest rooms with slanted ceilings are short on cat-swinging space, but the beach is nearby.

Carmel River Inn INN $$$
(Map p462; ☎831-624-1575, 800-966-6490; www.carmelriverinn.com; 26600 Oliver Rd; d $159-319;) Tucked off Hwy 1, this peaceful garden retreat south of Carmel's mission rents white-picket-fenced honeymooner and family cottages, many with fireplaces and kitchenettes, and simple country-style rooms. Pet fee $20.

Carmel Village Inn MOTEL $$
(Map p462; ☎831-624-3864, 800-346-3864; www.carmelvillageinn.com; cnr Ocean & Junípero Aves; d incl breakfast buffet $80-250;) With cheerful flowers decorating its exterior, this centrally located motel across from Devendorf Park has pleasant rooms, some with gas fireplaces, and nightly quiet hours.

Eating

Carmel's restaurant scene is more about old-world sidewalk atmosphere than sustenance. Most places open early for breakfast, and stop serving dinner before 9pm.

La Bicyclette FRENCH, ITALIAN $$$
(Map p462; www.labicyclетterestaurant.com; Dolores St at 7th Ave; lunch mains $7-16, 3-course prix-fixe dinner $28; ⊙11:30am-4pm & 5-10pm) Rustic European comfort food using seasonal local ingredients packs canoodling couples into this bistro, with an open kitchen baking wood-fired oven pizzas. Excellent local wines by the glass.

Mundaka TAPAS $$
(Map p462; www.mundakacarmel.com; San Carlos St btwn Ocean & 7th Aves; small plates $4-19; ⊙5:30-10pm Sun-Wed, 5:30-11pm Thu-Sat) This stone courtyard hideaway is a svelte escape from Carmel's stuffy 'newly wed and nearly dead' crowd. Take Spanish tapas plates for a spin and sip the house-made sangria while DJs or flamenco guitars play.

Carmel Belle CALIFORNIAN $$
(Map p462; www.carmelbelle.com; Doud Craft Studios, cnr Ocean Ave & San Carlos St; brunch mains $5-12; ⊙8am-5pm) Fresh, often organic ingredients flow from Carmel Valley farms onto mini-mall tables at this charcuterie, cheese and wine shop.

Bruno's Market & Deli DELI, GROCERIES $
(Map p462; www.brunosmarket.com; cnr 6th & Junípero Aves; sandwiches $5-8; ⊙7am-8pm) This small supermarket deli counter makes a saucy tri-trip beef sandwich and stocks all the accoutrements for a beach picnic, including Sparky's root beer from Pacific Grove.

Drinking & Entertainment

Forest Theater THEATER
(Map p462; ☎831-626-1681; www.foresttheaterguild.org; cnr Mountain View Ave & Santa Rita St; ⊙May-Jul) Founded in 1910 and now the oldest community theater west of the Rockies, here musicals, drama, comedies and film screenings take place under the stars by flickering firepits.

Jack London's PUB
(Map p462; www.jacklondons.com; Su Vecino Court, Dolores St, btwn 5th & 6th Aves; ⊙11am-late) Knock back a few drinks with the caddies from Pebble Beach next to the crackling fireplace at this Carmel institution.

Information

Downtown buildings have no street numbers, so addresses specify the street and nearest intersection only.

Carmel Chamber of Commerce (☎831-624-2522, 800-550-4333; www.carmelcalifornia.org; San Carlos St, btwn 5th & 6th Aves; ⊙10am-5pm) Free maps and information, including about local art galleries.

Carmel Pine Cone (www.pineconearchive.com) Free weekly newspaper packed with local personality and color – the police log is a comedy of manners.

Getting There & Around

Carmel is 5 miles south of Monterey via Hwy 1. Find free unlimited parking in a **municipal lot** (cnr 3rd & Junípero Aves) behind the Vista Lobos building.

MST (☎888-678-2871; www.mst.org) bus 5 ($2, every 30 minutes) and bus 7 ($2, hourly) connect Carmel with Monterey. Bus 4 runs between downtown Carmel and the mission ($1, every 30 minutes). Bus 22 ($3) passes through en route to/from Big Sur three times daily between late May and early September, and twice daily on Saturday and Sunday only the rest of the year.

Big Sur

Big Sur is more a state of mind than a place you can pinpoint on a map. There are no traffic lights, banks or strip malls, and when the sun goes down, the moon and the stars are the only streetlights – if summer's dense fog hasn't extinguished them, that is. Much ink has been spilled extolling the raw beauty

Big Sur

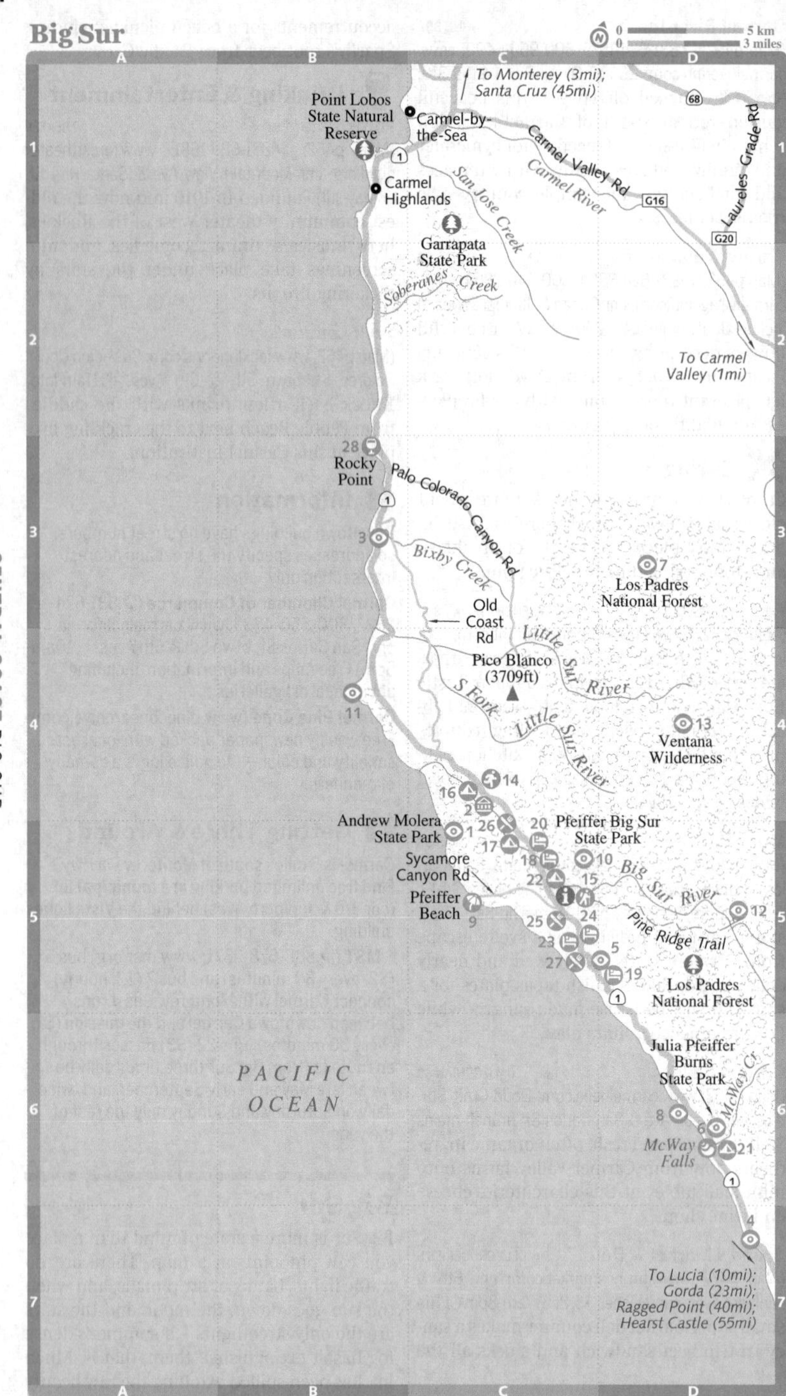

To Monterey (3mi); Santa Cruz (45mi)
Point Lobos State Natural Reserve
Carmel-by-the-Sea
Carmel Valley Rd
Carmel River
Laureles Grade Rd
San Jose Creek
Carmel Highlands
Garrapata State Park
Soberanes Creek
To Carmel Valley (1mi)
Rocky Point
Palo Colorado Canyon Rd
Bixby Creek
Old Coast Rd
Los Padres National Forest
Little Sur River
Pico Blanco (3709ft)
S Fork
Ventana Wilderness
Andrew Molera State Park
Pfeiffer Big Sur State Park
Sycamore Canyon Rd
Pfeiffer Beach
Big Sur River
Pine Ridge Trail
Los Padres National Forest
PACIFIC OCEAN
Julia Pfeiffer Burns State Park
McWay Cr
McWay Falls
To Lucia (10mi); Gorda (23mi); Ragged Point (40mi); Hearst Castle (55mi)

and energy of this precious piece of land shoehorned between the Santa Lucia Range and the Pacific Ocean, but nothing quite prepares you for your first glimpse of the craggy, unspoiled coastline.

In the 1950s and '60s, Big Sur – so named by Spanish settlers living on the Monterey Peninsula, who referred to the wilderness as *el país grande del sur* ('the big country to the south') – became a retreat for artists and writers, including Henry Miller and Beat Generation visionaries such as Lawrence Ferlinghetti. Today Big Sur attracts self-proclaimed artists, new-age mystics, latter-day hippies and city slickers seeking to unplug and reflect more deeply on this emerald-green edge of the continent.

Sights & Activities

All of the following places are listed north to south. Most parks are open from a half-hour before sunrise until a half-hour after sunset, with 24-hour campground access. At state parks, your parking fee ($10) receipt is valid for same-day entry to all except Limekiln; don't skip paying the entry fee by parking illegally outside along Hwy 1.

Bixby Bridge LANDMARK

Under 15 miles south of Carmel, this landmark spanning Rainbow Canyon is one of the world's highest single-span bridges. Completed in 1932, it was built by prisoners eager to lop time off their sentences. There's a perfect photo-op pull-off on the bridge's north side. Before Bixby Bridge was constructed, travelers had to trek inland on what's now called the **Old Coast Rd**, which heads off opposite the pull-off, reconnecting after 11 miles with Hwy 1 near Andrew Molera State Park. When the weather is dry enough, this route is usually navigable by 4WD or a mountain bike.

Point Sur State Historic Park LIGHTHOUSE

(☎831-625-4419; www.pointsur.org; adult/child 6-17yr $10/5, moonlight tour $15/10; ⏲tour schedules vary) Just over 6 miles south of Bixby Bridge, Point Sur rises like a green velvet fortress. This imposing volcanic rock looks like an island, but is actually connected to land by a sandbar. Atop the rock is the 1889 stone lightstation, which operated until 1974. Ocean views and tales of the lighthouse keepers' family lives are engrossing. Meet your tour guide at the locked gate a ¼-mile north of Point Sur Naval Facility, usually at 10am

Big Sur

Sights

1 Andrew Molera State Park....C5
2 Big Sur Discovery Center....C4
3 Bixby Bridge....B3
4 Esalen Institute....D7
5 Henry Miller Library....D5
6 Julia Pfeiffer Burns State Park....D6
7 Los Padres National Forest....D3
8 Partington Cove....D6
9 Pfeiffer Beach....C5
10 Pfeiffer Big Sur State Park....C5
11 Point Sur State Historic Park....B4
12 Sykes Hot Springs....D5
13 Ventana Wilderness....D4

Activities, Courses & Tours

14 Molera Horseback Tours....C4
15 Pine Ridge Trailhead....C5

Sleeping

16 Andrew Molera State Park Campground....C4
17 Big Sur Campground & Cabins....C5
18 Big Sur Lodge....C5
19 Deetjen's Big Sur Inn....D5
20 Glen Oaks Motel....C5
21 Julia Pfeiffer Burns State Park Campground....D6
22 Pfeiffer Big Sur State Park Campground....C5
23 Post Ranch Inn....C5
Ripplewood Resort....(see 20)
24 Ventana Inn & Spa....C5

Eating

25 Big Sur Bakery & Restaurant....C5
Big Sur Lodge....(see 18)
26 Big Sur River Inn....C5
Big Sur Roadhouse....(see 26)
Deetjen's Big Sur Inn....(see 19)
27 Nepenthe & Café Kevah....C5
Restaurant at Ventana....(see 24)

Drinking

Maiden Publick House....(see 26)
28 Rocky Point....B3

Entertainment

Henry Miller Library....(see 5)

Saturday and Sunday year-round, and 1pm Wednesday from November through March. Tours also depart at 2pm Wednesday and Saturday from April to October, when monthly full-moon tours are also available. Call ahead to confirm tour schedules. Arrive early because space is limited (no reservations).

Andrew Molera State Park PARK

(☎831-667-2315; www.parks.ca.gov; per vehicle $10) Named after the farmer who first planted artichokes in California, this oft-overlooked park is a trail-laced pastiche of grassy meadows, waterfalls, ocean bluffs and rugged beaches offering excellent wildlife watching. Look for the turn-off just over 8 miles south of Bixby Bridge.

From the parking lot, a half-mile walk along the beach-bound trail leads to a first-come, first-served campground, from where a gentle quarter-mile spur trail leads past the 1861 redwood **Cooper Cabin**, Big Sur's oldest building. Otherwise, keep hiking on the main trail out toward a beautiful beach where the Big Sur River runs into the ocean and condors can occasionally be spotted circling overhead.

South of the parking lot, learn all about endangered California condors at the park's **Big Sur Discovery Center** (☎831-620-0702; www.ventananaws.org; admission free; ⊙9am-4pm Fri-Sun late May–mid-Sep). At the nearby bird banding lab, inside a small shed which operates when funding allows, the public is welcome to watch naturalists at work carrying out long-term species monitoring programs.

Across Hwy 1 from the park entrance, **Molera Horseback Tours** (☎831-625-5486, 800-942-5486; http://molerahorsebacktours.com; per person $40-70; 👪) offers guided trail rides on the beach. Walk-ins and novices are welcome; children must be at least six years old.

Pfeiffer Big Sur State Park PARK

(☎831-667-2315; www.parks.ca.gov; per vehicle $10) Named after Big Sur's first European settlers, who arrived in 1869, Pfeiffer Big Sur is the largest state park in Big Sur. Hiking trails loop through redwood groves and head into the adjacent Ventana Wilderness. The most popular trail – to 60ft-high **Pfeiffer Falls**, a delicate cascade hidden in the forest, which usually runs from December to May – is an easy 1.4-mile round-trip. Built in the 1930s by the Civilian Conservation Corps (CCC), the rustic Big Sur Lodge is near the park entrance, about 13 miles south of Bixby Bridge.

Pfeiffer Beach BEACH

(www.fs.usda.gov; per vehicle $5; ⊙9am-8pm; 🐾) This phenomenal, crescent-shaped and dog-friendly beach is known for its huge double rock formation, through which waves crash with life-affirming power. It's often windy, and the surf is too dangerous for swimming. But dig down into the wet sand – it's purple! That's because manganese garnet washes down from the craggy hillsides above.

To get here from Hwy 1, make a sharp right onto Sycamore Canyon Rd, marked by a small yellow sign that says 'narrow road' at the top. It's about half a mile south of Big Sur Station, or 2 miles south of Pfeiffer Big Sur State Park. From the turnoff, it's two more narrow, twisting miles (RVs and trailers prohibited) down to the beach.

Henry Miller Library ARTS CENTER

(☎831-667-2574; www.henrymiller.org; admission by donation; ⊙11am-6pm Wed-Mon; @📶) 'It was here in Big Sur I first learned to say Amen!' wrote Henry Miller, a Big Sur denizen for 17 years. More of a living memorial, alt-cultural venue and bookshop, this community gathering spot was never Miller's home. The house belonged to Miller's friend, painter Emil White, until his death and is now run by a nonprofit group. Inside are copies of all of Miller's written works, many of his paintings and a collection of Big Sur and Beat Generation material, including copies of the top 100 books Miller said most influenced him. Stop by to browse and hang out on the front deck. It's about 0.4 miles south of Nepenthe restaurant.

Partington Cove BEACH

A raw and breathtaking spot where crashing surf salts your skin, this hidden cove is named for a settler who built a dock here in the 1880s. Originally used for loading freight, Partington Cove allegedly became a landing spot for Prohibition-era bootleggers. On the steep, half-mile dirt hike down to the cove, you'll cross a cool bridge and go through an even cooler tunnel. The water in the cove is unbelievably aqua and within it grow tangled kelp forests. There's no real beach access and ocean swimming isn't safe, but some people scamper on the rocks and look for tidepools as waves splash ominously.

Look for the unmarked trailhead turnoff inside a large hairpin turn on the west side of Hwy 1, about 6 miles south of Nepenthe restaurant or 2 miles north of Julia Pfeiffer

Burns State Park. The trail starts just beyond the locked vehicle gate.

Julia Pfeiffer Burns State Park PARK
(☎831-667-2315; www.parks.ca.gov; per vehicle $10) Named for another Big Sur pioneer, this park hugs both sides of Hwy 1. The big attraction is California's only coastal waterfall, **McWay Falls**, which drops 80ft straight into the sea – or onto the beach, depending on the tide. This is *the* classic Big Sur postcard shot, with tree-topped rocks jutting above a golden, crescent-shaped beach next to swirling blue pools and crashing white surf. To reach this spectacular viewpoint, take the short Overlook Trail west from the parking lot and cross underneath Hwy 1 via a tunnel. From trailside benches, you might spot migrating gray whales between mid-December and mid-April.

The park entrance is on the east side of Hwy 1, about 8 miles south of Nepenthe restaurant.

Esalen Institute HOT SPRINGS
(☎831-667-3000; www.esalen.org; 55000 Hwy 1;) Marked only by a lighted sign reading 'Esalen Institute – By Reservation Only,' this infamous spot is like a new-age hippie camp for adults. Esoteric workshops treat anything 'relating to our greater human capacity,' from shapeshifting to Thai massage. Things have sure changed a lot since Hunter S Thompson was the gun-toting caretaker here in the 1960s.

Esalen's famous **baths** (☎831-667-3047; per person $20, credit cards only; ⊙public entry 1-3am nightly, reservations accepted 8am-8pm Mon-Thu & Sat, 8am-noon Fri & Sun) are fed by a natural hot spring and sit on a ledge above the ocean. Dollars to donuts you'll never take another dip that compares panorama-wise with the one here, especially on stormy winter nights. Only two small outdoor pools perch directly over the waves, so once you've stripped down (bathing is clothing-optional) and taken a quick shower, head outside immediately to score the best views. Otherwise, you'll be stuck with a tepid, no-view pool or even worse, a rickety bathtub.

Esalen is just over 11 miles south of Nepenthe restaurant and 10 miles north of Lucia.

Limekiln State Park PARK
(☎831-667-2403; www.parks.ca.gov; per vehicle $8; ⊙8am-sunset) Two miles south of Lucia, this petite park gets its name from the four remaining wood-fired kilns originally built here in the 1870s and '80s to smelt quarried limestone into powder, a key ingredient in cement used to construct buildings from Monterey to San Francisco. Tragically, pioneers chopped down the steep canyon's old-growth redwood forests to fuel the kilns' fires. A one-mile round-trip trail through a redwood grove leads to the historic site, passing a quarter-mile spur trail to a gorgeous 100ft-high waterfall.

At press time, the future of this park was uncertain – it may close in 2012.

DRIVING HIGHWAY 1

Driving this narrow two-lane highway through Big Sur and beyond is very slow going. Allow about three hours to cover the distance between the Monterey Peninsula and San Luis Obispo, much more if you want to explore the coast. Traveling after dark can be risky and more to the point, it's futile, since you'll miss out on the seascapes. Watch out for cyclists and always use signposted roadside pullouts to let faster-moving traffic pass.

Los Padres National Forest FOREST
The tortuously winding 40-mile stretch of Hwy 1 south of Lucia to Hearst Castle is even more sparsely populated, rugged and remote, mostly running through national forest lands. Make sure you've got at least enough fuel in the tank to reach the expensive gas station at Gorda, around 11 miles south of Limekiln State Park.

About 5 miles south of Nacimiento-Fergusson Rd, almost opposite Plaskett Creek Campground, is **Sand Dollar Beach Picnic Area** (www.fs.usda.gov; per vehicle $5; ⊙9am-8pm), from where it's a five-minute walk down to southern Big Sur's longest sandy beach, a crescent-shaped strip of sand protected from winds by high bluffs.

In 1971, in the waters of **Jade Cove**, local divers recovered a 9000lb jade boulder that measured 8ft long and was valued at $180,000. People still comb the beach today. The best time to find jade, which is black or blue-green and looks dull until you dip it in water, is during low tide or after a big storm. Keep an eye out for hang gliders flying in for a dramatic landing on the beach. Trails down to the water start from roadside pulloffs immediately south of Plaskett Creek Campground.

CALIFORNIA'S COMEBACK CONDORS

When it comes to endangered species, one of the state's biggest success stories is the California condor. These gigantic, prehistoric birds weigh over 20lb with a wingspan of up to 10ft, letting them fly great distances in search of carrion. They're easily recognized by their naked pink head and large white patches on the underside of each wing.

This big bird became so rare that in 1987 there were only 27 left in the world – all were removed from the wild to special captive-breeding facilities. There are almost 400 California condors alive today, with increasing numbers of captive birds being released back into the wild, where it's hoped they will begin breeding naturally.

Pinnacles National Monument (p491) and the Big Sur coast both offer excellent opportunities to view this majestic bird.

If you have any sunlight left, keep trucking down the highway to **Salmon Creek Falls**, which usually flows from December through May. Tucked up a forested canyon, the double-drop waterfall can be glimpsed from the hairpin turn on Hwy 1, about 8 miles south of Gorda. Roadside parking gets very crowded, as everyone takes the 10-minute walk up to the falls to splash around in the pools, where kids shriek and dogs happily yip and yap.

Ragged Point LANDMARK

Your last – or first – taste of Big Sur's rocky grandeur comes at this craggy cliff outcropping with fabulous views of the coastline in both directions, about 15 miles north of Hearst Castle. Once part of the Hearst empire, it's now taken over by a sprawling, ho-hum resort with a pricey gas station. Heading south, the land grows increasingly wind-swept as Hwy 1 rolls gently down to the water's edge.

Sleeping

With few exceptions, Big Sur's lodgings do not have TVs and rarely have telephones. This is where you come to escape the world. There aren't a lot of rooms overall, so demand often exceeds supply and prices can be outrageous. Bigger price tags don't necessarily buy you more amenities either. In summer and on weekends, reservations are essential, whether for resort rooms or campsites.

TOP CHOICE **Post Ranch Inn** RESORT **$$$**

(831-667-2200, 888-524-4787; www.postranchinn.com; 47900 Hwy 1; d from $595;) The last word in luxurious coastal getaways, the legendary Post Ranch pampers guests with exclusive accommodations featuring slate spa tubs, fireplaces, private decks and walking sticks for coastal hikes. Ocean-view rooms celebrate the sea, while the treehouses without views have a bit of sway. Paddle around the clifftop infinity pool after your shamanic healing session in the spa or a group yoga, meditation or tai chi chuan class. One sour note: disappointing food from the panoramic sea-view restaurant.

Ventana Inn & Spa RESORT **$$$**

(831-667-2331, 800-628-6500; www.ventanainn.com; 48123 Hwy 1; d from $450;) Almost at odds with Big Sur's hippie-alternative vibe, Ventana manages to inject a little soul into its luxury digs. Honeymooning couples and paparazzi-fleeing celebs pad from yoga class to the Japanese baths and clothing-optional pool, or hole up all day next to the wood-burning fireplace in their villa or ocean-view cottage.

Glen Oaks Motel MOTEL **$$$**

(831-667-2105; www.glenoaksbigsur.com; Hwy 1; d $175-350;) At this 1950s redwood-and-adobe motor lodge, rustic rooms and cabins seem effortlessly chic. Dramatically transformed by eco-conscious design, these snug romantic hideaways all have gas fireplaces. The woodsy studio cottage has a kitchenette and walk-in shower built for two, or retreat to the one-bedroom house equipped with a full kitchen.

Treebones Resort YURTS **$$$**

(877-424-4787; www.treebonesresort.com; 71895 Hwy 1; d $170-285;) Don't let the word 'resort' throw you. Yes, they've got an ocean-view hot tub, heated pool and massage treatments available. But noisy yurts with polished pine floors, quilt-covered beds, sink vanities and redwood decks are actually like 'glamping,' with little privacy. Bathrooms and showers are a short stroll away. Rates include a make-your-own waffle breakfast.

Look for the signposted turnoff a mile north of Gorda.

Big Sur Lodge LODGE $$$
(☎831-667-3100, 800-424-4787; www.bigsurlodge.com; 47225 Hwy 1; d $189-369;) What you're really paying for is a peaceful location, right inside Pfeiffer Big Sur State Park. Fairly rustic duplexes each have a deck or balcony looking out into the redwood forest, while family-sized rooms may have kitchens or wood-burning fireplaces. The outdoor swimming pool is usually open from March until October.

Big Sur Campground & Cabins CABINS, CAMPGROUND $$
(☎831-667-2322; www.bigsurcamp.com; 47000 Hwy 1; cabins $90-345, tent/RV sites from $40/50;) Right on the Big Sur River and shaded by redwoods, cozy housekeeping cabins come with full kitchens and fireplaces, while canvas-sided tent cabins are dog-friendly (pet fee $15). The riverside campground is especially popular with RVs. There are hot showers, a coin-op laundry, playground and general store.

Ripplewood Resort CABINS $$
(☎831-667-2242; www.ripplewoodresort.com; 47047 Hwy 1; cabins $95-195;) North of Pfeiffer Big Sur State Park, Ripplewood has struck a blow for fiscal equality by asking the same rates year-round. Throwback Americana cabins all have kitchens and private baths, while some sport fireplaces. Quiet riverside cabins are surrounded by redwoods, but roadside cabins can be noisy. Wi-fi works in the restaurant only.

Deetjen's Big Sur Inn LODGE $$
(☎831-667-2377; www.deetjens.com; 48865 Hwy 1; d $90-250) Nestled among redwoods and wisteria, this creekside conglomeration of rustic, thin-walled rooms and cottages was built by Norwegian immigrant Helmuth Deetjen in the 1930s. Some rooms are warmed by wood-burning fireplaces, while cheaper ones share bathrooms.

Ragged Point Inn MOTEL $$
(☎805-927-4502; www.raggedpointinn.net; 19019 Hwy 1; r $129-269;) Split-level motel rooms are nothing special, except for ocean views; pet fee $50.

Lucia Lodge MOTEL $$
(☎831-688-4884, 866-424-4787; www.lucialodge.com; 62400 Hwy 1; d $150-275;) Dreamy clifftop views from tired 1930s cabin rooms.

Public Campgrounds

Camping is currently available at four of Big Sur's **state parks** (☎reservations 916-638-5883, 800-444-7275; www.reserveamerica.com) and two **United States Forest Service (USFS) campgrounds** (☎reservations 518-885-3639, 877-444-6777; www.recreation.gov) along Hwy 1.

Pfeiffer Big Sur State Park CAMPGROUND $
(www.parks.ca.gov; Hwy 1; tent & RV sites $35-50, hike-and-bike sites $5) Over 200 sites nestle in a redwood-shaded river valley. Facilities include drinking water, coin-op showers and laundry, but no RV hookups.

Andrew Molera State Park CAMPGROUND $
(www.parks.ca.gov; Hwy 1; tent sites $25) Two dozen first-come, first-served primitive walk-in sites with fire pits and drinking water, but no ocean views.

Julia Pfeiffer Burns State Park CAMPGROUND $
(www.parks.ca.gov; Hwy 1; tent sites $30) Two small walk-in campsites on a semi-shaded ocean bluff; register at Big Sur Station (10.5 miles north) or Pfeiffer Big Sur State Park (11 miles north).

Limekiln State Park CAMPGROUND $
(www.parks.ca.gov; Hwy 1; tent & RV sites $35) Near the park entrance, two dozen sites huddle under a Hwy 1 bridge next to the ocean; showers are available.

USFS Kirk Creek Campground CAMPGROUND
(www.campone.com; Hwy 1; tent & RV sites $22) Over 30 beautiful, if exposed ocean-view blufftop campsites with drinking water and BBQ grills, 2 miles south of Limekiln.

USFS Plaskett Creek Campground CAMPGROUND
(www.campone.com; Hwy 1; tent & RV sites $22) Almost 40 spacious, shaded campsites with drinking water in a forested meadow near Sand Dollar Beach, about 5 miles south of Nacimiento-Fergusson Rd.

Eating

Like Big Sur's lodgings, restaurants and cafes are often overpriced, overcrowded and underwhelming.

Restaurant at Ventana CALIFORNIAN $$$
(☎831-667-4242; www.ventanainn.com; 48123 Hwy 1; lunch mains $10-18, dinner mains $29-38; ⊙11:30am-9pm;) The old truism about the better the views, the worse the food just doesn't seem to apply here. The resort's

ocean-view terrace restaurant and cocktail bar is hands down the happiest place for foodies anywhere along Hwy 1. Dig into tender bison steaks with truffled mac 'n cheese, curried chicken salad or roasted vegetable pastas flavored with herbs grown in the garden right outside.

Nepenthe & Café Kevah CALIFORNIAN $$$
(831-667-2345; www.nepenthebigsur.com 48510 Hwy 1; cafe mains $11-17, restaurant mains $15-39; restaurant 11:30am-10pm, cafe 9am-4pm;) Nepenthe comes from a Greek word meaning 'isle of no sorrow,' and indeed, it's hard to feel blue while sitting by the firepit on this clifftop terrace. Just-okay California bistro cuisine (try the renowned Ambrosia burger) takes a backseat to the views and Nepenthe's history – Orson Welles and Rita Hayworth briefly owned a cabin here in the 1940s. Downstairs, Café Kevah serves light, casual brunches and has head-spinning ocean views from its own outdoor patio (closed in winter and bad weather).

Big Sur Bakery & Restaurant CALIFORNIAN $$$
(831-667-0520; www.bigsurbakery.com; 47540 Hwy 1; snacks & drinks from $4, mains $14-36; bakery from 8am daily, restaurant 11am-2:30pm Tue-Fri, 10:30am-2:30pm Sat & Sun, dinner from 5:30pm Tue-Sat) Behind the Shell station, this warmly lit, funky house has seasonally changing menus; wood-fired pizzas share space with more refined dishes like butter-braised halibut. Fronted by a pretty patio, the bakery pours Big Sur's priciest espresso. Expect long waits and standoffish service.

Deetjen's Big Sur Inn CALIFORNIAN $$$
(831-667-2377; www.deetjens.com; 48865 Hwy 1; breakfast mains $10-12, dinner mains $24-36; 8-11:30am & 6-9pm) This quaint yesteryear lodge has a cozy, candle-lit dining room serving up steaks, cassoulets and other hearty country fare from a daily changing menu, primarily sourced from organic local produce, hormone-free meat and sustainable seafood. Breakfast is a much better bet than dinner.

Big Sur Lodge AMERICAN, GROCERIES $$$
(831-667-3100; www.bigsurlodge.com; 47225 Hwy 1; breakfast & lunch mains $8-15, dinner mains $8-27; restaurant 7:30am-9pm, general store 8am-9pm;) Inside Pfeiffer Big Sur State Park, pull up a wooden table in this cabin-esque dining room and fill up on rainbow trout, pasta primavera, roast chicken and trail-mix salads, all made with hungry hikers in mind. The lodge's small general store stocks camping supplies, snacks, drinks and ice-cream treats.

Big Sur River Inn AMERICAN, GROCERIES $$$
(831-667-2700; www.bigsurriverinn.com; Hwy 1; mains $9-29; restaurant 8am-9pm, general store 11am-7pm;) Woodsy old supper club with a deck overlooks a creek teeming with throaty frogs. The wedding reception–quality food is mostly classic American seafood, grilled meats and pastas, but diner-style breakfasts and lunches – from berry pancakes to BLT sandwiches – satisfy. The nearby general store has limited packaged foods and produce, but also a made-to-order fruit smoothie and burrito bar at the back.

Big Sur Roadhouse MEXICAN, AMERICAN $$
(831-667-2264; www.bigsurroadhouse.com; 47080 Hwy 1; mains $14-26; 5:30-9pm Wed-Mon) This Latin-flavored roadhouse fairly glows with its coppertop bar and corner fireplace. At outdoor riverside tables, fork into hearty adobo-marinated skirt steak, stuffed pasilla peppers or barbecue chicken with jicama salad.

Drinking & Entertainment

Henry Miller Library PERFORMING ARTS
(831-667-2574; www.henrymiller.org; Hwy 1) Just south of Nepenthe, this nonprofit performance space hosts a bohemian carnival of live-music concerts, author readings, open-mic nights and indie film screenings outdoors.

Maiden Publick House BAR
(831-667-2355; Hwy 1) Near the Big Sur River Inn, this dive has an encyclopedic beer bible and motley local musicians jamming, mostly on weekends.

Rocky Point BAR
(www.rocky-point.com; 36700 Hwy 1; 9am-9pm) Come for the dizzying ocean-view terrace, where Bloody Marys are served all day, 2.5 miles north of Bixy Bridge.

Information

Visitors often wander into businesses along Hwy 1 and ask, 'How much further to Big Sur?' In fact, there is no town of Big Sur as such, though you may see the name on maps. Commercial activity is concentrated along the stretch north of Pfeiffer Big Sur State Park. Sometimes called 'the Village,' this is where you'll find most of the lodging, restaurants and shops, some of which offer free wi-fi, although cellphone reception is rare.

Big Sur Chamber of Commerce (☎831-667-2100; www.bigsurcalifornia.org; ⌚9am-1pm Mon, Wed & Fri) Pick up the free *Big Sur Guide* newspaper (also downloadable online) at local businesses.

Big Sur Station (☎831-667-2315; www.parks.ca.gov; Hwy 1; ⌚8am-4pm, closed Mon & Tue Nov-Mar) About 1.5 miles south of Pfeiffer Big Sur State Park, this multiagency ranger station has information and maps for state parks, Los Padres National Forest and Ventana Wilderness.

Henry Miller Library (www.henrymiller.org; Hwy 1; ⌚11am-6pm Wed-Mon; @📶) Free wi-fi and public internet terminals (donation requested).

Pacific Valley Station (☎805-927-4211; www.fs.usda.gov; Hwy 1; ⌚8am-4:30pm) South of Nacimiento-Fergusson Rd, USFS ranger station has limited visitor information.

Post office (www.usps.com; 47500 Hwy 1; ⌚10:30am-2:30pm Mon-Fri) Just north of Big Sur Bakery.

ℹ Getting There & Around

Big Sur is best explored by car, since you'll be itching to stop frequently and take in the rugged beauty and vistas that reveal themselves after every hairpin turn. Even if your driving skills are up to these narrow switchbacks, others' aren't: expect to average 35mph or less along the route. Parts of Hwy 1 are battle-scarred, evidence of a continual struggle to keep them open after landslides and washouts. Call ☎800-427-7623 to check current highway conditions, and fill up your gas tank beforehand.

MST (☎888-678-2871; www.mst.org) bus 22 ($3, 1¼ hours) travels from Monterey via Carmel as far south as Nepenthe restaurant three times daily between late May and early September, and twice daily on Saturdays and Sundays only the rest of the year.

Point Piedras Blancas

Many lighthouses still stand along California's coast, but few offer such a historically evocative seascape. Federally designated an outstanding natural area, the jutting, windblown grounds of this 1875 **lightstation** (☎805-927-7361; www.piedrasblancas.org; tour adult/child 6-17yr $10/5; ⌚tour schedules vary) – one of the tallest on the West Coast – have been laboriously replanted with native flora. Picturesquely, everything looks much the way it did when the first lighthouse keepers helped ships find safe harbor at the whaling station at San Simeon Bay. Guided tours currently meet at 9:45am on Tuesdays, Thursdays and Saturdays at the old Piedras Blancas Motel, about 1.5 miles north of the lightstation. No reservations are taken, but call ahead to check tour schedules.

At a signposted vista point 4.5 miles north of Hearst Castle, you can observe a colony of elephant seals bigger than the one at Anõ Nuevo State Reserve. During peak winter season, about 16,000 seals seek shelter in the coves and beaches along this stretch of coast. On sunny days the seals usually 'lie around like banana slugs,' in the words of one docent. Interpretative panels and blue-jacketed **Friends of the Elephant Seal** (www.elephantseal.org) docents demystify the behavior of these beasts.

Hearst Castle

The most important thing to know about William Randolph Hearst (1863–1951) is that he did not live like *Citizen Kane*. Not that Hearst wasn't bombastic, conniving and larger than life, but the moody recluse of the movie he was definitely not. Hearst also didn't call his 165-room monstrosity a castle, preferring its official name, *La Cuesta Encantada* ('The Enchanted Hill'), or more often calling it simply 'the ranch.' From the 1920s into the '40s, Hearst and Marion Davies, his longtime mistress (Hearst's wife refused to grant him a divorce), adored entertaining a steady stream of the era's biggest movers and shakers. Invitations were highly coveted, but Hearst had his quirks – he despised drunkenness, and guests were forbidden to speak of death.

Hearst Castle is a wondrous, historic (Winston Churchill penned anti-Nazi essays here in the 1930s), over-the-top homage to material excess, perched high on a hill; a visit is practically a must. Architect Julia Morgan based the main building, Casa Grande, on the design of a Spanish cathedral, and over the decades catered to Hearst's every design whim, deftly integrating the spoils of his fabled European shopping sprees (ancient artifacts, monasteries etc). The estate sprawls across acres of lushly landscaped gardens, accentuated by shimmering pools and fountains, statues from ancient Greece and Moorish Spain and the ruins of what was in Hearst's day the world's largest private zoo (drivers along Hwy 1 can sometimes still spot the remnant zebra herd).

WORTH A TRIP

VENTANA WILDERNESS

The 200,000-acre **Ventana Wilderness** (www.ventanawild.org) is Big Sur's wild backcountry. It lies within the northern Los Padres National Forest, which straddles the Santa Lucia Range and runs parallel to the coast. Most of this wilderness is covered with oak and chaparral, though canyons cut by the Big Sur and Little Sur Rivers support virgin stands of coast redwoods. The endemic Santa Lucia fir grows upslope in rocky outcroppings.

Partly reopened after devastating wildfires in 2008, the wilderness remains popular with adventurous backpackers. A favorite overnight destination is **Sykes Hot Springs**, natural 100°F (35°C) mineral pools framed by redwoods, but don't expect solitude during peak season (April through September). It's a moderately strenuous 10-mile one-way hike along the **Pine Ridge Trail**, starting from **Big Sur Station** (831-667-2315; www.parks.ca.gov; Hwy 1; 8am-4pm, closed Mon & Tue Nov-Mar), where you can get free campfire permits and pay for overnight trailhead parking ($5).

Much like Hearst's construction budget, the castle will devour as much of your time and money as you let it. To see anything of this **state historic monument** (info 805-927-2020, reservations 800-444-4445; www.hearstcastle.org; tours adult/child from $25/12; daily, hr vary), you have to take a tour. In peak summer months, show up early enough and you might be able to get a same-day ticket for later that afternoon. For special holiday and evening tours, book at least two weeks in advance.

Tours usually start daily at 8:20am, with the last leaving the visitor center for the 10-minute ride to the hilltop at 3:20pm (later in summer and during December). There are three main tours: the guided portion of each lasts about 45 minutes, after which you're free to wander the gardens and terraces, photograph the iconic Neptune and Roman Pools and soak up views. Tour guides are almost preternaturally knowledgeable – just try and stump 'em. Best of all are Christmas holiday evening tours, featuring living-history reenactors who escort you back in time to the castle's 1930s heyday.

Facilities at the visitor center (no eating or drinking is allowed on the hilltop) are geared for industrial-sized mobs of visitors. It's better to grab lunch at Sebastian's General Store by the beach across Hwy 1, or in Cambria. Before you leave the castle, take a moment to visit the often-overlooked museum area at the back of the visitors center. The center's five-story-high **theater** shows a 40-minute historical film (admission included with tour tickets) about the castle and the Hearst family.

Dress with plenty of layers: gloomy fog at the sea-level visitors center can turn into sunny skies at the castle's hilltop location, and vice versa. **RTA** (805-541-2228; www.slorta.org) bus 12 makes three or four daily round-trips to Hearst Castle from San Luis Obispo ($3, two hours) via Morro Bay, Cayucos and Cambria.

San Simeon

Little San Simeon Bay sprang to life as a whaling station in 1852. Shoreline whaling was practiced to catch gray whales migrating between Alaskan feeding grounds and birthing waters in Baja California, while sea otters were hunted here by Russian fur traders. In 1865 Senator George Hearst purchased 45,000 acres of ranch land and established an oceanfront settlement on the western side of Hwy 1. Designed by architect Julia Morgan, the historic 19th-century houses are now rented to employees of the Hearst Corporation's 80,000-acre free-range cattle ranch.

Sights & Activities

FREE **William Randolph Hearst Memorial State Beach** BEACH
(www.parks.ca.gov; dawn-dusk) Across Hwy 1 from Hearst Castle, this bayfront beach has a pleasant sandy stretch with rock outcroppings, kelp forests, a rickety wooden pier (fishing permitted) and picnic areas with barbecue grills.

Sea for Yourself Kayak Tours KAYAKING
(805-927-1787, 800-717-5225; www.kayakcambria.com; rentals $20-65, tours from $50) Right on the beach, you can rent sea kayaks, wet-

suits, bodyboards and surfboards, or take a guided paddle around San Simeon Cove.

FREE **Coastal Discovery Center** MUSEUM
(805-927-6575; Hwy 1; 11am-5pm Fri-Sun mid-Mar–Oct, 10am-4pm Fri-Sun Nov–mid-Mar;) Educational displays include a talking artificial tidepool that kids can touch and videos of deep-sea diving and a WWII-era shipwreck just offshore.

Sleeping & Eating

A few miles south of the original whaling station, the modern town of San Simeon is nothing more than a strip of unexciting motels and restaurants. There are better places to stay in Cambria and beach towns further south like Cayucos.

San Simeon State Park CAMPGROUND $
(reservations 800-444-7275; www.reserveamerica.com; Hwy 1; tent & RV sites $20-35) About 4.5 miles south of Hearst Castle are two popular campgrounds: **San Simeon Creek**, with hot showers and flush toilets; and undeveloped **Washburn**, located along a dirt road. Drinking water is available at both.

Sebastian's General Store DELI, GROCERIES $
(442 San Simeon Rd, off Hwy 1; mains $7-12; 11am-5pm Tue-Sun, kitchen to 4pm) Down a side road across Hwy 1 from the castle, this tiny historic market sells cold drinks, Hearst Ranch beef burgers, giant deli sandwiches and salads for beach picnics at San Simeon Cove. Hearst Ranch Winery tastings are available at the copper-top bar.

Cambria

With a whopping dose of natural beauty, the coastal idyll of Cambria is a lone pearl cast along the coast. Built on lands that once belonged to Mission San Miguel, one of the village's first nicknames was Slabtown, after the rough pieces of wood pioneer buildings were constructed from. Today, just like at neighboring Hearst Castle, money is no object in this wealthy retirement community, whose motto 'Pines by the Sea' is affixed to the back of BMWs that toodle around town.

Sights & Activities

Although its milky-white moonstones are long gone, **Moonstone Beach** still attracts romantics with its oceanfront boardwalk and truly picturesque rocky shoreline. For solitude, take the Windsor Rd exit off Hwy 1 and drive down to where the road dead-ends, then follow a 2-mile round-trip blufftop hiking trail across **East West Ranch**.

A 10-minute drive south of Cambria, past the Hwy 46 turnoff to Paso Robles' wine country, tiny **Harmony** is a slice of rural Americana, with an 1865 creamery now housing local artists' workshops and a hillside winery, **Harmony Cellars** (www.harmonycellars.com; 3255 Harmony Valley Rd; 10am-5pm).

Sleeping

Cambria's choicest motels and hotels line Moonstone Beach Dr, while quaint B&Bs cluster around the village.

Blue Dolphin Inn HOTEL $$$
(805-927-3300, 800-222-9157; www.cambriainns.com; 6470 Moonstone Beach Dr; d incl breakfast basket $159-239;) This sand-colored two-story, slat-sided building may not look as upscale as other oceanfront motels, but rooms do have romantic fireplaces, pillowtop mattresses and rich linens. Pet fee $25.

Fogcatcher Inn HOTEL $$$
(805-927-1400, 800-425-4121; www.fogcatcherinn.com; 6400 Moonstone Beach Dr; d incl breakfast $129-379;) Motels along Moonstone Beach Dr are nearly identical, but this one is a standout for its hot tub. Faux English Tudor–style cottages harbor luxurious modern rooms, some with fireplaces and ocean views.

Cambria Shores Inn MOTEL $$$
(805-927-8644, 800-433-9179; www.cambriashores.com; 6276 Moonstone Beach Dr; d incl breakfast $150-290;) A stone's throw from Moonstone Beach, this ocean-view motel offers pampering amenities for pooches (pet fee $15), including a welcome doggie basket. Rates include a breakfast basket delivered to your door.

Bluebird Inn MOTEL $$
(805-927-4634, 800-552-5434; http://bluebirdmotel.com; 1880 Main St; d $70-220;) With peaceful gardens, this friendly East Village motel offers basic, budget-conscious rooms, some with fireplaces and private creekside patios or balconies. Wi-fi in lobby only.

HI Cambria Bridge Street Inn HOSTEL $
(805-927-7653; www.bridgestreetinncambria.com; 4314 Bridge St; dm $22-25, r $45-80; check-in

5-9pm;) Inside a 19th-century parsonage, this tiny hostel sleeps more like a grandmotherly B&B. It has floral charm and a communal kitchen, but the shabby-chic rooms are thin-walled. Book ahead.

Eating & Drinking

It's a short walk between several cafes and eateries in the East Village.

Indigo Moon CALIFORNIAN **$$**
(www.indigomooncafe.com; 1980 Main St; lunch mains $6-13, dinner mains $13-29; 10am-4pm & 5-9pm Mon-Sat, 10am-3pm & 5-9pm Sun) Inside this artisan cheese and wine shop, breezy bistro tables complement market-fresh salads, toasty sandwiches and sweet-potato fries. Local luminaries gossip over lunch on the back patio, while dinner dates order lemon risotto, crab-stuffed trout or coriander-encrusted chicken.

Sow's Ear AMERICAN **$$$**
(805-927-4865; www.thesowsear.com; 2248 Main St; dinner mains $11-30; 5-9pm) For over a decade, the old-school Sow's Ear has been whipping up haute comfort food inside a cozy house on the East Village's main drag. Make reservations to dine on traditional lobster pot pie, pork tenderloin with olallieberry chutney and fresh bread baked in terracotta flowerpots.

Linn's Easy as Pie Cafe DELI, BAKERY **$**
(www.linnsfruitbin.com; 4251 Bridge St; items $4-10; 10am-6pm Oct-Apr, to 7pm May-Sep;) If you don't have time to visit Linn's Fruit Bin, the original farm store out on Santa Rosa Creek Rd (a 20-minute drive east via Main St), you can fork into their famous olallieberry pies and preserves at this take-out counter delivering salads, sandwiches and comfort fare to a sunny East Village patio.

Wild Ginger FUSION **$$**
(www.wildgingercambria.com; 2380 Main St; mains $12-17; 11am-2:30pm Mon-Wed, Fri & Sat & 5-9pm Fri-Wed;) This bright, cheery chef-owned cafe dishes up garden-fresh, pan-Asian fare, perfectly seasoned and presented, plus housemade sorbets in exotic flavors like pomegranate and pineapple-coconut. Expect long waits.

Lily's Coffeehouse CAFE **$**
(www.lilyscoffee.com; 2028 Main St; coffee & snacks $2-8; 8:30am-5pm Wed-Mon;) Francophilic Lily's has a peaceful garden patio and brews robust coffees and teas. Drop in on Saturday between 11am and 4pm for made-to-order crepes.

Information

Cambria has three distinct parts: the tourist-choked East Village, a half-mile from Hwy 1, where antiques shops, art galleries and coffeehouses line Main St; the newer West Village, further west along Main St, is where you'll find the **chamber of commerce** (805-927-3624; www.cambria-chamber.org; 767 Main St; 9am-5pm Mon-Fri, noon-4pm Sat & Sun); and motel-lined Moonstone Beach, off Hwy 1.

Getting There & Around

From San Luis Obispo, **RTA** (805-541-2228; www.slorta.org) bus 12 makes three or four daily round trips via Morro Bay and Cayucos to Cambria ($3, 1¾ hours), running along Moonstone Beach Dr and Main St through the East and West Villages.

Cayucos

With its historic storefronts housing antiques shops and eateries, the main drag of amiable, slow-paced Cayucos calls to mind an Old West frontier town. But just one block west of Ocean Ave, surf's up!

Sights & Activities

At downtown's north end, fronting a broad white-sand beach, Cayucos' long wooden pier is popular with fishers – it's also a sheltered spot for beginning surfers.

Cayucos Surf Company SURFING
(805-995-1000; www.surfcompany.com; 95 Cayucos Dr; board & wetsuit rental $8-38, 2hr lesson $80-100; 9am-6pm) Near the pier, this fun local surf shop rents surfboards, boogie boards and wetsuits. Call ahead for learn-to-surf lessons.

Sleeping

Cayucos doesn't lack for motels or beachfront inns, most higher-priced than in Morro Bay, 6 miles south.

TOP CHOICE **Cass House Inn** B&B **$$$**
(805-995-3669; www.casshouseinn.com; 222 N Ocean Ave; d incl breakfast $165-325;) Inside a charmingly renovated 1867 Victorian inn, five truly luxurious rooms await, some with ocean views, deep-soaking tubs and antique fireplaces to ward off chilly coastal fog. All have plush beds, flat-screen TVs with DVD

players and tasteful, romantic accents. Reservations are essential.

Seaside Motel MOTEL $$
(☎805-995-3809, 800-549-0900; www.seasidemotel.com; 42 S Ocean Ave; d $80-160;) Expect a warm welcome from the hands-on owners of this vintage motel. Country-kitsch rooms may be on the small side, but some have kitchenettes. Cross your fingers for quiet neighbors.

Cayucos Beach Inn MOTEL $$
(☎805-995-2828, 800-482-0555; www.cayucosbeachinn.com; 333 S Ocean Ave; d $85-175;) A remarkably pet-friendly motel, where even the doors have special peepholes for your canine (pet fee $10). Spacious rooms are nothing special, but you'll find invitingly grassy picnic areas and BBQ grills out front.

Cypress Tree Motel MOTEL $$
(☎805-995-3917, 800-241-4289; www.cypresstreemotel.com; 125 S Ocean Ave; d $50-120;) Retro motor court has lovingly cared-for, but kinda hokey theme rooms, like 'Nautical Nellie' with a net of seashells suspended behind the bed. Pet fee $10.

Eating

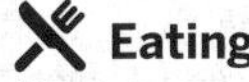
Cass House Restaurant EURASIAN $$$
(☎805-995-3669; www.casshouseinn.com; 222 N Ocean Ave; 4-course prix-fixe dinner $64, incl wine pairings $92; 5-9pm Thu-Mon) The inn's flawless chef-driven restaurant defies expectations. Linger over the locally sourced, seasonally inspired menu that ambitiously ranges from finger-lime snapper ceviche and artisan cheeses to heritage pork loin in cherry jus and black cod with lemongrass beurre blanc, all paired with top-notch regional wines.

Hoppe's Bistro & Wine Bar CALIFORNIAN $$$
(☎805-995-1006; www.hoppesbistro.com; 78 N Ocean Ave; dinner mains $18-35; 11am-10pm Wed-Sun) This slightly kitschy dining rooms features fresh seafood on its respectable coastal, often organic menu – don't skip the incredible red-abalone dishes. The sommelier really knows local wines.

Ruddell's Smokehouse SEAFOOD $
(www.smokerjim.com; 101 D St; items $5-12; 11am-6pm;) 'Smoker Jim' transforms fresh-off-the-boat seafood into succulently smoked slabs and sandwiches, while fish tacos come slathered in a unique apple-celery relish. Squeeze yourself in the door to order. Dogs allowed at sidewalk tables.

Sea Shanty DINER $
(www.seashantycayucos.com; 296 S Ocean Ave; mains $7-25; 8am-9pm Sep-May, to 10pm Jun-Aug;) At this family joint, where a bazillion baseball caps hang from the ceiling, just-OK breakfasts and fish and chips take a back seat to killer desserts.

Brown Butter Cookie Co BAKERY $
(www.brownbuttercookies.com; 250 N Ocean Ave; snacks from $2; 10am-5pm) Seriously addictive cookies, worth the shocking price.

Schooner's Wharf BAR & GRILL $$
(www.schoonerswharf.com; 171 N Ocean Ave; mains $9-42; 11am-9pm Sun-Thu, to 10pm Fri & Sat) Come for the ocean-view bar, not necessarily the food.

Getting There & Away

From San Luis Obispo, **RTA** (☎805-541-2228; www.slorta.org) bus 12 travels three or four times daily along Hwy 1 to Cayucos ($2.50, one hour) via Morro Bay, continuing north to Cambria ($2, 25 minutes) and Hearst Castle ($2, 40 minutes).

Morro Bay

Home to a commercial fishing fleet, Morro Bay's biggest claim to fame is Morro Rock, a volcanic peak jutting dramatically from the ocean floor. It's one of the Nine Sisters, a 21-million-year-old chain of rocks stretching all the way south to San Luis Obispo. Morro Bay's less boast-worthy landmark comes courtesy of the power plant, which threw up three cigarette-shaped smokestacks by the bay. Along this humble, working-class stretch of coast are fantastic opportunities for kayaking, hiking and camping, all within easy reach of San Luis Obispo, where Hwy 1 meets Hwy 101.

Sights & Activities

This town harbors natural riches, easily worth a half day's exploration. The bay itself is a deep inlet separated from the ocean by a 5-mile-long sand spit. Leading south from Morro Rock is the Embarcadero, a small waterfront boulevard jam-packed with seafood eateries and souvenir shops that's also a launching point for boat trips.

Morro Rock LANDMARK
Chumash tribespeople are the only people legally allowed to climb this volcanic rock, now the protected nesting ground of peregrine falcons. You can laze at the small beach on the rock's north side, but you

can't drive all the way around – instead, rent a kayak. The waters below are a giant estuary inhabited by two dozen threatened and endangered species, including brown pelicans, snowy plovers and sea otters.

Morro Bay State Park PARK
(info 805-772-2560, museum 805-772-2694; www.parks.ca.gov; Morro Bay State Park Rd; park entry free, museum adult/child $2/free; park sunrise-sunset, museum 10am-5pm;) Inside this woodsy waterfront park, a small natural-history **museum** has cool interactive exhibits geared toward kids that demonstrate how the forces of nature affect us all. Just north of the museum is a eucalyptus grove harboring one of California's last remaining great blue heron rookeries.

Kayak Horizons KAYAKING
(805-772-6444; www.kayakhorizons.com; 551 Embarcadero; kayak & canoe rentals $12-44, tours & lessons $65) One of several places on the Embarcadero offering kayak rentals and tours for novices. When paddling out on your own, be aware of the tide schedules. Ideally, you'll want to ride the tide out and then back in. Winds are generally calmest in the mornings.

Morro Bay Golf Course GOLF
(805-782-8060; www.slocountyparks.com; green fees $15-50) South of the Embarcadero, adjacent to the state park, this 18-hole golf course boasts tree-lined fairways and ocean views. A driving range and rental clubs and carts are available.

Tours

Sub-Sea Tours BOAT TRIPS
(805-772-9463; www.subseatours.com; 699 Embarcadero; 45min tour adult/child 3-12yr $14/7; hourly departures 10am-4pm Jun-Sep, 11am-3pm Sat & Sun & 1pm Mon-Fri Oct-May;) For pint-sized views of kelp forests and schools of fish, take the kids on a spin on a yellow semi-submersible.

Virg's Landing FISHING
(805-772-1222, 800-762-5263; www.morrobaysportfishing.com; 1169 Market St; tours $65-250) Salty dogs ready for a little sportfishing can book half-day or all-day trips with this long-running local outfit.

Central Coast Outdoors OUTDOOR SPORTS
(805-528-1080, 888-873-5610; www.centralcoastoutdoors.com; tours $65-150) Leads kayaking tours (including sunset and full-moon paddles), guided hikes and cycling trips along the coast and in nearby wine countries.

Festivals & Events

Morro Bay Winter Bird Festival OUTDOORS
(www.morrobaybirdfestival.org) Every January, bird-watchers flock together for guided hikes, kayaking trips and naturalist-led events, during which over 200 species can be spotted along the Pacific Flyway.

Sleeping

Dozens of motels cluster along Hwy 1 and around Harbor and Main Sts, between downtown and the Embarcadero.

Anderson Inn INN $$$
(805-772-3434, 866-950-3434; www.andersoninnmorrobay.com; 897 Embarcadero; d $239-349;) Like a small boutique hotel, this waterfront inn has just a handful of spacious, soothingly earth-toned rooms with flat-screen TVs, mini-fridges and if you're lucky, a gas fireplace, your own hot tub and harbor views.

La Serena Inn MOTEL $$
(805-772-5665, 800-248-1511; www.laserenainn.com; 990 Morro Ave; d $89-169;) Large, well-kept rooms at this bland three-story motel each have a microwave and minifridge. If you're feeling flush, request one with views of Morro Rock and a private balcony to hear the gentle clank-clank of boats in the harbor below.

Morro Bay State Park Campground CAMPGROUND $
(reservations 800-444-7275; www.reserveamerica.com; tent & RV sites without/with hookups $35/50) Less than 2 miles south of downtown and the Embarcadero, over 115 woodsy sites are fringed by eucalyptus and cypress trees, with trails leading down to the beach. Facilities include fire pits, showers and an RV dump station.

Beach Bungalow Inn & Suites MOTEL $$
(805-772-9700; www.morrobaybeachbungalow.com; 1050 Morro Ave; d $100-250;) This butter-yellow motor court's chic, contemporary rooms have mod-cons; pet fee $20.

Inn at Morro Bay MOTEL $$
(805-772-5651, 800-321-9566; www.innatmorrobay.com; 60 State Park Rd; d $115-275;) Dated two-story waterfront lodge inside the state park set for renovations.

Eating & Drinking

More predictable seafood shacks line the Embarcadero.

Taco Temple CALIFORNIAN $$
(2680 Main St, off Hwy 1; mains $7-13; ⏲11am-9pm Mon & Wed-Sat, to 8:30pm Sun;) Overlook the frontage-road location for huge helpings of Cal-Mex fusion flavor. At the next table, there might be fishers talking about the good ole' days or starving surfer buddies. Try one of the specials – they deserve the name. Cash only.

Giovanni's Fish Market & Galley SEAFOOD $$
(www.giovannisfishmarket.com; 1001 Front St; mains $7-13; ⏲9am-6pm;) This family-run joint on the Embarcadero is a classic California seafood shack. Folks line up for batter-fried fish and chips and killer garlic fries. Inside there's a market with all the fixin's for a beach campground fish fry.

Shine Cafe & Sunshine Health Foods VEGETARIAN $
(www.sunshinehealthfoods-shinecafe.com; 415 Morro Bay Blvd; mains $5-14; ⏲11am-5pm Mon-Fri, 9am-5pm Sat, 10am-4pm Sun;) Hidden inside a small natural-foods market, the mostly organic Shine Cafe serves karma-cleansing grub like tempeh tacos, garden-fresh salads and blueberry smoothies.

Stax Wine Bar TAPAS $$
(www.staxwine.com; 1099 Embarcadero; shared plates $6-10; ⏲noon-8pm Sun-Thu, to 10pm Fri & Sat) Perch on barstools in front of the harbor-view windows for a hand-selected tasting flight of local California wines. Tapas-sized bites such as artisan cheese and cured-meat plates keep revelers fueled, especially on live-music nights.

Last Stage West BARBECUE $$
(www.laststagewest.net; 15050 Morro Rd, Atascadero; mains $6-20; ⏲noon-9pm) At this Old West roadhouse and boot-stomping live-music venue, say 'Howdy, pardner!' to smoked tri-tip barbecue, slow-cooked pork ribs and rib-eye steak. To get here, drive Hwy 41 about 10 miles northeast of its intersection with Hwy 1 in Morro Bay.

Information

Morro Bay Chamber of Commerce (☎805-772-4467, 800-231-0592; www.morrobay.org; 845 Embarcadero; ⏲9am-5pm Mon-Fri, 10am-4pm Sat, 10am-2pm Sun) is in the thick of everything. A few blocks uphill, Main St is the less touristy downtown.

Getting There & Around

From San Luis Obispo, **RTA** (☎805-541-2228; www.slorta.org) bus 12b travels hourly on weekdays and a few times daily on weekends along Hwy 1 to Morro Bay ($2.50, 40 minutes). Three or four times daily, bus 12b continues north from Morro Bay to Cayucos ($1.50, 15 minutes), Cambria ($2, 45 minutes) and Hearst Castle ($2, one hour). From late May to early October, a **trolley** (single ride $1.25, day pass $3) loops around the waterfront and downtown, operating varying hours (no service Tuesday to Thursday).

Montaña de Oro State Park

In spring the hillsides are blanketed by bright California native poppies, wild mustard and other wildflowers, giving this park its Spanish name, meaning 'mountain of gold.' Wind-tossed coastal bluffs with wild, wide-open sea views make it a favorite spot with hikers, mountain bikers and horseback riders. The northern half of the park features sand dunes and an ancient marine terrace visible due to seismic uplifting. **Spooner's Cove**, once used by smugglers, is now a postcard-perfect sandy beach and picnic area. If you go tidepooling, remember to only touch the marine creatures like sea stars, limpets and crabs with the back of one hand to avoid disturbing them, and never remove them from their aquatic homes. You can hike along the beach and the grassy ocean bluffs, or drive uphill past the visitors center to the start of the exhilarating 7-mile loop trail tackling **Valencia** and **Oats Peaks**.

Sleeping

Montaña de Oro State Park Campground CAMPGROUND $
(☎reservations 800-444-7275; www.reserveamerica.com; tent & RV sites $20-25, hike-and-bike sites $5) Tucked into a small canyon by the visitor center, this minimally developed campground has pleasantly cool drive-up and environmental walk-in sites. Limited amenities include vault toilets, drinking water and firepits.

Information

Montaña de Oro State Park (☎805-772-7434; www.parks.ca.gov; 3550 Pecho Valley Rd, Los Osos; admission free; ⏲sunrise-sunset)

Getting There & Away

From the north, exit Hwy 1 in Morro Bay at South Bay Blvd; after 4 miles, turn right onto Los Osos Valley Rd (which runs into Pecho Valley Rd) for 6 miles. From the south, exit Hwy 101 in San Luis Obispo at Los Osos Valley Rd, then drive northwest 16 miles.

ALONG HIGHWAY 101

Driving inland along Hwy 101 is a quicker way to travel between the Bay Area and Southern California. Although it lacks the striking scenery of coastal Hwy 1, the historic El Camino Real (the King's Highway), established by Spanish conquistadors and missionaries, has a beauty of its own, ranging from the fertile fields of Salinas, immortalized by novelist John Steinbeck, to the oak-dappled golden hills of San Luis Obispo and beyond to seaside Santa Barbara. Along the way are ghostly missions, jaw-dropping Pinnacles National Monument and standout wineries.

Gilroy

About 30 miles south of San Jose, the self-proclaimed 'garlic capital of the world' puts on the jam-packed **Gilroy Garlic Festival** (www.gilroygarlicfestival.com) over the last full weekend in July. Show up for carnival-quality chow – garlicky fries, garlic-flavored ice cream and more – and for cooking contests under the blazing-hot sun.

Unusual **Gilroy Gardens** (408-840-7100; www.gilroygardens.org; 3050 Hecker Pass Hwy/Hwy 152; adult/child 3-10yr $45/35; 11am-5pm Mon-Fri mid-Jun–mid-Aug, 11am-6pm Sat & Sun late Mar-Nov;) is a nonprofit family-oriented theme park focused on food and plants rather than Disney-esque cartoon characters. You've got to really love flowers, fruit and veggies to get your money's worth. Rides like the 'Mushroom Swing' are mostly tame.

Heading east on Hwy 152 toward I-5, **Casa de Fruta** (408-842-7282; www.casadefruta.com; 10021 Pacheco Pass Hwy, Hollister; admission free;) is a commercialized farm stand with some hokey, old-fashioned rides ($2.50 to $4) for youngsters, including carousels and choo-choo trains. Opening hours vary.

San Juan Bautista

In atmospheric old San Juan Bautista, where you can practically hear the whispers of the past, California's 15th mission is fronted by the only original Spanish plaza remaining in the state. Along 3rd St, evocative historic buildings mostly shelter antiques shops and petite garden restaurants. Hark! That cock you hear crowing is one of the town's roosters, which are allowed by tradition to stroll the streets at will.

Sights

Mission San Juan Bautista MISSION
(www.oldmissionsjb.org; 406 2nd St; adult/child 5-17yr $4/2; 9:30am-4:30pm) Founded in 1797, this mission has the largest church among California's original 21 missions. As it was unknowingly built directly atop the San Andreas Fault, the mission has been rocked by earthquakes. Bells hanging in the tower today include chimes that were salvaged after the 1906 San Francisco earthquake toppled the original mission. Parts of Alfred Hitchcock's thriller *Vertigo* were shot here, although the bell tower in the climactic scene is just a special effect. Below the cemetery, a section of El Camino Real, the Spanish colonial road built to link the missions, can still be seen.

WHAT THE...?

'Oh, my!' is one of the more printable exclamations overheard from visitors at the **Madonna Inn** (805-543-3000, 800-543-9666; www.madonnainn.com; 100 Madonna Rd; r $179-449;), a garish confection visible from Hwy 101. You'd expect outrageous kitsch like this in Las Vegas, not SLO, but here it is, in all its campy extravagance. Japanese tourists, vacationing Midwesterners and hipster, irony-loving urbanites all adore the 110 themed rooms – including Yosemite Rock, Caveman and hot-pink Floral Fantasy. Check out photos of the different rooms online, or wander the halls and spy into the ones being cleaned. The urinal in the men's room is a bizarre waterfall. But the most irresistible reason to stop here? Old-fashioned cookies from the storybook-esque bakery.

San Juan Bautista State Historic Park PARK

(☎831-623-4881; www.parks.ca.gov; 2nd St, btwn Washington & Mariposa Sts; park entry free, museum adult/child $3/free; ⏰10am-4:30pm) Buildings around the old Spanish plaza opposite the mission anchor this historical park. The large plaza stables hint at San Juan Bautista in its 1860s heyday as a stagecoach stop. In 1876 the railroad bypassed the town, which has been a sleepy backwater ever since.

Across 2nd St is the 1858 **Plaza Hotel**, which started life as a single-story adobe building, and now houses a little historical museum. Next door, the **Castro-Breen Adobe** once belonged to Mexican general José Castro, who led a successful revolt against an unpopular governor. In 1848 it was bought by the Breen family, survivors of the Donner Party disaster.

Sleeping

Fremont Peak State Park CAMPGROUND $

(☎831-623-4255; www.parks.ca.gov; San Juan Canyon Rd, off Hwy 156; per car $6, tent & RV sites $25; ⏰park 8am-30min after sunset, campground 24hr) Eleven miles south of town, this park has a pretty, but primitive, 20-site campground shaded by oak trees on a hilltop with distant views of Monterey Bay. Equipped with a 30in telescope, the park's **astronomical observatory** (☎831-623-2465; 👪) is usually open to the public on moonless Saturday nights between April and October, starting around 8pm.

Eating & Drinking

Jardines de San Juan MEXICAN $$

(www.jardinesrestuarant.com; 115 3rd St; mains $8-18; ⏰11:30am-9pm Sun-Thu, to 10pm Fri & Sat; 👪) Here at the longest-running contender in the town's long lineup of touristy Mexican eateries, it's all about the pretty outdoor garden, not necessarily authentic food. Sunday dinner brings out *pollos borrachos* ('drunken chickens').

San Juan Bakery BAKERY $

(319 3rd St; snacks $2-4; ⏰7:30am-3pm) Pick up fresh loaves of cinnamon bread, hot-cross buns and guava turnovers to sustain you during the long drive south. Get there early, as it often sells out.

Vertigo Coffee COFFEESHOP $

(www.vertigocoffee.com; 81 4th St; snacks & drinks $2-5; ⏰6:30am-4pm Mon, 6:30am-5:30pm Tue-Thu, 6:30am-7pm Fri, 8am-7pm Sat, 8am-4pm Sun) Rich espresso, pour-over brews and sticky bear claws make this coffee roaster's cafe a find.

Getting There & Away

San Juan Bautista is on Hwy 156, a 3.5-mile detour east of Hwy 101, south of Gilroy en route to Monterey or Salinas. Further south, Hwy 101 enters the sun-dappled eucalyptus grove that James Stewart and Kim Novak drove through in *Vertigo*.

Salinas

Best known as the birthplace of John Steinbeck and nicknamed the 'Salad Bowl of the World,' Salinas is a working-class agricultural center with down-and-out, even mean streets. It makes a thought-provoking contrast with the affluence of the Monterey Peninsula, a fact of life that helped shape Steinbeck's novel *East of Eden*. The historic center stretches along Main St, with the National Steinbeck Center at its northern end.

Sights

National Steinbeck Center MUSEUM

(☎831-775-4721; www.steinbeck.org; 1 Main St; adult/child 6-12yr/youth 13-17yr $11/6/8; ⏰10am-5pm; 👪) This museum will enthrall almost anyone, even if you don't know a lick about Salinas' Nobel Prize–winning native son, John Steinbeck (1902–68), a Stanford University dropout. Tough, funny and brash, he sensitively portrayed the troubled spirit of rural, working-class Americans in such novels as *The Grapes of Wrath*. Interactive, kid-accessible exhibits and short video clips chronicle the writer's life and works in an engaging way. Gems include Rocinante, the customized camper in which Steinbeck traveled around America while researching *Travels with Charley*. Take a moment and listen to Steinbeck's Nobel acceptance speech – it's grace and power combined.

Admission also includes the small **Rabobank Agricultural Museum**, which takes visitors on a journey through the modern agricultural industry, from water to pesticides to transportation – it's way more interesting than it sounds, trust us.

Steinbeck House HISTORIC BUILDING

(132 Central Ave) Steinbeck was born and spent much of his boyhood in this house, three blocks west of the center. It's now a twee lunch cafe; we're not sure he'd approve.

Garden of Memories Memorial Park CEMETERY
(768 Abbott St, west of Hwy 101 exit Sanborn Rd) Steinbeck is buried in the Hamilton family plot, about 2 miles south of the center via Main, John and Abbott Sts.

Tours

Farm TOURS
(831-455-2575; www.thefarm-salinasvalley.com; admission free, tours adult/child 2-15yr $8/6; 10am-5pm early Nov–mid-Mar, to 6pm mid-Mar–early Nov) This family-owned organic fruit-and-veggie stand offers educational 45-minute walking tours of its fields, usually at 1pm on Tuesdays and Thursdays. On the drive in, watch for the kinda-creepy giant sculptures of farm workers by local artist John Cerney, which also stand along Hwy 101. The farm is off Hwy 68 at Spreckels Blvd, about 3.5 miles south of the center.

Ag Venture Tours TOURS
(831-761-8463; http://agventuretours.com; half-day minivan tours from adult/child 7-20yr $70/55) Take a more in-depth look at commercial and organic farm fields and vineyards around the Salinas Valley and Monterey County.

Festivals & Events

California Rodeo Salinas RODEO
(www.carodeo.com) Bull riding, calf roping, horse shows and cowboy poetry in late July.

Steinbeck Festival CULTURE
(www.steinbeck.org) Four-day festival in early August features films, lectures, guided bus and walking tours, music and a literary pub crawl.

California International Airshow OUTDOORS
(www.salinasairshow.com) Professional stunt flying and vintage and military aircraft take wing in late September.

Sleeping

Salinas has plenty of budget motels off Hwy 101, including at the Market St exit.

Best Western Plus Salinas Valley Inn & Suites MOTEL $$
(831-751-6411, 800-780-7234; www.bestwestern.com; 187 Kern St; r incl breakfast $99-299) As posh as you can get next to the freeway, this chain has newer, tasteful rooms (pet fee $20) and an outdoor pool and hot tub. Don't confuse it with the less appealing Best Western Salinas Monterey Hotel.

Laurel Inn MOTEL $
(831-449-2474, 800-354-9831; www.laurelinnmotel.com; 801 W Laurel Dr; r $60-100) If chains don't do it for you, this sprawling, family-owned cheapie has predictable motel rooms that are nevertheless spacious. There's a swimming pool, whirlpool tub and dry sauna for relaxing.

Eating & Drinking

Habanero Cocina Mexicana MEXICAN $$
(157 Main St; mains $5-15; 11am-9pm Sun-Thu, to 10pm Fri & Sat) On downtown's Restaurant Row just south of the National Steinbeck Center, this storefront Mexican kitchen gets a stamp of approval for its handmade tortillas, a rainbow of fresh salsas and chile-spiked carne asada tacos.

First Awakenings DINER $$
(www.firstawakenings.net; 171 Main St; mains $5-12; 7am-2pm) Fork into oversized diner breakfasts of fruity pancakes and egg crepes, or turn up later in the day for hand-crafted deli sandwiches, BBQ bacon burgers and market-fresh salads.

Monterey Coast Brewing Co BREWPUB $$
(165 Main St; mains $8-25; 11am-11pm Tue-Sun, to 9pm Mon) This microbrewery is a welcome sign of life downtown; the nine-beer tasting sampler costs just 10 bucks.

A Taste of Monterey WINE BAR
(www.atasteofmonterey.com; tasting fee $5; 127 Main St; 11am-5pm Mon-Wed, to 6pm Thu-Sat) This downtown tasting room pours Monterey Co wines. Ask for a free map to find local vineyards along Hwy 101.

Information

Salinas Valley Chamber of Commerce (831-751-7725; www.salinaschamber.com; 119 E Alisal St; 8am-5pm Mon & Wed-Fri, 9:30am-5pm Tue) Hands out free tourist information and maps, five blocks east of Main St.

Getting There & Away

Amtrak (www.amtrak.com; 11 Station Pl, off W Market St) runs daily trains on the Seattle–LA *Coast Starlight* route via Oakland ($16, three hours), Paso Robles ($24, two hours), San Luis Obispo ($31, 3½ hours) and Santa Barbara ($49, 6½ hours).

Greyhound (www.greyhound.com; 19 W Gabilan St, cnr Salinas St) has a few daily buses to Santa Cruz ($14, 65 minutes), and along Hwy 101 north to San Francisco ($25, four hours) or south to San Luis Obispo ($30, 2½ hours) and Santa Barbara ($50, 4¾ hours).

From the nearby **Salinas Transit Center** (110 Salinas St), **MST** (☎888-678-2871; www.mst.org) buses 20 and 21 leave every 30 to 60 minutes daily for Monterey ($3, one hour).

Pinnacles National Monument

Named for the towering spires that rise abruptly out of the chaparral-covered hills east of Salinas Valley, this off-the-beaten-path **park** (☎831-389-4486; www.nps.gov/pinn; per vehicle $5) protects the remains of an ancient volcano. A study in stunning geological drama, its craggy monoliths, sheer-walled canyons and twisting caves are the result of millions of years of erosion.

Sights & Activities

Besides **rock climbing** (for route information, surf www.pinnacles.org), the park's biggest attractions are its two talus caves, formed by piles of boulders. **Balconies Cave** is always open for exploration. Scrambling through it is not an exercise recommended for claustrophobes, as it's pitch-black inside, making a flashlight essential. Be prepared to get lost a bit, too. The cave is found along a 2.5-mile hiking loop from the west entrance. Nearer the east entrance, **Bear Gulch Cave** is closed seasonally, so as not to disturb a resident colony of Townsend's big-eared bats.

To really appreciate Pinnacles' stark beauty, you need to hike. Moderate loops of varying lengths and difficulty ascend into the **High Peaks** and include thrillingly narrow clifftop sections. In the early morning or late afternoon, you may spot endangered California condors (see p478) soaring overhead. Rangers lead guided full-moon and dark-sky hikes, as well as cool bat-viewing and star-gazing programs, on select Friday and Saturday nights from spring through fall. Reservations are required for these programs; call ☎831-389-4486, ext 243.

Sleeping

Pinnacles Campground CAMPGROUND $
(☎info 831-389-4485, reservations 877-444-6777; www.recreation.gov; tent & RV sites without/with hookups $23/36;) On the park's east side, this popular family-oriented campground has over 130 sites (some with shade), plus drinking water, firepits and a seasonal outdoor pool.

Information

The best time to visit Pinnacles National Monument is during spring or fall; summer's heat is extreme. Information, maps, books and bottled water are available on the park's east side from the small **NPS visitor center** (9:30am-5pm) inside the **campground store** (3-6pm Mon-Fri, 9am-6pm Sat & Sun).

Getting There & Away

There is no road connecting the two sides of the park. To reach the less-developed **west entrance** (7:30am-8pm mid-Mar–early Nov, to 6pm early Nov–mid-Mar), exit Hwy 101 at Soledad and follow Hwy 146 northeast for 14 miles. The **east entrance** (24hr), where you'll find the visitor center and campground, is accessed via lonely Hwy 25 in San Benito County, southeast of Hollister and northeast of King City.

Mission San Antonio De Padua

Remote, tranquil and evocative, this **mission** (☎831-385-4478; www.missionsanantonio.net; end of Mission Rd, Jolon; adult/child under 13yr $5/3; 10am-4pm) sits in the Valley of the Oaks, once part of the sprawling Hearst Ranch land holdings. It's now inside the boundaries of active Fort Hunter Liggett.

The mission was founded in 1771 by Franciscan priest Junípero Serra. Built with Native American labor, the church has been restored to its early 19th-century appearance, with a wooden pulpit, canopied altar and decorative flourishes on whitewashed walls. A creaky door leads to a cloistered garden anchored by a fountain. The museum has a small collection of such utilitarian items as an olive press and a weaving loom once used in the mission's workshops. Around the grounds, you can inspect the remains of a grist mill and irrigation system with aqueducts.

It's seldom crowded here, and you may have this vast site all to yourself, except during **Mission Days** in late April and **La Fiesta** on the second Sunday of June. Pick up a visitor's pass from a military checkpoint on the way in; bring photo ID and proof of your vehicle's registration. From the north, take the Jolon Rd exit off Hwy 101 before King City and follow Jolon Rd (County Rte G14) about 18 miles south to Mission Rd. From the south, take the Jolon Rd (County Rte G18) exit off Hwy 101 and drive 22 miles northwest to Mission Rd.

San Miguel

San Miguel is a small farming town right off Hwy 101, where life seems to have remained almost unchanged for decades. **Mission San Miguel Arcángel** (805-467-3256; www.missionsanmiguel.org; 775 Mission St; suggested donation per person/family $2/5; 10am-4:30pm) suffered heart-breaking damage during the 2003 Paso Robles earthquake. Although repairs are still underway, the restored mission church, cemetery, museum and gardens have since re-opened. An enormous cactus out front was planted around the same time as the mission was built in 1818.

Hungry? Inside a retro converted gas station downtown, **Station 3** (1199 Mission St; items $2-6; 6am-2:30pm Mon-Fri, 7am-2:30pm Sat & Sun) vends live-wire espresso and cups o' coffee, breakfast burritos, pulled-pork sandwiches and whopping good brownies.

Paso Robles

In northern San Luis Obispo County, Paso Robles is the heart of an agricultural region where grapes are now the biggest money-making crop. Scores of wineries along Hwy 46 produce a brave new world of more-than-respectable bottles. The Mediterranean climate is yielding another bounty, too: a fledging olive-oil industry. Paso's historic downtown centers on Park and 12th Sts, where boutique shops and wine-tasting rooms await.

Sights & Activities

You could spend days wandering country back roads off Hwy 46, both east and west of Hwy 101. Most wineries have tasting rooms and a few offer vineyard tours. For anything else you might want to know, check www.pasowine.com.

EASTSIDE

FREE **Tobin James Cellars** WINERY
(www.tobinjames.com; 8950 Union Rd; 10am-6pm) Boisterous Old West saloon pours bold reds, including an outlaw 'Ballistic' zinfandel and 'Liquid Love' late-harvest dessert wine. No tasting fee.

FREE **Eberle** WINERY
(www.eberlewinery.com; 3810 E Hwy 46; 10am-5pm Oct-Mar, 10am-6pm Apr-Sep) Offers lofty vineyard views, bocce ball courts and daily tours of its wine caves. No-fee tastings run the gamut of white and red varietals and blends, plus port.

Clautiere WINERY
(www.clautiere.com; 1340 Penman Springs Rd; noon-5pm Thu-Mon) Don't let the fantastical tasting room, where you can try on Dr Seuss-ian hats, fool you: serious Rhône-style blends will delight connoisseurs.

Cass WINERY
(www.casswines.com; 7350 Linne Rd; noon-5pm Mon-Fri, 11am-6pm Sat & Sun) All that rich Rhône wine-tasting, from Roussanne to Syrah, going straight to your head? Light lunches are served in the market cafe until 4pm daily.

WESTSIDE

Tablas Creek WINERY
(www.tablascreek.com; 9339 Adelaida Rd; 10am-5pm) Breathe easy at this organic estate vineyard in the rolling hillsides. Known for their Rhône varietals, signature blends also rate highly. Tours are usually offered at 10:30am and 2pm daily (reservations advised).

Castoro WINERY
(www.castorocellars.com; 1315 N Bethel Rd; 10am-5:30pm) Husband-and-wife team produces 'dam fine wine' (the mascot is a beaver, get it?), including from custom-crushed and organic grapes. Outdoor vineyard concerts in summer.

Zenaida WINERY
(www.zenaidacellars.com; 1550 W Hwy 46; 11am-5pm) Rustic tasting room that's simply zen for sampling estate zins and a signature 'Fire Sign' blend. Overnight vineyard accommodations (from $250 per night) are tempting too.

Dark Star WINERY
(www.darkstarcellars.com; 2985 Anderson Rd; 10:30am-5pm Fri-Sun) If you're lucky, you might meet the winemaker in this family-run tasting room, pouring big, bold red varietals and blends like 'Left Turn.'

Festivals & Events

Wine Festivals FOOD & WINE
(www.pasowine.com) Oenophiles crowd the Zinfandel Festival in mid-March, Wine Festival in mid-May and Harvest Wine Weekend in mid-October.

California Mid-State Fair CULTURE
(www.midstatefair.com) In late July and early August, 12 days of live rock and country-

and-western concerts, farm exhibits, carnival rides and a rodeo draw huge crowds.

Sleeping

Chain motels and hotels line Hwy 101. B&Bs and vacation rentals are scattered among the vineyards outside town.

Hotel Cheval BOUTIQUE HOTEL **$$$**
(805-226-9995, 866-522-6999; www.hotelcheval.com; 1021 Pine St; d incl breakfast $300-400;) Cocoon with your lover inside an art-splashed aerie downtown. A dozen stylish, modern rooms all come with California king beds, spa-worthy amenities and plantation shutters; some have gas fireplaces and sundecks with teak furniture. Staff can be snobby. Pet fee $30.

Wild Coyote Estate Winery B&B **$$$**
(805-610-1311; www.wildcoyote.biz; 3775 Adelaida Rd; d incl breakfast $225-275;) Steal yourself away among the stellar vineyards of Paso Robles' west side, where just five romantic adobe-walled casitas echo the Southwest and a complimentary bottle of wine awaits by your kiva-style fireplace. There's an outdoor hot tub and barbecue grills too.

Inn Paradiso B&B **$$**
(805-239-2800; www.innparadiso.com; 975 Mojave Ln; d incl breakfast from $265;) At an intimate B&B with only three contemporary rooms, amiable hosts pull out all the luxury stops, with gas fireplace sitting areas, deep soaking tubs, canopy king-sized beds and French balcony doors. Vegetarian breakfasts available.

Melody Ranch Motel MOTEL **$**
(805-238-3911, 800-909-3911; 939 Spring St; r $63-78;) There's just one story and only 19 basic rooms at this small, family-owned, 1950s motor court downtown, which translates into prices that are almost as small as the outdoor pool.

Courtyard Marriott HOTEL **$$**
(805-239-9700, 888-236-2427; www.courtyardpasorobles.com; 120 S Vine St, off Hwy 101; r $129-259;) Contemporary hotel with immaculate rooms and full amenities.

Adelaide Inn MOTEL **$$**
(805-238-2770, 800-549-7276; www.adelaideinn.com; 1215 Ysabel Ave, off Hwy 101; r $85-135;) Fresh-baked cookies and mini golf keep kids happy at this family motel.

JAMES DEAN MEMORIAL

In Cholame, about 25 miles east of Paso Robles via Hwy 46, there's a memorial near the spot where *Rebel Without a Cause* star James Dean fatally crashed his Porsche on September 30, 1955, at the age of 24. Ironically, the actor had recently filmed a public-safety campaign TV spot, in which he said, 'The road is no place to race your car. It's real murder. Remember, drive safely. The life you save might be mine.' Look for the shiny silver memorial wrapped around an oak tree outside the truck-stop Jack Ranch Cafe, which has old photographs and movie-star memorabilia inside.

Eating & Drinking

Restaurants, cafes and bars surround downtown's City Park, a grassy central square off Spring St between 11th and 12th Sts.

Artisan CALIFORNIAN **$$$**
(805-237-8084; www.artisanpasorobles.com; 1401 Park St; lunch mains $10-22, dinner mains $26-31; 11am-9pm Sun-Thu, to 10pm Fri & Sat) Eco-conscious chef Chris Kobayashi often ducks out of the kitchen just to make sure you're loving his impeccable contemporary renditions of modern American cuisine, featuring sustainably farmed meats, wild-caught seafood and artisan California cheeses. Make reservations and expect long waits.

Thomas Hill Organics Market Bistro ECLECTIC **$$$**
(805-226-5888; www.thomashillorganics.com; 1305 Park St; mains $18-26; lunch 11am-3pm Mon & Wed-Sat, 10am-3pm Sun, dinner 5-9pm Wed, Thu, Sun & Mon, to 10pm Fri & Sat) Hidden down a side alley, this farm-fresh gourmands' kitchen has only a few tables, so book ahead. On the eclectic fusion menu, which ranges from Vietnamese pork sandwiches to roasted duck breast with harissa sauce, most ingredients are locally sourced. Service is sloooow.

Villa Creek CALIFORNIAN **$$$**
(805-238-3000; 1144 Pine St; mains $22-35; 5:30-10pm) Perch casually at the wine bar and spin tapas plates or dine like a don in the formal restaurant, which marries early Spanish-colonial mission cooking traditions

with sustainable, organic ingredients in shepherd's plates of artisan cheese, sausages and olives, or rancho-style cassoulet with duck. Reservations recommended.

Firestone Walker Brewing Co BREWERY
(www.firestonebeer.com; 1400 Ramada Dr; ⊙noon-7pm) Bring your buddies to the taproom to sample famous brews like Double Barrel Ale.

Vinoteca WINE BAR
(www.vinotecawinebar.com; 835 12th St; ⊙4-9pm Mon-Thu, to 11pm Fri & Sat) Sends you soaring with its wine flights and Wednesday meet-the-winemaker nights.

Information

Paso Robles Chamber of Commerce (☎805-238-0506; www.pasoroblesschamber.com; 1225 Park St; ⊙8:30am-4:30pm Mon-Fri, 10am-2pm Sat) Information and free winery maps.

Getting There & Away

With **Amtrak** (www.amtrak.com; 800 Pine St), daily *Coast Starlight* trains head north to Salinas ($19, two hours) and Oakland ($29, five hours) or south to Santa Barbara ($26, 4¾ hours) and Los Angeles ($45, 7½ hours). Several daily Thruway buses link to more-frequent regional trains, including the *Pacific Surfliner.*

From the train station, **Greyhound** (www.greyhound.com; 800 Pine St) runs a few daily buses along Hwy 101 south to Santa Barbara ($40, three hours) and LA ($58, six hours) or north to San Francisco ($54, 6½ hours) via Santa Cruz ($40, 3¼ hours).

RTA (☎805-541-2228; www.slorta.org) bus 9 travels between San Luis Obispo and Paso Robles ($2.50, 70 minutes) hourly on weekdays, and three or four times daily on weekends.

San Luis Obispo

Almost halfway between LA and San Francisco, San Luis Obispo is the classic stopover point for road trippers. With no must-see attractions, SLO might not seem to warrant much of your time. That said, this lively yet low-key town has an enviably high quality of life – in fact, talk-show diva Oprah once deemed it America's happiest city. For travelers, SLO's proximity to beaches, state parks and Hearst Castle make it a convenient coastal hub. CalPoly university students inject a healthy dose of hubbub into the city's streets, pubs and cafes throughout the school year. Nestled at the base of the Santa Lucia foothills, SLO is just a grape's throw from thriving Edna Valley wineries, known for their crisp chardonnays and subtle syrahs and pinot noirs.

Sights

San Luis Obispo Creek, once used to irrigate mission orchards, flows through downtown. Uphill from Higuera St, **Mission Plaza** is a shady oasis with restored adobe buildings and fountains overlooking the creek. Look for the **Moon Tree**, a coast redwood grown from a seed that journeyed on board Apollo 14's lunar mission.

Mission San Luis Obispo de Tolosa MISSION
(www.missionsanluisobispo.org; 751 Palm St; suggested donation $2; ⊙9am-4pm) Those satisfyingly reverberatory bells heard around downtown emanate from this active parish. The fifth California mission, it was established in 1772 and named for a 13th-century French saint. Nicknamed the 'Prince of the Missions,' its modest church has an unusual L-shape and whitewashed walls depicting Stations of the Cross. An adjacent building contains an old-fashioned museum about daily life during the Chumash tribal and Spanish colonial periods.

FREE **San Luis Obispo Museum of Art** MUSEUM
(www.sloma.org; 1010 Broad St; ⊙11am-5pm, closed Tue Sep-Jun) Near the creek, this small gallery showcases local painters, sculptors, printmakers and fine-art photographers, as well as traveling California art exhibitions.

Bubblegum Alley QUIRKY
(off 700 block of Higuera St) SLO's weirdest sight is colorfully plastered with thousands of wads of ABC ('already been chewed') gum. Watch where you step!

Activities

The most popular local hiking trail summits **Bishop Peak** (1546ft), the tallest of the Nine Sisters, a chain of volcanic peaks that stretches north to Morro Bay. The 2.2-mile one-way trail starts in a grove of live oaks (watch out for poison oak, too) and heads uphill along rocky, exposed switchbacks. Scramble up boulders at the tippy-top for panoramic views. To get to the trailhead, drive northwest from downtown on Santa Rosa St (Hwy 1), turn left onto Foothill Dr, then right onto Patricia Dr; after 0.8 miles,

TOP FIVE EDNA VALLEY WINERIES

For a winery map and more vineyards to explore, visit www.slowine.com.

» **Edna Valley Vineyard** (ednavalleyvineyard.com; 2585 Biddle Ranch Rd; 10am-5pm) Sip Paragon Vineyard estate chardonnay by panoramic windows.

» **Kynsi** (www.kynsi.com; 2212 Corbett Canyon Rd; 11am-5pm Thu-Mon) Small, family-run vineyard pours cult-worthy pinot noirs.

» **Niven Family Wine Estates** (www.baileyana.com; 5828 Orcutt Rd; 10am-5pm) Tastings from five premium labels inside an early-20th-century wooden schoolhouse.

» **Talley** (www.talleyvineyards.com; 3031 Lopez Dr; 10:30am-4:30pm) Unpretentious, value-priced wines set among rolling hillsides, with vineyard tours daily.

» **Tolosa** (www.tolosawinery.com; 4910 Edna Rd; 11am-4:45pm) Classic no-oak chardonnay, soft pinot noir and bold red blends; guided tours and barrel tastings by appointment.

look for three black posts with a trailhead sign on your left.

For more peak hikes with ocean views, visit nearby Montaña de Oro State Park (p487).

Festivals & Events

TOP CHOICE **San Luis Obispo Farmers Market** FOOD, CULTURE
(www.downtownslo.com; 6-9pm Thu) The county's biggest and best weekly farmers market turns downtown's Higuera St into a giant street party, with smokin' barbecues, overflowing fruit and veggie stands, live music of all stripes and free sidewalk entertainment, from salvation peddlers to wackadoodle political activists. It's one of the liveliest evenings out anywhere along the Central Coast.

Concerts in the Plaza MUSIC, FOOD
(www.downtownslo.com) From early June until early September, Friday night concerts in downtown's Mission Plaza rock out with local bands and food vendors.

Savor the Central Coast FOOD, WINE
(www.savorcentralcoast.com) Behind-the-scenes farm and ranch tours, wine-tasting competitions and celebrity chefs' dinners happen in late September and early October.

Sleeping

Motels cluster off Hwy 101, especially at the northeast end of Monterey St and around Santa Rosa St (Hwy 1).

San Luis Creek Lodge HOTEL $$
(805-541-1122, 800-593-0333; www.sanluiscreeklodge.com; 1941 Monterey St; r incl breakfast $139-239;) Although it rubs shoulders a little too closely with neighboring motels, this boutique inn has fresh, spacious rooms with divine beds (some with gas fireplaces and jetted tubs) in three whimsically mismatched buildings built in Tudor, Arts and Crafts, and Southern Plantation styles. Fluffy robes, DVDs, chess sets and board games are free to borrow.

Peach Tree Inn MOTEL $$
(805-543-3170, 800-227-6396; www.peachtreeinn.com; 2001 Monterey St; r incl breakfast $79-200;) The folksy, nothing-fancy motel rooms here are inviting, especially those right by the creek or with rocking chairs on wooden porches overlooking grassy lawns, eucalyptus trees and rose gardens. A hearty breakfast features homemade breads.

Petit Soleil INN $$
(805-549-0321; www.petitsoleilslo.com; 1473 Monterey St; r incl breakfast $159-299;) This French-themed, gay-friendly 'bed et breakfast' is a mostly charming retrofit of a courtyard motel. Each room is tastefully decorated with Provençal flair, and breakfast is a gourmet feast. The front rooms catch some street noise, though.

HI Hostel Obispo HOSTEL $
(805-544-4678; www.hostelobispo.com; 1617 Santa Rosa St; dm $24-27, r from $45; check-in 4:30-10pm;) On a tree-lined street near the train station, this solar-empowered, avocado-colored hostel inhabits a converted Victorian, which gives it a bit of a B&B feel. Amenities include a kitchen and bike rentals (from $10 per day); BYOT (bring your own towel). No credit cards.

San Luis Obispo

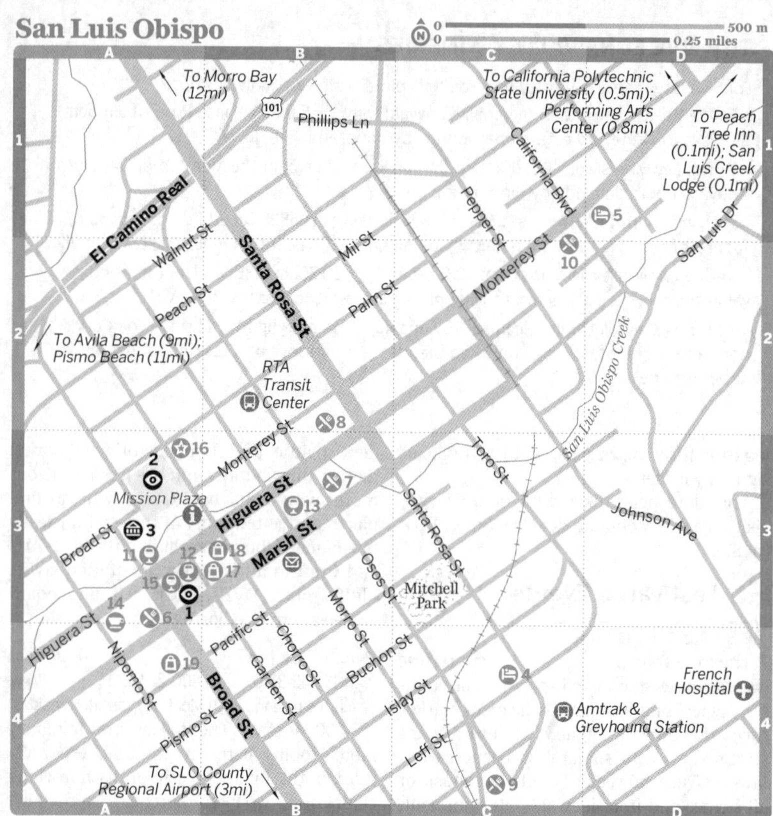

Eating

Luna Red FUSION $$$

(☎805-540-5243; www.lunaredslo.com; 1009 Monterey St; small plates $4-15, dinner mains $18-26; ⊙11am-9pm Mon-Thu, 11am-10pm Fri, 4-10pm Sat, 5-9pm Sun) An inspired chef spins recherché Californian, Mediterranean and Asian tapas, with a keen eye towards freshness and spice. Local bounty from the land and sea rules the menu, including house-smoked salumi and artisan cheeses. Stiff cocktails enhance the sophisticated ambience, with glowing lanterns and polished parquet floors.

Big Sky Café CALIFORNIAN $$

(www.bigskycafe.com; 1121 Broad St; mains $6-22; ⊙7am-9pm Mon-Wed, 7am-10pm Thu-Fri, 8am-10pm Sat, 8am-9pm Sun;) Big Sky is a big room, and still the wait can be long – its tagline is 'analog food for a digital world.' Vegetarians have almost as many options as carnivores, and many of the ingredients are sourced locally. Big-plate dinners can be bland, but breakfast (until 1pm daily) gets top marks.

Meze Wine Café & Market MEDITERRANEAN $$

(www.mezemarket.com; 1880 Santa Barbara Ave; sandwiches $8-10, shared plates $5-25; ⊙10am-9:30pm Mon-Sat, 11:30am-8:30pm Sun) Hidden downhill from the Amtrak station, this tiny Mediterranean and North African epicurean market, wine shop and tapas bar is an eclectic gem. Gather with friends around the cheese and charcuterie board, or stop in for a hand-crafted sandwich accompanied by couscous salad.

Firestone Grill BARBECUE $

(www.firestonegrill.com 1001 Higuera St; mains $5-12; ⊙11am-10pm Sun-Wed, 11am-11pm Thu-Sun;) If you can stomach huge lines, long waits for

San Luis Obispo

Sights

1 Bubblegum Alley........A3
2 Mission San Luis Obispo de Tolosa........A3
3 San Luis Obispo Museum of Art........A3

Sleeping

4 HI Hostel Obispo........C4
5 Petit Soleil........D1

Eating

Bel Frites........(see 12)
6 Big Sky Café........A3
7 Firestone Grill........B3
8 Luna Red........B2
9 Meze Wine Café & Market........C4
10 Splash Cafe........C2

Drinking

11 Creekside Brewing Co........A3
12 Downtown Brewing Co........A3
13 Granada Bistro........B3
14 Kreuzberg........A3
15 Mother's Tavern........A3

Entertainment

16 Palm Theatre........A3

Shopping

17 Finders Keepers........B3
18 Hands Gallery........B3
19 Mountain Air Sports........A4

a table and sports bar–style service, you'll get to sink your teeth into an authentic Santa Maria–style tri-tip steak sandwich on a toasted garlic roll, or a rack of succulent pork ribs.

Splash Cafe CAFE $
(www.splashbakery.com; 1491 Monterey St; dishes $3-10; ⏲7am-8:30pm Sun-Thu, to 9:30pm Fri & Sat;) Fresh soups and salads, sandwiches on house-made bread and tempting bakery treats are reason enough to kick back inside this airy uptown cafe, not far from motel row. The organic, hand-made Sweet Earth Chocolates shop is nearby.

New Frontiers Natural Marketplace GROCERIES, FAST FOOD $
(http://newfrontiers.com; 1531 Froom Ranch Way, off Hwy 101 exit Los Osos Valley Rd; ⏲8am-9pm) For organic groceries, deli picnic meals and a hot-and-cold salad bar. It's a 15-minute drive from downtown via Hwy 101 southbound.

SLO Donut Company SNACKS $
(www.slodonutcompany.com; 793 E Foothill Blvd; snacks from $2; ⏲24hr;) Home of bizarrely tasty donuts like bacon-maple or PB&J and organic, fair-trade, locally roasted coffee. It's a five-minute drive north of downtown off Santa Rosa St (Hwy 1).

Bel Frites SNACKS $
(www.belfrites.com; 1127 Garden St; snacks $4-8; ⏲3pm-2:30am Tue-Thu, noon-2:30am Fri & Sat, noon-6pm Sun) Belgian fries with New World seasonings and dipping sauces for late-night bar hoppers.

Drinking

Downtown, Higuera St is littered with college student–jammed bars and clubs.

Downtown Brewing Co BREWPUB
(www.slobrew.com; 1119 Garden St) More often called just SLO Brew, this study in rafters and exposed brick has plenty of craft beers to go with filling pub grub. Downstairs, you'll find DJs spinning or live bands with names like 'Atari Teenage Riot' playing most nights.

Creekside Brewing Co BREWPUB
(www.creeksidebrewing.com; 1040 Broad St) Kick back at a breezy patio overhanging the bubbling creek. It has got its own fairly respectable brews on tap, plus bottled Belgian beers. On Mondays, all pints are usually just three bucks.

Kreuzberg COFFEE SHOP
(www.kreuzbergcalifornia.com; 685 Higuera St; ⏲6:30am-midnight;) SLO's newest coffeehouse has earned a fervent following, with comfy couches, sprawling bookshelves, local art splashed on the walls and occasionally live music.

Mother's Tavern BAR
(www.motherstavern.com; 729 Higuera St;) Cavernous two-story 'MoTav' pub that draws in the party-hardy CalPoly student masses with its no-cover DJ-driven dance floor and frequent live-music shows.

Granada Bistro LOUNGE
(www.granadabistro.com; 1126 Morro St; ⏲Thu-Sun) Like a celebutante's living room, this swank lounge classes up the downtown scene, with imported wines and beers and live acoustic tunes.

Entertainment

Palm Theatre CINEMA
(805-541-5161; www.thepalmtheatre.com; 817 Palm St) In SLO's blink-and-you'll-miss-it Chinatown, this small-scale movie house showing foreign and indie flicks happens to be the USA's first solar-powered cinema. Look for the San Luis Obispo International Film Festival in mid-March.

Sunset Drive-In CINEMA
(805-544-4475; www.fairoakstheatre.net; 255 Elks Lane, off S Higuera St;) Recline your seat, put your feet up on the dash and munch on bottomless bags of popcorn at this classic Americana drive-in. Sticking around for the second feature (usually a B-list Hollywood blockbuster) doesn't cost extra. It's off Higuera St, about a 10-minute drive south of downtown.

Performing Arts Center PERFORMING ARTS
(PAC; 805-756-2787, 888-233-2787; www.pacslo.org; 1 Grand Ave) On the CalPoly campus, this state-of-the-art theater is SLO's biggest cultural venue, presenting a variety of concerts, theater, dance recitals, stand-up comedy and other shows by big-name performers. Event parking costs $6.

Shopping

Downtown, Higuera and Marsh Sts, along with all of the arcades and cross streets in between, are stuffed full of unique boutiques. Take a wander and find something wonderful.

Hands Gallery ART, JEWELRY
(www.handsgallery.com; 777 Higuera St; 10am-6pm Mon-Wed, 10am-8pm Thu, 10am-7pm Fri & Sat, 11am-5pm Sun) Brightly lit gallery sells fine contemporary craftwork by vibrant California artisans, including jewelry, fiber arts, metal sculptures, ceramics and blown glass, perfect for gifts or souvenirs.

Mountain Air Sports OUTDOORS
(www.mountainairsports.com; 667 Marsh St; 10am-6pm Mon-Sat, to 8pm Thu, 11am-4pm Sun) Almost the only outdoor outfitter between Monterey and Santa Barbara, here you can pick up anything from campstove fuel and tents to brand-name active clothing and hiking boots.

Finders Keepers CLOTHING
(www.finderskeepersconsignment.com; 1124 Garden St; 10am-5pm) Seriously stylish second-hand women's fashions that match SLO's breezy, laid-back coastal lifestyle, plus hand-picked handbags, coats and jewelry.

Information

SLO's compact downtown is bisected by the parallel one-way arteries of Higuera St and Marsh St. Banks with 24-hour ATMs are off Marsh St, near the post office. Most downtown coffee shops offer free wi-fi.

FedEx Office (www.fedex.com; 1127 Chorro St; per min 20-30¢; 7am-11pm Mon-Fri, 9am-9pm Sat & Sun;) Pay-as-you-go internet workstations and free wi-fi.

French Hospital (805-543-5353; www.frenchmedicalcenter.org; 1911 Johnson Ave; 24hr) Emergency room.

Public library (www.slolibrary.org; 995 Palm St; 10am-5pm Wed-Sat, to 8pm Tue;) Free wi-fi and public internet terminals.

San Luis Obispo Chamber of Commerce (805-781-2777; www.visitslo.com; 1039 Chorro St; 10am-5pm Sun-Wed, 10am-7pm Thu-Sat) Free maps and information.

Getting There & Around

Off Broad St, over 3 miles southeast of downtown, **SLO County Regional Airport** (SBP; www.sloairport.com;) offers commuter flights with United (LA and San Francisco) and US Airways (Phoenix).

Amtrak (www.amtrak.com; 1011 Railroad Ave) runs daily Seattle–LA *Coast Starlight* and twice-daily SLO–San Diego *Pacific Surfliner* trains. Both routes head south to Santa Barbara ($29, 2¾ hours) and Los Angeles ($34, 5½ hours). Only the *Coast Starlight* connects north to Salinas ($31, 3½ hours) and Oakland ($34, six hours). Several daily Thruway buses link to more regional trains.

From the train station, about 0.6 miles east of downtown, **Greyhound** (www.greyhound.com; 1023 Railroad Ave) operates a few daily buses along Hwy 101 south to Los Angeles ($38, 5¼ hours) via Santa Barbara ($26, 2¼ hours) and north to San Francisco ($48, 6½ hours) via Santa Cruz ($39, four hours).

San Luis Obispo's **Regional Transit Authority** (RTA; 805-541-2228; www.slorta.org) operates daily county-wide buses with limited weekend services; one-way fares are $1.50 to $3 (day pass $5). All buses are equipped with two-bicycle racks. Lines converge on downtown's **transit center** (cnr Palm & Osos Sts).

SLO Transit (805-541-2877; www.slocity.org) runs local city buses and the downtown trolley (50¢), which loops around every 15 to 20 minutes between 3pm and 10pm on Thursday

WORTH A TRIP

CARRIZO PLAIN NATIONAL MONUMENT

Hidden in eastern SLO County, **Carrizo Plain National Monument** (www.ca.blm.gov/bakersfield; admission free; ⏲24hr) is a geological wonderland, where you can walk or drive atop the San Andreas Fault. This peaceful wildlife preserve also protects a diversity of species including endangered California condors and jewel flowers, tule elk, pronghorn antelope and the San Joaquin kit fox. Pick up 4WD and hiking maps at the **Goodwin Education Center** (☎805-475-2131; ⏲9am-4pm Thu-Sun Dec-May), past the dazzling white salt flats of Soda Lake, near the trailhead for Painted Rock, which displays Native American pictographs. The monument is about 55 winding miles east of Hwy 101, or 55 miles west of the I-5 Freeway, via Hwy 58 and Soda Lake Rd. Two primitive **Bureau of Land Management (BLM) Campgrounds** offer free, first-come, first-served campsites.

year-round, and 3pm to 10pm Friday and 1pm to 10pm Saturday from April through October.

Avila Beach

Quaint, sunny Avila Beach lures crowds with its strand of golden sand and a freshly built seafront commercial district lined by restaurants, shops and cafes. Two miles west of downtown, Port San Luis is a working fishing harbor.

Sights & Activities

For a lazy summer day at the beach, rent beach chairs and umbrellas, surfboards, boogie boards and wetsuits underneath **Avila Pier**, off downtown's waterfront promenade. At the port, the barking of sea lions accompanies you as you stroll **Harford Pier**, one of the Central Coast's most authentic fishing piers.

Point San Luis Lighthouse LIGHTHOUSE
(Map p500; www.sanluislighthouse.org; lighthouse admission adult/family $5/10, trolley tour incl lighthouse admission per person $20; ⏲guided hikes 9am-1pm Wed & Sat, trolley tours noon, 1pm & 2pm on 1st & 3rd Sat of the month) Just getting to this scenic 1890 lighthouse, overshadowed by Diablo Canyon nuclear power plant, is an adventure. The cheapest way to reach the lighthouse is via a rocky, crumbling, 3.75-mile trail. Weather permitting, it's open only for **guided hikes** (☎805-541-8735) led by Pacific Gas & Electric docents. Children under nine years old are not allowed to hike; call for reservations at least two weeks in advance and bring plenty of water. If you'd rather take it easy and ride out to the lighthouse, which harbors an original Fresnel lens and authentic Victorian period furnishings, join a Saturday afternoon **trolley tour** (☎805-540-5771). Reservations are required.

Avila Valley Barn FARM
(Map p500; http://avilavalleybarn.com; 560 Avila Beach Dr; ⏲9am-6pm daily Jun-Oct, 9am-5pm Thu-Mon Nov-May; 👪) At this rural farmstand and pick-your-own berry farm, park alongside the sheep and goat pens, lick an ice-cream cone, then grab a basket and walk out into the fields to harvest jammy olallieberries and strawberries in late spring, midsummer peaches and nectarines or apples and pumpkins in autumn.

Sycamore Mineral Springs HOT SPRINGS
(Map p500; ☎805-595-7302, 800-234-5831; www.sycamoresprings.com; 1215 Avila Beach Dr; per person per hr $12.50-17.50; ⏲8am-midnight, last reservation 10:45pm) Make time for a luxuriant soak, where private redwood hot tubs are discreetly laddered up a woodsy hillside. Call in advance for reservations, as it's often fully booked, especially during summer and on weekends after dark.

Avila Hot Springs HOT SPRINGS
(Map p500; ☎805-595-2359; www.avilahotsprings.com; 250 Avila Beach Dr; adult/child under 16yr $10/8; ⏲8am-9pm Sun-Thu, to 10pm Fri & Sat; 👪) For families, this slightly sulfuric, lukewarm public swimming pool has a pretty cool waterslide (open noon to 5pm daily).

Central Coast Kayaks KAYAKING
(Map p500; ☎805-773-3500; www.centralcoastkayaks.com; 1879 Shell Beach Rd, Shell Beach; kayak or SUP rentals $20-60, 2hr kayaking tour $70) Paddle out among sea otters and seals and through mesmerizing sea caves, arches and kelp forests.

San Luis Obispo Bay

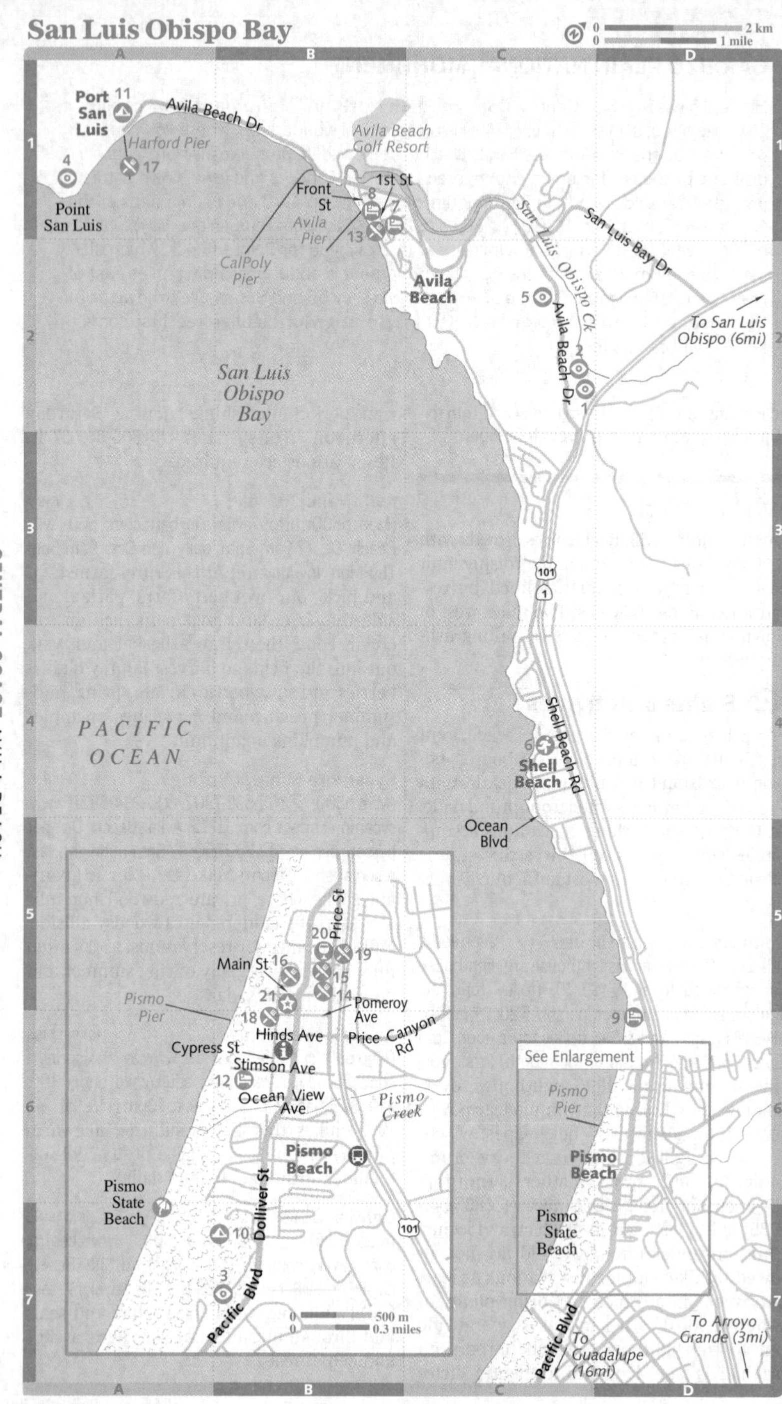

San Luis Obispo Bay

Patriot Sportfishing BOAT TOURS

(Map p500; ☎805-595-7200, 800-714-3474; www.patriotsportfishing.com; Harford Pier, off Avila Beach Dr; tours adult/child 4-12yr/child under 4yr from $35/15/10) This long-running local biz organizes deep-sea fishing trips and tournaments, as well as whale-spotting cruises between December and April.

Sleeping

Avila La Fonda BOUTIQUE HOTEL $$$

(Map p500; ☎805-595-1700; www.avilalafonda.com; 101 San Miguel St; ste $250-800;) Downtown, this small inn evinces a harmonious mix of Mexican and Spanish colonial styles, with hand-painted tiles, stained-glass windows, wrought iron and rich wood. The deck has barbecue grills, a wet bar and a sociable fireplace for nightly wine and hors d'oeuvres. With vibrant colors, the sprawling rooms and suites have all mod cons (except air-con), plus hot tubs and some kitchens. Pet fee $50.

Avila Lighthouse Suites HOTEL $$$

(Map p500; ☎805-627-1900, 800-372-8452; www.avilalighthousesuites.com; 550 Front St; ste incl breakfast $229-479;) Any closer to the ocean, and your bed would actually be sitting on the sand. Made with families in mind, this apartment-style hotel offers suites and villas with kitchenettes. But it's the giant heated outdoor pool, ping-pong tables, putting green and life-sized checkers board that keeps kids amused.

Port San Luis CAMPGROUND $

(Map p500; RV sites without/with hookups from $30/45) First-come, first-served parking spaces by the side of the road have ocean views; RVs only (no tents).

Avila Hot Springs Campground CAMPGROUND $

(Map p500; ☎805-595-2359; www.avilahotsprings.com; 250 Avila Beach Dr; tent & RV sites without/with hookups from $30/45) Crowded campground off Hwy 101 has hot showers and flush toilets; reservations essential in summer.

Eating

At Port San Luis, Harford Pier is home to seafood shops that sell rockfish, sole, salmon and other fresh catch right off the boats.

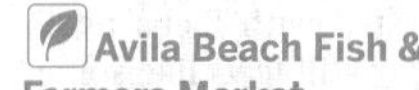

Avila Beach Fish & Farmers Market MARKET $

(Map p500; www.avilabeachpier.com; ⏲4-8pm Fri Apr–mid-Sep) With finger-lickin' food booths (seafood is a specialty, of course) and live music and entertainment, this outdoor street party takes over downtown's oceanfront promenade weekly in spring and summer.

Avila Grocery & Deli AMERICAN, FAST FOOD $
(Map p500; http://avilagrocery.com; 354 Front St; mains $5-11; ⏲7am-7pm; 👪) Gather everything you'll need for a beach picnic at this family-owned deli and general store on the ocean-front promenade. The chipotle tri-tip steak wrap is a gold-medal winner; so are bang-up breakfasts.

Pete's Pierside Cafe SEAFOOD, FAST FOOD $
(Map p500; www.petespiersidecafe.com; Harford Pier, off Avila Beach Dr; mains $5-12; ⏲11am-5pm) Hit this unpretentious seafood shack for crispy fish and chips, fresh oysters and crab legs, and an excellent salsa bar to doctor your fish taco with.

Olde Port Inn SEAFOOD $$$
(Map p500; ☎805-595-2515; www.oldeportinn.com; Harford Pier, off Avila Beach Dr; mains $10-38; ⏲11:30am-9pm Sun-Thu, to 10pm Fri & Sat) Clam chowder and cioppino are standouts at this seriously old-school seafood restaurant at the tip of Harford Pier. A few tables have glass tops, so lucky diners can peer down into the ocean.

Getting There & Around

From late May through September, a free **trolley** loops around downtown Avila Beach and Port San Luis, and out to Hwy 101. It usually operates hourly from 10am to 8pm on Saturday and 10am to 5pm on Sunday. In Shell Beach, the trolley connects with **South County Regional Transit** (SCAT; ☎805-781-4472; www.slorta.org) bus 21, which runs hourly to Pismo Beach ($1.25, 15 minutes).

Pismo Beach

The largest of San Luis Obispo Bay's 'Five Cities,' this 1950s-retro California beach town fronts a more commercial pier than neighboring Avila, but its beach is invitingly wide and sandy. Backed by a wooden pier that stretches toward the setting sun, here James Dean once trysted with Pier Angeli, and Pismo Beach today still feels like somewhere straight out of *Rebel Without a Cause* or *American Graffiti*. If you're looking for a sand-and-surf respite from road tripping, break your journey here.

Sights & Activities

Pismo likes to call itself the 'Clam Capital of the World,' but these days the **beach** is pretty much clammed out. You'll have better luck catching something fishy off the **pier**, where you can rent rods. To rent a wetsuit, boogie board or surfboard, cruise the nearby surf shops.

FREE **Monarch Butterfly Grove** PARK
(Map p500; www.monarchbutterfly.org; ⏲sunrise-sunset) From late October until February, over 25,000 black-and-orange monarchs make their winter home here. Forming dense clusters in the tops of eucalyptus trees, they might easily be mistaken for leaves. Volunteers can tell you all about the insects' incredible journey, which outlasts any single generation of butterflies. Look for a gravel parking pull-out on the west side of Pacific Blvd (Hwy 1), just south of Pismo State Beach's North Beach Campground.

Festivals & Events

Classic at Pismo Beach CULTURE
(www.thepismobeachclassic.com) Show up in mid-June when hot rods and muscle cars line the main drags off Hwy 1.

Clam Festival FOOD
(www.classiccalifornia.com) In mid-October, celebrate the formerly abundant and still tasty mollusk with a clam dig, chowder cookoff, food vendors and live music.

Sleeping

Pismo Beach has dozens of motels, but rooms fill up quickly and prices skyrocket in summer, especially on weekends. Resort hotels roost on cliffs north of town via Price St and Shell Beach Rd, while motels cluster near the beach and along Hwy 101.

Pismo Lighthouse Suites HOTEL $$$
(Map p500; ☎805-773-2411, 800-245-2411; www.pismolighthousesuites.com; 2411 Price St; ste incl breakfast $149-329; ❄@📶🏊👪) With everything a vacationing family needs – from in-room Nintendo and kitchenettes, to a life-sized outdoor chessboard, a putting green, table tennis and badminton courts – this contemporary all-suites hotel is hard to tear yourself away from.

Sandcastle Inn HOTEL $$$
(Map p500; ☎805-773-2422, 800-822-6606; www.sandcastleinn.com; 100 Stimson Ave; r incl breakfast $169-435; 📶) Many of these Eastern Seaboard–styled rooms are mere steps from the sand. The best suite in the house is perfect for getting engaged after cracking open a bottle of wine at sunset on the ocean-view patio. Wi-fi in lobby only.

WORTH A TRIP

GUADALUPE

Hwy 1 ends its brief relationship with Hwy 101 just south of Pismo Beach, as it veers off toward the coast. Over 15 miles further south, you almost expect to have to dodge Old West tumbleweeds as you drive into the one-road agricultural town of Guadalupe.

In 1923 a huge Hollywood crew descended on this remote outpost for the filming of the silent version of the *Ten Commandments*. Enormous Egyptian sets were constructed in Guadalupe's oceanfront sand dunes, complete with huge sphinxes and more. Afterward, director Cecil B DeMille saved money by leaving the magnificent sets – albeit ones constructed of hay, plaster and paint – in place and simply burying them in the sand. Over the following decades knowledge of the exact location of the vast sets was lost.

In 1983 film and archaeology buffs started looking for the 'Lost City of DeMille.' Many artifacts have been found and the locations of main structures pinpointed. Learn loads more about these oddball archaeological excavations online at www.lostcitydemille.com.

Back in town, inspect some of the recovered movie-set pieces at the tiny **Dunes Visitor Center** (www.dunescenter.org; 1055 Guadalupe St; admission by donation; ⌚10am-4pm Tue-Sat), which has exhibits about the ecology of North America's largest coastal dunes and also about the Dunites, mystical folks who called the dunes home during the 1930s.

The dunes preserve, which is a state-protected archaeological site (no digging or taking away souvenirs, sorry!) is about 5 miles west of town via Hwy 166. More recent movies shot here include *Pirates of the Caribbean: At World's End* (2007).

Pismo State Beach CAMPGROUND $
(Map p500; ☎reservations 800-444-7275; www.reserveamerica.com; tent & RV sites $25-35) About a mile south of downtown, off Dolliver St (Hwy 1), the state park's **North Beach Campground** has over 100 well-spaced, grassy sites, in the shade of eucalyptus trees. The campground offers easy beach access, flush toilets and hot showers.

Eating

TOP CHOICE **Cracked Crab** SEAFOOD $$$
(Map p500; www.crackedcrab.com; 751 Price St; mains $9-50; ⌚11am-9pm Sun-Thu, 11am-10pm Fri & Sat; 👪) Fresh seafood is the staple at this super-casual, family-owned grill. When the famous bucket o'seafood, full of flying bits of fish, Cajun sausage, red potatoes and cob corn, gets dumped on your butcher-paper-covered table, make sure you're wearing one of those silly-looking plastic bibs. Excellent regional wine list.

Giuseppe's ITALIAN $$$
(Map p500; www.guiseppesrestaurant.com; 891 Price St; lunch mains $9-15, dinner mains $12-32; ⌚lunch 11:30am-3pm Mon-Fri, dinner 4:30-10pm Sun-Thu, to 11pm Fri & Sat) Occasionally outstanding Southern Italian fare is served at this date-worthy *cucina*, which brims with the owner's personality – just eyeball the lineup of Vespa scooters parked out front. Safe bets are wood-fired pizzas and traditional pastas like spicy prawn spaghettini. Show up early, or expect a long wait (no reservations).

Splash Cafe SEAFOOD $
(Map p500; www.splashcafe.com; 197 Pomeroy Ave; dishes $4-10; ⌚8am-9pm; 👪) Uphill from the pier, lines go out the door to wrap around this scruffy surf-style hole-in-the-wall, famous for its award-winning clam chowder in a home-baked sourdough bread bowl, and a long lineup of grilled and fried briny fare. It keeps shorter hours in winter.

Klondike Pizza PIZZA $$
(www.klondikepizza.com; 104 Bridge St; pizzas $12-26; ⌚11am-9pm Sun-Thu, to 10pm Fri & Sat; 👪) Across Hwy 101 in small-town Arroyo Grande, this subterranean Alaskan-run pizzeria is littered with peanut shells and has checkers and other board games to play while you wait for your reindeer-sausage pie. Hum along with a kazoo during twice-monthly Saturday-night sing-alongs.

Doc Burnstein's Ice Cream Lab ICE CREAM $
(www.docburnsteins.com; 114 W Branch St; snacks $3-8; ⌚11am-9:30pm Sun-Thu, to 10:30pm Fri & Sat; 👪) On Arroyo Grande's main drag, Doc's scoops up fantastical flavors like Petite Syrah sorbet and the 'Elvis Special' (peanut butter with banana swirls). Live ice-cream lab shows start at 7pm sharp on Wednesday.

Old West Cinnamon Rolls BAKERY $
(Map p500; www.oldwestcinnamon.com; 861 Dolliver St; snacks & drinks $2-5; ⊙6:30am-5:30pm) Really, the name says it all at this gobsmacking bakery by the beach.

Utopia Bakery Cafe BAKERY $
(Map p500; www.utopiabakery.com; 950 Price St; snacks & sandwiches $2-8; ⊙6am-6pm) Corner stop for cookies, croissants, chocolate-chip scones and espresso drinks.

Drinking & Entertainment

Taste of the Valleys WINE BAR
(Map p500; www.pismowineshop.com; 911 Price St; ⊙noon-9pm Mon-Thu, to 10pm Fri & Sat, to 8pm Sun) Inside a quiet wine shop stacked floor to ceiling with California vintages; ask for a taste of anything they've got open today, or sample from the astounding list of 500 wines poured by the glass.

Pismo Bowl BOWLING ALLEY
(Map p500; www.pismobeachbowl.com; 277 Pomeroy Ave; ⊙noon-10pm Sun-Thu, to midnight Fri & Sat;) Epitomizing Pismo Beach's retro vibe, this old-fashioned bowling alley is just a short walk uphill from the pier. Rockin' blacklight 'cosmic bowling' rules on Friday and Saturday nights.

Information

Pismo Beach Visitors Information Center (☎805-773-4382, 800-443-7778; www.classiccalifornia.com; 581 Dolliver St, cnr Hinds Ave; ⊙9am-5pm Mon-Fri, 11am-4pm Sat) Free tourist maps and brochures.

Getting There & Around

Operating hourly on weekdays, and a few times daily on weekends, **RTA** (☎805-541-2228; www.slorta.org) bus 10 links Pismo's Premium Outlets mall, about a mile from the beach, with San Luis Obispo ($2, 25 minutes). **South County Regional Transit** (SCAT; ☎805-781-4472; www.slorta.org) runs hourly local buses ($1.25) connecting Pismo Beach with Shell Beach and Arroyo Grande.

La Purísima Mission State Historic Park

Surrounded by colorful commercial flower fields, this pastoral valley **mission** (www.lapurisimamission.org, www.parks.ca.gov; 2295 Purisima Rd, Lompoc; per car $6; ⊙9am-5pm) was extensively restored by the Civilian Conservation Corps (CCC) in the 1930s. Today it's one of the most evocative of California's original 21 Spanish colonial missions, with atmospheric adobe buildings that include a church, living quarters and shops. The mission's fields still support grazing livestock, while nearby flowering gardens are planted with medicinal plants used by Chumash tribespeople.

The mission is 15 miles west of Hwy 101 via Hwy 246. Past the golf course, take the turnoff for Purisima Rd on the north (right) side of the highway, then drive about another mile.

Santa Barbara Wine Country

Oak-dotted hillsides, winding country lanes, rows of sweetly heavy grapevines stretching as far as the eye can see – it's hard not to gush about the Santa Maria and Santa Ynez Valleys. Maybe you've been inspired to visit by the Oscar-winning film *Sideways,* an ode to the joys and hazards of wine-country living, as seen through the misadventures of middle-aged buddies Miles and Jack. The movie is like real life in one respect: this wine country is ideal for do-it-yourself-exploring with friends.

With more than 100 wineries spread out across the landscape, it can seem daunting at first. But the wine country's five small towns – Buellton, Solvang, Santa Ynez, Ballard and Los Olivos – are all clustered within 10 miles of one another, so it's easy to stop, shop and eat whenever and wherever you happen to feel like it. Don't worry about sticking to a regimented plan or following prescriptive wine guides. Just soak up the scenery and pull over where the signs look welcoming and the vibe feels right.

Sights & Activities

Nearer the coast, pinot noir – a particularly fragile grape – flourishes in the fog. Further inland, sun-loving Rhône varietals like Syrah thrive. Tasting fees average $10, and some wineries give vineyard tours (reservations may be required).

FOXEN CANYON

The pastoral **Foxen Canyon Wine Trail** (www.foxencanyonwinetrail.com) runs north from Hwy 154, just west of Los Olivos, into the rural Santa Maria Valley.

WORTH A TRIP

HIDDEN BEACHES OFF HIGHWAY 1

West of Lompoc lie some truly wild beaches worth the trouble of visiting.

Ocean Beach County Park (www.countyofsb.org/parks; ⏲8am-sunset) and **Surf Beach**, with its remote Amtrak train stop, are really one beach sidling up to Vandenberg Air Force Base. During the 10-mile drive west of Lompoc via Ocean Ave, you'll pass mysterious-looking structures supporting spy and commercial satellite launches. The dunes are untrammeled and interpretive signs explain the estuary's ecology. Because endangered snowy plovers nest here, vast areas of the beach are often closed between March and September.

Leaving Hwy 1 around 5 miles east of Lompoc, Jalama Rd follows 14 miles of twisting tarmac across ranch and farmlands, leading to **Jalama Beach County Park** (www.countyofsb.org/parks; per car/dog $10/3;). Utterly isolated, it's home to a crazy-popular **campground** (☎805-736-3504; www.jalamabeach.com; tent & RV sites without/with hookups from $25/40, cabins $100-220; ⏲campground store & cafe 7am-9pm) that only accepts reservations for its newly built cabins. Otherwise, you should arrive by 8am to get on the waiting list for a campsite – look for the 'campground full' sign, a half-mile south of Hwy 1, to avoid a wasted trip.

Firestone WINERY
(☎805-688-3940; www.firestonewine.com; 5000 Zaca Station Rd; tour $5; ⏲tasting room 10am-5pm, tour schedules vary) Firestone Vineyard is Santa Barbara's oldest estate winery, founded in 1972. Sweeping views of the vineyard from the sleek, wood-paneled tasting room are as impressive as the value-priced Syrah, pinot noir and Bordeaux-style blends.

Foxen WINERY
(www.foxenvineyard.com; 7600 Foxen Canyon Rd; ⏲11am-4pm) Crafts full-fruited pinot noirs, steel-cut chardonnays and Rhône-style reds inside a solar-powered tasting room on a former cattle ranch. Down the road, its rustic tin-roofed 'shack' pours Bordeaux-style and Cal-Ital varietals under the boutique 'Foxen 7200' label.

Zaca Mesa WINERY
(www.zacamesa.com; 6905 Foxen Canyon Rd; ⏲10am-4pm, to 5pm Fri & Sat late May-early Sep) Known not only for its sustainably-grown estate Rhône varietals and signature Z Cuvée red blend, but also a life-sized outdoor chessboard, shady picnic area and walking trails overlooking the vineyards.

Kenneth Volk WINERY
(www.volkwines.com; 5230 Tepusquet Rd; ⏲10:30am-4:30pm) Only an established cult winemaker could convince oenophiles to drive this far out of their way to taste standard-bearing pinot noir and heritage varietals like floral-scented Malvasia or inky Negrette.

SANTA RITA HILLS

The **Santa Rita Hills Wine Trail** (www.santaritahillswinetrail.com) shines brightly when it comes to ecoconscious farming practices and top-notch pinot noir. Country tasting rooms line a scenic loop west of Hwy 101 via Santa Rosa Rd and Hwy 246.

Alma Rosa WINERY
(www.almarosawinery.com; 7250 Santa Rosa Rd; ⏲11am-4:30pm) Cacti and cobblestones welcome you to the ranch, reached via a long, winding gravel driveway. Knock-out vineyard-designated pinot noirs and a fine pinot blanc made with California-certified organic grapes are poured.

Melville WINERY
(www.melvillewinery.com; 5185 E Hwy 146; ⏲11am-4pm) Mediterranean hillside villa offers estate-grown, small-lot bottled pinot noir, Syrah and chardonnay made by folks who believe in talking about pounds per plant, not tons per acre. Over a dozen different clones of pinot noir alone grow here.

Babcock WINERY
(www.babcockwinery.com; 5175 E Hwy 146; ⏲10:30am-4pm, to 5pm Apr-Oct) Family-owned vineyards overflowing with different varietals – chardonnay, sauvignon blanc, pinot noir, Syrah, cabernet sauvignon and more – let an innovative small-lot winemaker be the star. The Fathom red blend is pilgrimage-worthy.

Santa Barbara Wine Country

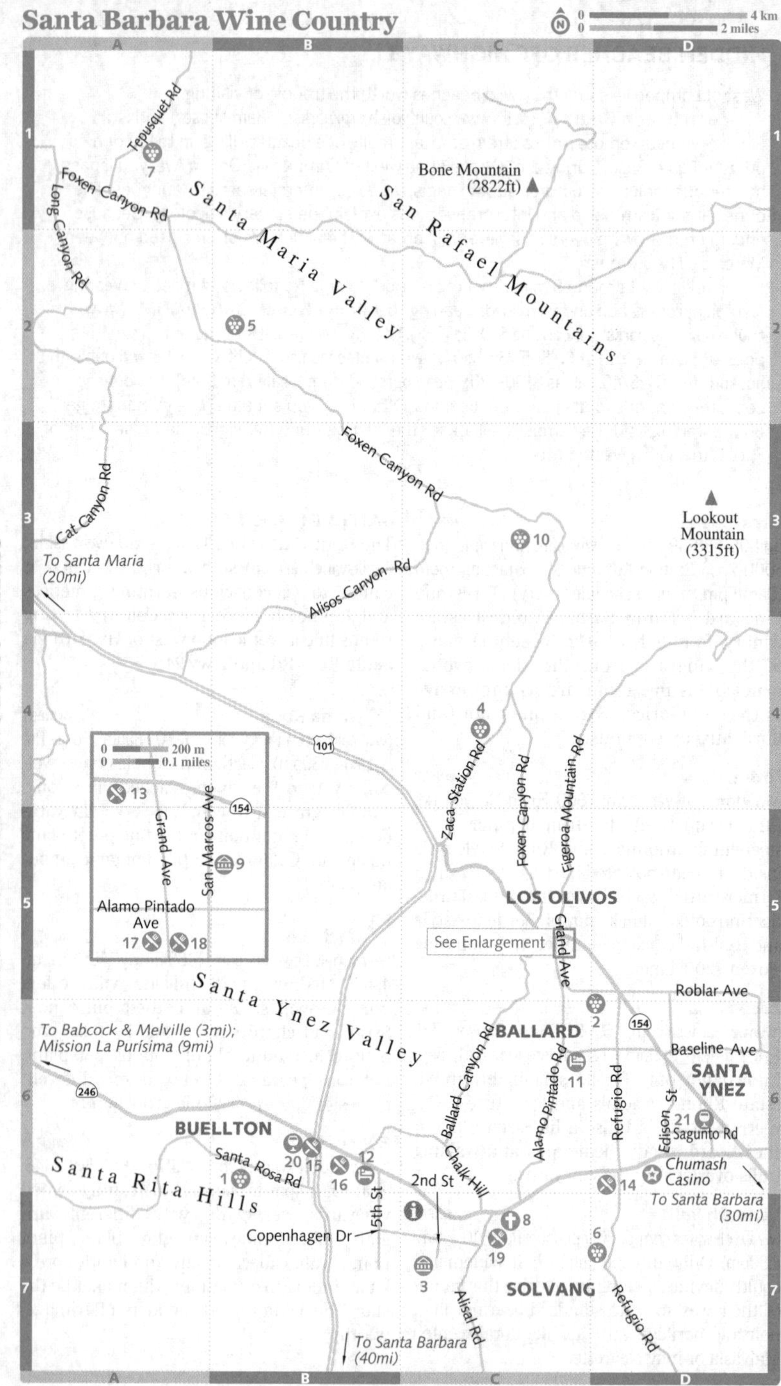

Santa Barbara Wine Country

Sights
1 Alma Rosa B6
2 Beckmen D6
3 Elverhøj Museum C7
4 Firestone C4
5 Foxen B2
6 Kalyra D7
7 Kenneth Volk A1
8 Mission Santa Inés C7
9 Wildling Art Museum B5
10 Zaca Mesa C3

Sleeping
11 Ballard Inn & Restaurant C6
12 Hadsten House Inn B6

Eating
13 Brothers' Restaurant at Mattei's Tavern A4
14 El Rancho Market D6
15 Ellen's Danish Pancake House B6
16 Hitching Post II B6
17 Los Olivos Café A5
18 Petros A5
19 Solvang Bakery C7

Drinking
20 Avant Tapas & Wine B6
21 Maverick Saloon D6

SANTA YNEZ VALLEY

You'll find dozens of wineries inside the triangle of Hwys 154, 246 and 101, including in downtown Los Olivos and Solvang. Noisy tour groups, harried staff and stingy pours too often disappoint at many popular places, but not at these welcoming wineries.

Beckmen WINERY
(www.beckmenvineyards.com; 2670 Ontiveros Rd; ⏲11am-5pm) Bring a picnic to the duck-pond gazebos at this tranquil winery, where biodynamically farmed, estate-grown Rhône varietals flourish on the unique terroir of Purisima Mountain. Follow Roblar Ave west of Hwy 154.

Kalyra WINERY
(www.kalyrawinery.com; 343 Refugio Rd; ⏲11am-5pm Mon-Fri, 10am-5pm Sat & Sun) An Australian surfer traveled halfway around the world to combine his two loves: surfing and wine making. Try his unique Shiraz–cabernet sauvignon blend made from Australian grapes or more locally grown varietals, all in bottles with Aboriginal art–inspired labels.

AROUND THE WINE COUNTRY TOWNS

Cap'n, we've hit a windmill! **Solvang** is a touristy Danish village founded in 1911 on what was once a 19th-century Spanish colonial mission, later a Mexican *rancho* land grant. With its knickknack stores and cutesy motels, the town is almost as sticky-sweet as the Scandinavian pastries foisted upon the wandering hordes. Solvang's **Elverhøj Museum** (www.elverhoj.org; 1624 Elverhoy Way; adult/child under 13 $3/free; ⏲1-4pm Wed & Thu, noon-4pm Fri-Sun) uncovers the roots of real Danish life in the area, while **Mission Santa Inés** (www.missionsantaines.org; 1760 Mission Dr; adult/child under 12 $5/free; ⏲9am-4:30pm) witnessed an 1824 Chumash revolt against Spanish colonial cruelty.

Farther northwest, the posh ranching town of **Los Olivos** has a four-block-long main street lined with wine-tasting rooms and bars, art galleries, cafes and surprisingly fashionable shops seemingly airlifted straight out of Napa. The petite **Wilding Art Museum** (www.wildingmuseum.org; 2928 San Marcos Ave; admission by donation; ⏲11am-5pm Wed-Sun) exhibits nature-themed California and American Western art.

ALONG HIGHWAY 154 (SAN MARCOS PASS RD)

The **Los Padres National Forest** (www.r5.fs.fed.us/lospadres) offers several good hiking trails off Paradise Rd, which crosses Hwy 154 north of San Marcos Pass. Try the 2-mile round-trip **Red Rock Trail**, where the Santa Ynez River deeply pools among rocks and waterfalls, a tempting spot for swimming and sunbathing. En route to the trailhead, which lies beyond the river crossing, drop by the **ranger station** (☎805-967-3481; 3505 Paradise Rd; ⏲8:30am-4:30pm Mon-Fri) for posted trail maps and information and a National Forest Adventure Pass for parking ($5 per day).

Just northwest, **Cachuma Lake Recreation Area** (www.cachuma.com; per car $10; ⏲sunrise-sunset) is a county-park haven for fishers, canoers and kayakers, with wildlife-watching **cruises** (☎805-686-5050/5055; adult/child 4-12yr $15/7) and a kid-friendly nature center (805-693-0691; 2265 Hwy 154; daily Jun-Aug, weekends only Sep-May;).

Tours

Sustainable Vine Wine Tours WINERY TOURS
(805-698-3911; www.sustainablevine.com; full-day tour incl lunch $125) Biodiesel van tours of wineries implementing organic and sustainable agricultural practices.

Santa Barbara Wine Country Cycling Tours WINERY TOURS
(888-557-8687; www.winecountrycycling.com; bike rentals per day $45-85, half-/full-day tours from $70/135) Cycling tours leave from Santa Ynez; quality road and hybrid mountain bike rentals also available.

Sleeping

Avoid the price-gouging by taking a day trip from Santa Barbara. Otherwise, Buellton has bland chains right off Hwy 101. A few miles east along Hwy 246, Solvang has many more motels and hotels, but don't expect any bargains, especially not on weekends. Smaller wine-country towns offer a handful of historic inns.

Ballard Inn & Restaurant B&B $$$
(805-688-7770, 800-638-2466; www.ballardinn.com; 2436 Baseline Ave, Ballard; r incl breakfast $269-345;) For honeymooners and romantics, this contemporary-built inn awaits in the 19th-century stagecoach town of Ballard, flung between Los Olivos and Solvang. Wood-burning fireplaces make private en-suite rooms even more cozy. Rates include wine tastings. Reservations essential.

Hadsten House Inn BOUTIQUE HOTEL $$
(805-688-3210, 800-457-5373; www.hadstenhouse.com; 1450 Mission Dr; r incl breakfast $150-255;) This revamped motel has glammed up everything except an uninspiring exterior. Inside, you'll find a heated pool and rooms that are surprisingly plush, with flatscreen TVs, triple-sheeted beds and L'Occitane bath products. Rates include afternoon wine-and-cheese tasting.

Cachuma Lake Recreation Area CAMPGROUND, CABINS $
(info 805-686-5055, yurt & cabin reservations 805-686-5050; www.cachuma.com; tent & RV sites without/with hookups from $20/40, yurts $80-105, cabins $100-220) First-come, first-served campsites with access to hot showers fill quickly, especially in summer and on weekends. Book ahead for ecofriendly canvas-sided yurts and knotty pine-paneled cabins (no air-con).

Los Padres National Forest CAMPGROUND $
(reservations 877-444-6777; www.recreation.gov; tent & RV sites $19-35) First-come, first-served and reservable sites include Fremont, Paradise and Los Prietos before the ranger station and Upper Oso at the end of Paradise Rd, off Hwy 154.

Eating

Petros MEDITERRANEAN $$$
(805-686-5455; www.petrosrestaurant.com; Fess Parker Wine Country Inn & Spa, 2860 Grand Ave, Los Olivos; shared plates $6-18, dinner mains $22-36; 7am-10pm Sun-Thu, to 11pm Fri & Sat) In a sunny, modern clean-lined dining room, sophisticated Greek cuisine makes for a refreshing change from Italianate wine-country kitsch. Grilled pita with sweet-and-savory dips, flatbread pizzas and feta-crusted rack of lamb will satisfy even picky foodies. Reservations recommended.

Los Olivos Café CALIFORNIAN $$$
(805-688-7265; www.losolivoscafe.com; 2879 Grand Ave, Los Olivos; mains $12-30; 11:30am-8:30pm) With white canopies and a wisteria-covered trellis, this Cal-Mediterranean bistro swirls up a casual-chic ambience that adds a nice finish to a long day of touring. The menu gets mixed marks; stick with antipasto platters, hearty salads and crispy pizzas, and wine flights at the bar. Reservations essential.

Brothers Restaurant at Mattei's Tavern AMERICAN $$$
(805-688-4820; www.matteistavern.com; 2350 Railway Ave, Los Olivos; mains $18-44; 5-9pm) You half expect a stagecoach to come thundering up in time for dinner at this authentic late-19th-century tavern. At checkered-tablecloth tables, dine on bold American country flavors like hickory-smoked salmon and oven-roasted rack of lamb. Get gussied up, pardner! Reservations advisable.

Hitching Post II STEAKHOUSE $$$
(805-688-0676; www.hitchingpost2.com; 406 E Hwy 246, Buellton; mains $22-48; 5-9:30pm Mon-Fri, 4-9:30pm Sat & Sun) You'll be hard-pressed to find better steaks and chops than at this legendary, old-guard country steakhouse, which serves oak-grilled steaks and baby back ribs and makes its own pinot noir

(which is damn good, by the way). Reservations essential.

El Rancho Market FAST FOOD, GROCERIES $
(www.elranchomarket.com; 2886 Mission Dr (Hwy 246), Solvang; ⌚6am-10pm) If you want to fill a picnic basket, not to mention reintegrate into society after a day of windmills, clogs and *abelskiver*, this supermarket has a fantastic deli case; take-out barbecue, soups and salads; bargain wine racks; and an espresso bar.

Ellen's Danish Pancake House BREAKFAST $$
(www.ellensdanishpancakehouse.com; 272 Ave of the Flags, Buellton; mains $6-12; ⌚6am-8pm Tue-Sun, to 2pm Mon; 👪) Who needs Solvang? Locals know to come here for the wine country's best Danish pancakes, Danish sausages and not-so-Danish Belgian waffles.

Solvang Bakery BAKERY $
(www.solvangbakery.com; 460 Alisal Rd, Solvang; items from $2; ⌚7am-6pm) Solvang's bakeries prove an irresistible draw, but most aren't especially good. This tasty exception vends Danish cookies, iced almond butter rings and more.

Drinking & Entertainment

Avant Tapas & Wine WINE BAR
(www.avantwines.com; 35 Industrial Way, Buellton; ⌚11am-8pm Thu & Sun, to 10pm Fri & Sat) Hidden upstairs in an industrial-chic space, this under-the-radar gathering spot tempts with hot and cold tapas, pizzas and DIY tastes of over 30 boutique wines barreled on-site.

Maverick Saloon BAR, NIGHTCLUB
(www.mavericksaloon.org; 3687 Sagunto St, Santa Ynez; ⌚noon-2am) In the one-horse town of Santa Ynez, en route to Chumash Casino, this Harley-friendly honky-tonk stages live country-and-western and rock bands, late-night DJs and dancing on weekends.

Information

The **Santa Barbara County Vintners' Association** (www.sbcountywines.com) publishes a self-guided winery touring map, available free at tasting rooms and the **Solvang Visitors Center** (☎805-688-6144, 800-468-6765; www.solvangusa.com; 1639 Copenhagen Dr, Solvang; ⌚9am-5pm).

Getting There & Around

The wine country is northwest of Santa Barbara; drive there in under an hour via Hwy 101 or more scenic, narrow and winding Hwy 154 (San Marcos Pass Rd). Hwy 246 runs east–west across the bottom of the Santa Ynez Valley, passing Solvang (where it's called Mission Dr) between Santa Ynez (off Hwy 154) and Buellton (off Hwy 101).

Santa Barbara

Frankly put, this area is damn pleasant to putter around. Just a 90-minute drive north of Los Angeles, tucked between mountains and the Pacific, Santa Barbara basks smugly in its near-perfection. Founded by a Spanish mission, the city's signature red-tile roofs, white stucco buildings and Mediterranean vibe have long given credence to its claim to the title of the 'American Riviera.' Santa Barbara is blessed with almost freakishly good weather, and no one can deny the appeal of those beaches that line the city tip to toe either. Just ignore those pesky oil derricks out to sea.

History

For hundreds of years before the arrival of the Spanish, the Chumash people thrived here, setting up trading routes over to the Channel Islands, which they reached in redwood canoes called *tomols*. In 1542 explorer Juan Rodríguez Cabrillo sailed into the channel and claimed it for Spain, then quickly met his doom on a nearby island.

The Chumash had little reason for concern until the permanent return of the Spanish in the late 1700s, when priests and soldiers arrived to establish military outposts and to convert the tribe to Christianity. The Spaniards forced the Chumash to evacuate the Channel Islands, construct the missions and presidios and provide subsequent labor. Many Native Americans changed their diet and clothing, and died of European diseases, ill treatment and culture shock.

Mexican ranchers arrived after wining independence from Spain in 1821. Easterners began arriving en masse with the 1849 Gold Rush, and by the late 1890s the city was an established vacation spot for the wealthy. After a massive earthquake in 1925, laws were passed requiring much of the city to be rebuilt in its now characteristic faux-Spanish style of white-stucco buildings with red-tiled roofs.

Sights

Mission Santa Barbara MISSION
(www.sbmission.org; 2201 Laguna St; adult/child 6-15yr $5/1; ⌚9am-4:30pm) Reigning from a hilltop above town, the 'Queen of the Missions' became the 10th California mission

Downtown Santa Barbara

Downtown Santa Barbara

Top Sights
- El Presidio de Santa Barbara State Historic Park C3
- Santa Barbara County Courthouse B3
- Santa Barbara Historical Museum B4
- Santa Barbara Museum of Art B3

Sights
- 1 Karpeles Manuscript Library B3
- 2 Santa Barbara Maritime Museum A6
- 3 Stearns Wharf B6
- 4 Ty Warner Sea Center B6

Activities, Courses & Tours
- 5 Condor Express A6
- 6 Los Baños del Mar A6
- 7 Paddle Sports A6
- 8 Santa Barbara Sailing Center A6
- 9 Santa Barbara Trolley (Main Stop) B6
- 10 Wheel Fun B5
- 11 Wheel Fun B5

Sleeping
- 12 Brisas del Mar A5
- 13 Canary Hotel B3
- 14 Harbor House Inn B5
- 15 Inn of the Spanish Garden C3
- 16 James House B1
- 17 Marina Beach Motel A5
- 18 Presidio Motel B2
- 19 Santa Barbara Tourist Hostel B5

Eating
- 20 Bouchon B2
- 21 Brophy Bros A6
- 22 D'Angelo Pastry & Bread B5
- 23 El Buen Gusto D3
- 24 Lilly's Taquería B5
- 25 Metropulos C5
- Olio Pizzeria .... (see 20)
- 26 Palace Grill B4
- 27 Santa Barbara Farmers Market B4
- 28 Santa Barbara Shellfish Company B6
- 29 Silvergreens B4
- 30 Sojourner C3

Drinking
- 31 Blenders in the Grass B4
- 32 Brewhouse B5
- 33 French Press B3
- 34 Press Room B4

Entertainment
- 35 Santa Barbara Bowl D2
- 36 Soho B3
- 37 Velvet Jones B4

Shopping
- 38 Channel Island Surfboards B5
- 39 CRSVR B4
- 40 REI B5

on the feast day of Saint Barbara in 1786. Occupied by Catholic priests ever since, the mission escaped Mexico's policy of forced secularization. Today it functions as a Franciscan friary, parish church and historical museum. The 1820 stone church has Chumash artwork and beautiful cloisters; its imposing Doric facade, an homage to a chapel in ancient Rome, is topped by twin bell towers. Behind the church is an extensive cemetery – look for skull carvings over the door leading outside – with 4000 Chumash graves and the elaborate mausoleums of early settlers.

El Presidio de Santa Barbara State Historic Park HISTORIC SITE
(☎805-965-0093; www.sbthp.org; 123 E Cañon Perdido St; adult/child under 17yr $5/free; ⊙10:30am-4:30pm) Founded in 1782 to protect missions between San Diego and Monterey, this fort was Spain's last military stronghold in Alta California. But its mission wasn't solely to protect – the presidio also served as a social and political hub, and as a stopping point for traveling Spanish military. Today this small urban park shelters some of the city's oldest structures, which seem to be in constant need of propping up and restoring. Be sure to stop by the chapel, its interior radiant with kaleidoscopic color. Tickets also include admission to **Casa de la Guerra** (15 E De La Guerra St; ⊙noon-4pm Sat & Sun), a 19th-century colonial adobe displaying Spanish-American heritage exhibits.

FREE **Santa Barbara County Courthouse** HISTORIC BUILDING
(1100 Anacapa St; ⊙8:30am-4:45pm Mon-Fri, 10am-4:45pm Sat & Sun) Built in Spanish-Moorish Revival style, it's an absurdly beautiful place to be on trial. The magnificent 1929

courthouse features hand-painted ceilings, wrought-iron chandeliers and tiles from Tunisia and Spain. Step inside the hushed 2nd-floor mural room depicting Spanish colonial history, then climb the 85ft clocktower for arch-framed panoramas of the city, ocean and mountains. Docent-led tours are usually offered at 2pm daily and 10:30am on Monday, Tuesday, Wednesday and Friday.

Santa Barbara Historical Museum MUSEUM
(www.santabarbaramuseum.com; 136 E De La Guerra St; admission by donation; ⏲10am-5pm Tue-Sat, noon-5pm Sun) Embracing a romantic cloistered adobe courtyard, this off-the-beaten-path museum has an endlessly fascinating collection of local memorabilia, ranging from simply beautiful, like Chumash woven baskets and colonial-era textiles, to intriguing, such as an intricately carved coffer once belonging to Junípero Serra. Learn about Santa Barbara's involvement in toppling the last Chinese monarchy, among other interesting footnotes in local history.

Santa Barbara Botanic Garden GARDEN
(www.sbbg.org; 1212 Mission Canyon Rd; adult/child 2-12yr/student $8/4/6; ⏲9am-5pm Nov-Feb, to 6pm Mar-Oct;) Take a soul-satisfying jaunt around this 40-acre botanic garden, devoted to California's native flora. Over 5 miles of partly wheelchair-accessible trails meander through cacti, redwoods and wildflowers past the old mission dam, originally built by Chumash tribespeople. Guided tours are available at 2pm daily and 11am on Saturday and Sunday. Ask for a 'Family Discovery Sheet' from the admission kiosk. Leashed dogs are welcome. See the website or call ahead for directions; it's about a 10-minute drive uphill from the mission.

Santa Barbara Museum of Art MUSEUM
(www.sbma.net; 1130 State St; adult/child 6-17yr $9/6; ⏲11am-5pm Tue-Sun;) Culture vultures delight in these downtown galleries, which hold an impressive, well-edited collection of contemporary Californian artists, modern masters like Matisse and Chagall, 20th-century photography and Asian art, with provocative special exhibits, an interactive children's gallery and a cafe. Sundays are pay-what-you-wish admission.

Santa Barbara Maritime Museum MUSEUM
(www.sbmm.org; 113 Harbor Way; adult/child 1-5yr/youth 6-17yr $7/2/4, all free 3rd Thu of the month; ⏲10am-5pm Thu-Tue Sep-May, to 6pm Jun-Aug;) Even li'l cap'ns will get a kick out of this museum by the yacht harbor. A two-level exhibition hall celebrates Santa Barbara's briny history with historical artifacts and memorabilia, hands-on and virtual-reality exhibits, and a small theater for documentary videos.

FREE **Karpeles Manuscript Library** MUSEUM
(www.rain.org/~karpeles; 21 W Anapamu St; ⏲10am-4pm) Stuffed with historical written artifacts, this museum is an embarrassment of riches for history nerds, science geeks and literary and music lovers. Rotating exhibits often spotlight literary masterworks, from Shakespeare to Sherlock Holmes.

Stearns Wharf LANDMARK
(www.stearnswharf.org) At its southern end, State St runs into Stearns Wharf, once co-owned by tough-guy actor Jimmy Cagney. Built in 1872, it's the West Coast's oldest continuously operating wooden pier. There's 90 minutes of free parking with validation from any shop or restaurant, but it's more fun to walk atop the very bumpy wooden slats.

Beaches

The long, sandy stretch between Stearns Wharf and Montecito is **East Beach**, Santa Barbara's largest and most crowded. At its far end, near the Biltmore hotel, Armani swimsuits and Gucci sunglasses abound at chic, but narrow **Butterfly Beach**.

Between Stearns Wharf and the harbor, **West Beach** is popular with tourists. There **Los Baños del Mar** (☎805-966-6110; 401 Shoreline Dr; admission $6;), a municipal heated outdoor pool complex, is good for recreational and lap swimming, plus a kids' wading pool. Call for opening hours. West of the harbor, **Leadbetter Beach** is the spot for beginning surfers and windsurfers. Climbing the stairs on the west end takes you to **Shoreline Park**, with picnic tables and awesome kite-flying conditions.

Further west, near the junction of Cliff Dr and Las Positas Rd, family-friendly **Arroyo Burro (Hendry's) Beach** has free parking and a restaurant and bar. Above the beach is the **Douglas Family Preserve**, offering cliffside romps for dogs.

Outside town off Hwy 101 you'll find even more spacious, family-friendly **state beaches** (☎805-958-1033; www.parks.ca.gov; per car $10; ⏲sunrise-sunset;), including **Carpinteria State Beach**, about 12 miles southeast of

TOP 5 SANTA BARBARA SPOTS FOR CHILDREN

Museum of Natural History (www.sbnature.org; 2559 Puesta del Sol; adult/child 3-12yr/youth 13-17yr $11/7/8; ⏲10am-5pm; 👪) Stuffed wildlife mounts, glittering gems and a pitch-dark planetarium captivate kids' imaginations. It's about a 10-minute drive uphill from the mission.

Arroyo Burro (Hendry's) Beach (p512) Wide sandy beach, away from the tourist crowds, popular with local families.

Ty Warner Sea Center (www.sbnature.org/seacenter; 211 Stearns Wharf; adult/child 2-12yr/youth 13-17yr $8/5/7; ⏲10am-5pm; 👪) Gawk at a gray whale skeleton, touch tide-pool critters and crawl through a 1500-gallon surge tank.

Santa Barbara Sailing Center (below) Short, one-hour harbor sails let young 'uns see sea lions up close.

Santa Barbara Maritime Museum (p512) Peer through a periscope, reel in a virtual fish or check out the gorgeous model ships.

Santa Barbara, and **Refugio & El Capitán State Beaches**, over 20 miles west in Goleta.

Activities

Surfing, Kayaking, Sailing & Whale-Watching

Santa Barbara's proximity to the windbreaking Channel Islands makes it a good spot to learn how to ride the waves. Unless you're a novice, conditions are too mellow in summer; swells kick back up in winter. Pro-level **Rincon Point** in Carpinteria has long, glassy, point-break waves, while **Leadbetter Point** is best for beginners. From spring through fall, kayakers can paddle the calm waters of the harbor or the coves of the Gaviota coast, or hitch a ride out to the Channel Islands for more solitude and sea caves. Meanwhile, stand-up paddle boarders can get their feet wet in the city's harbor.

Santa Barbara Sailing Center KAYAKING, SAILING
(☎805-962-2826, 800-350-9090; www.sbsail.com; 133 Harbor Way; rental per hr single/double kayak $10/15, kayaking lessons & tours $55-95, catamaran cruises $10-65) Rents kayaks and leads guided paddles, teaches sailing and offers sunset cocktail and wildlife-watching cruises.

Santa Barbara Adventure Co KAYAKING, SURFING
(☎805-884-9283; www.sbadventureco.com; kayaking tours $50-105, surfing & SUP lessons $99-125) Offers traditional board-surfing and SUP lessons, and leads guided coastal kayaking tours – ask about stargazing floats.

Paddle Sports KAYAKING, SURFING
(☎805-899-4925; www.kayaksb.com; 117b Harbor Way; surfboard rentals $10-30, kayak rentals $25-120, SUP rentals $40-65, 1hr SUP lesson $65, 2hr kayak tour $50) Friendly community-based outfitter, conveniently positioned right at the harbor.

Condor Express BOAT TOURS
(☎805-882-0088, 888-779-4253; www.condorcruises.com; 301 W Cabrillo Blvd; adult/child 5-12yr from $48/25) Runs year-round narrated whale-watching tours, including out to the Channel Islands, aboard a smooth-sailing catamaran.

Cycling

A paved recreational path stretches for 3 miles along the waterfront between Leadbetter Beach and Andrée Clark Bird Refuge, passing Stearns Wharf. **Santa Barbara Bicycle Coalition** (www.sbbike.org) offers free cycling tour maps online.

Wheel Fun CYCLING
(www.wheelfunrentals.com; ⏲8am-8pm) Cabrillo (23 E Cabrillo Blvd); State St (22 State St) Rents beach cruisers, hybrid mountain bikes and cheesy pedal-powered surreys with the fringe on top (local kids like to bomb 'em with water balloons!).

Hang-Gliding & Paragliding

For condor's-eye ocean views, **Eagle Paragliding** (☎805-968-0980; www.eagleparagliding.com) and **Fly Above All** (☎805-965-3733; www.flyaboveall.com) offer paragliding lessons (from $200) and tandem flights ($60 to $200). For hang-gliding lessons and tandem flights, contact **Fly Away** (805-403-8487; www.flyawayhanggliding.com).

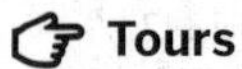

Tours

Architectural Foundation of Santa Barbara WALKING TOURS
(805-965-6307; www.afsb.org; adult/child under 12yr $10/free) Nonprofit organization offers 90-minute fascinating guided small-group walking tours of downtown's art, history and architecture, usually on Saturday and Sunday mornings.

Santa Barbara Trolley BUS TOURS
(805-965-0353; www.sbtrolley.com; adult/child 3-12yr $19/8; 10am-5:30pm) Biodiesel trolley buses make a narrated 90-minute one-way loop around major tourist attractions, starting at Stearns Wharf (last departure 4pm). Hop-on, hop-off tickets are valid all day and qualify for small discounts at select attractions.

Festivals & Events

First Thursday CULTURE
(www.santabarbaradowntown.com) On the first Thursday evening of every month, downtown art galleries, museums and theaters come alive for a big street party with live entertainment.

Santa Barbara International Film Festival CINEMA
(http://sbiff.org) Film buffs arrive in droves for screenings of independent US and foreign films in late January and early February.

I Madonnari Italian Street Painting Festival CULTURE
(www.imadonnarifestival.com) Chalk drawings adorn Santa Barbara's mission sidewalks over Memorial Day weekend.

Summer Solstice Celebration CULTURE
(www.solsticeparade.com) Wacky, wildly popular – and just plain wild – performance-art parade and outdoor fun in late June.

Old Spanish Days Fiesta CULTURE
(www.oldspanishdays-fiesta.org) The city gets packed in early August for this long-running but slightly overrated heritage festival featuring rodeos, music and dancing.

Avocado Festival FOOD
(www.avofest.com) In small-town Carpinteria, witness the world's largest guacamole vat in early October, with food and arts-and-crafts vendors and live bands.

Sleeping

Prepare for sticker shock: basic motel rooms by the beach command over $200 in summer. Don't show up without reservations, especially on weekends. Cheaper motels and hotels cluster along upper State St and Hwy 101 between Goleta and Carpinteria.

TOP CHOICE **Inn of the Spanish Garden** BOUTIQUE HOTEL $$$
(805-564-4700, 866-564-4700; http://spanishgardeninn.com; 915 Garden St; d incl breakfast $259-519;) At this elegant Spanish Revival-style downtown hotel, two dozen romantic rooms and suites have balconies and patios overlooking a gracious fountain courtyard. Beds have luxurious linens, bathrooms boast deep soaking tubs and concierge service is top-notch.

Four Seasons Resort – The Biltmore RESORT $$$
(805-969-2261, 800-819-5053; www.fourseasons.com/santabarbara; 1260 Channel Dr; d from $595;) Wear white linen and live like Jay Gatsby at the oh-so-cushy 1927 Biltmore, Santa Barbara's iconic Spanish Colonial–style hotel and spa, overlooking Butterfly Beach. Every detail is perfect, from bathrooms with Mediterranean tiles to hideaway garden cottages for honeymooners. Wi-fi in lobby and poolside only. The resort is a 15-minute drive from downtown via Hwy 101 southbound.

El Capitan Canyon CABINS, CAMPGROUND $$
(805-685-3887, 866-352-2729; www.elcapitancanyon.com; 11560 Calle Real, off Hwy 101; safari tents $155, cabins $225-350;) Go 'glamping' in this woodsy car-free zone near El Capitán State Beach, a 20-mile drive west of Santa Barbara via Hwy 101. Enjoy the great outdoors by day, and rustic safari tents or creekside cedar cabins with heavenly mattresses, gas fireplaces and backyard firepits by night.

Canary Hotel HOTEL $$$
(805-884-0300, 877-468-3515; www.canarysantabarbara.com; 31 W Carrillo St; d from $299;) Downtown's sleekest multi-story hotel has a rooftop pool and a sunset-watching perch for cocktails. Posh accommodations have four-poster Spanish-framed beds and all mod cons, but 'suites' are just over-

sized rooms. Ambient street noise may leave you sleepless. Pet fee $35.

James House B&B **$$$**
(☎805-569-5853; www.jameshousesantabarbara.com; 1632 Chapala St; r incl breakfast $190-240;) For a traditional B&B experience, revel in this stately Queen Anne Victorian run by a charmingly hospitable owner. All of the antique-filled rooms are sheer elegance, with lofty ceilings, some fireplaces and none of that shabby-chic look. Full sit-down breakfast served.

Harbor House Inn MOTEL **$$**
(☎805-962-9745, 888-474-6789; www.harborhouseinn.com; 104 Bath St; r $129-335;) All of these brightly lit studios inside a converted motel have hardwood floors, small kitchens and a cheery design scheme. Rates include a welcome basket of breakfast goodies, a DVD library and three-speed bikes to borrow. Pet fee $15.

Agave Inn MOTEL **$$**
(☎805-687-6009; www.agaveinnsb.com; 3222 State St; r $79-209;) While it's still just a motel at heart, this boutique-on-a-budget property's 'Mexican pop meets modern' motif livens things up with a color palette out of a Frieda Kahlo painting. Family-sized rooms come with kitchenettes and pull-out sofabeds. It's a 10-minute drive north of downtown.

Presidio Motel MOTEL **$$**
(☎805-963-1355; http://thepresidiomotel.com; 1620 State St; r incl breakfast $119-220;) Presidio is to lodging what H&M is to shopping: a cheap, trendy alternative. Just north of downtown, these crisp, modern motel rooms have panache, with dreamy bedding and art-splashed walls. Noise can be an issue, though. Free loaner beach cruisers.

Brisas del Mar HOTEL **$$**
(☎805-966-2219, 800-468-1988; www.sbhotels.com; 223 Castillo St; r incl breakfast $145-290; @) Big kudos for the freebies (DVDs, wine and cheese, milk and cookies) and the Mediterranean-style front section, although the motel wing is unlovely. Its sister properties away from the beach may be lower-priced.

State Park Campgrounds CAMPGROUND **$**
(☎reservations 800-444-7275; www.reserveamerica.com; tent & RV sites $35-50, hike-and-bike sites $10) Under a 30-minute drive from Santa Barbara, Carpinteria, Refugio and El Capitán State Beaches each offer a jam-packed, popular campground with flush toilets, hot showers, BBQ grills and picnic tables. Reserve ahead.

> **SANTA BARBARA'S URBAN WINE TRAIL**
>
> No wheels to head up to Santa Barbara's wine country? No problem! Walk between almost a dozen wine-tasting rooms (and a killer microbrewery, too) near the beach, southeast of downtown. You can join the burgeoning **Urban Wine Trail** (www.urbanwinetrailsb.com) anywhere along its route. Most wine-tasting rooms are open from 11am to 6pm daily.

Marina Beach Motel MOTEL **$$**
(☎805-963-9311, 877-627-4621; www.marinabeachmotel.com; 21 Bath St; r $115-289; @) Flower-festooned, one-story motor lodge by the sea, with some kitchenettes; pet fee $10.

Blue Sands Motel MOTEL **$$**
(☎805-965-1624; www.thebluesands.com; 421 S Milpas St; r $99-259;) Kinda kitschy two-story motel just steps from East Beach, with some kitchens; pet fee $10.

Motel 6 Santa Barbara MOTEL **$$**
(☎805-564-1392, 800-466-8356; www.motel6.com; 443 Corona del Mar; r $85-185;) The very first Motel 6, remodeled with Ikea-esque design; pet fee $10.

Santa Barbara Tourist Hostel HOSTEL **$**
(☎805-963-0154; www.sbhostel.com; 134 Chapala St; dm $25-43, r $79-139; ⏲check-in 2:30-11:15pm; @) Traveling strangers, trains rumbling by and a rowdy bar just steps from your door – it's either the perfect country-and-western song or this low-slung, tattered hostel.

Eating

TOP CHOICE **Bouchon** FRENCH **$$$**
(☎805-730-1160; www.bouchonsantabarbara.com; 9 W Victoria St; mains $28-36; ⏲5:30-9pm Sun-Thu, to 10pm Fri & Sat) Flavorful French cooking with a seasonal California influence is on the menu at convivial Bouchon (meaning 'wine cork'). Locally grown farm produce and ranched meats marry beautifully with more than 30 regional wines by the glass. Lovebirds, book a table on the candlelit patio.

TOP CHOICE **Santa Barbara Shellfish Company** SEAFOOD $$
(www.sbfishhouse.com; 230 Stearns Wharf; dishes $5-19; 11am-9pm) 'From sea to skillet to plate' best describes this end-of-the-wharf crab shack that's more of a counter joint. Great lobster bisque, ocean views and the same location for 25 years.

Olio Pizzeria ITALIAN $$
(805-899-2699; www.oliopizzeria.com; 11 W Victoria St; dishes $3-24; 11:30am-2pm Mon-Sat, 5-10pm Sun-Thu, to 11pm Fri & Sat) Cozy, high-ceilinged pizzeria and enoteca with a happening wine bar. It proffers a tempting selection of crispy pizzas, imported cheeses and meats, traditional antipasti and *dolci* (desserts).

Palace Grill SOUTHERN $$$
(www.palacegrill.com; 8 E Cota St; lunch mains $8-15, dinner mains $16-30; 11:30am-3pm daily, 5:30-10pm Sun-Thu, to 11pm Fri & Sat;) With all the exuberance of Mardi Gras, this N'awlins grill dishes up delectable biscuits and ginormous (if only so-so) plates of jambalaya, gumbo ya-ya and blackened catfish. Act unsurprised if the staff lead diners in a rousing sing-along.

Silvergreens HEALTHY $$
(www.silvergreens.com; 791 Chapala St; dishes $4-10; 7:30am-10pm Mon-Fri, 11am-10pm Sun;) Who says fast food can't be fresh and tasty? With the tag line 'Eat smart, live well,' this sun-drenched cafe makes nutritionally sound (check the calorie counts on your receipt) salads, soups, sandwiches and breakfast burritos.

Brophy Bros SEAFOOD $$
(www.brophybros.com; 119 Harbor Way; mains $9-20; 11am-10pm Sun-Thu, to 11pm Fri & Sat) A longtime favorite for its fresh-off-the-dock seafood, rowdy atmosphere, salty harborside setting and sunset-view deck. Skip the long lines for a table and start knocking back oyster shooters and Bloody Marys at the bar.

El Buen Gusto MEXICAN $
(836 N Milpas St; dishes $3-8; 8am-9pm) While waiting for authentic south-of-the-border tacos, kick back at plasticky booths with an *agua fresca* or cold Pacifico as Mexican music videos and soccer games blare on TVs. *Menudo* (tripe soup) and *birria* (spicy stew) are weekend specials.

D'Angelo Pastry & Bread CAFE $
(25 W Gutierrez St; dishes $2-8; 7am-2pm) This retrolicious downtown bakery with shiny-silver sidewalk bistro tables is a perfect quick breakfast or brunch spot, whether for a buttery croissant and rich espresso or Iron Chef Cat Cora's favorite 'Eggs Rose.'

Sojourner HEALTH FOOD $$
(www.sojournercafe.com; 134 E Cañon Perdido St; mains $8-15; 11am-11pm Mon-Sat, to 10pm Sun;) This granola-flavored favorite has been doing its all-natural, mostly meatless magic since 1978. Chili-spiced tempeh tacos and ginger tofu wonton pillows are tasty. Fair-

WORTH A TRIP

OJAI

Hollywood director Frank Capra chose the Ojai Valley to represent mythical Shangri-La in his 1937 movie *Lost Horizon*. Today Ojai (pronounced '*oh*-hi', meaning 'moon' to the Chumash) attracts artists, organic farmers, spiritual seekers and anyone ready to indulge in spa-style pampering. Start by wandering around Arcade Plaza, a maze of Mission Revival–style buildings on Ojai Ave (downtown's main drag), alive with arty boutiques and cafes.

Ojai is famous for the rosy glow that emanates from its mountains at sunset, the so-called 'Pink Moment.' The ideal vantage point for catching it is the peaceful lookout **Meditation Mount** (www.meditationmount.org; 10340 Reeves Rd; admission free). Head east of downtown on Ojai Ave (Hwy 150), then take a left at Boccali's farm-stand pizzeria. For hiking trail maps to hot springs, waterfalls and more mountaintop viewpoints, visit the **Ojai Ranger Station** (805-646-4348; www.fs.fed.us/r5/lospadres; 1190 E Ojai Ave; 8am-4:30pm Mon-Fri).

Ojai is about 35 miles east of Santa Barbara via Hwys 101 and 150, or 15 miles inland from Ventura via Hwy 33.

trade coffee, local beers and wines and delish desserts.

Lilly's Taquería MEXICAN $
(www.lillystacos.com; 310 Chapala St; dishes from $2; ⌚11am-9pm Mon & Wed-Thu, to 10pm Fri & Sat, to 9:30pm Sun) Almost always a line out the door for *adobada* (marinated pork) tacos.

Metropulos DELI $
(www.metrofinefoods.com; 216 E Yanonali St; dishes $6-10; ⌚8:30am-5:30pm Mon-Fri, 10am-4pm Sat) Artisan breads, cheeses and cured meats, hand-crafted sandwiches and market-fresh salads.

Santa Barbara Farmers Market MARKET $
(www.sbfarmersmarket.org; cnr Santa Barbara & Cota Sts; ⌚8:30am-1pm Sat) Farmers and food vendors also set up along lower State St on Tuesday afternoons.

Drinking

Santa Barbara's after-dark scene revolves around college-age bars and nightclubs on lower State St. Saturday nights here get rowdy.

Brewhouse BREWPUB
(www.brewhousesb.com; 229 W Montecito St; ⌚11am-11pm Sun-Thu, to midnight Fri & Sat; 📶) This rowdy dive down by the railroad tracks crafts its own unique small-batch beers (Saint Bar's Belgian-style rules!) and has cool art and rockin' live music Wednesday to Saturday nights.

Press Room PUB
(http://pressroomsb.com; 15 E Ortega St) This downtown pub attracts a slew of students and European travelers. There's no better place to watch the footie, stuff quarters in the jukebox and be jovially abused by the British bartender.

French Press COFFEE SHOP
(1101 State St; ⌚6am-7pm Mon-Fri, 7am-7pm Sat, 8am-5pm Sun; 📶) This State St coffee shop shames the chains with beans roasted in Santa Cruz, shiny silver espresso machines from Italy and baristas that know how to pull their shots and mix spicy chais.

Blenders in the Grass JUICE, SMOOTHIES $
(www.drinkblenders.com; 720 State St; drinks $3-6; ⌚7am-9pm Mon-Thu, 7am-10pm Fri, 8am-10pm Sat, 8am-9pm Sun) For a quick, healthy burst of energy, pop by this locally owned juice and smoothie bar for a wheatgrass shot or date milkshake.

Hollister Brewing Co BREWPUB
(www.hollisterbrewco.com; Camino Real Marketplace, 6980 Marketplace Dr, off Hwy 101 exit Glen Annie Rd; ⌚11am-10pm) Beer geeks won't regret making the trip out near the UCSB campus to sample unique brews like White Star XPA or Hip Hopimperial ale. It's about a 20-minute drive from downtown via Hwy 101 northbound.

☆ Entertainment

For a calendar of events and live shows, including in downtown's historic movie palaces and theaters, pick up the free weekly *Santa Barbara Independent* (www.independent.com) or Friday's 'Scene' guide from the *Santa Barbara News-Press* (www.sbnewspress.com).

Santa Barbara Bowl MUSIC, COMEDY
(☎805-962-7411; www.sbbowl.org; 1122 N Milpas St) Built by the 1930s New Deal–era WPA labor, this outdoor stone amphitheater grants ocean views from the highest cheap seats. Kick back in the summer sunshine or under the stars during live rock, jazz and folk concerts and stand-up comedy shows, including big-name acts.

Soho MUSIC
(☎805-962-7776; www.sohosb.com; 1221 State St, 2nd level) An unpretentious brick room hosts live music almost nightly, upstairs inside a downtown office complex. Lineups range from indie rock, jazz, folk, funk and world beats to DJs.

Velvet Jones MUSIC, COMEDY
(☎805-965-8676; www.velvet-jones.com; 423 State St) Long-running downtown punk and indie dive for rock, hip-hop, comedy and 18+ DJ nights for the city's college crowd. Many bands stop here between gigs in LA and San Francisco.

Zodo's Bowling & Beyond BOWLING, BILLIARDS
(☎805-967-0128; www.zodos.com; 5925 Calle Real, off Hwy 101 exit Fairview Rd; 👪) With over 40 beers on tap, pool tables and a video arcade (Skee-Ball!), this bowling alley near UCSB is good ol' family fun. Call for schedules of open-play lanes and 'glow bowling' nights. It's a 15-minute drive from downtown via Hwy 101 northbound.

CAR-FREE SANTA BARBARA

If you use public transportation to get to Santa Barbara, you can get valuable hotel discounts, plus get a nice swag bag of coupons for various activities and attractions, all courtesy of **Santa Barbara Car Free** (www.santabarbaracarfree.org).

Shopping

Downtown's **State St** is packed with shops, from vintage clothing to brand-name boutiques; cheapskates stick to lower State St, while trust-fund babies head uptown. For indie shops, dive into the **Funk Zone**, east of State St, just south of Hwy 101.

Channel Islands Surfboards OUTDOORS
(www.cisurfboards.com; 36 Anacapa St) Dying to take home a handcrafted, authentic SoCal surfboard? Down in the Funk Zone, this contempo surf shack turns out innovative pro-worthy board designs, cool surfer threads and beanie hats.

CRSVR SHOES, CLOTHING
(www.crsvr.com; 632 State St) Check this downtown sneaker boutique run by DJs, not just for rare, limited-edition Nikes and other athletic-shoe brands, but also trendy T-shirts, hats and other men's urban styles.

REI OUTDOORS
(www.rei.com; 321 Anacapa St; 10am-9pm Mon-Fri, 10am-7pm Sat, 11am-6pm Sun) West Coast's biggest independent co-op outdoor retailer is the place to pick up active clothing, shoes, sports gear and topographic recreational maps.

Information

Several downtown coffee shops offer free wi-fi.

FedEx Office (www.fedex.com; 1030 State St; per min 20-30¢; 7am-11pm Mon-Fri, 9am-9pm Sat & Sun; @) Pay-as-you-go internet workstations and free wi-fi.

Post office (www.usps.com; 836 Anacapa St; 9:30am-6pm Mon-Fri, 10am-2pm Sat) Full-service.

Public library (www.sbplibrary.org; 40 E Anapamu St; 10am-8pm Mon-Thu, 10am-5:30pm Fri & Sat, 1-5pm Sun; @) Public internet terminals and free wi-fi.

Santa Barbara Cottage Hospital (805-682-7111; http://cottagehealthsystemc.org; cnr Pueblo & Bath Sts; 24hr) Emergency room.

Visitor center (805-965-3021; www.santabarbaraca.com; 1 Garden St; 9am-5pm Mon-Sat, 10am-5pm Sun) Maps, brochures and tourist information at the waterfront.

Getting There & Away

About 10 miles west of downtown off Hwy 101, small **Santa Barbara Airport** (SBA; www.flysba.com; 500 Fowler Rd) is served by American (LA), Frontier (Denver), Horizon (Seattle), United (Denver, LA and San Francisco) and US Airways (Phoenix).

Santa Barbara Airbus (805-964-7759, 800-423-1618; www.sbairbus.com) shuttles between Los Angeles International Airport (LAX) and Santa Barbara (one way/round trip $48/90, 2½ to three hours, eight daily).

Amtrak (www.amtrak.com; 209 State St) is a stop on the daily Seattle–LA *Coast Starlight*. Regional *Pacific Surfliner* trains head south to LA ($25, three hours, six daily) and San Diego ($35, six hours, four daily), or north to San Luis Obispo ($29, 2¾ hours, twice daily). Connecting Amtrak Thruway buses also head north along Hwy 101 via San Luis Obispo and Paso Robles to the San Francisco Bay Area.

Greyhound (www.greyhound.com; 34 W Carrillo St) has a few daily services along Hwy 101 south to LA ($18, three hours) or north to San Francisco ($53, nine hours) via San Luis Obispo ($26, 2¼ hours).

Getting Around

Equipped with front-loading bicycle racks, local buses operated by **Metropolitan Transit District** (MTD; 805-963-3366; www.sbmtd.gov; 1020 Chapala St) cost $1.75 per ride; ask for a free transfer when boarding.

MTD's electric **Downtown Shuttle** runs along State St to Stearns Wharf every 10 to 15 minutes, while the **Waterfront Shuttle** travels from Stearns Wharf west to the harbor and east to the zoo every 15 to 30 minutes. Both routes operate 10am to 6pm daily (also from 6pm to 10pm on Fridays and Saturdays between late May and early September). The fare is 25¢ (transfers free).

In 10 municipal lots and garages around downtown parking is free for the first 75 minutes; each additional hour costs $1.50.

Channel Islands National Park

Don't let this remote park, part of an island chain lying off the SoCal coast, loiter too long on your bucket list. Imagine hiking, kayaking, scuba diving, camping and whale-watching, all amid a raw, end-of-the-world landscape. Rich in unique species of flora and fauna, tide pools and kelp forests, the islands are home to 145 species found nowhere else in the world, earning them the nickname 'California's Galapagos.'

Sights & Activities

Most tourists arrive during summer, when island conditions are hot, dusty and bone-dry. Better times to visit are during the spring wildflower bloom or in early fall, when the fog clears and kayaking conditions are ideal. Winter can be stormy, but it's also great for wildlife watching, especially whales.

Before you shove off from the mainland, stop by Ventura Harbor's NPS Visitor Center (p520) for educational natural-history exhibits, a short video and ranger-led family activity programs on weekends and holidays.

Anacapa Island — ISLAND

If you're short on time, Anacapa Island, which is actually three separate islets, gives a memorable introduction to the islands' ecology. Boats dock on the East Island and after a short climb you'll find 2 miles of trails offering fantastic views of island flora, a historic lighthouse, and rocky Middle and West Islands. Kayaking, diving, tidepooling and seal-watching are popular activities here. After checking out the small museum at the visitors center, ask about ranger-led programs. In summer, scuba divers with videocameras may broadcast live images to TV monitors you can watch.

Santa Cruz Island — ISLAND

The park's largest island (96 sq mi) boasts two mountain ranges. The western three-quarters of the island is managed by the Nature Conservancy and can only be accessed with a permit (apply online at www.nature.org/cruzpermit). But the remaining eastern quarter, managed by the NPS, packs a wallop – ideal if you want an action-packed day trip or overnight camping trip. You can swim, snorkel, scuba dive and kayak. There are rugged hikes too, which are best not attempted midday – there's little shade. It's a 1-mile climb to captivating, but windy Cavern Point.

Santa Rosa Island — ISLAND

Snowy white-sand beaches and a chance to spot hundreds of bird and plant species are among the highlights of Santa Rosa, where seals and sea lions haul out. Hiking trails through grasslands and canyons and along beaches abound, but high winds typically make swimming, diving and kayaking tough for everyone but experts.

San Miguel Island — ISLAND

The most remote of the park's northern islands offers solitude and a wilderness experience, but it's often shrouded in fog and is very windy. Some sections are off-limits to prevent disruption of the fragile ecosystem, which includes a ghostly caliche forest (made of the hardened calcium-carbonate castings of trees and vegetation) and seasonal colonies of seals and sea lions.

Santa Barbara Island — ISLAND

Only 1 sq mile in size, this isolated island is for nature lovers. Big, blooming coreopsis, cream cups and chicory are just a few of the island's memorable plant species. It's also a thriving playground for seabirds and marine wildlife, including humongous elephant

PARADISE LOST & FOUND

Humans have left a heavy footprint on the Channel Islands, originally inhabited by Chumash and Gabrieleño tribespeople. In the 19th century, ranching livestock overgrazed, causing erosion, while rabbits fed on native plants. The US military even used San Miguel as a mid-20th–century practice bombing range. In 1969, an offshore oil spill engulfed the northern islands in an 800-sq-mi slick, killing off uncountable seabirds and mammals. Meanwhile, deep-sea fishing has caused the destruction of three-quarters of the islands' kelp forests.

Despite past abuses, the islands' future is not bleak. Brown pelicans, once decimated by the effects of DDT and reduced to one chick on Anacapa in 1970, have rebounded, and bald eagles were recently reintroduced. On San Miguel, native vegetation has returned a half century after overgrazing sheep were removed. On Santa Cruz, the National Park Service (NPS) and the Nature Conservancy have implemented ambitious multi-year plans to eliminate invasive plants and feral pigs. Information is available from the NPS (805-658-5730; www.nps.gov/chis; 1901 Spinnaker Dr, off Harbor Blvd, Ventura; 8:30am-5pm;) and from **Nature Conservancy** (www.nature.org)..

seals and Xantus' murrelets, a bird that nests in cliff crevices. Ask at the island's visitor center about the best diving, snorkeling and kayaking spots.

Tours

Most trips require a minimum number of participants, and may be canceled due to surf and weather conditions.

Island Packers WHALE-WATCHING
(805-642-1393; www.islandpackers.com; 1691 Spinnaker Dr, Ventura Harbor; adult/child 3hr cruise from $33/24, full-day trip from $72/54) Offers whale-watching excursions from late December to early April (gray whales) and in summer (blue and humpback whales).

Paddle Sports of Santa Barbara KAYAKING, HIKING
(805-899-4925, 888-254-2094; www.kayaksb.com; 117b Harbor Way, Santa Barbara; day trips from $175) Organizes kayaking and hiking excursions to all five islands.

Santa Barbara Adventure Co KAYAKING
(805-899-4925, 888-254-2094; www.kayaksb.com; 720 Bond Ave, Santa Barbara; day trips adult/child from $170/150;) Offers both day and overnight sea-kayaking trips to the islands.

Sleeping

Each island has a primitive year-round **campground** (reservations 518-885-3639, 877-444-6777; www.recreation.gov; tent sites $15) with pit toilets and picnic tables. Water is available on Santa Cruz and Santa Rosa islands only. Campers must pack everything in and out, including trash. Due to fire danger, campfires are not allowed (enclosed gas campstoves are OK). Advance camping reservations are required.

Information

NPS Visitor Center (805-658-5730; www.nps.gov/chis; 1901 Spinnaker Dr, off Harbor Blvd, Ventura; 8:30am-5pm;) On the mainland, at the far end of Ventura Harbor, it's a one-stop shop for books, maps and trip-planning information.

Getting There & Away

Trips may be canceled anytime due to surf and weather conditions. Reservations are essential for weekends, holidays and summer trips.

AIR **Channel Islands Aviation** (805-987-1301; www.flycia.com; day trips adult/child from $160/135, campers from $300) runs half-day beach excursions, surf-fishing trips and camper shuttles to Santa Rosa Island, departing from Camarillo or Santa Barbara.

BOAT **Island Packers** (805-642-1393; www.islandpackers.com; 1691 Spinnaker Dr, Ventura Harbor; day trips adult/child from $56/39) provides regularly scheduled boat service to all of the islands; campers pay extra. Some departures from Oxnard.

Ventura

The primary departure point for Channel Islands trips, Ventura may not look at first like the most enchanting coastal city, but it has its seaside charms, especially along the beaches and in the historic downtown corridor along Main St, north of Hwy 101.

CHANNEL ISLANDS NPS CAMPGROUNDS

CAMPGROUND NAME	NO OF SITES	ACCESS FROM BOAT LANDING AREA	DESCRIPTION
Anacapa	7	0.5-mile walk with 154 stairs	High, rocky, sun-exposed & isolated
San Miguel	9	Steep 1-mile walk uphill	Windy, often foggy with volatile weather
Santa Barbara	10	Steep 0.5-mile walk uphill	Large, grassy & surrounded by trails
Santa Cruz (Scorpion Ranch)	40	Flat, 0.5-mile walk	Popular with groups, often crowded & partly shady
Santa Rosa	15	Flat, 1.5-mile walk	Eucalyptus grove in a windy canyon

Sights & Activities

San Buenaventura State Beach BEACH
(☎805-968-1033; www.parks.ca.gov; per car $10; ⊙dawn-dusk; ♿) Off Hwy 101, this long, golden strand is perfect for swimming, surfing or just lazing on the sand. Recreational cycling paths connect to more nearby beaches.

Mission San Buenaventura MISSION
(www.sanbuenaventuramission.org; 211 E Main St; adult/child $2/50¢; ⊙10am-5pm Mon-Fri, 9am-5pm Sat, 10am-4pm Sun) Ventura's Spanish colonial roots are in evidence at the final California mission founded by Junípero Serra in 1782. A stroll around this petite parish church is a tranquil experience, leading through a small museum, past statues of saints, centuries-old religious paintings and unusual wooden bells, and around a garden courtyard.

Limoneira AGROTOURISM
(☎805-525-5541; www.limoneira.com; 1141 Cummings Rd, Santa Paula; tours $20-40) A 20-minute drive outside town, this working ranch and farm is the place to get up close and smell the citrus that Ventura is famous for: lemons. Drop by the historical ranch store and play bocce ball on outdoor courts, or reserve a guided tour of the ranch, the modern packing house and the sea-view fruit and avocado orchards. Call for opening hours.

California Oil Museum MUSEUM
(☎805-933-0076; www.oilmuseum.net; 1001 E Main St, off Hwy 126, Santa Paula; adult/child 6-17yr/senior $4/1/3; ⊙10am-4pm Wed-Sun) If you've seen the Oscar-winning movie *There Will Be Blood*, then you already know that SoCal's early oil boom was a bloodthirsty business. Examine SoCal's 'black bonanza' with modest historical exhibits that include an authentic 1890s drilling rig and vintage gas pumps. To reach downtown Santa Paula, drive about 13 miles east of Ventura via Hwy 126.

Sleeping & Eating

Midrange motels and high-rise beachfront hotels cluster off Hwy 101 and by Ventura Harbor. Alternatively, keep driving on Hwy 101 southbound to Camarillo, where cheaper roadside chains abound. Back in downtown Ventura, Main St is chock-a-block with taco shops, healthy SoCal-style cafes and globally flavored kitchens.

Brooks CALIFORNIAN $$$
(☎805-652-7070; www.restaurantbrooks.com; 545 E Thompson Blvd; mains $17-34; ⊙5-9pm Tue-Thu & Sun, to 10pm Fri & Sat) Just off Hwy 101, this chef-driven restaurant serves such high-flying New American cuisine as cornmeal-fried oysters, jalapeño cheddar grits and Maytag blue cheesecake with seasonal berries.

Anacapa Brew Pub BREWPUB $$
(www.anacapabrewing.com; 472 E Main St; mains $9-20; ⊙11:30am-9pm Sun-Wed, to midnight Thu-Sun) Right downtown, this casual brewpub crafts its own microbrews – props to the Pierpoint IPA – and makes a fine pulled-pork sandwich too.

Mary's Secret Garden VEGETARIAN $
(☎805-641-3663; 100 S Fir St; mains $5-12; ⊙4-9:30pm Tue-Thu, 11am-9:30pm Fri & Sat; ✎) Two blocks east of California St by a pretty park, this internationally spiced vegan haven mixes up fresh juices, smoothies and out-of-this-world cakes.

Drinking

Wine Rack WINE BAR
(www.weaverwines.com; 14 S California St; ⊙4-9pm Mon & Tue, 2-9pm Wed & Thu, noon-10pm Fri & Sat, 2-8pm Sun) At this upbeat wine shop, novices can sidle up to the unpretentious tasting bar, loiter over a tasty cheese plate and listen to live music.

Zoey's Café CAFE $$
(☎805-652-1137; www.zoeyscafe.com; 185 E Santa Clara St; mains $9-15; ⊙6-9pm Tue-Sat, later on show nights) Cozy coffeehouse that makes pizzas and paninis, and showcases live acts almost nightly, mostly bluegrass, folk and acoustic singer-songwriters.

Shopping

Downtown on Main St, you'll find a terrific assortment of antiques, vintage, secondhand thrift and indie boutique shops.

Patagonia OUTDOOR EQUIPMENT
(www.patagonia.com; 235 W Santa Clara St; ⊙10am-6pm Mon-Sat & 11am-5pm Sun) Ventura is the birthplace of this pioneering outdoor-gear and clothing outfitter, known for its commitment to sustainable, environmentally progressive practices.

Real Cheap Sports OUTDOOR EQUIPMENT
(www.realcheapsports.com; 36 W Santa Clara St; ⊙10am-6pm Mon-Sat, to 5pm Sun) Shh, don't

tell anyone but you can get that brand-name outdoors stuff for less here, including Patagonia factory seconds.

Camarillo Premium Outlets MALL
(www.premiumoutlets.com; 740 E Ventura Blvd, Camarillo; ⏲10am-9pm Mon-Sat & 10am-8pm Sun) For steeply discounted designer duds, drive about 20 minutes from downtown via Hwy 101 southbound to this mall.

ℹ Information

Ventura Visitors & Convention Bureau (☎805-648-2075, 800-483-6214; www.ventura-usa.com; 101 S California St; ⏲8:30am-5pm Mon-Fri, 9am-5pm Sat, 10am-4pm Sun) Free information and maps downtown.

ℹ Getting There & Away

Ventura's unstaffed **Amtrak station** (www.amtrak.com; cnr Harbor Blvd & Figueroa St) has five daily trains north to Santa Barbara ($12, 40 minutes) and south to Los Angeles ($20, 2¼ hours). **Vista** (☎800-438-112; www.goventura.org) runs several daily Coastal Express buses between Ventura and Santa Barbara ($3, 35 minutes).

Understand Northern California

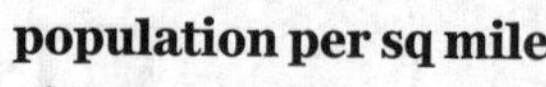

California

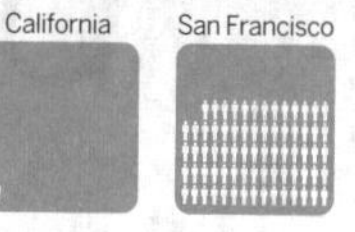

≈ 240 people

Northern California Today

NorCal in a Nutshell

Before you let your mind wander to suntanned, traffic-jammed, bikini-clad visions of California, remember that NorCal bears little cultural resemblance to Orange County. Although nobody can agree on exactly where to draw the dividing line, there's something that happens along the drive through the Central Valley, a salt-of-the-earth place that filters out much of the cultural static. The interest in Hollywood is replaced by one in redwood. The relationship to technology is as essential as the relationship to nature. There's always some kind of protest going on.

Natural Wonders

Highest point: Mt Whitney (14,497ft)

Lowest point: Death Valley (-282ft)

Area of national and state parks: 6.5 million acres

Miles of coastline: 1100

Medical marijuana is old news – the state allowed its use back in 1996 – but the myriad social and economic effects of the marijuana industry is a hot topic, particularly along the North Coast, where it grows like, um, weeds. The federal government, which had previously turned a blind eye to the gray area of medical marijuana, began to crack down on large for-profit growers in Northern California in fall 2011.

Since the 1960s, Northern California has relished political demonstrations. In 2011, several thousand protesters associated with the 'Occupy Wall St' movement grabbed national headlines by closing the Port of Oakland, America's fifth largest port.

Roots of Environmentalism

Californians originally helped kick-start the world's conservation movement in the midst of the 19th-century industrial revolution, creating laws curbing industrial dumping, setting aside swaths of prime real estate as urban green space, and protecting pristine wilderness in national and state parks. It's no surprise that Northern Californians lead the nation by choosing sustainable food and low-impact lifestyles, preserving old-growth forests, declaring nuclear-free zones, pushing for environmentally

NorCal Films

The Birds (1963)
Dirty Harry (1971)
American Graffiti (1973)
Chinatown (1974)
Big Trouble In Little China (1986)
The Joy Luck Club (1993)
Sideways (2004)
The Pursuit of Happiness (2006)

Essential Records

Workingman's Dead – The Grateful Dead
Green River – Creedence Clearwater Revival
My Ghetto Report Card – E-40
Time Out – Dave Brubeck Quartet
Stand! – Sly and the Family Stone
Dookie – Green Day
Crooked Rain, Crooked Rain – Pavement
Mama Tried – Merle Haggard

belief systems

(% of population)

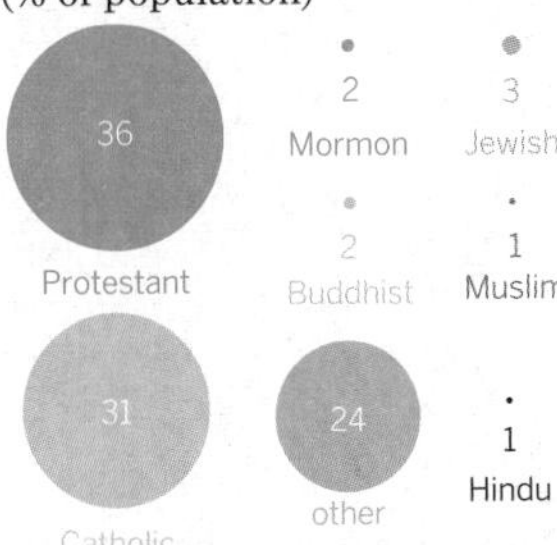

if California were 100 people

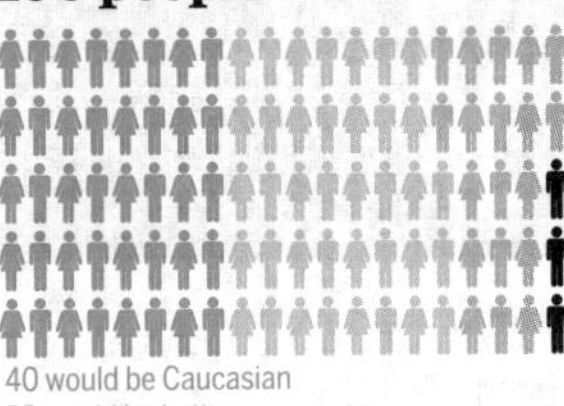

40 would be Caucasian
38 would be Latino
13 would be Asian American
6 would be African American
3 would be other

progressive legislation and establishing the USA's biggest market for hybrid vehicles.

Today, even conservative Californian politicians prioritize environmental issues on their agendas, as ex-Governor Arnold Schwarzenegger sometimes did. That said, the state's current budget crisis has resulted in deep cuts in environmental protections, as well as social services and education.

Fast Companies, Slow Food

The technology boom changed the cultural DNA of this place and the internet is cultural necessity. Northern California provides significant contributions to the state's economy through Silicon Valley and a burgeoning biotech industry, but has also birthed internet services such as Google, Amazon and Facebook.

If talking tech is over your head, try asking someone for a good place to have dinner. Northern Californians obsess about what goes into their mouths. They shop at farmers markets and follow the opening of restaurants with the rapt attention usually reserved for sports teams.

Many view their food choices through a political lens, and menus are loaded with organic, vegan, grass-fed, biodynamic and fair-trade foods. It's no accident that the term 'locavore' – meaning people who eat food grown locally – was invented here.

California by Numbers

Population: 37.3 million

Proportion of US GDP: 13% ($1.9 trillion)

Annual taxes earned from medical marijuana sales: $105 million

New World Religions

Despite proportionately small numbers, California's alternative religions and utopian communities dominate the popular imagination, from pagans to new-age healers. The Summer of Love imported gurus from India, the 1970s saw the rise of Jim Jones' People's Temple, and an Oakland radio minister proselytized that the Rapture was about to happen in 2010.

Dos & Don'ts

- » Don't get tanked wine tasting.
- » Don't call San Francisco 'Frisco.' Locals call it 'the City.'
- » Do slather on the sunblock, even on cloudy days.
- » Do drink plenty of water at high elevations.
- » Don't smoke indoors.

Myth

There's a rivalry between Northern and Southern California. True, but it's mostly on the Northern side. Southern Californians are too busy to care about what's going on in the north. One major exception: when the LA Dodgers play the San Francisco Giants.

Tribal Casinos

Though Native Californian tribal reservations account for less than 1% of the total land in the state, voter-approved 1998 state Proposition 5, allowing gambling on reservations, generates almost $7 billion annually.

History

Don't be distracted by the glittering stuff in the creek bed – the discovery of gold was merely one page in a very long story about the explosive intersection of natural grandeur, human desire and improbable coincidence. Sure, gold brought the Spanish north in the 16th century followed by a stampede of immigrants from around the world some 300 years later, but there's something about Northern California that's always drawn people to the edge. Leave Southern California's paved-over sprawl for those who prefer a tidy Hollywood story; Northern California's visceral timelessness – a place with the oldest and tallest trees on Earth, a place littered with glacier-carved granite and seething volcanoes, a place with fault lines that could literally open up and swallow us whole – is a hell of a tale.

Before the Ghosts

In some Central Californian Native American communities, mothers-in-law were traditionally so revered that you dared not speak to yours, and obeyed her without question.

Imagine California as a continent made up of many countries. In 1500 its population consisted of around 300,000 Native Americans, with somewhere between 100 and 300 languages in existence. Although this population is the subject of constant revision by historians, Northern California was certainly filled with a wide diversity of tribes.

On a day-to-day level the tribes had little in common. The Ahwahneechee, who lived in Yosemite's rugged hills in cone-shaped houses made from bark, scrupulously avoided eating bear meat and had elaborate ceremonial cremations. North Coast tribes such as the Yurok ate shellfish, wove baskets from ferns and grasses, and lived in partially underground longhouses. Central Coast fishing communities such as the Ohlone, Miwok and Pomo, built subterranean roundhouses and saunas, where they held ceremonies, told stories and gambled for fun. Most political leaders were men, but women shamans summoned dream-world powers to cure illness, control the weather and bring victories in hunting and war.

TIMELINE

6000–10,000 BC

Native American communities settle across the state, from the Yurok in gabled redwood houses in the north to the Tipai-Ipai in thatched domed dwellings in the south.

1542–43 AD

Juan Rodríguez Cabrillo becomes the first European explorer to navigate the California coast. After stumbling against a jagged rock, his journey ends with a gangrenous wound that causes his death.

1769

Padre Junípero Serra and Captain Gaspar de Portolá lead a Spanish expedition to establish missions, rounding up Native Americans as converts and conscripted labor.

These tribes had no written language but observed oral contracts and zoning laws, and expected that newcomers would likewise respect these contracts. When English pirate Sir Francis Drake harbored briefly on Miwok land north of San Francisco, the English were believed to be the dead returned from the afterworld, and shamans saw their arrival as a warning of the apocalypse. Story and gift exchanges eased tensions between the Native Americans and the Spanish and English adventurers, but the omens weren't entirely wrong. Within a century of the arrival of the Spanish colonists in 1769, California's Native American population would be reduced to just 20,000 people, their population decimated by European diseases, slavery and famine.

NATIVE AMERICANS

Traces of a Native American culture dating from the 1st century remain at Chumash Painted Cave State Historic Park, which features the most elaborate indigenous rock designs outside of the deserts of the Southwest.

Spain's Mission Impossible

When 18th-century Russian and English trappers began trading valuable otter pelts along the California coast, Spain concocted a plan for colonization. For the glory of God and the tax coffers of Spain, missions would be built across the state. This 'Sacred Expedition' was approved by Spain's quixotic visitor general, José de Gálvez of Mexico, who was full of grand schemes – including controlling Sonora province with a trained army of apes.

Almost immediately after Spain's missionizing plan was approved in 1769, it began to fail. Franciscan padres were undersupplied and poorly received. Soldiers entrusted to protect the missions weren't paid regularly, so they looted and pillaged local communities. Native Americans tasked with building the missions were promised one meal a day (when available) and a place in God's kingdom – but the later came much sooner than expected, due to the smallpox the Spanish brought with them. Native Americans often rebelled against the 21 Spanish missions and by 1784, the plan had failed, leaving only a handful of skittish Spanish soldiers on duty.

California Under Mexico

Spain wasn't sorry to lose California to Mexico in the 1810–21 Mexican War for Independence.

As long as missions had the best grazing land, *rancheros* (ranchers) couldn't compete in the growing market for cowhides and tallow (for use in soap). But Spanish, Mexican and American settlers who intermarried with Native Americans were now a sizable constituency, and together these *Californios* convinced Mexico to secularize the missions in 1834.

Californios snapped up deeds to privatized mission property, but since few were literate, boundary disputes that arose were settled with muscle, not paper. By law, half the lands were supposed to go to Native Americans who worked at the missions, but few actually received their entitlements.

1821

Mexican independence ends Spanish colonization of California. Mexico inherits 21 missions in various states of disrepair, along with unruly Californio cowboys and a decimated Native American population.

1835

An emissary of President Andrew Jackson makes a formal offer to buy Northern California, but Mexico tries to sell California as a package deal to England instead.

1846

Sierra Nevada blizzards strand the Donner Party of settlers, who avoid starvation by cannibalism. Five women and two men snowshoe 100 miles for help; half of the party of 87 survives.

» Donner Memorial

In her bestselling book *The Joy Luck Club,* Amy Tan weaves the stories of four Chinese-born women and their American-born daughters into a textured history of immigration and aspiration in San Francisco's Chinatown.

CHINATOWN

Through marriage and mergers, most of California was held by just 46 families by 1846. The average *rancho* (ranch) expanded to 16,000 acres, often presided over by elegant haciendas. Though women were supposedly confined to quarters at night, female ranchers cut a bold path during this period, and owned 13% of Californian ranches.

Meanwhile, settlers from the east were flowing into California via the relatively easy Santa Fe Trail or the tough northern passes through the Sierras. Of those parties who chose to take the northern route, none was more infamous than the Donner Party (see p378), tragically discovered in 1846; stranded in a desolate mountain pass, they resorted to cannibalism.

The US saw potential in California, but when US President Andrew Jackson offered financially strapped Mexico $500,000 for the territory, the offer was tersely rejected. After the USA annexed the Mexican territory of Texas in 1845, Mexico broke off diplomatic relations and ordered all foreigners without proper papers to be deported from California.

The Mexican-American War was declared in 1846 and lasted two years, with very little fighting in California. Hostilities ended with the *Treaty of Guadalupe Hidalgo*, ceding California and the present-day southwest to the USA. Mexico could not have had worse timing: within days of signing away California, gold was discovered.

Eureka!

The Gold Rush began with a bluff. Real-estate speculator, lapsed Mormon and tabloid publisher Sam Brannan was looking to unload some California swampland in 1848 when he heard rumors of gold flakes found near Sutter's Mill, 120 miles from San Francisco. Figuring this news should sell some newspapers and raise real-estate values, Brannan published the rumor as fact. Initially the story didn't generate excitement so Brannan ran another story, this time verified by Mormon employees at Sutter's Mill who had sworn him to secrecy. Brannan kept his word by running through the San Francisco streets, brandishing gold entrusted to him as tithes for the Mormon church, shouting, 'Gold on the American River!'

Newspapers around the world picked up stories of 'gold mountains' near San Francisco and by 1850, the year California was fast-tracked for admission as the 31st US state, California's non-native population had ballooned from 15,000 to 93,000 – a multicultural mix of Peruvians, Australians, Chileans and Mexicans, as well as Chinese, Irish, native Hawaiian and French prospectors.

Early arrivals panned for gold side by side, slept in close quarters, drank firewater with Chinese takeout, and splurged on French food and Australian wines. But with each wave of arrivals, profits dropped and

1848

Gold is discovered near present-day Placerville by mill employees. Sometime San Francisco newspaper publisher and full-time bigmouth Sam Brannan lets word out, and the Gold Rush is on.

1850

With hopes of solid-gold tax revenues, the US dubs California the 31st state. When miners find tax loopholes, SoCal ranchers are left carrying the tax burden, creating early north–south rivalries.

1851

The discovery of gold in Australia means cheering in the streets of Melbourne and panic in the streets of San Francisco, as the price of California gold plummets.

May 10, 1869

The Golden Spike is nailed in place, completing the first transcontinental railroad and connecting California to the East Coast.

gold became harder to find. The work was grueling and dangerous, and injuries often proved fatal. The cost of living in cold, filthy camps was sky-high: in 1849 a cot in a drafty flophouse among men who rarely washed could run to $10 a night (about $250 in today's terms), and such culinary abominations as a jelly omelet cost $2 (about $50 today). With one woman per 400 men in some camps, many turned to paid company, drink and opium for consolation.

Vigilantes & Robber Barons

Prospectors who did best arrived early and got out quick; those who stayed too long either lost fortunes searching for the next nugget or became targets for resentment. When foreign miners turned up better results than inexperienced white miners from the east, discriminatory laws such as the Foreign Miners Tax were enacted and vigilante justice was commonplace (see p320). Successful Peruvians and Chileans were harassed and denied renewals to their mining claims, and most left California by 1855. Native American laborers who helped the '49ers strike it rich were denied the right to hold claims. Also at the receiving end of hostilities were the Chinese, the most populous minority group in California by 1860. Frozen out of mining claims, many Chinese opened service-based businesses that survived when mining ventures went bust – incurring resentment among miners.

Such rivalries obscured the real competitive threat posed not by fellow miners or service workers, but by those who controlled the means of production: California's 'robber barons'. These speculators hoarded the industrial machinery necessary for deep-mining operations at the Comstock silver lode, discovered in 1860. As mining became industrialized, fewer miners were needed, and jobless prospectors turned their anger toward a convenient target: Chinese dockworkers. Discriminatory Californian laws restricting housing, employment and citizenship for anyone born in China were reinforced in the 1882 US Chinese Exclusion Act, which remained law until 1943.

Laws limiting work options for Chinese arrivals served the needs of robber barons, who needed cheap labor to build railroads to their claims and reach East Coast markets. To blast tunnels through the Sierras, workers were lowered down sheer mountain faces in wicker baskets, planted lit sticks of dynamite in rock crevices, and urgently tugged the rope to be hoisted out of harm's way. Those who survived the day's work were confined to bunkhouses under armed guard in cold, remote mountain regions. With little other choice of legitimate employment, an estimated 12,000 Chinese laborers blasted through the Sierra Nevada, meeting the westbound end of the railroad in 1869.

1882

The US Chinese Exclusion Act suspends new immigration from China, denies citizenship to those already in the country and sanctions racially targeted laws that stay on the books until 1943.

1906

An earthquake levels entire blocks of San Francisco in 47 seconds flat, setting off fires that rage for three days. Survivors start rebuilding immediately.

1927

After a year of tinkering, San Francisco inventor Philo Farnsworth transmits the first successful TV broadcast of…a straight line.

1934

A longshoremen's strike ends with 34 San Francisco strikers and sympathizers shot and 40 beaten by police. After mass funeral processions and a citywide strike, shipping magnates meet union demands.

Oil & Water

During the American Civil War (1861–65), California couldn't rely on food shipments from the East Coast so started growing its own. California recruited Midwestern homesteaders to farm the Central Valley with shameless propaganda. 'Acres of Untaken Government Land for a Million Farmers Without Cyclones or Blizzards,' trumpeted one California-boosting poster, neglecting to mention earthquakes or ongoing land disputes with rancheros and Native American groups. It worked: more than 120,000 homesteaders came to California in the 1870s and '80s.

Homesteaders discovered that California's gold rush had left the land badly tarnished. Hills were bare, vegetation wiped out, streams silted up and mercury washed into water supplies. Cholera spread through the open sewers in camps and claimed many lives. Because mining claims leased by the US government were granted significant tax exemptions, there were insufficient public funds for clean-up programs or public water works.

Frustrated Californian farmers south of San Luis Obispo voted to secede from California in 1859, but appeals for secession were shelved during the Civil War. In 1884 Southern Californians passed a pioneering law preventing dumping into Californian rivers and, with the support of budding agribusiness and real-estate concerns, passed bond measures to build aqueducts and dams that made large-scale farming and real-estate development possible. By the 20th century, the lower one-third of the state took two-thirds of available water supplies, inspiring Northern Californian calls for secession.

WATER WARS

Chinatown (1974) is the fictionalized yet surprisingly accurate account of the brutal water wars that were waged to build both San Francisco and Los Angeles.

While bucolic Southern California was urbanizing after the discovery of oil in the Central Valley, Northern Californians were forming the nation's first conservation movement. Naturalist John Muir founded the Sierra Club in 1892 and campaigned for the federal government to establish the first national park in Yosemite. Muir was instrumental in the grassroots political movement which would eventually establish the National Park Service in 1916.

Reforming the Wild West

When the great earthquake and fire hit San Francisco in 1906, it signaled change for California. With public funds for citywide water mains and fire hydrants siphoned off by corrupt bosses, there was only one functioning water source in San Francisco. When the smoke lifted, one thing was clear: the Wild West had to change its ways.

While San Francisco was rapidly rebuilt, California's reformers set to work on improving city, state and national politics, one plank at a time. Those concerned about public health and the trafficking of women

November 17, 1941

Five timber- and mineral-rich counties in Northern California and Southern Oregon begin a succession effort to form the State of Jefferson. Plans are halted when Japan bombs Pearl Harbor.

February 1942

Executive Order 9066 sends 120,000 Japanese Americans to internment camps. California's Japanese American Citizens' League files civil rights lawsuits, providing legal support for the 1964 Civil Rights Act.

1957

At the height of McCarthyism, City Lights wins a landmark ruling against book banning over the publication of Allen Ginsberg's *Howl*.

January 14, 1967

The Summer of Love kicks off at the Human Be-In in Golden Gate Park with blown conch shells and brain cells, and draft cards used as rolling papers.

pushed for the passage of the 1914 statewide Red Light Abatement Act. Mexico's revolution from 1910 to 1921 brought a new wave of migrants and revolutionary ideas, including ethnic pride and worker solidarity. As California's ports grew, longshoremen's unions coordinated a historic 83-day strike in 1934 along the entire West Coast that forced concessions for safer working conditions and fair pay.

At the height of the Depression in 1935, some 200,000 farming families fleeing the drought-struck Dust Bowl in Texas and Oklahoma arrived in California, where they found scant pay and deplorable working conditions at major farming concerns. California's artists alerted middle America to the migrants' plight, and the nation rallied around Dorothea Lange's haunting documentary photos of famine-struck families and John Steinbeck's harrowing fictionalized account in his 1939 novel, *The Grapes of Wrath*. The book was widely banned and Steinbeck was accused of harboring Communist sympathies, however he won both the Pulitzer and Nobel Prizes for his masterwork, and the public sympathy he generated for farm workers helped launch the United Farm Workers' Union.

California's workforce permanently changed in WWII, when women and African Americans were recruited for wartime industries and Mexican workers were brought in to fill labor shortages. Contracts in military communications and aviation attracted an international elite of engineers, who would launch California's high-tech industry. Within the decade after the war, California's population grew by 40%, reaching almost 13 million.

NORTHERN CALIFORNIA'S FIGHT FOR CIVIL RIGHTS

Before the 1963 march on Washington, DC, the Civil Rights movement was well under way in California. When 110,000 Japanese Americans along the West Coast were ordered into internment camps by President Roosevelt in 1942, San Francisco–based Japanese American Citizens' League immediately filed suits that eventually made their way to the Supreme Court. These lawsuits established groundbreaking civil rights legal precedents; in 1992 internees received reparations and an official letter of apology for internment signed by George W Bush. Adopting the nonviolent resistance practices of Mahatma Gandhi and Martin Luther King Jr, labor leaders César Chávez and Dolores Huerta formed United Farm Workers in 1962 to champion the rights of underrepresented immigrant laborers. While civil-rights leaders marched on Washington, Chávez and Californian grape pickers marched on Sacramento, bringing the issue of fair wages and the health risks of pesticides to the nation's attention. When Bobby Kennedy was sent to investigate, he sided with Chávez, bringing Latinos into the US political fold.

November 20, 1969

Native American activists symbolically reclaim Alcatraz as native land until ousted by the FBI in 1971. Public support for protesters strengthens self-rule concessions for native territories.

RICHARD LANSON/LONELY PLANET IMAGES ©

» Alcatraz (p75)

1977

San Francisco Supervisor Harvey Milk becomes the first openly gay man elected to US public office. Milk sponsors a gay-rights bill before his murder by political opponent Dan White.

October 17, 1989

The Loma Prieta earthquake hits 6.9 on the Richter scale near Santa Cruz, destroying a two-level section of Interstate 880 and resulting in 63 deaths and thousands of injuries.

The Seeds of Counterculture

It's appropriate that San Francisco is on the far left edge of the country – a position that's long underscored its political inclinations. It started during WWII, when sailors discharged in San Francisco for insubordination and homosexuality found themselves at home in North Beach's bebop jazz clubs, Bohemian coffeehouses and City Lights Bookstore. San Francisco became the home of free speech and free spirits, and soon everyone who was anyone was getting arrested: Beat poet Lawrence Ferlinghetti for publishing Allen Ginsberg's epic poem *Howl,* comedian Lenny Bruce for uttering the F-word onstage and Carol Doda for going topless. When the CIA made the mistake of using writer and willing test subject Ken Kesey to test psychoactive drugs intended to create the ultimate soldier, it inadvertently kicked off the psychedelic era. At the January 14, 1967 Human Be-In in Golden Gate Park, trip-master Timothy Leary urged a crowd of 20,000 hippies to dream a new American dream and 'turn on, tune in, drop out.' When Flower Power faded, other Bay Area rebellions grew in its place: Black Power, Gay Pride and medical marijuana clubs.

California is America's top technology hub, accounting for one-third of all US venture capital, half of biotech employment and half of all FDA-approved medical therapies since 1985.

Geeking Out

When Silicon Valley introduced the first personal computer in 1968, advertisements breathlessly gushed that Hewlett-Packard's 'light' (40lb) machine could 'take on roots of a fifth-degree polynomial' – for just $4900 (about $29,000 today). It wasn't until 21-year-old Steve Jobs and Steve Wozniak introduced the Apple II at the 1977 West Coast Computer Faire that computers seemed plausible for everyday people.

After a decade of expanding networks, things took off during the mid-1990s, when a dot-com industry boomed in Silicon Valley with online start-ups dedicated to delivering mail, news, politics, pet food and, yes, sex online. But when venture funding dried up, fortunes in stock-options disappeared on one nasty Nasdaq-plummeting day: March 10, 2000. Overnight, 26-year-old vice-presidents and Bay Area service-sector employees alike found themselves jobless. But as online users continued to look for useful information among billions of web pages, search engines and social media boomed.

Meanwhile, California biotech has been making strides. In 1976, an upstart company called Genentech was founded over beer at a San Francisco bar, and quickly got to work cloning human insulin and introducing the hepatitis B vaccine. California voters approved a $3 billion bond measure in 2004 for stem-cell research, and by 2008 the state had become the biggest funder of this research and the focus of Nasdaq's new Biotech Index. Now all that's missing is the actual boom – but if history is any indication, Northern California will make good on its talk, no matter how outlandish.

To read more about the garage-workshop culture of Silicon Valley go to www.folklore.org, which covers the crashes and personality clashes that made geek history.

March 10, 2000

The Nasdaq crashes, ending the dot-com era. Traditional industry wonks gloat over the burst bubble, until knock-on effects lead to a devalued dollar and NYSE slide beginning in 2002.

2003

Republican Arnold Schwarzenegger (aka The Governator) is elected governor of California. Schwarzenegger breaks party ranks on environmental issues and is reelected in 2007.

2004

Google's IPO raises a historic $1.67 billion at $85 per share. Share prices have since septupled, and the company's worth is valued at $111 billion.

November 2008

California voters pass Proposition 8, defining legal marriage as between a man and a woman. Courts ruled the law unconstitutional, due to California's civil-rights protections; further appeals are pending.

The People: Tree Huggers to Techies

It's fine to believe everything you've ever heard about Northern Californians, as long as the stereotypes are taken with a grain of salt. Sure, burnouts, *nuevo* hippies and Rastafarians patter away in drum circles in San Francisco's Golden Gate Park. Sure, tree huggers rhapsodize on hydroponic growing techniques and pass around doobies in the North Coast woods. Sure, young millionaires zip around the Google campus on Segways.

Even so, it's easy to see that people in Northern California are a different breed. Mostly, they espouse a live-and-let-live sensibility, which explains how both ultra-left hippies and ultra-right libertarians coexist in the far north. And although it may seem absurd to ponder the similarities between young tech execs from San Jose and grizzled lumberjacks from the northeast corner, both pride themselves on being fiercely independent thinkers.

There's truth in at least one outdoorsy stereotype: over 60% of Californians admit to having hugged a tree.

Regional Identity

In the Bay Area the politics are liberal and the people are generally open-minded, with a strong sense of social justice and a passionate devotion to the outdoors. Over the years, real-estate prices have made many of San Francisco's most desirable neighborhoods resemble the overwhelmingly wealthy and white demographics of Marin County, just over the Golden Gate Bridge. Both areas have a tremendous sense of civic pride that sometimes borders on narcissism and San Francisco, despite its all-embracing image, suffers from a lack of integration of its neighborhoods. The East Bay and Alameda County, which covers Oakland and Berkeley, have more ethnic diversity and middle-class blending.

Far north of San Francisco, it's a different scene altogether. The far north of California is a place people go to get away from other people, making for a small, self-selecting population. There aren't a lot of people way up here – and there's not a lot of money floating around either. At least not legal money.

California is defined as a 'minority majority' state, with 58% of its population Asian, Hispanic or Native American.

Despite the fact that medical marijuana is legal in California, the remote woods of the far north still harbor enormous illegal marijuana farms, and the culture of growers and itinerate pickers is impossible to overlook. The state's most progressive liberals also live up north and have fostered a strong and innovative culture of sustainability. (If you spot a beat-up old diesel Mercedes-Benz chugging along the highway, chances are it's running on biodiesel or recycled French-fry grease.) This faction is firmly entrenched against another sizable voting block: the conservative contingent in the northeast, who are still largely dependent on logging and mining.

The Central Coast, with its smaller pockets of population, starts near wacky, left-of-center Santa Cruz and stretches all the way south to the laid-back, liberal college town of San Luis Obispo. Along the way, Hwy 1 winds past working-class Monterey, made famous in John Steinbeck's novels; the bohemian Big Sur coast; the conservative upper-crust villages of Carmel-by-the-Sea; and Cambria, where the 'newly wed and nearly dead' have multimillion-dollar homes.

The Central Valley is the most socially conservative part of the state, with a largely agricultural economy. This is the land of cowboys, farmers and fruit barons. The identity of the region is also dramatically impacted by the presence of a Latino workforce that harvests the vast agricultural plains, and the echoes of the so-called 'Okies,' who fled the Oklahoma dustbowl a generation ago.

Finally, there are the foothills of the Sierra Nevada and the mountains surrounding Lake Tahoe. Many of these places have two distinct personalities: the quiet, relatively small populations of locals, who are tough as nails and deeply connected to the mountain environment, and the hordes of seasonal tourists who flock from California's cities to ski, hike and escape.

Sacramento was cited by *Time* magazine and the Civil Rights Project at Harvard University as America's most diverse and integrated city.

Lifestyle

According to a recent Cambridge University study, creativity, imagination, intellectualism and mellowness are all defining characteristics of Californians compared with inhabitants of other states.

Northern Californians are proud of their 'green' reputation and are sensitive to environmental issues. On the whole, Californians have zoomed ahead of the national energy-use curve, buying more hybrid and fuel-efficient cars than any other state.

Few Californians can afford a beach dream home, and most rent their homes, rather than own them, on a median household income of $56,134 per year. Eight of the 10 most expensive US housing markets are in California. Almost half of all Californians reside in cities, but much of the other half live in the suburbs, where the cost of living is just as high, if not higher: Marin County, outside San Francisco, is currently the most costly place to live in America. Yet San Francisco consistently tops national quality-of-life indexes.

Among adult Californians, one in four lives alone, and almost 50% are unmarried. Of those who are currently married, 33% won't be in 10 years. Increasingly, Californians are shacking up: the number of unmarried cohabiting couples has increased 40% since 1990.

Politically, Northern California is among the most liberal places in the US, particularly in the coastal areas. Voters favored Barack Obama in the 2008 presidential election with a historic 24% margin of victory. In San Francisco County, he won 83% of the vote. Those numbers probably

MARRIAGE: EQUAL RIGHTS FOR ALL

Forty thousand Californians were already registered as domestic partners when, in 2004, San Francisco Mayor Gavin Newsom issued marriage licenses to same-sex couples in defiance of a California same-sex marriage ban. Four thousand same-sex couples promptly got hitched. The state ban was nixed by California courts in June 2008 but in November of the same year, a proposition was passed amending the state's constitution to prohibit same-sex marriage. Civil-rights activists are challenging the constitutionality of the proposition, but meanwhile California's reputation as a haven of GLBT (gay/lesbian/bisexual/transgender) tolerance is lagging behind other states that have already legalized same-sex marriage, including Massachusetts, New Hampshire, Vermont, Connecticut, Iowa and New York, as well as the District of Columbia.

WHO'S UP IN THAT TREE?

Although many people in Northern California are active defenders of the environment, few demonstrate the zeal of Julia Butterfly Hill, who protested the deforestation of Northern California's redwood forests by climbing into a 180ft tree near Scotia on December 10, 1997, and stayed there. Hill's tree, a 1500-year-old coast redwood which she named 'Luna', was under threat from the Pacific Lumber Company. In an astonishing act of civil disobedience, Hill lived on a 6ft-by-6ft platform, weathering cold weather and persistent harassment from lumberjacks, for 738 days – over two full years.

Hill's actions captured the nation's imagination, and she became both the face of radical environmental action and a punch line for late-night talk-show hosts. In the end, Luna was spared, and a $50,000 deal was brokered with the Pacific Lumber Company. Not that the campaign to protect old-growth redwood is over – a current proposition to widen and straighten Hwy 101 by CalTrans threatens to bring chainsaws to over 40 trees in Richardson Grove State Park.

would have been even larger if not for the fact that California voters also turned out in the nation's largest numbers for Peace and Freedom candidate Ralph Nader, whose running mate was longtime San Francisco City Council member Matt Gonzalez.

Self-help, fitness and body modification are major industries throughout California, successfully marketed since the 1970s as 'lite' versions of religious experience – all the agony and ecstasy of the major religious brands, without those heavy commandments. Exercise and good food help keep Californians among the fittest in the nation. Yet almost 250,000 Californians are apparently ill enough to merit prescriptions for medical marijuana.

The Homeless

Homelessness is not part of the California dream, but it is a reality for at least 160,000 Californians. With the additional impacts of the global economic crisis, the housing boom and recent unemployment numbers, some suggest that the numbers are much higher. The sheer visibility of homeless people in Northern California, particularly in San Francisco, is a shock for many visitors.

Understanding the causes and demographics of Northern California's homeless is not easy. Some are teens who have run away or been kicked out by their families, but the largest contingent of homeless Californians are US military veterans – almost 30,000 in all. In the 1970s mental health programs were cut, while state-funded drug-treatment programs were dropped in the 1980s, leaving many Californians with mental illnesses and substance-abuse problems no place to go.

Also standing in line at homeless shelters are the working poor, unable to cover medical care and high rent on minimum-wage salaries. Rather than addressing the underlying causes of homelessness, some California cities have criminalized loitering, panhandling and even sitting on sidewalks. Since empathy has not yet been outlawed, feel free to give to local charities doing their part to keep California alive and dreaming.

If Southern California is *totally* known for its surfer drawl, Northern California has its own mix of idiosyncratic slang. The most iconic example? 'Hella' and 'hecka' which are technically defined as an intensifier by linguists.

Sports

California has more professional sports teams than any other state, and loyalties to local NFL football, NBA basketball and major-league baseball teams run deep. Still, San Francisco doesn't necessarily have the sports nuts in large numbers like other American cities. That said, people in the Bay Area do get worked up before a big game – just go ahead and try to find tickets to see the San Francisco 49ers. After a dizzying season in

SURFING

Surfing is the coastal spectator sport of choice, with waves reaching 100ft at the annual Mavericks competition near Half Moon Bay.

2010, the San Francisco Giants won the baseball World Series and transformed San Francisco's typically apathetic population into rabid fans in orange and black.

A recent study found Californians are less likely to be couch potatoes than other Americans, but when one Californian team plays another, the streets are deserted and all eyes are glued to the tube. The biggest grudge matches are between the San Francisco 49ers and the Oakland Raiders, the San Francisco Giants and the LA Dodgers, and baseball's Oakland A's and Anaheim's Angels. Sometimes tensions explode at these games. In August, 2011, at a match between San Francisco's 49ers and the Oakland Raiders, an enormous brawl broke out in the parking lot and three people were shot.

To see small but dedicated crowds of hometown fans (and score cheaper tickets more easily), watch pro men's or women's (WNBA) basketball in Sacramento, or pro hockey or soccer in San Jose. Or catch minor league baseball teams up and down the state, especially the winning San Jose Giants.

Except for championship play-offs, the regular season for major-league baseball runs from April to September, soccer from April to October, WNBA basketball from late May to mid-September, NFL football from September to early January, NHL ice hockey from October to March, and NBA basketball from November to April.

The Land & Sustainability

From soaring snowcapped peaks to misty coastal forests Northern California has a stunning variety of landscapes. Its pleasant Mediterranean climate is characterized by dry summers and mild, wet winters with snow falling only in the high north and at the highest elevations, making it an easy destination to travel to at any time of the year. Despite all these blessings, there's an uneasy relationship between Northern Californians and the land on which they live. Though the north of California is more sparsely populated than the south, the state as a whole has the largest human population of any US state and the nation's highest projected growth rate, which puts a tremendous strain on its many precious natural resources. The forests and rivers of the north, while a blissful retreat for people who live in the dense urban areas, as well as numerous animals and plants, are under constant threat from the growing population through logging, water diversion and urban sprawl.

California claims both the highest point in contiguous US (Mt Whitney, 14,505ft) and the lowest elevation in North America (Badwater, Death Valley, 282ft below sea level) – plus they're only 90 miles apart, as the condor flies.

Lay of the Land

The third-largest state after Alaska and Texas, California covers more than 155,000 sq miles, making it larger than 85 of the world's smallest nations. Northern California is bordered to the north by Oregon and the east by Nevada and to the west by miles of Pacific shoreline.

Geology & Earthquakes

As a whole, California is a complex geologic landscape formed from fragments of rock and earth crust scraped together as the North American continent drifted westward over hundreds of millions of years. Northern California has crumpled coastal ranges, the downward-bowing Central Valley and the still-rising Sierra Nevada, and all provide evidence of the gigantic forces exerted as the continental and ocean plates crushed together.

Everything changed about 25 million years ago, when the ocean plates stopped colliding and instead started sliding against each other, creating the massive San Andreas Fault. Because this contact zone doesn't slide

ALMOST AN ISLAND

Much of California is a biological island cut off from the rest of North America by the soaring heights of the Sierra Nevada. As on other 'islands' in the world, evolution has created unique plants and animals under these biologically isolated conditions. As a result, California ranks first in the nation for its number of endemic plants, amphibians, reptiles, freshwater fish and mammals. Even more impressive, 30% of all the plant species found in the USA, 50% of all bird species and 50% of all mammal species occur in California.

smoothly, but catches and slips irregularly, it rattles California with an ongoing succession of tremors and earthquakes.

The armchair explanation of what's happening is that the San Andreas Fault is where the Pacific Plate, which runs under the Pacific Ocean floor and much of California's coastline, meets the continental North American Plate. The fault runs for over 650 miles and has spawned numerous smaller faults that extend their fingers toward the shoreline. Walk the Earthquake Trail at Point Reyes National Seashore (p123) for an up-close lesson in plate tectonics. Earthquakes are common, although most are too small or too remote to be detected without sensors. For safety advice, see p560.

The state's most famous earthquake, in 1906, measured 7.8 on the Richter scale and demolished San Francisco, leaving more than 3000 people dead. The Bay Area made headlines again in 1989 when the Loma Prieta earthquake (7.1) caused a section of the Bay Bridge to collapse. The last 'big one' was in 1994, in Southern California, when the Northridge quake (6.7) caused parts of the Santa Monica Fwy to fall down, making it the most costly quake in US history – so far.

EARTHQUAKE

According to the US Geological Survey, the odds of a magnitude 6.7 or greater earthquake hitting California in the next 30 years is 99.7%.

The Coast to the Central Valley

Much of Northern California's coast is fronted by rugged coastal mountains that capture winter's water-laden storms. San Francisco divides the Coast Ranges roughly in half, with the foggy North Coast remaining sparsely populated, while the Central and lower regions of the Bay Area have a balmier climate and many more people.

Over 120in of rain falls each year in the northernmost reaches of the Coast Ranges and, in some places, persistent summer fog contributes another 12in of precipitation. Nutrient-rich soils and abundant moisture foster forests of giant trees, including stands of towering redwoods growing as far south as Big Sur all the way north to Oregon. Because of this unique arrangement of mountains and weather, the most reliably sunny time to visit the North Coast is in the fall, when moisture (in the form of fog) isn't being sucked in by the blisteringly hot Central Valley.

On their eastern flanks, the Coast Ranges subside into gently rolling hills that give way to the sprawling Central Valley. Once an inland sea, this flat inland basin is now an agricultural powerhouse producing about half of America's fruits, nuts and vegetables, valued at over $14 billion a year. Its bounty is evident when driving through the region – large fields of edibles stretch out into the horizon. The productivity of the region is a modern agricultural feat: about 450 miles long and 50 miles wide, the Central Valley gets about as much rainfall as a desert, but receives huge volumes of water running off the Sierra Nevada. Before the arrival of Europeans the valley was a natural wonderland – a region of vast marshes and flocks of geese that blackened the sky, not to mention grasslands carpeted with countless flowers and grazed on by millions of antelopes, elk and grizzly bears. Virtually this entire landscape has been plowed and replaced with alien weeds (including agricultural crops) and livestock.

Mountain Highs

Bordering the Central Valley on its eastern side looms California's most prominent topographic feature, the world-famous ridges of the Sierra Nevada mountain range. At 400 miles long and 50 miles wide, this is not only one of the largest mountain ranges in the world, it is also home to vast wilderness areas and 13 peaks over 14,000ft. In fact, the entire 150-mile region from Sonora Pass south to Mt Whitney lies mostly above 9000ft and is known as the High Sierra; this is a stunning and remote landscape of glaciers, sculpted granite peaks and lonely canyons. It's beautiful to look at but difficult to access, and crossing it posed one of the greatest challenges for settlers attempting to reach California in the 1800s.

The soaring Sierra Nevada captures storm systems and drains them of their water, with most of the precipitation over 3000ft falling as snow. Snowfalls average 38ft at mid-elevations on the west slope, with a record of 73.5ft at one location, making this a premier skiing and winter-sports destination. These waters eventually flow into 11 major river systems on the west slope and several on the east slope, providing the vast majority of water for agriculture in the Central Valley and meeting the needs of major metropolitan areas from San Francisco to Los Angeles.

Most of the Sierra Nevada is cloaked in dense conifer forests with stands of oaks taking over in the western foothills and in dry canyons. Twenty-three species of conifer occur in the Sierra Nevada, ranging from the scraggly twisting gray pines of the western foothills to tiny wind-sculpted whitebark pines at 12,000ft. In between, mid-elevation forests are home to massive Douglas firs, ponderosa pines and, biggest of all, the giant sequoia.

At its northern end the Sierra Nevada merges imperceptibly into the southern tip of the volcanic Cascade Mountains that continue north into Oregon and Washington. This wet mountainous region extends westward to the coast through a tangle of ancient and geologically complex ranges that are sparsely populated and also heavily cloaked with conifer forests.

California's Top Parks

» Point Reyes National Seashore p123

» Redwood National & State Parks p256

» Yosemite National Park p396

» Sequoia & Kings Canyon National Parks p414

National & State Parks

The majority of Californians rank outdoor recreation as vital to their quality of life, and the number of preserved lands has steadily grown due to important pieces of legislation passed since the 1960s, including the landmark 1976 California Coastal Act, which saved the coastline from further development. Today, **California State Parks** (www.parks.ca.gov) protect nearly a third of the state's coastline, along with redwood forests, mountain lakes, desert canyons, waterfalls, wildlife preserves and historical sites.

In recent years, both federal and state budget shortfalls and chronic underfunding have been partly responsible for widespread park closures,

THE BIG ONES

Although the San Andres Fault has apparently been rumbling for millennia, the earliest recorded earthquake in California dates to 1769, when it shook members of the Spanish Portola Expedition near LA. Here are some of the largest rattlers in Northern California since then:

» 1868 Hayward earthquake – Mentioned by Mark Twain in *Roughing It*, this 7.0 magnitude quake destroyed every building in the Bay Area suburb of Hayward.

» 1872 Lone Pine earthquake – Although it was unmeasured, scientists think that this earthquake in the Owens Valley rivaled the intensity of the 1906 event. It apparently woke John Muir, who ran out of his Yosemite cabin shouting 'A noble quake!'

» 1906 San Francisco earthquake – The granddaddy of them all, this quake and the subsequent fires leveled San Francisco and was felt as far north as Oregon, leaving almost 75% of the city homeless.

» 1964 Good Friday earthquake – Although the epicenter of this quake was near Anchorage, Alaska, it sent tsunami waves down the coast and destroyed much of downtown Crescent City.

» 1989 Loma Prieta earthquake – Centered in the Santa Cruz mountains, this shook players warming up for the 1989 World Series and caused the collapse of a section of the bridge connecting Oakland and San Francisco.

more limited visitor services and steadily rising park-entry and outdoor recreation fees. In May 2011, the State of California announced that it planned to close 70 state parks – about 25% of the system – and in the months since, nonprofit organizations, environmentalists and park advocates have scrambled to save them. Many believe that it's in California's economic interests to protect the wilderness, as recreational tourism consistently outpaces competing 'resource extraction' industries such as mining.

Take a virtual field trip courtesy of the myriad links put together by the California Geological Survey at www.conservation.ca.gov/cgs/geotour.

Unfortunately, some of Northern California's parks are also being loved to death. Overcrowding severely impacts the environment, and it's increasingly difficult to balance public access with the principles of conservation. If possible, try visiting big-name parks like Yosemite in the shoulder seasons (ie not summer) to avoid the biggest crowds. Alternatively, lesser-known natural areas managed by the **National Park Service** (www.nps.gov/state/CA) may go relatively untouched most of the year, which means you won't have to reserve permits, campsites or accommodations months in advance.

There are 18 national forests in California run by the **US Forest Service** (USFS; www.fs.fed.us/r5/), including lands around Mt Whitney, Mt Shasta and Big Bear Lake, and many other areas worth exploring. National wildlife refuges (NWR), favored by bird-watchers, are managed by the **US Fish & Wildlife Service** (USFWS; www.fws.gov/refuges). More wilderness tracts are overseen by the **Bureau of Land Management** (BLM; www.blm.gov/ca/st/en.html).

Northern California Water

As you travel through Northern California, the interconnected water systems that move in naturally occurring and human-built systems are evident at every turn. Start at the top, with those big clouds that come in weather patterns off the Pacific and get caught on the ridges of the Sierra Nevada, resulting in a thick blanket of snow in the winter. The Sierra snowmelt moves across the landscape drop by drop all year, down the rivers that support white-water rafting, though irrigation systems that grow the food that makes the cuisine here so fresh, and through giant aqueducts and a web of water pipes that provide fresh water to the dense urban Bay Area. Water is a basic ingredient of life, sure, but its profound effect on all aspects of culture in Northern California is only now a topic of discussion, one which quickly heats up with the contentious mention of population growth, protection and global climate change.

Moving through the inland territory of Northern California, you'll almost certainly encounter one or both of the region's two major rivers, the Sacramento and the San Joaquin. These are the aquatic highways into which so many other river systems feed – rivers such as the Kern, which runs through Bakersfield; the Tuolumne, which rushes through

CALIFORNIA'S CAP & TRADE

In October of 2011, California lawmakers adopted a cap-and-trade system for air emissions, in order to help the state achieve its ambitious goals to reduce greenhouse gas by 2020. The complex market system fixes a price on heat-trapping pollution by California's dirtiest industries – coal, oil and manufacturing – and allows them to trade carbon credits. Beginning in 2013, the state's largest carbon emitters will be required by law to meet the caps or buy credits. The legislation, originally endorsed by former governor Arnold Schwarzenegger, had to overcome a number of legal challenges and a 2010 ballot initiative that aimed to suspend it. The first of its kind in the US, the system promises to establish a model that could be adopted at national level.

Yosemite's High Country; and the American, which crosses the Gold Country. For these rivers, the end of the line is the San Francisco Bay, where their fresh water meets the salty Pacific. In the redwood-dotted north, there are another set of six rivers which are the subjects of major recreational interest – the Trinity, Smith, Klamath, Mad, Eel and Van Duzen.

Aside from rivers, Northern California's lakes are a major draw for travelers. Lake Tahoe, the deepest natural lake in the US, and Clear Lake, north of the Wine Country, are two of the region's major natural lakes, but other engineered lakes, such as Shasta Lake and Whiskeytown Lake, host a suite of recreational activities.

Northern California's struggle to protect and maintain these bodies of water is a major environmental, political and social issue. Perhaps few topics capture the multifaceted nuances of this struggle more succinctly than that of Hetch Hetchy, a man-made reservoir in Yosemite National Park. Once a deep natural gorge described by conservationist John Muir as 'one of nature's rarest and most precious mountain temples,' Hetch was flooded to create a water reservoir. Although even in its flooded state Hetch Hetchy provides a beautiful setting for camping and hiking, in recent years environmentalists have been fighting local governments to drain the reservoir and restore Hetch Hetchy to its natural state. Opponents argue this would endanger San Francisco's water supply in the event of an emergency.

WATER

The San Francisco airport introduced green 'hydration stations' at its state-of-the-art airport terminal to decrease waste from bottled water. The stations came with a snappy slogan, offering a drink from the 'pristine Sierra snowmelt.'

Conserving California

Although California is in many ways a success story, development and growth have come at great environmental cost. Starting in 1849, Gold Rush miners tore apart the land in their frenzied quest for the 'big strike,' ultimately sending more than 1.5 billion tons of debris, and uncalculated amounts of poisonous mercury, downstream into the Central Valley where rivers and streams became clogged and polluted.

Water, or the lack thereof, has long been at the heart of California's epic environmental struggles and catastrophes. Despite campaigning by California's greatest environmental champion, John Muir, in the 1920s the Tuolumne River was damned at Hetch Hetchy, to provide San Francisco with drinking water. Likewise, the diversion of water to LA has contributed to the destruction of Owens Lake and its fertile wetlands, and the degradation of Mono Lake (see boxed text, p431). Statewide, the damming of rivers and capture of water for houses and farms has destroyed countless salmon runs and drained marshlands. The Central Valley, for example, today resembles a dust bowl, and its underground aquifer is in poor shape.

Altered and compromised habitats, both on land and water, make easy targets for invasive species, including highly aggressive species that wreak havoc on both California's economy and ecosystems. In San Francisco Bay, one of the most important estuaries in the world, there are now over 230 alien species choking the aquatic ecosystem and in some areas they already comprise as much as 95% of the total biomass.

Although air quality in California has improved markedly in past decades, it's still among the worst in the country. Auto exhaust and fine particulates generated by the wearing down of vehicle tires, along with industrial emissions, are the chief culprits. An even greater health hazard is ozone, the principal ingredient in smog, which makes sunny days around the Central Valley look hazy.

But there's hope. Low-emission vehicles are becoming one of the most sought-after types of car in the state, and rapidly rising fuel costs are keeping more gas guzzling SUVs off the road. Californians recently voted to fund construction of solar-power plants, and there's even talk of harnessing the tremendous tidal flows of the Pacific to generate more 'clean' energy. By law California's utilities must get 33% of their energy from renewable resources by 2020, the most ambitious target yet set by any US state.

Browse through over 1200 aerial photos covering almost every mile of California's gorgeously rugged coastline, from Oregon to the Mexican border, at www.californiacoastline.org.

Also, some of the most visionary sustainability practices in the world are unfolding throughout Northern California. The wine regions north of San Francisco are the greenest in the world, maximizing their water and energy usage and pioneering techniques that have all but eliminated the use of pesticides. The city government of Arcata has world-leading sustainability practices. The city purchased tracts of forest land to protect the integrity of their water supply and developed a revolutionary marsh-based sewer treatment system. Built on a solid waste, the marsh processes wastewater through a series of oxidation ponds and wetlands that also serve as a wildlife sanctuary. Additionally, citizens in towns of the far north such as McCloud and Shasta have fought to protect their natural resources in landmark civic action. In 2009, they blocked multinational Nestle from tapping the Shasta watershed for a water-bottling facility.

Wild, Wildlife

Let's start with the bad news: with five distinct climatic zones, Northern California has such an overwhelming variety of plants and animals that it would take several lifetimes to explore. The good news, especially for time-crunched travelers: many exist within a short drive of one another. This is a place where, without much effort, a visitor can laze on a sunny beach during the morning, spend the afternoon under the dripping canopy of the coast redwood and catch a sunset over a snowcapped mountain. There are (mountain) lions, tigers (or at least California tiger salamanders) and bears. There are whales, sharks and rays. Even travelers uninterested in the wild kingdom have little choice but to confront it: herds of Roosevelt elk stop traffic, curious deer graze at the edge of motel parking lots and flocks of migratory birds are constantly overhead.

Pick up one of the excellent *California Natural History Guides* published by the University of California Press (www.ucpress.edu), which are compact enough to carry in a daypack.

Wild Things

Much of California is a biological island cut off from the rest of North America by the soaring heights of the Sierra Nevada and, as on other 'islands' in the world, evolution creates unique plants and animals under these conditions. As a result, California ranks first in the nation for its number of endemic plants, amphibians, reptiles, freshwater fish and mammals.

Although the staggering numbers of animals that greeted the first European settlers are now a thing of the past, it is still possible to see wildlife thriving in Northern California in the right places and at the right times of year. You're likely to spot at least a few iconic species, such as coyotes, bobcats and eagles, during your travels. Unfortunately, some of these are but shadow populations, hovering at the edge of survival, pushed up against the burgeoning human population.

Whales & Other Marine Animals

Spend even one day along Northern California's coast and you'll get a crash course in marine wildlife – from the gulls overhead (or eyeing your picnic) to tide pools of starfish. Still, the king of the Northern California coast is much, much bigger: the magnificent gray whale. Gray whales migrate in growing numbers along California's coast, and visitors to coastal bluffs in the north should scan the horizons for their clouds of spray. Adult whales live up to 70 years, are longer than a city bus and can weigh up to 40 tons, making quite a splash when they dive below or leap out of the water. In summer, the whales feed in the Arctic waters between Alaska and Siberia. In the fall, they move south down the Pacific coast of Canada and the USA to sheltered lagoons in the Gulf of California, by the Mexican state of Baja California. During this 6000-mile migration, the whales pass by California between December and April. Traveling night and day at a clip of about 3mph, this is thought to be the longest migration of any mammal. (Sooty shearwaters, seabirds that resemble a dark gray seagull, hold the record for the longest migration of anything in the

Peak mating season for northern elephants seals along the Pacific coast just happens to coincide with Valentine's Day (February 14).

animal kingdom, and they also can be seen in Northern California.) The best way to see whales is by getting right out on the water. During the season of their migration, visitors can depart from many cities along the North Coast on whale-watching expeditions, which often last two hours. These have no guarantees, but visitors can ask the boat operators about recent sightings to get an idea of what to expect.

Even if you don't spot the big guys, you'll likely see other charming little creatures, including playful sea otters and harbor seals. These species especially like to crowd around public piers and protected bays. Since the 1989 earthquake, the air of San Francisco's Pier 39 has been filled by the distinct sound (and distinct odor) of barking sea lions, much to the delight of ogling tourists. Other places to see wild pinnipeds include Point Lobos State Natural Reserve near Monterey, and the Channel Islands National Park.

California's mountain forests are home to an estimated 25,000 to 35,000 black bears, whose fur actually ranges in color from black to dark brown, cinnamon or even blond.

Almost hunted to extinction by the late 19th century, northern elephant seals have made a remarkable comeback along California's coast. Año Nuevo State Reserve, north of Santa Cruz, is a major breeding ground for northern elephant seals. But California's biggest elephant seal colony is found at Piedras Blancas near Hearst Castle, south of Big Sur. There's a smaller rookery at Point Reyes National Seashore.

Mountain Kings

There's some irony in the fact that California's most symbolic animal is the grizzly bear. The brown beast that graces the state flag is long gone. Extirpated in the early 1900s, grizzlies once roamed California's beaches and grasslands in large numbers, eating everything from whale carcasses to acorns. Grizzlies were particularly abundant in the Central Valley, but retreated upslope into the mountains as they were hunted out. There's occasionally chatter from conservationists about reintroducing the grizzly population to California, but it seems unlikely.

All that remains now are the grizzlies' relatively diminutive cousins, black bears, which typically weigh under 400lb. These burly omnivores feed on berries, nuts, roots, grasses, insects, eggs, small mammals and fish, but can become a nuisance around campgrounds and mountain cabins where food is not stored properly (for safety tips, see p560). Remember the old adage that 'a fed bear is a dead bear' – people invite the destruction of these beautiful animals by carelessly leaving food unattended in their cars and campsites. It's a wonderful complement to a trip in the woods to see a black bear foraging in a high mountain

EYEING ELEPHANT SEALS

Northern elephant seals follow a precise calendar. In November and December, adult male 'bull seals' return to their colony's favorite California beaches and start the ritual struggles to assert superiority; only the largest, strongest and most aggressive 'alpha' males gather a harem. In January and February, adult females, already pregnant from last year's beach antics, give birth to their pups and soon mate with the dominant males, who promptly depart on their next feeding migration. The bull seals' motto seems to be 'love 'em and leave 'em'!

At birth an elephant seal pup weighs about 75lb, and while being fed by its mother it puts on about 10lb a day. Female seals leave the beach in March, abandoning their offspring. For up to two months the young seals, now known as 'weaners,' lounge around in groups, gradually learning to swim, first in tidal pools, then in the sea. Then they, too, depart by May, having lost 20% to 30% of their weight during this prolonged fast.

Between June and October, elephant seals of all ages and both sexes return in smaller numbers to the beaches to molt.

WILDFLOWER WATCHING

The famous 'golden hills' of California are actually the result of many plants drying up in preparation for the long dry summer. Many plants have adapted to long periods of almost no rain by growing prolifically during California's mild wet winters, springing to life with the first rains of autumn and blooming as early as February. As snows melt later at higher elevations in the Sierra Nevada, Yosemite National Park's Tuolumne Meadows is a prime spot for wildflower walks and photography, with peak blooms usually in late June or early July.

meadow, but sadly they're most often scrounging around in the campground dumpster.

Northern California's other fearsome mammal is the mountain lion. Sometimes called cougars, they hunt throughout the mountains and forests of Northern California, especially in areas teeming with deer. Solitary lions, which can grow to 8ft in length and weigh 175lb, are formidable predators, but they are very, very seldom seen. Although they incite a panic in many urbanites (and you'll see warning signs at many trailheads), these large cats are very skittish and attacks on humans are extremely rare. Most human encounters have occurred where encroachment has pushed hungry lions to their limits – for example, at the boundaries between wilderness and rapidly developing suburbs.

Feathered Friends & Butterflies

Northern California lies on major migratory routes for over 350 species of birds, which either pass through the state or linger through the winter. This is one of the top birding destinations in North America. Witness, for example, the congregation of one million ducks, geese and swans at the Klamath Basin National Wildlife Refuges every November. During winter, these water birds head south into the refuges of the Central Valley, another area to observe huge numbers of native and migratory species.

Year-round you can see birds at California's beaches, estuaries and bays, where herons, cormorants, shorebirds and gulls gather at places such as Point Reyes National Seashore and the shores near Redwood National and State Parks. Monarch butterflies are gorgeous orange creatures that follow long-distance migration patterns in search of milkweed, their only source of food. They winter in California by the tens of thousands, mostly on the Central Coast, including at Santa Cruz, Pacific Grove and Pismo Beach.

The Audubon Society's free California chapter website (http://ca.audubon.org) has helpful birding checklists, a newsy blog, and descriptions of key species and important birding areas statewide.

As you drive along the Big Sur coast, look skyward to spot endangered California condors (see p478), which also soar over inland Pinnacles National Monument. Condors are the largest flying birds in the hemisphere, with a wingspan that can reach 9ft. They're easy to mistake with the wobbly, and common, turkey vulture, who are also frequent guests above the shorelines. You can tell the difference by their coasting pattern: turkey vultures are poorly balanced and seem to soar drunkenly, where condors glide much more smoothly. Also keep an eye out for regal bald eagles, which can be seen in the Sierra Nevada and along the North Coast.

Going Native: Wildflowers & Trees

Plant life in Northern California is both flamboyant and subtle. Many species are so obscure and similar that only a dedicated botanist could tell them apart, but add them all together in the spring and you end up with riotous carpets of wildflowers that can take your breath away. The state flower is the orange-yellow native California poppy.

California is also a land of superlative trees: the tallest (coast redwoods approaching 380ft), the largest (giant sequoias of the Sierra Nevada over 36ft across at the base) and the oldest (bristlecone pines of the White Mountains that are almost 5000 years old; see p441). The giant sequoia, which is unique to California, survives in isolated groves scattered on the Sierra Nevada's western slopes, including in Yosemite, Sequoia and Kings Canyon National Parks.

In 2006 the world's tallest tree was discovered in Redwood National Park (its location is being kept secret). It's named Hyperion and stands a whopping 379ft tall.

An astounding 20 native species of oak grow in California, including live, or evergreen, oaks with hollylike leaves and scaly acorns, which thrive in coastal ranges. More rare native species include the Monterey pine, gnarly trees that have adapted to harsh coastal conditions such as high winds, sparse rainfall and sandy, stony soils. You can find groves of them near Monterey.

Heading inland, the Sierra Nevada has three distinct ecozones: the dry western foothills covered with oak and chaparral, conifer forests starting from about 2000ft, and an alpine zone above 8000ft. Twenty-three species of conifer occur in the Sierra Nevada, with midelevation forests home to massive Douglas firs, ponderosa pines and, biggest of all, the giant sequoia. Deciduous trees include the delightful quaking aspen, a white-trunked tree whose shimmering leaves brighten many mountain meadow edges. Its large, rounded leaves turn pale yellow in the fall, creating some of the most spectacular scenery you'll see, notably around June Lake in the Eastern Sierra.

Arts & Architecture

You'll be sitting in a San Francisco *taqueria* (Mexican fast-food restaurant), just about to tuck into a heavenly, overstuffed burrito and minding your own business when – apropos of absolutely nothing – a posse of mariachis saunter in from the street and break into a brassy ballad. *This* is the essence of Northern California's relationship with the arts: deeply woven into the fabric of everyday life, unexpected and utterly unavoidable. Northern California has been a bastion for creative thinkers, contrarians and crackpots from the very beginning and visitors will encounter the thriving creative culture that they've created: broadly independent, highly spirited and marching to its own beat.

Music

The essential sounds of Northern California would be a schizophrenic playlist. It would lead with a track from Summer of Love icons like Jefferson Airplane, Janis Joplin or the Grateful Dead, include a few choice cuts from twanging, heartbroken country heroes from the Central Valley, and eventually make its way to the distinctive thump of the East Bay's 'hyphy' hip-hop movement. You'd also have to have a sample of haute folk nuevo acts like Joanna Newsom and a couple of lilting *norteño* ballads, which dominate the region's AM radio, and round things out with the San Francisco Symphony, now one of the nation's most exciting orchestral bodies under the baton of Michael Tilson Thomas.

San Francisco is the seat of most of the musical action, but even away from the twinkling city lights Northern California is an earful, with fantastic outdoor festivals and spunky music scenes in college towns such as Arcata and Chico. Come with open ears and be prepared to be impressed.

OPERA

When the 1906 earthquake hit San Francisco, the visiting Metropolitan Opera lost all its costumes and tenor Enrico Caruso was thrown from his bed. Caruso never returned, but the Met played free shows in the rubble-choked streets.

Golden Oldies

The guy crooning in the corner of the taco shop represents one of California's longest musical traditions – Mexican folk music. This sound arrived even before the Gold Rush introduced Western bluegrass, bawdy dancehall ragtime and Chinese classical music and is still an essential sound of the region. Still, by the turn of the 20th century, opera had become California's favorite sound. San Francisco alone had 20 concert and opera halls before the 1906 earthquake literally brought down the houses. Among San Francisco's first public buildings to be completed was the War Memorial Opera House, now home to the second-largest US opera company after New York's Metropolitan. Although the San Francisco Opera still rolls out the same chestnuts that entertained fans after the quake, today its program includes a number of visionary modern works, including recent premiere *The Bonesetter's Daughter,* which had a libretto written by Bay Area author Amy Tan.

It Don't Mean a Thing...

Swing – imported from black neighborhoods in the East and dance halls of the South – swept Northern California in the 1930s and '40s. Big bands packed houses in the Bay Area and Western Swing (the country kind) filled Central Valley dancehalls. Swing's arty edge flourished on the stages of San Francisco's underground, integrated jazz clubs. These scenes might sound like estranged cousins, but swing's essential feel – lilting, often up-tempo rhythmic underpinnings – was the colorblind common thread.

Still, the era swung in two distinctly segregated ways in Northern California: the black communities that arrived via the 'Great Migration' to work in the Bay Area's WWII shipping and manufacturing boom, and satin-clad Western Swing outfits that modeled themselves after Texas fiddler Bob Wills. While both San Francisco and Oakland fostered working-class blues scenes throughout the 1940s and '50s, championed by guitarists Pee Wee Crayton from Texas and Oklahoma-born Lowell Fulson, the most happening scene was in San Francisco's Fillmore district, known as the 'Harlem of the West' – which is rumored to have hosted the only gig where jazz icons Charlie Parker and Louis Armstrong ever played together. By marrying Western Swing and a rural working-class aesthetic, the Central Valley minted the Bakersfield Sound, a hard-edged, honky-tonk genre that would see the rise of Buck Owens and Merle Haggard.

While Beat poets riffed over improvised bass-lines and audiences snapped along San Francisco's North Beach neighborhood, the cool West Coast Jazz movement emerged from the 1950s, with champions in trumpeter Chet Baker and pianist Dave Brubeck. In the 1950s and '60s, doo-wop, rhythm and blues, and soul music were all in steady rotation at nightclubs in San Francisco, while the nexus of pop music became firmly established in the studios of Los Angeles.

JAZZ

The Monterey Jazz Festival is among the longest-running jazz festivals in the world and has been swinging along on the Central Coast since 1958. Its organizers have included pianist Dave Brubeck and actor, former Carmel mayor (and occasional composer) Clint Eastwood. It is held annually at the end of September.

The San Francisco Sound & Summer of Love

No tune captures the psychedelic San Francisco sound better than the brilliant, twisted, totally bizarre trip of Jefferson Airplane's musical take of Lewis Carroll's *Alice's Adventures in Wonderland*, 'White Rabbit.' After the building waves of musical rebellion manifested in the form of a sassy, sultry, salty singer named Janis Joplin, all ears were on San Francisco during the '60s. The Grateful Dead would emerge as the most enduring Bay Area ambassadors, but they were only a sliver of the scene. A seething, psychedelic mess of musical exploration, sexual liberation and mind-altering expression, it was a sound presented in vivid Technicolor by groups like Moby Grape, Quicksilver Messenger Service and Santana. This movement was cranked up to 11 during 1967, when the Summer of Love brought 10,000 pilgrims to San Francisco's Haight-Ashbury neighborhood. Golden Gate Park's 'Human Be-In' in January of that year kicked things off with a free-form festival of good vibes, LSD and live music. At the end of the '60s, Sly and the Family Stone – a funky, interracial group lead by the so-called 'Black Prince of Woodstock', Sly Stone – perfectly captured the all-embracing, edgy, revolutionary spirit of the times with their hit 'I Want to Take You Higher'.

Wider social tensions, civic unrest and an increasingly volatile discourse on the Civil Rights movement later boiled over and changed the vanguard players of San Francisco's sound, and many musicians instrumental in the Summer of Love entered a period of decline hastened by over-exposure and overdoses. Those that survived cleaned up and cashed out (lookin' at you, Mr Santana), though the Grateful Dead soldiered on until Jerry Garcia's passing in a Marin County rehabilitation clinic in 1995.

Alternative NorCal

Forget the '80s, the spandex, the commercial synth pop and hair metal. While these trends wafted north from LA like a noxious cloud of Aquanet, Northern California's music scene slumbered. Aside from a couple of marginal mainstream acts, like Huey Lewis & the News, Tesla and MC Hammer, Northern California was relatively quiet and its influence relatively minor. But there's something in the cultural DNA of Northern California that delights in swimming against the stream, so when the cultural backlash against mainstream movements began in earnest with college radio, late-night MTV programming and the emergence of arty, post-punk underground, Northern California was back in the action.

As so-called 'alternative music' found larger and larger audiences, well-packaged Bay Area folk rockers like Counting Crows, Chris Isaak and 4 Non Blondes crossed over and enjoyed a moment of Top 40 success. Still, the most interesting music of the '90s was produced by a group of quietly influential, genre-bending groups like Jawbreaker, Pavement, Primus and Faith No More.

The dot-com boom was the death knell of San Francisco's underground music in the 2000s; escalating rents were bankrolled by venture-capital firms, and artists watched their venues and rehearsal spaces transformed into offices, sushi restaurants and boutiques.

Over the last decade, Northern California's music has flourished across the bay in Oakland, where there are plucky scenes of underground rock and hip-hop. Even farther afield, unlikely musical centers have flourished – like Nevada City, home to harp-playing indie darling Joanna Newsom.

Rap & Hip-Hop Rhythms

Los Angeles' Compton neighborhood was the epicenter of the West Coast rap and hip-hop movements throughout the 1980s and '90s, but Northern California maintained a healthy grassroots hip-hop scene in the heart of the black-power movement in Oakland. One of the primary figures of West Coast rap, Tupac Shakur, spent his high-school years on the mean streets of Marin County. It wasn't until the 1990s that the Bay Area sound came into its own with the 'hyphy movement.' Like the Bay Area's punk and rock movements, its roots were also contrarian – a reaction against the increasing commercialization of hip-hop. Its most enduring and influential players were underground Oakland artists like

PUNKS OF THE NORTH

In the 1970s, when American airwaves were jammed with commercial arena rock, California rock critics like Lester Bangs and Greil Marcus formed the cultural front line to fight back. Sick of the prepackaged anthems, teenagers across the US and across Northern California plugged secondhand guitars into crappy, distorted amplifiers and articulated their fury with three chords and unvarnished rage. Punk was born.

San Francisco's punk scene was arty and absurdist, in rare form with Dead Kennedy's singer (and future San Francisco mayoral candidate) Jello Biafra howling 'Holiday in Cambodia.' The Avengers opened for the Sex Pistols' 1978 San Francisco show, which Sid Vicious celebrated with an OD in the Haight that broke up the band.

In the mid-'90s a fresh wave of influential punks grew out of all-ages, DIY venues like Berkeley's (now defunct) Gillman Street Project, including bands like Operation Ivy and Rancid. Of these, none had more sustained success than the Berkeley trio Green Day, who churned out catchy pop-punk hooks about suburban doldrums, masturbation and teen ennui. While Green Day grew into arena-sized audiences through the next decade, their 2004 LP *American Idiot* was a mainstream success with Bay Area ideals: its songs derided war, capitalism and conservative politics.

Keak Da Sneak, Mac Dre and E-40. Also from Oakland, Michael Franti & Spearhead blended hip-hop with funk, reggae, folk, jazz and rock stylings into messages for social justice and peace in 2010's *The Sound of Sunshine*. Meanwhile, Korn from Bakersfield combined hip-hop with rap and metal to popularize 'nu metal.'

Architecture

There's more to Northern California than bungalows and boardwalks, and buildings here have often adapted imported styles to the climate and available materials – just look at the fog-resistant redwood-shingle houses in Mendocino. But after a century and a half of grafting on inspired influences and eccentric details as the mood strikes, the element of the unexpected is everywhere: tiled Maya deco facades in Oakland, English thatched roofs in Carmel, chinoiserie streetlamps in San Francisco. California's architecture was postmodern before the word even existed.

Oddball California Architecture

- Hearst Castle, San Simeon
- Tor House, Carmel-by-the-Sea
- Sea Ranch Chapel, Sea Ranch
- Winchester House, San Jose

Spanish Missions & Victorian Queens

The first Spanish missions were built around courtyards, using materials that Native Californians and colonists found on hand: adobe, limestone and grass. Many missions crumbled into disrepair as the church's influence waned, but the style remained practical for the climate. Early California settlers later adapted it into the rancho adobe style, as in the San Carlos Borroméo de Carmelo Mission in Monterey.

Once the mid-19th-century Gold Rush was on, Northern California's nouveau riche imported materials to construct grand mansions matching European fashions, and raised the stakes with ornamental excess. Many millionaires favored the gilded Queen Anne style. Outrageous examples of Victorian architecture, including 'Painted Ladies' and 'gingerbread' houses, can be found in such Northern California towns as San Francisco, Ferndale and Eureka.

Art Deco & Arts & Crafts

Like much of the rest of the state, simplicity was the hallmark of Northern California's Arts and Crafts style. Influenced by both Japanese design principles and England's Arts and Crafts movement, its woodwork and handmade touches marked a deliberate departure from the Industrial Revolution. SoCal architects Charles and Henry Greene and Bernard Maybeck in Northern California popularized the versatile one-story bungalow, which became trendy at the turn of the 20th century. Today you'll spot them all over Sacramento and Berkeley with their overhanging eaves, terraces and sleeping porches, harmonizing indoors and outdoors.

In 1915, newspaper magnate William Randolph Hearst commissioned California's first licensed female architect, Julia Morgan, to build his Hearst Castle. The commission would take decades.

California was cosmopolitan from the start, and couldn't be limited to any one set of international influences. In the 1920s, the international art deco style took elements from the ancient world – Mayan glyphs, Egyptian pillars, Babylonian ziggurats – and flattened them into modern motifs to cap stark facades and outline streamlined skyscrapers, most notably in downtown Oakland and Sacramento. Streamline moderne kept decoration to a minimum and mimicked the aerodynamic look of ocean liners and airplanes, as seen at San Francisco's Cathedral of Saint Mary of the Assumption.

Postmodern Evolutions

True to its mythic nature, California can't help wanting to embellish the facts a little, veering away from strict high modernism to add unlikely postmodern shapes to the local landscape. Following in the footsteps of Southern California buildings like Richard Meier's Getty Center, and Frank Gehry's Walt Disney Concert Hall in Los Angeles, San Francisco has become home to a brave new crop of buildings in the new millennium.

San Francisco's brand of postmodernism is emblematic in Pritzker Prize-winning architects that magnify and mimic California's great outdoors, especially in Golden Gate Park. Swiss architects Herzog & de Meuron clad the MH de Young Memorial Museum in copper, which will eventually oxidize green to match its park setting. Nearby, Renzo Piano literally raised the roof on sustainable design at the LEED platinum-certified California Academy of Sciences, capped by a living garden.

Literature

For a traveler, there's much to love about Northern California's duo of great early literary icons, Jack London and Mark Twain. After all, it was Twain whose thoughts on travel are just so quotable: 'The World is a book, and those who do not travel read only a page.' Both men were avid adventurers, vivid storytellers and iconic literary stylists.

Long before Huck Finn, Twain got his break with a story called *The Celebrated Jumping Frog of Calaveras County,* which he wrote while living in a cabin in the California foothills. Every year the central event of Twain's story still sees the competition of little green contestants at the Calaveras County Fair in Angels Camp. Jack London was also a restless vagabond. Born in San Francisco, London shipped in and out of the ports of Oakland, which informed sea-faring stories and adventure novels like *White Fang, The Call of the Wild* and *Sea Wolf.* London's old neighborhood isn't the turf of salty dogs any more; the waterfront area is now a dining and entertainment district in Oakland which bears his name.

In the North Coast community of Sea Ranch, buildings are subject to rigorous zoning guidelines that require simple timber-frame structures clad in wooden siding or shingles and a harmonious relationship with the surroundings.

A generation later came the Beats, a collection of poets, novelists and alternative thinkers who populated San Francisco's North Beach neighborhood. The cast of characters who drifted in and out of the scene are household names in American literature: Jack Kerouac, Alan Ginsberg and Lawrence Ferlinghetti. Ferlinghetti's City Lights bookstore published many of the generation's most definitive titles, including Ginsberg's *Howl and Other Poems,* which won a landmark 1957 obscenity case during the oppressive era of McCarthyism.

More recently, a number of Northern California authors have enjoyed attention on the international stage. Chinese American novelist Amy Tan's *Joy Luck Club* was a celebrated work about the dynamics of families in San Francisco's Chinatown. Writer, editor and publisher Dave Eggers was a Pulitzer Prize finalist for his 2000 memoir *A Heartbreaking Work of Staggering Genius,* and two literary ventures have earned national attention: a literary magazine *The Believer* and a nonprofit literary advocacy program, 826 Valencia, which is named for its Mission District address.

Some of the most eloquent modern writing on Northern California, the Summer of Love, the Central Valley and the California political circus is by the hand of Sacramento native essayist Joan Didion. Didion's *White Album* is a collection of essays that goes deep into the psyche of California in the late '60s, and discussion of the Central Valley in *Where I Was*

FILM IN SAN FRANCISCO

Although San Francisco can't hold a candle to the cinematic clout of its neighbor to the south, the city hosts a number of internationally renowned film festivals. The annual San Francisco International Film Festival, held each spring, is the oldest continuously running film festival in the Americas and the city also hosts several other notable film festivals each year, including the Asian American Film Festival in March and the International Lesbian and Gay Film Festival in June as part of the city's Pride Month. Film fans who come at other times of the year should look into UC Berkeley's Pacific Film Archive.

The Bay Area is also home to some notable film houses, including animation giant Pixar and George Lucas' Skywalker Ranch.

From takes a thoughtful look at Ronald Regan's governor mansion, water wars, and the odysseys of California's mythmakers.

Visual Arts & Theater

Although the earliest European artists were trained cartographers accompanying Western explorers, their images of California as an island show more imagination than scientific rigor. This exaggerated, mythologizing tendency of depicting California continued throughout the Gold Rush era, as Western artists alternated between caricatures of Wild West debauchery and manifest-destiny propaganda that urged pioneers to settle in the golden West. The completion of the Transcontinental Railroad in 1869 brought an influx of romantic painters, who produced epic California wilderness landscapes. In the early 1900s, homegrown colonies of California Impressionist *plein-air* painters emerged, particularly at Carmel-by-the-Sea.

Timeless, rare Ansel Adams photographs are paired with excerpts from canonical Californian writers such as Jack Kerouac and Joan Didion *in With Classic California Writings*, edited by Andrea Gray Stillman.

With the invention of photography, the improbable truth of California's landscape and its inhabitants was revealed. Pirkle Jones saw expressive potential in California landscape photography after WWII, while San Francisco native Ansel Adams' sublime photographs had already started doing justice to Yosemite. Adams founded Group f/64 with Edward Weston from Carmel and Imogen Cunningham in San Francisco. Berkeley-based Dorothea Lange turned her unflinching lens on the plight of Californian migrant workers in the Great Depression and Japanese Americans forced to enter internment camps in WWII, producing poignant documentary photos.

As the postwar American West became crisscrossed with freeways and divided into planned communities, Californian painters captured the abstract forms of manufactured landscapes on canvas. In San Francisco Richard Diebenkorn and David Park became leading proponents of Bay Area Figurative Art, while San Francisco sculptor Richard Serra captured urban aesthetics in massive, rusting monoliths resembling ship prows and industrial Stonehenges. San Francisco also developed its own brand of pop art, with the rough-and-readymade 1950s Beat collage, 1960s psychedelic Fillmore posters, earthy '70s funk and beautiful-mess punk, and '80s graffiti and skate culture. This tradition remains alive at the Fillmore Auditorium, which distributes show posters after most of its concerts.

Due to cuts in the California Arts Council budget, Californians now invest only about 3¢ per capita in the arts – a minuscule amount compared with Canadians, who each contribute over $5 annually toward their arts.

The contemporary art scene in Northern California is a blend of all these influences, informed by the international community and augmented by muralist-led social commentary. There's also an obsessive dedication to craft and a new-media milieu pierced by Silicon Valley's cutting-edge technology. To see California-made art at its most experimental, check out independent NorCal art spaces in San Francisco's Mission District and the laboratory-like galleries of SOMA's Yerba Buena Arts District. The Yerba Buena Center for the Arts is at the center of it all, and has excellent modern art programs.

San Francisco's priorities have been obvious since the great earthquake of 1906, when survivors were entertained in tents set up amid the smoldering ruins, and its famous theaters were rebuilt well before City Hall. Major productions destined for the lights of Broadway and London premiere at the American Conservatory Theater, and San Francisco's answer to Edinburgh is the annual SF Fringe Festival at the Exit Theatre. The Magic Theatre gained a national reputation in the 1970s, when Sam Shepard was the theater's resident playwright, and still today it premieres innovative California playwrights. Across the Bay, the Berkeley Repertory Theatre has launched acclaimed productions based on such unlikely subjects as the rise and fall of Jim Jones Peoples Temple.

Survival Guide

DIRECTORY A–Z 554

TRANSPORTATION. .563

Directory A–Z

Accommodations

» Budget-conscious accommodations include campgrounds, hostels and motels. Because midrange properties generally offer better value for money, most of our accommodations fall into this category.

» At midrange motels and hotels, expect clean, comfortable and decent-sized double rooms with a private bath and amenities including cable TV, direct-dial telephone, a coffeemaker and perhaps a microwave and minifridge.

» Top-end lodgings offer more amenities and the possibility for designer decor or historical ambience. Pools, fitness rooms, business centers, full-service restaurants and bars and other convenient facilities are all standard.

» Where an indoor or outdoor pool is available, the swimming icon (≋) appears with the review.

» In Northern California, where it rarely gets hot, air-con may not be provided. Where air-con is available, the air-con (❄) icon appears with the review.

» Accommodations offering online computer terminals for guests are designated with the internet icon (@). A fee may apply (eg at full-service business centers inside hotels).

» When wireless internet access is offered, the wi-fi icon (wi-fi) appears with the review. There may be a fee, especially for in-room access. Look for free wi-fi hot spots in hotel public areas (eg lobby, poolside).

» Many lodgings are now exclusively nonsmoking. Where they still exist, smoking rooms are often left unrenovated and in less desirable locations. Expect a hefty 'cleaning fee' ($100 or more) if you light up in designated nonsmoking rooms.

Rates

This guide lists accommodations in order of author recommendation. Rates quoted are for high season: June to August everywhere, except the deserts and mountain ski areas, where December through April are the busiest months. Demand and prices spike even higher around major holidays (see p559) and for festivals (p23), when some properties may impose multiday minimum stays. Generally, midweek rates are lower, except in hotels geared toward weekday business travelers. Unless noted, rates do not include taxes, averaging more than 10%.

Rates are categorized in the following way:

Budget ($) Under $100
Midrange ($$) $100-200
Top End ($$$) Over $200

» Discount cards (p556) and auto-club membership (p566) may get you 10% or more off standard rates at participating hotels and motels.

» You might get a better deal by booking through discount-travel websites like **Priceline** (www.priceline.com), **Hotwire** (www.hotwire.com) or **Hotels.com** (www.hotels.com).

PRACTICALITIES

» **Electricity:** 110/120V AC, 50/60Hz

» **Newspapers:** *San Francisco Chronicle* (www.sfgate.com), *San Jose Mercury News* (www.mercurynews.com), *Sacramento Bee* (www.sacbee.com), *Oakland Tribune* (www.insidebayarea.com)

» **Radio:** National Public Radio (NPR), lower end of FM dial

» **Video:** NTSC standard (incompatible with PAL or SECAM); DVDs coded region 1 (USA & Canada only)

» **Weights & Measures:** Imperial (to convert between metric and imperial, see the inside front cover of this guide)

GREEN HOTELS & MOTELS

Surprisingly many of California's hotels and motels haven't yet jumped on the environmental bandwagon. Apart from offering you the option of reusing your towels and sheets, even such simple eco-initiatives as switching to bulk soap dispensers or replacing plastic and Styrofoam cups and dropping prepackaged breakfast items are pretty rare. Some hotels and motels now put recycling baskets in guestrooms, and a few loan or rent bicycles to guests. We've marked listings that espouse particularly admirable sustainability initiatives with the icon.

» Bargaining may be possible for walk-in guests without reservations, especially during off-peak times.

Reservations

» Reservations are recommended for weekend and holiday travel year-round, and every day during high season.

» If you plan to arrive late in the evening, call ahead on the day of your stay. Hotels overbook, but if you've guaranteed the reservation with your credit card, they should accommodate you somewhere else.

B&Bs

If you want an atmospheric or perhaps romantic alternative to impersonal motels and hotels, bed-and-breakfast inns typically inhabit fine old Victorian houses or other heritage buildings, bedecked with floral wallpaper and antique furnishings. People who like privacy may find Northern California B&Bs too intimate.

Rates often include a home-cooked breakfast, but occasionally breakfast is *not* included (never mind what the name 'B&B' suggests!). Amenities vary widely. Standards are high at places certified by the **California Association of Bed & Breakfast Inns** (www.cabbi.com).

Most B&Bs require advance reservations, although some will accommodate the occasional drop-in guest. Minimum-stay requirements are common, especially on weekends and in high season.

Camping

In California, camping is much more than just a cheap way to spend the night. The best campsites will have you waking up on the beach, next to an alpine lake or underneath a canopy of redwood trees. The California State Parks website, www.parks.ca.gov, is a good place to start.

Hostels

Northern California has a number of hostels affiliated with **Hostelling International USA** (HI-USA; ☎301-495-1240; www.hiusa.org). Dorms in HI hostels are typically gender-segregated and alcohol and smoking are prohibited. HI-USA membership cards (adult/senior $28/18 per year, free for under-18s) entitle you to $3 off per night.

There are also scores of independent hostels, particularly in coastal cities. They generally have more relaxed rules, often no curfew and frequent guest parties and activities. Some hostels include a light breakfast in their rates, arrange local tours or offer pick-ups at transportation hubs. No two hostels are alike but facilities typically include mixed dorms, semiprivate rooms with shared bathrooms, communal kitchens, lockers, internet access, laundry and TV lounges.

Dorm-bed rates average $20 to $40 per night, including tax. Reservations are always a good idea, especially in high season. Most hostels take reservations online or by phone. Many independent hostels belong to reservation services like www.hostels.com, www.hostelz.com and www.hostelworld.com, which sometimes offer lower rates than the hostels directly.

Hotels & Motels

» Rooms are often priced by the size and number of beds, rather than the number of occupants. A room with one double or queen-size bed usually costs the same for one or two people, while a room with a king-size bed or two double beds costs more.

» There is often a small surcharge for the third and fourth person, but children under a certain age (this varies) may stay free. Cribs or rollaway cots usually incur a surcharge.

» Beware that suites or 'junior suites' may simply be oversized rooms; ask about the layout when booking.

» Recently renovated or larger rooms, or those with a view, are likely to cost more. Descriptors like 'oceanfront' and 'oceanview' are too liber-

BOOK YOUR STAY ONLINE

For more accommodations reviews by Lonely Planet authors, check out hotels.lonelyplanet.com/California. You'll find independent reviews, as well as recommendations on the best places to stay. Best of all, you can book online.

ally used, and may require a periscope to spot the surf.

» Rates may include breakfast, which could be just a stale donut and wimpy coffee, an all-you-can-eat hot and cold buffet, or anything in-between.

» If you arrive without a reservation, ask to see a room before paying for it, especially at motels.

Business Hours

Unless otherwise noted with reviews, standard opening hours for listings in this guide are as follows.

Banks 8:30am-4:30pm Mon-Fri, some to 5:30pm Fri, 9am-12:30pm Sat

Bars 5pm-midnight daily

Business hours (general) 9am-5pm Mon-Fri

Nightclubs 10pm-2am Thu-Sat

Post offices 9am-5pm Mon-Fri, some 9am-noon Sat

Restaurants 7am-10:30am, 11:30am-2:30pm & 5-9:30pm daily, some later Fri & Sat

Shops 10am-6pm Mon-Sat, noon-5pm Sun (malls open later)

Discount Cards

For discounts for children and families, see p45.

America the Beautiful Interagency Annual Pass (http://store.usgs.gov/pass; $80) The price admits four adults and all children under 16 years old free to all national parks and federal recreational lands – eg US Forest Service (USFS) and Bureau of Land Management (BLM) lands – for one year. It can be purchased online or at any national park entrance station. US citizens and permanent residents 62 years and older are eligible for a lifetime Senior Pass ($10) that grants free entry and some discounts.

American Association of Retired Persons (AARP; ☎888-687-2277; www.aarp.org; annual membership $16). Advocacy group for Americans 50 years and older offers member discounts (usually 10%) on hotels, car rentals and more.

American Automobile Association (AAA; ☎877-428-2277; www.aaa.com; annual membership from $48) Members of AAA and its foreign affiliates (eg CAA, AA) qualify for small discounts (usually 10%) on Amtrak trains, car rentals and accommodations.

Go San Francisco Card ($55/40) This covers museums, bicycle rental and a bay cruise. Note that you've got to do *a lot* of sightseeing over multiple days to make this pay off. For the best prices, buy online in advance at www.smartdestinations.com.

Student Advantage Card (☎877-256-4672; www.studentadvantage.com; $23) For international and US students, offers 15% savings on Amtrak and Greyhound, plus discounts of 10% to 20% on some airlines and chain shops, hotels and motels.

Electricity

Food

In this guide, restaurant prices usually refer to an average main course at dinner.

Budget ($) Dinner mains under $10

Midrange ($$) Most dinner mains $10-20

Top End ($$$) Dinner mains over $20

These prices don't include drinks, appetizers, desserts, taxes or tip. Note the same dishes at lunch will usually be cheaper, maybe even half-price.

Lunch is generally served between 11:30am and 2:30pm, and dinner between 5pm and 9:30pm daily, though some restaurants close later, especially on Friday and Saturday nights. If breakfast is served, it's usually between 7am and 10:30am; some diners and coffee shops keep serving breakfast into the afternoon, or all day. Weekend brunch is a laidback affair, usually available from 9am until 2pm on Saturdays and Sundays. Full opening hours are given with all restaurant reviews in this guide.

Like all things Northern Californian, restaurant etiquette tends to be informal. Other things to keep in mind:

» Tipping 15% to 20% is expected anywhere you receive table service.

» Smoking is illegal indoors; some restaurants have patios or sidewalk tables where lighting up is tolerated, though don't expect your neighbors to be happy about secondhand smoke.

» You can bring your own wine to most restaurants, but expect to pay a 'corkage' fee of $15 to $30. Lunches rarely include booze, though a glass of wine or beer, while uncommon, is usually acceptable.

» Vegetarians and travelers with food allergies are in luck – most restaurants are used to catering to specific dietary needs.

» If you're dining out with kids, see p45.

Gay & Lesbian Travelers

Northern California is extremely gay friendly and a magnet for lesbian, gay, bisexual and transgender travelers. California offers gays and lesbians extensive domestic rights but currently stops short of the legalization of same-sex marriage and civil unions. Despite widespread tolerance, make no mistake: homophobic bigotry still exists, especially away from the coast.

Helpful Resources

Advocate (www.advocate.com/travel) Online news articles, gay travel features and destination guides.

Gay.com Daily Travel (daily.gay.com/travel) City guides, blog-style travel news and special events.

Gay & Lesbian Yellow Pages (www.glyp.com) Includes ads for local restaurants, bars and clubs; 'Gay Yellow Pages' mobile app now available.

Gay Travelocity (www.travelocity.com/gaytravel) LGBT travel articles with hotel, guided-tour and activity bookings.

Out Traveler (www.outtraveler.com) Free online magazine, trip planner, destination guides and a mobile app.

Purple Roofs (www.purpleroofs.com) Online directory of LGBT accommodations.

Health

» For medical emergencies, call ☎911 or go to the nearest 24-hour hospital emergency room, or ER.

» Medical treatment in the USA is of the highest caliber, but the expense could kill you. Many health-care professionals demand payment at the time of service, especially from out-of-towners or international visitors.

» Except for medical emergencies, phone around to find a doctor who will accept your insurance.

» Overseas visitors with travel health-insurance policies may need to contact a call center for an assessment by phone before getting medical treatment.

» Carry any medications you may need in their original containers, clearly labeled. Bring a signed, dated letter from your doctor describing all medical conditions and medications (including generic names).

Insurance

See p566 for car insurance.

Getting travel insurance to cover theft, loss and medical problems is highly recommended. Some policies do not cover 'risky' activities such as scuba diving, motorcycling and skiing so read the fine print. Make sure the policy at least covers hospital stays and an emergency flight home.

Paying for your airline ticket or rental car with a credit card may provide limited travel accident insurance. If you already have private health insurance or a homeowners or renters policy, find out what those policies cover and only get supplemental insurance. If you have prepaid a large portion of your vacation, trip cancellation insurance may be a worthwhile expense.

Worldwide travel insurance is available at www.lonelyplanet.com/travel_services. You can buy, extend and claim online anytime – even if you're already on the road.

Internet Access

» Internet cafes listed throughout this guide typically charge $6 to $12 per hour for online access.

» Accommodations, cafes, restaurants, bars etc that provide guest computer terminals for going online are identified in this guide by the internet icon (@); the wi-fi icon (wi-fi) indicates that wireless access is available. There may be a charge for either service.

» Wi-fi hot spots (free or fee-based) can be found at major airports; many hotels, motels and coffee shops (eg Starbucks); and some tourist information centers, RV parks (eg KOA), museums, bars, restaurants (including fast-food chains such as McDonalds) and stores (eg Apple).

» Free public wi-fi is proliferating and even some state parks are now wi-fi–enabled (for a list, go to www.parks.ca.gov/wifi).

» Public libraries have internet terminals, but online time may be limited, advance sign-up may be required and a nominal fee charged for out-of-network visitors. Increasingly libraries offer free wi-fi access.

INTERNATIONAL VISITORS

Entering the USA

Currently, non-US citizens and permanent residents may import:

» 1L of alcohol (if you're over 21 years old)

» 200 cigarettes (one carton) or 50 (non-Cuban) cigars (if you're over 18)

» $100 worth of gifts

Amounts higher than $10,000 in cash, traveler's checks, money orders and other cash equivalents must be declared. Don't even consider bringing in illegal drugs. For more complete, current information, check with **US Customs and Border Protection** (www.cbp.gov).

For info on passports, see p563; for visas, see p562.

Under the US Department of Homeland Security (DHS) registration program, **US-VISIT** (www.dhs.gov/us-visit), almost all visitors (excluding, for now, many Canadian citizens, some Mexican citizens and children under age 14) will be digitally photographed and have their electronic (inkless) fingerprints scanned upon arrival; the process typically takes less than a minute.

Regardless of your visa status, US immigration officers have absolute authority to refuse entry to the USA. They may ask about your plans and whether you have sufficient funds; it's a good idea to list an itinerary, produce an onward or round-trip ticket and have at least one major credit card. Don't make too much of having friends, relatives or business contacts in the US – officers may decide this makes you more likely to overstay your visa.

Post

» The **US Postal Service** (USPS; ☎800-275-8777; www.usps.com) is inexpensive and reliable.

» For sending important letters or packages overseas, try **Federal Express** (FedEx; ☎800-463-3339; www.fedex.com) or **UPS** (☎800-782-7892; www.ups.com).

Telephone

CELL (MOBILE) PHONES

» You'll need a multiband GSM phone in order to make calls in the US.

» SIM cards are sold at telecommunications and electronics stores. These stores also sell inexpensive prepaid phones.

» You can rent a cell phone at San Francisco airport from **TripTel** (☎877-874-7835; www.triptel.com); pricing plans vary, but typically are expensive.

DIALING CODES

» US phone numbers consist of a three-letter area code followed by a seven-digit local number.

» When dialing a number within the same area code, use the seven-digit number.

» If you are calling long distance, dial ☎1 plus the area code plus the phone number.

» Toll-free numbers begin with ☎800, ☎866, ☎877 or ☎888 and must be preceded by ☎1.

» For direct international calls, dial ☎011 plus the country code plus the area code (usually without the initial '0') plus the local phone number.

» For international call assistance, dial ☎00.

» If you're calling from abroad, the country code for the US is ☎1.

PAYPHONES & PHONECARDS

» Where payphones still exist, they are usually coin-operated, although some may only accept credit cards (eg in national parks).

» Local calls usually cost 50¢ minimum.

» For long-distance calls, you're usually better off buying a prepaid phonecard, sold at convenience stores, supermarkets, newsstands and electronics stores.

Legal Matters

Drugs & Alcohol

» Possession of under 1oz of marijuana is a misdemeanor in California. Possession of any other drug or more than an ounce of weed is a felony punishable by lengthy jail time. For foreigners, conviction of any drug offense is grounds for deportation.

» Police can give roadside sobriety checks to assess if you've been drinking or using drugs. If you fail, they'll require you to take a breath, urine or blood test to determine if your blood-alcohol is over the legal limit (0.08%). Refusing to be tested is treated as failing the test.

» Penalties for driving under the influence (DUI) can include license suspension, fines and jail time.

» It's illegal to carry open containers of alcohol inside a vehicle. Unless they're full and sealed, store them in the trunk.

» Consuming alcohol anywhere other than at a private residence or licensed premises is illegal, which puts most parks and beaches off-limits (although many campgrounds allow it).

» Bars, clubs and liquor stores often ask for photo ID as proof of age.

Police & Security

» For police, fire and ambulance emergencies, dial ☎911. For nonemergency police assistance, call directory assistance (☎411) for the number of the nearest local police station.

» If you are stopped by the police, be courteous. Don't get out of the car unless asked. Keep your hands where the officer can see them (eg on the steering wheel).

» There is no system of paying fines on the spot.

» For traffic violations the ticketing officer will explain the options to you. Most matters can be handled by mail.

» If you are arrested, you have the right to remain silent and are presumed innocent until proven guilty. Everyone has the right to make one phone call. If you don't have a lawyer, one will be appointed to you free of charge. Foreign travelers should call their embassy or consulate.

» Due to security concerns, never leave your bags unattended, especially not at airports or bus and train stations.

Smoking

» Smoking is generally prohibited inside all public buildings, including airports, shopping malls and train and bus stations.

» No smoking is allowed inside restaurants.

» At hotels, you must specifically request a smoking room, but note some properties are entirely nonsmoking by law.

Money

For US dollar exchange rates and setting your trip budget, see p18.

ATMs

» ATMs are available 24/7 at most banks, shopping malls, airports, and grocery and convenience stores.

» Expect a minimum surcharge of $2 to $3 per transaction, in addition to any fees charged by your home bank.

» Most ATMs are connected to international networks and offer decent foreign-exchange rates.

» Withdrawing cash from an ATM using a credit card usually incurs a hefty fee and high interest rates; check with your credit-card company for a PIN number.

Cash

» Most people do not carry large amounts of cash for everyday use, relying instead on credit cards, ATMs and debit cards. Some businesses refuse to accept bills over $20.

Credit Cards

Major credit cards are almost universally accepted. In fact, it's almost impossible to rent a car, book a room or buy tickets over the phone without one. Visa, MasterCard and American Express are the most widely accepted.

Moneychangers

» You can exchange money at major airports, some banks and all currency-exchange offices such as **American Express** (www.americanexpress.com) or **Travelex** (www.travelex.com). Always inquire about rates and fees.

Taxes

» A California state sales tax of 8.25% is added to the retail price of most goods and services (gasoline is an exception).

» Local and city sales taxes may tack on an additional 1.5% or more.

» Tourist lodging taxes vary statewide, but currently average over 10%.

Traveler's Checks

» Traveler's checks have pretty much fallen out of use.

» Larger restaurants, hotels and department stores will still often accept traveler's checks (in US dollars only), but small businesses, markets and fast-food chains may refuse them.

» Visa and American Express are the most widely accepted issuers of traveler's checks.

Public Holidays

On the following national holidays, banks, schools and government offices (including post offices) are closed, and transportation, museums and other services operate on a Sunday schedule.

TIPPING

Tipping is *not* optional. Only withhold tips in cases of outrageously bad service.

Airport skycaps & hotel bellhops	$2 per bag, minimum per cart $5
Bartenders	10% to 15% per round, minimum $1 per drink
Concierges	Nothing for simple information, up to $20 for securing last-minute restaurant reservations, sold-out show tickets etc
Housekeeping staff	$2 to $4 daily, left under the card provided; more if you're messy
Parking valets	At least $2 when handed back your car keys
Restaurant servers & room service	15% to 20%, unless a gratuity is already charged
Taxi drivers	10% to 15% of metered fare, rounded up to the next dollar

Holidays falling on a weekend are usually observed the following Monday.

New Year's Day January 1

Martin Luther King Jr Day Third Monday in January

Presidents' Day Third Monday in February

Easter Sunday March/April

Memorial Day Last Monday in May

Independence Day July 4 (aka Fourth of July)

Labor Day First Monday in September

Columbus Day Second Monday in October

Veterans' Day November 11

Thanksgiving Day Fourth Thursday in November

Christmas Day December 25

School Holidays

Colleges take a one- or two-week 'spring break' around Easter, sometime in March or April. Some hotels and resorts, especially along the coast and in the deserts, raise their rates during this time. School summer vacations run from early June to late August, making July and August the busiest travel months.

Safe Travel

Despite its seemingly apocalyptic list of dangers – guns, violent crime, riots, earthquakes – California is a reasonably safe place to visit. The greatest danger is posed by car accidents (buckle up – it's the law), while the biggest annoyances are city traffic and crowds. Wildlife poses some small threats, and of course there is the dramatic, albeit unlikely, possibility of a natural disaster.

Earthquakes

Earthquakes happen all the time but most are so tiny they are detectable only by sensitive seismological instruments. If you're caught in a serious shaker:

» If indoors, get under a desk or table or stand in a doorway.

» Protect your head and stay clear of windows, mirrors or anything that might fall.

» Don't head for elevators or go running into the street.

» If you're in a shopping mall or large public building, expect the alarm and/or sprinkler systems to come on.

» If outdoors, get away from buildings, trees and power lines.

» If you're driving, pull over to the side of the road away from bridges, overpasses and power lines. Stay inside the car until the shaking stops.

» If you're on a sidewalk near buildings, duck into a doorway to protect yourself from falling bricks, glass and debris.

» Prepare for aftershocks.

» Turn on the radio and listen for bulletins.

» Use the telephone only if absolutely necessary.

Riptides

If you find yourself being carried offshore by a dangerous ocean current called a riptide, the important thing is to just keep afloat. Don't panic or try to swim against the current, as this will quickly exhaust you and you could drown. Instead, swim parallel to the shoreline and once the current stops pulling you out, swim back to shore.

Wildlife

» Never feed or approach wild animals – it causes them to lose their innate fear of humans, which in turn makes them more aggressive.

» Disturbing or harassing specially protected species (eg many marine mammals) is a crime, subject to enormous fines.

» Black bears are often attracted to campsites, where they may find food, trash and any other scented items left out on picnic tables or stashed in tents and cars. Always use bear-proof containers where provided.

Visit http://sierrawild.gov/bears for more bear-country travel tips.

» If you encounter a black bear in the wild, don't run. Stay together, keeping small children next to you and picking up little ones. Keep back at least 100yd. If the bear starts moving toward you, back away slowly off-trail and let it pass by, being careful not to block any of the bear's escape routes or to get caught between a mother and her cubs. Sometimes a black bear will 'bluff charge' to test your dominance. Stand your ground by making yourself look as big as possible (eg waving your arms above your head) and shouting menacingly.

» Mountain lion attacks on humans are rare. If you encounter one, stay calm, pick up small children, face the animal and retreat slowly. Try to appear larger by raising your arms or grabbing a stick. If the lion becomes aggressive, shout or throw rocks at it. If attacked, fight back aggressively.

» Snakes and spiders are common throughout California, not just in wilderness areas. Always look inside your shoes before putting them back on outdoors, especially when camping. Snake bites are rare, but occur most often when a snake is stepped on or provoked (eg picked up or poked with a stick). The only venomous snake in region is the Northern Pacific rattlesnake, and its bite, while painful, is very rarely deadly. If you are bitten, seek medical attention at a hospital immediately.

Tourist Information

» For pretrip planning, peruse the information-packed website of the **California Travel and Tourism Commission** (www.visitcalifornia.com).

» This state-run agency also operates several **California Welcome Centers** (www.visitcwc.com), where staff dispense maps and brochures and help find accommodations.

» Almost every city and town has a local visitors center or a chamber of commerce where you can pick up maps, brochures and information; these are listed in the relevant destination chapters.

» For helpful tourist information websites, see p19.

Travelers with Disabilities

Northern California is reasonably well-equipped for travelers with disabilities.

Communications

» Telephone companies provide relay operators (dial ☎711) for the hearing impaired.

» Many banks provide ATM instructions in Braille.

Mobility & Accessibility

» Most intersections have dropped curbs and sometimes audible crossing signals.

» The Americans with Disabilities Act (ADA) requires public buildings built after 1993 to be wheelchair-accessible, including restrooms.

» Motels and hotels built after 1993 must have at least one ADA-compliant accessible room; state your specific needs when making reservations.

» For nonpublic buildings built prior to 1993, including hotels, restaurants, museums and theaters, there are no accessibility guarantees; call ahead to find out what to expect.

» Most national and many state parks and some other outdoor recreation areas offer paved or boardwalk-style nature trails accessible for wheelchairs; for a free national parks pass, consult http://store.usgs.gov/pass/access.html.

Public Transportation

» All major airlines, Greyhound buses and Amtrak trains can accommodate people with disabilities, usually with 48 hours of advance notice (for details, see the Transportation chapter, p566).

» Major car-rental agencies offer hand-controlled vehicles and vans with wheelchair lifts at no extra charge, but you must reserve these well in advance.

» For wheelchair-accessible van rentals, try **Wheelchair Getaways** (☎800-642-2042; www.wheelchairgetaways.com) in San Francisco.

» Local buses, trains and subway lines usually have wheelchair lifts.

» Seeing-eye dogs are permitted to accompany passengers on public transportation.

» Taxi companies should have at least one wheelchair-accessible van, but you'll usually need to call ahead to inquire about availability.

Helpful Resources

Access Northern California (www.accessnca.com) Extensive links to accessible-travel resources, publications, tours and transportation, including outdoor recreation opportunities and car and van rentals, plus a searchable lodgings database and an events calendar.

Access San Francisco (www.onlyinsanfrancisco.com/plan_your_trip/access_guide.asp) Free downloadable accessible travel info (somewhat dated, but still useful).

Access Santa Cruz County (www.sharedadventures.com/access_guide.htm) Bilingual (English/Spanish) accessible-travel guide (US shipping $3).

California State Parks (http://access.parks.ca.gov)

Online searchable map and database to find accessible features at parks statewide.

Coastal Conservancy (www.scc.ca.gov) Offers free downloadable wheelchair riders' guides to the San Francisco, Los Angeles and Orange County coasts, covering beaches, parks, aquariums, museums and more.

Disabled Sports Eastern Sierra (disabledsportseasternsierra.org) Offers summer and winter outdoor activities around Mammoth Mountain and Lakes.

Disabled Sports USA Far West (www.dsusafw.org) Organizes summer and winter sports and outdoor recreation programs (annual membership $30).

Flying Wheels Travel (www.flyingwheelstravel.com) Full-service travel agency.

MossRehab Resource Net (www.mossresourcenet.org/travel.htm) Useful links and general advice about accessible travel.

Yosemite Access Guide (www.nps.gov/yose/planyourvisit/upload/access.pdf) Detailed, if somewhat dated, downloadable information for Yosemite National Park.

Visas

» All of the following information is highly subject to change. Depending on your country of origin, the rules for entering the USA keep changing. Double-check current visa requirements *before* coming to the USA.

» Currently, under the US Visa Waiver Program (VWP), visas are not required for citizens of 36 countries for stays of up to 90 days (no extensions) as long as your passport meets current US standards. For more information, visit the US Customs and Border Patrol website at www.cbp.gov/xp/cgov/travel.

» Citizens of VWP countries must also register with the **Electronic System for Travel Authorization** (ESTA; $14) online (https://esta.cbp.dhs.gov/) at least 72 hours before travel. Once approved, the registration is valid for up to two years.

» Citizens from all other countries or whose passports don't meet US standards will need to apply for a visa in their home country. The process costs a nonrefundable $140, involves a personal interview and can take several weeks, so apply as early as possible.

» For more information, consult http://travel.state.gov/visa.

Volunteering

Casual drop-in volunteer opportunities are most common in cities, where you can socialize with locals while helping out nonprofit organizations. Browse upcoming projects and sign up online with local organizations such as San Francisco's **One Brick** (www.onebrick.org) or **HandsOn Bay Area** (www.handsonbayarea.org). For more opportunities, check local alternative weekly newspapers and **Craigslist** (www.craigslist.org).

Helpful Resources

California Volunteers (www.californiavolunteers.org) State volunteer directory and matching service, with links to national service days and long-term AmeriCorps programs.

Habitat for Humanity (www.habitat.org) Nonprofit organization helps build homes for impoverished families, including weekend and week-long projects.

Idealist.org (www.idealist.org) Free searchable database includes both short- and long-term volunteer opportunities.

Sierra Club (www.sierraclub.org) Day or weekend projects and longer volunteer vacations (including for families) focusing on conservation; annual membership $25.

Wilderness Volunteers (www.wildernessvolunteers.org) Week-long trips help maintain national parks, wildlands and outdoor recreation areas.

Worldwide Opportunities on Organic Farms (www.wwoofusa.org) Long-term volunteering opportunities on local organic farms; online membership fee $30.

Transportation

GETTING THERE & AWAY

Getting to Northern California by air or overland by bus, car or train is easy, although it's not always cheap. Flights, tours and train tickets can be booked online at www.lonelyplanet.com/bookings.

Entering the Region

California's importance as an agricultural state is evident in the sprawling fields of the Central Valley. Because of this, expect some border controls. To prevent the spread of pests and diseases, certain food items (including meats and fresh fruit and vegetables) may not be brought into the state. Bakery items, chocolates and hard-cured cheeses are admissible. If you're driving into California across the border from Mexico, or from the neighboring states of Oregon, Nevada or Arizona, you may have to stop for a quick inspection and questioning by California Department of Food and Agriculture agents.

Passports

» Under the Western Hemisphere Travel Initiative (WHTI), all travelers must have a valid machine-readable passport (MRP) when entering the USA by air, land or sea.

» The only exceptions are for most US citizens and some Canadian and Mexican citizens traveling *by land* who can present other WHTI-compliant documents (eg pre-approved 'trusted traveler' cards). For details, check www.getyouhome.gov.

» All foreign passports must meet current US standards and be valid for at least six months longer than your intended stay.

» MRPs issued or renewed after October 26, 2006 must be e-passports (ie have a digital photo and integrated chip with biometric data). For more information, consult www.cbp.gov/travel.

» See also US Visa entry requirements on p562.

Air

» To get through airport security checkpoints (30-minute wait times are standard), you'll need a boarding pass and photo ID.

» Some travelers may be required to undergo a secondary screening, involving hand pat-downs and carry-on bag searches.

» Airport security measures restrict many common items (eg pocket knives) from being carried on planes. Check current restrictions with the **Transportation Security Administration** (TSA; ☎866-289-9673; www.tsa.gov).

» Currently, TSA requires that all carry-on liquids and gels be stored in 3oz or smaller bottles placed inside a quart-sized clear plastic zip-top bag. Exceptions, which must be declared to checkpoint security officers, include medications.

» All checked luggage is screened for explosives. TSA may open your suitcase for visual confirmation, breaking the lock if necessary. Leave your bags unlocked or use a TSA-approved lock like **Travel Sentry** (www.travelsentry.org).

Airports

Northern California's has several international airports:

San Francisco International Airport (SFO; www.flysfo.com) Northern California's major hub, 14 miles south of downtown, on San Francisco Bay. This is the likely point of entrance for international travelers.

Oakland International Airport (OAK; www.flyoakland.com) In San Francisco's East Bay, easily connected to San Francisco by local public transport.

Mineta San José International Airport (SJC; www.flysanjose.com) In San Francisco's South Bay.

Sacramento International Airport (SMF; www.sacairports.org/int) In the Gold Country. Flights here can be cheaper than those in the Bay Area and it makes an excellent launching point for Northern California wilderness areas.

CLIMATE CHANGE & TRAVEL

Every form of transport that relies on carbon-based fuel generates CO_2, the main cause of human-induced climate change. Modern travel is dependent on aeroplanes, which might use less fuel per kilometer per person than most cars but travel much greater distances. The altitude at which aircraft emit gases (including CO_2) and particles also contributes to their climate change impact. Many websites offer 'carbon calculators' that allow people to estimate the carbon emissions generated by their journey and, for those who wish to do so, to offset the impact of the greenhouse gases emitted with contributions to portfolios of climate-friendly initiatives throughout the world. Lonely Planet offsets the carbon footprint of all staff and author travel.

For more regional airports handling domestic flights, see opposite.

Land

Border Crossings

It's relatively easy crossing from the USA into Canada or Mexico; it's crossing back into the USA that can pose problems if you haven't brought all of the required documents. Check the ever-changing passport and visa requirements with the **US Department of State** (http://travel.state.gov) beforehand.

US Customs & Border Protection (http://apps.cbp.gov/bwt/) tracks wait times at every Mexico border crossing.

Bus

» **Greyhound** (☎800-231-2222; www.greyhound.com) is the major long-distance bus company, with routes throughout the USA, including to/from California.

» Greyhound has recently stopped service to many small towns; routes trace major highways and stop at larger population centers.

» Greyhound also connects to Canada and Mexico, though usually riders will have to change buses at the border.

» For more details about Greyhound, including onboard amenities, costs and reservations, see p565.

BUS PASSES

» Greyhound's **Discovery Pass** (www.discoverypass.com) is good for unlimited travel throughout the US and Canada for seven ($246), 15 ($356), 30 ($456) or 60 ($556) consecutive days.

» If you're starting your trip in the US, passes may be bought at Greyhound terminals or online (for terminal pick-up) up to two hours before travel.

Car & Motorcycle

» If you're driving your own car, carry your vehicle's registration papers, liability insurance and driver's license; an international driving permit (IDP) is a good supplement, but not required.

» If you're renting a car or a motorcycle, ask if the agency allows its vehicles to be taken across the Mexican or Canadian border; chances are it doesn't.

Train

» **Amtrak** (☎800-872-7245; www.amtrak.com) operates a rail system throughout the USA.

» Fares vary according to the type of train and seating (eg reserved or unreserved coach seats, business class, sleeping compartments).

» Trains are comfortable, if slow, and are equipped with dining and lounge cars on long-distance routes.

» Amtrak operates twice-daily Cascades rail service and several daily Thruway buses from Vancouver, British Columbia in Canada to Seattle, Washington.

» US/Canadian customs and immigration inspections happen at the border, not upon boarding.

» From Seattle, Amtrak's *Coast Starlight* connects south to several destinations in Northern California en route to LA.

» Currently no train services connect California and Mexico.

» Amtrak routes to/from California:

California Zephyr Daily service between Chicago and Emeryville (from $149, 52 hours), near San Francisco, via Denver, Salt Lake City, Reno and Sacramento.

Coast Starlight Travels the West Coast daily from Seattle to LA (from $104, 35 hours) via Portland, Sacramento, Oakland and Santa Barbara; wi-fi may be available.

Capital Corridor Connects Sacramento with San Jose (from $36, three hours) via Berkeley, Oakland and San Francisco (via coach); wi-fi may be available.

For more details about Amtrak trains, including costs, reservations, onboard amenities and intra-California routes, see p569.

GETTING AROUND

Most people drive around Northern California, although you can also fly (if time is limited) or save money by taking buses or often scenic trains. Public transportation routes can be very difficult to stitch together.

Air

Besides Northern California's major international airports, domestic flights also depart from smaller regional airports, including:

Arcata/Eureka Airport (ACV; www.co.humboldt.ca.us/aviation) On the North Coast.

Fresno Yosemite International Airport (FYI; www.flyfresno.org) In the Central Valley.

Monterey Peninsula Airport (MRY; www.montereyairport.com) On the Central Coast.

Redding Municipal Airport (RDD; http://ci.redding.ca.us/transeng/airports/rma.htm) In the Northern Mountains.

San Luis Obispo County Regional Airport (SBP; www.sloairport.com) On the Central Coast.

Santa Barbara Municipal Airport (SBA; www.flysba.com) On the Central Coast.

Several major US carriers fly within California. Flights are often operated by their regional subsidiaries.

American Eagle and Horizon Air (www.aa.com) Affiliated with American Airlines; connects to regional airports in Mammoth Lakes, Santa Rosa, Fresno and Reno.

United Express (www.united.com) Connects to Crescent City, Redding, Chico, Modesto, Mammoth Lakes and Fresno.

Alaska Airlines (www.alaskaair.com) Connects to Reno, Mammoth Lakes and Fresno.

Popular low-cost airlines Southwest and JetBlue also serve destinations in Northern California.

Bicycle

Although it's a nonpolluting 'green' way to travel, the distances involved in cycling around Northern California demand a high level of fitness and make it hard to cover much ground. Forget the mountains in winter.

Some helpful resources for cyclists:

Adventure Cycling Association (www.adventurecycling.org) Excellent online resource for purchasing bicycle-friendly maps, long-distance route guides and gadgets.

Better World Club (☎866-238-1137; www.betterworldclub.com) Annual membership ($40, plus $12 enrollment fee) entitles you to two 24-hour emergency roadside pickups with transportation to the nearest bike repair shop within a 30-mile radius.

California Department of Transportation (www.dot.ca.gov/hq/tpp/offices/bike) Road rules, safety tips and links to statewide bicycle advocacy groups.

Road Rules

» Cycling is allowed on all roads – and even along some freeways if there's no suitable alternative. In this case, rules are clearly marked.

» Many cities, including San Francisco, Oakland and Sacramento, have designated bicycle lanes.

» Cyclists must follow the same rules of the road as vehicles. Don't expect drivers to always respect your right of way.

» Wearing a helmet is mandatory for riders under 18 years old.

» Ensure you have proper lights and reflective gear, especially if you're pedaling at night or in fog.

Rental & Purchase

» You can rent bikes by the hour, the day or the week in most cities and major towns.

» Rentals start around $10 per day for beach cruisers and up to $45 or more for mountain bikes; ask about multiday and weekly discounts.

» Most rental companies require a credit-card security deposit of $200 or more.

» To buy or sell used bikes, check online bulletin boards like **Craigslist** (www.craigslist.org).

Transporting Bicycles

» If you tire of pedaling, some local buses and trains are equipped with bicycle racks.

» Greyhound buses transport bicycles as luggage (surcharge $30 to $40), provided the bicycle is disassembled and placed in a box ($10, available at some terminals).

» Most of Amtrak's *Capital Corridor* and *San Joaquin* trains feature onboard racks for bikes; try to reserve a spot when making your ticket reservation (surcharge $5 to $10).

» Before flying, you'll need to disassemble your bike and box it as checked baggage; contact the airline directly for details, including applicable surcharges (typically $50 to $100, sometimes more).

Boat

Boats won't get you around California, but in San Francisco Bay, regular ferry routes operate between San Francisco and Sausalito, Larkspur, Tiburon, Angel Island, Oakland, Alameda and Vallejo.

Bus

Greyhound (☎800-231-2222; www.greyhound.com) buses are an economical way to travel between major cities and to points along the coast, but won't get you off the beaten path or to national parks. Frequency of service varies from 'rarely' to 'constantly,' but the main routes have service several times daily.

Greyhound buses are usually clean, comfortable and reliable. The best seats are typically near the front away from the bathroom. Limited on-board amenities include freezing air-con (bring a sweater) and slightly reclining seats; an increasing number of buses have electrical outlets and wi-fi. Long-distance buses stop for meal breaks and driver changes.

Bus stations are typically dreary places, often in dodgy areas. In small towns where there is no station, know exactly where and when the bus arrives, be obvious as you flag it down and pay the driver with exact change.

Costs

For lower fares, purchase tickets seven to 14 days in advance. Round trips and Monday through Thursday travel may be cheaper.

Discounts (on unrestricted fares only) are available for seniors over 62 (5% off), students with a Student Advantage Card (p556, 20%) and children aged 2 to 11 (25%).

Special promotional discounts, such as 50% off companion fares, are often available on the Greyhound website, though they may come with restrictions.

Reservations

It's easy to buy tickets online with a credit card, then pick them up (bring photo ID) at the terminal. You can also buy tickets over the phone or in person from a ticket agent. Most boarding is done on a first-come, first-served basis.

Travelers with disabilities who need special assistance should call ☎800-752-4841 (TDD/TTY ☎800-345-3109) at least 48 hours before traveling. Wheelchairs are accepted as checked baggage and service animals are allowed on board.

Car, Motorcycle & RV

America's weak network of public transportation can't cover Northern California; a car is nearly essential. Beware that rental rates and gas prices can eat up a good chunk of your trip budget.

Automobile Associations

For 24-hour emergency roadside assistance, free maps and discounts on lodging, attractions, entertainment, car rentals and more:

American Automobile Association (AAA; ☎877-428-2277; www.aaa.com) Walk-in offices throughout California, add-on coverage for RVs and motorcycles, and reciprocal agreements with some international auto clubs (eg CAA in Canada, AA in the UK) – bring your membership card from home.

Better World Club (☎866-238-1137; www.betterworldclub.com) Ecofriendly alternative supports environmental causes and also offers cyclists' emergency roadside assistance.

Driver's License

- Visitors may legally drive a car in California for up to 12 months with their home driver's license.
- To drive a motorcycle, you'll need a valid US state motorcycle license or a specially endorsed IDP.
- International automobile associations can issue IDPs, valid for one year, for a fee. Always carry your home license together with the IDP.

Fuel

- Gas stations in Northern California, nearly all of which are self-service, are ubiquitous near the cities, though sparse near national parks and sparsely populated mountain areas.
- Gas is sold in gallons (one US gallon equals 3.78L). At press time, the cost for mid-grade fuel ranged from $3.75 to $4.25.

Insurance

California law requires liability insurance for all vehicles. When renting a car, check your auto-insurance policy from home or your travel-insurance policy (p557) to see if you're already covered. If not, expect to pay about $20 per day.

Insurance against damage to the car itself, called Collision Damage Waiver (CDW) or Loss Damage Waiver (LDW), costs another $20 per day; the deductible may require you to pay the first $100 to $500 for any repairs. Some credit cards cover this, provided you charge the entire cost of the car rental to the card. If there's an accident you may have to pay the rental-car company first, then seek reimbursement from the credit-card company. Check your credit card's policy carefully before renting.

Parking

- Parking is usually plentiful and free in small towns and rural areas, but scarce and expensive in cities.

SAMPLE GREYHOUND FARES

ROUTE	FARE ($)	DURATION (HR)	FREQUENCY
San Francisco-LA	55	7½-12¼	14 daily
San Francisco-Sacramento	21	2-2¾	7 daily
San Francisco-San Luis Obispo	48	6½-7¼	5 daily
San Francisco-Arcata	47	7	1 daily

FURTHER AFIELD: LOS ANGELES & LAS VEGAS

For muscle beaches, celebrity sightings and camera-ready wackiness, head south from San Francisco on coastal Hwy 1 to Los Angeles. It'll take 12 hours depending on traffic and how often you stop. A quicker jaunt is less-scenic Hwy 101 (nine hours); the fastest route is boring inland I-5, which takes about six hours. Las Vegas, Nevada, is a nine-hour nonstop drive from San Francisco. Cross the Bay Bridge to 580 east, to I-5 south, veering off towards 99 south (at exit 278), to 58 east, then I-15 the last 160 miles. A slower, gloriously scenic option is to go east through Yosemite National Park on Hwy 120 (summer only; verify by calling 800-GAS-ROAD) and south on Hwy 395, east on Hwy 190 through Death Valley National Park then south on Hwy 95 straight into Sin City.

» Look for the free-parking icon (P) used in San Francisco.

» You can pay municipal parking meters with coins (eg quarters) or sometimes credit cards.

» Expect to pay at least $25 to park overnight in a city lot or garage.

» When parking on the street, read all posted regulations and restrictions and pay attention to colored curbs, or you may be ticketed or towed.

Rental

CARS

To rent your own wheels, you'll typically need to be at least 25 years old, hold a valid driver's license and have a major credit card, *not* a check or debit card. A few companies may rent to drivers under 25 but over 21 for a surcharge (around $25 per day). If you don't have a credit card, you may occasionally be able to make a large cash deposit instead.

With advance reservations, you can often get an economy-size vehicle with unlimited mileage from around $30 per day, plus insurance, taxes and fees. Weekend and weekly rates are usually more economical. Airport locations may have cheaper rates but higher fees. City-center branches may offer free pick-ups and drop-offs.

Rental rates generally include unlimited mileage, but expect surcharges for additional drivers and one-way rentals. Child or infant safety seats are compulsory (reserve them at time of booking), costing about $10 per day (maximum $50 per rental).

Major international car-rental companies:

Alamo (☎877-222-9075; www.alamo.com)

Avis (☎800-331-1212; www.avis.com)

Budget (☎800-527-0700; www.budget.com)

Enterprise (☎800-261-7331; www.enterprise.com)

Fox (☎800-225-4369; www.foxrentacar.com)

Hertz (☎800-654-3131; www.hertz.com)

Thrifty (☎800-847-4389; www.thrifty.com)

You might get a better deal by booking through websites like **Priceline** (www.priceline.com), **Hotwire** (www.hotwire.com), **Expedia** (www.expedia.com), **Orbitz** (www.orbitz.com) or **Travelocity** (www.travelocity.com).

If you'd like to minimize your carbon footprint, a few major car-rental companies (including Avis, Budget, Enterprise, Fox, Hertz and Thrifty) offer 'green' fleets of hybrid or biofueled rental cars, but they're in short supply. Reserve well in advance and expect to pay significantly more for these models. Also try:

Zipcar (☎866-494-7227; www.zipcar.com) Currently available in 19 California cities (mostly along the coast), this car-sharing club charges usage fees (per hour or daily), including free gas, insurance and limited mileage. Apply online (foreign drivers OK); annual membership $50, application fee $25.

Independent companies that may rent to drivers under 25 include:

Rent-a-Wreck (☎877-877-0700; www.rentawreck.com) Minimum rental age and surcharges vary by location. Ten locations, mostly around the San Francisco Bay Area.

Super Cheap Cars (www.supercheapcar.com) Normally there's a surcharge for drivers aged 21 to 24; daily fee applies for drivers aged 18 to 21. Located in San Francisco.

For wheelchair-accessible van rentals, see p561

MOTORCYCLES

Motorcycle rentals and insurance are not cheap, especially if you've got your eye on a Harley. Depending on the model, renting a motorcycle costs $100 to $200 per day plus taxes and fees. Discounts may be available for three-day and weekly rentals. Security deposits range from $1000 to $3000 (credit card required).

Motorcycle and scooter rental agencies include:

Dubbelju (☎415-495-2774, 866-495-2774; www.dubbelju.com; 698a Bryant St, San Francisco) Harley-Davidson,

BMW, Japanese-import and electric motorcycles for rent.

Eagle Rider (☎888-900-9901; www.eaglerider.com) Nationwide company with 12 locations in California, as well as Reno, Nevada. One-way rental surcharge $250.

RVs

RVs (recreational vehicles) are a popular, if not ecologically friendly, option for families, though the cost of RV campsites and poor gas mileage can be significant. Also, note that rental prices fluctuate by season and there are additional charges for miles. No special license is necessary to operate an RV, though, like rental cars, there is typically an additional fee for drivers under 25.

Cruise America (☎800 671 8042; www.cruiseamerica.com) is the largest rental agency in Northern California. You'll see these vehicles at every national park. Typically, the rental fee during peak season is $100 to $150 per night. These vehicles get between seven and 13 miles per gallon of gasoline.

Road Conditions & Hazards

For up-to-date highway conditions in Northern California, including road closures and construction updates, dial ☎800-427-7623 or visit www.dot.ca.gov.

In places where winter driving is an issue, such as mountain areas, snow tires and tire chains may be required. Ideally, carry your own chains and learn how to use them before you hit the road. Otherwise, chains can usually be bought (but not cheaply) on the highway, at gas stations or in the nearest town. Most car-rental companies don't permit the use of chains. Driving off-road, or on dirt roads, is also prohibited by most rental-car companies, and it can be dangerous in wet weather.

In rural areas, livestock and grazing deer can be hazards – look for cautionary road signs. In coastal areas thick fog may impede driving – slow down and if it's too soupy, get off the road. Along coastal cliffs and in the mountains, watch out for falling rocks, mudslides and avalanches that could damage or disable your car if struck.

Road Rules

» Drive on the right-hand side of the road.

» Talking and texting on a cell phone while driving is illegal.

» The use of seatbelts is required for drivers, front-seat passengers and children under age 16.

» Infant and child safety seats are required for children under six years old or weighing less than 60lb.

» All motorcyclists must wear a helmet. Scooters are not allowed on freeways.

» High-occupancy vehicle (HOV) lanes marked with a diamond symbol are reserved for cars with multiple occupants, sometimes only during morning and afternoon rush hours.

» Unless otherwise posted, the speed limit is 65mph on freeways, 55mph on two-lane undivided highways, 35mph on major city streets and 25mph in business and residential districts and near schools.

» It's forbidden to pass a school bus when its rear red lights are flashing.

» Except where indicated, turning right at red lights after coming to a full stop is permitted, although intersecting traffic still has the right of way.

» At four-way stop signs, cars proceed in the order in which they arrived. If two cars arrive simultaneously, the one on the right has the right of way. When in doubt, politely wave the other driver ahead.

» When emergency vehicles (ie police, fire or ambulance) approach from either direction, carefully pull over to the side of the road.

» California has strict anti-littering laws; throwing trash from a vehicle may incur a $1000 fine. Like Woody says, 'Give a hoot, don't pollute'.

» Driving under the influence of alcohol or drugs is illegal (see p559).

» It's illegal to carry open containers of alcohol inside a vehicle, even empty ones. Unless containers are full and still sealed, store them in the trunk.

Local Transportation

Except in cities, public transportation is rarely the most convenient option, and coverage to outlying towns and suburbs can be sparse. However, it is usually cheap, safe and reliable. See the regional chapters for details.

Bicycle

» Davis, San Francisco, San Luis Obispo, Santa Barbara and Santa Cruz are among California's most bike-friendly communities, as rated by the **League of American Bicyclists** (www.bikeleague.org).

» For more information see p565.

Bus, Cable Car, Streetcar & Trolley

» Most cities and larger towns have reliable local bus systems (average $1 to $3 per ride), but they may be designed for commuters and provide only limited evening and weekend service.

» San Francisco's extensive Municipal Railway (MUNI) network includes not only buses and trains, but also historic streetcars and those famous cable cars.

Train

» To get around the San Francisco Bay Area, hop aboard Bay Area Rapid Transit (BART) or Caltrain.

Sacramento also offers a limited light-rail system.

Taxi

» Taxis are metered, with flag-fall fees of $2.50 to $3.50 to start, plus $2 to $3 per mile. Credit cards may be accepted.

» Taxis may charge extra for baggage and/or airport pick-ups.

» Drivers expect a 10% to 15% tip, rounded up to the next dollar.

» Taxis cruise the busiest areas in large cities, but elsewhere you may need to call a cab company.

For quickest service in San Francisco, try these large cab companies:

Yellow Cab (415-333-3333; www.yellowcabsf.com)

Luxor Cab (415-282-4141; www.luxorcab.com)

Train

Amtrak (800-872-7245; www.amtrak.com) runs comfortable, if occasionally tardy, trains to major California cities and limited towns. At some stations Thruway buses provide onward connections. Smoking is prohibited on board trains and buses.

Amtrak routes within California:

Capitol Corridor Links San Francisco's East Bay (including Oakland, Emeryville and Berkeley) and San Jose with Davis and Sacramento several times daily. Thruway buses connect west to San Francisco, north to Auburn in the Gold Country and east to Truckee (near Lake Tahoe) and Reno, Nevada.

California Zephyr Daily service from Emeryville (near San Francisco) via Davis and Sacramento to Truckee (near Lake Tahoe) and Reno, Nevada.

Coast Starlight Chugs north–south almost the entire length of the state. Daily stops include LA, Santa Barbara, San Luis Obispo, Paso Robles, Salinas, San Jose, Oakland, Emeryville, Davis, Sacramento, Chico, Redding and Dunsmuir. Wi-fi may be available.

San Joaquin Several daily trains between Bakersfield and Oakland or Sacramento. Thruway bus connections include San Francisco, LA, Palm Springs and Yosemite National Park.

SAMPLE AMTRAK FARES

ROUTE	FARE ($)	DURATION (HR)
Oakland/San Francisco–LA	54	12
San Luis Obispo–LA	$33	5½
San Francisco/Emeryville–Sacramento	28	2¼
San Francisco/Emeryville–Truckee	44	5½

Costs

Purchase tickets at train stations, by phone or online. Fares depend on the day of travel, the route, the type of seating etc. Fares may be slightly higher during peak travel times (eg summer). Round-trip tickets cost the same as two one-way tickets.

Usually seniors over 62 and students with an ISIC or Student Advantage Card (p556) receive a 15% discount, while up to two children aged two to 15 who are accompanied by an adult get 50% off. AAA members save 10%. Special promotions can become available any time, so check Amtrak's website for details.

Reservations

Reservations can be made any time from 11 months in advance to the day of departure. In summer and around holidays, trains sell out quickly, so book tickets as early as possible. The cheapest coach fares are usually for unreserved seats; business-class fares typically come with reserved seats.

Train Passes

» Amtrak's California Rail Pass costs $159 ($80 for children aged two to 15). The pass is valid on all trains (except certain long-distance routes) and most connecting Thruway buses for seven days of travel within a 21-day period.

» Passholders must make advance reservations for each leg of travel and obtain hard-copy tickets prior to boarding.

behind the scenes

SEND US YOUR FEEDBACK

We love to hear from travelers – your comments keep us on our toes and help make our books better. Our well-traveled team reads every word on what you loved or loathed about this book. Although we cannot reply individually to postal submissions, we always guarantee that your feedback goes straight to the appropriate authors, in time for the next edition. Each person who sends us information is thanked in the next edition – and the most useful submissions are rewarded with a free book.

Visit **lonelyplanet.com/contact** to submit your updates and suggestions or to ask for help. Our award-winning website also features inspirational travel stories, news and discussions.

Note: We may edit, reproduce and incorporate your comments in Lonely Planet products such as guidebooks, websites and digital products, so let us know if you don't want your comments reproduced or your name acknowledged. For a copy of our privacy policy visit lonelyplanet.com/privacy.

OUR READERS

Many thanks to the travelers who used the last edition of the California guidebook and wrote to us with helpful hints, useful advice and interesting anecdotes:
Martina Alpeza, Gino Assaf, Collette Beuther, Lalimarie Bhagwani, Dr Andrew Brandeis, Rob Brehant, Thor Brisbin, Scott Broc, Alison Cant, Dave Carlisle, Deric Carner, Roe Cheung, Michael Chien, Ted Choi, May Chu, Eileen Connery, Gerald Crosby, Christine Dauer, Cindy De Groot, Jason Dibler, Silke Diedenhofen, Robert Douthit, Richard Edwards, Keith Endean, Kenneth Endo, Edgar Ennen, Damian Ennis, Behrooz Farahani, Gerhard Faul, Gentry Fischer, Judy Fried, Pierre Garapon, Peter Garvey, Marg Gibson, Sven Gold, Monica Griffin, Michael Gullo, Caroline Hall, Chris Hardman, Henrik Hiltunen, Bobbi Lee Hitchon, TJ Huffman, Mary Jenn, Winnie Kaplan, Marijn Kastelein, S Keizer, Christine Klerian, Ali Komiha, Harish Kumar, April Kummrow, Jason Kwon, Tom Laufer, Jennifer Lee, Ali Lemer, Gillian Lomax, Bo Lorentzen, Diderik Lund, Megan MacDonald, Melissa MacNabb, Stephanie Magalhaes, Ara Martirosyan, Victoria Mascord, Trevor Mazzucchelli, Kevin McElroy, Jimmy McGill, Steve McInnes, Ben Miller, Molly Mitoma, Jacqui Monaghan, Heather Monell, Kirsty Moore, Bradford Nordeen, Junhui Park, Jerry Patel, Sudha Patel, Sheri Peters, Celeste Perez, Juliana Pesavento, Charlotte Pothuizen, Louisa Ramshaw, Mona Reed, Christine Rice, Bobby Richards, Raphael Richards, Julia Ringma, Daniel Roberts, Matthew Roder, Danny Roman, Elizabeth Saenger, Karen Sams, Art Sandoval, Elie Sasson, Matthew Scharpnick, Hannah Schmidt, Scott Schmidt, David Schnur, Geoff Shepherd, Joe Silins, Aimee Smith, Allie Smith, Mike Smith, Renee Stuart, Susan Sueiro, Estrella Tadeo, Emanuela Tasinato, Mona Telega, Hans Ter Beek, Amanda Thomas, Aaron Tomas, Carton Tsutomu, Christian Utzman, Ophelie Vantournout, Luka Vidovic, Lorna Visser, Ira Vouk, Gordon Waggoner, Cyndi Wish, Alex Wong, Dr Felix Z, Greta Zeit

AUTHOR THANKS

Nate Cavalieri

Thanks tons to Suki Gear, my commissioning editor, for her support during the long duration of work. Thanks also to Florence Chien for joining me during the epic road trip.

Sara Benson

Thanks to everyone at Lonely Planet and all of my California co-authors. I'm grateful to those folks I met on the road who shared their local expertise and tips. Big thanks to all of my friends and family across the Golden

State, especially the Picketts for their Lake Tahoe hospitality and Jai for road-tripping humor (cowbears!). PS to MSC Jr: glad that avalanche didn't kill us. Whew! Here's hoping we're invincible.

Alison Bing

Suki Gear and Sam Benson, whose guidance, insight and support make any tricky mental backbend possible. Shameless California bear hugs to John Vlahides and Robert Landon for setting giddily high writing standards, to fearless leaders Brice Gosnell and Heather Dickson at Lonely Planet, to the Sanchez Writers' Grotto and, above all, to Marco Flavio Marinucci, whose kindness and bracing espresso make everything possible.

Beth Kohn

All the usual suspects get thanks again, especially the fabulous multi-tasking Suki Gear and the dynamo known as Sam Benson. California cohorts and experts this time around included Agent 'Pedal-to-the-metal' Moller, Felix 'Hella Loves Oakland' Thomson, Jenny 'Stink' G, Dillon 'The Scientist' Dutton and Julia 'Wawona' Brashares, plus all the helpful and patient rangers at Yosemite National Park.

John A Vlahides

I owe heartfelt thanks to my commissioning editor, Suki Gear, and co-authors Sam Benson and Alison Bing, for their wonderful help and always-sunny dispositions. Kate Brady, Steven Kahn, Karl Soehnlein, Kevin Clarke, Jim Aloise and Adam Young – you kept me upbeat and laughing when things seemed impossible. And to you, the readers: thank you for letting me be your guide to Wine Country. Have fun. I know you will.

ACKNOWLEDGMENTS

Climate map data adapted from Peel MC, Finlayson BL & McMahon TA (2007) 'Updated World Map of the Köppen-Geiger Climate Classification', *Hydrology and Earth System Sciences*, 11, 163344.

Cover photograph: Hikers above Yosemite National Park and El Capitan, California, John Mock/LPI. Many of the images in this guide are available for licensing from Lonely Planet Images: www.lonelyplanetimages.com.

THIS BOOK

This 1st edition of Northern California was coordinated by Nate Cavalieri. This guidebook was also researched and written by Sara Benson, Alison Bing, Beth Kohn and John A Vlahides. It was commissioned in Lonely Planet's Oakland office, and produced by the following:

Commissioning Editor Suki Gear

Coordinating Editors Sarah Bailey, Bella Li, Karyn Noble

Coordinating Cartographer Valentina Kremenchutskaya

Coordinating Layout Designer Carlos Solarte

Managing Editors Bruce Evans, Annelies Mertens

Senior Editor Angela Tinson

Managing Cartographers Alison Lyall, Diana Von Holdt

Managing Layout Designer Chris Girdler

Assisting Editors Alice Barker, Lauren Hunt, Fionnuala Twomey

Assisting Layout Designers Virginia Moreno, Wibowo Rusli

Cover Research Naomi Parker

Internal Image Research Sabrina Dalbesio

Thanks to Sasha Baskett, Lucy Birchley, Ryan Evans, Yvonne Kirk, Kirsten Rawlings, Gerard Walker

index

D

000 Map pages
000 Photo pages

000 Map pages
000 Photo pages

N

000 Map pages
000 Photo pages

S

T

000 Map pages
000 Photo pages

U

V

W

Y

Z

how to use this book

These symbols will help you find the listings you want:

- Sights
- Beaches
- Activities
- Courses
- Tours
- Festivals & Events
- Sleeping
- Eating
- Drinking
- Entertainment
- Shopping
- Information/ Transport

These symbols give you the vital information for each listing:

- Telephone Numbers
- Opening Hours
- Parking
- Nonsmoking
- Air-Conditioning
- Internet Access
- Wi-Fi Access
- Swimming Pool
- Vegetarian Selection
- English-Language Menu
- Family-Friendly
- Pet-Friendly
- Bus
- Ferry
- Metro
- Subway
- Tram
- Train

Reviews are organised by author preference.

Look out for these icons:

Our author's recommendation

FREE No payment required

A green or sustainable option

Our authors have nominated these places as demonstrating a strong commitment to sustainability – for example by supporting local communities and producers, operating in an environmentally friendly way, or supporting conservation projects.

Map Legend

Sights
Beach
Buddhist
Castle
Christian
Hindu
Islamic
Jewish
Monument
Museum/Gallery
Ruin
Winery/Vineyard
Zoo
Other Sight

Activities, Courses & Tours
Diving/Snorkelling
Canoeing/Kayaking
Skiing
Surfing
Swimming/Pool
Walking
Windsurfing
Other Activity/ Course/Tour

Sleeping
Sleeping
Camping

Eating
Eating

Drinking
Drinking
Cafe

Entertainment
Entertainment

Shopping
Shopping

Information
Post Office
Tourist Information

Transport
Airport
Border Crossing
Bus
Cable Car/ Funicular
Cycling
Ferry
Metro
Monorail
Parking
S-Bahn
Taxi
Train/Railway
Tram
Tube Station
U-Bahn
Other Transport

Routes
Tollway
Freeway
Primary
Secondary
Tertiary
Lane
Unsealed Road
Plaza/Mall
Steps
Tunnel
Pedestrian Overpass
Walking Tour
Walking Tour Detour
Path

Boundaries
International
State/Province
Disputed
Regional/Suburb
Marine Park
Cliff
Wall

Population
Capital (National)
Capital (State/Province)
City/Large Town
Town/Village

Geographic
Hut/Shelter
Lighthouse
Lookout
Mountain/Volcano
Oasis
Park
Pass
Picnic Area
Waterfall

Hydrography
River/Creek
Intermittent River
Swamp/Mangrove
Reef
Canal
Water
Dry/Salt/ Intermittent Lake
Glacier

Areas
Beach/Desert
Cemetery (Christian)
Cemetery (Other)
Park/Forest
Sportsground
Sight (Building)
Top Sight (Building)

John A Vlahides

Napa & Sonoma Wine Country John A Vlahides co-hosts the TV series *Lonely Planet: Roads Less Travelled,* screening on National Geographic Channels International. John studied cooking in Paris, with the same chefs who trained Julia Child, and is a former luxury-hotel concierge and member of *Les Clefs d'Or,* the international union of the world's elite concierges. He lives in San Francisco, where he sings tenor with the San Francisco Symphony, and spends free time skiing the Sierra Nevada. For more, see johnvlahides.com and @JohnVlahides on Twitter.

Read more about John at:
lonelyplanet.com/members/johnvlahides

OUR STORY

A beat-up old car, a few dollars in the pocket and a sense of adventure. In 1972 that's all Tony and Maureen Wheeler needed for the trip of a lifetime – across Europe and Asia overland to Australia. It took several months, and at the end – broke but inspired – they sat at their kitchen table writing and stapling together their first travel guide, *Across Asia on the Cheap*. Within a week they'd sold 1500 copies. Lonely Planet was born.

Today, Lonely Planet has offices in Melbourne, London and Oakland, with more than 600 staff and writers. We share Tony's belief that 'a great guidebook should do three things: inform, educate and amuse'.

OUR WRITERS

Nate Cavalieri

Coordinating Author, North Coast & Redwoods, Northern Mountains, Gold Country & Central Valley, A Taste of Northern California A native of central Michigan, Nate Cavalieri lives in Northern California and has crisscrossed the region's back roads by bicycle, bus and rental car on a quest for the biggest trees, the best camping and the hoppiest pints of beer. In addition to authoring guides on California and Latin America for Lonely Planet, he writes about music and professional cycling. He's the Jazz Editor at Rhapsody Music Service. Photos from his travels in Northern California and other writing can be found at www.natecavalieri.com.

Read more about Nate at:
lonelyplanet.com/members/natecavalieri

Sara Benson

Central Coast, Lake Tahoe After graduating from college, Sara jumped on a plane to California with just one suitcase and $100 in her pocket. She has bounced around the Golden State ever since, especially between San Francisco and Los Angeles, and in the Sierra Nevada Mountains, where she has worked as a national park ranger. The author of over 40 travel and nonfiction books, Sara has also contributed to Lonely Planet's *USA* and *Coastal California* guides. Follow more of her adventures online at www.indietraveler.blogspot.com, www.indietraveler.net and @indie_traveler on Twitter.

Read more about Sara at:
lonelyplanet.com/members/sara_benson

Alison Bing

San Francisco Author, arts commentator and adventurous eater, Alison Bing was adopted by California 16 years ago. By now she has done everything you're supposed to do here and a few things you're definitely not, including talking up Los Angeles bands in San Francisco bars and falling in love on the 7 Haight bus. Alison holds a graduate degree in international diplomacy, which she regularly undermines with opinionated commentary on public radio and in magazines, newspapers and more than 20 books.

Beth Kohn

Marin County & the Bay Area, Yosemite & the Sierra Nevada A lucky long-time resident of San Francisco, Beth lives to be playing outside or splashing in big puddles of water. For this guide, she hiked and bicycled Bay Area byways, lugged a bear canister along the John Muir Trail and selflessly soaked in hot springs – for research purposes, of course. An author of Lonely Planet's *Yosemite, Sequoia & Kings Canyon National Parks* and *Mexico* guides, you can see more of her work at www.bethkohn.com.

OVER PAGE MORE WRITERS

Published by Lonely Planet Publications Pty Ltd
ABN 36 005 607 983
1st edition – April 2012
ISBN 978 1 74220 590 8

10 9 8 7 6 5 4 3 2
Printed in China